Communications
in Computer and Information Science     300

Salvatore Greco   Bernadette Bouchon-Meunier
Giulianella Coletti   Mario Fedrizzi
Benedetto Matarazzo   Ronald R. Yager (Eds.)

# Advances in Computational Intelligence

14th International Conference
on Information Processing and Management
of Uncertainty in Knowledge-Based Systems
IPMU 2012
Catania, Italy, July 9-13, 2012
Proceedings, Part IV

Springer

Volume Editors

Salvatore Greco
University of Catania, Italy
E-mail: salgreco@unict.it

Bernadette Bouchon-Meunier
University Pierre et Marie Curie, Paris, France
E-mail: bernadette.bouchon-meunier@lip6.fr

Giulianella Coletti
University of Perugia, Italy
E-mail: coletti@dmi.unipg.it

Mario Fedrizzi
University of Trento, Italy
E-mail: mario.fedrizzi@unitn.it

Benedetto Matarazzo
University of Catania, Italy
E-mail: matarazz@unict.it

Ronald R. Yager
IONA College, New Rochelle, NY, USA
E-mail: ryager@iona.edu

ISSN 1865-0929                          e-ISSN 1865-0937
ISBN 978-3-642-31723-1                  e-ISBN 978-3-642-31724-8
DOI 10.1007/978-3-642-31724-8
Springer Heidelberg Dordrecht London New York

Library of Congress Control Number: Applied for

CR Subject Classification (1998): I.2, H.3, F.1, H.4, I.5, I.4, C.2

*Typesetting:* Camera-ready by author, data conversion by Scientific Publishing Services, Chennai, India

Printed on acid-free paper

Springer is part of Springer Science+Business Media (www.springer.com)

# Preface

We are glad to present the proceedings of the IPMU 2012 conference (International Conference on Information Processing and Management of Uncertainty in Knowledge-Based Systems) held in Catania, Italy, during July 9–13, 2012. The IPMU conference is organized every two years with the focus of bringing together scientists working on methods for the management of uncertainty and aggregation of information in intelligent systems. This conference provides a medium for the exchange of ideas between theoreticians and practitioners in these and related areas. This was the 14th edition of the IPMU conference, which started in 1986 and has been held every two years in the following locations in Europe: Paris (1986), Urbino (1988), Paris (1990), Palma de Mallorca (1992), Paris (1994), Granada (1996), Paris (1998), Madrid (2000), Annecy (2002), Perugia (2004), Paris (2006), Malaga (2008), Dortmund (2010). Among the plenary speakers of past IPMU conferences there are three Nobel Prize winners: Kenneth Arrow, Daniel Kahneman, Ilya Prigogine.

The program of IPMU 2012 consisted of six invited talks together with 258 contributed papers, authored by researchers from 36 countries, including the regular track and 35 special sessions. The invited talks were given by the following distinguished researchers: Kalyanmoy Deb (Indian Institute of Technology Kanpur, India), Antonio Di Nola (University of Salerno, Italy), Christophe Marsala (Université Pierre et Marie Curie, France), Roman Slowinski (Poznan University of Technology, Poland), Tomohiro Takagi (Meiji University, Japan), Peter Wakker (Erasmus University, The Netherlands). Michio Sugeno received the Kampé de Fériet Award, granted every two years on the occasion of the IPMU conference, in view of his eminent research contributions to the handling of uncertainty through fuzzy measures and fuzzy integrals, and fuzzy control using fuzzy systems.

The success of such an event is mainly due to the hard work and dedication of a number of people and the collaboration of several institutions. We want to acknowledge the help of the members of the International Program Committee, the additional reviewers, the organizers of special sessions, and the volunteer students. All of them deserve many thanks for having helped to attain the goal of providing a balanced event with a high level of scientific exchange and a pleasant environment. A special mention is deserved by Silvia Angilella, Salvatore Corrente, Fabio Rindone, and Giuseppe Vaccarella, who contributed greatly to the organization of the conference and especially to the review process.

We acknowledge the use of the EasyChair conference system for the paper submission and review. We would also like to thank Alfred Hofmann and Leonie Kunz, and Springer, for providing continuous assistance and ready advice whenever needed.

May 2012

Salvatore Greco
Bernadette Bouchon-Meunier
Giulianella Coletti
Mario Fedrizzi
Benedetto Matarazzo
Ronald R. Yager

# Organization

## Conference Committee

### General Chair

Salvatore Greco                    University of Catania, Italy

### Co-chairs

Giulianella Coletti                University of Perugia, Italy
Mario Fedrizzi                     University of Trento, Italy
Benedetto Matarazzo                University of Catania, Italy

### Executive Directors

Bernadette Bouchon-Meunier         LIP6, Paris, France
Ronald R. Yager                    Iona College, USA

## Special Session Organizers

Alessandro Antonucci
Michal Baczynski
Edurne Barrenechea
Sebastiano Battiato
Jan Bazan
Abdelhamid Bouchachia
Humberto Bustine
David Carfi
Davide Ciucci
Jesus Chamorro
Giulianella Coletti
Didier Coquin
Alfredo Cuzzocrea
Giovanni Battista
 Dagnino
Didier Dubois
Fabrizio Durante
Zied Eloudi
Macarena Espinilla
Gisella Facchinetti
Javier Fernandez
Tommaso Flaminio
Giovanni Gallo

Roberto Ghiselli
 Ricci
Karina Gibert
Giovanni Giuffrida
Michel Grabisch
Przemyslaw
 Grzegorzewski
Maria Letizia Guerra
Francisco Herrera
Balasubramaniam
 Jayaram
Janusz Kacprzyk
Cengiz Kahraman
Cristophe Labreuche
Ioana Leustean
Edwin Lughofer
Enrico Marchioni
Nicolas Marin
Luis Martinez
Pedro Melo-Pinto
Radko Mesiar
Enrique Miranda
Antonio Moreno

Moamar Sayed
 Mouchaweh
Guillermo
 Navarro-Arribas
Vesa Niskanen
Miguel Pagola
Olga Pons
Ana Pradera
Anca Ralescu
Daniel Sanchez
Miquel Sanchez-Marré
Rudolf Seising
Andrzej Skowron
Dominik Slezak
Hung Son Nguyen
Carlo Sempi
Luciano Stefanini
Eulalia Szmidt
Marco Elio Tabacchi
Vicenc Torra
Gracian Trivino
Lionel Valet
Aida Valls

# International Program Committee

J. Aczel (Canada)
J. Bezdek (USA)
P. Bonissone (USA)
G. Chen (China)
V. Cross (USA)
B. De Baets (Belgium)
T. Denoeux (France)
M. Detyniecki (France)
A. Di Nola (Italy)
D. Dubois (France)
F. Esteva (Spain)
J. Fodor (Hungary)
S. Galichet (France)
P. Gallinari (France)
M.A. Gil (Spain)
F. Gomide (Brazil)
M. Grabisch (France)
S. Grossberg (USA)
P. Hajek
  (Czech Republic)

L. Hall (USA)
F. Herrera (Spain)
K. Hirota (Japan)
F. Hoffmann (Germany)
J. Kacprzyk (Poland)
A. Kandel (USA)
J. Keller (USA)
F. Klawonn (Germany)
E.P. Klement (Austria)
L. Koczy (Hungary)
V. Kreinovich (USA)
R. Kruse (Germany)
H. Larsen (Denmark)
M.-J. Lesot (France)
T. Martin (UK)
J. Mendel (USA)
R. Mesiar (Slovakia)
S. Moral (Spain)
H.T. Nguyen (USA)
S. Ovchinnikov (USA)

G. Pasi (Italy)
W. Pedrycz (Canada)
V. Piuri (Italy)
O. Pivert (France)
H. Prade (France)
A. Ralescu (USA)
D. Ralescu (USA)
M. Ramdani (Maroc)
E. Ruspini (Spain)
S. Sandri (Brasil)
M. Sato (Japan)
G. Shafer (USA)
P. Shenoy (USA)
P. Sobrevilla (Spain)
M. Sugeno (Japan)
E. Szmidt (Poland)
S. Termini (Italy)
I.B. Turksen (Canada)
S. Zadrozny (Poland)

We thank the precious support of all the referees, which helped to improve the scientific quality of the papers submitted to the conference:

Daniel Abril
Tofigh Allahviranloo
Cecilio Angulo
Alessandro Antonucci
Luca Anzilli
Raouia Ayachi
Michal Baczynski
Valentina Emilia Balas
Rosangela Ballini
Adrian Ban
Mohua Banerjee
Carlos D. Barranco
Sebastiano Battiato
Jan Bazan
Benjamin Bedregal
Gleb Beliakov
Nahla Ben Amor
Sarah Ben Amor
Alessio Benavoli

Ilke Bereketli
Veronica Biazzo
Isabelle Bloch
Fernando Bobillo
Andrea Boccuto
Gloria Bordogna
Silvia Bortot
Imen Boukhris
Juergen Branke
Werner Brockmann
Antoon Bronselaer
Matteo Brunelli
Alberto Bugarín
Humberto Bustince
Tomasa Calvo
Domenico Candeloro
Andrea Capotorti
Marta Cardin
Fabrizio Caruso

Bice Cavallo
Nihan Çetin Demirel
Emre Cevikcan
Mihir Chakraborty
Davide Ciucci
Lavinia Corina Ciungu
Vincent Clivillé
Giulianella Coletti
Dante Conti
Didier Coquin
Giorgio Corani
Chris Cornelis
Miguel Couceiro
Pedro Couto
Alfredo Cuzzocrea
Nuzillard Danielle
Bernard De Baets
Gert De Cooman
Yves De Smet

David Picado Muino
Olivier Pivert
Olga Pons
Henri Prade
Ana Pradera
Mahardhika Pratama
Giovanni Puglisi
Antonio Punzo
Barbara Pękala
Anca Ralescu
Fahimeh Ramezani
Daniele Ravì
Mohammad Rawashdeh
Renata Reiser
Magdalena Rencova
Silja Renooij
Hana Rezankova
Angela Ricciardello
Maria Rifqi
J. Tinguaro Rodríguez
Rosa M. Rodríguez
Antoine Rolland
Nils Rosemann
Rafael Rumi
Nobusumi Sagara
Antonio Salmeron

Giuseppe Sanfilippo
Jose Santamaria
José Antonio Sanz
   Delgado
Moamar
   Sayed-Mouchaweh
Florence Sedes
Rudolf Seising
Carlo Sempi
Jesus Serrano-Guerrero
Prakash Shenoy
Marek Sikora
Andrzej Skowron
Damjan Skulj
Dominik Slezak
Zdenko Sonicki
Luca Spada
Anna Stachowiak
Ivana Stajner-Papuga
Daniel Stamate
Luciano Stefanini
Jaroslaw Stepaniuk
Martin Stepnicka
Marcin Szczuka
Miquel Sànchez-Marrè
Marco Elio Tabacchi

Settimo Termini
Vicenc Torra
Joan Torrens
Krzysztof Trawinski
Gracian Trivino
Alessandra Trunfio
Mayumi Ueda
Ziya Ulukan
Alp Ustundag
İrem Uçal Sarı
Lionel Valet
Aida Valls
Arthur Van Camp
Linda Van Der Gaag
Barbara Vantaggi
Jirina Vejnarova
Thomas Vetterlein
Maria-Amparo Vila
Doretta Vivona
Marcin Wolski
Yu-Lung Wu
Slawomir Zadrozny
Calogero Zarba
Pawel Zielinski
Michele Zito

# Table of Contents – Part IV

## Fuzzy Uncertainty in Economics and Business

## New Trends in De Finetti's Approach

## Fuzzy Measures and Integrals

## Multicriteria Decision Making

## Uncertainty in Privacy and Security

## Uncertainty in the Spirit of Pietro Benvenuti

## Coopetition

# Game Theory

# Probabilistic Approach

# Supplier Selection Decisions: A Fuzzy Logic Model Based on Quality Aspects of Delivery

Margaret F. Shipley and Gary L. Stading

University of Houston Downtown
326 North Main Street
Houston, Texas 77002
{Shipleym,stadingg}@uhd.edu

**Abstract.** This paper presents a decision making model to address uncertainty in requirement planning. The model proposes a DSS to evaluate the quality of suppliers where quality is categorized into three primary areas dealing with delivery specifics, front office quality, and support specific quality. The application of the model is restricted to delivery specifics with two quality criteria illustrated of on-time delivery and accuracy of shipping. Results of the model provide ranking of suppliers based on belief that each supplier can provide average or greater performance. Extension of the model will determine overall fuzzy-set based rankings based upon all considered quality parameters.

**Keywords:** Fuzzy Set Theory, Fuzzy Probability, Supplier Selection.

## 1 Introduction

Various applications of fuzzy logic based modeling for supply chain management have been utilized in areas of inventory, purchasing, and specifically quality management. Inventory modeling traces back to 1999 when Lui, [1] proposed a fuzzy model for partial backording models. Little was done with inventory considerations until fully five years later when inventory discounting considered the buyer-seller relationships [2], and location aspects for inventory control became fuzzy considerations [3]. Supply chain decisions for integrated just-in-time inventory systems recognized the fuzzy nature of annual demand and production rates as being no longer statistically based. The signed distance, a ranking method for fuzzy numbers, was used to estimate fuzzy total cost of JIT production. Such a fuzzy-set based method derived the optimal buyer's quantity and number of lots from the vendor [4]. Some standard OR decision making models as fuzzy set-based models appeared when fuzzy programming was used for optimal product mix based on ABC analysis [5], fuzzy multi-objective linear programming minimized total production and transportation costs, the number of rejected items and total delivery time as related to labor and budget constraints [6], and fuzzy goal programming considered supply chain management from the perspective of activity-based costing with mathematically derived optimization for evaluating performance of the value –chain relationship [7].

S. Greco et al. (Eds.): IPMU 2012, Part IV, CCIS 300, pp. 1–9, 2012.

The attainment of quality further led to attempts to balance production processes of assembly lines with precise and fuzzy goals as an instrument and product for measuring, displaying and controlling industrial process variables [5]. Manufacturing processes as related to business logistics looked at the data itself as fuzzy in Quality Function Deployment's relationship to quality customer service [8]. Considering different quality standards in a supply chain network a fuzzy neural approach was utilized to suggest the appropriate adjustment of product quantity from various suppliers [9].

Overall, the fuzzy Analytic Hierarchy Process (AHP) has become the most widely used SCM decision making modeling process (see [10],[11],[12],[13], for example). Che [10] looked at both production and delivery where each component in the supply chain was weighted using fuzzy AHP based on the theory that a supply chain is not a balanced system but incurs processing damages or delivery losses. Cigolini and Rossi [14] recognized that fuzzy sets had been used in inventory planning, to improve organizational effectiveness and to evaluate suppliers but their contribution focused upon the partnerships within the chain of both design and management policies.

Bevilacqua and Petroni used linguistic variables provided by three decision makers for 9 criteria upon which suppliers would be rated. The linguistic variables were translated to triangular numbers by an algorithm called the Fuzzy Suitability Index (FSI) which aggregated rankings and multiplied, by weight, each criterion [15]. Five years later another fuzzy expression for importance weights, and a fuzzy preference index were aggregated to rank order suppliers [16]. In the same time period, supplier selection was approached from a rule-based perspective, again considering that these decisions are dynamic and ill-structured. The approach selected was fuzzy associated rule mining from the database for supplier assessment [17].

Ultimately, the question is whether the fuzzy logic-based approaches are effective for supplier selection. Sevkli [18] in his comparison of a recognized crisp ELECTRE model versus a fuzzy ELECTRE model, reached the conclusion that fuzzy sets for multi-criteria supplier selection decisions is superior.

## 2     Methodology

### 2.1     Description of Survey

A pilot study was used to identify a filtered list of potential attributes buyers evaluated when selecting their suppliers. The pilot study collected data through initial questionnaires with subsequent follow-up discussions. This information was then used to build a survey instrument that was sent to a large industry data base of buyers of electronic parts. Since the purpose of this paper is a DSS for ranking suppliers based on quality aspects important to the buyers, the following modeling application (section 3) will be based on specific questions (numbered 20-32) in the survey instrument. Delivery specific questions related to on-time performance, availability of inventory, shipping accuracy and return authorization process were queried in 20,21,22, and 27. Front office quality was assessed based on quote completeness, credit and payment terms, cancelled/non-returnable letters, and contract processing (questions 23,25,26 and 28). Finally, support specific quality assessment dealt with customized processing, knowledgeable specialists, technical design services, e-business services and sales management (24, 29,30,31 and 32).

## 2.2     Fuzzy Model Development

The model utilizes fuzzy set theory basic concepts and extension principles with fuzzy probabilities that determine a belief-weighted score for each criterion.

### 2.2.1     Fuzzy Logic Basics

Fuzzy logic addresses the ambiguity of data and uncertainty in this decision making situation, where a fuzzy subset A of a set X is a function of X into [0,1]. For a brief foundation in the basics, see [19],[20], [21], [22]. While a new class of implication operators has been proposed [23], the more traditionally utilized fuzzy operations are used in this research. Thus, if A and B denote two fuzzy sets, then the intersection, union, and complement are defined by:

$$A \cap B = \Sigma\, \gamma_i / x_i \text{ where } \gamma_i = \text{Min } \{\alpha_i, \beta_i\}$$

$$A \cup B = \Sigma\, \gamma_i / x_i \text{ where } \gamma_i = \text{Max } \{\alpha_i, \beta_i\}$$

$$\neg A = \Sigma\, \gamma_i / x_i \text{ where } \gamma_i = 1 - \alpha_i$$

and it is assumed that $B = \Sigma\, \beta_i / x_i$. For a general discussion of the fuzzy logic concepts above, see [24], [25], [26], [27].

Extension principles (see [28], [21] and [29] ) often guide the computations when dealing with fuzzy sets. Letting $f$ be a function from X into Y, with Y as any set and A as above, then $f$ can be extended to fuzzy subsets of X by:

$$f(A) = \Sigma_y\, u_{f(A)}(y) / y \text{ where}$$

$$u_{f(A)}(y) = \text{Max } A(x)$$
$$x \varepsilon f^{-1}(y)$$

Thus, $f(A)$ is a fuzzy subset of Y. In particular, if $f$ is a mapping from a Cartesian product such as X x Y to any set, Z, then $f$ can be extended to objects of the form (A,B) where A and B are fuzzy subsets of X and Y by:

$$f(A,B) = \Sigma\, u_{f(A,B)} (z) / z, \text{ where}$$

$$u_{f(A,B)}(z) = \text{Max } \text{Min } \{A(x), B(x)\}.$$
$$(x,y) \varepsilon f^{-1}(z)$$

The above formula shows how binary operations may be extended to fuzzy sets. Furthermore, a fuzzy set P whose elements all lie on the interval [0,1] can be expressed as a fuzzy probability.

### 2.2.2     Fuzzy Probability Distributions

Consider a set of n fuzzy probabilities each having r elements, $\quad p_i = \displaystyle\sum_{j=1}^{r} a_{ij} / p_{ij} \quad$ for i

= 1, 2, ..., n, where $a_{ij}$ denotes the degree of belief that a possible value of $p_i$ is $p_{ij}$.

Then $(p_1, p_2,...p_n)$ constitutes a finite fuzzy probability distribution if and only if there are n-tuples $p_i$, i = 1,2,...,n such that $\sum_{j=1}^{n} p_i = 1$.

In order to qualify as a finite fuzzy probability distribution, each fuzzy probability in the distribution must have the same number of elements (some of the a's may be zero), and these elements should be ordered in the sense that the sum of the elements in each specific position must equal one. So the n-tuples $(p_{ij})$, i=1,2,...,n form probability distributions in the crisp sense. This type of probability distribution can be transformed such that the resulting distribution has entropy at least as great as the original [30].

### 2.2.3    Fuzzy Expected Value

A version of fuzzy expected values was first used by Zebda [29] when he defined $Q_{ijk} = \Sigma\ \alpha_{ijk} / a_k$ as the fuzzy probability that if we are at a state i and make a decision j, we go to state k. Associated with this are fuzzy benefits $B_{ijk}$ where $B_{ijk} = \Sigma\ \beta_{ijk} / b_k'$

Then the averaged benefit is defined by $E\ (B_{ijk}) = \Sigma\ c_{ijl} / b_l$ where

$c_{ijl} = $ Max $\qquad\qquad$ Min $\ \{\alpha_{ijk}, \beta_{ijk}\}$
$\quad (a_1,...a_p, b_{1'},...b_p')\varepsilon f^{-1}(b_l)$ k

For $b_l\ =\quad \Sigma_k\ a_x\ b_x$ if $\Sigma_k\ a_x = 1$ and 0 otherwise.

Here, $f(a_1, ...,a_p, b_1',....,b_p') = \Sigma\ a_x b_x'$

### 2.2.4    Algorithm

1. For each supplier, $A_i$, assign a score, $s_{ki}$ (k=1,2,3),   defining Average $(s_{1i})$, Above Average $(s_{2i})$, and   Excellent $(s_{3i})$ ratings.  Then supplier rating, $s_{Ai}$ , is given by:

$$s_{Aki} = \Sigma\ \tau_{ki} / s_{ki} \text{ for all } A_i \text{ where } \tau_{ki} = 1 \qquad (i=1,2,...,m \text{ and } k= 1,2,3)$$

2. Define fuzzy probability, $Q_{A\ ki}$, for each $A_i$ in terms of each $s_{ki}$ as:

$Q_{A\ k\ j} = \Sigma\ \alpha_{kij} / a_{kij}$ for all $s_{ki}$   where each $\alpha_{kij}$ represents belief in the probability $a_{kij}$ that $A_i$ will be scored $s_{ki}$. (k=1,2,3; i =1,2,...,m and j = 1,2,...,n)

3. Consider all $a_{kij}$ such that $\Sigma\ a_{kij} = 1.00$ for some set H of  k's. We assign automatically, $a_{kij} = 0$ for k$\notin$ H.

4. Compute $b_{il} = \{$ $\qquad\Sigma\ a_{kij}\ s_{ki}$ if $\Sigma\ a_{kij} = 1$
$\qquad\qquad\qquad 0 \qquad\qquad$ otherwise

(k=1,2,3) and p = distinct no. of $\Sigma\ a_{kij} = 1$

5. Determine $c_{il} = $ Min $\{\tau_{ki}, \alpha_{kij}\}$ for all $\alpha_{kij} \neq 0$   where $c_{il}$ is degree of belief that expected value is $b_{il}$; $1 \leq l \leq$ p

6. Defuzzify the expected activity time to yield   $E(t_A) = \Sigma\ c_{il}\ b_{il} / \Sigma\ c_{il}$

# 3    Application

To illustrate the model, we consider the operational parameters for Delivery Specific Questions (20, 21, 22 and 27) for hypothetical 4 suppliers A,B,C, and D. The model considers the uncertainty of the person providing the rating scaled to some range such as [1,5] or use of linguistic variables such as Poor, Below Average, Average, Above Average and Excellent. Assuming that no Poor, or Below Average on-time supplier should be considered, we begin the algorithm, by defining fuzzy probabilities for Supplier A as:

$$Q_{A\,1} = 0.7/0.3 + 0.9/0.4 \qquad \text{for } s_{11} = \text{Average}$$
$$Q_{A\,2} = 0.8/0.4 + 0.5/0.3 \qquad \text{for } s_{21} = \text{Above Average}$$
$$Q_{A\,3} = 0.6/0.2 + 0.7/0.3 \qquad \text{for } s_{31} = \text{Excellent}$$

Here $s_A = 1.0/3 + 1.0/4 + 1.0/5$.

Then beliefs and the corresponding probabilities are respectively defined as:

$$\alpha_{11} = 0.7 \quad \alpha_{12} = 0.9 \qquad\qquad a_{11} = 0.3 \quad a_{12} = 0.4$$

$$\alpha_{21} = 0.8 \quad \alpha_{22} = 0.5 \qquad\qquad a_{21} = 0.4 \quad a_{22} = 0.3$$

$$\alpha_{31} = 0.6 \quad \alpha_{32} = 0.7 \qquad\qquad a_{31} = 0.2 \quad a_{32} = 0.3$$

According to Step 3, all combinations are considered for each ranking outcome that sums to one which yields:

$$a_{11} + a_{21} + a_{32} = 0.3 + 0.4 + 0.3 = 1.00$$
$$a_{12} + a_{21} + a_{31} = 0.4 + 0.4 + 0.2 = 1.00$$
$$a_{12} + a_{22} + a_{32} = 0.4 + 0.3 + 0.3 = 1.00$$

Looking at these values, it can be observed that possible n-tuples are (0.3,0.4,0.3), (0.4,0.4,0.2), and (0.4,0.3,0.3). Intuitively, we assess belief in each triplet at its minimum value. For A, the belief in each triplet (0.7,0.8,0.7), (0.9,0.8,0.6) and (0.9,0.5,0.7) is, respectively, 0.7, 0.6, and 0.5. For a definitive expected on-time delivery performance score, we need to incorporate expected values of all triplets with corresponding belief measures .

Following Step 4, a weighted measure  for each of these three combinations, is derived. Although any score can be assigned to the linguistic variables, the range [1,5] was used in the survey, so 3 can be designated as "Average", 4 as "Above average" and 5 as "Excellent" such that the following is determined.

$$b_{11} = (0.3)(3) + (0.4)(4) + (0.3)(5) = 4.0$$
$$b_{12} = (0.4)(3) + (0.4)(4) + (0.2)(5) = 3.8$$
$$b_{13} = (0.4)(3) + (0.3)(4) + (0.3)(5) = 3.9$$

The degree of belief in the expected on-time delivery then assessed according to Step 5 is:

$$c_{11} = Min \{0.7, 1; 0.8, 1; 0.7, 1\} = 0.7$$
$$c_{12} = Min \{ 0.9, 1; 0.8, 1; 0.6, 1\} = 0.6$$
$$c_{13} = Min \{0.9, 1; 0.5, 1; 0.7, 1\} = 0.5$$

where $s = 1.0/3 + 1.0/4 + 1.0/5$ for average, above average and excellent in $[1,5]$.
Using Step 6, we defuzzify the expected time such that:

$$E(A) = [(0.7)(4)+(0.6)(3.8)+(0.5)(3.9)] / [(0.7+0.6+0.5)] \quad = 3.91$$

Continuing for the three other suppliers we define:

$$Q_{B\,1} = 0.6/0.4 + 0.7/0.3 \qquad \text{for } s_{11} = \text{Average}$$
$$Q_{B\,2} = 0.4/0.6 + 0.5/0.7 \qquad \text{for } s_{21} = \text{Above Average}$$
$$Q_{B\,3} = 0.9/0.1 + 0.7/0.3 \qquad \text{for } s_{31} = \text{Excellent}$$

$$Q_{C\,1} = 0.1/0.1 + 0.1/0.2 \qquad \text{for } s_{11} = \text{Average}$$
$$Q_{C\,2} = 0.2/0.6 + 0.1/0.3 \qquad \text{for } s_{21} = \text{Above Average}$$
$$Q_{C\,3} = 0.8/0.6 + 0.9/0.7 \qquad \text{for } s_{31} = \text{Excellent}$$

$$Q_{D\,1} = 0.3/0.8 + 0.5/0.7 \qquad \text{for } s_{11} = \text{Average}$$
$$Q_{D\,2} = 0.6/0.1 + 0.7/0.2 \qquad \text{for } s_{21} = \text{Above Average}$$
$$Q_{D\,3} = 0.4/0.2 + 0.3/0.1 \qquad \text{for } s_{31} = \text{Excellent}$$

It should be noted that membership in these performance measures may sometimes be zero then the zero case becomes part of the n-tuple calculations. For example, Supplier B combinations over the set of Average, Above Average and Excellent on-time delivery are: (0.4,0.6); (0.3,0.7); (0.7,0.3); and (0.3,0.6,0.1) which with the addition of the zero case equate respectively to: (0.4,0.6,0.0), (0.3,0.7,0.0), (0.0,0.7,0.3), and, (0.3,0.6,0.1) and beliefs (0.6,0.4,0.4), (0.7,0.5,0.5), (0.5,0.5,0.7), and of course (0.7,0.4,0.9), respectively. The resulting belief-weighted expected value for B would be 3.67.

Based on the scores from the experts and allowing zero to be supplied by the decision maker the four suppliers would score as follows based on $[1.5]$:

Fuzzy Probability Scores for On-Time Delivery Performance

| Supplier | Mean Score |
|----------|-----------|
| A | 3.91 |
| B | 3.67 |
| C | 3.68 |
| D | 3.10 |

By using the fuzzy probability approach achieving Average, Above Average or Excellent on-time delivery performance provides a better ranking than by using simple means. Based on the expert opinions of users and decision makers, Supplier A would be selected on this one criterion; Supplier D would definitely not be selected.

## 4     Discussion

However, delivery quality is not measured by only one criterion so each supplier must be ranked on the criteria specified in section 2.1. To continue the illustration,  we consider shipping accuracy as well as on-time performance with results given below:

| Supplier | On-time Delivery | Shipping Accuracy |
|----------|------------------|-------------------|
| A        | 3.91             | 3.37              |
| B        | 3.67             | 3.7               |
| C        | 3.68             | 3.6               |
| D        | 3.1              | 3.906             |

The decision maker can rule out those with high and low scores and compromise with Suppliers B and C. But this overlooks the strength of Supplier A for on-time delivery and now Supplier D for shipping accuracy. Instead, a method needs to be developed to combine these scores. A simple average would yield: Supplier A scores 3.64,Supplier B scores 3.675.Supplier C scores 3.64 and Supplier D scores 3.503, such that  Supplier B would be selected. But, again it becomes obvious that a simple mean has its limitations. Instead, the decision maker may consider one criterion more important than another. While this can be solved with a standard scoring model, the goals of the decision maker would not be as obvious.

## 5     Future Research

The database described in section 2.1  is rich in that it includes multiple dimensions of quality to be assessed. Also, the respondents were asked for not only the score of each supplier based on scaling Poor, Below Average, Average, Above Average and Excellent but also the importance of each criterion for each supplier. Thus, the experts provide the beliefs in each supplier's quality but also weight the criteria. These aspects will be combined when the entire database is considered. In addition, instead of focusing solely upon the delivery quality parameters all quality parameters also described in section 2.1 will be considered. A fuzzy set based scoring model is being developed to handle this very large decision making problem.

## References

1. Lui, B.: Fuzzy criterion models for inventory systems with partial backorders. Annals of Operations Research 87(1-4), 117–126 (1999)
2. Das, K., Roy, T.K., Maiti, M.: Buyer-seller fuzzy inventory model for a deteriorating item with discount. International Journal of Systems Science 35(8), 457–466 (2004)

3. Usenik, J., Bogata, M.: A fuzzy set approach for a location-inventory model. Transportation Planning & Technology 28(6), 447–464 (2005)
4. Pan, J.C.-H., Yang, M.-F.: Integrated inventory models with fuzzy annual demand and fuzzy production rate in a supply chain. International Journal of Production Research 46(3), 753–770 (2008)
5. Kara, Y., Gokcen, H., Atasagun, Y.: Balancing parallel assembly lines with precise and fuzzy goals. International Journal of Production Research 48(6), 1685–1703 (2010)
6. Liang, T.-F.: Integrating production-transportation planning decision with fuzzy multiple goals in supply chains. International Journal of Production 46(6), 1477–1494 (2008)
7. Tsai, W.-H., Hung, S.-J.: A fuzzy goal programming approach for green supply chain optimization under activity based costing and performance evaluation with a value-chain structure. International Journal of Production Research 47(18), 4991–5017 (2009)
8. Shu, M.H., Wu, H.-C.: Measuring the manufacturing process yield based on fuzzy data. International Journal of Production Research 48(6), 1627–1638 (2010)
9. Lau, H.C.W., Hui, I.K., Chan, F.T.S., Wong, C.W.Y.: Monitoring the supply of products in a supply chain environment: a fuzzy neural approach. Expert Systems 19(4), 235–243 (2002)
10. Che, Z.H.: Using fuzzy analytic hierarchy process and particle swarm optimization for balanced and defective supply chain problems considering WEEE/RoHS directives. International Journal of Production Research 46(11), 3355–3381 (2010)
11. Sen, C.G., Sen, S., Basligil, H.: Pre-selection of suppliers through an integrated fuzzy analytic hierarchy process and max-min methodology. International Journal of Production Research 48(6), 1603–1625 (2010)
12. Chan, F.T.S., Kumar, N., Tiwari, M.K., Lau, H.C., Choy, K.L.: Global supplier selection: a fuzzy AHP approach. International Journal of Production Research 46(14), 3825–3857 (2008)
13. Chan, F.T.S., Kumar, N., Choy, K.L.: Decision-making approach for the distribution centre location problem in a supply chain network using the fuzzy-based hierarchical concept. Proceedings of the Institute of Mechanical Engineers-Part B- Engineering Manufacture 221(4), 725–739 (2007)
14. Cigolini, R., Rossi, T.: Evaluating supply chain integration: A case study using fuzzy logic. Production Planning & Control 19(3), 242–255 (2008)
15. Bevilacqua, M., Petroni, A.: From traditional purchasing to supplier management: A fuzzy logic-based approach to supplier selection. International Journal of Logistics: Research and Applications 5(3), 235–255 (2002)
16. Bayrak, M.Y., Celebi, N., Taskin, H.: A fuzzy approach for supplier selection. Production Planning & Control 18(1), 54–63 (2007)
17. Jain, V., Wadhwa, S., Deshmukh, S.G.: Supplier selection using fuzzy association rules mining approach. International Journal of Production Research 45(6), 1323–1353 (2007)
18. Sevkli, M.: An application of the fuzzy ELECTRE method for supplier selection. International Journal of Production Research 48(12), 3393–3405 (2010)
19. Zadeh, L.: Generalized Theory of Uncertainty (GTU)-Principal Concepts and Ideas. Computational Statistics & Data Analysis 51(1), 15046 (2007)
20. Bellman, R., Zadeh, L.: Decision making in a fuzzy environment. Management Science 17, 141–164 (1970)
21. Dubois, D., Prade, H.: Fuzzy Sets and Systems: Theory and Applications. Academic Press, New York (1980)
22. Freeling, A.: Fuzzy sets and decision analysis. IEEE Transactions on Systems, Man, and Cybernetics SMC-10, 1341–1354 (1980)

23. Yager, R.: On Some Classes of Implication Operators and Their Role in Approximate Reasoning. Information Sciences 167(1-4), 193–216 (2004)
24. Kaufmann, A., Gupta, M.: An introduction to fuzzy sets arithmetic. Nosfrand Reinhold Co., New York (1985)
25. Klir, G., Folger, T.: Fuzzy Sets, Uncertainty and Information. Prentice Hall, Englewood Cliffs (1988)
26. Zadeh, L.: Fuzzy sets. Information and Control 8, 338–353 (1965)
27. Zadeh, L.: Fuzzy logic and approximate reasoning. Syntheses 30, 407–428 (1975)
28. Dubois, D., Prade, H.: Decision making under fuzziness. In: Gupta, M., Ragade, R., Yager, R. (eds.) Advances in Fuzzy Set Theory and Applications. North Holland, Amsterdam (1979)
29. Zebda, A.: The investigation of cost variances: A fuzzy set theory approach. Decision Sciences 15, 359–389 (1984)
30. Yager, R., Kreinovich, V.: Entropy Conserving Probability Transforms and the Entailment Principle. Fuzzy Sets & Systems 158(12), 1397–1405 (2007)

# Modified Net Present Value under Uncertainties: An Approach Based on Fuzzy Numbers and Interval Arithmetic

Antonio Carlos Sampaio Filho[1], Marley Vellasco[2], and Ricardo Tanscheit[2]

[1] Petróleo Brasileiro S.A., Rio de Janeiro, Brazil
acsampaio@petrobras.com.br
[2] Pontifícia Universidade Católica do Rio de Janeiro, Rio de Janeiro, Brazil
{marley,ricardo}@ele.puc-rio.br

**Abstract.** This paper presents an alternative approach to capital budgeting, named fuzzy modified net present value (*fuzzy MNPV*) method, for evaluation of investment projects under uncertainty. Triangular fuzzy numbers are used to represent uncertainty of cash flows and of reinvestment, financing and risk-adjusted discount rates. Due to the complexity of the calculations involved, a new financial function for MS-Excel has been developed (*MNPVfuzzy*). To illustrate the use of the model and of the function, numerical examples are supplied. Results show that the proposed method is more advantageous and simpler to use than other methods for evaluation of investment under uncertainty.

**Keywords:** Capital Budgeting, Modified Net Present Value, Triangular Fuzzy Numbers, Interval Arithmetic.

## 1 Introduction

The evaluation of projects, involving the technological innovations and the expansion of the production capacity, constitutes one of the most critical areas of decision-making in companies. Therefore, increasingly sophisticated models for capital budgeting have been developed.

In the last decades the net present value (*NPV*) and the internal rate of return (*IRR*) have replaced the old payback method [1]. There has also been an increasing academic interest in the modified internal rate of return (*MIRR*) [2-4] and the modified net present value (*MNPV*) methods, which make use of different assumptions to the cost of capital of companies [5], [6].

An essential assumption common to the techniques of *NPV, IRR, MIRR* and *MNPV* is that it is possible to foresee investments and operational expenses, as well as revenues and net incomes throughout the useful life of the projects. The estimates must be made within a small error range in order to allow the comparison of alternatives, including short term and long term investment projects. Moreover, capital budgeting techniques also require estimates of the discount rates that are applicable through the entire duration of the project.

S. Greco et al. (Eds.): IPMU 2012, Part IV, CCIS 300, pp. 10–19, 2012.
© Springer-Verlag Berlin Heidelberg 2012

Alternatives to those deterministic approaches, such as the Monte Carlo me-thod and, more recently, methods based on fuzzy sets concepts, have been often used to deal with uncertainty in capital budgeting.

This paper proposes an alternative method for capital budgeting under uncertainty, where the uncertain parameters are specified as triangular fuzzy numbers (TFNs). It takes as a basis the modified net present value (*MNPV*) [5], which provides an alter-native structure to project analysis when the company's financing and reinvestment opportunity rates are different.

## 2     The Modified Net Present Value Method

The conventional *NPV* method has some deficiencies which can lead to interpretation errors in companies' investment decisions. These deficiencies are related, mainly, to the fact that the *NPV* method is based on the following assumptions:

- intermediate cash inflows of the project are reinvested at a rate of return equal to the risk-adjusted discount rate (*RDAR*) of the project, instead of the reinvestment opportunity rate of the company;
- cash outflows, after the initial investment, are discounted at the *RDAR*, instead of at the financing rate (weighted average cost of capital – *WACC*) of the company.

These problems have been investigated and some authors have proposed alternative models to the conventional *NPV* method, known as modified *NPV* methods. In prac-tice, these methods are improved versions of the traditional *NPV* method, eliminating problems regarding the reinvestment rate, and different versions are known by differ-ent names and acronyms [5], [6].

Despite being more recent, the model proposed in [6] is a simplification of the one presented in [5]. The latter is used in this paper, since it is a more comprehen-sive proposal and totally compatible with the *MIRR* method proposed in [2]. The use of financing and reinvestment rates is more suitable for analysis, since in practice there are differences between those rates (they are associated to the return of institu-tions that do financial intermediation).

According to the McClure and Girma [5], the general equation of the modified net present value is:

$$MNPV = \frac{\sum_{t=1}^{n} CF_{it}(1+k_{rr})^{n-t}}{(1+k_{radr})^{n}} - \sum_{t=0}^{n} \frac{CF_{ot}}{(1+k_{wacc})^{t}} \tag{1}$$

where, $CF_{it}$ is the net cash inflow at the end of period $t$, $n$ is the lifetime of the project, $k_{rr}$ is the reinvestment rate, $k_{radr}$ is the risk-adjusted discount rate (*RDAR*), $CF_{ot}$ is the net cash outflow at the end of the period $t$, and $k_{wacc}$ is the financing rate (*WACC*).

The numerator of the first term in the right-hand side of equation (1) is the sum of all cash inflows capitalized at the reinvestment rate until the last period ($n$) of the project. This sum, called terminal value (*TV*), is discounted at the risk-adjusted discount rate until period zero. The second term in the right-hand side is the sum of all the cash outflows discounted at the financing rate until period zero of the project. This sum is called present value (PV). Thus, TV and PV can be written as:

$$TV = \sum_{t=1}^{n} CF_{it}(1+k_{rr})^{n-t} \tag{2}$$

$$PV = \sum_{t=0}^{n} \frac{CF_{ot}}{(1+k_{wacc})^{t}} \tag{3}$$

With cash outflows and cash inflows concentrated at periods zero (PV) and n (TV), respectively, the MNPV becomes:

$$MNPV = \frac{TV}{(1+k_{radr})^{n}} - PV \tag{4}$$

The decision criterion associated to the MNPV method is identical to that of the traditional NPV: accept projects if the MNPV is positive and reject projects if the MNPV is negative. A MNPV equal to zero indicates indifference.

**Example 1.** Consider the financing problem [7] of the net cash flows associated with an investment project for oil extraction. The project can be defined as an outgoing cash flow of $1,600 in the year zero for the installation of a larger pump in an operating oil well. The new pump allows the additional extraction of $10,000 in oil in year 1. However, as a consequence of this installation, the capacity of the well is partially depleted within this year. As a result, the production in year 2 decreases by $10,000 in oil. The net cash flows are –$1,600, $10,000 and –$10,000 in years 0, 1 and 2, respectively. Admitting that the project is of low risk and that the reinvestment rate ($k_{rr}$), financing rate ($k_{wacc}$) and risk adjusted discount rate ($k_{radr}$) are of 12%, 10% and 5% per year, respectively, the MNPV is 294.27. As this value is positive, the project should be approved. On the other hand, the use of the conventional NPV method results in an NPV equal to –$1,146.49, which would lead to the rejection of the project. The MNPV calculation is shown in Table 1.

**Table 1.** Calculation of the MNPV for the oil pump problem

| | Year | | |
|---|---|---|---|
| | 0 | 1 | 2 |
| Net Cash Flows | −1,600.00 | 10,000.00 | −10,000.00 |
| Cash Outflows @ 10% | −8,264.46 | | |
| Cash Inflows @ 12% | | | 11,200.00 |
| Present Value | −9,864.46 | Terminal Value | 11,200.00 |
| Risk-adjusted discount rate: 5% | | | |
| $MNPV = 11,200/(1+0.05)^{2} - 9,846.46 = 294,27$ | | | |

# 3    The MNPV Method under Uncertainties

In equation (1) it is assumed that the cash flows, the reinvestment rate, the financing rate and the risk-adjusted discount rate are precisely established. However, it is not easy to determine the precise value of those parameters, and unforeseen variations may even make impractical a project initially considered as of high return.

In traditional modeling of capital budgeting problems, uncertain parameters are generally represented by probability distributions. This approach is appropriate to represent the statistical nature of uncertainties and the Monte Carlo method is often used for practical calculations. However, there are many situations where statistical data cannot be established and the parameters are determined subjectively. Moreover, the uncertainty does not always come from the parameters' random character. For example, in the sentence "this project will provide a high return in the next 10 or 15 years", different interpretations of the term "high" and the uncertainty on the useful life of the project can be a source of ambiguity and imprecision.

In such situations, modeling of capital budgeting problems can be improved by the use of an alternative approach. Fuzzy sets concepts [8] are very useful for dealing with uncertain or imprecise parameters in the form of linguistic variables. Fuzzy numbers are especially useful for the quantification of imprecise or ambiguous information. Several authors have investigated the use of fuzzy sets in decision making under uncertainty and a wide revision of the literature can be found in [9], [10].

## 3.1    The *MNPV* with Fuzzy Cash Flows and Fuzzy Rates

Let's assume that cash flows, reinvestment and financing rates and the risk-adjusted discount rate of an investment project under uncertainty are represented by triangular fuzzy numbers. Such fuzzy numbers take the form shown in Fig. 1, where a hypothetical α-cut is also shown.

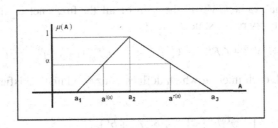

**Fig. 1.** Triangular fuzzy number

An L-R fuzzy number can be expressed as:

$$A^\alpha = [a^{l(\alpha)}, a^{r(\alpha)}] \tag{5}$$

where, $l(\alpha)$ represents the line segment to the left of the fuzzy number and $r(\alpha)$, the line segment to the right.

The α-cut notation is also used very often. In this:

$$\frac{a^{l(\alpha)} - a_1}{a_2 - a_1} = \alpha, \quad \frac{a_3 - a^{r(\alpha)}}{a_3 - a2} = \alpha \tag{6}$$

Such that:

$$a^{l(\alpha)} = a_1 + (a_2 - a_1)\alpha, \quad a^{r(\alpha)} = a_3 + (a_2 - a_3)\alpha \tag{7}$$

Hence,

$$A^{\alpha} = [a^{l(\alpha)}, a^{r(\alpha)}] = [a_1 + (a_2 - a_1)\alpha, a_3 + (a_2 - a_3)\alpha] \tag{8}$$

From equation (8), the mathematical notations for triangular fuzzy numbers corresponding to cash flows $(CF_t)$, reinvestment $(k_{rr})$, financing $(k_{wacc})$ and risk-adjusted discount $(k_{radr})$ rates can be established.

$$FC_t{}^{\alpha} = [FC_t{}^{l} + (FC_t - FC_t{}^{l})\alpha, \; FC_t{}^{r} - (FC_t{}^{r} - FC_t)\alpha] \qquad \alpha \in [0,1] \tag{9}$$

$$k_{rr}{}^{\alpha} = [k_{rr}{}^{l} + (k_{rr} - k_{rr}{}^{l})\alpha, \; k_{rr}{}^{r} - (k_{rr}{}^{r} - k_{rr})\alpha] \qquad \alpha \in [0,1] \tag{10}$$

$$k_{wacc}{}^{\alpha} = [k_{wacc}{}^{l} + (k_{wacc} - k_{wacc}{}^{l})\alpha, \; k_{wacc}{}^{r} - (k_{wacc}{}^{r} - k_{wacc})\alpha] \qquad \alpha \in [0,1] \tag{11}$$

$$k_{radr}{}^{\alpha} = [k_{radr}{}^{l} + (k_{radr} - k_{radr}{}^{l})\alpha, \; k_{radr}{}^{r} - (k_{radr}{}^{r} - k_{radr})\alpha] \qquad \alpha \in [0,1] \tag{12}$$

To simplify, the computation of the *MNPV* with fuzzy cash flows and discount rates will be divided into three stages:

*Step 1: Calculation of the fuzzy Terminal Value (TV$^{\alpha}$).*
The fuzzy terminal value $(TV^{\alpha})$ is the sum of all the fuzzy net cash inflows $(CF_i{}^{\alpha})$ capitalized at the fuzzy reinvestment rate $(k_{rr}{}^{\alpha})$:

$$TV^{\alpha} = CF_{i1}^{\alpha}(1 + k_{rr}^{\alpha})^{n-1} + CF_{i2}^{\alpha}(1 + k_{rr}^{\alpha})^{n-2} + \ldots + CF_{in}^{\alpha}(1 + k_{rr}^{\alpha})^{0} \qquad CF_{it}^{\alpha} > 0 \tag{13}$$

According to [11], each interval which defines a fuzzy number satisfies the following conditions:

$$\begin{aligned}
[a^l, a^r] + [b^l, b^r] &= [a^l + b^l, a^r + b^r] \\
[a^l, a^r] \times [b^l, b^r] &= [a^l x b^l, a^r x b^r] \\
[a^l, a^r] \div [b^l, b^r] &= [a^l / b^r, a^r / b^l] \qquad n^l > 0 \\
[1,1] \div [b^l, b^r] &= [1/b^r, 1/b^l]
\end{aligned} \tag{14}$$

Applying the conditions established in (14) to expression (13):

$$TV^{\alpha} = [CF_{i1}^{l(\alpha)} x(1+k_{rr}^{l(\alpha)})^{n-1}, \; CF_{i1}^{r(\alpha)} x(1+k_{rr}^{r(\alpha)})^{n-1}] +$$
$$[CF_{i2}^{l(\alpha)} x(1+k_{rr}^{l(\alpha)})^{n-2}, \; CF_{i2}^{r(\alpha)} x(1+k_{rr}^{r(\alpha)})^{n-2}] + ... + [CF_{in}^{l(\alpha)}, \; CF_{in}^{r(\alpha)}] \tag{15}$$

where:

$$TV^{l(\alpha)} = CF_{i1}^{l(\alpha)} x(1+k_{rr}^{l(\alpha)})^{n-1} + CF_{i2}^{l(\alpha)} x(1+k_{rr}^{l(\alpha)})^{n-2} + ... + CF_{in}^{l(\alpha)} \tag{16}$$

$$TV^{r(\alpha)} = CF_{i1}^{r(\alpha)} x(1+k_{rr}^{r(\alpha)})^{n-1} + CF_{i2}^{r(\alpha)} x(1+k_{rr}^{r(\alpha)})^{n-2} + ... + CF_{in}^{r(\alpha)} \tag{17}$$

**Step 2**: *Calculation of the fuzzy Present Value ($PV^{\alpha}$).*
The fuzzy present value ($PV^{\alpha}$) is the sum of all net cash outflows discounted at the fuzzy financing rate ($k_{wacc}^{\alpha}$):

$$PV^{\alpha} = CF_{o0}^{\alpha} + \frac{CF_{o1}^{\alpha}}{\left(1+k_{wacc}^{\alpha}\right)^{1}} + \frac{CF_{o2}^{\alpha}}{\left(1+k_{wacc}^{\alpha}\right)^{2}} + ... + \frac{CF_{on}^{\alpha}}{\left(1+k_{wacc}^{\alpha}\right)^{n}} \qquad CF_{ot}^{\alpha} < 0 \tag{18}$$

Applying the conditions established in (14) to expression (18):

$$PV^{\alpha} = [CF_{o0}^{l(\alpha)}, CF_{o0}^{r(\alpha)}] + [\frac{CF_{o1}^{l(\alpha)}}{1+k_{wacc}^{r(\alpha)}}, \frac{CF_{o1}^{r(\alpha)}}{1+k_{wacc}^{l(\alpha)}}] + ... + [\frac{CF_{on}^{l(\alpha)}}{\left(1+k_{wacc}^{r(\alpha)}\right)^{n}}, \frac{CF_{on}^{r(\alpha)}}{\left(1+k_{wacc}^{l(\alpha)}\right)^{n}}] \tag{19}$$

where:

$$PV^{l(\alpha)} = CF_{o0}^{l(\alpha)} + \frac{CF_{o1}^{l(\alpha)}}{\left(1+k_{wacc}^{r(\alpha)}\right)^{1}} + \frac{CF_{o2}^{l(\alpha)}}{\left(1+k_{wacc}^{r(\alpha)}\right)^{2}} + ... + \frac{CF_{on}^{l(\alpha)}}{\left(1+k_{wacc}^{r(\alpha)}\right)^{n}} \tag{20}$$

$$PV^{r(\alpha)} = CF_{o0}^{r(\alpha)} + \frac{CF_{o1}^{r(\alpha)}}{\left(1+k_{wacc}^{l(\alpha)}\right)^{1}} + \frac{CF_{o2}^{r(\alpha)}}{\left(1+k_{wacc}^{l(\alpha)}\right)^{2}} + ... + \frac{CF_{on}^{r(\alpha)}}{\left(1+k_{wacc}^{l(\alpha)}\right)^{n}} \tag{21}$$

**Step 3**: *Calculation of the Modified Net Present Value ($MNPV^{\alpha}$).*
From equation (4), $MNPV^{\alpha}$ can be represented as:

$$MNPV^{\alpha} = \frac{TV^{\alpha}}{(1+k_{radr}^{\alpha})^{n}} - PV^{\alpha} \tag{22}$$

Applying the conditions established in (14) to the expression (22):

$$MNPV^{\alpha} = [\frac{TV^{l(\alpha)}}{(1+k_{radr}^{r(\alpha)})^{n}}, \frac{TV^{r(\alpha)}}{(1+k_{radr}^{l(\alpha)})^{n}}] - [PV^{l(\alpha)}, PV^{r(\alpha)}] \tag{23}$$

where:

$$MNPV^{l(\alpha)} = \frac{TV^{l(\alpha)}}{(1+k_{radr}^{r(\alpha)})^n} - PV^{l(\alpha)} \tag{24}$$

$$MNPV^{r(\alpha)} = \frac{TV^{r(\alpha)}}{(1+k_{radr}^{l(\alpha)})^n} - PV^{r(\alpha)} \tag{25}$$

**Example 2.** Assume that in example 1 the cash flows, the reinvestment rate, the financing rate and the risk-adjusted discount rate are established by an expert as the following triangular fuzzy numbers: $FC_0^\alpha$ = (-1600, -1600, -1600), $FC_1^\alpha$ = (9000, 10000, 11000), $FC_2^\alpha$ = (-9000, -10000, -11000), $k_{rr}^\alpha$ = (11%, 12%, 13%), $k_{wacc}^\alpha$ = (9%, 10%, 11%) and $k_{radr}^\alpha$ = (4%, 5%, 6%).

a) Calculation of the values of the $CF_i^\alpha$:

The fuzzy cash flows are expressed as:

$$FC_0^\alpha = [-1600 + (-1600 + 1600)\alpha, \ -1600 - (1600 + 1600)\alpha] = [-1600, \ -1600]$$

$$FC_1^\alpha = [9000 + (10000 - 9000)\alpha, \ 11000 - (11000 - 10000)\alpha]$$
$$= [9000 + 1000\alpha, \ 11000 - 1000\alpha]$$

$$FC_2^\alpha = [-9000 + (-10000 + 9000)\alpha, \ -11000 - (-11000 + 10000)\alpha]$$
$$= [-9000 - 1000\alpha, \ -11000 + 1000\alpha]$$

For $\alpha = 0$:

$$FC_0^{\alpha=0} = [-1600, \ -1600]$$

$$FC_1^{\alpha=0} = [9000 + 1000x0, \ 11000 - 1000x0] = [9000, \ 11000]$$

$$FC_2^{\alpha=0} = [-9000 - 1000x0, \ -11000 + 1000x0] = [-9000, \ -11000]$$

The values of $FC_0^\alpha$, $FC_1^\alpha$ and $FC_2^\alpha$ are shown in Table 2 for different values of $\alpha$.

**Table 2.** Values of $CF_0^\alpha$, $CF_1^\alpha$ and $CF_2^\alpha$

| $\alpha$ | $FC_0^\alpha$ | | $FC_1^\alpha$ | | $FC_2^\alpha$ | |
| --- | --- | --- | --- | --- | --- | --- |
| | $FC_0^{l(\alpha)}$ | $FC_0^{r(\alpha)}$ | $FC_1^{l(\alpha)}$ | $FC_1^{r(\alpha)}$ | $FC_2^{l(\alpha)}$ | $FC_2^{r(\alpha)}$ |
| 0 | -1,600 | -1,600 | 9,000 | 11,000 | -9,000 | -11,000 |
| 0,1 | -1,600 | -1,600 | 9,100 | 10,900 | -9,100 | -10,900 |
| 0,2 | -1,600 | -1,600 | 9,200 | 10,800 | -9,200 | -10,800 |
| 0,3 | -1,600 | -1,600 | 9,300 | 10,700 | -9,300 | -10,700 |
| 0,4 | -1,600 | -1,600 | 9,400 | 10,600 | -9,400 | -10,600 |
| 0,5 | -1,600 | -1,600 | 9,500 | 10,500 | -9,500 | -10,500 |
| 0,6 | -1,600 | -1,600 | 9,600 | 10,400 | -9,600 | -10,400 |
| 0,7 | -1,600 | -1,600 | 9,700 | 10,300 | -9,700 | -10,300 |
| 0,8 | -1,600 | -1,600 | 9,800 | 10,200 | -9,800 | -10,200 |
| 0,9 | -1,600 | -1,600 | 9,900 | 10,100 | -9,900 | -10,100 |
| 1,0 | -1,600 | -1,600 | 10,000 | 10,000 | -10,000 | -10,000 |

b) Calculation of the values of $k_{rr}{}^{\alpha}$, $k_{wacc}{}^{\alpha}$ and $k_{radr}{}^{\alpha}$

Using the same procedures above for the calculation of fuzzy cash flows, different values of $k_{rr}{}^{\alpha}$, $K_{wacc}{}^{\alpha}$ and $k_{radr}{}^{\alpha}$ are calculated and shown in Table 3.

**Table 3.** Values of $k_{rr}{}^{\alpha}$, $k_{wacc}{}^{\alpha}$ and $k_{radr}{}^{\alpha}$

| $\alpha$ | $k_{rr}{}^{\alpha}$ (%) | | $k_{wacc}{}^{\alpha}$ (%) | | $k_{radr}{}^{\alpha}$ (%) | |
|---|---|---|---|---|---|---|
| | $k_{rr}{}^{l(\alpha)}$ | $k_{rr}{}^{r(\alpha)}$ | $k_{wacc}{}^{l(\alpha)}$ | $k_{wacc}{}^{r(\alpha)}$ | $k_{radr}{}^{l(\alpha)}$ | $k_{radr}{}^{r(\alpha)}$ |
| 0 | 11.0 | 13.0 | 9.0 | 11.0 | 4.0 | 6.0 |
| 0,1 | 11.1 | 12.9 | 9.1 | 10.9 | 4.1 | 5.9 |
| 0,2 | 11.2 | 12.8 | 9.2 | 10.8 | 4.2 | 5.8 |
| 0,3 | 11.3 | 12.7 | 9.3 | 10.7 | 4.3 | 5.7 |
| 0,4 | 11.4 | 12.6 | 9.4 | 10.6 | 4.4 | 5.6 |
| 0,5 | 11.5 | 12.5 | 9.5 | 10.5 | 4.5 | 5.5 |
| 0,6 | 11.6 | 12.4 | 9.6 | 10.4 | 4.6 | 5.4 |
| 0,7 | 11.7 | 12.3 | 9.7 | 10.3 | 4.7 | 5.3 |
| 0,8 | 11.8 | 12.2 | 9.8 | 10.2 | 4.8 | 5.2 |
| 0,9 | 11.9 | 12.1 | 9.9 | 10.1 | 4.9 | 5.1 |
| 1,0 | 12.0 | 12.0 | 10.0 | 10.0 | 5.0 | 5.0 |

c) Calculation of the values of the fuzzy Terminal Value ($TV^{\alpha}$)

From equations (16) and (17), $TV^{\alpha}$ for $\alpha = 0$ is expressed as:

$$TV^{l(\alpha=0)} = CF_{i1}^{l(\alpha=0)} x(1+k_{rr}^{l(\alpha=0)})^1 = 9{,}000x(1+0.11) = 9{,}990$$

$$TV^{r(\alpha=0)} = CF_{i1}^{r(\alpha=0)} x(1+k_{rr}^{r(\alpha=0)})^1 = 11{,}000x(1+0.13) = 12{,}430$$

d) Calculation of the values of the fuzzy Present Value ($PV^{\alpha}$)

From equations (20) and (21), $PV^{\alpha}$ for $\alpha = 0$ is expressed as:

$$PV^{l(\alpha=0)} = CF_{o0}^{l(\alpha=0)} + \frac{CF_{o2}^{l(\alpha=0)}}{\left(1+k_{wacc}^{r(\alpha=0)}\right)^2} = -1{,}600 + \frac{-9{,}000}{(1+0.11)^2} = -8{,}904.60$$

$$PV^{r(\alpha=0)} = CF_{o0}^{r(\alpha=0)} + \frac{CF_{o2}^{r(\alpha=0)}}{\left(1+k_{wacc}^{l(\alpha=0)}\right)^2} = -1{,}600 + \frac{-11{,}000}{(1+0.9)^2} = -10{,}858.48$$

e) Calculation of the values of fuzzy Modified Net Present Value ($MNPV^{\alpha}$)

From equations (24) and (25), $MNPV^{\alpha}$ for $\alpha = 0$ is:

$$MNPV^{l(\alpha=0)} = \frac{TV^{l(\alpha=0)}}{(1+k_{radr}^{r(\alpha=0)})^2} - PV^{l(\alpha=0)} = \frac{9{,}990.00}{(1+0.06)^2} - 8{,}904.60 = -13.54$$

$$MNPV^{r(\alpha=0)} = \frac{TV^{r(\alpha=0)}}{(1+k_{radr}^{l(\alpha=0)})^2} - PV^{r(\alpha=0)} = \frac{12{,}430.00}{(1+0.04)^2} - 10{,}858.48 = 633.75$$

The values of $TV^{\alpha}$, $PV^{\alpha}$ and $MNPV^{\alpha}$ are shown in Table 4, for the different values of $\alpha$. A graphical representation of $MNPV^{\alpha}$ is shown in Figure 2.

**Table 4.** Values of $TV^{\alpha}$, $PV^{\alpha}$ and $MNPV^{\alpha}$

| | $TV^{\alpha}$ | | $PV^{\alpha}$ | | $MNPV^{\alpha}$ | |
|---|---|---|---|---|---|---|
| $\alpha$ | $TV^{l(\alpha)}$ | $TV^{r(\alpha)}$ | $PV^{l(\alpha)}$ | $PV^{r(\alpha)}$ | $MNPV^{l(\alpha)}$ | $MNPV^{r(\alpha)}$ |
| 0 | 9,990.00 | 12,430.00 | -8,904.60 | -10,858.48 | -13.54 | 633.75 |
| 0,1 | 10,110.10 | 12,306.10 | -8,999.09 | -10,757.50 | 15.86 | 598.33 |
| 0,2 | 10,230.40 | 12,182.40 | -9,093.91 | -10,656.88 | 45.57 | 563.24 |
| 0,3 | 10,350.90 | 12,058.90 | -9,189.06 | -10,556.61 | 75.58 | 528.48 |
| 0,4 | 10,471.60 | 11,935.60 | -9,284.54 | -10,456.69 | 105.89 | 494.05 |
| 0,5 | 10,592.50 | 11,812.50 | -9,380.35 | -10,357.12 | 136.51 | 459.94 |
| 0,6 | 10,713.60 | 11,689.60 | -9,476.50 | -10,257.89 | 167.44 | 426.17 |
| 0,7 | 10,834.90 | 11,566.90 | -9,572.98 | -10,159.02 | 198.68 | 392.71 |
| 0,8 | 10,956.40 | 11,444.40 | -9,669.80 | -10,060.49 | 230.23 | 359.58 |
| 0,9 | 11,078.10 | 11,322.10 | -9,766.96 | -9,962.30 | 262.09 | 326.76 |
| 1,0 | 11,200.00 | 11,200.00 | -9,864.46 | -9,864.46 | 294.27 | 294.27 |

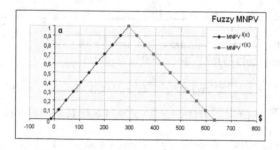

**Fig. 2.** Fuzzy $MNPV$

The area with negative $MNPV$ indicates that there is a very small possibility that the project will not to be indicated as acceptable. According to Chiu and Park [12], this possibility can be computed by dividing the negative area by the total area, which in this case results in 0.1%.

## 3.2    The MNPVfuzzy Function

As the calculation of the $MNPV$ under uncertainty, for an investment project with cash flows and rates represented by triangular fuzzy numbers, is quite hard and complex, a new financial function, called $MNPVfuzzy$, was developed in Visual Basic for Applications of MS-Excel. The use of this function is shown in Example 3.

**Example 3.** Admitting that the initial investment and the values of fuzzy cash flows for Example 2 are inserted in *B3:D3*, *B4:D4* and *B5:D5* cells; that the reinvestment, financing and risk-adjusted discount rates are inserted in *G3:I3*, *G4:I4* and *G5:I5* cells; and that $\alpha$ = zero is inserted in the *G8* cell of a MS-Excel spread sheet, the fuzzy modified net present value is calculated, from the *MNPVfuzzy* function, as follows:

*MNPVfuzzy*$^{left}$:
=*MNPVfuzzy(B3:B5;C3:C5;D3:D5;G3:I3;G4:I4;G5:I5;G8;0)*

*NPVfuzzy*$^{right}$:
=*MNPVfuzzy((B3:B5;C3:C5;D3:D5;G3:I3;G4:I4;G5:I5;G8;1)*

This results in $MNPV^{l(\alpha=0)}$ = -$13.54 and $MNPV^{r(\alpha=0)}$ = $633.75, which are the same as those obtained manually.

## 4 Conclusions

The association of fuzzy numbers to the modified net present value method proved to be appropriate for solving problems of evaluation of investments. The proposed approach is simple and makes fewer assumptions than the traditional models for treatment of uncertainty regarding the behavior of related variables, which is very useful for decision makers. The fuzzy *MNPV* function showed good performance and is user friendly, which is an essential feature for professional use.

## References

1. Graham, J.R., Harvey, C.R.: The Theory and Practice of Corporate Finance: Evidence from the Field. Journal of Financial Economics 60, 187–243 (2001)
2. Plath, D.A., Kennedy, W.F.: Teaching Return-Based Measures of Project Evaluation. Financial Practice & Education 4, 77–86 (1994)
3. Biondi, Y.: The Double Emergence of the Modified Internal Rate of Return: The Neglected Financial Work of Duvillard (1755-1832) in a Comparative Perspective. European Journal of the History of Economic Thought 13, 311–335 (2006)
4. Kierulff, H.: MIRR: A Better Measure. Business Horizons 51, 321–329 (2008)
5. McClure, K.G., Girma, P.B.: Modified Net Present Value (MNPV): A New Technique for Capital Budgeting. Zagreb International Review of Economics and Business 7, 67–82 (2004)
6. Chandra, P.: Projects: Planning, Analysis, Selection, Financing, Implementation, and Review, 7th edn. Tata McGraw-Hill, New Delhi (2009)
7. Solomon, E.: The Arithmetic of Capital-Budgeting Decisions. The Journal of Business 29(2), 124–129 (1956)
8. Zadeh, L.A.: Fuzzy Sets. Information and Control 8, 338–353 (1965)
9. Kahraman, C. (ed.): Fuzzy Engineering Economics with Applications. Springer, Heidelberg (2008)
10. Ulukan, Z., Ucuncuoglu, C.: Economic Analyses for the Evaluation of IS Projects. Journal of Information Systems and Technology Management 7(2), 233–260 (2010)
11. Gutiérrez, I.: Fuzzy Numbers and Net Present Value. Scandinavian Journal of Management 5, 149–159 (1989)
12. Chiu, C.Y., Park, C.S.: Fuzzy Cash Flow Analysis Using Present Worth Criterion. The Engineering Economist 39(2), 113–137 (1994)

# Evolving Fuzzy Modeling
# for Stock Market Forecasting

Leandro Maciel[1], Fernando Gomide[1], and Rosangela Ballini[2]

[1] Department of Computer Engineering and Automation
School of Electrical and Computer Engineering, University of Campinas
São Paulo, Brazil 13.083-852
{maciel,gomide}@dca.fee.unicamp.br
[2] Department of Economic Theory
Institute of Economics, University of Campinas
São Paulo, Brazil 13.083-857
ballini@eco.unicamp.br

**Abstract.** Stock market forecasting plays an important role in risk management, asset pricing and portfolio analysis. Stock prices involve non-linear dynamics and uncertainties due to their high volatility and noisy environments. Forecasting modeling with adaptive and high performance accuracy is a major requirement in this case. This paper addresses a new approach for stock market forecast within the framework of evolving fuzzy rule-based modeling, a form of adaptive fuzzy modeling. US and Brazilian stock market data are used to evaluate modeling characteristics and forecasting performance. The results show the high potential of evolving fuzzy models to describe stock market behavior accurately. The evolving modeling approach reveals the essential capability to detect structural changes arising from complex dynamics and instabilities like financial crisis.

**Keywords:** Evolving Fuzzy Systems, Stock Price Forecasting, Rule-Based Models, Adaptive Systems.

# 1 Introduction

Prediction of stock market returns is a challenging task due to volatility, complex and noisy nonlinear dynamical environment. Information regarding a stock is uncertain, vague and normally incomplete, since factors such as politics, economic status, and expectations of traders influence the stock prices. Accurate forecasts of stock markets is an important issue for investors, professional analysts and for all market participants in general. Hedge operations against potential market risks, buy or sell strategies, portfolio analysis and asset options pricing are examples in which stock prices forecasts play a relevant role.

Regression and ARIMA models have been extensively applied for stock marketing forecasting [4]. However, their linear structures and some other limitations imply in failures to provide accurate results. In the past few years, computational

S. Greco et al. (Eds.): IPMU 2012, Part IV, CCIS 300, pp. 20–29, 2012.

intelligence tools such as artificial neural networks (ANN) have been successfully used for stock price modeling due to their capability to handle complex systems [6,8]. Lack of interpretability is the main ANNs drawback once no mechanism for understanding market relationships is provided. To overcome this limitation, models based on fuzzy inference systems have recently been used to forecast stock prices because they help to explain the relations in the system [9,13].

The price movement of a stock market is non-stationary, inherently noisy, and chaotic [13], requiring an adaptive and flexible model to describe its behavior. The purpose of this paper is to study stock market forecast using evolving functional models and their application for US and Brazilian market data. Evolving fuzzy systems use data streams to continuously adapt the structure and functionality of fuzzy models to improve their performance, ensuring high generality. The evolving mechanism translates into an adaptive procedure to continuously capture gradual changes of models structure and parameters [10].

Recently, applications of fuzzy systems for stock market forecasting include fuzzy decision trees [11], fuzzy neural networks [15] and hypernetwork models [5]. These are not evolving approaches in the sense of adaptive modeling from the point of view of structural and parametric learning. In this paper, we suggest an evolving functional fuzzy modeling framework in the form of Takagi-Sugeno (TS) models. Here, the rule base, rules membership functions and consequent parameters continually evolve by adding new rules with higher summarization power, modifying existing rules and parameters to match current knowledge [14]. We emphasize the evolving Takagi-Sugeno (eTS+) [1] and compare it against the evolving participatory learning (ePL) [12] using US and Brazilian stock markets data. eTS+ includes extensions to the original eTS version [2] and the eXtended evolving model (xTS) [3] in which the adjustments of antecedent parameters and the structure of the rule-bases are based on criteria such as age, utility, local density and zone of influence.

Forecasting performance of eTS+, eTS, xTS and ePL are evaluated using data from January 2000 through November 2011 of the US S&P 500 and Brazilian Ibovespa stock indexes, and compared against some benchmarks such as ARIMA process and neural networks. Performance is given in terms of accuracy and model size (number of rules).

After this introduction, the paper proceeds as follows. Section 2 summarizes the eTS+ and ePL approaches and algorithms. Computational experiments and results analysis for stock market forecasts are reported in Section 3. Section 4 concludes the paper and suggests issues for further investigation.

## 2   Evolving Functional Fuzzy Inference Systems

The evolving Takagi-Sugeno fuzzy system (eTS+) assumes functional rule-based models in the form of Takagi-Sugeno fuzzy rules:

$$\mathcal{R}_i : \textbf{IF } x_1 \textit{ is } \Lambda_{i,1} \textbf{ AND } \ldots \textbf{ AND } x_n \textit{ is } \Lambda_{i,n} \textbf{ THEN } y_i = \alpha_{0,i} + \sum_{j=1}^{n} \alpha_{j,i} x_j \quad (1)$$

where $\mathcal{R}_i$ denotes the $i^{th}$ fuzzy rule ($i = 1, 2, \ldots, R$), $\mathbf{x} = [x_1, x_2, \ldots, x_n]^T$ is the input vector, $\Lambda_{i,j}$ are the antecedent fuzzy sets ($j = 1, 2, \ldots, n$), $y_i$ is the output of the $i^{th}$ rule, and $\alpha_{l,i}$ the consequent parameters ($l = 0, 1, \ldots, n$).

eTS+ assumes antecedent fuzzy sets with Gaussian membership functions since a fuzzy system with Gaussian membership function has been shown to be a universal approximator of any nonlinear functions on a compact set [16]:

$$\mu_{i,j}\left(x_j^k\right) = e^{-\frac{\left(x_{j,i}^* - x_j^k\right)^2}{2\sigma_{i,j}^2}} \tag{2}$$

where $\mu_{i,j}$ denotes the membership degree of input $x_j^k$, ($k = 1, 2, \ldots$), $x_{j,i}^*$ is the focal point of the $j^{th}$ fuzzy set of the $i^{th}$ fuzzy rule, and $\sigma_{i,j}$ is the projection of the zone of influence of the $i^{th}$ cluster on the axis of the $j^{th}$ input variable [1].

The firing level of the $i^{th}$ rule, assuming the product $T$-norm of the antecedent fuzzy sets is:

$$\pi_i\left(x^k\right) = \prod_{j=1}^{n} \mu_{i,j}\left(x_j^k\right) \tag{3}$$

The model output at step $k$ is found as the weighted average of the individual rule contributions:

$$y^k = \sum_{i=1}^{R} \gamma_i y_i^k = \sum_{i=1}^{R} \gamma_i x_e^T \Psi_i, \quad \gamma_i = \frac{\pi_i}{\sum_{l=1}^{R} \pi_l} \tag{4}$$

where $\gamma_i$ is the normalized firing level of the $i^{th}$ rule, $x_e = \begin{bmatrix} 1 & x^T \end{bmatrix}^T$ is the expanded data vector, and $\Psi_i = [\alpha_{0,i}, \alpha_{1,i}, \alpha_{2,i}, \ldots, \alpha_{n,i}]^T$ is the vector of parameters of the $i^{th}$ linear consequent.

There are essentially two sub-tasks related to the problem of identification of a TS model [2]: learning of the antecedents to determine the focal points of the rules, and identification the parameters of the linear consequents. These sub-tasks are described as follows.

## 2.1   Learning Antecedents by e*Clustering*+

The learning procedure in eTS+ model, e*Clustering*, considers *streaming* data, which are collected continuously. This mechanism ensures that the new data reinforce and confirm the information contained in previous data [2,1]. In off line situations, the learning procedure can be viewed as a recursive mechanism to process data. The judgment related to form a new rule or to modify an existing one is take considering the density at a data point using a Cauchy functions [1,2].

The density is evaluated recursively and information related to the spatial distribution of all data is accumulated by variables $\varphi^k$ e $\delta_j^k$ as follows:

$$D^k\left(z^k\right) = \frac{k-1}{(k-1)\left(\sum_{j=1}^{n}(z_j^k)^2 + 1\right) + \varphi^k - 2\sum_{j=1}^{n} z_j^k \delta_j^k} \tag{5}$$

where $D^k\left(z^k\right)$ is the density of the data around the last data point of the data stream provides to the algorithm, $z^k = ([x^T, y^T]^T)^k$ is an input/output pair at step $k$ $(k = 2, 3, \ldots)$, $\varphi^k = \varphi^{k-1} + \sum_{j=1}^{n}(z_j^{k-1})^2$, $\varphi^1 = 0$, $\delta_j^k = \delta_j^{k-1} + z_j^{k-1}$ and $\delta_j^1 = 0$.

This clustering mechanism ensures a gradual change of the rule-base. Data points with high density are potential candidates to became focal points of antecedents of fuzzy rules. The density of a data point selected to be a cluster focal point have its density calculated by Equation (5) and is updated according to new information available, since any data point coming from the data stream will influence the data density. Therefore, the focal points density is recursively updated by:

$$D^k\left(z^{i^*}\right) = \frac{k-1}{k-1+(k-2)\left(\frac{1}{D^{k-1}(z^{i^*})}-1\right)+\sum_{j=1}^{n}\left(z_j^{i^*}-z_j^k\right)} \qquad (6)$$

where $D^1\left(z^{i^*}\right) = 1$, $k = 2, 3, \ldots$, and $i^*$ denotes the focal points of the $i^{th}$ fuzzy rule. It must be noted that the initialization $(k = 1)$ includes: $z^{1^*} \leftarrow z^1$, $R \leftarrow 1$, i.e. the first data point is considered as a cluster center, forming the first rule.

The recursive density estimation clustering approach does not rely on user- or problem-specific thresholds, differently as in methods like subtractive clustering or participatory learning, for example. Moreover, the density is evaluated recursively and the whole information that concerns the spatial distribution of all data is accumulated in a small number of variables [1].

In the e*Clustering* procedure, representative clusters with high generalization capability are formed considering the data points with the highest value of $D$. Therefore, the Condition (I) is formulated [2,1]: *if* $D^k\left(z^k\right) > \max_{i=1}^{R} D^k\left(z^{i^*}\right)$ *or* $D^k\left(z^k\right) < \min_{i=1}^{R} D^k\left(z^{i^*}\right)$ *then* $z^{(R+1)^*} \leftarrow z^k$ *and* $R \leftarrow R+1$.

If a current data point satisfies Condition (I) then the new data point is accepted as a new center and a new rule is formed with focal point based on the new data point $(R \leftarrow R+1; z^{R^*} = z^k)$. This condition ensures good convergence, but it is more sensitive to outliers. Influence of outliers can be avoided using quality clusters indicators [1].

To control the level of overlap and to avoid redundant clusters, Condition (II) is also considered [3]: *if* $\exists\, i : \mu_{i,j}(x^k) > e^{-1}$, $\forall j$ *then* $R \leftarrow R-1$.

Condition (II) remove highly overlapping clusters, avoiding contradictory rules, which means that the new candidate cluster focal point describes any of the existing cluster focal points. The previously existing focal point(s) for which this condition holds is(are) removed. These mechanisms simplify the rule-base and the number of rules grow according to the system information availability only.

Quality measures for *online/recursive* monitoring the clusters includes support, age, utility, zone of influence and local density [1]. Here in this paper, similarly as in [1], the quality of the clusters are constantly monitored using the accumulated relative firing level of a particular antecedent [3]:

$$U_i^k = \frac{\sum_{l=1}^{k} \gamma_l}{k - T^{i*}}, \quad i = 1, 2, \ldots, R; \quad k = 2, 3, \ldots \tag{7}$$

where $T^{i*}$ denotes the time tag which indicates when a fuzzy rule is generated.

The utility of the clusters is evaluated according to the Condition (III): *if* $U_i^k < \varepsilon$ *then* $R \leftarrow R - 1$, where $\varepsilon$ is a threshold related to the minimum utility of a cluster (typically, threshold values are in the range $[0.03, 0.1]$) [1].

This condition means that if some cluster has low utility (lower than an threshold $\varepsilon$), the data pattern has shifted away from the focal point of that rule, then the rule that satisfies Condition III is removed. This quality measure evaluates the importance of the fuzzy rules and assists the evolving process.

## 2.2   Participatory Learning Clustering

The ePL approach joins the concept of participatory learning with the evolving fuzzy modeling idea. In evolving systems, the PL concept is viewed as an unsupervised clustering algorithm and is a natural candidate to find rule base structures in dynamic environments [14]. ePL uses participatory learning fuzzy clustering instead of scattering, density or information potential as in eTS models. In ePL, the object of learning are cluster structures. The cluster structure is updated if the arousal index is greater than a threshold value $\tau$, which changes according each new data by a control arousal rate parameter $\beta$. Moreover, if a compatibility index among cluster centers, computed by a distance measure, is higher than a threshold $\lambda$, redundant clusters are removed. Details about ePL model and its control parameters see [12,14].

The parameters of the rule consequents are computed using the recursive least squares algorithm as in eTS+ systems, described bellow.

## 2.3   Recursive Consequent Parameters Identification

Equation (4) can be put into the following vector form:

$$y = \Gamma^T \Phi \tag{8}$$

where $y$ is the output, $\Gamma = \left[\gamma_1 x_e^T, \gamma_2 x_e^T, \ldots, \gamma_n x_e^T\right]^T$ denotes the fuzzily weighted extended inputs vector, and $\Phi = \left[\Psi_1^T, \Psi_2^T, \ldots, \Psi_R^T\right]^T$ the vector of parameters of the rule base.

Since at each step the real/target output is given, the parameters of the consequents can be updated using the recursive least squares algorithm RLS [7] considering locally or globally optimization. In this paper we apply a locally optimal error criterion which is given by:

$$\min E_L^i = \min \sum_{l=1}^{k} \gamma_i(x_l) \left(y_l - x_{e,l}^T \Psi_{i,l}\right)^2 \tag{9}$$

In eTS+ there are not only fuzzily coupled linear subsystems and streaming data, but also structure evolution. Thus, the optimal update of the parameters of the $i^{th}$ rule is [2,3,1]:

$$\Psi_i^{k+1} = \Psi_i^k + \Sigma_i^k x_e^k \gamma_i^k \left( y^k - (x_e^k)^T \Psi_i^1 \right), \ \Psi_i^1 = 0 \tag{10}$$

$$\Sigma_i^{k+1} = \Sigma_i^k - \frac{\gamma_i^k \Sigma_i^k x_e^k (x_e^k)^T \Sigma_i^k}{1 + \gamma_i^k (x_e^k)^T \Sigma_i^k x_e^k}, \ \Sigma_i^1 = \Omega I_{(n+1) \times (n+1)} \tag{11}$$

where $I$ is a $(n+1) \times (n+1)$ identity matrix, $\Omega$ denotes a large number, usually $\Omega = 1000$, and $\Sigma$ a dispersion matrix. [1] performed simulations on several benchmarks and verified the stability and convergence of the RLS updating formulas (10) and (11).

When a new fuzzy rule is added, a new dispersion matrix is computed $\Sigma_{R+1}^k = I\Omega$. Parameters of the new rules are approximated from the parameters of the existing $R$ fuzzy rules as follows:

$$\Psi_{R+1}^k = \sum_{i=1}^{R} \gamma_i \Psi_i^{k-1} \tag{12}$$

Otherwise, parameters of all other rules are inherited from the previous step, while the dispersion matrices are updated independently.

However, when a focal points is replaced by another rule due to Condition (II), the parameters and the dispersion matrix are inherited by the fuzzy rule being replaced [1]:

$$\Psi_{R+1}^k = \Psi_{i^*}^{k-1}, \ \mu_{i^*,j}(x^k) > e^{-1}, \ \forall j, \ j = 1,2,\ldots,n \tag{13}$$

$$\Sigma_{R+1}^k = \Sigma_{i^*}^{k-1}, \ \mu_{i^*,j}(x^k) > e^{-1}, \ \forall j, \ j = 1,2,\ldots,n \tag{14}$$

Finally, once the consequent parameters are found, the model output is computed using Equation (4).

## 3 Computational Results and Analysis for Stock Market Forecast

This section investigates the effectiveness of using the eTS+ modeling to forecast stock prices for the US and Brazilian markets. The accuracy performance of eTS+ is compared against eTS, xTS, and ePL fuzzy models, as well as against ARIMA process and neural networks, considered as benchmarks.

### 3.1 Data

The US stock market is represented by the S&P 500 index, which is a free-float capitalization-weighted index published since 1957 of the prices of 500 large-cap common stocks actively traded in the New York Stock Exchange. The Bovespa Index (Ibovespa) represents the Brazilian stock market. Ibovespa reflects the variation of the Brazilian Stock Market Exchange most traded stocks since 1968. Daily stock indexes from $3^{rd}$ Jan 2000 through $30^{th}$ Sept 2011 for both markets were collected from the Yahoo finance website. It should be noted that since evolving fuzzy modeling deals with streaming data, processing is done recursively and thus we may assume that no *a priori* training data is available, different from ARIMA and ANN models. Therefore, the first one third of total data was used as the training set for all methodologies.

## 3.2   Implementation of Evolving Models

Input selection considers the sample autocorrelation function analysis to determine the number of lags for the indexes considered. Therefore, five lags of S&P 500 and three lags of Ibovespa are used as input variables and evolving models outputs give one step ahead forecast of the index.

As stated previously, the eTS+ was evaluated against alternative evolving fuzzy modeling approaches. In particular, here we focus on the eTS original version [2], the xTS model [3], and the ePL model [12]. The control parameters of all evolving models were selected based on simulation results to choose the most appropriated values for each model. The $ARIMA(4, 1, 1)$ model was selected based on Bayesian information criteria, and the neural network performed was a feedforward type trained with the gradient algorithm. The network is composed by one hidden layer with five neurons and a linear neuron in the output layer.

## 3.3   Results and Analysis

The values of the control parameters for eTS+ are $\sigma = 0.05$, $\Omega = 1000$, and $\varepsilon = 0.1$. The eTS uses $\sigma = 0.05$ and $\Omega = 1000$, whereas for the xTS model $\Omega = 1000$. The ePL model adopts $\alpha = 0.01$ as learning rate, $\beta = \tau = 0.16$, $\sigma = 0.05$ (same interpretation as in eTS+ model), and $\lambda = 0.84$.

To evaluate the forecasting accuracy given by the models outputs we use the root mean squared error ($RMSE$) and mean absolute error ($MAE$):

$$RMSE = \sqrt{\left(\frac{1}{N}\right) \sum_{k=1}^{N} (y^k - \hat{y}^k)^2}, \quad MAE = \frac{1}{N} \sum_{k=1}^{n} |y^k - \hat{y}^k| \qquad (15)$$

where $y$ is the desired output, $\hat{y}$ the model output, and $N$ the sample size.

Figure 1 displays the evolution of the number of rules for the US and Brazilian markets for the eTS+ model.

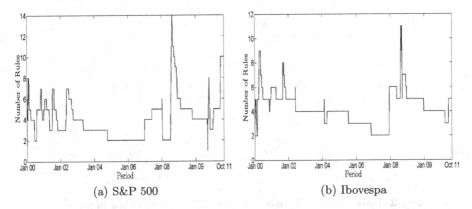

**Fig. 1.** Evolution of the number of rules for S&P 500 and Ibovespa indexes

It shows the continuous model structure adaptation through changes in the rule base structure. It is interesting to note that the number of rules increases significantly between 2008 and 2009, revealing the capability of eTS+ to capture crises instabilities. This period corresponds to the US *subprime* mortgage crisis which has led to plunging property prices, a slowdown in the US economy, and billions in banks losses, affecting the main financial markets over the world, Brazil included.

Table 1 summarizes the computational results of the forecasts in terms of final number of rules, forecasting errors, and correlation coefficient ($\rho$) between real and forecasts values. One can note that eTS+ and ePL performed better than the remaining models in terms of accuracy. The eTS+ and ePL models reported the lowest number of final rules for both markets, whereas eTS and xTS required higher number of rules to model stock market index. Moreover, the ANN applied reports similar results as evolving systems, whereas the ARIMA process presents poor forecasts, for both US and Brazilian markets. Figure 2 shows actual and eTS+ predicted values of the US and Brazilian markets.

**Table 1.** Computational results for S&P 500 and Ibovespa indexes

| | S&P 500 | | | | Ibovespa | | | |
|---|---|---|---|---|---|---|---|---|
| Models | RMSE | MAE | $\rho$ | No. of Rules | RMSE | MAE | $\rho$ | No. of Rules |
| eTS+ | 0.0141 | 0.0096 | 0.9977 | 10 | 0.0051 | 0.0043 | 0.9998 | 5 |
| eTS | 0.0170 | 0.0120 | 0.9966 | 19 | 0.0118 | 0.0076 | 0.9993 | 15 |
| xTS | 0.0183 | 0.0128 | 0.9961 | 13 | 0.0120 | 0.0080 | 0.9992 | 11 |
| ePL | 0.0162 | 0.0115 | 0.9969 | 8 | 0.0112 | 0.0074 | 0.9993 | 4 |
| ARIMA | 0.0289 | 0.0144 | 0.8951 | – | 0.0226 | 0.0124 | 0.8672 | – |
| ANN | 0.0188 | 0.0124 | 0.9764 | – | 0.0131 | 0.0085 | 0.9778 | – |

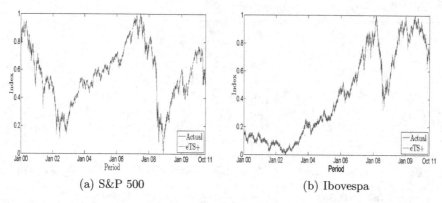

(a) S&P 500                    (b) Ibovespa

**Fig. 2.** Forecasts of eTS+ model for S&P 500 and Ibovespa indexes

One can note the high capability of the evolving models to deal with the stock market forecasting. One must also note the high volatility of the S&P 500 index during the period of the recent crisis, compared against the Ibovespa index. The Brazilian stock market also suffered from the crisis, however the contamination was less persistent because the US economy was the focus of the crisis. The lower variability in the Ibovespa index helps to explain the small forecasting errors of Table 1. One may also infer that, in terms of short-term horizons, the higher the market volatility, the greater the number of rules requires to model market movements.

## 4    Conclusion

In this paper we have addressed evolving fuzzy modeling for stock market forecasting. Evolving fuzzy models were evaluated to forecast future trends in the US and Brazilian markets. Actual data from January 2000 to October 2011 were used for evaluation. Since stock prices mirrors the behavior of nonstationary nonlinear environments, evolving models have shown to be quite suitable to capture its behavior. Computational results have shown that evolving models have high forecast accuracy and are capable to capture stock markets movements by adapting the rule-base properly, overperforming traditional benchmarks. This includes periods with high instabilities such as the recent subprime mortgage crisis. Future work shall consider analysis of evolving fuzzy modeling in actual financial decision making instances and its capability to predict structural breaks in economies.

**Acknowledgments.** The authors would like to thank the Brazilian Ministry of Education (CAPES), the Brazilian National Research Council (CNPq) grant 304596/2009-4, and the Foundation for Research Support of the State of São Paulo (FAPESP) for their support.

# References

1. Angelov, P.: Evolving Takagi-Sugeno fuzzy systems from streaming data (eTS+). In: Angelov, P., Filev, D.P., Kasabov, N. (eds.) Evolving Systems: Methodology and Applications. John Wiley & Sons, Inc., Hoboken (2010)
2. Angelov, P., Filev, D.: An approach to online identification of Takagi-Sugeno fuzzy models. IEEE Transactions on Systems, Man, and Cybernetics – Part B: Cybernetics 4(1), 484–498 (2004)
3. Angelov, P., Zhou, X.: Evolving fuzzy systems from data streams in real-time. In: 2006 International Symposium on Evolving Fuzzy Systems, Ambleside, September 7-9, pp. 29–35 (2006)
4. Atsalakis, G.S., Valavanis, K.P.: Surveying stock market forecasting techniques - Part II: Soft computing methods. Expert Systems with Applications 36(3), 5931–5941 (2009)
5. Bautu, E., Kim, S., Bautu, A., Luchian, H., Zhang, B.: Evolving hypernetwork models of binary time series for forecasting price movements on stock markets. In: IEEE Congress on Evolutionary Computation (CEC 2009), Trondheim, May 18-21, pp. 166–173 (2009)
6. Chen, A.S., Leuny, M.T., Daoun, H.: Application of neural networks to an emerging financial market: Forecasting and trading the Taiwan stock index. Computers and Operations Research 30(6), 901–923 (2003)
7. Chiu, S.L.: Fuzzy model identification based on clustering estimation. Journal of Intelligent Fuzzy Systems 2(3), 267–278 (1994)
8. Conner, N.O., Madden, M.: A neural network approach to prediction stock exchange movements using external factor. Knowledge Based System 19(5), 371–378 (2006)
9. Jilani, T.A., Burney, S.M.A.: A refined fussy time series model for stock market forecasting. Physica A: Statistical Mechanics and its Applications 387(12), 2857–2862 (2008)
10. Kasabov, N., Song, Q.: DENFIS: Dynamic evolving neural-fuzzy inference system and its application for time series prediction. IEEE Transactions on Fuzzy Systems 10(2), 144–154 (2002)
11. Lai, R.K., Fan, C., Huang, W., Chang, P.: Evolving and clustering fuzzy decision tree for financial time series data forecasting. Expert Systems with Applications 36(2), 3761–3773 (2009)
12. Lima, E., Hell, M., Ballini, R., Gomide, F.: Evolving fuzzy modeling using participatory learning. In: Angelov, P., Filev, D.P., Kasabov, N. (eds.) Evolving Systems: Methodology and Applications. John Wiley & Sons, Inc., Hoboken (2010)
13. Liu, X.: Modified TSK fuzzy system in stock price forecasting. In: 2nd IEEE International Conference on Information and Financial Engineering, Chongqing, September 17-19, pp. 621–624 (2010)
14. Maciel, L., Lemos, A.P., Gomide, F., Ballini, R.: Evolving fuzzy systems for pricing fixed income options. Evolving Systems 3(1), 5–18 (2012)
15. Nguyen, N.N., Quek, C.: Stock market prediction using Generic Self-Evolving Takagi-Sugeno-Kang (GSETSK) fuzzy neural network. In: The 2010 International Joint Conference on Neural Networks (IJCNN), Barcelona, July 18-23, pp. 1–8 (2010)
16. Wang, L.X., Mendel, J.M.: Fuzzy basis functions, universal approximation, and orthogonal least-squares learning. IEEE Transactions on Neural Networks 3(5), 724–740 (1992)

# Distance–Based Characterization
# of Inconsistency in Pairwise Comparisons

Michele Fedrizzi

University of Trento, Department of Computer and Management Sciences,
via Inama 5, 38122 Trento, Italy
michele.fedrizzi@unitn.it

**Abstract.** This paper deals with the evaluation of preference consistency in decision making, assuming that decision makers express their preferences by means of pairwise comparisons in the set of alternatives. Preferences can be expressed using one of the various known representations, such as fuzzy preference relations or multiplicative pairwise comparison matrices. A geometrical characterization of inconsistency evaluation is proposed by considering a pairwise comparison matrix as a point in the vector space of square matrices of order $n$ and by using different metrics to measure deviation of this matrix from full consistency. An inconsistency index is defined as the minimum distance of a pairwise comparison matrix from a consistent one, according to a fixed metric. Consequently, to each choice of a particular metric corresponds an inconsistency index. Geometrical properties of the subset of consistent matrices are investigated.

**Keywords:** consistency, pairwise comparison matrix, inconsistency index.

## 1 Introduction

Pairwise comparisons over a set of alternatives $X = \{x_1, \ldots, x_n\}$ is a well known and powerful method for preference elicitation in a decision problem. An important characteristic of this method is the capability of dealing with the imprecision of the collected data due to the unavoidable inconsistency of human judgements. Each entry $a_{ij}$ of a pairwise comparison matrix $\mathbf{A} = (a_{ij})_{n \times n}$ quantifies the degree of preference of alternative $x_i$ over alternative $x_j$. Different meanings of entries $a_{ij}$ correspond to different assumptions in preference quantification. For example, in the so called multiplicative approach [23], $a_{ij}$ is the relative preference of $x_i$ over $x_j$ and, therefore, estimates the *ratio* between the weight of $x_i$ and the weight of $x_j$, $a_{ij} \approx \frac{w_i}{w_j}$. Conversely, in the additive approaches, $a_{ij}$ represents preference *difference* between $x_i$ and $x_j$. Although different preference representations has been considered so far, included so called fuzzy preference relations, this paper focuses mainly on multiplicative representation, since the equivalence with the other representations has been widely studied [4, 6, 12]

In the multiplicative approach, a pairwise comparison matrix, *PCM*, is a positive real valued matrix $\mathbf{A} = (a_{ij})_{n \times n}$ with $a_{ii} = 1 \ \forall i$ and $a_{ij} a_{ji} = 1 \ \forall i, j$.

S. Greco et al. (Eds.): IPMU 2012, Part IV, CCIS 300, pp. 30–36, 2012.

Multiplicative reciprocity $a_{ij}a_{ji} = 1$ derives from $\frac{w_i}{w_j}\frac{w_j}{w_i} = 1$ and it is a property always required. A *PCM* is said consistent if

$$a_{ij}a_{jk} = a_{ik}, \quad i,j,k = 1,\ldots,n. \tag{1}$$

Consistency condition (1) corresponds to the ideal situation where the decision maker is perfectly coherent in her/his judgements but, in general, this property is not required, since it is well known that in making paired comparisons people do not have the intrinsic logical ability to always be consistent [22]. Although a violation of (1) to some extent is necessarily accepted, consistency has always been regarded as a desirable property, since coherent judgements are clearly considered more preferable and reliable than contradictory ones. Therefore, a correct inconsistency evaluation is regarded as a crucial task, and several indices have been proposed in order to quantify the deviation from the condition of full consistency (1) [1, 4, 8, 11, 13, 17, 18, 20, 21, 23–25]. The problem of compatibility among the numerous different methods proposed for evaluating the same notion of inconsistency degree has been addressed in some recent studies. In [3] ten known indices have been numerically compared, while in [2] a more theoretical approach is proposed, defining four characterizing properties for inconsistency indices. In [4], [5] and in some preceding papers by the same authors, a general framework for inconsistency evaluation is proposed, based on the algebraic structure of group. This paper proposes a more geometric–oriented point of view, trying to unify inconsistency evaluation by means of the notion of distance in matrix spaces. This approach is justified by the assumption that distance is the most suitable mathematical tool to evaluate how much two objects are different. Several open questions remain for future researches.

## 2    Inconsistency as Distance in Matrix Space

For a fixed $n > 2$, let $\mathbb{R}^{n \times n}$ be the vector space of real matrices of order $n$. Let $\mathcal{A} \subset \mathbb{R}^{n \times n}$ be the set of all pairwise comparison matrices of order $n$,

$$\mathcal{A} = \{\mathbf{A} = (a_{ij})_{n \times n} | a_{ij} > 0, a_{ij}a_{ji} = 1 \; \forall i,j\}.$$

Similarly, the set of *consistent* pairwise comparison matrices $\mathcal{A}^* \subset \mathcal{A}$ is defined as

$$\mathcal{A}^* = \{\mathbf{A} = (a_{ij})_{n \times n} | \mathbf{A} \in \mathcal{A}, a_{ik} = a_{ij}a_{jk} \; \forall i,j,k\}$$

An inconsistency index is a function which associates a real number to each *PCM* $\mathbf{A} \in \mathcal{A}$,

$$I : \mathcal{A} \to \mathbb{R}$$

The number $I(\mathbf{A})$ quantifies the inconsistency of $\mathbf{A}$.

The inconsistency of a *PCM* is usually viewed as a deviation from the condition of full consistency (1) and an inconsistency index as a numerical evaluation of this deviation. From a geometrical point of view, a *PCM* $\mathbf{A} = (a_{ij})_{n \times n}$ can be viewed as a point in the vector space $\mathbb{R}^{n \times n}$. Closeness to consistency condition

(1) can therefore be interpreted as closeness of $\mathbf{A}$ to a consistent matrix $\mathbf{A}_C$ in the same space. It is interesting to observe that choosing the 'closest' consistent matrix $\mathbf{A}_C$ exactly corresponds to compute the weight vector $\mathbf{w}$ from $\mathbf{A}$. In fact, $\mathbf{A}_C$ is consistent if and only if there exists a weight vector $\mathbf{w} = (w_1, ..., w_n)$ such that $\mathbf{A}_C = (\frac{w_i}{w_j})_{n \times n}$. In [7] 18 methods for deriving a weight vector $\mathbf{w} = (w_1, ..., w_n)$ from an inconsistent $PCM$ $\mathbf{A}$ are discussed. Most of them are based on the minimization of a 'distance–like' function, but only 8 over 18 are minimization methods of a true distance function. These observations suggest the following characterization of an inconsistency index.

## 2.1   Distance Induced Inconsistency

By the following definition, the inconsistency degree of a $PCM$ is characterized by its distance to the 'closest' consistent matrix according to a fixed metric, or distance, in $\mathbb{R}^{n \times n}$.

**Definition 1.** *Let $d : \mathbb{R}^{n \times n} \times \mathbb{R}^{n \times n} \longrightarrow \mathbb{R}$ be a metric in $\mathbb{R}^{n \times n}$. Given a PCM $\mathbf{A}$, let $\hat{\mathbf{B}} \in \mathcal{A}^*$ be a consistent matrix, solution of the optimization problem*

$$\min_{B \in \mathcal{A}^*} d(\mathbf{A}, \mathbf{B}). \tag{2}$$

*The inconsistency index of $\mathbf{A}$ induced by the metric $d$ is defined as*

$$I_d(\mathbf{A}) = d(\mathbf{A}, \hat{\mathbf{B}}). \tag{3}$$

Note that the above definition could also be given more shortly as $I_d(\mathbf{A}) = d(\mathbf{A}, \mathcal{A}^*)$. Several questions naturally arise from definition 1. Are the known inconsistency indices induced by a suitable distance, so that they could be defined in an equivalent way according to definition 1? Which type of inconsistency indices are induced by the most popular distances in $\mathbb{R}^{n \times n}$? In particular, which type of inconsistency indices are induced by the distances used for deriving a weight vector $\mathbf{w} = (w_1, ..., w_n)$ from an inconsistent $PCM$? As pointed out above, a number of these distances or distance–like functions are discussed in [7]. Does an inconsistency index defined by definition 1 satisfy the four characterizing properties introduced in [2]?

For some known inconsistency indices it is easy to identify which metric induces them through definition 1. For example, the discrete metric

$$d_{discrete}(\mathbf{A}, \mathbf{B}) = \begin{cases} 0 & \text{if } \mathbf{A} = \mathbf{B}, \\ 1 & \text{if } \mathbf{A} \neq \mathbf{B} \end{cases}$$

induces the discrete inconsistency index

$$I_{discrete}(\mathbf{A}) = \begin{cases} 0 & \text{if } \mathbf{A} \in \mathcal{A}^*, \\ 1 & \text{if } \mathbf{A} \notin \mathcal{A}^*. \end{cases}$$

In fact, $I_{discrete}(\mathbf{A}) = d_{discrete}(\mathbf{A}, \mathcal{A}^*) = 1 \Leftrightarrow \mathbf{A} \notin \mathcal{A}^*$.

In [15] it is proved that every method for deriving a priority vector from a *PCM*, which is correct in the consistent case, defines a somewhat 'artificial' metric which leads to the discrete topology. The corresponding $0 - 1$ inconsistency measure is nothing but the poorly satisfactory discrete inconsistency index described above.

The usual Euclidean distance

$$d_E(\mathbf{A}, \mathbf{B}) = \|\mathbf{A} - \mathbf{B}\|_2 = \left( \sum_{i=1}^{n} \sum_{j=1}^{n} \left(a_{ij} - b_{ij}\right)^2 \right)^{\frac{1}{2}}, \tag{4}$$

induces the Least Squares index $LS$ [8], except for the square root,

$$LS = \min_{w_1,\ldots,w_n} \sum_{\substack{i=1 \\ }}^{n} \sum_{\substack{j=1 \\ j \neq i}}^{n} \left(a_{ij} - \frac{w_i}{w_j}\right)^2 \quad \text{s.t.} \quad \sum_{i=1}^{n} w_i = 1, \quad w_i > 0. \tag{5}$$

The logarithmic distance

$$d_{ln}(\mathbf{A}, \mathbf{B}) = \|\ln(\mathbf{A}) - \ln(\mathbf{B})\|_2, \tag{6}$$

where $\ln(\mathbf{A})$ is defined componentwise, $\ln(\mathbf{A}) = (\ln(a_{ij}))_{n \times n}$, induces the Geometric Consistency Index GCI [11] (see proposition 1) except for the square root and a numerical factor,

$$GCI = \frac{2}{(n-1)(n-2)} \sum_{i=1}^{n} \sum_{j=i+1}^{n} \ln^2 a_{ij} \frac{w_j}{w_i}. \tag{7}$$

It can be noted that even indices introduced with no reference to the notion of distance can be characterized by means of definition 1. A relevant example is the well known consistency index $CI(\mathbf{A}) = \frac{\lambda_{max} - n}{n-1}$, defined by Saaty [23] without involving any optimization. Nevertheless, Fichtner [14] provided a metric that is minimized by the consistent matrix defined by the principal eigenvector and such that the distance of $\mathbf{A}$ from the nearest consistent matrix in this metric is exactly $CI(\mathbf{A})$.

## 2.2   Geometrical Properties

It is interesting to remark some geometrical properties of the subset $\mathcal{A}^*$ of consistent matrices [1, 9, 19]. By componentwise applying a logarithmic function to a consistent matrix $\mathbf{A_C} = (a_{ij})_{n \times n}$, a matrix $\mathbf{B} = \ln(\mathbf{A_C}) = (\ln(a_{ij}))_{n \times n} = (b_{ij})_{n \times n}$ is obtained satisfying

$$b_{ij} + b_{jk} = b_{ik}, \quad i, j, k = 1, \ldots, n. \tag{8}$$

Property (8) clearly follows from (1) and proves that the image set of $\mathcal{A}^*$ through the logarithmic function is given by a homogeneous linear system (8) and it is therefore a linear subspace of $\mathbb{R}^{n \times n}$, say $\mathcal{L} = \{\ln(\mathbf{B}); \mathbf{B} \in \mathcal{A}^*\} = \ln(\mathcal{A}^*)$. Linear spaces are simple structures and allow working with tools of linear algebra.

In [19] it is proposed to compute a consistent approximation of an inconsistent $PCM$ $\mathbf{A}$ by the orthogonal projection of the transformed matrix $\ln(\mathbf{A}) = (\ln(a_{ij}))_{n \times n}$ onto the linear subspace $\mathcal{L}$. Orthogonality refers to the usual dot product in $\mathbb{R}^{n \times n}$. The method is based on the projection theorem (see [16] for details) and is proposed, under a slightly different point of view, also in [1]. A way to obtain the orthogonal projection of $\ln(\mathbf{A})$ onto $\mathcal{L}$ is to consider first an orthogonal basis of $\mathcal{L}$. Then, project $\ln(\mathbf{A})$ on the one–dimensional subspaces of $\mathcal{L}$ generated by each vector in the orthogonal basis of $\mathcal{L}$ and, finally, sum these projections. A relevant property of the orthogonal projection is that it identifies the minimum Euclidean distance of the transformed inconsistent matrix $\ln(\mathbf{A})$ from the linear subspace $\mathcal{L}$. It is possible to prove that this method is equivalent to the one proposed in [11].

**Proposition 1.** *Orthogonal projection method described in [1, 19] is equivalent to the geometric mean method.*

*Proof.* It is known that the weight vector $\mathbf{w} = (w_1, ..., w_n)$ obtained by the geometric mean method [11] is the solution of the problem

$$\min_{\mathbf{w}} \sum_{i,j=1}^{n} (\ln a_{ij} - \ln w_i + \ln w_j)^2. \tag{9}$$

Since $\ln(\frac{w_i}{w_j}) = \ln w_i - \ln w_j$, problem (9) can be interpreted as the minimization of the Euclidean distance between $\ln(\mathbf{A})$ and the logarithmic image $\ln(\mathbf{A}_C) = (\ln(\frac{w_i}{w_j}))_{n \times n} \in \mathcal{L}$ of a consistent matrix. Then, the solution of (9) can be obtained by orthogonally projecting $\ln(\mathbf{A})$ on $\mathcal{L}$.

From the relevant fact that $\mathcal{L} = \ln(\mathcal{A}^*)$ is a linear subspace of $\mathbb{R}^{n \times n}$, it follows that $\mathcal{A}^*$ is the image of $\mathcal{L}$ through the inverse function $\exp(\cdot)$, where the function is again defined componentwise on matrix elements. Therefore, $\mathcal{A}^* = \exp(\mathcal{L})$ is a differentiable connected manifold in the positive orthant of $\mathbb{R}^{n \times n}$.

A visualization of the subset $\mathcal{A}^*$ of $3 \times 3$ consistent $PCMs$ can be given as follows. Since the three elements above the diagonal, $a_{12}$, $a_{13}$ and $a_{23}$, completely identify an arbitrary $3 \times 3$ $PCM$, such a matrix can also be represented by a point $(a_{12}, a_{13}, a_{23}) \in \mathbb{R}^3$ instead of being represented by a point in $\mathbb{R}^{3 \times 3}$. The 2–dimensional subset $\mathcal{A}^*$ of $3 \times 3$ consistent $PCMs$ is characterized (see (1)) by the equation

$$a_{13} = a_{12}a_{23}, \tag{10}$$

whose graphical image is the hyperbolic paraboloid shown in Figure 1.

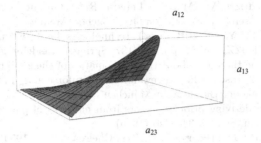

**Fig. 1.** parameterized visualization of $\mathcal{A}^*$ for $3 \times 3$ consistent matrices

# References

1. Barzilai, J.: Consistency measures for pairwise comparison matrices. Journal of Multi-Criteria Decision Analysis 7, 123–132 (1998)
2. Brunelli, M., Fedrizzi, M.: Characterizing properties of inconsistency indices for pairwise comparison matrices. Submitted to European Journal of Operational Research (2011)
3. Brunelli, M., Canal, L., Fedrizzi, M.: Inconsistency indices for pairwise comparison matrices: a numerical study. Submitted to Annals of Operations Research (2011)
4. Cavallo, B., D'Apuzzo, L.: Characterizations of Consistent Pairwise Comparison Matrices over Abelian Linearly Ordered Groups. International Journal of Intelligent Systems 25, 1035–1059 (2010)
5. Cavallo, B., D'Apuzzo, L., Squillante, M.: About a consistency index for Pairwise Comparison Matrices over a divisible alo-group. International Journal of Intelligent Systems 27, 153–175 (2012)
6. Chiclana, F., Herrera, F., Herrera-Viedma, H.: Integrating multiplicative preference relations in a multipurpose decision-making model based on fuzzy preference relations. Fuzzy Sets and Systems 122, 277–291 (2001)
7. Choo, E.U., Wedley, W.C.: A common framework for deriving preference values from pairwise comparison matrices. Computers and Operations Research 31, 893–908 (2004)
8. Chu, A.T.W., Kalaba, R.E., Springarn, K.: A comparison of two methods for determining the weights of belonging to fuzzy sets. Journal of Optimization Theory and Applications 27, 321–538 (1979)
9. Chu, M.T.: On the optimal consistent approximation to pairwise comparison matrices. Linear Algebra and its Applications 272, 155–168 (1998)
10. Cook, W.D., Kress, M.: Deriving weights from pairwise comparison ratio matrices: An axiomatic approach. European Journal of Operational Research 37, 355–362 (1988)
11. Crawford, G., Williams, C.: A note on the analysis of subjective judgement matrices. Journal of Mathematical Psychology 29, 25–40 (1985)
12. Fedrizzi, M.: On a consensus measure in a group MCDM problem. In: Kacprzyk, J., Fedrizzi, M. (eds.) Multiperson Decision Making Models using Fuzzy Sets and Possibility Theory, Theory and Decision Library. Series B: Mathematical and Statistical Methods, vol. 18, pp. 231–241. Kluwer Academic Publ., Dortrecht (1990), http://www.unitn.it/files/download/10528/9_2010.pdf

13. Fedrizzi, M., Fedrizzi, M., Marques Pereira, R.A.: On the issue of consistency in dynamical consensual aggregation. In: Bouchon Meunier, B., Gutierrez Rios, J., Magdalena, L., Yager, R.R. (eds.) Technologies for Constructing Intelligent Systems. STUDFUZZ, vol. 89, pp. 129–137. Springer, Heidelberg (2002)
14. Fichtner, J.: Some thoughts about the mathematics of the analytic hierarchy process. Report 8403, Institut für Angewandte Systemforschung und Operations Research, Hochschule der Bundeswehr München (1984)
15. Fichtner, J.: On deriving priority vectors from matrices of pairwise comparisons. Socio–Econ. Plann. Sci. 20, 341–345 (1986)
16. Gantmacher, F.R.: The theory of matrices, Chelsea, vol. 1 (1959)
17. Golden, B.L., Wang, Q.: An alternate measure of consistency. In: Golden, B.L., Wasil, E.A., Harker, P.T. (eds.) The Analythic Hierarchy Process, Applications and Studies, pp. 68–81. Springer, Heidelberg (1989)
18. Koczkodaj, W.W.: A new definition of consistency or pairwise comparisons. Mathematical & Computer Modelling 18, 79–84 (1993)
19. Koczkodaj, W.W., Orlowski, M.: An orthogonal basis for computing a consistent approximation to a pairwise comparison matrix. Computers Math. Applic. 34, 41–47 (1997)
20. Peláez, J.I., Lamata, M.T.: A new measure of consistency for positive reciprocal matrices. Computers and Mathematics with Applications 46, 1839–1845 (2003)
21. Ramík, J., Korviny, P.: Inconsistency of pair-wise comparison matrix with fuzzy elements on the geometric mean. Fuzzy Sets and Systems 161, 1604–1613 (2010)
22. Saaty, T.L.: Highlights and critical points in the theory and application of the Analytic Hierarchy Process. European Journal of Operational Research 74, 426–447 (1994)
23. Saaty, T.L.: A scaling method for priorities in hierarchical structures. Journal of Mathematical Psychology 15, 234–281 (1977)
24. Shiraishi, S., Obata, T., Daigo, M.: Properties of a positive reciprocal matrix and their application to AHP. Journal of the Operations Research Society of Japan 41, 404–414 (1998)
25. Stein, W.E., Mizzi, P.J.: The harmonic consistency index for the analythic hierarchy process. European Journal of Operational Research 177, 488–497 (2007)

# A Fuzzy Method for the Assessment of the Scientific Production

Marta Cardin and Silvio Giove

Department of Economics,
University Cà Foscari of Venice

**Abstract.** The problem of measuring the impact of a scientific output of a researcher has attracted significant interest in recent years. Most of the methodologies actual in use focus the attention to bibliometric indices and features of the journals. In this note we propose a new approach based on *class of assignment* and a fuzzy extension to asses the research output of a scholar.

**Keywords:** Aggregation, axioms, scientometrics, bibliometric index.

## 1 Introduction

Evaluating research is an important issue, especially when cuts in government spending forces to rank and discriminate among projects and researchers.

Moreover, finding an appropriate, not discretionary, evaluation method is not an easy task and about this problem there is a vast debate in literature (see for example [1] and [2]).

In effect, there is no a perfect research evaluation approach. On the one hand the traditional method based on peer review may be accurate but subjective and often very time consuming and expensive ([6] and [7]). On the other hand, each bibliometric indicator such as total number of publications, total number of citations, citations per paper, number of highly cited papers and so on, highlight only a particular dimension of the research output, but suffers of many drawbacks. Conceptually, a good approach should combine different indicators and items together, in order to take into account the multidimensional nature of research output. Nevertheless, in practice, only some quantitative data, such as the number of publications, the number of citation for each paper, the journal impact factor etc., are used in order to rank authors, papers, departments or journals. This is mainly due to the fact that other kind of information may be harder to obtain, whereas publications and citations are provided also by some international databases such as Scopus, ISI Web of Sciences or Google Scholar.

Anywise, that statistics collected on individuals' research output should be correctly and wisely used, as the 2009 Report from the International Mathematical Union [1] underlines. Similarly, the citations count is often considered the prevalent measure of research quality, but the meaning of citations can be

S. Greco et al. (Eds.): IPMU 2012, Part IV, CCIS 300, pp. 37–43, 2012.

ambiguous, thus citation-based statistics are not as objective as sometimes af-
firmed (see [1]). At present, there is a huge number of indexes that have been
proposed to evaluate scientists' research output and many of them are based
also on citation statistics.

In the literature on the assessment of the quality of research, fuzzy reasoning
have been used in different ways and applications. For example, to rank scientific
journals [3] uses fuzzy measures, while in [16] a fuzzy set based group decision
support system is proposed in order to integrate objective and subjective judgments. Again in [14] a fuzzy inference model is considered to rank journals,
conferences and authors, while a general approach based on a fuzzy inference
system is proposed in [8] to ranking scientists productivity.

In this paper we discuss a procedure to asses the scientific production of scholars. An important property of our approach is that we characterize the scientific
production of a individual by two factors that are the number of published papers and the quality of the journals where the articles are published. We rank
the journals according to some bibliometric indices and we group them in some
classes of decreasing importance.

The rest of the paper is organized as follows. Section 2 provides some basic
definitions, Section 3 introduces the class assignment approach and its axiomatic
characterization, while Section 4 proposes a fuzzy extension. Finally, Section 5
reports some conclusive remarks.

## 2   Preliminaries

To characterize convexity of real valued functions by difference operators, we
consider the approach proposed in [12].

Given any $a \in \mathbb{R}$ a *difference operator* $D_a \colon \mathbb{R}^{\mathbb{R}} \to \mathbb{R}^{\mathbb{R}}$ is defined by

$$(D_a f)(x) = f(x + a) - f(x), \qquad x \in \mathbb{R},\ a \in \mathbb{R},\ f \in \mathbb{R}^{\mathbb{R}}.$$

If $a \in \mathbb{N}$, $D_a$ operates from $\mathbb{R}^{\mathbb{N}}$ to $\mathbb{R}^{\mathbb{N}}$ and we shall use the same symbol for its
restriction to $\mathbb{R}^{\mathbb{N}}$.

We consider also the second- order difference operator $D_b D_a$ that is defined by

$$(D_b D_a f)(x) = f(x+a+b) - f(x+a) - f(x+b) + f(x) \qquad x \in \mathbb{R},\ a, b \in \mathbb{R},\ f \in \mathbb{R}^{\mathbb{R}}.$$

Using the well known fact that a continuous function $f \colon \mathbb{R} \to \mathbb{R}$ is convex if and
only if $(D_b D_a f)(x) \geqslant 0$ for all $a, b > 0$, we adfirm that a function $f \colon \mathbb{N} \to \mathbb{R}$ is
*convex*  if $(D_1 D_1 f)(n) \geqslant 0$ for all $n \in \mathbb{N}$.

Moreover a function $f \colon \mathbb{N} \to \mathbb{R}$ is said to be *concave*  if $(D_1 D_1 f)(n) \leqslant 0$ for
all $n \in \mathbb{N}$ and *linear* if $(D_1 D_1 f)(n) = 0$ for all $n \in \mathbb{N}$ .

It can be proved (see Theorem 4.1 in [12] ) that a function $f \colon \mathbb{N} \to \mathbb{R}$ is convex
(concave)if and only if $(D_b D_a f)(n) \geqslant 0$ $((D_b D_a f)(n) \leqslant 0)$ for all $a, b > 0$ and
$n \in \mathbb{N}$. Theorem 4.1 in [12] states also that a function $f \colon \mathbb{N} \to \mathbb{R}$ is linear if and
only if $(D_b D_a f)(n) = 0$ for all for all $a, b > 0$ and $n \in \mathbb{N}$ and if and only if there
are real constants $a, b$ such that $f(n) = an + b$.

We introduce an order relation between discrete functions which may be used to describe our aggregation procedure.

If $f, g$ are functions defined in $\mathbb{N}$ with values in $\mathbb{R}$, $f$ is said to be *more increasing* than $g$, $f \gg g$, if

$$(D_1 f)(n) \geqslant (D_1 g)(m) \qquad \text{for all } n, m \in \mathbb{N}.$$

If $f$ and $g$ are functions defined in $\mathbb{N}$ with values in $\mathbb{R}$, $g$ is an *asymptotically tight bound* for $f$ if there exists two positive real numbers $c_1, c_2$ such that

$$c_1 g(n) \leqslant f(n) \leqslant c_2 g(n) \quad \text{for all } n \in \mathbb{N}.$$

Namely, $g$ is an asymptotically tight bound for $f$ if $f(n)$ is "sandwiched" between $c_1 g_n$ and $c_2 g(n)$.

If $f$ is a function defined in $\mathbb{N}$ with values in $\mathbb{R}$, we say that $f$ is *asymptotically linear* if there exists a linear function $g$ defined in $\mathbb{N}$ with values in $\mathbb{R}$, such that $g$ is an asymptotically tight bound for $f$.

## 3   The Class Assignment Problem for Publications

Two factors mainly characterize the scientific production of an individual: the number of scientific papers and the "importance" of the journals where the papers have been published, so we suppose that if a paper appears in a "top" journal, it is a "top" paper. The journals are ranked accordingly to their Impact Factor or taking account of some other bibliometric indices. In a class assignment approach, one of the most applied in practical cases, each publication will be assigned to one (and only one) class of merit. The set $\mathcal{A}$ formed by the classes of merit, is thus a set of pre-ordered classes $\mathcal{A} = \{C_1, C_2 \ldots, C_M\}$, where the classes are listed in descending order.

Despite the marginal of bibliometric evaluation system, in our approach, the marginal contribution of an added paper (for a single author) sums up not in a linear fashion. This item, which characterizes the main contribution of our proposal, as to be intended as follows: the marginal gain depends not only on the intrinsic value of the added publication classified in one of the three aforementioned classes of merit, but even on the number of papers previously assigned to the same class. Adding a publication to the lowest level class produces a *subadditive* effect; this implies that one (or more) high-level (or intermediate level) publications cannot be compensated by (possibly many) low-level ones, thus discouraging an author to produce even many and many, but low-level, papers. Conversely, adding a publication in the highest level class has a *super-additive* effect, while the effect becomes naturally linear for an intermediate contribution. Permitting only a partial compensation between low, intermediate and high level papers, highlights and encourage the *quality* with respect to the *quantity*. We finally remark that the order by which a publication is assigned to one of the three classes of merit has no influence on the procedure, it is only the *accumulation* effect which is important, and not the *time* of the publication.

Another property of this models is that adding an high-level publication to a pre-existing set of high level papers, the score will increase *more than linearly*; conversely, adding a low-level publication to a pre-existing set of low- level papers, the score will increase *less than linearly*. So doing, the *marginal* gain of a new publication depends not only on its own quality, as in a linear model, but even on the quality of the previously published ones.

Thus we can suppose that the set $\mathcal{A}$ can be partitioned into three sets, $\mathcal{A} = A_I \cup A_L \cup A_D$ , with $A_I$ containing the classes of "increasing merit " of publications, $A_D$ the "decreasing merit" one, and $A_L$ containing the linearly increasing set of classes. Note that one of the above three sets of classes can be empty. A researcher is formally described by a vector $x = (x_1, \ldots, x_n)$ with non-negative integer components where $x_i$ is the number of papers in class $C_i$.

In our framework we consider the set $\mathcal{F}$ of strictly increasing functions $f \colon \mathbb{N} \to \mathbb{R}$ such that $f(0) = 0$.

We define a *scientific evaluation system* as a set of classes $\mathcal{A} = \{C_1, C_2 \ldots, C_n\}$ that is partitioned in three sets $\mathcal{A} = A_I \cup A_L \cup A_D$ and a for every class in $A_I$ a convex and not asymptotically linear function $f_i \in \mathcal{F}$, for every class in $A_L$ a linear function $f_i \in \mathcal{F}$ and for every class in $A_D$ a concave and not asymptotically linear function $f_i \in \mathcal{F}$.

Moreover we suppose that the functions that characterize the elements in $A_I$ and in $A_D$ are in descending order with respect to the preorder $\gg$.

The *scientific evaluation function* associated with the scientific evaluation system is defined as

$$F(x_1, \ldots, x_n) = \sum_{i=1}^{n} f_i(x_i).$$

Then we can prove the following result.

**Proposition 1.** *Both the sets $A_I$ and $A_D$ contains at most one class only.*

This result follows immediately from the following proposition.

**Proposition 2.** *If $f, g$ are convex functions in $\mathcal{F}$ such that $f \gg g$, then $g$ is asymptotically linear. If $f, g$ are concave functions in $\mathcal{F}$ such that $f \gg g$ then $f$ is asymptotically linear.*

*Proof.* We have that

$$f(n+1) - f(n) \geqslant g(m+1) - g(m) \qquad \text{for all } n, m \in \mathbb{N}.$$

Then we have for all $m \in \mathbb{N}$, $g(m+1) - g(m) \leqslant f(1) - f(0) = f(1)$ and so we can prove that for all $n \in \mathbb{N}$, $g(n) \leqslant nf(1)$. Since the function $g$ is convex the difference $g(n+1) - g(n)$ is increasing with respect to $n$ and so we can prove that $g(n+1) - g(n) \geqslant g(1) - g(0) = g(1)$ and then for all $n \in \mathbb{N}$, $g(n) \geqslant ng(1)$. We can conclude that for all $n \in \mathbb{N}$, $g(n) \geqslant ng(1)$. By the fact that $f(1), g(1) \neq 0$ we can prove that $g$ is asymptotically linear.

If $f, g$ are concave functions in $\mathcal{F}$ such that $f(n+1) - f(n) \geqslant g(m+1) - g(m)$ for all $n, m \in \mathbb{N}$, it follows that $f(n+1) - f(n) \geqslant g(1)$. Then for all

$n \in \mathbb{N}$, $f(n) \geqslant ng(1)$ and being $f$ concave, the difference $g(n+1) - g(n)$ is decreasing with respect to $n$, thus $f(n+1) - f(n) \leqslant f(1)$. As a consequence, for all $n \in \mathbb{N}$, $f(n) \leqslant nf(1)$, and then $f$ is asymptotically linear.

Now we consider a particular case of a scientific evaluation system: a *three-classes scientific evaluation system*, i.e. the sets $A_I$, $A_L$ and $A_D$ are singleton sets and so the system is characterized by three functions in $\mathcal{F}$, $f_i, i = 1, 2, 3$, with $f_1$ convex, $f_2$ linear and $f_3$ concave. Then we consider a *three-classes scientific evaluation function* $F: \mathbb{N}^3 \to \mathbb{R}$ defined by

$$F(x_1, x_2, x_3) = \sum_{i=1}^{3} f_i(x_i) \tag{1}$$

The following Axioms characterize certain properties of a three-classes scientific evaluation system, as can be easily proved.

**A1** If the vectors $x, y$ are such that $x \leqslant y$ with respect to the componentwise order then $F(x) \leqslant F(y)$.

This is clearly a additivity property with respect to different classes.

**A2** If the vectors $x$ and $y$ are such that $\min\{x_i, y_i\} = 0$ for every $i = 1, 2, 3$ then $F(x + y) = F(x) + F(y)$.

The following axiom states the importance of the classes.

**A3** If the vectors $y$ and $z$ are obtained from vector $x$ by adding a new pubblication respectively in class $i, j$ with $1 \leqslant i \leqslant j \leqslant 3$ then $F(y) \geqslant F(z)$.

The next axioms characterize the proposed evaluation system, based on the property of *increasing, constant,* or *decreasing* marginal gains for the three ordered classes.

**A4** $F(x_1 + 2, x_2, x_3) - F(x_1 + 1, x_2, x_3) \geqslant F(x_1 + 1, x_2, x_3) - F(x_1, x_2, x_3)$ for every vector $x$.

**A5** $F(x_1, x_2 + 2, x_3) - F(x_1, x_2 + 1, x_3) = F(x_1, x_2 + 1, x_3) - F(x_1, x_2, x_3)$ for every vector $x$.

**A6** $F(x_1, x_2, x_3 + 2) - F(x_1, x_2, x_3 + 1) \leqslant F(x_1, x_2, x_3 + 1) - F(x_1, x_2, x_3)$ for every vector $x$.

## 4  The Fuzzy Model

In any classification system, a *rigid* border between two consecutive classes introduces undesired discontinuity, i.e., in the neighborhood of the border, even a very small variation moves the object to be classified from one class to an other one. Is is commonly recognized that fuzzy logic by-passes this undesired effect, introducing a *smooth* border between classes, using suitable membership function, see [8]. To this purpose, formula 1 used for the *crisp* evaluation will be consequently modified. Let $B^a\{p_1^a, p_2^a, ..., p_N^a\}$ be the set of publications of author $a$, which contains the performance score $p_i^a$ of his $N^a$ publications, i.e. the result of an aggregation of some characterizing parameters (the impact factor of the Journal, the citation counts, the number of co-authors, the date of publication, and so on)[1]. Given the $j$-th publication, we can compute its belonging degree to one of the three classes of merit using a suitably *membership function*[2] $\mu_k(p_j)$, the *degree of truth* of the proposition: *The j-th publication belongs to the class $C_k$, given the value $p_j$*, or equivalently $\equiv Prob(p_j \in C_k|p)$, the *coherent* conditional probability that a paper belong to the $k$-th class, given the performance score $p_i^a$. The identification of the fuzzy memberships $\mu_k$ is beyond the scope of our work, we limit to observe that a wide family of parametric functions could be used; for a general approach based on Fuzzy Inference System, see [8].

Following the above described approach, the scoring rule consists into summing up the fuzzy scores of the 3 classes, respectively filtered by $f_1$, a convex function (for the *excellence* class, by $f_2$, a concave one (for the *low* class), and by the linear function $f_3$ for the *intermediate* class. Being $\mu_k(p_i)$ the membership degree to the $k$-th class of the $i$-th publication, we can write:

$$\pi^a = \sum_{k=1}^{3} f_k \left( \sum_{i=1}^{N_p^a} \mu_k(p_i^a) \right) \tag{2}$$

In contrast with the widely used methods like to the *h-index* and similar, this method uses all the available information, and includes the concept of *classes of merit*, widely in use in many real evaluation systems. Finally, the border between two consecutive classes is smoothed, avoiding discontinuity in the classification procedure. This method can be applied to rank a set of authors on the basis of the score $\pi^a$.

## 5   Final Remarks and Conclusions

Defining an index that quantify the research production of an author is a challenging task, and many proposal appeared in the specialized literature. In this contribution we propose an approach based on different classes of merit, a commonly used categorization in many University Departments. The classes are determined by the *importance* of the journals where the papers have been published. The main strength of our indicator is that it considers both the quantity and quality of the scientific production of an author, as well as the fact that it properly encourages authors to selective publication strategies, given that the

---

[1] The way to obtain $p_i^a$ is not here considered, supposing that the performance scores were previously computed, see for instance [8].

[2] A deep discussion about the nature of a membership as *conditional coherent* probability can be found in [9].

marginal contribution of an added paper increases only for high level one. In addition, the index is simple to be calculated and it can be used to compare researchers of different scientific fields, despite other methods based, for instance, on the citation count, strongly dependent on the research field. However, our index depends on the length of the scientific career, and, in this preliminary proposal, does not take the number of coauthors into account. We intend to extend our approach to explicitly consider these items in a future extension.

# References

1. Adler, R., Ewing, J., Taylor, P.: Citation Statistics. A Report from the International Mathematical Union (IMU) in Cooperation with the International Council of Industrial and Applied Mathematics (ICIAM) and the Institute of Mathematical Statistics (IMS). Statistical Science 24, 1–14 (2009)
2. Alonso, S., Cabrerizo, F.J., Herrera-Viedma, E., Herrera, F.: h-Index: A review focused in its variants, computation and standardization for different scientific fields. Journal of Informetrics 3, 273–289 (2009)
3. Beliakov, G., James, S.: Citation-based journal ranks: the use of fuzzy measure. Fuzzy Sets and Systems 167, 101–119 (2011)
4. Bouyssou, D., Marchant, T.: Consistent bibliometric rankings of authors and of journals. Journal of Infometrics 4, 365–378 (2010)
5. Bouyssou, D., Marchant, T.: Bibliometric rankings of journals based on Impact Factors: An axiomatic approach. Journal of Infometrics 5, 75–86 (2011)
6. Campanario, J.M.: Peer review for journals as it stands today, part 1. Science Communication 19, 181–211 (1998)
7. Campanario, J.M.: Peer review for journals as it stands today, part 2. Science Communication 19, 277–306 (1998)
8. Cardin, M., Corazza, M., Funari, S., Giove, S.: A Fuzzy-based Scoring Rule for Author Ranking - an alternative of h-index. In: Apolloni, B., Bassis, S., Morabito, C.F. (eds.) Neural Nets, WIRN 2011, vol. 234, pp. 36–45. IOS Press (2011)
9. Coletti, G., Scozzafava, R.: Conditional probability, fuzzy sets, and possibility: a unifying view. Fuzzy Sets and Systems 144, 227–249 (2004)
10. Franceschet, M., Costantini, A.: The first Italian research assessment excercise: A bibliometric perspective. Journal of Informetrics 5, 275–291 (2011)
11. Hirsch, J.: An index to quantify an individuals scientific research output. Proceedings of the National Academy of Sciences 102, 16569–16572 (2005)
12. Kiselman, C.O.: Chararcterizing digital straightness and digital convexity by means of difference operators. Mathematika 57, 355–380 (2011)
13. Klement, E.P., Mesiar, R., Pap, E.: Triangular norms. Journal of Cybernetics (2000)
14. Hussain, S., Grahn, H.: Ranking journals, conferences and authors in computer graphics: a fuzzy reasoning. In: IADIS International Conference Informatics, pp. 75–82 (2008)
15. Terano, T., Asai, K., Sugeno, M.: Applied Fuzzy Systems. Academic Press Inc., Boston (1994)
16. Turban, E., Zhou, D., Ma, J.: A group decision support approach to evaluating journals. Information & Management 42, 31–44 (2004)
17. Vincke, P., Gassner, M., Roy, B.: Multicriteria Decision Aid. John Wiley & Sons, New York (1989)

# A Possibilistic Approach to Evaluating Equity-Linked Life Insurance Policies

Luca Anzilli

Department of Economics, Mathematics and Statistics
University of Salento, Italy
luca.anzilli@unisalento.it

**Abstract.** We deal with the problem of pricing equity-linked life insurance policies under uncertainty of randomness and fuzziness. Firstly, we propose an evaluation method for general life insurance, with stochastic representation of mortality and fuzzy quantification of financial present values, by defining the actuarial value of the liabilities as the expectation of a fuzzy random variable. Then, we apply the suggested methodology to the fair valuation of an equity-linked policy. In such a contract policyholder's benefits are linked to the performance of a reference fund. We perform the risk neutral valuation in a fuzzy binomial-tree model. The crisp value of the policy is obtained by means of a "defuzzification method" based on possibilistic mean values. A numerical example illustrates how the proposed method allows the actuary to model the fuzziness in the parameters according to his subjective judgement.

**Keywords:** Fuzzy numbers, Fuzzy random variables, Possibilistic mean values, Life insurance.

## 1 Introduction

Fuzzy set theory has been applied to incorporate vague or incomplete information into insurance pricing, because of its ability to deal with vagueness and imprecision [1]. This type of information is reflected in the subjective judgment of the actuary and cannot be handled by probability theory. In traditional life insurance, characterized by deterministic benefits, the main application of fuzzy logic has been to model the discount rates as fuzzy numbers. The fuzzy premium of term insurance, deferred annuities and pure endowment policies has been studied in [2–4] using the fuzzy financial model developed in [5]. A comprehensive review of the use of fuzzy logic in insurance can be found in [6].

Modern life insurance contracts incorporate demographic and financial uncertainty, since the date of payment of benefit is determined by demographic events and the amount of benefit is linked to financial markets. In equity-linked life insurance policies [7] some or all of the premium is invested in a reference fund and benefits depend on the performance of the underlying asset (equity). An equity-linked endowment policy with a minimum guaranteed is an insurance policy whose benefit payable on death or at maturity is given by the grater of some guaranteed amount and the value of the investment in the reference fund.

S. Greco et al. (Eds.): IPMU 2012, Part IV, CCIS 300, pp. 44–53, 2012.

In a fair valuation approach [8] this contract is treated like an European-type derivative [9] and the premium, i.e. the value of the policy, is computed by using standard actuarial tools for demographic risk and an appropriate stochastic pricing model for financial risk.

In this paper we propose a fuzzy pricing model for equity-linked life insurance contracts. The asset price evolution is described using a binomial-tree model ([10]) where the stock price at each node of the tree takes imprecise values. This approach incorporates random and fuzzy uncertainty since the future lifetime of the insured is a random variable and the up and down factors that determine the movements of the asset price are fuzzy numbers. Therefore, in order to deal with both randomness and fuzziness we model the present value of the liabilities as a fuzzy random variable [11–14]. Related to our approach, fuzzy random variables are applied in [15] for pricing life annuities (with deterministic benefits and fuzzy discount rates). Since the expectation of a fuzzy random variable is a fuzzy number, in order to associate to the value of the policy a crisp number we suggest a "defuzzification method" based on the possibilistic mean values introduced in [16]. Moreover, to provide more flexibility, we describe fuzziness by means of a nonlinear-type of fuzzy number (introduced in [18]) and we show that this choice, in a possibilistic framework, allows the actuary to modify possibility distributions according to his subjective judgement.

In Section 2 we give basic definitions and notations and introduce the concept of fuzzy random variable. In Section 3 we propose a fuzzy pricing model for general life insurance policies and suggest a possibilistic approach to defuzzification problem. In Section 4 we apply our methodology to equity-linked life insurance contracts. Finally, in Section 5 we present a numerical example.

## 2   Fuzzy Random Variables

Let $X$ denote a universe of discourse. A fuzzy set $\tilde{A}$ in $X$ is defined by a membership function $\mu_{\tilde{A}} : X \to [0, 1]$ which assigns to each element of $X$ a grade of membership to the set $\tilde{A}$. The support and the core of $\tilde{A}$ are defined, respectively, as the crisp sets $supp(\tilde{A}) = \{x \in X; \mu_{\tilde{A}}(x) > 0\}$ and $core(\tilde{A}) = \{x \in X; \mu_{\tilde{A}}(x) = 1\}$. A fuzzy set $\tilde{A}$ is normal if its core is nonempty. A fuzzy number $\tilde{A}$ is a fuzzy set of the real line with a normal, convex and upper-semicontinuous membership function of bounded support. The $\alpha$-cut of $\tilde{A}$, $0 \leq \alpha \leq 1$, is defined as the crisp set $\tilde{A}_{\alpha} = \{x \in X; \mu_{\tilde{A}}(x) \geq \alpha\}$ if $0 < \alpha \leq 1$ and as the closure of the support if $\alpha = 0$. Each $\alpha$-cut of a fuzzy number is a closed interval $\tilde{A}_{\alpha} = [\underline{a}_{\alpha}, \overline{a}_{\alpha}]$, for $0 \leq \alpha \leq 1$, where $\underline{a}_{\alpha} = \inf \tilde{A}_{\alpha}$ and $\overline{a}_{\alpha} = \sup \tilde{A}_{\alpha}$.

Fuzzy random variables were introduced to combine both random and fuzzy uncertainty, but different approaches to this concept have been developed in the literature (see [11, 12, 14]). In the following we use the definition given by Puri and Ralescu [14].

**Definition 1.** *Let $(\Omega, \mathcal{A})$ be a measurable space, $(\mathbb{R}, \mathcal{B})$ the Borel measurable space and $\mathcal{F}(\mathbb{R})$ denote the set of fuzzy numbers. A mapping $\tilde{\mathcal{X}} : \Omega \to \mathcal{F}(\mathbb{R})$ is said to be a fuzzy random variable if*

$$\forall \alpha \in [0,1] \quad \forall B \in \mathcal{B} \qquad \{\omega \in \Omega \,;\, \tilde{\mathcal{X}}(\omega)_\alpha \cap B \neq \emptyset\} \in \mathcal{A}$$

*where* $\tilde{\mathcal{X}}(\omega)_\alpha = [\underline{\mathcal{X}(\omega)}_\alpha, \overline{\mathcal{X}(\omega)}_\alpha]$ *are the $\alpha$-cuts of the fuzzy number* $\tilde{\mathcal{X}}(\omega)$.

A fuzzy random variable $\tilde{\mathcal{X}}$ defines for any $\alpha \in [0,1]$ the random variables $\underline{\mathcal{X}}_\alpha$ and $\overline{\mathcal{X}}_\alpha$ whose realisations are, respectively, the lower and upper extremes of $\alpha$-cuts of $\tilde{\mathcal{X}}(\omega)$ (see [19]). Thus $\underline{\mathcal{X}}_\alpha : \Omega \to \mathbb{R}$ is a random variable such that $\underline{\mathcal{X}}_\alpha(\omega) = \underline{\mathcal{X}(\omega)}_\alpha$ for all $\omega \in \Omega$ and $\overline{\mathcal{X}}_\alpha : \Omega \to \mathbb{R}$ is a random variable defined by $\overline{\mathcal{X}}_\alpha(\omega) = \overline{\mathcal{X}(\omega)}_\alpha$. A fuzzy random variable $\tilde{\mathcal{X}}$ is said to be discrete if $\Omega$ is a countable set. Let $(\Omega, \mathcal{A}, P)$ be a probability space and $\tilde{\mathcal{X}} : \Omega \to \mathcal{F}(\mathbb{R})$ a discrete fuzzy random variable. The expectation of $\tilde{\mathcal{X}}$ is the fuzzy number $E(\tilde{\mathcal{X}})$ whose $\alpha$-cuts, for $\alpha \in [0,1]$, are given by (see [14, 15])

$$E(\tilde{\mathcal{X}})_\alpha = [\underline{E(\tilde{\mathcal{X}})}_\alpha, \overline{E(\tilde{\mathcal{X}})}_\alpha] = [E(\underline{\mathcal{X}}_\alpha), E(\overline{\mathcal{X}}_\alpha)].$$

## 3   A Fuzzy Pricing Model for Life Insurance Policies

In this section we propose an evaluation model for general life insurance contracts. We develop our methodology for endowment policies but it can be adapted to other contracts like pure endowment policies, life annuities, whole life insurance, etc. An *endowment policy* is a life insurance contract in which the insurance company agrees to pay a specified benefit to the beneficiary if the insured dies within the term of the contract or survives the maturity date [20]. We assume that the policy is paid by a single premium.

Consider an endowment policy issued at time 0 and maturing $T$ years later. We choose the year as time unit and assume $T$ as an integer. Let $x$ be the age (measured in years) of the insured at time 0. We denote by $b_t$, $t = 1, 2, \ldots, T$, the benefit payable at the end of year $t$ in case of death of the insured in the year $t$, and by $c_T$ the benefit payable at maturity $T$ if the insured is still alive.

Adopting the classical equivalence principle the single premium, i.e. the value of the policy, is given by the expected present value (or actuarial value) of benefits (liabilities). Furthermore, in a fair valuation approach, the value of the policy is computed by using standard actuarial tools for demographic risk and an appropriate financial pricing model for the financial risk. In order to introduce a fair pricing model incorporating the imprecision or lack of knowledge on financial markets, we consider uncertainty of randomness and fuzziness: random uncertainty, since the future lifetime of the insured is a random variable and fuzzy uncertainty, since the present values of benefits are described by fuzzy numbers.

For an insured aged $x$ we denote by $_{t-1/1}q_x$ the probability to die between ages $x + t - 1$ and $x + t$ and by $_T p_x$ the probability to survive until maturity $T$. These probabilities can be obtained from life tables. Moreover, we denote by $\tilde{v}_0(y_t)$ the financial value at time 0 of a contract that pays $y_t$ at time $t$ and assume that $\tilde{v}_0(y_t)$ is a fuzzy number with $\alpha$-cuts $\tilde{v}_0(y_t)_\alpha = [\underline{v_0(y_t)}_\alpha, \overline{v_0(y_t)}_\alpha]$.

To combine both randomness and fuzziness we model the present value of the liabilities as a fuzzy random variable. We define the space of events as

$$\Omega = \{\omega_0, \omega_1, \omega_2, \ldots, \omega_T\}$$

where $\omega_m$="the insured dies within the $(m+1)$-th year of the contract", $m = 0, \ldots, T-1$, and $\omega_T$="the insured is still alive at maturity $T$". Then $P(\omega_m) = {}_{m/1}q_x$ if $m = 0, 1, \ldots, T-1$ and $P(\omega_T) = {}_Tp_x$ if $m = T$.

**Definition 2.** *We define the fuzzy random present value of the liabilities of an endowment life insurance policy as a fuzzy random variable* $\tilde{\mathcal{L}} : \Omega \to \mathcal{F}(\mathbb{R})$ *such that for any* $m = 0, 1, \ldots, T$ *the fuzzy number* $\tilde{\mathcal{L}}(\omega_m)$ *is given by*

$$\tilde{\mathcal{L}}(\omega_m) = \sum_{t=1}^{T} \phi_t(\omega_m)\,\tilde{v}_0(b_t) + \psi_T(\omega_m)\,\tilde{v}_0(c_T) \tag{1}$$

*where the random variables* $\phi_t$, $t = 1, \ldots, T$, *are defined by* $\phi_t(\omega_m) = 1$ *if* $m + 1 = t$ *and* $\phi_t(\omega_m) = 0$ *otherwise and the random variable* $\psi_T$ *is defined by* $\psi_T(\omega_m) = 1$ *if* $m = T$ *and* $\psi_T(\omega_m) = 0$ *otherwise (for the arithmetic operations on fuzzy numbers we refer to [21]).*

Thus, for $m = 0, \ldots, T-1$ (i.e. if the insured dies within the $(m+1)$-th year of the contract) $\tilde{\mathcal{L}}(\omega_m) = \tilde{v}_0(b_{m+1})$; for $m = T$ (i.e. if the insured is still alive at maturity) $\tilde{\mathcal{L}}(\omega_T) = \tilde{v}_0(c_T)$ . The $\alpha$-cuts $\tilde{\mathcal{L}}(\omega_m)_\alpha = [\underline{\mathcal{L}(\omega_m)}_\alpha, \overline{\mathcal{L}(\omega_m)}_\alpha]$ are given by

$$\underline{\mathcal{L}(\omega_m)}_\alpha = \sum_{t=1}^{T} \phi_t(\omega_m)\,\underline{v_0(b_t)}_\alpha + \psi_T(\omega_m)\,\underline{v_0(c_T)}_\alpha,$$

$$\overline{\mathcal{L}(\omega_m)}_\alpha = \sum_{t=1}^{T} \phi_t(\omega_m)\,\overline{v_0(b_t)}_\alpha + \psi_T(\omega_m)\,\overline{v_0(c_T)}_\alpha.$$

The fuzzy random variable $\tilde{\mathcal{L}}$ defines for any $\alpha \in [0,1]$ the random variables $\underline{\mathcal{L}}_\alpha$ and $\overline{\mathcal{L}}_\alpha$ whose realisations are, respectively, $\underline{\mathcal{L}(\omega_m)}_\alpha$ and $\overline{\mathcal{L}(\omega_m)}_\alpha$. The *fuzzy actuarial value* of the liabilities is given by the expectation $E(\tilde{\mathcal{L}})$. From the above discussion, we can easily deduce the following result.

**Proposition 1.** *The expectation* $E(\tilde{\mathcal{L}})$ *of the fuzzy random present value* $\tilde{\mathcal{L}}$ *is the fuzzy number with* $\alpha$-*cuts,* $\alpha \in [0,1]$,

$$E(\tilde{\mathcal{L}})_\alpha = \left[\underline{E(\tilde{\mathcal{L}})}_\alpha, \overline{E(\tilde{\mathcal{L}})}_\alpha\right] = [E(\underline{\mathcal{L}}_\alpha), E(\overline{\mathcal{L}}_\alpha)]$$

*where*

$$\underline{E(\tilde{\mathcal{L}})}_\alpha = E(\underline{\mathcal{L}}_\alpha) = \sum_{m=0}^{T} \underline{\mathcal{L}(\omega_m)}_\alpha\, P(\omega_m) = \sum_{t=1}^{T} \underline{v_0(b_t)}_\alpha\, {}_{t-1/1}q_x + \underline{v_0(c_T)}_\alpha\, {}_Tp_x$$

$$\overline{E(\tilde{\mathcal{L}})}_\alpha = E(\overline{\mathcal{L}}_\alpha) = \sum_{m=0}^{T} \overline{\mathcal{L}(\omega_m)}_\alpha\, P(\omega_m) = \sum_{t=1}^{T} \overline{v_0(b_t)}_\alpha\, {}_{t-1/1}q_x + \overline{v_0(c_T)}_\alpha\, {}_Tp_x.$$

$$\tag{2}$$

*Example 1.* In traditional life insurance policies, where benefits are deterministic amounts, the present values are computed by discounting future payments at an appropriate interest rate. Therefore, if we assume, as is usually done in fuzzy actuarial mathematics (see e.g. [2]), that the annual interest rate is a fuzzy number $\tilde{r}$, we get $\tilde{v}_0(b_t) = b_t \, (1+\tilde{r})^{-t}$, $t = 1, 2, \ldots, T$ and $\tilde{v}_0(c_T) = c_T \, (1+\tilde{r})^{-T}$. Hence, denoting the $\alpha$-cuts of $\tilde{r}$ by $\tilde{r}_\alpha = [\underline{r}_\alpha, \overline{r}_\alpha]$, we obtain

$$\underline{E(\tilde{\mathcal{L}})}_\alpha = \sum_{t=1}^{T} b_t \, (1+\overline{r}_\alpha)^{-t} \,\, _{t-1/1}q_x + c_T \, (1+\overline{r}_\alpha)^{-T} \,\, _T p_x \,,$$

$$\overline{E(\tilde{\mathcal{L}})}_\alpha = \sum_{t=1}^{T} b_t \, (1+\underline{r}_\alpha)^{-t} \,\, _{t-1/1}q_x + c_T \, (1+\underline{r}_\alpha)^{-T} \,\, _T p_x \,.$$

## 3.1   A Possibilistic Approach to Defuzzification

Since the expectation $E(\tilde{\mathcal{L}})$ is a fuzzy number, it is convenient to find a crisp number that synthesises the value of the liabilities and thus the value of the policy. To this end, we suggest a "defuzzification method" based on the possibilistic mean values introduced in [16, 17]. The $w$-weighted interval-valued possibilistic mean of $E(\tilde{\mathcal{L}})$ is defined as $M_w(E(\tilde{\mathcal{L}})) = [M_w^-(E(\tilde{\mathcal{L}})), M_w^+(E(\tilde{\mathcal{L}}))]$ where

$$M_w^-(E(\tilde{\mathcal{L}})) = \int_0^1 \underline{E(\tilde{\mathcal{L}})}_\alpha w(\alpha) \, d\alpha \,, \qquad M_w^+(E(\tilde{\mathcal{L}})) = \int_0^1 \overline{E(\tilde{\mathcal{L}})}_\alpha w(\alpha) \, d\alpha \,.$$

The weighting function $w : [0, 1] \to \mathbb{R}$ is a non-negative and monotone increasing function satisfying the normalization condition $\int_0^1 w(\alpha) \, d\alpha = 1$. The $w$-weighted possibilistic mean value of the liabilities is the crisp number

$$\bar{M}_w(E(\tilde{\mathcal{L}})) = \int_0^1 \frac{\underline{E(\tilde{\mathcal{L}})}_\alpha + \overline{E(\tilde{\mathcal{L}})}_\alpha}{2} w(\alpha) \, d\alpha = \frac{M_w^-(E(\tilde{\mathcal{L}})) + M_w^+(E(\tilde{\mathcal{L}}))}{2} \,.$$

## 4   Equity-Linked Life Insurance Policies

In this section we apply our proposed model to evaluate an equity-linked life insurance contract. In such a policy a part of the premium is invested in a reference fund and benefits depend on the performance of the underlying asset.

Consider an equity-linked endowment policy issued at time 0 and maturing at time $T$. Let $S_t$ denote the unit price of the reference fund at time $t$. Assume that at time 0 an amount $C_0$ is invested in the reference fund. Thus the value of this investment at time $t$ is $F_t = (C_0/S_0)S_t$. We assume that the benefits are given by

$$b_t = f_t(F_t), \quad t = 1, 2, \ldots, T \,, \qquad\qquad c_T = g_T(F_T),$$

where $f_t, g_T$ are suitable functions. For example, if the benefit is the current value of the investment then $f_t(F_t) = F_t$. If the policy offers a minimum guarantee then $f_t(F_t) = \max\{F_t, H_t\}$.

## 4.1  The Fuzzy Binomial-Tree Model

Pricing equity-linked policies requires modelling two sources of uncertainty: the behaviour of mortality and the evolution of underlying asset price. To model the dynamics of the asset price we adopt the Cox, Ross and Rubinstein binomial model [10]. We discretize each unit-length period (one year) into $N$ subintervals of equal length $\Delta = 1/N$. Hence the interval $[0, T]$ is divided into $NT$ subintervals $[k\Delta, (k + 1)\Delta]$, $k = 0, 1, \ldots, TN - 1$. We consider a fuzzy version of binomial model (see [22–25]). Assume that at each step the asset price can only move up by an up jump factor, or down by a down jump factor. Since up and down factors depend on the volatility of the asset and it is often hard to give a precise estimate of the volatility, we model the up and down jump factors as fuzzy numbers $\tilde{u}$ and $\tilde{d}$, respectively, with $\alpha$-cuts $\tilde{u}_\alpha = [\underline{u}_\alpha, \overline{u}_\alpha]$ and $\tilde{d}_\alpha = [\underline{d}_\alpha, \overline{d}_\alpha]$, $\alpha \in [0, 1]$. Thus, given the price of the underlying asset $\tilde{S}_{k\Delta}$ at time $k\Delta$, the price of the asset $\tilde{S}_{(k+1)\Delta}$ at time $(k + 1)\Delta$ can take only two possible values $\tilde{u}\tilde{S}_{k\Delta}$ and $\tilde{d}\tilde{S}_{k\Delta}$. We assume that the risk-free interest rate is a crisp number and denote by $r$ the annual risk-free interest rate and by $\rho$ the risk-free interest rate over one step of length $\Delta = 1/N$. Thus $\rho = (1 + r)^\Delta - 1$. Assuming that financial markets are perfectly competitive, frictionless and arbitrage-free, the no-arbitrage condition $\overline{d}_0 < 1 + \rho < \underline{u}_0$ must be satisfied [9, 22].

In this framework, the price at time 0 of a contract that pays the payoff $y_t = f(S_t)$ at time $t$, $t = 1, 2, \ldots, T$, is equal to the expected value of $y_t$, under the risk-neutral probabilities [9], discounted at the risk-free interest rate. The risk neutral probabilities can be computed as solution of the following fuzzy system

$$\begin{cases} \tilde{q}_d + \tilde{q}_u = 1 \\ \tilde{d}\,\tilde{q}_d + \tilde{u}\,\tilde{q}_u = 1 + \rho \end{cases} \tag{3}$$

where the fuzzy numbers $\tilde{q}_u$ and $\tilde{q}_d$ are the fuzzy up and down probabilities. Using the methodology proposed in [26] the solution of the fuzzy system (3) is found to be (see [22–24] for details) $\tilde{q}_u, \tilde{q}_d$ with $\alpha$-cuts given, respectively, by

$$(\tilde{q}_u)_\alpha = [\underline{q}_\alpha, \overline{q}_\alpha], \qquad (\tilde{q}_d)_\alpha = [1 - \overline{q}_\alpha, 1 - \underline{q}_\alpha] \tag{4}$$

where

$$\underline{q}_\alpha = \frac{1 + \rho - \overline{d}_\alpha}{\overline{u}_\alpha - \overline{d}_\alpha}, \qquad \overline{q}_\alpha = \frac{1 + \rho - \underline{d}_\alpha}{\underline{u}_\alpha - \underline{d}_\alpha}. \tag{5}$$

The price at time 0 of a contract that pays $y_t = f(S_t)$ at time $t$ is

$$\tilde{v}_0(y_t) = (1 + r)^{-t} \sum_{k=0}^{tN} \binom{tN}{k} \tilde{q}_u^k \tilde{q}_d^{tN-k} \tilde{f}(S_0\,\tilde{u}^k\,\tilde{d}^{tN-k}) \tag{6}$$

where $\tilde{f}$ is defined by Zadeh's extension principle. We assume that $f$ is an increasing continuous function. Then from Nguyen's theorem if $\tilde{A}$ is a fuzzy number we have $\tilde{f}(\tilde{A})_\alpha = f(\tilde{A}_\alpha) = f([\underline{a}_\alpha, \overline{a}_\alpha]) = [f(\underline{a}_\alpha), f(\overline{a}_\alpha)]$. Thus the $\alpha$-cuts $\tilde{v}_0(y_t)_\alpha = [\underline{v_0(y_t)}_\alpha, v_0(y_t)_\alpha]$, $\alpha \in [0, 1]$, are given by

$$\underline{v_0(y_t)}_\alpha = (1+r)^{-t} \sum_{k=0}^{tN} \binom{tN}{k} \underline{q}_\alpha^k (1-\overline{q}_\alpha)^{tN-k} f(S_0 \underline{u}_\alpha^k \underline{d}_\alpha^{tN-k})$$

$$\overline{v_0(y_t)}_\alpha = (1+r)^{-t} \sum_{k=0}^{tN} \binom{tN}{k} \overline{q}_\alpha^k (1-\underline{q}_\alpha)^{tN-k} f(S_0 \overline{u}_\alpha^k \overline{d}_\alpha^{tN-k}).$$
(7)

## 4.2    Evaluation of Equity-Linked Life Endowment Policies

From (1), by using (6), we obtain that the fuzzy random present value of the liabilities of an equity-linked endowment policy is the fuzzy random variable $\tilde{\mathcal{L}} : \Omega \to \mathcal{F}(\mathbb{R})$ such that for all $m = 0, 1, \ldots, T$

$$\tilde{\mathcal{L}}(\omega_m) = \sum_{t=1}^{T} (1+r)^{-t} \phi_t(\omega_m) \sum_{k=0}^{tN} \binom{tN}{k} \tilde{q}_u^k \tilde{q}_d^{tN-k} \tilde{f}_t(C_0 \tilde{u}^k \tilde{d}^{tN-k})$$

$$+ (1+r)^{-T} \psi_T(\omega_m) \sum_{k=0}^{TN} \binom{TN}{k} \tilde{q}_u^k \tilde{q}_d^{TN-k} \tilde{g}_T(C_0 \tilde{u}^k \tilde{d}^{TN-k})$$

where $\tilde{f}_t$, $\tilde{g}_T$ are defined by Zadeh's extension principle. Assume that $f_t$, $t = 1, \ldots, T$ and $g_T$ are increasing continuous functions. From (2), by using (7), the fuzzy actuarial value of the liabilities is the expectation $E(\tilde{\mathcal{L}})$ with $\alpha$-cuts $E(\tilde{\mathcal{L}})_\alpha = \left[ \underline{E(\tilde{\mathcal{L}})}_\alpha, \overline{E(\tilde{\mathcal{L}})}_\alpha \right]$, $\alpha \in [0,1]$, given by

$$\underline{E(\tilde{\mathcal{L}})}_\alpha = \sum_{t=1}^{T} {}_{t-1/1}q_x (1+r)^{-t} \sum_{k=0}^{tN} \binom{tN}{k} \underline{q}_\alpha^k (1-\overline{q}_\alpha)^{tN-k} f_t(C_0 \underline{u}_\alpha^k \underline{d}_\alpha^{tN-k})$$

$$+ {}_T p_x (1+r)^{-T} \sum_{k=0}^{TN} \binom{TN}{k} \underline{q}_\alpha^k (1-\overline{q}_\alpha)^{TN-k} g_T(C_0 \underline{u}_\alpha^k \underline{d}_\alpha^{TN-k})$$

$$\overline{E(\tilde{\mathcal{L}})}_\alpha = \sum_{t=1}^{T} {}_{t-1/1}q_x (1+r)^{-t} \sum_{k=0}^{tN} \binom{tN}{k} \overline{q}_\alpha^k (1-\underline{q}_\alpha)^{tN-k} f_t(C_0 \overline{u}_\alpha^k \overline{d}_\alpha^{tN-k})$$

$$+ {}_T p_x (1+r)^{-T} \sum_{k=0}^{TN} \binom{TN}{k} \overline{q}_\alpha^k (1-\underline{q}_\alpha)^{TN-k} g_T(C_0 \overline{u}_\alpha^k \overline{d}_\alpha^{TN-k}).$$

*Remark 1.* Note that if $\tilde{u}, \tilde{d}$ are crisp numbers we get the same result of the standard model (see [27, 28]).

## 5    Application

As an application, we compute the single premium of an equity-linked endowment policy with a minimum annual rate of return guarantee $h$.

**Table 1.** Expected values for different values of $n$ and $\alpha$

| $\alpha$ | $n = 1$ | | $n = 5$ | | $n = 10$ | |
|---|---|---|---|---|---|---|
| | $\underline{E(\tilde{\mathcal{L}})}_\alpha$ | $\overline{E(\tilde{\mathcal{L}})}_\alpha$ | $\underline{E(\tilde{\mathcal{L}})}_\alpha$ | $\overline{E(\tilde{\mathcal{L}})}_\alpha$ | $\underline{E(\tilde{\mathcal{L}})}_\alpha$ | $\overline{E(\tilde{\mathcal{L}})}_\alpha$ |
| 0.5 | 6.65 | 2315.13 | 51.81 | 243.80 | 74.96 | 167.19 |
| 0.6 | 11.19 | 1260.06 | 62.69 | 200.53 | 83.02 | 150.77 |
| 0.7 | 19.39 | 686.09 | 74.13 | 169.10 | 90.66 | 137.96 |
| 0.8 | 34.31 | 373.83 | 86.12 | 145.29 | 97.96 | 127.62 |
| 0.9 | 61.63 | 204.04 | 98.68 | 126.69 | 104.99 | 119.05 |
| 1 | 111.80 | 111.80 | 111.80 | 111.80 | 111.80 | 111.80 |

Thus $H_t = C_0(1 + h)^t$, $b_t = \max\{F_t, C_0(1 + h)^t\}$, $t = 1, 2, \ldots, T$ and $c_T = b_T$. We suppose $C_0 = 100$, $T = 15$, $h = 0.02$, $x = 45$. The annual risk-free rate is $r = 0.05$. Death and survival probabilities are derived from the Italian Statistics for Males Mortality in 1991. For the discretization we set $N = 20$ (i.e. $\Delta = 0.05$). We model up and down factors by using *triangular adaptive fuzzy numbers* (see [18, 29]) $\tilde{A} = < a_1, a_2, a_3 >_n$, $n > 0$, defined by

$$\mu_{\tilde{A}}(x) = \begin{cases} \left(\frac{x-a_1}{a_2-a_1}\right)^n & a_1 \le x \le a_2 \\ 1 & x = a_2 \\ \left(\frac{a_3-x}{a_3-a_2}\right)^n & a_2 \le x \le a_3 \\ 0 & \text{otherwise.} \end{cases}$$

If $n = 1$, $\tilde{A} = < a_1, a_2, a_3 >$ is a triangular fuzzy number; if $n > 1$, $\tilde{A} = < a_1, a_2, a_3 >_n$ is a concentration of the triangular fuzzy number $< a_1, a_2, a_3 >$; if $0 < n < 1$ it is a dilation. Concentration by $n = 2$ is interpreted as the linguistic hedge *very*, dilation by $n = 0.5$ as *more or less* [29]. Thus we assume $\tilde{u} = < u_1, u_2, u_3 >_n$ and $\tilde{d} = < d_1, d_2, d_3 >_n$ with $\alpha$-cuts

$$\tilde{u}_\alpha = [\underline{u}_\alpha, \overline{u}_\alpha] = [u_1 + (u_2 - u_1)\alpha^{1/n}, u_3 - (u_3 - u_2)\alpha^{1/n}]$$
$$\tilde{d}_\alpha = [\underline{d}_\alpha, \overline{d}_\alpha] = [d_1 + (d_2 - d_1)\alpha^{1/n}, d_3 - (d_3 - d_2)\alpha^{1/n}]. \tag{8}$$

The use of adaptive fuzzy numbers allows the actuary to modify the shape of the membership functions, and thus the possibility distributions, without

**Table 2.** Possibilistic mean values

| $n$ | $M^-(E(\tilde{\mathcal{L}}))$ | $M^+(E(\tilde{\mathcal{L}}))$ | $\bar{M}(E(\tilde{\mathcal{L}}))$ |
|---|---|---|---|
| 5 | 71.77 | 228.50 | 150.14 |
| 10 | 86.87 | 155.66 | 121.26 |
| 15 | 93.66 | 138.45 | 116.05 |
| 20 | 97.53 | 130.90 | 114.21 |
| 25 | 100.04 | 126.67 | 113.36 |
| 30 | 101.80 | 123.97 | 112.89 |

having to change the support or the core. Indeed, he can increase or decrease the fuzziness by adjusting the parameter $n$ according to his subjective estimation. In accordance with the classical model [10] we assume that jump factors are determined by three volatility parameters, $\sigma_1 < \sigma_2 < \sigma_3$, as follows: $u_1 = e^{\sigma_1 \sqrt{\Delta}}$, $u_2 = e^{\sigma_2 \sqrt{\Delta}}$, $u_3 = e^{\sigma_3 \sqrt{\Delta}}$, $d_1 = e^{-\sigma_3 \sqrt{\Delta}}$, $d_2 = e^{-\sigma_2 \sqrt{\Delta}}$, $d_3 = e^{-\sigma_1 \sqrt{\Delta}}$. Assuming that the annual volatility is "approximately 20%", we set $\sigma_1 = 0.197$, $\sigma_2 = 0.20$, $\sigma_3 = 0.205$. Note that the no-arbitrage condition $e^{-\sigma_1 \sqrt{\Delta}} < (1+r)^{\Delta} < e^{\sigma_1 \sqrt{\Delta}}$ is satisfied. Substituting (8) in (5) we get

$$\underline{q}_\alpha = \frac{1 + \rho - d_3 + (d_3 - d_2)\, \alpha^{1/n}}{u_3 - (u_3 - u_2)\, \alpha^{1/n} - d_3 + (d_3 - d_2)\, \alpha^{1/n}}$$

$$\overline{q}_\alpha = \frac{1 + \rho - d_1 - (d_2 - d_1)\, \alpha^{1/n}}{u_1 + (u_2 - u_1)\, \alpha^{1/n} - d_1 - (d_2 - d_1)\, \alpha^{1/n}}$$

and so, from (4), we obtain the risk neutral probabilities. The numerical results for different values of $n$ and $\alpha$ are shown in Table 1. For example, setting $n = 5$, the degree of belief for a single premium of 169.10 is 0.7. Furthermore, for a given $\alpha$-level, we obtain the value of the policy as an interval. For instance, if we have a degree of belief of 0.9 then the single premium lies within the confidence interval [98.68, 126.69]. Note that $\alpha = 1$ gives the same result of the standard model with crisp jump factors. Moreover, in Table 2 we compute, for different values of parameter $n$, the interval-valued possibilistic mean $[M^-(E(\tilde{\mathcal{L}})), M^+(E(\tilde{\mathcal{L}}))]$ and the possibilistic mean value $\bar{M}(E(\tilde{\mathcal{L}}))$ with weighting function $w(\alpha) = 2\alpha$. For example, the single premium corresponding to $n = 10$ is 121.26.

# 6   Conclusions

In literature fuzzy set theory has been applied to traditional life insurance with deterministic benefits in order to model the discount rates as fuzzy numbers. In this paper we have proposed a fuzzy pricing model for modern life insurance products with benefits linked to the performance of a reference fund. The suggested methodology incorporates uncertainty of randomness and fuzziness. Randomness concerns the uncertainty related to lifetime and fuzziness is due to imprecision or a lack of knowledge regarding the financial markets. Although we have discussed the evaluation of equity-linked policies, in our view the proposed method can be applied to other life insurance contracts like unit-linked or participating policies even in the case of periodic premiums. Furthermore, we believe that this model could be a useful tool to study the fuzzy price of the options embedded in life insurance products.

# References

1. Zadeh, L.A.: Fuzzy sets. Inform. Control 8, 338–353 (1965)
2. Lemaire, J.: Fuzzy insurance. ASTIN Bull. 20, 33–55 (1990)

3. Terceno, A., De Andres, J., Belvis, C., Barbera, G.: Fuzzy methods incorporated to the study of personal insurances. In: Int. Symp. Neuro-Fuzzy Syst., pp. 187–202 (1996)
4. Ostaszewski, K.: An Investigation into Possible Applications of Fuzzy Sets Methods in Actuarial Science. Society of Actuaries, Schaumburg (1993)
5. Buckley, J.J.: The fuzzy mathematics of finance. Fuzzy Sets and Systems 21, 257–273 (1987)
6. Shapiro, A.F.: Fuzzy logic in insurance. Insurance: Mathematics and Economics 35, 399–424 (2004)
7. Hardy, M.: Investment guarantees: Modelling and risk management for equity-linked life insurance. Wiley (2003)
8. Brennan, M.J., Schwartz, E.S.: The pricing of equity-linked life insurance policies with an asset value guarantee. J. Finan. Econ. 3, 195–213 (1976)
9. Hull, J.C.: Options, Futures, and Other Derivatives. Prentice Hall (2003)
10. Cox, J.C., Ross, S.A., Rubinstein, M.: Option Pricing: A Simplified Approach. Journal of Financial Economics 7, 229–263 (1979)
11. Kwakernaak, H.: Fuzzy random variables. Part I: definitions and theorems. Inform. Sci. 15, 1–29 (1978)
12. Kwakernaak, H.: Fuzzy random variables. Part II: algorithms and examples for the discrete case. Inform. Sci. 17, 253–278 (1979)
13. Kruse, R., Meyer, K.D.: Statistics with Vague Data. Reidel Publ. Co. (1987)
14. Puri, M.L., Ralescu, D.A.: Fuzzy random variables. Journal of Mathematical Analysis and Applications 114, 409–422 (1986)
15. de Andrés-Sánchez, J., González-Vila Puchades, L.: Using fuzzy random variables in life annuities pricing. Fuzzy Sets and Systems 188, 27–44 (2012)
16. Carlsson, C., Fuller, R.: On possibilistic mean value and variance of fuzzy numbers. Fuzzy Sets and Systems 122, 315–326 (2001)
17. Fuller, R., Majlender, P.: On weighted possibilistic mean and variance of fuzzy numbers. Fuzzy Sets and Systems 136, 363–374 (2003)
18. Bodjanova, S.: Median value and median interval of a fuzzy number. Information Sciences 172, 73–89 (2005)
19. Gil, M.Á., López-Díaz, M., Ralescu, D.A.: Overview on the Development of Fuzzy Random Variables. Fuzzy Sets and Systems 157, 2546–2557 (2006)
20. Gerber, H.U.: Life Insurance Mathematics. Springer, Berlin (1995)
21. Kaufmann, A., Gupta, M.M.: Introduction to fuzzy arithmetic. Theory and applications. Van Nostrand Reinhold Company Inc. (1985)
22. Muzzioli, S., Torricelli, C.: A multiperiod binomial model for pricing options in a vague world. Journal of Economic Dynamics and Control 28, 861–887 (2004)
23. Muzzioli, S., Reynaerts, H.: The solution of fuzzy linear systems by non linear programming: a financial application. European Journal of Operational Research 177, 1218–1231 (2007)
24. Muzzioli, S., Reynaerts, H.: American option pricing with imprecise risk-neutral probabilities. International Journal of Approximate Reasoning 49, 140–147 (2008)
25. Yoshida, Y.: A discrete-time model of American put option in an uncertain environment. European Journal of Operational Research 151, 153–166 (2003)
26. Buckley, J.J., Qu, Y.: Solving systems of linear fuzzy equations. Fuzzy Sets and Systems 43, 33–43 (1991)
27. Melnikov, A.: Risk Analysis in Finance and Insurance. Chapman & Hall (2003)
28. Bacinello, A.R.: Endogenous model of surrender conditions in equity-linked life insurance. Insurance: Mathematics and Economics 37, 270–296 (2005)
29. Zadeh, L.A.: A fuzzy-set-theoretic interpretation of linguistic hedge. Journal of Cybernetics 2, 4–34 (1972)

# A Political Scenario Faced by a New Evaluation of Intuitionistic Fuzzy Quantities

Luca Anzilli[1] and Gisella Facchinetti[2]

[1] Department of Economics, Mathematics and Statistics, University of Salento, Italy
luca.anzilli@unisalento.it
[2] Department of Economics, Mathematics and Statistics, University of Salento, Italy
gisella.facchinetti@unisalento.it

**Abstract.** We deal with the problem of evaluating and ranking intuitionistic fuzzy quantitities (IFQs). We call IFQ an intuitionistic fuzzy set (IFS) described by a pair of fuzzy quantities, where a fuzzy quantity is defined as the union of two, or more, generalized fuzzy numbers. We suggest an evaluation defined by a pair index based on "value" & "ambiguity" and a ranking method based on them.

**Keywords:** Intuitionistic fuzzy sets, Intuitionistic fuzzy numbers, Ranking, Defuzzification, Ambiguity, Opinion poll.

## 1  Introduction

Classical fuzzy set theory assigns to each element of the universe of discourse a degree of belongingness to the set under consideration from the unit interval. The degree of non-belongingness is the complement to one of the membership degree. In many practical applications the available information corresponding to a fuzzy concept may be incomplete, that is the sum of the membership degree and the non-membership degree may be less than one. A possible solution is to use IFSs introduced by Atanassov in [1, 2]. Atanassov's IFSs are characterized by two functions, membership and non-membership, which are not necessarily complementary and thus they can be applied for modelling situations with missing information or hesitance. Hence they may express more abundant and flexible information as compared with the fuzzy set. Severals proposals of intuitionistic fuzzy numbers (IFNs) evaluation and ranking are present in literature [3–10].

In this paper we don't deal of IFNs but of IFQs that is an IFS described by a pair of fuzzy quantities. A fuzzy quantity is a fuzzy set obtained by the union of two or more fuzzy numbers not necessarily normal, called generalized fuzzy numbers. Thus a fuzzy quantity is usually a non-convex and non-normal fuzzy set. In classical fuzzy logic it is known that evaluation and ranking may be obtained by a unique procedure or not. Here we follow the first line and suggest an evaluation defined by a pair index based on "value" & "ambiguity" and a ranking that uses a lexicographic order based on them. The evaluation we propose depends on three subjective parameters, one reflecting the optimistic/pessimistic point

S. Greco et al. (Eds.): IPMU 2012, Part IV, CCIS 300, pp. 54–63, 2012.

of view of the decision maker, a second representing the decision maker's preferences and a third related to the decision maker's belief about the hesitation margin. Several properties of these new concepts are proposed and a possible application to opinion poll on political election is presented.

## 2   Fuzzy Quantities

Let $X$ denote a universe of discourse. A fuzzy set $A$ in $X$ is characterized by a membership function $\mu_A : X \to [0,1]$ which assigns to each element of $X$ a grade of membership to the set $A$. The support and the core of $A$ are defined, respectively, as the crisp sets $supp(A) = \{x \in X; \mu_A(x) > 0\}$ and $core(A) = \{x \in X; \mu_A(x) = 1\}$. A fuzzy set $A$ is normal if its core is nonempty. A fuzzy number $A$ is a fuzzy set of the real line with a normal, convex and upper-semicontinuous membership function of bounded support. The $\alpha$-cut of $A$, $0 \leq \alpha \leq 1$, is defined as the crisp set $A_\alpha = \{x \in X; \mu_A(x) \geq \alpha\}$ if $0 < \alpha \leq 1$ and as the closure of the support if $\alpha = 0$. Every $\alpha$-cut of a fuzzy number is a closed interval $A_\alpha = [a_L(\alpha), a_R(\alpha)]$, for $0 \leq \alpha \leq 1$, where $a_L(\alpha) = \inf A_\alpha$ and $a_R(\alpha) = \sup A_\alpha$. A generalized fuzzy number is a fuzzy number whose height can be different from 1.

**Definition 1.** *We call fuzzy quantity the union of two, or more, generalized fuzzy numbers with non-disjoint supports [11, 12].*

A fuzzy quantity is usually non-convex and non-normal since the union operation on fuzzy sets may produce fuzzy quantities that are non-convex.

In [11] the authors introduced an evaluation for fuzzy quantities based on $\alpha$-cut levels and depending on two parameters: a real number connected with the optimistic/pessimistic point of view of the decision maker and an additive measure that allows the decision maker to attribute different weights to each level, according to his preference. Their definition can be utilized for defuzzification since the evaluation lies in the support of the fuzzy quantity and this is a fundamental property from the point of view of defuzzification problem. In [12] we introduced a notion of ambiguity for fuzzy quantities and proposed a ranking method based on the value-ambiguity pair. In the following we review some of those results. We refer to [11, 12] for more details.

Let $S$ be an additive measure on $[0,1]$ reflecting the subjective attribution of weights to each level $\alpha$ by decision maker and $\lambda \in [0,1]$ be an optimistic/pessimistic parameter. We assume that $S$ is a normalized Stieltjes measure on $[0,1]$ defined through the function $s$, i.e. $S(]a,b]) = s(b) - s(a)$, $0 \leq a < b \leq 1$, where $s : [0,1] \to [0,1]$ is a strictly increasing and continuous function such that $s(0) = 0$ and $s(1) = 1$.

**Definition 2.** *Let $A$ be a generalized fuzzy number with height $A = w_A \leq 1$, and $\alpha$-cuts $A_\alpha = [a_L(\alpha), a_R(\alpha)]$, $\alpha \in [0, w_A]$. We define the lower and upper values of $A$ as*

$$V_*(A; S) = \frac{1}{s(w_A)} \int_0^{w_A} a_L(\alpha) \, dS(\alpha), \qquad V^*(A; S) = \frac{1}{s(w_A)} \int_0^{w_A} a_R(\alpha) \, dS(\alpha),$$

*and the value of $A$, for $\lambda \in [0, 1]$,*

$$V_\lambda(A; S) = \frac{1}{s(w_A)} \int_0^{w_A} \phi_\lambda(A_\alpha) \, dS(\alpha) = (1 - \lambda)V_*(A; S) + \lambda V^*(A; S)$$

*where $\phi_\lambda([x_1, x_2]) = (1 - \lambda)x_1 + \lambda x_2$, $x_1 \leq x_2$, is an evaluation function. If the measure $S$ is generated by $s(\alpha) = \alpha^r$, $r > 0$, we denote the value of $A$ as*

$$V_\lambda(A; r) = \frac{r}{w_A^r} \int_0^{w_A} \phi_\lambda(A_\alpha) \, \alpha^{r-1} \, d\alpha.$$

We observe that $V_*(A; S)$, $V^*(A; S)$ and $V_\lambda(A; S)$ belong to the support of $A$. In the following we denote by $\overline{supp}\, B$ the closure of the support of the generalized fuzzy number $B$.

**Definition 3.** *Let $B, C$ be two generalized fuzzy numbers with height $w_B$ and $w_C$, respectively, such that $\overline{supp}\, B \cap \overline{supp}\, C \neq \emptyset$. The value of the fuzzy quantity $A = B \cup C$ is*

$$V_\lambda(A; S) = V_\lambda(B \cup C; S) = \sigma_1 V_\lambda(B; S) + \sigma_2 V_\lambda(C; S) - \sigma_3 V_\lambda(B \cap C; S) \quad (1)$$

*where $\sigma_i = \sigma_i(w_B, w_C, w_{B \cap C}) = \psi_i(s(w_B), s(w_C), s(w_{B \cap C}))$, $i = 1, 2, 3$, with $\psi_i(z_1, z_2, z_3) = z_i/(z_1 + z_2 - z_3)$, $z_1 + z_2 - z_3 \neq 0$. Note that $\sigma_i \geq 0$ and $\sigma_1 + \sigma_2 - \sigma_3 = 1$.*

We call evaluation interval of $A = B \cup C$ the interval $[V_*(A; S), V^*(A; S)]$ where the lower and upper values are defined by

$$V_*(A; S) = V_*(B \cup C; S) = \sigma_1 V_*(B; S) + \sigma_2 V_*(C; S) - \sigma_3 V_*(B \cap C; S)$$
$$V^*(A; S) = V^*(B \cup C; S) = \sigma_1 V^*(B; S) + \sigma_2 V^*(C; S) - \sigma_3 V^*(B \cap C; S).$$

Note that $V_\lambda(A; S) = (1 - \lambda)V_*(A; S) + \lambda V^*(A; S)$.

**Definition 4.** *We call ambiguity of the fuzzy quantity $A$ the real number ([12])*

$$Amb(A; S) = \frac{1}{2} \int_0^{w_A} m(A_\alpha) \, dS(\alpha)$$

*where $w_A$ is the height of $A$ and $m(\cdot)$ is the Lebesgue measure on the real line. If $s(\alpha) = \alpha^r$, $r > 0$, we denote $Amb(A; r) = Amb(A; S)$.*

For the fuzzy quantity $A = B \cup C$ the ambiguity can be expressed as

$$Amb(B \cup C; S) = Amb(B; S) + Amb(C; S) - Amb(B \cap C; S).$$

Moreover, by denoting $h(w_B, w_C, w_{B \cap C}; S) = s(w_B) + s(w_C) - s(w_{B \cap C})$,

$$Amb(B \cup C; S) = \frac{V^*(B \cup C; S) - V_*(B \cup C; S)}{2} h(w_B, w_C, w_{B \cap C}; S).$$

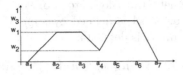

**Fig. 1.** Fuzzy quantity $A = (a_1, a_2, a_3, a_4, a_5, a_6, a_7; w_1, w_2, w_3)$

**Proposition 1.** $A, B$ *fuzzy quantities,* $A \subset B \implies Amb(A; S) \leq Amb(B; S)$.

*Example 1.* If $A = (a_1, a_2, a_3, a_4, a_5, a_6, a_7; w_1, w_2, w_3)$, with $w_2 < \min\{w_1, w_3\}$, is the fuzzy quantity defined by the membership function (see Fig. 1)

$$\mu_A(x) = \begin{cases} \dfrac{w_1}{a_2 - a_1}(x - a_1) & a_1 \leq x \leq a_2 \\ w_1 & a_2 \leq x \leq a_3 \\ \dfrac{w_1 - w_2}{a_4 - a_3}(a_4 - x) + w_2 & a_3 \leq x \leq a_4 \\ \dfrac{w_3 - w_2}{a_5 - a_4}(x - a_4) + w_2 & a_4 \leq x \leq a_5 \\ w_3 & a_5 \leq x \leq a_6 \\ \dfrac{w_3}{a_7 - a_6}(a_7 - x) & a_6 \leq x \leq a_7 \\ 0 & \text{otherwise} \end{cases} \tag{2}$$

$$V_*(A; r) = \gamma_1 \left[ a_1 + \frac{r}{r+1}(a_2 - a_1) \right] - \gamma_2 a_4 + \gamma_3 \left[ a_4 + \frac{r}{r+1} g(w_3; w_2, r)(a_5 - a_4) \right]$$

$$V^*(A; r) = \gamma_1 \left[ a_4 - \frac{r}{r+1} g(w_1; w_2, r)(a_4 - a_3) \right] - \gamma_2 a_4 + \gamma_3 \left[ a_7 - \frac{r}{r+1}(a_7 - a_6) \right]$$

with $\gamma_i = w_i^r / (w_1^r + w_3^r - w_2^r)$, $i = 1, 2, 3$, and

$$g(w; w_2, r) = 1 - \frac{w_2}{r(w - w_2)} \left[ 1 - \left( \frac{w_2}{w} \right)^r \right], \qquad w = w_1, w_3.$$

## 3   Intuitionistic Fuzzy Quantities

An IFS $A$ in $X$ is given by $A = \{< x, \mu_A(x), \nu_A(x) >; x \in X\}$ where $\mu_A : X \to [0, 1]$ and $\nu_A : X \to [0, 1]$ with the condition

$$0 \leq \mu_A(x) + \nu_A(x) \leq 1. \tag{3}$$

The numbers $\mu_A(x), \nu_A(x) \in [0, 1]$ denote the degree of membership and a degree of non-membership of $x$ to $A$, respectively. For each IFS $A$ in $X$, we call $\pi_A(x) = 1 - \mu_A(x) - \nu_A(x)$ the degree of the indeterminacy membership of the element $x$ in $A$, that is the hesitation margin (or intuitionistic index) of $x \in A$ which expresses a lack of information of whether $x$ belongs to $A$ or not. We have $0 \leq \pi_A(x) \leq 1$ for all $x \in X$. The support of $A$ is defined by $supp\,A = \{x \in X; \nu_A(x) < 1\}$. Inclusion for two IFSs $A$ and $B$ is defined as

$$A \subset B \iff \forall x \in X \quad \mu_A(x) \leq \mu_B(x), \quad \nu_A(x) \geq \nu_B(x). \tag{4}$$

There are different approaches to define IFNs (see [13]). We adopt the concept given in [3]. An IFS $A$ of the real line is called an *IFN* if $\mu_A$ and $1 - \nu_A$ are membership functions of fuzzy numbers.

## 3.1   Evaluation of Intuitionistic Fuzzy Quantities

We now propose a definition of IFQ based on the concept of fuzzy quantity.

**Definition 5.** *We call IFQ an IFS* $A = \langle \mu_A, \nu_A \rangle$ *such that* $\mu_A$ *and* $1 - \nu_A$ *are membership functions of fuzzy quantities.*

If $A$ is an IFQ we denote by $A^+$ the fuzzy quantity with membership function $\mu_{A^+} = \mu_A$ and by $A^-$ the fuzzy quantity with membership function $\mu_{A^-} = 1 - \nu_A$. In the following an IFQ $A$ will be indifferently denoted by $A = \langle \mu_A, \nu_A \rangle$ or $A = (A^+, A^-)$.

**Definition 6.** *We define the evaluation interval* $[V_\rho^L(A; S), V_\rho^U(A; S)]$ *of* $A$ *by*

$$V_\rho^L(A; S) = (1 - \rho)V_*(A^+; S) + \rho V_*(A^-; S)$$
$$V_\rho^U(A; S) = (1 - \rho)V^*(A^+; S) + \rho V^*(A^-; S).$$

**Definition 7.** *We define the value of* $A$ *with respect to the additive measure* $S$, *the parameter* $\lambda \in [0, 1]$ *and the parameter* $\rho \in [0, 1]$ *as*

$$V_{\rho,\lambda}(A; S) = (1 - \lambda)V_\rho^L(A; S) + \lambda V_\rho^U(A; S).$$

The parameter $\rho \in [0, 1]$ is a weight reflecting the decision maker's belief about the hesitation margin. Taking into account that $\mu_A(x)$, $\nu_A(x)$ and $\pi_A(x)$ express the parts of membership, non-membership and hesitation, respectively, the parameter $\rho$ reflects the subjective opinion of decision maker about a lack of information.

*Remark 1.* The value $V_{\rho,\lambda}(A; S)$ belongs to the support of $A$. Indeed, for the fuzzy quantities $A^+, A^-$ we have $supp\,A^- = \{x \in X; 1 - \nu_A(x) > 0\} = supp\,A$ and $supp\,A^+ = \{x \in X; \mu_A(x) > 0\} \subset supp\,A^- = supp\,A$ since $\mu_A(x) \leq 1 - \nu_A(x)$ (from (3)). Taking into account that the value of a fuzzy quantity belongs to its support (see [11]) we can argue that $V_{\rho,\lambda}(A; S) = (1 - \rho)V_\lambda(A^+; S) + \rho V_\lambda(A^-; S)$, $\rho \in [0, 1]$, belongs to the support of $A$.

*Remark 2.* An alternative evaluation approach may consider the operator defined, for $\alpha \in [0, 1]$, as (see [2])

$$D_\alpha(A) = \{\langle x, \mu_A(x) + \alpha\,\pi_A(x), \nu_A(x) + (1 - \alpha)\pi_A(x)\rangle; \ x \in X\}$$

for any IFS $A$, where $\alpha$ and $1 - \alpha$ represent the proportion of redistribution of hesitation between membership and non-membership, respectively. However, $D_\alpha(A)$ is a (standard) fuzzy set since $\mu_A(x) + \alpha\,\pi_A(x) + \nu_A(x) + (1-\alpha)\pi_A(x) = 1$ but, in general, it is not a fuzzy quantity in the sense of our definition.

*Example 2.* We consider the evaluation of the IFQ $A = \langle \mu_A, \nu_A \rangle$ defined by the membership function

$$
\mu_A(x) = \begin{cases}
\dfrac{w_1}{a_2 - a_1}(x - a_1) & a_1 \le x \le a_2 \\[2mm]
w_1 & a_2 \le x \le a_3 \\[2mm]
\dfrac{w_1 - w_2}{a_4 - a_3}(a_4 - x) + w_2 & a_3 \le x \le a_4 \\[2mm]
\dfrac{w_3 - w_2}{a_5 - a_4}(x - a_4) + w_2 & a_4 \le x \le a_5 \\[2mm]
w_3 & a_5 \le x \le a_6 \\[2mm]
\dfrac{w_3}{a_7 - a_6}(a_7 - x) & a_6 \le x \le a_7 \\[2mm]
0 & \text{otherwise}
\end{cases}
$$

with $w_2 < \min\{w_1, w_3\}$ and by the non-membership function

$$
\nu_A(x) = \begin{cases}
\dfrac{b_2 - x + u_1(x - b_1)}{b_2 - b_1} & b_1 \le x \le b_2 \\[2mm]
u_1 & b_2 \le x \le b_3 \\[2mm]
\dfrac{u_2 - u_1}{b_4 - b_3}(x - b_3) + u_1 & b_3 \le x \le b_4 \\[2mm]
\dfrac{u_2 - u_3}{b_5 - b_4}(b_5 - x) + u_3 & b_4 \le x \le b_5 \\[2mm]
u_3 & b_5 \le x \le b_6 \\[2mm]
\dfrac{x - b_6 + u_3(b_7 - x)}{b_7 - b_6} & b_6 \le x \le b_7 \\[2mm]
1 & \text{otherwise}
\end{cases}
$$

with $u_2 > \max\{u_1, u_3\}$ (see Fig. 2).

Then $A = (A^+, A^-)$ with $A^+ = (a_1, a_2, a_3, a_4, a_5, a_6, a_7; w_1, w_2, w_3)$ and $A^- = (b_1, b_2, b_3, b_4, b_5, b_6, b_7; 1 - u_1, 1 - u_2, 1 - u_3)$,

$$
V_*(A^+; r) = \gamma_1^+ \left[ a_1 + \frac{r}{r+1}(a_2 - a_1) \right] - \gamma_2^+ a_4 + \gamma_3^+ \left[ a_4 + \frac{r}{r+1}g^+(w_3; w_2, r)(a_5 - a_4) \right]
$$

$$
V^*(A^+; r) = \gamma_1^+ \left[ a_4 - \frac{r}{r+1}g^+(w_1; w_2, r)(a_4 - a_3) \right] - \gamma_2^+ a_4 + \gamma_3^+ \left[ a_7 - \frac{r}{r+1}(a_7 - a_6) \right]
$$

$$
V_*(A^-; r) = \gamma_1^- \left[ b_1 + \frac{r}{r+1}(b_2 - b_1) \right] - \gamma_2^- b_4 + \gamma_3^- \left[ b_4 + \frac{r}{r+1}g^-(u_3; u_2, r)(b_5 - b_4) \right]
$$

$$
V^*(A^-; r) = \gamma_1^- \left[ b_4 - \frac{r}{r+1}g^-(u_1; u_2, r)(b_4 - b_3) \right] - \gamma_2^- b_4 + \gamma_3^- \left[ b_7 - \frac{r}{r+1}(b_7 - b_6) \right]
$$

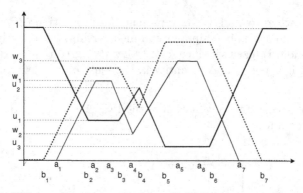

**Fig. 2.** IFQ: $\mu_A$ (continuous line), $\nu_A$ (bold line), $1 - \nu_A$ (dashed line)

$$g^+(w; w_2, r) = 1 - \frac{w_2}{r(w - w_2)}\left[1 - \left(\frac{w_2}{w}\right)^r\right], \qquad w = w_1, w_3$$

$$g^-(u; u_2, r) = 1 - \frac{1 - u_2}{r(u_2 - u)}\left[1 - \left(\frac{1 - u_2}{1 - u}\right)^r\right], \qquad u = u_1, u_3$$

$$\gamma_i^+ = \frac{w_i^r}{w_1^r + w_3^r - w_2^r}, \quad \gamma_i^- = \frac{(1 - u_i)^r}{(1 - u_1)^r + (1 - u_3)^r - (1 - u_2)^r}, \qquad i = 1, 2, 3.$$

## 3.2   Ambiguity of Intuitionistic Fuzzy Quantities

We now introduce the definition of ambiguity for an IFQ by using the notion of ambiguity of fuzzy quantities.

**Definition 8.** *We define the ambiguity of the IFQ $A = (A^+, A^-)$ as*

$$Amb_\rho(A; S) = (1 - \rho)Amb(A^+; S) + \rho Amb(A^-; S).$$

**Proposition 2.** *Let $A = (A^+, A^-)$ and $B = (B^+, B^-)$ be two IFQs. Then $A \subset B \implies Amb_\rho(A; S) \le Amb_\rho(B; S)$.*

*Proof.* If $A \subset B$ then from (4) we have, for any $x \in X$, $\mu_A(x) \le \mu_B(x)$ and $\nu_A(x) \ge \nu_B(x)$. So we get $A^+ \subset B^+$ and $A^- \subset B^-$, since $1 - \nu_A(x) \le 1 - \nu_B(x)$, and thus from Proposition 1 we obtain $Amb(A^+; S) \le Amb(B^+; S)$ and $Amb(A^-; S) \le Amb(B^-; S)$. Then for $\rho \in [0, 1]$

$$Amb_\rho(A; S) = (1 - \rho)\, Amb(A^+; S) + \rho\, Amb(A^-; S)$$
$$\le (1 - \rho)\, Amb(B^+; S) + \rho\, Amb(B^-; S) = Amb_\rho(B; S). \qquad \square$$

*Example 3.* If $A = (A^+, A^-)$ where $A^+ = (a_1, a_2, a_3, a_4, a_5, a_6, a_7; w_1, w_2, w_3)$ and $A^- = (b_1, b_2, b_3, b_4, b_5, b_6, b_7; 1 - u_1, 1 - u_2, 1 - u_3)$ then

$$Amb(A^+; r) = \frac{V^*(A^+; r) - V_*(A^+; r)}{2} h(w_1, w_3, w_2; r)$$

$$Amb(A^-; r) = \frac{V^*(A^-; r) - V_*(A^-; r)}{2} h(1 - u_1, 1 - u_3, 1 - u_2; r)$$

where $h(v_1, v_2, v_3; r) = v_1^r + v_3^r - v_2^r$.

### 3.3   Ranking Intuitionistic Fuzzy Quantities

In order to compare two or more IFQs we introduce a function that maps the set of IFQs into $\mathbb{R}^2$ by assigning to every IFQ $A$ the pair $(V(A), Amb(A))$ where $V(A)$ and $Amb(A)$ are, respectively, the value and ambiguity of $A$ with respect to parameters $\rho, \lambda, S$ (fixed). The ranking method we propose can be summarized into the following steps:

1. For two IFQs $A$ and $B$
   if $V(A) > V(B)$ then $A \succ B$; if $V(A) < V(B)$ then $A \prec B$;
   if $V(A) = V(B)$ then go to the next step.
2. Compare $Amb(A)$ and $Amb(B)$:
   if $Amb(A) < Amb(B)$ then $A \succ B$; if $Amb(A) > Amb(B)$ then $A \prec B$;
   if $Amb(A) = Amb(B)$ then $A \sim B$, that is $A$ and $B$ are indifferent.

The proposed ranking method satisfies axioms $A1 - A5$ proposed in [14] as reasonable properties for the rationality of a ranking method.

## 4   Voters Application

In a political scenario (S1) two opposite political lines are present: LA and LB. Every voters has a political position in between. We propose an analytical representation of the voters' political position on real axe in the interval [0,100], where the first extreme "0" correspond to the political line LA and "100" for LB. The point "50" individuates the zone in which the moderate voters are placed oneself, while the two extremists are placed near to "0" and "100". The principal candidates are A1,A2,B1,B2,C1 where A1,B1 are the candidates of the two extreme political position, C1 is the moderate candidate and A2,B2 are the candidates of the two most important coalitions. We organize an opinion

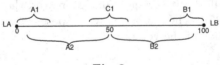

**Fig. 3.**

poll in a previous period of vote day with this question: "would you vote for leader A2 or B2?". We may repeat the same survey in several different moments obtaining different scenarios S2, S3 and so on and their evaluations may offer a way to control how the voters change their positions getting close the vote day. To present their replay in a Cartesian product we put on $x$-axis the interval $[0, 100]$. In this domain we define two functions $\mu(x)$ and $\nu(x)$, where the former is the vote distribution for LA and LB, the second is the vote distribution of who votes neither for LA nor LB. We represent the distributions of vote by an IFQ $A = (A^+, A^-)$, where $\mu_{A^+} = \mu$ and $\mu_{A^-} = 1 - \nu$, as shown in Fig. 4. Note that in the picture we see not $\nu$, but $1 - \nu$. The zone between the two graphs contains the wavering ones. For a concrete evaluation we set

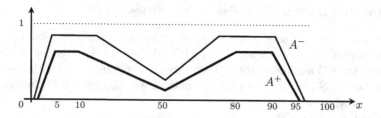

**Fig. 4.** IFQ for vote distribution

$$A^+ = (3, 5, 10, 50, 80, 90, 95; 0.6; 0.2; 0.6)$$
$$A^- = (2, 4, 15, 50, 75, 91, 96; 0.8, 0.3, 0.8).$$

We assume $s(\alpha) = \alpha$ $(r = 1)$ and denote by $V_*(A^+) = V_*(A^+; 1)$, $V^*(A^+) = V^*(A^+; 1)$, $V_*(A^-) = V_*(A^-; 1)$, $V^*(A^-) = V^*(A^-; 1)$. By calculation, we obtain $[V_*(A^+), V^*(A^+)] = [28.4, 67.5]$ and $[V_*(A^-), V^*(A^-)] = [25.9, 70.0]$. The evaluation we propose, depends on two parameters $\rho$ and $\lambda$ both in $[0, 1]$. When $\rho$ is zero we evaluate only the fuzzy quantity $A^+$ till when $\rho$ is one in which we evaluate $A^-$. An intermediate value of $\rho$ suggests the will to consider some part of the wavering ones. In Fig. 5 we have plotted as a function of parameter $\rho$ the lower value $V_\rho^L(A)$ and the upper value $V_\rho^U(A)$. For example, if $\rho = 0.6$ then the corresponding evaluation interval $[V_\rho^L(A), V_\rho^U(A)]$ is $[26.9, 69.0]$. We observe from the graph that as the value of $\rho$ increases, the interval evaluation increases. The choice of $\lambda$ depends on the will to obtain a pessimistic ($\lambda = 0$) or optimistic ($\lambda = 1$) evaluation of the two leader politic performance. Fig. 5 also shows the defuzzification value $V_{\rho,\lambda}(A)$ (dashed line) as a function of $\rho$, for different values of the parameter $\lambda$. Therefore, setting $\rho = 0.6$, if $\lambda = 0.2$ then the defuzzification value is 35.3 whereas if $\lambda = 0.8$ we get 60.6. Moreover, the ambiguity of $A$ for $\rho = 0.6$ is $Amb(A) = 25.1$. The evaluation we propose is an aggregated outcome of the political allocation of the voters.

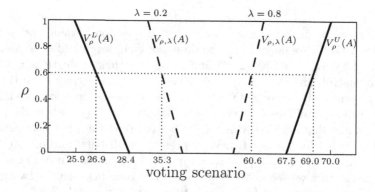

**Fig. 5.** Evaluation intervals and defuzzification values

# 5   Conclusions

In this paper we have proposed two different definitions. The first concerns the introduction of IFSs in which $\mu_A$ and $1 - \mu_A$ are not quasi-concave functions. The second concerns an evaluation definition that produces a ranking method. A political example is presented as possible application of both.

The recent developement of Intuitionistic Fuzzy Expert Systems (IFES) has shown as there will be their possible application to real world problems. The output of a IEFS frequently will be an IFQ and it evaluation, that is, its defuzzification will be necessary. Our proposal would be one idea to reach a real value as final output of a IFES [15].

# References

1. Atanassov, K.: Intuitionistic fuzzy sets. Fuzzy Sets and Systems 20, 87–96 (1986)
2. Atanassov, K.: Intuitionistic fuzzy sets. Theory and Applications. Physica-Verlag, Heidelberg (1999)
3. Grzegorzewski, P.: Distances and orderings in a family of intuitionistic fuzzy numbers. In: Proceedings of the Third Conference on Fuzzy Logic and Technology (Eusflat 2003), pp. 223–227 (2003)
4. Dubey, D., Mehra, A.: Linear programming with Triangular intuitionistic fuzzy number. In: EUSFLAT-LFA, pp. 563–569 (2011)
5. Li, D.-F.: A ratio ranking method of triangular intuitionistic fuzzy numbers and its application to MADM problems. Computers and Mathematics with Applications 60, 1557–1570 (2010)
6. Mitchell, H.B.: Ranking intuitionistic fuzzy numbers. International Journal of Uncertainity, Fuzziness and Knowledge-Based Systems 12, 377–386 (2004)
7. Nan, J.X., Li, D.F.: A lexicographic method for matrix games with payoffs of triangular intuitionistic fuzzy numbers. International Journal of Computational Intelligence Systems 3, 280–289 (2010)
8. Nayagam, V.L., Vankateshwari, G., Sivaraman, G.: Ranking of intuitionistic fuzzy numbers. In: IEEE International Conference on Fuzzy Systems, pp. 1971–1974 (2008)
9. Nehi, H.M.: A new ranking method for intuitionistic fuzzy numbers. International Journal of Fuzzy Systems 12, 80–86 (2010)
10. Su, J.S.: Fuzzy programming based on intervalvalued fuzzy numbers and ranking. International Journal of Contempraroy Mathematical Sciences 2, 393–410 (2007)
11. Facchinetti, G., Pacchiarotti, N.: Evaluations of fuzzy quantities. Fuzzy Sets and Systems 157, 892–903 (2006)
12. Anzilli, L., Facchinetti, G.: Fuzzy quantities and their ranking: a new proposal. Discussion Paper no. 673, Economics Department, University of Modena and Reggio Emilia (2011)
13. Atanassov, K.: Intuitionistic fuzzy sets: past, present and future. In: Proceedings of the Third Conference on Fuzzy Logic and Technology (Eusflat 2003), pp. 12–19 (2003)
14. Wang, X., Kerre, E.E.: Reasonable properties for the ordering of fuzzy quantities (I). Fuzzy Sets and Systems 118, 375–385 (2001)
15. Chountas, P., Sotirova, E., Kolev, B., Atanassov, K.: On Intuitionistic Fuzzy Expert Systems With Temporal Parameters. Computational Intelligence, Theory and Applications 38, 241–249 (2006)

# Average Rate of Return with Uncertainty

Maria Letizia Guerra[1], Carlo Alberto Magni[2], and Luciano Stefanini[3]

[1] Department of Mathematics, University of Bologna
mletizia.guerra@unibo.it
[2] Department of Economics, University of Modena and Reggio Emilia
magni@unimo.it
[3] Department of Economics, Society and Politics, and University of Urbino
"Carlo Bo"
lucste@uniurb.it

**Abstract.** In investment appraisal, uncertainty can be managed through intervals or fuzzy numbers. The arithmetical properties and the extension principle are well established and can be successfully applied in a rigorous way. The investments ranking is preferably performed when the decision maker dispone of an interest.

**Keywords:** investment appraisal, Interval Arithmetic, Fuzzy Number Arithmetic.

## 1 Introduction

In this paper we introduce uncertainty in the investment appraisal managed through a new criterion called Average Internal Rate of Return (AIRR), introduced in [6]. The consistency of the arithmetic of variables represented with intervals of fuzzy numbers makes possible the application of the extension principle and a rigorous analysis of the investment decisions handled under uncertainty conditions. This approach for uncertainty modelling is not new in literature: Chiu and Park propose in [2] a decision model in which the uncertain cash flows and discounted rates are defined as fuzzy numbers. They study the difference between the present and the approximated present worth formula and they observe that the range of periodic cash flows is not a key feature. Kuchta in [4] proposes generalized fuzzy equivalents in order to incorporate uncertainty into the most frequently used techniques for capital budgeting. In [3] we develop the Kuchta approach with careful attention to the parametric representation of fuzzy numbers. In a second paper [5], Kuchta assumes a fuzzy Net Present Value for some projects and she shows that the common realization of them, may allow savings in the resource utilization. In [1] it is possible to find a detailed description of the possibilistic theory involved when taking decisions.

## 2 Basic Notions in Interval Arithmetic

In interval arithmetic the standard addition is not an invertible operation and in particular the algebraic difference $A - B = \{a - b | a \in A, b \in B\}$ is such that

S. Greco et al. (Eds.): IPMU 2012, Part IV, CCIS 300, pp. 64–73, 2012.

$A - A \neq 0$. The Hukuhara difference $A \ominus B = C$, if it exists, is defined to be the set $C$ such that $A = B + C$

$$A \ominus B = C \iff A = B + C$$

and we have $A \ominus A = 0$ but $A \ominus B \neq A - B$.

The equation $A + X = B$ is not equivalent to $A = B - X$ :the non equivalence is due to the way in which the uncertainty propagates, the position of $X$ at the left or at the right modify the magnitude of the propagation.

Given an interval $A = [a^-, a^+]$ with $a^- \leq a^+$, we can represent $A$ in terms of

$$\widehat{a} = \frac{a^+ + a^-}{2}, \ \overline{a} = \frac{a^+ - a^-}{2} \tag{1}$$

and we obtained the so called midpoint-radius representation $A = (\widehat{a}, \overline{a})$.

The fundamental notion in the rest of the paper is the generalization of the Hukuhara difference, introduced in [7] and detailed in [9], that is defined as:

$$A \ominus_{gH} B = C \Leftrightarrow \begin{cases} (i) \ A = B + C \\ or \\ (ii) \ B = A - C \end{cases}.$$

The generalized addition, the interval multiplication, the division $\oslash$ and the generalized division can be properly defined and the notation $\bigcirc_{gH}$ is simplified as $\bigcirc$.

The following property will be used:

**Lemma 1.** *Let* $A_k = [a_k^-, a_k^+]$ *and* $B_k = [b_k^-, b_k^+]$ *be given intervals for* $k = 1, 2, ..., n$; *if the* $n$ *gH-differences* $C_k = A_k \ominus B_k$ *are all of the same type (i) (i.e.,* $A_k = B_k + C_k$ *for all* $k$) *or all of the same type (ii) (i.e.,* $B_k = A_k - C_k$ *for all* $k$), *then we have*

$$\left( \sum_{k=1}^{n} A_k \right) \ominus \left( \sum_{k=1}^{n} B_k \right) = \sum_{k=1}^{n} (A_k \ominus B_k) = \sum_{k=1}^{n} C_k$$

Given a continuous real-valued function $y = f(x_1, ..., x_n)$ of $n$ real variables $x_1, ..., x_n$, its extension to intervals $X_j = [x_j^-, x_j^+]$ for $j = 1, ..., n$ is defined as the interval-valued function $Y = f(X_1, ..., X_n)$ such that the interval $Y$ is

$$Y = \{f(x_1, ..., x_n) | \ x_j \in X_j = [x_j^-, x_j^+] \text{ for all } j = 1, ..., n\}.$$

The resulting interval $Y = [y^-, y^+]$ is obtained by solving the box-constrained optimization problems

$$(EP) : \begin{cases} y^- = \min \{f(x_1, ..., x_n) | x_j \in [x_j^-, x_j^+], \ j = 1, ..., n\} \\ y^+ = \max \{f(x_1, ..., x_n) | x_j \in [x_j^-, x_j^+], \ j = 1, ..., n\} \end{cases}. \tag{2}$$

The direct application of *(EP)* may be difficult and computationally expensive, we use an implementation of a multiple population differential evolution (DE) algorithm detailed in [10].

# 3   The Average Internal Rate of Return (AIRR)

The Internal Rate of Return (IRR) has been strongly accepted in the economic literature and in real-life applications also if it implies many theoretical and empirical critical points. Recently IRR problems have been solved in [6] where the author states that a rate of return is not a function of cash flows but a function of capital.

Consider the sets of dates $\mathbb{T}_0 = \{0, 1, 2, ..., T\}$, $\mathbb{T}_1 = \{1, 2, ..., T\}$ and $\mathbb{T}_2 = \{1, ..., T - 1\}$. Let $(x_t)_{t \in \mathbb{T}_0}$ be the stream of cash flows, $(b_t)_{t \in \mathbb{T}_1}$ be the stream of returns, $(c_t)_{t \in \mathbb{T}_2}$ be the stream of invested capitals.

The three variables are connected each other via a fundamental economic relation:

$$c_{t-1} + b_t = x_t + c_t \quad \text{for all } t \in \mathbb{T}_1 \tag{3}$$

with the boundary conditions $c_0 = -x_0$ and $c_T = 0$. Three different situations may arise in applications:

(i) cash flow $(x_t)_{t \in \mathbb{T}_0}$ and capital $(c_t)_{t \in \mathbb{T}_2}$ are known, return $(b_t)_{t \in \mathbb{T}_1}$ is derived:

$$b_t = x_t + c_t - c_{t-1} \quad \text{for all } t \in \mathbb{T}_1 \tag{4}$$

(ii) return $(b_t)_{t \in \mathbb{T}_1}$ and capital $(c_t)_{t \in \mathbb{T}_2}$ are known, including $c_0$, cash flow $(x_t)_{t \in \mathbb{T}_0}$ is derived:

$$x_t = c_{t-1} - c_t + b_t \quad \text{for all } t \in \mathbb{T}_1 \tag{5}$$
$$x_0 = -c_0$$

(iii) cash flow $(x_t)_{t \in \mathbb{T}_0}$ and return $(b_t)_{t \in \mathbb{T}_1}$ are known, capital $(c_t)_{t \in \mathbb{T}_2}$ is derived:

$$c_t = c_{t-1} + b_t - x_t \quad \text{for all } t \in \mathbb{T}_1 \tag{6}$$
$$c_0 = -x_0.$$

An investment fund is an example of the first case because the investor invests an amount of money in a fund investment and periodically deposits additional amounts into the fund or withdraws some money from it; at the terminal date the investor receives the liquidation value of the fund. An example of the second case is given by a capital budgeting investment. Prospective returns are estimated, as well as prospective capitals, so that cash flows are finally derived. A loan where installments are fixed by the lender can be an example of the third case.

The three equations (i)-(iii) are logically equivalent in 'crisp' arithmetic. In interval arithmetic they differ and depending on which variable is known and which is unknown, the extension-principle approach or the generalized Hukuhara arithmetic are applied.

For a fixed market rate $r \in \mathbb{R}$, the NPVs of $(x_t)_{t\in T_0}$ and $(c_{t-1})_{t\in T_1}$ are defined, respectively, as

$$pv((x_t)_{t\in T_0}|r) = \sum_{t=0}^{T} x_t(1+r)^{-t} \tag{7}$$

$$pv((c_{t-1})_{t\in T_1}|r) = \sum_{t=1}^{T} c_{t-1}(1+r)^{-t} \tag{8}$$

$$pv((b_t)_{t\in T_1}|r) = \sum_{t=1}^{T} b_t(1+r)^{-t} \tag{9}$$

The IRR is defined as that rate $k^*$ such that $pv((x_t)_{t\in T_0}|k^*) = 0$. The Average Internal Rate of Return is defined as the ratio of the aggregate return generated by the project to the aggregate capital invested in the project:

$$k = \frac{\sum_{t=1}^{T} b_t(1+r)^{-(t-1)}}{\sum_{t=1}^{T} c_{t-1}(1+r)^{-(t-1)}} = \frac{pv((b_t)_{t\in T_1}|r)(1+r)}{pv((c_{t-1})_{t\in T_1}|r)} \tag{10}$$

It can be shown that, for any capital stream $(c_{t-1})_{t\in T_1}$ the following relation holds:

$$pv((x_t)_{t\in T_0}|r) = \sum_{t=1}^{T}(b_t - rc_{t-1})(1+r)^{-t}. \tag{11}$$

The amount $b_t - rc_{t-1}$ represents a residual return: if it is positive, then value is created; if it is negative, then value is destroyed. Replacing each $b_t$ with the product $kc_{t-1}$ in (11), one finds

$$(1+r)pv((x_t)_{t\in T_0}|r) = pv((c_{t-1})_{t\in T_1}|r)(k-r). \tag{12}$$

The right-hand side of (12) has a strong economic meaning: the investor invests an aggregate capital equal to $pv((c_{t-1})_{t\in T_1}|r)$ at a return rate equal to $k$, so foregoing the opportunity of investing the same capital at the market rate $r$. Note that the sign of the NPV equals the sign of $k-r$, so the project is acceptable (value is created) if and only if the AIRR is greater than the market rate. Also, note that $k = r$ if and only if $pv((x_t)_{t\in T_0}|r) = 0$, so project is value-neutral if the AIRR and the market rate coincide. The result holds for any capital stream, so that there are infinitely many AIRRs, each one associated with an aggregate capital $pv((c_{t-1})_{t\in T_1}|r)$. Among these, the correct rate of return is the one that makes use of the capital *actually* invested in the project. From (12) a computational shortcut is derived: solving for $k$ as a function of the $2T+1$ independent values $(x_t)_{t\in T_0}$, $(c_t)_{t\in T_2}$ and $r$, we obtain:

$$k(\boldsymbol{x}, \boldsymbol{c}, r) = (1+r)\frac{pv((x_t)_{t\in T_0}|r) + pv((c_{t-1})_{t\in T_1}|r)}{pv((c_{t-1})_{t\in T_1}|r))} - 1 \tag{13}$$

$$= (1+r)\frac{pv((x_t)_{t\in T_0}|r)}{pv((c_{t-1})_{t\in T_1}|r)} + r.$$

The streams $(x_t)_{t\in\mathbb{T}_0}, (c_t)_{t\in\mathbb{T}_1}, (b_t)_{t\in\mathbb{T}_1}, (d_t)_{t\in\mathbb{T}_0}$ are represented as the vectors $\mathbf{x}\in\mathbb{R}^{T+1}, \mathbf{c}\in\mathbb{R}^{T-1}, \mathbf{b}\in\mathbb{R}^T, \mathbf{d}\in\mathbb{R}^T$ respectively.

If we have nonzero capitals, then the AIRR may be framed as a weighted average of holding period rates. To show it, consider the stream of holding period rates $(k_t)_{t\in\mathbb{T}_1}$ defined as

$$k_1 := -\frac{x_1 + c_1}{x_0} - 1 \tag{14}$$

$$k_t := \frac{(x_t + c_t)}{c_{t-1}} - 1, t = 2, ..., T - 1$$

$$k_T := \frac{x_T}{c_{T-1}} - 1$$

where $c_t \neq 0$, $t \in \mathbb{T}_1$ is assumed. Therefore,

$$b_t = k_t c_{t-1} \tag{15}$$

and equation (11) may also be written in terms of holding period rates:

$$pv((x_t)_{t\in\mathbb{T}_0}|r) = \sum_{t=1}^{T}(k_t - r)c_{t-1}(1+r)^{-t}. \tag{16}$$

The AIRR is then found back as a Chisini mean of the period rates: replacing each $k_t$ with a constant $a$, and solving

$$\sum_{t=1}^{T}(k_t - r)c_{t-1}(1+r)^{-t} = \sum_{t=1}^{T}(a - r)c_{t-1}(1+r)^{-t}$$

for $a$, one gets

$$a = \alpha_1 k_1 + \alpha_2 k_2 + ... + \alpha_T k_T \tag{17}$$

where $\alpha_t := \frac{c_{t-1}(1+r)^{-(t-1)}}{pv((c_{t-1})_{t\in\mathbb{T}_1}|r)}$. From (15) one obtains $a = k$.

## 4   Interval Investment Appraisal

The basic variables and equations valid for any investment are:

$$c_0 = -x_0, \quad d_0 = x_0, \quad c_T = 0$$

$$b_t + c_{t-1} = x_t + c_t, \quad t = 1, ..., T$$

$$b_t = k_t c_{t-1}, \quad t = 1, ..., T$$

$$d_t = c_t - c_{t-1}, \quad t = 1, ..., T$$

$$b_t = x_t + d_t, \quad t = 1, ..., T$$

$$(1 + k_t)c_{t-1} = x_t + c_t, \quad t = 1, ..., T.$$

The equation $\sum_{t=0}^{T} x_t = \sum_{t=1}^{T} b_t$ is always valid, equivalent to $c_T = 0$.

To write the equations in matrix notation, we define the following arrays

$$\boldsymbol{x}' = (x_0, ..., x_T) \in \mathbb{R}^{T+1}$$
$$\boldsymbol{c}' = (c_1, ..., c_{T-1}) \in \mathbb{R}^{T-1}$$
$$\boldsymbol{b}', \boldsymbol{d}', \boldsymbol{k}' \in \mathbb{R}^T$$

and introduce the two rectangular matrices $\boldsymbol{M}$ and $\boldsymbol{N}$

$$\boldsymbol{M} = \begin{bmatrix} 1 & 1 & 0 & 0 & ... & 0 \\ 0 & 0 & 1 & 0 & ... & 0 \\ 0 & 0 & 0 & 1 & ... & 0 \\ & & & ... & & \\ 0 & 0 & 0 & 0 & ... & 1 \end{bmatrix} \text{ of order } (T, T+1) \text{ and rank } T$$

$$\boldsymbol{N} = \begin{bmatrix} 1 & 0 & 0 & ... & 0 \\ -1 & 1 & 0 & ... & 0 \\ 0 & -1 & 1 & ... & 0 \\ & & ... & ... & \\ 0 & 0 & 0 & ... & 1 \\ 0 & 0 & 0 & ... & -1 \end{bmatrix} \text{ of order } (T, T-1) \text{ and rank } T-1.$$

such that $\boldsymbol{b} = \boldsymbol{M}\boldsymbol{x} + \boldsymbol{N}\boldsymbol{c}$.

The interval-valued cash flow stream is denoted by $(X_t)_{t \in \mathbb{T}_0}$ where, at time $t$, we have $X_t = [x_t^-, x_t^+]$. The interval-valued investment stream is denoted by $(C_t)_{t \in \mathbb{T}_0}$ where $C_t = [c_t^-, c_t^+]$; considering that $(C_t)_{t \in \mathbb{T}_0}$ is constrained to have $C_0 = -X_0 = [-x_0^+, -x_0^-]$ and $C_T = 0$, we consider $C_t$ for $t \in \mathbb{T}_2$ and write $(C_t)_{t \in \mathbb{T}_2}$. The interval-valued interest rate will be $R = [r^-, r^+]$; we will generally assume that $1 + r^- > 0$.

A real-valued realization of $(X_t)_{t \in \mathbb{T}_0}$ will be any sequence $(x_t)_{t \in \mathbb{T}_0}$ with $x_t \in X_t$ for all $t \in \mathbb{T}_0$; analogously, a real valued realization of $(C_t)_{t \in \mathbb{T}_2}$ will be any $(c_t)_{t \in \mathbb{T}_2}$ with $c_t \in C_t$ for all $t \in \mathbb{T}_2$ and we will obtain its extension to all $t \in \mathbb{T}_0$ by $c_0 = -x_0$ and $c_T = 0$.

The interval-valued present values of the streams $(X_t)_{t \in \mathbb{T}_0}$, $(C_{t-1})_{t \in \mathbb{T}_1}$, $(D_t)_{t \in \mathbb{T}_0}$, $(B_t)_{t \in \mathbb{T}_0}$ are defined, for a fixed real $r \in R$, using the extension principle, to be the sets of present values obtained by any real-valued realizations of any pair of the stream flows. We use the following notations

$$PV((X_t)_{t \in \mathbb{T}_0} | r) = \{pv((x_t)_{t \in \mathbb{T}_0} | r); x_t \in X_t, t \in \mathbb{T}_0\} \tag{18}$$
$$\text{where } C_0 = -X_0.$$

and for an interval-valued market rate $R = [r^-, r^+]$, the interval present values corresponding to the streams $(X_t)_{t \in \mathbb{T}_0}$, $(C_{t-1})_{t \in \mathbb{T}_1}$, $(B_t)_{t \in \mathbb{T}_1}$, $(D_t)_{t \in \mathbb{T}_0}$ are

$$PV((X_t)_{t \in \mathbb{T}_0}|R) = \bigcup_{r \in R} PV((X_t)_{t \in \mathbb{T}_0}|r) \tag{19}$$

$$PV((C_{t-1})_{t \in \mathbb{T}_1}|R) = \bigcup_{r \in R} PV((C_{t-1})_{t \in \mathbb{T}_1}|r) \tag{20}$$

$$PV((B_t)_{t \in \mathbb{T}_1}|R) = \bigcup_{r \in R} PV((B_t)_{t \in \mathbb{T}_1}|r) \tag{21}$$

$$PV((D_t)_{t \in \mathbb{T}_0}|R) = \bigcup_{r \in R} PV((D_t)_{t \in \mathbb{T}_0}|r). \tag{22}$$

Clearly, the interval-valued $PV((X_t)_{t \in \mathbb{T}_0}|R)$, $PV((C_{t-1})_{t \in \mathbb{T}_1}|R)$, $PV((B_t)_{t \in \mathbb{T}_1}|R)$ and $PV((D_t)_{t \in \mathbb{T}_0}|R)$ are not independent. This fact is to be taken into account when using them in interval arithmetic operations. In particular, there is not a simple way of using (18-**??**) or (19-20) to define the interval-valued counterpart of the AIRR.

In this paper we discuss deeply the first situation, where cash flows $(x_t)_{t \in \mathbb{T}_0}$ and capitals $(c_t)_{t \in \mathbb{T}_2}$ are known in terms of intervals of "possible values":

$$x_t \in X_t = [x_t^-, x_t^+], \; t = 0, 1, ..., T$$
$$c_t \in C_t = [c_t^-, c_t^+], \; t = 1, ..., T - 1$$

and returns $(b_t)_{t \in \mathbb{T}_1}$ are derived by applying the extension principle to

$$\begin{cases} b_1 = x_1 + c_1 + x_0 \\ b_t = x_t + c_t - c_{t-1} & \text{for } t = 2, ..., T-1 \\ b_T = x_T - c_{T-1} \end{cases} \tag{23}$$

We can write $b = Mx + Nc$ and the set of arrays $b$ are obtained by the extension principle

$$\mathbb{B} = \{Mx + Nc| \; x \in X, c \in C\}. \tag{24}$$

**Proposition 1.** *If the streams $(X_t)_{t \in \mathbb{T}_0}$ and $(C_{t-1})_{t \in \mathbb{T}_1}$ are given independent intervals, then the sets $B_t = \{b_t; b \in \mathbb{B}\}$ with $\mathbb{B}$ in (24) satisfy $B_t = X_t + C_t - C_{t-1}$ for all $t = 1, ..., T$ (here, $C_T = 0$ and $C_0 = -X_0$).*

*Remark 1.* Starting with independent intervals $(X_t)_{t \in \mathbb{T}_0}$ and $(C_t)_{t \in \mathbb{T}_2}$ we can easily compute the intervals $B_t$ and define the interval-valued period rate $K_t$ by the extension of equation (14), i.e. $1 + K_t = (X_t + C_t)/C_{t-1}$. We also have the following interval identities

$$B_t \oplus C_{t-1} = X_t + C_t, \quad t = 1, ..., T$$

But, in terms of interval arithmetic, it is not true that $B_t = K_t C_{t-1}$. If we compute $K_t^B = B_t \oslash C_{t-1}$, we have, in terms of intervals, $K_t^B \neq K_t$ and if we compute $B_t^K = K_t C_{t-1}$ by interval multiplication, this will produce overestimation of $B_t$ because $K_t$ and $C_{t-1}$ are not independent, and $B_t \neq B_t^K$.

In order to obtain an interval extension of equations (11), consider $x_0 \in X_0$ and denote the interval-valued PV of the stream $\{x_0\}, X_1, ..., X_T$ by

$$PV_{x_0}((X_t)_{t \in T_0}|r) = x_0 + \sum_{t=1}^{T} X_t(1+r)^{-t}.$$

We have the following

**Theorem 1.** *Let* $(X_t)_{t \in T_0}$, $(C_t)_{t \in T_2}$ *be given interval-valued streams,* $x_0 \in X_0$ *and* $C_0 = \{-x_0\}$; *assuming* $0 \leq r < 1$, *the intervals* $B_t = X_t + C_t - C_{t-1}$ *satisfy the interval inclusion*

$$PV_{x_0}((X_t)_{t \in T_0}|r) \subseteq \sum_{t=1}^{T} (B_t \ominus rC_{t-1})(1+r)^{-t}. \tag{25}$$

*If the differences* $B_t \ominus rC_{t-1}$ *are all of the same type, then inclusion (25) holds also for* $r \geq 1$.

From Theorem 1 we obtain the following inclusion for $PV((X_t)_{t \in T_0}|r)$:

**Corollary 1.** *Let* $(X_t)_{t \in T_0}$, $(C_t)_{t \in T_2}$ *be given interval-valued streams; assuming the conditions of theorem (1) we have the interval inclusion*

$$PV((X_t)_{t \in T_0}|r) \subseteq X_0 + (C_1 + X_1)(1+r)^{-1} + \sum_{t=2}^{T} (B_t \ominus rC_{t-1})(1+r)^{-t}. \tag{26}$$

*Considering that* $B_1 = X_0 + C_1 + X_1$ *and* $1 + r > 0$, *we finally obtain* $(B_1 + rX_0)(1+r)^{-1} = X_0 + (C_1 + X_1)(1+r)^{-1}$.

We obtain the interval version of the AIRR by using the well known extension principle; it is denoted by $K_{EP}(U, V, r)$, where $(U, V)$ will denote $(X, C)$ and $r$ will be the actual real-valued market rate $R = [r^-, r^+]$, i.e. for $r \in R$, defined by

$$K_{EP}(U, V, R) = \bigcup_{r \in R} K_{EP}(U, V, r).$$

It follows that $K_{EP}(U, V, R)$ is itself an interval, assuming that each $K_{EP}(U, V, r)$ is an interval for all $r \in R$.

The AIRR as a function of $X = (X_0, X_1, ..., X_T)$ and $C = (C_1, ..., C_{T-1})$ is the extension of the function $k(x, c, r)$, i.e.

$$K_{EP}(X, C, r) = \{k(x, c, r); x \in X, c \in C\} \text{ for a real-valued } r$$

$$K_{EP}(X, C, R) = \bigcup_{r \in R} K_{EP}(X, C, r) \text{ for an interval-valued } R.$$

An interesting interpretation of equation (12) is that

$$r = k \implies pv((x_t)_{t \in T_0}|r) = 0$$

and in the interval-valued case, we are interested to have a similar property, or at least that

$$r \in K \implies 0 \in PV((X_t)_{t \in \mathbb{T}_0} | r)$$

and similarly for the $\alpha - cuts$ of the fuzzy AIRR $\widetilde{k}$.

We obtain an estimation of the interval-valued AIRR satisfying the property above, if we compute $K_{gH}$ by solving the following interval equation, analogous to (12)

$$(K_{gH} - r)PV((C_{t-1})_{t \in \mathbb{T}_1} | r) = (1 + r)PV((X_t)_{t \in \mathbb{T}_0} | r) \tag{27}$$

and it also holds

$$r \in K_{gH}(\boldsymbol{X}, \boldsymbol{C}, r) \implies 0 \in PV((X_t)_{t \in \mathbb{T}_0} | r).$$

We can prove that

$$K_{gH}(\boldsymbol{X}, \boldsymbol{C}, r) \subseteq K_{EP}(\boldsymbol{X}, \boldsymbol{C}, r) \tag{28}$$

Aa an example, consider the interval data $(X_t, C_t)$ obtained from the following crisp data

| $t = 0$ | $t = 1$ | $t = 2$ | $t = 3$ | $t = 4$ | $t = 5$ | $t = 6$ | $t = 7$ | $t = 8$ |
|---------|---------|---------|---------|---------|---------|---------|---------|---------|
| $x_t$ | $-4.0$ | $3.0$ | $2.25$ | $1.5$ | $0.75$ | $0.0$ | $-0.75$ | $-1.5$ | $-2.25$ |
| $c_t$ | | $3.0$ | $5.0$ | $6.0$ | $1.0$ | $8.0$ | $3.0$ | $1.745$ | |

and the corresponding returns

| $t = 1$ | $t = 2$ | $t = 3$ | $t = 4$ | $t = 5$ | $t = 6$ | $t = 7$ | $t = 8$ |
|---------|---------|---------|---------|---------|---------|---------|---------|
| $b_t$ | $2.0$ | $4.25$ | $2.25$ | $0.75$ | $0.0$ | $-0.75$ | $-1.5$ | $-2.25$ |

with a rate $r = 1\%$, then we find the picture that shows (28).

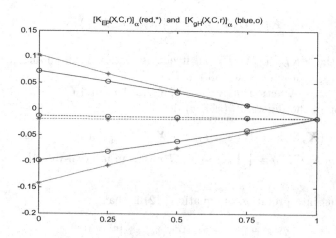

$[K_{EP}(X,C,r)]_\alpha$ (red,*)  and  $[K_{gH}(X,C,r)]_\alpha$ (blue,o)

# 5 Conclusions

We can argue that the interpretation of (3) plays a leading role in the definition of a method for investment appraisal based on the AIRR criterion, including the possibility for investors to deal with uncertainty modelled through intervals. In a very next future we are going to extend the analysis to all the possible cases relevant in applications and to a comparison index helpful in making the final decision.

# References

1. Carlsson, C., Fullér, R.: Possibility for decision. STUDFUZZ. Springer (2011)
2. Chiu, C.Y., Park, C.S.: Fuzzy cash flow analysis using present worth criterion. The Engineering Economist 39(2), 113–138 (1994)
3. Guerra, M.L., Sorini, L., Stefanini, L.: Fuzzy Investment Decision Making. In: Magdalena, L., Ojeda-Aciego, M., Verdegay, J.L. (eds.) Proceedings of IPMU 2008, pp. 745–750 (2008) ISBN: 978-84-612-3061-7
4. Kuchta, D.: Fuzzy Capital Budgeting. Fuzzy Sets and Systems 111, 367–385 (2000)
5. Kuchta, D.: A fuzzy model for R&D project selection with benefit, outcome and resource interactions. The Engineering Economist 46, 164–180 (2001)
6. Magni, C.A.: Average internal rate of return and investment decisions: a new perspective. The Engineering Economist 55(2), 150–180 (2010) Updated version available at SSN: http://ssrn.com/abstract=1542690
7. Markov, S.: Extended interval arithmetic. Compt. Rend. Acad. Bulg. Sci. 30(9), 1239–1242 (1977)
8. Pohjola, V.J., Turunen, I.: Estimating the interval rate of return from fuzzy data. Engineering Costs and Production Economics 18, 215–221 (1990)
9. Stefanini, L.: A generalization of Hukuhara difference and division for interval and fuzzy arithmetic. Fuzzy Sets and Systems 161(11), 1564–1584 (2010)
10. Stefanini, L., Sorini, L., Guerra, M.L.: Fuzzy Numbers and Fuzzy Arithmetics. In: Pedrycz, W., Skowron, A., Kreinovich, V. (eds.) Handbook of Granular Computing, pp. 249–283. John Wiley & Sons (2008)

# Parallel Machine Scheduling under Uncertainty

Adam Kasperski[1], Adam Kurpisz[2], and Paweł Zieliński[2]

[1] Institute of Industrial Engineering and Management, Wrocław University
of Technology, Wybrzeże Wyspiańskiego 27, 50-370, Wrocław, Poland
`adam.kasperski@pwr.wroc.pl`
[2] Faculty of Fundamental Problems of Technology, Wrocław University of
Technology, Wybrzeże Wyspiańskiego 27, 50-370, Wrocław, Poland
`{adam.kurpisz,pawel.zielinski}@pwr.wroc.pl`

**Abstract.** In this paper a parallel machine scheduling problem with
uncertain processing times is discussed. This uncertainty is modeled by
specifying a scenario set containing $K$ distinct processing time scenarios. The ordered weighted averaging aggregation (OWA) operator, whose
special cases are the maximum and Hurwicz criteria, is applied to compute the best schedule. Some new positive and negative approximation
results concerning the problem are shown.

**Keywords:** scheduling, parallel machines, uncertain processing times,
OWA operator, robust optimization.

## 1 Introduction and Motivation

Scheduling under uncertainty is a wide and important area of operations research
and computer science. In real life, the values of some parameters which appear
in scheduling problems, for example processing times, are often uncertain. Every
possible realization of the parameters which may occur is called a *scenario* and all
the scenarios form a *scenario set*. Under uncertainty, no additional information
in the scenario set, such as a *probability* or *possibility distribution*, is known (see,
e.g., [11]). In the traditional robust approach to scheduling (see, e.g., [8,9]) we
wish to minimize a schedule cost in a worst case, for example its maximum cost
over all scenarios. Hence the resulting solution can be very conservative and is
appropriate if a decision maker is risk-averse. In this paper we generalize the
min-max approach by using the *ordered weighted averaging aggregation operator*
(shortly OWA) proposed in [13], which is well known in decision theory. The
OWA operator allows a decision maker to take his/her attitude towards risk
into account. In particular, the well known Hurwicz criterion under which we
minimize a convex combination of the maximal (pessimistic) and the minimal
(optimistic) cost is also a special case of the OWA operator.

In this paper we consider the parallel machine scheduling problem denoted as
$P||C_{max}$ in the commonly used Graham's notation. This is one of the basic and
most extensively studied scheduling problems (see, e.g., [2]). The classical deter-
ministic $P||C_{max}$ problem is known to be NP-hard. Therefore, its version with

S. Greco et al. (Eds.): IPMU 2012, Part IV, CCIS 300, pp. 74–83, 2012.

uncertain parameters cannot be easier and is also NP-hard. If an optimization problem turns out to be NP-hard, then we would like to design some efficient approximation algorithms for it. An algorithm $\mathcal{A}$ is a *k-approximation algorithm* for a minimization problem if it runs in polynomial time and for every instance of this problem it returns a solution whose cost is at most $k \cdot OPT$, where $OPT$ is the cost of an optimal solution. If an optimization problem admits a $k$-approximation algorithm, then we say that it is approximable within $k$. Sometimes it is possible to design a family of $(1 + \epsilon)$-approximation algorithms for $\epsilon > 0$. Such a family is called a *polynomial time approximation scheme* (PTAS) or a *fully polynomial time approximation scheme* (FPTAS) if it is also polynomial in $1/\epsilon$. This is the best one could expect if P$\neq$NP.

In this paper, we show some new positive and negative results concerning the approximation of the $P||C_{\max}$ problem with uncertain processing times and the OWA criterion. In particular, we prove that, contrary to the deterministic problem, the uncertain version of $P||C_{\max}$ with unbounded scenario set cannot have a PTAS if P$\neq$NP. We also show that if the number of machines and scenarios are constant, then the problem with the min-max criterion admits an FPTAS and the problem with the OWA criterion can be solved in a pseudopolynomial time. Finally, we propose a mixed integer programming based approach (MIP) to get an optimal schedule for the Hurwicz criterion. In order to make the presentation clear, we place all the technical proofs in Appendix.

## 2    Parallel Machine Scheduling under Uncertainty

Let $J = \{1, \ldots, n\}$ be a set of jobs which must be processed on $m$ identical parallel machines $M_1, \ldots, M_m$. Each machine can process at most one job at a time. In the deterministic case, each job $j \in J$ has a nonnegative processing time $p_j$. We wish to assign each job to exactly one machine so that the maximum job completion time of the resulting schedule, called a *makespan*, is minimal. This problem is denoted as $P||C_{\max}$ in the commonly used Graham's notation (see, e.g., [2]). It is well known [10] that the deterministic problem with only two machines, is already NP-hard. However, if the number of machines is constant, then the problem admits an FPTAS [12]. On the other hand, if the number of machines is unbounded (it is a part of the input), then the problem becomes strongly NP-hard [4] but it admits a PTAS [1,7]. The problem has also an efficient $(\frac{4}{3} - \frac{1}{3m})$-approximation algorithm based on a *list scheduling* according to the LPT rule [6].

Suppose that the job processing times are uncertain and $\Gamma = \{S_1, \ldots, S_K\}$ contains $K \geq 1$ distinct processing time scenarios. Thus each scenario $S \in \Gamma$ is a vector $(p_1^S, p_2^S, \ldots, p_n^S)$ of job processing times, which may appear with a positive but unknown probability. Let $\Pi$ be the set of all schedules. We denote by $C_{\max}(\pi, S)$ the makespan of schedule $\pi \in \Pi$ under scenario $S$. We also use $\overline{C}_{\max}(\pi) = \max_{S \in \Gamma} C_{\max}(\pi, S)$ and $\underline{C}_{\max}(\pi) = \min_{S \in \Gamma} C_{\max}(\pi, S)$ to denote the maximal and the minimal makespans of schedule $\pi$ over all scenarios in $\Gamma$, respectively. The OWA of a schedule $\pi$ with respect to weights $\boldsymbol{w} = (w_1, \ldots, w_K)$,

$w_1 + \cdots + w_K = 1, w_i \geq 0, i = 1, \ldots, K$, is defined as follows:

$$\mathrm{OWA}_{\boldsymbol{w}}(\pi) = \sum_{i=1}^{K} w_i C_{\max}(\pi, S_{\sigma(i)}), \tag{1}$$

where $\sigma$ is a permutation of the set $\{1, \ldots, K\}$ such that $C_{\max}(\pi, S_{\sigma(1)}) \geq C_{\max}(\pi, S_{\sigma(2)}) \geq \cdots \geq C_{\max}(\pi, S_{\sigma(K)})$.

In the OWA $P||C_{\max}$ problem, we seek a schedule $\pi$ minimizing $\mathrm{OWA}_{\boldsymbol{w}}(\pi)$ for a given vector of weights $\boldsymbol{w}$. It can be easily verified that if $w_1 = 1$ and $w_i = 0$ for $i = 2, \ldots, K$, then $\mathrm{OWA}_{\boldsymbol{w}}(\pi) = \overline{C}_{\max}(\pi)$ and the problem reduces to computing a min-max schedule, which is a typical goal in the *robust optimization* (see, e.g., [9]). We denote such a problem as MIN-MAX $P||C_{\max}$. We get another important case when $w_1 = \alpha$ and $w_K = (1 - \alpha)$ for $\alpha \in [0, 1]$. Then

$$\mathrm{OWA}_{\boldsymbol{w}}(\pi) = (1 - \alpha)\underline{C}_{\max}(\pi) + \alpha\overline{C}_{\max}(\pi) = H_\alpha(\pi)$$

is the well known Hurwicz criterion (see, e.g., [11]), which is a compromise between the best (optimistic) and the worst (pessimistic) case. We will denote the problem with the Hurwicz criterion as HUR $P||C_{\max}$. Obviously, if $\alpha = 1$, then we again get the MIN-MAX $P||C_{\max}$ problem.

## 3    Approximation Results for the General Problem

It is obvious that OWA $P||C_{\max}$, MIN-MAX $P||C_{\max}$ and HUR $P||C_{\max}$ are NP-hard even if $m = 2$ and $K = 1$, which follows from the fact that their deterministic versions with only one scenario and two machines are already NP-hard [10,4]. Furthermore, it turns out that MIN-MAX $P||C_{\max}$ is equivalent to the *vector scheduling problem* discussed in [3]. So, all the results obtained in [3] applies to MIN-MAX $P||C_{\max}$ as well. In particular, if $m$ is unbounded and $K$ is constant, then the problem admits a PTAS but if both $m$ and $K$ are unbounded, then the problem is not approximable within any constant factor unless NP=ZPP [3] (if we use the results presented in [14], the we can state the above hardness approximation result assuming only P≠NP). Since both OWA $P||C_{\max}$ and HUR $P||C_{\max}$ include MIN-MAX $P||C_{\max}$ as a special case, they are also not approximable within any constant factor if $m$ and $K$ are unbounded unless P=NP.

In this section we wish to investigate the case when the number of machines $m$ is constant (in particular $m = 2$) and the number of scenarios $K$ is unbounded. The following theorem is the main result of this section:

**Theorem 1.** *If the number of scenarios $K$ is unbounded and $m = 2$, then OWA $P||C_{\max}$ with $w_K = \alpha$, $w_{\lceil K/2 \rceil+1} = 1 - \alpha$ and $w_i = 0$, for all $i \neq 1, \lceil K/2 \rceil + 1$, $\alpha \in [0, 1]$, is not approximable within $\frac{3\alpha + \frac{3}{2}(1-\alpha)}{2\alpha + \frac{3}{4}(1-\alpha)} - \epsilon$ for any $\epsilon > 0$ unless $P = NP$.*

*Proof.* See Appendix.    □

Theorem 1 applied to the extreme values of $\alpha$ leads to the following corollary:

**Corollary 1.** *If the number of scenarios $K$ is unbounded and $m = 2$, then* MIN-MAX $P||C_{\max}$ *and* HUR $P||C_{\max}$ *are not approximable within $3/2 - \epsilon$ and* OWA $P||C_{\max}$ *is not approximable within $2 - \epsilon$ for any $\epsilon > 0$ unless $P = NP$. Hence all these problems do not admit a PTAS.*

The following theorem establishes a positive approximation result for the general problem:

**Theorem 2.** *For any schedule $\pi \in \Pi$ it holds $\mathrm{OWA}_{\boldsymbol{w}}(\pi) \leq m \cdot \mathrm{OWA}_{\boldsymbol{w}}(\pi^*)$, where $\pi^*$ is an optimal schedule. Hence OWA $P||C_{\max}$ is approximable within $m$.*

*Proof.* See Appendix.    □

Corollary 1 and Theorem 2 allow us to close the approximation gap for the OWA $P||C_{\max}$ problem.

**Corollary 2.** OWA $P||C_{\max}$ *with two machines ($m = 2$) is approximable within 2 but not approximable within $2 - \epsilon$ for any $\epsilon > 0$ if $P \neq NP$.*

## 4   Approximation Results for Min-Max $P||C_{\max}$

In this section, we discuss the approximation of MIN-MAX $P||C_{\max}$. Let us first consider the case, when $m$ and $K$ are unbounded. In [3] a very simple $O(\ln Km/\ln\ln Km)$-approximation randomized algorithm and a deterministic $(K+1)$-approximation algorithm for the *vector scheduling problem* have been proposed. This problem is equivalent to MIN-MAX $P||C_{\max}$. Hence, both algorithms can also be applied to MIN-MAX $P||C_{\max}$. The first one simply assigns each job to a machine chosen uniformly at random (see Algorithm 1).

---

**Algorithm 1.** Randomized algorithm for MIN-MAX $P||C_{\max}$.

---
**foreach** $j \in J$ **do**
    ⌞ assign job $j$ to exactly one machine $M_1, \ldots, M_m$, with the probability $1/m$;

---

Notice that the random mechanism in Algorithm 1 can be realized by casting for each job $j \in J$ a symmetric $m$-faced dice whose face probabilities are $1/m$. Since each job is assigned to exactly one machine, Algorithm 1 returns a feasible schedule. The idea of the second algorithm, proposed in [3], (Algorithm 2) is to apply the classical list scheduling algorithm (see e.g., [6]) to a particular processing time scenario.

The following theorems give approximation bounds for schedules constructed by Algorithm 1 and Algorithm 2:

**Theorem 3 ([3]).** *Algorithm 1 returns an $O(\ln(Km)/\ln\ln(Km))$-approximate schedule with high probability.*

---

**Algorithm 2.** Approximation algorithm for MIN-MAX $P||C_{\max}$.

---

**foreach** $j \in J$ **do**

$\quad \lfloor \; p_j^{\widehat{S}} \leftarrow \sum_{S \in \Gamma} p_j^S$ /*Construct an auxiliary scenario $\widehat{S}$      */

/*Apply List Scheduling Algorithm for jobs in $J$ with $p_j^{\widehat{S}}, j \in J$      */
**foreach** $j \in J$ **do**

$\quad \lfloor$ assign $j$ to the machine with the smallest load;

---

**Theorem 4 ([3]).** *Algorithm 2 returns a $(K+1)$-approximate schedule.*

Since MIN-MAX $P||C_{\max}$ is a special case of OWA $P||C_{\max}$ with $\alpha = 1$, Theorems 2 and 4 immediately imply MIN-MAX $P||C_{\max}$ is approximable within $\min\{m, K+1\}$. Thus in particular it is approximable within 2 for two machines. There is still and open gap, because we know (see Corollary 1) that the two-machine case is not approximable within $3/2 - \epsilon$ for any $\epsilon > 0$.

We now discuss the case in which both the number of machines $m$ and the number of scenarios $K$ are constant. We first show that the general OWA $P||C_{max}$ problem can be solved in pseudopolynomial time. Let us define a *load vector*:

$$L = (L_{11}, \ldots, L_{m1}, L_{12}, \ldots, L_{m2}, \ldots, L_{1K}, \ldots, L_{mK}),$$

where $L_{ik}$ is the load of machine $M_i$ under scenario $S_k$ for some partial schedule. Let $L_{\max} = \max_{S \in \Gamma} \sum_{j \in J} p_j^S$. Clearly $L_{ik} \leq L_{\max}$ for all $i = 1, \ldots, m$ and $k = 1, \ldots, K$. Therefore, the number of distinct load vectors is bounded by $l = (L_{\max})^{mK}$. We can now use a simple dynamic algorithm to compute an optimal schedule. An idea of that algorithm is illustrated in Fig. 1.

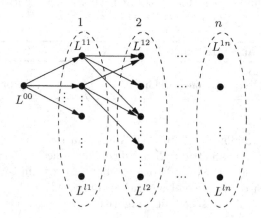

**Fig. 1.** An illustration of the exact algorithm

We first build a directed acyclic network composed of node $\boldsymbol{L}^{00} = (0, \ldots, 0)$ and $n$ layers, where the $j$th layer is composed of nodes $\boldsymbol{L}^{1j}, \ldots, \boldsymbol{L}^{lj}$. The arc between $L^{uj-1}$ and $L^{vj}$ exists if and only if the load vector $L^{vj}$ can be obtained from $L^{uj-1}$ by placing the job $j$ on some machine. This network can be built in $O(nml) = O(nm(L_{\max})^{mK})$ time, since it contains $nl + 1$ nodes and each node has at most $m$ outgoing arcs. The last, $n$th, layer contains the load vectors of at most $l$ complete schedules and the vector corresponding to schedule $\pi$ with the minimum value of $\mathrm{OWA}_{\boldsymbol{w}}(\pi)$ is optimal. This optimal schedule can be obtained by using simple backward computations in the network constructed. The overall running time of the algorithm is $O(nm(L_{\max})^{mK}) = O(nm(np_{\max})^{mK}) = O(n^{mK+1}m(p_{\max})^{mK})$. Theorem 5 summarizes this result:

**Theorem 5.** OWA $P||C_{\max}$ *can be solved in* $O(n^{mK+1}m(p_{\max})^{mK})$ *time, which is pseudopolynomial if $m$ and $K$ are constant.*

Using theorem 5 we get the following result:

**Theorem 6.** *For any instance of the* MIN-MAX $P||C_{\max}$ *problem with constant $m$ and $K$ and any $\epsilon \in (0,1)$, there is an $(1 + \epsilon)$-approximation algorithm which runs in* $O(n^{2mK+1}m(1/\epsilon)^{mK})$ *time. Hence,* MIN-MAX $P||C_{\max}$ *with constant $m$ and $K$ admits and FPTAS.*

*Proof.* see Appendix.                                                                 □

## 5   Some Results for Hur $P||C_{\max}$

It is not difficult to see that HUR $P||C_{\max}$ can be represented as follows:

$$
\begin{aligned}
H_\alpha(\pi^*) = \min\ & (1 - \alpha)u + \alpha v \\
\text{s.t.}\ & u \ge C_{\max}(\pi, S_k) - M(1 - \delta_k),\ k = 1, \ldots, K, \\
& v \ge C_{\max}(\pi, S_k), \qquad\qquad k = 1, \ldots, K, \\
& \pi \in \Pi, \\
& \textstyle\sum_{k=1}^{K} \delta_k = 1, \\
& \delta_k \in \{0,1\}, \qquad\qquad\qquad k = 1, \ldots, K,
\end{aligned}
\tag{2}
$$

where $M$ is a number greater than all the possible values of $C_{\max}(\pi, S_k)$ for $k = 1, \ldots, K$. The first $K$ constraints ensure that $u = \underline{C}_{\max}(\pi)$ and the next $K$ constraints set $v = \overline{C}_{\max}(\pi)$. Let $x_{ij} \in \{0,1\}$ and $x_{ij} = 1$ if job $j$ is placed on machine $M_i$. Then problem (2) can be represented as the following mixed integer linear programming problem, which can be solved by some standard off-the-shelf MIP solvers.:

$$
\begin{aligned}
\min\ & (1 - \alpha)u + \alpha v \\
\text{s.t.}\ & u \ge \textstyle\sum_{j=1}^{n} x_{ij}p_j^{S_k} - M(1 - \delta_k),\ i = 1, \ldots, m, k = 1, \ldots, K, \\
& v \ge \textstyle\sum_{j=1}^{n} x_{ij}p_j^{S_k}, \qquad\qquad i = 1, \ldots, m, k = 1, \ldots, K, \\
& \textstyle\sum_{i=1}^{m} x_{ij} = 1, \qquad\qquad\qquad j = 1, \ldots, n, \\
& \textstyle\sum_{k=1}^{K} \delta_k = 1, \\
& \delta_k \in \{0,1\}, \qquad\qquad\qquad\qquad k = 1, \ldots, K, \\
& x_{ij} \in \{0,1\}, \qquad\qquad\qquad i = 1, \ldots, m, j = 1, \ldots, n.
\end{aligned}
\tag{3}
$$

Clearly, if $\alpha = 1$, then we get the Min-max $P||C_{\max}$ problem to which all the approximation results shown in Section 4 can be applied. The second extreme case, when $\alpha = 0$, is even easier. Because $H_0(\pi^*) = \min_{\pi \in \Pi} \min_{S \in \Gamma} C_{\max}(\pi, S) = \min_{S \in \Gamma} \min_{\pi \in \Pi} C_{\max}(\pi, S)$, we get an optimal solution by solving $K$ deterministic problems for scenarios $S_1, \ldots, S_K$. Furthermore, each deterministic problem can be approximated within $(4/3 - 1/(3m))$ by applying the list scheduling algorithm according to LPT rule. In consequence the case $\alpha = 0$ is also approximable within $(4/3 - 1/(3m))$.

Theorem 2 shows that Hur $P||C_{max}$ with two machines is approximable within 2 even if the number of scenarios is unbounded. On the other hand this problem is not approximable within $3/2 - \epsilon$ for any $\epsilon > 0$ (see Corollary 1). So closing this gap is an interesting open problem.

# 6    Conclusions

In this paper, we have discussed one of the basic scheduling problems denoted as $P||C_{\max}$. We have considered the situation in which the job processing times are uncertain and all the possible vectors of the processing times form a given scenario set. Then an additional criterion is required to choose a solution. We have adopted the well known OWA operator, which is commonly used in decision theory. This operator generalizes the min-max criterion typically used in robust optimization and allows us to model various attitudes towards the risk. The deterministic version of the problem is already NP-hard, even for two machines. So, the problem with uncertain processing times cannot be easier. In fact, we have shown that the general problem with the OWA criterion is hard to approximate even for two machines. However, we have also provided some positive results. In particular, we have strengthen approximation results for the min-max criterion if the number of machines and scenarios are constant. Under this criterion only a randomized approximation algorithm and a simple version of the list scheduling algorithm have been proposed so far. We have shown that in this case the problem with the min-max criterion admits an FPTAS and the problem with the OWA criterion can be solved in a pseudopolynomial time. For the Hurwicz criterion we have proposed a mixed integer programming based approach that gives us an optimal schedule.

There are a number of open problems concerning the considered problem. There are still some gaps between the positive and negative results which should be closed. Also, no approximation algorithm for the general OWA criterion is known. One can try to transform the pseudopolynomial time algorithm into an FPTAS. We can also consider some generalization of the $P||C_{\max}$ problem, for example by assuming that the machines are not identical. We believe that it is an interesting area of further research.

**Acknowledgments.** The first and the third author of the paper were partially supported by Polish Committee for Scientific Research, grant N N206 492938.

# References

1. Alon, N., Azar, Y., Woeginger, G.J., Yadid, T.: Approximation Schemes for Scheduling on Parallel Machines. Journal of Scheduling 1, 55–66 (1998)
2. Brucker, P.: Scheduling Algorithms, 5th edn. Springer, Heidelberg (2007)
3. Chekuri, C., Khanna, S.: On Multi-dimensional Packing Problems. SIAM Journal on Computing 33, 837–851 (2004)
4. Garey, M.R., Johnson, D.S.: "Strong" NP-Completeness Results: Motivation, Examples, and Implications. Journal of the ACM 25, 499–508 (1978)
5. Garey, M.R., Johnson, D.S.: Computers and Intractability. A Guide to the Theory of NP-Completeness. W. H. Freeman and Company (1979)
6. Graham, R.L.: Bounds on Multiprocessing Timing Anomalies. SIAM Journal of Applied Mathematics 17, 416–429 (1969)
7. Hochbaum, D.S., Shmoys, D.B.: Using dual approximation algorithms for scheduling problems: theoretical and practical results. Journal of the ACM 34, 144–162 (1987)
8. Kouvelis, P., Daniels, R.L., Vairaktarakis, G.: Robust scheduling of a two-machine flow shop with uncertain processing times. IIE Transactions 32, 421–432 (2000)
9. Kouvelis, P., Yu, G.: Robust Discrete Optimization and its applications. Kluwer Academic Publishers (1997)
10. Lenstra, J.K., Rinnooy Kan, A., Brucker, P.: Complexity of Machine Scheduling Problems. In: Hammer, P., Johnson, E.L., Korte, B.H., Nemhauser, G.L. (eds.) Studies in Integer Programming, Annals of Discrete Mathematics, vol. 1, pp. 343–363. North-Holland Publishing Company (1977)
11. Luce, R., Raiffa, H.: Games and Decisions: Introduction and a Critical Survey. Wiley (1957)
12. Sahni, S.K.: Algorithms for Scheduling Independent Tasks. Journal of the ACM 23, 116–127 (1976)
13. Yager, R.R.: On Ordered Weighted Averaging Aggregation Operators in Multi-Criteria Decision Making. IEEE Transactions on Systems, Man and Cybernetics 18, 183–190 (1988)
14. Zuckerman, D.: Linear Degree Extractors and the Inapproximability of Max Clique and Chromatic Number. Theory of Computing 3, 103–128 (2007)

# Appendix

*Proof of Theorem 1.* We show a gap-introducing reduction from the following NAE-3SAT problem, which is known to be NP-hard [5]:

NAE-3SAT: *Input:* A set of Boolean variables $x_1, \ldots, x_q$ and a set of clauses $\mathcal{C} = \{C_1, \ldots, C_r\}$, where each clause contains at most three literals.
*Question:* Is there a truth assignment to the variables such that each clause in $\mathcal{C}$ has at least one true literal and at least one false literal?

Given an instance of NAE-3SAT, we define for each literal $l_i$, where $l_i = x_i$ or $l_i = \overline{x}_i$, a job $J_{l_i}$. For each clause $(l_1 \vee l_2 \vee l_3) \in \mathcal{C}$, we create four *clause scenarios*: $S$ such that $p_{l_1}^S = p_{l_2}^S = p_{l_3}^S = 1$ and three scenarios $S', S'', S'''$, corresponding to all pairs of the literals in the clause, such that $p_{l_1}^{S'} = p_{l_2}^{S'} = \frac{3}{4}$, $p_{l_1}^{S''} = p_{l_3}^{S''} = \frac{3}{4}$,

$p_{l_2}^{S'''} = p_{l_3}^{S'''} = \frac{3}{4}$. The processing times of all the remaining jobs under $S$, $S'$, $S''$ and $S''''$ are equal to 0. For each variable $x_i$, we create *variable scenarios* $\overline{S}$, $\overline{S}'$ such that $p_{x_i}^{\overline{S}} = p_{\overline{x}_i}^{\overline{S}} = \frac{3}{2}$, $p_{x_i}^{\overline{S}'} = p_{\overline{x}_i}^{\overline{S}'} = \frac{3}{4}$ and the processing times of all the remaining jobs under $\overline{S}$ and $\overline{S}'$ are equal to 0. A sample reduction is shown in Table 1. Obviously, $|\Gamma| = K = 4r + 2q$ and $|J| = 2q$ and thus the instance of OWA $P||C_{\max}$ can be constructed in polynomial time. Finally, we set $m = 2$, $w_1 = \alpha$ and $w_{2r+q+1} = 1 - \alpha$, where $\alpha \in [0,1]$ is fixed, and $w_k = 0$, for all $k \neq 1, 2r + q + 1$.

**Table 1.** The reduction for $\mathcal{C} = \{(\overline{x}_1 \vee x_2 \vee \overline{x}_3), (x_1 \vee \overline{x}_2 \vee \overline{x}_4), (x_1 \vee x_2 \vee \overline{x}_4), (\overline{x}_1 \vee x_3 \vee x_4)\}$

| | $S_1$ | $S_1'$ | $S_1''$ | $S_1'''$ | $S_2$ | $S_2'$ | $S_2''$ | $S_2'''$ | $S_3$ | $S_3'$ | $S_3''$ | $S_3'''$ | $S_4$ | $S_4'$ | $S_4''$ | $S_4''''$ | $\overline{S}_1$ | $\overline{S}_1'$ | $\overline{S}_2$ | $\overline{S}_2'$ | $\overline{S}_3$ | $\overline{S}_3'$ | $\overline{S}_4$ | $\overline{S}_4'$ |
|---|---|---|---|---|---|---|---|---|---|---|---|---|---|---|---|---|---|---|---|---|---|---|---|---|
| $J_{x_1}$ | 0 | 0 | 0 | 0 | 1 | $\frac{3}{4}$ | $\frac{3}{4}$ | 0 | 1 | $\frac{3}{4}$ | $\frac{3}{4}$ | 0 | 0 | 0 | 0 | 0 | $\frac{3}{2}$ | $\frac{3}{4}$ | 0 | 0 | 0 | 0 | 0 | 0 |
| $J_{\overline{x}_1}$ | 1 | $\frac{3}{4}$ | $\frac{3}{4}$ | 0 | 0 | 0 | 0 | 0 | 0 | 0 | 0 | 0 | 1 | $\frac{3}{4}$ | $\frac{3}{4}$ | 0 | $\frac{3}{2}$ | $\frac{3}{4}$ | 0 | 0 | 0 | 0 | 0 | 0 |
| $J_{x_2}$ | 1 | $\frac{3}{4}$ | 0 | $\frac{3}{4}$ | 0 | 0 | 0 | 0 | 1 | $\frac{3}{4}$ | 0 | $\frac{3}{4}$ | 0 | 0 | 0 | 0 | 0 | 0 | $\frac{3}{2}$ | $\frac{3}{4}$ | 0 | 0 | 0 | 0 |
| $J_{\overline{x}_2}$ | 0 | 0 | 0 | 0 | 1 | $\frac{3}{4}$ | 0 | $\frac{3}{4}$ | 0 | 0 | 0 | 0 | 0 | 0 | 0 | 0 | 0 | 0 | $\frac{3}{2}$ | $\frac{3}{4}$ | 0 | 0 | 0 | 0 |
| $J_{x_3}$ | 0 | 0 | 0 | 0 | 0 | 0 | 0 | 0 | 0 | 0 | 0 | 0 | 1 | $\frac{3}{4}$ | 0 | $\frac{3}{4}$ | 0 | 0 | 0 | 0 | $\frac{3}{2}$ | $\frac{3}{4}$ | 0 | 0 |
| $J_{\overline{x}_3}$ | 1 | 0 | $\frac{3}{4}$ | $\frac{3}{4}$ | 0 | 0 | 0 | 0 | 0 | 0 | 0 | 0 | 0 | 0 | 0 | 0 | 0 | 0 | 0 | 0 | $\frac{3}{2}$ | $\frac{3}{4}$ | 0 | 0 |
| $J_{x_4}$ | 0 | 0 | 0 | 0 | 0 | 0 | 0 | 0 | 0 | 0 | 0 | 0 | 1 | 0 | $\frac{3}{4}$ | $\frac{3}{4}$ | 0 | 0 | 0 | 0 | 0 | 0 | $\frac{3}{2}$ | $\frac{3}{4}$ |
| $J_{\overline{x}_4}$ | 0 | 0 | 0 | 0 | 1 | 0 | $\frac{3}{4}$ | $\frac{3}{4}$ | 1 | 0 | $\frac{3}{4}$ | $\frac{3}{4}$ | 0 | 0 | 0 | 0 | 0 | 0 | 0 | 0 | 0 | 0 | $\frac{3}{2}$ | $\frac{3}{4}$ |

If the answer to NAE-3SAT is *yes*, then according to a satisfying truth assignment, we form a schedule $\pi$ by assigning the jobs corresponding to the true literals to machine $M_1$ and the jobs corresponding to the false literals to machine $M_2$. Let us sort the scenarios in nonincreasing order with respect to the values of the makespans for $\pi$, $C_{\max}(\pi, S_{\sigma(1)}) \geq C_{\max}(\pi, S_{\sigma(2)}) \geq \cdots \geq C_{\max}(\pi, S_{\sigma(K)})$. The jobs associated with the contradictory literals are placed on different machines and each clause has at least one truth and at least one false literal, which implies $C_{\max}(\pi, S_{\sigma(2r+q)}) \leq \cdots \leq C_{\max}(\pi, S_{\sigma(1)}) \leq 2$. The same reasoning yields $C_{\max}(\pi, S_{\sigma(2r+q+1)}) = \cdots = C_{\max}(\pi, S_{\sigma(K)}) = \frac{3}{4}$. So, $\mathrm{OWA}_{\boldsymbol{w}}(\pi) \leq 2\alpha + \frac{3}{4}(1 - \alpha)$. On the other hand, if the answer to NAE-3SAT is *no*, then for all schedules $\pi$ at least two jobs corresponding to the contradictory literals are executed on the same machine, $C_{\max}(\pi, S_{\sigma(1)}) = 3$, $C_{\max}(\pi, S_{\sigma(2r+q+1)}) = \frac{3}{2}$ thus $\mathrm{OWA}_{\boldsymbol{w}}(\pi) = 3\alpha + \frac{3}{2}(1 - \alpha)$, or for at least one clause all three jobs corresponding to this clause are executed on the same machine, $C_{\max}(\pi, S_{\sigma(1)}) = 3$, $C_{\max}(\pi, S_{\sigma(2r+q+1)}) = \frac{3}{2}$ thus $\mathrm{OWA}_{\boldsymbol{w}}(\pi) = 3\alpha + \frac{3}{2}(1 - \alpha)$, where the permutation $\sigma$ is such that $C_{\max}(\pi, S_{\sigma(1)}) \geq C_{\max}(\pi, S_{\sigma(2)}) \geq \cdots \geq C_{\max}(\pi, S_{\sigma(K)})$. So, OWA $P||C_{\max}$ is not approximable within $\frac{3\alpha + \frac{3}{2}(1-\alpha)}{2\alpha + \frac{3}{4}(1-\alpha)} - \epsilon$ for any $\epsilon > 0$ unless P=NP. □

*Proof of Theorem 2.* Under each scenario $S$, it holds $C_{\max}(\pi, S) \leq \sum_{j \in J} p_j^S$ and $C_{\max}(\pi^*, S) \geq \frac{1}{m} \sum_{j \in J} p_j^S$. This implies $C_{\max}(\pi, S) \leq m \cdot C_{\max}(\pi^*, S)$ for all $S \in \Gamma$. Let $\sigma$ and $\rho$ be two permutations of $\{1, \ldots, K\}$ such that $C_{\max}(\pi, S_{\sigma(1)}) \geq \cdots \geq C_{\max}(\pi, S_{\sigma(K)})$ and $C_{\max}(\pi^*, S_{\rho(1)}) \geq \cdots \geq C_{\max}(\pi^*, S_{\rho(K)})$. We now show that $C_{\max}(\pi, S_{\sigma(i)}) \leq m \cdot C_{\max}(\pi^*, S_{\rho(i)})$ for all $i = 1, \ldots, K$. Suppose by contradiction that this is not the case and $C_{\max}(\pi, S_{\sigma(j)}) > m \cdot C_{\max}(\pi^*, S_{\rho(j)})$ for some $j \in \{1, \dots, K\}$. Suppose that there is a scenario $S$ such that $S \in \{S_{\sigma(1)}, \dots, S_{\sigma(j)}\}$ and $S \in \{S_{\rho(j+1)}, \dots, S_{\rho(K)}\}$. Then it holds

$$C_{\max}(\pi, S) \geq C_{\max}(\pi, S_{\sigma(j)}) > m \cdot C_{\max}(\pi^*, S_{\rho(j)}) \geq m \cdot C_{\max}(\pi^*, S),$$

a contradiction. In consequence, each scenario which is in $\{S_{\sigma(1)}, \dots, S_{\sigma(j)}\}$ must also be in $\{S_{\rho(1)}, \dots, S_{\rho(j)}\}$ and $\{S_{\sigma(1)}, \dots, S_{\sigma(j)}\} = \{S_{\rho(1)}, \dots, S_{\rho(j)}\}$. Thus, in particular $S_{\rho(j)} \in \{S_{\sigma(1)}, \dots, S_{\sigma(j)}\}$ and

$$C_{\max}(\pi, S_{\rho(j)}) \geq C_{\max}(\pi, S_{\sigma(j)}) > m \cdot C_{\max}(\pi^*, S_{\rho(j)}),$$

a contradiction. We thus get

$$\mathrm{OWA}_{\boldsymbol{w}}(\pi) = \sum_{i=1}^{K} w_i C_{\max}(\pi, S_{\sigma(i)}) \leq m \sum_{i=1}^{K} w_i C_{\max}(\pi^*, S_{\rho(i)}) = m \cdot \mathrm{OWA}_{\boldsymbol{w}}(\pi^*),$$

which completes the proof.    □

*Proof of Theorem 6.* Let us fix $\epsilon \in (0, 1)$. For each scenario $S \in \Gamma$ define a *scaled scenario* $\widehat{S}$ under which $p_j^{\widehat{S}} = \left\lfloor \frac{n p_j^S}{\epsilon p_{\max}} \right\rfloor$, $j \in J$, where $p_{\max} = \max_{S \in \Gamma, j \in J} p_j^S$. If $L_{ik}$ is the load of machine $M_i$ under $S_k$ for some schedule $\pi$, then $\widehat{L}_{ik}$ is the load of machine $M_i$ under $\widehat{S}_k$ for $\pi$. Similarly, $\widehat{C}_{\max}(\pi)$ is the maximal makespan of $\pi$ over the set of scaled scenarios. It holds:

$$\frac{\epsilon p_{\max}}{n} p_j^{\widehat{S}} \leq p_j^S \leq \frac{\epsilon p_{\max}}{n} (p_j^{\widehat{S}} + 1).$$

Thus, for each $i = 1, \dots, m$ and $k = 1, \dots, K$:

$$\frac{\epsilon p_{\max}}{n} \widehat{L}_{ik} \leq L_{ik} \leq \frac{\epsilon p_{\max}}{n} \widehat{L}_{ik} + \epsilon p_{\max},$$

which implies that for any schedule $\pi$:

$$\frac{\epsilon p_{\max}}{n} \widehat{C}_{\max}(\pi) \leq \overline{C}_{\max}(\pi) \leq \frac{\epsilon p_{\max}}{n} \widehat{C}_{\max}(\pi) + \epsilon p_{\max}. \tag{4}$$

If $\widehat{\pi}$ is an optimal schedule for the scaled scenario set and $\pi^*$ is an optimal schedule for the original scenario set, then $\widehat{C}_{\max}(\widehat{\pi}) \leq \widehat{C}_{\max}(\pi^*)$, $\overline{C}_{\max}(\pi^*) = OPT$, $OPT \geq p_{\max}$ and inequalities (4) imply:

$$\overline{C}_{\max}(\widehat{\pi}) \leq \frac{\epsilon p_{\max}}{n} \widehat{C}_{\max}(\widehat{\pi}) + \epsilon p_{\max} \leq \frac{\epsilon p_{\max}}{n} \widehat{C}_{\max}(\pi^*) + \epsilon p_{\max} \leq (1 + \epsilon) OPT.$$

Hence the cost of $\widehat{\pi}$ is within $(1 + \epsilon) OPT$. We can find $\widehat{\pi}$ by applying the exact pseudopolynomial time algorithm for the scaled scenarios (see Theorem 5). Since the maximal scaled processing time is not greater than $n/\epsilon$, the schedule $\widehat{\pi}$ can be computed in $O(n^{2mK+1} m (1/\epsilon)^{mK})$ time.    □

# An Application in Bank Credit Risk Management System Employing a BP Neural Network Based on *sfloat24* Custom Math Library Using a Low Cost FPGA Device

Maria Cristina Miglionico[1] and Fernando Parillo[2]

[1] Department of Culture of the Project, Second University of Napoli
Via S. Lorenzo, Monastero di San Lorenzo, I-81031 Aversa (CE), Italy
BENECON Scarl, Member of UNESCO
mcristina.miglionico@unina2.it
[2] Department of Electrical Engineering and Information, University of Cassino
Via G. Di Biasio 43, I-03043 Cassino (FR), Italy
f.parillo@unicas.it

**Abstract.** Artificial Neural Networks (ANN$_S$) base their processing capabilities in parallel architectures. This makes them useful to solve pattern recognition, system identification and control problems. In particular, it is extremely important for commercial banks to set up an early bank credit risk warning system. The authors set up early warning indicators for commercial bank credit risk, and carry out the warning for the credit risk in advance with the help of the ANN$_S$.

A three layer ANN has been implemented, using a custom developed *sfloat24* math library, on a low cost FPGA device.

**Keywords:** Artificial Neural Network, Field Programmable Gate Array ((FPGA), *sfloat24* math library.

## 1    Introduction

Artificial Neural Networks (ANN$_S$) are used with success in pattern recognition problems, function approximation, control, etc. There are different kind of electronic implementation of ANN$_S$, digital, analog and hybrid [1] and each one has specific advantage and disadvantages depending on the type and configuration of the network, training method and application.

For a digital implementation of ANN$_S$ there are different alternatives, custom design, digital signal processors, programmable logic, etc. Programmable logic offers low cost, powerful software tools and true parallel implementations.

As well known the digital systems, in particular the FPGA devices have the following fundamental properties [2]:

- *Insensitivity to environment.* Digital systems are considered less sensitive to environmental conditions than analog systems. In contrast, digital system's operations do not depend on its environment.

S. Greco et al. (Eds.): IPMU 2012, Part IV, CCIS 300, pp. 84–93, 2012.

- *Insensitivity to component tolerances.* Analog components are manufactured to particular tolerances. The overall response of an analog system depends on the actual values of all the analog used components.

ANN$_s$ are nonlinear self-adaptive dynamic systems, which simulate human's neural system structure. They are ideal to solve early warning system of the commercial bank credit risk [3], [4].

Traditionally to solve early warning problems the following methods could be used:

- *Fuzzy logic* technique has been in its wide-ranging use in modelling of uncertainties, vagueness, impreciseness and the human thought process. The main problem of this approach is the fact that the credit analyst needs to analyse and assume a large number of differently valuated factors in a short time.
- *Monte Carlo* method usually takes a long time to simulate rare event, the failure event of repaying loans is treated as rare event due to the relatively low probability, and the failure probability of repaying loans is taken as the criterion to measure the level of credit risk [5].

The commercial bank's credit risk management could be analysed also adopting the following most recent, methods:

- *Bayesian Network* is a graphical representation of statistical relationships between random variables, through a Direct Acyclic Graph (DAG), widely used for statistical inference and machine learning. This method consists in two parts: in the first part is implemented a function that scores each DAG based on how accurately it represents the probabilistic relation between variables based on the realization in a generic dataset. In the second part a search procedure, that selects which DAG$_s$ to score within the set of all possible DAG$_s$ [6].
- *Support Vector Machine* (SVM) is an excellent method used to solve this kind of problem. This theory was initially developed by Vapnik. It is a learning machine based on statistical theory, and is used for classification and regression. The SVM is used to solve the over-fitting problem. Empirical risk is defined to be just the measured mean error rate on the training set [7].

To implement the bank credit risk management system, depicted in the section 3, an ANN is sufficiently suitable. Their usage avoids the very difficult task to implement one of the above mentioned methods on a low cost FPGA device.

In this paper the authors present the design and the implementation of a complete ANN on an ALTERA® Cyclone III EP3C25F324C8 FPGA evaluation board.

The implementation of an Artificial Neuron is widely described in [8].

The authors have developed a floating point math library for FPGA$_s$, called *sfloat24* [9], [10]. This library has been used, in this paper, for the Artificial Neural Network implementation. Respect to the classical IEEE 754 [11], [12] floating point number format, the numbers are stored in a 24 bit word length [13].

Using this library the smallest number, neglecting the sign (Most Significant Bit), is represented by the following word:

86      M.C. Miglionico and F. Parillo

S      **Exponent field** BIAS=63          **Fractional part of mantissa** [15 ... 0]

that correspond to a decimal value of $1.08423e^{-19}$, the greatest value is represented by:

S      **Exponent field** BIAS=63          **Fractional part of mantissa** [15 ... 0]

that corresponds to: $18.4467e^{+18}$.


## 2    Artificial Neural Network — Back Propagation Algorithm Operating Principle

The back-propagation (BP) learning process is widely adopted as a successful learning rule to find appropriate values of the weights for ANNs. The BP learning process requires that the activation function is derivable. An example of a derivable function is the sigmoid.

A sigmoid function has the following expression:

$$f(x) = \frac{1}{(1+e^{-x})} \tag{1}$$

This function has been implemented using the CORDIC theory [14].

Here is discusses only the application of the CORDIC theory to implement the hyperbolic functions in order to show an optimized version of the algorithm used to implement this kind of math functions and consequently to implement the sigmoid function.

As said in [8] the hyperbolic functions can be formulated using the following expressions:

$$\vartheta_i = \tanh^{-1}(2^{-i}) \tag{2}$$

$$x_{i+1} = x_i + y_i d_i 2^{-i}$$
$$y_{i+1} = y_i + x_i d_i 2^{-i} \tag{3}$$
$$\vartheta_{i+1} = \vartheta_i - d_i \vartheta_i$$

where $d_i = -1$ if $\vartheta_i < 0$, +1 otherwise.

The hyperbolic functions are present in the $x_i$ and $y_i$ variables. In this case, the steps of *for ... loop* construct are 24, because the input variable can assume any value; the hyperbolic are not circular math functions.

The exponential functions can be easily derived from the hyperbolic functions as following:

$$e^x = \sinh(\vartheta) + \cosh(\vartheta) \quad e^{-x} = -(\sinh(\vartheta) + \cosh(\vartheta)) \tag{4}$$

At this point it easy to formulate the expression (1) using the second expression (4).

With reference to the Fig. 1, the output value of the hidden-layer and the output-layer should meet the following conditions:

$$a_j = f(\sum_{i=0}^{n} w_{[j][i]} - W_{[i][n+1]}) \quad \forall i \in N \quad y_j = f(\sum_{i=0}^{j} w_{h[j][i]} - W_{h[j][n+1]}) \quad \forall i \in K \quad (5)$$

where the quantities $W_{[i][n+1]}$ and $W_{[j][n+1]}$ are the thresholds of the input and the hidden layer respectively.

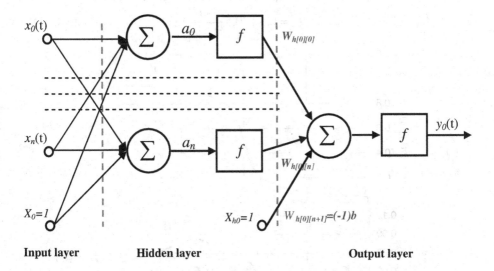

**Input layer**        **Hidden layer**                    **Output layer**

**Fig. 1.** Schematic diagram of a generic neural network

The hidden layer node and the output layer node's transfer function uses, in general, the expression (1).

The purpose of the network training is to find a set of weights that minimize the following quantity:

$$E = \frac{1}{2}\sum_{i=0}^{k-1}(\overline{y}_i - y_i)^2 \qquad (6)$$

where $\overline{y}_i$ is the desired output and $y_i$ is the actual output of the trained network.

In a BP ANN, the performances are heavily influenced by the weights correction method.

## 3    FPGA Implementation – Simulation Results

It is possible, on the basis of the expressions (2), (3) and (4), to build the sigmoid function.

The code of the hyperbolic functions has been written in VHDL. If the VHDL code is written similar to the C code depicted in [8], using, the *for* ..... *loop* instruction the *sfloat24* sigmoid activation function occupies the 44% of total logic elements of the

ALTERA® Cyclone III EP3C25F324C8 device. In this case, the compilation, the synthesis and the fitting process are very expensive in terms of requested time to perform all the mentioned operations.

Using the expression (1) to implement a full Artificial Neural Network similar to the one shown in Fig. 1, any Cyclone® III FPGA device family is not capable to perform this operation. In this case an ALTERA® Stratix FPGA could be required [8].

To avoid this, to reduce the occupation of the device logic elements, the authors have considered [15] the following approximation of the sigmoid function:

$$f_{ss} = 0.5 + (0.5 \cdot \frac{a}{1+|a|}) \qquad (7)$$

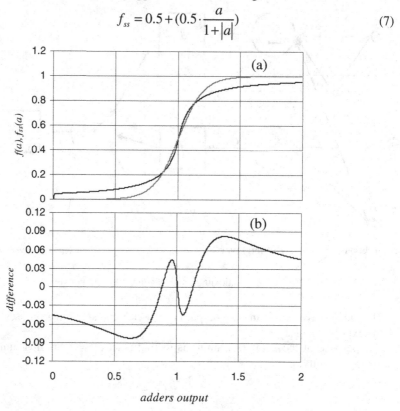

**Fig. 2.** Simulation results – (a) Sigmoid activation function and the approximation of the same, blue line. (b) The absolute difference between two math functions.

Implementing the (7), always using the *sfloat24* math library, the occupation the logic elements on the same FPGA device is only 7%, the optimization is obtained also during simulation phase.

The shortcoming of this approximation is that the BP algorithm numeric convergence time is greater respect to the case of an ANN that use as activation function a pure sigmoid. The BP algorithm has been written in MS® Visual Studio 2008. In Fig. 2 (b) is depicted the error between the expressions (1) and (7).

To improve the sigmoid function algorithm performances and to reduce its occupation into FPGA device, the *for ... loop* construct has been substituted by a counting event of an external counter. This operation allows faster compilation, synthesis and fitting device operations under ALTERA® Quartus II environment and with the same number of iterations.

In order to perform 25 iterations a 5 bit external counter is required, an auto-reset operation occurs when its value is greater of 24.

The counter is implemented on the same FPGA device, the term "external" means that it is not a component of the sigmoid code, but gives only the event (rising edge) to execute the implemented optimized code, as depicted in Fig.3.

In this case, considering 25 iterations, the device occupation of the sigmoid function VHDL code is 15%, instead 44% relative to the case of usage of the algorithm depicted in [15].

Using this version of the algorithm instead that described in [15] the compilation, synthesis and fitting operation in to FPGA device is 20 time faster.

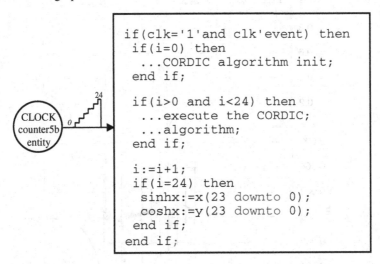

```
if(clk='1'and clk'event) then
  if(i=0) then
    ...CORDIC algorithm init;
  end if;

  if(i>0 and i<24) then
    ...execute the CORDIC;
    ...algorithm;
  end if;

  i:=i+1;
  if(i=24) then
    sinhx:=x(23 downto 0);
    coshx:=y(23 downto 0);
  end if;
end if;
```

**Fig. 3.** Operating principle of the sigmoid optimized algorithm obtained using an external counter

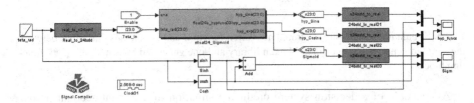

**Fig. 4.** Hyperbolic and Sigmoid functions Simulink® simulation layout

In the following is shown the obtained sigmoid function compared to the same function built with Simulink® blocks. It is important to underline that the Matlab® operates with double precision floating (64 bit) point numbers. The simulations have been performed using the ALTERA® DSP Builder tool, in particular using the HDL import block, as depicted in Fig. 4.

Fig. 5 shows the simulation results when the sampling time $T_s$ has been fixed to a 2.56 µS, in this case the output error varies in the range ±0.006 about. Other simulations have been performed with different sampling times. In all the tests, results that the entire system has latency time at maximum of 6 clock cycles.

The system presents a stable performance comparing to the any external disturbance.

Two additional routines, green blocks depicted in Fig. 4, allow to test the Artificial Neuron performances. These routine, convert respectively a given floating point number in to *sfloat24* number layout format and vice versa.

These routine, due to their complexity, have been written in C/C++ language and implemented as S-Function as depicted in [10].

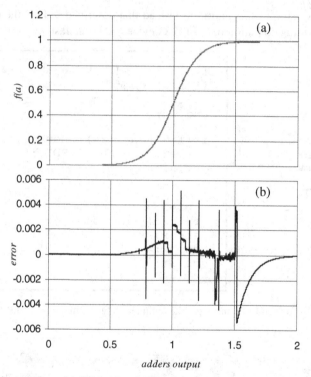

**Fig. 5.** Simulation results – (a) Sigmoid activation function and (b) the absolute error between the sigmoid generated by the *sfloat24* math library and one generated by Simulink® math function block

As example of a decision system credit the situation of a current account holder that requires a loan at proper credit institute with its risk evaluation has been taken into consideration.

The risk is represented by the variable $R$. The variable $x_0$ indicates whether the current account holder has got (value = 1) a real estate property or hasn't (value = -1). The current account holder has got a mortgage loan ($x_1 = 1$) or hasn't ($x_1 = -1$), or ($x_1 = 0$) if he does not own any property. The variable $x_2$ represents the availability of a profit (value = 1) or not (value = -1) if the profit is non-existent or insignificant ($x_2 = $

0). The loan applicant has a good behaviour $(x_3 = 1)$, middle $(x_3 = 0)$ or bad $(x_3 = -1)$ with the credit institute. The case study is summarized in the following table:

**Table 1.** Training set of the implemented ANN, in this case, only for simplicity, are considered 12 examples, 13 and 14 represent the validation sets

| N. | $x_0$ | $x_1$ | $x_2$ | $x_3$ | $O$ | $R$ |
|----|-------|-------|-------|-------|-----|-----|
| 1 | 1 | 1 | 0 | 1 | 0.5 | 0.5 |
| 2 | 1 | 1 | 1 | 0 | 0.5 | 0.5 |
| 3 | 1 | 1 | -1 | 0 | 0 | 1 |
| 4 | 1 | 1 | 0 | -1 | 0 | 1 |
| 5 | 1 | -1 | 0 | 1 | 1 | 0 |
| 6 | 1 | -1 | 1 | 0 | 1 | 0 |
| 7 | -1 | 0 | 1 | 0 | 0.5 | 0.5 |
| 8 | 1 | -1 | -1 | -1 | 0 | 1 |
| 9 | -1 | 0 | 1 | 1 | 1 | 0 |
| 10 | 1 | -1 | -1 | 0 | 0.5 | 0.5 |
| 11 | 1 | -1 | 1 | -1 | 0.5 | 0.5 |
| 12 | -1 | 0 | -1 | 1 | 0.5 | 0.5 |
| 13 | -1 | 0 | 0 | 0 | 0 | 1 |
| 14 | -1 | 0 | -1 | -1 | 0 | 1 |

where $O$ represents the desired output of the implemented ANN.

Training, using the first 12 examples of Table 1, an ANN constituted only by 3 neurons in the hidden layer and 1 neuron in the output layer, the maximum error, difference between desired output and the actual ones, reached is 0.1%.

The examples 13 and 14 are used as validation set.

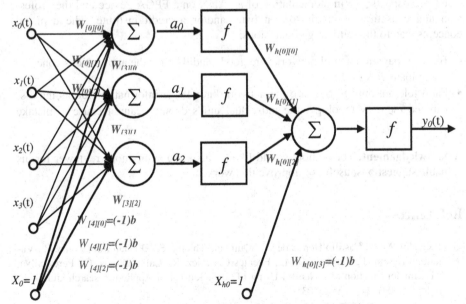

**Fig. 6.** ANN used for the case study depicted in the Table 1

The device occupation of the entire ANN of Fig. 6, on the above mentioned FPGA device, is equal to 92% of logic elements.

The risk of the credit institute is simply evaluated as the opposite of the desired output as depicted in the last column of the Table 1.

**Table 2.** ALTERA® Quartus II report of the implemented ANN

| | |
|---|---|
| Total logic elements | 22,757/24,624 (92%) |
| • Total combinational functions | 22,734/24,624 (92%) |
| • Dedicated logic registers | 2,236 (9%) |
| Total registers | 2236 |

To examine more complex situations it is necessary to implement ANN with a major number of neurons. With the used low cost FPGA device this operation is not possible, because it is not capable to accommodate other neurons; this is depicted in the Table 2.

## 4     Conclusions

The obtained results show, through an optimized algorithm of the sigmoid function, the validity and the feasibility of the implementation of a complete trained ANN, using the developed *sfloat24* math library.

The speed execution or latency of the ANN can be precisely controlled with the amount of reuse of *sfloat24* arithmetic elements.

From the angle of theory combined with the practice, in this paper have been analysed two aspects: the implementation of an ANN on a FPGA device and the profession and causation of credit risk in bank and/or a credit institute. The depicted concepts lead to the following conclusions:

- Back-propagation neural networks are good candidate for the applications concerning in loans risk evaluation.
- Fault-tolerant ability. Because the network knowledge information adopts the distributed memory topology, the individual unit's damage cannot cause a mistake output.

**Acknowledgement.** The authors would like to thank the anonymous reviewer for his valuable suggestions, useful to improve this work.

## References

1. Banuelos, M.A., Castillo Hernandez, J., Quintana Thierry, S., Damian Zamacoma, R., Valeriano Assem, J., Cervantes, R.E., Fuentes Conzalez, R., Calva Olmos, G., Perez Silva, J.L.: Implementation of a Neuron Using FPGAS. Journal of Applied Research and Technology I(003), 248–255 (2003)

2. Lapskey, P., Bier, J., ShoHam, A., Lee, E.A.: DSP Processor Fundamentals – Architecture and features. IEEE Press (1997)

3. Zhao, S.-F., Chen, L.-C.: The BP Neural Networks applications in Bank Credit Risk Management System. In: 8th IEEE International Conference on Cognitive Informatics, ICCI 2009, pp. 527–532 (2009)

4. Wang, Y., Yan, H., Meng, X.: Matching Decision Model for Self-adaptability of Knowledge manufacturing System. In: International Conference on Information Science and Technology (ICIST), pp. 891–895 (2011)

5. Zhou, H., Wang, J., Qiu, Y.: Application of the Cross Entropy Method to the Credit Risk Assessment in an Early Warning System. In: International Symposiums on Information Processing (ISIP), May 23-25, pp. 728–732 (2008)

6. Quer, G., Meenakshisundaram, H., Tamma, B., Manoj, B.S., Rao, R., Zorzi, M.: A Cognitive Network Inference through Bayesan Network Analysis. In: 2010 IEEE Global Telecommunications Conference (GLOBECOM 2010), December 06-10, pp. 1–6 (2010)

7. Pang, X.-L., Feng, Y.-Q.: An Improved Economic Early Warning Based on Rough Set and Support Vector Machine. In: International Conference on Machine Learning and Cybernetics, August 13-16, pp. 2444–2449 (2006)

8. Miglionico, M.C., Parillo, F.: Modelling a neuron using a custom math library *sfloat24* – Implementation of a sigmoid function on a FPGA device. In: Proceedings of the International Symposium on the Analytic Hierarchy Process for Multicriteria Decision Making, ISHAP Conference, Sorrento Italy, June15-18 (2011) ISSN 1556-8296,
http://204.202.238.22/isahp2011/dati/autor.html

9. Miglionico, M.C., Parillo, F.: A Current Hysteresis Controller for Reduction of Switching Losses in a Full-Bridge Inverter – FPGA implementation by using a custom developed 24 bit Floating Point Math Library. In: IEEE Conference UPEC 2011, Soest, Germany, September 05-08, pp. 1–6 (2011)

10. Miglionico, M.C., Parillo, F.: FPGA implementation of *sfloat24* digital PI. In: IEEE Conference PEDES 2010 Power India, New Delhi, December 20-23 (2010)

11. IEEE Standard for Binary Floating-Point Arithmetic, ANSI/IEEE 754 (1985)

12. Kahan, W.: Lecture notes on the Status of IEEE Standard 754 for Binary Floating Point Arithmetic. Electrical Engineering and Computer Science. University of California, Berkeley (May 31,1996)

13. Attaianese, C., Parillo, F., Tomasso, G.: Dual Boost High Performances control strategy on a Power Factor Correction (PFC) implementation by using a 24 bit custom floating point library. Journal of Electrical Engineering 10 (December 23, 2010),
http://www.jee.ro

14. Ginsberg, S.: Compact and Efficient Generation of Trigonometric Functions using a CORDIC algorithm, Cape Town, South Africa (January 2002)

15. Miglionico, M.C., Parillo, F.: A BP Neural Network Application in Bank Credit Risk Management System using a sfloat24 custom math library – FPGA implementation. In: A.M.A.S.E.S. Meeting, XXXV edn., Pisa, Italy, September 15-17 (2011)

# Concentration Measures
# in Portfolio Management

Ghassan Chammas and Jaap Spronk

Rotterdam School of Management, Erasmus University, Rotterdam, The Netherlands
ghchammas@gmail.com, jspronk@rsm.nl
http://www.rsm.nl

**Abstract.** The allocation of wealth in an investment portfolio can be viewed as finding a proper weight allocation vector while obeying investment constraints and preferences, as risk aversion, expected returns, investment sector preferences and regulatory and/or preferential limits on allocation per stock. It is these constraints and preferences that make the stock (or wealth) allocation problem a multiple criteria problem.

We link these allocations to the theory of inequality and related concentration measurements, focusing on weight concentration as an other criterion for investment portfolio management. In this paper, we will discuss the Gini and the Herfindhal concentration measures of weights and relate them to the portfolio allocation problem using a hypothetical investment portfolio.

**Keywords:** Portfolio management, Concentration measures, Pretension level, Gini index, Herfindhal index, Weights allocation.

## 1 Introduction

The basic characteristics used in the market today hinge on the risk and return method first discussed by Markowitz. Despite the similar foundation, various ratios are actually used to describe and manage a selected portfolio. Nevertheless, nearly all ratios are based on the average, historic return of the stock and the deviation of those returns from the average standardized per unit of average return. Both measures, which are estimates, are used to predict the possible future performance of the portfolio (or more precisely the stocks that constitute it). As these estimates are based on assumptions, including the symmetry of information, both rational markets and investors and a normal distribution of returns, these estimates are not error free. In fact, portfolio managers talk about estimation error which is the difference between the return estimated for time $t_1$ and the true return realized and observed at time $t_1$. The greater this estimation error is, the riskier the stock, because the magnitude of the deviation from the estimated average is bigger than expected. This deviation can be very costly if a heavy weight (a high amount of the total wealth) was invested in this particular stock. Thus, the weights also play a very important role in investment and allocation decisions.

S. Greco et al. (Eds.): IPMU 2012, Part IV, CCIS 300, pp. 94–103, 2012.
© Springer-Verlag Berlin Heidelberg 2012

The two-step process of first identifying the sub-universe of investments, followed by the allocation of resources to these investments, has a concentrating effect on the portfolio. The first concentration comes in the selection (as per investor preferences) of potential investments with a further concentration arising through the assignment of weights (as per the investors desired levels of risk and return).

In this paper, we explore two concentration measures, inspired by economic theory related to income inequality and poverty concentration. The Hirschmann-Herfindahl Index (HHI) and its reverse (rHHI) along with the GINI index are explored in this paper and applied to an investment portfolio.

The paper is organized as follows. Section two will define and describe the HHI and the GINI indices with their basic characteristics pertinent to portfolio management. Section three will apply those two indices to investment, defining a pretension level and using the HHI and Gini indices as descriptors of an investment portfolio. Section four will conclude .

## 2 Concentration Measures: Gini and Hirschmann-Herfindahl (HHI) Indices

The literature available on concentration primarily addresses the concentration of income or the inequality of income.

In our research we did not find substantial research on concentration within an investment portfolio, except the work of Benedetto et al. on pretension level in a portfolio and Simonelli (2005) working on the indeterminacy in portfolio selection. Important portfolio approaches were made by Mussard et al. (2004) by arguing that the concentration of returns of a particular security around a certain value is a measure of the risk of this security, since it defines the dispersion of the values of returns and hence their standard deviation. Mussard et al. used the Gini index and its decomposition suggested in the central work of Camilo Dagum (1997) where the Gini index was decomposed into concentration within a subgroup of the set, the concentration of the whole set and the distance between the concentrations between each subgroup. An interesting development in portfolio management and concentration was presented by Brands et al. (2003) suggesting the usage of a divergence index to measure the amount of divergence between the concentration of the portfolio and the market concentration, that they use a s a benchmark.

From his side, Ogryczak (2007) dealt with allocating resources among competitive activities using inequality measures approach, which suggests using the same logic to allocate the wealth in different securities to form a portfolio.

The concentration measures used and researched in the past literature focus primarily on *equality* which suggests a natural wealth allocation of $1/n$ within a portfolio. But logically this is not the case in real life investment situation. In fact investors *pretend* to invest in a certain direction that they believe would maximize their return for the risk they accept to take, which automatically suggest a bias to the $1/n$ allocation strategy. This *pretension* of the investor will be the base of our research to quantify it through the concentration indices.

## 2.1 The Hirschmann-Herfindahl Index, HHI

The Hirschmann-Herfindahl Index, HHI is defined as the sum of the square of the weights of each element of the universe, the weights taken as a percentage of the total. In a universe of n stocks, we assign the value $x_i$ as the market cap of stock i (where i= 1 to n), then we can define $s_i$ as the market cap share of stock i relative to the universe of stocks:

$$s_i = x_i / (\textstyle\sum_1^n x_i) \tag{1}$$

Considering that $x_i$ is the market cap of stock i , it is clear from equation (1) above that $s_i$ represents also the weight of stock i in a portfolio of n stocks where the asset allocation is based on market cap share., and hence, if $w_i$ denotes the weight of stock $i$ (where $i = 1$ to $n$) in a portfolio of $n$ assets then we can write: $s_i = x_i / (\sum_1^n x_i) = w_i$ , with $\sum w_i = 1$ as the budget constraint.

We define the HHI as the sum of the squares of the market cap shares, i.e.

$$\mathrm{HHI} = \textstyle\sum_1^n s_i^2 = \sum_i (x_i / (\sum_1^n x_i))^2 = \sum w_i^2 \tag{2}$$

Notice that the HHI represents the concentration level of the descriptor chosen. In the exposition above, it denoted the concentration of market cap weighted stocks. In general, the HHI can be used to calculate the concentration of any descriptor of the portfolio such as returns, standard deviation etc ...

The maximum value possible for the HHI is one; this occurs when all of the weights except one are equal to zero. The minimum possible value of HHI in a portfolio is $\mathrm{HHI}_{min} = 1/n$.

The index cannot be lower then this value for a given portfolio of n stocks. This extreme case would represent the situation of no concentration; all stocks are equally concentrated. In this case, the higher the n, then the lower the HHI and theoretically $\mathrm{HHI}_{min} = lim_{(n \to \infty)} 1/n = 0$.

The HHI is sensitive to large weight values in a portfolio. The bigger that some weights are, then the smaller the effect of the small weights on the index. In short, HHI is an index that emphasizes the presence of stocks with relatively big weights. As an example consider Tab.1

An Interesting variation of the HHI is the reverse HHI or rHHI. The rHHI represents the equivalent total number of elements in a universe with equal weights. This is derived from the boundary conditions of the HHI discussed above. When HHI is 1, it means that the concentration is on one stock among all the others possible stocks; in turn, an rHHI of one says that the equivalent universe of 1 stock is representative of the universe under study. Consequently,

**Table 1.** Three different portfolios P1,P2 and P3 consisting of 5 stocks with their associated weights $w_i$ and their respective HHI. Please note the effect on HHI of transferring 0.02 from $w_5$ to $w_4$ and from $w_2$ to $w_1$. Strikingly HHI reflects more value when the same amount is transferred to a big player.

| Portfolio | | | |
|---|---|---|---|
| | 1 | 2 | 3 |
| $w_1$ | 0.32 | 0.32 | 0.34 |
| $w_2$ | 0.23 | 0.23 | 0.21 |
| $w_3$ | 0.2 | 0.2 | 0.2 |
| $w_4$ | 0.13 | 0.15 | 0.13 |
| $w_5$ | 0.12 | 0.1 | 0.12 |
| HHI | 0.2266 | 0.2278 | 0.231 |

when the HHI is at its minimum value of HHI $= 1/n$ , the rHHI equals $n$ which indicates that this concentration can only be achieved with an equivalent number of stocks of equal weights.

## 2.2  The Gini Coeficient

The Gini coefficient has been widely used in the field of inequality measurement. It is closely related to the Lorenz curve, by which the cumulative share of each element of the universe is plotted against the rank of each share, sorted from the smallest to the largest. If all stocks have the same market share,, then the Lorenz curve is a straight diagonal line, called the line of equality. If there is any inequality in size, then the Lorenz curve falls below the line of equality.

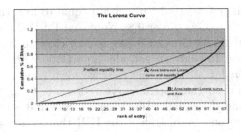

**Fig. 1.** The Lorez curve, showing the line of perfect equality

The Gini coefficient is usually defined mathematically based on the Lorenz curve as shown in Fig. 1. Geometrically, the coefficient is the ratio of the area that lays between the line of equality and the Lorenz curve to the total area under the equality line.

The Gini index is included in the close interval [0,1] and is expressed as:

$$G = \sum_{i=1}^{n} ((2i - n - 1)w_i)/n$$

Where $n$ is the number of observations, $i$ is the rank of the observation in an ascending series, and $w_i$ is the weight vector with $s_i = x_i/(\sum_1^n x_i) = w_i$ and $\sum w_i = 1$ as the budget constraint.

As G tends towards one, the distribution of $w_i$ is unequal; when G tends towards zero, the distribution of $w_i$ is equal. Consider a portfolio with $n$ stocks where $w_1$ equals one and all remaining weights are equal to zero. In this case, we have the maximum inequality possible and the Gini coefficient becomes: G= $(n - 1)/n$ , and when $n$ is big enough then $lim_{(n\to\infty)}G = 1$. Consider the following table which illustrates the Gini coefficient. Note that the formula of

**Table 2.** Gini coefficient

| Portfolio | | | |
|---|---|---|---|
| | 1 | 2 | 3 |
| $w_1$ | 0.3 | 0.46 | 0.9 |
| $w_2$ | 0.23 | 0.46 | 0.03 |
| $w_3$ | 0.2 | 0.03 | 0.03 |
| $w_4$ | 0.14 | 0.03 | 0.02 |
| $w_5$ | 0.13 | 0.02 | 0.02 |
| HHI | 0.2194 | 0.4254 | 0.8126 |
| rHHI | 4.5578 | 2.3507 | 1.2306 |
| Gini | 0.172 | 0.524 | 0.708 |

total inequality, namely G=$(n - 1)/n$ , with $n$ equal to five, then the maximum inequality happens when G is 4/5 or 0.8 . Note that Portfolio 3 is highly concentrated in the first stock, its Gini, at 0.708, is very close to the maximum of 0.8 attainable in this case. In contrast, consider a portfolio with $n$ equally weighted stocks, i.e. $w_i$ is $1/n$ for all $i$. In this case we have total equality. Intuitively since the straight line in the Lorenz curve represents total equality, the area between the curve and the equality line becomes zero and we should expect the Gini coefficient to become zero. Unlike the HHI that emphasizes the presence of stocks with relatively big weights, the Gini coefficient is sensitive to small transfers of weights between the small weighted stocks. In other words, HHI is less sensitive to changes in weights among the small weighted elements, whereas the Gini coefficient senses this change. To illustrate this characteristic consider Tab. 3. The Gini index is an index that emphasizes the presence of stocks with relatively small weights. In this narrow sense it can be used to complement the HHI index which emphasizes the presence of relatively big stocks.

It should be noted however that, for a given value of n, and a given matrix of $[w_i]$ there exists one value of HHI and one single value of GINI index.

**Table 3.** Three different portfolios consisting of five stocks with wieghts $w_1$ to $w_5$ and their respective HHI and Gini coeficient. note the effect on the HHI of transferring 0.02 from stock 5 to stock 4 and from Stock 2 to Stock 1. Strikingly HHI is higher when the same amount is transferred to a big player. In contrast, the Gini coefficient does not sense the same transfer when it comes to big weighted elements (Gini=0.208 for both Portfolio 2 and Portfolio 3). Rather, the Gini coefficient senses the transfer when it happens between small weighted elements, hence Gini moves from 0.2 to 0.208 between Portfolio 1 and Portfolio 2 , when the smallest weighted stock is altered, as shown.

| Portfolio | | | |
|---|---|---|---|
| | 1 | 2 | 3 |
| $w_1$ | 0.32 | 0.32 | 0.34 |
| $w_2$ | 0.23 | 0.23 | 0.21 |
| $w_3$ | 0.2 | 0.2 | 0.2 |
| $w_4$ | 0.13 | 0.15 | 0.13 |
| $w_5$ | 0.12 | 0.1 | 0.12 |
| HHI | 0.2266 | 0.2278 | 0.231 |
| Gini | 0.200 | 0.208 | 0.208 |

# 3    Application of Concentration Measures in Portfolio Allocation

Intuitively, if we choose n stocks from a larger then n investment universe, we are concentrating our investment strategy on those n stocks, compared with the N stocks of the wider universe. If we choose a weight matrix $[w_i]$ where $i$ belongs to $[1, n]$ with the budget constraint of $\sum w_i = 1$, then we can define a concentration measure related to the components of the weight matrix. We will call this a weight matrix concentration measure; this measure, in fact, is best captured by the HHI and Gini indices of the weight matrix of this particular portfolio.

If we measure the concentration of weights at time zero, this measure will stay the same as long as the matrix of weights $[w_i]$ is not changed, i.e. the components and weights of the portfolio remain the same. However, it is not generally the case, because markets are not completely homogeneous and as such, the concentration is always changing. We will monitor the concentration indices or level in order to describe the concentration of the investment portfolio across time.

## 3.1    Pretension Level

If we choose to invest equal wealth in each stock, i.e. $w_1 = w_2 = w_3 \ldots = w_n = 1/n$, then we assume that we do not have any preference of one stock or sector over the other, and we define this as a zero pretension level of investment . The more we deviate from the $1/n$ allocation strategy, the more we invest in one stock against the others within the $n$ stock universe. This indicates a higher pretension level, in the sense that we assume that our choice, different from the lowest possible level of pretension $1/n$, will eventually outperform the $1/n$ portfolio. Note, the equal distribution portfolio will serve as the reference portfolio in our subsequent analysis. Although we placed more weight on some stocks and less on others, hence creating a pretension level and equivalently a higher HHI and GINI indices, the choice remains a pretension or ex-ante prognostic. Ex-post results could be different from our pretension and therefore a higher pretension level is definitely not a guarantee of higher or better performance.

1. We define a pretentious portfolio as one with a weight matrix $[w_i]$ such that its HHI is greater than the $1/n$ concentration level of the minimum pretension portfolio.
2. The minimum pretension portfolio is a unique portfolio (a $1/n$ or equally weighted portfolio).
3. A given pretension level, i.e. a given value of HHI can be generated by various matrices $[w_i]$, hence a given pretension level does not impose a unique portfolio, but rather an isometric HHI Portfolio Opportunity Set: POS. We further define the Portfolio Pretension Set (PPS) as the POS that satisfies a unique pretension level, a chosen HHI value, or the ISO-HHI-POS.
4. From 3. above we conclude that for a given pretension level HHI, we have a variety of resulting POS (i.e. the several sets of $[w_i]$ satisfying HHI=h), and hence a given HHI value or level does not specify a unique return value. In fact, the return of a portfolio is $R = [w_i]^T.[r_i]$, where $[r_i] = [r_1, r_2, r_3, r_4, \ldots r_n]$ is the return vector of each individual stock included in the chosen universe. It is clear that the value of $R$ is not unique for a given HHI, since the given HHI does not define a unique weight vector $[w_i]$.

### 3.2  HHI of Weights and Return of Portfolios

Thus far, we have defined two concentration measures dependent on a chosen set of weights, $w_i$. We have also shown that for a given HHI $> 1/n$ we have various portfolios that will satisfy the value of the HHI, the pretension of the investor; these sets make up the PPS defined earlier. Intuitively, we can state that since $[w_i]$ for a given pretension is not unique, the return from the corresponding portfolios will vary. The same argument holds for the variance or the standard deviation of the resulting PPS if we fix a value of pretension, i.e. an HHI $> 1/n$. The following graph depicts a plot of the value of HHI versus the resulting return and standard deviation of a hypothetical PPS of $n = 3$ stocks.

The first conclusion that we can draw from this graph is that at the point of no pretension, corresponding to the $\mathrm{HHI}_{min} = 1/n = 0.1$, we observe that the return of this portfolio is not the highest and the standard deviation of the same is not the lowest, which means the $1/n$ portfolio obtained randomly in this case is far from being an ex-ante optimum portfolio. Nevertheless, this portfolio does not necessarily lay on the efficient frontier. Furthermore, knowing that the portfolio of maximum return is the one containing the stock of highest return

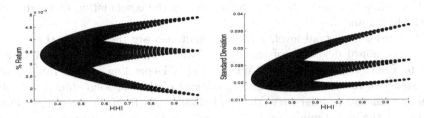

**Fig. 2.** Relationship between the HHI or pretension level (horizontal axis) and Total return and Standard deviation of the resulting portfolios. Please note that these graphs were obtained by using a hypothetical n=3 stocks (hence the min HHI=0.33 as shown) with random values for their respective returns and standard deviation. We generated a POS of around 10,000 portfolios, calculated the portfolio HHI, return and standard deviation. The graphs shows the HHI sorted values against the resulting portfolio return and standard deviation.

with weight $w_1 = 1$, and consequently the portfolio of minimum return is the one containing the stock of the lowest return with a weight of 1, we observe these special portfolios on the right tip of the curve towards HHI=1.

We also know from portfolio theory that the portfolio of minimum variance or standard deviation is obtained by the effect of correlation between the individual stocks. This minimum variance portfolio has a weight matrix $[w_i]$ that corresponds to an HHI which is not necessarily at the extreme end of the curve. In fact, the standard deviation versus HHI plot is tilted to the top right due to the effect of covariance between the individual stocks that will cause the curve to reach a minimum point somewhere in the middle and not on the tip as with the return (the right side curve in Fig. 2).

From Fig. 2 above, we see that any pretension level gives infinite variety of values for corresponding returns, because we have an infinite number of $[w_i]$ that satisfy the HHI chosen.

When we have three stocks the system of equations becomes:

HHI= $w_1^2 + w_2^2 + w_3^2 = h$ (a chosen pretension level greater than $1/n = 1/3$),

With the budget constraint: $w_1 + w_2 + w_3 = 1$,

then the set of $[w_i]$ vectors that satisfy these two equations is in fact the intersection between the 1/8 of sphere $w_1^2 + w_2^2 + w_3^2 = h$ of radius $h^{1/2}$ (since all $w_i$ should be positive, by definition no short selling is considered) and the plane defined by $w_1 + w_2 + w_3 = 1$. This intersection is a circular plane and hence the set of vectors $[w_i]$ solving this system of equations is infinite since it is the set of points existing on the intersection plane.

### 3.3   HHI and the Efficient Frontier

Initially, plotting the resulting returns against their standard deviations of our 3-stocks PPS will show the efficient frontier as the envelope of the cloud plotted. The perimeter we refer to is also called *the minimum variance set*. each point on this perimeter represents a portfolio made of the combination of weights of the stocks 1,2 and 3.

On a two-dimensional level, plotting simultaneously the HHI on the x-axis and the standard deviation of the PPS on the y-axis, and superimposing the efficient frontier will yield the graphs in Fig.3. Depending on the ranking of the respective returns and standard deviations of the portfolio stocks, we will obtain an efficient frontier curve that will always start from the set of minimum variance or the global minimum variance set, and later will end up in a point of HHI=1 with the individual stock contained in the portfolio having the maximum return. Please note that the equally weighted portfolio $1/n$ is not necessarily on the efficient frontier, as it is clear on Fig.3, where this equally weighted portfolio is not on the efficient frontier of the right hand side graph.

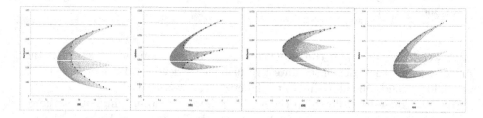

**Fig. 3.** HHI vs. Return and standard deviation of TWO 3-stocks portfolio, showing the efficient frontier points. Note that the efficient frontier on the left graphs is not continuously defined, because the highest return stock we chose does not have the lowest standard deviation as it is the case of the graphs to the right hand side..

## 4   Conclusion

The HHI and Gini indices are a tool to describe a portfolio. A portfolio can be equally weighted or highly concentrated in one single stock. This concentration level describes the *state* of the portfolio and can be used to compare two or more portfolios with respect to their concentration also.

In a rather graphical way, we showed that the concentration of the weights is related directly to the return of the portfolio as well as to its standard deviation. The concentration is also in direct relation with the efficient set, and the allocation strategy would relate to the concentration of the portfolio ,or to its *pretension*, to dynamically mange the investment allocation through time. This study suggests that the Gini index must be used to fine tune the allocated weights corresponding to the initial pretension level so as to draw as near as possible to the efficient set.

**Acknowledgments.** The authors wish to thank Dr Faith Jordan Srour for her valuable input and guidance. Her editing techniques and Latex knowledge made our task much easier.

We also wish to thank Mr Michel Kamel and Mr. Roy Nehme for their help in the technical and computational techniques involved in this paper.

# References

1. Bourguignon, F., Morrisson, C.: Inequality and Development: the role of dualism. J. Dev. Eco. 57 (1988)
2. Brands, S., Brown, S.J., Gallagher, D.R.: Portfolio Concentration and Investment Manager Performance. NYU Working Paper No. (March 2004)
3. Cowell, F.: Measuring Inequality. Oxford University Press (2009)
4. Dagum, C.: A new Approach to the Decomposition of the Gini Income Inequality Ratio. Emp. Eco. 22 (1997)
5. Greco, S., Matarazzo, B., Slowinski, R.: Rough Sets Methodology for Sorting Problems in Presence of Multiple Attributes and Criteria. Eur. J. Op. Res. (2002)
6. Mussard, S., Terraza, V.: Methodes de Decomposition de la Volatilite 'd'un Portefeuille. Une Nouvelle Approche d'Estimation des Risques par l'Indice de Gini. Rev. Eco. Pol. 114, 557–571 (2004)
7. Ogryczak, W.: Multicriteria Models for Fair Resource Allocation. Con. Cyb. Rev. 36 (2007)
8. Simonelli, M.R.: Indeterminacy in Portfolio Selection. Eur. J. Op. Res. 163, 170–176 (2005)
9. Yitzhak, S., Lerman, R.: Income Inequality Effects by Income Source: A New Approach and Applications to the United States. Rev. Eco. Stat. 67(1), 151–156 (1985)

# Decision Making under Scenario Uncertainty in a Requirement Planning

Romain Guillaume[1] and Paweł Zieliński[2,*]

[1] Université de Toulouse-IRIT, 5, Allées A. Machado 31058 Toulouse Cedex 1, France
Guillaum@irit.fr
[2] Faculty of Fundamental Problems of Technology, Wrocław University of
Technology, Wybrzeże Wyspiańskiego 27, 50-370, Wrocław, Poland
pawel.zielinski@pwr.wroc.pl

**Abstract.** The paper deals with a collaborative supply chain, where actors use Material Requirement Planning (MRP) with uncertain demands. The demand uncertainty is modeled by a scenario set containing all possible demand realizations. Three scenario based uncertainty representations are examined. The min-max and the Hurwicz criterion and the ordered weighted averaging aggregation(OWA) are adopted to choose a best production or procurement plan under the assumed uncertainty models. Efficient solution methods for finding optimal plans with respect to each optimization criterion are provided.

**Keywords:** supply chain, requirement planning, uncertain demands, scenarios, robust optimization.

## 1 Introduction

In real life, there is an uncertainty in supply chains. Uncertainty in demands creates a risk in supply chains as backordering, obsolete inventory due to the bullwhip effect [12]. To reduces this risk, it is necessary to integrate the demand uncertainty in decision processes of supply chain actors. Another way to reduce the risk in a supply chain is sharing information between supply chain actors [8]. This supply chain is so-called *collaborative supply chain*. In this paper, we analyze collaborative supply chains, where actors use *Material requirement planning* (MRP) [3] under uncertain demands. Our purpose is to help the decision maker to compute required quantities subject to *capacity constraints* (supplier capacity or production capacity constraints). This problem is equivalent to a certain version of the *lot sizing problem* with ill-known demands. The uncertainty is modeled by specifying a set of all possible realizations of the demands (states of the world) called *scenarios*. In the literature, two types of demand uncertainty are distinguished: the uncertainty in a quantity for a given period and the uncertainty in a date [4]. In the first type, the uncertainty is defined by intervals and the corresponding scenario set is the Cartesian product of these uncertainty intervals. In the second type, the uncertainty is described by a scenario set defined

* This work was partially supported by Polish Committee for Scientific Research, grant
N N206 492938.

by explicitly listing all possible scenarios. We consider three models of such uncertainty representation. In the first two models, it is assumed that each demand scenario is equally likely. In order to choose a *robust* plan (decision making under "complete ignorance"), three optimization criteria called the *min-max* (see, e.g., [11]), the *Hurwicz criterion* (see, e.g., [13]) and the *ordered weighted averaging aggregation* (OWA) [16] are adopted. Under the min-max criterion, we seek a plan that minimizes the largest cost over all scenarios. A less conservative criterion is the Hurwicz one under which, we wish to find a plan that minimizes a convex combination of its pessimistic and optimistic costs. A more general criterion that takes into account decision maker's personal attitude toward risk is the OWA criterion. It is a generalization of the conservative min-max and the Hurwicz criteria, since it includes them as particular cases. In the third demand uncertainty model, it is assumed that the decision maker has some partial information about more likely scenarios in the form of a *possibility distribution* (decision making under "partial ignorance"). Furthermore, it is assumed that the decision maker knows her/his preferences about a cost of a production plan expressed by a *fuzzy goal*. In order to choose a robust plan, in the setting of possibility theory [5], we apply a criterion in which, we maximize the degree of *necessity* (certainty) that costs of the plan fall within the fuzzy goal.

In this paper, we provide efficient linear or mixed integer programming based methods for finding robust production plans with respect to the proposed models of the demand uncertainty and the assumed optimization criteria.

## 2    Preliminaries

In this section, we formally define a deterministic version of the problem, which is under consideration, i.e. the problem in which all demands are known in advance. Suppose that we are given $T$ periods. For period $t$, $t = 1, \ldots, T$, let $d_t$ be the precise demand in period $t$, $d_t \geq 0$, $x_t$ the production amount in period $t$, $x_t \geq 0$, $l_t$, $u_t$ the production capacity limits on $x_t$. Let $\mathcal{X} = \{(x_1, \ldots, x_T) : l_t \leq x_t \leq u_t, t = 1, \ldots, T\} \subseteq \mathbb{R}_+^T$ be the set of feasible production amounts. Set $\mathbf{D}_t = \sum_{i=1}^{t} d_i$ and $\mathbf{X}_t = \sum_{i=1}^{t} x_i$, $\mathbf{D}_t$ and $\mathbf{X}_t$ stand for the cumulative demand up to period $t$ and the production level up to period $t$, respectively. Obviously, $\mathbf{X}_{t-1} \leq \mathbf{X}_t$ and $\mathbf{D}_{t-1} \leq \mathbf{D}_t$, $t = 2, \ldots, T$. The costs of carrying one unit of inventory from period $t$ to period $t + 1$ is given by $c_t^I \geq 0$ and the costs of backordering one unit from period $t + 1$ to period $t$ is given by $c_t^B \geq 0$. The nonnegative real function $L_t(u, v)$ represents either the cost of storing inventory from period $t$ to period $t+1$ or the cost of backordering quantity from period $t+1$ to period $t$, namely $L_t(\mathbf{X}_t, \mathbf{D}_t) = c_t^I(\mathbf{X}_t - \mathbf{D}_t)$ if $\mathbf{X}_t \geq \mathbf{D}_t$; $c_t^B(\mathbf{D}_t - \mathbf{X}_t)$ otherwise. The function has the form $L_t(\mathbf{X}_t, \mathbf{D}_t) = \max\{c_t^I(\mathbf{X}_t - \mathbf{D}_t), c_t^B(\mathbf{D}_t - \mathbf{X}_t)\}$. The optimization problem with the precise demands consists in finding a feasible production plan $\boldsymbol{x} = (x_1, \ldots, x_T)$, $\boldsymbol{x} \in \mathcal{X}$, that minimizes the total cost of storage and backordering subject to the conditions of satisfying each demand, namely

$$\mathcal{P} : \min_{x \in \mathcal{X}} F(\boldsymbol{x}) = \min_{\boldsymbol{x} \in \mathcal{X}} \sum_{t=1}^{T} L_t \left( \sum_{i=1}^{t} x_i, \sum_{i=1}^{t} d_i \right) = \min_{\boldsymbol{x} \in \mathcal{X}} \sum_{t=1}^{T} L_t(\mathbf{X}_t, \mathbf{D}_t). \quad (1)$$

The problem $\mathcal{P}$ is a version of the *classical lot sizing with backordering* (see, e.g., [7]). Without loss of generality, we can assume that an initial inventory $I_0$ and an initial backorder $B_0$ are equal to zero. Otherwise, one can append period 0 and assign $x_0 = I_0$ and $d_0 = 0$ with zero inventory cost if $I_0 > 0$ or assign $x_0 = 0$ and $d_0 = B_0$ with zero backorder cost if $B_0 > 0$. The problem $\mathcal{P}$ can be formulated as the minimum cost flow problem:

$$\begin{aligned}
\min \ & \textstyle\sum_{t=1}^{T} (c_t^I I_t + c_t^B B_t) \\
\text{s.t. } & B_t - I_t = \textstyle\sum_{j=1}^{t} (d_j - x_j), \ t \in [T], \\
& l_t \leq x_t \leq u_t, \qquad\qquad\qquad t \in [T], \\
& B_t, I_t \geq 0, \qquad\qquad\qquad\quad t \in [T],
\end{aligned} \quad (2)$$

where $[N]$, for any nonnegative integer $N$, stands for the set $\{1, 2, \ldots, N\}$. Problem (2) can efficiently solved, for instance, by an algorithm presented in [2].

In this section, we have assumed the all input parameters in problem (1) are precisely known. However, in real life this is rarely the case. Section 3 will investigate the case, when some parameters are uncertain.

## 3    Decisions under Uncertainty in Requirement Planning

In practice, the precise values of demands $d_t$, $t \in [T]$, in problem (1) may be not well known. This uncertainty can be modeled by specifying a set of all possible realizations of the demands (states of the world) called *scenarios*. We denote by $\Gamma$ the set of all the scenarios. Formally, a scenario is a vector $S = (d_1, \ldots, d_T)$, $d_t \geq 0$, that represents an assignment of demands $d_t$ to periods $t$, $t \in [T]$. The demand and the cumulative demand in period $t$ under scenario $S$ are denoted by $d_t(S)$ and $\mathbf{D}_t(S)$, respectively, $\mathbf{D}_t(S) = \sum_{i=1}^{t} d_i(S)$. Clearly, for every $S \in \Gamma$ it holds $\mathbf{D}_{t-1}(S) \leq \mathbf{D}_t(S)$, $t = 2, \ldots, T$. The function $L_t(\mathbf{X}_t, \mathbf{D}_t(S)) = \max\{c_t^I(\mathbf{X}_t - \mathbf{D}_t(S)), c_t^B(\mathbf{D}_t(S) - \mathbf{X}_t)\}$, represents either the cost of storing inventory from period $t$ to period $t+1$ or the cost of backordering quantity from period $t+1$ to period $t$ under scenario $S$. Now $F(\boldsymbol{x}, S)$ denotes the total cost of a production plan $\boldsymbol{x} \in \mathcal{X}$ under scenario $S$, i.e. $F(\boldsymbol{x}, S) = \sum_{t=1}^{T} L_t(\mathbf{X}_t, \mathbf{D}_t(S))$.

We consider two ways of describing the set of scenarios $\Gamma$. In the *discrete scenario uncertainty representation*, the scenario set is defined by explicitly listing all possible scenarios that express realizations of the demands. So, $\Gamma = \{S^1, \ldots, S^K\}$ is finite and contains exactly $K$ scenarios, $S^k \in \Gamma$ is a vector $S^k = (d_t(S^k))_{t \in [T]}$, $k \in [K]$ (see Table 1a). In the *interval uncertainty representation* demands are only known to belong to intervals $D_t = [d_t^-, d_t^+]$, $d_t^- \geq 0$. This means that we neither know the exact demands, nor can set them precisely. It is assumed that the demands are unrelated to one another. Thus, the set of scenarios is the Cartesian product of these intervals, i.e. $\Gamma = [d_1^-, d_1^+] \times \cdots \times [d_T^-, d_T^+]$, scenario $S \in \Gamma$ is a vector $S = (d_t(S))_{t \in [T]}$, $d_t(S) \in D_t = [d_t^-, d_t^+]$ (see Table 1b).

In this paper, we consider decision making under the scenario uncertainty representation in the case of "complete ignorance" and in the case of "partial ignorance" (see, e.g., [13]). In the first case it is assumed that each demand scenario $S \in \Gamma$ is equally likely (the models presented in Table 1a and b). In the second one, it is assumed that the decision maker has some partial information about more likely scenarios, here in the form of a *possibility distribution* (see [5] for more details about possibility theory). A possibility distribution $\pi$ is specified on the set of scenarios $\Gamma$, which describes more or less plausible scenarios (see Table 1c). Hence for each scenario $S \in \Gamma$ a number $\pi(S) \in [0,1]$ is provided, which is a possibility of the event that scenario $S$ will occur. In particular, $\pi(S) = 0$ means that $S$ is impossible and $\pi(S) > 0$ means that $S$ is plausible. Moreover, the value of $\pi(S)$ can be also seen as an upper bound on a probability of occurring $S$ [6].

**Table 1.** Different scenario representations of the uncertain demands

a)

| period | $\Gamma$ | | | |
|---|---|---|---|---|
| $t$ | $S_1$ | $S_2$ | ... | $S_K$ |
| 1 | $d_1(S^1)$ | $d_1(S^2)$ | ... | $d_1(S^K)$ |
| 2 | $d_2(S^1)$ | $d_2(S^2)$ | ... | $d_2(S^K)$ |
| $\vdots$ | $\vdots$ | $\vdots$ | $\vdots$ | $\vdots$ |
| T | $d_T(S^1)$ | $d_T(S^2)$ | ... | $d_T(S^K)$ |

b)

| period | $\Gamma$ |
|---|---|
| $t$ | |
| 1 | $[d_1^-, d_1^+]$ |
| 2 | $[d_2^-, d_2^+]$ |
| $\vdots$ | $\vdots$ |
| T | $[d_T^-, d_T^+]$ |

c)

| period | $\Gamma$ | | | |
|---|---|---|---|---|
| $t$ | $S_1$ | $S_2$ | ... | $S_K$ |
| 1 | $d_1(S^1)$ | $d_1(S^2)$ | ... | $d_1(S^K)$ |
| 2 | $d_2(S^1)$ | $d_2(S^2)$ | ... | $d_2(S^K)$ |
| $\vdots$ | $\vdots$ | $\vdots$ | $\vdots$ | $\vdots$ |
| T | $d_T(S^1)$ | $d_T(S^2)$ | ... | $d_T(S^K)$ |
| $\pi$ | $\pi(S^1)$ | $\pi(S^2)$ | ... | $\pi(S^K)$ |

In the following sections, we examine several criteria, which allow us to find a robust plan of the planning problem $\mathcal{P}$ under uncertain demands (Table 1a, b and c) and propose efficient methods for such solutions (some of them are polynomial ones). The first three criterion (the min-max, the pessimism-optimism index criterion of Hurwicz, the ordered weighted averaging aggregation) refer to "complete ignorance". The last criterion based on the *necessity measure* refers to "partial ignorance" - it is a decision making in the setting of possibility theory.

### 3.1  Min-Max Optimization

In this section, we model the uncertain demands in the planning problem $\mathcal{P}$ by explicitly listing all possible demand scenarios and so $\Gamma = \{S^1, \ldots, S^K\}$ (see Table 1a). In order to choose a robust solution the *min-max criterion* can be applied (see, e.g. [11]). In the min-max version of problem $\mathcal{P}$, we wish to find among all production plans the one, $\boldsymbol{x}^* \in \mathcal{X}$, that minimizes the maximum total production plan cost over all scenarios, that is:

$$\text{MIN-MAX } \mathcal{P}: \; \min_{\boldsymbol{x} \in \mathcal{X}} \max_{S \in \Gamma} F(\boldsymbol{x}, S) = \min_{\boldsymbol{x} \in \mathcal{X}} \max_{S \in \Gamma} \sum_{t=1}^{T} L_t(\mathbf{X}_t, \mathbf{D}_t(S)). \tag{3}$$

An optimal plan $\boldsymbol{x}^*$ to (3) has the best worst total cost $F(\boldsymbol{x}^*, S^w)$, where $S^w$ is a worst case scenario. Furthermore, we are sure that for any $S \in \Gamma$ the total cost of $\boldsymbol{x}^*$ never exceed $F(\boldsymbol{x}^*, S^w)$. Hence, we have no doubts that $\boldsymbol{x}^*$ is a robust plan.

Fortunately, MIN-MAX $\mathcal{P}$ can be solved efficiently, in polynomial time. Let us formulate the problem by the following mathematical programming problem:

$$\min v$$
$$\text{s.t. } v \geq F(\boldsymbol{x}, S^k), k \in [K], \tag{4}$$
$$\boldsymbol{x} \in \mathcal{X}.$$

Note that the constraint $v \geq F(\boldsymbol{x}, S^k)$, called *scenario cut*, associated with $S^k$ is not a linear constraint. The following statement helps us to linearize it.

**Statement 1.** *Scenario cut $v \geq F(\boldsymbol{x}, S)$, where $S = (d_t(S))_{t \in [T]}$, $\boldsymbol{x} = (x_t)_{t \in [T]}$, can be linearized by replacing it with the following $T + 1$ constraints and $2T$ new decision variables:*

$$v \geq \sum_{t=1}^{T}(c_t^I I_t^S + c_t^B B_t^S),$$
$$B_t^S - I_t^S = \sum_{j=1}^{t}(d_j(S) - x_j), t \in [T],$$
$$B_t^S, I_t^S \geq 0, \qquad\qquad t \in [T].$$

Applying Statement 1 to (4) leads to the following linear program:

$$\min v$$
$$\text{s.t. } v \geq \sum_{t=1}^{T}(c_t^I I_t^{S^k} + c_t^B B_t^{S^k}), \qquad\qquad k \in [K],$$
$$B_t^{S^k} - I_t^{S^k} = \sum_{j=1}^{t}(d_j(S^k) - x_j), t \in [T], k \in [K], \tag{5}$$
$$B_t^{S^k}, I_t^{S^k} \geq 0, \qquad\qquad t \in [T], k \in [K],$$
$$l_t \leq x_t \leq u_t \qquad\qquad t \in [T].$$

The linear program (5) can be efficiently solved by using a specially-tuned method for this kind of problems [1] or by some standard off-the-shelf LP solvers.

We have not considered here the case of MIN-MAX $\mathcal{P}$ with uncertain demands under the interval scenario uncertainty representation (Table 1b), since it has been studied in [10].

## 3.2  Hurwicz-Based Optimization

The min-max criterion presented in Section 3.1 can be seen as ultraconservative. We now apply to problem $\mathcal{P}$ with the uncertain demands less conservative criterion. The criterion concentrates both on pessimistic and optimistic scenarios that lead to the maximal and minimal total costs. This criterion is the *Hurwicz criterion* (see, e.g., [13]). In Hurwicz version of problem $\mathcal{P}$, we seek a production plan $\boldsymbol{x}^*$ that minimizes the convex combination of the best and worst performance (the total cost) over all scenarios, i.e. we solve the following problem:

$$\text{HUR } \mathcal{P}: \min_{\boldsymbol{x} \in \mathcal{X}}\{\alpha \min_{S \in \Gamma} F(\boldsymbol{x}, S) + (1 - \alpha) \max_{S \in \Gamma} F(\boldsymbol{x}, S)\} \tag{6}$$
$$= \min_{\boldsymbol{x} \in \mathcal{X}}\{\alpha \min_{S \in \Gamma} \sum_{t=1}^{T} L_t(\mathbf{X}_t, \mathbf{D}_t(S)) + (1 - \alpha) \max_{S \in \Gamma} \sum_{t=1}^{T} L_t(\mathbf{X}_t, \mathbf{D}_t(S))\},$$

where $\alpha \in [0, 1]$ is given (fixed) called *optimism-pessimism index*. Clearly, $\alpha = 1$ then we seek a plan which minimizes minimal total cost over the scenario set; if

$\alpha = 0$ then HUR $\mathcal{P}$ is MIN-MAX $\mathcal{P}$. Hence, $\alpha \in [0,1]$ controls which of two extremes is preferred.

We first study HUR $\mathcal{P}$, where the scenario set is $\Gamma = [d_1^-, d_1^+] \times \cdots \times [d_T^-, d_T^+]$ (the interval uncertainty representation, see Table 1b) and propose an iterative algorithm for based on on iterative relaxation scheme for min-max problems proposed in [15]. Let us consider a relaxation of HUR $\mathcal{P}$ that consists in replacing a given scenario set $\Gamma$ with a discrete scenario set $\Gamma_{\mathrm{dis}} = \{S^1, \ldots, S^K\}$, $\Gamma_{\mathrm{dis}} \subseteq \Gamma$:

$$
\begin{aligned}
\hat{z} = \min \ & \alpha u + (1 - \alpha) v \\
\text{s.t.} \quad & u \geq F(\boldsymbol{x}, S), && S \in \Gamma = [d_1^-, d_1^+] \times \cdots \times [d_T^-, d_T^+], \\
& v \geq F(\boldsymbol{x}, S^k), && S^k \in \Gamma_{\mathrm{dis}} = \{S^1, \ldots, S^K\}, \\
& \boldsymbol{x} \in \mathcal{X},
\end{aligned}
\tag{7}
$$

where $S^k = (d_t(S^k))_{t \in [T]}$, $\boldsymbol{x} = (x_t)_{t \in [T]}$. Obviously $\hat{z}$ is a lower bound on the optimal value of HUR $\mathcal{P}$. One can easy transform (7) into a linear program by applying Statement 1 to scenario cuts $u \geq F(\boldsymbol{x}, S)$ and $v \geq F(\boldsymbol{x}, S^k)$ (see also (5)). Our algorithm (Algorithm 1) starts with zero lower bound $LB = 0$, a candidate $\hat{\boldsymbol{x}} \in \mathcal{X}$ for an optimal solution for HUR $\mathcal{P}$ (any solution for $\mathcal{X}$) and empty discrete scenario set, $\Gamma_{\mathrm{dis}} = \emptyset$. At each iteration, an optimistic scenario $S^o$, $S^o = \arg\min_{S \in \Gamma} F(\hat{\boldsymbol{x}}, S)$, a worst case scenario $S^w$, $S^w = \arg\max_{S \in \Gamma} F(\hat{\boldsymbol{x}}, S)$, for $\hat{\boldsymbol{x}}$ are computed. $S^w$ may be determined by a mixed integer model presented in [10]. The value of $\alpha F(\hat{\boldsymbol{x}}, S^o) + (1 - \alpha) F(\hat{\boldsymbol{x}}, S^w)$ is an upper bound on the optimal value of HUR $\mathcal{P}$. If a termination criterion is fulfilled (Step 3), for a given precision $\epsilon > 0$, then algorithm stops with production plan $\hat{\boldsymbol{x}}$. Otherwise the worst case scenario $S^w = (s_t^w)_{t \in [T]}$ is added to $\Gamma_{\mathrm{dis}}$, the scenario cut corresponding to $S^w$ is appended to problem (7). Next the updated linear programming problem (7) is solved to obtain a better candidate $\hat{\boldsymbol{x}}$ for an optimal solution for HUR $\mathcal{P}$ and new lower bound $LB = \hat{z}$. Since set $\Gamma_{\mathrm{dis}}$ is updated during the course of the algorithm, the computed values of lower bounds $\{\hat{z}\}$ form a nondecreasing sequence of their values. Then new iteration is started.

---

**Algorithm 1.** Solving HUR $\mathcal{P}$.

---

**Step 0.** $k := 0$, $LB := 0$, $\Gamma_{\mathrm{dis}} := \emptyset$.

**Step 1.** $\boldsymbol{x}^k := \hat{\boldsymbol{x}}$.

**Step 2.** Compute a worst case scenario $S^w$ and optimistic scenario $S^o$ for $\boldsymbol{x}^k$.

**Step 3.** $\Delta := \alpha F(\boldsymbol{x}^k, S^o) + (1 - \alpha) F(\boldsymbol{x}^k, S^w) - LB$. If $LB > 1$ then $\Delta := \Delta / LB$. If $\Delta \leq \epsilon$ then output $\boldsymbol{x}^k$ and STOP.

**Step 4.** $k := k + 1$, $S^k := S^w$, $\Gamma_{\mathrm{dis}} := \Gamma_{\mathrm{dis}} \cup \{S^k\}$ and append scenario cut $v \geq F(\boldsymbol{x}, S^k)$ to problem (7).

**Step 5.** Compute an optimal solution $(\hat{\boldsymbol{x}}, \hat{z})$ for (7), $LB := \hat{z}$, and go to Step 1.

---

The following theorem justifies Algorithm 1.

**Theorem 1.** *Algorithm 1 terminates in a finite number of steps for any given $\epsilon > 0$.*

*Proof.* The proof is almost the same as those given in [9, Theorem 2.5] and [15, Theorem 3]. $\qquad\square$

Let us turn to the case $\Gamma = \{S^1, \ldots, S^K\}$ in HUR $\mathcal{P}$ (the discrete scenario uncertainty representation, see Table 1a). For such uncertainty representation HUR $\mathcal{P}$ can be modeled by the following mathematical programming problem:

$$
\begin{aligned}
\min \; & \alpha u + (1 - \alpha)v \\
\text{s.t.} \; & u \geq F(\boldsymbol{x}, S^k) - M(1 - \delta_k) \; k \in [K], \\
& v \geq F(\boldsymbol{x}, S^k), & k \in [K], \\
& \boldsymbol{x} \in \mathcal{X}, \\
& \delta_1 + \ldots + \delta_K = 1, \\
& \delta_k \in \{0, 1\}, & k \in [K],
\end{aligned}
\tag{8}
$$

where $S^k = (d_t(S^k))_{t \in [T]}$, $\boldsymbol{x} = (x_t)_{t \in [T]}$ and $M$ is a sufficiently large number. In order to obtain an equivalent mixed integer programming problem (MIP), we again linearize the scenario cuts $u \geq F(\boldsymbol{x}, S^k) - M(1 - \delta_k)$ and $v \geq F(\boldsymbol{x}, S^k)$ in (8) using Statement 1 (see also (5)). The obtained MIP can be then efficiently solved, especially when the number of scenario $K$ is not too large (not too many binary variables $\delta_k$, $k \in [K]$), by using some standard off-the-shelf MIP solvers.

### 3.3  OWA-Based Optimization

In this section, in order to find a production plan under uncertain demands in the problem $\mathcal{P}$, we apply a more general criterion based on the so-called *ordered weighted averaging aggregation* (OWA) proposed in [16]. This criterion allows to take a risk into account in a decision making. It is a generalization of the conservative criteria presented in Sections 3.1 and 3.2, the min-max and the Hurwicz criteria, since it includes them as particular cases.

We assume the discrete scenario representation of the uncertain demands (Table 1a), i.e. $\Gamma = \{S^1, \ldots, S^K\}$. The OWA of a production plan $\boldsymbol{x}$ is defined as follows: $\text{OWA}_{\boldsymbol{w}}(\boldsymbol{x}) = \sum_{k=1}^{K} w_k F(\boldsymbol{x}, S^{\sigma(k)}) = \sum_{k=1}^{K} w_k \sum_{t=1}^{T} L_t(\mathbf{X}_t, \mathbf{D}_t(S^{\sigma(k)}))$, where $\boldsymbol{w} = (w_1, \ldots, w_K)$ is a vector of weights such that $w_k \geq 0$, $k \in [K]$, and $\sum_{k=1}^{K} w_k = 1$ and $\sigma$ is a permutation of the set $\{1, \ldots, K\}$ such that $F(\boldsymbol{x}, S^{\sigma(1)}) \geq F(\boldsymbol{x}, S^{\sigma(2)}) \geq \cdots \geq F(\boldsymbol{x}, S^{\sigma(K)})$.

In OWA version of problem $\mathcal{P}$, we seek a production plan $\boldsymbol{x} \in \mathcal{X}$ that minimize $\text{OWA}_{\boldsymbol{w}}(\boldsymbol{x})$ for a given weight vector $\boldsymbol{w}$:

$$
\text{OWA } \mathcal{P}: \quad \min_{\boldsymbol{x} \in \mathcal{X}} \text{OWA}_{\boldsymbol{w}}(\boldsymbol{x}) = \min_{\boldsymbol{x} \in \mathcal{X}} \sum_{k=1}^{K} w_k F(\boldsymbol{x}, S^{\sigma(k)}).
\tag{9}
$$

It is easily seen that OWA $\mathcal{P}$ is a generalization of HUR $\mathcal{P}$. It suffices to set: $w_1 = 1 - \alpha$, $w_K = \alpha$ and the rest weights to zero.

We focus on OWA $\mathcal{P}$ with the nonincreasing weights, $w_1 \geq \cdots \geq w_K \geq 0$. This assumption allows us to propose a linear program for OWA $\mathcal{P}$. It is worth pointing out that OWA $\mathcal{P}$ includes MIN-MAX $\mathcal{P}$ as a special case. Indeed, it is enough to set $w_1 = 1$ and the rest weights to zero.

To give a linear program for OWA $\mathcal{P}$ with the nonincreasing weights, we first need to linearize the objective function. A clever linearization, under the assumption that the weights in OWA are nonincreasing, has been proposed in [14]. Let $\Theta_k(\boldsymbol{x}) = \sum_{i=1}^{k} F(\boldsymbol{x}, S^{\sigma(k)})$. Obviously, $F(\boldsymbol{x}, S^{\sigma(1)}) = \Theta_1(\boldsymbol{x})$ and $F(\boldsymbol{x}, S^{\sigma(k)}) = \Theta_k(\boldsymbol{x}) - \Theta_{k+1}(\boldsymbol{x})$, $k = 2, \ldots, K$. Thus OWA can rewritten as:

$$\text{OWA}_{\boldsymbol{w}}(\boldsymbol{x}) = \sum_{k=1}^{K} (w_k - w_{k+1}) \Theta_k(\boldsymbol{x}), \tag{10}$$

where $w_{K+1} = 0$. Coefficient $\Theta_k(\boldsymbol{x})$ for a given $\boldsymbol{x}$ can be found as the optimal value of the following linear problem (see [14, Theorem 1]):

$$\begin{aligned}
\Theta_k(\boldsymbol{x}) = \min \; & k r_k + \sum_{i=1}^{K} d_{ik} \\
\text{s.t.} \; & r_k + d_{ik} \geq F(\boldsymbol{x}, S^i), \quad i \in [K], \\
& d_{ik} \geq 0, \qquad\qquad\quad i \in [K],
\end{aligned} \tag{11}$$

where $r_k$ and $d_{ik}$ are new decision variables. Combining (10) with (11) yields a model for OWA $\mathcal{P}$:

$$\begin{aligned}
\min \; & \sum_{k=1}^{K} (w_k - w_{k+1})(k r_k + \sum_{i=1}^{K} d_{ik}) \\
\text{s.t.} \; & r_k + d_{ik} \geq v_i, && i, k \in [K], \\
& v_i = F(\boldsymbol{x}, S^i), && i \in [K], \\
& \boldsymbol{x} \in \mathcal{X}, \\
& d_{ik} \geq 0, && i, k \in [K].
\end{aligned}$$

To obtain a linear program (LP) for OWA $\mathcal{P}$, it remains to linearize constraints: $v_i = F(\boldsymbol{x}, S^i)$. This can be easily done by Statement 1 (see also (5)). The resulting linear program may be efficiently solved by LP solver even for large sizes.

### 3.4 Possibilistic Optimization

We now assume that the decision maker has some partial information about more likely scenarios in the form of a possibility distribution $\pi$ specified on the set of scenarios $\Gamma = \{S^1, \ldots, S^K\}$, $\pi(S^k) \in [0, 1]$, $k \in [K]$, that describes more or less plausible scenarios (see Table 1c). Let $\mathcal{F}(\boldsymbol{x})$ denote uncertain cost of a production plan $\boldsymbol{x}$, i.e. a real valued variable whose possibility distribution $\pi_{\mathcal{F}(\boldsymbol{x})}$, induced by $\pi$, has the form: $\pi_{\mathcal{F}(\boldsymbol{x})}(z) = \max_{\{k \in [K] : F(\boldsymbol{x}, S^k) = z\}} \pi(S^k)$, $z \in \mathbb{R}$, and $\pi_{\mathcal{F}(\boldsymbol{x})}(z) = 0$ if $F(\boldsymbol{x}, S^k) \neq z$ for all $k \in [K]$. The value of $\pi_{\mathcal{F}(\boldsymbol{x})}(z)$ represents the possibility degree of the assignment $\mathcal{F}(\boldsymbol{x}) = z$. In particular, $\pi_{\mathcal{F}(\boldsymbol{x})}(z) = 0$ means that $\mathcal{F}(\boldsymbol{x}) = z$ is impossible and $\pi_{\mathcal{F}(\boldsymbol{x})}(z) > 0$ means that $\mathcal{F}(\boldsymbol{x}) = z$ is plausible (a more detailed description of possibility theory can be found in [5]).

Suppose that the decision maker knows her/his preferences about a cost of a production plan $\mathcal{F}(\boldsymbol{x})$ and expresses it by a *fuzzy goal* $\widetilde{G}$, which is a fuzzy interval with a bounded support and a nonincreasing upper semicontinuous membership function $\mu_{\widetilde{G}} : \mathbb{R} \rightarrow [0, 1]$ such that $\mu_{\widetilde{G}}(z) = 1$ for $v \in [0, g]$. The value of $\mu_{\widetilde{G}}(\mathcal{F}(\boldsymbol{x}))$ is the extent to which cost $\mathcal{F}(\boldsymbol{x})$ of $\boldsymbol{x}$ satisfies the decision maker. We follow [5] in determining the *necessity* that event "$\mathcal{F}(\boldsymbol{x}) \in \widetilde{G}$" holds, denoted by $N(\mathcal{F}(\boldsymbol{x}) \in \widetilde{G})$:

$$N(\mathcal{F}(\boldsymbol{x}) \in \widetilde{G}) = 1 - \sup_{z \in \mathbb{R}} \min\{\pi_{\mathcal{F}(\boldsymbol{x})}(z), 1 - \mu_{\widetilde{G}}(z)\} \tag{12}$$

$$= \max_{k \in [K]} \min\{\pi(S^k), \mu_{\widetilde{G}^c}(F(\boldsymbol{x}, S^k))\},$$

where $\widetilde{G}^c$ stands for the complement of $\widetilde{G}$ with the membership function $1 - \mu_{\widetilde{G}}$. Observe that if $N(\mathscr{F}(\boldsymbol{x}) \in \widetilde{G}) = 1$, then we are sure that the cost of a plan $\boldsymbol{x}$ under every scenario $S \in \Gamma$ such that $\pi(S) > 0$ is totally accepted. If $N(\mathscr{F}(\boldsymbol{x}) \in \widetilde{G}) = 1 - \lambda$ means that for all scenarios $S$ such that $\pi(S) > \lambda$, the degree of necessity (the degree of certainty) that costs of plan $\boldsymbol{x}$ fall within fuzzy goal $\widetilde{G}$, is not less than $1 - \lambda$. Thus, it is natural to find a production plan which maximizes the necessity degree that costs of the plan fall within fuzzy goal $\widetilde{G}$. We have no doubts that such production plan is a robust one. Therefore, we need to solve the following optimization problem (see (12)):

$$\text{POSS } \mathcal{P} : \max_{\boldsymbol{x} \in \mathcal{X}} N(\mathscr{F}(\boldsymbol{x}) \in \widetilde{G}) = \min_{\boldsymbol{x} \in \mathcal{X}} \max_{k \in [K]} \min\{\pi(S^k), \mu_{\widetilde{G}^c}(F(\boldsymbol{x}, S^k))\}. \quad (13)$$

We check at once that POSS $\mathcal{P}$ is equivalent to the following mathematical programming problem (see also (12)):

$$\begin{aligned} &\min v \\ \text{s.t.} \quad &v \geq \min\{\pi(S^k), \mu_{\widetilde{G}^c}(F(\boldsymbol{x}, S^k))\}, \, k \in [K], \quad (14) \\ &\boldsymbol{x} \in \mathcal{X}. \end{aligned}$$

If fuzzy goal $\widetilde{G}$ is given by a trapezoidal fuzzy interval $\widetilde{G} = (0, 0, g, g + \beta)$ whose membership function is defined as follows:

$$\mu_{\widetilde{G}}(z) = \begin{cases} 1 & \text{if } z \leq g, \\ 1 - \frac{g-z}{\beta} & \text{if } g < z < g + \beta, \\ 0 & \text{if } z \geq g + \beta, \end{cases}$$

and each constraint $v \geq \min\{\pi(S^k), \mu_{\widetilde{G}^c}(F(\boldsymbol{x}, S^k))\}$ is replaced with linear constraints, similarly like in Statement 1, together with introducing variables $\delta_k \in \{0, 1\}$, $k \in [K]$, then problem (14) has the following linear form:

$$\begin{aligned} &\min v \\ \text{s.t.} \quad &v \geq \pi(S^k) - \delta_k, & k \in [K], \\ &v \geq \frac{1}{\beta} \sum_{t=1}^{T} (c_t^I I_t^{S^k} + c_t^B B_t^{S^k}) - \frac{g}{\beta} - M(1 - \delta_k), & k \in [K], \\ &B_t^{S^k} - I_t^{S^k} = \sum_{j=1}^{t} (d_j(S^k) - x_j), & t \in [T], k \in [K], \quad (15) \\ &v, B_t^{S^k}, I_t^{S^k} \geq 0, & t \in [T], k \in [K], \\ &\delta_k \in \{0, 1\}, & k \in [K], \\ &l_t \leq x_t \leq u_t, & t \in [T], \end{aligned}$$

where $M$ is a sufficiently number. The above final model for POSS $\mathcal{P}$ may be efficiently solved by MIP solvers.

## 4    Conclusions

In this paper, we have investigated the decision making in collaborative supply chains, where the customer uses a version of MRP (Material Requirement Planning) with ill-known demands to plan a production. The demand uncertainty has been modeled by a scenario set. We have analyzed three models, with different descriptions of the scenario set: the interval uncertainty representation, the discrete scenario uncertainty representation without, and with, a possibility distribution on the scenario set, and different criteria: the min-max, the Hurwicz and the OWA criterion, that lead to choose robust procurement plans. We have proposed iterative, LP and MIP based methods to compute optimal procurement plans efficiently with respected to each assumed optimization criterion (some of these methods are polynomial).

# References

1. Ahuja, R.K.: Minimax linear programming problem. Operations Research Letters 4, 131–134 (1985)
2. Ahuja, R.K., Hochbaum, D.S.: Solving Linear Cost Dynamic Lot Sizing Problems in O(n log n) Time. Operations Research 56, 255–261 (2008)
3. Arnold, J.R.T., Chapman, S.N., Clive, L.M.: Introduction to Materials Management, 7th edn. Prentice Hall (2011)
4. Dolgui, A., Prodhon, C.: Supply planning under uncertainties in MRP environments: A state of the art. Annual Reviews in Control 31, 269–279 (2007)
5. Dubois, D., Prade, H.: Possibility theory: an approach to computerized processing of uncertainty. Plenum Press, New York (1988)
6. Dubois, D., Prade, H.: When upper probabilities are possibility measures. Fuzzy Sets and Systems 49, 65–74 (1992)
7. Florian, M., Lenstra, K.J., Rinnooy Kan, A.H.G.: Deterministic Production Planning: Algorithms and Complexity. Management Science 26, 669–679 (1980)
8. Galasso, F., Thierry, C.: Design of cooperative processes in a customer-supplier relationship: An approach based on simulation and decision theory. Engineering Applications of Artificial Intelligence 22, 865–881 (2009)
9. Geoffrion, A.M.: Generalized Benders Decomposition. Journal of Optimization Theory and Applications 10, 237–260 (1972)
10. Guillaume, R., Kobylański, P., Zieliński, P.: Production Planning with Uncertain Demands. In: Proceedings of the 2011 IEEE International Conference on Fuzzy Systems, pp. 2644–2649 (2011)
11. Kouvelis, P., Yu, G.: Robust Discrete Optimization and its applications. Kluwer Academic Publishers (1997)
12. Lee, H.L., Padmanabhan, V., Whang, S.: Information Distortion in a Supply Chain: The Bullwhip Effect. Management Science 43, 546–558 (1997)
13. Luce, R.D., Raiffa, H.: Games and decisions. Introduction and critical survey. Dover Publications, Inc., New York (1989)
14. Ogryczak, W., Śliwiński, T.: On solving linear programs with ordered weighted averaging objective. European Journal of Operational Research 148, 80–91 (2003)
15. Shimizu, K., Aiyoshi, E.: Necessary Conditions for Min-Max Problems and Algorithms by a Relaxation Procedure. IEEE Transactions on Automatic Control 25, 62–66 (1980)
16. Yager, R.R.: On Ordered Weighted Averaging Aggregation Operators in Multi-Criteria Decision Making. IEEE Transactions on Systems, Man and Cybernetics 18, 183–190 (1988)

# Finitely Additive FTAP under an Atomic Reference Measure

Patrizia Berti[1], Luca Pratelli[2], and Pietro Rigo[3]

[1] Dipartimento di Matematica Pura ed Applicata "G. Vitali", Università di Modena
e Reggio-Emilia, via Campi 213/B, 41100 Modena, Italy
patrizia.berti@unimore.it
[2] Accademia Navale, viale Italia 72, 57100 Livorno, Italy
pratel@mail.dm.unipi.it
[3] Dipartimento di Matematica "F. Casorati", Università di Pavia, via Ferrata 1,
27100 Pavia, Italy
pietro.rigo@unipv.it

**Abstract.** Let $L$ be a linear space of real bounded random variables on
the probability space $(\Omega, \mathcal{A}, P_0)$. A finitely additive probability $P$ on $\mathcal{A}$
such that

$$P \sim P_0 \quad \text{and} \quad E_P(X) = 0 \text{ for each } X \in L$$

is called EMFA (equivalent martingale finitely additive probability). In
this note, EMFA's are investigated in case $P_0$ is atomic. Existence of
EMFA's is characterized and various examples are given. Given $y \in \mathbb{R}$
and a bounded random variable $Y$, it is also shown that $X_n + y \xrightarrow{a.s.} Y$,
for some sequence $(X_n) \subset L$, provided EMFA's exist and $E_P(Y) = y$ for
each EMFA $P$.

**Keywords:** Equivalent martingale measure, Finitely additive probability, Fundamental theorem of asset pricing, Price uniqueness.

**2000 Mathematics Subject Classification:** 60A05, 60A10, 28C05, 91B25,
91G10.

## 1 Introduction

In the sequel, $(\Omega, \mathcal{A}, P_0)$ is a probability space and $L$ a linear space of real bounded
random variables. We let $\mathbb{P}$ denote the set of finitely additive probabilities on $\mathcal{A}$ and
$\mathbb{P}_0 = \{P \in \mathbb{P} : P \text{ is } \sigma\text{-additive}\}$. In particular, $P_0 \in \mathbb{P}_0$. We also say that $P \in \mathbb{P}$ is
an *equivalent martingale finitely additive probability* (EMFA) if

$$P \sim P_0 \quad \text{and} \quad E_P(X) = 0 \text{ for each } X \in L.$$

Here, $P \sim P_0$ means that $P$ and $P_0$ have the same null sets. Further, the term
"martingale" (attached to $P$) is motivated as follows.

S. Greco et al. (Eds.): IPMU 2012, Part IV, CCIS 300, pp. 114–123, 2012.
© Springer-Verlag Berlin Heidelberg 2012

Let $\mathcal{F} = (\mathcal{F}_t : t \in T)$ be a filtration and $S = (S_t : t \in T)$ a real $\mathcal{F}$-adapted process on $(\Omega, \mathcal{A}, P_0)$, where $T \subset \mathbb{R}$ is any index set. Suppose $S_t$ a bounded random variable for each $t \in T$ and define

$$L(\mathcal{F}, S) = \text{Span}\{I_A (S_t - S_s) : s, t \in T, \ s < t, \ A \in \mathcal{F}_s\}.$$

If $P \in \mathbb{P}_0$, then $S$ is a $P$-martingale (with respect to $\mathcal{F}$) if and only if $E_P(X) = 0$ for all $X \in L(\mathcal{F}, S)$. If $P \in \mathbb{P}$ but $P \notin \mathbb{P}_0$, it looks natural to *define* $S$ a $P$-martingale in case $E_P(X) = 0$ for all $X \in L(\mathcal{F}, S)$.

Thus, the process $S$ is a martingale under the probability $P$ if and only if $E_P(X) = 0$ for each $X$ in a suitable linear space $L(\mathcal{F}, S)$. Basing on this fact, given *any* linear space $L$ of bounded random variables, $P$ is called a martingale probability whenever $E_P(X) = 0$ for all $X \in L$.

Existence of EMFA's is investigated in [5]. The main results are recalled in Subsection 2.2. Here, we try to motivate EMFA's and we describe the content of this note.

Quoting from [5], we list some reasons for dealing with EMFA's. As usual, a $\sigma$-additive EMFA is called *equivalent martingale measure* (EMM).

(i) Dating from de Finetti, the finitely additive theory of probability is well founded and developed, even if not prevailing. Finitely additive probabilities can be always extended to the power set and have a solid motivation in terms of coherence. Also, there are problems which can not be solved in the usual countably additive setting, while admit a finitely additive solution. Examples are in conditional probability, convergence in distribution of non measurable random elements, Bayesian statistics, stochastic integration and the first digit problem. See e.g. [4] and references therein. Moreover, in the finitely additive approach, one can clearly use $\sigma$-additive probabilities. Merely, one is not obliged to do so.

(ii) Martingale probabilities play a role in various financial frameworks. Their economic motivations, however, do not depend on whether they are $\sigma$-additive or not. See e.g. Chapter 1 of [8]. In option pricing, for instance, EMFA's give arbitrage-free prices just as EMM's. Note also that many underlying ideas, in arbitrage price theory, were anticipated by de Finetti and Ramsey.

(iii) It may be that EMM's fail to exist and yet EMFA's are available. See Examples 1 and 5. In addition, existence of EMFA's can be given simple characterizations; see Theorems 2, 3 and 4.

(iv) Each EMFA $P$ can be written as $P = \alpha P_1 + (1 - \alpha) Q$, where $\alpha \in [0, 1)$, $P_1 \in \mathbb{P}$ is purely finitely additive and $Q \in \mathbb{P}_0$ is equivalent to $P_0$; see Theorem 2. Even if one does not like finitely additive probabilities, when EMM's do not exist one may be content with an EMFA $P$ whose $\alpha$ is small enough. In other terms, a fraction $\alpha$ of the total mass must be sacrificed for having equivalent martingale probabilities, but the approximation may look acceptable for small $\alpha$. An extreme situation of this type is exhibited in Example 5. In such example, EMM's do not exist and yet, for each fixed $\epsilon > 0$, there is an EMFA $P$ with $\alpha \le \epsilon$.

In connection with points (iii)-(iv) above, and to make the notion of EMFA more transparent, we report a simple example from [5].

**Example 1. (Example 7 of [5]).** Let $\Omega = \{1, 2, \ldots\}$, $\mathcal{A}$ the power set of $\Omega$, and $P_0\{\omega\} = 2^{-\omega}$ for all $\omega \in \Omega$. For each $n \geq 0$, define $A_n = \{n+1, n+2, \ldots\}$. Define also $L = L(\mathcal{F}, S)$, where

$$\mathcal{F}_0 = \{\emptyset, \Omega\}, \quad \mathcal{F}_n = \sigma(\{1\}, \ldots, \{n\}), \quad S_0 = 1, \quad \text{and}$$

$$S_n(\omega) = \frac{1}{2^n} I_{A_n}(\omega) + \frac{\omega^2 + 2\omega + 2}{2^\omega} (1 - I_{A_n}(\omega)) \quad \text{for all } \omega \in \Omega.$$

The process $S$ has been introduced in [1]. Loosely speaking, $\omega$ could be regarded as a (finite) stopping time and $S_n(\omega)$ as a price at time $n$. Such a price falls by 50% at each time $n < \omega$. Instead, for $n \geq \omega$, the price is constant with respect to $n$ and depends on $\omega$ only.

If $P \in \mathbb{P}$ is a martingale probability, then

$$1 = E_P(S_0) = E_P(S_n) = \frac{P(A_n)}{2^n} + \sum_{j=1}^n \frac{j^2 + 2j + 2}{2^j} P\{j\}.$$

Letting $n = 1$ in the above equation yields $P\{1\} = 1/4$. By induction, one obtains $2 P\{n\} = 1/n(n+1)$ for all $n \geq 1$. Since $\sum_{n=1}^\infty P\{n\} = 1/2$, then $P \notin \mathbb{P}_0$. Thus, EMM's do not exist. Instead, EMFA's are available. Define in fact

$$P = \frac{P_1 + Q}{2}$$

where $P_1$ and $Q$ are probabilities on $\mathcal{A}$ such that $P_1\{n\} = 0$ and $Q\{n\} = 1/n(n+1)$ for all $n \geq 1$. (Note that $Q \in \mathbb{P}_0$ while $P_1$ is purely finitely additive). Clearly, $P \sim P_0$. Given $X \in L(\mathcal{F}, S)$, since $S_{n+1} = S_n$ on $A_n^c$, one obtains

$$X = \sum_{j=0}^k b_j I_{A_j} (S_{j+1} - S_j) \quad \text{for some } k \geq 0 \text{ and } b_0, \ldots, b_k \in \mathbb{R}.$$

Since $A_j = \{j+1\} \cup A_{j+1}$ and $S_{j+1} - S_j = -1/2^{j+1}$ on $A_{j+1}$, it follows that

$$E_{P_1}(X) = \sum_{j=0}^k \frac{b_j}{2^{j+1}} \left\{ ((j+1)^2 + 2(j+1)) P_1\{j+1\} - P_1(A_{j+1}) \right\} = - \sum_{j=0}^k \frac{b_j}{2^{j+1}}$$

and

$$E_Q(X) = \sum_{j=0}^k \frac{b_j}{2^{j+1}} \left\{ ((j+1)^2 + 2(j+1)) Q\{j+1\} - Q(A_{j+1}) \right\}$$

$$= \sum_{j=0}^k \frac{b_j}{2^{j+1}} \left\{ \frac{(j+1)^2 + 2(j+1)}{(j+1)(j+2)} - \frac{1}{(j+2)} \right\} = \sum_{j=0}^k \frac{b_j}{2^{j+1}}.$$

Therefore $E_P(X) = 0$, that is, $P$ is an EMFA.

This note investigates EMFA's when the reference probability measure $P_0$ is *atomic*. There are essentially two reasons for focusing on atomic $P_0$. One is that $P_0$ is actually atomic in several real situations. The other reason is a version of the FTAP (fundamental theorem of asset pricing). Indeed, when $P_0$ is atomic, existence of EMFA's amounts to

$$\overline{L - L_\infty^+} \cap L_\infty^+ = \{0\} \quad \text{with the closure in the norm-topology;}$$

we refer to Subsection 2.2 for details.

Three results are obtained for atomic $P_0$. First, existence of EMFA's is given a new characterization (Theorem 4). Such a characterization looks practically more useful than the existing ones. Second, the extreme situation mentioned in point (iv) is realized (Example 5). Third, the following problem is addressed (Theorem 6 and Example 8). Suppose EMFA's exist and fix a bounded random variable $Y$. If

$$E_P(Y) = y \quad \text{for some } y \in \mathbb{R} \text{ and all EMFA's } P,$$

does $Y - y$ belong to the closure of $L$ in some topology ? Or else, if $E_P(Y) \geq 0$ for all EMFA's $P$, can $Y$ be approximated by random variables of the form $X + Z$ with $X \in L$ and $Z \geq 0$ ? Indeed, with EMM's instead of EMFA's, these questions are classical; see [6], [9], [10], [13] and references therein. For instance, if $Y$ is regarded as a contingent claim, $E_P(Y) = y$ for all EMFA's $P$ means that $y$ is the unique arbitrage-free price of $Y$. Similarly $Y - y \in \overline{L}$, with the closure in a suitable topology, can be seen as a weak form of completeness for the underlying market.

A last note deals with the assumption that $L$ consists of *bounded* random variables. Even if strong, such an assumption can not be dropped. In fact, while de Finetti's coherence principle (our main tool) can be extended to unbounded random variables, the extensions are very far from granting an integral representation; see [2], [3] and references therein.

## 2    Known Results

### 2.1    Notation

For each essentially bounded random variable $X$, we let

$$\text{essup}(X) = \inf\{a \in \mathbb{R} : P_0(X > a) = 0\} = \inf\{\sup_A X : A \in \mathcal{A}, P_0(A) = 1\},$$

$$\|X\| = \|X\|_\infty = \text{essup}(|X|).$$

Given $P, T \in \mathbb{P}$, we write $P \ll T$ if $P(A) = 0$ whenever $A \in \mathcal{A}$ and $T(A) = 0$, and $P \sim T$ if $P \ll T$ and $T \ll P$. We also write

$$E_P(X) = \int X \, dP$$

whenever $P \in \mathbb{P}$ and $X$ is a real bounded random variable.

A probability $P \in \mathbb{P}$ is *pure* if it does not have a non trivial $\sigma$-additive part. Precisely, if $P$ is pure and $\Gamma$ is a $\sigma$-additive measure such that $0 \leq \Gamma \leq P$, then $\Gamma = 0$. By a result of Yosida-Hewitt, any $P \in \mathbb{P}$ can be written as $P = \alpha P_1 + (1 - \alpha) Q$ where $\alpha \in [0, 1]$, $P_1 \in \mathbb{P}$ is pure (unless $\alpha = 0$) and $Q \in \mathbb{P}_0$.

A $P_0$-*atom* is a set $A \in \mathcal{A}$ with $P_0(A) > 0$ and $P_0(\cdot \mid A) \in \{0, 1\}$; $P_0$ is *atomic* if there is a countable partition $A_1, A_2, \ldots$ of $\Omega$ such that $A_n$ is a $P_0$-atom for all $n$.

## 2.2   Existence of EMFA's

We next state a couple of results from [5]. Let

$$M = \{P \in \mathbb{P} : P \sim P_0 \text{ and } E_P(X) = 0 \text{ for all } X \in L\}$$

be the set of EMFA's. Note that $M \cap \mathbb{P}_0$ is the set of EMM's.

**Theorem 2.** *Each $P \in M$ admits the representation $P = \alpha P_1 + (1-\alpha) Q$ where $\alpha \in [0, 1)$, $P_1 \in \mathbb{P}$ is pure (unless $\alpha = 0$), $Q \in \mathbb{P}_0$ and $Q \sim P_0$. Moreover, $M \neq \emptyset$ if and only if*

$$E_Q(X) \leq k \, \mathrm{essup}(-X), \quad X \in L, \tag{1}$$

*for some constant $k > 0$ and $Q \in \mathbb{P}_0$ with $Q \sim P_0$. In particular, under condition (1), one obtains*

$$\frac{k P_1 + Q}{k + 1} \in M \quad \text{for some } P_1 \in \mathbb{P}.$$

In addition to characterizing $M \neq \emptyset$, Theorem 2 provides some information on the weight $1 - \alpha$ of the $\sigma$-additive part $Q$ of an EMFA. Indeed, under (1), there is $P \in M$ such that $\alpha \leq k/(k + 1)$. On the other hand, condition (1) is not very helpful in real problems, for it requires to have $Q$ in advance. A characterization independent of $Q$ would be more effective. We will come back to this point in the next section.

We next turn to separation theorems. Write $U - V = \{u - v : u \in U, v \in V\}$ whenever $U, V$ are subsets of a linear space. Let $L_p = L_p(\Omega, \mathcal{A}, P_0)$ for all $p \in [1, \infty]$. We regard $L$ as a subspace of $L_\infty$ and we let $L_\infty^+ = \{X \in L_\infty : X \geq 0\}$. Since $L_\infty$ is the dual of $L_1$, it can be equipped with the weak-star topology $\sigma(L_\infty, L_1)$. Thus, $\sigma(L_\infty, L_1)$ is the topology on $L_\infty$ generated by the maps $X \mapsto E_{P_0}(X Y)$ for all $Y \in L_1$.

By a result of Kreps [11] (see also [12]) existence of EMM's amounts to

$$\overline{L - L_\infty^+} \cap L_\infty^+ = \{0\} \quad \text{with the closure in } \sigma(L_\infty, L_1).$$

On the other hand, it is usually argued that the norm topology on $L^\infty$ is geometrically more transparent than $\sigma(L_\infty, L_1)$, and results involving the former are often viewed as superior. Thus, a (natural) question is what happens if the closure is taken in the norm-topology.

**Theorem 3.** $\mathbb{M} \neq \emptyset$ *if and only if*

$$L_\infty^+ \subset U \cup \{0\} \quad and \quad (L - L_\infty^+) \cap U = \emptyset$$
*for some norm-open convex set* $U \subset L_\infty$.

*In particular, a necessary condition for* $\mathbb{M} \neq \emptyset$ *is*

$$\overline{L - L_\infty^+} \cap L_\infty^+ = \{0\} \quad \text{with the closure in the norm-topology.} \qquad (2)$$

*If* $P_0$ *is atomic, condition (2) is sufficient for* $\mathbb{M} \neq \emptyset$ *as well.*

Note that, in the particular case where $L$ is a suitable class of stochastic integrals (in a fixed time interval and driven by a fixed semi-martingale), condition (2) agrees with the *no free lunch with vanishing risk* condition of [7]. See also [8]. The main difference with [7] is that, in this note, $L$ is an arbitrary subspace of $L_\infty$.

It is still open whether condition (2) implies $\mathbb{M} \neq \emptyset$ for arbitrary $P_0 \in \mathbb{P}_0$. However, (2) is equivalent to $\mathbb{M} \neq \emptyset$ when $P_0$ is atomic. This is a first reason for paying special attention to the latter case. A second (and more important) reason is that $P_0$ is actually atomic in various real situations. Accordingly, in the sequel we focus on the atomic case.

## 3   New Results in Case of Atomic $P_0$

In this section, $P_0$ *is atomic*. Everything is well understood if $P_0$ has finitely many atoms only (such a case can be reduced to that of $\Omega$ finite). Thus, the $P_0$-atoms are assumed to be *infinitely many*. Let $A_1, A_2, \ldots$ be a countable partition of $\Omega$ such that $A_n$ is a $P_0$-atom for each $n$. Also, $X|A_n$ denotes the a.s.-constant value of the random variable $X$ on $A_n$.

Theorem 2 gives a general characterization of existence of EMFA's. As already noted, however, a characterization not involving $Q$ would be more usable in real problems. In case $P_0$ is atomic, one such characterization is actually available.

**Theorem 4.** *Suppose that, for each $n \geq 1$, there is a constant $k_n > 0$ such that*

$$X|A_n \leq k_n \, essup(-X) \quad for \; each \; X \in L. \qquad (3)$$

*Letting* $\beta = \inf_n k_n$, *for each* $\alpha \in \left(\frac{\beta}{1+\beta}, 1\right)$ *one obtains*

$$\alpha \, P_1 + (1 - \alpha) \, Q \in \mathbb{M} \quad for \; some \; P_1 \in \mathbb{P} \; and \; Q \in \mathbb{P}_0 \; with \; Q \sim P_0.$$

*Moreover, condition (3) is necessary for* $\mathbb{M} \neq \emptyset$ *(so that* $\mathbb{M} \neq \emptyset$ *if and only if (3) holds).*

*Proof.* Suppose first $\mathbb{M} \neq \emptyset$. Fix $P \in \mathbb{M}$, $n \geq 1$ and $X \in L$. Since $E_P(X) = 0$,

$$P(A_n) \, X|A_n \leq P(A_n) \, X^+|A_n \leq E_P(X^+)$$
$$= E_P(X) + E_P(X^-) = E_P(X^-) \leq essup(-X).$$

Therefore, condition (3) holds with $k_n = 1/P(A_n)$. Conversely, suppose (3) holds. Fix any sequence $(q_n : n \geq 1)$ satisfying $q_n > 0$ for all $n$, $\sum_n q_n = 1$ and $\sum_n (q_n/k_n) < \infty$. For each $A \in \mathcal{A}$, define

$$I(A) = \{n : P_0(A \cap A_n) > 0\} \quad \text{and} \quad Q(A) = \frac{\sum_{n \in I(A)}(q_n/k_n)}{\sum_n (q_n/k_n)}.$$

Then, $Q \in \mathbb{P}_0$ and $Q \sim P_0$. Also, for each $X \in L$, condition (3) yields

$$E_Q(X) = \sum_n Q(A_n) X | A_n \leq \operatorname{essup}(-X) \sum_n Q(A_n) k_n = \frac{\operatorname{essup}(-X)}{\sum_n (q_n/k_n)}.$$

Thus, condition (1) holds with $k = \{\sum_n (q_n/k_n)\}^{-1}$. By Theorem 2, there is $P_1 \in \mathbb{P}$ such that $(k\, P_1 + Q)/(k+1) \in \mathbb{M}$. Finally, fix $\alpha \in (\frac{\beta}{1+\beta}, 1)$. Condition (3) remains true if the $k_n$ are replaced by arbitrary constants $k_n^* \geq k_n$. Thus, it can be assumed $\sup_n k_n = \infty$. In this case, it suffices to note that

$$k = \frac{1}{\sum_n (q_n/k_n)} = \frac{\alpha}{1-\alpha}$$

for a suitable choice of $(q_n : n \geq 1)$.

Next example has been discussed in point (iv) of Section 1.

**Example 5.** Let $\Omega = \{1, 2, \ldots\}$. Take $\mathcal{A}$ to be the power set and $P_0\{n\} = 2^{-n}$ for all $n \in \Omega$. Define $T = (2P_0 + P^* - \delta_1)/2$, where $P^* \in \mathbb{P}$ is any pure probability and $\delta_1$ the point mass at 1. Since $P^*\{n\} = 0$ for all $n \in \Omega$, then $T\{1\} = 0$ and $T \in \mathbb{P}$. Let $B = \{2, 3, \ldots\}$ and define $L$ to be the linear space generated by $\{I_A - T(A) I_B : A \subset B\}$. If $P \in \mathbb{P}$ is a martingale probability, then

$$P\{n, n+1, \ldots\} = T\{n, n+1, \ldots\} P(B) \geq \frac{P(B)}{2} \quad \text{for all } n > 1.$$

Thus, $P \notin \mathbb{P}_0$ as far as $P(B) > 0$, so that $\mathbb{M} \cap \mathbb{P}_0 = \emptyset$. On the other hand, $P_\epsilon := \epsilon T + (1 - \epsilon) \delta_1 \in \mathbb{M}$ for all $\epsilon \in (0, 1)$. In fact, $P_\epsilon\{n\} > 0$ for all $n \in \Omega$ (so that $P_\epsilon \sim P_0$) and

$$E_{P_\epsilon}(X) = \epsilon\, E_T(X) + (1 - \epsilon)\, X(1) = 0 \quad \text{for all } X \in L.$$

To sum up, in this example, EMM's do not exist and yet, for each $\epsilon > 0$, there is $P \in \mathbb{M}$ such that $\alpha(P) \leq \epsilon$. Here, $\alpha(P)$ denotes the weight of the pure part of $P$, in the sense that $P = \alpha(P) P_1 + (1 - \alpha(P)) Q$ for some pure $P_1 \in \mathbb{P}$ and $Q \in \mathbb{P}_0$ with $Q \sim P_0$.

The rest of this note is concerned with the following problem. Suppose $\mathbb{M} \neq \emptyset$ and fix $Y \in L_\infty$. If $E_P(Y) = y$ for some $y \in \mathbb{R}$ and all $P \in \mathbb{M}$, does $Y - y$ belong to the closure of $L$ in some reasonable topology ? Or else, if $E_P(Y) \geq 0$ for all $P \in \mathbb{M}$, can $Y$ be approximated by random variables of the form $X + Z$ with

$X \in L$ and $Z \in L_\infty^+$ ? Up to replacing EMFA's with EMM's, questions of this type are classical; see [6], [9], [10], [13] and references therein. Indeed, regarding $Y$ as a contingent claim, $E_P(Y) = y$ for all $P \in \mathbb{M}$ means that $y$ is the unique arbitrage-free price of $Y$. Similarly $Y - y \in \overline{L}$, with the closure in a suitable topology, can be seen as a weak form of completeness for the underlying market.

In what follows, $L_\infty$ is equipped with the norm topology. Accordingly, for each $H \subset L_\infty$, $\overline{H}$ denotes the closure of $H$ in the norm topology.

**Theorem 6.** *Suppose* $\mathbb{M} \neq \emptyset$ *and fix* $Y \in L_\infty$. *Then,*

*(a)* $Y \in \overline{L - L_\infty^+} \iff E_P(Y) \leq 0$ *for each* $P \in \mathbb{M}$,

*(b)* $Y \in \bigcap_{P \in \mathbb{M}} \overline{L}^P \iff E_P(Y) = 0$ *for each* $P \in \mathbb{M}$,

*where* $\overline{L}^P$ *denotes the closure of* $L$ *in the* $L_1(P)$*-topology. In addition, if* $E_P(Y) = 0$ *for each* $P \in \mathbb{M}$*, then* $X_n \xrightarrow{a.s.} Y$ *for some sequence* $(X_n) \subset L$.

*Proof.* First note that "$\implies$" is obvious in both (a) and (b). Suppose $Y \notin \overline{L - L_\infty^+}$. Fix $A \in \mathcal{A}$ with $P_0(A) > 0$ and define

$$U = \overline{L - L_\infty^+}, \quad V = \{\alpha I_A + (1 - \alpha)Y : 0 \leq \alpha \leq 1\}.$$

Then, $U \cap V = \emptyset$. In fact, $I_A \notin U$ because of $\mathbb{M} \neq \emptyset$ and Theorem 3. If $\alpha I_A + (1 - \alpha)Y \in U$ for some $\alpha < 1$, there are $(X_n) \subset L$ and $(Z_n) \subset L_\infty^+$ such that $X_n - Z_n \xrightarrow{L_\infty} \alpha I_A + (1 - \alpha)Y$, which in turn implies

$$\frac{X_n - (Z_n + \alpha I_A)}{1 - \alpha} \xrightarrow{L_\infty} Y.$$

But this is a contradiction, as $Y \notin U$. Next, since $U$ and $V$ are convex and closed with $V$ compact, some linear (continuous) functional $\Phi : L_\infty \to \mathbb{R}$ satisfies

$$\inf_{f \in V} \Phi(f) > \sup_{f \in U} \Phi(f).$$

It is routine to verify that $\Phi$ is positive and $\Phi(1) > 0$. Hence, $\Phi(f) = \Phi(1) E_{P_A}(f)$ for all $f \in L_\infty$ and some $P_A \in \mathbb{P}$ with $P_A \ll P_0$. Since $L$ is a linear space and $\sup_{f \in L} \Phi(f) \leq \sup_{f \in U} \Phi(f) < \infty$, then $\Phi = 0$ on $L$. To sum up, $P_A$ satisfies $P_A \ll P_0$, $P_A(A) > 0$, $E_{P_A}(Y) > 0$, and $E_{P_A}(X) = 0$ for all $X \in L$. It follows that

$$P := \sum_n \frac{1}{2^n} P_{A_n} \in \mathbb{M} \quad \text{and} \quad E_P(Y) > 0.$$

This concludes the proof of (a). Suppose now that $E_P(Y) = 0$ for all $P \in \mathbb{M}$. By (a), there are sequences $(X_n) \subset L$ and $(Z_n) \subset L_\infty^+$ such that $X_n - Z_n \xrightarrow{L_\infty} Y$. For each $P \in \mathbb{M}$, since $Z_n \in L_\infty^+$ and $E_P(X_n) = E_P(Y) = 0$, one obtains

$$E_P|X_n - Y| \leq E_P|X_n - Z_n - Y| + E_P(Z_n)$$
$$= E_P|X_n - Z_n - Y| - E_P(X_n - Z_n - Y) \leq 2\|X_n - Z_n - Y\| \longrightarrow 0.$$

This proves (b). Finally, take $P \in \mathbb{M}$, say $P = \alpha P_1 + (1 - \alpha) Q$ where $\alpha \in [0, 1)$, $P_1 \in \mathbb{P}$, $Q \in \mathbb{P}_0$ and $Q \sim P_0$. Arguing as above,

$$E_Q(Z_n) \leq \frac{E_P(Z_n)}{1 - \alpha} \leq \frac{\|X_n - Z_n - Y\|}{1 - \alpha} \longrightarrow 0.$$

Thus, $Z_{n_j} \xrightarrow{a.s.} 0$ and $X_{n_j} = Z_{n_j} + (X_{n_j} - Z_{n_j}) \xrightarrow{a.s.} Y$ for some subsequence $(n_j)$.

As regards part (b) of Theorem 6, a question is whether $E_P(Y) = 0$ for all $P \in \mathbb{M}$ implies $Y \in \overline{L}$. We now prove that the answer is no. The following lemma is useful.

**Lemma 7.** *Let $P \in \mathbb{P}$. If $P \ll P_0$ and $P(A_n) = P_0(A_n)$ for all $n$, then $P = P_0$.*

*Proof.* Fix $A \in \mathcal{A}$ and $n \geq 1$. If $P_0(A \cap A_n) = 0$, then $P(A \cap A_n) = 0 = P_0(A \cap A_n)$. If $P_0(A \cap A_n) > 0$, then $P_0(A^c \cap A_n) = 0$, and thus

$$P(A \cap A_n) = P(A_n) = P_0(A_n) = P_0(A \cap A_n).$$

It follows that $P(A) \geq \sum_{i=1}^{n} P(A \cap A_i) = \sum_{i=1}^{n} P_0(A \cap A_i)$. As $n \to \infty$, one obtains $P(A) \geq P_0(A)$. Finally, taking complements yields $P = P_0$.

**Example 8.** Let $L$ be the linear space generated by $\{I_{A_n} - P_0(A_n) : n \geq 1\}$ and

$$Y = \frac{I_A}{P_0(A)} - \frac{I_{A^c}}{P_0(A^c)} \quad \text{where } A = \cup_{n=1}^{\infty} A_{2n}.$$

Each $P \in \mathbb{M}$ meets $P \ll P_0$ and $P(A_n) = P_0(A_n)$ for all $n$. Thus, Lemma 7 yields $\mathbb{M} = \{P_0\}$. Further, $E_{P_0}(Y) = 0$. However, $Y \notin \overline{L}$. Fix in fact $X \in L$. Since $X = x$ a.s. on the set $\left(\cup_{i=1}^{n} A_i\right)^c$, for some $n \geq 1$ and $x \in \mathbb{R}$, one obtains

$$\|Y - X\| = \sup_i |(Y - X)|A_i| \geq \sup_{i>n} |(Y - x)|A_i| \geq \frac{1}{P_0(A)} \wedge \frac{1}{P_0(A^c)}.$$

In Example 8, $\mathbb{M}$ is quite small (its cardinality is 1). It looks reasonable to conjecture that, with $\mathbb{M}$ large enough, $E_P(Y) = 0$ for all $P \in \mathbb{M}$ could imply $Y \in \overline{L}$. One more question is whether Theorem 6 holds in case $P_0$ is not atomic. Incidentally, this question is related to the open problem mentioned after Theorem 3: is condition (2) equivalent to $\mathbb{M} \neq \emptyset$ when $P_0$ is not atomic ?

# References

1. Back, K., Pliska, S.R.: On the fundamental theorem of asset pricing with an infinite state space. J. Math. Econ. 20, 1–18 (1991)
2. Berti, P., Rigo, P.: Integral representation of linear functionals on spaces of unbounded functions. Proc. Amer. Math. Soc. 128, 3251–3258 (2000)

3. Berti, P., Regazzini, E., Rigo, P.: Strong previsions of random elements. Statist. Methods Appl. 10, 11–28 (2001)
4. Berti, P., Rigo, P.: Convergence in distribution of non measurable random elements. Ann. Probab. 32, 365–379 (2004)
5. Berti, P., Pratelli, L., Rigo, P.: Finitely additive equivalent martingale measures. J. Theoret. Probab. (to appear, 2012), http://economia.unipv.it/pagp/pagine_personali/prigo/arb.pdf
6. Dalang, R., Morton, A., Willinger, W.: Equivalent martingale measures and no-arbitrage in stochastic securities market models. Stoch. and Stoch. Reports 29, 185–201 (1990)
7. Delbaen, F., Schachermayer, W.: A general version of the fundamental theorem of asset pricing. Math. Annalen 300, 463–520 (1994)
8. Delbaen, F., Schachermayer, W.: The mathematics of arbitrage. Springer (2006)
9. Harrison, J.M., Kreps, D.M.: Martingales and arbitrage in multiperiod securities markets. J. Econom. Theory 20, 381–408 (1979)
10. Jacka, S.D.: A martingale representation result and an application to incomplete financial markets. Math. Finance 2, 23–34 (1992)
11. Kreps, D.M.: Arbitrage and equilibrium in economics with infinitely many commodities. J. Math. Econ. 8, 15–35 (1981)
12. Stricker, C.: Arbitrage et lois de martingale. Ann. Inst. Henri Poincaré −Probab. et Statist. 26, 451–460 (1990)
13. Tehranchi, M.R.: Characterizing attainable claims: a new proof. J. Appl. Probab. 47, 1013–1022 (2010)

# A Further Empirical Study
# on the Over-Performance of Estimate Correction
# in Statistical Matching

Andrea Capotorti

Dip. Matematica e Informatica, Università di Perugia, Italy
capot@dmi.unipg.it

**Abstract.** Usual estimates inside the statistical matching problem can encounter consistency problem whenever logical constraints are present among categorical variables. Inconsistencies correction through a specific discrepancy minimization has already shown, in terms of goodness-of-fit test, an empirical over-performance with respect to originally coherent assessments. This behavior is now confirmed also with respect to distances between imprecise estimates and imprecise models represented by credal sets of joint distributions.

**Keywords:** Incoherence correction, statistical matching, informative distance, credal sets.

## 1 Introduction

Statistical matching deals with the problem of integration of different sources of information about a common population. Whenever the population is described through categorical variables, the problem reduces to estimate cell probabilities from different samples with some overlapping variables and some others observed only in one of them. Except to the case of forced assumptions like conditional independence, in general there are many joint distributions on the population compatible with the available partial information carried by the different samples. Hence any reasonable approach will lead to imprecise models, i.e. there will be more than one reasonable joint distribution over the population of interest. The main goal is to estimate such set of joint distributions, usually named *credal set* [10,13]. Because of the presence of the overlapping variables in the different samples, a quite natural way to obtain indirect estimation of the searched credal set is through assessments on the parameters represented by conditional and marginal probabilities. Nevertheless the aggregation of the assessments based on the different sources, even being separately consistent, could be jointly incoherent whenever in the underlaying population there is some logical constraint. For this, in previous contributions [2,3] the statistical matching problem has been embedded into a coherent framework to find reasonable incoherence correction procedures. Among the proposed methods, the corrected assessments obtained through the minimization of a specific discrepancy measure have shown goodness-of-fit performances even better than those obtained

S. Greco et al. (Eds.): IPMU 2012, Part IV, CCIS 300, pp. 124–133, 2012.

with assessments originally coherent. The doubt was that such result strongly depended on the comparison target: a unique known joint distribution for the underlying population. Since, as previously mentioned, the available information would never permit a precise estimation of the joint distribution, in this paper the performance comparison is done with respect to the more reasonable target of the credal set of joints compatible with the parameters really estimable, represented by conditional and marginal probabilities.

The study at the moment is limited to empirical results based on simulations from the prototypical example already used in the aforementioned papers. Nevertheless, in such a case comparisons between credal sets, based on both the purely geometrical Hausdorff and the uncertainty based Informative [1] distances, support the conjecture that the correction procedure adds to the estimates implicit information about the population otherwise absent in the separate assessments.

The rest of the paper is organized as follows: in the next Sec.2 a concise reformulation of the statistical matching inside the coherence setting is given. In the successive Sec.3 the incoherence correction method based on pseudo-distances minimization is reported, with particular emphasis about the discrepancy specifically tailored for the statistical matching. The generalization of the estimation target to credal sets of joint distributions is shortly motivated in Sec.4. Section 5 reports the empirical comparisons between credal sets, performed with both Hausdorff and Informative distances.

## 2   Statistical Matching in a Coherent Setting

We recall the problem of integration of sources in a coherent conditional probability setting. For the sake of simplicity we will limit here to the case of a population described simply by a triplet of categorical variables $(X, Y, Z)$ and of two sources of information, namely sample $A$ and sample $B$, providing observations about the couples $(X, Y)$ and $(X, Z)$, respectively. Obviously, results can be straightforwardly generalized to higher dimensions, both for the variables in the populations and for the number of separate sources of information, as already done in [12].

Let $(X, Y, Z)$ be categorical variables with respectively $I, J$, and $K$ finite categories index sets and denote by $(X_1, Y_1), ..., (X_{n_A}, Y_{n_A})$ and by $(X_{n_A+1}, Z_{n_A+1}), ..., (X_{n_A+n_B}, Z_{n_A+n_B})$ two random samples related to the two sources $A$ and $B$. We suppose that the two samples are related to the same population of interest and that $(X_1, Y_1), ..., (X_{n_A}, Y_{n_A})$ and $(X_{n_A+1}, Z_{n_A+1}), ..., (X_{n_A+n_B}, Z_{n_A+n_B})$ can be regarded exchangeable, as well as the sequence $X_1, ..., X_{n_A}, X_{n_A+1}, ..., X_{n_A+n_B}$. The following relevant population parameters, representing conditional probability values, can be assessed from the two files:

$$\boldsymbol{y}_{j|i} = P(Y = y_j | X = x_i), \quad \boldsymbol{z}_{k|i} = P(Z = z_k | X = x_i). \tag{1}$$

Moreover, by collecting data from both files we can elicit the marginal probability

$$\boldsymbol{x}_i = P(X = x_i). \tag{2}$$

Usually, such assessments are elicited through the (unconstrained) partial maximum likelihood evaluations, that in this case coincide with the following frequencies

$$y_{j|i} = \frac{n_A^{ij}}{n_A^{i\cdot}} \quad , \quad z_{k|i} = \frac{n_B^{ik}}{n_B^{i\cdot}} \quad , \quad x_i = \frac{n_A^{i\cdot} + n_B^{i\cdot}}{n_A + n_B} \quad , \tag{3}$$

where $n_A^{i\cdot}$ and $n_B^{i\cdot}$ represent the number of units expressing $(X = x_i)$ in samples A and B, respectively, while $n_A^{ij}$ stands for the number of units in A with $(X = x_i, Y = y_j)$ and $n_B^{ik}$ the number of units in B with $(X = x_i, Z = z_k)$.

Now, we should deal with the whole assessment $(\mathcal{E}, p)$ with

$$\mathcal{E} = \{(X = x_i),\ (Y = y_j | X = x_i),\ (Z = z_k | X = x_i)\}_{i \in I, j \in J, k \in K} \tag{4}$$

$$p = \{x_i, y_{j|i}, z_{k|i}\}_{i \in I, j \in J, k \in K} \quad .$$

Then, first of all we need to check its coherence, that means the compatibility of $p$ with a full conditional probability [5]. Such compatibility is equivalent to the existence of a suitable class of joint probability distributions $\alpha_1, \ldots, \alpha_l$ agreeing with $p$ (see for more details [4]). Note that coherence is crucial being a prerequisite for a sound inference, that means extension of $p$ to any new event, conditional or not.

In [12] it has been proved that when there is not any logical constraint between $Y$ and $Z$ for any given value $x_i$ of $X$ (i.e. for any $i \in I$, if $(X = x_i, Y = y_j) \neq \emptyset$ and $(X = x_i, Z = z_k) \neq \emptyset$, then $(X = x_i, Y = y_j, Z = z_k) \neq \emptyset$ for all $j \in J$ and $k \in K$) coherence is assured; otherwise, whenever there is some logical constraint between the variables $Y$ and $Z$, the coherence of the whole assessment (4) is not assured by the separate coherence of the single assessments (1-2). Note that the need of managing logical constraints arises from practical applications [6]. In [12] it has also been proved that incoherences must be localized among conditional events with the same conditioning event $(X = x_i)$. Hence, the check of coherence of the whole assessments (4) can be reduced to the check of coherence for sub-assessments

$$\{y_{j|i}, z_{k|i} : \text{for a given } i \text{ and any } j \in J, k \in K\} . \tag{5}$$

Since the check of coherence is in general an NP-hard problem, its segmentation in several subproblems is a great advantage.

Thus, it is possible to proceed in two ways: a supervised procedure, where not coherent sub-assessments of type (5) are detected and attention is focused only on them; or a unsupervised approach that adjusts the whole assessment (4).

In any case, adjustment can be performed by finding coherent estimates that derive from the minimization of some pseudo-distance, as shown in the next section.

## 3   Removing Inconsistencies in Statistical Matching

Estimate correction has been already studied, but this approach does not seem suitable in the context of statistical matching because of the lack of information due to the fact that $Y$ and $Z$ are not jointly observed, so the prior distribution cannot be updated and the likelihood function has a flat ridge (as already noted in [11]). A possible correction method is to find coherent assessments as "close" as possible to the available information represented by the whole elicitation (4). This approach implies the choice of some pseudo-distance. Given two probability assessments $\boldsymbol{p} = [p_1, \ldots, p_n]$ and $\boldsymbol{q} = [q_1, \ldots, q_n]$ on $\mathcal{E}$, where hence $n$ represents now the cardinality of $\mathcal{E}$, the most widely adopted divergencies among them are

$$L1(\boldsymbol{p}, \boldsymbol{q}) = \sum_{i=1}^{n} |q_i - p_i|, \tag{6}$$

$$L2(\boldsymbol{p}, \boldsymbol{q}) = \sum_{i=1}^{n} (q_i - p_i)^2, \tag{7}$$

$$KL(\boldsymbol{p}, \boldsymbol{q}) = \sum_{i=1}^{n} (q_i \ln(q_i/p_i) - q_i + p_i). \tag{8}$$

$L1$ and $L2$ are usual metric distances, endowed with all their geometric properties, but until now they remain without an intuitive probabilistic interpretation for conditional assessments. $KL$ is the so-called logarithmic Bregman divergence and, in the unconditional case, it is deeply used for its information theoretic properties. In fact $KL(p, q) = d_f(q, p)$, where $d_f(q, p)$ is the (generalized) Kullback-Leibler divergence or I-divergence, however in some cases it presents some unpleasant situation since it is based on a scoring rule which takes into account only the events which occur and not those which do not occur.

Note that $L1$, $L2$ and $KL$ homogenously operate on the whole domain $\mathcal{E}$, so that correction of $\boldsymbol{p}$ through their minimizations would induce changes also on the marginal assessments $\{x_i\}_{i \in I}$ that, being surely coherent, could be valuable to avoid to change. Hence, to encompass this need and to provide a tool that could more specifically deal with conditional assessments, recently in [2] the following modified discrepancy (9) has been introduced:

$$\Delta_{mix}(\boldsymbol{p}, \{\boldsymbol{\alpha}_i\}_i) = \sum_i x_i \left[ \sum_j \left( q_{j|i}^{\alpha_i} \ln \frac{q_{j|i}^{\alpha_i}}{y_{j|i}} + (1 - q_{j|i}^{\alpha_i}) \ln \frac{(1 - q_{j|i}^{\alpha_i})}{(1 - y_{j|i})} \right) + \right.$$
$$\left. + \sum_k \left( q_{k|i}^{\alpha_i} \ln \frac{q_{k|i}^{\alpha_i}}{z_{k|i}} + (1 - q_{k|i}^{\alpha_i}) \ln \frac{(1 - q_{k|i}^{\alpha_i})}{(1 - z_{k|i})} \right) \right]. \tag{9}$$

For any $i \in I$, each probability distribution $\alpha_i$ on the sample space spanned by $(Y = y_j)|(X = x_i)$ and $(Z = z_k)|(X = x_i)$ should fulfill the normalizing condition $\alpha_i(X = x_i) = x_i$, and generates the conditional probabilities

$$q_{j|i}^{\alpha_i} = \frac{\alpha_i(X = x_i, Y = y_j)}{\alpha_i(X = x_i)} \qquad q_{k|i}^{\alpha_i} = \frac{\alpha_i(X = x_i, Z = z_k)}{\alpha_i(X = x_i)}. \tag{10}$$

Note that the generated assessment $\boldsymbol{q} = \{x_i, q_{j|i}^{\alpha_i}, q_{k|i}^{\alpha_i}\}_{i,j,k}$ is surely coherent (see e.g. [12]).

Discrepancy $\Delta_{mix}$ derives from the adoption of a specific scoring rule that is an extension to partial and conditional probability assessments of the "total-log" for probability distributions proposed by Lad in [9, p.355] and it has been considered in [7] as an example of equivalence between the coherence of a partial conditional probability $p$ and its admissibility with respect to a proper scoring rule.

In order to correct an estimation $p$ we need to look for the assessment $q_p$, that is solution of the following nonlinear optimization program, with $\delta(p, q)$ any pseudo-distance (if $\delta \equiv \Delta_{mix}$ then $q$ are those induced by $\{\alpha_i\}_i$ as in (10)):

$$\min_q \delta(p, q). \tag{11}$$

Note that minimization of discrepancy (9) will leave, as required, unchanged the marginal values $\{x_i\}_{i \in I}$. This characteristic differs such specialized discrepancy from the other pseudo-distances, so that its use in the unsupervised approach let it actually work as in a supervised context.

## 4   On the Estimate Target

Going back to the primary statistical matching problem, through the two samples $A$ and $B$ we can evaluate the whole assessment $(\mathcal{E}, p)$ as in (4), and if $p$ would result not coherent it can be replaced by a corrected assessment $q_p$ solution of (11). Let us denote with $e$ the final coherent assessment on $\mathcal{E}$, i.e. $e \equiv p$ if $p$ is coherent, $e \equiv q_p$ otherwise. As already sketched in the introduction, the goal is to have an estimate of the joint distribution over the sample space $\Omega$ of $(X, Y, Z)$ by profiting from $e$. Because of the coherence of $e$, it is possible to extend it (for details refer again to [4, §13]) to each population cell, obtaining a credal set of admissible joint distributions. In our context, the bounds of the coherent extension can be analytically determined for any $(x_i, y_j, z_k) \in \Omega$:

$$\max\{y_{j|i}x_i + z_{k|i}x_i - 1, 0\} \leq P(X = x_i, Y = y_j, Z = z_k) \leq \min\{y_{j|i}x_i, z_{k|i}x_i\}. \tag{12}$$

Note that any single value inside these bounds would be coherent for an extension of $e$ to a single possible event $(X = x_i, Y = y_j, Z = z_k)$, while the whole set of bounds (12) for all $(x_i, y_j, z_k) \in \Omega$ represent just a part of the constraints. In fact, not all joint distribution with values inside bounds (12) are automatically coherent, since coherence will mainly depend on the numerical constraints induced by $e$. The credal set of probability distributions $\beta$ both fulfilling (12) and compatible with $e$ will be denoted as $\mathcal{K}_e$ and represents an imprecise estimate of the joint distribution of the population of interest.

To compare the performances of the estimates stemming from the different incoherence correction methods, in [2,3] chi-squared goodness-of-fit tests have been performed among the estimated joint distributions of the various credal sets $\mathcal{K}_e$ against a known real joint distribution $\alpha$. From these comparisons it emerges that $L2$ and $\Delta_{mix}$ minimizations perform better than the others corrections techniques, and that the latter could be preferred because of its implicit supervised behavior. Quite surprisingly estimations based on corrected assessments, i.e. with $e \equiv q_p$, show an over-performance with respect to those based on originally coherent assessments, i.e. with $e \equiv p$. A reasonable doubt is that such phenomenon could be influenced by the non-homogeneity between the imprecise estimates, represented by the credal sets $\mathcal{K}_e$, and the precise target, represented by the known joint distribution $\alpha$. Hence we extend now such comparisons by taking as reference the imprecise target $\mathcal{K}_o$ represented by the credal set of all the joint distributions compatible with marginal and conditional probabilities $\pi$ on $\mathcal{E}$ induced by the known distribution $\alpha$. Because of the homogeneity of the terms under comparisons, it is possible now to test the goodness of the estimates by computing some kind of distance between the estimated credal set $\mathcal{K}_e$ and the original one $\mathcal{K}_o$. Empirical results of such comparisons will be reported in the next section by continuing the simulations study presented in [2,3].

## 5   Empirical Comparison of Credal Sets

We report the aforementioned prototypical example already used to compare the goodness-of-fit of credal sets $\mathcal{K}_e$. We have a finite population described through three categorical variables $(X, Y, Z)$, with $I = \{1,2\}, J = \{1,2,3\}, K = \{1,2,3\}$, distributed over the 12-dimensional sample space $\Omega$ as in Table 1, where the $(-)$ represent the impossible cells implied by the logical constraints

$$(Z = z_1) \wedge ((Y = y_1) \vee (Y = y_2)) = \emptyset \quad , \quad (Z = z_2) \wedge (Y = y_1) = \emptyset. \quad (13)$$

From each couple of samples A and B, as described in Sec. 2, we can obtain an assessment $p$ on

$$\begin{aligned}
\mathcal{E} = \{&(X = x_1), (X = x_2), (Y = y_1)|(X = x_1), (Y = y_2|X = x_1), (Y = y_3|X = x_1), \\
&(Z = z_1|X = x_1), (Z = z_2|X = x_1), (Z = z_3|X = x_1), \\
&(Y = y_1|X = x_2), (Y = y_2|X = x_2), (Y = y_3|X = x_2), \\
&(Z = z_1|X = x_2), (Z = z_2|X = x_2), (Z = z_3|X = x_2)\}
\end{aligned} \quad (14)$$

**Table 1.** Finite population with $(X, Y, Z)$ endowed with logical constraints (-)

| X Y | Z | $z_1$ | $z_2$ | $z_3$ |
|---|---|---|---|---|
| $x_1$ $y_1$ | | (-) | (-) | 116 |
| $y_2$ | | (-) | 26 | 5 |
| $y_3$ | | 54 | 108 | 25 |
| | | | | |
| $x_2$ $y_1$ | | (-) | (-) | 277 |
| $y_2$ | | (-) | 65 | 1 |
| $y_3$ | | 321 | 1 | 1 |

In [2] there were simulated 1000 couples of samples $A$ and $B$, each one with dimensions $n_A = 1148$ and $n_B = 1165$, respectively, obtaining 565 not coherent assessments $\boldsymbol{p}$. Incoherence corrections were performed by minimizing the four pseudo-distances reported in Sec. 3. For each associated credal set $\mathcal{K}_e$ there were computed minimal chi-squared goodness-of-fit values, obtaining the results reported in Fig. 1. Notice the over-performance of estimates induced by corrected

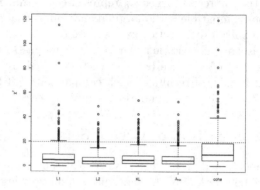

**Fig. 1.** Minimal $\chi^2$ "goodnes-of-fit" for credal sets induced by pseudo-distances minimizations "L1", "L2", "KL", "$\Delta_{mix}$" and coherent frequencies (label "cohe") estimates. The dashed line corresponds to the 95% confidence threshold.

assessments with respect to those induced by the not changed ones and the best behavior of the minimization of $L2$ and $\Delta_{mix}$ with respect to the other pseudo-distances. We will privilege $\Delta_{mix}$ for its already noted implicit capacity of sub-domains localization where changes are needed.

As already depicted in Sec.4, we can extend the study with the comparisons between credal sets. For computational complexity reasons, we will limit to consider corrected assessments obtained through the $\Delta_{mix}$ minimization and we will randomly select 20 of such $\boldsymbol{q_p}^s$ and other 20 of originally coherent assessments $\boldsymbol{p}^s$, among the 1000 simulated. Consequently, in the following the exponent $s = 1, \ldots, 20$ will refer to the associated selected simulation. We have hence to compare the credal set $K_o$, derived from the coherent extension of the probabilities on $\mathcal{E}$ stemming from the cell counts of Tab. 1, against each one of the 20 credal sets $K_{\boldsymbol{q_p}^s}$, $s = 1, \ldots, 20$, extensions of the corrected estimates, and against the other 20 credal sets $K_{\boldsymbol{p}^s}$, $s = 1, \ldots, 20$, extensions of the originally coherent assessments.

Comparisons between credal sets can be done by measuring some kind of distance, and in the next subsections we will propose two of them.

## 5.1   Hausdorff Distance

Since the credal sets $K_o$ and $K_{e^s}$, where $e^s \equiv \boldsymbol{q_p}^s$ or $e^s \equiv \boldsymbol{p}^s$, are convex sets, a first comparison of the "goodness" of the estimations can be performed by computing the different Hausdorff distances

$$d_H(K_o, K_{e^s}) = \max\{h(K_o, K_{e^s}), h(K_{e^s}, K_o)\} \tag{15}$$

where $h(K_1, K_2)$ denotes the asymmetric Hausdorff difference defined as

$$h(K_1, K_2) = \max_{\zeta \in K_1} \min_{\eta \in K_2} L2(\zeta, \eta). \tag{16}$$

As proved e.g. in [8], distributions for which (16) occurs are always one on the vertices and the other on the borders of the convex sets. Hence, because of our implicit representation of credal sets through constraints (12), to operationally compute the distances (15) we firstly perform the following 48 non-linear optimization problems

$$\min_{\eta} L2(\overline{\zeta}, \eta), \tag{17}$$

where each distribution $\overline{\zeta}$ is coerced to fit exactly with a specific extreme cell probability (12) characterizing one of the two credal sets and to be compatible with the associated assessment ($o$ or $e^s$), while the other distribution $\eta$ varies in the second credal set. Hence we have two optimization problems, one whenever $\overline{\zeta} \in K_o$ and an other whenever $\overline{\zeta} \in K_{e^s}$, for each extreme in (12). Since we have a 12-dimensional sample space $\Omega$, and consequently 24 extremes on bounds (12), we end up with 48 values whose maximization gives us the final Hausdorff distance.

In this way we obtain a first group of 20 Hausdorff distances computed between $K_o$ and each credal set $K_{q_{p^s}}$, $s = 1, \ldots, 20$, extension of one corrected estimate, and an other group of 20 Hausdorff distances computed between $K_o$ and each credal set $K_{p^s}$, $s = 1, \ldots, 20$, extension of one originally coherent assessment. The two separate distributions of these distances are described with the boxplots in Fig. 2(left). It is evident a more concentrated and systematically closer to the zero distribution for the distances of the credal sets induced by the corrected estimates with respect to those induced by the originally coherent ones. This confirms, from a geometrical point of view, the over-performance of the corrected estimates already observed with the goodness-of-fit test.

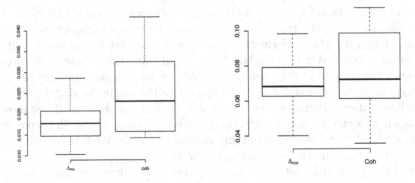

**Fig. 2.** Distributions of the Hausdorff (left) and Informative (right) distances between credal sets

## 5.2  Informative Distance

Differently, we can quantify the difference of information based uncertainty between the credal set $K_o$ and the different $K_{e^s}$ with the Informative distance proposed in [1]:

$$\Theta(K_o, K_{e^s}) = 1 - \min\{\phi(K_o, K_{e^s}), \phi(K_{e^s}, K_o)\} \qquad (18)$$

with $\phi(\cdot, \cdot)$ being the inclusion index between compatible non-degenerated credal sets $K_1$ and $K_2$

$$\phi(K_1, K_2) = \frac{IG(K_1 \cap K_2)}{IG(K_1)} \qquad (19)$$

where for the non-specificity measure $IG(K_*)$ of a credal set $K_*$ the general one proposed by the same authors has been chosen:

$$IG(K_*) = \sum_{E \subseteq \Omega} m_{K_*}(E) \ln(|E|), \qquad (20)$$

which is based on the Möebius inverse

$$m_{K_*}(E) = \sum_{F \subseteq E} (-1)^{|E-F|} f_{K_*}(F), \quad \forall E \in \mathcal{P}(\Omega) \qquad (21)$$

of the lower-probability function associated to $K_*$

$$f_{K_*}(F) = \inf_{\xi \in K_*} \xi(F), \quad \forall F \in \mathcal{P}(\Omega). \qquad (22)$$

Authors in [1] underline that $m_{K_*}(E)$ as in (21) can be negative for some $E \in \mathcal{P}(\Omega)$ but that it anyhow fulfil the normalization condition $\sum_{E \subseteq \Omega} m_{K_*}(E) = 1$, and that $IG(K_*)$ as in (20) is a general Hartley measure which gives the same value for credal sets with equal lower probabilities.

By computing the Informative distances (18) between the credal set $K_o$ and each credal set $K_{e^s}$ of the two groups, we obtain the values summarized in the boxplots of Fig. 2(right). Informative distances of the first group result quite more concentrated and with a slightly lesser mean value than those of the second group. Hence, also in this case we can observe an over-performance of the corrected imprecise estimates $K_{q_p^s}$ with respect to the originally coherent ones $K_{p^s}$, although more attenuate than the results based on the Hausdorff distance. Once again it seems that the corrections performed through the discrepancy minimization introduce some kind of information about the joint distribution of the population that the crude estimates can miss.

Note that all the credal sets $K_{e^s}$ induced by estimates, both corrected or originally coherent, are quite close to the original one $K_o$, since we have Informative distances that range between 0.040 and 0.098 in the first case, and between 0.035 and 0.113 in the second case.

# References

1. Abellan, J., Gomez, M.: Measures of divergence on credal sets. Fuzzy Sets and Systems 157, 1514–1531 (2006)
2. Brozzi, A., Capotorti, A., Vantaggi, B.: Incoherence Correction Strategies in Statistical Matching. Int. Journ. of Approximate Reasoning (in press) (extended version of the omonimous paper by Capotorti, A. Vantaggi, B.: Proc. of 7th Int. Symp. on Imprecise Probability, ISIPTA 2011, pp.109–118 (2011))
3. Capotorti, A., Vantaggi, B.: Correction of Incoherences in Statistical Matching. In: Cerciello, P., Tarantola, C. (eds.) CLADAG 2011 Book of Abstract, p. 5. Pavia University Press, Pavia (2011) ISBN: 978-88-96764-22-0
4. Coletti, G., Scozzafava, R.: Probabilistic Logic in a Coherent Setting. Trends in Logic. Kluwer, Dordrecht (2002)
5. de Finetti, B.: Sull'Impostazione Assiomatica del Calcolo delle Probabilità. Annali Univ. Trieste 19, 3–55 (1949); Engl. transl. in: ch. 5 of Probability, Induction, Statistics. Wiley, London (1972)
6. D'Orazio, M., Di Zio, M., Scanu, M.: Statistical Matching: Theory and Practice. Wiley (2006)
7. Gilio, A., Sanfilippo, G.: Coherent Conditional Probabilities and Proper Scoring Rules. In: Proc. of 7th Int. Symp. on Imprecise Probability, ISIPTA 2011, pp. 189–198 (2011)
8. Irpino, A., Tontodonato, V.: Clustering Reduced Interval Data Using Hausdorff Distance. Computational Statistics 21, 241–288 (2006)
9. Lad, F.: Operational Subjective Statistical Methods: a mathematical, philosophical, and historical introduction. Wiley, New York (1996)
10. Levi, I.: The Enterprise of Knowledge. MIT Press, London (1980)
11. Rubin, D.B.: Statistical Matching Using File Concatenation with Adjusted Weights and Multiple Imputations. J. of Business & Economic Statistics 2, 87–94 (1986)
12. Vantaggi, B.: Statistical Matching of Multiple Sources: A look through coherence. Int. J. of Approx. Reasoning 49(3), 701–711 (2008)
13. Walley, P.: Measures of Uncertainty in Expert Systems. Artificial Intelligence 83(1), 1–58 (1996)

# Claims Reserving in Non-life Insurance: A Fully Bayesian Model

Gilberto Castellani[1], Massimo De Felice[1], and Franco Moriconi[2]

[1] Sapienza, Università di Roma, Dip. di Scienze Statistiche, Rome, Italy
[2] Università di Perugia, Dip. di Economia, Finanza e Statistica, Perugia, Italy
moriconi@unipg.it

**Abstract.** Stochastic claims reserving has been developed mostly using models defined in the framework of the classical statistics. The recently proposed Time Series Chain Ladder (TSCL) is one of these models. In order to allow for a comparison with the Bayesian point of view, we propose a fully Bayesian model having the property of reproducing TSCL if improper priors are assumed. With "informative" priors the Bayesian model allows for incorporating into the reserving process relevant external data, e.g. expert opinions, which are largely used by the actuaries. We provide numerical examples using Markov Chain Monte Carlo methods.

**Keywords:** Claims reserving, Chain Ladder, Reserve Risk, Bayesian modelling, Markov Chain Monte Carlo, Solvency II.

## 1 Introduction

Claims reserving (loss reserving) in non-life insurance is a difficult valuation problem, requiring to insurance companies to make predictions on futures claims payments – the outstanding loss liabilities –, which are affected by a large degree of uncertainty, both in amount and in timing. In the last two decades, especially under new solvency regimes, a number of stochastic loss reserving models have been developed (see [7] for a review). Most of these models are specified in the framework of the classical statistics. An important example is the "Time Series Chain Ladder" model (TSCL), which has been introduced in 2006 [1] as a stochastic version of the popular Chain Ladder method (CL), a traditional deterministic approach to claims reserving.

To allow for a comparison with the Bayesian point of view, we introduce a fully Bayesian approach to loss reserving, the "Normal Bayesian Chain Ladder" model (NBCL). NBCL has the property of producing results very close to those of TSCL in the case of improper prior distributions. In particular, the variance in NBCL and the mean square error of prediction in TSCL have very similar expressions. For proper ("informative") priors NBCL allows for incorporating into the reserving process relevant external data, e.g. expert opinions, which are largely used by the actuaries. In these cases the posterior distributions provided by NBCL have no closed form expression and a simulation approach

S. Greco et al. (Eds.): IPMU 2012, Part IV, CCIS 300, pp. 134–145, 2012.

is needed. We provide numerical examples using Markov Chain Monte Carlo methods (MCMC) in the package winBUGS.

The probabilistic structure of NBCL is characterized by normality assumptions on the data and by (log-)uniform assumptions on the parameters distributions. From this point of view the mathematical structure of the model is similar to that of the classical problem of estimating from a normal sample with unknown mean and variance. This framework has also been chosen by de Finetti ([2] Vol. 2, pp. 234-240) for illustrating his criticism to the classical statistics approach. However, in the NBCL the technical details are more complex, because it is a multiperiod model having a Markov chain structure and the normality assumptions only conditionally hold.

Currently TSCL is largely used by the insurance industry. Moreover, in the new European supervisory framework "Solvency II", TSCL seems to have been accepted by the Supervisors as a "standardized method" for measuring uncertainty in loss reserving. This should make more easy for an insurance company to obtain its validation as an internal model. A Bayesian model like NBCL hence lends itself as a proper choice for an internal model under the Solvency II regime. On one hand the regulator should appreciate that NBCL generalizes TSCL while preserving its basic structure. On the other hand, through the choice of the prior distribution and its parameters, NBCL allows flexibility to catch the special conditions which the specific insurance company might wish to emphasize. Of course, other Bayes models extending TSCL can be thought of. Such an alternative attempt called "Gamma-Gamma Bayes CL" is proposed in [6].

## 2   The Claims Reserving Problem in Non-life Insurance

Let us consider a non-life insurance company and the payments for claims incurred in the past in a specified line of business. We refer to the usual *claims development table*, where claims payments are organized by *accident year* (AY) and *development year* (DY). The index $i \in \{0, \ldots, I\}$ denotes the AY and $j \in \{0, \ldots, J\}$ the DY ($J \leq I$). We denote by $X_{i,j}$ the amount paid in DY $j$ for all claims of AY $i$. The sequence $\{X_{i,j}; j = 0, \ldots, J\}$ represents the claims cost development of AY $i$, $J$ is the *run-off* year and $C_{i,J} = \sum_{j=0}^{J} X_{i,j}$ is the *ultimate cost* of claims incurred in AY $i$.

We assume that we are at time $I$ (a year-end). Moreover, to fix the ideas, we pose $J = I$. Therefore the claims development table $\{X_{i,j}; 0 \leq i, j \leq I\}$, can be split into two parts: the "upper triangle" $\mathcal{D}_I = \{X_{i,j}; i+j \leq I\}$, containing the payments observed up to time $I$, and the "lower triangle" $\mathcal{D}_I^c = \{X_{i,j}; i+j > I\}$, containing the payments arising in the future.

As a general solvency principle, a money amount $R$ must be held by the company in order to be able to meet all future claims arising from policies currently in force and policies written in the past. The amount $R$ is referred to as the *outstanding claims reserve* or *loss reserve*. Referring to the claims development table, the insurance company has to set the reserve $R$ for the random variables in $\mathcal{D}_I^c$. In the traditional approach, a point estimate $\widehat{C}_{i,I}$ for the ultimate loss of AY $i \in \{1, \ldots, I\}$ is provided and the corresponding reserve is obtained as $R_i = \widehat{C}_{i,I} - \sum_{j=0}^{I-i} X_{i,j}$.

The new insurance regulatory framework ("Solvency II") is also interested in adverse claims reserve developments, prescribing that the insurance companies shall protect against possible shortfalls in these reserve assessments with risk bearing capital. Therefore the insurers have both to justify the reserve estimates and also to quantify the uncertainties in these estimates. This requires the introduction of stochastic models for loss reserving. In principle, stochastic models should provide the joint probability distribution of $\mathcal{D}_I^c$. In a simplified approach, at least the variance of the total ultimate costs has to be specified. In any case, claims reserving is a challenging predictive problem, where observation in the upper trapezoid $\mathcal{D}_I$ can be used as data to make inference on $\mathcal{D}_I^c$.

In the following we shall denote by:

$$C_{i,j} = \sum_{k=0}^{j} X_{i,k}, \quad i,j \in \{0, \ldots, I\},$$

the *cumulative payments* for AY $i$ up to DY $j$. The "individual development factors" are defined, as

$$Y_{i,j} = \frac{C_{i,j+1}}{C_{i,j}}, \quad i \in \{0, \ldots, I\}, j \in \{0, \ldots, I-1\}.$$

We also define the set of the cumulative payments

$$\mathcal{B}_j = \{C_{i,k}; i+k \leq I, 0 \leq k \leq j\}, \quad j \in \{0, \ldots, I\}, \tag{1}$$

and the "column sum"

$$S_j = \sum_{i=0}^{I-j-1} C_{i,j}, \quad j \in \{0, \ldots, I-1\}. \tag{2}$$

The cumulative payments $C_{i,I-i}$ are the total losses currently paid for AY $i$, while the random variables $C_{i,I}$ are the corresponding ultimate costs. The total outstanding loss liabilities for AY $i \in \{1, \ldots, I\}$ are given by

$$L_i = C_{i,I} - C_{i,I-i},$$

and the reserve $R_i$ for AY $i$ can be defined as an estimate for $L_i$, that is an estimate for $C_{i,I}$ net of the claims just paid.

For ease of exposition in the following we limit our attention to the prediction of the random variables $\{C_{i,I}; 1 \leq i \leq I\}$.

## 3    The Chain Ladder Approach: The Classical Framework

### 3.1    The Chain Ladder as a Method for Point Estimates

The Chain Ladder (CL) is probably the most popular deterministic method for claims reserving, providing point estimates of the ultimate costs. A purely algorithmic definition of CL can be given as follows.

**CL1.** *For $j \in \{0, \ldots, I-1\}$ there exist constants $f_j$ (the chain ladder factors, or development factors), such that the future cumulative payments $C_{i,j}$ ($1 \leq i \leq I$, $I - i + 1 \leq j \leq I$), are estimated by*

$$\widehat{C}_{i,j} = C_{i,I-i} \prod_{k=I-i}^{j-1} f_k. \tag{3}$$

**CL2.** *The chain ladder factors are estimated as the weighted averages*

$$\widehat{f}_j = \sum_{i=0}^{I-j-1} Y_{i,j} \frac{C_{i,j}}{S_j}. \tag{4}$$

By assumptions CL1 and CL2, the chain ladder estimator for $C_{i,I}$, $i \in \{1, \ldots, I\}$, is defined as

$$\widehat{C}_{i,I}^{\mathrm{CL}} = C_{i,I-i} \prod_{k=I-i}^{I-1} \widehat{f}_k. \tag{5}$$

## 3.2 A Stochastic CL Model: The Time Series Chain Ladder

The Time Series Chain Ladder model (TSCL) has been introduced in 2006 by Buchwalder et al. [1] as a revisitation of the Distribution Free Chain Ladder (DFCL) provided by Mack in 1993 [5].

The TSCL: a) provides an assessment of the statistical quality of the CL reserve estimates; b) provides a closed form expression for a quadratic measure (MSEP) of the total prediction uncertainty of the reserves; c) allows for producing the predictive distribution of future payments by simulation.

### Model Assumptions

**TS1.** *Cumulative claims $C_{i,j}$ of different accident years are independent.*

**TS2.** *There exist constants $f_j > 0$, $\sigma_j > 0$ and random variables $\varepsilon_{i,j+1}$ such that for $i \in \{0, \ldots, I\}$ and $j \in \{0, \ldots, I-1\}$*

$$C_{i,j+1} = f_j C_{i,j} + \sigma_j \sqrt{C_{i,j}} \, \varepsilon_{i,j+1}, \tag{6}$$

*where $\varepsilon_{i,j+1}$ are independent with $\mathbf{E}(\varepsilon_{i,j+1}) = 0$ and $\mathbf{E}(\varepsilon_{i,j+1}^2) = 1$.*

When the distribution of the $\varepsilon_{i,j+1}$ is specified, the model is no more distribution free and the time series assumption (6) provides a mechanism for generating future payments by Monte Carlo simulation. Of course, if the $\varepsilon_{i,j+1}$ are normal, assumption TS2 implies $C_{i,j+1}|C_{i,j} \sim \mathcal{N}(f_j C_{i,j}, \sigma_j^2 C_{i,j})$.

*Remark 1.* Theoretically, the process generated by assumption TS2 could have negative values for the cumulative payments $C_{i,j}$. This "negativity problem" could be avoided reformulating the properties of $\varepsilon_{i,j+1}$ conditional on $C_{i,j}$. This would lead however to a model with a more complex dependency structure. Since the negativity problem is usually irrelevant in practical applications, in the TSCL one takes the pragmatic position of ignoring this theoretical inconsistency.

**Estimators for $f_j$ and $\sigma_j^2$.** The parameters $f_j$ and $\sigma_j^2$ must be estimated. One finds that under assumptions TS1 and TS2 the CL estimator $\widehat{f}_j$ given by (4) is unbiased for $f_j$. The CL estimator is also minimum variance among all linear estimators.

For the variance parameters one finds that the appropriate estimator is

$$\widehat{\sigma}_j^2 = \frac{1}{I-j-1} \sum_{i=0}^{I-j-1} C_{i,j}\left(Y_{i,j} - \widehat{f}_j\right)^2, \qquad 0 \leq j \leq I-2. \tag{7}$$

It can be shown that $\widehat{\sigma}_j^2$ is unbiased for $\sigma_j^2$. For normal $\varepsilon_{i,j+1}$ the estimator $\widehat{\sigma}_j^2$ is also minimum variance. The last estimator $\widehat{\sigma}_{I-1}^2$ is not defined by (7). Usually this estimator is determined by the extrapolation

$$\widehat{\sigma}_{I-1}^2 = \min\left\{\widehat{\sigma}_{I-2}^4/\widehat{\sigma}_{I-3}^2, \widehat{\sigma}_{I-3}^2, \widehat{\sigma}_{I-2}^2\right\}. \tag{8}$$

**Estimators for the Ultimate Costs.** It can be immediately shown that under model assumption TS2 the conditional expectation, given $\mathcal{D}_I$, of the ultimate costs $C_{i,I}$, $i \in \{1, \ldots, I\}$, is given by

$$\mathbf{E}(C_{i,I}|\mathcal{D}_I) = C_{i,I-i} \prod_{k=I-i}^{I-1} f_k. \tag{9}$$

It results that, given $C_{i,I-i}$, the CL estimator $\widehat{C}_{i,I}^{\mathrm{CL}}$ given by (5) is conditionally unbiased for $\mathbf{E}(C_{i,I}|\mathcal{D}_I)$. Moreover $\widehat{C}_{i,I}^{\mathrm{CL}}$ is an unbiased estimator for $\mathbf{E}(C_{i,I})$.

**The Mean Square Error of Prediction of Ultimate Costs.** The TSCL also provides a method for determining the total prediction uncertainty of the ultimate costs. As usual in the framework of classical statistics, this is made by introducing the concept of *mean square error of prediction* (MSEP). We use the definitions in [7], pp. 33-34.

The CL estimator $\widehat{C}_{i,I}^{\mathrm{CL}}$ for $\mathbf{E}(C_{i,I}|\mathcal{D}_I)$ given by (5) is a $\mathcal{D}_I$-measurable predictor for $C_{i,I}$. The conditional (i.e. given $\mathcal{D}_I$) MSEP of the predictor $\widehat{C}_{i,I}^{\mathrm{CL}}$ for $C_{i,I}$ is given by

$$\begin{aligned}
\mathrm{msep}_{C_{i,I}|\mathcal{D}_I}(\widehat{C}_{i,I}^{\mathrm{CL}}) &:= \mathbf{E}\left[\left(C_{i,I} - \widehat{C}_{i,I}^{\mathrm{CL}}\right)^2 \middle| \mathcal{D}_I\right] \\
&= \mathbf{E}\left[\left(C_{i,I} - \mathbf{E}(C_{i,I}|\mathcal{D}_I)\right)^2 \middle| \mathcal{D}_I\right] + \left[\mathbf{E}(C_{i,I}|\mathcal{D}_I) - \widehat{C}_{i,I}^{\mathrm{CL}}\right]^2.
\end{aligned} \tag{10}$$

The first term is the conditional *process variance*, the second represents the conditional *estimation error*. In order to obtain an estimate for the MSEP we need estimates of both these terms.

*Process Variance.* One finds that the (conditional) process variance of the ultimate costs, for $1 \leq i \leq I$, can be estimated as

$$\widehat{\mathbf{E}}^{\mathrm{CL}}\left([C_{i,I} - \mathbf{E}(C_{i,I}|\mathcal{D}_I)]^2|\mathcal{D}_I\right) = C_{i,I-i} \sum_{k=I-i}^{I-1} \prod_{l=I-i}^{k-1} \widehat{f}_l \cdot \widehat{\sigma}_k^2 \cdot \prod_{l=k+1}^{I-1} \widehat{f}_l^2. \quad (11)$$

*Estimation Error.* For the (conditional) estimation error of the ultimate costs one obtains $(1 \leq i \leq I)$

$$\left[\widehat{C}_{i,I}^{\mathrm{CL}} - \mathbf{E}(C_{i,I}|\mathcal{D}_I)\right]^2 = C_{i,I-i}^2 \left(\prod_{k=I-i}^{I-1} \widehat{f}_k^2 + \prod_{k=I-i}^{I-1} f_k^2 - 2 \prod_{k=I-i}^{I-1} \widehat{f}_k f_k\right). \quad (12)$$

In the framework of classical statistics the estimation of this quantity requires to determine the volatility of $\widehat{f}_k$ around its "true value" $f_k$. This can be made with the help of resampled observations for $\widehat{f}_k$. However different approaches are possible for resampling the time series (6) (see [1], [7] pp. 44-53). In the TSCL the *conditional resampling* approach is chosen, which leads to the estimator

$$\widehat{\mathbf{E}}_{\mathcal{D}_I}\left([\widehat{C}_{i,I}^{\mathrm{CL}} - \mathbf{E}(C_{i,I}|\mathcal{D}_I)]^2\right) = C_{i,I-i}^2 \left[\prod_{k=I-i}^{I-1} \left(\widehat{f}_k^2 + \frac{\widehat{\sigma}_k^2}{S_k}\right) - \prod_{k=I-i}^{I-1} \widehat{f}_k^2\right], \quad (13)$$

where $\mathbf{E}_{\mathcal{D}_I}$ is the expectation taken with respect to the probability measure of the conditionally resampled CL estimates.

**Generating the Predictive Distribution.** As for the MSEP, the simulation procedure for the full predictive distribution of the ultimate costs must include both the process uncertainty, which is modelled by the time series equations (6), and the estimation uncertainty. The latter will be simulated by resampling data, e.g. using a *bootstrap* technique. For consistency, the same resampling method adopted for the MSEP calculation has to be used in the bootstrap procedure. In this paper the conditional resampling approach has been chosen.

## 4    A Bayesian Model: The Normal Bayesian Chain Ladder

A normal Bayesian CL model with stochastic factors $f_j$ and deterministic variance parameters $\sigma_j^2$ has been introduced by Gisler [3] for discussing the estimation error in the TSCL model. A distribution free Bayesian version of CL has also been proposed in [4]. We propose here a fully Bayesian version of Gisler's model – the Normal Bayesian Chain Ladder (NBCL) –, where also the variance parameters are stochastic.

The NBCL: a) allows for incorporating prior opinions in a stochastic CL framework, producing the predictive distribution of future claims payments by simulation methods; b) produces a Bayesian version of TSCL in case of improper priors, providing closed form expressions for the variance of future payments.

### 4.1   Model Assumptions

**Model for Claims Payments**

**NB1.** *There exist random vectors* $\boldsymbol{F} = \{F_0, \ldots, F_{I-1}\}$ *and* $\boldsymbol{V} = \{V_0, \ldots, V_{I-1}\}$ *such that for* $i \in \{0, \ldots, I\}$ *and* $j \in \{0, \ldots, I-1\}$ *the random variables* $C_{i,j+1}$ *are conditionally independent and normally distributed, given* $\boldsymbol{F}, \boldsymbol{V}$ *and* $\mathcal{B}_j$, *with mean*

$$\mathbf{E}(C_{i,j+1}|\boldsymbol{F}, \boldsymbol{V}, C_{i,0}, C_{i,1}, \ldots, C_{i,j}) = \mathbf{E}(C_{i,j+1}|\boldsymbol{F}, \boldsymbol{V}, C_{i,j}) = F_j\, C_{i,j}\,, \quad (14)$$

*and variance*

$$\mathbf{Var}(C_{i,j+1}|\boldsymbol{F}, \boldsymbol{V}, C_{i,0}, C_{i,1}, \ldots, C_{i,j}) = \mathbf{Var}(C_{i,j+1}|\boldsymbol{F}, \boldsymbol{V}, C_{i,j}) = V_j\, C_{i,j}\,. \quad (15)$$

We shall denote by $\boldsymbol{f} = \{f_0, \ldots, f_{I-1}\}$ and $\boldsymbol{\sigma}^2 = \{\sigma_0^2, \ldots, \sigma_{I-1}^2\}$ the realization of $\boldsymbol{F}$ and $\boldsymbol{V}$, respectively.

*Remark 2.* By assumptions NB1 the CL factors are a realization $\boldsymbol{f}$ of the random vector $\boldsymbol{F}$. Also in this case we have a negativity problem: as with the time series assumption (6), under NB1 some $C_{i,j}$ could become negative, providing a negative value for the conditional variance of $C_{i,j+1}$. From this point of view assumptions NB1 are a bit questionable.

**Model for Parameters**

**NB2.1** *The random variables* $F_0, \ldots, F_{I-1}$ *are independent and uniformly distributed in* $(a_j, b_j)$ *with* $a_j \le b_j \in \mathbb{R}$, $j \in \{0, \ldots, I-1\}$.
**NB2.2** *The random variables* $V_0, \ldots, V_{I-1}$ *are independent, independent of* $\boldsymbol{F}$ *and log-uniform, that is with logarithm uniformly distributed in* $(a'_j, b'_j)$ *with* $a'_j \le b'_j \in \mathbb{R}$, $j \in \{0, \ldots, I-1\}$.

### 4.2   Implementing the Model

By assumption NB2.1 and NB2.2, the joint prior distribution of all parameters $(\boldsymbol{F}, \boldsymbol{V})$ has the form

$$\pi_0(\boldsymbol{f}, \boldsymbol{\sigma}^2) = \prod_{j=0}^{I-1} \pi_0(f_j) \prod_{j=0}^{I-1} \pi_0(\sigma_j^2) \propto \prod_{j=0}^{I-1} \frac{1}{\sigma_j^2}\, \mathbf{1}_{(a_j < f_j < b_j)}\, \mathbf{1}_{(a'_j < \log \sigma_j^2 < b'_j)}\,, \quad (16)$$

where $\mathbf{1}_A$ is the indicator function of the event $A$.

Given the realizations $\boldsymbol{F} = \boldsymbol{f}$ and $\boldsymbol{V} = \boldsymbol{\sigma}^2$ and given $\mathcal{B}_0$, the joint density of the observations $\mathcal{C}_I = \mathcal{D}_I \setminus \mathcal{B}_0 = \{C_{i,j};\ i+j \le I, 1 \le j \le I\}$ (the likelihood function) can be written as

$$u_0(\mathcal{C}_I|\boldsymbol{f}, \boldsymbol{\sigma}^2, \mathcal{B}_0) = \prod_{j=0}^{I-1} (2\pi)^{-(I-j)/2} \frac{\sigma_j^{-(I-j)}}{\prod_{i=0}^{I-j-1} \sqrt{C_{i,j}}}\, e^{-\frac{1}{2\sigma_j^2}\left[\Sigma_j^2 + \left(f_j - \hat{f}_j\right)^2 S_j\right]}\,,$$

$$(17)$$

where $\Sigma_j^2 := \sum_{i=0}^{I-j-1} C_{i,j}(Y_{i,j} - \widehat{f}_j)^2$. The product form of this density is due to the fact that $C_{i,j}$, $i \in \{0, \dots, I - j\}$, are independent and the sequences $\{C_{i,0}, C_{i,1}, \dots, C_{i,I}\}$ have the Markov property.

Using (16) and (17), the joint posterior parameters distribution has the form:

$$\pi(\boldsymbol{f}, \boldsymbol{\sigma}^2 | \mathcal{D}_I) = u_0(C_I | \boldsymbol{f}, \boldsymbol{\sigma}^2, \mathcal{B}_0)\, \pi_0(\boldsymbol{f}, \boldsymbol{\sigma}^2) = \prod_{j=0}^{I-1} \pi(f_j, \sigma_j^2 | \mathcal{D}_I), \qquad (18)$$

with

$$\pi(f_j, \sigma_j^2 | \mathcal{D}_I) \propto (\sigma_j^2)^{-\frac{I-j+2}{2}} e^{-\frac{1}{2\sigma_j^2}\left[\Sigma_j^2 + \left(f_j - \widehat{f}_j\right)^2 S_j\right]} \mathbf{1}_{(a_j < f_j < b_j)} \mathbf{1}_{(a'_j < \log \sigma_j^2 < b'_j)} \cdot \qquad (19)$$

The product form of expression (18) shows that, given the observations $\mathcal{D}_I$, the random pairs $(F_j, V_j)$ and $(F_k, V_k)$, for $j, k \in \{0, \dots, I - 1\}$ and $j \neq k$, are independent.

The mean of the marginal posterior distribution $\pi(f_j | \mathcal{D}_I)$ and $\pi(\sigma_j^2 | \mathcal{D}_I)$, respectively, provides the "Bayesian estimator" for $F_j$ and $V_j$ ($0 \leq j \leq I - 1$)

$$\widehat{F}_j^{\text{Bayes}} = \mathbf{E}(F_j | \mathcal{D}_I), \quad \widehat{V}_j^{\text{Bayes}} = \mathbf{E}(V_j | \mathcal{D}_I).$$

By the independence, for the Bayesian estimator of the ultimate costs one has

$$\widehat{C}_{i,I}^{\text{Bayes}} := \mathbf{E}(C_{i,I} | \mathcal{D}_I) = C_{i,I-i} \prod_{k=I-i}^{I-1} \mathbf{E}(F_k | \mathcal{D}_I) = C_{i,I-i} \prod_{k=I-i}^{I-1} \widehat{F}_k^{\text{Bayes}}.$$

We derive all these posterior distributions by simulation, using MCMC methods. The predictive distribution of the ultimate costs $\{C_{i,I}; 1 \leq i \leq I\}$ can be obtained by the simulated values $\{F_j^*; 0 \leq j \leq I - 1\}$ computing the products $C_{i,I}^* = C_{i,I-i} \prod_{k=I-i}^{I-1} F_k^*$. The sample mean of the empirical distribution for each AY $i \in \{1, \dots, I\}$ provides the Bayesian estimator $\widehat{C}_{i,I}^{\text{Bayes}}$.

## 4.3 Variance of the Ultimate Costs

It is useful to derive a general expression for the variance of the ultimate costs. Because of the general property $\mathbf{Var}(X) = \mathbf{E}[\mathbf{Var}(X|Y)] + \mathbf{Var}[\mathbf{E}(X|Y)]$, the conditional variance, given $\mathcal{D}_I$, of future payments $C_{i,j}$ ($i + j > I$) is written as

$$\mathbf{Var}(C_{i,j} | \mathcal{D}_I) = \mathbf{E}\left[(C_{i,j} - \widehat{C}_{i,j}^{\text{Bayes}})^2 \Big| \mathcal{D}_I\right]$$

$$= \mathbf{E}\left[\mathbf{Var}(C_{i,j} | \boldsymbol{F}, \boldsymbol{V}, \mathcal{D}_I) \Big| \mathcal{D}_I\right] + \mathbf{Var}\left[\mathbf{E}(C_{i,j} | \boldsymbol{F}, \boldsymbol{V}, \mathcal{D}_I) \Big| \mathcal{D}_I\right]. \qquad (20)$$

This representation highlights all the uncertainty affecting $C_{i,j}$, including that on the unknown parameters $\boldsymbol{F}, \boldsymbol{V}$. Comparing (20) with the representation of the MSEP (10), one can try a similar interpretation of the two components, taking into account however that now $\boldsymbol{F}$ and $\boldsymbol{V}$ are random vectors. Mimicking discussions of similar expressions in [3,4], one could interpret the first term in (20) as some kind of an "average" process error (averaged over the set of possible values of $\boldsymbol{F}, \boldsymbol{V}$) and the second term as some kind of an "average" estimation error. We conventionally adopt this terminology here, observing however that the meaning of both the two variance components, the "average process error" and the "average estimation error", is completely clear in the present Bayesian setting. In particular no additional assumption is required for evaluating the average estimation error.

*Average Process Error.* After some manipulations one has, for $i + j > I$

$$\mathbf{Var}\left(C_{i,j}|\boldsymbol{F},\boldsymbol{V},\mathcal{D}_I\right) = C_{i,I-i} V_{j-1} \prod_{k=I-i}^{j-2} F_k + F_{j-1}^2 \mathbf{Var}\left[C_{i,j-1}|\boldsymbol{F},\boldsymbol{V},\mathcal{D}_I\right].$$

By iterating one obtains $(1 \leq i \leq I)$

$$\mathbf{Var}\left(C_{i,I}|\boldsymbol{F},\boldsymbol{V},\mathcal{D}_I\right) = C_{i,I-i} \sum_{k=I-i}^{I-1} \prod_{l=I-i}^{k-1} F_l \cdot V_k \cdot \prod_{l=k+1}^{I-1} F_l^2$$

(with the usual assumption $\prod_{k=l}^m x_k = 1$ if $m < l$). Taking the conditional expectation, since the pairs $(F_j, V_j)$ are conditionally independent given $\mathcal{D}_I$, one has

$$\mathbf{E}\left[\mathbf{Var}\left(C_{i,I}|\boldsymbol{F},\boldsymbol{V},\mathcal{D}_I\right)\Big|\mathcal{D}_I\right] =$$

$$C_{i,I-i} \sum_{k=I-i}^{I-1} \prod_{l=I-i}^{k-1} \mathbf{E}(F_l|\mathcal{D}_I) \cdot \mathbf{E}(V_k|\mathcal{D}_I) \cdot \prod_{l=k+1}^{I-1} \mathbf{E}(F_l^2|\mathcal{D}_I). \tag{21}$$

*Average estimation error.* Here one accounts for the variance effects on $C_{i,I}$ given by the randomness of $F_j$ and $V_j$ (of which $f_j$ and $\sigma_j^2$ are realizations). Since $\mathbf{E}\left[\mathbf{E}(C_{i,I}|\boldsymbol{F},\boldsymbol{V},\mathcal{D}_I)\big|\mathcal{D}_I\right] = \mathbf{E}\left(C_{i,I}|\mathcal{D}_I\right) = \widehat{C}_{i,I}^{\mathrm{Bayes}}$, one obtains

$$\mathbf{Var}\left[\mathbf{E}(C_{i,I}|\boldsymbol{F},\boldsymbol{V},\mathcal{D}_I)\big|\mathcal{D}_I\right] = C_{i,I-i}^2 \left[\prod_{k=I-i}^{I-1} \mathbf{E}(F_k^2|\mathcal{D}_I) - \prod_{k=I-i}^{I-1} \left(\widehat{F}_k^{\mathrm{Bayes}}\right)^2\right]. \tag{22}$$

## 5   The Case of Improper Priors

Let us consider the case of improper priors. Precisely, for the development factors we consider the limiting case $a_j \to -\infty$, $b_j \to \infty$ for $j \in \{0, \ldots, I-1\}$, while for the variances we consider the limiting case $a_j' \to -\infty$, $b_j' \to \infty$ for $j \in \{0, \ldots, I-4\}$, assuming that $V_j$ has a known value equal to $\widehat{\sigma}_j^2$ for $j \in \{I-3, \ldots, I-1\}$.

The posterior distributions of the parameters can be now derived in closed form, using standard calculations in Bayesian analysis. In particular, one finds

$$\widehat{F}_j^{\text{Bayes}} = \mathbf{E}(F_j|\mathcal{D}_I) = \widehat{f}_j, \qquad \mathbf{Var}(F_j|\mathcal{D}_I) = \frac{\widetilde{\sigma}_j^2}{S_j}, \tag{23}$$

where

$$\widetilde{\sigma}_j^2 := \mathbf{E}(V_j|\mathcal{D}_I) = \begin{cases} \dfrac{I-j-1}{I-j-3}\,\widehat{\sigma}_j^2, & j \in \{0, \dots, I-4\}, \\ \widehat{\sigma}_j^2, & j \in \{I-3, \dots, I-1\}. \end{cases}$$

Using (23) expressions (21) and (22) take the form

$$\mathbf{E}\left[\mathbf{Var}\left(C_{i,I}|\mathbf{F},\mathbf{V},\mathcal{D}_I\right)\Big|\mathcal{D}_I\right] = C_{i,I-i}\sum_{k=I-i}^{I-1}\prod_{l=I-i}^{k-1}\widehat{f}_l\cdot\widetilde{\sigma}_k^2\cdot\prod_{l=k+1}^{I-1}\left(\widehat{f}_l^2 + \frac{\widetilde{\sigma}_l^2}{S_l}\right), \tag{24}$$

$$\mathbf{Var}\left[\mathbf{E}(C_{i,I}|\mathbf{F},\mathbf{V},\mathcal{D}_I)\Big|\mathcal{D}_I\right] = C_{i,I-i}^2\left[\prod_{k=I-i}^{I-1}\left(\widehat{f}_k^2 + \frac{\widetilde{\sigma}_k^2}{S_k}\right) - \prod_{k=I-i}^{I-1}\widehat{f}_k^2\right]. \tag{25}$$

These formulas have a similar structure to the expressions (11) and (13) derived in the TSCL model for the process error and the estimation error, respectively. Here, however, a positive term $\widetilde{\sigma}_j^2/S_j$ is added to the squared estimators $\widehat{f}_j^2$. Moreover the estimator $\widehat{\sigma}_j^2$ is replaced by $\widetilde{\sigma}_j^2$, which is larger than $\widehat{\sigma}_j^2$ for $j < I-3$. This increased value of the variance can be considered a consequence of the fact that in the Bayesian approach also the variability of the random vectors $\mathbf{F},\mathbf{V}$ is included in the valuation of the ultimate costs.

## 6 Example of Application

We use data taken from an insurance company operating on the "Motor Third Party Liability" line of business. The set $\mathcal{D}_I$ is triangular with $I = 11$.

The CL estimates for $f_j$ and $\sigma_j^2$ provided by (4), (7) and (8) are reported in Table 1.

We implemented the NBCL model using winBUGS, a freely downloadable specialized software for implementing MCMC methods. Our simulations used an initial burn-in of $10,000$ updates, followed by a sample of $50,000$ updates.

In a first run we assumed improper priors for $\mathbf{F}$ and $\mathbf{V}$. The results of the simulation are summarized in Table 2, where also the overall reserve $R = \sum_{i=1}^{I} R_i$ is considered. The reserve estimates with NBCL obtained by simulation (Sim.) result to be very close to the corresponding closed form estimates (C.F.). Also the simulated reserve standard errors in the Bayesian model are similar to the

**Table 1.** Parameter estimates $\widehat{f}_j$ and $\widehat{\sigma}_j^2$

| $j$ | 0 | 1 | 2 | 3 | 4 | 5 | 6 | 7 | 8 | 9 | 10 |
|---|---|---|---|---|---|---|---|---|---|---|---|
| $\widehat{f}_j$ | 2.10 | 1.21 | 1.09 | 1.06 | 1.04 | 1.04 | 1.02 | 1.02 | 1.02 | 1.01 | 1.01 |
| $\widehat{\sigma}_j^2$ | 3,059.76 | 186.44 | 114.37 | 152.13 | 159.24 | 96.09 | 14.39 | 2.98 | 0.50 | 14.21 | 0.50 |

**Table 2.** Results on reserve estimates (thousand Euros) by TSCL and by NBCL with improper priors

| | Reserve Estimates | | | Standard Errors | | | | |
|---|---|---|---|---|---|---|---|---|
| AY | TSCL C.F. (a) | NBCL Sim. (b) | Δ% (b-a) | TSCL C.F. (c) | NBCL C.F. (d) | Δ% (d-c) | NBCL Sim. (e) | Δ% (e-d) |
| 1 | 2,470 | 2,472 | 0.09 | 747 | 747 | 0.00 | 747 | 0.03 |
| 2 | 9,501 | 9,500 | -0.01 | 3,718 | 3,718 | 0.00 | 3,726 | 0.19 |
| 3 | 18,522 | 18,520 | -0.01 | 3,824 | 3,824 | 0.00 | 3,793 | -0.82 |
| 4 | 30,301 | 30,287 | -0.05 | 4,116 | 4,649 | 12.95 | 4,595 | -1.16 |
| 5 | 41,344 | 41,362 | 0.04 | 5,093 | 6,367 | 25.03 | 6,289 | -1.22 |
| 6 | 59,931 | 59,945 | 0.02 | 9,701 | 12,415 | 27.98 | 12,476 | 0.49 |
| 7 | 85,736 | 85,814 | 0.09 | 14,921 | 18,649 | 24.99 | 18,668 | 0.10 |
| 8 | 99,720 | 99,695 | -0.03 | 17,052 | 20,931 | 22.75 | 20,985 | 0.25 |
| 9 | 129,058 | 129,287 | 0.18 | 18,487 | 22,421 | 21.27 | 22,405 | -0.07 |
| 10 | 207,457 | 207,348 | -0.05 | 22,093 | 26,370 | 19.36 | 26,233 | -0.52 |
| 11 | 374,962 | 375,319 | 0.10 | 42,941 | 48,879 | 13.83 | 48,506 | -0.76 |
| overall | 1,059,002 | 1,059,550 | 0.05 | 67,542 | 79,420 | 17.59 | 78,918 | -0.63 |

corresponding theoretical values obtained by (24), (25). The differences between the theoretical NBCL standard errors and the square root of MSEP provided in TSCL by (11), (13) are also shown. The standard deviation of the overall reserve[1] with NBCL is 17.6% larger than the corresponding figure with TSCL.

In a second simulation of NBCL we included a proper prior reflecting an expert opinion on the level of the first development factor $F_0$. As shown in Table 1 the CL estimate for this factor is $\widehat{f}_0 = 2.1$. Here we assumed that $F_0$ is uniformly distributed in ($a_0 = 1.5, b_0 = 1.9$), maintaining improper priors for all the other parameters (including $V_0$). In Table 3 the new reserve estimates (Sim. 2) are compared with the previous results (Sim. 1). One finds that with the inclusion of the expert opinion the overall reserve decreases by 58.2 million Euros (−5.5%) while the corresponding standard deviation increases by 23.8 million Euros (+29.3%). As a "rule of thumb" for valuing the trade-off between these two effects, one can consider that in the Solvency II regime the capital requirement for the reserve risk is about three times the standard deviation of the claims reserve. However, if NBCL would be included into a proprietary internal model validated by the Insurance Supervisors, the solvency capital requirement could be exactly computed using the details of the predictive distribution of future payments provided by the simulation procedure.

---

[1] In the derivation of the overall estimation error in the TSCL model, the correlations across different AY induced by the data has been taken into account (see [1]).

**Table 3.** Results on reserve estimates (thousand Euros) by NBCL with improper priors (Sim. 1) and with expert opinion on $F_0$ (Sim. 2)

| AY | Reserve Estimates | | | Standard Errors | | |
|---|---|---|---|---|---|---|
| | NBCL Sim. 1 (a) | NBCL Sim. 2 (b) | $\Delta\%$ (b–a) | NBCL Sim. 1 (c) | NBCL Sim. 2 (d) | $\Delta\%$ (d–c) |
| 1 | 2,472 | 2,469 | -0.13 | 747 | 745 | -0.27 |
| 2 | 9,500 | 9,501 | 0.01 | 3,726 | 3,714 | -0.31 |
| 3 | 18,520 | 18,531 | 0.06 | 3,793 | 3,798 | 0.14 |
| 4 | 30,287 | 30,337 | 0.16 | 4,595 | 4,897 | 6.57 |
| 5 | 41,362 | 41,325 | -0.09 | 6,289 | 6,742 | 7.19 |
| 6 | 59,945 | 59,898 | -0.08 | 12,476 | 12,602 | 1.01 |
| 7 | 85,814 | 85,674 | -0.16 | 18,668 | 18,805 | 0.73 |
| 8 | 99,695 | 99,688 | -0.01 | 20,985 | 21,009 | 0.12 |
| 9 | 129,287 | 129,056 | -0.18 | 22,405 | 22,488 | 0.37 |
| 10 | 207,348 | 207,378 | 0.01 | 26,233 | 26,356 | 0.47 |
| 11 | 375,319 | 317,483 | -15.41 | 48,506 | 80,747 | 66.47 |
| overall | 1,059,550 | 1,001,340 | -5.49 | 78,918 | 101,998 | 29.25 |

# References

1. Buchwalder, M., Bühlmann, H., Merz, M., Wüthrich, M.V.: The mean square error of prediction in the chain ladder reserving method (Mack and Murphy revisited). ASTIN Bulletin 36, 521–542 (2006)
2. de Finetti, B.: Theory of Probability. A critical introductory treatment. Wiley, New York (1975)
3. Gisler, A.: The Estimation Error in the Classical Chain-Ladder Reserving Method: a Bayesian Approach. ASTIN Bulletin 36, 554–565 (2006)
4. Gisler, A., Wüthrich, M.V.: Credibility for the Chain Ladder Method. ASTIN Bulletin 38, 565–600 (2008)
5. Mack, T.: Distribution-free calculation of the standard error of chain ladder reserve estimates. ASTIN Bulletin 23, 213–225 (1993)
6. Salzmann, R., Wüthrich, M.V., Merz, M.: Higher Moments of the Claims Development Result in General Insurance (preprint) (to appear in ASTIN Bulletin) (2010)
7. Wüthrich, M.V., Merz, M.: Stochastic Claims Reserving Methods in Insurance. Wiley, New York (2008)

# Coherent Conditional Previsions
# and Proper Scoring Rules

Veronica Biazzo[1], Angelo Gilio[2], and Giuseppe Sanfilippo[3]

[1] University of Catania, Italy
vbiazzo@dmi.unict.it
[2] University of Rome "La Sapienza", Italy
angelo.gilio@sbai.uniroma1.it
[3] University of Palermo, Italy
giuseppe.sanfilippo@unipa.it

**Abstract.** In this paper we study the relationship between the notion of coherence for conditional prevision assessments on a family of finite conditional random quantities and the notion of admissibility with respect to bounded strictly proper scoring rules. Our work extends recent results given by the last two authors of this paper on the equivalence between coherence and admissibility for conditional probability assessments. In order to prove that admissibility implies coherence a key role is played by the notion of Bregman divergence.

**Keywords:** Conditional prevision assessments, coherence, proper scoring rules, conditional scoring rules, weak dominance, strong dominance, admissibility, Bregman divergence.

## 1 Introduction

Proper scoring rules have been largely studied in many fields, such as probability, statistics and decision theory. The notion of proper scoring rules was central to de Finetti's ideas about assessing the relative values of different subjective probability assessments ([4]). A review of the general theory, with applications, has been given in [6,7]; an application to sequential forecasting of economic indices has been given in [1]. The connections between the notions of coherence and of admissibility have been investigated in many works (see, e.g., [4,8,9,10,11]). In [5] the last two authors of this paper extended the results given in [9] to the case of conditional probability assessments. In this paper we further extend the work made in [5], by considering the case of conditional prevision assessments on arbitrary families of finite conditional random quantities. We prove the equivalence between the coherence of a conditional prevision assessment on an arbitrary family of finite conditional random quantities and the admissibility of the assessment with respect to any given bounded strictly proper scoring rule. The paper is organized as follows: In Section 2 we give some preliminary notions on conditional prevision assessments; then, we recall some results on the checking of coherence for conditional prevision assessments; in Section 3 we illustrate

S. Greco et al. (Eds.): IPMU 2012, Part IV, CCIS 300, pp. 146–156, 2012.
© Springer-Verlag Berlin Heidelberg 2012

the notions of strictly proper scoring rules and admissibility for conditional prevision assessments; we also give a list of properties for the conditional prevision of strictly proper scoring rules; finally, in Section 4 we prove that a conditional prevision assessment on an arbitrary family of finite conditional random quantities is coherent if and only if it is admissible with respect to any bounded strictly proper scoring rule.

## 2    Some Preliminary Notions

We denote by $A^c$ the negation of $A$ and by $A \vee B$ (resp., $AB$) the logical union (resp., intersection) of $A$ and $B$. We use the same symbol to denote an event and its indicator. For each integer $n$, we set $J_n = \{1, 2, \ldots, n\}$. Given a prevision function $\mathbb{P}$ defined on an arbitrary family $\mathcal{K}$ of finite conditional random quantities, let $\mathcal{F}_n = \{X_i | H_i, i \in J_n\}$ be a finite subfamily of $\mathcal{K}$ and $\mathcal{M}_n$ the vector $(\mu_i, i \in J_n)$, where $\mu_i = \mathbb{P}(X_i | H_i)$ is the assessed prevision for the conditional random quantity $X_i | H_i$. With the pair $(\mathcal{F}_n, \mathcal{M}_n)$ we associate the random gain $\mathcal{G}_n = \sum_{i \in J_n} s_i H_i (X_i - \mu_i)$, where $s_1, \ldots, s_n$ are arbitrary real numbers and $H_1, \ldots, H_n$ denote the indicators of the corresponding events. We set $\mathcal{H}_n = H_1 \vee \cdots \vee H_n$; moreover, we denote by $\mathcal{G}_n | \mathcal{H}_n$ the restriction of $\mathcal{G}_n$ to $\mathcal{H}_n$. Then, using the *betting scheme* of de Finetti, we have

**Definition 1.** The function $\mathbb{P}$ is coherent if and only if, $\forall n \geq 1, \forall \mathcal{F}_n \subseteq \mathcal{K}, \forall s_1, \ldots, s_n \in \mathbb{R}$, it holds: $\sup \mathcal{G}_n | \mathcal{H}_n \geq 0$.

Given a family of $n$ conditional random quantities $\mathcal{F}_n = \{X_1 | H_1, \ldots, X_n | H_n\}$, for each $i \in J_n$ we assume $X_i \in \{x_{i1}, \ldots, x_{ir_i}\}$; then, for each $i \in J_n$ and $j = 1, \ldots, r_i$, we set $A_{ij} = (X_i = x_{ij})$. Of course, for each $i \in J_n$, the family $\{A_{ij}, j = 1, \ldots, r_i\}$ is a partition of the sure event $\Omega$. Moreover, for each $i \in J_n$, the family $\{H_i^c, A_{ij} H_i, j = 1, \ldots, r_i\}$ is a partition of $\Omega$ too. Then, the constituents generated by the family $\mathcal{F}_n$ are (the elements of the partition of $\Omega$) obtained by expanding the expression $\bigwedge_{i \in J_n} (A_{i1} H_i \vee \cdots \vee A_{ir_i} H_i \vee H_i^c)$. We set $C_0 = H_1^c \cdots H_n^c$ (it may be $C_0 = \emptyset$); moreover, we denote by $C_1, \ldots, C_m$ the constituents contained in $\mathcal{H}_n = H_1 \vee \cdots \vee H_n$. Hence

$$\bigwedge_{i \in J_n} (A_{i1} H_i \vee \cdots \vee A_{ir_i} H_i \vee H_i^c) = \bigvee_{h=0}^{m} C_h .$$

With each $C_h$, $h \in J_m$, we associate a vector $Q_h = (q_{h1}, \ldots, q_{hn})$, where

$$q_{hi} = \begin{cases} x_{i1}, & C_h \subseteq A_{i1} H_i, \\ \ldots\ldots & \ldots\ldots\ldots\ldots\ldots \\ x_{ir_i}, & C_h \subseteq A_{ir_i} H_i, \\ \mu_i, & C_h \subseteq H_i^c. \end{cases} \tag{1}$$

In more explicit terms, for each $j \in \{1, \ldots, r_i\}$ the condition $C_h \subseteq A_{ij} H_i$ amounts to $C_h \subseteq A_{i1}^c \cdots A_{i,j-1}^c A_{ij} A_{i,j+1}^c \cdots A_{ir}^c A_{ir_i}^c H_i$.

Given any vector $(\lambda_h\,,\ h \in J_m)$ and any event $A$, we set $\sum_{h:C_h \subseteq A} \lambda_h = \sum_A \lambda_h$. Then, by observing that $H_i = \bigvee_{j=1}^{r_i} A_{ij}H_i$, for each $i \in J_n$ we have

$$\sum_{h \in J_m} \lambda_h q_{hi} = \sum_{H_i} \lambda_h q_{hi} + \sum_{H_i^c} \lambda_h q_{hi} = \sum_{j=1}^{r_i} x_{ij} \sum_{A_{ij}H_i} \lambda_h + \mu_i \sum_{H_i^c} \lambda_h \,. \qquad (2)$$

Denoting by $\mathcal{I}_n$ the convex hull of the points $Q_1, \ldots, Q_m$, we examine the satisfiability of the condition $\mathcal{M}_n \in \mathcal{I}_n$; that is we check the existence of a vector $(\lambda_1, \ldots, \lambda_m)$ such that: $\sum_{h \in J_m} \lambda_h Q_h = \mathcal{M}_n$, $\sum_{h \in J_m} \lambda_h = 1$, $\lambda_h \geq 0$, $\forall h$. More explicitly, we check the solvability of the following system $\Sigma$ associated with the pair $(\mathcal{F}, \mathcal{M})$, in the nonnegative unknowns $\lambda_1, \ldots, \lambda_m$,

$$\Sigma: \qquad \sum_{h \in J_m} \lambda_h q_{hi} = \mu_i\,, \ i \in J_n\,; \ \sum_{h \in J_m} \lambda_h = 1\,, \ \lambda_h \geq 0\,, \ \forall h. \qquad (3)$$

We remark that $X_i H_i = \sum_{j=1}^{r_i} x_{ij} A_{ij} H_i$; hence, by interpreting the vector $(\lambda_h\,, h \in J_m)$ as a probability assessment on the family $\{C_1|\mathcal{H}_n, \ldots, C_m|\mathcal{H}_n\}$, one has: $\mathbb{P}(X_i H_i|\mathcal{H}_n) = \sum_{j=1}^{r_i} x_{ij} \sum_{A_{ij}H_i} \lambda_h = \mathbb{P}(X_i|H_i)P(H_i|\mathcal{H}_n)$, where $P(H_i|\mathcal{H}_n) = \sum_{H_i} \lambda_h$. Then in system (3), by decomposition formula (2), the equality $\sum_{h \in J_m} \lambda_h q_{hi} = \mu_i$ represents the condition $\mathbb{P}(X_i H_i|\mathcal{H}_n) = \mu_i P(H_i|\mathcal{H}_n)$. Given a subset $J \subseteq J_n$, we set $\mathcal{F}_J = \{X_i|H_i\,, i \in J\}$, $\mathcal{M}_J = (\mu_i\,, i \in J)$; then, we denote by $\Sigma_J$, where $\Sigma_{J_n} = \Sigma$, the system like (3) associated with the pair $(\mathcal{F}_J, \mathcal{M}_J)$. Then, it can be proved the following ([2])

**Theorem 1.** [*Characterization of coherence*]. Given a family of $n$ conditional random quantities $\mathcal{F} = \{X_1|H_1, \ldots, X_n|H_n\}$ and a vector $\mathcal{M} = (\mu_1, \ldots, \mu_n)$, the conditional prevision assessment $\mathbb{P}(X_1|H_1) = \mu_1$, $\ldots$, $\mathbb{P}(X_n|H_n) = \mu_n$ is coherent if and only if, for every subset $J \subseteq J_n$, defining $\mathcal{F}_J = \{X_i|H_i\,, i \in J\}$, $\mathcal{M}_J = (\mu_i\,, i \in J)$, the system $\Sigma_J$ associated with the pair $(\mathcal{F}_J, \mathcal{M}_J)$ is solvable.

## 3  Scoring Rules and Admissibility for Conditional Prevision Assessments

In this section we consider scoring rules for conditional prevision assessments and we illustrate the notions of weak and strong dominance, and of admissibility with respect to a scoring rule. A score may represent a reward or a penalty; we think of scores as penalties, so that to improve the score means to reduce it. We now extend the notion of strictly proper scoring rule in the following way.

**Definition 2.** A function $\sigma : (-\infty, +\infty) \times (-\infty, +\infty) \to [0, +\infty)$ is said to be a strictly proper scoring rule if the following conditions are satisfied:
(a) given any real numbers $x_1, \ldots, x_r, z, p_1, \ldots, p_r$, with

$$\sum_{i=1}^r p_i = 1\,, \ \sum_{i=1}^r p_i x_i = \mu \neq z\,, \ p_i \geq 0\,, \forall i\,,$$

it holds

$$\sum_{i=1}^r p_i\, \sigma(x_i, z) > \sum_{i=1}^r p_i\, \sigma(x_i, \mu)\,; \qquad (4)$$

(b) for every real number $x$, the function $\sigma(x, z)$ is a continuous function of $z$.

In this paper we focus our attention on strictly proper scoring rules which are bounded. Given a scoring rule $\sigma$, with any (finite) conditional random quantity $X|H$, we associate the *conditional scoring rule* $\sigma(X|H, z)$ defined as $\sigma(X|H, z) = H\sigma(X, z)$. Consider any conditional random quantity $X|H$, with $X \in \{x_1, \ldots, x_r\}$, and any probability distribution $\mathcal{P} = (p_1, \ldots, p_r) \in \mathcal{V}^{r-1}$, where $p_i = P(X = x_i|H)$ and $\mathcal{V}^{r-1} = \{\mathcal{P} = (p_1, \ldots, p_r) : \sum_{i=1}^{r} p_i = 1, \ p_i \geq 0\}$. We denote by $\overline{\mathcal{P}}$ the subvector $(p_1, p_2, \ldots, p_{r-1})$ of $\mathcal{P}$ and by $\mathcal{S}^{r-1} \subset \mathbb{R}^{r-1}$ the convex set

$$\mathcal{S}^{r-1} = \{\overline{\mathcal{P}} = (p_1, \ldots, p_{r-1}) \in \mathbb{R}^{r-1} : \mathcal{P} = (\overline{\mathcal{P}}, 1 - \sum_{i=1}^{r-1} p_i) \in \mathcal{V}^{r-1}\}.$$

For any given real number $z$ and for any proper scoring rule $\sigma$ the conditional prevision of $\sigma(X|H, z)$ w.r.t. $\mathcal{P}$ is given by

$$s(\overline{\mathcal{P}}, z) = \mathbb{P}_{\mathcal{P}}(\sigma(X|H, z)|H) = \sum_{i=1}^{r-1} p_i \sigma(x_i, z) + (1 - \sum_{i=1}^{r-1} p_i)\sigma(x_r, z). \quad (5)$$

We give below, without proof, some properties of the function $s(\overline{\mathcal{P}}, z)$.

**Proposition 1.** The function $s(\overline{\mathcal{P}}, z) : \mathcal{S}^{r-1} \times (-\infty, +\infty) \to [0, +\infty)$ satisfies the following properties:

1. $s(\alpha\overline{\mathcal{P}}' + (1 - \alpha)\overline{\mathcal{P}}'', z) = \alpha\, s(\overline{\mathcal{P}}', z) + (1 - \alpha)\, s(\overline{\mathcal{P}}'', z)$ for every $\alpha \in [0, 1]$;
2. we have $s(\overline{\mathcal{P}}, z) \geq s(\overline{\mathcal{P}}, \mu)$, where $\mu = \sum_{i=1}^{r-1} p_i x_i + (1 - \sum_{i=1}^{r-1} p_i)x_r$, with $s(\overline{\mathcal{P}}, z) = s(\overline{\mathcal{P}}, \mu)$ if and only if $z = \mu$;
3. $s(\overline{\mathcal{P}}, \mu)$, with $\mu = \sum_{i=1}^{r-1} p_i x_i + (1 - \sum_{i=1}^{r-1} p_i)x_r$, is a strictly concave function of $\overline{\mathcal{P}}$;
4. given any $\overline{\mathcal{P}} = (p_1, \ldots, p_{r-1})$, with $\sum_{i=1}^{r-1} p_i x_i + (1 - \sum_{i=1}^{r-1} p_i)x_r = \mu$, $s(\overline{\mathcal{P}}, z)$ is partially derivable with respect to $z$, $\forall\, z$, and it holds $\frac{\partial s(\overline{\mathcal{P}}, z)}{\partial z}|_{z=\mu} = 0$;
5. given any interior point $\overline{\mathcal{P}}$ of $\mathcal{S}^{r-1}$, with $\sum_{i=1}^{r-1} p_i x_i + (1 - \sum_{i=1}^{r-1} p_i)x_r = \mu$, for each $j = 1, \ldots, r - 1$, we have $\frac{\partial s(\overline{\mathcal{P}}, \mu)}{\partial p_j} = \sigma(x_j, \mu) - \sigma(x_r, \mu)$. Moreover, $s(\overline{\mathcal{P}}, \mu)$ is differentiable in the interior of $\mathcal{S}^{r-1}$;
6. for any interior point $\overline{\mathcal{P}}$ of $\mathcal{S}^{r-1}$, with $\sum_{i=1}^{r-1} p_i x_i + (1 - \sum_{i=1}^{r-1} p_i)x_r = \mu$, and for every $\overline{\mathcal{P}}' \in \mathcal{S}^{r-1}$, we have

$$s(\overline{\mathcal{P}}', \mu) = s(\overline{\mathcal{P}}, \mu) + \nabla s(\overline{\mathcal{P}}, \mu) \cdot (\overline{\mathcal{P}}' - \overline{\mathcal{P}}).$$

Given a prevision assessment $\mathcal{M}_n = (\mu_1, \mu_2, \ldots, \mu_n)$ on a family of conditional random quantities $\mathcal{F}_n = \{X_1|H_1, X_2|H_2, \ldots, X_n|H_n\}$, where $\mu_i = \mathbb{P}(X_i|H_i)$, and a proper scoring rule $\sigma$, let $C_0, C_1, \ldots, C_m$ be the constituents generated by $\mathcal{F}_n$ and $Q_1, \ldots, Q_m$ the points associated with the pair $(\mathcal{F}_n, \mathcal{M}_n)$, as defined by formula (1). The penalty $\mathcal{L}$ associated with the pair $(\mathcal{F}_n, \mathcal{M}_n)$ is given by

$$\mathcal{L} = \sum_{i=1}^{n} \sigma(X_i|H_i, \mu_i) = \sum_{i=1}^{n} H_i\sigma(X_i, \mu_i).$$

We denote by $L_k$ the value of $\mathcal{L}$ associated with $C_k$, $k = 0, 1, \ldots, m$. Of course, $L_0 = 0$; moreover, by defining the quantities

$$h_{ki} = \begin{cases} 1, \ C_k \subseteq H_i, \\ 0, \ C_k \subseteq H_i^c, \end{cases} \qquad e_{kij} = \begin{cases} 1, \ C_k \subseteq A_{ij}, \\ 0, \ C_k \subseteq A_{ij}^c, \end{cases}$$

we have

$$L_k = \sum_{i=1}^n h_{ki} \sum_{j=1}^{r_i} e_{kij} \sigma(x_{ij}, \mu_i), \ k = 1, \ldots, m. \tag{6}$$

We give below the notions of weak and strong dominance and admissibility with respect to scoring rules.

**Definition 3.** Let $\sigma$ be a scoring rule and $\mathcal{M}_n$ be a prevision assessment on a family $\mathcal{F}_n$ of $n$ conditional random quantities. Given any assessment $\mathcal{M}_n^*$ on $\mathcal{F}_n$, with $\mathcal{M}_n^* \neq \mathcal{M}_n$, we say that $\mathcal{M}_n$ is *weakly dominated* by $\mathcal{M}_n^*$, with respect to $\sigma$, if denoting by $\mathcal{L}$ (resp., $\mathcal{L}^*$) the penalty associated with the pair $(\mathcal{F}_n, \mathcal{M}_n)$ (resp., $(\mathcal{F}_n, \mathcal{M}_n^*)$), it holds $\mathcal{L}^* \leq \mathcal{L}$, that is: $L_k^* \leq L_k$, for every $k = 0, 1, \ldots, m$. Moreover, by observing that $L_0 = L_0^* = 0$, we say that $\mathcal{M}_n$ is *strongly dominated* by $\mathcal{M}_n^*$, with respect to $\sigma$, if $L_k^* < L_k$, for every $k = 1, \ldots, m$.

We observe that $\mathcal{M}_n$ is not weakly dominated by $\mathcal{M}_n^*$ if and only if $L_k^* > L_k$ for at least a subscript $k$.

**Definition 4.** Let $\sigma$ be a scoring rule and $\mathcal{M}_n$ be a prevision assessment on a family $\mathcal{F}_n$ of $n$ conditional random quantities. We say that $\mathcal{M}_n$ is *admissible* w.r.t. $\sigma$ if $\mathcal{M}_n$ is not weakly dominated by any $\mathcal{M}_n^* \neq \mathcal{M}_n$. Moreover, given a prevision assessment $\mathcal{M}$ on an arbitrary family of conditional random quantities $\mathcal{K}$, we say that $\mathcal{M}$ is admissible w.r.t. $\sigma$ if, for every finite subfamily $\mathcal{F}_n \subseteq \mathcal{K}$, the restriction $\mathcal{M}_n$ of $\mathcal{M}$ to $\mathcal{F}_n$ is admissible w.r.t. $\sigma$.

*Remark 1.* We observe that, by Definition 4, it follows:
- If the assessment $\mathcal{M}_n$ on $\mathcal{F}_n$ is admissible, then for every subfamily $\mathcal{F}_J \subset \mathcal{F}_n$ the sub-assessment $\mathcal{M}_J$ associated with $\mathcal{F}_J$ is admissible.

## 4    Coherence and Admissibility of Conditional Prevision Assessments

In this section we give the main result of the paper, by showing the equivalence between the coherence of conditional prevision assessments and admissibility with respect to proper scoring rules. Given the assessment $\mathcal{M}_n = (\mu_1, \ldots, \mu_n)$ on $\mathcal{F}_n = \{X_1|H_1, X_2|H_2, \ldots, X_n|H_n\}$ and a bounded strictly proper scoring rule $\sigma$, we set $S(\overline{P}, \mathcal{Z}_n) = S(\overline{\mathcal{P}}_1, \ldots, \overline{\mathcal{P}}_n, \mathcal{Z}_n) = \sum_{i=1}^n s(\overline{\mathcal{P}}_i, z_i)$, where $\overline{P} = (\overline{\mathcal{P}}_1, \ldots, \overline{\mathcal{P}}_n)$, $\overline{\mathcal{P}}_i = (p_{i1}, \ldots, p_{ir_i-1})$, $\sum_{j=1}^{r_i-1} p_{ij} x_{ij} + (1 - \sum_{j=1}^{r_i-1} p_{ij}) x_{ir_i} = \mu_i$ and $\mathcal{Z}_n = (z_1, \ldots, z_n)$. Given any vector $\overline{P}' = (\overline{\mathcal{P}}_1', \ldots, \overline{\mathcal{P}}_n') \in \Pi$, with $\overline{\mathcal{P}}_i' = (p_{i1}', \ldots, p_{ir_i-1}')$ and $\Pi = \prod_{i=1}^n \mathcal{S}^{r_i-1} \subset \mathbb{R}^{r-n}$, $r = \sum_{i=1}^n r_i$, from the properties 5 and 6 in Proposition 1 we have $S(\overline{P}', \mathcal{M}_n) = S(\overline{P}, \mathcal{M}_n) + \nabla S(\overline{P}, \mathcal{M}_n) \cdot (\overline{P}' - \overline{P})$. We set $\Phi(\overline{P}) = -S(\overline{P}, \mathcal{M}_n) = -\sum_{i=1}^n s(\overline{\mathcal{P}}_i, \mu_i)$. Then, we have $S(\overline{P}', \mathcal{M}_n) = -\Phi(\overline{P}) - \nabla\Phi(\overline{P}) \cdot (\overline{P}' - \overline{P})$, that is

$$S(\overline{P}', \mathcal{M}_n) - S(\overline{P}, \mathcal{M}_n) = -\nabla\Phi(\overline{P}) \cdot (\overline{P}' - \overline{P}). \tag{7}$$

We observe that the function $\Phi(\overline{P})$ is continuous on $\Pi$ and strictly convex in the interior of $\Pi$. Moreover, $\Phi(\overline{P})$ has continuous partial derivatives on the interior of $\Pi$, so that $\Phi(\overline{P})$ is differentiable in the interior of $\Pi$ and the gradient $\nabla\Phi(\overline{P})$ is a continuous function on the interior of $\Pi$. As the functions $\sigma(x_{ij}, z_i)$ are assumed bounded, then $\nabla\Phi(\overline{P})$ extends to a bounded continuous function on $\Pi$. The Bregman divergence ([3,9]) associated with the function $\Phi$ is given by

$$d_\Phi(\overline{P}', \overline{P}) = \Phi(\overline{P}') - \Phi(\overline{P}) - \nabla\Phi(\overline{P}) \cdot (\overline{P}' - \overline{P}).$$

Then, from (7) it follows

$$d_\Phi(\overline{P}', \overline{P}) = \Phi(\overline{P}') - \Phi(\overline{P}) + S(\overline{P}', \mathcal{M}_n) + \Phi(\overline{P}) = S(\overline{P}', \mathcal{M}_n) - S(\overline{P}', \mathcal{M}_n'). \quad (8)$$

We illustrate now the relationship between the notion of coherence and the property of non dominance, by first examining a single assessment $\mathbb{P}(X|H) = \mu$.

**Lemma 1.** Given any event $H \neq \emptyset$, any finite random quantity $X \in \{x_1, \ldots, x_r\}$ and any strictly proper continuous and bounded scoring rule $\sigma$, the assessment $\mathbb{P}(X|H) = \mu$ is coherent if and only if $\mu$ is admissible with respect to $\sigma$.

*Proof.* ($\Rightarrow$) Assume that $\mu$ is coherent. With no loss of generality, we can suppose $x_1 < \cdots < x_r$ and $A_i H \neq \emptyset$ where $A_i = (X = x_i)$, $i = 1, \ldots, r$; then coherence of $\mu$ amounts to $x_1 \leq \mu \leq x_r$, so that there exist $p_1, \ldots, p_r$ such that $\sum_i p_i x_i = \mu$, with $\sum_i p_i = 1$, $p_i \geq 0$, for every $i$. Then, for any given $\mu^* \neq \mu$, by recalling (4) we have $\sum_i p_i \sigma(x_i, \mu) < \sum_i p_i \sigma(x_i, \mu^*)$, so that $\sigma(x_k, \mu) < \sigma(x_k, \mu^*)$ for at least an index $k$; hence, $\mu$ is not weakly dominated by $\mu^*$.

($\Leftarrow$) Assume that $\mu$ is not coherent; that is $\mu \notin [x_1, x_r]$. We consider the random quantity $Y = XH + \mu H^c$ with possible values: $x_1, \ldots, x_r, \mu$, which are associated with the $r+1$ constituents: $A_1 H, \ldots, A_r H, H^c$. Let $P = (p_1, p_2, \ldots, p_{r+1})$ be a probability distribution on $Y$; we set $\overline{P} = (p_1, p_2, \ldots, p_r)$. Then, the prevision of the score $\sigma(Y, \mu)$ is $s(\overline{P}, \mu)$. We observe that particular choices of $P$ are the vectors $W_k = (w_{k1}, \ldots, w_{kr}, w_{k\,r+1})$, $k = 1, 2, \ldots, r + 1$, with $W_1 = (1, 0, \ldots, 0)$, $W_2 = (0, 1, 0, \ldots, 0)$, $\ldots, W_{r+1} = (0, \ldots, 0, 1)$. We set $\overline{W}_k = (w_{k1}, \ldots, w_{kr})$; then $s(\overline{W}_k, \mu) = \sum_{j=1}^r w_{kj} \sigma(x_j, \mu) + (1 - \sum_{j=1}^r w_{kj}) \sigma(\mu, \mu) = \sigma(x_k, \mu)$, $k = 1, \ldots, r$, with $s(\overline{W}_{r+1}, \mu) = \sigma(\mu, \mu)$. As $s(\overline{W}_k, x_k) = \sigma(x_k, x_k)$, $k = 1, \ldots, r$, we obtain $L_k = \sigma(x_k, \mu) = s(\overline{W}_k, \mu) - s(\overline{W}_k, x_k) + \alpha_k$, $k = 1, \ldots, r$, with $\alpha_k = \sigma(x_k, x_k)$ and $L_{r+1} = \sigma(\mu, \mu)$. We set $\mathcal{C} = [0, 1]^r$; then, we consider the function $\Phi(\overline{P}) : \mathcal{C} \to R$, defined as $\Phi(\overline{P}) = -s(\overline{P}, \mu(\overline{P}))$, with $\overline{P} = (p_1, \ldots, p_r)$, $\mu(\overline{P}) = p_1 x_1 + \ldots + p_r x_r + p_{r+1}\mu$, $p_{r+1} = 1 - \sum_{j=1}^r p_j$. Based on (8), we have $d_\Phi(\overline{P}', \overline{P}) = s(\overline{P}, \mu(\overline{P})) - s(\overline{P}', \mu(\overline{P}'))$ and, by observing that $\mu(\overline{W}_k) = x_k$ and $\mu(\overline{W}_{r+1}) = \mu$, we obtain

$$L_k = s(\overline{W}_k, \mu) - s(\overline{W}_k, x_k) + \alpha_k = d_\Phi(\overline{W}_k, \overline{W}_{r+1}) + \alpha_k, \quad k = 1, \ldots, r.$$

Denoting by $\mathcal{I}_W$ the convex hull of $\overline{W}_1, \ldots, \overline{W}_r$, for each $\overline{P} = (p_1, \ldots, p_r) \in \mathcal{I}_W$ we have $\overline{P} = \sum_{i=1}^r p_i \overline{W}_i$, with $\sum_{i=1}^r p_i = 1$, so that $p_{r+1} = 0$. Then $\mu(\overline{P}) \in [x_1, x_r]$ and, as $\mu \notin [x_1, x_r]$, we have $\mu(\overline{P}) \neq \mu, \forall \overline{P} \in \mathcal{I}_W$. Then, for every $\overline{P}_\mu \in \mathcal{C}$ such that $\mu(\overline{P}_\mu) = \mu$, it holds that $\overline{P} \notin \mathcal{I}_W$; thus, there exists a projection point

$\overline{P}_\mu^* \in \mathcal{I}_W$, with $\mu(\overline{P}_\mu^*) = \mu^*$, such that: $d_\Phi(\overline{W}_k, \overline{P}_\mu^*) + d_\Phi(\overline{P}_\mu^*, \overline{P}_\mu) \le d_\Phi(\overline{W}_k, \overline{P}_\mu)$, and, as $\overline{P}_\mu^* \ne \overline{P}_\mu$, one has: $d_\Phi(\overline{W}_k, \overline{P}_\mu^*) < d_\Phi(\overline{W}_k, \overline{P}_\mu)$, $k = 1, \ldots, r$, that is $\sigma(x_k, \mu^*) < \sigma(x_k, \mu)$, $k = 1, \ldots, r$. Now, by considering the alternative assessments $\mu^*$ and $\mu$ for the prevision of $X|H$, we have

$$L_0^* = L_0 = 0 \text{ and } L_k^* = \sigma(x_k, \mu^*) < \sigma(x_k, \mu) = L_k, \; k = 1, \ldots, r;$$

thus, $\mu$ is (strictly) dominated by $\mu^*$ with respect to $\sigma$.    □

Based on the previous Lemma, given any prevision assessment $\mathcal{M}_n = (\mu_1, \ldots, \mu_n)$, in what follows we can assume $\mu_i \in [min\,X_i|H_i, max\,X_i|H_i,]$ for every $i$. We have

**Theorem 2.** Let $\mathcal{M}$ be a prevision assessment on a family $\mathcal{K}$ of conditional random quantities, with $\mu_{X|H} = \mathbb{P}(X|H) \in [minX|H, maxX|H]$ for every $X|H \in \mathcal{K}$; moreover, let $\sigma$ be any bounded strictly proper scoring rule. $\mathcal{M}$ is coherent if and only if $\mathcal{M}$ is admissible with respect to $\sigma$.

*Proof.* ($\Rightarrow$) Assuming $\mathcal{M}$ coherent, let $\sigma$ be a bounded proper scoring rule. Given any subfamily $\mathcal{F}_n = \{X_1|H_1, \ldots, X_n|H_n\}$ of $\mathcal{K}$, let $\mathcal{M}_n = (\mu_1, \ldots, \mu_n)$ be the restriction to $\mathcal{F}_n$ of $\mathcal{M}$. Now, given any $\mathcal{M}_n^* = (\mu_1^*, \ldots, \mu_n^*) \ne \mathcal{M}_n$, we distinguish two cases:

(a) $\mu_i^* \ne \mu_i$, for every $i = 1, \ldots, n$; (b) $\mu_i^* = \mu_i$, for at least one index $i$. Case (a). We still denote by $C_0, C_1, \ldots, C_m$, where $C_0 = H_1^c \wedge \cdots \wedge H_n^c$, the constituents generated by $\mathcal{F}_n$ and by $Q_k = (q_{k1}, \ldots, q_{kn})$ the point associated with $C_k, k = 1, \ldots, m$. With the assessment $\mathcal{M}_n$ we associate the loss

$$\mathcal{L} = \sum_{i=1}^n \sigma(X_i|H_i, \mu_i) = \sum_{i=1}^n H_i \sigma(X_i, \mu_i),$$

with $L_0 = 0$ and, recalling (6), $L_k = \sum_{i=1}^n h_{ki} \sum_{j=1}^{r_i} e_{kij} \sigma(x_{ij}, \mu_i)$, $k = 1, \ldots, m$. Of course, with any other assessment $\mathcal{M}_n^*$ on $\mathcal{F}_n$ we associate the loss

$$\mathcal{L}^* = \sum_{i=1}^n \sigma(X_i|H_i, \mu_i^*) = \sum_{i=1}^n H_i \sigma(X_i, \mu_i^*),$$

with $L_0^* = 0$ and $L_k^* = \sum_{i=1}^n h_{ki} \sum_{j=1}^{r_i} e_{kij} \sigma(x_{ij}, \mu_i^*)$, $k = 1, \ldots, m$. As $L_0 = L_0^* = 0$, in what follows we will only refer to the values $L_k, L_k^*, k = 1, \ldots, m$. As $\mathcal{M}_n$ is coherent, there exists a vector $(\lambda_1, \ldots, \lambda_m)$, with $\lambda_k \ge 0$ and $\sum_k \lambda_k = 1$, which is a coherent extension of $\mathcal{M}_n$ on the family of conditional events $\{C_1|\mathcal{H}_n, \ldots, C_m|\mathcal{H}_n\}$, with $\lambda_h = P(C_h|\mathcal{H}_n)$. We have

$$P(H_i|\mathcal{H}_n) = \sum_{C_k \subseteq H_i} P(C_k|\mathcal{H}_n) = \sum_k \lambda_k h_{ki},$$

with $\sum_{i=1}^n P(H_i|\mathcal{H}_n) \ge P(\mathcal{H}_n|\mathcal{H}_n) = 1$, so that $P(H_i|\mathcal{H}_n) > 0$ for at least an index $i$. Moreover

$$P(A_{ij}H_i|\mathcal{H}_n) = \sum_{C_k \subseteq A_{ij}H_i} P(C_k|\mathcal{H}_n) = \sum_k \lambda_k h_{ki} e_{kij} = P(A_{ij}|H_i)P(H_i|\mathcal{H}_n).$$

We set: $I' = \{i : \sum_k \lambda_k h_{ki} > 0\} \subseteq \{1, 2, \ldots, n\}$. Of course, $I' \neq \emptyset$. We set $P(A_{ij}|H_i) = p_{ij}$; then, by observing that

$$\sum_{j=1}^{r_i}(\sum_k \lambda_k h_{ki} e_{kij})x_{ij} = \sum_{j=1}^{r_i} P(A_{ij}H_i|\mathcal{H}_n)x_{ij} =$$
$$= \sum_{j=1}^{r_i} P(A_{ij}|H_i)P(H_i|\mathcal{H}_n)x_{ij} = P(H_i|\mathcal{H}_n)\sum_{j=1}^{r_i} p_{ij}\,x_{ij} = \mu_i P(H_i|\mathcal{H}_n),$$

for each $i \in I'$ it holds

$$\sum_{j=1}^{r_i}(\sum_k \lambda_k h_{ki} e_{kij})\sigma(x_{ij}, \mu_i) = P(H_i|\mathcal{H}_n)\sum_{j=1}^{r_i} p_{ij}\sigma(x_{ij}, \mu_i) <$$
$$< P(H_i|\mathcal{H}_n)\sum_{j=1}^{r_i} p_{ij}\sigma(x_{ij}, \mu_i^*).$$

It follows:

$$\sum_k \lambda_k L_k = \sum_k \lambda_k \sum_{i=1}^{n} h_{ki} \sum_{j=1}^{r_i} e_{kij}\sigma(x_{ij}, \mu_i) = \sum_{i\in I'}\sum_{j=1}^{r_i}(\sum_k \lambda_k h_{ki} e_{kij})\sigma(x_{ij}, \mu_i) =$$
$$\sum_{i\in I'} P(H_i|\mathcal{H}_n)\sum_{j=1}^{r_i} p_{ij}\sigma(x_{ij}, \mu_i) < \sum_{i\in I'} P(H_i|\mathcal{H}_n)\sum_{j=1}^{r_i} p_{ij}\sigma(x_{ij}, \mu_i^*) =$$
$$= \sum_k \lambda_k \sum_{i=1}^{n} h_{ki} \sum_{j=1}^{r_i} e_{kij}\sigma(x_{ij}, \mu_i^*) = \sum_k \lambda_k L_k^* .$$

The inequality $\sum_k \lambda_k L_k < \sum_k \lambda_k L_k^*$ implies that there exists an index $k$ such that $L_k < L_k^*$; that is $\mathcal{L}^* > \mathcal{L}$ in at least one case. Hence $\mathcal{M}_n$ is admissible. Since $\mathcal{F}_n$ is arbitrary, it follows that $\mathcal{M}$ is admissible.

Case **(b)**. Let $\mathcal{M}_n^* \neq \mathcal{M}_n$, with $\mu_i^* = \mu_i$, for at least one index $i$. We set $J = \{i : \mu_i^* \neq \mu_i\} \subset J_n = \{1, \ldots, n\}$. We denote by $\mathcal{M}_J$ (resp., $\mathcal{M}_{J_n\setminus J}$) the subvector of $\mathcal{M}_n$ associated with $J$ (resp., $J_n \setminus J$). Analogously, we can consider the subvectors $\mathcal{M}_J^*$ and $\mathcal{M}_{J_n\setminus J}^*$ of $\mathcal{M}_n^*$. Then, we have

$$\mathcal{L} = \mathcal{L}_J + \mathcal{L}_{J_n\setminus J}, \quad \mathcal{L}^* = \mathcal{L}_J^* + \mathcal{L}_{J_n\setminus J}^*, \quad \mathcal{L}_{J_n\setminus J} = \mathcal{L}_{J_n\setminus J}^*.$$

By the same reasoning as in case (a), it holds that $\mathcal{L}_J^* > \mathcal{L}_J$ in at least one case. Then, by observing that $\mathcal{L} - \mathcal{L}^* = \mathcal{L}_J - \mathcal{L}_J^*$, it is $\mathcal{L}^* > \mathcal{L}$ in at least one case; hence $\mathcal{M}_n$ is admissible. Since $\mathcal{F}_n$ is arbitrary, $\mathcal{M}$ is admissible.

($\Leftarrow$). We will prove that, given any bounded proper scoring rule $\sigma$, if $\mathcal{M}$ is not coherent, then $\mathcal{M}$ is not admissible with respect to $\sigma$. Assume that $\mathcal{M}$ is not coherent. Then, there exists a subfamily $\mathcal{F}_n = \{X_1|H_1, \ldots, X_n|H_n\} \subseteq \mathcal{K}$ such that, for the restriction $\mathcal{M}_n = (\mu_1, \ldots, \mu_n)$ of $\mathcal{M}$ to $\mathcal{F}_n$, denoting by $\mathcal{I}_n$ the associated convex hull, we have $\mathcal{M}_n \notin \mathcal{I}_n$. For each constituent $C_k$ we set $\Gamma_k = \{i : C_k \subseteq H_i\}$, $I_k = \{i : C_k \subseteq H_i^c\} = J_n \setminus \Gamma_k$. As for each $i$ it holds $minX_i|H_i \leq \mu_i \leq maxX_i|H_i$, with each quantity $q_{ki}$, defined as in (1), we associate a vector $W_{ki} = (w_{ki1}, \ldots, w_{kir_i}) \in \mathcal{V}^{r_i-1}$, with

$$w_{kij} = \begin{cases} 1, & C_k \subseteq A_{ij}H_i, \\ 0, & C_k \subseteq A_{ij}^c H_i, \\ p_{ij}, & C_k \subseteq H_i^c, \end{cases} \tag{9}$$

where $\sum_{j=1}^{r_i} p_{ij}x_{ij} = \mu_i$, $\sum_{j=1}^{r_i} p_{ij} = 1$, $p_{ij} \geq 0$. We denote by $\overline{W}_{ki}$ the subvector $(w_{ki1}, \ldots, w_{ki(r_i-1)})$ of $W_{ki}$. As $W_{ki} \in \mathcal{V}^{r-1}$ it follows $\overline{W}_{ki} \in \mathcal{S}^{r-1}$. We observe that, if $C_k \subseteq H_i$, that is $i \in \Gamma_k$, then

$$s(\overline{W}_{ki}, q_{ki}) = \sum_{j=1}^{r_i-1} w_{kij}\sigma(x_{ij}, q_{ki}) + (1 - \sum_{j=1}^{r_i-1} w_{kij})\sigma(x_{ir}, q_{ki}) = \sigma(q_{ki}, q_{ki}) ;$$
$$s(\overline{W}_{ki}, \mu_i) = \cdots = \sigma(q_{ki}, \mu_i) .$$

If $C_k \subseteq H_i^c$, that is $i \in I_k$, then:

$$s(\overline{W}_{ki}, q_{ki}) = s(\overline{W}_{ki}, \mu_i) = \sum_{j=1}^{r_i-1} p_{ij}\sigma(x_{ij}, \mu_i) + (1 - \sum_{j=1}^{r_i-1} p_{ij})\sigma(x_{ir}, \mu_i) .$$

Then, by taking into account that $\sum_{i \in I_k}[s(\overline{W}_{ki}, \mu_i) - s(\overline{W}_{ki}, q_{ki})] = 0$ and defining $\overline{W}_k = (\overline{W}_{k1}, \ldots, \overline{W}_{kn})$, for the value $L_k$ of the penalty $\mathcal{L}$, we obtain

$$L_k = \sum_{i=1}^{n} h_{ki} \sum_{j=1}^{r_i} e_{kij}\sigma(x_{ij}, \mu_i) = \sum_{i \in \Gamma_k} \sigma(q_{ki}, \mu_i) =$$
$$= \sum_{i \in \Gamma_k} \sigma(q_{ki}, \mu_i) - \sum_{i \in \Gamma_k} \sigma(q_{ki}, q_{ki}) + \sum_{i \in \Gamma_k} \sigma(q_{ki}, q_{ki}) =$$
$$= \sum_{i \in \Gamma_k}[\sigma(q_{ki}, \mu_i) - \sigma(q_{ki}, q_{ki})] + \alpha_k = \sum_{i \in \Gamma_k}[s(\overline{W}_{ki}, \mu_i) - s(\overline{W}_{ki}, q_{ki})] + \alpha_k =$$
$$= \sum_{i \in \Gamma_k}[s(\overline{W}_{ki}, \mu_i) - s(\overline{W}_{ki}, q_{ki})] + \sum_{i \in I_k}[s(\overline{W}_{ki}, \mu_i) - s(\overline{W}_{ki}, q_{ki})] + \alpha_k =$$
$$= \sum_{i=1}^{n}[s(\overline{W}_{ki}, \mu_i) - s(\overline{W}_{ki}, q_{ki})] + \alpha_k = S(\overline{W}_k, \mathcal{M}_n) - S(\overline{W}_k, Q_k) + \alpha_k,$$

where $\alpha_k = \sum_{i \in \Gamma_k} \sigma(q_{ki}, q_{ki})$. Then, by applying (8) with $\overline{P}' = \overline{W}_k$, so that $\mathcal{M}'_n = Q_k$, we have

$$L_k = S(\overline{W}_k, \mathcal{M}_n) - S(\overline{W}_k, Q_k) + \alpha_k = d_\Phi(\overline{W}_k, \overline{P}) + \alpha_k . \qquad (10)$$

We recall that for the probability assessment $P = (\mathcal{P}_1, \ldots, \mathcal{P}_n)$ on the family $\mathcal{A} = \{A_{ij}|H_i, j = 1, \ldots, r_i; i \in J_n\}$ it holds that $\sum_{j=1}^{r_i} p_{ij}x_{ij} = \mu_i$, $i = 1, \ldots, n$. We recall that $\mathcal{M}_n \notin \mathcal{I}_n$; then, denoting by $\mathcal{I}_{\overline{P}}$ the convex hull associated with the pair $(\overline{\mathcal{A}}, \overline{P})$, where $\overline{\mathcal{A}} = \{A_{ij}|H_i, j = 1, \ldots, (r_i - 1); i \in J_n\}$, $\overline{P} = (\overline{\mathcal{P}}_1, \ldots, \overline{\mathcal{P}}_n)$ and $\overline{\mathcal{P}}_i = (p_{i1}, \ldots, p_{i(r_i-1)})$, we have $\overline{P} \notin \mathcal{I}_{\overline{P}}$. Then, by recalling the projection lemma associated with Bregman divergences ([9], see also [5], Proposition 2), for the projection $\overline{P}^*$ of $\overline{P}$ on $\mathcal{I}_{\overline{P}}$ we have

$$d_\Phi(\overline{W}_k, P^*) + d_\Phi(\overline{P}^*, \overline{P}) \leq d_\Phi(\overline{W}_k, \overline{P}) .$$

Moreover, as $\overline{P}^* \neq \overline{P}$, we have $d_\Phi(\overline{P}^*, \overline{P}) > 0$; therefore

$$d_\Phi(\overline{W}_k, \overline{P}^*) < d_\Phi(\overline{W}_k, \overline{P}), \ k = 1, \ldots, m .$$

Now, with the point $\overline{P}^*$ we associate the probability assessment $P^* = (\mathcal{P}_1^*, \ldots, \mathcal{P}_n^*)$, where $\mathcal{P}_i^* = (p_{i1}^*, \ldots, p_{i(r_i-1)}^*, 1 - \sum_{j=1}^{r-1} p_{ij}^*)$, and the (possibly not coherent) prevision assessment $\mathcal{M}_n^* = (\mu_1^*, \ldots, \mu_n^*)$, with $\sum_{j=1}^{r_i-1} p_{ij}^*x_{ij} + (1 - \sum_{j=1}^{r_j-1} p_{ij}^*)x_{ir_i} = \mu_i^*$, $i = 1, \ldots, n$. For each constituent $C_k$ we consider the vector $Q_k^*$ associated with the pair $(\mathcal{F}_n, \mathcal{M}_n^*)$; moreover, based on (9), with the pair $(P^*, Q_k^*)$ we associate the vector $W_k^*$. Then, for the values of the penalty $\mathcal{L}^*$, we have

$$L_k^* = S(\overline{W}_k^*, \mathcal{M}_n^*) - S(\overline{W}_k^*, Q_k^*) + \alpha_k^* = d_\Phi(\overline{W}_k^*, \overline{P}^*) + \alpha_k^*, \ k = 1, \ldots, m, \quad (11)$$

with $L_0^* = 0$ and $\alpha_k^* = \alpha_k = \sum_{i \in \Gamma_k} \sigma(q_{ki}, q_{ki})$. We observe that

$$\overline{W}_{ki} = \overline{W}_{ki}^*, \quad q_{ki} = q_{ki}^*, \ \forall i \in \Gamma_k, \ \forall k = 1, \ldots, m.$$

Then, by virtue of the property 2 of the function $s(\overline{P}, z)$ (which is connected with condition (a) in Definition 2), for each $k = 1, \ldots, m$ we have

$$
\begin{aligned}
d_\Phi(\overline{W}_k, \overline{P}^*) - d_\Phi(\overline{W}_k^*, \overline{P}^*) = \\
= S(\overline{W}_k, \mathcal{M}_n^*) - S(\overline{W}_k, Q_k) - [S(\overline{W}_k^*, \mathcal{M}_n^*) - S(\overline{W}_k^*, Q_k^*)] = \\
= \sum_{i=1}^n [s(\overline{W}_{ki}, \mu_i^*) - s(\overline{W}_{ki}, q_{ki})] - \sum_{i=1}^n [s(\overline{W}_{ki}^*, \mu_i^*) - s(\overline{W}_{ki}^*, q_{ki}^*)] = \\
= \sum_{i=1}^n [s(\overline{W}_{ki}, \mu_i^*) - s(\overline{W}_{ki}^*, \mu_i^*)] - \sum_{i=1}^n [s(\overline{W}_{ki}, q_{ki}) - s(\overline{W}_{ki}^*, q_{ki}^*)] = \\
= \sum_{i \in I_k} [s(\overline{P}_i, \mu_i^*) - s(\overline{P}_i^*, \mu_i^*)] - \sum_{i \in I_k} [s(\overline{P}_i, \mu_i) - s(\overline{P}_i^*, \mu_i^*)] = \\
= \sum_{i \in I_k} [s(\overline{P}_i, \mu_i^*) - s(\overline{P}_i, \mu_i)] \geq 0.
\end{aligned}
$$

Therefore, $d_\Phi(\overline{W}_k^*, \overline{P}^*) \leq d_\Phi(\overline{W}_k, \overline{P}^*) < d_\Phi(\overline{W}_k, \overline{P})$, for each $j = 1, 2, \ldots, m$. Then, recalling (10) and (11), for each $k = 1, \ldots, m$ we obtain

$$L_k^* = d_\Phi(\overline{W}_k^*, \overline{P}^*) + \alpha_k < d_\Phi(\overline{W}_k, \overline{P}) + \alpha_k = L_k;$$

that is, $\mathcal{M}_n$ is strongly dominated (and hence weakly dominated) by $\mathcal{M}_n^*$; hence $\mathcal{M}_n$ is not admissible. This implies that $\mathcal{M}$ is not admissible. $\square$

**Acknowledgments.** The authors thank the anonymous referees for their very useful comments and suggestions.

# References

1. Agró, G., Lad, F., Sanfilippo, G.: Sequentially forecasting economic indices using mixture linear combinations of EP distributions. Journal of Data Science 8(1), 101–126 (2010)
2. Biazzo, V., Gilio, A., Sanfilippo, G.: Generalized coherence and connection property of imprecise conditional previsions. In: Proceedings of IPMU 2008, Malaga, Spain, June 22-27, pp. 907–914 (2008)
3. Censor, Y., Zenios, S.A.: Parallel Optimization: Theory, Algorithms, and Applications. Oxford Univ. Press, Oxford (1997)
4. de Finetti, B.: Does it make sense to speak of 'good probability appraisers'? In: Good, I.J. (ed.) The Scientist Speculates: An Anthology of Partly-Baked Ideas, pp. 357–364. Heinemann, London (1962)
5. Gilio, A., Sanfilippo, G.: Coherent conditional probabilities and proper scoring rules. In: Proc. of ISIPTA 2011, Innsbruck, Austria, July 25-28, pp. 189–198 (2011)
6. Gneiting, T., Raftery, A.: Strictly proper scoring rules, prediction and estimation. J. Amer. Statist. Assoc. 102(477), 359–378 (2007)
7. Lad, F.: Operational Subjective Statistical Methods: a mathematical, philosophical, and historical introduction. John Wiley, New York (1996)

8. Lindley, D.V.: Scoring rules and the inevitability of probability. Int. Statist. Rev. 50, 1–11 (1982)
9. Predd, J.B., Seiringer, R., Lieb, E.H., Osherson, D.N., Poor, H.V., Kulkarni, S.R.: Probabilistic Coherence and Proper Scoring Rules. IEEE T. Inform. Theory 55, 4786–4792 (2009)
10. Savage, L.J.: Elicitation of personal probabilities and expectations. J. Amer. Statist. Assoc. 66, 783–801 (1971)
11. Schervish, M.J., Seidenfeld, T., Kadane, J.B.: Proper Scoring Rules, Dominated Forecasts, and Coherence. Decision Analysis 6(4), 202–221 (2009)

# Exchangeability in Probability Logic

Christian Wallmann and Gernot D. Kleiter*

Department of Psychology,
University of Salzburg, Salzburg, Austria
{christian.wallmann2,gernot.kleiter}@sbg.ac.at

**Abstract.** The paper investigates exchangeability in the context of probability logic. We study generalizations of basic inference rules and inferences involving cardinalities. We compare the results with those obtained in the case in which only identical probabilities are assumed.

**Keywords:** Exchangeability, Probability logic, Generalized inference rules, Interval probabilities.

## 1  Introduction

Exchangeability is one of several symmetry properties in probability theory. It is fundamental for the treatment of frequencies in Bayesian statistics. The concept was first introduced by de Finetti around 1928. It is the basic principle in his work on the logic of induction and foresight [4,3] and in the famous "de Finetti Theorem" first presented in his Henri Poincaré lecture given in Paris in 1935.

In the present paper we investigate exchangeability in the context of conditional probability logic. The main aim of conditional probability logic is to determine the set of all coherent probability values of an event (the conclusion) if a specific coherent probability assessment on other events (the premises) is given. De Finettis Fundamental Theorem [2] states that this set has to be an interval or a point value. An elementary example is Modus Ponens. It licenses the inference from the premises $\{A, A \to B\}$ to the conclusion $B$. Within conditional probability logic conditionals are represented by conditional events, so that the probabilistic version of Modus Ponens [9] licenses the inference from $P(A) = \alpha$ and $P(B|A) = \beta$ to $P(B) \in [\alpha\beta, \alpha\beta + 1 - \alpha]$ .

Gilio [6] has shown that conditional probability logic is a weak logic (see also [10]). In many cases the width of the interval of the conclusion increases as the number of some premises increases. It seems plausible that probability logic becomes stronger if further constraints are added. In many cases stochastic independence leads to point probabilities but it is a too restrictive and often implausible requirement [1]. Exchangeability is a weaker but more realistic assumption. We investigate whether exchangeability strengthens conditional probability

* Supported by the Austrian Science Foundation (FWF, I 141-G15) within the LogICCC Programme of the European Science Foundation. We want to thank three anonymous referees for their valuable and detailed comments.

S. Greco et al. (Eds.): IPMU 2012, Part IV, CCIS 300, pp. 157–167, 2012.

logic. For that purpose we treat generalizations of Modus Ponens, Conjunction, and Predictive Inference and compare our results with those recently presented by Gilio [6]. These argument forms may be considered as special cases of the rules of SYSTEM P, a well-known system of defeasible reasoning [8]. Conjunction corresponds to And, Modus Ponens to Cut, and Predictive Inference to Cautious Monotonicity. We furthermore study inferences involving cardinalities, the generalization of Modus Tollens, and the rule Or of SYSTEM P .

The probability of a composed event is the sum of the probabilities of the constituents verifying it. Let $\{E_1, \ldots, E_n\}$ be a set of binary events. A composed event $\pm E_1 \wedge \ldots \wedge \pm E_n$, where $\pm E_i$ is either $E_i$ or $E_i^c$, is called a constituent. We denote the set of all constituents generated by $\{E_1, \ldots, E_n\}$ by $\mathcal{C}$. If three logically independent events $A, B, C$ are given, then there are eight constituents:

$$E_1 = A \wedge B \wedge C, \ E_2 = A \wedge B \wedge C^c, \ E_3 = A \wedge B^c \wedge C, \ E_4 = A \wedge B^c \wedge C^c,$$
$$E_5 = A^c \wedge B \wedge C, \ E_6 = A^c \wedge B \wedge C^c, \ E_7 = A^c \wedge B^c \wedge C, \ E_8 = A^c \wedge B^c \wedge C^c.$$

We denote by $x_i$ the probability of $E_i$, so that for example $P(A) = x_1 + x_2 + x_3 + x_4$. Exchangeability requires that constituents with the same number of negated (failures) and non-negated (successes) events have the same probability. For the following definition compare, e.g., [7, p. 179].

**Definition 1 (Exchangeability).** *A sequence of events* $(E_1, E_2, \cdots, E_n)$ *is exchangeable iff for* $r = 1, 2, \ldots, n$ *and every permutation of the subscripts* $\pi$, *it holds that*
$$P(E_1 \wedge \ldots \wedge E_r \wedge E_{r+1}^c \wedge \ldots \wedge E_n^c) = P(E_{\pi(1)} \wedge \ldots \wedge E_{\pi(r)} \wedge E_{\pi(r+1)}^c \wedge \ldots \wedge E_{\pi(n)}^c).$$

If the events $A, B, C$ are exchangeable, then $x_2 = x_3 = x_5$ and $x_4 = x_6 = x_7$. Therefore the number of unknown probabilities reduces from eight to four. If we denote by $\omega_i$ the probability of a constituent with $i$ successes, then it holds that $P(A) = \omega_1 + 2\omega_2 + \omega_3$.

The following lemma states that every composed event resulting in the substitution of permutations of exchangeable events has the same probability as the initial event (compare also [7, Corollary 3.10.1]). Let $(E_1, \ldots, E_n)$ be an exchangeable sequence, $\pi$ be a permutation and $B$ be a composed event. We denote by $\pi(B)$ the event obtained from $B$ by substitution of every occurrence of $E_i$ by $\pi(E_i)$, for $i = 1, \ldots, n$.

**Lemma 1.** *Let* $\mathcal{E} = (E_1, \ldots, E_n)$ *be a sequence of exchangeable events and* $B, D$ *be Boolean combinations of members of* $\mathcal{E}$. *Then* $P(B) = P(\pi(B))$ *for every permutation* $\pi$ *on* $\mathcal{E}$. *Furthermore, if* $P(B) > 0$, *then* $P(D|B) = P(\pi(D|B))$.

*Proof.* It is a common fact in propositional logics that

$$E \models B \quad \text{if and only if} \quad \pi(E) \models \pi(B) \quad \text{for every Boolean combination } E. \quad (1)$$

We have $\pi(C) \in \mathcal{C}$ for every $C \in \mathcal{C}$. From exchangeability it follows that $P(\pi(C)) = P(C)$ for every $C \in \mathcal{C}$ and consequently by (1)

$$P(B) = \sum_{\substack{C \in \mathcal{C} \\ C \models B}} P(C) = \sum_{\substack{C \in \mathcal{C} \\ C \models B}} P(\pi(C)) = \sum_{\substack{\pi(C) \in \mathcal{C} \\ \pi(C) \models \pi(B)}} P(\pi(C)) = \sum_{\substack{E \in \mathcal{C} \\ E \models \pi(B)}} P(E) = P(\pi(B)).$$

For $P(D|B) = P(\pi(D|B))$ observe that if $P(B) \neq 0$, then

$$P(D|B) = \frac{P(D \wedge B)}{P(B)} = \frac{P(\pi(D \wedge B))}{P(\pi(B))} = \frac{P(\pi(D) \wedge \pi(B))}{P(\pi(B))} = P(\pi(D|B)).$$

## 2  Generalized Conjunction

The Generalized Conjunction rule determines the coherent probability interval of a conjunction $P(E_1 \wedge \ldots \wedge E_r \wedge E_{r+1}^c \wedge \ldots \wedge E_n^c)$ if the probabilities $P(E_i)$ for $i = 1, \ldots, n$ are given. We distinguish the cases $r = n$, $r = 0$, and $0 < r < n$. We first consider the case $r = n$. The case $r = 0$ is obtained by symmetrical considerations. We illustrate the use of exchangeability in probability logic for the conjunction of two and three events.

If $E_1$ and $E_2$ are exchangeable events and consequently have the same probability $P(E_1) = P(E_2) = \alpha$, then for every coherent extension $P'$ of $P$ it holds that $P'(E_1 \wedge E_2) \in [\gamma', \gamma'']$, with $\gamma' = \max\{0, 2\alpha - 1\}$ and $\gamma'' = \alpha$.

If $E_1, E_2, E_3$ are exchangeable and $P(E_1) = P(E_2) = P(E_3) = \alpha$, then $P(E_1 \wedge E_2 \wedge E_3) \in [\max\{0, 3\alpha - 2\}, \alpha]$. The result is obtained by minimizing (maximizing) $\omega_3$ in the linear system

$$\omega_1 + 2\omega_2 + \omega_3 = \alpha$$
$$\omega_0 + 3\omega_1 + 3\omega_2 + \omega_3 = 1$$
$$\omega_k \geq 0 \ .$$

The first equation expresses that the sum of probabilities of all constituents verifying $E_1$ is $\alpha$. The analog equations obtained for $E_2$ and $E_3$ are completely redundant since $E_1$, $E_2$, and $E_3$ are exchangeable. The second equation states that the sum of all probabilities of constituents has to be 1. The third equation states that the probability of each constituent is nonnegative.

If $n$ logically independent events are given, then there are $2^n$ constituents. If the $n$ events are exchangeable, we have $n + 1$ different probabilities $\omega_k$, $k = 0, \ldots, n$, each occurring $\binom{n}{k}$ times; hence $\sum_{k=0}^{n} \binom{n}{k}\omega_k = 1$. It follows from elementary combinatorics that for every conjunction of the length $i$, $i = 1, \ldots, n$, it holds that

$$P(E_1 \wedge \ldots \wedge E_i) = \sum_{k=i}^{n} \binom{n-i}{k-i}\omega_k \ . \tag{2}$$

This gives the following linear system

$$\sum_{k=1}^{n} \binom{n-1}{k-1}\omega_k = \alpha \tag{3}$$

$$\sum_{k=0}^{n} \binom{n}{k}\omega_k = 1 \tag{4}$$

$$\omega_k \geq 0 \ .$$

The lower (upper) bound of $P(\bigwedge_{i=1}^{n} E_i)$ is obtained by minimizing (maximizing) $\omega_n$.

Observe that because exchangeability imposes additional constraints on the linear system the lower (upper) bound cannot be smaller (greater) than that in the case of identical probabilities $P(E_i) = \alpha$ for $i = 1, \ldots, n$. Gilio [6] has shown that if $P(E_i) = \alpha$ for $i = 1, \ldots, n$, then $P(\bigwedge_{i=1}^{n} E_i) \in [\max\{0, n\alpha - (n-1)\}, \alpha]$. Therefore, the following solutions of the linear system yield the lower (upper) bound for the conjunction. For the minimum we distinguish two cases $\alpha > \frac{n-1}{n}$ and $\alpha \leq \frac{n-1}{n}$. In the first case $\omega_n = n\alpha - (n-1)$, $\omega_{n-1} = 1 - \alpha$, $\omega_i = 0$ for $i = 0, \ldots, n-2$ yields the minimum. In the second case the solution $\omega_n = 0$, $\omega_{n-1} = \frac{\alpha}{n-1}$, $\omega_0 = 1 - n\frac{\alpha}{n-1}$, $\omega_i = 0$ for $i = 1, \ldots, n-2$ yields the minimum.

The solution $\omega_n = \alpha$, $\omega_0 = 1 - \alpha$, $\omega_i = 0$ for $i = 1, \ldots, n-1$ yields the maximum.

As a result, we obtain

**Theorem 1 (Conjunction of $n$ events).**
*If $(E_1, \ldots, E_n)$ is an exchangeable sequence and $P(E_i) = \alpha$, then*

$$P(\bigwedge_{i=1}^{n} E_i) \in [\max\{0, n\alpha - (n-1)\}, \alpha] \ .$$

As already pointed out, for the case in which the assumption of exchangeability is dropped and only identical probabilities $P(E_i) = \alpha$ for $i = 1, \ldots, n$ are assumed, Gilio derived the same result. Consequently exchangeability has no other impact on the interval of the conjunction of $n$-successes than identifying the probabilities of the premises. Observe that in both cases, if $\alpha < 1$, then as the number of premises increases, the lower bound decreases. If $n \geq 1/(1 - \alpha)$ premises are given, then the lower bound is zero.

Next we consider the probability of $r$ successes ($0 < r < n$) and $n - r$ failures. First we determine the interval for the probability of a particular constituent with $r$ successes and $n - r$ failures and in a second step we determine the probability for $r$ successes and $n - r$ failures.

Since the lower bound of $P(E_r \wedge E_{r+1}^c)$ is 0 and $P(E_1 \wedge \ldots \wedge E_r \wedge E_{r+1}^c \wedge \ldots \wedge E_n^c) \leq P(E_r \wedge E_{r+1}^c)$, the minimum of $\omega_r$ is also 0. For the maximum subtracting (3) from (4) and observing that $1 - P(E_i) = P(E_i^c)$ gives

$$\sum_{k=0}^{n-1} \binom{n-1}{k} \omega_k = 1 - \alpha \ . \tag{5}$$

We may maximize $\omega_r$ in two ways. We may set the probability of all constituents, except $\omega_r$, in (3) to 0. This gives $\omega_r = \frac{\alpha}{\binom{n-1}{r-1}}$. Alternatively we may set the probability of all constituents, except $\omega_r$, in (5) to 0. This leads to $\omega_r = \frac{1-\alpha}{\binom{n-1}{r}}$. In order to satisfy both, (3) and (5), we have to take the minimum of both values. As a result, we obtain

**Theorem 2 (Constituent of $r$ successes and $n - r$ failures).**
*If $(E_1, E_2, \ldots, E_n)$ is an exchangeable sequence, $P(E_i) = \alpha$, and $0 < r < n$, then $\omega_r \in [\gamma', \gamma'']$, with $\gamma' = 0$ and*

$$\gamma'' = \min \left\{ \frac{1 - \alpha}{\binom{n-1}{r}} \, , \, \frac{\alpha}{\binom{n-1}{r-1}} \right\} .$$

If we denote the event that exactly $r$ successes and $n - r$ failures occur by $E_r^n$, then $P(E_r^n) = \omega_r \cdot \binom{n}{r}$. By reducing the fraction we obtain

**Theorem 3 (Probability of $r$ successes and $n - r$ failures).**
*If $(E_1, E_2, \ldots, E_n)$ is an exchangeable sequence, $P(E_i) = \alpha$, and $0 < r < n$, then $P(E_r^n) \in [\gamma', \gamma'']$, with $\gamma' = 0$ and*

$$\gamma'' = \min \left\{ \frac{(1 - \alpha)n}{n - r} \, , \, \frac{\alpha n}{r} \right\} .$$

Here $\gamma'' \leq 1$. To show this we have to distinguish between (i) $\alpha \leq \frac{r}{n}$ and (ii) $\alpha > \frac{r}{n}$. If (i), then since $\alpha n \leq r$, we have $\frac{\alpha n}{r} \leq 1$. If (ii), then since $(1 - \alpha)n < (n - r)$, we have $\frac{(1-\alpha)n}{n-r} < 1$. So that in both cases $\gamma'' \leq 1$.

Note that the upper bound does not monotonically increase as the number of premises increases. As long as (i) holds, the upper bound is increasing. However, since if $\frac{r}{n}$ tends to 0 as $n$ tends to infinity, at some point (ii) must be the case. Since $\frac{n}{n-r}$ tends to one, the upper bound is decreasing from that point onward and tends to $1 - \alpha$.

Comparing the results obtained in this section with the results for identical probabilities only, shows that exchangeability has no impact on the conjunction of $n$ successes. If $0 < r < n$, then the two assumptions lead to different results, because if the assumption of exchangeability is dropped, we obtain the interval $[0, \min\{\alpha, 1 - \alpha\}]$ for a constituent with $r$ successes and for $P(E_r^n)$.

## 3 Predictive Inference

The probability $P(E_{n+1} | E_1 \wedge \ldots \wedge E_r \wedge E_{r+1}^c \wedge \ldots \wedge E_n^c)$ of a success in trial $n + 1$ after having observed $r$ successes and $n - r$ failures in the preceding $n$ trials, is called *predictive probability*. If the denominator is not zero, it is obtained from the ratio

$$P(E_{n+1} | E_1 \wedge \ldots \wedge E_r \wedge E_{r+1}^c \wedge \ldots \wedge E_n^c) = \frac{P(E_1 \wedge \ldots \wedge E_r \wedge E_{r+1}^c \wedge \ldots \wedge E_n^c \wedge E_{n+1})}{P(E_1 \wedge \ldots \wedge E_r \wedge E_{r+1}^c \wedge \ldots \wedge E_n^c)} \tag{6}$$

We distinguish the cases $r = n$ and $0 \leq r < n$. The following theorem states the result for the case $r = n$, i.e., that all preceding $n$ trials were successes.

**Theorem 4 (Predictive probability given $n$ successes).**
If $(E_1, \ldots, E_{n+1})$ is an exchangeable sequence and $P(E_i) = \alpha$, then
$P(E_{n+1}|E_1 \wedge \ldots \wedge E_n) \in [\gamma', \gamma'']$, with $\gamma'' = 1$ and

$$\gamma' = \frac{(n+1)\alpha - n}{n\alpha - (n-1)}, \; \text{if } (n+1)\alpha - n > 0, \; \text{and } \gamma' = 0 \text{ otherwise} .$$

This can be shown as follows. By assuming that $(n+1)\alpha - n > 0$, it follows that $\omega_n > 0$. The lower bound for $P(E_{n+1}|E_1 \wedge \cdots \wedge E_n)$ is $\frac{\max\{0, \alpha + \omega_n - 1\}}{\omega_n}$. Such a lower bound increases as $\omega_n$ increases. Then, by setting $\omega_n$ to its minimum (Theorem 1) we have $\gamma' = \frac{\alpha + n\alpha - (n-1) - 1}{n\alpha - (n-1)}$. If $(n+1)\alpha - n \leq 0$, the lower bound of $P(E_1 \wedge \ldots \wedge E_{n+1})$ is 0 (Theorem 1). Then every value of the predictive probability is coherent, so that the lower bound is 0. The upper bound is obtained by setting $\omega_{n+1}$ to its maximum $\alpha$ (Theorem 1).

Predictive inference for $n$ observed successes is a special case of Generalized Cautious Monotonicity, obtained by conditionalizing on the sure event. Gilio [6] obtained in that case the same result as we did. In both cases if $\alpha < 1$, then as the number of premises increases, the lower bound decreases. If $n \geq \alpha/(1 - \alpha)$ premises are given, the lower bound is zero.

The interval for the predictive probability in the case $0 \leq r < n$, i.e., at least one observed failure, is not informative.

**Theorem 5 (Predictive probability given $r$ successes and $n-r$ failures).**
If $(E_1, \ldots, E_{n+1})$ is an exchangeable sequence, $P(E_i) = \alpha$, and $0 \leq r < n$, then
$P(E_{n+1}|E_1 \wedge \ldots \wedge E_r \wedge E_{r+1}^c \wedge \ldots \wedge E_n^c) \in [0, 1]$.

For the lower bound 0 note that according to Theorem 2 the lower bound for the numerator in (6) is 0 and that the upper bound of the denominator is different from 0. For the upper bound set the probability $P(E_1 \wedge \ldots \wedge E_r \wedge E_{r+1}^c \wedge \ldots \wedge E_n^c \wedge E_{n+1}^c)$ of $r$ successes in $n + 1$ trials equal to 0. Setting of $P(E_1 \wedge \ldots \wedge E_r \wedge E_{r+1}^c \wedge \ldots \wedge E_n^c \wedge E_{n+1})$ to its maximum, which is according to Theorem 2 different from 0 yields the upper bound 1.

Comparing these results with the results for identical probabilities only, shows that exchangeability has no impact on predictive inference.

## 4   Modus Ponens

In the introduction we already considered the Modus Ponens with two events. In this section we study its generalization. Suppose $(E_1, \ldots, E_n)$ is an exchangeable sequence, $P(E_i) = \alpha$ for $i = 1, \ldots, n$ and $P(H| \bigwedge_{i=1}^{n} E_i) = \beta$. We do not assume that $H$ is exchangeable with any of the other events. $H$ may be a hypothesis and $\{E_i\}_{i=1}^n$ a set of data, so that both are clearly not exchangeable.

We determine the interval for $P(H)$ with the help of the theorem of total probability

$$P(H) = P(H| \bigwedge_{i=1}^{n} E_i)P(\bigwedge_{i=1}^{n} E_i) + P(H|(\bigwedge_{i=1}^{n} E_i)^c)P((\bigwedge_{i=1}^{n} E_i)^c) . \tag{7}$$

Since the value of $P(H|(\bigwedge_{i=1}^{n} E_i)^c)$ is not given, it may attain any value between 0 and 1. To obtain the lower bound we set $P(H|(\bigwedge_{i=1}^{n} E_i)^c)$ to 0 and $P(\bigwedge_{i=1}^{n} E_i)$ to its minimum. To obtain the upper bound we set $P(H|(\bigwedge_{i=1}^{n} E_i)^c)$ to 1 and $P(\bigwedge_{i=1}^{n} E_i)$ to its minimum. According to the Conjunction rule (Theorem 1) it follows that

$$P(\bigwedge_{i=1}^{n} E_i) \in [\delta', \delta''], \text{with } \delta'' = \alpha \text{ and}$$

$$\delta' = \max\{0, n\alpha - (n - 1)\} \ .$$

The next theorem follows from this result.

**Theorem 6 (Modus Ponens).** *If $(E_1, \ldots, E_n)$ is an exchangeable sequence, $P(E_i) = \alpha$, and $P(H| \bigwedge_{i=1}^{n} E_i) = \beta$, then*

$$P(H) \in [\beta\delta' , \ \beta\delta' + 1 - \delta'] \ .$$

Modus Ponens is a special case of Cut rule, which is prominent in SYSTEM P. The interval obtained by Gilio [6] for identical probabilities of the premises is the same as the interval obtained in Theorem 6. In both cases, if $\alpha < 1$, then as the number of premises increases, the lower bound decreases and the upper bound increases. Moreover, if $n \geq 1/(1 - \alpha)$, the unity interval is obtained.

## 5    Cardinalities

Imagine that a person is $\alpha \cdot 100\%$ sure that an urn contains exactly $r$ red balls and $n - r$ black balls. Without replacement the person draws $k$ balls at random. What is the lower (upper) probability, that at least one of them is or that all of them are red? We determine the probability of a disjunction or a conjunction of a fixed length if the probability of $E_r^n$ is given. Suppose that $(E_1, \ldots, E_n)$ is an exchangeable sequence and $P(E_r^n) = \alpha$.

What is the probability $P(E_1 \vee \ldots \vee E_k)$, i.e., that at least one of $k$ events is true? Suppose that $k \leq (n - r)$. There are $\binom{n}{r}$ constituents verifying $E_r^n$. $\binom{n-k}{r}$ of these verify none of the events $E_1, \ldots, E_k$. Therefore $\binom{n}{r} - \binom{n-k}{r}$ of these $\binom{n}{r}$ constituents verify at least one of the events $E_1, \ldots, E_k$ and consequently $E_1 \vee \ldots \vee E_k$. From exchangeability it follows that each of the $\binom{n}{r}$ constituents has the same probability and therefore it holds that

$$P(E_1 \vee \ldots \vee E_k) \geq P((E_1 \vee \ldots \vee E_k) \wedge E_r^n) = P(E_r^n) - P(E_1^c \wedge \ldots \wedge E_k^c \wedge E_r^n) =$$

$$(1 - P(E_1^c \wedge \ldots \wedge E_k^c | E_r^n))P(E_r^n) = \frac{\left(\binom{n}{r} - \binom{n-k}{r}\right) \cdot \alpha}{\binom{n}{r}}.$$

If $r \neq 0$, the lower bound is obtained by setting $\omega_0 = 1 - \alpha$. The upper bound is obtained by setting $\omega_n = 1 - \alpha$. The result is summarized in

**Theorem 7.** *If* $(E_1, \ldots, E_n)$ *is an exchangeable sequence and* $P(E_r^n) = \alpha$, *and* $r = 1, \ldots, n$, *then for* $k = 1, \ldots, n$ *it holds that*

$$P(E_1 \vee \ldots \vee E_k) \in \left[ \alpha - \frac{\alpha \cdot \binom{n-k}{r}}{\binom{n}{r}} \ , \ 1 - \frac{\alpha \cdot \binom{n-k}{r}}{\binom{n}{r}} \right] .$$

If the assumption of exchangeability is dropped, we distinguish the following cases:

- If $k > n - r$, then we obtain the interval $[\alpha, 1]$. Since if $k > n - r$, then none of the constituents verifying $E_r^n$ falsifies each of the events $E_1, \ldots, E_k$. We obtain the lower bound by setting $\omega_0 = 1 - \alpha$. By setting $\omega_n = 1 - \alpha$ we obtain the upper bound. The result obtained in this case is the same as the result obtained in Theorem 7.
- If $r = n = k$, then we obtain the interval $[\alpha, 1]$. The result obtained in this case is the same as the result obtained in Theorem 7.
- If $k \le n - r$ and $r < n$, then we obtain the interval $[0, 1]$. Since if $k \le n - r$ there is a constituent verifying $E_r^n$ that falsifies each of the events $E_1, \ldots, E_k$. If the probability of this constituent is $\alpha$ and $\omega_0 = 1 - \alpha$, the lower bound 0 is obtained. For the upper bound 1 choose a constituent that verifies at least one of the events and assign probability $\alpha$ to this constituent and set $\omega_n = 1 - \alpha$. The result obtained in this case is rather different from the result obtained in Theorem 7.

What is the probability $P(E_1 \wedge \ldots \wedge E_k)$, i.e., that all $k$ events are true? From elementary combinatorics it follows that $\binom{n-k}{r-k}$ of the $\binom{n}{r}$ constituents with exactly $r$ successes verify $E_1 \wedge \ldots \wedge E_k$. Since each of them has the same probability it holds that

$$P(E_1 \wedge \ldots \wedge E_k) \ge P(E_1 \wedge \ldots \wedge E_k \wedge E_r^n) = P(E_1 \wedge \ldots \wedge E_k | E_r^n) P(E_r^n) = \frac{\binom{n-k}{r-k} \cdot \alpha}{\binom{n}{r}}$$

If it is not the case that $r = k = n$, then the lower bound is obtained by setting $\omega_0 = 1 - \alpha$. The upper bound is obtained by setting $\omega_n = 1 - \alpha$. The result is summarized in

**Theorem 8.** *If* $(E_1, \ldots, E_n)$ *is an exchangeable sequence,* $P(E_r^n) = \alpha$, *and if it is not the case that* $r = k = n$, *then for* $k = 1, \ldots, n$ *it holds that*

$$P(E_1 \wedge \ldots \wedge E_k) \in \left[ \frac{\binom{n-k}{r-k} \cdot \alpha}{\binom{n}{r}} \ , \ \frac{\binom{n-k}{r-k} \cdot \alpha}{\binom{n}{r}} + (1 - \alpha) \right] .$$

If the assumption of exchangeability is dropped, we distinguish the following cases:

- If $k > r$, then $P(E_1 \wedge \ldots \wedge E_k) \in [0, 1 - \alpha]$. The result obtained in this case is the same as the result obtained in Theorem 8.
- If $r = n \ne k$, then $P(E_1 \wedge \ldots \wedge E_k) \in [\alpha, 1]$. The result obtained in this case is the same as the result obtained in Theorem 8.

– If $k \leq r$ and $r \neq n$, then $P(E_1 \wedge \ldots \wedge E_k) \in [0, 1]$. The result obtained in this case is rather different from the result obtained in Theorem 8.

We conclude that exchangeability has a strong impact on inferences concerning cardinalities. The reason for this is that $E_r^n$ refers explicitly to the set of all constituents verifying exactly $r$ of the events $E_1, \ldots, E_n$. Exchangeability requires that each of these constituents has the same probability.

## 6    Or Rule

The Or rule is the only SYSTEM P rule for which the assumption of exchangeability yields an interval that is different from that in the case of identical probabilities of the premises only. Gilio [5] has shown that, if $P(E_3|E_1) = \alpha$ and $P(E_3|E_2) = \alpha$, then $P(E_3|E_1 \vee E_2) \in [\gamma', \gamma'']$, with

$$\gamma' = \begin{cases} \frac{\alpha^2}{2\alpha - \alpha^2}, & \text{if } \alpha \neq 0 \\ 0, & \text{if } \alpha = 0 \end{cases} , \quad \gamma'' = \begin{cases} \frac{2\alpha - 2\alpha^2}{1 - \alpha^2}, & \text{if } \alpha \neq 1 \\ 1, & \text{if } \alpha = 1 \end{cases} . \quad (8)$$

If $E_1, E_2, E_3$ are exchangeable events such that $P(E_i) \neq 0$ and $P(E_3|E_1) = \alpha$, then it follows from Lemma 1 that $P(E_3|E_2) = \alpha$.

To obtain the lower (upper) bound we minimize (maximize) $\frac{\omega_3 + 2\omega_2}{\omega_3 + 3\omega_2 + 2\omega_1}$ in the following linear system

$$\omega_0 + 3\omega_1 + 3\omega_2 + \omega_3 = 1$$

$$\alpha \cdot (\omega_1 + 2\omega_2 + \omega_3) = \omega_2 + \omega_3$$

$$\omega_k \geq 0 .$$

Observe that

$$P(E_3|E_1 \vee E_2) = \frac{P(E_3 \wedge (E_1 \vee E_2))}{P(E_1 \vee E_2)} = \frac{P((E_3 \wedge E_1) \vee (E_3 \wedge E_2))}{P(E_1 \vee E_2)} =$$

$$\frac{P(E_3 \wedge E_1) + P(E_3 \wedge E_2) - P(E_3 \wedge E_1 \wedge E_2)}{P(E_1 \vee E_2)} .$$

We consequently consider for the lower (upper) bound the maximum (minimum) of $P(E_3|E_1 \wedge E_2)$.

From exchangeability—but not from the assumption of identical probabilities of the premises only—it follows by Lemma 1 that $P(E_2|E_1) = \alpha$. We can therefore apply Cautious Monotonicity which licenses the inference from $E_2|E_1$ and $E_3|E_1$ to $E_3|E_1 \wedge E_2$.

For the lower bound observe that according to Cautious Monotonicity [5] the maximum of $P(E_3|E_1 \wedge E_2)$ is 1. Because of $P(E_3|E_1 \wedge E_2) = \frac{\omega_3}{\omega_3 + \omega_2}$, we obtain $\omega_2 = 0$. Setting $\omega_0 = 0$ and solving the linear system we obtain $\omega_3 = \frac{1-\alpha}{3-2\alpha}$ and $\omega_1 = \frac{\alpha}{3-2\alpha}$ and consequently $P(E_3|E_1 \vee E_2) = \frac{\alpha}{2-\alpha}$.

For the upper bound consider the minimum of $P(E_3|E_1 \wedge E_2)$. This minimum is according to Cautious Monotonicity rule $\max\{0, \frac{2\alpha-1}{\alpha}\}$. We distinguish consequently the cases $\alpha \leq \frac{1}{2}$ and $\alpha > \frac{1}{2}$.

1. If $\alpha \leq \frac{1}{2}$, then $P(E_3|E_1 \wedge E_2) = 0$ and consequently $\omega_3 = 0$. Setting $\omega_0 = 0$ and solving the linear system we obtain $\omega_2 = \frac{\alpha}{3(1-\alpha)}$ and $\omega_1 = \frac{1-2\alpha}{3(1-\alpha)}$ and consequently $P(E_3|E_1 \vee E_2) = \frac{2\alpha}{2-\alpha}$.

2. If $\alpha > \frac{1}{2}$, then $P(E_3|E_1 \wedge E_2) = \frac{2\alpha-1}{\alpha}$ and consequently $\omega_3 \neq 0$. Setting $\omega_1 = 0$ (instead of setting $\omega_3 = 0$), $\omega_0 = 0$ and solving the linear system we obtain $\omega_2 = \frac{1-\alpha}{2-\alpha}$ and $\omega_3 = \frac{-1+2\alpha}{2-\alpha}$ and consequently $P(E_3|E_1 \vee E_2) = \frac{1}{2-\alpha}$.

As a result we obtain

**Theorem 9 (Or Rule).** *Let $(E_1, E_2, E_3)$ be an exchangeable sequence such that $P(E_i) \neq 0$. If $P(E_3|E_1) = \alpha$, then $P(E_3|E_1 \vee E_2) \in [\gamma', \gamma'']$, with*

$$\gamma' = \frac{\alpha}{2-\alpha} \quad , \quad \gamma'' = \begin{cases} \frac{2\alpha}{2-\alpha}, & \text{if } \alpha \leq \frac{1}{2} \\ \frac{1}{2-\alpha}, & \text{if } \alpha > \frac{1}{2} \end{cases}.$$

We compare our result with (8). Since $\frac{\alpha}{2-\alpha} = \frac{\alpha^2}{2\alpha-\alpha^2}$ for $\alpha \neq 0$, exchangeability has no additional impact on the lower bound than identifying the probabilities of the premises. The result for the upper bound is different from that obtained in the case of identical probabilities of the premises. The reason is that exchangeability constrains certain probabilities. For obtaining the upper bound we can not set $P(E_3|E_1 \wedge E_2)$ equal to 0, because this contradicts Cautious Monotonicity. However, this is possible if the assumption of exchangeability is dropped.

## 7    Modus Tollens

We finally give the result for the Generalized Modus Tollens. For reasons of space we omit the derivation of

**Theorem 10 (Modus Tollens).** *If $P(E_i^c) = \alpha$, for $i = 1, 2, \ldots, n$, and if $P(E_1 \wedge E_2 \wedge \ldots \wedge E_n|H) = \beta$, then $P(H^c)$ is in the interval $[\gamma', \gamma'']$, with $\gamma'' = 1$ and*

$$\gamma' = \begin{cases} \max\{0, 1 - \frac{n\alpha}{1-\beta}\} & \text{if } \alpha + \beta \leq 1 \\ 1 - \frac{1-\alpha}{\beta} & \text{if } \alpha + \beta > 1 \end{cases} \tag{9}$$

The theorem is special because if the sum of $\alpha$ and $\beta$ is small, the lower probability of the conclusion depends on the number $n$ of events in the sequence $E_1, \ldots, E_n$ while if the sum of $\alpha$ and $\beta$ is large, the lower probability is invariant with respect to the number $n$ of events in the sequence.

## 8    Conclusions

Like all inferences in conditional probability logic the assumption of exchangeability leads to conclusions with interval probabilities. In most inferences exchangeability does not prevent a degradation of these intervals. Even if exchangeability is assumed, the width of the intervals of the conclusion of the

Conjunction of $n$ successes, Modus Ponens, and Predictive inference increases as the number of categorical premises increases. There are, however, several cases in which this degradation does not occur. An example for this is the Conjunction of $r$ successes and $n - r$ failures. A very special case is Modus Tollens. While the upper bound of its conclusion is always 1 its lower bound may be invariant with respect to the number of categorical premises, or it may be sensitive to their number. This depends on the probabilities of the premises. The property that more information may increase imprecision seems to be counter intuitive. However, the introduction of more and more data without stating anything about their interdependence may increase noise.

That does not imply that exchangeability has a negligible impact on conditional probability logic. Above all it often identifies the probabilities of certain premises. In some cases it even leads to rather different intervals than in the case of identical probabilities of the premises. This holds for inferences referring to particular cardinalities. It is surprising that the Or rule is the only SYSTEM P rule, where such a difference shows up.

Exchangeability may be investigated in other fields of probabilistic inference. We have started to look at models which are analog to conditional independence models, for example, Bayesian networks.

# References

1. Capotorti, A., Lad, F., Sanfilippo, G.: Reassessing accuracy rates of median decisions. The American Statistician 61(2), 132–138 (2007)
2. De Finetti, B.: Theory of Probability. A Critical Introductory Treatment, vol. 1. Wiley, New York (1974)
3. De Finetti, B.: Theory of Probability. A Critical Introductory Treatment, vol. 2. Wiley, New York (1975)
4. De Finetti, B.: Foresight: Its logical laws, its subjective sources. In: Kotz, S., Johnson, N.L. (eds.) Breakthroughs in Statistics, vol. 1, pp. 134–174. Springer, New York (1992 orig. 1937)
5. Gilio, A.: Probabilistic reasoning under coherence in System P. Ann. Math. Artif. Intell. 34, 5–34 (2002)
6. Gilio, A.: Generalization of inference rules in coherence-based probabilistic default reasoning. International Journal of Approximate Reasoning 53, 413–434 (2012)
7. Lad, F.: Operational Subjective Statistical Methods. Wiley, New York (1996)
8. Kraus, S., Lehmann, D., Magidor, M.: Nonmonotonic reasoning, preferential models and cumulative logics. Artificial Intelligence 44, 167–207 (1990)
9. Pfeifer, N., Kleiter, G.D.: Inference in conditional probability logic. Kybernetika 42, 391–404 (2006)
10. Tweney, R.D., Doherty, M.E., Kleiter, G.D.: The pseudodiagnosticity trap: Should subjects consider alternative hypotheses? Thinking and Reasoning 16, 332–345 (2010)

# Coherence for Uncertainty Measures Given through ⊕-Basic Assignments Ruled by General Operations

Giulianella Coletti[1], Romano Scozzafava[2], and Barbara Vantaggi[2]

[1] Università di Perugia
via Vanvitelli 1, Perugia, Italy
[2] Università La Sapienza di Roma
via Scarpa 16, Roma, Italy
coletti@dmi.unipg.it, romscozz@dmmm.uniroma1.it,
barbara.vantaggi@sbai.uniroma1.it

**Abstract.** In order to deal with partial assessments and their extensions, we give a characterization of some measures (such as capacities, belief functions, possibilities) in terms of basic assignments ruled by a general operation ⊕. The notion of coherence introduced by de Finetti in the probabilistic setting is generalized to non additive measures and we study the upper and lower envelopes of all possible extensions.

**Keywords:** Decomposable measures, basic assignment, coherence, lower and upper envelopes.

## 1  Introduction

A measure of uncertainty is a function whose domain is an algebra (or $\sigma$-algebra) and satisfying a set of axioms, which are strictly dependent on that structure (closure with respect to Boolean operations). When the measure is not assessed on the whole domain, it is necessary to strengthen the relevant axioms.

A well–known example is the coherence of a probabilistic assessment, introduced by de Finetti in terms of a betting scheme; the dual version asserts that the assessment on a set $\mathcal{E}$ of events is coherent if it is the restriction of a probability defined on the algebra $\mathcal{A}$ spanned by $\mathcal{E}$. Thus coherence amounts to check consistence by solving a linear system. We note that the dual version is strictly related to the fact that the composition rule for probability is the sum, and this feature is peculiar for this situation; this fact must be taken into account in generalizing the concept of coherence in frameworks different from the probabilistic one.

Given an assessment on an arbitrary set $\mathcal{E}$ of events, we say that it is *coherent* with respect to an uncertainty measure (belonging to a certain class) if there exists a measure $\mu$ of this class, agreeing with the given assessment, on the algebra $\mathcal{A}$ spanned by $\mathcal{E}$. This notion is simple, but it is not operative. To this aim and to look for an algorithm for checking coherence (as in the case of probability),

S. Greco et al. (Eds.): IPMU 2012, Part IV, CCIS 300, pp. 168–177, 2012.

it is useful trying to express the uncertainty measures $\mu$ by means of a function $k : \mathcal{A} \to [0,1]$, which is defined through a suitable binary operation $\oplus$ from $[0,1]^2$ into $\mathbf{R}$ ($k$ will be called a $\oplus$-basic assignment).

In this paper we restrict to $\oplus$-basic assignments taking values on $[0,1]$, even if this condition could be removed in order to deal with other measures such as the 2-monotone ones (see [2]).

In probability theory, a relevant aspect concerning coherence is the possibility of extending a coherent assessment to a new set of events preserving coherence. In other words, we deal with the general concept of inference, consisting on the extension of a coherent assessment to other events without introducing fictitious or non relevant information. For every new event, coherent values belong to an interval whose extremes are computed by solving a linear programming problem (the same extension problem has been studied in [8] for possibility measures; see also [1]). Proceeding step by step by considering at each steep one event of the new family, if we choose for its probability a value on the relevant interval, we get a coherent probability, but the final result obviously depends on the choice of the sequence of events and on the values chosen in the intervals. So we should avoid intermediate choices of the possible values during the process: it follows that it is better to study the properties of the functions obtained as lower and upper envelopes of the possible extensions, which are, in general, upper and lower coherent probabilities [4,18]. In some particular cases, due to specific logical conditions between the initial and final class of events, these envelopes can be belief and plausibility functions ([5,12,16]), k–order additive functions [15,17] or even possibilities and necessities ([6,10,14]).

In this paper we are interested in extending the above inferential process to the case of an assessment that is coherent with respect to a non additive measure. We give a characterization of the uncertainty measures admitting an $\oplus$-basic assignment (focusing on $\oplus = +$ or $\oplus = \max$) showing the peculiarities of the upper and lower bounds of the possible coherent extensions.

## 2    $\oplus$-Basic Assignment

Let $\mathcal{A}$ be a finite Boolean algebra and $\mathcal{A}_o = \{A_1, ..., A_m\}$ the set of atoms of $\mathcal{A}$.

**Definition 1.** *Given an uncertainty measure* $\varphi : \mathcal{A} \to [0,1]$, *the function* $k : \mathcal{A} \to [0,1]$ *is an $\oplus$-basic assignment for $\varphi$ if there exists a commutative, associative and increasing function* $\oplus : [0,1]^2 \to \mathbf{R}$ *such that* $\oplus_{A \in \mathcal{A}} k(A) = 1$ *and for every $A \in \mathcal{A}$ either*

$$\varphi(A) = \oplus_{B \subseteq A} k(B) \tag{1}$$

*or*

$$\varphi(A) = \oplus_{B \wedge A \neq \emptyset} k(B). \tag{2}$$

Actually, any measure $\varphi$ satisfying condition (1) for any $B \in \mathcal{A}$, has a dual measure $\varphi'$ satisfying condition (2) for any $B \in \mathcal{A}$. We note that either by choosing different operations $\oplus$ or by requiring further properties to the function

$k$ (for instance, that of being null for some class of events), we obtain particular measures: as it is well known, if we require that $k(C) = 0$ for every $C \in \mathcal{A} \setminus \mathcal{A}_o$ we obtain a probability for $\oplus = +$ and a possibility for $\oplus = \max$. Since in these cases $k$ is different from zero only on the atoms, we trivially obtain, for both operations, that the measure $\varphi$ satisfies

$$\varphi(A) = \oplus_{B \subseteq A} k(B) = \oplus_{B \wedge A \neq \emptyset} k(B).$$

Obviously, depending on the operation $\oplus$ we obtain measures with different properties.

As recalled in the Introduction, for the measures $\varphi$ admitting an $\oplus$-basic assignment, to check that an assessment $\varphi$ on an arbitrary set $\mathcal{E} = \{E_1, ..., E_n\}$ of events is coherent with respect to a specific measure it is sufficient to look for a (not unique, in general) function $k$ on the algebra $\mathcal{A}$ spanned by $\mathcal{E}$, such that for every $E_i \in \mathcal{E}$ one has $\varphi(E_i) = \oplus_{B \subseteq E_i} k(B)$ (or $\varphi(E_i) = \oplus_{B \wedge E_i \neq \emptyset} k(B)$), consisting in solving a system, with some constraints on the unknowns.

We first recall the definition of weakly $\oplus$-decomposable measure (see [3]).

**Definition 2.** *Given a finite algebra $\mathcal{A}$, a function $\varphi : \mathcal{A} \to [0,1]$ and a commutative binary operation $\oplus$ on $\{\varphi(A_i)\}_{A_i \in \mathcal{A}}$ with $\varphi(\emptyset)$ neutral element, $\varphi$ is a weakly $\oplus$-decomposable measure if the restriction of $\oplus$ to the pairs $\{\varphi(A_i), \varphi(A_j)\}$, with $A_i \wedge A_j = \emptyset$ is associative and increasing and moreover*

$$\varphi(A_i \vee A_j) = \varphi(A_i) \oplus \varphi(A_j).$$

We note that for this uncertainty measure the function $k$ coincides with $\varphi$ on $\mathcal{A}_0$ and it is null in $\mathcal{A} \setminus \mathcal{A}_o$. Nevertheless, the difficulty in checking coherence for this kind of measures depends on the operation $\oplus$. In the following we focus mainly on the measures admitting an $\oplus$-basic assignment with $\oplus$ coinciding with the usual sum or the max.

## 2.1   Additive Basic Assignments

In this section we consider the case $\oplus = +$. As it is well known, if we do not require constraints for $k$ (except those in Definition 1.), then we obtain a characterization of belief functions and plausibilities, respectively, as

$$\varphi(A) = \sum_{B \subseteq A} k(B)$$

and

$$\varphi(A) = \sum_{B \wedge A \neq \emptyset} k(B).$$

Then to check that an assessment on an arbitrary set $\mathcal{E} = \{E_1, ..., E_n\}$ of events is a coherent belief (or plausibility) assessment we must prove the existence of a non negative solution of a linear system with $n + 1$ equations and $2^m$ unknowns

$x_j = k(B_j)$(where $m$ is the number of atoms generated by $\mathcal{E}$ and $B_j$ are the elements of the relevant algebra).

By the same formulas and adding conditions of partial nullity for $k$, we characterize specific belief functions and plausibilities, which are $h$-order additive [15] (with $1 \leq h \leq n$): we must require the following conditions

$$k(\bigvee_1^r A_j) = 0, \; A_j \in \mathcal{A}_o, \text{ for every } r > h$$

and there is $B \in \mathcal{A}$ with $B = \bigvee_{j=1}^h A_{i_j}$ such that

$$k(B) > 0 \,.$$

In this case the number of equations is again $n+1$, but the number of unknowns is less than $2^m$, and the minimum $m$ is reached for probability. This fact puts in evidence that in general checking coherence of an assessment with a measure is (computationally) harder when the rules defining the measure are weaker. In any case the general problem is np-hard; moreover the computability problem does not change by considering the dual problem through Mobius inverse characterization.

## 2.2   Maxitive Basic Assignments

In this section we consider the case $\oplus = \max$. The results obtained are completely different from those of the previous section. The main difference is due to the fact that possibility functions are characterized not only by means of a max-basic function $k$ which is null in $\mathcal{A} \setminus \mathcal{A}_o$, but by any other $k$, as the following result shows.

**Theorem 1.** *For a function $\varphi : \mathcal{A} \to [0,1]$ the following statements are equivalent:*

**(i)** *the function $\varphi$ is a possibility;*
**(ii)** *there exists a max-basic function $k$ such that, for every $A \in \mathcal{A}$*

$$\varphi(A) = \max_{B \wedge A \neq \emptyset} k(B).$$

*Proof.* To prove the implication **(ii)**$\Rightarrow$ **(i)** it is sufficient to consider that for every $A$ and $C$ in $\mathcal{A}$, we have

$$\max_{(B \vee C) \wedge A \neq \emptyset} k(B) = \max[\max_{B \wedge A \neq \emptyset} k(B), \max_{C \wedge A \neq \emptyset} k(B)]$$

To prove the implication **(i)** $\Rightarrow$ **(ii)** it is sufficient to consider that, for instance, every function $k$ such that $k(A_r) = \varphi(A_k)$ for every $A_r \in \mathcal{A}_o$ and $k(B) \leq \min_{A_r \in B}\{k(A_r)\}$ satisfies condition **(ii)**.

For dual measures (necessities) we have instead the following characterization:

**Corollary 1.** *For a function* $\varphi : \mathcal{A} \to [0,1]$ *the following statements are equivalent:*

**(i)** *the function* $\varphi$ *is a necessity;*
**(ii)** *there exists a function* $h : \mathcal{A} \to [0,1]$, *with* $\min_{B \in \mathcal{A}} h(B) = 0$ *such that, for every* $A \in \mathcal{A}$

$$\varphi(A) = \min_{B \subseteq A^c} h(B);$$

*Proof.* The proof easily follows by characterizations of possibilities and duality.

Now we are able to give a complete characterization of capacities, that is uncertainty measures monotone with respect to the partial order induced by the inclusion $\subseteq$.

**Theorem 2.** *For a function* $\varphi : \mathcal{A} \to [0,1]$ *the following statements are equivalent:*

**(i)** *the function* $\varphi$ *is a capacity;*
**(ii)** *there exists a* max-*basic function* $k$ *such that, for every* $A \in \mathcal{A}$

$$\varphi(A) = \max_{B \subseteq A} k(B).$$

*Proof.* To prove the implication **(ii)** $\Rightarrow$ **(i)** it is sufficient to consider that if $A \subseteq C$, we have $B \subseteq A \Rightarrow B \subseteq C$ and so

$$\varphi(A) = \max_{B \subseteq A} k(B) \leq \max_{B \subseteq C} k(B).$$

To prove the implication **(i)** $\Rightarrow$ **(ii)** we start from a capacity $\varphi$ and build a (not unique) max-basic function $k$. We put $k(A_r) = \varphi(A_r)$ for every $A_r \in \mathcal{A}_o$. For every $A \in \mathcal{A} \setminus \mathcal{A}_o$, if $\varphi(A) = \max_{B \subseteq A} \varphi(B)$ give to $k(A)$ any number in $[0, \varphi(A)]$, if $\varphi(A) > \max_{B \subseteq A} \varphi(B)$ put $k(A) = \varphi(A)$.
    It is easy to see that $\max_{B \in \mathcal{A}} k(B) = 1$ and $k(\cdot)$ satisfies condition **(ii)**.

## 3    Inference

In coherent probability theory one of the most important results (known as the *fundamental theorem of probability* [9]) assures that, given a coherent assessment $P$ on an arbitrary family $\mathcal{E}$ of events, it can be extended (possibly not in a unique way) to any set $\mathcal{E}'$. Moreover, for each event $E \in \mathcal{E}'$ there exist two events $E_*$ and $E^*$ in the algebra spanned by $\mathcal{E}$ (possibly $E_* = \emptyset$ and $E^* = \Omega$) that are, respectively, the "maximum" and the "minimum" union of atoms $A_r$ (generated by the initial family $\mathcal{E}$) such that $E_* \subseteq E \subseteq E^*$ (in particular, $E_* = E = E^*$ if $E$ is logically dependent on $\mathcal{E}$). When $\mathcal{E}$ is finite, given the set $\mathcal{P} = \{\tilde{P}\}$ of all possible extensions of $P$, coherent assessments of $\tilde{P}(E)$ are all real numbers of a closed interval $[p_*(E), p^*(E)]$, with

$$p_*(E) = \inf_{\mathcal{P}} \tilde{P}(E_*) = \inf_{\mathcal{P}} \sum_{A_r \subseteq E_*} \tilde{P}(A_r), \qquad (3)$$

$$p^*(E) = \sup_{\mathcal{P}} \tilde{P}(E^*) = \sup_{\mathcal{P}} \sum_{A_r \subseteq E^*} \tilde{P}(A_r). \tag{4}$$

This extension problem can be reformulated on the basis of $\oplus$-basic assignments, and it is useful in order to extend any other measure characterized by means of an $\oplus$-basic assignment.

In Section 2 we showed that for all the measures admitting an $\oplus$-basic assignment, given an assessment $\varphi$ on $\mathcal{E}$, coherent with respect to a specific measure (such as probability, possibility etc.), then there is (at least) an $\oplus$-basic assignment $k(\cdot)$ defined on the minima algebra $\mathcal{A}$ generated by $\mathcal{E}$ satisfying (1) or (2) for any $E \in \mathcal{E}$. Therefore, if the measure taken into account is extendible on any algebra containing $\mathcal{A}$, then for any $F \in \mathcal{E}' \setminus \mathcal{E}$ we look for

$$\varphi_*(F) = \inf_{k \in \mathcal{K}} \oplus_{A \subseteq F_*, \, A \in \mathcal{A}} k(A) \quad \text{and} \quad \varphi^*(F) = \sup_{k \in \mathcal{K}} \oplus_{A \subseteq F^*, \, A \in \mathcal{A}} k(A) \tag{5}$$

or

$$\varphi_*(F) = \inf_{k \in \mathcal{K}} \oplus_{A \wedge F_* \neq \emptyset, \, A \in \mathcal{A}} k(A) \quad \text{and} \quad \varphi^*(F) = \sup_{k \in \mathcal{K}} \oplus_{A \wedge F^* \neq \emptyset, \, A \in \mathcal{A}} k(A) \tag{6}$$

where $\mathcal{K}$ is the set of $\oplus$-basic assignments $k(\cdot)$ agreeing with $\varphi$. Then the aim now is to show that the measures considered in Section 2 are extendible.

Actually, for possibilities, analogously to the probabilistic case, in [8] we proved that coherence of a possibility assessment assures its extendibility to a new set $\mathcal{E}'$ of events, and for any event $E \in \mathcal{E}'$ the coherent possibility values belong to a closed interval whose extremes are computed as above with $\oplus = \max$.

The following results show that capacities, belief functions and weakly $\oplus$-decomposable measures can be extended to a super-algebra.

**Theorem 3.** *Let $\varphi$ be a capacity on a finite algebra $\mathcal{A}$ and let $\mathcal{A}'$ be an algebra such that $\mathcal{A} \subseteq \mathcal{A}'$. Then there exists a capacity $\varphi'$ on $\mathcal{A}'$ whose restriction on $\mathcal{A}$ coincides with $\varphi$ (i.e. $\varphi'_{|\mathcal{A}} = \varphi$).*

*Proof.* Define $\varphi'$ on $\mathcal{A}'$ as follows: for any $B \in \mathcal{A}'$, $\varphi'(B) = \sup_{A \subseteq B} \varphi(A)$. Since $\emptyset \subseteq B$ for any possible event $B$, then for those events $B \in \mathcal{A}'$ such that no possible event $A \in \mathcal{A}$ is included in $B$, we have $\varphi'(B) = 0$. Moreover, by construction $\varphi'$ is a capacity on $\mathcal{A}'$ and $\varphi'_{|\mathcal{A}} = \varphi$.

**Theorem 4.** *Let $\varphi$ be a weakly $\oplus$-decomposable measure on a finite algebra $\mathcal{A}$ and let $\mathcal{A}'$ be an algebra such that $\mathcal{A} \subseteq \mathcal{A}'$. Then there exists a weakly $\oplus$-decomposable measure $\varphi'$ on $\mathcal{A}'$ whose restriction on $\mathcal{A}$ coincides with $\varphi$.*

*Proof.* Define $\varphi'$ on $\mathcal{A}'$ as follows: for any $B \in \mathcal{A}'$, $\varphi'(B) = \sup_{A \subseteq B} \varphi(A)$. Since $\emptyset \subseteq B$ for any possible event $B$, then for those events $B \in \mathcal{A}'$ such that no possible event $A \in \mathcal{A}$ is included in $B$, we have $\varphi'(B) = 0$. Then $\oplus$ on $\{\varphi(A)\}_{A \in \mathcal{A}}$ is extendible on $\{\varphi(B)\}_{B \in \mathcal{A}'}$ as a commutative binary operation. Note that by construction $\oplus$ on the pairs $\varphi'(B_i), \varphi'(B_j)$ with $B_i \wedge B_j = \emptyset$ is associative and increasing, since $\varphi'(B_i) = \varphi(A_i)$ and $\varphi'(B_j) = \varphi(A_j)$ with

$$A_i = \bigcup_{A \subseteq B_i; \, A \in \mathcal{A}} A \quad \text{and} \quad A_j = \bigcup_{A \subseteq B_j; \, A \in \mathcal{A}} A$$

and $\oplus$ satisfies the same properties for $\varphi(A_i), \varphi(A_j)$, since $A_i \wedge A_j = \emptyset$. Moreover,

$$\varphi'(B_i \vee B_j) = \varphi(A_i \vee A_j) = \varphi(A_i) \oplus \varphi(A_j) = \varphi'(B_i) \oplus \varphi'(B_j).$$

Then $\varphi'$ is a weakly $\oplus$-decomposable measure on $\mathcal{A}'$ and, by construction, one has $\varphi'_{|\mathcal{A}} = \varphi$.

The following result already proved in [11,16] is an immediate consequence of Theorem 4.

**Corollary 2.** *Let $\varphi$ be a belief function on a finite algebra $\mathcal{A}$ and let $\mathcal{A}'$ be an algebra such that $\mathcal{A} \subseteq \mathcal{A}'$. Then, there exists a belief function $\varphi'$ on $\mathcal{A}'$ whose restriction on $\mathcal{A}$ coincides with $\varphi$.*

Concerning assignment coherent with capacities, belief functions or weakly $\oplus$-decomposable, the above results imply, due to the convexity of the set $\mathcal{K}$ of all possible $\oplus$-basic assignments agreeing with $\varphi$, that coherence assures its extendibility to a new set $\mathcal{E}'$ of events, and for any event $E \in \mathcal{E}'$ the coherent possibility values belong to a closed interval $[\varphi_*(E), \varphi^*(E)]$ with $\varphi_*(E)$ and $\varphi^*(E)$ computed as in equation (5) and (6).

### 3.1   Lower and Upper Extensions

We consider now the following inferential problem: given an assessment $\varphi$ on $\mathcal{E}$ coherent with a measure given by an $\oplus$-basic assignment, by extending it to a new set $\mathcal{E}'$ of events and computing all the intervals associated to the events in $\mathcal{E}'$, and then choosing for any event $E \in \mathcal{E}'$ the minimum or the maximum value, we get the upper envelope and the lower envelope of the coherent extensions. The aim is to characterize such measures.

In the probabilistic context, the functions $p_*(\cdot)$ and $p^*(\cdot)$ are, respectively, a coherent lower and upper probability on $\mathcal{E}'$ respectively (see for instance [4,18]). As it is well known the above lower and upper probability are generally not 2-monotone or 2-alternating respectively, but, when $\mathcal{A}'$ and $\mathcal{A}$ are algebras, then $p_*(\cdot)$ and $p^*(\cdot)$ are, respectively, a belief and a plausibility (see for instance [13]). The above result is true for any algebra $\mathcal{A}'$, even if it is not necessarily a super-algebra of the initial one.

Concerning possibilities, the upper envelope is still a possibility [8], while the lower envelope is in general neither a possibility nor a necessity, but only a capacity, as shown in the next result.

Actually, Theorem 5 shows also that both the lower and the upper envelope of the extensions of a capacity are still a capacity. The next result proves that the lower envelope of the extensions of a possibility does not satisfy further properties when we start from an assessment given on an algebra.

**Theorem 5.** *Given an algebra $\mathcal{A}$, consider a possibility $\Pi$ on $\mathcal{A}$ and let $\underline{\Pi}$ and $\overline{\Pi}$ be the lower and upper envelope of all the coherent extensions of $\Pi$ on an algebra $\mathcal{A}'$. Then the following statements hold:*

1. $\overline{\Pi}$ *is a possibility on* $\mathcal{A}'$;
2. $\underline{\Pi}$ *is a capacity on* $\mathcal{A}'$.

*Moreover for any* $A \in \mathcal{A}'$ *the functions* $\underline{\Pi}$ *and* $\overline{\Pi}$ *are such that*

$$\max\{\underline{\Pi}(A), \overline{\Pi}(A^c)\} = 1.$$

*Proof.* Statement *1* has been proved in [8]. Statement *2* follows from the fact that the lower envelope of a set of capacities is a capacity. To prove that $\max\{\underline{\Pi}(A), \overline{\Pi}(A^c)\} = 1$, it is sufficient to consider that

$$\underline{\Pi}(A) = \inf_{\Pi' \in \Pi} \Pi'(A) = \max_{B \subseteq A, B \in \mathcal{A}'} \Pi(B)$$

$$\overline{\Pi}(A^c) = \sup_{\Pi' \in \Pi} \Pi'(A^c) = \max_{B \wedge A^c \neq \emptyset, B \in \mathcal{A}} \Pi(B).$$

This result points out the differences between probabilistic and possibilistic settings arising under inferential processes. In particular, the classical duality relation between $\underline{\Pi}$ and $\overline{\Pi}$ does not hold. Actually, in [7] we show that $\underline{\Pi}$ can even be a possibility. Moreover, under a logical condition (called weak logical independence in [7]) between the two algebras, also the lower envelope is still a possibility.

As a consequence of Theorem 5 we obtain the following result:

**Corollary 3.** *Consider a necessity* $N$ *on an algebra* $\mathcal{A}$ *and let* $\underline{N}$ *and* $\overline{N}$ *be the lower and upper envelope of all the coherent extensions on* $\mathcal{A}'$. *Then, the following statements hold:*

1. $\overline{N}$ *is a capacity on* $\mathcal{A}'$;
2. $\underline{N}$ *is a necessity on* $\mathcal{A}'$.

*Moreover,* $\min\{\overline{N}(A), \underline{N}(A^c)\} = 0$ *for any* $A \in \mathcal{A}'$.

*Proof.* Property *2* is proved in [7]. Property *1* holds since the upper envelope of the set of capacities is a capacity.

To prove that $\min\{\overline{N}(A), \underline{N}(A^c)\} = 0$ let us consider the set **N** of necessities $N'$ extending $N$ on $\mathcal{A}$ and let $\boldsymbol{\Pi}$ be the set of the dual possibilities $\Pi'$. Then, from Theorem 5, one has, for every $A \in \mathcal{A}$:

$$\overline{N}(A) = \sup_{N' \in \mathbf{N}} N'(A) = 1 - \inf_{\Pi' \in \boldsymbol{\Pi}} \Pi'(A^c) = 1 - \underline{\Pi}(A^c)$$

and

$$\underline{N}(A^c) = \inf_{\mathbf{N}} N'(A^c) = 1 - \sup_{\boldsymbol{\Pi}} \Pi'(A) = 1 - \overline{\Pi}(A)$$

for any $A \in \mathcal{A}'$. Then, the statement follows again from Theorem 5.

The condition that the initial assessment is given on an algebra is essential for the above result: given an assessment on an arbitrary set of events, coherent with respect to a belief function, neither the lower envelope nor the upper envelope of its extensions are belief functions, as the following example shows:

*Example 1.* Consider a partition $\{C_1, C_2, C_3\}$ and let $\mathcal{A}$ be the algebra generated by it. It is easy to check that the following assessment

$$\varphi(C_1 \vee C_2) = \varphi(C_2 \vee C_3) = 0.4, \; \varphi(C_1 \vee C_3) = 0.3$$

is coherent with respect to a belief function and that the set of agreeing $\oplus$-basic assignments is such that the lower envelope $k_*$ satisfies $k_*(C_i) = 0$ for $i = 1, 2, 3$, and so the lower envelope $\underline{Bel}$ of the belief extending $\varphi$ is such that

$$\underline{Bel}(C_i) = 0, \underline{Bel}(C_1 \vee C_2) = \underline{Bel}(C_2 \vee C_3) = 0.4, \; \underline{Bel}(C_1 \vee C_3) = 0.3, \; \underline{Bel}(\Omega) = 1$$

$(i = 1, 2, 3)$ and it is not a belief.

Analogously, the upper envelope $\overline{Bel}$ of the belief extending $\varphi$ is such that

$$\underline{Bel}(C_i) = 0.3 \, (i = 1, 3), \overline{Bel}(C_2) = \overline{Bel}(C_1 \vee C_2) = \underline{Bel}(C_2 \vee C_3) = 0.4,$$

$$\underline{Bel}(C_1 \vee C_3) = 0.3, \; \underline{Bel}(\Omega) = 1$$

and it is neither a belief nor a plausibility.

Example 1 shows also that the lower (upper) envelope of the agreeing $\oplus$-basic assignments is not an $\oplus$-basic assignment. Examples in the same line can be given for assessments coherent with respect to weakly $\oplus$-decomposable measures.

However the following result shows that the lower (upper) envelope of the belief functions extending a coherent belief is a capacity.

**Theorem 6.** *Consider an assessment $\varphi$ on $\mathcal{E}$ coherent with respect to a belief and let $\underline{\varphi}$ and $\overline{\varphi}$ be the lower and upper envelope of all the coherent extensions on an algebra $\mathcal{E}'$. Then, both $\overline{\varphi}$ and $\underline{\varphi}$ are coherent capacities on $\mathcal{E}'$.*

*Proof.* From coherence of $\varphi$, it can be extended on the algebra $\mathcal{A}$ generated by $\mathcal{E}$ as a belief function. Let $V$ be the set of belief functions extending $\varphi$. Given the algebra $\mathcal{A}'$ generated by $\mathcal{E} \bigcup \mathcal{E}'$, it is sufficient to consider that for the lower envelope $\underline{\varphi}$ we have, for every $A \in \mathcal{A}'$,

$$\underline{\varphi}(A) = \inf_{\varphi' \in \mathbf{V}} \varphi'(A) = \oplus_{B \subseteq A, B \in \mathcal{A}'} \varphi(B).$$

So it follows that $\underline{\Pi}(\cdot)$ is monotone with respect to the inclusion.

The proof for $\overline{\varphi}$ goes along the same lines.

Results similar to Theorem 6 can be proved also for assessments coherent with respect to capacities or weakly $\oplus$-decomposable measures.

# References

1. Baioletti, M., Coletti, G., Petturiti, D., Vantaggi, B.: Inferential models and relevant algorithms in a possibilistic framework. Inter. J. of Approximate Reasoning 52(5), 580–598 (2011)

2. Chateauneuf, A., Jaffray, J.Y.: Some characterizations of lower probabilities and other monotone capacities through the use of Mobius inversion. Mathematical Social Sciences 17(3), 263–283 (1989)
3. Coletti, G., Scozzafava, R.: From conditional events to conditional measures: a new axiomatic approach. Annals of Mathematics and Artificial Intelligence 32, 373–392 (2001)
4. Coletti, G., Scozzafava, R.: Probabilistic Logic in a Coherent Setting. Trends in Logic, vol. 15. Kluwer Academic Publishers, Dordrecht (2002)
5. Coletti, G., Scozzafava, R.: Toward a general theory of conditional beliefs. Int. J. of Intelligent Systems 21, 229–259 (2006)
6. Coletti, G., Scozzafava, R., Vantaggi, B.: Possibility measures through a probabilistic inferential process. In: Proc. Int. Conf. of NAFIPS. IEEE CN: CFP08750-CDR Omnipress, New York (2008)
7. Coletti, G., Scozzafava, R., Vantaggi, B.: Inferential processes leading to possibility and necessity. Submitted to Information Sciences
8. Coletti, G., Vantaggi, B.: T-conditional possibilities: coherence and inference. Fuzzy Sets and Systems 160(3), 306–324 (2009)
9. de Finetti, B.: Problemi determinati e indeterminati nel calcolo delle probabilitá. Rendiconti della R.Accademia Nazionale dei Lincei 12, 367–373 (1930)
10. de Cooman, G., Aeyels, D.: Supremum-preserving upper probabilities. Information Sciences 118, 173–212 (1999)
11. de Cooman, G., Miranda, E., Couso, I.: Lower previsions induced by multi-valued mappings. J. of Statistical Planning and Inference 133, 173–197 (2005)
12. de Cooman, G., Troffaes, M., Miranda, E.: n-monotone lower previsions. J. of Intelligent and Fuzzy Systems 16(4), 253–263 (2005)
13. Denneberg, D.: Non-Additive Measure and Integral. Kluwer, Berlin (1997)
14. Dubois, D., Prade, H.: When upper probabilities are possibility measures. Fuzzy Sets and Systems 49, 65–74 (1992)
15. Grabisch, M.: k-order additive discrete fuzzy measures and their representation. Fuzzy Sets and Systems 92(2), 167–189 (1997)
16. Halpern, J.: Reasoning about uncertainty. The MIT Press (2003)
17. Mesiar, R.: k-order additivity and maxitivity. Atti Sem. Mat. Fis. Univ. Modena 51, 179–189 (2003)
18. Walley, P.: Statistical reasoning with Imprecise Probabilities. Chapman and Hall, London (1991)

# Quasi-Lovász Extensions and Their Symmetric Counterparts

Miguel Couceiro and Jean-Luc Marichal

University of Luxembourg, Mathematics Research Unit
6, rue Richard Coudenhove-Kalergi
L–1359 Luxembourg, G.-D. Luxembourg
{miguel.couceiro,jean-luc.marichal}@uni.lu

**Abstract.** We introduce the concept of quasi-Lovász extension as being a mapping $f\colon I^n \to \mathbb{R}$ defined over a nonempty real interval $I$ containing the origin, and which can be factorized as $f(x_1,\ldots,x_n) = L(\varphi(x_1),\ldots,\varphi(x_n))$, where $L$ is the Lovász extension of a pseudo-Boolean function $\psi\colon \{0,1\}^n \to \mathbb{R}$ (i.e., the function $L\colon \mathbb{R}^n \to \mathbb{R}$ whose restriction to each simplex of the standard triangulation of $[0,1]^n$ is the unique affine function which agrees with $\psi$ at the vertices of this simplex) and $\varphi\colon I \to \mathbb{R}$ is a nondecreasing function vanishing at the origin. These functions appear naturally within the scope of decision making under uncertainty since they subsume overall preference functionals associated with discrete Choquet integrals whose variables are transformed by a given utility function.

To axiomatize the class of quasi-Lovász extensions, we propose generalizations of properties used to characterize the Lovász extensions, including a comonotonic version of modularity and a natural relaxation of homogeneity. A variant of the latter property enables us to axiomatize also the class of symmetric quasi-Lovász extensions, which are compositions of symmetric Lovász extensions with 1-place nondecreasing odd functions.

**Keywords:** Aggregation function, discrete Choquet integral, Lovász extension, comonotonic modularity, invariance under horizontal differences.

MSC Classes: 39B22, 39B72 (Primary) 26B35 (Secondary).

## 1   Introduction

Aggregation functions arise wherever merging information is needed: applied and pure mathematics (probability, statistics, decision theory, functional equations), operations research, computer science, and many applied fields (economics and finance, pattern recognition and image processing, data fusion, etc.). For recent references, see Beliakov et al. [1] and Grabisch et al. [7].

The discrete Choquet integral has been widely investigated in aggregation theory due to its many applications, for instance, in decision making (see the edited book [8]). A convenient way to introduce the discrete Choquet integral is

S. Greco et al. (Eds.): IPMU 2012, Part IV, CCIS 300, pp. 178–187, 2012.
© Springer-Verlag Berlin Heidelberg 2012

via the concept of Lovász extension. An $n$-place Lovász extension is a continuous function $L\colon \mathbb{R}^n \to \mathbb{R}$ whose restriction to each of the $n!$ subdomains

$$\mathbb{R}_\sigma^n = \{\mathbf{x} = (x_1, \ldots, x_n) \in \mathbb{R}^n : x_{\sigma(1)} \leqslant \cdots \leqslant x_{\sigma(n)}\}, \qquad \sigma \in S_n,$$

is an affine function, where $S_n$ denotes the set of permutations on $[n] = \{1, \ldots, n\}$. An $n$-place Choquet integral is simply a nondecreasing (in each variable) $n$-place Lovász extension which vanishes at the origin. For general background, see [7, §5.4].

The class of $n$-place Lovász extensions has been axiomatized by the authors [4] by means of two noteworthy aggregation properties, namely comonotonic additivity and horizontal min-additivity (for earlier axiomatizations of the $n$-place Choquet integrals, see, e.g., [2,6]). Recall that a function $f\colon \mathbb{R}^n \to \mathbb{R}$ is said to be *comonotonically additive* if, for every $\sigma \in S_n$, we have

$$f(\mathbf{x} + \mathbf{x}') = f(\mathbf{x}) + f(\mathbf{x}'), \qquad \mathbf{x}, \mathbf{x}' \in \mathbb{R}_\sigma^n.$$

The function $f$ is said to be *horizontally min-additive* if

$$f(\mathbf{x}) = f(\mathbf{x} \wedge c) + f(\mathbf{x} - (\mathbf{x} \wedge c)), \qquad \mathbf{x} \in \mathbb{R}^n, \ c \in \mathbb{R},$$

where $\mathbf{x} \wedge c$ denotes the $n$-tuple whose $i$th component is $x_i \wedge c = \min(x_i, c)$.

In this paper we consider a generalization of Lovász extensions, which we call quasi-Lovász extensions, and which are best described by the following equation

$$f(x_1, \ldots, x_n) = L(\varphi(x_1), \ldots, \varphi(x_n))$$

where $L$ is a Lovász extension and $\varphi$ a nondecreasing function such that $\varphi(0) = 0$. Such an aggregation function is used in decision under uncertainty, where $\varphi$ is a utility function and $f$ an overall preference functional. It is also used in multi-criteria decision making where the criteria are commensurate (i.e., expressed in a common scale). For a recent reference, see Bouyssou et al. [3].

To axiomatize the class of quasi-Lovász extensions, we propose the following generalizations of comonotonic additivity and horizontal min-additivity, namely comonotonic modularity and invariance under horizontal min-differences (as well as its dual counterpart), which we now briefly describe. We say that a function $f\colon \mathbb{R}^n \to \mathbb{R}$ is *comonotonically modular* if, for every $\sigma \in S_n$, we have

$$f(\mathbf{x}) + f(\mathbf{x}') = f(\mathbf{x} \wedge \mathbf{x}') + f(\mathbf{x} \vee \mathbf{x}'), \qquad \mathbf{x}, \mathbf{x}' \in \mathbb{R}_\sigma^n,$$

where $\mathbf{x} \wedge \mathbf{x}'$ (resp. $\mathbf{x} \vee \mathbf{x}'$) denotes the $n$-tuple whose $i$th component is $x_i \wedge x_i' = \min(x_i, x_i')$ (resp. $x_i \vee x_i' = \max(x_i, x_i')$). We say that $f$ is *invariant under horizontal min-differences* if

$$f(\mathbf{x}) - f(\mathbf{x} \wedge c) = f([\mathbf{x}]_c) - f([\mathbf{x}]_c \wedge c), \qquad \mathbf{x} \in \mathbb{R}^n, \ c \in \mathbb{R},$$

where $[\mathbf{x}]_c$ denotes the $n$-tuple whose $i$th component is 0, if $x_i \leqslant c$, and $x_i$, otherwise.

The outline of this paper is as follows. In Section 2 we recall the definitions of Lovász extensions, discrete Choquet integrals, as well as their symmetric versions, and present representations for these functions. In Section 3 we define the concept of quasi-Lovász extension and its symmetric version, introduce natural relaxations of homogeneity, namely weak homogeneity and odd homogeneity, and present characterizations of those quasi-Lovász extensions (resp. symmetric quasi-Lovász extensions) that are weakly homogeneous (resp. oddly homogeneous). In Section 4 we define the concepts of comonotonic modularity, invariance under horizontal min-differences and invariance under horizontal max-differences, and present a complete description of those function classes axiomatized by each of these properties. In Section 5 we give axiomatizations of the class of quasi-Lovász extensions by means of the properties above, and give all possible factorizations of quasi-Lovász extensions into compositions of Lovász extensions with 1-place functions. Finally, in Section 6 we present analogous results for the symmetric quasi-Lovász extensions.

We employ the following notation throughout the paper. Let $\mathbb{B} = \{0,1\}$, $\mathbb{R}_+ = [0, +\infty[$, and $\mathbb{R}_- = ]-\infty, 0]$. The symbol $I$ denotes a nonempty real interval, possibly unbounded, containing 0. We also introduce the notation $I_+ = I \cap \mathbb{R}_+$, $I_- = I \cap \mathbb{R}_-$, and $I_\sigma^n = I^n \cap \mathbb{R}_\sigma^n$. A function $f\colon I^n \to \mathbb{R}$, where $I$ is centered at 0, is said to be *odd* if $f(-\mathbf{x}) = -f(\mathbf{x})$. For any function $f\colon I^n \to \mathbb{R}$, we define $f_0 = f - f(\mathbf{0})$. For every $A \subseteq [n]$, the symbol $\mathbf{1}_A$ denotes the $n$-tuple whose $i$th component is 1, if $i \in A$, and 0, otherwise. Let also $\mathbf{1} = \mathbf{1}_{[n]}$ and $\mathbf{0} = \mathbf{1}_\varnothing$. The symbols $\wedge$ and $\vee$ denote the minimum and maximum functions, respectively. For every $\mathbf{x} \in \mathbb{R}^n$, let $\mathbf{x}^+ = \mathbf{x} \vee 0$ and $\mathbf{x}^- = (-\mathbf{x})^+$. For every $\mathbf{x} \in \mathbb{R}^n$ and every $c \in \mathbb{R}_+$ (resp. $c \in \mathbb{R}_-$) we denote by $[\mathbf{x}]_c$ (resp. $[\mathbf{x}]^c$) the $n$-tuple whose $i$th component is 0, if $x_i \leqslant c$ (resp. $x_i \geqslant c$), and $x_i$, otherwise.

In order not to restrict our framework to functions defined on $\mathbb{R}$, we consider functions defined on intervals $I$ containing 0, in particular of the forms $I_+$, $I_-$, and those centered at 0.

A full version of the current paper appeared as [5].

## 2    Lovász Extensions and Symmetric Lovász Extensions

We now recall the concepts of Lovász extension and symmetric Lovász extension.

Consider an $n$-place *pseudo-Boolean function*, i.e. a function $\psi\colon \mathbb{B}^n \to \mathbb{R}$, and define the set function $v_\psi\colon 2^{[n]} \to \mathbb{R}$ by $v_\psi(A) = \psi(\mathbf{1}_A)$ for every $A \subseteq [n]$. Hammer and Rudeanu [9] showed that such a function has a unique representation as a multilinear polynomial of $n$ variables

$$\psi(\mathbf{x}) = \sum_{A \subseteq [n]} a_\psi(A) \prod_{i \in A} x_i \,,$$

where the set function $a_\psi\colon 2^{[n]} \to \mathbb{R}$, called the *Möbius transform* of $v_\psi$, is defined by

$$a_\psi(A) = \sum_{B \subseteq A} (-1)^{|A|-|B|} \, v_\psi(B).$$

The *Lovász extension* of a pseudo-Boolean function $\psi\colon \mathbb{B}^n \to \mathbb{R}$ is the function $L_\psi\colon \mathbb{R}^n \to \mathbb{R}$ whose restriction to each subdomain $\mathbb{R}^n_\sigma$ ($\sigma \in S_n$) is the unique affine function which agrees with $\psi$ at the $n+1$ vertices of the $n$-simplex $[0,1]^n \cap \mathbb{R}^n_\sigma$ (see [10,12]). We then have $L_\psi|_{\mathbb{B}^n} = \psi$.

It can be shown (see [7, §5.4.2]) that the Lovász extension of a pseudo-Boolean function $\psi\colon \mathbb{B}^n \to \mathbb{R}$ is the continuous function

$$L_\psi(\mathbf{x}) = \sum_{A \subseteq [n]} a_\psi(A) \bigwedge_{i \in A} x_i, \qquad \mathbf{x} \in \mathbb{R}^n.$$

Its restriction to $\mathbb{R}^n_\sigma$ is the affine function

$$L_\psi(\mathbf{x}) = \psi(\mathbf{0}) + \sum_{i \in [n]} x_{\sigma(i)} \left(v_\psi(A^\uparrow_\sigma(i)) - v_\psi(A^\uparrow_\sigma(i+1))\right), \qquad \mathbf{x} \in \mathbb{R}^n_\sigma, \qquad (1)$$

or equivalently,

$$L_\psi(\mathbf{x}) = \psi(\mathbf{0}) + \sum_{i \in [n]} x_{\sigma(i)} \left(L_\psi(\mathbf{1}_{A^\uparrow_\sigma(i)}) - L_\psi(\mathbf{1}_{A^\uparrow_\sigma(i+1)})\right), \qquad \mathbf{x} \in \mathbb{R}^n_\sigma, \qquad (2)$$

where $A^\uparrow_\sigma(i) = \{\sigma(i), \ldots, \sigma(n)\}$, with the convention that $A^\uparrow_\sigma(n+1) = \varnothing$. Indeed, for any $k \in [n+1]$, both sides of each of the equations (1) and (2) agree at $\mathbf{x} = \mathbf{1}_{A^\uparrow_\sigma(k)}$. It is noteworthy that $L_\psi$ can also be represented by

$$L_\psi(\mathbf{x}) = \psi(\mathbf{0}) + \sum_{i \in [n]} x_{\sigma(i)} \left(L_\psi(-\mathbf{1}_{A^\downarrow_\sigma(i-1)}) - L_\psi(-\mathbf{1}_{A^\downarrow_\sigma(i)})\right), \qquad \mathbf{x} \in \mathbb{R}^n_\sigma,$$

where $A^\downarrow_\sigma(i) = \{\sigma(1), \ldots, \sigma(i)\}$, with the convention that $A^\downarrow_\sigma(0) = \varnothing$. Indeed, for any $k \in [n+1]$, by (2) we have $L_\psi(-\mathbf{1}_{A^\downarrow_\sigma(k-1)}) = \psi(\mathbf{0}) + L_\psi(\mathbf{1}_{A^\uparrow_\sigma(k)}) - L_\psi(\mathbf{1}_{A^\uparrow_\sigma(1)})$.

Let $\psi^d$ denote the *dual* of $\psi$, that is the function $\psi^d\colon \mathbb{B}^n \to \mathbb{R}$ defined by $\psi^d(\mathbf{x}) = \psi(\mathbf{0}) + \psi(\mathbf{1}) - \psi(\mathbf{1} - \mathbf{x})$. The next result provides further representations for $L_\psi$.

**Proposition 1.** *The Lovász extension of a pseudo-Boolean function $\psi\colon \mathbb{B}^n \to \mathbb{R}$ is given by*

$$L_\psi(\mathbf{x}) = \psi(\mathbf{0}) + \sum_{A \subseteq [n]} a_{\psi^d}(A) \bigvee_{i \in A} x_i,$$

*and*

$$L_\psi(\mathbf{x}) = \psi(\mathbf{0}) + L_\psi(\mathbf{x}^+) - L_{\psi^d}(\mathbf{x}^-).$$

A function $f\colon \mathbb{R}^n \to \mathbb{R}$ is said to be a *Lovász extension* if there is a pseudo-Boolean function $\psi\colon \mathbb{B}^n \to \mathbb{R}$ such that $f = L_\psi$.

An $n$-place *Choquet integral* is a nondecreasing Lovász extension $L_\psi\colon \mathbb{R}^n \to \mathbb{R}$ such that $L_\psi(\mathbf{0}) = 0$. It is easy to see that a Lovász extension $L\colon \mathbb{R}^n \to \mathbb{R}$ is an $n$-place Choquet integral if and only if its underlying pseudo-Boolean function $\psi = L|_{\mathbb{B}^n}$ is nondecreasing and vanishes at the origin (see [7, §5.4]).

The *symmetric Lovász extension* of a pseudo-Boolean function $\psi\colon \mathbb{B}^n \to \mathbb{R}$ is the function $\check{L}\colon \mathbb{R}^n \to \mathbb{R}$ defined by $\check{L}_\psi(\mathbf{x}) = \psi(\mathbf{0}) + L_\psi(\mathbf{x}^+) - L_\psi(\mathbf{x}^-)$ (see [4]). In particular, we see that $\check{L}_\psi - \check{L}_\psi(\mathbf{0}) = \check{L}_\psi - \psi(\mathbf{0})$ is an odd function. It is easy to see that the restriction of $\check{L}_\psi$ to $\mathbb{R}_\sigma^n$ is the function

$$\check{L}_\psi(\mathbf{x}) = \psi(\mathbf{0}) + \sum_{1 \leqslant i \leqslant p} x_{\sigma(i)} \left( L_\psi(\mathbf{1}_{A_\sigma^\downarrow(i)}) - L_\psi(\mathbf{1}_{A_\sigma^\downarrow(i-1)}) \right)$$

$$+ \sum_{p+1 \leqslant i \leqslant n} x_{\sigma(i)} \left( L_\psi(\mathbf{1}_{A_\sigma^\uparrow(i)}) - L_\psi(\mathbf{1}_{A_\sigma^\uparrow(i+1)}) \right), \qquad \mathbf{x} \in \mathbb{R}_\sigma^n,$$

where the integer $p \in \{0, \ldots, n\}$ is such that $x_{\sigma(p)} < 0 \leqslant x_{\sigma(p+1)}$.

A function $f\colon \mathbb{R}^n \to \mathbb{R}$ is said to be a *symmetric Lovász extension* if there is a pseudo-Boolean function $\psi\colon \mathbb{B}^n \to \mathbb{R}$ such that $f = \check{L}_\psi$. Nondecreasing symmetric Lovász extensions vanishing at the origin, also called *discrete symmetric Choquet integrals*, were introduced by Šipoš [13] (see also [7, §5.4]).

## 3   Quasi-Lovász Extensions and Symmetric Quasi-Lovász Extensions

In this section we introduce the concepts of quasi-Lovász extension and symmetric quasi-Lovász extension. We also introduce natural relaxations of homogeneity, namely weak homogeneity and odd homogeneity, and present a characterization of those quasi-Lovász extensions (resp. symmetric quasi-Lovász extensions) that are weakly homogeneous (resp. oddly homogeneous). Recall that $I$ is a real interval containing 0.

A *quasi-Lovász extension* is a function $f\colon I^n \to \mathbb{R}$ defined by

$$f = L \circ (\varphi, \ldots, \varphi),$$

also written $f = L \circ \varphi$, where $L\colon \mathbb{R}^n \to \mathbb{R}$ is a Lovász extension and $\varphi\colon I \to \mathbb{R}$ is a nondecreasing function satisfying $\varphi(0) = 0$. Observe that a function $f\colon I^n \to \mathbb{R}$ is a quasi-Lovász extension if and only if $f_0 = L_0 \circ \varphi$, where $f_0 = f - f(\mathbf{0})$ and $L_0 = L - L(\mathbf{0})$.

**Lemma 2.** *Assume* $I \subseteq \mathbb{R}_+$. *For every quasi-Lovász extension* $f\colon I^n \to \mathbb{R}$, $f = L \circ \varphi$, *we have*

$$f_0(x\mathbf{1}_A) = \varphi(x)L_0(\mathbf{1}_A), \qquad x \in I, \ A \subseteq [n]. \tag{3}$$

Observe that if $[0, 1] \subseteq I \subseteq \mathbb{R}_+$ and $\varphi(1) = 1$, then the equation in (3) becomes $f_0(x\mathbf{1}_A) = \varphi(x)f_0(\mathbf{1}_A)$. This motivates the following definition. We say that a function $f\colon I^n \to \mathbb{R}$, where $I \subseteq \mathbb{R}_+$, is *weakly homogeneous* if there exists a nondecreasing function $\varphi\colon I \to \mathbb{R}$ satisfying $\varphi(0) = 0$ such that $f(x\mathbf{1}_A) = \varphi(x)f(\mathbf{1}_A)$ for every $x \in I$ and every $A \subseteq [n]$. Clearly, every weakly homogeneous function $f$ satisfies $f(\mathbf{0}) = 0$ (take $x = 0$ in the definition).

**Proposition 3.** *Assume* $[0,1] \subseteq I \subseteq \mathbb{R}_+$. *Let* $f\colon I^n \to \mathbb{R}$ *be a nonconstant quasi-Lovász extension,* $f = L \circ \varphi$. *Then the following are equivalent.*

(i) $f_0$ *is weakly homogeneous.*
(ii) *There exists* $A \subseteq [n]$ *such that* $f_0(\mathbf{1}_A) \neq 0$.
(iii) $\varphi(1) \neq 0$.

*In this case we have* $f_0(x\mathbf{1}_A) = \frac{\varphi(x)}{\varphi(1)} f_0(\mathbf{1}_A)$ *for every* $x \in I$ *and every* $A \subseteq [n]$.

*Remark 4.* (a) If $[0,1] \subsetneq I \subseteq \mathbb{R}_+$, then the quasi-Lovász extension $f\colon I^n \to \mathbb{R}$ defined by $f(\mathbf{x}) = \bigwedge_{i \in [n]} \varphi(x_i)$, where $\varphi(x) = 0 \vee (x-1)$, is not weakly homogeneous.
(b) When $I = [0,1]$, the assumption that $f$ is nonconstant implies immediately that $\varphi(1) \neq 0$. We then see by Proposition 3 that $f_0$ is weakly homogeneous. Note also that, if $f$ is constant, then $f_0 \equiv 0$ is clearly weakly homogeneous. Thus, for any quasi-Lovász extension $f\colon [0,1]^n \to \mathbb{R}$, the function $f_0$ is weakly homogeneous.

Assume now that $-x \in I$ whenever $x \in I$, that is, $I$ is centered at 0. A *symmetric quasi-Lovász extension* is a function $f\colon I^n \to \mathbb{R}$ defined by $f = \check{L} \circ \varphi$, where $\check{L}\colon \mathbb{R}^n \to \mathbb{R}$ is a symmetric Lovász extension and $\varphi\colon I \to \mathbb{R}$ is a nondecreasing odd function.

We say that a function $f\colon I^n \to \mathbb{R}$, where $I$ centered at 0, is *oddly homogeneous* if there exists a nondecreasing odd function $\varphi\colon I \to \mathbb{R}$ such that $f(x\mathbf{1}_A) = \varphi(x)f(\mathbf{1}_A)$ for every $x \in I$ and every $A \subseteq [n]$. Clearly, for every oddly homogeneous function $f$, the functions $f|_{I_+^n}$ and $f|_{I_-^n}$ are weakly homogeneous.

**Proposition 5.** *Assume that* $I$ *is centered at* 0 *with* $[-1,1] \subseteq I$. *Let* $f\colon I^n \to \mathbb{R}$ *be a symmetric quasi-Lovász extension,* $f = \check{L} \circ \varphi$, *such that* $f|_{I_+^n}$ *or* $f|_{I_-^n}$ *is nonconstant. Then the following are equivalent.*

(i) $f_0$ *is oddly homogeneous.*
(ii) *There exists* $A \subseteq [n]$ *such that* $f_0(\mathbf{1}_A) \neq 0$.
(iii) $\varphi(1) \neq 0$.

*In this case we have* $f_0(x\mathbf{1}_A) = \frac{\varphi(x)}{\varphi(1)} f_0(\mathbf{1}_A)$ *for every* $x \in I$ *and every* $A \subseteq [n]$.

*Remark 6.* Similarly to Remark 4(b), we see that, for any symmetric quasi-Lovász extension $f\colon [-1,1]^n \to \mathbb{R}$, the function $f_0$ is oddly homogeneous.

## 4  Comonotonic Modularity

Recall that a function $f\colon I^n \to \mathbb{R}$ is said to be *modular* (or a *valuation*) if

$$f(\mathbf{x}) + f(\mathbf{x}') = f(\mathbf{x} \wedge \mathbf{x}') + f(\mathbf{x} \vee \mathbf{x}') \tag{4}$$

for every $\mathbf{x}, \mathbf{x}' \in I^n$. It was proved (see Topkis [14, Thm 3.3]) that a function $f\colon I^n \to \mathbb{R}$ is modular if and only if it is *separable*, that is, there exist $n$ functions

$f_i: I \to \mathbb{R}$, $i \in [n]$, such that $f = \sum_{i \in [n]} f_i$. In particular, any 1-place function $f: I \to \mathbb{R}$ is modular.

Two $n$-tuples $\mathbf{x}, \mathbf{x}' \in I^n$ are said to be *comonotonic* if there exists $\sigma \in S_n$ such that $\mathbf{x}, \mathbf{x}' \in I^n_\sigma$. A function $f: I^n \to \mathbb{R}$ is said to be *comonotonically modular* (or a *comonotonic valuation*) if (4) holds for every comonotonic $n$-tuples $\mathbf{x}, \mathbf{x}' \in I^n$. This notion was considered in the special case when $I = [0, 1]$ in [11]. We observe that, for any function $f: I^n \to \mathbb{R}$, condition (4) holds for every $\mathbf{x}, \mathbf{x}' \in I^n$ of the forms $\mathbf{x} = x \mathbf{1}_A$ and $\mathbf{x}' = x' \mathbf{1}_A$, where $x, x' \in I$ and $A \subseteq [n]$. Observe also that, for every $\mathbf{x} \in \mathbb{R}^n_+$ and every $c \in \mathbb{R}_+$, we have $\mathbf{x} - \mathbf{x} \wedge c = [\mathbf{x}]_c - [\mathbf{x}]_c \wedge c$. This motivates the following definition. We say that a function $f: I^n \to \mathbb{R}$, where $I \subseteq \mathbb{R}_+$, is *invariant under horizontal min-differences* if, for every $\mathbf{x} \in I^n$ and every $c \in I$, we have

$$f(\mathbf{x}) - f(\mathbf{x} \wedge c) = f([\mathbf{x}]_c) - f([\mathbf{x}]_c \wedge c). \tag{5}$$

Dually, we say that a function $f: I^n \to \mathbb{R}$, where $I \subseteq \mathbb{R}_-$, is *invariant under horizontal max-differences* if, for every $\mathbf{x} \in I^n$ and every $c \in I$, we have

$$f(\mathbf{x}) - f(\mathbf{x} \vee c) = f([\mathbf{x}]^c) - f([\mathbf{x}]^c \vee c). \tag{6}$$

We observe that, for any function $f: I^n \to \mathbb{R}$, where $I \subseteq \mathbb{R}_+$, condition (5) holds for every $\mathbf{x} \in I^n$ of the form $\mathbf{x} = x \mathbf{1}_A$, where $x \in I$ and $A \subseteq [n]$. Dually, for any function $f: I^n \to \mathbb{R}$, where $I \subseteq \mathbb{R}_-$, condition (6) holds for every tuple $\mathbf{x} \in I^n$ of the form $\mathbf{x} = x \mathbf{1}_A$, where $x \in I$ and $A \subseteq [n]$. We also observe that a function $f$ is comonotonically modular (resp. invariant under horizontal min-differences, invariant under horizontal max-differences) if and only if so is the function $f_0$.

**Theorem 7.** *Assume $I \subseteq \mathbb{R}_+$ and let $f: I^n \to \mathbb{R}$ be a function. Then the following are equivalent.*

(i) *$f$ is comonotonically modular.*
(ii) *$f$ is invariant under horizontal min-differences.*
(iii) *There exists a function $g: I^n \to \mathbb{R}$ such that, for every $\sigma \in S_n$ and every $\mathbf{x} \in I^n_\sigma$, we have*

$$f(\mathbf{x}) = g(\mathbf{0}) + \sum_{i \in [n]} \big( g(x_{\sigma(i)} \mathbf{1}_{A^\uparrow_\sigma(i)}) - g(x_{\sigma(i)} \mathbf{1}_{A^\uparrow_\sigma(i+1)}) \big).$$

*In this case, we can choose $g = f$.*

*Remark 8.* The equivalence between (i) and (iii) in Theorem 7 generalizes Theorem 1 in [11], which describes the class of comonotonically modular functions $f: [0, 1]^n \to [0, 1]$ under the additional conditions of symmetry and idempotence.

We observe that if $f: I^n \to \mathbb{R}$ is comonotonically modular then necessarily

$$f_0(\mathbf{x}) = f_0(\mathbf{x}^+) + f_0(-\mathbf{x}^-) \quad \text{(take } \mathbf{x}' = \mathbf{0} \text{ in (4))}.$$

We may now present a characterization of the class of comonotonically modular functions on an arbitrary interval $I$ containing 0.

**Theorem 9.** *For any function* $f\colon I^n \to \mathbb{R}$, *the following are equivalent.*

(i) $f$ *is comonotonically modular.*

(ii) *There exist* $g\colon I_+^n \to \mathbb{R}$ *comonotonically modular (or invariant under horizontal min-differences) and* $h\colon I_-^n \to \mathbb{R}$ *comonotonically modular (or invariant under horizontal max-differences) such that* $f_0(\mathbf{x}) = g_0(\mathbf{x}^+) + h_0(-\mathbf{x}^-)$ *for every* $\mathbf{x} \in I^n$. *In this case, we can choose* $g = f|_{I_+^n}$ *and* $h = f|_{I_-^n}$.

(iii) *There exist* $g\colon I_+^n \to \mathbb{R}$ *and* $h\colon I_-^n \to \mathbb{R}$ *such that, for every* $\sigma \in S_n$ *and every* $\mathbf{x} \in I_\sigma^n$,

$$f_0(\mathbf{x}) = \sum_{1 \leqslant i \leqslant p} \left( h(x_{\sigma(i)} \mathbf{1}_{A_\sigma^\downarrow(i)}) - h(x_{\sigma(i)} \mathbf{1}_{A_\sigma^\downarrow(i-1)}) \right)$$

$$+ \sum_{p+1 \leqslant i \leqslant n} \left( g(x_{\sigma(i)} \mathbf{1}_{A_\sigma^\uparrow(i)}) - g(x_{\sigma(i)} \mathbf{1}_{A_\sigma^\uparrow(i+1)}) \right),$$

*where* $p \in \{0, \ldots, n\}$ *is such that* $x_{\sigma(p)} < 0 \leqslant x_{\sigma(p+1)}$. *In this case, we can choose* $g = f|_{I_+^n}$ *and* $h = f|_{I_-^n}$.

*Remark 10.* Observe that using condition (iii) in Theorems 7 and 9, we can easily derive characterizations of Choquet integrals and of symmetric Choquet integrals given in terms of comonotonic modularity. Indeed, we simply need to suppose that $f\colon I^n \to \mathbb{R}$ is nondecreasing and satisfies

$$f(x\mathbf{1}_A) = xf(\mathbf{1}_A), \quad \text{for every } x \in I \text{ and every } A \subseteq [n],$$

and assume that $[0,1] \subseteq I \subseteq \mathbb{R}_+$ (in Theorem 7) and that $I$ is centered at 0 with $[-1,1] \subseteq I \subseteq \mathbb{R}$ (in Theorem 9).

From Theorem 9 we obtain the "comonotonic" analogue of Topkis' characterization [14] of modular functions as separable functions, and which provides an alternative description of comonotonically modular functions.

**Corollary 11.** *Let* $J$ *be any nonempty real interval, possibly unbounded. A function* $f\colon J^n \to \mathbb{R}$ *is comonotonically modular if and only if it is comonotonically separable, that is, for every* $\sigma \in S_n$, *there exist functions* $f_i^\sigma\colon J \to \mathbb{R}$, $i \in [n]$, *such that*

$$f(\mathbf{x}) = \sum_{i=1}^n f_i^\sigma(x_{\sigma(i)}) = \sum_{i=1}^n f_{\sigma^{-1}(i)}^\sigma(x_i), \quad \mathbf{x} \in J^n \cap \mathbb{R}_\sigma^n.$$

# 5 Axiomatization and Representation of Quasi-Lovász Extensions and Their Symmetric Counterparts

We now present axiomatizations of the class of quasi-Lovász extensions and describe all possible factorizations of quasi-Lovász extensions into compositions of Lovász extensions with 1-place nondecreasing functions. Similarly, we provide analogous results concerning the class of symmetric quasi-Lovász extensions.

**Theorem 12.** *Assume* $[0,1] \subseteq I \subseteq \mathbb{R}_+$ *and let* $f \colon I^n \to \mathbb{R}$ *be a nonconstant function. Then the following are equivalent.*

(i) $f$ *is a quasi-Lovász extension and there exists* $A \subseteq [n]$ *such that* $f_0(\mathbf{1}_A) \neq 0$.

(ii) $f$ *is comonotonically modular (or invariant under horizontal min-differences) and* $f_0$ *is weakly homogeneous.*

(iii) *There is a nondecreasing function* $\varphi_f \colon I \to \mathbb{R}$ *satisfying* $\varphi_f(0) = 0$ *and* $\varphi_f(1) = 1$ *such that* $f = L_{f|_{\mathbb{B}^n}} \circ \varphi_f$.

Let $f \colon I^n \to \mathbb{R}$ be a quasi-Lovász extension, where $[0,1] \subseteq I \subseteq \mathbb{R}_+$, for which there exists $A^* \subseteq [n]$ such that $f_0(\mathbf{1}_{A^*}) \neq 0$. Then the inner function $\varphi_f$ introduced in Theorem 12 is unique. Indeed, by Proposition 3, we have $f_0(x\mathbf{1}_A) = \varphi_f(x)f_0(\mathbf{1}_A)$ for every $x \in I$ and every $A \subseteq [n]$. The function $\varphi_f$ is then defined by $\varphi_f(x) = \frac{f_0(x\mathbf{1}_{A^*})}{f_0(\mathbf{1}_{A^*})}$, $x \in I$.

**Theorem 13.** *Assume* $[0,1] \subseteq I \subseteq \mathbb{R}_+$ *and let* $f \colon I^n \to \mathbb{R}$ *be a quasi-Lovász extension,* $f = L \circ \varphi$. *Then there exists* $A^* \subseteq [n]$ *such that* $f_0(\mathbf{1}_{A^*}) \neq 0$ *if and only if there exists* $a > 0$ *such that* $\varphi = a\,\varphi_f$ *and* $L_0 = \frac{1}{a}(L_{f|_{\mathbb{B}^n}})_0$.

We now present an axiomatization of the class of symmetric quasi-Lovász extensions and describe all possible factorizations of symmetric quasi-Lovász extensions into compositions of symmetric Lovász extensions with 1-place non-decreasing odd functions.

**Theorem 14.** *Assume that* $I$ *is centered at* $0$ *with* $[-1,1] \subseteq I$ *and let* $f \colon I^n \to \mathbb{R}$ *be a function such that* $f|_{I_+^n}$ *or* $f|_{I_-^n}$ *is nonconstant. Then the following are equivalent.*

(i) $f$ *is a symmetric quasi-Lovász extension and there exists* $A \subseteq [n]$ *such that* $f_0(\mathbf{1}_A) \neq 0$.

(ii) $f$ *is comonotonically modular and* $f_0$ *is oddly homogeneous.*

(iii) *There is a nondecreasing odd function* $\varphi_f \colon I \to \mathbb{R}$ *satisfying* $\varphi_f(1) = 1$ *such that* $f = \check{L}_{f|_{\mathbb{B}^n}} \circ \varphi_f$.

Assume again that $I$ is centered at $0$ with $[-1,1] \subseteq I$ and let $f \colon I^n \to \mathbb{R}$ be a symmetric quasi-Lovász extension for which there exists $A^* \subseteq [n]$ such that $f_0(\mathbf{1}_{A^*}) \neq 0$. Then the inner function $\varphi_f$ introduced in Theorem 14 is unique. Indeed, by Proposition 5, we have $f_0(x\mathbf{1}_A) = \varphi_f(x)f_0(\mathbf{1}_A)$ for every $x \in I$ and every $A \subseteq [n]$. The function $\varphi_f$ is then defined by $\varphi_f(x) = \frac{f_0(x\mathbf{1}_{A^*})}{f_0(\mathbf{1}_{A^*})}$, $x \in I$.

**Theorem 15.** *Assume that* $I$ *is centered at* $0$ *with* $[-1,1] \subseteq I$ *and let* $f \colon I^n \to \mathbb{R}$ *be a symmetric quasi-Lovász extension,* $f = \check{L} \circ \varphi$. *Then there exists* $A^* \subseteq [n]$ *such that* $f_0(\mathbf{1}_{A^*}) \neq 0$ *if and only if there exists* $a > 0$ *such that* $\varphi = a\,\varphi_f$ *and* $\check{L}_0 = \frac{1}{a}(\check{L}_{f|_{\mathbb{B}^n}})_0$.

*Remark 16.* If $I = [-1,1]$, then the "nonconstant" assumption and the second condition in assertion (i) of Theorem 14 can be dropped off.

**Acknowledgments.** This research is supported by the internal research project F1R-MTH-PUL-09MRDO of the University of Luxembourg.

# References

1. Beliakov, G., Pradera, A., Calvo, T.: Aggregation Functions: A Guide for Practitioners. STUDFUZZ. Springer, Berlin (2007)
2. Benvenuti, P., Mesiar, R., Vivona, D.: Monotone set functions-based integrals. In: Handbook of Measure Theory, vol. II, pp. 1329–1379. North-Holland, Amsterdam (2002)
3. Bouyssou, D., Dubois, D., Prade, H., Pirlot, M. (eds.): Decision-Making Process - Concepts and Methods. ISTE/John Wiley, London (2009)
4. Couceiro, M., Marichal, J.-L.: Axiomatizations of Lovász extensions and symmetric Lovász extensions of pseudo-Boolean functions. Fuzzy Sets and Systems 181(1), 28–38 (2011)
5. Couceiro, M., Marichal, J.-L.: Axiomatizations of quasi-Lovász extensions of pseudo-Boolean functions. Aequationes Mathematicae 82, 213–231 (2011)
6. de Campos, L.M., Bolaños, M.J.: Characterization and comparison of Sugeno and Choquet integrals. Fuzzy Sets and Systems 52(1), 61–67 (1992)
7. Grabisch, M., Marichal, J.-L., Mesiar, R., Pap, E.: Aggregation functions. Encyclopedia of Mathematics and its Applications, vol. 127. Cambridge University Press, Cambridge (2009)
8. Grabisch, M., Murofushi, T., Sugeno, M. (eds.): Fuzzy measures and integrals - Theory and applications. STUDFUZZ, vol. 40. Physica-Verlag, Heidelberg (2000)
9. Hammer, P., Rudeanu, S.: Boolean methods in operations research and related areas. Springer, Heidelberg (1968)
10. Lovász, L.: Submodular functions and convexity. In: 11th Int. Symp., Mathematical programming, Bonn 1982, pp. 235–257 (1983)
11. Mesiar, R., Mesiarová-Zemánková, A.: The ordered modular averages. IEEE Trans. Fuzzy Syst. 19(1), 42–50 (2011)
12. Singer, I.: Extensions of functions of 0-1 variables and applications to combinatorial optimization. Numer. Funct. Anal. Optimization 7, 23–62 (1984)
13. Šipoš, J.: Integral with respect to a pre-measure. Mathematica Slovaca 29(2), 141–155 (1979)
14. Topkis, D.M.: Minimizing a submodular function on a lattice. Operations Research 26(2), 305–321 (1978)

# Choquet Integration and the AHP: Inconsistency and Non-additivity

Silvia Bortot and Ricardo Alberto Marques Pereira

Dipartimento di Informatica e Studi Aziendali,
Università degli Studi di Trento
Via Inama 5, TN 38122 Trento, Italy
{silvia.bortot,ricalb.marper}@unitn.it

**Abstract.** We propose to extend the aggregation scheme of the AHP, from the standard weighted averaging to the more general Choquet integration. In our model, a measure of dominance inconsistency between criteria is derived from the main pairwise comparison matrix of the AHP and it is used to construct a non-additive capacity, whose associated Choquet integral reduces to the standard weighted mean of the AHP in the consistency case. In the general inconsistency case, however, the new AHP aggregation scheme based on Choquet integration tends to attenuate (resp. emphasize) the priority weights of the criteria with higher (resp. lower) average dominance inconsistency with the other criteria.

**Keywords:** Aggregation functions, multiple criteria analysis, AHP, inconsistency, 2-additive capacities, Choquet integral, and Shapley values.

## 1 Introduction

The Analytic Hierarchy Process (AHP) introduced by Thomas L. Saaty [28], [29], [30], [31] is a well-known multicriteria aggregation model based on pairwise comparison matrices at two fundamental levels: the lower level encodes pairwise comparison matrices between alternatives (one such matrix for each criterion), and the higher level encodes a single pairwise comparison matrix between criteria. In its most general form, the higher level of the AHP can itself be structured hierarchically, with several layers of criteria, but in this paper we focus on the single layer case, with a single pairwise comparisons matrix between criteria.

The AHP extracts from the main pairwise comparison matrix **A** between criteria, at the higher level, a vector of priority weights corresponding to the principal eigenvector, or, alternatively, to the geometric mean vector. The positive components of the priority vector are usually taken normalized to unit sum.

Analogously, for each criterion at the lower level, the model extracts from the corresponding pairwise comparison matrix between alternatives a priority vector, whose components represent the evaluations of the alternatives accordingly to that criterion.

Finally, we associate to each alternative a vector containing its evaluations according to the various criteria, and we obtain an aggregated multicriteria

S. Greco et al. (Eds.): IPMU 2012, Part IV, CCIS 300, pp. 188–197, 2012.

evaluation of each alternative using the weighted mean with the priority weights derived from the main matrix **A**.

In this paper we consider only the geometric mean method, because its structural properties are more suited for our study. Moreover, we focus on the question of inconsistency and how it can be used to modulate the priority values of the various criteria. Pairwise comparison matrices are typically inconsistent and in fact consistency is not required by the AHP. However, it is in many respects useful to estimate and possibly compensate for the degree of inconsistency involved in any decision making model which is based on pairwise comparison matrices.

In order to take into account some appropriate measure of the dominance inconsistency between criteria which may be present in the main matrix **A**, for the purpose of modulating the weighted averaging scheme of the AHP, it is natural to extend the standard weighted mean aggregation to the more general framework of Choquet integration. Comprehensive reviews of Choquet integration can be found in Grabisch and Labreuche [13], [14], [15], Grabisch, Kojadinovich, and Meyer [12], plus also Wang and Klir [33], Grabisch, Nguyen and Walker [18], Grabisch, Murofushi and Sugeno [17]. The Choquet integral is defined with respect to a non-additive capacity and corresponds to a large class of aggregation functions, including the classical weighted means - the additive capacity case - and the ordered weighted means (OWA) - the symmetric capacity case. General reviews of aggregation functions can be found in Calvo, Mayor, and Mesiar [5], Beliakov, Pradera, and Calvo [2], Grabisch, Marichal, Mesiar, and Pap [16].

In the framework of Choquet integration, in order to control the exponential complexity in the construction of the capacity ($2^n - 2$ degrees of freedom), Grabisch [10] introduced the so called k-additive capacities, see also Grabisch [11], and Miranda and Grabisch [25]. The 2-additive case, in particular (see Miranda, Grabisch, and Gil, [26]; Mayag, Grabisch, and Labreuche, [23], [24]), provides a good trade-off between the range of the model and its complexity (only $n(n+1)/2$ real coefficients are required to define a 2-additive capacity). The Choquet integral with respect to a 2-additive capacity is a rich and effective modelling tool, see for instance Berrah and Clivillé [3], Clivillé, Berrah, and Maurice [7], Berrah, Maurice, and Montmain [4], Marques Pereira, Ribeiro, and Serra [22].

In this paper we focus on the main matrix **A** and we propose an extension of the AHP based on Choquet integration with respect to a 2-additive capacity. This capacity is defined on the basis of an appropriate transformation of the totally inconsistent matrix introduced by Barzilai [1]. The aggregation scheme is then redefined in terms of the Choquet integral associated to such capacity, thereby extending the usual weighted averaging scheme of the AHP. A preliminary version of this paper was presented in [21].

An important effect of the new aggregation scheme based on Choquet integration is that of emphasizing (resp. attenuating) the effective priority weights of those criteria which have a lower (resp. higher) level of dominance inconsistency with the remaining ones. This compensatory mechanism that emphasizes some effective priority weights and attenuates others is nicely illustrated by the Shapley values associated with the capacity, which correspond to the mean value of the effective Choquet priority weights taken over all comonotonicity cones. In our model, therefore, the Shapley values encode the mean effective priority weights of the various criteria and, under consistency, they coincide with the standard AHP priority weights.

## 2  Choquet Integration

Consider a finite set $N = \{1, 2, \ldots, n\}$ of interacting criteria. The subsets $S, T \subseteq N$ are usually called coalitions. A *capacity* [6] on the set $N$ is a set function $\mu : 2^N \longrightarrow [0, 1]$ satisfying

(i) $\mu(\emptyset) = 0$, $\mu(N) = 1$
(ii) $S \subseteq T \subseteq N \;\Rightarrow\; \mu(S) \leq \mu(T)$.

Given two coalitions $S, T \subseteq N$, with $S \cap T = \emptyset$, the capacity $\mu$ is said to be

- subadditive for $S, T$ if $\mu(S \cup T) < \mu(S) + \mu(T)$,
- additive for $S, T$ if $\mu(S \cup T) = \mu(S) + \mu(T)$,
- superadditive for $S, T$ if $\mu(S \cup T) > \mu(S) + \mu(T)$.

If any of these properties holds for all coalitions $S, T \subseteq N$, with $S \cap T = \emptyset$, the capacity $\mu$ is said to be additive, subadditive, or superadditive, respectively.

Given a capacity $\mu$, we can define the *Choquet integral* [6], [8], [9] of a vector $\mathbf{x} = (x_1, \ldots, x_n) \in [0, 1]^n$ with respect to $\mu$ as

$$\mathcal{C}_\mu(\mathbf{x}) = \sum_{i=1}^n [\mu(A_{(i)}) - \mu(A_{(i+1)})] \, x_{(i)} \tag{1}$$

where $x_{(1)} \leq x_{(2)} \leq \ldots \leq x_{(n)}$. Moreover $A_{(i)} = \{(i), \ldots, (n)\}$ for $i = 1, \ldots, n$ and $A_{(n+1)} = \emptyset$.

Notice that the Choquet integral with respect to an additive capacity $\mu$ reduces to a weighted arithmetic mean, whose weights $w_i$ are given by the $\mu(i)$ values.

A capacity $\mu$ can be equivalently represented by its *Möbius transform* $m_\mu$ [27], which is defined as

$$m_\mu(T) = \sum_{S \subseteq T} (-1)^{t-s} \mu(S) \qquad T \subseteq N \tag{2}$$

where $s$ and $t$ denote the cardinality of the coalitions $S$ and $T$, respectively.

Conversely, given the Möbius transform $m_\mu$, the associated capacity $\mu$ is obtained as

$$\mu(T) = \sum_{S \subseteq T} m_\mu(S) \qquad T \subseteq N. \tag{3}$$

A capacity $\mu$ is said to be *2-additive* [10] if its Möbius transform satisfies $m_\mu(T) = 0$ for all $T \subseteq N$ with $t > 2$, and there exists at least one coalition $T \subseteq N$ with $t = 2$ such that $m_\mu(T) \neq 0$. For 2-additive capacities we have

$$\mu(T) = \sum_{i \in T} m_\mu(i) + \sum_{\{i, j\} \subseteq T} m_\mu(ij) \qquad T \subseteq N. \tag{4}$$

The Choquet integral can be expressed in terms of the Möbius transform in the following way [20],

$$\mathcal{C}_\mu(x_1,\ldots,x_n) = \sum_{T \subseteq N} m_\mu(T) \min_{i \in T}(x_i) . \qquad (5)$$

and in the case of 2-additive capacity we have simply

$$\mathcal{C}_\mu(x_1,\ldots,x_n) = \sum_{i \in N} m_\mu(i)\, x_i \; + \sum_{\{i,j\} \subseteq N} m_\mu(ij) \min(x_i, x_j) . \qquad (6)$$

The *importance index* or *Shapley value* [19], [32] of criterion $i \in N$ with respect to a capacity $\mu$ is defined as

$$\phi_\mu(i) = \sum_{T \subseteq N \setminus i} \frac{(n-1-t)!\,t!}{n!} \left[\mu(T \cup i) - \mu(T)\right], \qquad \sum_{i=1}^{n} \phi_\mu(i) = 1. \qquad (7)$$

The Shapley value $\phi_\mu(i)$ amounts to a weighted average of the marginal contribution of element $i$ with respect to all coalitions $T \subseteq N \setminus i$ and can be interpreted as an effective importance weight. The Shapley values can be expressed in terms of the Möbius transform in the following way [10],

$$\phi_\mu(i) = \sum_{T \subseteq N \setminus i} \frac{m_\mu(T \cup i)}{t+1} \qquad i = 1,\ldots,n. \qquad (8)$$

and in the case of 2-additive capacity we have simply

$$\phi_\mu(i) = m_\mu(i) + \frac{1}{2} \sum_{j \in N \setminus i} m_\mu(ij) \qquad i = 1,\ldots,n. \qquad (9)$$

## 3   A Measure of Dominance Consistency in the AHP

Consider a positive reciprocal $n \times n$ matrix $\mathbf{A} = [a_{ij}]$,

$$a_{ij} > 0 \qquad a_{ji} = 1/a_{ij} \qquad i,j = 1,\ldots,n \qquad (10)$$

where $a_{ij}$ is the dominance of criterion $i$ over criterion $j$, as in the main pairwise comparison matrix at the higher level. In fact all pairwise comparison matrices in the AHP are of this form. However, our model regards only the single pairwise comparison matrix $\mathbf{A}$ between criteria at the higher level of the AHP. This is because the main matrix $\mathbf{A}$ is the one that controls the aggregation process: in the AHP, the aggregation is performed by means of weighted averaging, in which the weights are the components of the higher level priority vector.

In general, the positive reciprocal matrix above is inconsistent, where consistency means

$$a_{ij} = a_{ik} a_{kj} \qquad i,j,k = 1,\ldots,n. \qquad (11)$$

Given a general positive reciprocal matrix $\mathbf{A}$, typically inconsistent, we can define an associated consistent matrix $\mathbf{C} = [c_{ij}]$ in the following way, see for instance Barzilai [1],

$$c_{ij} = w_i/w_j \qquad w_i = u_i/\Sigma_{j=1}^n u_j \qquad i, j = 1, \ldots, n \qquad (12)$$

where $u_i$ is the geometric mean of the matrix elements in row $i$,

$$u_i = \sqrt[n]{\Pi_{j=1}^n a_{ij}} \qquad i, j = 1, \ldots, n \qquad (13)$$

and the priority weights $w_i > 0$ are normalized to unit sum, $\Sigma_{i=1}^n w_i = 1$.

Given an element $a_{ij}$ of the matrix $\mathbf{A}$, we define the *neighborhood* $U(a_{ij})$ as the set of matrix elements in row $i$ and column $j$,

$$U(a_{ij}) = \{a_{ik}, a_{kj} \mid k = 1, \ldots, n\}. \qquad (14)$$

A matrix $\mathbf{A}$ is said to be *locally consistent* at $(ij)$ if, on average, $a_{ij}$ is consistent with the matrix elements in its neighborhood,

$$a_{ij} = c_{ij} = \sqrt[n]{\Pi_{k=1}^n a_{ik} a_{kj}} \qquad i, j = 1, \ldots, n. \qquad (15)$$

The local consistency is a weak form of the (full) consistency. In fact, it can be shown that the matrix $\mathbf{A}$ is (fully) consistent if and only if it is locally consistent at every $(ij)$, for $i, j = 1, \ldots, n$.

Given a general positive reciprocal matrix $\mathbf{A}$, we now consider the associated *totally inconsistent matrix* $\mathbf{E} = [e_{ij}]$ introduced by Barzilai [1],

$$e_{ij} = a_{ij}/c_{ij} \qquad i, j = 1, \ldots, n \qquad (16)$$

The general element $e_{ij} \in (0, \infty)$ of the totally inconsistent matrix $\mathbf{E}$ associated with $\mathbf{A}$ is a natural local consistency measure of the matrix $\mathbf{A}$ at $(ij)$. The more $e_{ij}$ is close to 1, the more $\mathbf{A}$ is locally consistent at $(ij)$. On the basis of this notion, we now wish to define a $(0, 1]$ measure of local consistency by means of an appropriate transformation of the matrix elements of $\mathbf{E}$.

We now define the *scaling function* $f : (0, \infty) \to (0, 1]$ as

$$f(x) = \frac{2}{x + x^{-1}} \qquad \text{for } x > 0. \qquad (17)$$

The scaling function $f$ has the important property

$$f(x) = f(x^{-1}) \qquad \text{for } x > 0 \qquad (18)$$

and its graph is shown in Fig. 1. Notice that the scaling function $f$ has a single critical point at $x = 1$, where it reaches the maximum value $f(1) = 1$, and $f(x)$ tends monotonically to 0 as $x$ moves away from $x = 1$, towards 0 or infinity.

By means of the scaling function $f$, we can associate a positive symmetric $n \times n$ matrix $\mathbf{V} = [v_{ij}]$ to the matrix $\mathbf{A} = [a_{ij}]$ in the following way,

$$v_{ij} = f(e_{ij}) = f(a_{ij}/c_{ij}) \qquad v_{ij} \in (0, 1] \qquad v_{ij} = v_{ji} \qquad i, j = 1, \ldots, n. \qquad (19)$$

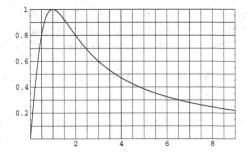

**Fig. 1.** The graph of the scaling function $f$

The fact that the $n \times n$ matrix $\mathbf{V} = [v_{ij}]$ is symmetric is due to the reciprocity of the positive matrix $\mathbf{A}$, plus the fact that $f(x) = f(x^{-1})$ for $x > 0$,

$$v_{ji} = f(e_{ji}) = f(a_{ji}/c_{ji}) = f(c_{ij}/a_{ij}) = f(a_{ij}/c_{ij}) = f(e_{ij}) = v_{ij} \ . \qquad (20)$$

Notice that $v_{ij} = 1$ if and only if $a_{ij} = c_{ij}$, otherwise $v_{ij} \in (0,1)$, and the more $a_{ij}/c_{ij}$ differs from 1 the more $v_{ij}$ gets closer to 0. Therefore, we can consider the element $v_{ij}$ as a $(0,1]$ measure of local consistency of the matrix $\mathbf{A}$ at $(ij)$.

On the basis of the local dominance consistency measure $v_{ij}$, $i, j = 1, \ldots, n$, we introduce the notation $v_i = \sum_{j=1}^{n} v_{ij} w_j$ and $v = \sum_{i=1}^{n} w_i v_i$. We obtain

$$w_i < v_i \leq 1 \qquad i = 1, \ldots, n \qquad \sum_{i=1}^{n} w_i^2 < v \leq 1 \qquad (21)$$

where the value $v_i$ measures the degree of dominance consistency of criterion $i$ with respect to the other criteria, and the value $v$ measures the global degree of dominance consistency between the various criteria.

## 4    Extending the Aggregation Scheme of the AHP

In this section we present an extension of the AHP based on Choquet integration with respect to a 2-additive capacity. On the basis of the dominance consistency measure constructed above, we define the interaction coefficients of a 2-additive capacity and then we reconsider the aggregation scheme in terms of Choquet integration, thereby extending the usual weighted averaging scheme of the AHP.

Given a general positive reciprocal $n \times n$ matrix $\mathbf{A} = [a_{ij}]$, typically inconsistent, we now wish to define a 2-additive capacity $\mu : 2^N \longrightarrow [0,1]$ by associating to each criterion $i = 1, \ldots, n$ its standard AHP priority weight $w_i$, and to each pair of criteria $i, j = 1, \ldots, n$ a negative interaction proportional to the corresponding dominance inconsistency $1 - v_{ij}$. In this way, the capacity $\mu$ will be subadditive and the deviation from the standard additive AHP is due to the amount of dominance inconsistency present in the criteria coalitions considered. The capacity $\mu$ in our model is constructed as follows: making use of the Möbius transform $m_\mu$ of the capacity $\mu$, we define $m_\mu(i) = w_i/D$ for each singlet $\{i\}$ and

$m_\mu(ij) = -w_i(1-v_{ij})w_j/D$ for each doublet $\{i,j\}$ , with null higher order terms. On that basis, we define the value of the 2-additive capacity $\mu$ on a coalition $T$ as the sum of the singletons and the pairs contained in the coalition $T$

$$\mu(T) = \sum_{\{i\}\subseteq T} w_i/D + \sum_{\{i,j\}\subseteq T} (-w_i(1-v_{ij})w_j)/D \qquad (22)$$

where the normalization factor $D$ is the sum of all singlets and pairs in $N$

$$D = \sum_{\{i\}\subseteq N} w_i + \sum_{\{i,j\}\subseteq N} -w_i(1-v_{ij})w_j = 1 - \frac{1}{2}\sum_{i,j=1}^{n} w_i(1-v_{ij})w_j = \frac{1}{2}(1+v). \quad (23)$$

In particular, we have

$$\mu(i) = 2w_i/(1+v) \qquad\qquad i,j = 1,\ldots,n$$

$$\mu(ij) = (2w_i + 2w_j - 2w_i(1-v_{ij})w_j)/(1+v) . \qquad (24)$$

The capacity $\mu$ satisfies the boundary conditions $\mu(\emptyset) = 0$ and $\mu(N) = 1$, and is monotonic and subadditive. The (strict) monotonicity of the capacity is due to the fact that

$$w_i - \sum_{j=1}^{n} w_i(1-v_{ij})w_j = w_i - w_i(1-v_i) = w_i v_i > w_i^2 > 0 \qquad i = 1,\ldots,n . \quad (25)$$

This means that the positive value $w_i/D$ associated to each criterion dominates (in absolute value) the sum of the non positive values $-w_i(1-v_{ij})w_j/D \leq 0$ associated to the $n-1$ pairwise interactions between that criterion and the other criteria, which implies the strict monotonicity of the capacity,

$$\mu(T\cup i) = \mu(T) + w_i/D - \sum_{j\in T} w_i(1-v_{ij})w_j/D > \mu(T). \qquad (26)$$

In turn, subadditivity is due to

$$\mu(S\cup T) = \mu(S) + \mu(T) - \sum_{i\in S, j\in T} w_i(1-v_{ij})w_j/D \leq \mu(S) + \mu(T). \qquad (27)$$

The non-additive capacity introduced in (22), (23) is the basis of our extension of the AHP. In our model, the aggregated evaluations of an alternative with respect to the $n$ criteria are obtained through Choquet integration with respect to the 2-additive capacity $\mu$. Our model is thus an extension of the AHP, in the sense that our model coincides with the AHP in the case of consistency (additive capacity), but differs slightly from the AHP in the case of inconsistency (non-additive capacity). In fact, if the matrix $\mathbf{A}$ is consistent then $v_{ij} = 1$ for all $i,j = 1,\ldots,n$ and $D = 1$. In such case, $m_\mu(i) = w_i = \mu(i)$ and $m_\mu(ij) = 0$, which means that the capacity $\mu$ is additive, and $\mu(T) = \sum_{i\in T} m_\mu(i) = \sum_{i\in T} w_i$.

Accordingly, the Choquet integral reduces to the standard weighted mean of the AHP

$$\mathcal{C}_\mu(\mathbf{x}) = \sum_{i=1}^{n} w_i x_i. \tag{28}$$

In the general inconsistency case, the Shapley values $\phi_i$, $i = 1, \ldots, n$ associated with the capacity $\mu$ in our model are given by

$$\phi_i = m_\mu(i) + \frac{1}{2} \sum_{j \in N \setminus i} m_\mu(ij) = w_i(1 + v_i)/(1 + v). \tag{29}$$

In our multicriteria aggregation model the Shapley values encode the effective priority weights of the various criteria. When the matrix $\mathbf{A}$ is consistent, we have $v_{ij} = 1$ for all $i, j = 1, \ldots, n$ and equation above implies that the Shapley values are simply $\phi_i = w_i$. Otherwise, we have $\phi_i > w_i$ if $v_i > v$ and $\phi_i < w_i$ if $v_i < v$. In general, the fact that $\mathbf{A}$ is inconsistent changes the original distribution of priority weights, attenuating the importance weights of the more dominance inconsistent criteria (those with lower dominance consistency $v_i$) and emphasizing the importance weights of the more dominance consistent criteria. For instance consider the following main pairwise comparison matrix $\mathbf{A}$,

$$\mathbf{A} = \begin{pmatrix} 1 & 15/2 & 3/2 & 1/5 \\ & 1 & 1 & 10/3 \\ & & 1 & 2/3 \\ & & & 1 \end{pmatrix} \tag{30}$$

The standard priority weighting vector of the AHP associated with this pairwise comparison matrix (using the geometric mean method) is

$$\mathbf{w} = [w_i] = (0.3, 0.2, 0.2, 0.3). \tag{31}$$

The consistent matrix $\mathbf{C}$ associated with the pairwise comparison matrix $\mathbf{A}$ in (30) can easily be obtained from the standard AHP priority weights in (31),

$$\mathbf{C} = [c_{ij} = w_i/w_j] = \begin{pmatrix} 1 & 3/2 & 3/2 & 1 \\ & 1 & 1 & 2/3 \\ & & 1 & 2/3 \\ & & & 1 \end{pmatrix} \tag{32}$$

The two matrices $\mathbf{A}$, $\mathbf{C}$ share the same priority vector $\mathbf{w}$. However, the matrix $\mathbf{A}$ in (30) is not locally consistent at positions (12), (14), (24), because the matrix elements $a_{12}$, $a_{14}$, $a_{24}$ are different than the corresponding elements in the consistent matrix $\mathbf{C}$. This means that with respect to the consistent matrix $\mathbf{C}$, matrix $\mathbf{A}$ emphasizes the relative dominance of criterion 1 over criterion 2, attenuates the relative dominance of criterion 1 over criterion 4, and emphasizes the relative dominance of criterion 2 over criterion 4. These changes produce an inconsistent pairwise comparison matrix but preserve the standard AHP priority weights $\mathbf{w}$ obtained by the geometric mean method.

If we compute the dominance consistency degrees $v_i$, we obtain

$$v_1 = v_4 \simeq 0.6923\,, \quad v_2 \simeq 0.6308\,, \quad v_3 = 1\,, \qquad v \simeq 0.7415\,. \tag{33}$$

Note that $v_3 > v$, and thus $\phi_3 > w_3$, as explained above. On the other hand, $v_i < v$ for $i = 1, 2, 4$ and thus in these cases we have $\phi_i < w_i$. In fact, the Shapley values associated with the inconsistent main pairwise comparison matrix $\mathbf{A}$ are $\phi_1 \simeq 0.2915$, $\phi_2 \simeq 0.1873$, $\phi_3 \simeq 0.2297$, $\phi_4 \simeq 0.2915$. In this example, therefore, our extended AHP aggregation scheme emphasizes the priority weight of criterion 3 with respect to the priority weights of the other criteria.

# References

1. Barzilai, J.: Consistency measures for pairwise comparison matrices. Journal of Multi-Criteria Decision Analysis 7(3), 123–132 (1998)
2. Beliakov, G., Pradera, A., Calvo, T.: Aggregation Functions: A Guide for Practitioners. STUDFUZZ, vol. 221. Springer, Heidelberg (2007)
3. Berrah, L., Clivillé, V.: Towards an aggregation performance measurement system model in a supply chain context. Computers in Industry 58(7), 709–719 (2007)
4. Berrah, L., Mauris, G., Montmain, J.: Monitoring the improvement of an overall industrial performance based on a Choquet integral aggregation. Omega 36(3), 340–351 (2008)
5. Calvo, T., Mayor, G., Mesiar, R.: Aggregation Operators: New Trends and Applications. STUDFUZZ, vol. 97. Physica-Verlag, Heidelberg (2002)
6. Choquet, G.: Theory of capacities. Annales de l'Institut Fourier 5, 131–295 (1953)
7. Clivillé, V., Berrah, L., Mauris, G.: Quantitative expression and aggregation of performance measurements based on the MACBETH multi-criteria method. International Journal of Production Economics 105(1), 171–189 (2007)
8. Grabisch, M.: Fuzzy integral in multicriteria decision making. Fuzzy Sets and Systems 69(3), 279–298 (1995)
9. Grabisch, M.: The application of fuzzy integrals in multicriteria decision making. European Journal of Operational Research 89(3), 445–456 (1996)
10. Grabisch, M.: k-order additive discrete fuzzy measures and their representation. Fuzzy Sets and Systems 92(2), 167–189 (1997)
11. Grabisch, M.: Alternative representations of discrete fuzzy measures for decision making. International Journal of Uncertainty, Fuzzyness and Knowledge-Based Systems 5(5), 587–607 (1997)
12. Grabisch, M., Kojadinovich, I., Meyer, P.: A review of methods for capacity identification in Choquet integral based multi-attribute utility theory: Applications of the Kappalab R package. European Journal of Operational Research 186(2), 766–785 (2008)
13. Grabisch, M., Labreuche, C.: Fuzzy measures and integrals in MCDA. In: Figueira, J., Greco, S., Ehrgott, M. (eds.) Multiple Criteria Decision Analysis, pp. 563–604. Springer, Heidelberg (2005)
14. Grabisch, M., Labreuche, C.: A decade of application of the Choquet and Sugeno integrals in multi-criteria decision aid. 4OR 6(1), 1–44 (2008)
15. Grabisch, M., Labreuche, C.: A decade of application of the Choquet and Sugeno integrals in multi-criteria decision aid. Annals of Operations Research 175(1), 247–286 (2010)

16. Grabisch, M., Marichal, J.L., Mesiar, R., Pap, E.: Aggregation Functions, Encyclopedia of Mathematics and its Applications, vol. 127. Cambridge University Press (2009)
17. Grabisch, M., Murofushi, T., Sugeno, M.: Fuzzy Measure and Integrals: Theory and Applications. Physica-Verlag (2000)
18. Grabisch, M., Nguyen, H.T., Walker, E.A.: Fundamentals of Uncertainty Calculi with Applications to Fuzzy Inference. Kluwer Academic Publishers, Dordrecht (1995)
19. Grabisch, M., Roubens, M.: An axiomatic approach to the concept of interaction among players in cooperative games. Int. J. of Game Theory 28(4), 547–565 (1999)
20. Marichal, J.L.: Aggregation operators for multicriteria decision aid. Ph.D. Thesis, University of Liège, Liège, Belgium (1998)
21. Marques Pereira, R.A., Bortot, S.: Choquet measures, Shapley values, and inconsistent pairwise comparison matrices: an extension of Saaty's A.H.P. In: Proc. 25th Linz Seminar on Fuzzy Set Theory: Mathematics of Fuzzy Systems, Linz, Austria, pp. 130–135 (2004)
22. Marques Pereira, R.A., Ribeiro, R.A., Serra, P.: Rule correlation and Choquet integration in fuzzy inference systems. International Journal of Uncertainty, Fuzzyness and Knowledge-Based Systems 16(5), 601–626 (2008)
23. Mayag, B., Grabisch, M., Labreuche, C.: A representation of preferences by the Choquet integral with respect to a 2-additive capacity. Theory and Decision 71(3), 297–324 (2011)
24. Mayag, B., Grabisch, M., Labreuche, C.: A characterization of the 2-additive Choquet integral through cardinal information. Fuzzy Sets and Systems 184(1), 84–105 (2011)
25. Miranda, P., Grabisch, M.: Optimization issues for fuzzy measures. International Journal of Uncertainty, Fuzzyness and Knowledge-Based Systems 7(6), 545–560 (1999)
26. Miranda, P., Grabisch, M., Gil, P.: Axiomatic structure of k-additive capacities. Mathematical Social Sciences 49(2), 153–178 (2005)
27. Rota, G.C.: On the foundations of combinatorial theory I. Theory of Möbius functions. Zeitschrift für Wahrscheinlichkeitstheorie und Verwandte Gebeite 2(4), 340–368 (1964)
28. Saaty, T.L.: A scaling method for priorities in hierarchical structures. Journal of Mathematical Psychology 15(3), 234–281 (1977)
29. Saaty, T.L.: Axiomatic foundation of the analytic hierarchy process. Management Science 32(7), 841–855 (1986)
30. Saaty, T.L.: Multicriteria Decision Making: The Analytic Hierarchy Process. RWS Publications, Pittsburgh (1988); Original version published by McGraw-Hill (1980)
31. Saaty, T.L., Vargas, L.G.: Prediction, Projection and Forecasting. Kluwer Academic Publishers, Norwell (1991)
32. Shapley, L.S.: A value for n-person games. In: Kuhn, H.W., Tucker, A.W. (eds.) Contributions to the Theory of Games. Annals of Mathematics Studies, vol. II, pp. 307–317. Princeton University Press, NJ (1953)
33. Wang, Z., Klir, G.J.: Fuzzy Measure Theory. Springer, New York (1993)

# Minimax Regret Capacity Identification

Mikhail Timonin

National Nuclear Research University MEPhI,
31 Kashirskoe Shosse, Moscow 115409, Russian Federation
mikhail.timonin@gmail.com

**Abstract.** We study the minimax-regret version of the Choquet integral maximization problem. Our main result is to show that there always exist a capacity such that the robust solution is also a maximizer of the Choquet integral with respect to this capacity. However, in contrast to additive decision models (the case of several priors) it is not always a global one.

## 1 Introduction

A critical factor for successful application of the Choquet integral to decision problems is the identification of the capacity representing the preferences of the decision maker (DM). Quite commonly, the DM has only a limited knowledge of the problem being modelled, thus introducing some aspects of uncertainty. In such situation the numerical representation (i.e. the capacity) of her preferences is usually not unique, so making a decision by maximizing the Choquet integral with respect to some fixed capacity over the set of admissible actions is not possible anymore. The DM has to either perform a further clarification of the model, which is not always possible, or to adopt some sort of robust strategy which would provide performance guarantees for the whole range of potential scenarios. Two widespread approaches to providing robustness are the minimax criterion and its minimax-regret variation. In this paper we analyze how the latter can complement the Choquet integral in MCDA problems. In particular, we will be interested in the question whether the "robust" solution is also "optimal" with respect to any of the capacities compliant with the preferences of the DM.

## 2 Basic Definitions

The following notations will be used throughout the paper:

- $N = \{1, \ldots, n\}$ - the set of criteria;
- $Z_i = [0, \bar{z}_i] \subset \mathbb{R}, i \in N$ - sets of criteria values, where "0" is the least preferred value and $\bar{z}_i$ the most preferred.
- $Z = Z_1 \times \ldots \times Z_n$ - set of alternatives;
- $\mathcal{Z}_0 \subset Z$ - feasible alternatives.

S. Greco et al. (Eds.): IPMU 2012, Part IV, CCIS 300, pp. 198–207, 2012.

**Definition 1.** *Let $N$ be a finite set and $2^N$ its power set. Capacity (non-additive measure, fuzzy measure) is a set function $\nu : 2^N \to \mathbb{R}_+$ such that:*

1. *$\nu(\varnothing) = 0$;*
2. *$A \subseteq B \Rightarrow \nu(A) \leq \nu(B), \ \forall A, B \in 2^N$.*

*In this article, it is assumed that capacity is normalized, i.e. $\nu(N) = 1$.*

**Definition 2.** *The Choquet integral of a function $\mathcal{G} : N \to \mathbb{R}_+$ with range $\{g_1, \ldots, g_n\}$ with respect to a capacity $\nu$ is defined as*

$$C_\nu(g_1, \ldots, g_n) = \sum_{i=1}^{n} (g_{(i)} - g_{(i-1)}) \nu(j | \mathcal{G}(j) \geqslant g_{(i)})$$

*where $g_{(1)}, \ldots, g_{(n)}$ is a permutation of $g_1, \ldots, g_n$ such that $g_{(1)} \leq g_{(2)} \leq \cdots \leq g_{(n)}$, and $g_{(0)} = 0$.*

In contrast to decision problems under uncertainty, in multicriteria setting the criteria might be non-commensurable. Therefore, the values $z_i \in Z_i = [0, \overline{z}_i]$ should be mapped onto a common scale by means of the value functions.

- $f_i : \mathbb{R} \to \mathbb{R}$ - value functions, and $f_i(Z_i) \subset [0, 1]$ (see below);
- Note, that according to the introduced notions the function $\mathcal{G} : N \to \mathbb{R}$ in the definition of the Choquet integral is obtained as $\mathcal{G} = F \circ H$, where $F = f_1 \times \ldots \times f_n$ and $H : N \to Z$ is an "alternative selection" function (analogue of "act" in decision making under uncertainty).

A modification of MACBETH approach [4] allowing to construct the value functions for Choquet integral-based models has been proposed in [12]. In this paper we assume that the functions have already been determined and meet certain requirements. Namely, we require the functions $f_i(z_i)$ to be:

- Concave on $\mathbb{R}$;
- Non-decreasing on $[0, \overline{z}_i]$.
- $f_i(0) = 0, f_i(\overline{z}_i) = 1$, where $\overline{z}_i$ is the most preferred value of criterion $i$.

The assumption of concavity is not of course met in all possible applications, however, we believe it should be appropriate in the majority of cases. The limitation has to be made in order to improve the tractability of the model and connect it with the classic applications of the Choquet integral in MCDA.

## 3  Problem Statement

When the information provided by the decision maker is sufficient to narrow down the set of capacities compliant with her preferences to a single point, the decision problem can be formulated in the following way:

$$C(\nu, f(z)) \to \max_z$$
$$z \in Z_0,$$

$$(1)$$

where $C(\nu, f(z))$ is the Choquet integral with regard to capacity $\nu$, $z$ is the decision variable and $\mathcal{Z}_0$ is the set of admissible alternatives, which we restrict to be closed, bounded, and convex. Optimal decisions are then the ones maximizing the value of the integral (refer to [22] for solutions to this problem). However, once the capacity is not unique but can only be identified down to some set $\mathcal{U}$, the form (1) is not valid anymore, and an additional criterion must be introduced in order to distinguish between solutions corresponding to different capacities. There are two major approaches to this problem. The first one is "value agnostic", in the sense that decision is made using a single capacity selected from the uncertainty set without taking the value functions into account. A recent review of such methods in relation to models employing the Choquet integral can be found in [9]. The second approach utilizes the information about the value functions as well. The most prominent example of the second class of methods is the minimax criterion (see [16,6] for axiomatization). See also [13] for a recent example of the second type approach related to the Choquet integral.

An important question arising is whether the result obtained by the methods of the second type complies with the initial preferences of the DM. In particular, would the resulting solution also maximize $C(\nu^r, f(z)), z \in \mathcal{Z}_0$ for some $\nu^r \in \mathcal{U}$? In this paper we would investigate the minimax regret criterion [19] (for axiomatizations see [16,21]). Let $z^r$ be the "robust decision", and $\nu^{real}$ the capacity which describes the factual state of the world. Since the DM is ignorant about what capacity is actually "real"[1], the optimization problem would have the following form:

$$\max_{\nu}(\max_{z} C(\nu, f(z)) - C(\nu, f(z^r))) \;\; \to \min_{z^r}$$

$$\nu \in \mathcal{U}$$
$$z \in \mathcal{Z}_0 \quad\quad\quad\quad\quad\quad\quad\quad\quad\quad (RP)$$
$$z^r \in \mathcal{Z}_0,$$

where $\mathcal{U}$ is the set of capacities compliant with the preferences of the DM. We aim to minimize the maximal deviation from the optimum for all possible scenarios. This is a continuous minimax problem in variables $\nu, z$, and $z^r$.

The main problem we try to answer in this paper is whether there exist a capacity $\nu^r \in \mathcal{U}$ such that the solution $z_*^r$ of (RP) is also a solution of

$$C(\nu^r, f(z)) \to \max_{z}$$
$$z \in \mathcal{Z}_0. \quad\quad\quad\quad\quad\quad\quad\quad (2)$$

## 4   Capacity Identification Problem

The capacity identification process involves expressing informal knowledge, obtained from the DM, as constraints on the set of capacities. Listed below are the types of information which can be incorporated into the model [15].

---

[1] In fact, there is most likely no single "real" capacity. In practical problems system parameters are constantly changing under the influence of environment, so this notion is just an abstraction.

**Criteria Importance.** The most intuitive way to describe a multicriteria model is, perhaps, to define the relative weights of its components. In capacity identification problems this is performed via the Shapley value [20].

**Criteria Interaction.** A more complicated type of knowledge about criteria is the character of their combined influence. In particular, criteria can complement each other, which is also known under the name of positive synergy, or else be redundant (resp. negative synergy).The measure of criteria interaction was introduced in [17] for pairs of elements and later generalized in [8].

**Veto and Favor Criteria.** Proposed in [7] "veto" criteria are those of an immense importance, so that the alternatives having low valuations on them will also inevitably receive low overall judgements. The opposite is a "favor" criterion (or criteria) which, when has a high valuation, automatically justifies a high overall mark.

**Learning Set.** In some situations the decision maker might be able to express his judgements about a small number of objects. This type of knowledge usually corresponds to some qualitative rating of alternatives.

Having the preferences of the DM expressed as a set of constraints we obtain the set $\mathcal{U}$. In accordance to the robust programming terminology, we will refer to it as the *uncertainty set*. $\mathcal{U}$ can then be written down as

$\mathcal{U}$ :

**The information from the DM**

$$\phi_\nu(i) - \phi_\nu(j) \geqslant \delta_{SH}, \quad i,j \in 1,\ldots,n$$
$$-\delta_{SH} \geqslant \phi_\nu(i) - \phi_\nu(j) \leqslant \delta_{SH}, \quad i,j \in 1,\ldots,n$$
$$I_\nu(i,j) - I_\nu(k,l) \geqslant \delta_I, \quad i,j \in 1,\ldots,n$$
$$-\delta_I \geqslant I_\nu(i,j) - I_\nu(k,l) \leqslant \delta_I, \quad i,j \in 1,\ldots,n$$
$$C(\nu,f(z_i)) - C(\nu,f(z_j)) \geqslant \delta_{LS}, \quad i,j \in 1,\ldots,n$$
$$-\delta_{LS} \geqslant C(\nu,f(z_i)) - C(\nu,f(z_j)) \leqslant \delta_{LS}, \quad i,j \in 1,\ldots,n \tag{3}$$
$$\nu(A) = 1, \forall A \supset \text{favor criteria}$$
$$\nu(A) = 0, \forall A \not\supset \text{veto criteria}$$

**Technical constraints**

$$\nu(\emptyset) = 0$$
$$\nu(N) = 1$$
$$\nu(B) \geq \nu(A) \quad \forall B \subset A \subset N$$

**Additional constraints**

$k - additivity\ constraints.$ (Not always applicable.)

Where $\phi_\nu(i)$ is the Shapley value for criterion $i$, $\delta_{SH}$ is the indifference threshold for representing preference between criteria, $I_\nu(i,j)$ is the interaction index for criteria $i$ and $j$, $\delta_I$ is the indifference threshold for interaction index ordering, and $\delta_{LS}$ is the indifference threshold for ordering alternatives from the learning set.

All of the constraints above are linear, thus the uncertainty set is a polyhedron in $\mathbb{R}_+^{2^n}$. The dimension can be reduced to $2^n - 2$ if we exclude the $\emptyset$ and $N$ coordinates, which have fixed values. If the constraints are such that the set $\mathcal{U}$ is empty, the DM should be asked to review his preferences (see [9] for detailed discussion). Apparently, the set $\mathcal{U}$ can also contain more than one capacity which induces the problem discussed in the beginning of the article.

## 5   Main Results

**Definition 3.** *A capacity $\nu$ is called k-monotone for some $k \geqslant 2$, if, for all families $k$ of subsets $A_1, \ldots, A_k$, it holds that*

$$\nu\left(\bigcup_{i=1}^k A_i\right) \geqslant \sum_{\emptyset \neq I \subset 1, \ldots, k} (-1)^{|I|+1} \nu\left(\bigcap_{i \in I} A_i\right).$$

*A capacity is called totally monotone if it is k-monotone for all $k \geqslant 2$.*

An important property of totally monotone capacities (also called belied functions) is that their Mobius transform includes only non-negative coefficients [1].

**Theorem 1.** *Assume, that all $\nu \in \mathcal{U}$ are 2-monotone. In this case, the solution $z_*^r$ of (RP) is also a global maximum of $C(\nu^r, f(z)), z \in \mathcal{Z}_0$ for some $\nu^r \in \mathcal{U}$.*

*Proof.* The function $\mathcal{R}(\nu) = \max_{z \in \mathcal{Z}_0} C(\nu, f(z)) - C(\nu, f(z^r))$ is convex in $\nu$ and hence reaches its maximum at an extreme point of $\mathcal{U}$. The latter is a polyhedron, so the problem (RP) can thus be rewritten as

$$\max_{\lambda \in \Lambda} \sum_i \lambda_i \left[ \max_{z \in \mathcal{Z}_0} C(\nu_i, f(z)) - C(\nu_i, f(z^r)) \right] \quad \to \min_{z^r \in \mathcal{Z}_0},$$

where $\Lambda = \{\lambda | \lambda \geq 0, \sum_i \lambda_i = 1\}$ is a simplex, $|\Lambda| = |\mathcal{U}_{ext}|$, $\nu_i \in \mathcal{U}_{ext}$ - the set of vertices of $\mathcal{U}$. The function

$$\mathcal{F}(\lambda, z^r) = \sum_i \lambda_i \left[ \max_{z \in \mathcal{Z}_0} C(\nu_i, f(z)) - C(\nu_i, f(z^r)) \right]$$

is concave in $\lambda$ for every $z^r \in \mathcal{Z}_0$, and convex in $z^r$ for every $\lambda \in \Lambda$ [14]. The sets $\Lambda$ and $\mathcal{Z}_0$ are compact. Therefore,

$$\min_{z^r \in \mathcal{Z}_0} \max_{\lambda \in \Lambda} \mathcal{F}(\lambda, z^r) = \max_{\lambda \in \Lambda} \min_{z^r \in \mathcal{Z}_0} \mathcal{F}(\lambda, z^r),$$

and we obtain the following dual problem:

$$\min_{z^r \in \mathcal{Z}_0} \sum_i \lambda_i \left[ \max_{z \in \mathcal{Z}_0} C(\nu_i, f(z)) - C(\nu_i, f(z^r)) \right] \quad \to \max_{\lambda \in \Lambda}, \qquad \text{(DP)}$$

or, equivalently

$$\sum_i \lambda_i \max_{z \in \mathcal{Z}_0} C(\nu_i, f(z)) - \max_{z^r \in \mathcal{Z}_0} C(\sum_i \lambda_i \nu_i, f(z^r)) \quad \to \max_{\lambda \in \Lambda}, \tag{4}$$

It follows, that $z_*^r$ minimizing (4) is also a maximum of $C(\sum_i \lambda_i^* \nu_i, f(z^r))$, where $\lambda^*$ is a maximizer of (4). Defining $\nu^r = \sum_i \lambda_i^* \nu_i$ and noticing that due to 2-monotonicity of $\nu^r$ the integral $C(\sum_i \lambda_i^* \nu_i, f(z^r))$ is concave [14], we obtain the required result.    □

It is easy to see that Theorem 1 also holds for probabilities (since any probability is a 2-monotone capacity). So for minimax regret in additive models, the robust solution is always a global maximizer of the expected value. The situation is however different for capacities, since in general the integral $C(\nu, f(z^r))$ is not concave in $z^r$.

Another observation to be made is more of a semantic flavour. In terms of [18] the expression (4) is referred to as *expected value of perfect information*, with the difference that in (4) the distribution $\lambda$ is not fixed. In this context, minimizing the regret can be viewed as minimization of maximal expected value of information.

**Theorem 2.** *Solution* $z_*^r$ *of (RP) is also a local maximum of* $C(\nu^r, f(z)), z \in \mathcal{Z}_0$ *for some* $\nu^r \in \mathcal{U}$.

In other words, for the general case $z_*^r$ is a *locally* optimal solution for some capacity $\nu^r$ belonging to $\mathcal{U}$, but not always a global one.

**Lemma 1 ([5]).** *The Choquet integral w.r.t an arbitrary capacity $\nu$ can be represented as*

$$C(\nu, f(z)) = \bigvee_{\mathcal{N}_i \in \mathcal{B}(\nu)} C(\mathcal{N}_i, f(z)), \tag{5}$$

*where* $\mathcal{N}_i \in \mathcal{B}(\nu)$ *are totally monotone chain measures given by (via their Mobius transform):*

$$m^{\mathcal{N}}(A) = \begin{cases} 0, & A \notin \mathcal{C} \\ \nu(Y_i) - \nu(Y_{i-1}), & A = Y_i \in \mathcal{C}, \end{cases} \tag{6}$$

*where* $\mathcal{C} = \{\emptyset \subset Y_1 \subset \cdots \subset Y_n = N\}$ *is a maximal chain. Note that measures* $\mathcal{N}_i$ *bijectively correspondent to sets* $L_i = \{z | f_{(1)}(z_{(1)}) \leq \cdots \leq f_{(n)}(z_{(n)})\}$ *and*

$$C(\nu, f(z)) = C(\mathcal{N}_i, f(z)), \forall z \in L_i$$
$$C(\nu, f(z)) \geq C(\mathcal{N}_i, f(z)), \forall z \notin L_i.$$

**Lemma 2.** *The global solution of the problem (RP) can be found by solving at most n! problems with sets $\mathcal{U}$ containing only 2-monotone capacities.*

*Proof.* By Lemma 1 and due to convexity of $\mathcal{R}(\nu) = \max_z C(\nu, f(z)) - C(\nu, f(z^r))$, problem (RP) can be rewritten as

$$t \qquad\qquad\qquad\qquad \rightarrow \min$$
$$\max_z C(\nu, f(z)) - \max_{\mathcal{N}_i \in \mathcal{B}(\nu)} C(\mathcal{N}_i, F(z^r)) \leq t, \quad \forall \nu \in \mathcal{U}_{ext}$$
$$z \in \mathcal{Z}_0$$
$$z^r \in \mathcal{Z}_0, \tag{7}$$

which for points $z^r$ lying within every set $L_i$ is equivalent to

$$t \qquad\qquad\qquad\qquad \rightarrow \min$$
$$\max_z C(\nu, f(z)) - C(\mathcal{N}_i, f(z^r)) \leq t, \quad \forall (\nu, \mathcal{N}_i) \in (\mathcal{U}_{ext}, \aleph_i(\mathcal{U}_{ext}))$$
$$z \in \mathcal{Z}_0$$
$$z^r \in \mathcal{Z}_0, \tag{8}$$

where $\aleph_i(\mathcal{U}_{ext})$ is constructed from chains measures $\mathcal{N}_i$ corresponding to $L_i$ for each $\nu$ from $\mathcal{U}_{ext}$ (see (6)).

Let $z_i^r$ be a solution of problem (8), and $t_i^*$ the corresponding value of the objective function. Two cases are possible. Either $z_i^r \in L_i$ and then $z_i^r$ is also a local solution of (RP) according to the arguments above, or $z_i^r$ belongs to some other subset $L_j$. In this case, for the set of corresponding chain measures $\aleph_j(\mathcal{U}_{ext})$ and all constraints of (8) it holds

$$\max_z C(\nu, f(z)) - C(\mathcal{N}_i, f(z)) \geq \max_z C(\nu, f(z)) - C(\mathcal{N}_j, f(z)).$$

Hence, the value of objective function of (RP) at $z_i^r$ *does not exceed* $t_i^*$. In other words, solving (8) for all possible $\aleph_j(\mathcal{U}_{ext})$ (corresponding to $n!$ sets $L_i$) and choosing solutions with the least $t_i^*$ will elicit all global minima of the problem (8) and only them.    □

Solution of (RP) can be found more efficiently (i.e. by solving less than $n!$ problems) if a coarser partition of $\nu$ can be used. For details of obtaining such partition refer to [22].

*Proof (Theorem 2).* Note, that the proof of Theorem 2 entails that the "robust" capacity lies within a polyhedron with vertices $\mathcal{N}_i^1, \mathcal{N}_i^2, \ldots \in \aleph_i(\mathcal{U}^k)$ (cf. (8) and (4)). It can be thus represented as

$$\mathcal{N}^r = \sum_j \lambda_j^* \mathcal{N}_i^j.$$

$\mathcal{N}^r$ generally lies outside the uncertainty set $\mathcal{U}$. However, it is possible to construct a capacity $\nu^r \in \mathcal{U}$ such that $\mathcal{N}^r$ is one of the chain measures constituting $\nu^r$. Recall, from the definition of $\mathcal{N}$ measures, that $\nu_i(A) = \mathcal{N}_i(A)$ for all $A \in \mathcal{C}$. Thus, for $\mathcal{N}^r$ we can find a corresponding measure $\nu^r \in \mathcal{U}$, by setting $\nu^r = \sum_i \lambda_i^* \nu_i$. Lemma 2 also guarantees that $z_*^r = \arg\max C(\mathcal{N}^r, f(z^r))$ is a maximum of $C(\nu^r, f(z^r))$, albeit only a local one.    □

Consider the following example [2]

$$N = \{1, 2, 3, 4\}$$
$$\mathcal{U} = \{\nu | \phi_\nu(1) = 0.2, I_\nu(1, 2) - I_\nu(2, 3) > 0.05\}$$
$$\mathcal{Z}_0 = \{z | z \geq 0, \sum z = 1\}$$
$$f_i(z_i) = 1 - e^{-3z_i}$$

In this case the solution of the problem (RP) is [3]

$$z_*^r = (0.4620, 0.0785, 0.0285, 0.4309)$$
$$\mathcal{N}^r = (0, 0.4, 0, 0.4, 0, 0.4, 0, 0.4, 0, 0.7644, 0, 0.89105, 0, 0.76446, 0, 1)$$
$$\nu^r = (0, 0.4, 0.1993, 0.5993, 0.0585, 0.4585, 0.2297, 0.6297, 0.7645,$$
$$0.7645, 0.8911, 0.8911, 0.9015, 0.9015, 1, 1)$$

$$\arg \max_{z \in \mathcal{Z}_0} C(\mathcal{N}^r, f(z^r)) = z_*^r$$
$$\max_{z \in \mathcal{Z}_0} C(\nu^r, f(z_*^r)) = C(\mathcal{N}^r, f(z_*^r)) = \mathbf{0.5999}$$
$$\arg \max_{z \in \mathcal{Z}_0} C(\nu^r, f(z)) = (0, 0.0688, 0.1791, 0.7520)$$
$$\max_{z \in \mathcal{Z}_0} C(\nu^r, f(z)) = \mathbf{0.7597}$$

## 5.1   Finding the Robust Capacity

The problem (DP) might be hard to solve directly if the number of extreme points of $\mathcal{U}$ is very high. Unfortunately, due to a large dimensionality of the uncertainty set this is usually the case. A detailed research of the question can be found in [2,10]. The results in [3], although not being directly applicable, allow to conjecture that direct enumeration approach might be used if capacities in $\mathcal{U}$ are of low additivity order (2 or 3). This has been frequently observed by the author while solving practical problems.

Providing $\mathcal{U}$ has a low number of extreme points which can be easily found, the solution of (DP) is straightforward and can be found by standard minimax methods (see also Lemma 1 for the case of non-convex capacities). In case when the number of extreme points is high, the following approach can be used. In [23] we have proposed an algorithm for finding the solution of (RP). The algorithm builds successive finite approximations $\mathcal{U}^k$ of the set $\mathcal{U}$ such that

$$\mathcal{U}^0 \subset \mathcal{U}^1 \subset \ldots \subset \mathcal{U}.$$

---

[2] Shapley values should not be directly set in practical problems, we have also slightly relaxed the requirements to the value functions.

[3] Capacities are given in binary ordering, i.e. 0, 1, 2, 12, 3...

This allows to reduce the problem (RP) to a sequence of problems:

$$t \qquad\qquad\qquad\qquad\qquad \to \min$$
$$\max_{z} C(\nu, f(z)) - C(\nu, f(z^r)) \le t, \quad \forall \nu \in \mathcal{U}^k$$
$$z \in \mathcal{Z}_0 \tag{RP-F}$$
$$z^r \in \mathcal{Z}_0.$$

The problem (RP-F) is a finite one, and can be solved easier than the problem (RP) The sequence is built in the following way. Assume, we have found the solution $z_k^r$ and the value of the objective function $t^k$ of (RP-F) for some approximation $\mathcal{U}^k$. The algorithm then looks for the solution(s) $\nu^{k+1}$ of the "inner" problem:

$$\mathcal{R}(\nu^{k+1}, z_k^r) = \max_{z \in \mathcal{Z}_0} C(\nu, z) - C(\nu, z_k^r) \quad \to \max_{\nu \in \mathcal{U}}. \tag{InP}$$

In case when there exist maximizers $\nu^{k+1} \in \mathcal{U}$ of (InP) such that $\mathcal{R}(\nu^{k+1}, z_k^r) > t^k$ a better approximation $\mathcal{U}^{k+1}$ is formed by adding these maximizers to $\mathcal{U}^k$, and the algorithm proceeds onto the next iteration. If on contrary $\mathcal{R}(\nu^{k+1}, z_k^r) \le t^k$, the algorithm stops, and the point $z_k^r$ is the solution of the problem (RP). The convergence proof for algorithms of this type can be found in e.g. [11].

Apparently, the approximation $\mathcal{U}^F$ obtained on the final iteration can be used in (DP) instead of $\mathcal{U}$. Indeed, according to (InP) there are no capacities in $\mathcal{U}$ for which the value of $\max_{z \in \mathcal{Z}_0} C(\nu, z) - C(\nu, z_k^r)$ is larger than $t^F$ but which are not in $\mathcal{U}^F$. At the same time, it is easy to see that the maximizer of (DP) would have non-zero $\lambda_i$ only for $\nu_i$ having maximal values of $\max_{z \in \mathcal{Z}_0} C(\nu, z) - C(\nu, z_k^r)$.

## 6  Conclusion

In this paper, we have analyzed the usage of minimax regret criterion in capacity identification problems. We have shown that for 2-monotone capacities the solution minimizing the regret value is a also a maximizer of the Choquet integral w.r.t. some "robust" capacity from the uncertainty set, i.e. the set of capacities compliant with preferences of the DM. This mirrors the situation when the preferences are represented by a probability distribution. However, the situation is somehow different for the general case, where the minimax regret solution can be only a local maximum of the Choquet integral w.r.t. some capacity from the uncertainty set. We have also discussed the algorithms for finding such capacity.

## References

1. Chateauneuf, A., Jaffray, J.: Some characterizations of lower probabilities and other monotone capacities through the use of möbius inversion. Mathematical Social Sciences 17(3), 263–283 (1989)
2. Combarro, E., Miranda, P.: On the polytope of non-additive measures. Fuzzy Sets and Systems 159(16), 2145–2162 (2008)

3. Combarro, E., Miranda, P.: On the structure of the k-additive fuzzy measures. Fuzzy Sets and Systems 161(17), 2314–2327 (2010)
4. Costa, C., Vansnick, J.: MACBETH–An Interactive Path Towards the Construction of Cardinal Value Functions. International Transactions in Operational Research 1(4), 489–500 (1994)
5. Denneberg, D.: Totally monotone core and products of monotone measures. International Journal of Approximate Reasoning 24(2-3), 273–281 (2000)
6. Gilboa, I., Schmeidler, D.: Maxmin expected utility with non-unique prior. Journal of Mathematical Economics 18(2), 141–153 (1989)
7. Grabisch, M.: Alternative representations of discrete fuzzy measures for decision making. International Journal of Uncertainty Fuzziness and Knowledge-Based Systems 5(5), 587–607 (1997); 4th International Conference on Soft Computing (IIZUKA 1996), Iizuka, Japan (September 1996)
8. Grabisch, M.: k-order additive discrete fuzzy measures and their representation. Fuzzy Sets and Systems 92(2), 167–189 (1997)
9. Grabisch, M., Kojadinovic, I., Meyer, P.: A review of methods for capacity identification in Choquet integral based multi-attribute utility theory:Applications of the Kappalab R package. European Journal of Operational Research 186(2), 766–785 (2008)
10. Grabisch, M., Miranda, P.: On the vertices of the k-additive core. Discrete Mathematics 308(22), 5204–5217 (2008)
11. Hettich, R., Kortanek, K.O.: Semi-infinite programming: theory, methods, and applications. SIAM Review, 380–429 (1993)
12. Labreuche, C., Grabisch, M.: The Choquet integral for the aggregation of interval scales in multicriteria decision making. Fuzzy Sets and Systems 137(1), 11–26 (2003)
13. Labreuche, C., Miranda, P., Lehuede, F.: Computation of the robust preference relation combining a Choquet integral and utility functions. In: 5th Multidisciplinary Workshop on Advances in Preference Handling, Lisbon, Portugal (August 2010)
14. Lovász, L.: Submodular functions and convexity. In: Mathematical Programming: The State of the Art, pp. 235–257 (1983)
15. Marichal, J.L., Roubens, M.: Determination of weights of interacting criteria from a reference set. European Journal of Operational Research 124(3), 641–650 (2000)
16. Milnor, J.: Games against nature. Decision Processes, 49 (1954)
17. Murofushi, T., Soneda, S.: Techniques for reading fuzzy measures (iii): interaction index. In: 9th Fuzzy System Symposium, pp. 693–696 (1993)
18. Raiffa, H., Schlaifer, R.: Applied statistical decision theory. MIT Press (1968)
19. Savage, L.J.: The theory of statistical decision. Journal of the American Statistical Association 46(253), 55–67 (1951)
20. Shapley, L.: A value for n-person games. Contributions to the Theory of Games 2, 307–317 (1953)
21. Stoye, J.: Axioms for minimax regret choice correspondences. Journal of Economic Theory 146(6), 2226–2251 (2011)
22. Timonin, M.: Maximization of the Choquet integral over a convex set and its application to resource allocation problems. Annals of Operations Research (2012), http://dx.doi.org/10.1007/s10479-012-1147-9
23. Timonin, M.: Robust maximization of the Choquet integral. Fuzzy Sets and Systems (2012), http://dx.doi.org/10.1016/j.fss.2012.04.014

# A Characterization of Fuzzy Integrals Invariant with Respect to Permutation Groups*

Antonín Dvořák and Michal Holčapek

Centre of Excellence IT4Innovations
Division of UO, Institute for Research and Applications of Fuzzy Modeling
30. dubna 22, 70103 Ostrava, Czech Republic
antonin.dvorak@osu.cz, michal.holcapek@osu.cz
http://irafm.osu.cz

**Abstract.** This contribution studies isomorphisms of fuzzy measure spaces and related notions, namely cardinal fuzzy measure spaces and fuzzy measure spaces closed under isomorphisms with respect to permutation groups. By these special fuzzy measure spaces, a characterization of ⊙-fuzzy integrals that are for a given function invariant with respect to permutations from a group of permutations is provided.

## 1 Introduction and Motivation

In [6], we introduced fuzzy measurable spaces, fuzzy measure spaces and appropriate ⊙-fuzzy integrals (fuzzy integrals for short). All foregoing concepts were designed to introduce fuzzy quantifiers of type $\langle 1, 1 \rangle$ determined by fuzzy measures [3]. For example, the natural language quantifiers *many*, *at least half* and *few* may be modeled by the proposed type of fuzzy integral. Note that the first argument of $\langle 1, 1 \rangle$ fuzzy quantifier is called *restriction* and the second one is called *scope* (i.e., in "Nearly every young man has hair", "to be a young man" is the restriction and "to have hair" is the scope). It is natural to think of the restriction as a *new universe* for the fuzzy quantifier (in our example, for the determination of the truth value of this sentence, only those objects fulfilling the restriction condition are important, i.e., young men). Because we are working with fuzzy subsets of some universe $M$, the restriction is represented by a *fuzzy* set, and we should in effect be able to define quantifiers on *fuzzy universes*. Therefore, in [6] we defined a new type of fuzzy measure spaces defined on algebras of subsets of a *fuzzy* set $A$ (on some crisp universal set $M$).

When we investigated semantic properties of $\langle 1, 1 \rangle$ fuzzy quantifiers, we ran into problems to provide a satisfactory answer related to permutation and isomorphism invariances. This motivated us to study fuzzy measure spaces (fuzzy integrals) that are closed (invariant) with respect to permutation groups. Hence, this paper presents some of the results on isomorphisms of fuzzy measure spaces and a characterization of fuzzy integrals that are, for a given function, invariant with respect to permutations from a permutation group.

---

* This work was supported by the European Regional Development Fund in the IT4Innovations Centre of Excellence project (CZ.1.05/1.1.00/02.0070).

S. Greco et al. (Eds.): IPMU 2012, Part IV, CCIS 300, pp. 208–217, 2012.

## 2 Preliminaries

### 2.1 Structures of Truth Values

In this paper, we suppose that the structure of truth values is a *complete residuated lattice* [1,8,9], i.e., an algebra $\mathbf{L} = \langle L, \wedge, \vee, \rightarrow, \otimes, \bot, \top \rangle$ with four binary operations and two constants such that $\langle L, \wedge, \vee, \bot, \top \rangle$ is a complete lattice, where $\bot$ is the least element and $\top$ is the greatest element of $L$, respectively, $\langle L, \otimes, \top \rangle$ is a commutative monoid (i.e., $\otimes$ is associative, commutative and the identity $a \otimes \top = a$ holds for any $a \in L$) and the adjointness property is satisfied, i.e., $a \leq b \rightarrow c$ iff $a \otimes b \leq c$ holds for each $a, b, c \in L$, where $\leq$ denotes the corresponding lattice ordering. A residuated lattice is *divisible*, if $a \otimes (a \rightarrow b) = a \wedge b$ holds for arbitrary $a, b \in L$, and satisfies the *law of double negation*, if $(a \rightarrow \bot) \rightarrow \bot = a$ holds for any $a \in L$. A divisible residuated lattice satisfying the law of double negation is called an *MV-algebra*.

### 2.2 Fuzzy Sets

Let $\mathbf{L}$ be a complete residuated lattice and $M$ be a universe of discourse (possibly empty). A mapping $A : M \rightarrow L$ is called a *fuzzy set on* $M$. A value $A(m)$ is called a *membership degree of* $m$ *in the fuzzy set* $A$. The set of all fuzzy sets on $M$ is denoted by $\mathcal{F}(M)$. A fuzzy set $A$ on $M$ is called *crisp*, if there is a subset $Z$ of $M$ such that $A = 1_Z$, where $1_Z$ denotes the characteristic function of $Z$. Particularly, $1_\emptyset$ denotes the empty fuzzy set on $M$, i.e., $1_\emptyset(m) = \bot$ for any $m \in M$. This convention will be also kept for $M = \emptyset$. The set of all crisp fuzzy sets on $M$ is denoted by $\mathcal{P}(M)$. A fuzzy set $A$ is *constant*, if there is $c \in L$ such that $A(m) = c$ for any $m \in M$. For simplicity, a constant fuzzy set is denoted by the corresponding element of $L$, e.g., $a, b, c$. A fuzzy set $A$ is a *fuzzy subset* of a fuzzy set $B$ (denoted by $A \subseteq B$) if $A(x) \leq B(x)$ for all $x \in M$.

To refer to the universe of discourse $M$ of $A$, we will sometimes write $\text{Dom}(A)$ instead of $M$. Let us denote $\text{Supp}(A) = \{m \mid m \in M \ \& \ A(m) > \bot\}$ the *support* of a fuzzy set $A$. The set of all fuzzy subsets of $A$ on $M$ is denoted by $\mathcal{F}(A)$. Thus

$$\mathcal{F}(A) = \{B \mid B \in \mathcal{F}(M) \text{ and } B \subseteq A\}. \tag{1}$$

Let $A \in \mathcal{F}(M)$ and $Z$ be a set (not necessary a subset of $M$). Then $A \upharpoonright Z$ denotes the common restriction of $A : M \rightarrow L$ to the set $Z$. Let $\{A_i \mid i \in I\}$ be a non-empty family of fuzzy sets on $M$. Then the *union* and the *intersection of* $A_i$ are defined by

$$\left( \bigcup_{i \in I} A_i \right)(m) = \bigvee_{i \in I} A_i(m) \quad \text{and} \quad \left( \bigcap_{i \in I} A_i \right)(m) = \bigwedge_{i \in I} A_i(m) \tag{2}$$

for any $m \in M$, respectively. Let $A, B$ be fuzzy sets on $M$. The *difference of* $A$ and $B$ is a fuzzy set $A \setminus B$ on $M$ defined by

$$(A \setminus B)(m) = A(m) \otimes (B(m) \rightarrow \bot) \tag{3}$$

for any $m \in M$ and the *complement* of $A$ is a fuzzy set $\overline{A} = 1_M \setminus A$. Let $f : M \to M'$ be a mapping. A mapping $f^\to : \mathcal{F}(M) \to \mathcal{F}(M')$ defined by $f^\to(A)(m) = \bigvee_{m' \in f^{-1}(m)} A(m')$ is called the *fuzzy extension* of the mapping $f$. Obviously, if $f$ is a one-to-one mapping from $M$ onto $M'$, then $f^\to(A)(f(m)) = A(m)$ for any $m \in M$.

# 3   Fuzzy Measure Spaces, Integrals and Isomorphisms

In this section, we will first recall the basic notions of the theory of fuzzy measure spaces that have been proposed and investigated in [6]. Then we will concentrate on the notion of isomorphism between fuzzy measure spaces and related notions. Finally, we will present a characterization of fuzzy integrals that are for a given function invariant with respect to permutations from a group of permutations. This characterization is substantial in the proofs of the permutation and isomorphism invariances of fuzzy quantifiers (see [4]).

## 3.1   Isomorphisms of Fuzzy Measure Spaces

**Definition 1.** *[6] Let $A$ be a non-empty fuzzy set on $M$. A subset $\mathcal{F}$ of $\mathcal{F}(A)$ is an* algebra of fuzzy sets on $A$*, if the following conditions are satisfied*

*(i)* $1_\emptyset, A \in \mathcal{F}$,
*(ii) if $X \in \mathcal{F}$, then $A \setminus X \in \mathcal{F}$,*
*(iii) if $X, Y \in \mathcal{F}$, then $X \cup Y \in \mathcal{F}$.*

*A pair $(A, \mathcal{F})$ is called a* fuzzy measurable space *(on $A$), if $\mathcal{F}$ is an algebra of fuzzy sets on $A$.*

*Example 1.* Let us say that a fuzzy set $A$ on $M$ is a *simple fuzzy set* on $M$ if its range is a finite set. Obviously, the set of all simple fuzzy sets on $M$ is an algebra of fuzzy sets on $1_M$.

A fuzzy measure is defined as a normalized one.

**Definition 2.** *A mapping $\mu : \mathcal{F} \to L$ is called a* fuzzy measure *on $(A, \mathcal{F})$, if*

*(i) $\mu(1_\emptyset) = \bot$ and $\mu(A) = \top$,*
*(ii) if $B, C \in \mathcal{F}$ such that $B \subseteq C$, then $\mu(B) \leq \mu(C)$.*

*A triplet $(A, \mathcal{F}, \mu)$ is called a* fuzzy measure space*, if $(A, \mathcal{F})$ is a fuzzy measurable space and $\mu$ is a fuzzy measure on $(A, \mathcal{F})$.*

We use $\mathbf{Fms}(M)$ to denote the set of all fuzzy measure spaces on a universe $M$, i.e., $(A, \mathcal{F}, \mu) \in \mathbf{Fms}(M)$ if $A \in \mathcal{F}(M)$ and $A \neq 1_\emptyset$.

In our investigation of semantic properties of fuzzy quantifiers defined by fuzzy measures and integrals, we need to construct isomorphisms between fuzzy measurable spaces and fuzzy measure spaces.

**Definition 3.** *Let $(A, \mathcal{F})$ and $(B, \mathcal{G})$ be fuzzy measurable spaces. We say that a mapping $g : \mathcal{F} \to \mathcal{G}$ is an* isomorphism *between $(A, \mathcal{F})$ and $(B, \mathcal{G})$, if*

*(i) $g$ is a bijective mapping with $g(1_\emptyset) = 1_\emptyset$,*
*(ii) $g(X \cup Y) = g(X) \cup g(Y)$ and $g(A \setminus X) = B \setminus g(X)$ hold for any $X, Y \in \mathcal{F}$,*
*(iii) there exists a bijective mapping $f : \mathrm{Dom}(A) \to \mathrm{Dom}(B)$ with $X(m) = g(X)(f(m))$ for any $X \in \mathcal{F}$ and $m \in \mathrm{Dom}(A)$.*

The following theorem shows that each isomorphism of fuzzy measurable spaces is derived from a bijective mapping by the Zadeh's extension principle and its restriction to the algebra of fuzzy sets.

**Theorem 1 ([6]).** *Let $(A, \mathcal{F})$, $(B, \mathcal{G})$ be fuzzy measurable spaces and $g : \mathcal{F} \to \mathcal{G}$ be a surjective mapping. Then $g$ is an isomorphism between $(A, \mathcal{F})$ and $(B, \mathcal{G})$ if and only if there exists a bijective mapping $f : \mathrm{Dom}(A) \to \mathrm{Dom}(B)$ such that $g = f^\to \restriction \mathcal{F}$.*

**Definition 4.** *Let $(A, \mathcal{F}, \mu)$ and $(B, \mathcal{G}, \mu')$ be fuzzy measure spaces. We say that a mapping $g : \mathcal{F} \to \mathcal{G}$ is an* isomorphism *between $(A, \mathcal{F}, \mu)$ and $(B, \mathcal{G}, \mu')$, if*

*(i) $g$ is an isomorphism between $(A, \mathcal{F})$ and $(B, \mathcal{G})$,*
*(ii) $\mu(X) = \mu'(g(X))$ for any $X \in \mathcal{F}$.*

If $g$ is an isomorphism between fuzzy measure spaces $\mathbf{A} = (A, \mathcal{F}, \mu)$ and $\mathbf{B} = (B, \mathcal{G}, \mu')$, then we will write $g(A, \mathcal{F}, \mu) = (B, \mathcal{G}, \mu')$ or shortly $g(\mathbf{A}) = \mathbf{B}$. If an isomorphism $g$ between $\mathbf{A}$ and $\mathbf{B}$ is determined by a bijective mapping $f : \mathrm{Dom}(A) \to \mathrm{Dom}(B)$ (see Theorem 1), then we will write $f^\to(\mathbf{A}) = \mathbf{B}$.[1]

**Definition 5.** *Let $\mathbf{A} = (A, \mathcal{F}, \mu)$ be a fuzzy measure space and $f$ be a bijection from $M = \mathrm{Dom}(A)$ to a set $M'$. Then a* fuzzy measure space generated by $\mathbf{A}$ and $f$ *is the measure space $\mathbf{A}_f = (f^\to(A), \mathcal{F}_f, \mu_f)$, where $\mathrm{Dom}(f^\to(A)) = M'$, $\mathcal{F}_f = \{f^\to(X) \mid X \in \mathcal{F}\}$ and $\mu_f(X) = \mu((f^{-1})^\to(X))$ for all $X \in \mathcal{F}_f$.*

It is easy to see that $\mathbf{A}_f$ is a fuzzy measure space and it holds that $f^\to(\mathbf{A}) = \mathbf{A}_f$. We will often refer to $\mathbf{A}_f$ by $f^\to(\mathbf{A})$.

## 3.2   Fuzzy Measure Spaces Closed under Isomorphisms

We say that a system $\mathcal{A}$ of fuzzy measure spaces from $\mathbf{Fms}(M)$ is *closed under isomorphisms* in $\mathbf{Fms}(M)$ if the following holds: if $\mathbf{A} \in \mathcal{A}$ and $\mathbf{B} \in \mathbf{Fms}(M)$ are isomorphic, then $\mathbf{B} \in \mathcal{A}$. This notion is very important in proving the permutation invariance of fuzzy quantifiers determined by fuzzy measure spaces. In the following text, we will, for the sake of simplicity, omit the term "under isomorphisms" in "closed under isomorphisms" and say only "closed system of fuzzy measure spaces in $\mathbf{Fms}(M)$". Note that there are closed systems of fuzzy

---

[1] Note that $f^\to(\mathbf{A}) = \mathbf{B}$ is an imprecise expression, since the domain of $g$ is $\mathcal{F}$, but $f^\to : \mathcal{F}(M) \to \mathcal{G}(M)$. Nevertheless, the precise expression $(f^\to \restriction \mathcal{F})(\mathbf{A}) = \mathbf{B}$ can lead, in our opinion, to unnecessarily complicated formulations.

measure spaces containing non-isomorphic fuzzy measure spaces. If a system $\mathcal{A}$ of mutually isomorphic fuzzy measure spaces in $\mathbf{Fms}(M)$ is closed, then we say that $\mathcal{A}$ is a *closed system of mutually isomorphic fuzzy measure spaces in* $\mathbf{Fms}(M)$. Obviously, each closed system is a union of closed systems of mutually isomorphic fuzzy measure spaces.

**Lemma 1 ([6]).** *A system $\mathcal{A}$ of fuzzy measure spaces in* $\mathbf{Fms}(M)$ *is closed if and only if $f^{\rightarrow}(\mathbf{A}) \in \mathcal{A}$ for any $\mathbf{A} \in \mathcal{A}$ and any permutation $f$ on* $\mathrm{Dom}(A)$.

In [6], we defined the concept of a cardinal fuzzy measure space. The denotation "cardinal" means that these measures are invariant under the same cardinality of fuzzy sets. Let $A$ be a non-empty fuzzy set. Then we can say that two fuzzy sets $X, Y \in \mathcal{F}(A)$ have the same cardinality if there exists a permutation $f$ on $\mathrm{Dom}(A)$ such that $f^{\rightarrow}(X) = Y$. In the following, the set of all permutations on a set $M$ will be denoted by $\mathrm{Perm}(M)$. Cardinal fuzzy measure spaces are used to define so-called *cardinal fuzzy quantifiers* which are determined by them (see [4]). A cardinal fuzzy measure space is defined as follows.

**Definition 6.** *We say that $(A, \mathcal{F}, \mu)$ is a cardinal fuzzy measure space if*

*(i) if $X \in \mathcal{F}$, then $f^{\rightarrow}(X) \in \mathcal{F}$,*
*(ii) $\mu(X) = \mu(f^{\rightarrow}(X))$*

*hold for any $X \in \mathcal{F}$ and for any permutation $f$ on* $\mathrm{Dom}(A)$.

**Lemma 2 ([6]).** *If $\mathbf{A}$ is a cardinal fuzzy measure space, then $A$ is a constant fuzzy set.*

The following two examples present cardinal as well as non-cardinal fuzzy measure spaces. Notice that an isomorphism of fuzzy measurable spaces do not guarantee an isomorphism of fuzzy measure spaces. The invariance of a fuzzy measure under the isomorphism has to be verified, too (see Definition 4). All examples are constructed over a complete residuated lattice with the support $[0, 1]$.

*Example 2.* Let $N$ be the set of natural numbers. Let $F : (\mathcal{F}(N) \times N) \times N \to \mathcal{F}(N)$ be given by

$$F(A, n)(m) = \begin{cases} A(m), & \text{if } m \leq n; \\ 0, & \text{otherwise.} \end{cases} \tag{4}$$

Let $A$ be a non-empty fuzzy set on $N$ and $\mathcal{F}_A \subseteq \mathcal{F}(A)$ be an algebra of fuzzy sets on $A$. Put $n_A = \min(\mathrm{Supp}(A))$ and define a fuzzy measure $\mu_{A,n} : \mathcal{F}_A \to [0, 1]$ with respect to $n$ for any $n \geq n_A$ by

$$\mu_{A,n}(X) = \frac{\sum_{m \in \mathrm{Supp}(X)} F(X, n)(m)}{\sum_{m \in \mathrm{Supp}(A)} F(A, n)(m)}. \tag{5}$$

For $n < n_A$, define $\mu_{A,n}(X) = 0$ for any $X \neq A$ and $\mu_{A,n}(A) = 1$. It is easy to see that $(A, \mathcal{F}_A, \mu_{A,n})$ is a fuzzy measure space for any $n \in N$.

Let us consider $A = 1_N$, $\mathcal{F}_{1_N} = \mathcal{F}(1_N)$ and $f \neq 1_N$ be a permutation on $N$. Then there exist $n \in N$ and $X \in \mathcal{F}_{1_N}$ such that $\mu_n(X) \neq \mu_n(f^{\rightarrow}(X))$. In fact, put $K = \{m \mid m \in N \ \& \ f(m) \neq m\}$ and denote $n_K = \min(K)$. Since $f(m) = m$ for any $m < n_K$, we have $n_K < f(n_K)$. Consider

$$X = \{1/0, \dots, 1/n_K\}.$$

Clearly, $f^{\rightarrow}(X) = \{1/0, \dots, 1/n_K - 1, 1/f(n_K)\}$ and we obtain

$$\mu_{1_N, n_K}(X) = 1 > 1 - \frac{1}{n_K} = \mu_{1_N, n_K}(f^{\rightarrow}(X)).$$

Hence, $(1_N, \mathcal{F}_{1_N}, \mu_{1_N, n})$ is not cardinal for any $n \in N$. Let us define

$$\underline{\mu_A}(X) = \liminf_{n \to \infty} \mu_{A,n}(X),$$
$$\overline{\mu_A}(X) = \limsup_{n \to \infty} \mu_{A,n}(X). \tag{6}$$

Obviously, if $A$ is a non-empty fuzzy set with a finite support, then $\mu_{A,n}(X) = \mu_{A,m}(X)$ for any $m \geq n$, where $n = \max(\mathrm{Supp}(A))$. Hence, $\underline{\mu_A}$ and $\overline{\mu_A}$ are defined for any non-empty fuzzy set $A$. Note that $\underline{\mu_A}$ and $\overline{\mu_A}$ (for $A = 1_N$ and $\mathcal{F}_{1_N} = \mathcal{F}(1_N)$) are examples of lower and upper weighted asymptotic densities, respectively, well known in the number theory (see [7] and the references therein). Again, neither $(1_N, \mathcal{F}_{1_N}, \underline{\mu_{1_N}})$ nor $(1_N, \mathcal{F}_{1_N}, \overline{\mu_{1_N}})$ are cardinal fuzzy measure spaces. In fact, it is well known that the set of even numbers has the measure ($\underline{\mu_{1_N}}$ or $\overline{\mu_{1_N}}$) equal to $\frac{1}{2}$ and the set of prime numbers equal to 0. Now, it is sufficient to consider a permutation on $M$ such that the set of even numbers is transformed to the set of prime numbers.

*Example 3.* Here, we will propose an extension of the fuzzy measures $\mu_{A,n}$, $\underline{\mu_A}$ and $\overline{\mu_A}$ provided for fuzzy sets on $N$ to fuzzy sets on an arbitrary countable universe $M$. Let $M$ be an arbitrary countable set (finite or denumerable) and $h : \mathcal{F}(M) \to \mathcal{F}(N)$ be a mapping such that $h(A) \subseteq h(B)$, whenever $A \subseteq B$, $h(1_\emptyset) = 1_\emptyset$. Then, for any non-empty fuzzy set $A \in \mathcal{F}(M)$ such that $h(A) \neq 1_\emptyset$ and any algebra $\mathcal{F}_A \subseteq \mathcal{F}(A)$, we can define an $h$-fuzzy measure $\mu^h_{A,n} : \mathcal{F}_A \to [0,1]$ with respect to $n \in N$ by

$$\mu^h_{A,n}(X) = \mu_{h(A),n}(h(X)), \tag{7}$$

where $\mu_{h(A),n}$ is the fuzzy measure defined in the previous example. The extension of the $h$-fuzzy measure for $n$ going to the infinity may be done by

$$\underline{\mu^h_A}(X) = \liminf_{n \to \infty} \mu^h_{A,n}(X) = \underline{\mu_{h(A)}}(h(X)), \tag{8}$$

$$\overline{\mu^h_A}(X) = \limsup_{n \to \infty} \mu^h_{A,n}(X) = \overline{\mu_{h(A)}}(h(X)). \tag{9}$$

If $M = N$, then putting $h = 1_N$ we obtain the definitions of $\mu_{A,n}$, $\underline{\mu_A}$ and $\overline{\mu_A}$ from the previous example. One way how to define $h$ is to consider an injective mapping $f : M \to N$ and to put $h = f^{\to}$. Another way is, for example, to define $h$ by

$$h^{\star}(X)(n) = \bigvee_{\substack{Y \subseteq M \\ |Y| = n}} \bigwedge_{m \in Y} X(m), \tag{10}$$

for any $n \in N$. Note that $h^{\star}(A)$ is a generalized cardinal number in the sense of Wygralak's cardinal theory for vaguely defined objects (see [10,11]). One can simply check that $(A, \mathcal{F}_A, \mu_A^{h^{\star}})$, for $\mu_A^{h^{\star}} \in \{\mu_{A,n}^{h^{\star}}, \underline{\mu_A^{h^{\star}}}, \overline{\mu_A^{h^{\star}}}\}$, is a fuzzy measure space for any non-empty fuzzy set $A \in \mathcal{F}(M)$ and

$$\mu_A^{h^{\star}}(X) = \mu_{f^{\to}(A)}^{h^{\star}}(f^{\to}(X)) \tag{11}$$

for any $X \in \mathcal{F}_A$ (this fact immediately follows from the equality $h^{\star}(A) = h^{\star}(f^{\to}(A))$). Moreover, for example, $(1_N, \mathcal{F}_{1_N}, \underline{\mu_{1_N}^{h^{\star}}})$ is a cardinal fuzzy measure space in contrast to $(1_N, \mathcal{F}_{1_N}, \underline{\mu_{1_N}})$ defined in the previous example.[2]

A relation between closed systems of fuzzy measure spaces and cardinal fuzzy measure spaces is stated in the following lemma.

**Lemma 3 ([6]).** *A set $\{\mathbf{A}\}$ forms a closed system of fuzzy measure spaces in* **Fms**$(M)$ *if and only if* $\mathbf{A}$ *is a cardinal fuzzy measure space.*

One may see that the set of all permutations on a set with the composition as the operation on it forms a maximal permutation group. Then a natural generalization of the concept of cardinal fuzzy measure space can be done by considering an arbitrary permutation group instead of the maximal one.

**Definition 7.** *Let* $\mathbf{A} = (A, \mathcal{F}, \mu)$ *be a fuzzy measure space and $G$ be a group of permutations on* Dom$(A)$*. We say that* $\mathbf{A}$ *is closed under isomorphisms with respect to $G$, if* $g^{\to}(\mathbf{A}) = \mathbf{A}$ *for any* $g \in G$.

The following example shows fuzzy measure spaces being closed under isomorphism with respect to a permutation group.

*Example 4.* Recall that $(1_N, \mathcal{F}(1_N), \overline{\mu_{1_N}})$ defined in Example 2 is not closed under isomorphisms with respect to the group of all permutations on $N$ (i.e., it is not a cardinal fuzzy measure space). Now, let $X$ be a crisp subset of $N$ such that $\overline{\mu_{1_N}}(1_X) = 0$ (e.g. $X$ is a finite subset of $N$ or an infinite subset as the set of prime numbers) and $G$ be a group of all permutations $g$ on $N$ with $g(n) = n$ for any $n \in N \setminus X$. It is easy to see that $G$ is a permutation group and, trivially, $g^{\to}(\mathcal{F}(1_N)) = \mathcal{F}(1_N)$ for any $g \in G$. To show that $(1_N, \mathcal{F}(1_N), \overline{\mu_{1_N}})$ is closed under isomorphisms with respect to $G$ we have to check that $\overline{\mu_{1_N}}(Y) = \overline{\mu_{1_N}}(g^{\to}(Y))$ holds for any $Y \in \mathcal{F}(1_N)$. But this immediately follows from the fact that $\overline{\mu_{1_N}}(X) = 0$ and $\overline{\mu_{1_N}}$ is null-additive, i.e., $\overline{\mu_{1_N}}(A \cup B) = \overline{\mu_{1_N}}(A)$

---

[2] For example, if $P$ and $E$ denote the sets of prime and even numbers, respectively, then $h^{\star}(1_P) = h^{\star}(1_E) = 1_N$ and $\underline{\mu_{1_N}^{h^{\star}}}(1_P) = \underline{\mu_{1_N}^{h^{\star}}}(1_N) = \underline{\mu_{1_N}^{h^{\star}}}(1_E) = 1$, but $\underline{\mu_{1_N}}(1_P) = 0 < \underline{\mu_{1_N}}(1_E) = 0.5 < \underline{\mu_{1_N}}(1_N) = 1$.

holds for any $A, B \in \mathcal{F}(1_N)$ with $\overline{\mu_{1_N}}(B) = 0$.[3] In fact, let $Y \in \mathcal{F}(1_N)$ and put $Y_1 = Y \upharpoonright (\mathrm{Supp}(Y) \cap \mathrm{Supp}(X))$ and $Y_2 = Y \upharpoonright (\mathrm{Supp}(Y) \setminus \mathrm{Supp}(X))$. Since $\overline{\mu_{1_N}}(X) = 0$ then, from the monotony of $\overline{\mu_{1_N}}$ and $Y_1 \subseteq X$, we also have $\overline{\mu_{1_N}}(Y_1) = 0$. Moreover, for any $g \in G$ we have $g^{\rightarrow}(Y) = g^{\rightarrow}(Y_1 \cup Y_2) = g^{\rightarrow}(Y_1) \cup Y_2$ and $g^{\rightarrow}(Y_1) \subseteq X$ which implies $\overline{\mu_{1_N}}(g^{\rightarrow}(Y_1)) = 0$. From the null-additivity of $\overline{\mu_{1_N}}$, we obtain $\overline{\mu_{1_N}}(Y) = \overline{\mu_{1_N}}(Y_1 \cup Y_2) = \overline{\mu_{1_N}}(Y_2)$ and similarly $\overline{\mu_{1_N}}(g^{\rightarrow}(Y)) = \overline{\mu_{1_N}}(g^{\rightarrow}(Y_1) \cup Y_2) = \overline{\mu_{1_N}}(Y_2)$. Hence, we have $\overline{\mu_{1_N}}(Y) = \overline{\mu_{1_N}}(g^{\rightarrow}(Y))$. Note that the same result cannot be obtained for an arbitrary fuzzy set $X$ with $\overline{\mu_{1_N}}(X) = 0$ and also for the lower asymptotic weighted density $\underline{\mu_{1_N}}$ which is not null-additive.

*Example 5.* One can verify that each fuzzy measure space $(A, \mathcal{F}(A), \mu_A^{h^*})$ for $h^*$ defined by (10) in Example 3 is closed under isomorphisms with respect to $G = \{f \mid f \in \mathrm{Perm}(M) \; \& \; f^{\rightarrow}(A) = A\}$, where $M = \mathrm{Dom}(A)$.

The following theorem is a generalization of Lemma 3.9 in [6] showing a construction of a cardinal fuzzy measure space from a closed system of fuzzy measure spaces in **Fms**$(M)$ (see Lemma 1) and provides a more general construction of fuzzy measure spaces closed under isomorphisms with respect to a permutation group. This construction is then used for a characterization of fuzzy integrals that are invariant with respect to permutations from a permutation group.

**Theorem 2.** *Let $(A, \mathcal{F}, \mu)$ be a fuzzy measure space and $G$ be a group of permutations on $\mathrm{Dom}(A)$. Then $(B, \mathcal{G}, \nu)$ defined as follows: $B = \bigcup_{g \in G} g^{\rightarrow}(A)$, $\mathcal{G}$ is the least algebra of fuzzy sets on $B$ containing the set*

$$\mathcal{T} = \bigcup_{g \in G} g^{\rightarrow}(\mathcal{F}) \tag{12}$$

*and*

$$\nu(X) = \bigvee_{g \in G} \bigvee_{Y \in \mathcal{F}_{g,X}} \mu_g(Y),$$

*where $\mathcal{F}_{g,X} = \{Y \mid Y \in g^{\rightarrow}(\mathcal{F}) \text{ and } Y \subseteq \dot{X}\}$, is a fuzzy measure space closed under isomorphisms with respect to $G$.*

*Example 6.* Let us consider $(1_N, \mathcal{F}(1_N), \overline{\mu_{1_N}})$ defined in Example 2 and discussed in Example 4. As it has been shown this fuzzy measure space need not be closed under isomorphisms with respect to some permutation group over $N$. Let $X \subseteq N$ and $G = \{g \mid g \in \mathrm{Perm}(N) \; \& \; g^{\rightarrow}(1_X) = 1_X\}$. According to the previous theorem, we can construct a fuzzy measure space $(B, \mathcal{G}, \nu)$ closed under isomorphisms with respect to $G$ as follows:

---

[3] From the definition of $\overline{\mu_{1_N}}$, we have $\overline{\mu_{1_N}}(A \cup B) \leq \limsup_{n \to \infty} (\mu_{1_N,n}(A) + \mu_{1_N,n}(B)) \leq \limsup_{n \to \infty} \mu_{1_N,n}(A) + \limsup_{n \to \infty} \mu_{1_N,n}(B) = \overline{\mu_{1_N}}(A) + \overline{\mu_{1_N}}(B) = \overline{\mu_{1_N}}(A)$, where $\sup_i(a_i + b_i) \leq \sup_i a_i + \sup_i b_i$ is applied. Since $\overline{\mu_{1_N}}(A) \leq \overline{\mu_{1_N}}(A \cup B)$ follows from the monotony of $\overline{\mu_{1_N}}$, we obtain the desired equality.

(i) put $B = \bigcup_{g \in G} g^{\to}(1_N) = 1_N$;
(ii) put $\mathcal{G}$ the least algebra of fuzzy sets that contains the set

$$\mathcal{T} = \bigcup_{g \in G} g^{\to}(\mathcal{F}(1_N)),$$

since $g^{\to}(\mathcal{F}(1_N)) = \mathcal{F}(1_N)$ for any $g \in G$, then $\mathcal{G} = \mathcal{F}(1_N)$;
(iii) define

$$\nu(A) = \bigvee_{g \in G} \bigvee_{Y \in \mathcal{F}_{g,A}} \overline{\mu_{g,1_N}}(Y) = \bigvee_{g \in G} \bigvee_{B \in \mathcal{F}_A} \overline{\mu_{1_N}}(g^{\to}(Y)).$$

One may simply check that if $X = N$, then $\nu(A) = 1$, whenever there exists an infinite crisp set $Y$ such that $1_Y \subseteq A$. For example, the fuzzy measure of the set $P$ of prime numbers is under $\nu$ equal to 1 (in contrast to 0 for $\overline{\mu_{1_N}}$). In fact, it is sufficient to consider a permutation $g$ on $N$ such that $g^{\to}(1_P) = 1_{N \setminus P}$ and, from the null-additivity of $\overline{\mu_{1_N}}$, we obtain $\overline{\mu_{1_N}}(1_{N \setminus P}) = 1$. On the other hand, fuzzy sets with finite supports have the measure under $\nu$ equal to 0.

### 3.3   Invariant Fuzzy Integrals with Respect to Permutation Groups

Let $\odot$ be either $\wedge$ or $\otimes$, i.e., $\odot \in \{\wedge, \otimes\}$. In [6], we proposed the following definition of fuzzy integral with respect to $\odot$ that reflects our needs related to the development of a theory of $\langle 1, 1 \rangle$ fuzzy quantifiers determined by fuzzy measures.

**Definition 8.** *[6] Let $(A, \mathcal{F}, \mu)$ be a fuzzy measure space, $M = \mathrm{Dom}(A)$, $Z : M \to L$ and $X$ be an $\mathcal{F}$-measurable fuzzy set. The $\odot$-fuzzy integral of $Z$ on $X$ is given by*

$$\int_X^{\odot} Z \, d\mu = \bigvee_{Y \in \mathcal{F}_X^-} \bigwedge_{m \in \mathrm{Supp}(Y)} (Z(m) \odot \mu(Y)), \tag{13}$$

*where $\mathcal{F}_X^- = \{B \mid B \in \mathcal{F} \setminus \{1_\emptyset\} \text{ and } B \subseteq X\}$. If $X = A$, then we write $\int^{\odot} Z \, d\mu$.*

It should be noted that the $\odot$-fuzzy integral is a Sugeno-like type of fuzzy integral and its basic properties can be found in [6] and some results related to convergence in [2]. An isomorphism theorem for $\odot$-fuzzy quantifiers is as follows.

**Theorem 3.** *[6] Let $g^{\to}$ be an isomorphism between $(A, \mathcal{F}, \mu)$ and $(B, \mathcal{G}, \nu)$, $Z : \mathrm{Dom}(A) \to L$ be a mapping and $X$ be a $\mathcal{F}$-measurable fuzzy set. Then*

$$\int_X^{\odot} Z \, d\mu = \int_{g^{\to}(X)}^{\odot} Z \circ g^{-1} \, d\nu. \tag{14}$$

The following theorem characterizes fuzzy integrals that are invariant with respect to permutations from a group of permutations for a given function, i.e., the values of fuzzy integrals remain unchanged, when the integrated functions are transformed by the permutations from a group of permutations. It should be noted that the proof of this theorem needs a presumption on the distributivity of $\odot$ over arbitrary meets and joins in the complete residuated lattice. For instance, this presumption for $\odot = \wedge$ is ensured in the divisible complete residuated lattices and for $\odot = \otimes$ in the complete MV-algebras.

**Theorem 4.** *Let* **L** *be a complete residuated lattice such that* $\odot$ *is distributive over* $\bigwedge$ *and* $\bigvee$, $(A, \mathcal{F}, \mu)$ *be a fuzzy measure space and* $Z : \mathrm{Dom}(A) \to L$. *If* $G$ *is a group of permutations on* $\mathrm{Dom}(A)$ *such that* $\int^{\odot} Z \, d\mu = \int^{\odot} Z \circ g \, d\mu$ *for any* $g \in G$, *then there exists a fuzzy measure space* $(B, \mathcal{G}, \nu)$ *closed under isomorphisms with respect to* $G$ *for which* $\int^{\odot} Z \, d\mu = \int^{\odot} Z \, d\nu$.

As it has been pointed above, the cardinal fuzzy measure spaces form a subfamily of the family of all fuzzy measure spaces closed under isomorphisms with respect to permutation groups. Hence, Theorem 4.22 in [6] becomes a simple consequence of the previous theorem.

**Corollary 1.** *Let* **L** *be a complete residuated lattice such that* $\odot$ *is distributive over* $\bigwedge$ *and* $\bigvee$, $(A, \mathcal{F}, \mu)$ *be a fuzzy measure space and* $Z : \mathrm{Dom}(A) \to L$. *If* $\int^{\odot} Z \, d\mu = \int^{\odot} Z \circ g \, d\mu$ *holds for any permutation* $g$ *on* $\mathrm{Dom}(A)$, *then there exists a cardinal fuzzy measure space* $(B, \mathcal{G}, \nu)$ *for which* $\int^{\odot} Z \, d\mu = \int^{\odot} Z \, d\nu$.

# References

1. Bělohlávek, R.: Fuzzy Relational Systems: Foundations and Principles. Kluwer Academic Publisher, New York (2002)
2. Dvořák, A., Holčapek, M.: On convergence of fuzzy integrals over complete residuated lattices. In: Proceedings of EUSFLAT-LFA, Aix-les-Bains, France, July 18-22, pp. 98–105 (2011)
3. Dvořák, A., Holčapek, M.: Type ⟨1,1⟩ fuzzy quantifiers determined by fuzzy measures, Part I: Basic definitions and examples. Submitted to Fuzzy Sets and Systems
4. Dvořák, A., Holčapek, M.: Type ⟨1,1⟩ fuzzy quantifiers determined by fuzzy measures, Part II: Permutation and isomorphism invariances. Submitted to Fuzzy Sets and Systems
5. Dvořák, A., Holčapek, M.: Type ⟨1, 1⟩ fuzzy quantifiers determined by fuzzy measures. In: Proceedengs of WCCI 2010 IEEE World Congress on Computational Intelligence, CCIB, Barcelona, Spain, July 18-23, pp. 3168–3175 (2010)
6. Dvořák, A., Holčapek, M.: Fuzzy measures and integrals defined on algebras of fuzzy subsets over complete residuated lattices. Information Sciences 185(1), 205–229 (2012)
7. Mišík, L., Tóth, J.: On asymptotic behaviour of universal fuzzy measure. Kybernetika 42(3), 379–388 (2006)
8. Novák, V., Perfilieva, I., Močkoř, J.: Mathematical principles of fuzzy logic. Kluwer Academic Publisher, Boston (1999)
9. Ward, M., Dilworth, R.: Residuated lattices. Transactions of the American Mathematical Society 45, 335–354 (1939)
10. Wygralak, M.: Generalized cardinal numbers and operations on them. Fuzzy Sets and Systems 53(1), 49–85 (1993)
11. Wygralak, M.: Vaguely defined objects. Representations, fuzzy sets and nonclassical cardinality theory. Theory and Decision Library. Series B: Mathematical and Statistical Methods, vol. 33. Kluwer Academic Publisher, Dordrecht (1996)

# Vector-Valued Choquet Integrals
# for Set Functions and Bi-capacities

Eiichiro Takahagi

Senshu University, Kawasaki, 2148580, Japan
takahagi@isc.senshu-u.ac.jp
http://www.isc.senshu-u.a.jp/~thc0456/

**Abstract.** Logical vector-valued Choquet integral models are vector-valued functions calculated by $m$ times Choquet integral calculations with respect to the $m$-th set functions to the interval $[0, 1]$. By placing restrictions on the set functions, we can get some good properties, such as a normalized output. To introduce a symmetric difference expression, some set functions are transformed into monotone set functions, and they can be interpreted by using fuzzy measure tools such as Shapley values. Similarly, we introduce a vector-valued Choquet integral for bi-capacities and their symmetric difference expressions. Despite from the vector-valued Choquet integral for set functions, the output values match with original and symmetric difference expressions.

**Keywords:** vector-valued Choquet integral, bi-capacities, symmetric difference, classification.

## 1 Introduction

Vector-valued Choquet integrals are proposed to deal with classification models. Fuzzy measures and set functions are used as classification rules. Each element of the output vector calculated using vector-valued Choquet integrals indicates the degree of belonging to a class. By introducing restrictions on the set functions, we can obtain good properties such as a normalized output. If a classification model has a reference point, bi-capacities are useful tools. Therefore, vector-valued Choquet integrals for bi-capacities are proposed in this paper.

In [12] and [13], vector-valued Choquet integral models and symmetric difference representations of set functions were proposed. Using the symmetric difference representations, some non-monotone set functions can be transformed to monotone set functions and be interpreted by using monotone fuzzy measure tools such as Shapley values. In general, the output values of Choquet integrals do not match with the original set function and its symmetric representations. Therefore, the AV-type Choquet integral model is defined as the average value of all symmetric representations.

In this paper, vector-valued Choquet integral models for bi-capacities, a symmetric representation for bi-capacities, and their interpretations are proposed. In the case of bi-set functions, the output values of the Choquet integrals match with those of the original bi-set functions and its symmetric representations.

S. Greco et al. (Eds.): IPMU 2012, Part IV, CCIS 300, pp. 218–227, 2012.

# 2   Fuzzy Measure, Bi-capacities, and Choquet Integrals

## 2.1   Fuzzy Measure

$X = \{1, \ldots, n\}$ is the set of evaluation items ($n$: number of evaluation items), $x_i \in \mathbf{R}^+$ is the input value of the $i^{\text{th}}$ item, and $y$ is the comprehensive evaluation value.

**Definition 1.** *A non-monotone fuzzy measure $\mu$ is defined as*

$$\mu : 2^X \to \mathbf{R}, \quad \mu(\emptyset) = 0. \tag{1}$$

**Definition 2.** *A monotone fuzzy measure $\mu$ is defined as*

$$\mu : 2^X \to \mathbf{R}, \quad \mu(\emptyset) = 0, \quad \mu(A) \leq \mu(B) \quad if \quad A \subseteq B \subseteq X. \tag{2}$$

**Definition 3.** *The Choquet integral for $\mu$ [1],[2] is defined as*

$$y = f^C_\mu(x_1, \ldots, x_n) \equiv \sum_{i=1}^{n} [x_{\sigma(i)} - x_{\sigma(i+1)}] \mu(\{\sigma(1), \ldots, \sigma(i)\}), \tag{3}$$

*where $\sigma$ is a permutation such that $x_{\sigma(1)} \geq \ldots \geq x_{\sigma(n)}$ and $X = \{\sigma(1), \ldots, \sigma(n)\}$. Let $x_{\sigma(n+1)} = 0$.*

## 2.2   Set Function

The Choquet integral for a set function (logical Choquet integral) [5] was introduced to deal with fuzzy values (in the interval $[0,1]$) and fuzzy switching functions. The input and output values, the domain of fuzzy measures (set functions), and the integration range are in the interval $[0,1]$.

**Definition 4.** *The set function to $[0,1]$, $\mu^\sharp$, is defined as*

$$\mu^\sharp : 2^X \to [0,1]. \tag{4}$$

**Definition 5.** *A monotone set function to $[0,1]$, $\mu^\sharp$, is defined as*

$$\mu^\sharp : 2^X \to [0,1], \tag{5}$$

$$\mu^\sharp(A) \leq \mu^\sharp(B) \quad if \quad A \subseteq B \subseteq X. \tag{6}$$

The input values for the Choquet integral for a set function are $x_i^\sharp \in [0,1], \forall i$.

**Definition 6 (Logical Choquet integral [5]).** *The logical Choquet integral, that is, the Choquet integral for $\mu^\sharp$ [5], is defined as*

$$y^\sharp = f^{EC}_{\mu^\sharp}(x_1^\sharp, \ldots, x_n^\sharp) \equiv \sum_{i=0}^{n} [x_{\sigma(i)}^\sharp - x_{\sigma(i+1)}^\sharp] \mu^\sharp(\{\sigma(1), \ldots, \sigma(i)\}), \tag{7}$$

*where $\sigma$ is a permutation such that $x_{\sigma(1)} \geq \ldots \geq x_{\sigma(n)}$ and $X = \{\sigma(1), \ldots, \sigma(n)\}$. Let $x_{\sigma(0)} = 1$, $x_{\sigma(n+1)} = 0$ and $\{\sigma(1), \ldots, \sigma(i)\} = \emptyset$ when $i = 0$.*

The summation index $i$ starts at 0 in equation (7), because $\mu^\sharp(\emptyset) \neq 0$, therefore $\mu^\sharp(\emptyset)[1 - x^\sharp_{\sigma(1)}]$ is added to $y^\sharp$. In [12], monotone increaseness of $\mu^\sharp$ for an element $i(\in X)$ is defined as

$$\mu^\sharp(A \cup \{i\}) \geq \mu^\sharp(A), \forall A \not\ni i. \tag{8}$$

If $\mu^\sharp$ is a monotone increasing set function, $y^\sharp = f^{EC}_{\mu^\sharp}(x^\sharp_1, \ldots, x^\sharp)$ is an increasing function with $x^\sharp_i$ [12]. If the inequality sign of equation (8) is strict, $f^{EC}_{\mu^\sharp}(x^\sharp_1, \ldots, x^\sharp)$ is a strictly increasing function. If the inequality sign is reversed, $f^{EC}_{\mu^\sharp}(x^\sharp_1, \ldots, x^\sharp)$ is a decreasing function [12]. If $\mu^\sharp$ is monotone increasing for all $i \in X$, then $\mu^\sharp$ is a monotone set function [12].

## 2.3   Bi-capacity

Bi-capacities [6] are defined to deal with the situation when the evaluation methods are difference between among upper and under from the reference point and express the interactions among both areas.

**Definition 7.** *Let $Q(X) = \{(A, B) \in 2^X \times 2^X | A \cap B = \emptyset\}$. Bi-capacities are functions $\nu : Q(X) \to [-1, 1]$ such that*
*$\nu(A, B) \leq \nu(A', B)$ if $A \subset A'$ and $\nu(A, B) \geq \nu(A, B')$ if $B \subset B'$ (monotonicity),*
*$\nu(\emptyset, \emptyset) = 0$ (neutral element),*
*$\nu(X, \emptyset) = 1, \nu(\emptyset, X) = -1$ (normality).*

The input value of the bi-capacities is $x_i \in \mathbf{R}, i = 1, \ldots, n$.

**Definition 8 (The Choquet integral for bi-capacities [7]).**

$$f^{BC}_\nu(x_1, \ldots, x_n) \equiv \sum_{i=1}^n [(|x_{\sigma(i)}| - |x_{\sigma(i+1)}|)\nu(A_{\sigma(i)} \cap X^+, A_{\sigma(i)} \cap X^-)], \tag{9}$$

*where $\sigma$ is a permutation such that $|x_{\sigma(1)}| \geq \ldots \geq |x_{\sigma(n)}|$ and $x_{\sigma(n+1)} = 0$. Let $A_{\sigma(i)} = \{\sigma(1), \ldots, \sigma(i)\}$, $A_{\sigma(0)} = \emptyset$, $X^+ = \{i | x_i \geq 0\}$, and $X^- = \{i | x_i < 0\}$.*

## 3   Bi-set Functions

The neutral element, monotonicity, and normality of bi-capacities correspond to $\mu(\emptyset) = 0$, similar to the monotonicity and normality of fuzzy measures. In definition 4, fuzzy measures are extended to set functions to $[0, 1]$ and their integrals are defined in definition 6. In [8], the bi-set function is defined as a real-valued mapping on $Q(X)$ and "particular cases of interest are bi-cooperative games, where it is required that $\nu(\emptyset, \emptyset) = 0$, and bi-capacities which require in addition monotonicity." In this study, we consider the case $\nu(\emptyset, \emptyset) \neq 0$ and define the bi-set functions as follows.

**Definition 9 (Bi-set function to $[-1,1]$).** *The bi-set function to $[-1,1]$ is the real-valued mapping $\nu^b : Q(X) \to [-1,1]$.*

No assumptions are made for the monotonicity, neutral element, and normality of the bi-set functions to $[-1,1]$. The input values $x_i^b$ for the bi-set functions are in the interval $[-1,1]$, that is, $x_i^b \in [-1,1], i = 1, \ldots, n$.

**Definition 10 (Choquet integral for a bi-set function to $[0,1]$).**

$$f_{\nu^b}^{EBC}(x_1^b, \ldots, x_n^b) \equiv \sum_{i=0}^{n}[(|x_{\sigma(i)}^b| - |x_{\sigma(i+1)}^b|)\nu^b(A_{\sigma(i)} \cap X^+, A_{\sigma(i)} \cap X^-)], \quad (10)$$

*where $\sigma$ is a permutation on $X$ such that $|x_{\sigma(1)}^b| \geq \ldots \geq |x_{\sigma(n)}^b|$. Let $x_{\sigma(0)}^b = 1$, $x_{\sigma(n+1)}^b = 0$, $A_{\sigma(i)} = \{\sigma(1), \ldots, \sigma(i)\}$, $A_{\sigma(0)} = \emptyset$, $X^+ = \{i|x_i^b \geq 0\}$, and $X^- = \{i|x_i^b < 0\}$.*

This Choquet integral has close relations to k-ary bi-capacities [10].

By the extension, it is easy to do various evaluations. Table 1 presents an example of an evaluation for $n = 2$; the output values are high when the input values are close to the reference point. Figure 1 shows a graph of $f_{\nu^b}^{EBC}(x_1^b, x_2^b)$.

**Table 1.** Bi-set functions

| $(A,B)$ | $(\emptyset,\emptyset)$ | $(\{1\},\emptyset)$ | $(\emptyset,\{1\})$ | $(\{2\},\emptyset)$ | $(\{1,2\},\emptyset)$ | $(\{2\},\{1\})$ | $(\emptyset,\{2\})$ | $(\{1\},\{2\})$ | $(\emptyset,\{1,2\})$ |
|---|---|---|---|---|---|---|---|---|---|
| Value | 1 | 0 | 1 | 0 | 0 | 0.5 | 1 | 0.5 | 0 |

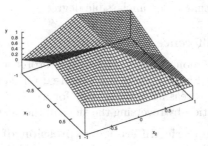

**Fig. 1.** Graph of $f_{\nu^b}^{EBC}(x_1^b, x_2^b)$

# 4 Logical Vector-Valued Choquet Integrals

## 4.1 Vector-Valued Choquet Integrals

A vector-valued Choquet integral model [11], [13] is an extension of the product of a matrix and a vector. Let the input vectors be $\mathbf{x}^\sharp = (x_1^\sharp, \ldots, x_n^\sharp)$, the output vectors be $\mathbf{y}^\sharp = (y_1^\sharp, \ldots, y_m^\sharp)$, and the set function vectors be $\mu^\sharp = (\mu_1^\sharp, \ldots, \mu_m^\sharp)$. A logical vector-valued Choquet integral for a set function [11],[12] is defined as follows.

**Definition 11 (Logical vector-valued Choquet integral).**

$$\mathbf{y}^\sharp = f_{\boldsymbol{\mu}^\sharp}^{EC}(\mathbf{x}^\sharp), \ where \ y_j^\sharp = f_{\mu_j^\sharp}^{EC}(x_1^\sharp, \ldots, x_n^\sharp). \tag{11}$$

As $\mu^\sharp(\emptyset) = 0$ is not assumed, it is possible that $\sum_{j=1}^m \mu_j^\sharp(\emptyset) > 0$.

**Theorem 1.** *For any* $c(\in [0, 1])$, *if*

$$\sum_{j=1}^m \mu_j^\sharp(A) = c, \forall A \in 2^X, \tag{12}$$

*then for any* $\mathbf{x}^\sharp \in [0,1]^n$, $\mathbf{y}^\sharp = f_{\boldsymbol{\mu}^\sharp}^{EC}(\mathbf{x}^\sharp)$ *for* $y_j^\sharp \in [0,1], j = 1, \ldots, m$, *and*

$$\sum_{j=1}^m y_j^\sharp = c . \tag{13}$$

*Proof.*

$$\sum_{j=1}^m y_j^\sharp = \sum_{j=1}^m f_{\mu_j^\sharp}^{EC}(x_1^\sharp, \ldots, x_n^\sharp) = \sum_{j=1}^m [\sum_{i=0}^n [(x_{\sigma(i)}^\sharp - x_{\sigma(i+1)}^\sharp)\mu_j^\sharp(\{\sigma(1), \ldots, \sigma(i)\})]]$$

$$= \sum_{i=0}^n [(x_{\sigma(i)}^\sharp - x_{\sigma(i+1)}^\sharp)\sum_{j=1}^m \mu_j^\sharp(\{\sigma(1), \ldots, \sigma(i)\})] = c\sum_{i=0}^n [x_{\sigma(i)}^\sharp - x_{\sigma(i+1)}^\sharp] = c. \quad \square$$

The output vector $\mathbf{y}^\sharp$, where $\sum_{j=1}^m y_j^\sharp = 1$, is called normalized output vector. The condition of theoren 1 is strong. But if $\sum_{j=1}^m \mu_j^\sharp(A) \leq c$, by placing $\mu_{m+1}^\sharp(A) = c - \sum_{j=1}^m \mu_j^\sharp(A)$, $\sum_{j=1}^{m+1} y_j^\sharp = c$. $y_{m+1}^\sharp$ shows the degree not belonging to any of the classes, that is the unclassible degree.

## 4.2    Symmetric Difference Expression

If a set function is not monotone, it is hard to interpret it. Because some fuzzy measure tools such as Shapley value are premised on monotonicity. If the set function is monotone increasing or decreasing for all $i \in X$, then we can obtain the monotone set function by reversing the signs of the decreasing elements [12].

**Definition 12 (Symmetric difference expression of a set function to** $[0, 1]$ **[12]).** *For* $T \subseteq X$, *the symmetric difference expression of a set function to* $[0, 1]$, $\mu^{T^\sharp}$, *is defined as*

$$\mu^{T^\sharp}(A) \equiv \mu^\sharp((A \setminus T) \cup (T \setminus A)), \forall A \in 2^X. \tag{14}$$

$\mu^\sharp$ is monotone increasing (resp. decreasiong) on $i$ if $\mu^\sharp(S \cup \{i\}) \geq \mu^\sharp(S)$ (resp. $\mu^\sharp(S \cup i) \leq \mu^\sharp(S)$) for all $S \subseteq X \setminus i$. If all elements of $X$ are monotone increasing or decreasing, using the symmetric difference expression, we can convert the set function to monotone.

**Theorem 2 ([12]).** *If a set function* $\mu^\sharp$ *is monotone increasing or decreasing for all* $i \in X$ *and if* $T$ *is the set of decreasing elements, then* $\mu^{T^\sharp}$ *is a monotone set function.*

### 4.3 Interpretation of Symmetric Difference Expression

By theorem 2, some non-monotone set functions may be converted to monotone symmetric difference expressions. If a set function is monotone, we may use fuzzy measure tools such as Shapley values. The Shapley values of a monotone set function $\mu^{T^\sharp}$ are

$$sh_i(\mu^{T^\sharp}) \equiv \sum_{S \subseteq X} \frac{(n-\mid S \mid)!(\mid S \mid -1)!}{n!}[\mu^{T^\sharp}(S) - \mu^{T^\sharp}(S \setminus \{i\})], \qquad (15)$$

$i = 1, \ldots, n$, where $\sum_i sh_i(\mu^{T^\sharp}) = \mu^{T^\sharp}(X) - \mu^{T^\sharp}(\emptyset)$.

### 4.4 AV-Type Logical Choquet Integral

The input value of the Choquet integral of the symmetric difference expression $x_i^{T^\sharp}$ is

$$x_i^{T^\sharp} = \begin{cases} x_i^\sharp & \text{if } i \notin T \\ 1 - x_i^\sharp & \text{otherwise.} \end{cases} \qquad (16)$$

However, it is not always true that $f_{\mu^\sharp}^{EC}(x_1^\sharp, \ldots, x_n^\sharp) = f_{\mu^{T^\sharp}}^{EC}(x_1^{T^\sharp}, \ldots, x_n^{T^\sharp})$. In $f^{EC}$, the output values change with the cases for selecting the $T$, that is the direction of input values. For this equality to always hold true, an AV-type logical Choquet integral is introduced.

**Definition 13 (AV-type logical Choquet integral [5]).**

$$y^\sharp = f_{\mu^\sharp}^{AV}(x_1^\sharp, \ldots, x_n^\sharp) \equiv \underset{T \subseteq X}{\text{Average}} \, f_{\mu^{T^\sharp}}^{EC}(x_1^{T^\sharp}, \ldots, x_n^{T^\sharp}). \qquad (17)$$

**Theorem 3.** *For any $\mu^\sharp$, $T \subseteq X$, and $\mathbf{x}^\sharp \in [0,1]^n$,*

$$f_{\mu^\sharp}^{AV}(x_1^\sharp, \ldots, x_n^\sharp) = f_{\mu^{T^\sharp}}^{AV}(x_1^{T^\sharp}, \ldots, x_n^{T^\sharp}). \qquad (18)$$

*Proof.* Trivial.  □

AV-type logical Choquet integral have corresponding properties with the theorem 1 and 2 [12].

## 5 Vector-Valued Choquet Integrals for Bi-set Functions

### 5.1 Vector-Valued Choquet Integrals for Bi-set Functions

In section 4, logical vector-valued Choquet integrals are discussed. Further, vector-valued Choquet integrals for bi-set functions are introduced.

**Definition 14 (Vector-valued Choquet integrals for bi-set functions).**

$$\mathbf{y}^b = f_{\nu^b}^{EBC}(\mathbf{x}^b), \quad where \ y_j^b = f_{\nu_j^b}^{EBC}(x_1^b,\ldots,x_n^b). \tag{19}$$

**Theorem 4.** *For any* $c(\in [-1,1])$, *if*

$$\sum_{j=1}^m \nu_j^b(A,B) = c, \ \forall(A,B) \in Q(X), \tag{20}$$

*then for any* $\mathbf{x}^b \in [-1,1]^n$,

$$\mathbf{y}^b = f_{\nu^b}^{EBC}(\mathbf{x}^b) \tag{21}$$

*for* $y_j^b \in [-1,1], j = 1,\ldots,m$, *and*

$$\sum_{j=1}^m y_j^b = c. \tag{22}$$

*Proof.* This theorem can be proved in a similar manner as theorem 1.     □

By considering $c = 0$, we can obtain the neutral output model, that is, the sum of the output values is 0.

## 5.2   Symmetric Difference Expression for Bi-set Functions

**Definition 15 (Symmetric difference expression for bi-set functions).**
*For a bi-set function to* $[-1,1]$, $\nu^b$, *and* $T \subseteq X$, *the symmetric difference expression* $\nu^{T^b}$ *is defined as*

$$\nu^{T^b}(A,B) \equiv \nu^b(((A \setminus T) \cup (B \cap T)), ((B \setminus T) \cup (A \cap T))), \forall(A,B) \in Q(X). \tag{23}$$

In this expression, the whole set of symmetric differences is $A \cup B$. The symmetric difference expression is exchanged the element of $T$ between $A$ and $B$. The symmetric difference expressions are also bi-set functions to $[-1,1]$.
   The input values of symmetric difference expressions $x_i^{T^b}$ are

$$x_i^{T^b} = \begin{cases} x_i^b & if \ i \notin T \\ -x_i^b & otherwise. \end{cases} \tag{24}$$

Unlike the logical Choquet integral, the output values match with the original bi-set functions and the symmetric expressions.

**Theorem 5.** *For any* $T \subseteq X$, *for any bi-set function* $\nu^b$ *and for all* $x_i^b \in [-1,1], i = 1,\ldots,n$, *let* $\nu^{T^b}$ *be the symmetric difference expression for* $\nu^b$,

$$f_{\nu^b}^{EBC}(x_1^b,\ldots,x_n^b) = f_{\nu^{T^b}}^{EBC}(x_1^{T^b},\ldots,x_n^{T^b}). \tag{25}$$

*Proof.* As $\sigma(i), i = 1, \ldots, n$, is common between $x_{\sigma(i)}^b$ and $x_{\sigma(i)}^{T^b}$, $|x_{\sigma(i)}^b| = |x_{\sigma(i)}^{T^b}|$ and $A_{\sigma(i)}$. Let $X^{T^+} = \{i \mid x_i^{T^b} \geq 0\}$ and $X^{T^-} = \{i \mid x_i^{T^b} < 0\}$. Therefore, $\nu^b(A_{\sigma(i)} \cap X^+, A_{\sigma(i)} \cap X^-) = \nu^{T^b}(A_{\sigma(i)} \cap X^{T^+}, A_{\sigma(i)} \cap X^{T^-}), i = 0, \ldots, n.$

$$f_{\nu^{T^b}}^{EBC}(x_1^{T^b}, \ldots, x_n^{T^b}) = \sum_{i=0}^{n}(|x_{\sigma(i)}^{T^b}| - |x_{\sigma(i+1)}^{T^b}|)\nu^{T^b}(A_{\sigma(i)} \cap X^{T^+}, A_{\sigma(i)} \cap X^{T^-})$$

$$= \sum_{i=0}^{n}(|x_{\sigma(i)}^b| - |x_{\sigma(i+1)}^b|)\nu^b(A_{\sigma(i)} \cap X^+, A_{\sigma(i)} \cap X^-) = f_{\nu^b}^{EBC}(x_1^b, \ldots, x_n^b). \qquad \square$$

### 5.3 Interpretation of Symmetric Difference Expression

Using the symmetric difference expression of bi-set functions, we can use bi-capacity tools such as Shapley importance index for bi-capacities [6] and bipolar Möbius transforms [9]

## 6 Numerical Examples

### 6.1 Set Functions

Table 2 presents an example of a logical vector-valued Choquet integral model for $n = 3$ and $m = 3$. $\mu_1^{T_1^{\sharp}}$, $\mu_2^{T_2^{\sharp}}$, and $\mu_3^{T_3^{\sharp}}$ are monotone and weakly super-additive fuzzy measures. $\mu_3^{\emptyset^{\sharp}}$ is a 2-additive fuzzy measure [3]. In this example, the direction of input values depends on $\mu_1^{\sharp}$, that is, $f_{\mu_1^{\sharp}}^{EC}(x_1^{\sharp}, x_2^{\sharp}, x_3^{\sharp})$ is an increasing function of $x_1^{\sharp}$, $x_2^{\sharp}$, and $x_3^{\sharp}$ and $T_1 = \emptyset$. Let $f_{\mu_2^{\sharp}}^{EC}(x_1^{\sharp}, x_2^{\sharp}, x_3^{\sharp})$ be an increasing function of $x_1^{\sharp}$ and $x_3^{\sharp}$ and a decreasing function of $x_2^{\sharp}$ and $T_2 = \{2\}$. Let $f_{\mu_3^{\sharp}}^{EC}(x_1^{\sharp}, x_2^{\sharp}, x_3^{\sharp})$ be an increasing function of $x_2^{\sharp}$ and a decreasing function of $x_1^{\sharp}$ and $x_3^{\sharp}$ and let $T_3 = \{1, 3\}$. However, the output values do not match with those of the original set functions and symmetric expressions. For example, $f_{\mu_2^{\sharp}}^{EC}(0.2, 0.1, 0.8) = 0.47$ and $f_{\mu_2^{T_2^{\sharp}}}^{EC}(0.2, 1 - 0.1, 0.8) = 0.5$.

$\mu_1^{\sharp}$, $\mu_2^{\sharp}$, and $\mu_3^{\sharp}$ are the original expressions of $\mu_1^{T_1^{\sharp}}$, $\mu_2^{T_2^{\sharp}}$, and $\mu_3^{T_3^{\sharp}}$. As $\mu_1^{\sharp}(A) + \mu_2^{\sharp}(A) + \mu_3^{\sharp}(A) = 1, \forall A$, $f_{\mu_1^{\sharp}}^{EC}(x_1^{\sharp}, x_2^{\sharp}, x_3^{\sharp}) + f_{\mu_2^{\sharp}}^{EC}(x_1^{\sharp}, x_2^{\sharp}, x_3^{\sharp}) + f_{\mu_3^{\sharp}}^{EC}(x_1^{\sharp}, x_2^{\sharp}, x_3^{\sharp}) = 1$ and $f_{\mu_1^{\sharp}}^{AV}(x_1^{\sharp}, x_2^{\sharp}, x_3^{\sharp}) + f_{\mu_2^{\sharp}}^{AV}(x_1^{\sharp}, x_2^{\sharp}, x_3^{\sharp}) + f_{\mu_3^{\sharp}}^{AV}(x_1^{\sharp}, x_2^{\sharp}, x_3^{\sharp}) = 1, \forall x_i^{\sharp}, i = 1, 2, 3$.

Table 3 shows Shapely values of fuzzy measures. These values show that $x_3^{\sharp}$ has a relatively strong impact on the three output values. Figure 2 shows the graph of the set functions when $x_1^{\sharp} = 0.2$ and $x_3^{\sharp} = 0.8$.

### 6.2 Bi-set Functions

Table 4 shows an example of a bi-set function model for $n = 2$ and $m = 3$. $y_1^b$ and $y_2^b$ denote the degrees of classes 1 and 2, and $y_3^b$ is the rest value, that is

**Table 2.** Example of set functions

| $A$ | $\mu_1^{T_1^\sharp}(A)$ | $\mu_2^{T_2^\sharp}(A)$ | $\mu_3^{T_3^\sharp}(A)$ | $\mu_1^\sharp(A)$ | $\mu_2^\sharp(A)$ | $\mu_3^\sharp(A)$ | Sum |
|---|---|---|---|---|---|---|---|
| $\{\}$ | 0 | 0 | 0 | 0 | 0.2 | 0.8 | 1 |
| $\{1\}$ | 0.1 | 0 | 0.1 | 0.1 | 0.5 | 0.4 | 1 |
| $\{2\}$ | 0.2 | 0.2 | 0 | 0.2 | 0 | 0.8 | 1 |
| $\{1,2\}$ | 0.3 | 0.5 | 0.4 | 0.3 | 0 | 0.7 | 1 |
| $\{3\}$ | 0.3 | 0.1 | 0.4 | 0.3 | 0.6 | 0.1 | 1 |
| $\{1,3\}$ | 0.4 | 0.1 | 0.8 | 0.4 | 0.6 | 0 | 1 |
| $\{2,3\}$ | 0.5 | 0.6 | 0.7 | 0.5 | 0.1 | 0.4 | 1 |
| $\{1,2,3\}$ | 0.9 | 0.6 | 0.8 | 0.9 | 0.1 | 0 | 1 |

**Table 3.** Shapley values

| | $\mu_1^{T_1^\sharp}$ | $\mu_2^{T_2^\sharp}$ | $\mu_3^{T_3^\sharp}$ | Sum |
|---|---|---|---|---|
| $sh_1$ | 0.2 | 0.05 | 0.2 | 0.45 |
| $sh_2$ | 0.3 | 0.4 | 0.1 | 0.8 |
| $sh_3$ | 0.4 | 0.15 | 0.5 | 1.05 |
| Sum | 0.9 | 0.6 | 0.8 | 2.3 |

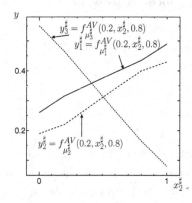

**Fig. 2.** Graph of table 2

**Fig. 3.** Graph of table 4

unclassable degree. In this example, as we set $y_1^\flat$ to increase with $x_1^\flat$ and $x_2^\flat$, $T_1 = \emptyset$. Since $y_2^\flat$ increases with an increase in $x_1^\flat$ and a decrease in $x_2^\flat$, $T_2 = \{2\}$. $\nu_1^{T_1^\flat}$ and $\nu_2^{T_2^\flat}$ are super-additive in a positive area and sub-additive in a negative area. To earn neutral outputs, that is, $y_1^\flat + y_2^\flat + y_3^\flat = 0$, we set the bi-set function values as $\nu_1^\flat(A,B) + \nu_2^\flat(A,B) + \nu_3^\flat(A,B) = 0, \forall(A,B) \in Q(X)$. The Shapley values are $sh_1(\nu_1^{T_1^\flat}) = 1$, $sh_2(\nu_1^{T_1^\flat}) = 0.5$, $sh_1(\nu_2^{T_2^\flat}) = 1$, and $sh_2(\nu_2^{T_2^\flat}) = 0.5$.

**Table 4.** Example of bi-set functions

| $(A,B)$ | $\nu_1^{T_1^\flat}$ | $\nu_2^{T_2^\flat}$ | $\nu_1^\flat$ | $\nu_2^\flat$ | $\nu_3^\flat$ | sum | $(A,B)$ | $\nu_1^{T_1^\flat}$ | $\nu_2^{T_2^\flat}$ | $\nu_1^\flat$ | $\nu_2^\flat$ | $\nu_3^\flat$ | sum |
|---|---|---|---|---|---|---|---|---|---|---|---|---|---|
| $(\{\},\{\})$ | 0 | 0 | 0 | 0 | 0 | 0 | $(\{1\},\{\})$ | 0.2 | 0.3 | 0.2 | 0.3 | $-0.5$ | 0 |
| $(\{\},\{1\})$ | $-0.5$ | $-0.5$ | $-0.5$ | $-0.5$ | 1 | 0 | $(\{2\},\{\})$ | 0.3 | 0.2 | 0.3 | 0 | $-0.3$ | 0 |
| $(\{1,2\},\{\})$ | 1 | 1 | 1 | 0 | $-1$ | 0 | $(\{2\},\{1\})$ | $-0.5$ | $-0.5$ | $-0.5$ | $-0.5$ | 1 | 0 |
| $(\{\},\{2\})$ | 0 | 0 | 0 | 0.2 | $-0.2$ | 0 | $(\{1\},\{2\})$ | 0 | 0 | 0 | 1 | $-1$ | 0 |
| $(\{\},\{1,2\})$ | $-0.5$ | $-0.5$ | $-0.5$ | $-0.5$ | 1 | 0 | | | | | | | |

Figure 3 shows the $y_1^b$, $y_2^b$, and $y_3^b$ graphs for the case in which $x_2^b = 0.4$. As $x_2^b > 0$, $y_1^b$ increases in $[-1, 1]$ and $y_2^b$ increases slightly. For any $\mathbf{x}^b \in [-1, 1]^3$, $y_1^b + y_2^b + y_3^b = 0$. A negative $y_3^b$ is interpreted as the degree of overlap classification, while a positive $y_3^b$ is interpreted as the degree of unclassification if positive.

# 7 Conclusion

We extend the Choquet integral for bi-capacities to a vector-valued model and show the condition that sum of output values set a constant. Symmetric difference expressions are introduced so that we can interpret bi-set functions by using bi-capacities tools. The output value of the logical Choquet integral may not match with those of the original set function and its symmetric difference expression. In the case of bi-set functions, the output values match with the original bi-set function and symmetric difference expressions.

# References

1. Choquet, G.: Theory of capacities. Annales de l'Institut Fourier 5, 131–295 (1954)
2. Murofushi, T., Sugeno, M.: A theory of fuzzy measure: Representation, the Choquet integral and null sets. J. Math. Anal. Appl. 159, 532–549 (1991)
3. Grabisch, M.: k-Order additive discrete fuzzy measures and their representation. Fuzzy Sets and Systems 92, 167–189 (1999)
4. Takahagi, E.: Fuzzy three-valued switching functions using Choquet integral. Journal of Advanced Computational Intelligence and Intelligent Informatics 7(1), 47–52 (2003)
5. Takahagi, E.: Fuzzy Integral Based Fuzzy Switching Functions. In: Peters, J.F., Skowron, A., Dubois, D., Grzymała-Busse, J.W., Inuiguchi, M., Polkowski, L. (eds.) Transactions on Rough Sets II. LNCS, vol. 3135, pp. 129–150. Springer, Heidelberg (2004)
6. Grabisch, M., Labreuche, C.: Bi-capacities — Part I: Definition, Möbius transform and interaction. Fuzzy Sets and Systems 151, 211–236 (2005)
7. Grabisch, M., Labreuche, C.: Bi-capacities — Part II: The Choquet integral. Fuzzy Sets and Systems 151, 237–259 (2005)
8. Grabisch, M., Lange, F.: Interaction transform for bi-set functions over a finite set. Information Sciences 176(16), 2279–2303 (2006)
9. Fujimoto, K., Murofushi, T., Sugeno, M.: k-additivity and C-decomposability of bi-capacities and its integral. Fuzzy Sets and Systems 158, 1698–1712 (2007)
10. Grabisch, M., Labreuche, C.: Bipolarization of posets and natural interpolation. Journal of Mathematical Analysis and Applications 343(2), 1080–1097 (2008)
11. Takahagi, E.: A Choquet integral model with multiple outputs and its application to classifications. Journal of Japan Society for Fuzzy Theory and Intelligent Informatics 22(4), 481–484 (2010) (in Japanese)
12. Takahagi, E.: Vector-valued Choquet integral models: Relations among set functions and properties. Journal of Japan Society for Fuzzy Theory and Intelligent Informatics 23(4), 596–603 (2011) (in Japanese)
13. Takahagi, E.: Multiple-output Choquet integral models and their applications in classification methods. International Journal of Intelligent Technologies and Applied Statistics 4(4), 519–530 (2011)

# A Probabilistic Representation
# of Exact Games on $\sigma$-Algebras

Nobusumi Sagara*

Faculty of Economics, Hosei University,
4342, Aihara, Machida, Tokyo, 194–0298, Japan
nsagara@hosei.ac.jp

**Abstract.** The purpose of this paper is to establish the intrinsic relations between the cores of exact games on $\sigma$-algebras and the extensions
of exact games to function spaces. Given a probability space, to derive
a probabilistic representation for exact functionals, we endow them with
two probabilistic conditions: law invariance and the Fatou property. The
representation theorem for exact functionals lays a probabilistic foundation for nonatomic scalar measure games. Based on the notion of
$P$-convexity, we also investigate the equivalent conditions for the representation of anonymous convex games.

**Keywords:** Exact game, Core, Exact functional, Choquet integral, Law
invariance, Fatou property, Anonymity, $P$-convex measure.

## 1 Introduction

One of the most fundamental solution concepts of transferable utility (TU) games
is the core, defined as the set of feasible payoffs upon which no coalition can
improve. When the number of players is infinite, an element of the core is a
finitely additive signed measure of bounded variation that dominates an underlying game. Among the classes of TU games, the class of exact games is central
to the characterization of the cores, because they are defined as the setwise
minimum of the dominating measures in the cores.

   The purpose of this paper is to establish the intrinsic relations between the
cores of exact games on $\sigma$-algebras and the extensions of exact games to function
spaces. While our focus is confined to exploring an appropriate notion of integrals
for nonadditive set functions that is especially suitable for the analysis of TU
games, the problem under consideration belongs to the scope of fuzzy integration
([6, 13, 22]), imprecise probabilities ([7, 23]) and decision theory ([10]), on which
rapid progress has been made over the past few decades.

   There are several approaches to formulating nonadditive integrals as a nonlinear functional on a function space. One of the most prevalent extensions of

---

* This research is supported by Grants-in-Aid for Scientific Research (No. 21530277
  and No. 23530230) from the Ministry of Education, Culture, Sports, Science and
  Technology, Japan.

S. Greco et al. (Eds.): IPMU 2012, Part IV, CCIS 300, pp. 228–237, 2012.

nonadditive set functions to the space of measurable functions is a Choquet integral (see [6, 22]), which is significant for cooperative game theory because convex games have an intimate relation between their Choquet integral and their core. It is well known that the Choquet integral of a bounded convex game is the support functional of its core. Along another line of research, [3] introduced *na-*continuous extensions of nonatomic vector measure games to axiomatize the values of TU games with an infinite number of players, which have recently turned out to be useful for a characterization of an exact game with the norm compact core, as demonstrated by [1].

In the next section, we propose exact functionals on the space $B(\Omega, \mathcal{F})$ of bounded measurable functions as an extension of exact games on a $\sigma$-algebra $\mathcal{F}$, which are originated in [14, 21]. An exact functional is a functional satisfying upper semicontinuity, superadditivity, positive homogeneity and translation invariance. These conditions are naturally embodied in Choquet integrals of convex games. This observation suggests that exact functionals are suitable extensions of exact games. Moreover, they are imposed as axioms for coherent risk measures proposed by [2, 8]. While the extension of an exact game in terms of an exact functional is not unique, exact games are fully characterized by their minimal exact extension, which coincides with the support functional of the core. To this end, superdifferential calculus for concave functions on infinite-dimensional vector spaces plays a crucial role.

The support functionals of the cores are weakly upper semicontinuous and concave on $B(\Omega, \mathcal{F})$, which is a nice property in conformity with traditional convex analysis. However, it is difficult to obtain weak compact sets in $B(\Omega, \mathcal{F})$ which are useful for many applications. Under the continuity hypothesis, exact games are extended to the space $L^\infty(\Omega, \mathcal{F}, P)$ of essentially bounded functions for some appropriate probability measure $P$ as a support functional of the core that is weakly* upper semicontinuous and concave. Weakly* compact sets in $L^\infty(\Omega, \mathcal{F}, P)$ are easily obtained because they are just bounded, weakly* closed sets. On the contrary, Choquet integrals of nonconvex games extended to $L^\infty(\Omega, \mathcal{F}, P)$ necessarily lack concavity. This is the reason we propose the use of the support functionals of the cores as suitable extensions of exact games.

In Section 3, given a probability space $(\Omega, \mathcal{F}, P)$, exact functionals are defined on $L^\infty(\Omega, \mathcal{F}, P)$ as an extension of exact games on a $\sigma$-algebra. To derive probabilistic representation for exact functionals, we exploit the axiomatization of coherent risk measures, along the lines of [8, 12], and endow exact functionals with two probabilistic conditions: law invariance and the Fatou property. A new characterization of exact functionals in terms of the support functionals and the quantile functions is formulated.

Section 4 is the main part of this paper. The representation theorem for exact functionals lays the probabilistic foundation of nonatomic scalar measure games $\nu$ of the form $\nu = f \circ P$, where $f$ is a real-valued function on the unit interval with $f(0) = 0$ and $f(1) = 1$, and $P$ is a nonatomic probability measure, which is a special case of nonatomic vector measure games studied by [3, 4, 9, 15, 16]. A game of this form is regarded as a distortion of a probability measure, capturing imprecise probabilities for decision making (see [5]). We introduce the concept of anonymity of games and provide the equivalent conditions on exact games for the representation of the form $\nu = f \circ P$. Based on the notion of $P$-convexity proposed by [19, 20], we also investigate the equivalent conditions for the representation of anonymous convex games of the form $\nu = f \circ P$ with $f$ a convex function.

## 2    Exact Functionals and Exact Games

### 2.1    Exact Games

Let $(\Omega, \mathcal{F})$ be a measurable space, where $\mathcal{F}$ is a $\sigma$-algebra of subsets of a nonempty set $\Omega$. Let $B(\Omega, \mathcal{F})$ denote the vector space of bounded measurable functions on $\Omega$ with the sup norm and let $ba(\Omega, \mathcal{F})$ denote the vector space of finitely additive set functions on $\mathcal{F}$ of bounded variation, which is the dual space of $B(\Omega, \mathcal{F})$. The space $ba(\Omega, \mathcal{F})$ is endowed with the weak* topology, under which its dual space is $B(\Omega, \mathcal{F})$. Let $ca(\Omega, \mathcal{F})$ be the vector subspace of $ba(\Omega, \mathcal{F})$ consisting of all countably additive set functions on $\mathcal{F}$ of bounded variation.

**The Core of an Exact Game.** A set function $\nu : \mathcal{F} \to \mathbb{R}$ with $\nu(\emptyset) = 0$ is a *game*. The *core* $\mathcal{C}(\nu)$ of a game $\nu$ is defined by:

$$\mathcal{C}(\nu) = \{\mu \in ba(\Omega, \mathcal{F}) \mid \nu \leq \mu \text{ and } \mu(\Omega) = \nu(\Omega)\}.$$

A game is *balanced* if its core is nonempty. A bounded game $\nu$ is balanced if and only if $\sum_{i=1}^{k} \alpha_i \mathbb{1}_{A_i} = \mathbb{1}_{\Omega}$ with $\alpha_1, \ldots, \alpha_k \geq 0$ and $A_1, \ldots, A_k \in \mathcal{F}$ implies $\sum_{i=1}^{k} \alpha_i \nu(A_i) \leq \nu(\Omega)$. A balanced game $\nu : \mathcal{F} \to \mathbb{R}$ is *exact* if $\nu(A) = \min_{\mu \in \mathcal{C}(\nu)} \mu(A)$ for every $A \in \mathcal{F}$. A game $\nu$ is *convex* (or *supermodular*) if $\nu(A) + \nu(B) \leq \nu(A \cup B) + \nu(A \cap B)$ for every $A, B \in \mathcal{F}$. A bounded convex game is exact.

A game $\nu : \mathcal{F} \to \mathbb{R}$ is *continuous from above* at $A$ if $\nu(A_n) \to \nu(A)$ for every sequence $\{A_n\}$ in $\mathcal{F}$ with $A_n \downarrow A$; $\nu$ is *continuous from below* at $A$ if $\nu(A_n) \to \nu(A)$ for every sequence $\{A_n\}$ in $\mathcal{F}$ with $A_n \uparrow A$; $\nu$ is *continuous* if it is both continuous from above and continuous from below at every $A \in \mathcal{F}$.

Given a game $\nu$, a set $N \in \mathcal{F}$ is $\nu$-*null* if $\nu(A \cup N) = \nu(A)$ for every $A \in \mathcal{F}$. A game $\nu$ is *nonatomic* if, for every $\nu$-nonnull set $A \in \mathcal{F}$, there exists a subset $B$ of $A$ in $\mathcal{F}$ such that both $A \setminus B$ and $B$ are $\nu$-nonnull.

**Proposition 2.1 ([21]).** *Let $\nu : \mathcal{F} \to \mathbb{R}$ be an exact game. Then, the following conditions are equivalent.*

(i) *$\nu$ is continuous.*
(ii) *$\mathcal{C}(\nu) \subset ca(\Omega, \mathcal{F})$.*
(iii) *There exists a probability measure $P$ such that:*

$$\lim_{P(A) \to 0} \sup_{\mu \in \mathcal{C}(\nu)} \mu(A) = 0.$$

A probability measure $P$ satisfying condition (iii) is called a *control measure* for $\mathcal{C}(\nu)$, which asserts that the countable additivity is uniform with respect to $\mu$ in $\mathcal{C}(\nu)$ and, hence, with respect to $P$, every element in $\mathcal{C}(\nu)$ is absolutely continuous. It is obvious from Proposition 2.1 that a discontinuous exact game does not possess a control measure.

## 2.2   Exact Functionals

In view of the definition of an exact game $\nu : \mathcal{F} \to \mathbb{R}$, the support functional $\Gamma_\nu : B(\Omega, \mathcal{F}) \to \mathbb{R}$ of the core $\mathcal{C}(\nu)$ defined by $\Gamma_\nu(X) = \min_{\mu \in \mathcal{C}(\nu)} \langle \mu, X \rangle$ for $X \in B(\Omega, \mathcal{F})$ gives rise to a possible extension of $\nu$. As $\Gamma_\nu$ is a pointwise minimum of a family of continuous linear functionals $X \mapsto \langle \mu, X \rangle$ over $\mu$ in $\mathcal{C}(\nu)$, it is upper semicontinuous, superadditive, positively homogeneous and translation invariant. This observation suggests that it is quite natural to introduce the functionals possessing these properties as suitable extensions of exact games.

**Definition 2.1.** *A functional $\Gamma : B(\Omega, \mathcal{F}) \to \mathbb{R}$ is exact if the following conditions are satisfied.*

*(Upper semicontinuity): $\Gamma$ is upper semicontinuous.*
*(Superadditivity): $\Gamma(X + Y) \geq \Gamma(X) + \Gamma(Y)$ for every $X, Y \in B(\Omega, \mathcal{F})$.*
*(Positive homogeneity): $\Gamma(\alpha X) = \alpha \Gamma(X)$ for every $X \in B(\Omega, \mathcal{F})$ and $\alpha \geq 0$.*
*(Translation invariance): $\Gamma(X + \alpha 1_\Omega) = \Gamma(X) + \alpha \Gamma(1_\Omega)$ for every $X \in B(\Omega, \mathcal{F})$ and $\alpha \geq 0$.*

**Representation of Exact Functionals.** The next theorem asserts that there is a one-to-one correspondence between exact functionals on $B(\Omega, \mathcal{F})$ and weakly* compact, convex subsets of $ba(\Omega, \mathcal{F})$ with the same mass.

**Theorem 2.1.** *A functional $\Gamma : B(\Omega, \mathcal{F}) \to \mathbb{R}$ is exact if and only if there exists a unique, weakly* compact, convex subset $\mathcal{C}$ of $ba(\Omega, \mathcal{F})$ such that:*

$$\Gamma(X) = \min_{\mu \in \mathcal{C}} \langle \mu, X \rangle \quad \text{for every } X \in B(\Omega, \mathcal{F}),$$

*where $\mathcal{C}$ is of the form:*

$$\mathcal{C} = \{\mu \in ba(\Omega, \mathcal{F}) \mid \Gamma(X) \leq \langle \mu, X \rangle \ \forall X \in B(\Omega, \mathcal{F}), \ \mu(\Omega) = \Gamma(1_\Omega)\}.$$

**Extension of Exact Games**

**Definition 2.2.** *A functional $\Gamma_\nu : B(\Omega, \mathcal{F}) \to \mathbb{R}$ is an exact extension of a game $\nu : \mathcal{F} \to \mathbb{R}$ if it is exact and $\Gamma_\nu(1_A) = \nu(A)$ for every $A \in \mathcal{F}$. The minimal exact extension $\underline{\Gamma}_\nu$ of $\nu$ is an exact extension of $\nu$ such that $\underline{\Gamma}_\nu \leq \Gamma_\nu$ for every exact extension $\Gamma_\nu$ of $\nu$.*

Let $\Gamma : B(\Omega, \mathcal{F}) \to \mathbb{R}$ be a functional. The *superdifferential* $\partial\Gamma(X)$ of $\Gamma$ at $X \in B(\Omega, \mathcal{F})$ is given by:

$$\partial\Gamma(X) = \{\mu \in ba(\Omega, \mathcal{F}) \mid \Gamma(Y) - \Gamma(X) \leq \langle \mu, Y - X \rangle \ \forall Y \in B(\Omega, \mathcal{F})\},$$

where an element in $\partial\Gamma(X)$ is called a *supergradient* of $\Gamma$ at $X$. The *directional derivative* $\Gamma'(X; h)$ of $\Gamma$ at $X \in B(\Omega, \mathcal{F})$ in the direction $h \in B(\Omega, \mathcal{F})$ is defined by:

$$\Gamma'(X; h) = \lim_{t \downarrow 0} \frac{\Gamma(X + th) - \Gamma(X)}{t}.$$

It follows from the standard argument of convex analysis that if $\Gamma$ is continuous and concave, then $\partial\Gamma(X)$ is a nonempty, weakly* compact, convex subset of $ba(\Omega, \mathcal{F})$ for every $X \in B(\Omega, \mathcal{F})$ and $\Gamma'(X; h)$ exists at every $X \in B(\Omega, \mathcal{F})$ in any direction $h \in B(\Omega, \mathcal{F})$.

**Theorem 2.2.** *Let $\nu : \mathcal{F} \to \mathbb{R}$ be a balanced game. Then, the following conditions are equivalent.*

(i) *$\nu$ is exact.*
(ii) *$\nu$ has the minimal exact extension $\underline{\Gamma}_\nu : B(\Omega, \mathcal{F}) \to \mathbb{R}$ such that:*

$$\mathcal{C}(\nu) = \partial\underline{\Gamma}_\nu(\alpha 1_\Omega) \quad \text{for every } \alpha \geq 0.$$

(iii) *$\nu$ has the minimal exact extension $\underline{\Gamma}_\nu : B(\Omega, \mathcal{F}) \to \mathbb{R}$ such that:*

$$\underline{\Gamma}_\nu(X) = \underline{\Gamma}_\nu'(\alpha 1_\Omega; X) = \langle \mu, X \rangle = \min_{\mu \in \mathcal{C}(\nu)} \langle \mu, X \rangle$$

*for every $X \in B(\Omega, \mathcal{F})$, $\mu \in \partial\underline{\Gamma}_\nu(X)$ and $\alpha \geq 0$.*

Condition (ii) of Theorem 2.2 involves a "core representation" result for exact games. Indeed, the core can be characterized by the local behavior of the superdifferential of the minimal exact extension of an exact game only at any nonnegative constant in the real line.

**The Choquet Extension.** One of the most prevalent extensions of games on $\mathcal{F}$ to $B(\Omega, \mathcal{F})$ is a Choquet integral, the definition of which is as follows.

**Definition 2.3.** *A functional $\Gamma_\nu^C : B(\Omega, \mathcal{F}) \to \mathbb{R}$ is a Choquet extension of a game $\nu : \mathcal{F} \to \mathbb{R}$ of bounded variation to $B(\Omega, \mathcal{F})$ if it is of the form:*

$$\Gamma_\nu^C(X) = \int_0^{+\infty} \nu(X \geq t)dt + \int_{-\infty}^0 [\nu(X \geq t) - \nu(\Omega)]dt.$$

*Here, $(X \geq t)$ denotes the measurable set $\{\omega \in \Omega \mid X(\omega) \geq t\}$ in $\mathcal{F}$.*

**Proposition 2.2.** *The minimal exact extension $\underline{\Gamma}_\nu : B(\Omega, \mathcal{F}) \to \mathbb{R}$ of a bounded convex game $\nu : \mathcal{F} \to \mathbb{R}$ is given by:*

$$\underline{\Gamma}_\nu(X) = \Gamma_\nu^C(X) = \min_{\mu \in \mathcal{C}(\nu)} \langle \mu, X \rangle \quad \text{for every } X \in B(\Omega, \mathcal{F}).$$

*Remark 2.1.* A support functional of the core of a game is both strongly and weakly upper semicontinuous, and concave on $B(\Omega, \mathcal{F})$. However, it is difficult to obtain compact sets in $B(\Omega, \mathcal{F})$ which are useful for many applications. In particular, if $\Omega$ is a compact Hausdorff topological space, then both norm compact sets and weakly compact sets in $B(\Omega, \mathcal{F})$ must be a subset of continuous functions on $\Omega$. Compact sets in $B(\Omega, \mathcal{F})$ are in general restricted severely both in the norm and the weak topologies. This observation leads to the need for the extension of exact functionals to $L^\infty$ because weakly* compact sets in $L^\infty$ are easily obtained in that they are just bounded, weakly* closed sets.

*Remark 2.2.* Although Choquet integrals of continuous exact games are extended to $L^\infty(\Omega, \mathcal{F}, P)$, they are not concave if and only if the continuos exact games are not convex. For a probabilistic representation of exact functionals developed in the next section, the effective use of the techniques in infinite-dimensional convex analysis is required. This is the reason we propose the use of the support functionals of the cores as extension of exact games.

## 3    A Probabilistic Characterization of Exact Functionals

### 3.1    Law Invariance and the Fatou Property

The (*probability*) *law* (or *distribution*) of a random variable $X : \Omega \to \mathbb{R}$ is a probability measure $P \circ X^{-1}$ on the Borel space $(\mathbb{R}, \mathcal{B})$. When a random variable $X$ has the same law as $Y$, we denote it by $X \sim Y$. The *distribution function* of $X$ is given by $F_X(x) = P(X \le x)$. The (*upper*) *quantile function* $q_X : [0, 1) \to \mathbb{R} \cup \{-\infty\}$ of $X$ is defined by $q_X(t) = \inf\{x \in \mathbb{R} \mid F_X(x) > t\}$, which is nondecreasing, right-continuous and satisfies $q_{-X}(t) = q_X(1 - t)$ a.e. $t \in (0, 1)$. For each $\alpha \in [0, 1]$, we define the functional $q_\alpha : L^\infty(\Omega, \mathcal{F}, P) \to \mathbb{R}$ by:

$$q_\alpha(X) = \begin{cases} \frac{1}{\alpha} \int_0^\alpha q_X(t)dt & \text{for } \alpha \in (0, 1], \\ \text{ess.inf } X & \text{for } \alpha = 0, \end{cases}$$

where $\text{ess.inf } X = \sup\{t \in \mathbb{R} \mid P(X \ge t) = 1\}$.

Let $ca([0, 1])$ be the vector space of countably additive bounded set functions of the Borel space $([0, 1], \mathcal{B})$ and let $C([0, 1])$ be the vector space of continuous functions on $[0, 1]$ with the sup norm. The dual space of $C([0, 1])$ is $ca([0, 1])$. The space $ca([0, 1])$ is endowed with the weak* topology. Let $p([0, 1]) \subset ca([0, 1])$ denote the set of probability measures of $([0, 1], \mathcal{B})$.

**Definition 3.1.**    (i) *A functional* $\Gamma : L^\infty(\Omega, \mathcal{F}, P) \to \mathbb{R}$ *is law invariant if* $\Gamma(X) = \Gamma(Y)$ *whenever* $X \sim Y$.
   (ii) *A subset* $C$ *of* $L^1(\Omega, \mathcal{F}, P)$ *is law invariant whenever* $Y \in C$ *and* $\tilde{Y} \sim Y$ *imply that* $\tilde{Y} \in C$.
   (iii) *A subset* $C$ *of* $ca(\Omega, \mathcal{F}, P)$ *is law invariant whenever the set:*

$$C = \left\{ \frac{d\mu}{dP} \in L^1(\Omega, \mathcal{F}, P) \mid \mu \in \mathcal{C} \right\}$$

*is law invariant.*

**Definition 3.2.** *A functional* $\Gamma : L^\infty(\Omega, \mathcal{F}, P) \to \mathbb{R}$ *has the Fatou property whenever* $X_n \to X$ *a.e. with* $\sup_n \|X_n\|_\infty < \infty$ *implies that* $\limsup_n \Gamma(X_n) \leq \Gamma(X)$.

**Representation Theorem.** The next result is a generalization of [8, 12], which dispenses with the monotonicity assumption on $\Gamma$.

**Theorem 3.1.** *Let* $\Gamma : L^\infty(\Omega, \mathcal{F}, P) \to \mathbb{R}$ *be a functional. Then, the following conditions are equivalent.*

(i) $\Gamma$ *is a law invariant exact functional with the Fatou property.*
(ii) *There exists a unique, law invariant, weakly compact, convex subset* $\mathcal{C}$ *of* $ca(\Omega, \mathcal{F}, P)$ *such that:*

$$\Gamma(X) = \min_{\mu \in \mathcal{C}} \langle \mu, X \rangle \quad \text{for every } X \in L^\infty(\Omega, \mathcal{F}, P),$$

*where* $\mathcal{C}$ *is of the form:*

$$\mathcal{C} = \left\{ \mu \in ca(\Omega, \mathcal{F}, P) \middle| \begin{matrix} \Gamma(X) \leq \langle \mu, X \rangle \ \forall X \in L^\infty(\Omega, \mathcal{F}, P) \\ \mu(\Omega) = \Gamma(\mathbf{1}_\Omega) \end{matrix} \right\}.$$

(iii) $\Gamma$ *is superadditive and there exists a subset* $\mathcal{M}$ *of* $ca([0,1])$ *such that* $m([0,1]) = \Gamma(\mathbf{1}_\Omega)$ *for every* $m \in \mathcal{M}$ *and:*

$$\Gamma(X) = \inf_{m \in \mathcal{M}} \int_0^1 q_\alpha(X) dm(\alpha) \quad \text{for every } X \in L^\infty(\Omega, \mathcal{F}, P).$$

### 3.2    Choquet Integral Representation

Let $f : [0,1] \to \mathbb{R}$ be of bounded variation with $f(0) = 0$. The set function $f \circ P : \mathcal{F} \to \mathbb{R}$ is a distortion of a probability measure $P$. We define the Choquet extension $\Gamma^C_{f \circ P} : L^\infty(\Omega, \mathcal{F}, P) \to \mathbb{R}$ of a set function $f \circ P : \mathcal{F} \to \mathbb{R}$ by:

$$\Gamma^C_{f \circ P}(X) = \int_0^\infty f(P(X \geq t))dt + \int_{-\infty}^0 [f(P(X \geq t)) - f(1)]dt.$$

As $f \circ P$ is of bounded variation whenever $f$ is, the Choquet integral of $f \circ P$ is well defined. In particular, if $f$ is nondecreasing, then it is of bounded variation.

**Theorem 3.2.** *A functional* $\Gamma : L^\infty(\Omega, \mathcal{F}, P) \to \mathbb{R}$ *is a law invariant exact functional with the Fatou property if and only if it is superadditive and there exists a family* $\Pi$ *of functions* $f : [0,1] \to \mathbb{R}$ *with* $f(0) = 0$ *that are written as a difference of two nondecreasing concave functions on* $[0,1]$, *vanishing at 0, such that:*

$$\Gamma(X) = \inf_{f \in \Pi} \left[ -\Gamma^C_{f \circ P}(-X) \right] \quad \text{for every } X \in L^\infty(\Omega, \mathcal{F}, P).$$

# 4  Anonymous Exact Games

## 4.1  Representation of Anonymous Exact Games

A transformation $\tau : \Omega \to \Omega$ is an *automorphism* if it is a bijection such that both $\tau$ and $\tau^{-1}$ are measurable mappings. A transformation $\tau$ is *measure-preserving* if it is a measurable mapping such that $P \circ \tau^{-1} = P$. Let $\mathcal{T}(\Omega, \mathcal{F}, P)$ denote the group of measure-preserving automorphisms on $(\Omega, \mathcal{F}, P)$, where the group action is, as usual, given by the composition in $\mathcal{T}(\Omega, \mathcal{F}, P)$.

An interpretation behind the measure-preserving automorphisms is that every $\tau \in \mathcal{T}(\Omega, \mathcal{F}, P)$ maps each coalition $A \in \mathcal{F}$ to another coalition $\tau(A) \in \mathcal{F}$ such that their population is invariant: $P(A) = P(\tau(A))$. This motivates us to introduce the following notions of anonymity.

**Definition 4.1.**  (i)  *A game $\nu : \mathcal{F} \to \mathbb{R}$ is anonymous if there exists a probability measure $P$ such that $\nu \circ \tau = \nu$ for every $\tau \in \mathcal{T}(\Omega, \mathcal{F}, P)$.*
(ii)  *A game $\nu : \mathcal{F} \to \mathbb{R}$ has the anonymous core if there exists a probability measure $P$ such that $\mu \in \mathcal{C}(\nu)$ implies $\mu \circ \tau \in \mathcal{C}(\nu)$ for every $\tau \in \mathcal{T}(\Omega, \mathcal{F}, P)$.*

When it is necessary to emphasize that the underlying measure is $P$, we say that $\nu$ is *P-anonymous* and that $\nu$ has the *P-anonymous core*.

The anonymity of games states that the coalitional worths of a game do not depend on the names of players, but exclusively on the population size of coalitions. On the other hand, given a feasible payoff $\mu \in ba(\Omega, \mathcal{F})$ of a game, $\mu \circ \tau \in ba(\Omega, \mathcal{F})$ is a rearrangement of $\mu$ among the players in terms of a "population-invariant transformation" $\tau \in \mathcal{T}(\Omega, \mathcal{F}, P)$. Thus, the payoff $\mu(A)$ to coalition $A \in \mathcal{F}$ is transformed into the payoff $\mu(\tau(A))$ to coalition $\tau(A) \in \mathcal{F}$. The anonymity of the core means that if $\mu$ is in $\mathcal{C}(\nu)$, then the rearrangement $\mu \circ \tau$ of $\mu$ is also in $\mathcal{C}(\nu)$.

**Theorem 4.1.** *Let $\nu : \mathcal{F} \to \mathbb{R}$ be an exact game. Then, the following conditions are equivalent.*

(i)  *There exists a nonatomic control measure $P$ for $\mathcal{C}(\nu)$ such that $\nu$ is P-anonymous.*
(ii)  *There exists a nonatomic control measure $P$ for $\mathcal{C}(\nu)$ such that $\nu$ has the P-anonymous core.*
(iii)  *There exists a nonatomic probability measure $P$ such that $\nu$ has the law invariant, minimal, exact extension $\underline{\Gamma}_\nu : L^\infty(\Omega, \mathcal{F}, P) \to \mathbb{R}$ with the Fatou property of the form:*

$$\underline{\Gamma}_\nu(X) = \min_{\mu \in \mathcal{C}(\nu)} \langle \mu, X \rangle \quad \text{for every } X \in L^\infty(\Omega, \mathcal{F}, P).$$

(iv)  *There exists a nonatomic probability measure $P$ and a unique continuous function $f : [0,1] \to \mathbb{R}$ satisfying $f(0) = 0$ and $f(1) = \nu(\Omega)$ such that $\nu = f \circ P$.*

By Propositions 2.1, an exact game $\nu$ has a nonatomic control measure for $\mathcal{C}(\nu)$ if it is continuous and nonatomic. It follows from the proof of Theorem 4.1 that every anonymous game has the anonymous core and that, especially for exact games, anonymity is equivalent to possessing the anonymous core.

## 4.2    Representation of Anonymous Convex Games

For an arbitrarily given $A \in \mathcal{F}$ and $t \in [0,1]$, we define the family $\mathcal{K}_t^P(A)$ of measurable subsets of $A$ by:

$$\mathcal{K}_t^P(A) = \{E \in \mathcal{F} \mid E \subset A \text{ and } P(E) = tP(A)\}.$$

By the nonatomicity of $P$, it is evident that $\mathcal{K}_t^P(A)$ is nonempty for every $A \in \mathcal{F}$ and $t \in [0,1]$. For an arbitrarily given $A, B \in \mathcal{F}$ and $t \in [0,1]$, we define the family $\mathcal{K}_t^P(A, B)$ of measurable sets by:

$$\mathcal{K}_t^P(A, B) = \left\{ C \in \mathcal{F} \middle| \begin{array}{l} \exists (E, F) \in \mathcal{K}_t^P(A) \times \mathcal{K}_{1-t}^P(B) : \\ C = E \cup F \text{ and } E \cap F = \emptyset \end{array} \right\}.$$

It can be shown that $\mathcal{K}_t^P(A, B)$ is nonempty for every $A, B \in \mathcal{F}$ and $t \in [0,1]$ (see [19]).

**Definition 4.2.** *A game* $\nu : \mathcal{F} \to \mathbb{R}$ *is a convex measure if there exists a nonatomic probability measure* $P$ *such that for every* $A, B \in \mathcal{F}$ *and* $t \in [0,1]$, *we have:*

$$\nu(C) \leq t\nu(A) + (1-t)\nu(B) \quad \text{for every } C \in \mathcal{K}_t^P(A, B).$$

When the underlying measure is $P$, we say that a game $\nu$ is $P$-convex. A nonatomic signed measure $\frac{\nu(\Omega)}{P(\Omega)}P$ belongs to the core of a $P$-convex game $\nu$ and, moreover, $P$-convex games are totally balanced (see [20]).

**Theorem 4.2.** *Let* $\nu : \mathcal{F} \to \mathbb{R}$ *be a bounded game. Then, the following conditions are equivalent.*

(i) *$\nu$ is convex (or supermodular) and there exists a nonatomic control measure $P$ for $\mathcal{C}(\nu)$ such that $\nu$ is $P$-anonymous.*

(ii) *$\nu$ is convex (or supermodular) and there exists a nonatomic control measure $P$ for $\mathcal{C}(\nu)$ such that $\nu$ has the $P$-anonymous core.*

(iii) *There exists a nonatomic probability measure $P$ such that $\nu$ is $P$-convex.*

(iv) *There exists a nonatomic probability measure $P$ and a unique, continuous, convex function $f : [0,1] \to \mathbb{R}$ satisfying $f(0) = 0$ and $f(1) = \nu(\Omega)$ such that $\nu = f \circ P$.*

**Corollary 4.1.** *Let $P$ be a nonatomic probability measure. For every continuous $P$-convex game $\nu : \mathcal{F} \to \mathbb{R}$, there exists a unique, continuous, convex function $f : [0,1] \to \mathbb{R}$ satisfying $f(0) = 0$ and $f(1) = \nu(\Omega)$, such that $\nu$ has the minimal exact extension $\underline{\Gamma}_\nu : L(\Omega, \mathcal{F}, P) \to \mathbb{R}$, such that:*

$$\underline{\Gamma}_\nu(X) = \Gamma_{f \circ P}^C(X) = \min_{\mu \in \mathcal{C}(\nu)} \langle \mu, X \rangle \quad \text{for every } X \in L^\infty(\Omega, \mathcal{F}, P).$$

# References

[1] Amarante, M., Maccheroni, F., Marinacci, M., Montrucchio, L.: Cores of non-atomic market games. Int. J. Game Theory 34, 399–424 (2006)

[2] Artzner, P., Delbaen, F., Eber, J.-M., Heath, D.: Coherent measures of risk. Math. Finance 9, 203–228 (1999)

[3] Aumann, R.J., Shapley, L.S.: Values of Non-Atomic Games. Princeton University Press, Princeton (1974)

[4] Carlier, G.: Representation of the core of convex measure games via Kantorovich potentials. J. Math. Econom. 41, 898–912 (2005)

[5] Carlier, G., Dana, R.A.: Core of convex distortions of a probability. J. Econom. Theory 113, 199–222 (2003)

[6] Choquet, G.: Theory of capacities. Ann. Inst. Fourier (Grenoble) 5, 131–295 (1955)

[7] de Cooman, G., Troffaes, M., Miranda, E.: $n$-Monotone exact functionals. J. Math. Anal. Appl. 347, 143–156 (2008)

[8] Delbaen, F.: Coherent risk measures on general probability spaces. In: Sandmann, K., Schönbucher, P.J. (eds.) Advances in Finance and Stochastics, pp. 1–37. Springer, Berlin (2002)

[9] Epstein, L.G., Marinacci, M.: The core of large TU games. J. Econom. Theory 100, 235–273 (2001)

[10] Gilboa, I., Schmeidler, D.: Maximin expected utility with non-unique prior. J. Math. Econom. 18, 141–153 (1989)

[11] Hüsseinov, F., Sagara, N.: Concave measures and the fuzzy core in exchange economies with heterogeneous divisible commodities. Fuzzy Sets and Systems (in press, 2012), doi:10.1016/j.fss.2011.12.021

[12] Kusuoka, S.: On law invariant coherent risk measures. Adv. Math. Econ. 3, 83–95 (2001)

[13] Lehrer, E., Tepper, R.: The concave integral over large spaces. Fuzzy Sets and Systems 159, 2130–2144 (2008)

[14] Maaß, S.: Exact functionals and their core. Statist. Papers 43, 75–93 (2002)

[15] Marinacci, M., Montrucchio, L.: Subcalculus for set functions and cores of TU games. J. Math. Econom. 39, 1–25 (2003)

[16] Marinacci, M., Montrucchio, L.: A characterization of the core of convex games through Gateaux derivatives. J. Econom. Theory 116, 229–248 (2004)

[17] Marinacci, M., Montrucchio, L.: Introduction to the mathematics of ambiguity. In: Gilboa, I. (ed.) Uncertainty in Economic Theory, pp. 46–107. Routledge, New York (2004)

[18] Sagara, N., Vlach, M.: Representation of preference relations on $\sigma$-algebras of nonatomic measure spaces: convexity and continuity. Fuzzy Sets and Systems 160, 624–634 (2009)

[19] Sagara, N., Vlach, M.: Convexity of the lower partition range of a concave vector measure. Adv. Math. Econ. 13, 155–160 (2010)

[20] Sagara, N., Vlach, M.: A new class of convex games and the optimal partitioning of measurable spaces. Int. J. Game Theory 40, 617–630 (2011)

[21] Schmeidler, D.: Cores of exact games, I. J. Math. Anal. Appl. 40, 214–225 (1972)

[22] Schmeidler, D.: Integral representation without additivity. Proc. Amer. Math. Soc. 97, 255–261 (1986)

[23] Walley, P.: Statistical Reasoning with Imprecise Probabilities. Chapman and Hall, London (1991)

# Elicitation of a 2-Additive Bi-capacity through Cardinal Information on Trinary Actions

Brice Mayag[1], Antoine Rolland[2], and Julien Ah-Pine[2]

[1] LAMSADE, University Paris Dauphine, Place du Maréchal de Lattre de Tassigny
75116 Paris, France
brice.mayag@dauphine.fr
[2] ERIC, University Lumière Lyon 2, 5 avenue Pierre Mendes-France
F-69676 BRON Cedex, France
{antoine.rolland,julien.ah-pine}@univ-lyon2.fr

**Abstract.** In the context of MultiCriteria Decision Aid, we present new properties of a 2-additive bi-capacity by using a bipolar Möbius transform. We use these properties in the identification of a 2-additive bi-capacity when we represent a cardinal information by a Choquet integral with respect to a 2-additive bi-capacity.

**Keywords:** MCDA, Preference modeling, bi-capacity, Choquet integral.

## 1 Introduction

Multi-criteria decision analysis aims at representing the preferences of a decision maker (DM) over options. One possible model is the transitive decomposable one where an overall utility is determined for each option. The Choquet integral has been proved to be a versatile aggregation function to construct overall scores [3,9,10] and is based on the notion of the capacity or fuzzy measure. The definition of Choquet integral in this case is based on unipolar scales [13]. Because these scales are not always appropriate (See the motivating example in [13]), the bipolar general Choquet integral have been introduced [8,12] for bipolar scales and in particular the bipolar Choquet integral w.r.t. a 2-additive capacity. Grabisch and Labreuche studied in [12] the expressions of a 2-additive bi-capacity according to their definition of 2-additivity via a Möbius transform. But, the identification of a 2-additive bi-capacities is not yet studied in the literature in details.

In this paper, we studied in details properties of a 2-additive bi-capacity by using the bipolar Möbius transform defined by Fujimoto et al. [8]. Hence we obtain here some simple expressions of monotonicity conditions of a 2-additive bi-capacity. We propose also an identification or elicitation of a 2-additive bi-capacity by asking to DM to express his preferences over a set of alternatives called here a set of trinary actions. A trinary action is an (fictitious) alternative representing a prototypical situation where on a given subset of at most two criteria, the attributes reach a satisfactory level $1$ or unsatisfactory level $-1$,

S. Greco et al. (Eds.): IPMU 2012, Part IV, CCIS 300, pp. 238–247, 2012.

while on the remaining ones, they are at a neutral level (neither satisfactory nor unsatisfactory) $\mathbf{0}$.

After some basic notions and properties of a 2-additive capacity given in the next section, we present in Section 3 how to identify a 2-additive capacity by using a linear program.

## 2    Basic Concepts

Let us denote by $N = \{1, \ldots, n\}$ a finite set of $n$ criteria and $X = X_1 \times \cdots \times X_n$ the set of actions (also called alternatives or options), where $X_1, \ldots, X_n$ represent the point of view or attributes. For all $i \in N$, the function $u_i : X_i \to \mathbb{R}$ is called a utility function. Given an element $x = (x_1, \ldots, x_n)$, we set $U(x) = (u_1(x_1), \ldots, u_n(x_n))$. For a subset $A$ of $N$ and actions $x$ and $y$, the notation $z = (x_A, y_{N-A})$ means that $z$ is defined by $z_i = x_i$ if $i \in A$, and $z_i = y_i$ otherwise. We will often write $ij$, $ijk$ instead of $\{i,j\}$ and $\{i,j,k\}$ respectively.

### 2.1    2-Additive Bi-capacities

Let us denote by $2^N := \{S \subseteq N\}$ the set of subsets of $N$ and $3^N := \{(A,B) \in 2^N \times 2^N | A \cap B = \emptyset\}$ the set of couples of subsets of $N$ with an empty intersection. We define on $3^N$ the following relation $\sqsubseteq$: for all $(A_1, A_2), (B_1, B_2) \in 3^N$

$$(A_1, A_2) \sqsubseteq (B_1, B_2) \Leftrightarrow [A_1 \subseteq B_1 \text{ and } B_2 \subseteq A_2]. \tag{1}$$

**Definition 1 (Bi-capacity [12,13]).** *A function $\nu : 3^N \to \mathbb{R}$ is a bi-capacity on $3^N$ if it satisfies:*

1. $\nu(\emptyset, \emptyset) = 0$;
2. *For all $(A_1, A_2), (B_1, B_2) \in 3^N$,*

$$[(A_1, A_2) \sqsubseteq (B_1, B_2) \Rightarrow \nu(A_1, A_2) \leq \nu(B_1, B_2)].$$

In addition, a bi-capacity $\nu : 3^N \to \mathbb{R}$ is said to be

- normalized if

$$\nu(N, \emptyset) = 1 \text{ and } \nu(\emptyset, N) = -1;$$

- additive if for all $(A_1, A_2) \in 3^N$,

$$\nu(A_1, A_2) = \sum_{i \in A_1} \nu(i, \emptyset) + \sum_{j \in A_2} \nu(\emptyset, j).$$

**Definition 2 (Möbius transform of a bi-capacity [11]).** *Let $\nu$ a bi-capacity on $3^N$. A Möbius transform of $\nu$ is a set function $m^\nu : 3^N \to \mathbb{R}$ such that for all $(A_1, A_2) \in 3^N$*

$$m^\nu(A_1, A_2) := \sum_{\substack{B_1 \subseteq A_1 \\ A_2 \subseteq B_2 \subseteq A_1{}^c}} (-1)^{|A_1 \setminus B_1| + |B_2 \setminus A_2|} \nu(B_1, B_2). \tag{2}$$

When $m^\nu$ is given, it is possible to recover the original $\nu$ by the following expression:

$$\nu(A_1, A_2) := \sum_{(B_1, B_2) \sqsubseteq (A_1, A_2)} m^\nu(B_1, B_2), \quad \forall (A_1, A_2) \in 3^N \qquad (3)$$

Fujimoto [6,8] has proposed another equivalent definition of a Möbius transform of a bi-capacities as follows:

**Definition 3 (Bipolar Möbius transform of a bi-capacity).** *Let $\nu$ a bi-capacity on $3^N$. The (bipolar) Möbius transform of $\nu$ is a set function $b^\nu : 3^N \to \mathbb{R}$ defined by*

$$b^\nu(A_1, A_2) := \sum_{\substack{B_1 \subseteq A_1 \\ B_2 \subseteq A_2}} (-1)^{|A_1 \setminus B_1| + |A_2 \setminus B_2|} \nu(B_1, B_2) \qquad (4)$$

$$= \sum_{(\emptyset, A_2) \sqsubseteq (B_1, B_2) \sqsubseteq (A_1, \emptyset)} (-1)^{|A_1 \setminus B_1| + |A_2 \setminus B_2|} \nu(B_1, B_2)$$

$\forall (A_1, A_2) \in 3^N$.

*Conversely, for any $(A_1, A_2) \in 3^N$, it holds that*

$$\nu(A_1, A_2) := \sum_{\substack{B_1 \subseteq A_1 \\ B_2 \subseteq A_2}} b^\nu(B_1, B_2). \qquad (5)$$

There is a link, given by Fujimoto and Murofushi [7],between these two definitions of a Möbius transform of a bi-capacity:

**Proposition 1.** *Let $\nu$ be a bi-capacity on $3^N$, $m^\nu$ the Möbius transform of $\nu$, and $b^\nu$ the bipolar Möbius transform of $\nu$. Then, it holds, for any $(A_1, A_2) \in 3^N$, that*

$$m^\nu(A_1, A_2) = (-1)^{|A_1{}^c \setminus A_2|} \sum_{A_1{}^c \setminus A_2 \subseteq C_2 \subseteq A_1{}^c} b^\nu(A_1, C_2) \qquad (6)$$

*and*

$$b^\nu(A_1, A_2) = (-1)^{|A_2|} \sum_{C_2 \subseteq A_1{}^c \setminus A_2} m^\nu(A_1, C_2) \qquad (7)$$

*Proof.* See [7].

If there is no confusion, we will use the notation $m$ for $m^\nu$ and $b$ for $b^\nu$.

Bi-capacities on $3^N$ generally require $3^n - 1$ parameters. In order to reduce this number, Grabisch and Labreuche [11,12,13] proposed the notion of $k$-additivity of bi-capacity as follows:

**Definition 4.** *Given a positive integer $k < n$, a bi-capacity $\nu$ is said to be k-additive iff*

1. $m^\nu(A_1, A_2) = 0$ *whenever* $|A_2{}^c| > k$;
2. *There exists* $(A_1, A_2) \in 3^N$ *such that* $|A_2{}^c| = k$ *and* $m^\nu(A_1, A_2) \neq 0$

An alternative and equivalent concept of $k$-additivity is proposed by Fujimoto et al. [8] by using bipolar Möbius transform.

**Proposition 2.** *Given a positive integer $k < n$, a bi-capacity $\nu$ is k-additive iff*

1. $b^\nu(A_1, A_2) = 0$ *whenever* $|A_1 \cup A_2| > k$;
2. *There exists* $(A_1, A_2) \in 3^N$ *such that* $|A_1 \cup A_2| = k$ *and* $b^\nu(A_1, A_2) \neq 0$

*Proof.* See [8].

To avoid a heavy notation, for a bi-capacity $\nu$, its Möbius transform $m$ and its bipolar Möbius transform $b$, we use the following shorthand for all $i, j \in N$, $i \neq j$:

- $\nu_{i|} := \nu(i, \emptyset)$, $\nu_{|j} := \nu(\emptyset, j)$, $\nu_{i|j} := \nu(i, j)$, $\nu_{ij|} := \nu(ij, \emptyset)$, $\nu_{|ij} := \nu(\emptyset, ij)$,
- $m_{i|} := m(i, \emptyset)$, $m_{|j} := m(\emptyset, j)$, $m_{i|j} := m(i, j)$, $m_{ij|} := m(ij, \emptyset)$, $m_{|ij} := m(\emptyset, ij)$,
- $b_{i|} := b(i, \emptyset)$, $b_{|j} := b(\emptyset, j)$, $b_{i|j} := b(i, j)$, $b_{ij|} := b(ij, \emptyset)$, $b_{|ij} := b(\emptyset, ij)$.

Whenever we use $i$ and $j$ together, it always means that they are different.

Using the above definitions, we propose the following properties of a 2-additive bi-capacity $\nu$ and its bipolar Möbius transform $b$:

**Proposition 3.** *1. Let $\nu$ be a 2-additive bi-capacity and $b$ its bipolar Möbius transform. For any $(A_1, A_2) \in 3^N$ we have:*

$$\nu(A_1, A_2) = \sum_{i \in A_1} b_{i|} + \sum_{j \in A_2} b_{|j} + \sum_{\substack{i \in A_1 \\ j \in A_2}} b_{i|j} + \sum_{\{i,j\} \subseteq A_1} b_{ij|} + \sum_{\{i,j\} \subseteq A_2} b_{|ij} \quad (8)$$

*2. If the coefficients $b_{i|}$, $b_{|j}$, $b_{i|j}$, $b_{ij|}$, $b_{|ij}$ are given for all $i, j \in N$, then the necessary and sufficient conditions to get a 2-additive bi-capacity generated by (8) are: for any $(A, B) \in 3^N$ and $k \in A$,*

$$b_{k|} + \sum_{j \in B} b_{k|j} + \sum_{i \in A \setminus k} b_{ik|} \geq 0 \quad (9)$$

$$b_{|k} + \sum_{j \in B} b_{j|k} + \sum_{i \in A \setminus k} b_{|ik} \leq 0 \quad (10)$$

*3. The inequalities (9) and (10) can be rewritten in terms of bi-capacity $\nu$ as follows: for any $(A, B) \in 3^N$ and $k \in A$, such that $|B| + |A| \geq 2$,*

$$\sum_{j \in B} \nu_{k|j} + \sum_{i \in A \setminus k} \nu_{ik|} \geq (|B| + |A| - 2)\nu_{k|} + \sum_{j \in B} \nu_{|j} + \sum_{i \in A \setminus k} \nu_{i|} \quad (11)$$

$$\sum_{j\in B} \nu_{j|k} + \sum_{i\in A\backslash k} \nu_{|ik} \leq (|B|+|A|-2)\nu_{|k} + \sum_{j\in B} \nu_{j|} + \sum_{i\in A\backslash k} \nu_{|i} \qquad (12)$$

*Proof.* 1. Because $\nu$ is 2-additive, the proof of the equation (8) is given by using the relation (5) between $\nu$ and $b$.

2. The proof of the second point of the proof is based on the expression of $\nu(A_1, A_2)$ given in (8) and on these equivalent monotonicity properties (which are easy to check): $\forall (A, B) \in 3^N$ and $\forall A \subseteq A'$,
   (i)  $\nu(A, B) \leq \nu(A', B) \Leftrightarrow \nu(A \backslash k, B) \leq \nu(A, B) \; \forall k \in A$;
   (ii) $\nu(B, A') \leq \nu(B, A) \Leftrightarrow \nu(B, A) \leq \nu(B, A \backslash k) \; \forall k \in A$.

3. The inequalities (11) and (12) are obtained by using the relation (5) between $\nu$ and $b$.

Hence, Proposition 3 shows that the computation of a 2-additive bi-capacity $\nu$ can be done by knowing only the values of $\nu$ on the elements $(i, \emptyset)$, $(\emptyset, i)$, $(i, j)$, $(ij, \emptyset)$, $(\emptyset, ij)$ for all $i, j \in N$ such that the inequalities (11) and (12), which correspond to the 2-additive monotonicity of a bi-capacity, are satisfied. In addition, we can add these normalized conditions:

$$\nu_{N|} = \sum_{i\in N} b_{i|} + \sum_{\{i,j\}\subseteq N} b_{ij|} = 1 \qquad (13)$$

$$\nu_{|N} = \sum_{i\in N} b_{|i} + \sum_{\{i,j\}\subseteq N} b_{|ij} = -1$$

## 2.2   Choquet Integral W.R.T. a 2-Additive Bi-capacity

**Definition 5 (Grabisch and Labreuche [12]).** *Let $\nu$ be a bi-capacity on $3^N$ and $x = (x_1, \ldots, x_n) \in \mathbb{R}^n$. The expression of Choquet of $x$ w.r.t. $\nu$ is given by*

$$\mathcal{C}_\nu(x) := \sum_{i=1}^{n} |x_{\sigma(i)}| \left[ \nu(N_{\sigma(i)} \cap N^+, N_{\sigma(i)} \cap N^-) - \nu(N_{\sigma(i+1)} \cap N^+, N_{\sigma(i+1)} \cap N^-) \right],$$
$$(14)$$

*where*

- $N^+ = \{i \in N | x_i \geq 0\}$ *and* $N^- = N \backslash N^+$;
- $N_{\sigma(i)} := \{\sigma(i), \ldots, \sigma(n)\}$ *and $\sigma$ is a permutation on $N$ such that* $|x_{\sigma(i)}| \leq |x_{\sigma(i+1)}| \leq \ldots \leq |x_{\sigma(n)}|$.

We have also the following equivalent expression of Choquet integral w.r.t. $\nu$, given by Fujimoto and Murofushi [7]:

$$\mathcal{C}_\nu(x) = \sum_{(A_1, A_2)\in 3^N} b(A_1, A_2)\left( \bigwedge_{i\in A_1} x_i^+ \wedge \bigwedge_{j\in A_2} x_j^- \right) \qquad (15)$$

where $\begin{cases} x_i^+ = x_i & \text{if } x_i > 0 \\ x_i^+ = 0 & \text{if } x_i \leq 0 \end{cases}$ and $\begin{cases} x_i^- = x_i & \text{if } x_i < 0 \\ x_i^- = 0 & \text{if } x_i \geq 0 \end{cases}$

Therefore the Choquet integral of $x$ w.r.t. a 2-additive bi-capacity $\nu$ is given by:

$$\mathcal{C}_\nu(x) = \sum_{i=1}^{n} b_{i|} \, x_i^+ + \sum_{i=1}^{n} b_{|i} \, x_i^- + \sum_{\{i,j\} \subseteq N} b_{i|j} \, (x_i^+ \wedge x_j^-) \tag{16}$$

$$+ \sum_{\{i,j\} \subseteq N} b_{ij|} \, (x_i^+ \wedge x_j^+) + \sum_{\{i,j\} \subseteq N} b_{|ij} \, (x_i^- \wedge x_j^-)$$

## 3   Elicitation of a 2-Additive Bi-capacity

### 3.1   The Set of Trinary Actions and Relations

We assume that the DM is able to identify for each criterion $i$ three reference levels:

1. A reference level $\mathbf{1}_i$ in $X_i$ which he considers as good and completely satisfying if he could obtain it on criterion $i$, even if more attractive elements could exist. This special element corresponds to the *satisficing level* in the theory of bounded rationality of Simon [16].
2. A reference level $\mathbf{0}_i$ in $X_i$ which he considers neutral on $i$. The neutral level is the absence of attractiveness and repulsiveness. The existence of this neutral level has roots in psychology [17], and is used in bipolar models [18].
3. A reference level $-\mathbf{1}_i$ in $X_i$ which he considers completely unsatisfying.

We set for convenience $u_i(\mathbf{1}_i) = 1$, $u_i(\mathbf{0}_i) = 0$ and $u_i(-\mathbf{1}_i) = -1$.

We call a *trinary action or trinary alternative*, an element of the set

$$\mathcal{T} = \{(\mathbf{1}_\emptyset, -\mathbf{1}_\emptyset), (\mathbf{1}_i, -\mathbf{1}_\emptyset), (\mathbf{1}_\emptyset, -\mathbf{1}_j), (\mathbf{1}_i, -\mathbf{1}_j), (\mathbf{1}_{ij}, -\mathbf{1}_\emptyset), (\mathbf{1}_\emptyset, -\mathbf{1}_{ij}), i, j \in N\} \subseteq X$$

where

- $(\mathbf{1}_\emptyset, -\mathbf{1}_\emptyset) =: a_{0|0}$ is an action considered neutral on all criteria.
- $(\mathbf{1}_i, -\mathbf{1}_\emptyset) =: a_{i|}$ is an action considered satisfactory on criterion $i$ and neutral on the other criteria.
- $(\mathbf{1}_\emptyset, -\mathbf{1}_j) =: a_{|j}$ is an action considered unsatisfactory on criterion $j$ and neutral on the other criteria.
- $(\mathbf{1}_i, -\mathbf{1}_j) =: a_{i|j}$ is an action considered satisfactory on criteria $i$, unsatisfactory on $j$ and neutral on the other criteria.
- $(\mathbf{1}_{ij}, -\mathbf{1}_\emptyset) := a_{ij|}$ is an action considered satisfactory on criteria $i$ and $j$ and neutral on the other criteria.
- $(\mathbf{1}_\emptyset, -\mathbf{1}_{ij}) := a_{|ij}$ is an action considered unsatisfactory on criteria $i$ and $j$ and neutral on the other criteria.

The number of binary actions is $1 + n + \dfrac{n \times (n-1)}{2} = 1 + \dfrac{n \times (n+1)}{2}$. On the other hand, the number of trinary actions is: $1 + 2 \times n + \dfrac{2 \times n \times (n-1)}{2} = 1 + 2 \times n^2$. Roughly speaking there are 4 times as much trinary actions for 2 additive bi-capacities compare to the 2 additive capacities.

Using the expression (16) of the Choquet integral w.r.t. a 2-additive bi-capacity $\nu$, we get the following consequences:

$C_\nu(U(a_{0|0})) = 0$, $C_\nu(U(a_{i|})) = \nu_{i|}$,
$C_\nu(U(a_{|j})) = \nu_{|j}$, $C_\nu(U(a_{i|j})) = \nu_{i|j}$,
$C_\nu(U(a_{ij|})) = \nu_{ij|}$ and $C_\nu(U(a_{|ij})) = \nu_{|ij}$.

To entirely determine the 2-additive bi-capacity, as shown by Proposition 3, it should be sufficient to get some preferential information from the DM only on trinary actions. We assume that, given two trinary actions $x$ and $y$ the DM is able to judge the difference of attractiveness between $x$ and $y$ when he strictly prefers $x$ to $y$. Like in MACBETH [2,4], 2-additive MACBETH [15] and GRIP [5], MCDA methodologies, the difference of attractiveness[1] will be provided under the form of semantic categories $d_s$, $s = 1, \ldots, q$ defined so that, if $s < t$, any difference of attractiveness in the class $d_s$ is smaller than any difference of attractiveness in the class $d_t$. If there is no ambiguity, a category $d_s$ will be simply designated by $s$.

Under these hypotheses, the preferences given by the DM is expressed by the following relations:

- $P = \{(x, y) \in \mathcal{T} \times \mathcal{T} :$ the DM strictly prefers $x$ to $y\}$,
- $I = \{(x, y) \in \mathcal{T} \times \mathcal{T} :$ the DM is indifferent between $x$ and $y\}$,
- For the semantic categories "$d_s$", "$d_t$", $s, t \in \{1, ..., q\}$, $s \le t$, $P_{st} = \{(x, y) \in P$ such that the DM judges the difference of attractiveness between $x$ and $y$ as belonging from the class "$d_s$" to the class "$d_t$" $\}$. When $s < t$, $P_{st}$ expresses some hesitation.

We will suppose always $P$ nonempty ("non-trivial axiom") and use the notation $\mathbb{N}_{st} = \{s, s+1, \ldots, t-1, t\}$ for $s \le t$.

*Remark 1.* In this paper, the relation $P \cup I$ is not necessarily complete.

**Definition 6.** *1. The ordinal information on $\mathcal{T}$ is the structure $\{P, I\}$.*
*2. The cardinal information on $\mathcal{T}$ is the structure $\{P, I, \{P_{st}\}_{s \le t}\}$.*

### 3.2    The Representation and the Linear Program to Solve

A cardinal information $\{P, I, \{P_{st}\}_{s \le t}\}$ is said to be *representable by a Choquet integral w.r.t. a 2-additive bi-capacity* $\nu : 3^N \to \mathbb{R}$ if the following conditions are satisfied: $\forall x, y, z, w \in \mathcal{T}$, $\forall s, t, u, v \in \{1, \ldots, q\}$ such that $u \le v < s \le t$,

---

[1] MACBETH approach uses the following six semantic categories: $d_1$ = very weak, $d_2$ = weak, $d_3$ = moderate, $d_4$ = strong, $d_5$ = very strong, $d_6$ = extreme.

$$x \ I \ y \Rightarrow C_\nu(U(x)) = C_\nu(U(y)), \tag{17}$$

$$x \ P \ y \Rightarrow C_\nu(U(x)) > C_\nu(U(y)), \tag{18}$$

$$\left.\begin{array}{l}(x,y) \in P_{st} \\ (z,w) \in P_{uv}\end{array}\right\} \Rightarrow C_\nu(U(x)) - C_\nu(U(y)) > C_\nu(U(z)) - C_\nu(U(w)) \tag{19}$$

De Corte [2] proved that the previous conditions are equivalent to the existence of $q$ thresholds $\sigma_1, \ldots, \sigma_q$ such that:

$$\forall(x,y) \in I : C_\nu(U(x)) = C_\nu(U(y)), \tag{20}$$

$$\forall s,t \in \mathbb{N}_{1q}, s \leq t, \forall(x,y) \in P_{st} : \sigma_s < C_\nu(U(x)) - C_\nu(U(y)), \tag{21}$$

$$\forall s,t \in \mathbb{N}_{1(q-1)}, s \leq t, \forall(x,y) \in P_{st} : C_\nu(U(x)) - C_\nu(U(y)) < \sigma_{t+1}, \tag{22}$$

$$0 < \sigma_1 < \sigma_2 < \cdots < \sigma_q \tag{23}$$

In order to identify a 2-additive bi-capacity $\nu$ such that a cardinal information $\{P, I, \{P_{st}\}_{s \leq t}\}$ on $\mathcal{T}$ is representable by $C_\nu$, we use the following linear program (PL) where the variables to determine are $\nu(i, \emptyset)$, $\nu(\emptyset, i)$, $\nu(i, j)$, $\nu(ij, \emptyset)$ and $\nu(\emptyset, ij)$ for all $i, j \in N$:

$$\min C_\nu(U(x_0))$$

$$C_\nu(U(x)) = C_\nu(U(y)), \forall(x,y) \in I \tag{24}$$

$$\sigma_i + d_{\min} \leq C_\nu(U(x)) - C_\nu(U(y)), \forall(x,y) \in P_{ij}, \forall i,j \in \mathbb{N}_{1q}, \ i \leq j \tag{25}$$

$$C_\nu(U(x)) - C_\nu(U(y)) \leq \sigma_{j+1} - d_{\min}, \forall(x,y) \in P_{ij}, \forall i,j \in \mathbb{N}_{1(q-1)}, i \leq j \tag{26}$$

$$d_{\min} \leq \sigma_1 \tag{27}$$

$$\sigma_{i-1} + d_{\min} \leq \sigma_i, \forall i \in \{2, \ldots, q\} \tag{28}$$

$$\forall(A,B) \in 3^N, \forall k \in A \text{ such that } (|A| + |B| - 2) \geq 0$$

$$\sum_{j \in B} \nu_{k|j} + \sum_{i \in A \setminus k} \nu_{ik|} \geq (|B| + |A| - 2)\nu_{k|} + \sum_{j \in B} \nu_{|j} + \sum_{i \in A \setminus k} \nu_{i|} \tag{29}$$

$$\sum_{j \in B} \nu_{j|k} + \sum_{i \in A \setminus k} \nu_{|ik} \leq (|B| + |A| - 2)\nu_{|k} + \sum_{j \in B} \nu_{j|} + \sum_{i \in A \setminus k} \nu_{|i} \tag{30}$$

where $x_0$ is an alternative of $\mathcal{T}$ arbitrarily chosen, and $d_{\min}$ an arbitrary strictly positive constant. The variables $\sigma_i$ in this linear program are thresholds of categories.

**Example 1.** $N = \{1, 2, 3\}$, $q = 6$,
$3^N = \{(\emptyset, \emptyset), (\emptyset, N), (N, \emptyset), (1, \emptyset), (2, \emptyset), (3, \emptyset), (\emptyset, 1), (\emptyset, 2), (\emptyset, 3),$
$(1, 2), (1, 3), (2, 3), (2, 1), (3, 1), (3, 2), (12, \emptyset), (23, \emptyset), (13, \emptyset), (\emptyset, 12), (\emptyset, 23),$
$(\emptyset, 13), (12, 3), (23, 1), (3, 12), (2, 13), (1, 23), (13, 2)\}$

$\mathcal{T} = \{a_{0,0}; a_{1|}; a_{2|}; a_{3|}; a_{|1}; a_{|2}; a_{|3}; a_{1|2}; a_{2|1}; a_{1|3}; a_{3|1}; a_{3|2}; a_{2|3}; a_{13|}; a_{12|};$
$a_{23|}; a_{|12}; a_{|23}; a_{|13}\}$

*Let us suppose that the DM gives the following preferences:* $I = \{(a_{1|3}; a_{3|1}); (a_{2|}, a_{|3})\}$; $P_3 = \{(a_{23|}, a_{|1})\}$; $P_{24} = \{(a_{1|}, a_{|3})\}$;

*To look for a 2-additive capacity such that the cardinal information* $\{I, P_3, P_{24}\}$ *is representable by* $C_\mu$, *we solve the following linear program:*

$\min C_\nu(U(a_{0,0}))$

$C_\nu(U(a_{1|3})) - C_\nu(U(a_{3|1})) = 0 \Leftrightarrow \nu(1,3) - \nu(3,1) = 0$

$C_\nu(U(a_{2|})) - C_\nu(U(a_{|3})) = 0 \Leftrightarrow \nu(2,\emptyset) - \nu(\emptyset,3) = 0$

$\sigma_3 + 0.01 \leq C_\nu(U(a_{23|})) - C_\nu(U(a_{|1})) \Leftrightarrow \sigma_3 + 0.01 \leq \nu(23,\emptyset) - \nu(\emptyset,1)$

$C_\nu(U(a_{23|})) - C_\nu(U(a_{|1})) \leq \sigma_4 - 0.01 \Leftrightarrow \nu(23,\emptyset) - \nu(\emptyset,1) \leq \sigma_4 - 0.01$

$\sigma_2 + 0.01 \leq C_\nu(U(a_{1|})) - C_\nu(U(a_{|3})) \Leftrightarrow \sigma_2 + 0.01 \leq \nu(1,\emptyset) - \nu(\emptyset,3)$

$C_\nu(U(a_{1|})) - C_\nu(U(a_{|3})) \leq \sigma_5 - 0.01 \Leftrightarrow \nu(1,\emptyset) - \nu(\emptyset,3) \leq \sigma_5 - 0.01$

$0.01 \leq \sigma_1; \sigma_{i-1} + 0.01 \leq \sigma_i, \forall i \in \{2, \ldots, 6\}$

$\nu(1,2) \geq \nu(\emptyset,2); \nu(1,3) \geq \nu(\emptyset,3);$

$\nu(2,3) \geq \nu(\emptyset,3); \nu(2,1) \geq \nu(\emptyset,1); \nu(3,2) \geq \nu(\emptyset,2); \nu(3,1) \geq \nu(\emptyset,1);$

$\nu(1,2) \leq \nu(1,\emptyset); \nu(2,1) \leq \nu(2,\emptyset); \nu(1,3) \leq \nu(1,\emptyset); \nu(3,1) \leq \nu(3,\emptyset);$

$\nu(3,2) \leq \nu(3,\emptyset); \nu(2,3) \leq \nu(2,\emptyset); \nu(\emptyset,12) \leq \nu(\emptyset,1); \nu(\emptyset,12) \leq \nu(\emptyset,2);$

$\nu(\emptyset,13) \leq \nu(\emptyset,1); \nu(\emptyset,13) \leq \nu(\emptyset,3); \nu(\emptyset,23) \leq \nu(\emptyset,2); \nu(\emptyset,23) \leq \nu(\emptyset,3);$

$\nu(12,\emptyset) \geq \nu(1,\emptyset); \nu(12,\emptyset) \geq \nu(2,\emptyset); \nu(13,\emptyset) \geq \nu(1,\emptyset); \nu(13,\emptyset) \geq \nu(3,\emptyset);$

$\nu(23,\emptyset) \geq \nu(2,\emptyset); \nu(23,\emptyset) \geq \nu(3,\emptyset); \nu(\emptyset,1) + \nu(\emptyset,2) \leq 0; \nu(1,\emptyset) + \nu(2,\emptyset) \geq 0;$

$\nu(\emptyset,1) + \nu(\emptyset,3) \leq 0; \nu(1,\emptyset) + \nu(3,\emptyset) \geq 0; \nu(\emptyset,2) + \nu(\emptyset,3) \leq 0; \nu(2,\emptyset) + \nu(3,\emptyset) \geq 0;$

$\nu(1,2) + \nu(1,3) \geq \nu(1,\emptyset) + \nu(\emptyset,2) + \nu(\emptyset,3); \nu(2,1) + \nu(2,3) \geq \nu(2,\emptyset) + \nu(\emptyset,1) + \nu(\emptyset,3);$

$\nu(3,1) + \nu(3,2) \geq \nu(3,\emptyset) + \nu(\emptyset,1) + \nu(\emptyset,2); \nu(2,1) + \nu(2,3) \geq \nu(2,\emptyset) + \nu(\emptyset,1) + \nu(\emptyset,3);$

$\nu(2,1) + \nu(3,1) \leq \nu(\emptyset,1) + \nu(2,\emptyset) + \nu(3,\emptyset); \nu(1,2) + \nu(3,2) \leq \nu(\emptyset,2) + \nu(1,\emptyset) + \nu(3,\emptyset);$

$\nu(2,3) + \nu(1,3) \leq \nu(\emptyset,3) + \nu(1,\emptyset) + \nu(2,\emptyset); \nu(2,3) + \nu(1,3) \leq \nu(\emptyset,3) + \nu(1,\emptyset) + \nu(2,\emptyset);$

$\nu(1,3) + \nu(12,\emptyset) \geq \nu(1,\emptyset) + \nu(\emptyset,3) + \nu(2,\emptyset); \nu(2,3) + \nu(12,\emptyset) \geq \nu(2,\emptyset) + \nu(\emptyset,3) + \nu(1,\emptyset);$

$\nu(1,2) + \nu(13,\emptyset) \geq \nu(1,\emptyset) + \nu(\emptyset,2) + \nu(3,\emptyset); \nu(3,2) + \nu(13,\emptyset) \geq \nu(3,\emptyset) + \nu(\emptyset,2) + \nu(1,\emptyset);$

$\nu(2,1) + \nu(23,\emptyset) \geq \nu(2,\emptyset) + \nu(\emptyset,1) + \nu(3,\emptyset); \nu(3,1) + \nu(23,\emptyset) \geq \nu(3,\emptyset) + \nu(\emptyset,1) + \nu(2,\emptyset);$

$\nu(3,1) + \nu(\emptyset,12) \leq \nu(\emptyset,1) + \nu(3,\emptyset) + \nu(\emptyset,2); \nu(3,2) + \nu(\emptyset,12) \leq \nu(\emptyset,2) + \nu(3,\emptyset) + \nu(\emptyset,1);$

$\nu(2,1) + \nu(\emptyset,13) \leq \nu(\emptyset,1) + \nu(2,\emptyset) + \nu(\emptyset,3); \nu(2,3) + \nu(\emptyset,13) \leq \nu(\emptyset,3) + \nu(2,\emptyset) + \nu(\emptyset,1);$

$\nu(1,2) + \nu(\emptyset,23) \leq \nu(\emptyset,2) + \nu(1,\emptyset) + \nu(\emptyset,3); \nu(1,3) + \nu(\emptyset,23) \leq \nu(\emptyset,3) + \nu(1,\emptyset) + \nu(\emptyset,2);$

If (PL) is feasible, then a 2-additive bi-capacity is computed by using the equation (8) in Proposition 3. Of course it can exist several bi-capacities compatible with the cardinal information provided by the DM. To compute a robust bi-capacity, one can use the approach of Angilella et al. [1] based on the concept of possible and necessary relation. To deal with inconsistencies when (PL) is infeasible, we can use the interactive algorithm of Mayag et al. [14] which generates recommendations for the DM to retrieve consistent cardinal information. This simple and intuitive algorithm identifies the minimal number of constraints we can relax in this infeasible linear problem. In order to retrieve consistent information, the preferences associated to these constraints are relaxed by an augmentation or diminution of categories.

Because the identification of a 2-additive bi-capacity is an interesting problem to investigate, we will look for in the future works necessary and sufficient conditions such that a cardinal information is representable by a Choquet integral w.r.t. a 2-additive bi-capacity.

# References

1. Angilella, S., Greco, S., Matarazzo, B.: Non-additive robust ordinal regression: A multiple criteria decision model based on the Choquet integral. European Journal of Operational Research 41(1), 277–288 (2009)
2. Bana e Costa, C.A., De Corte, J.-M., Vansnick, J.-C.: On the mathematical foundations of MACBETH. In: Figueira, J., Greco, S., Ehrgott, M. (eds.) Multiple Criteria Decision Analysis: State of the Art Surveys, pp. 409–437. Springer, Heidelberg (2005)
3. Choquet, G.: Theory of capacities. Annales de l'Institut Fourier 5, 131–295 (1953)
4. De Corte, J.M.: Un logiciel d'Exploitation d'Information Préférentielles pour l'Aide à la Décision. Bases Mathématiques et Algorithmiques. PhD thesis, University of Mons-Hainaut, Mons (2002)
5. Figueira, J.R., Greco, S., Slowinski, R.: Building a set of additive value functions representing a reference preorder and intensities of preference: Grip method. European Journal of Operational Research 195(2), 460–486 (2009)
6. Fujimoto, K.: New characterizations of $k$-additivity and $k$-monotonicity of bi-capacities. In: SCIS-ISIS 2004, 2nd Int. Conf. on Soft Computing and Intelligent Systems and 5th Int. Symp. on Advanced Intelligent Systems, Yokohama, Japan (September 2004)
7. Fujimoto, K., Murofushi, T.: Some characterizations of $k$-monotonicity through the bipolar möbius transform in bi-capacities. J. of Advanced Computational Intelligence and Intelligent Informatics 9(5), 484–495 (2005)
8. Fujimoto, K., Murofushi, T., Sugeno, M.: $k$-additivity and $C$-decomposability of bi-capacities and its integral. Fuzzy Sets and Systems 158, 1698–1712 (2007)
9. Grabisch, M.: $k$-order additive discrete fuzzy measures and their representation. Fuzzy Sets and Systems 92, 167–189 (1997)
10. Grabisch, M., Labreuche, C.: Fuzzy measures and integrals in MCDA. In: Figueira, J., Greco, S., Ehrgott, M. (eds.) Multiple Criteria Decision Analysis: State of the Art Surveys, pp. 565–608. Springer (2005)
11. Grabisch, M., Labreuche, C.: Bi-capacities. Part I: definition, Möbius transform and interaction. Fuzzy Sets and Systems 151, 211–236 (2005)
12. Grabisch, M., Labreuche, C.: Bi-capacities. Part II: the Choquet integral. Fuzzy Sets and Systems 151, 237–259 (2005)
13. Grabisch, M., Labreuche, C.: A decade of application of the Choquet and Sugeno integrals in multi-criteria decision aid. 4OR 6, 1–44 (2008)
14. Mayag, B., Grabisch, M., Labreuche, C.: An Interactive Algorithm to Deal with Inconsistencies in the Representation of Cardinal Information. In: Hüllermeier, E., Kruse, R., Hoffmann, F. (eds.) IPMU 2010. CCIS, vol. 80, pp. 148–157. Springer, Heidelberg (2010)
15. Mayag, B., Grabisch, M., Labreuche, C.: A characterization of the 2-additive Choquet integral through cardinal information. Fuzzy Sets and Systems 184(1), 84–105 (2011)
16. Simon, H.: Rational choice and the structure of the environment. Psychological Review 63(2), 129–138 (1956)
17. Slovic, P., Finucane, M., Peters, E., MacGregor, D.G.: The affect heuristic. In: Gilovitch, T., Griffin, D., Kahneman, D. (eds.) Heuristics and Biases: The Psychology of Intuitive Judgment, pp. 397–420. Cambridge University Press (2002)
18. Tversky, A., Kahneman, D.: Advances in prospect theory: cumulative representation of uncertainty. J. of Risk and Uncertainty 5, 297–323 (1992)

# SMAA-Choquet: Stochastic Multicriteria Acceptability Analysis for the Choquet Integral

Silvia Angilella, Salvatore Corrente, and Salvatore Greco

Department of Economics and Business, University of Catania,
Corso Italia 55, I-95129 Catania, Italy
{angisil,salvatore.corrente,salgreco}@unict.it

**Abstract.** In this paper, we extend the Choquet integral decision model in the same spirit of the Stochastic Multicriteria Acceptability Analysis (SMAA) method that takes into account a probability distribution over the preference parameters of multiple criteria decision methods. In order to enrich the set of parameters (the capacities) compatible with the DM's preference information on the importance of criteria and interaction between couples of criteria, we put together Choquet integral with SMAA. The sampling of the compatible preference parameters (the capacities) is obtained by a Hit-and-Run procedure. Finally, we evaluate a set of capacities contributing to the evaluation of the rank acceptability indices and of the central preference parameters as done in the SMAA methods.

**Keywords:** Multiple criteria decision analysis, SMAA, Choquet integral.

## 1 Introduction

In a multiple criteria decision problem (see [7] for a recent state of the art), an alternative $a_j$, belonging to a finite set of $m$ alternatives $A = \{a_1, a_2, \ldots, a_m\}$, is evaluated on the basis of a consistent family of $n$ criteria $G = \{g_1, g_2, \ldots, g_n\}$. In our approach we make the assumption that each criterion $g_i \colon A \to \mathbb{R}$ is an interval scale of measurement. From here on, we will use the terms criterion $g_i$ or criterion $i$ interchangeably ($i = 1, 2, \ldots, n$). Without loss of generality, we assume that all the criteria have to be maximized.

We define a marginal weak preference relation as follows:

$a_r$ is at least as good as $a_s$ with respect to criterion $i \iff g_i(a_r) \geq g_i(a_s)$.

The purpose of Multi-Attribute Utility Theory (MAUT) [13] is to represent the preferences of a Decision Maker (DM) on a set of alternatives $A$ by an overall value function $U \colon \mathbb{R}^n \to \mathbb{R}$ with $U(g_1(a_r), \ldots, g_n(a_r)) = U(a_r)$:

- $a_r$ is indifferent to $a_s \iff U(a_r) = U(a_s)$,
- $a_r$ is preferred to $a_s \iff U(a_r) > U(a_s)$.

S. Greco et al. (Eds.): IPMU 2012, Part IV, CCIS 300, pp. 248–257, 2012.

The principal aggregation model of value function is the multiple attribute additive utility [13]:

$$U(a_j) = u_1(g_1(a_j)) + u_2(g_2(a_j)) + \ldots + u_n(g_n(a_j)) \text{ with } a_j \in A,$$

where $u_i$ are non-decreasing marginal value functions for $i = 1, 2, \ldots, n$.

As it is well-known in literature, the underlying assumption of the preference independence of the multiple attribute additive utility is unrealistic since it does not permit to represent interaction between the criteria under consideration. In a decision problem we, usually, distinguish between positive and negative interaction among criteria, representing synergy and redundancy among criteria respectively. In particular, two criteria are synergic (redundant) when the comprehensive importance of these two criteria is greater (smaller) than the importance of the two criteria considered separately.

Within Multiple Criteria Decision Analysis (MCDA), the interaction of criteria has been considered in a decision model based upon a non-additive integral, *viz.* the Choquet integral [6] (see [9] for a comprehensive survey on the use of non-additive integrals in MCDA).

One of the main drawbacks of the Choquet integral decision model is the elicitation of its parameters representing the importance and interaction between criteria.

In literature, many multicriteria disaggregation procedures have been proposed to infer such parameters from the DM (see for example, [16] and [1]). Recently, an approach based on the determination of necessary and possible preference relations within the so-called *Robust Ordinal Regression* has been extended to the Choquet integral decision model (see [2]).

The principal aim of the paper is to include eventual DM's uncertain preference information on the importance and interaction among criteria.

In this direction, we propose an extension of the Stochastic Multiobjective Acceptability Analysis (SMAA) [14,15] to the Choquet integral decision model.

The paper is organized as follows. In Section 2, we present the basic concepts relative to interaction between criteria and to the Choquet integral. In Section 3, we briefly describe the SMAA methods. An extension of the SMAA method to the Choquet integral decision model is introduced in Section 4 and illustrated by a didactic example in Section 5. Some conclusions and future directions of research are presented in Section 6.

## 2   The Choquet Integral Decision Model

Let $2^G$ be the power set of $G$ (*i.e.* the set of all subsets of $G$); a fuzzy measure (capacity) on $G$ is defined as a set function $\mu : 2^G \to [0,1]$ satisfying the following properties:

**1a)** $\mu(\emptyset) = 0$ and $\mu(G) = 1$ (boundary conditions),

**2a)** $\forall T \subseteq R \subseteq G,\ \mu(T) \leq \mu(R)$ (monotonicity condition).

A fuzzy measure is said to be additive if $\mu(T \cup R) = \mu(T) + \mu(R)$, for any $T, R \subseteq G$ such that $T \cap R = \emptyset$. An additive fuzzy measure is determined uniquely by $\mu(\{1\}), \mu(\{2\}) \ldots, \mu(\{n\})$. In fact, in this case, $\forall T \subseteq G$, $\mu(T) = \sum_{i \in T} \mu(\{i\})$. In the other cases, we have to define a value $\mu(T)$ for every subset $T$ of $G$, obtaining $2^{|G|}$ coefficients values. Therefore, we have to calculate the values of $2^{|G|} - 2$ coefficients, since we know that $\mu(\emptyset) = 0$ and $\mu(G) = 1$.

The Möbius representation of the fuzzy measure $\mu$ (see [19]) is defined by the function $a : 2^G \to \mathbb{R}$ (see [20]) such that:

$$\mu(R) = \sum_{T \subseteq R} a(T).$$

Let us observe that if $R$ is a singleton, i.e. $R = \{i\}$ with $i = 1, \cdots, n$ then $\mu(\{i\}) = a(\{i\})$. If $R$ is a couple (non-ordered pair) of criteria, i.e. $R = \{i, j\}$, then $\mu(\{i, j\}) = a(\{i\}) + a(\{j\}) + a(\{i, j\})$.

In general, the Möbius representation $a(R)$ is obtained by $\mu(R)$ in the following way:

$$a(R) = \sum_{T \subseteq R} (-1)^{|R-T|} \mu(T).$$

In terms of Möbius representation (see [5]), properties 1a) and 2a) are, respectively, formulated as:

1b) $a(\emptyset) = 0$, $\displaystyle\sum_{T \subseteq G} a(T) = 1$,

2b) $\forall R \subseteq G$, $\displaystyle\sum_{T \subseteq R} a(T) \geq 0$.

Let us observe that in MCDA, the importance of any criterion $g_i \in G$ should be evaluated considering all its global effects in the decision problem at hand; these effects can be "decomposed" from both theoretical and operational points of view in effects of $g_i$ as single, and in combination with all other criteria. Therefore, a criterion $i \in G$ is important with respect to a fuzzy measure $\mu$ not only when it is considered alone, i.e. for the value $\mu(\{i\})$ in itself, but also when it interacts with other criteria from $G$, i.e. for every value $\mu(T \cup \{i\})$, $T \subseteq G \setminus \{i\}$.

Given $x \in A$ and $\mu$ being a fuzzy measure on $G$, then the Choquet integral [6] is defined by:

$$C_\mu(x) = \sum_{i=1}^{n} \left[ \left( g_{(i)}(x) \right) - \left( g_{(i-1)}(x) \right) \right] \mu(A_i), \tag{1}$$

where $_{(.)}$ stands for a permutation of the indices of criteria such that:
$g_{(1)}(x) \leq g_{(2)}(x) \leq \cdots \leq g_{(n)}(x)$, with $A_i = \{(i), \ldots, (n)\}$, $i = 1, \ldots, n$, and $g_{(0)} = 0$.

The Choquet integral can be redefined in terms of the Möbius representation [8], without reordering the criteria, as:

$$C_\mu(x) = \sum_{T \subseteq G} a(T) \min_{i \in T} g_i(x). \tag{2}$$

One of the main drawbacks of the Choquet integral is the necessity to elicitate and give an adequate interpretation of $2^{|G|} - 2$ parameters. In order to reduce the number of parameters to be computed and to eliminate a too strict description of the interactions among criteria, which is not realistic in many applications, the concept of fuzzy $k$-additive measure has been considered [10].

A *fuzzy measure* is called $k$-*additive* if $a(T) = 0$ with $T \subseteq G$, when $|T| > k$. We observe that a 1-additive measure is the common additive fuzzy measure. In many real decision problems, it suffices to consider 2-additive measures. In this case, positive and negative interactions between couples of criteria are modeled without considering the interaction among triples, quadruplets and generally $n$-tuples, (with $n > 2$) of criteria. From the point of view of MCDA, the use of 2-additive measures is justified by observing that the information on the importance of the single criteria and the interactions between couples of criteria are noteworthy. Moreover, it could be not easy or not straightforward for the DM to provide information on the interactions among three or more criteria during the decision procedure. From a computational point of view, the interest in the 2-additive measures lies in the fact that any decision model needs to evaluate a number $n + \binom{n}{2}$ of parameters (in terms of Möbius representation, a value $a(\{i\})$ for every criterion $i$ and a value $a(\{i,j\})$ for every couple of distinct criteria $\{i,j\}$.) With respect to a 2-additive fuzzy measure, the inverse transformation to obtain the fuzzy measure $\mu(R)$ from the Möbius representation is defined as:

$$\mu(R) = \sum_{i \in R} a(\{i\}) + \sum_{\{i,j\} \subseteq R} a(\{i,j\}), \ \forall R \subseteq G. \tag{3}$$

With regard to 2-additive measures, properties **1b)** and **2b)** have, respectively, the following formulations:

**1c)** $a(\emptyset) = 0, \ \sum_{i \in G} a(\{i\}) + \sum_{\{i,j\} \subseteq G} a(\{i,j\}) = 1,$

**2c)** $a(\{i\}) \geq 0, \ \forall i \in G, a(\{i\}) + \sum_{j \in T} a(\{i,j\}) \geq 0, \forall i \in G \text{ and } \forall T \subseteq G \setminus \{i\}.$

In this case, the representation of the Choquet integral of $x \in A$ is given by:

$$C_\mu(x) = \sum_{\{i\} \subseteq G} a(\{i\})(g_i(x)) + \sum_{\{i,j\} \subseteq G} a(\{i,j\}) \min\{g_i(x), g_j(x)\}. \tag{4}$$

Finally, we recall the definitions of the importance and interaction indices for a couple of criteria.

The Shapley value [21] expressing the importance of criterion $i \in G$, is given by:

$$\varphi(\{i\}) = a(\{i\}) + \sum_{j \in G \setminus \{i\}} \frac{a(\{i,j\})}{2}, \quad i \in G, \tag{5}$$

The *interaction index* [17] expressing the sign and the magnitude of the sinergy in a couple of criteria $\{i,j\} \subseteq G$, in case of a 2-additive capacity $\mu$, is given by:

$$\varphi(\{i,j\}) = a(\{i,j\}). \tag{6}$$

## 3   SMAA

A utility function gives a value to an alternative in order to represent its degree of desirability with respect to the decision problem under consideration; in its easiest form

$$u(a_j, w) = \sum_{i=1}^{n} w_i g_i(a_j)$$

this function depends on two sets of parameters: the set $W$ of weight vectors relative to the set of criteria $G = \{g_1, g_2, \ldots, g_n\}$ and the set of evaluations $g_i(a_j)$ of alternative $a_j$ with respect to the set of the considered criteria $g_i \in G$. In order to find a vector of weights of the model, in literature two different techniques are used: direct and indirect. The direct technique consists of asking the DM to provide directly all these parameters; the indirect technique consists of asking the DM a set of information from which a set of parameters of the model can be elicited. In this context two situations can occur:

- the DM can not provide or does not want to provide this information,
- different DMs can provide different sets of parameters.

Stochastic Multiobjective Acceptability Analysis (SMAA) [14,15] is a multicriteria decision support method taking into account this uncertainty or lack of information. These methods are based on exploring the set $W$ of weight vectors and the space of alternatives' evaluations in order to state recommendation regarding a possible ranking obtained by the considered alternatives. For each weight vector $w \in W$, and for each set of alternatives' evaluations $\xi \in X$, where $X$ is the set of all vectors of possible evaluations with respect to considered criteria, SMAA computes the rank of an alternative $a_j$:

$$rank(j, \xi, w) = 1 + \sum_{k \neq j} \rho\left(u(\xi_k, w) > u(\xi_j, w)\right)$$

where $\rho(false) = 0$ and $\rho(true) = 1$;

Then, for each alternative $a_j$, for each alternatives' evaluations $\xi \in X$ and for each rank $r$, SMAA computes the set of weights of criteria for which alternative $a_j$ assumes rank $r$:

$$W_j^r(\xi) = \{w \in W : rank(j, \xi, w) = r\}.$$

Imprecision and uncertainty are represented in SMAA as probability distributions: one $f_W$ regarding weights of the set $W$ and one $f_X$ regarding evaluations of the set $X$.

The SMAA methodology is mainly based on the computation of three indices:

- the rank acceptability index:

$$b_j^r = \int_{\xi \in X} f_X(\xi) \int_{w \in W_j^r(\xi)} f_W(w) \, dw \, d\xi$$

measuring for each alternative $a_j$ and for each rank $r$ the variety of different DM's preferences information giving to $a_j$ the rank $r$. $b_j^r$ is a real number bounded between 0 and 1; obviously, an alternative presenting large acceptability index for the best ranks will be preferred to an alternative having lower acceptability index for the same best ranks;

- the central weight vector:

$$w_j^c = \frac{1}{b_j^1} \int_{\xi \in X} f_X(\xi) \int_{w \in W_j^1(\xi)} f_W(w) w \, dw d\xi$$

describing the middle preferences of the DMs giving to $a_j$ the best position;

- the confidence factor:

$$p_j^c = \int_{\xi \in X : u(\xi_j, w_j^c) \geq u(\xi_k, w_j^c) \atop \forall k=1,\dots,m} f_X(\xi) \, d\xi$$

defined as the probability of an alternative to be the preferred one with the preferences expressed by its central weight vector.

From a computational point of view, the considered indices are evaluated by the multidimensional integrals approximated by using the Monte Carlo method.

All these sets of indices are considered simultaneously in order to help the DM to choose the better solution of the decision problem under consideration.

The first paper on SMAA [14], appeared in 1998, is a generalization to the $n$-dimensional case of two works of Bana and Costa [3,4] providing an acceptability index only for the first rank; that is it calculates which weights configurations give to each alternative the best rank; its generalization is SMAA 2 [15] in which for each alternative it is computed not only the acceptability index corresponding to the best rank, but also the acceptability indices for all the other possible ranks. For a detailed survey on SMAA methods see [23].

# 4 An Extension of the **SMAA** Method to the Choquet Integral Decision Model

As explained in Section 2, adopting the Choquet integral in terms of Möbius representation with a 2-additive measure as utility value of every alternative $a_j$, we need to estimate $n + \binom{n}{2}$ parameters (the Möbius measures).

Following a multicriteria disaggregation paradigm, preference information about importance and interaction of criteria given by the DM can be represented by the following system of linear constraints on $G$, denoted by $E^{DM}$:

$$\left.\begin{cases} \varphi(\{g_i\}) > \varphi(\{g_j\}), & \text{if criterion } i \text{ is more important than criterion } j, \\ \varphi(\{g_i, g_j\}) > 0, & \text{if criteria } i \text{ and } j \text{ are synergic with } i, j \in G, \\ \varphi(\{g_i, g_j\}) < 0, & \text{if criteria } i \text{ and } j \text{ are redundant with } i, j \in G, \\[2mm] a(\{\emptyset\}) = 0, \displaystyle\sum_{g_i \in G} a(\{g_i\}) + \sum_{\{g_i, g_j\} \subseteq G} a(\{g_i, g_j\}) = 1, \\ a(\{g_i\}) \geq 0, \ \forall g_i \in G, a(\{g_i\}) + \displaystyle\sum_{g_j \in T} a(\{g_i, g_j\}) \geq 0, \forall g_i \in G \text{ and } \forall T \subseteq G \setminus \{g_i\}, \end{cases}\right\} (*)$$

where $(*)$ denotes the set of boundary and monotonicity constraints on the Möbius measures.

In order to explore the preferences induced by the Choquet integral within the set of compatible parameters, we integrate Choquet integral with **SMAA**. The sampling of compatible preference parameters (Möbius measures) is obtained by a Hit-and-Run procedure [22] on the set of constraints $E^{DM}$ (see also [24] for a recent application of the above algorithm in multiple criteria decision analysis).

The rank acceptability index of every alternative is evaluated by considering the variety of different compatible preference parameters (the Möbius measures obtained after each iteration) giving to alternative $a_j \in A$ the rank $r$ on the basis of a utility function expressed in terms of a Choquet integral. At the same time as preference parameters we compute the Möbius measures corresponding to the capacities for which the Choquet integral ranks every alternative $a_j$ as the best.

# 5 A Didactic Example

In this Section, an example inspired from Pomerol and Barba-Romero [18] illustrates the multicriteria model explained in Section 4. We consider an executive manager (the DM) that has to hire an employee in her company. She evaluates a set $A = \{a_1, a_2, a_3, a_4, a_5, a_6, a_7, a_8, a_9\}$ of nine candidates, on the basis of the following four criteria: educational degree (criterion $g_1$), professional experience (criterion $g_2$), age (criterion $g_3$), job interview (criterion $g_4$).

The evaluation performance matrix of the candidates is presented in Table 1.

The scores of every criterion are on a $[0, 10]$ scale and are supposed to be maximized.

Let us consider the following DM's partial preference information on the set of criteria $G$:

- criterion $g_1$ is more important than criterion $g_2$;
- criterion $g_2$ is more important than criterion $g_3$;
- criterion $g_3$ is more important than criterion $g_4$;
- there is a positive interaction between criteria $g_1$ and $g_2$;
- there is a positive interaction between criteria $g_2$ and $g_3$;
- there is a negative interaction between criteria $g_2$ and $g_4$.

The DM's preference constraints jointly with the boundary and monotonicity conditions are summarized in the following system:

$$
\begin{cases}
\varphi(\{g_1\}) > \varphi(\{g_2\}), \\
\varphi(\{g_2\}) > \varphi(\{g_3\}), \\
\varphi(\{g_3\}) > \varphi(\{g_4\}), \\
\varphi(\{g_1, g_2\}) > 0, \\
\varphi(\{g_2, g_3\}) > 0, \\
\varphi(\{g_2, g_4\}) < 0, \\
a(\{\emptyset\}) = 0, \ \sum_{g_i \in G} a(\{g_i\}) + \sum_{\{g_i, g_j\} \subseteq G} a(\{g_i, g_j\}) = 1, \\
a(\{g_i\}) \geq 0, \ \forall g_i \in G, a(\{g_i\}) + \sum_{g_j \in T} a(\{g_i, g_j\}) \geq 0, \forall g_i \in G \text{ and } \forall T \subseteq G \setminus \{g_i\}.
\end{cases}
$$

Then, as explained in Section 4, we apply a Hit-and-Run sampling [22] for a number maximum of iterations denoted by MaxIter.

We evaluate the rank acceptabilities of every alternative, measuring on the basis of a Choquet integral the utility value of each alternative $a_j$ and for each rank $r$, the variety of preference parameters (the Möbius measures obtained after each iteration) giving to $a_j$ the rank $r$.

Considering MaxIter equal to $100,000$, in the example the rank acceptabilities of the nine alternatives are displayed in Table 2.

**Table 1.** Evaluation matrix

| | **Alternatives** | | | | | | | | |
|---|---|---|---|---|---|---|---|---|---|
| **Criteria** | $a_1$ | $a_2$ | $a_3$ | $a_4$ | $a_5$ | $a_6$ | $a_7$ | $a_8$ | $a_9$ |
| $g_1$ | 8 | 3 | 10 | 5 | 8 | 5 | 8 | 5 | 0 |
| $g_2$ | 6 | 1 | 9 | 9 | 0 | 9 | 10 | 7 | 10 |
| $g_3$ | 7 | 10 | 0 | 2 | 8 | 4 | 5 | 9 | 2 |
| $g_4$ | 5 | 10 | 5 | 9 | 6 | 7 | 7 | 4 | 8 |

Then we compute as central preference parameters the Möbius measures which give the best position to every alternative (in our example only $a_1$, $a_3$, $a_7$, see Table 3).

According to the obtained first rank acceptability of every alternative and their corresponding central preference parameters summarized in Table 3, we can observe that:

- on average, $a_1$ is the most preferred alternative if *educational degree* ($g_1$) is the most important criterion and there is a synergy between *professional experience* ($g_2$) and *age* ($g_3$),

**Table 2.** Rank acceptabilities $(b_i)$ in percentages

| Alt | $b_j^1$ | $b_j^2$ | $b_j^3$ | $b_j^4$ | $b_j^5$ | $b_j^6$ | $b_j^7$ | $b_j^8$ | $b_j^9$ |
|---|---|---|---|---|---|---|---|---|---|
| $a_1$ | 0.03 | 51.32 | 43.64 | 4.35 | 0.66 | 0.00 | 0.00 | 0.00 | 0.00 |
| $a_2$ | 0.00 | 0.29 | 0.60 | 1.37 | 5.00 | 5.78 | 34.51 | 50.04 | 2.41 |
| $a_3$ | 13.28 | 34.08 | 20.51 | 12.25 | 9.62 | 5.49 | 3.94 | 0.83 | 0.01 |
| $a_4$ | 0.00 | 0.00 | 0.16 | 2.58 | 19.16 | 56.33 | 19.92 | 1.85 | 0.00 |
| $a_5$ | 0.00 | 0.00 | 0.48 | 4.60 | 5.29 | 7.94 | 36.55 | 44.50 | 0.65 |
| $a_6$ | 0.00 | 0.00 | 5.10 | 20.90 | 48.51 | 21.10 | 4.37 | 0.03 | 0.00 |
| $a_7$ | 86.70 | 13.15 | 0.15 | 0.00 | 0.00 | 0.00 | 0.00 | 0.00 | 0.00 |
| $a_8$ | 0.00 | 1.15 | 29.37 | 53.96 | 11.76 | 3.37 | 0.39 | 0.01 | 0.00 |
| $a_9$ | 0.00 | 0.00 | 0.00 | 0.00 | 0.00 | 0.00 | 0.32 | 2.75 | 96.94 |

**Table 3.** First rank acceptability $(b_1)$ and central weights

| Alt | $b_1$ | $a(\{1\})$ | $a(\{2\})$ | $a(\{3\})$ | $a(\{4\})$ | $a(\{1,2\})$ | $a(\{1,3\})$ | $a(\{1,4\})$ | $a(\{2,3\})$ | $a(\{2,4\})$ | $a(\{3,4\})$ |
|---|---|---|---|---|---|---|---|---|---|---|---|
| $a_1$ | 0.03 | 0.32799 | 0.1308 | 0.055755 | 0.18084 | 0.045792 | 0.1751 | -0.10253 | 0.25613 | -0.040672 | -0.029203 |
| $a_3$ | 13.28 | 0.4833 | 0.12818 | 0.19372 | 0.16042 | 0.21504 | -0.12405 | -0.044048 | 0.053126 | -0.049708 | -0.015979 |
| $a_7$ | 86.70 | 0.23032 | 0.15372 | 0.14022 | 0.1788 | 0.2164 | 0.053909 | 0.0067834 | 0.092624 | -0.063965 | -0.0088056 |

- on average, $a_3$ is the most preferred alternative if *educational degree* is the most important criterion and there is synergy between *educational degree* and *professional experience*,
- on average, $a_7$ is the most preferred alternative if all criteria are almost equally important except *educational degree* that is a bit more important than the other criteria, and there is synergy between *professional experience* and *age*, and redundancy between *age* and *job interview*.

## 6 Conclusions

In this paper, we have considered an extension of the SMAA method to the Choquet integral decision model.

As future work, we plan to extend the SMAA-Choquet by including some DM's preference information on the alternatives such as $a_i$ is preferred to $a_j$ and considering the criteria expressed in possible ranges of evaluations. Moreover, the SMAA-Choquet method could be enriched calculating an index that gives the probability that an alternative $a_r$ is better than an alternative $a_s$. Finally, the SMAA-Choquet method could be improved by coupling it with the approach of the *Robust Ordinal Regression* [12], and applying it to some more sophisticated fuzzy integrals such as the level dependent Choquet integral [11].

## References

1. Angilella, S., Greco, S., Lamantia, F., Matarazzo, B.: Assessing non-additive utility for multicriteria decision aid. European Journal of Operational Research 158(3), 734–744 (2004)

2. Angilella, S., Greco, S., Matarazzo, B.: Non-additive robust ordinal regression: A multiple criteria decision model based on the choquet integral. European Journal of Operational Research 201(1), 277–288 (2010)
3. Bana e Costa, C.A.: A multicriteria decision aid methodology to deal with conflicting situations on the weights. European Journal of Operational Research 26(1), 22–34 (1986)
4. Bana e Costa, C.A.: A methodology for sensitivity analysis in three-criteria problems: A case study in municipal management. European Journal of Operational Research 33(2), 159–173 (1988)
5. Chateauneuf, A., Jaffray, J.Y.: Some characterizations of lower probabilities and other monotone capacities through the use of möbius inversion. Mathematical Social Sciences 17, 263–283 (1989)
6. Choquet, G.: Theory of capacities. Ann. Inst. Fourier 5(54), 131–295 (1953)
7. Figueira, J., Greco, S., Ehrgott, M.: Multiple Criteria Decision Analysis: State of the Art Surveys. Springer, Berlin (2010)
8. Gilboa, I., Schmeidler, D.: Additive representations of non-additive measures and the choquet integral. Ann. Operational Research 52, 43–65 (1994)
9. Grabisch, M.: The application of fuzzy integrals in multicriteria decision making. European Journal of Operational Research 89, 445–456 (1996)
10. Grabisch, M.: k-order additive discrete fuzzy measures and their representation. Fuzzy Sets and Systems 92, 167–189 (1997)
11. Greco, S., Matarazzo, B., Giove, S.: The Choquet integral with respect to a level dependent capacity. Fuzzy Sets and Systems 175, 1–35 (2011)
12. Greco, S., Mousseau, V., Słowiński, R.: Ordinal regression revisited: multiple criteria ranking using a set of additive value functions. European Journal of Operational Research 191(2), 416–436 (2008)
13. Keeney, R.L., Raiffa, H.: Decisions with multiple objectives: Preferences and value tradeoffs. J. Wiley, New York (1976)
14. Lahdelma, R., Hokkanen, J., Salminen, P.: SMAA - stochastic multiobjective acceptability analysis. European Journal of Operational Research 106(1), 137–143 (1998)
15. Lahdelma, R., Salminen, P.: SMAA-2: Stochastic multicriteria acceptability analysis for group decision making. Operations Research 49(3), 444–454 (2001)
16. Marichal, J.L., Roubens, M.: Determination of weights of interacting criteria from a reference set. European Journal of Operational Research 124(3), 641–650 (2000)
17. Murofushi, S., Soneda, T.: Techniques for reading fuzzy measures (iii): interaction index. In: 9th Fuzzy Systems Symposium, Sapporo, Japan, pp. 693–696 (1993)
18. Barba Romero, S., Pomerol, J.C.: Choix multicritère dans l'enterprise. Heres. Collection Informatique (1993)
19. Rota, G.C.: On the foundations of combinatorial theory i. Theory of möbius functions. Wahrscheinlichkeitstheorie und Verwandte Gebiete 2, 340–368 (1964)
20. Shafer, G.: A Mathematical Theory of Evidence. Princeton University Press (1976)
21. Shapley, L.S.: A value for n-person games. In: Tucker, A.W., Kuhn, H.W. (eds.) Contributions to the Theory of Games II, p. 307. Princeton University Press, Princeton (1953)
22. Smith, R.L.: Efficient Monte Carlo procedures for generating points uniformly distributed over bounded regions. Operations Research 32, 1296–1308 (1984)
23. Tervonen, T., Figueira, J.: A survey on stochastic multicriteria acceptability analysis methods. Journal of Multi-Criteria Decision Analysis 15(1-2), 1–14 (2008)
24. Tervonen, T., Van Valkenhoef, G., Basturk, N., Postmus, D.: Efficient weight generation for simulation based multiple criteria decision analysis. In: EWG-MCDA, Tarragona, April 12-14 (2012)

# An Axiomatization of the Choquet Integral and Its Utility Functions without Any Commensurability Assumption

Christophe Labreuche[1]

Thales Research & Technology
1 avenue Augustin Fresnel
91767 Palaiseau Cedex - France

**Abstract.** We propose an axiomatization of global utility functions that can be factorized as a composition of a Choquet integral with local utility functions, without assuming any commensurability condition. This was an open problem in the literature. The main axiom, called *Commensurability Through Interaction (CTI)*, allows to construct commensurate sequences and by consequence, the utility functions, thanks to the presence of interaction between criteria.

## 1 Introduction

There exist several axiomatizations of the Choquet integral in the literature. The Choquet integral has been characterized as an aggregation function which has certain properties such as *comonotone additivity* [1], *horizontally min-additivity* [2,3] or *stability to positive linear transformations* [4]. In the context of Decision Under Uncertainty (all partial utility functions are similar), we can mention the axiomatization of the preference relation induced by a Choquet integral by Schmeidler [5], and of the Choquet integral and its utility function by Couceiro and Marichal [6]. The axiomatic characterization of the Choquet integral in the context of Multi-Criteria Decision Making has not been addressed so far. The difficulty comes from the fact that the partial utility functions are different, which entails commensurability issues.

The main idea of this paper is summarized as follows. Commensurability between the criteria is required for the Choquet integral since this aggregation function is based on a ranking of the values of the criteria. Yet, the Choquet integral is a piecewise weighted sum in which the weights of the criteria are the same whenever the criteria are ranked in the same order. Considering two criteria $i$ and $k$, the weight of criterion $i$ depends on the relative values of criteria $i$ and $k$. This means that, if the value of criterion $k$ varies while the other criteria are fixed, then one may observe that the weight of criterion $i$ suddenly changes when the value of criterion $k$ is equal to that of criterion $i$. From this remark, it is possible to construct from an element of attribute $i$, an element of attribute $k$ that is commensurate to the previous element. This construction does not work if the weight of criterion $i$ does not depend on criterion $k$. If this holds for

S. Greco et al. (Eds.): IPMU 2012, Part IV, CCIS 300, pp. 258–267, 2012.

any value of the other criteria, then it can be shown that criteria $i$ and $k$ are independent. An axiom called *Commensurability Through Interaction (CTI)* is derived from this idea.

The structure of the paper is as follows. The background on the Choquet integral is recalled in Section 2. Our major difficulty in the construction of the utility function is to construct two reference values on each attribute that are commensurate. This is done in Section 3, where the main axiom is presented. Axiomatic result is given in Section 4.

## 2   Notation and the Choquet Integral

A Multi-Criteria Decision Making problem consists in selecting one alternative among several, where each alternative is described by several attributes. $N = \{1, \ldots, n\}$ is the set of attributes and the set of possible values of attribute $i \in N$ is denoted by $X_i$. Alternatives are thus elements of the product set $X := X_1 \times \cdots \times X_n$. Preferences of a decision maker over the alternatives are characterized by an overall utility function $U : X \to \mathbb{R}$.

We wish to determine conditions on $U$ so that it takes the form

$$U(x) = C_v(\phi_1(x_1), \ldots, \phi_n(x_n)), \tag{1}$$

where functions $\phi_i : X_i \to \mathbb{R}$ are (partial) utility functions transforming the attributes into a commensurate scale (representing some satisfaction degree), and $C_v$ stands for the Choquet integral w.r.t. a capacity $v$.

A *capacity* (also called *fuzzy measure*) on a set $N$ of criteria is a set function $v : 2^N \to [0,1]$ satisfying monotonicity ($\forall A \subseteq B \subseteq N, v(A) \leq v(B)$) and normalization conditions ($v(\emptyset) = 0$ and $v(N) = 1$) [7].

The Choquet integral of $a = (a_1, \ldots, a_n) \in \mathbb{R}^n$ defined w.r.t. a capacity $v$ has the following expression [8] :

$$C_v(a_1, \ldots, a_n) = \sum_{i=1}^{n} \left(a_{\tau(i)} - a_{\tau(i-1)}\right) v\left(\{\tau(i), \cdots, \tau(n)\}\right), \tag{2}$$

where $\tau$ is a permutation on $N$ such that $a_{\tau(0)} := 0$ and $a_{\tau(1)} \leq a_{\tau(2)} \leq \cdots \leq a_{\tau(n)}$. The Choquet integral has been shown to model both importance of criteria and interaction between criteria. The *interaction index* [9] between criteria $i, j$ is defined by

$$I_{ij} := \sum_{A \subseteq N \setminus \{i,j\}} \frac{|A|!(n - |A| - 2)!}{(n-1)!} \delta_{i,j} v(A)$$

where $\delta_{i,j} v(A) := v(A \cup \{i, j\}) - v(A \cup \{i\}) - v(A \cup \{j\}) + v(A)$.

Considering two alternatives $x, y \in X$ and $S \subseteq N$, we use the notation $(x_S, y_{-S})$ to denote the compound alternative $w \in X$ such that $w_i = x_i$ if $i \in S$ and $y_i$ otherwise. Likewise, alternatives $(x_S, y_T, z_{-S \cup T})$ denotes the compound alternative $w \in X$ such that $w_i = x_i$ if $i \in S$, $w_i = y_i$ if $i \in T$, and $w_i = z_i$ otherwise.

# 3   Construction of Profiles of Commensurate Values

## 3.1   Basic Assumptions

From now on, we assume that we know the overall value $U(x)$ for all $x \in X$.
For the sake of simplicity, we assume that

$$X = \mathbb{R}^n.$$

We make the following increasingness assumption:

$$\forall x_i, y_i \in X_i \text{ with } x_i > y_i \quad \exists z_{-i} \in X_{-i} \quad \text{such that} \quad U(x_i, z_{-i}) > U(y_i, z_{-i}). \tag{3}$$

It is easy to show that, if $U$ takes the form (1), the previous relation is indeed
equivalent to the fact that $\phi_i$ is strictly increasing, provided that capacity $v$ does
not rule out one criterion.

## 3.2   Motivation of Our Main Axiom

The axiomatization by Schmeidler is based on comonotone additivity and
monotony [1]. Comonotone additivity means that the aggregation model becomes a simple weighted sum for all alternatives whose components are ranked
in the same way. Translating this property in terms of importance, one may say
that the importance of a criterion depends on the relative ordering of the criteria, but not on the precise values of the criteria. Let us consider the importance
of criterion $i$. We wish to understand how it is influenced by the other criteria.
To this end let us select another criterion $k$ and we fix the values of the remaining criteria. Hence if we vary the value of attribute $k$, the weight of criterion $i$
will take only two values: the first one is obtained when attribute $k$ is ranked
below attribute $i$, and the second one is reached when the opposite holds. We
also note that the weight of criterion $i$ is proportional to $\frac{\partial U(x)}{\partial x_i}$. This simple idea
is expressed in our main axiom.

   As we will see later, this axiom is crucial. It relates the notion of interaction to
the ability to make the attributes commensurate[1]. We will show that commensurability cannot be constructed when there is no interaction among criteria.
This is why this axiom is called *commensurability through interaction*. This idea
of interaction is hidden in this axiom through the number of values that the
importance of criterion $i$ can take when attribute $k$ varies: two when there is
some interaction among criteria $i$ and $k$, and only one otherwise.

## 3.3   Commensurability between Two Criteria

   **Regularity (R):** *$U$ is continuous, $U$ is piecewise continuously differentiable ($C^1$).*

---

[1] Two scales $u_i, u_j$ over criteria $i$ and $j$ are said to be *commensurate* if for every $x_i, x_j$
such that $u_i(x_i) = u_j(x_j)$, the degrees of satisfaction felt by the DM on criteria $i$
and $j$ are equal.

More precisely, we assume that there is a finite partition of the space $X = \mathbb{R}^N$ such that $U$ is $C^1$ in each subspace of the partition. More precisely, there exists $\{\Xi_m\}_{m \in M}$ such that $X = \cup_{m \in M} \Xi_m$ where $U$ is $C^1$ in each $\Xi_m$.

Let us consider in this section, two criteria $i, k \in N$ with $i \neq k$. As depicted in Section 3.2, we fix the values $x_{-k}$ on all attributes except attribute $k$, and we analyze the influence of $x_k$ on the partial derivative $\frac{\partial U(x)}{\partial x_i}$. The resulting variation is proportional to the weight of criterion $i$.

**Commensurability through Interaction (CTI)**: *Let $i, k \in N$ with $i \neq k$. We have the alternative:*

*(i) Either for all $x_i \in X_i$, there exist $x_k^* \in X_k$ and $\mathcal{X}_{-i,k} \subseteq X_{-i,k}$ non empty, such that for all $x_{-i,k} \in \mathcal{X}_{-i,k}$, the function $x_k \mapsto \frac{\partial U(x)}{\partial x_i}$ is not constant. More precisely, for all $x_{-i,k} \in \mathcal{X}_{-i,k}$, there exist $c_0, c_1 \in \mathbb{R}$ with $c_0 \neq c_1$ such that*

$$\forall x_k < x_k^* \quad \frac{\partial U}{\partial x_i}(x_i, x_k, x_{-i,k}) = c_0 \tag{4}$$

$$\forall x_k > x_k^* \quad \frac{\partial U}{\partial x_i}(x_i, x_k, x_{-i,k}) = c_1 \tag{5}$$

*Moreover, for all $x_{-i,k} \in X_{-i,k} \setminus \mathcal{X}_{-i,k}$, function $x_k \mapsto \frac{\partial U(x)}{\partial x_i}$ is constant.*

*(ii) Or for all $x_i \in X_i$ and all $x_{-i,k} \in X_{-i,k}$, function $x_k \mapsto \frac{\partial U(x)}{\partial x_i}$ is constant.*

As function $U$ is only piecewise $C^1$, one needs to specify more precisely the meaning of the derivative in (4) and (5). Indeed, for a point $x \in \Xi_{m^+} \cap \Xi_{m^-}$ (for $m^+, m^- \in M$), the derivative $\frac{\partial U}{\partial x_i}(x)$ may vary if we consider $x$ as an element of $\Xi_{m^+}$ or an element of $\Xi_{m^-}$. By **CTI**, the derivative $\frac{\partial U}{\partial x_i}$ is constant and thus continuous in the segment $S^+ = \{(x_i, x_k, x_{-i,k}) : x_k > x_k^*\}$ and also in $S^- = \{(x_i, x_k, x_{-i,k}) : x_k < x_k^*\}$. The derivative is defined as the limit of a divided difference. Hence $\frac{\partial U}{\partial x_i}$ shall be continuous above or below $S^-$ and $S^+$. More precisely, there exist $s \in \{-1, 1\}$ and two strictly positive functions $\varepsilon_0^+, \varepsilon_0^-$ of $x_k$ such that $\frac{\partial U}{\partial x_i}$ is continuous in $B^+$ and also in $B^-$, where (see Figure 1)

$$B^+ := \{(x_i + s\,\varepsilon, x_k, x_{-i,k}) : x_k^* \leq x_k \leq x_k^+ \text{ and } 0 \leq \varepsilon \leq \varepsilon_0^+(x_k)\} \tag{6}$$

$$B^- := \{(x_i + s\,\varepsilon, x_k, x_{-i,k}) : x_k^- \leq x_k \leq x_k^* \text{ and } 0 \leq \varepsilon \leq \varepsilon_0^-(x_k)\} \tag{7}$$

The meaning of (4) and (5) is given by

$$\forall x_k < x_k^* \quad \lim_{\varepsilon \to 0, \, 0 < \varepsilon < \varepsilon_0^-(x_k)} \frac{U(x_i + s\,\varepsilon, x_k, x_{-i,k}) - U(x_i, x_k, x_{-i,k})}{s\,\varepsilon} = c_0 \tag{8}$$

$$\forall x_k > x_k^* \quad \lim_{\varepsilon \to 0, \, 0 < \varepsilon < \varepsilon_0^+(x_k)} \frac{U(x_i + s\,\varepsilon, x_k, x_{-i,k}) - U(x_i, x_k, x_{-i,k})}{s\,\varepsilon} = c_1 \tag{9}$$

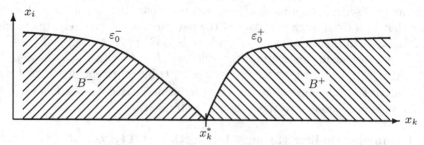

**Fig. 1.** Sets $B^-$ and $B^+$ from (6) and (7) – case when $s = +1$

Around $x_k^*$, one may have a domain in between $B^-$ and $B^+$ (see Figure 1). However, from **CTI**, for every $y_i$ with $sy_i > sx_i$, function $x_k \mapsto \frac{\partial U}{\partial x_i}(y_i, x_k, x_{-i,k})$ is discontinuous for at most one value of $x_k$. Hence $B^+$ and $B^-$ can be extended so that

$$\{(x_i + s\,\varepsilon, x_k, x_{-i,k}) \ : \ x_k \in X_k \text{ and } 0 \leq \varepsilon \leq \varepsilon_0\} \subseteq B^- \cup B^+ \qquad (10)$$

for some $\varepsilon_0 > 0$ (see Figure 2). Thus, function $x_k \mapsto \frac{\partial U(x)}{\partial x_i}$ is continuous in $B^+$ and also in $B^-$.

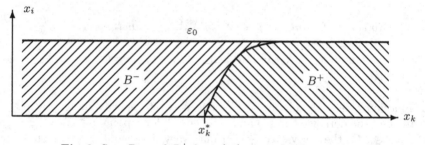

**Fig. 2.** Sets $B^-$ and $B^+$ from (10) – case when $s = +1$

The axiom characterizes the concept of interaction between two criteria. For a pair $(i, k)$, axiom **CTI** says that either an element $x_k^*$ of $X_k$ can always be construct from any $x_i \in X_i$, or such a construction can never be performed. If we are in the situation (i) in the previous axiom, the element $x_k^*$ that is constructed from $x_i$ is denoted by $\mathrm{Comm}_{i \to k}(x_i)$, where Comm stands for commensurability (we will indeed show later that this corresponds to commensurability w.r.t. the utility functions). We also write $i \rhd k$ in this case.

### 3.4   Some Properties of the Commensurability Function

We need some properties of the commensurability function $\mathrm{Comm}_{i \to k}$.

**Commensurability Properties (CP):**
- *Let $x_i, x_i' \in X_i$*

$$x_i \leq x_i' \quad \Longrightarrow \quad \mathrm{Comm}_{i \to k}(x_i) \leq \mathrm{Comm}_{i \to k}(x_i')$$

- *Function $\mathrm{Comm}_{i \to k}$ is Lipschitz continuous in any compact set.*

Let us comment the increasingness property. It can be shown that using only monotonicity of $U$. We can indeed imagine $U$ piecewise affine such that $\text{Comm}_{i \to k}(x_i) = -x_i$ (i.e. the transition in $k$ is decreasing w.r.t. $x_i$). This is the case with bi-capacities (or the Sipŏs integral).

We also need transitivity of the commensurability between subsets of criteria. For a triplet of attributes $i, j, k$, we can construct a sequence of commensurate values, starting from a value $x_i$ on attribute $i$, in two different ways: (i) from $i$ to $j$, and then from $j$ to $k$, or (ii) from $i$ to $k$, and then from $k$ to $j$. The following axiom essentially says that one obtains the same results in the previous two ways.

**Commensurability Among Three Criteria (C3):** *Let $i, j, k \in N$ such that $i \triangleright j$, $j \triangleright k$ and $i \triangleright k$.*
- *Then for all $z_{-i,j,k} \in X_{-i,j,k}$ and all $x_i \in X_i$,*

$$U(x_i, \text{Comm}_{i \to j}(x_i), \text{Comm}_{j \to k} \circ \text{Comm}_{i \to j}(x_i), z_{-i,j,k})$$
$$= U(x_i, \text{Comm}_{k \to j} \circ \text{Comm}_{i \to k}(x_i), \text{Comm}_{i \to k}(x_i), z_{-i,j,k})$$

- *For all $x_i \in X_i$, there exists $z_{-i,j,k} \in X_{-i,j,k}$ such that*

*If $s_j > t_j$ and $s_k > t_k$ then $U(x_i, s_j, s_k, z_{-i,j,k}) > U(x_i, t_j, t_k, z_{-i,j,k})$,*
*If $s_j < t_j$ and $s_k < t_k$ then $U(x_i, s_j, s_k, z_{-i,j,k}) < U(x_i, t_j, t_k, z_{-i,j,k})$*

*where $s_j = \text{Comm}_{i \to j}(x_i)$, $s_k = \text{Comm}_{j \to k}(s_j)$, $t_k = \text{Comm}_{i \to k}(x_i)$ and $t_j = \text{Comm}_{k \to j}(t_k)$.*

The second condition is the previous axiom is a monotonicity condition.

We can show that $\triangleright$ is symmetric. Moreover, for $i, k \in N$ such that $i \triangleright k$, $\text{Comm}_{i \to k} = \text{Comm}_{k \to i}^{-1}$. Finally, the Comm function is transitive in the sense that for all $i, j, k \in N$ such that $i \triangleright j$, $j \triangleright k$ and $i \triangleright k$, $\text{Comm}_{j \to k} \circ \text{Comm}_{i \to j} = \text{Comm}_{i \to k}$.

### 3.5   Construction of Commensurability Sequences

The strongly connected components[2] of $(N, \triangleright)$ are noted $\mathcal{T} = \{S_1, \ldots, S_p\}$. By definition, they form a partition of $N$.

For each $l \in \{1, \ldots, p\}$, there exists a sequence $i_1^l, \ldots, i_{s_l}^l$ with $s_l = |S_l|$ such that $S_l = \{i_1^l, \ldots, i_{s_l}^l\}$ and $i_1^l \triangleright i_2^l$, $i_2^l \triangleright i_3^l$, $\ldots$, $i_{s_l-1}^l \triangleright i_{s_l}^l$. Such a sequence always exists since $\triangleright$ is symmetric and $S_l$ is a strongly connected component of $(N, \triangleright)$.

Algorithm 1 returns an element of $X$ from values in attributes $i_1^1, i_1^2, \ldots, i_1^p$. The sequence that is so obtained is called *commensurate sequence*. We will state later that all elements in a sequence within a partition set $S_l$ are indeed commensurate.

---

[2] The strongly connected components of a directed graph are its maximal strongly connected subgraphs. A directed graph is said to be strongly connected if there is a path from each vertex in the graph to every other vertex.

Let $l \in \{1, \ldots, p\}$. We wish to construct a commensurate sequence not starting from criterion $i_1^l$ but starting from a criterion $i \in S_l$ with the value $x_i$. From the properties on the Commensurability function (see Section 3.4), for $x_i \in X_i$, we can easily define $\mathrm{Comm}_i^{S_l}(x_i)$ that returns a vector in $X_{S_l}$ of commensurate elements taking value $x_i$ on attribute $i$. This vector is independent from the order in which the sequence is constructed. Indeed, for $i, k \in S_l$, we have $\mathrm{Comm}_k^{S_l}\left(\left(\mathrm{Comm}_i^{S_l}(x_i)\right)_k\right) = \mathrm{Comm}_i^{S_l}(x_i)$. Algorithm 2 returns $\mathrm{Comm}_i^{S_l}(x_i)$.

---

**Function** getCommensurateSequence$(x_{i_1^1}, x_{i_1^2}, \ldots, x_{i_1^p})$ :

  **For** $l$ **from** 1 **to** $p$ **do**

    $z_{i_1^l} = x_{i_1^l}$;

    **For** $m$ **from** 2 **to** $s_l$ **do**

      $z_{i_m^l} = \mathrm{Comm}_{i_{m-1}^l \to i_m^l}(z_{i_{m-1}^l})$;

    **end For**

  **end For**

  **return** $z$;

**End**

**Algorithm 1.** Algorithm **getCommensurateSequence**

---

**Function** $\mathrm{Comm}_i^{S_l}(x_i)$ :

  $z_{i_k^l} = x_{i_k^l}$ where $k$ is such that $i_k^l = i$;

  **For** $m$ **from** $k+1$ **to** $s_l$ **do**

    $z_{i_m^l} = \mathrm{Comm}_{i_{m-1}^l \to i_m^l}(z_{i_{m-1}^l})$;

  **end For**

  **For** $m$ **from** $k-1$ **to** 1 **do**

    $z_{i_m^l} = \mathrm{Comm}_{i_{m+1}^l \to i_m^l}(z_{i_{m+1}^l})$;

  **end For**

  **return** $z$;

**End**

**Algorithm 2.** Algorithm $\mathrm{Comm}_i^{S_l}$

## 4   Axiomatization Result

### 4.1   Decomposition $U$ on $\mathcal{T}$ and Homogeneity Property

In order to define utility functions and a capacity, we usually need two reference levels denoted by $\mathbb{O}$ and $\mathbb{G}$ [10]. They are defined as commensurate sequences.

**Definition 1.** *The outcome of function "getCommensurateSequence" in Algorithm 1 on $\mathbb{O}_{i_1^1}, \mathbb{O}_{i_1^2}, \ldots, \mathbb{O}_{i_1^p}$ is denoted by $\mathbb{O}$, where $\mathbb{O}_{i_1^1}, \mathbb{O}_{i_1^2}, \ldots, \mathbb{O}_{i_1^p}$ takes any values in $X_{i_1^1}, X_{i_1^2}, \ldots, X_{i_1^p}$ respectively.*

*Function "getCommensurateSequence" in Algorithm 1 is used a second time on* $\mathbb{G}_{i_1^1}$, $\mathbb{G}_{i_1^2}$, ..., $\mathbb{G}_{i_1^p}$ *and its outcome is denoted by* $\mathbb{G}$, *where* $\mathbb{G}_{i_1^1} > \mathbb{O}_{i_1^1}$, $\mathbb{G}_{i_1^2} > \mathbb{O}_{i_1^2}$, ..., $\mathbb{G}_{i_1^p} > \mathbb{O}_{i_1^p}$.

We now state that the overall evaluation function $U$ is additive over the elements (coalitions) of $\mathcal{T}$.

**Lemma 1.** *We have for every* $x \in X$

$$U(x) - U(\mathbb{O}) = \sum_{p}^{p} \left[ U(x_{S_l}, \mathbb{O}_{-S_l}) - U(\mathbb{O}) \right]$$

We set $X_i^+ := \{x_i \in X_i \ : \ x_i \geq \mathbb{O}_i^!\}$ and $X_i^- := \{x_i \in X_i \ : \ x_i \leq \mathbb{O}_i\}$. We need now some homogeneity property in order to construct the utility functions. Homogeneity basically reads [3]: For all $l \in \{1, \dots, p\}$, all $i \in S_l$, all $\alpha \in X_i^+$ and all $A \subseteq S_l$ with $i \in A$,

$$\frac{U((\mathrm{Comm}_i^{S_l}(\alpha))_A, \mathbb{O}_{-A}) - U(\mathbb{O})}{U((\mathrm{Comm}_i^{S_l}(\mathbb{G}))_A, \mathbb{O}_{-A}) - U(\mathbb{O})}$$

is independent from the choice of $A$. A similar definition can be obtained for $\alpha \in X_i^-$.

**Homogeneity (H[$\mathbb{O}, \mathbb{G}$]):** *For all* $l \in \{1, \dots, p\}$, *all* $i \in S_l$:
  - *Let* $\varepsilon = \{+, -\}$. *For* $A \subseteq S_l$ *with* $i \in A$, *if for some* $\alpha \in X_i^\varepsilon \setminus \{\mathbb{O}_i\}$

$$U((\mathrm{Comm}_i^{S_l}(\alpha))_A, \mathbb{O}_{-A}) = U(\mathbb{O})$$

*then for all* $\beta_i \in X_i^\varepsilon \setminus \{\mathbb{O}_i\}$, $U((\mathrm{Comm}_i^{S_l}(\beta))_A, \mathbb{O}_{-A}) = U(\mathbb{O})$. *Let*

$$\mathcal{A}^\varepsilon(i) = \{A \subseteq S_l \text{ with } i \in A : \exists \alpha \in X_i^\varepsilon, \ U((\mathrm{Comm}_i^{S_l}(\alpha))_A, \mathbb{O}_{-A}) \neq U(\mathbb{O})\}.$$

*We have* $\mathcal{A}^\varepsilon(i) \neq \emptyset$ *(*$S_l \in \mathcal{A}^\varepsilon(i)$*).*
  - *For all* $\alpha \in X_i^+$ *and all* $A \in \mathcal{A}^+(i)$,

$$\frac{U((\mathrm{Comm}_i^{S_l}(\alpha))_A, \mathbb{O}_{-A}) - U(\mathbb{O})}{U(\mathbb{G}_A, \mathbb{O}_{-A}) - U(\mathbb{O})} \tag{11}$$

*is independent from the choice of* $A$.
  - *For all* $\alpha \in X_i^-$ *and all* $A \in \mathcal{A}^-(i)$,

$$\frac{U((\mathrm{Comm}_i^{S_l}(\alpha))_A, \mathbb{O}_{-A}) - U(\mathbb{O})}{U(\mathbb{G}_N) - U(\mathbb{O}_A, \mathbb{G}_{-A})} \tag{12}$$

*is independent from the choice of* $A$. *If* $A \notin \mathcal{A}^-(i)$ *then* $U(\mathbb{G}_N) - U(\mathbb{O}_A, \mathbb{G}_{-A}) = 0$.

Let $V := U(\mathbb{G}) - U(\mathbb{O}) = \sum_{l=1}^{p}(U(\mathbb{G}_{S_l}, \mathbb{O}_{-S_l}) - U(\mathbb{O}))$. Ratio (11) multiplied by $V$ (resp. (12)) in **H** depends only on $i$ and $\alpha$ (it is independent from the choice of $A$), and is denoted by $\phi_i(\alpha)$ for $\alpha \in X_i^+$ (resp. $\alpha \in X_i^-$). Moreover, we define the set function $v_l : 2^{S_l} \to \mathbb{R}$ by, for all $A \subseteq S_l$,

$$v_l(A) = \frac{U(\mathbb{G}_A, \mathbb{O}_{-A}) - U(\mathbb{O})}{V}.$$

## 4.2   Link between Comm and $\phi_i$

The next lemma states that function $\text{Comm}_{i \to k}$ constructs commensurate values w.r.t. the utility functions $\phi_i$, $\phi_k$.

**Lemma 2.** *We have:*

- *Let $i, k \in N$ such that $i \rhd k$. Then for every $x_i \in X_i$ and $x_k \in X_k$*

$$\text{Comm}_{i \to k}(x_i) \geq x_k \quad \Longleftrightarrow \quad \phi_i(x_i) \geq \phi_k(x_k).$$

- *Let $x$ be the outcome of the function "getCommensurateSequence" (see Algorithm 1). For every $S \in \mathcal{T}$, we have*

$$\forall i, k \in S \; \forall x_i \in X_i \; \forall x_k \in X_k \text{ with } \text{Comm}_{i \to k}(x_i) \geq x_k \,, \qquad \phi_i(x_i) = \phi_k(x_k).$$

The previous lemma proves that the set of criteria can be partitioned into disjoint sets such that all elements of $x$ in each coalition are commensurate (they have the same value), and each set is independent from the choice of the other ones (see Figure 3).

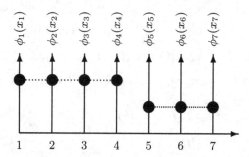

**Fig. 3.** Example $\mathcal{T} = \{\{1, 2, 3, 4\}, \{5, 6, 7\}\}$. We have $\phi_1(x_1) = \phi_2(x_2) = \phi_3(x_3) = \phi_4(x_4)$ and $\phi_5(x_5) = \phi_6(x_6) = \phi_7(x_7)$.

## 4.3   Interpretation of the CTI Axiom

We give an interpretation of **CTI**. To this end consider $U$ satisfying axiom **CTI**. Assume that $U$ is of the form (1).

**Lemma 3.** *Let $i, k \in N$ such that $i \not\rhd k$ (we are in the situation of Axiom **CTI** part (ii)). Then*

$$\forall A \subseteq N \setminus \{i, k\} \quad \delta_{i,k} v(A) = 0. \tag{13}$$

From Lemma 3, the interaction between $i$ and $k$ vanishes. Hence axiom **CTI** relates to the possibility to construct a value on attribute $k$ that is commensurate to some value of attribute $i$, to the presence of interaction between $i$ and $k$.

## 4.4    Characterization Result

**Theorem 1.** *Suppose that* $U: X \to \mathbb{R}$ *satisfies the assumptions (3). Then the following statements are equivalent:*

(i) *$U$ satisfies* **R, CTI, CP, C3** *and* **H**$[\mathbb{O}, \mathbb{G}]$, *where* $\mathbb{O}, \mathbb{G} \in X$ *are defined in Definition 1.*

(ii) *There exist strictly increasing functions* $\phi_1 : X_1 \to \mathbb{R}, \ldots, \phi_n : X_n \to \mathbb{R}$ *that are continuous and piecewise* $C^1$, *and a capacity* $v$ *such that (1) holds.*

*If* $\phi_1, \ldots, \phi_n, v$ *and* $\widehat{\phi}_1, \ldots, \widehat{\phi}_n, \widehat{v}$ *are two parameters sets satisfying (1), then for all* $S \in \mathcal{T}$, *there exist* $\alpha_S > 0$ *and* $\beta_S \in \mathbb{R}$ *such that*

$$\forall i \in S \; \forall x_i \in X_i \; , \quad \widehat{\phi}_i(x_i) = \alpha_S \, \phi_i(x_i) + \beta_S \tag{14}$$

$$\forall A \subseteq S \; , \quad \widehat{v}(A) = \frac{v(A)}{\alpha_S} \tag{15}$$

The second part of the theorem states that the representation is not unique in general. Yet the utility functions are unique up to an affine transformation. More precisely, the same affine transformation is applied to all criteria belonging to the same coalition of $\mathcal{T}$. The capacity is then modified by the inverse coefficient. Note that different transformations can be applied to different coalitions in $\mathcal{T}$. If $\mathcal{T}$ is composed of a single coalition (the grand coalition), then the capacity and utility functions are unique. Finally, if all criteria are independent, then all utility functions can be linearly transformed independently so that commensurability cannot be obtained. In this case, we recover the additive utility model.

# References

1. Schmeidler, D.: Integral representation without additivity. Proc. of the Amer. Math. Soc. 97(2), 255–261 (1986)
2. Benvenuti, P., Mesiar, R., Vivona, D.: Monotone set functions-based integrals. In: Pap, E. (ed.) Handbook of Measure Theory, pp. 1329–1379. Elsevier Science (2002)
3. Couceiro, M., Marichal, J.: Axiomatizations of lovász extensions of pseudo-Boolean functions. Fuzzy Sets and Systems 181, 28–38 (2011)
4. Marichal, J.L.: An axiomatic approach of the discrete Choquet integral as a tool to aggregate interacting criteria. IEEE Tr. on Fuzzy Systems 8(6), 800–807 (2000)
5. Schmeidler, D.: Subjective probability and expected utility without additivity. Econometrica 57(3), 571–587 (1989)
6. Couceiro, M., Marichal, J.: Axiomatizations of quasi-lovász extensions of pseudo-Boolean functions. Aequationes Mathematicae 82, 213–231 (2011)
7. Grabisch, M., Murofushi, T., Sugeno, M.: Fuzzy Measures and Integrals. Theory and Applications (edited volume). STUDFUZZ. Physica Verlag (2000)
8. Choquet, G.: Theory of capacities. Annales de l'Institut Fourier 5, 131–295 (1953)
9. Murofushi, T., Soneda, S.: Techniques for reading fuzzy measures (III): interaction index. In: 9th Fuzzy System Symposium, Sapporo, Japan, pp. 693–696 (May 1993)
10. Labreuche, C., Grabisch, M.: The Choquet integral for the aggregation of interval scales in multicriteria decision making. Fuzzy Sets & Systems 137, 11–26 (2003)

# Eliciting CPTS-Integrals on Bipolar Scale

Agnès Rico[1] and Michio Sugeno[2]

[1] ERIC, Université de Lyon, France
agnes.rico@univ-lyon1.fr
[2] European Centre for Soft Computing, Mieres-Asturias, Spain
michio.sugeno@softcomputing.es

**Abstract.** CPTS-integrals (Cumulative Prospect Theory Sugeno integral) are agregation functions that return a global rating when the evaluations are given on a bipolar scale. This paper presents the problem of the elicitation of CPTS-integrals agreeing with a data set composed of pairs concerning some criteria and a global evaluation. Moreover the set of fuzzy measures which are solutions of this inverse problem is identified. When the elicitation of one CPTS-integral is not possible, a set of family of CPTS-integrals is proposed.

**Keywords:** S-integral, CPTS-integral, fuzzy measures, bipolar scale.

## 1 Introduction

In decision making when the evaluation scale is an ordinal set, the S-integral [5,6] is an agregation function classicaly used. In the case that decisions are often based on positive and negative aspects, the scale should be bipolar. Moreover several areas exist in engineering in which positive and negative part are taken into account [7]. A bipolar scale consists of a positive part, a negative part and a neutral level which is a point considered neither positive nor negative. Copying the cardinal preference model, the S-integral is extended on the bipolar scale, leading to the definition of the CPTS-integral (Cumulative Prospect Theory Sugeno integral). In the CPTS model, first the positive and negative part are treated separetely. After they are mixed using the symmetric maximum introduced in [8].

When the evaluation scale is ordinal, an approach to elicit S-integrals agreeing with a data set was presented in [3]. Moreover the solution set of all the fuzzy measures is given, i.e., the lower bound and the upper bounds of the solutions are identified using the theoritical results presented in [2]. This paper extends these results for the CPTS-integrals defined on a bipolar scale.

The paper is organised as follows. The second section is devoted to the framework and notations. The section 3 summarizes the results concerning the elicitation of S-integrals in the ordinal context. The section 4 presents some technical results concerning the CPTS-integrals. The section 5 is devoted to the approach of the elicitation of CPTS-integrals agreeing with a data set. More precisely, this section identifies the constraints induced by the data on a CPTS-integral.

S. Greco et al. (Eds.): IPMU 2012, Part IV, CCIS 300, pp. 268–277, 2012.

Before the conclusion, the section 6 gives some ideas when all the data are not compatible, i.e., when they are not representable by a same CPTS-integral. In such a case a family of CPTS-integrals is proposed for partial compatibility.

## 2   Framework and Notations

### 2.1   The Data Set

Let $L^+ = \{0, \cdots, l\}$ be an ordinal scale. Define $L^- = \{-l, \cdots, -1\}$ and a bipolar scale $L = L^- \cup L^+$. The element 0 is the neutral level of the scale. The elements of $L^+$ are considered as good and the elements of $L^-$ as bad by the decision maker, respectively. The min $\wedge$ and the max $\vee$ operations are extended to $L$.

**Definition 1.** $a \otimes b = sign(a + b)(|a| \vee |b|)$ and $a \oslash b = sign(a \times b)(|a| \wedge |b|)$ where $|a| = a$ if $a \in L^+$, $|a| = -a$ if $a \in L^-$; $sign(a) = 1$ for $a > 0$, 0 for $a = 0$ and $-1$ for $a < 0$.

$\otimes$ is not associative on $L$ and $\oslash$ is not distributive over $\otimes$. These do not cause any difficulty since $\otimes$ and $\oslash$ coincide with $\vee$ and $\wedge$ on $L^+$.

We consider $\mathcal{C} = \{C_1, \ldots, C_n\}$ a set of $n$ evaluation criteria represented on the bipolar scale $L$. A fuzzy measure $\mu : \mathcal{C} \to L^+$ is an increasing set function such that $\mu(\emptyset) = 0$ and $\mu(\mathcal{C}) = l$. A set of objects are evaluated with respect to each criterion. Hence, an object is represented by a function $f : \mathcal{C} \to L$. An object can be also viewed as a vector $(f_1, \cdots, f_n)$ where $f_i$ is the evaluation of the object $f$ according to the criterion $C_i$. Two functions $f, g : \mathcal{C} \to L$ are said to be comonotone if $f_i \geq f_j \Leftrightarrow g_i \geq g_j$.

Here a data set is a collection of objects $f = (f_1, \cdots, f_n)$ associated with a global rating $a \in L$. Hence a pair of data is denoted $(f, a)$.

Note that the global ratings define a preference relation on the objects.

*Example 1.* Let us consider $L = \{-2, -1, 0, 1, 2\}$, three criteria $\{C_1, C_2, C_3\}$ and the following data set:

|        | $C_1$ | $C_2$ | $C_3$ | global rating |
|--------|-------|-------|-------|---------------|
| $f^1$  | -2    | 2     | 1     | 1             |
| $f^2$  | 0     | -1    | 2     | 0             |
| $f^3$  | -1    | -1    | 0     | -1            |

In such a case the data set represents the preference relation $(f^3, -1) \prec (f^2, 0) \prec (f^1, 1)$.

An equivalence class of objects is a set of objects which have the same global rating. We consider that the given data set defines $p$ equivalence classes of objects. Each of them is represented by an element in $L$: the common global rating of its objects. More precisely we consider $p$ elements of $L$ denoted $a^1 < \cdots < a^p$. The i-th class, denoted $[a^i]$, implies the set of all the objects which have $a^i$ as global evaluation.

The problem considered in this paper is the elicitation of CPTS-integrals that are compatible with a data set. Let us recall some definitions and some properties concerning these integrals.

## 2.2    S-Integrals and CPTS-Integrals: A Brief Reminder

**Definition 2.** *Let $f$ be a non-negative function such that $f : \mathcal{C} \to L^+$.*
*The S-integral of $f$ with respect to a fuzzy measure $\mu$ is $S_\mu(f) = \vee_{i=1}^n f_i \wedge \mu(A_i)$*
*where the values of $f$ are assumed to be such that $f_1 \leq \cdots \leq f_n$ and $A_i$ is the*
*set $\{C_i, \cdots C_n\}$.*

Note that, in the previous definition, if the values of $f$ are not well ordered we
can rearrange them in an increasing order.

With a function $f : \mathcal{C} \to L$ two non-negative functions can be defined as
follows: $f^+ = max(f, 0)$ and $f^- = max(-f, 0)$ where 0 denotes the function
equals to 0 everywhere and where the max is calculated on each coordinate.

**Definition 3.** *The Cumulative Prospect Theory S-integral of a function $f : \mathcal{C} \to$*
*$L$ with respect to a fuzzy measure $\mu^+$ and $\mu^-$ is defined as*

$$CPTS_{\mu^+,\mu^-}(f) = S_{\mu^+}(f^+) \otimes -S_{\mu^-}(f^-).$$

The following properties proved in [1] where the evaluation scale is $[-1, 1]$ are
still valid in our context:

**Proposition 1.** *The CPTS-integral is*

- *comonotone-$\otimes$-additive, i.e, for all comonotone functions $f$ and $g$*
  *$CPTS_{\mu^+,\mu^-}(f \otimes g) = CPTS_{\mu^+,\mu^-}(f) \otimes CPTS_{\mu^+,\mu^-}(g)$.*
- *monotone , i.e., $f \leq g \Rightarrow CPTS_{\mu^+,\mu^-}(f) \leq CPTS_{\mu^+,\mu^-}(g)$.*
- *weak $\otimes$-homogeneous, i.e, $CPTS_{\mu^+,\mu^-}(a \otimes 1_A) = a \otimes CPTS_{\mu^+,\mu^-}(1_A)$ and*
  *$CPTS_{\mu^+,\mu^-}(a \otimes (-1_A)) = a \otimes CPTS_{\mu^+,\mu^-}(-1_A)$ for all $a \in L^+$ and for all*
  *set $A$ (its characteristic function is $1_A$).*

In the following, given a set of objects $f$, we shall consider a data set consisting
of pairs of data $(f, a^i)$, and we want to identify the measures $\mu^+$ and $\mu^-$ such
that $CPTS_{\mu^+,\mu^-}(f) = a^i$ for all objects $f$ belonging to the i-th equivalence class
and for all the classes: $[a^i] = \{f | CPTS_{\mu^+,\mu^-}(f) = a^i\}$. If the fuzzy measures
can be identified then the data set is said to be compatible; otherwise the data set
set is incompatible.

Our approach to identify the fuzzy measures is based on the results concerning
the elicitation of a S-integral [2,3]. Let us briefly recall these results.

## 3    Elicitation of S-Integrals Agreeing with a Data Set

In this section the evaluations are assumed to be non-negative. Let $(f, a)$ be a
pair of data where $f$ is an object and $a \in L^+$. We are going to identify the
fuzzy measures $\mu$ such that $S_\mu(f) = a$. First two particular fuzzy measures are
defined:

**Definition 4.**

Let $i_{f,a}^{\geq}$ be the index such that $f_1 \leq \ldots \leq f_{i_{f,a}^{\geq}-1} < a \leq f_{i_{f,a}^{\geq}} \leq \ldots \leq f_n$ and $i_{f,a}^{>}$ be the index such that $f_1 \leq \ldots \leq f_{i_{f,a}^{>}-1} \leq a < f_{i_{f,a}^{>}} \leq \ldots \leq f_n$.

$$\forall X \in 2^C, X \neq \emptyset, C, \quad \check{\mu}_{f,a}(X) = \begin{cases} a & \text{if } A_{i_{f,a}^{\geq}} \subseteq X \\ 0 & \text{otherwise} \end{cases} \quad \text{and } \hat{\mu}_{f,a}(X) =$$
$$\begin{cases} a & \text{if } X \subseteq A_{i_{f,a}^{>}} \\ l & \text{otherwise} \end{cases}$$

where $A_{i_{f,a}^{\geq}} = \{C_{i_{f,a}^{\geq}}, \cdots, C_n\}$ and $A_{i_{f,a}^{>}} = \{C_{i_{f,a}^{>}}, \cdots, C_n\}$.

Hence the following result can be proved:

**Proposition 2.** $\{\mu \text{ s.t. } S_\mu(f) = a\} = \{\mu \text{ s.t. } \check{\mu}_{f,a} \leq \mu \leq \hat{\mu}_{f,a}\}$.

Here, $\check{\mu}_{f,a}$ and $\hat{\mu}_{f,a}$ are the least upper bound and the greatest lower bound of $\mu$, respectively. Note that to compare a fuzzy measure $\mu$ with $\check{\mu}_{f,a}$ or $\hat{\mu}_{f,a}$ we don't need to do it on each coordinate. More precisely, a fuzzy measure $\mu$ satisfies $\mu \leq \hat{\mu}_{f,a}$ if and only if $\mu(A_{i_{f,a}^{>}}) \leq a$ and $\mu$ satisfies $\mu \geq \check{\mu}_{f,a}$ if and only if $\mu(A_{i_{f,a}^{\geq}}) \geq a$.

We conclude this section with a result which characterises a data set compatible with a same S-integral.

**Proposition 3.** *There exists a common fuzzy measure for the different classes if and only if* $\forall i, j, a^i < a^j \Rightarrow A_{j_{g,a^j}^{\geq}} \not\subseteq A_{i_{f,a^i}^{>}}, \quad g \in [a^j], \quad f \in [a^i]$.

Moreover, the common fuzzy measure $\mu$ satisfies $\vee_{a^i} \vee_{f \in [a^i]} \check{\mu}_{f,a^i} \leq \mu \leq \wedge_{a^i} \wedge_{f \in [a^i]} \hat{\mu}_{f,a^i}$.

# 4  Technical Results Concerning CPTS-Integral

In this section we consider $(f, a)$ a pair of data where $f$ is an object and $a \in L$ is the global evaluation. In order to identify the fuzzy measures $\mu^-$ and $\mu^+$ such that $CPTS_{\mu^+,\mu^-}(f) = a$, there are three possible cases to study: $CPTS_{\mu^+,\mu^-}(f) = a$ for $a > 0$, $a < 0$ and $a = 0$.

**Proposition 4.** *Let* $a \in L^+$, $a \neq 0$, *then* $\{(\mu^-, \mu^+)|CPTS_{\mu^+,\mu^-}(f) = a\} = \{\check{\mu}_{f^+,a} \leq \mu^+ \leq \hat{\mu}_{f^+,a} \text{ and } \mu^-(\{C_i|f_i^- \geq a\}) < a\}$.

*Proof.* Since $CPTS_{\mu^+,\mu^-}(f) = a > 0$, it follows from the properties of the operation $\oslash$ that $S_{\mu^+}(f^+) = a$ and $S_{\mu^-}(f^-) < a$. So the identification of $\mu^-$ and $\mu^+$ such that $CPTS_{\mu^+,\mu^-}(f) = a$ is equivalent to find $\mu^+$ and $\mu^-$ such that $S_{\mu^+}(f^+) = a$ and $S_{\mu^-}(f^-) < a$. The last inequality is equivalent to $S_{\mu^-}(f^-) \not\geq a$, i.e., $\mu^-(\{C_i|f_i^- \geq a\}) \not\geq a$.

**Proposition 5.** *Let* $a \in L^-$, *then* $\{(\mu^-, \mu^+)|CPTS_{\mu^-,\mu^+}(f) = a\} = \{\check{\mu}_{f^-,-a} \leq \mu^- \leq \hat{\mu}_{f^-,-a} \text{ and } \mu^+(\{C_i|f_i^+ \geq -a\}) < -a\}$.

*Proof.* This proof is similar to the previous one. The resolution of $CPTS_{\mu^+,\mu^-}(f) = a$ is equivalent to find $\mu^+$ and $\mu^-$ such that $S_{\mu^+}(f^+) < -a$ and $S_{\mu^-}(f^-) = -a$.

**Proposition 6.** $\{(\mu^-, \mu^+) | CPTS_{\mu^-,\mu^+}(f) = 0\} = \cup_{a \in L^+} \{(\mu^-, \mu^+) | \check{\mu}_{f^-,a} \leq \mu^- \leq \hat{\mu}_{f^-,a} \text{ and } \check{\mu}_{f^+,a} \leq \mu^+ \leq \hat{\mu}_{f^+,a}\}$

*Proof.* $CPTS_{\mu^-,\mu^+}(f) = 0$ iff $\exists a \in L^+$ such that $S_{\mu^+}(f^+) = a$ and $S_{\mu^-}(f^-) = a$.

# 5   Elicitation of a CPTS-Integral Agreeing with a Data Set

We consider a data set with $p$ equivalence classes represented by $a^1 < \cdots < a^p$ where $a^i \in L$ for all $i \in \{1, \cdots, p\}$. We want to identify $\mu^-$ and $\mu^+$ such that $CPTS_{\mu^-,\mu^+}(f) = a^i$ for all $i$ and for all $f$ in the i-th class: $f \in [a^i]$.

We begin to study the constraints induced by a pair of data on the CPTS-integrals compatible with it. Assume $f \in [a^i]$ where $a^i \in L$: $CPTS_{\mu^-,\mu^+}(f) = a^i$.

- First let us assume $a^i \in L^+$ and $a^i \neq 0$.
  The definition of the symmetric maximum entails $S_{\mu^+}(f^+) = a^i$ and $S_{\mu^-}(f^-) < a^i$. In such a case $S_{\mu^-}(f^-)$ can be any value smaller than $a^i$.
- Next let us assume $a^i \in L^-$.
  The definition of the symmetric maximum entails $S_{\mu^+}(f^+) < |a^i|$ and $S_{\mu^-}(f^-) = |a^i|$. In such a case $S_{\mu^+}(f^+)$ can be any value smaller than $|a^i|$.

Let us consider a data set denoted $\{(f, a^i)_{i \in \{1, \cdots, n\}, f \in [a^i]}\}$.

- If $a^i \in L^+, a^i \neq 0$ then the pair of data $(f, a^i)$ entails the following set of possible data $(f^+, a^i)$ and $\{(f^-, b^j), \quad \forall b^j < a^i\}$.
- If $a^i = 0$ then $S_{\mu^+}(f^+) = S_{\mu^-}(f^-)$. Since the S-integral of a function is always between the minimum and the maximum of the function, this common value is between 0 and the minimum located between $\vee_{i=1}^n f_i$ and $- \wedge_{i=1}^n f_i$. Note that in such a case there exists $i, j$ such that $f_i \leq 0$ and $f_j \geq 0$. So the pair of data $(f, 0)$ entails the following possible data set $\{(f^+, a) \text{ and } (f^-, a), \quad \forall a \text{ s.t.} 0 \leq a \leq (\vee_{i=1}^n f_i) \wedge (- \wedge_{i=1}^n f_i)\}$.
- If $a^i \in L^-$ then $(f, a^i)$ entails $\{(f^+, b^j), \quad \forall b^j < |a^i|\}$ and $(f^-, |a^i|)$.

So many global evaluations are possible for $f^-$ or $f^+$. We can choose one value for each $f^-$ and $f^+$ whenever it is available. This selection defines a data set for the objects $f^-$ and $f^+$. So a data set can define several data sets on the objects $f^+$ and $f^-$. One of the data sets on the objects $f^+$ and one of the possible data sets on the objects $f^-$ are representable by a S-integral if and only if the data set on the objects $f$ is compatible with a CPTS-integral.

*Example 2.* We consider four criteria $C_1, C_2, C_3, C_4$ represented on the evaluation scale $L = \{5, 4, 3, 2, 1, 0, -1, -2, -3, -4, -5\}$ and six objects:

|   | $C_1$ | $C_2$ | $C_3$ | $C_4$ | global evaluation |
|---|---|---|---|---|---|
| $E$ | 5 | 0 | 5 | -4 | 4 |
| $D$ | -5 | 5 | 4 | 5 | 3 |
| $F$ | 0 | -3 | 1 | -4 | 0 |
| $B$ | 0 | -4 | 0 | -5 | -1 |
| $C$ | 5 | -5 | -5 | 5 | -2 |
| $A$ | -5 | 4 | -4 | 0 | -3 |

First, let us consider $E^+, \cdots, A^+$ and show their possible global evaluations. Since $E$ and $D$ have positive global evaluations, $E^+$ and $D^+$ keep the same evaluation. The evaluation of $B$ is $-1$ and so the global evaluation of $B^+$ must be smaller than 1, i.e., 0.

|   | $C_1$ | $C_2$ | $C_3$ | $C_4$ | possible g.e. |
|---|---|---|---|---|---|
| $E^+$ | 5 | 0 | 5 | 0 | 4 |
| $D^+$ | 0 | 5 | 4 | 5 | 3 |
| $F^+$ | 0 | 0 | 1 | 0 | 0 or 1 |
| $B^+$ | 0 | 0 | 0 | 0 | 0 |
| $C^+$ | 5 | 0 | 0 | 5 | 0 or 1 |
| $A^+$ | 0 | 4 | 0 | 0 | 0 or 1 or 2 |

|   | $C_1$ | $C_2$ | $C_3$ | $C_4$ | possible g.e. |
|---|---|---|---|---|---|
| $E^-$ | 0 | 0 | 0 | 4 | 0 or 1 or 2 or 3 |
| $D^-$ | 5 | 0 | 0 | 0 | 0 or 1 or 2 |
| $F^-$ | 0 | 3 | 0 | 4 | 0 or 1 |
| $B^-$ | 0 | 4 | 0 | 5 | 1 |
| $C^-$ | 0 | 5 | 5 | 0 | 2 |
| $A^-$ | 5 | 0 | 4 | 0 | 3 |

Next, let us consider $E^-, \cdots, A^-$ and show their possible global evaluations. Since $E$ has a positive evaluation 4, the evaluation of $E^-$ is smaller than 4: $0, 1, 2$ or $3$. We do the same for $D^-$. On the other hand, $B, C$ and $A$ have negative evaluations so $B^-, C^-$ and $A^-$ keep the same evaluations.

For each object $f$, we study the existence of $\mu^+$ for $f^+$ considering $A^{\geq}_{f^+, a}$ and $A^{>}_{f^+, a}$ where $a$ is one of the possible evaluation of $f^+$. In the following table $A^{\geq}$ and $A^{>}$ with respect to $a$ are shown.

|   | $C_1$ | $C_2$ | $C_3$ | $C_4$ | global evaluation | $A^{\geq}$ | $A^{>}$ |
|---|---|---|---|---|---|---|---|
| $E^+$ | 5 | 0 | 5 | 0 | 4 | $\{C_1, C_3\}$ | $\{C_1, C_3\}$ |
| $D^+$ | 0 | 5 | 4 | 5 | 3 | $\{C_2, C_3, C_4\}$ | $\{C_2, C_3, C_4\}$ |
| $F^+$ | 0 | 0 | 1 | 0 | 0 | $\{C_1, C_2, C_3, C_4\}$ | $\{C_3\}$ |
|   |   |   |   |   | or 1 | $\{C_3\}$ | $\emptyset$ |
| $B^+$ | 0 | 0 | 0 | 0 | 0 | $\{C_1, C_2, C_3, C_4\}$ | $\emptyset$ |
| $C^+$ | 5 | 0 | 0 | 5 | 0 | $\{C_1, C_2, C_3, C_4\}$ | $\{C_1, C_4\}$ |
|   |   |   |   |   | or 1 | $\{C_1, C_4\}$ | $\{C_1, C_4\}$ |
| $A^+$ | 0 | 4 | 0 | 0 | 2 or 1 | $\{C_2\}$ | $\{C_2\}$ |
|   |   |   |   |   | or 0 | $\{C_1, C_2, C_3, C_4\}$ | $\{C_2\}$ |

For any value for the global evaluation, a fuzzy measure $\mu^+$ can be identified since the conditions of the proposition 3 for $A^{\geq}$ and $A^{>}$. For example considering that the evaluation of $F^+, B^+, C^+$ and $A^+$ is 0, we can compute $\mu^+$ the fuzzy measure which is the greatest lower bound of the solution set. According to the sets $A^{\geq}$, $\mu^+(C_i) = 0$ for all $i$; $\mu^+(C_i, C_j) = 0$ except for $\mu^+(C_1, C_3) = 4$; $\mu^+(C_1, C_2, C_3) = 4$, $\mu^+(C_1, C_2, C_4) = 0$; $\mu^+(C_1, C_3, C_4) = 4$ and $\mu^+(C_2, C_3, C_4) = 3$. It is easy to prove that this fuzzy measure is compatible with the data set.

Similarly, we study the existence of the fuzzy measure $\mu^-$ for $f^-$.

| | $C_1$ | $C_2$ | $C_3$ | $C_4$ | global evaluation | $A^{\geq}$ | $A^{>}$ |
|---|---|---|---|---|---|---|---|
| $E^-$ | 0 | 0 | 0 | 4 | 3 or 2 or 1 or 0 | $\{C_4\}$ $\{C_1, C_2, C_3, C_4\}$ | $\{C_4\}$ $\{C_4\}$ |
| $D^-$ | 5 | 0 | 0 | 0 | 2 or 1 or 0 | $\{C_1\}$ $\{C_1, C_2, C_3, C_4\}$ | $\{C_1\}$ $\{C_1\}$ |
| $F^-$ | 0 | 3 | 0 | 4 | 0 or 1 | $\{C_1, C_2, C_3, C_4\}$ $\{C_2, C_4\}$ | $\{C_2, C_4\}$ $\{C_2, C_4\}$ |
| $B^-$ | 0 | 4 | 0 | 5 | 1 | $\{C_2, C_4\}$ | $\{C_2, C_4\}$ |
| $C^-$ | 0 | 5 | 5 | 0 | 2 | $\{C_2, C_3\}$ | $\{C_2, C_3\}$ |
| $A^-$ | 5 | 0 | 4 | 0 | 3 | $\{C_1, C_3\}$ | $\{C_1, C_3\}$ |

If $E^-$ has a global evaluation 0, a fuzzy mesure $\mu^-$ can be identified.

Note that both data set associated to $f^+$ and $f^-$ are compatible with the same S-integral if and only if the data set is compatible with a Symmetric S-integral, i.e., a CPTS-integral with $\mu^+ = \mu^-$.

If we look carefully at the conditions presented above, some data sets can be easily identified as cases not compatible with a CPTS-integral. For any pair of data $(f, a)$ we denote $A^{\leq}_{f,a} = \{C_i | f_i \leq a\}$ and $A^{<}_{f,a} = \{C_i | f_i < a\}$.

**Proposition 7.** *If $\exists a^i, a^j \in L^+$ such that $a^i < a^j$ and $A_{i^{\geq}_{f^j, a^j}} \subseteq A_{i^{>}_{f^i, a^i}}$ or if $\exists a^i, a^j \in L^-$ such that $a^i < a^j$ and $A_{i^{\leq}_{f^j, a^j}} \subseteq A_{i^{<}_{f^i, a^i}}$ then the data set is not compatible with a CPTS-integral.*

*Proof.* For all $a^i \in L^+$, we have $A_{i^{\geq}_{f^i, +, a^i}} = A_{i^{\geq}_{f^i, a^i}}$, $A_{i^{>}_{f^i, +, a^i}} = A_{i^{>}_{f^i, a^i}}$ and for all $a^j \in L^-$ we have $A_{i^{\geq}_{f^j, -, -a^j}} = A_{i^{\leq}_{f^j, a^j}}$, $A_{i^{>}_{f^j, -, -a^j}} = A_{i^{<}_{f^j, a^j}}$.

*Example 3.* Let us consider four objects $A, B, C, D$ evaluated with respect to four criteria. The evaluation scale is $\{2, 1, 0, -1, -2\}$.

| | $C_1$ | $C_2$ | $C_3$ | $C_4$ | global evaluation | $A^{\geq}$ | $A^{>}$ | $A^{\leq}$ | $A^{<}$ |
|---|---|---|---|---|---|---|---|---|---|
| $A$ | 2 | 2 | -1 | -1 | 2 | $\{C_1, C_2\}$ | $\emptyset$ | | |
| $B$ | 2 | 2 | -2 | -2 | 1 | $\{C_1, C_2\}$ | $\{C_1, C_2\}$ | | |
| $C$ | -2 | 0 | 2 | 2 | -1 | | | $\{C_1\}$ | $\{C_1\}$ |
| $D$ | -2 | 0 | 1 | 1 | -2 | | | $\{C_1\}$ | $\emptyset$ |

The data set is incompatible since $A^{\geq}_{A,2} \subseteq A^{\geq}_{B,1}$.

Moreover, it is not necessary to identify fuzzy measures for $f^+$ and $f^-$ for each act to prove the CPTS-compatibility. To begin let us define the positive and the negative point of view evaluation.

**Definition 5.** *Assume that $f \in [a^i]$.*

- *The positive point of view evaluation of $f$ is*
  - $a^i$ *if* $a^i \in L^+$
  - $\{a \in L | a \le |a^i|\}$ *if* $a^i \in L^-$.
- *The negative point of view evaluation of $f$ is*
  - $\{a \in L | a \le -a^i\}$ *if* $a^i \in L^+$.
  - $a^i$ *if* $a^i \in L^-$.

In the next example the global evaluation of $C$ is $-2$, and therefore the positive point of view evaluation can be 0 or 1.

For each possible values for the positive and the negative point of view evaluation the sets $A^{\ge}$, $A^{>}$, $A^{\le}$ and $A^{<}$ can be identified. Hence we check the following conditions:

**Proposition 8.** *We consider a data set which entails*

*positive point of view preferences denoted $\{(f^i, a^i)\}_{i \in P}$ where $a^i$ are some elements of $L^+$, $f^i$ represents any objects $f^i \in [a^i]$ and $P$ is a finite set of indexes;*

*negative point of view preferences denoted $\{(g^i, b^i)\}_{i \in Q}$ where $b^i$ are some elements of $L^-$, $g^i$ represents any objects $g^i \in [b^i]$ and $Q$ is a finite set of indexes.*

*There exist at least one family $\{(f^i, a^i)\}$ and one family $\{(g^i, b^i)\}$ such that*

- *for all $a^i, a^j$ present in the family $\{(f^i, a^i)\}$, $a^i < a^j \Rightarrow A^{\ge}_{f^j, a^j} \not\subseteq A^{>}_{f^i, a^i}$*
- *for all $b^i, b^j$ present in the family $\{(g^i, b^i)\}$, $b^i < b^j \Rightarrow A^{\le}_{g^j, b^j} \not\subseteq A^{<}_{g^i, b^i}$*

*if and only if the data set is compatible by a CPTS-integral.*

*Example 4.* Let $\{5, 4, 3, 2, 1, 0, -1, -2, -3, -4, -5\}$ be the evaluation scale, the following data set is representable by a CPTS-integral.

| | $C_1$ | $C_2$ | $C_3$ | $C_4$ | global eval. | positive point of view | $A^{\ge}$ | $A^{>}$ | negative point of view | $A^{\le}$ | $A^{<}$ |
|---|---|---|---|---|---|---|---|---|---|---|---|
| | | | | | | | | | | | 0 |
| $E$ | 5 | 0 | 5 | -4 | 4 | 4 | $\{C_1, C_3\}$ | $\{C_1, C_3\}$ | $-3, -2$ or $-1$ | $\{C_4\}$ | $\{C_4\}$ |
| | | | | | | | | | or 0 | $c$ | $\{C_4\}$ |
| $D$ | -5 | 5 | 4 | 5 | 3 | 3 | $\{C_2, C_3, C_4\}$ | $\{C_2, C_3, C_4\}$ | $-2$ or $-1$ | $\{C_1\}$ | $\{C_1\}$ |
| | | | | | | | | | or 0 | $c$ | $\{C_1\}$ |
| $B$ | 0 | -4 | 0 | -5 | -1 | 0 | $c$ | $\emptyset$ | $-1$ | $\{C_2, C_4\}$ | $\{C_2, C_4\}$ |
| $C$ | 5 | -5 | -5 | 5 | -2 | 0 | $c$ | $\{C_1, C_4\}$ | $-2$ | $\{C_2, C_3\}$ | $\{C_2, C_3\}$ |
| | | | | | | or 1 | $\{C_1, C_4\}$ | $\{C_1, C_4\}$ | | | |
| $A$ | -5 | 4 | -4 | 0 | -3 | 0 | $c$ | $\{C_2\}$ | $-3$ | $\{C_1, C_3\}$ | $\{C_1, C_3\}$ |
| | | | | | | 1 or 2 | $\{C_2\}$ | $\{C_2\}$ | | | |

## 6  How to Represent Incompatible Data

When the data set is not representable by a same CPTS-integral, a recovery containing maximal compatible subsets can be defined as follows. Using the sets

$A^{\geq}, A^{>}, A^{\leq}$ and $A^{<}$ the pairs of incompatible objects can be identified. The set of all these pairs is $I = \{((f, a^i), (g, a^j))| \; \not\exists \mu^-, \mu^+$ such that $CPTS_{\mu^+, \mu^-}(f) = a^i$ and $CPTS_{\mu^+, \mu^-}(g) = a^j\}$. $I^C$ is the set containing all the objects not present in $I$. That is, $I^C$ is a compatible data set.

*Example 5.* We consider four objects, four criteria and the evaluation scale $\{2, 1, 0, -1, -2\}$.

| | $C_1$ | $C_2$ | $C_3$ | $C_4$ | glo. eval. | positive eval. | $A^{\geq}$ | $A^{>}$ | negative eval. | $A^{\leq}$ | $A^{<}$ |
|---|---|---|---|---|---|---|---|---|---|---|---|
| $A$ | 2 | 2 | −1 | −1 | 2 | 2 | $\{C_1, C_2\}$ | $\emptyset$ | −1 | $\{C_3, C_4\}$ | $\emptyset$ |
| | | | | | | | | | or 0 | $\{C_3, C_4\}$ | $\{C_3, C_4\}$ |
| $B$ | 2 | 2 | −2 | −2 | 1 | 1 | $\{C_1, C_2\}$ | $\{C_1, C_2\}$ | 0 | $\{C_3, C_4\}$ | $\{C_3, C_4\}$ |
| $C$ | −2 | 0 | 2 | 2 | −1 | 0 | $\{C_2, C_3, C_4\}$ | $\{C_3, C_4\}$ | −1 | $\{C_1\}$ | $\{C_1\}$ |
| $D$ | −2 | 0 | 1 | 1 | −2 | 0 | $\{C_2, C_3, C_4\}$ | $\{C_3, C_4\}$ | −2 | $\{C_1\}$ | $\emptyset$ |
| | | | | | | or 1 | $\{C_3, C_4\}$ | $\emptyset$ | | | |

We select the evaluations to obtain a maximum number of compatible data:

| | $C_1$ | $C_2$ | $C_3$ | $C_4$ | g.e. | positive eval. | $A^{\geq}$ | $A^{>}$ | negative eval. | $A^{\leq}$ | $A^{<}$ |
|---|---|---|---|---|---|---|---|---|---|---|---|
| $A$ | 2 | 2 | −1 | −1 | 2 | 2 | $\{C_1, C_2\}$ | $\emptyset$ | −1 | $\{C_3, C_4\}$ | $\emptyset$ |
| $B$ | 2 | 2 | −2 | −2 | 1 | 1 | $\{C_1, C_2\}$ | $\{C_1, C_2\}$ | 0 | $\{C_3, C_4\}$ | $\{C_3, C_4\}$ |
| $C$ | −2 | 0 | 2 | 2 | −1 | 0 | $\{C_2, C_3, C_4\}$ | $\{C_3, C_4\}$ | −1 | $\{C_1\}$ | $\{C_1\}$ |
| $D$ | −2 | 0 | 1 | 1 | −2 | 0 | $\{C_2, C_3, C_4\}$ | $\{C_3, C_4\}$ | −2 | $\{C_1\}$ | $\emptyset$ |

Since $A^{\geq}_{A,2} \subseteq A^{\geq}_{B,1}$, the data set $\{(A, 2), (B, 1), (C, -1), (D, -2)\}$ is incompatible, where we have $I = \{((A, 2), (B, 1))\}$: incompatible and $I^c = \{(C, -1), (D, -2)\}$ : compatible.

Assume $((f, a^i), (g, a^j)) \in I$, a pair of incompatible objects, then $I^C \cup \{(f, a^i)\}$ is a compatible set because it satisfies the proposition 8.

- If there exists another pair of incompatible objects containing $(f, a^i)$:
  $((f, a^i), (h, a^k)) \in I$, then $I^C \cup \{(f, a^i), (h, a^k)\}$ is an incompatible set.
- If we consider another pair of incompatible objects which doesn't contain $(f, a^i)$: $((l, a^j), (h, a^k))$ then $I^C \cup \{(f, a^i), (h, a^k)\}$ or $I^C \cup \{(f, a^i), (l, a^j)\}$ is a compatible set.

The set $I$ has a finite number of elements. Therefore adding, as presented above, some objects from $I$ to $I^C$ we can obtain maximal sets of compatible objects, in other words, maximal compatible parts of the original set of data. Given a set of data, we call a compatible part of it a subset of data. After the construction of a subset od data denoted $I_{comp,1}$, we can further obtain $I_{comp,2}$ and so on.

*Example 6.* In the previous example there are two possible maximum sets: $I_{comp,1} = \{(A, 2), (C, -1), (D, -2)\}$ and $I_{comp,2} = \{(B, 1), (C, -1), (D, -2)\}$.

Assume that we have $p$ maximum compatible sets: $I_{comp,1}, \cdots, I_{comp,p}$ by construction $I_{comp,1} \cap \cdots \cap I_{comp,p} = I^C$; $I_{comp,1} \cup \cdots \cup I_{comp,p}$ is the data set.

For each set $I_{comp,k}$ we can identify $\mu_k^-$ and $\mu_k^+$ such that for all $(f, a^i)$ in $I_{comp,k}$, $CPTS_{\mu_k^+, \mu_k^-}(f) = a^i$.

In the above construction, each set $I_{comp,k}$ is a compatible set of data; so we identify a set of pairs of fuzzy measures $\{(\mu_k^-, \mu_k^+)\}$ such that $CPTS_{\mu_k^+, \mu_k^-}$ represents it. Note that for all element $(f, a)$ of the data set, there exists $k$ such that $(f, a) \in I_{comp,k}$, i.e., there exists $\mu_k^-$ and $\mu_k^+$ such that $CPTS_{\mu_k^+, \mu_k^-}(f) = a$.

In the previous example we can identify $(\mu_1^-, \mu_1^+)$ to represent $\{(A, 2), (C, -1), (D, -2)\}$ and $(\mu_2^-, \mu_2^+)$ to represent $\{(B, 1), (C, -1), (D, -2)\}$.

## 7 Concluding Remarks

We have presented an approach to elicit CPTS-integrals agreeing with a data set. Moreover the lower and upper bound of the fuzzy measures which are solutions of this inverse problem have been given. Often, in practice, the data set can't be modeled by a CPTS-integral. In such a case we have proposed a family of CPTS-integrals which can be seen as a covery of the data set.

In this paper we have considered the S-integral on a totally ordered set. On the other hand, the definition of the S-integral can be extended on bounded distributive lattice $(L, \vee, \wedge, 0, 1)$, where 0 is the bottom and 1 is the top. Moreover, a function $f : L^n \to L$ is a S-integral if and only if $f$ is a polynomial function satisfying $f(0, \cdots, 0) = 0$ and $f(1, \cdots, 1) = 1$. It would be interesting to extend our result on the symmetric lattices where the CPTS-integral can be generalized.

## References

1. Pap, E., Mihailović, B.P.: A representation of a comonotone-⊗-additive and monotone functional by two Sugeno integrals. Fuzzy Sets and Systems 155, 77–88 (2005)
2. Rico, A., Grabisch, M., Labreuche, C., Chateauneuf, A.: Preference modelling on totally ordered sets by the Sugeno integral. Discrete Applied Mathematics 147, 113–124 (2005)
3. Prade, H., Rico, A., Serrurier, M., Raufaste, E.: Elicitating Sugeno Integrals: Methodology and a Case Study. In: Sossai, C., Chemello, G. (eds.) ECSQARU 2009. LNCS, vol. 5590, pp. 712–723. Springer, Heidelberg (2009)
4. Sugeno, M.: Ordinal Preference Models Based on S-Integrals and Their Verification. In: Li, S., Wang, X., Okazaki, Y., Kawabe, J., Murofushi, T., Guan, L., et al. (eds.) Nonlinear Mathematics for Uncertainty and its Applications. AISC, vol. 100, pp. 1–18. Springer, Heidelberg (2011)
5. Sugeno, M.: Theory of fuzzy integrals and its applications, Ph.D. Thesis, Tokyo Institute of Technology (1974)
6. Grabisch, M., Labreuche, C.: A decade of application of the Choquet and Sugeno integrals in multi-criteria decision aid. Annals OR 175(1), 247–286 (2010)
7. Dubois, D., Prade, H.: Bipolar Representations in Reasoning, Knowledge Extraction and Decision Processes. In: Greco, S., Hata, Y., Hirano, S., Inuiguchi, M., Miyamoto, S., Nguyen, H.S., Słowiński, R. (eds.) RSCTC 2006. LNCS (LNAI), vol. 4259, pp. 15–26. Springer, Heidelberg (2006)
8. Grabisch, M.: The symmetric Sugeno integral. Fuzzy Sets and Systems 139, 473–490 (2003)
9. Marichal, J.-L.: Weighted lattice polynomials. Discrete Mathematics 309, 814–820 (2009)

# On Weak Null-Additivity of Monotone Measures

Jun Li[1,*], Radko Mesiar[2], and Hemin Wu[3]

[1] School of Science, Communication University of China,
Beijing 100024, China
lijun@cuc.edu.cn
[2] Department of Mathematics and Descriptive Geometry,
Faculty of Civil Engineering, Slovak University of Technology,
SK-81368 Bratislava, Slovakia
mesiar@math.sk
[3] College of Mathematics and Informational Technology,
Xinjiang Educational Institute, Urumqi, Xinjiang 830043, China
whm@xjei.cn

**Abstract.** In this note, the relations between weak null-additivity and pseudometric generating property of monotone measures are discussed. We show that on finite continuous monotone measure spaces $(X, \mathcal{F}, \mu)$, if measurable space $(X, \mathcal{F})$ is $S$-compact (especially, if X is countable), then the weak null-additivity is equivalent to pseudometric generating property. We put a question: abandoning the $S$-compactness condition, does the equivalence remain valid?

**Keywords:** Monotone measure, weak null-additivity, pseudometric generating property.

## 1 Introduction

In non-additive measure theory, various structure characteristics of set functions are proposed and investigated by many authors [1, 2, 7, 10, 11, 13–16, 18, 20–22]. The weak null-additivity and pseudometric generating property (for short, p.g.p.) of monotone measure are very important structure characteristics. They play important roles in the discussion of Egoroff's theorem ([3, 5, 9, 14, 19]), Lusin's theorem ([3, 5, 12, 14, 23]), Lebesgue Decomposition Theorem ([25]), regularity ([5, 8, 12, 14, 17]), absolute continuity ([4]), and atom ([24]) for non-additive measures. For example, Lusin's theorem, which is one of the most important theorems in classical measure theory, is generalized to finite continuous monotone measure space under the weak null-additivity condition [12], that is, the weak null-additivity is a sufficient condition for Lusin's theorem on finite continuous monotone measure spaces. In the same way, we showed that pseudometric generating property is a sufficient condition for Lusin's theorem on monotone measure spaces [14]. The weak null-additivity condition is really weaker than pseudometric generating property. In general, they are not equivalent without additional conditions.

---

* Corresponding author.

S. Greco et al. (Eds.): IPMU 2012, Part IV, CCIS 300, pp. 278–285, 2012.

The weak null-additivity condition is a weak requirement for monotone measure, for this reason, it is very important to clarify the relationship between the two concepts.

In this paper, we show that on finite continuous monotone measure spaces $(X, \mathcal{F}, \mu)$, if measurable space $(X, \mathcal{F})$ is $S$-compact (especially, if X is countable), then the weak null-additivity is equivalent to pseudometric generating property. Since countable measurable spaces with finite continuous monotone measures are often encountered in practice, our result is quite useful. On the other hand, we do no know whether the assumption of $S$-compactness can be abandoned. So an open problem is suggested: on general finite continuous monotone measure spaces, does the weak null-additivity imply pseudometric generating property?

## 2  Notation and Definitions

Let $X$ be a non-empty set, $\mathcal{F}$ a $\sigma$-algebra of subsets of $X$, and $(X, \mathcal{F})$ denotes the measurable space.

**Definition 1.** ([10, 18]) *Set function* $\mu : \mathcal{F} \to [0, +\infty]$ *is called a monotone measure on* $(X, \mathcal{F})$ *iff it satisfies the following requirements:*

(1)  $\mu(\emptyset) = 0$;                                                      *(vanishing at $\emptyset$)*
(2)  $A \subset B$ *and* $A, B \in \mathcal{F}$ $\Rightarrow$ $\mu(A) \leq \mu(B)$.               *(monotonicity)*

When $\mu$ is a monotone measure, the triple $(X, \mathcal{F}, \mu)$ is called a monotone measure space (Pap [18]).

*Note*: In some literature, a set function $\mu$ satisfying the conditions (1) and (2) of Definition 1 is called a fuzzy measure or a non-additive measure.

A monotone measure $\mu : \mathcal{F} \to [0, +\infty]$ is said to be *finite*, if $\mu(X) < \infty$; *continuous from below*, if $\lim_{n \to \infty} \mu(A_n) = \mu(A)$ whenever $A_n \nearrow A$; *continuous from above*, if $\lim_{n \to \infty} \mu(A_n) = \mu(A)$ whenever $A_n \searrow A$ and there exists $n_0$ with $\mu(A_{n_0}) < +\infty$; *continuous*, if $\mu$ is continuous from below and above; *strongly order continuous* [11], if $\lim_{n \to \infty} \mu(A_n) = 0$ whenever $A_n \searrow A$ and $\mu(A) = 0$.

Let $\mathbf{F}$ be the class of all finite real-valued measurable functions on $(X, \mathcal{F}, \mu)$, and let $f \in \mathbf{F}, f_n \in \mathbf{F}$ $(n = 1, 2, \ldots)$ and $\{f_n\}$ denote a sequence of measurable functions. We say that $\{f_n\}$ *converges almost everywhere to $f$ on $X$* , and denote it by $f_n \xrightarrow{a.e.} f \, [\mu]$ , if there is a subset $E \subset X$ such that $\mu(E) = 0$ and $f_n \to f$ on $X \setminus E$; $\{f_n\}$ *converges in measure to $f$ on $X$*, and denote it by $f_n \xrightarrow{\mu} f$, if for any given $\sigma > 0$, $\lim_{n \to +\infty} \mu(\{|f_n - f| \geq \sigma\}) = 0$.

In this paper, we always assume that $\mu$ is a monotone measure on $(X, \mathcal{F})$.

## 3  Weak Null-Additivity and Pseudometric Generating Property

The weak null-additivity and pseudometric generating property of monotone measure are very important structure characteristics (see [2–4, 9, 12, 14, 24, 25]). In this section, we discuss the relations between them.

**Definition 2.** ([22]) *A set function* $\mu : \mathcal{F} \to [0, +\infty]$ *is said to be weakly null-additive , if for any* $E, F \in \mathcal{F}$

$$\mu(E) = \mu(F) = 0 \implies \mu(E \cup F) = 0.$$

**Definition 3.** ([2]) *A set function* $\mu : \mathcal{F} \to [0, +\infty]$ *is said to have pseudometric generating property (for short p.g.p.), if for any* $\{E_n\} \subset \mathcal{F}$ *and* $\{F_n\} \subset \mathcal{F}$,

$$\mu(E_n) \vee \mu(F_n) \to 0 \implies \mu(E_n \cup F_n) \to 0.$$

*Note*: The concept of pseudometric generating property goes back to Dobrakov and Drewnowski in seventies, and this was related to Frechet-Nikodym topology [2, 18].

Obviously, we have the following result.

**Proposition 1.** *If* $\mu$ *has pseudometric generating property, then it is weakly null-additive.*

In general, the inverse statement in Proposition 1 does not hold without additional conditions. The weak null-additivity condition is really weaker than pseudometric generating property. We give the following examples to show it.

*Example 1.* Let $X = \{1, 2, \ldots\}, \mathcal{F} = \wp(X)$. Put

$$\mu(E) = \begin{cases} 1 & \text{if } \{n, n+1\} \subset E \text{ for some n} \\ & \text{or } |E| = \infty, \\ 0 & \text{if } E = \emptyset, \\ \sum\limits_{i \in E} \dfrac{1}{2^i} & \text{otherwise.} \end{cases}$$

It is easy to see that $\mu$ is monotone measure and weakly null-additive. However $\mu$ has not the p.g.p.. In fact, if we take $E_n = \{n\}$ and $F_n = \{n+1\}$, then $\mu(E_n) \vee \mu(F_n) = \frac{1}{2^n} \to 0 \ (n \to \infty)$. But $\mu(E_n \cup F_n) = \mu(\{n, n+1\}) = 1 \nrightarrow 0 \ (n \to \infty)$.

Note that the monotone measure $\mu$ in Example 1 is not strongly order continuous, and hence it is not continuous. In fact, we take $E_n = \{n, n+1, n+2, \cdots\}$, then $E_n \searrow \emptyset \ (n \to \infty)$. But $\mu(E_n) = 1 \nrightarrow 0 \ (n \to \infty)$.

*Example 2.* Let $X = \{1, 2, \ldots\}, \mathcal{F} = \wp(X)$. Put

$$\mu(E) = \begin{cases} 0 & \text{if } E = \{1\} \text{ or } E = \emptyset, \\ \sum\limits_{i \in E} \dfrac{1}{2^i} & \text{if } 1 \notin E, \\ +\infty & \text{otherwise.} \end{cases}$$

It is not difficult to verify that $\mu$ is a continuous monotone measure and $\mu$ is weakly null-additive. But $\mu$ has not the p.g.p.. In fact, we take $E_n = \{n, n+$

$1, n+2, \cdots\}$, $F_n = \{1\}(n = 1, 2, \cdots)$, then $\mu(E_n) = \sum_{i=n}^{\infty} \frac{1}{2^i} \to 0 \ (n \to \infty)$ and $\mu(F_n) = 0 \ (n = 1, 2, \cdots)$. But $\mu(E_n \cup F_n) = \mu(\{1\} \cup \{n, n+1, n+2, \cdots\}) = \infty \ (n = 1, 2, \cdots)$.

Note that the monotone measure $\mu$ in Example 2 is not strongly order continuous, but it is continuous. In fact, if we take $E_n = \{1\} \cup \{n, n+1, n+2, \cdots\}(n = 1, 2, \cdots)$ and $F = \{1\}$, then $E_n \searrow F \ (n \to \infty)$ and $\mu(F) = 0$. But $\mu(E_n) = \infty \ (n = 1, 2, \cdots)$, and hence $\mu(E_n) \nrightarrow 0 \ (n \to \infty)$.

In the following we show that on $S$-compact measurable spaces $(X, \mathcal{F})$ [22], if monotone measure $\mu$ is strongly order continuous, then weak null-additivity implies pseudometric generating property, i.e., weak null-additivity is equivalent to pseudometric generating property.

**Definition 4.** ([22])   A measurable space $(X, \mathcal{F})$ is said to be $S$-compact, if for any sequence of sets in $\mathcal{F}$ there exists some convergent subsequence, i.e., $\forall \{A_n\}_{n \in N} \subset \mathcal{F}$, $\exists \{A_{n_i}\}_{i \in N} \subset \{A_n\}_{n \in N}$ such that,

$$\limsup_{i \to \infty} A_{n_i} = \liminf_{i \to \infty} A_{n_i}.$$

**Theorem 1.** Let $(X, \mathcal{F})$ be $S$-compact. If $\mu$ is strongly order continuous, then weak null-additivity implies p.g.p..

*Proof.* We assume that $\mu$ has not p.g.p.. Then there exist $\epsilon_0 > 0$ and two sequences $\{E_n\}_{n \in N}$ and $\{F_n\}_{n \in N}$ such that

$$\mu(E_n) \vee \mu(F_n) \to 0 \quad \text{while} \quad \mu(E_n \cup F_n) \geq \epsilon_0, \quad \forall \, n \geq 1.$$

Now we show that there exists subsequence $\{E_{n_i}\}_{i \in N}$ of $\{E_n\}_{n \in N}$ such that $\mu\left(\bigcap_{s=1}^{\infty} \bigcup_{i=s}^{\infty} E_{n_i}\right) = 0$. In fact, since $(X, \mathcal{F})$ is $S$-compact, there exists subsequence $\{E_{n_i}\}_{i \in N}$ of $\{E_n\}_{n \in N}$ such that,

$$\limsup_{i \to \infty} E_{n_i} = \liminf_{i \to \infty} E_{n_i},$$

that is,

$$\bigcap_{s=1}^{\infty} \bigcup_{i=s}^{\infty} E_{n_i} = \bigcup_{s=1}^{\infty} \bigcap_{i=s}^{\infty} E_{n_i}.$$

For any fixed $s = 1, 2, \cdots$,

$$0 \leq \mu\left(\bigcap_{i=s}^{\infty} E_{n_i}\right) \leq \mu(E_{n_i}) \quad \forall i \geq s.$$

Noting $\lim_{i \to \infty} \mu(E_{n_i}) = 0$, so $\mu\left(\bigcap_{i=s}^{\infty} E_{n_i}\right) = 0, s = 1, 2, \cdots$. From Proposition 2.3 in [14], we can obtain $\mu\left(\bigcup_{s=1}^{\infty} \bigcap_{i=s}^{\infty} E_{n_i}\right) = 0$. Thus, $\mu\left(\bigcap_{s=1}^{\infty} \bigcup_{i=s}^{\infty} E_{n_i}\right) = 0$.

Similarly, we we can take the subsequence $\{F_{n_i}\}_{i \in N}$ of $\{F_n\}_{n \in N}$ such that $\mu\left(\bigcap_{s=1}^{\infty} \bigcup_{i=s}^{\infty} F_{n_i}\right) = 0$, without any loss of generality.

By the weak null-additivity of $\mu$, we have

$$\mu\left(\bigcap_{s=1}^{\infty}\bigcup_{i=s}^{\infty}(E_{n_i}\cup F_{n_i})\right) = \mu\left((\bigcap_{s=1}^{\infty}\bigcup_{i=s}^{\infty}E_{n_i})\cup(\bigcap_{s=1}^{\infty}\bigcup_{i=s}^{\infty}F_{n_i})\right) = 0.$$

Therefore, from the strong order continuity of $\mu$, we have

$$\limsup_{s\to\infty}\mu(E_{n_s}\cup F_{n_s}) \le \lim_{s\to\infty}\mu\left(\bigcup_{i=s}^{\infty}(E_{n_i}\cup F_{n_i})\right) = 0.$$

This is in contradiction with the fact that

$$\mu(E_{n_s}\cup F_{n_s}) \ge \epsilon_0, \quad \forall s \ge 1.$$

The proposition is now proved.    $\square$

A finite continuous monotone measure is strongly order continuous, from Theorem 1, we obtain the following result.

**Theorem 2.** *Let $(X, \mathcal{F})$ be $S$-compact. If $\mu$ is finite continuous monotone measure, then weak null-additivity implies p.g.p..*

Any countable measurable space is $S$-compact ([22]). As special result of Theorem 1 and 2, we have following consequence.

**Theorem 3.** *Let $(X, \mathcal{F})$ be countable measurable space. If $\mu$ is strongly order continuous or finite continuous, then weak null-additivity implies p.g.p..*

We point out that we do not know whether the assumption of $S$-compactness in Theorem 1, 2 and 3 can be abandoned. So we suggest an open problem, as follows:

**Problem:** Does the weak null-additivity imply pseudometric generating property on general finite continuous monotone measure spaces?

*Note*: On a continuous monotone measure space $(X, \mathcal{F}, \mu)$, if $\mu$ is not finite, then the weak null-additivity may not have pseudometric generating property (see Example 2).

## 4    Weak Null-Additivity and Convergence of Measurable Functions

The weak null-additivity and pseudometric generating property are closely related to the convergence of measurable function sequences. In this section, we describe the links between the two concepts by means of the convergence almost everywhere and the convergence in measure.

We can easily obtain the following proposition.

**Proposition 2.** *The following statements are equivalent:*

(1)  $\mu$ *is weakly null-additive;*

(2)  *for any* $f, g, f_n, g_n \in \mathbf{F}$, $\alpha, \beta \in R^1$,

$$f_n \xrightarrow{a.e} f \text{ and } g_n \xrightarrow{a.e} g \implies \alpha f_n + \beta g_n \xrightarrow{a.e} \alpha f + \beta g;$$

(3)  *for any* $f, g, f_n, g_n \in \mathbf{F}$, $\alpha, \beta \in R^1$,

$$f_n \xrightarrow{a.e} f \text{ and } g_n \xrightarrow{a.e} g \implies (\alpha \wedge f_n) \vee (\beta \wedge g_n) \xrightarrow{a.e} (\alpha \wedge f) \vee (\beta \wedge g);$$

Combining Proposition 2, Theorem 1, and Theorem 3.1 and 3.3 in [10], we can obtain the following result.

**Proposition 3.** *Let* $(X, \mathcal{F})$ *be S-compact (especially, $X$ is countable) and $\mu$ be strongly order continuous or finite continuous. The following statements are equivalent:*

(1)  $\mu$ *is weakly null-additive;*

(2)  $\mu$ *has p.g.p.;*

(3)  *for any* $f, g, f_n, g_n \in \mathbf{F}$, $\alpha, \beta \in R^1$,

$$f_n \xrightarrow{a.e} f \text{ and } g_n \xrightarrow{a.e} g \implies \alpha f_n + \beta g_n \xrightarrow{a.e} \alpha f + \beta g;$$

(4)  *for any* $f, g, f_n, g_n \in \mathbf{F}$, $\alpha, \beta \in R^1$,

$$f_n \xrightarrow{a.e} f \text{ and } g_n \xrightarrow{a.e} g \implies (\alpha \wedge f_n) \vee (\beta \wedge g_n) \xrightarrow{a.e} (\alpha \wedge f) \vee (\beta \wedge g);$$

(5)  *for any* $f, g, f_n, g_n \in \mathbf{F}$, $\alpha, \beta \in R^1$,

$$f_n \xrightarrow{\mu} f \text{ and } g_n \xrightarrow{\mu} g \implies \alpha f_n + \beta g_n \xrightarrow{\mu} \alpha f + \beta g;$$

(6)  *for any* $f, g, f_n, g_n \in \mathbf{F}$, $\alpha, \beta \in R^1$,

$$f_n \xrightarrow{\mu} f \text{ and } g_n \xrightarrow{\mu} g \implies (\alpha \wedge f_n) \vee (\beta \wedge g_n) \xrightarrow{\mu} (\alpha \wedge f) \vee (\beta \wedge g).$$

## 5  Concluding Remarks

In this note, we have discussed the relations between weak null-additivity and pseudometric generating property of monotone measure. For a monotone measure, pseudometric generating property implies weak null-additivity. In general, the inverse statement may not be true (Examples 1 and 2). We show that on finite continuous (or strongly order continuous) monotone measure spaces $(X, \mathcal{F}, \mu)$, if measurable space $(X, \mathcal{F})$ is $S$-compact (especially, X is countable), then the weak null-additivity is equivalent to pseudometric generating property (Theorem 1, 2 and 3). We do no know whether the assumption of $S$-compactness can be abandoned. An open problem is suggested: on general finite continuous monotone measure spaces, does the weak null-additivity imply pseudometric generating property?

**Acknowledgements.** The second author was supported by the grants APVV-0073-10.

# References

1. Asahina, S., Uchino, K., Murofushi, T.: Relationship among continuity conditions and null-additivity conditions in non-additive measure theory. Fuzzy Sets and Systems 157(2), 691–698 (2006)
2. Dobrakov, I., Farkova, J.: On submeasures II. Math. Slovaca 30, 65–81 (1980)
3. Jiang, Q., Wang, S., Ziou, D.: A further investigation for fuzzy measures on metric spaces. Fuzzy Sets and Systems 105(1), 293–297 (1999)
4. Jiang, Q., Wang, S., Ziou, D., Wang, Z., Klir, G.J.: Pseudometric generated preporty and autocontinuity of fuzzy measure. Fuzzy Sets and Systems 112(2), 207–216 (2000)
5. Kawabe, J.: Regularity and Lusin's theorem for Riesz space-valued fuzzy measures. Fuzzy Sets and Systems 158(8), 895–903 (2007)
6. Kawabe, J.: The Alexandroff theorem for Riesz space-valued non-additive measures. Fuzzy Sets and Systems 158(21), 2413–2421 (2007)
7. Kawabe, J.: Continuity and compactness of the indirect product of two non-additive measures. Fuzzy Sets and Systems 160(9), 1327–1333 (2009)
8. Kawabe, J.: Regularities of Riesz space-valued non-additive measures with applications to convergence theorems for Choquet integrals. Fuzzy Sets and Systems 161(5), 642–650 (2010)
9. Li, J., Yasuda, M., Jiang, Q., Suzuki, H., Wang, Z., Klir, G.J.: Convergence of sequence of measurable functions on fuzzy measure space. Fuzzy Sets and Systems 87(3), 385–387 (1997)
10. Li, J., Zhang, Q.: Asymptotic Structural Characteristics of Monotone Measure and Convergence in Monotone measure. The J. of Fuzzy Math. 9(2), 447–459 (2001)
11. Li, J.: Order continuous of monotone set function and convergence of measurable functions sequence. Applied Mathematics and Computation 135(2-3), 211–218 (2003)
12. Li, J., Yasuda, M.: Lusin's theorem on fuzzy measure spaces. Fuzzy Sets and Systems 146(1), 121–133 (2004)
13. Li, J., Yasuda, M.: On Egoroff's theorem on finite monotone non-additive measure space. Fuzzy Sets and Systems 153(1), 71–78 (2005)
14. Li, J., Mesiar, R.: Lusin's theorem on monotone measure spaces. Fuzzy Sets and Systems 175(1), 75–86 (2011)
15. Murofushi, T., Uchino, K., Asahina, S.: Conditions for Egoroff's theorem in non-additive measure theory. Fuzzy Sets and Systems 146, 135–146 (2004)
16. Murofushi, T.: Extensions of (weakly) null-additive, monotone set functions from rings of subsets to generated algebras. Fuzzy Sets and Systems 158(21), 2422–2428 (2007)
17. Narukawa, Y., Murofushi, T.: Choquet integral with respect to a regular non-additive measure. In: Proceedings of FUZZ-IEEE 2004 International Conference, vol. 1, pp. 517–521 (2004)
18. Pap, E.: Null-additive Set Functions. Kluwer Academic Press, Dordrecht (1995)
19. Precupanu, A., Gavrilut, A., Croitoru, A.: A set-valued Egoroff type theorem. Fuzzy Sets and Systems 175(1), 87–95 (2011)

20. Uchino, K., Murofushi, T.: Relations between mathematical properties of fuzzy measures. In: 10th IFSA World Congress, Istanbul, Turkey, pp. 27–30 (2003)
21. Wang, Z.: Asymptotic structural characteristics of fuzzy measure and their applications. Fuzzy Sets and Systems 16, 277–290 (1985)
22. Wang, Z., Klir, G.J.: Generalized Measure Theory. Springer (2009)
23. Watanabe, T., Kawasaki, T., Tanaka, T.: On a sufficient condition of Lusin's theorem for non-additive measures that take values in an ordered topological vector space. Fuzzy Sets and Systems 194, 66–75 (2012)
24. Wu, C., Sun, B.: Pseudo-atoms of fuzzy and non-fuzzy measure. Fuzzy Sets and Systems 158(11), 1258–1272 (2007)
25. Zhang, Q., Xu, Y., Du, W.: Lebesgue decomposition theorem for $\sigma$-finite signed fuzzy measures. Fuzzy Sets and Systems 101(3), 445–451 (1999)

# Some Comments to the Fuzzy Version of the Arrow-Sen Theorem[*]

Davide Martinetti[1], Susana Montes[1], Susana Díaz[1], and Bernard De Baets[2]

[1] Dept. Statistics and O.R., University of Oviedo, Oviedo, Spain
{martinettidavide.uo,montes,diazsusana}@uniovi.es
[2] Dept. Appl. Math., Biometrics and Process Control, University of Ghent,
Ghent, Belgium
Bernard.DeBaets@UGent.be

**Abstract.** The Arrow-Sen Theorem is one of the most important results concerning rationality of choice functions. It states that under suitable hypothesis, several definitions of rationality given by different authors can be considered equivalent. Following the same spirit, other authors have proved that further definitions can also be considered equivalent to rationality. In this work we consider the fuzzy version of this problem, using the most general definition of fuzzy choice function possible. Older results are recalled and in many cases improved and also new theorems are proposed.

**Keywords:** Fuzzy choice function, revealed preference, rationality, Arrow-Sen Theorem.

## 1 Introduction

Choice functions have been widely studied in the last century by several authors. They can be considered as the mathematical expression of the act of choice. A very important property for choice functions is *normality*, that corresponds to the possibility of constructing the choice function starting from a binary preference relation and vice versa, revealing a preference relation from a choice function: when these two processes are reversible, we can speak of a normal choice function. The advantage of having such a strong connection between choice functions and preference relations, is that we can pass interesting properties from one definition to the other. For example, we know that the transitivity of the preference relation is a good property when we speak of the coherence of a decision maker, but what can be considered a good property for a choice function? Several answers to the previous question have been proposed by different authors in different disciplines (see [1, 3, 4, 8–10, 12]). The so-called Arrow-Sen Theorem studies the connection between some rationality conditions and states that under suitable

---

[*] The research reported in this paper has been partially supported by project MTM2010-17844 and the Foundation for the promotion in Asturias of the scientific and technolologic research BP10-090.

S. Greco et al. (Eds.): IPMU 2012, Part IV, CCIS 300, pp. 286–295, 2012.

hypothesis, several of those proposals are equivalent! The significance of this theorem is evident: first of all it proves that different ideas of rationality given by different authors working in separate subjects are substantially equivalent and also mark a common point of departure for future developments in choice theory. This work is inspired by that theorem, but it faces the problem under a different (more general) point of view: the entire theory is revisited using *fuzzy* concepts of choice and preference, as it has been proposed by Banerjee [2] first and extended by Georgescu [5] later. Actually, we will use the notations and definitions proposed in [5], that, to date, are the most general possible. In particular we will try to improve the results contained in Chapter 6 of [5], that is dedicated to the conversion of the Arrow-Sen Theorem to the framework of fuzzy choice functions and fuzzy preference relations. In Section 2 we will recall the classic theory of choice and the Arrow-Sen Theorem, while Section 3 contains the original results of this work, divided into four subsections, one for every one of the subjects treated. Finally, Section 4 summarizes the results achieved and proposes a revised and more general version of the Fuzzy Arrow-Sen Theorem.

## 2    Classic Choice Theory

In this subsection we will briefly recall some notions of classic choice theory that will be re-interpreted in the fuzzy framework in Section 3.

### 2.1    Basic Definition

Let $X$ be a finite set of alternatives. There exist two main ways of representing the preferences of an individual: either through binary preference relations or through choice functions. The former represents the information about the preference by the comparison of any pair of alternatives, while the second indicates which are the chosen alternatives amongst a set of available ones. Hence a (crisp) binary weak preference relation $Q$ on $X$ is a function $Q : X^2 \to [0, 1]$, that can be understood in the following way: if $Q(x, y) = 1$, then the alternative $x$ is considered at least as good as alternative $y$, while $Q(x, y) = 0$ means the contrary. Obviously, $Q(x, x) = 1, \forall x \in X$ (reflexivity). Given a weak preference relation $Q$, a strong preference relation $P$ can be defined as follows $P(x, y) = Q(x, y) \wedge \neg Q(y, x)$, for any $x, y \in X$. Recall some basic properties of binary preference relations:

**completeness** $Q(x, y) \vee Q(y, x) = 1$, for every $x, y \in X$;
**transitivity** $Q(x, y) = 1$ and $Q(y, z) = 1$ imply $Q(x, z) = 1, \forall x, y, z \in X$;
**regularity** if $Q$ is reflexive, complete and transitive.

A choice function $C$ is a function from the family $\mathcal{B}_C$ of non-empty subsets of $X$ into the power set of $X$, denoted $2^X$, such that, for every $S \in \mathcal{B}_C$, it holds $\emptyset \neq C(S) \subseteq S$. Since the two concepts are intimately correlated, it is to be expected some kind of relation between them and in fact we can distinguish two procedures for passing from one definition to another and vice versa:

**rationalization:** given a preference relation $Q$, a choice function can be generated using one of the following procedures:

**G-rationalization:** $G(S,Q) = \{x \in S | Q(x,y) = 1, \forall y \in S\}$, $\forall S \in \mathcal{B}_C$;

**M-rationalization:** $M(S,Q) = \{x \in S | Q(x,y) > Q(y,x), \forall y \in S\}$, $\forall S \in \mathcal{B}_C$;

**revealing preferences:** given a choice function $C$, a preference relation can be revealed from it in one of the following ways:

**Revealed preference:** $R = \{(x,y) \in X^2 | x \in C(S), y \in S,$ for some $S \in \mathcal{B}_C\}$;

**Strong revealed preference:** $\tilde{P} = \{(x,y) \in X^2 | x \in C(S), y \in S$ and $y \notin C(S),$ for some $S \in \mathcal{B}_C\}$;

**Base revealed preference:** $\bar{R} = \{(x,y) \in X^2 | x \in C(\{x,y\})\}$.

**Definition 1.** *A choice function $C$ on $X$ is called G-rational (M-rational respectively) if there exists a weak preference relation $Q$ such that $C(S) = G(S,Q)$ ($C(S) = M(S,Q)$ resp.). A choice function is called G-normal (M-normal respectively) if it is G-rational (M-rational) and the revealed preference $R$ is equal to $Q$.*

The definition of normality is crucial because it entails the equivalence of the two *philosophies*: the preference relation and the choice function approach.

## 2.2 Arrow-Sen Theorem and Further Results on the Rationality Problem

The rationality of a choice function can be based on the notions of normality of a choice function and the regularity of the revealed preference relation. There are multiple attempts for establishing equivalent conditions to the normality of a choice function and the regularity of the revealed preference. Many authors have proposed different definitions, conditions or axioms that were supposed to be the *ultimate* definition of rationality. Here we propose a non-exhaustive list of these conditions:

**Definition 2** ([1, 8–11]). *A choice function $C$ on $X$ can satisfies the following conditions: for all $S, T \in \mathcal{B}_C$ and $x, y \in X$*

**WCA** *Weak Congruence Axiom: if $y \in C(S)$, $x \in S$ and $R(x,y) = 1$, then $x \in C(S)$;*

**SCA** *Strong Congruence Axiom: if $y \in C(S)$, $x \in S$ and $R^T(x,y) = 1$, then $x \in C(S)$, where $R^T$ is the transitive closure of $R$;*

**WARP** *Weak Axiom of Revealed Preference: if $\tilde{P}(x,y) = 1$, then $R(y,x) = 0$;*

**SARP** *Strong Axiom of Revealed Preference: if $\tilde{P}^T(x,y) = 1$, then $R(y,x) = 0$, where $\tilde{P}^T$ is the transitive closure of $\tilde{P}$;*

**Condition** $\alpha$ *if $S \subseteq T$, $x \in S$ and $x \in C(T)$ then $x \in C(S)$;*

**Condition** $\beta$ *if $S \subseteq T$ and $\{x,y\} \in C(S)$, then $x \in C(T)$ iff $y \in C(T)$;*

**Condition** $\delta$ *if $S \subseteq T$ and there exists $x \neq y$ such that $\{x,y\} \in C(S)$, then $C(T) \neq \{x\}$;*

For an intuitive explanation of the previous conditions, see [11]. One of the most interesting results in choice theory is the so-called *Arrow-Sen Theorem*, that states the equivalence of some of the previous conditions (and other that will be listed later). It constituted a milestone in classic choice theory, because any other attempt of definition of rationality since the theorem was proved, needed to be compared with the definitions contained in it. Unfortunately, such a beautiful result cannot be proved without imposing a (quite strong) condition on the domain of the choice function:

**Definition 3.** *A choice function $C$ satisfies hypothesis H iff the domain of $C$ contains all finite subsets of $X$, i.e. $\mathcal{B}_C = 2^X$.*

A deep discussion on hypothesis H can be found in Chapter 6 of [11], while weaker results have been proved without hypothesis H by Richter and Suzumura in [8, 12]. In the sake of brevity, we will report here a modified version of the original Arrow-Sen Theorem, including also those equivalent conditions that were not considered by Sen in [11], but have been added later by other authors:

**Theorem 4.** *Let $C$ be a choice function and $R$ its revealed preference. If hypothesis H is verified, then the condition $R$ regular and $C$ G-normal is equivalent to any one of the following conditions:*

1. *Conditions $\alpha$ and $\beta$;*     3. *WARP;*      5. *WCA;*
2. *$R = \tilde{R}$;*      4. *SARP;*      6. *SCA;*

# 3   Fuzzy Choice Theory

In this section we will present the fuzzy approach to choice theory. After recalling the definitions and basic properties that are characteristic of this new framework, we will present our original results.

## 3.1   Basic Definitions

The next paragraphs are dedicated to extend the classic definitions of logic connectives, preference relations, choice functions and rationality to the new framework. We follow the constructions and definitions proposed by Georgescu in [5].

*Fuzzy logic operators: t-norms, negators and residual implicators* In fuzzy theory the boolean logical operators AND, OR, NO and THEN are typically represented through t-norms, t-conorms, fuzzy negations and fuzzy implications respectively.

**Definition 5.** *A triangular norm (t-norm for short) is a commutative, associative, increasing in each component binary operator $*$ from the unit square to $[0, 1]$ with neutral element 1.*

The three most popular examples of t-norms are the minimum, $a *_M b = a \wedge b$, the product, $a *_P b = a \cdot b$ and the Łukasiewicz operator, $a *_L b = (a + b - 1) \vee 0$. A t-norm is continuous if it is a continuous two-place function. A t-norm is continuous if and only if all partial mappings are continuous. A t-norm is left-continuous if all partial mappings are left-continuous. A t-norm $*$ is said to have zero divisors if there exists at least one pair of values $(a, b) \in (0, 1)^2$, such that $a * b = 0$. A t-norm is called strict if it is continuous and strictly monotone. Associated to any t-norm we can define an implication operator (or residuum) and a negation:

**Definition 6.** *Let $*$ be a left-continuous t-norm. Then the implication operator associated to $*$ is a binary operator defined as $\rightarrow: [0, 1] \times [0, 1] \rightarrow [0, 1]$ and such that $a \rightarrow b = \sup(c \in [0, 1] | a * c \leq b)$. The negation operator associated to $*$ is defined by $\neg a = a \rightarrow 0$.*

Negations defined in this way are sometimes called *residual negators* or *induced negations*, like in [6, 7]. In those works is underlined the importance of rotation invariant property of the t-norm w.r.t. the negation: $x * y \leq z \Leftrightarrow y * \neg z \leq \neg x$. The relevance of the t-norms that satisfy rotation invariance property is that the induced negation is always a *strong negation*, i.e. a negation that is strictly decreasing and such that $\neg \neg x = x$. All along this work we are supposing that the t-norm is chosen first and then implication and negation operators are derived from it according to Definition 6. In no case we will work with one t-norm and an implication operator or an induced negation derived from another t-norm. For this reason we can avoid the classical notation of implication and negation operators ($\rightarrow_*$ and $\neg_*$) in which the dependence from the t-norm has to be exhibited. This also makes the difference with the work of [13], in which the negation is always the standard negation $\neg x = 1 - x$, independently of the t-norm considered.

*Fuzzy Preference Relations.* Fuzzy relations are a generalization of the classical (crisp) concept of binary relation. A fuzzy binary relation is a function from $X \times X \rightarrow [0, 1]$, such that if $x, y$ are two alternatives in $X$, then the value of $Q(x, y)$ stands for the degree up to which $x$ is connected to $y$ by $Q$. The fuzzy relation $Q$ can be easily represented through a matrix $Q = (q_{ij})_{i, j \in \{1, \ldots, N\}}$, where $q_{ij} = Q(x_i, x_j)$. In this work we are interested in fuzzy preference relations, i.e. reflexive fuzzy relations (for all $x \in X$, $Q(x, x) = 1$). If $Q$ is a fuzzy preference relation, $Q(x, y)$ can be interpreted as the degree up to which $x$ is considered at least as good as $y$. Given a fuzzy preference relation $Q$, its asymmetric part $P_Q$ that represents the degree of strict preference is computed as $P_Q(x, y) = Q(x, y) * \neg Q(y, x)$. Other properties that will be considered are:

**strong completeness** if $Q(x, y) \vee Q(y, x) = 1$, for all $x, y \in X$;
**$*$-transitivity** if $Q(x, y) * Q(y, z) \leq Q(x, z)$, for all $x, y, z \in X$;
**quasi-transitivity** if $P_Q(x, y) * P_Q(y, z) \leq P_Q(x, z)$, for all $x, y, z \in X$;
**regularity** if it is strongly complete, reflexive and $*$-transitive.

Given a fuzzy preference relation $Q$ we will denote by $Q^T$ its $*$-transitive closure, i.e. the smallest fuzzy preference relation $Q^T$ such that $Q^T(x,y) \geq Q(x,y)$, for every $x, y \in X$ and $Q^T$ is $*$-transitive.

*Fuzzy Choice Function.* Let $X$ be a set of alternatives and $\mathcal{F}(X)$ the set of all fuzzy subsets in $X$. Denote by $\mathcal{B}$ a subset of $\mathcal{F}(X) \setminus \{\emptyset\}$, which elements are called *criteria* or *available sets*. Given a set $S \in \mathcal{B}$, the value of $S(x)$ indicates the *degree of availability* of the alternative $x$ when the set $S$ is considered.

**Definition 7.** [5] *A fuzzy choice function in Georgescu sense (fuzzy choice function from now on) is a function $C : \mathcal{B} \to \mathcal{F}(X)$ that assigns to each available set $S$ a fuzzy set $C(S)$ (called chosen set) in such a way that, for every $S \in \mathcal{B}$ it holds that:*

1. *there exists at least one alternative $x \in X$, such that $C(S)(x) > 0$;*
2. *$C(S)(x) \leq S(x)$, for every $x \in X$.*

The former condition establishes that for every available set, at least one alternative has to be chosen to some positive degree, while the second entails that an element cannot be more *eligible* than *available*. Inclusion between fuzzy sets is expressed through the following operator (see [5]):

**subsethood degree** $I(S,T) = \bigwedge_{x \in X}(S(x) \to T(x))$, for every $S, T \in \mathcal{F}(X)$;

Given a fuzzy choice function $C$, the revealed preference $R$ associated to $C$ is defined by:

$$R(x,y) = \sup_{S \in \mathcal{B}}(C(S)(x) * S(y)), \text{ for every } x, y \in X. \tag{1}$$

The value of $R(x,y)$ measures the maximum degree up to which the alternative $x$ is chosen, when $y$ is also available. Other ways of deriving a preference relation from a fuzzy choice function can be found in [5]:

- $\bar{R}(x,y) = C(\{x,y\})(x)$, where $\{x,y\}$ is the crisp set containing $x$ and $y$;
- $\tilde{P}(x,y) = \sup_{S \in \mathcal{B}}(C(S)(x) * S(y) * \neg C(S)(y))$.

*The Rationality Problem in the Fuzzy Framework.* In [5], the author showed two ways of rationalizing a choice function given a fuzzy preference relation $Q$. Using the concepts of greatest and maximal elements of a set w.r.t. a preference relation $Q$, two functions can be defined:

**Definition 8.** [5] *Let $Q$ be a fuzzy preference relation on $X$, then for every $S \in \mathcal{B}$ and every $x \in X$, let us define the following functions $G : \mathcal{B} \to \mathcal{F}(X)$ such that, for every $S \in \mathcal{B}$ and $x \in X$, it holds*

$$G(S,Q)(x) = S(x) * \bigwedge_{y \in X}(S(y) \to Q(x,y))$$

*and $M : \mathcal{B} \to \mathcal{F}(X)$ such that, for every $S \in \mathcal{B}$ and $x \in X$, it holds*

$$M(S,Q)(x) = S(x) * \bigwedge_{y \in X}(S(y) \to (Q(y,x) \to Q(x,y))).$$

*A fuzzy choice function $C$ is called G-rational if there exists a fuzzy preference relation $Q$, such that $C(S)(x) = G(S,Q)(x)$, for every $S \in \mathcal{B}$ and $x \in X$. It is called M-rational if the same happens for the function $M(\cdot, Q)$. A fuzzy choice function $C$ is called G-normal (M-normal resp.) if it is G-rational (M-rational resp.) with the relation $Q$ and the revealed preference relation $R$ from $C$ is such that $Q = R$.*

Also the classical conditions of rationality here listed in Definition 2 have been modified in [5] to fit with the new fuzzy framework:

**Definition 9.** *A fuzzy choice function $C$ on $X$ can satisfy the following conditions*

- *Weak Fuzzy Congruence Axiom (WFCA): $R(x,y)*S(x)*C(S)(y) \leq C(S)(x)$, for any $S \in \mathcal{B}_C$ and $x,y \in X$;*
- *Strong Fuzzy Congruence Axiom (SFCA): $R^T(x,y) * S(x) * C(S)(y) \leq C(S)(x)$, for any $S \in \mathcal{B}_C$ and $x,y \in X$;*
- *Weak Axiom of Fuzzy Revealed Preference (WAFRP): $\tilde{P}(x,y) \leq \neg R(y,x)$, for any $x,y \in X$;*
- *Strong Axiom of Fuzzy Revealed Preference (SAFRP): $\tilde{P}^T(x,y) \leq \neg R(y,x)$, for any $x,y \in X$;*
- *F$\alpha$: $I(S,T) * S(x) * C(T)(x) \leq C(S)(x)$, for any $S,T \in \mathcal{B}_C$ and $x \in X$;*
- *F$\beta$: if for any $S,T \in \mathcal{B}_C$ and $x,y \in X$ it holds that*
  $I(S,T)*C(S)(x)*C(S)(y) \leq ((C(T)(x) \to C(T)(y)) \wedge (C(T)(y) \to C(T)(x)))$;
- *F$\delta$: for every pair of crisp sets $S = [a_1, \ldots, a_n]$, $T = [b_1, \ldots, b_m]$ in $\mathcal{B}$ and $x \neq y \in X$, the following holds:*

$$I(S,T) * C(S)(x) * C(S)(y) \leq \neg \left( C(T)(x) * \bigwedge_{t \neq x} (\neg C(T)(t)) \right)$$

Also hypothesis H of the classic theory needs to be modified, as in [5]:

H1 All $S \in \mathcal{B}$ and $C(S)$ are normal fuzzy sets, i.e. there exists $x \in X$ such that $S(x) = 1$;

H2 $\mathcal{B}$ contains all crisp subsets of $X$, except for the empty set.

## 3.2    G- and M- Normality and Rationality

In this section we investigate if there exist some implications among the four rationality conditions (G-rationality/normality and M-rationality/normality) of a fuzzy choice function. First of all, recall the implications that are valid in general (without H1 and H2): obviously, if the fuzzy choice function $C$ is G-normal (M-normal respectively) then it is G-rational (M-rational resp.). Furthermore, by Lemma 5.36 of [5], if $C$ is M-rational, then it is G-rational too. From now on, we will always assume that hypothesis H1 and H2 are verified and that the t-norm is at least left-continuous.

**Lemma 10.** *If a fuzzy choice function C is G-rational, it is also G-normal. Hence G-normality and G-rationality are equivalent.*

**Lemma 11.** *Any M-rational fuzzy choice function is also M-normal. Hence M-rationality and M-normality are equivalent conditions.*

Finally, using Lemmas 10 and 11, we can state the following result:

**Theorem 12.** *The following four conditions of rationality are equivalent:*
1. *M-rationality;*                                3. *M-normality;*
2. *G-rationality;*                                4. *G-normality.*

### 3.3 Fuzzy Revealed Preference and Fuzzy Congruence Axioms

This section is dedicated to the four conditions WAFRP, SAFRP, WFCA and SFCA. In Theorem 4 it has been proved that their crisp counterparts are equivalent. In [5] some implications between these conditions have been proved, but a strong condition was required ($* = *_L$). Here we extend those results to a larger family of t-norms, i.e. rotation invariant t-norms. Recall that also in this subsection hypothesis H1 and H2 are supposed to hold. Let us start by recalling those implications that are trivial or already proved for every t-norm:

- SAFRP implies WAFRP;
- SFCA implies WFCA;
- WFCA implies SFCA (see Proposition 6.1 in [5]);
- if $R$ is regular and $C$ is $G-$normal then $C$ satisfies WFCA, while the opposite implication holds only when the t-norm is the minimum operator (see [5]).

We have been able to prove additional connections:

**Theorem 13.** *The following statements are verified:*

1. *For any t-norm $*$, WAFRP is equivalent to SAFRP.*
2. *For any t-norm $*$, WFCA is equivalent to SFCA.*
3. *For any t-norm $*$, WFCA implies WAFRP.*
4. *If $*$ is rotation invariant, then WAFRP implies WFCA and hence the four conditions are equivalent.*

### 3.4 Expansion Contraction Conditions and Rationality

In this section we will analyse the so-called contraction/expansion conditions F$\alpha$ and F$\beta$ in relation with the problem of rationality of a fuzzy choice function. In [5] some results have already been proposed, as the following one

**Proposition 14 (Proposition 6.12 of [5]).** *Let $C$ be a fuzzy choice function on $X$ and $*$ the minimum t-norm. If $C$ satisfies conditions F$\alpha$ and F$\beta$, then it also satisfies WFCA.*

But those results impose too restrictive conditions on the t-norm as we have seen. We next present general results, valid for any t-norm except in one case:

**Theorem 15.** *Under hypothesis H1 and H2, the following statements are true for a fuzzy choice function C:*

1. *For any t-norm $*$, if C satisfies property WFCA, then $\bar{R} = R$;*
2. *For any t-norm $*$, if C satisfies property WFCA, then condition $F\alpha$ is verified;*
3. *If $*$ is the minimum t-norm and C satisfies property WFCA, then C satisfies property $F\beta$;*
4. *For any t-norm $*$, if C is G-normal and R is $*$-transitive, then property $F\beta$ holds;*

Moreover, we have two counterexamples which show that the conditions on the t-norm in Proposition 14 and Point 3 of Theorem 15 cannot be weakened.

### 3.5  Quasi-Transitivity and Condition F$\delta$

Sen proved in Theorem 10 of [11] that in the crisp case, for a normal choice function, condition $\delta$ is equivalent to quasi-transitivity of the revealed preference $R$. The aim of this subsection is to investigate if the result of Sen can be extended to the fuzzy framework. A first attempt can be found in [5], but the conditions over the t-norm were too restrictive. We have proven that one of the implications holds for any left-continuous t-norm, but the converse implication only holds for a more particular family of t-norms.

**Theorem 16.** *If hypothesis H1 and H2 are verified and the fuzzy choice function C is G-normal and satisfies property F$\delta$ with respect to any left-continuous t-norm, then the revealed preference relation R is quasi-transitive. The opposite implication holds true only when the t-norm is strict.*

We have a counterexample which shows that the restriction to strict t-norms in Theorem 16 cannot be weakened.

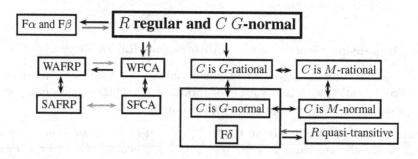

**Fig. 1.** Summary of the achieved results

# 4   Conclusions and Open Problems

The results obtained are summarized in Figure 1. An arrow going from one box to another indicates that the former condition implies the second, but not vice versa. The colors of the arrow are used to indicate for which t-norms the implications hold. Black arrows indicate no condition (apart from left-continuity), red arrows indicate that the t-norm is the minimum, green arrows indicate that the t-norm is rotation invariant, while the blue arrow indicates that the t-norm is strict. Recall that all the results are obtained under hypothesis H1 and H2.

# References

1. Arrow, K.J.: Rational choice functions and orderings. Economica 26, 121–127 (1959)
2. Banerjee, A.: Fuzzy preferences and arrow-type problems in social choice. Social Choice and Welfare 11, 121–130 (1994)
3. Cutello, V., Montero, J.: Equivalence and compositions of fuzzy rationality measures. Fuzzy Sets and Systems 85, 31–43 (1997)
4. Cutello, V., Montero, J.: Fuzzy rationality measures. Fuzzy Sets and Systems 62, 39–54 (1994)
5. Georgescu, I.: Fuzzy choice functions, A revealed Preference Approach. Springer, Berlin (2007)
6. Jenei, J.: Continuity of left-continuous triangular norms with strong induced negations and their boundary condition. Fuzzy Sets and Systems 124, 35–41 (2001)
7. Maes, K.C., De Baets, B.: Rotation-invariant t-norms: the rotation invariance property revisited. Fuzzy Sets and Systems 160, 44–51 (2009)
8. Richter, M.K.: Revealed preference theory. Econometrica 34, 635–645 (1966)
9. Samuelson, P.A.: A note on the pure theory of consumer's behavior. Economica 5, 61–71 (1938)
10. Sen, A.: Quasi-transitivity, rational choice and collective decisions. The Review of Economic Studies 36, 381–393 (1969)
11. Sen, A.: Choice function and revealed preference. Review of Economic Studies 38, 307–317 (1971)
12. Suzumura, K.: Rational choice and revealed preference. Review of Economic Studies 43, 149–159 (1976)
13. Wu, C., Wang, W., Hao, Y.: A further study on rationality conditions of fuzzy choice functions. Fuzzy Sets and Systems 176, 1–19 (2011)

# Product Triplets in Winning Probability Relations

Karel De Loof[1], Bernard De Baets[1], and Hans De Meyer[2]

[1] Department of Mathematical Modelling, Statistics and Bioinformatics, Ghent University, Coupure links 653, B-9000 Gent, Belgium
karel.deloof@ugent.be
[2] Department of Applied Mathematics and Computer Science, Ghent University, Krijgslaan 281 S9, B-9000 Gent, Belgium

**Abstract.** It is known that the winning probability relation of a dice model, which amounts to the pairwise comparison of a set of independent random variables that are uniformly distributed on finite integer multisets, is dice transitive. The condition of dice transitivity, also called the 3-cycle condition, is, however, not sufficient for an arbitrary rational-valued reciprocal relation to be the winning probability relation of a dice model. An additional necessary condition, called the 4-cycle condition, is introduced in this contribution. Moreover, we reveal a remarkable relationship between the 3-cycle condition and the number of so-called product triplets of a reciprocal relation. Finally, we experimentally count product triplets for several families of winning probability relations.

**Keywords:** dice representability, dice transitivity, independent random variables, product triplets, reciprocal relation, winning probability relation.

## 1 Introduction

We define a *dice model* $\mathcal{D}$ as a tuple $(D_1, \ldots, D_m, Q)$ consisting of $m \geq 2$ dice, where each dice $D_i$ is represented by the multiset of integers present on its $n_i$ faces, and a rational-valued reciprocal relation $Q$ expressing the winning probability of one dice over another, henceforth called the *winning probability relation* of $\mathcal{D}$, defined by:

$$Q(D_i, D_j) = \text{Prob}\{D_i > D_j\} + \frac{1}{2}\text{Prob}\{D_i = D_j\},$$

where

$$\text{Prob}\{D_i > D_j\} = \frac{\#\{(x,y) \in D_i \times D_j \mid x > y\}}{n_i n_j},$$

$$\text{Prob}\{D_i = D_j\} = \frac{\#\{(x,y) \in D_i \times D_j \mid x = y\}}{n_i n_j}.$$

S. Greco et al. (Eds.): IPMU 2012, Part IV, CCIS 300, pp. 296–305, 2012.
© Springer-Verlag Berlin Heidelberg 2012

Recall that a reciprocal relation $R$ on a set $A$ is a mapping from $A^2$ to $[0,1]$ such that for all $a, b \in A$ it holds that $R(a,b) + R(b,a) = 1$. Reciprocal relations serve as a popular representation in various preference models [1,6,9], where $R(x,y)$ expresses the degree of preference of alternative $x$ over alternative $y$. Note that we assume that each face of a dice has an equal likelihood of showing up when the corresponding dice is randomly rolled.

As an example, consider the three dice $E_1 = \{4,4,4,4,0,0\}$, $E_2 = \{3,3,3,3,3,3\}$, $E_3 = \{6,6,2,2,2,2\}$, and denote the winning probability relation as $Q_3$. One easily verifies that $Q_3(E_1, E_2) = Q_3(E_2, E_3) = 2/3$ and $Q_3(E_3, E_1) = 5/9$. If $Q_3(X,Y) > 1/2$, we say that dice $X$ is strictly preferred over dice $Y$ and write $X \triangleright Y$. This reflects the fact that dice $X$ wins from dice $Y$ in the long run. Since $E_1 \triangleright E_2$, $E_2 \triangleright E_3$ and $E_3 \triangleright E_1$, the relation $\triangleright$ is not transitive and forms a cycle. As a consequence, upon the selection of any of the dice $E_1, E_2$ or $E_3$, one of the remaining dice is always strictly preferred over it. The occurrence of such non-transitive dice is an intriguing phenomenon belonging to the popular non-transitivity paradoxes receiving considerable attention [7,8]. Note that the winning probability relation is closely related to the probability dominance relation [10], shown to be transitive for several distributions on the random variables.

Let us now consider a fourth dice $E_4 = \{5,5,5,1,1,1\}$ such that the winning probability relation $Q_4$ of a set of four dice is obtained. It holds that

$$Q_4(E_1, E_2) = Q_4(E_2, E_3) = Q_4(E_3, E_4) = Q_4(E_4, E_1) = 2/3 \,,$$

whence $E_1 \triangleright E_2$, $E_2 \triangleright E_3$, $E_3 \triangleright E_4$ and $E_4 \triangleright E_1$. These non-transitive dice are known as *Efron's dice* [7].

We can represent a reciprocal relation $Q$ on a set $A$ by a directed, weighted and complete graph. In this graph, called a *reciprocally weighted graph* and denoted as $G_Q$, the vertices are the elements of $A$ and the edges $(a,b) \in A^2$ have a weight $Q(a,b)$. We call the reciprocally weighted graph $G_Q$ representing the winning probability relation $Q$ of some dice model $\mathcal{D}$ the *winning probability graph* of $Q$. In Figure 1, the winning probability graph $G_{Q_4}$ of Efron's dice is shown. Note that for the sake of clarity only edges $(a,b)$ are drawn for which $Q_4(a,b) \geq 1/2$. Due to reciprocity, the weights of the inverse edges follow by complementation.

It is known that the winning probability relation of a dice model exhibits a type of cycle transitivity called dice transitivity [5]. In Section 2 of this contribution, the fundamentals of the cycle transitivity framework are briefly recalled. Section 3 introduces the notion of dice representability and explains why the condition of dice transitivity for rational-valued reciprocal relations to be dice representable is aptly called the 3-cycle condition. In the next section, an additional necessary condition for dice representability, called the 4-cycle condition, is given. In Section 4, we finally reveal a remarkable relationship between the 3-cycle condition and the number of so-called product triplets of a reciprocal relation. Furthermore, we experimentally determine the distribution of the number of product triplets for several families of winning probability relations.

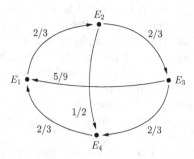

**Fig. 1.** The winning probability graph $G_{Q_4}$ representing winning probability relation $Q_4$ where only edges $(a, b)$ are drawn for which $Q_4(a, b) \geq 1/2$

## 2   The Cycle Transitivity Framework

The transitivity of winning probability relations has been studied extensively by some of the present authors [4,5], resulting in a new framework for studying transitivity of reciprocal relations in general, referred to as the cycle transitivity framework [2,3].

Consider a reciprocal relation $Q$ on an arbitrary set $A$. For any $(a, b, c) \in A^3$, let

$$\alpha_{abc} = \min(Q(a, b), Q(b, c), Q(c, a)),$$
$$\beta_{abc} = \text{median}(Q(a, b), Q(b, c), Q(c, a)),$$
$$\gamma_{abc} = \max(Q(a, b), Q(b, c), Q(c, a)).$$

It then obviously holds that $\alpha_{abc} \leq \beta_{abc} \leq \gamma_{abc}$, and also $\alpha_{abc} = \alpha_{bca} = \alpha_{cab}$, $\beta_{abc} = \beta_{bca} = \beta_{cab}$ and $\gamma_{abc} = \gamma_{bca} = \gamma_{cab}$. On the other hand, the reciprocity of $Q$ implies that $\alpha_{cba} = 1 - \gamma_{abc}$, $\beta_{cba} = 1 - \beta_{abc}$ and $\gamma_{cba} = 1 - \alpha_{abc}$. When no confusion is possible, we drop the indices $a$, $b$ and $c$.

**Definition 1.** *Let $\Delta = \{(x, y, z) \in [0,1]^3 \mid x \leq y \leq z\}$. A function $U : \Delta \to \mathbb{R}$ is called an upper bound function if it satisfies:*

*(i) $U(0, 0, 1) \geq 0$ and $U(0, 1, 1) \geq 1$;*
*(ii) for any $(\alpha, \beta, \gamma) \in \Delta$:*

$$U(\alpha, \beta, \gamma) + U(1 - \gamma, 1 - \beta, 1 - \alpha) \geq 1.$$

Note that the definition of an upper bound function does not include any monotonicity condition. The function $L : \Delta \to \mathbb{R}$ defined by

$$L(\alpha, \beta, \gamma) = 1 - U(1 - \gamma, 1 - \beta, 1 - \alpha)$$

is called the *dual lower bound function* of a given upper bound function $U$.

**Definition 2.** *A reciprocal relation $Q$ on a set $A$ is called cycle transitive w.r.t. an upper bound function $U$ if for any $(a, b, c) \in A^3$ it holds that*

$$L(\alpha_{abc}, \beta_{abc}, \gamma_{abc}) \leq \alpha_{abc} + \beta_{abc} + \gamma_{abc} - 1 \leq U(\alpha_{abc}, \beta_{abc}, \gamma_{abc}), \qquad (1)$$

*where $L$ is the dual lower bound function of $U$.*

Due to the built-in duality, it holds that if (1) is true for some $(a, b, c)$, then this is also the case for any permutation of $(a, b, c)$. In practice, it is therefore sufficient to check (1) for a single permutation of any $(a, b, c) \in A^3$. Alternatively, due to the same duality, it is also sufficient to verify the right-hand inequality (or equivalently, the left-hand inequality) for two permutations of any $(a, b, c) \in A^3$ (not being cyclic permutations of one another), e.g. $(a, b, c)$ and $(c, b, a)$.

For two upper bound functions such that $U_1 \leq U_2$, it clearly holds that cycle transitivity w.r.t. $U_1$ implies cycle transitivity w.r.t. $U_2$. It is clear that $U_1 \leq U_2$ is not a necessary condition for the latter implication to hold. Two upper bound functions $U_1$ and $U_2$ are called equivalent if cycle transitivity w.r.t. $U_1$ is equivalent to cycle transitivity w.r.t. $U_2$.

We finally mention that some of the present authors have shown that the winning probability relation of any dice model $\mathcal{D}$ exhibits a type of cycle transitivity called dice transitivity [5].

**Definition 3.** *A reciprocal relation $Q$ is called dice transitive if it is cycle transitive w.r.t. the upper bound function*

$$U(\alpha, \beta, \gamma) = \beta + \gamma - \beta\gamma. \tag{2}$$

**Proposition 1.** *The winning probability relation of any dice model $\mathcal{D}$ is dice transitive.*

# 3   Dice Representability of a Reciprocal Relation

As we will focus on necessary conditions for a rational-valued reciprocal relation $Q$ to be the winning probability relation of a dice model $\mathcal{D}$, we introduce the notion of dice representability.

**Definition 4.** *A rational-valued reciprocal relation $Q$ is called dice representable if it is the winning probability relation of some dice model $\mathcal{D}$.*

Let us now slightly reformulate the dice transitivity condition (2) to suit our purposes.

**Proposition 2.** *[4,5] A reciprocal relation $Q$ is dice transitive if and only if for the consecutive weights $(t_1, t_2, t_3)$ in any 3-cycle in the winning probability graph $G_Q$ it holds that*

$$t_1 + t_2 + t_3 - 1 \geq \min(t_1 t_2, t_2 t_3, t_3 t_1). \tag{3}$$

As dice transitivity imposes conditions on 3-cycles, we will call it the *3-cycle condition*. Remark the cyclic nature of this condition: imposing condition (3) on one permutation of $t_1, t_2, t_3$ is sufficient for all cyclic permutations of it to satisfy condition (3). Note that a 3-cycle with consecutive weights $(t_1, t_2, t_3)$ is said to fulfill the 3-cycle condition if it satisfies condition (3).

Adopting the above terminology, Proposition 1 can be rewritten as follows.

**Proposition 3.** [5] *The winning probability relation of any dice model satisfies the 3-cycle condition.*

Remarkably, some of the present authors [5] have been able to show that the 3-cycle condition is also sufficient for the dice representability of a rational-valued reciprocal relation on a set of three elements. In other words, a rational-valued reciprocal relation is the winning probability relation of a set of three dice (such as $Q_3$), *i.e.* a reciprocal relation obtained through pairwisely comparing three independent discrete random variables that are uniformly distributed on finite integer multisets, if and only if it satisfies the 3-cycle condition.

The following essential theorem summarizes the above findings.

**Theorem 1.** [5] *A rational-valued reciprocal relation $Q$ on a set of three elements is dice representable if and only if it satisfies the 3-cycle condition.*

Although the 3-cycle condition is fulfilled by the winning probability relation of an arbitrary set of dice (such as $Q_4$), *i.e.* by any dice representable relation, it is no longer sufficient for a rational-valued reciprocal relation on a set of four or more elements to be dice representable [5].

Note that, without loss of generality, we can assume that all numbers on the faces of the dice $D_i$ in a dice model $\mathcal{D}$ are unique and that $D_i \subseteq [1, n_1 + n_2 + \ldots + n_m] \cap \mathbb{N}$. We call such a dice model standardized. If a dice model is not standardized, it can be shown that the set of dice can be substituted by a new set that generates an identical winning probability relation for which the above assumption is valid [5]. From now on, we can therefore restrict to sets instead of multisets.

Finally, we remark that the transitivity results obtained for the dice model described in Section 1, which essentially amounts to the pairwise comparison of a set of independent random variables that are uniformly distributed on finite integer multisets, can be extrapolated to the pairwise comparison of independent discrete or continuous random variables with arbitrary probability distributions [4].

# 4    The 4-Cycle Condition for Dice Representability

Consider a dice model $\mathcal{D}$ with winning probability relation $Q$ and corresponding winning probability graph $G_Q$.

**Definition 5.** *A reciprocal relation $Q$ fulfills the 4-cycle condition if for the consecutive weights $(t_1, t_2, t_3, t_4)$ in any 4-cycle in $G_Q$ it holds that*

$$t_1 + t_2 + t_3 + t_4 - 1 \geq t_1 t_3 + t_2 t_4 + \min(t_1, t_3)\min(t_2, t_4). \tag{4}$$

A 4-cycle is said to fulfill the 4-cycle condition if its consecutive weights $(t_1, t_2, t_3, t_4)$ satisfy condition (4). Note that imposing condition (4) on one permutation of $t_1, t_2, t_3, t_4$ is sufficient for all cyclic permutations of it to satisfy condition (4). We remark that the 4-cycle condition is neither implied by the 3-cycle condition nor implies the 3-cycle condition.

A 3-cycle can be regarded as a special 4-cycle where one of the edges is a loop. Such a loop carries weight 1/2. We hence verify whether given a 3-cycle with consecutive weights $(t_1, t_2, t_3)$ that fulfills the 3-cycle condition, the 4-cycle condition is fulfilled by the 4-cycle with consecutive weights $(t_1, t_2, t_3, 1/2)$. Proposition 4 provides an affirmative answer.

**Proposition 4.** *Given a 3-cycle in a reciprocally weighted graph with consecutive weights $(t_1, t_2, t_3)$ that fulfills the 3-cycle condition, the 4-cycle condition is fulfilled by the 4-cycle with consecutive weights $(t_1, t_2, t_3, 1/2)$.*

The previous section learned us that the 3-cycle condition is necessary and sufficient for the dice representability of rational-valued reciprocal relations on a set of three elements, and necessary (but no longer sufficient) for the dice representability of rational-valued relations on four or more elements. The following theorem shows that the 4-cycle condition is a necessary condition for rational-valued reciprocal relations on four or more elements to be dice representable.

**Theorem 2.** *The winning probability relation $Q$ of any dice model satisfies the 4-cycle condition.*

The 4-cycle condition is only sufficient for rational-valued relations on a set of four elements in the sense that a given rational-weighted 4-cycle and reciprocally weighted inverse cycle, both fulfilling the 4-cycle condition, can be extended to a winning probability graph representing a dice-representable reciprocal relation on a set of four elements. This finding is summarized below in Theorem 3. As the 4-cycle condition imposes conditions on 4-cycles, and not on all six edges between those four elements simultaneously, the condition is possibly not yet characteristic for winning probability relations of four dice.

**Theorem 3.** *Given rational numbers $t_1, t_2, t_3$ and $t_4$ such that the 4-cycle condition (4) is satisfied for $(t_1, t_2, t_3, t_4)$ and $(1 - t_4, 1 - t_3, 1 - t_2, 1 - t_1)$, a reciprocally weighted graph can be constructed having a 4-cycle with consecutive weights $(t_1, t_2, t_3, t_4)$ representing a dice-representable reciprocal relation on four elements.*

We conclude this section by remarking that the above results can be extrapolated, in a similar way as the transitivity results in the previous section, to the pairwise comparison of independent discrete or continuous random variables with arbitrary probability distributions.

# 5   Product Triplets in Winning Probability Relations

Let us first define the notion of a product triplet in a reciprocal relation.

**Definition 6.** *Let $Q$ be a reciprocal relation on a set $A$. A permutation $(a, b, c) \in A^3$ is called a product triplet if*

$$Q(a, b)\, Q(b, c) \leq Q(a, c)\,.$$

Consider a reciprocal relation $Q$ on a set $A$ and let $\Delta(Q)$ denote the greatest number such that any subset $\{a, b, c\} \subseteq A$ has at least $\Delta(Q)$ product triplets. Note that it trivially holds that $\Delta(Q) \leq 6$. We are now in the position to formulate the following remarkable theorem.

**Theorem 4.** *A reciprocal relation $Q$ on a set $A$ satisfies the 3-cycle condition if and only if $\Delta(Q) \geq 4$.*

We remark that Theorem 1 can thus be rewritten as follows.

**Theorem 5.** *A rational-valued reciprocal relation $Q$ on a set $A$ of three elements is dice representable if and only if $\Delta(Q) \geq 4$, i.e. it contains at least 4 product triplets.*

Motivated by this interesting relationship between the number of product triplets and dice representability of rational-valued reciprocal relations on a set of three elements, we count the number of product triplets for various configurations.

First, we enumerate all standardized dice models with a set of three dice with $m$ faces for $m = 2, \ldots, 7$. For each dice model $\mathcal{D}$, the number of product triplets is derived from its winning probability relation $Q$. The results of this counting operation are summarized in Tables 1 and 2. In Table 1, the absolute number of standardized dice models with a set of three dice with a given number of faces for each number of product triplets $\Delta$ is shown, while in Table 2 the percentage of standardized dice models with a set of three dice with a given number of faces for each number of product triplets $\Delta$ is shown.

**Table 1.** Number of standardized dice models with a set of three dice with a given number of faces for each number of product triplets $\Delta$

| $\Delta$ | 2 faces | 3 faces | 4 faces | 5 faces | 6 faces | 7 faces |
|---|---|---|---|---|---|---|
| 4 | 0 | 1 | 5 | 21 | 93 | 398 |
| 5 | 4 | 66 | 809 | 10 064 | 120 343 | 1 539 726 |
| 6 | 11 | 213 | 4 961 | 116 041 | 2 738 420 | 64 972 036 |

From Table 2 it is clear that the fraction of dice models with the maximum number (6) of product triplets increases with the number of faces. Note that their winning probability relations are product transitive, *i.e.* they are cycle transitive w.r.t. $U(\alpha, \beta, \gamma) = \alpha + \beta - \alpha\beta$.

A similar experiment of counting product triplets is now repeated for standardized dice models with a set of four dice with $m$ faces for $m = 2, 3, \ldots, 7$. As it holds for a given dice model $\mathcal{D}$ with winning probability relation $Q$ that $4 \leq \Delta(Q) \leq 6$, a dice model with four dice has at least 16 product triplets and

**Table 2.** Percentage of standardized dice models with a set of three dice with a given number of faces for each number of product triplets $\Delta$

| $\Delta$ | 2 faces | 3 faces | 4 faces | 5 faces | 6 faces | 7 faces |
|---|---|---|---|---|---|---|
| 4 | 0 % | 0.36 % | 0.09 % | 0.02 % | 0.00 % | 0.00 % |
| 5 | 26.67 % | 23.57 % | 14.01 % | 7.98 % | 4.21 % | 2.31 % |
| 6 | 73.33 % | 76.07 % | 85.90 % | 92.00 % | 95.79 % | 97.68 % |
| models | 15 | 280 | 5 775 | 126 126 | 2 858 856 | 66 512 160 |

**Table 3.** Fraction of standardized dice models with a set of four dice with a given number of faces for each number of product triplets $\Delta$

| $\Delta$ | 2 faces | 3 faces | 4 faces | 5 faces | 6 faces | 7 faces |
|---|---|---|---|---|---|---|
| 16 | 0 | 0 | 0 | 0 | 0 | 0 |
| 17 | 0 | 0 | 0 | 0 | $1.02 \cdot 10^{-9}$ | $5.84 \cdot 10^{-11}$ |
| 18 | 0 | $1.30 \cdot 10^{-4}$ | $9.13 \cdot 10^{-6}$ | $4.44 \cdot 10^{-7}$ | $2.51 \cdot 10^{-8}$ | $1.97 \cdot 10^{-9}$ |
| 19 | 0 | $6.49 \cdot 10^{-4}$ | $1.00 \cdot 10^{-4}$ | $1.27 \cdot 10^{-5}$ | $1.28 \cdot 10^{-6}$ | $1.33 \cdot 10^{-7}$ |
| 20 | 0 | $6.56 \cdot 10^{-3}$ | $2.58 \cdot 10^{-3}$ | $7.98 \cdot 10^{-4}$ | $1.76 \cdot 10^{-4}$ | $3.96 \cdot 10^{-5}$ |
| 21 | $3.81 \cdot 10^{-2}$ | $6.29 \cdot 10^{-2}$ | $3.37 \cdot 10^{-2}$ | $1.51 \cdot 10^{-2}$ | $5.42 \cdot 10^{-3}$ | $2.01 \cdot 10^{-3}$ |
| 22 | $4.38 \cdot 10^{-1}$ | $3.21 \cdot 10^{-1}$ | $1.74 \cdot 10^{-1}$ | $9.48 \cdot 10^{-2}$ | $4.91 \cdot 10^{-2}$ | $2.62 \cdot 10^{-2}$ |
| 23 | $7.62 \cdot 10^{-2}$ | $1.10 \cdot 10^{-1}$ | $1.06 \cdot 10^{-1}$ | $8.23 \cdot 10^{-2}$ | $5.35 \cdot 10^{-2}$ | $3.40 \cdot 10^{-2}$ |
| 24 | $4.48 \cdot 10^{-1}$ | $4.99 \cdot 10^{-1}$ | $6.83 \cdot 10^{-1}$ | $8.07 \cdot 10^{-1}$ | $8.92 \cdot 10^{-1}$ | $9.38 \cdot 10^{-1}$ |
| models | $1.05 \cdot 10^{2}$ | $1.54 \cdot 10^{4}$ | $2.63 \cdot 10^{6}$ | $4.89 \cdot 10^{8}$ | $9.62 \cdot 10^{10}$ | $1.97 \cdot 10^{13}$ |

at most 24 product-triplets. The counting results are summarized in Table 3. The fraction of dice models with the maximum number of product triplets also turns out to increase with the number of faces for sets of four dice.

We furthermore exhaustively generate all $(N + 1)^3$ rational-valued reciprocal relations $Q$ on a set $A$ of three elements for which it holds that for any $x, y \in A$ a number $i \in \{0, 1, \ldots, N\}$ can be found such that $Q(x, y) = i/N$, for $N \in \{2^2, 3^2, \ldots, 7^2\}$ and $N = 1000$. Next, we retain only relations $Q$ that satisfy the 3-cycle condition, *i.e.* that are winning probability relations, and compute the number of product triplets $\Delta$ in these relations. As can be derived from Table 4, the distributions of the number of product triplets of these winning probability relations with $N = m^2$ differ considerably from the distributions in Table 2 that resulted from the generation of dice with $m$ faces. The probability of encountering a relation that has the maximal number of product triplets turns out to be much smaller in this new setting.

Note that the winning probability relations generated for $N = m^2$ are a superset of the winning probability relations corresponding to all sets of three dice with $m$ faces. Although the 3-cycle condition is sufficient for dice representability, dice with larger numbers of faces can be required to materialize such relations. Moreover, and more importantly, winning probability relations with a high number of product triplets seem to be overrepresented in the winning probability relations corresponding to dice with $m$ faces.

Similarly, we exhaustively generate all $(N + 1)^6$ rational-valued reciprocal relations $Q$ on a set $A$ of four elements for which it holds that for any $x, y \in A$

**Table 4.** Distribution of the number of product triplets $\Delta$ for reciprocal relations $Q$ on a set $A$ of three elements satisfying the 3-cycle condition, and for which it holds that for any $x, y \in A$ a number $i \in \{0, 1, \dots, N\}$ can be found such that $Q(x, y) = i/N$, for $N \in \{2^2, 3^2, \dots 7^2\}$ and $N = 1000$

| $\Delta$ | $N = 2^2$ | $N = 3^2$ | $N = 4^2$ | $N = 5^2$ | $N = 6^2$ | $N = 7^2$ | $N = 1000$ |
|---|---|---|---|---|---|---|---|
| 4 | 0 % | 3.91 % | 4.78 % | 5.70 % | 5.87 % | 6.14 % | 6.61 % |
| 5 | 45.57 % | 52.77 % | 52.34 % | 51.58 % | 50.35 % | 50.05 % | 47.85 % |
| 6 | 54.43 % | 43.32 % | 42.89 % | 42.72 % | 43.78 % | 43.81 % | 45.54 % |
| relations | 79 | 614 | $3.02 \cdot 10^3$ | $1.08 \cdot 10^4$ | $3.14 \cdot 10^4$ | $7.76 \cdot 10^4$ | $6.29 \cdot 10^8$ |

a number $i \in \{0, 1, \dots, N\}$ can be found such that $Q(x, y) = i/N$, for $N \in \{2^2, 3^2, \dots, 7^2\}$. When only retaining reciprocal relations that satisfy the 3-cycle and 4-cycle conditions, Table 5 clearly shows that also here the probability of encountering a large number of product triplets is much smaller than when generating dice with $m$ faces. We emphasize that it has not yet been proven that simultaneously imposing the 3-cycle and 4-cycle conditions on a rational-valued reciprocal relation on four elements is sufficient for its dice representability. Therefore, not necessarily all such reciprocal relations are winning probability relations.

**Table 5.** Distribution of the number of product triplets $\Delta$ for reciprocal relations $Q$ on a set $A$ of four elements satisfying the 3-cycle and 4-cycle conditions, and for which it holds that for any $x, y \in A$ a number $i \in \{0, 1, \dots, N\}$ can be found such that $Q(x, y) = i/N$, for $N \in \{2^2, 3^2, \dots, 7^2\}$

| $\Delta$ | $N = 2^2$ | $N = 3^2$ | $N = 4^2$ | $N = 5^2$ | $N = 6^2$ | $N = 7^2$ |
|---|---|---|---|---|---|---|
| 16 | 0 % | 0.01 % | 0.01 % | 0.01 % | 0.01 % | 0.01 % |
| 17 | 0 % | 0.03 % | 0.04 % | 0.05 % | 0.05 % | 0.05 % |
| 18 | 0 % | 0.49 % | 0.42 % | 0.47 % | 0.45 % | 0.48 % |
| 19 | 0 % | 1.52 % | 2.29 % | 2.82 % | 2.78 % | 2.93 % |
| 20 | 0 % | 10.30 % | 11.31 % | 12.29 % | 12.00 % | 12.22 % |
| 21 | 8.05 % | 24.61 % | 26.36 % | 26.49 % | 25.45 % | 25.33 % |
| 22 | 63.60 % | 44.44 % | 38.77 % | 36.51 % | 36.43 % | 36.06 % |
| 23 | 9.66 % | 8.96 % | 10.87 % | 11.45 % | 12.17 % | 12.27 % |
| 24 | 18.69 % | 9.64 % | 9.94 % | 9.93 % | 10.66 % | 10.64 % |
| relations | $1.56 \cdot 10^4$ | $1.80 \cdot 10^5$ | $4.41 \cdot 10^6$ | $5.78 \cdot 10^7$ | $4.88 \cdot 10^8$ | $2.99 \cdot 10^9$ |

Remark in Table 3 that there is no set of four dice with at most 7 faces that has the minimum number of product triplets. As it has been shown that dice transitivity is no longer characteristic for the type of transitivity exhibited by the winning probability relation of four dice, it is interesting to find out whether the theoretical lower bound on the number of product triplets can still be reached. This turns out to be the case, as the following example set of dice with 9 faces and exactly 16 product triplets illustrates: $D_1 = \{4 \to 10, 34 \to 35\}$,

$D_2 = \{11 \rightarrow 18, 36\}$, $D_3 = \{1, 19 \rightarrow 26\}$, $D_4 = \{2 \rightarrow 3, 27 \rightarrow 33\}$. Note that the notation $n \rightarrow m$ is used as a shorthand for the sequence $n, n+1, \ldots, m$. Moreover, the following example set shows that the lower bound of 40 product triplets for 5 dice also can be reached: $D_1 = \{2 \rightarrow 3, 54 \rightarrow 69\}$, $D_2 = \{4 \rightarrow 6, 70 \rightarrow 84\}$, $D_3 = \{7 \rightarrow 21, 85 \rightarrow 87\}$, $D_4 = \{22 \rightarrow 37, 88 \rightarrow 89\}$ $D_5 = \{1, 38 \rightarrow 53, 90\}$. Based on these examples, we formulate the following conjecture.

*Conjecture 1.* A dice model $\mathcal{D}$ of arbitrary size can always be constructed such that $\Delta(Q) = 4$, where $Q$ is the winning probability relation of $\mathcal{D}$.

Unfortunately, it is not clear how the above examples can be generalized to an arbitrary number of dice. Furthermore, due to the exponential computational complexity to enumerate (part of) the search space consisting of all standardized dice models with a set of dice of a given size, it is all but evident to search for examples with a larger number of dice to provide additional support for this conjecture.

# References

1. David, H.: The Method of Paired Comparisons. Griffin, London (1963)
2. De Baets, B., De Meyer, H.: Transitivity frameworks for reciprocal relations: cycle-transitivity versus FG-transitivity. Fuzzy Sets and Systems 152, 249–270 (2005)
3. De Baets, B., De Meyer, H., De Schuymer, B., Jenei, S.: Cyclic evaluation of transitivity of reciprocal relations. Social Choice and Welfare 26, 217–238 (2006)
4. De Schuymer, B., De Meyer, H., De Baets, B.: Cycle-transitive comparison of independent random variables. Journal of Multivariate Analysis 96, 352–373 (2005)
5. De Schuymer, B., De Meyer, H., De Baets, B., Jenei, S.: On the cycle-transitivity of the dice model. Theory and Decision 54, 261–285 (2003)
6. Fishburn, P.: Binary choice probabilities: on the varieties of stochastic transitivity. Journal of Mathematical Psychology 10, 327–352 (1973)
7. Gardner, M.: Mathematical games: The paradox of the nontransitive dice and the elusive principle of indifference. Scientific American 223, 110–114 (1970)
8. Savage, R.: The paradox of nontransitive dice. The American Mathematical Monthly 101, 429–436 (1994)
9. Switalski, S.: Rationality of fuzzy reciprocal preference relations. Fuzzy Sets and Systems 107, 187–190 (1999)
10. Wrather, C., Lu, P.: Probability dominance in random outcomes. Journal of Optimization Theory and Applications 36, 315–334 (1982)

# Opening Reciprocal Relations w.r.t. Stochastic Transitivity

Steven Freson[1], Hans De Meyer[1], and Bernard De Baets[2]

[1] Department of Applied Mathematics and Computer Science, Ghent University,
Krijgslaan 281 (S9), B-9000 Gent, Belgium
[2] Department of Mathematical Modelling, Statistics and Bioinformatics, Ghent
University, Coupure links 653, B-9000 Gent, Belgium
{steven.freson,hans.demeyer,bernard.debaets}@ugent.be

**Abstract.** For crisp as well as fuzzy relations, the results concerning transitive closures and openings are well known. For reciprocal relations transitivity is often defined in terms of stochastic transitivity. This paper focuses on stochastic transitive openings of reciprocal relations, presenting theoretical results as well as a practical method to construct such transitive openings.

**Keywords:** Preference relation, reciprocal relation, stochastic transitivity, transitive opening.

## 1 Introduction

In the context of crisp as well as fuzzy relations, a given relation is often evaluated on whether or not it satisfies different properties, such as transitivity, symmetry, ... If it does not satisfy the property under consideration, one often requires to find a relation that possesses the property and approximates the given relation. Having defined an order on the class of relations under consideration, an interesting question is whether there exists some minimal relation with the considered property containing the given relation, and whether there exists some maximal relation with the considered property contained by the given relation. These questions lead to the study of closures and openings with respect to the property under consideration. A detailed exposition of results concerning a number of properties of crisp and fuzzy relations has been given by Bandler and Kohout [1]. More recently, additional research has been devoted to theoretical as well as algorithmical results concerning $T$-transitivity of fuzzy relations in general and their min-transitivity in particular [4,6,9]. Also, we have investigated the generation of transitive reciprocal relations that approximate a given reciprocal relation [11].

Our intent is to enlarge the investigation to the domain of reciprocal relations. A reciprocal relation is a $[0,1]$-valued relation $Q$ that satisfies the reciprocity condition, i.e. $Q(x,y) + Q(y,x) = 1$ [3]. The concept of reciprocal relation has proven to be a useful tool in preference modelling, where it is used to express the intensities of preferences of alternatives, one over another. However, the

S. Greco et al. (Eds.): IPMU 2012, Part IV, CCIS 300, pp. 306–314, 2012.

resulting preferences might prove to be inconsistent. In a crisp context, consistency has been defined in terms of acyclicity [14], which is closely related to the property of transitivity. In a graded context, consistency properties have been proposed that extend the notion of boolean transitivity. Three interesting types of transitivity in the context of reciprocal relations are weak stochastic transitivity, moderate stochastic transitivity and strong stochastic transitivity [5,15]. Some of the present authors have recently presented the cycle-transitivity framework for describing and studying many types of transitivity of reciprocal relations [7,8].

In the present paper we first recall some results concerning the existence of stochastic transitive closures of reciprocal relations. Further, we examine the existence of stochastic transitive openings of reciprocal relations. We will show that only for a specific subclass of reciprocal relations a stochastic transitive opening can be found. The paper will start by recalling some basic notions and operations of reciprocal relations.

## 2 Definitions and Basic Results

### 2.1 Reciprocal Relations

A mapping $Q : X^2 \to [0, 1]$ is called a reciprocal $[0, 1]$-valued relation on $X$ if it satisfies

$$(\forall(x, y) \in X^2)(Q(x, y) + Q(y, x) = 1). \tag{1}$$

The class of all reciprocal $[0, 1]$-valued relations, or in short reciprocal relations, on a universe $X$ is denoted by $\mathcal{Q}_X$.

A 3-valued reciprocal relation is a reciprocal relation with values restricted to $\{0, \frac{1}{2}, 1\}$. The subclass of all 3-valued reciprocal relations is denoted by $\mathcal{Q}_X^*$. With any $Q \in \mathcal{Q}_X$ one can associate a $Q^* \in \mathcal{Q}_X^*$, defined by

$$Q^*(x, y) = \begin{cases} 1 & , \text{if } Q(x, y) > \frac{1}{2}, \\ \frac{1}{2} & , \text{if } Q(x, y) = \frac{1}{2}, \\ 0 & , \text{if } Q(x, y) < \frac{1}{2}. \end{cases} \tag{2}$$

**Definition 1.** Let $Q_1, Q_2 \in \mathcal{Q}_X$. $Q_1$ is smaller than $Q_2$, or $Q_2$ is larger than $Q_1$, denoted as $Q_1 \sqsubseteq Q_2$, if

$$(\forall(x, y) \in X^2) \left( \begin{cases} Q_1(x, y) \geqslant Q_2(x, y) & , \text{if } Q_2(x, y) > \frac{1}{2} \\ Q_1(x, y) \leqslant Q_2(x, y) & , \text{if } Q_2(x, y) < \frac{1}{2} \end{cases} \right) \tag{3}$$

It can be shown that $\sqsubseteq$ defines an order relation on $\mathcal{Q}_X$ and that $(\mathcal{Q}_X, \sqsubseteq)$ is a join-semilattice with greatest element $Q_T$, with $Q_T(x, y) = \frac{1}{2}$ for all $x, y \in X$, and set of minimal elements $\mathcal{Q}_\perp = \{Q \in \mathcal{Q}_X^* \mid (\forall(x, y) \in X^2)(Q(x, y) = 1 \vee Q(x, y) = 0 \vee x = y)\}$. Any two reciprocal relations have a common reciprocal relation that is greater, namely $Q_T$. Moreover, given two reciprocal relations, there exists a smallest reciprocal relation that is greater than the given relations, which is made explicit in the following proposition.

**Proposition 1.** *Let* $Q_1, Q_2 \in \mathcal{Q}_X$. *The* union *of* $Q_1$ *and* $Q_2$ *is the reciprocal relation* $Q_1 \sqcup Q_2$ *given by:*

$$Q_1 \sqcup Q_2(x, y) = \begin{cases} \min(Q_1(x,y), Q_2(x,y)) & , \text{ if } \min(Q_1(x,y), Q_2(x,y)) \geq \frac{1}{2}, \\ \max(Q_1(x,y), Q_2(x,y)) & , \text{ if } \max(Q_1(x,y), Q_2(x,y)) \leq \frac{1}{2}, \\ \frac{1}{2} & , \text{ else.} \end{cases}$$
(4)

Since $(\mathcal{Q}_X, \sqsubseteq)$ does not have a smallest element, a shared smaller reciprocal relation is not guaranteed. If, for two given reciprocal relations, there is a reciprocal relation that is smaller, there is a largest reciprocal relation with this property.

**Definition 2.** *Two reciprocal relations* $Q_1, Q_2 \in \mathcal{Q}_X$ *are called* compatible, *denoted as* $Q_1 \approx Q_2$, *if there exists a reciprocal relation* $Q \in \mathcal{Q}_X$ *such that*

$$Q \sqsubseteq Q_1 \text{ and } Q \sqsubseteq Q_2.$$

**Proposition 2.** *Let* $Q_1, Q_2 \in \mathcal{Q}_X$ *and* $Q_1 \approx Q_2$. *The intersection of* $Q_1$ *and* $Q_2$ *is the reciprocal relation* $Q_1 \sqcap Q_2$ *given by*

$$Q_1 \sqcap Q_2(x, y) = \begin{cases} \max(Q_1(x,y), Q_2(x,y)) & , \text{ if } \min(Q_1(x,y), Q_2(x,y)) \geq \frac{1}{2}, \\ \min(Q_1(x,y), Q_2(x,y)) & , \text{ else.} \end{cases}$$
(5)

## 2.2 Stochastic Transitivity

Different definitions of transitivity of reciprocal relations can be found in literature. We will focus on $g$-stochastic transitivity, a general definition proposed in [8].

**Definition 3.** *Let* $g$ *be an increasing* $[\frac{1}{2}, 1]^2 \to [0, 1]$ *mapping with* $g(\frac{1}{2}, \frac{1}{2}) \leq \frac{1}{2}$. *A reciprocal relation* $Q \in \mathcal{Q}_X$ *is called* $g$-stochastic transitive *if for any* $(x, y, z) \in X^3$ *it holds that:*

$$\left(Q(x, y) \geq \frac{1}{2} \wedge Q(y, z) \geq \frac{1}{2}\right) \Rightarrow Q(x, z) \geq g(Q(x, y), Q(y, z)).$$
(6)

This definition incorporates well-known types of stochastic transitivity, such as

- Weak stochastic transitivity for $g = \frac{1}{2}$ [13],
- Moderate stochastic transitivity for $g = \min$ [13],
- Strong stochastic transitivity for $g = \max$ [13],
- $\lambda$-transitivity, with $\lambda \in [0, 1]$, for $g = \lambda \max + (1 - \lambda) \min$ [2].

Clearly, strong stochastic (SS) transitivity implies $\lambda$-transitivity, which implies moderate stochastic (MS) transitivity, which again implies weak stochastic (WS) transitivity. Stochastic transitivity is described in more detail in [7,8].

Note that for any mapping $g \geq \frac{1}{2}$, $g$-stochastic transitivity on $\mathcal{Q}_X^*$ is equivalent to weak stochastic transitivity on $\mathcal{Q}_X^*$.

# 3   Closures and Openings

## 3.1   Closures in $\mathcal{Q}_X$

We recall that the closure of a given relation is the smallest relation that includes the given relation and satisfies the considered property.

**Definition 4.** *Let* $(\mathcal{S}, \subseteq_\mathcal{S})$ *be a partially ordered set. Given a property* $P$ *that elements of* $\mathcal{S}$ *can satisfy or fail to satisfy, the* $P$*-closure of* $S \in \mathcal{S}$*, if it exists, is the unique element* $\widehat{S}^{\mathrm{P}} \in \mathcal{S}$ *such that:*

*(i)* $\widehat{S}^{\mathrm{P}}$ *satisfies* $P$*,*
*(ii)* $S \subseteq_\mathcal{S} \widehat{S}^{\mathrm{P}}$*,*
*(iii) for* $S' \in \mathcal{S}$*, if* $S \subseteq_\mathcal{S} S'$ *and* $S'$ *satisfies* $P$*, then* $\widehat{S}^{\mathrm{P}} \subseteq_\mathcal{S} S'$*.*

Bandler and Kohout [1] have laid bare the necessary and sufficient conditions for the existence of closures as well as openings in the case of classical crisp relations as well as fuzzy relations. Although their theorems are based on a complete bounded lattice structure, since this is the structure that is found when dealing with crisp or fuzzy relations, with little effort, both theorems can be generalized to a class of relations in which the intersection, respectively the union, is defined for every family of relations that has a common lower, respectively upper, bound.

Based on these results, the present authors have shown [12] that for a given $Q \in \mathcal{Q}_X$, the weak stochastic transitive closure as well as the strong stochastic transitive closure always exist. For moderate stochastic transitivity, however, a closure does not exist due to the lack of a unique relation satisfying the conditions. In general, the following proposition states a necessary condition on the mapping $g$ for the existence of a $g$-stochastic transitive closure.

**Proposition 3.** *Let* $g$ *be an increasing* $\left[\frac{1}{2}, 1\right]^2 \to [0, 1]$ *mapping with* $g(\frac{1}{2}, \frac{1}{2}) \leqslant \frac{1}{2}$*. The* $g$*-stochastic transitive closure exists for every* $Q \in \mathcal{Q}_X$ *if* $g$ *satisfies*

$$\sup_{i \in I} g(a_i, b_i) \geqslant g(\sup_{i \in I} a_i, \sup_{i \in I} b_i)$$

*with* $a_i, b_i \in \left[\frac{1}{2}, 1\right], i \in I$*.*

It was shown in [12] that the well-known Floyd-Warshall algorithm [10] can be adjusted to generate the weak stochastic transitive closure $\widehat{Q}^{\mathrm{ws}}$ of a given reciprocal relation $Q \in \mathcal{Q}_X$, while a new algorithm was proposed that generates the strong stochastic transitive closure $\widehat{Q}^{\mathrm{ss}}$. We refer to [12] for more detail. In the following we will use the notation $\mathcal{Q}_X^{\mathrm{ws}}$ to denote the class of all weak stochastic transitive reciprocal relations.

## 3.2   Openings in $\mathcal{Q}_X$

The notion of opening is dual to that of closure, namely it is the largest relation satisfying the considered property that is included in the given relation.

**Definition 5.** *Given a property $P$ that elements of $S$ can satisfy or fail to satisfy, the $P$-opening of $S \in \mathcal{S}$, if it exists, is the unique element $\check{S}^{P} \in \mathcal{S}$ satisfying:*

*(i)* $\check{S}^{P}$ *satisfies $P$,*

*(ii)* $\check{S}^{P} \subseteq_{S} S$,

*(iii)* *for $S' \in \mathcal{S}$, if $S' \subseteq_{S} S$ and $S'$ satisfies $P$, then $S' \subseteq_{S} \check{S}^{P}$.*

It is easily shown that not all reciprocal relations have a transitive opening.

*Example 1.* Consider a relation $Q \in \mathcal{Q}_X$ such that $Q(x,y) = Q(y,z) = Q(z,x) = 1$ and $Q(x,z) = Q(z,y) = Q(y,x) = 0$, with $x,y,z \in X$. For $Q$ to be $g$-stochastic transitive, it should hold that $Q(x,z) = 0 \geqslant g(Q(x,y), Q(y,z)) = g(1,1)$. Any reciprocal relation $Q' \sqsubseteq Q$ will have the same values with respect to $x, y, z \in X$. From this it can be seen that there simply is no smaller reciprocal relation that satisfies transitivity for some $g \neq 0$.

This example can be generalised into the following proposition.

**Proposition 4.** *Let $Q \in \mathcal{Q}_X \backslash \mathcal{Q}_X^{ws}$ and $g \geqslant \frac{1}{2}$, then $Q$ does not have a $g$-stochastic transitive opening.*

For a weak stochastic transitive reciprocal relation, the following proposition holds.

**Proposition 5.** *For every $Q \in \mathcal{Q}_X^{ws}$ and $g \geqslant \frac{1}{2}$, $Q^*$ is $g$-stochastic transitive.*

In general, taking the union of reciprocal relations does not preserve $g$-stochastic transitivity.

**Proposition 6.** *Let $Q_1, Q_2 \in \mathcal{Q}_X^{ws}$ and $g \geqslant \frac{1}{2}$. If $Q_1^* = Q_2^*$ and $Q_1, Q_2$ are $g$-stochastic transitive, then $Q_1 \sqcup Q_2$ is $g$-stochastic transitive.*

The usefulness of the previous proposition becomes more evident in the light of the following proposition.

**Proposition 7.** *For $Q_0 \in \mathcal{Q}_X^{ws}$ and $Q_1 \in \mathcal{Q}_X$ with $Q_1 \sqsubseteq Q_0$ and $Q_1$ $g$-stochastic transitive, there exists a $Q_2 \in \mathcal{Q}_X$ that is $g$-stochastic transitive and*

$$Q_1 \sqsubseteq Q_2 \sqsubseteq Q_0, \quad Q_0^* = Q_2^*.$$

Combining these propositions, we find that for every weak stochastic transitive relation and a $g$-stochastic transitivity type with $g \geqslant \frac{1}{2}$, the $g$-stochastic transitive opening exists.

**Proposition 8.** *For every $Q \in \mathcal{Q}_X^{ws}$ the $g$-stochastic transitive opening, denoted by $\check{Q}^g$, exists and is given as*

$$\check{Q}^g = \bigsqcup \{Q' \in \mathcal{Q}_X^{ws} \mid Q' \sqsubseteq Q, Q' \text{ is } g\text{-stochastic transitive}\}. \tag{7}$$

As was noted in Sect. 3.1, given a reciprocal relation $Q$, there exists an algorithm that generates $\hat{Q}^{\mathrm{ws}}$. A different adaptation of the Floyd-Warshall algorithm can be used to construct the $g$-stochastic transitive opening of $Q$.

---

**Algorithm GSO**
Input: dimension $n$, $Q \in \mathcal{Q}_X^{\mathrm{ws}}$, $g$
Output: $\check{Q}^g$
**for** $i := 1$ **to** $n$ **do**
  **for** $j := 1$ **to** $n$ **do**
    **for** $k := 1$ **to** $n$ **do**
      **if** $q_{ji} \geqslant \frac{1}{2}$ **and** $q_{ik} \geqslant \frac{1}{2}$ **then**
        $q_{jk} := \max(g(q_{ji}, q_{ik}), q_{jk})$
        $q_{kj} := 1 - q_{jk}$
      **endif**
    **endfor** $k$
  **endfor** $j$
**endfor** $i$

---

**Proposition 9.** *Let $g$ be an associative increasing $[\frac{1}{2}, 1]^2 \to [\frac{1}{2}, 1]$ mapping with $g(\frac{1}{2}, \frac{1}{2}) = \frac{1}{2}$ and $\max(g(\frac{1}{2}, a), g(a, \frac{1}{2})) \leqslant a$ for all $a \in [\frac{1}{2}, 1]$. For any $Q \in \mathcal{Q}_X^{\mathrm{ws}}$ the algorithm GSO generates $\check{Q}^g$.*

When the algorithm **GSO** is applied for a mapping $g$ that is not associative, the outcome is not guaranteed to be $g$-stochastic transitive. However, if $\max(g(\frac{1}{2}, a), g(a, \frac{1}{2})) \leqslant a$ for all $a \in [\frac{1}{2}, 1]$, it can be shown that a finite number of applications of **GSO** will provide the $g$-stochastic transitive opening. This behaviour can be explained by the fact that if $g$ is not associative, the adjustments of the values of $Q$ should be applied in a specific order to result in a transitive relation.

In the following section we will give some examples illustrating the algorithm.

## 4   Examples

*Example 2.* Let $X = \{x, y, z\}$ and consider $Q_1 \in \mathcal{Q}_X^{\mathrm{ws}}$, given as

| $Q_1$ | $x$ | $y$ | $z$ |
|---|---|---|---|
| $x$ | 0.5 | 0.9 | 0.8 |
| $y$ | 0.1 | 0.5 | 1.0 |
| $z$ | 0.2 | 0 | 0.5 |

It is easily seen that the moderate stochastic transitive opening and the strong stochastic transitive opening of $Q_1$ are found by adjusting the value $Q_1(x, z)$:

| $\check{Q}_1^{\mathrm{MS}}$ | $x$ | $y$ | $z$ |
|---|---|---|---|
| $x$ | 0.5 | 0.9 | 0.9 |
| $y$ | 0.1 | 0.5 | 1.0 |
| $z$ | 0.2 | 0 | 0.5 |

| $\check{Q}_1^{\mathrm{SS}}$ | $x$ | $y$ | $z$ |
|---|---|---|---|
| $x$ | 0.5 | 0.9 | 1.0 |
| $y$ | 0.1 | 0.5 | 1.0 |
| $z$ | 0.2 | 0 | 0.5 |

*Example 3.* Let $X = \{x, y, z, u\}$ and consider $Q_2 \in \mathcal{Q}_X^{ws}$ given as

| $Q_2$ | $x$ | $y$ | $z$ | $u$ |
|---|---|---|---|---|
| $x$ | 0.5 | 0.8 | 0.6 | 0.65 |
| $y$ | 0.2 | 0.5 | 0.9 | 0.6 |
| $z$ | 0.4 | 0.1 | 0.5 | 0.7 |
| $u$ | 0.35 | 0.4 | 0.3 | 0.5 |

This relation is not moderate stochastic transitive due to

$$Q_2(x, z) < \min(Q_2(x, y), Q_2(y, z)),$$
$$Q_2(y, u) < \min(Q_2(y, z), Q_2(z.u)).$$

Note that, originally, for $Q_2$ the conditions

$$Q_2(x, u) \geqslant \min(Q_2(x, y), Q_2(y, u)),$$
$$Q_2(x, u) \geqslant \min(Q_2(x, z), Q_2(z, u))$$

are satisfied, but by changing either $Q_2(x, z)$ to 0.8 or $Q_2(y, u)$ to 0.7 it becomes necessary to adjust $Q_2(x, u)$ as well. Applying the algorithm for $g = \min$ and $g = \max$, we find the moderate stochastic transitive opening and the strong stochastic transitive opening of $Q_2$:

| $\breve{Q}_2^{MS}$ | $x$ | $y$ | $z$ | $u$ |
|---|---|---|---|---|
| $x$ | 0.5 | 0.8 | 0.8 | 0.7 |
| $y$ | 0.2 | 0.5 | 0.9 | 0.7 |
| $z$ | 0.2 | 0.1 | 0.5 | 0.7 |
| $u$ | 0.3 | 0.3 | 0.3 | 0.5 |

| $\breve{Q}_2^{SS}$ | $x$ | $y$ | $z$ | $u$ |
|---|---|---|---|---|
| $x$ | 0.5 | 0.8 | 0.9 | 0.9 |
| $y$ | 0.2 | 0.5 | 0.9 | 0.9 |
| $z$ | 0.1 | 0.1 | 0.5 | 0.7 |
| $u$ | 0.1 | 0.1 | 0.3 | 0.5 |

*Example 4.* Let $X = \{x, y, z, u, v\}$ and consider $Q_3 \in \mathcal{Q}_X$, given as

| $Q_3$ | $x$ | $y$ | $z$ | $u$ | $v$ |
|---|---|---|---|---|---|
| $x$ | 0.50 | 0.55 | 0.55 | 0.55 | 0.55 |
| $y$ | 0.45 | 0.50 | 1 | 0.81 | 0.63 |
| $z$ | 0.45 | 0 | 0.50 | 0.96 | 0.70 |
| $u$ | 0.45 | 0.19 | 0.04 | 0.50 | 0.59 |
| $v$ | 0.45 | 0.37 | 0.30 | 0.41 | 0.50 |

Applying the algorithm for $g = \min$ and $g = \max$, the moderate and strong stochastic transitivity openings of $Q_3$ are found.

| $\breve{Q}_3^{MS}$ | $x$ | $y$ | $z$ | $u$ | $v$ |
|---|---|---|---|---|---|
| $x$ | 0.50 | 0.55 | 0.55 | 0.55 | 0.55 |
| $y$ | 0.45 | 0.50 | 1 | 0.96 | 0.70 |
| $z$ | 0.45 | 0 | 0.50 | 0.96 | 0.70 |
| $u$ | 0.45 | 0.04 | 0.04 | 0.50 | 0.59 |
| $v$ | 0.45 | 0.30 | 0.30 | 0.41 | 0.50 |

| $\breve{Q}_3^{SS}$ | $x$ | $y$ | $z$ | $u$ | $v$ |
|---|---|---|---|---|---|
| $x$ | 0.50 | 0.55 | 1 | 1 | 1 |
| $y$ | 0.45 | 0.50 | 1 | 1 | 1 |
| $z$ | 0 | 0 | 0.50 | 0.96 | 0.96 |
| $u$ | 0 | 0 | 0.04 | 0.50 | 0.59 |
| $v$ | 0 | 0 | 0.04 | 0.41 | 0.50 |

*Example 5.* For any $\lambda \in ]0, 1[$, the mapping $g = \lambda \max + (1 - \lambda) \min$ corresponding to $\lambda$-transitivity is not associative. For instance, for $\lambda = \frac{1}{2}$ we have $g(x, y) = \frac{x+y}{2}$. Applying for the latter $g$ algorithm **GSO** to $Q_3$ as given in Ex. 4, the resulting relation $Q_3'$ is not $g$-stochastic transitive, as is seen from $Q_3'(x, v) = 0.7375 < g(Q_3'(x, z), Q_3'(z, v)) = \frac{0.775 + 0.775}{2} = 0.775$.

| $Q_3'$ | $x$ | $y$ | $z$ | $u$ | $v$ |
|---|---|---|---|---|---|
| $x$ | 0.5000 | 0.5500 | 0.7750 | 0.8675 | 0.7375 |
| $y$ | 0.4500 | 0.5000 | 1.0000 | 0.9800 | 0.8500 |
| $z$ | 0.2250 | 0.0000 | 0.5000 | 0.9600 | 0.7750 |
| $u$ | 0.1325 | 0.0200 | 0.0400 | 0.5000 | 0.5900 |
| $v$ | 0.2625 | 0.1500 | 0.2250 | 0.4100 | 0.5000 |

A second application of the algorithm is required to find the $g$-stochastic transitive opening of $Q_3$.

| $\widetilde{Q_3}^{g}$ | $x$ | $y$ | $z$ | $u$ | $v$ |
|---|---|---|---|---|---|
| $x$ | 0.5000 | 0.5500 | 0.7750 | 0.8675 | 0.7750 |
| $y$ | 0.4500 | 0.5000 | 1.0000 | 0.9800 | 0.8875 |
| $z$ | 0.2250 | 0.0000 | 0.5000 | 0.9600 | 0.7750 |
| $u$ | 0.1325 | 0.0200 | 0.0400 | 0.5000 | 0.5900 |
| $v$ | 0.2250 | 0.1125 | 0.2250 | 0.4100 | 0.5000 |

If we would rearrange the elements of $X$ such that the same relation $Q_3$ is represented as

| $Q_3$ | $z$ | $u$ | $x$ | $y$ | $v$ |
|---|---|---|---|---|---|
| $z$ | 0.5000 | 0.9600 | 0.4500 | 0.0000 | 0.7000 |
| $u$ | 0.0400 | 0.5000 | 0.4500 | 0.1900 | 0.5900 |
| $x$ | 0.5500 | 0.5500 | 0.5000 | 0.5500 | 0.5500 |
| $y$ | 1.0000 | 0.8100 | 0.4500 | 0.5000 | 0.6300 |
| $v$ | 0.3000 | 0.4100 | 0.4500 | 0.3700 | 0.5000 |

a single application of the algorithm yields $\widetilde{Q_3}^{g}$.

| $\widetilde{Q_3}^{g}$ | $z$ | $u$ | $x$ | $y$ | $v$ |
|---|---|---|---|---|---|
| $z$ | 0.5000 | 0.9600 | 0.2250 | 0.0000 | 0.7750 |
| $u$ | 0.0400 | 0.5000 | 0.1325 | 0.0200 | 0.5900 |
| $x$ | 0.7750 | 0.8675 | 0.5000 | 0.5500 | 0.7750 |
| $y$ | 1.0000 | 0.9800 | 0.4500 | 0.5000 | 0.8875 |
| $v$ | 0.2250 | 0.4100 | 0.2250 | 0.1125 | 0.5000 |

# 5   Conclusion

In the context of reciprocal relations, there are different ways to define transitivity. We have focused on stochastic transitivity types, in particular on weak stochastic transitivity, moderate stochastic transitivity and strong stochastic transitivity. Concerning closures, every reciprocal relation has a weak stochastic transitive closure and a strong stochastic transitive closure. A moderate stochastic transitive closure does not exist in general.

Concerning openings, we have shown that if the mapping $g$ satisfies $g \geqslant \frac{1}{2}$, a $g$-stochastic opening exists if and only if the reciprocal relation is weak stochastic transitive. Subsequently, we have provided an algorithm to construct the $g$-stochastic transitive opening of a given reciprocal relation, for any mapping $g$ satisfying $\max(g(a, \frac{1}{2}), g(\frac{1}{2}, a)) \leqslant a$, for all $a \in [\frac{1}{2}, 1]$.

# References

1. Bandler, W., Kohout, L.J.: Special properties, closures and interiors of crisp and fuzzy relations. Fuzzy Sets and Systems 26, 317–331 (1988)
2. Basu, K.: Fuzzy revealed preference theory. J. Econom. Theory 32, 212–227 (1984)
3. Bezdek, J., Spillman, B., Spillman, R.: A fuzzy relational space for group decision theory. Fuzzy Sets and Systems 1, 255–268 (1978)
4. Boixader, D., Recasens, J.: Transitive openings. In: Proceedings of the 7th conference of the European Society for Fuzzy Logic and Technology (EUSFLAT 2011) and LFA 2011, pp. 493–497 (2011)
5. Chiclana, F., Herrera-Viedma, E., Alonso, S., Herrera, F.: Cardinal consistency of reciprocal preference relations: a characterization of multiplicative transitivity. IEEE Transactions on Fuzzy Systems 17, 14–23 (2009)
6. De Baets, B., De Meyer, H.: On the existence and construction of $T$-transitive closures. Information Sciences 152, 167–179 (2003)
7. De Baets, B., De Meyer, H.: Transitivity frameworks for reciprocal relations: cycle-transitivity versus $FG$-transitivity. Fuzzy Sets and Systems 152, 249–270 (2005)
8. De Baets, B., De Meyer, H., De Schuymer, B., Jenei, S.: Cyclic evaluation of transitivity of reciprocal relations. Social Choice and Welfare 26, 217–238 (2006)
9. De Meyer, H., Naessens, H., De Baets, B.: Algorithms for computing the min-transitive closure and associated partition tree of a symmetric fuzzy relation. European Journal of Operational Research 155, 226–238 (2004)
10. Floyd, R.W.: Algorithm 97: shortest path. Communications of the ACM 5(6), 345 (1962)
11. Freson, S., De Meyer, H., De Baets, B.: An Algorithm for Generating Consistent and Transitive Approximations of Reciprocal Preference Relations. In: Hüllermeier, E., Kruse, R., Hoffmann, F. (eds.) IPMU 2010. LNCS, vol. 6178, pp. 564–573. Springer, Heidelberg (2010)
12. Freson, S., De Meyer, H., De Baets, B.: On the transitive closure of reciprocal [0, 1]-valued relations. In: Proceedings of the 7th Conference of the European Society for Fuzzy Logic and Technology (EUSFLAT 2011) and LFA 2011, pp. 1015–1021 (2011)
13. Monjardet, B.: A generalisation of probabilistic consistency: linearity conditions for valued preference relations. In: Kacprzyk, J., Roubens, M. (eds.) Non-conventional Preference Relations in Decision Making. LNEMS, vol. 301. Springer (1988)
14. Montero, F.J., Tejada, J.: Some problems on the definition of fuzzy preference relations. Fuzzy Sets and Systems 20, 45–53 (1986)
15. Tanino, T.: Fuzzy preference relations in group decision making. LNEMS, vol. 301, pp. 54–71 (1988)

# Investigating Properties of the ⊙-Consistency Index

Bice Cavallo and Livia D'Apuzzo

University Federico II,
Naples, Italy

**Abstract.** We consider pairwise comparison matrices on a real divisible and continuous abelian linearly ordered group $\mathcal{G} = (G, \odot, \leq)$, focusing on a proposed ⊙-consistency measure and its properties. We show that the proposed general ⊙-(in)consistency index satisfies some basic properties that can be considered naturally characterizing a consistency measure.

**Keywords:** Multi-Criteria Decision Making, Pairwise comparison matrices, consistency index, abelian linearly ordered group.

## 1 Introduction

Let $X = \{x_1, x_2, ..., x_n\}$ be a set of alternatives or criteria. In a multi-criteria evaluation context, an expert may state his/her preferences, for the set $X$, by means of a preference relation

$$\mathcal{A} : (x_i, x_j) \in X \times X \mapsto \mathcal{A}(x_i, x_j) = a_{ij} \in \mathbb{R},$$

where $a_{ij}$ represents the preference intensity of $x_i$ over $x_j$. The preference relation is represented by the *Pairwise Comparison Matrix* (PCM):

$$A = \begin{pmatrix} a_{11} & a_{12} & ... & a_{1n} \\ a_{21} & a_{22} & ... & a_{2n} \\ ... & ... & ... & ... \\ a_{n1} & a_{n2} & ... & a_{nn} \end{pmatrix}. \tag{1}$$

In literature, several kinds of PCMs are proposed, as the entry $a_{ij}$ assumes different meanings: in multiplicative PCMs it represents a preference ratio; in additive PCMs it is a preference difference; in fuzzy PCMs it quantifies in $[0,1]$ the distance from the value 0.5 expressing the indifference.

In an ideal situation, in which the expert is strongly coherent when stating his/her preferences, the PCM satisfies the consistency property, that, in the multiplicative case, is expressed as follows:

$$a_{ik} = a_{ij} \cdot a_{jk} \quad \forall \, i, j, k = 1, \ldots, n. \tag{2}$$

Under condition of consistency, the preference value $a_{ij}$ can be expressed by means of the components of a suitable vector, called consistent vector for $A =$

S. Greco et al. (Eds.): IPMU 2012, Part IV, CCIS 300, pp. 315–327, 2012.

$(a_{ij})$; for a multiplicative PCM, it is a positive vector $\underline{w} = (w_1, w_2, ..., w_n)$ verifying the condition

$$\frac{w_i}{w_j} = a_{ij} \quad \forall\, i, j = 1, \ldots, n.$$

The multiplicative PCMs play a basic role in the Analytic Hierarchy Process (AHP), a procedure developed by T.L. Saaty at the end of the 70s [20], [21], [22]. In [3], [4], [5], [6] and [15], properties of multiplicative PCMs are analyzed in order to determine a qualitative ranking on the set of alternatives and find vectors representing this ranking. Additive and fuzzy PCMs are investigated for instance by [2] and [17].

In order to unify the several approaches to the PCMs and remove some drawbacks linked to the possibility of the expert to be consistent, in [9] the authors introduce PCMs, whose entries belong to an abelian linearly ordered group (*alogroup*) $\mathcal{G} = (G, \odot, \leq)$. In this way, the consistency condition is expressed in terms of the group operation $\odot$. Under the assumption of divisibility of $\mathcal{G}$, for each $A = (a_{ij})$, a $\odot$-consistency measure $I_{\mathcal{G}}(A)$, expressed in terms of $\odot$-mean of $\mathcal{G}$-distances, is provided; furthermore a $\odot$-mean vector $\underline{w}_{m_\odot}(A)$, satisfying the independence of scale-inversion condition, is chosen as a weighting vector for the alternatives. Results related to this general unified framework are provided in [9], [10], [11], [12] and [13].

Since several consistency measures have been proposed in literature (see [1], [2], [14], [16], [18], [19], [8] and [20]), in [7], the authors address the following questions: "what is a (in)consistency index?", "which are the minimal characterizing properties that a proposed index must satisfy in order to be considered an (in)consistency index?"; then they introduce some characterizing properties for consistency indices that are very basic and hardly questionable.

In this paper, by investigating properties of the $\odot$-consistency index $I_{\mathcal{G}}(A)$, we prove that $I_{\mathcal{G}}(A)$ satisfies the characterizing properties proposed in [7].

The paper is organized as follows: Section 2 provides notation and preliminaries useful in the sequel; Section 3 introduces PCMs on real continuous divisible alo-groups; Section 4 focus on properties of the $\odot$-consistency index $I_{\mathcal{G}}(A)$; Section 5 provides concluding remarks and directions for future work.

## 2   Notation and Preliminaries

From now on, $\mathbb{R}$ will denote the set of real numbers, $\mathbb{Q}$ the subset of rational numbers, $\mathbb{Z}$ the subset of relative integers, $\mathbb{N}$ the subset of positive integers and $\mathbb{N}_0$ the set $\mathbb{N} \cup \{0\}$.

### 2.1   Alo-groups

$\mathcal{G} = (G, \odot, \leq)$ denotes an abelian linearly ordered group (alo-group), $e$ its *identity*, $a^{(-1)}$ the *inverse* of $a \in G$ with respect to $\odot$, $\div$ the *inverse operation* of $\odot$, defined by:

$$a \div b = a \odot b^{(-1)} \quad \forall a, b \in G. \tag{3}$$

**Proposition 1.** *[9] If $\mathcal{G} = (G, \odot, \leq)$ is a non-trivial alo-group then it has neither a greatest element nor a least element.*

**Proposition 2.** *[9] The operation*

$$d_\mathcal{G} : G \times G \to G$$
$$(a, b) \mapsto d_\mathcal{G}(a, b) = (a \div b) \vee (b \div a) \tag{4}$$

*is a $\mathcal{G}$-distance, that is satisfies the following properties:*

1. $d(a, b) \geq e$;
2. $d(a, b) = e \Leftrightarrow a = b$;
3. $d(a, b) = d(b, a)$;
4. $d(a, b) \leq d(a, c) \odot d(b, c)$.

**Definition 1.** *[9] Let $n \in \mathbb{N}_0$. The $(n)$-power $a^{(n)}$ of $a \in G$ is defined as follows:*

$$a^{(n)} = \begin{cases} e, & if \quad n = 0 \\ a^{(n-1)} \odot a, & if \quad n \geq 1. \end{cases}$$

**Definition 2.** *[12] Let $z \in \mathbb{Z}$. The $(z)$-power $a^{(z)}$ of $a \in G$ is defined as follows:*

$$a^{(z)} = \begin{cases} a^{(n)}, & if \quad z = n \in \mathbb{N}_0 \\ (a^{(n)})^{(-1)} & if \quad z = -n, \quad n \in \mathbb{N}. \end{cases}$$

### Divisible Alo-groups

**Definition 3.** *$\mathcal{G} = (G, \odot, \leq)$ is divisible if and only if $(G, \odot)$ is divisible, that is for each $n \in \mathbb{N}$ and each $a \in G$, the equation $x^{(n)} = a$ has at least a solution.*

If $\mathcal{G} = (G, \odot, \leq)$ is divisible, then the equation $x^{(n)} = a$ has a unique solution. Thus, it is reasonable provide the following definition:

**Definition 4.** *[9] Let $\mathcal{G} = (G, \odot, \leq)$ be divisible, $n \in \mathbb{N}$ and $a \in G$. Then, the $(n)$-root of $a$, denoted by $a^{(\frac{1}{n})}$, is the unique solution of the equation $x^{(n)} = a$, that is:*

$$(a^{(\frac{1}{n})})^{(n)} = a. \tag{5}$$

**Definition 5.** *[9] Let $\mathcal{G} = (G, \odot, \leq)$ be divisible. $\odot$-mean $m_\odot(a_1, a_2, ..., a_n)$ of the $n$ elements $a_1, a_2, ..., a_n$ of $G$ is the element $a \in G$ verifying the equality $a \odot a \odot ... \odot a = a_1 \odot a_2 \odot ... \odot a_n$; that is*

$$m_\odot(a_1, a_2, ..., a_n) = \begin{cases} a_1 & if \ n = 1, \\ (\bigodot_{i=1}^n a_i)^{(\frac{1}{n})} & if \ n \geq 2. \end{cases}$$

**Definition 6.** *[12] Let $(G, \odot, \leq)$ be divisible. For each $q = \frac{m}{n}$, with $m \in \mathbb{Z}$ and $n \in \mathbb{N}$, and for each $a \in G$, the $(q)$-power $a^{(q)}$ is defined as follows:*

$$a^{(q)} = (a^{(m)})^{(\frac{1}{n})}.$$

**Proposition 3.** *[12] Let $\mathcal{G} = (G, \odot, \le)$ be divisible. For each $a, b \in G$ and $q, q_1, q_2 \in \mathbb{Q}$, we have:*

1. $a^{(-q)} = (a^{(q)})^{(-1)} = (a^{(-1)})^{(q)}$;
2. $a^{(q_1)} \odot a^{(q_2)} = a^{(q_1 + q_2)}$;
3. $(a^{(q_1)})^{(q_2)} = a^{(q_1 q_2)} = (a^{(q_2)})^{(q_1)}$;
4. $(a \odot b)^{(q)} = a^{(q)} \odot b^{(q)}$;
5. $e^{(q)} = e$.

**Proposition 4.** *[12] Let $\mathcal{G} = (G, \odot, \le)$ be divisible. Let $q \in \mathbb{Q}$. Then, $(q)$-power function:*

$$f_{(q)} : x \in G \to x^{(q)} \in G$$

*is strictly increasing if $q > 0$, strictly decreasing if $q < 0$ and the constant function identically equal to identity element $e$ if $q = 0$.*

**Proposition 5.** *[12] Let $\mathcal{G} = (G, \odot, \le)$ be divisible and $a \in G$, with $a \ne e$. Then, $(q)$-exponential function*

$$g_{\mathbb{Q}} : x \in \mathbb{Q} \to a^{(x)} \in G$$

*is strictly increasing if $a > e$ and strictly decreasing if $a < e$.*

## 2.2 Real Divisible Alo-Groups

An alo-group $\mathcal{G} = (G, \odot, \le)$ is a *real* alo-group if and only if $G$ is a subset of the real line $\mathbb{R}$ and $\le$ is the total order on $G$ inherited from the usual order on $\mathbb{R}$. If $G$ is an interval of $\mathbb{R}$ then, by Proposition 1, it has to be an open interval.

Examples of real divisible continuous alo-groups are the following (see [10], [12] for details):

**Multiplicative alo-group.** $]0, +\infty[ = (]0, +\infty[, \cdot, \le)$, where $\cdot$ is the usual multiplication on $\mathbb{R}$;

**Additive alo-group.** $\mathcal{R} = (\mathbb{R}, +, \le)$, where $+$ is the usual addition on $\mathbb{R}$;

**Fuzzy group.** $]0, 1[ = (]0, 1[, \otimes, \le)$, where $\otimes : ]0, 1[^2 \to ]0, 1[$ is the operation defined by

$$x \otimes y = \frac{xy}{xy + (1 - x)(1 - y)}.$$

Two divisible continuous real alo-groups are isomorphic; in particular for each real divisible continuous alo-group $\mathcal{G} = (G, \odot, \le)$, there exists an isomorphism $h$ between $]0, +\infty[$ and $\mathcal{G}$ (see [9] for examples). Moreover, for each $a \in G$, we have:

$$a^{(q)} = h((h^{-1}(a))^q). \tag{6}$$

Let $\mathcal{G} = (G, \odot, \le)$ be a real divisible continuous alo-group. For each $a \in G$ and $r \in \mathbb{R}$, we set:

$$I_{a,r} = \{a^{(q)} : q \in Q \quad and \quad q < r\}, \quad S_{a,r} = \{a^{(q)} : q \in Q \quad and \quad q > r\}. \tag{7}$$

By Proposition 5, we can consider a separation point $c$; if $h$ is an isomorphism between $]0,+\infty[$ and $\mathcal{G}$, then, by (6), $h^{-1}(c) = (h^{-1}(a))^r$, that is the only one separation point between $h^{-1}(I_{a,r}) = \{(h^{-1}(a))^q : q \in Q \quad and \quad q < r\}$ and $h^{-1}(S_{a,r}) = \{(h^{-1}(a))^q : q \in Q \quad and \quad q > r\}$; as a consequence $c = h((h^{-1}(a))^r)$.

Thus, it is reasonable to extend the notion of $(q)$-power, with $q \in \mathbb{Q}$, in Definition 6, to the notion of $(r)$-power, with $r \in \mathbb{R}$, as follows:

**Definition 7.** *Let $\mathcal{G} = (G, \odot, \leq)$ be a real divisible continuous alo-group. For each $a \in G$ and $r \in \mathbb{R}$, $a^{(r)}$ is the separation point of sets in $(7)$, thus the following holds:*

$$a^{(r)} = h((h^{-1}(a))^r),$$

*with $h$ an isomorphism between $]0,+\infty[$ and $\mathcal{G}$.*

Properties of $a^{(q)}$, in Proposition 3, Proposition 4 and Proposition 5 can be extend to $a^{(r)}$, with $r \in \mathbb{R}$ instead of $q \in \mathbb{Q}$.

**Proposition 6.** *Let $\mathcal{G} = (G, \odot, \leq)$ be a real divisible continuous alo-group a. For each $a, b \in G$ and $r, r_1, r_2 \in \mathbb{R}$, we have:*

1. $a^{(-r)} = (a^{(r)})^{(-1)} = (a^{(-1)})^{(r)}$;
2. $a^{(r_1)} \odot a^{(r_2)} = a^{(r_1+r_2)}$;
3. $(a^{(r_1)})^{(r_2)} = a^{(r_1 r_2)} = (a^{(r_2)})^{(r_1)}$;
4. $(a \odot b)^{(r)} = a^{(r)} \odot b^{(r)}$;
5. $e^{(r)} = e$.

**Proposition 7.** *Let $\mathcal{G} = (G, \odot, \leq)$ be a real divisible continuous alo-group and $r \in \mathbb{R}$. Then, $(r)$-power function:*

$$f_{(r)} : x \in G \to x^{(r)} \in G$$

*is strictly increasing if $r > 0$, strictly decreasing if $r < 0$ and the constant function identically equal to identity element $e$ if $r = 0$.*

By property 4 of Proposition 6, $f_{(r)}$ is solution of the functional equation $f(x) \odot f(y) = f(x \odot y)$.

**Proposition 8.** *Let $\mathcal{G} = (G, \odot, \leq)$ be a real divisible continuous alo-group and $a \in G$, with $a \neq e$. Then, $(r)$-exponential function*

$$g : x \in \mathbb{R} \to a^{(x)} \in G$$

*is strictly increasing if $a > e$ and strictly decreasing if $a < e$.*

# 3   PCMs on Real Continuous Divisible Alo-groups

Let $X = \{x_1, x_2, \dots x_n\}$ be a set of alternatives, with $n \geq 3$, and $A = (a_{ij})$ in (1) the related PCM. We assume that $A = (a_{ij})$ is a PCM over a real continuous divisible alo-group $\mathcal{G} = (G, \odot, \leq)$, that is $a_{ij} \in G$, $\forall i, j \in \{1, \dots, n\}$ [9]. We assume that:

1. $\underline{a}_1, \underline{a}_2, \ldots, \underline{a}_n$ are the rows of $A$;
2. $\underline{a}^1, \underline{a}^2, \ldots, \underline{a}^n$ are the columns of $A$;
3. $A_{(ijk)}$ is the sub-matrix $\begin{pmatrix} a_{ii} & a_{ij} & a_{ik} \\ a_{ji} & a_{jj} & a_{jk} \\ a_{ki} & a_{kj} & a_{kk} \end{pmatrix}$;
4. $A_{ijk}$ denotes $A_{(ijk)}$ if $i < j < k$ (see [9]);
5. $A^{(r)} = (a_{ij}^{(r)})$.

**Definition 8.** *For each $A = (a_{ij})$ over $\mathcal{G} = (G, \odot, \leq)$, the $\odot$-mean vector associated to $A$ is:*

$$\underline{w}_{m_\odot}(A) = (m_\odot(\underline{a}_1), m_\odot(\underline{a}_2), \cdots, m_\odot(\underline{a}_n)), \tag{8}$$

*where $m_\odot(\underline{a}_i) = m_\odot(a_{i1}, a_{i2}, \ldots, a_{in})$.*

**Definition 9.** *$A = (a_{ij})$ is a $\odot$-reciprocal PCM if and only if verifies the condition:*
$$a_{ji} = a_{ij}^{(-1)} \quad \forall\, i, j \in \{1, \ldots, n\}., \qquad (\odot - reciprocity)$$
*so $a_{ii} = e \;\; \forall i \in \{1, \ldots, n\}$.*

**Definition 10.** *$RM(n)$ is the set of $\odot$-reciprocal PCMs of order $n$.*

Let us assume $A \in RM(n)$, then we set:

$$x_i \succ x_j \Leftrightarrow a_{ij} > e, \qquad x_i \sim x_j \Leftrightarrow a_{ij} = e, \tag{9}$$

where $x_i \succ x_j$ and $x_i \sim x_j$ stand for "$x_i$ is strictly preferred to $x_j$" and "$x_i$ and $x_j$ are indifferent", respectively; the relation $\succ$ is asymmetric and the strict preference of $x_i$ over $x_j$ is expressed also by the equivalence:

$$x_i \succ x_j \Leftrightarrow a_{ji} < e. \tag{10}$$

**Proposition 9.** *$A \in RM(n)$ if and only if $A^{(r)} \in RM(n)$, $\forall r \in \mathbb{R}$.*

*Proof.* By property 1 of Proposition 6.

### 3.1  $\odot$-*Consistent* PCMs

**Definition 11.** *[9] $A = (a_{ij})$ is a $\odot$-consistent PCM, if and only if verifies the condition:*

$$a_{ik} = a_{ij} \odot a_{jk} \qquad \forall i, j, k \in \{1, \ldots, n\}. \quad (\odot - consistency)$$

**Definition 12.** *$CM(n)$ is the set of $\odot$-consistent PCMs of order $n$.*

**Proposition 10.** *$A \in CM(n)$ if and only if $A^{(r)} \in CM(n)$, $\forall r \in \mathbb{R}$.*

*Proof.* By property 4 of Proposition 6.

**Proposition 11.** *[9], [10] $A \in CM(n)$ if and only if $A \in RM(n)$ and verifies the condition:*

$$a_{ik} = a_{ij} \odot a_{jk} \quad \forall\, i, j, k \in \{1, \ldots, n\} : i < j < k.$$

We stress that $CM(n) \subset RM(n)$ (see [13]).

**Definition 13.** *Let $A = (a_{ij}) \in CM(n)$. A vector $\underline{w} = (w_1, \ldots, w_n)$, with $w_i \in G$, is a ⊙-consistent vector for $A = (a_{ij})$ if and only if:*

$$w_i \div w_j = a_{ij} \quad \forall\, i, j \in \{1, \ldots, n\}.$$

**Proposition 12.** *[9] The following assertions related to $A = (a_{ij})$ are equivalent:*

1. $A = (a_{ij}) \in CM(n)$;
2. *there exists a ⊙-consistent vector $\underline{w}$ for $A$;*
3. *each column $\underline{a}^k$ is a ⊙-consistent vector;*
4. *the ⊙-mean vector $\underline{w}_{m_\odot}(A)$ is a ⊙-consistent vector.*

## 4   Properties of the ⊙-Consistency Index $I_{\mathcal{G}}(A)$

In order to measure the coherence of an expert when stating his/her preferences, in [9], we provide the following ⊙-consistency index:

**Definition 14.** *[9] Let $A \in RM(n)$ with $n \geq 3$, then the ⊙-consistency index $I_{\mathcal{G}}(A)$ is defined as follows:*

$$I_{\mathcal{G}}(A) = \Big( \bigodot_{(i,j,k) \in T} d_{\mathcal{G}}(a_{ik}, a_{ij} \odot a_{jk}) \Big)^{\left(\frac{1}{n_T}\right)}$$

*with $T = \{(i, j, k) : i < j < k\}$ and $n_T = |T| = \frac{n(n-2)(n-1)}{6}$.*

Thus:

$$I_{\mathcal{G}}(A) = \begin{cases} d_{\mathcal{G}}(a_{13}, a_{12} \odot a_{23}) & \text{if } n = 3, \\ \big( \bigodot_{(i,j,k) \in T} I_{\mathcal{G}}(A_{ijk}) \big)^{\left(\frac{1}{n_T}\right)} & \text{if } n > 3. \end{cases} \tag{11}$$

$I_{\mathcal{G}}(A)$ has an intuitive meaning, because is a ⊙-mean of $\mathcal{G}$-distances, and is suitable for several kinds of PCMs (e.g. multiplicative, additive and fuzzy). In this section, properties of $I_{\mathcal{G}}(A)$ are investigated.

**Proposition 13.** *[9] Let $A \in RM(n)$, then:*

$$I_{\mathcal{G}}(A) \geq e, \quad I_{\mathcal{G}}(A) = e \Leftrightarrow A \in CM(n).$$

Proposition 13 proves that there is a unique value of $I_{\mathcal{G}}(A)$ representing the ⊙-consistency, that is the identity element $e$ (property that a consistency index must satisfy as required in [7]).

### 4.1   Invariance under Permutation of Alternatives

Let $\pi : \{1, \ldots, n\} \to \{1, \ldots, n\}$ be a bijection, then $(\pi(1), \ldots, \pi(n))$ denotes the corresponding permutation of the $n$-tuple $(1, \ldots, n)$ and $\Pi : RM(n) \to RM(n)$ the function:

$$\Pi : A = \begin{pmatrix} a_{11} & a_{12} & \cdots & a_{1n} \\ a_{21} & a_{22} & \cdots & a_{2n} \\ \cdots & \cdots & \cdots & \cdots \\ a_{n1} & a_{n2} & \cdots & a_{nn} \end{pmatrix} \mapsto \Pi(A) = \begin{pmatrix} a_{\pi(1)\pi(1)} & a_{\pi(1)\pi(2)} & \cdots & a_{\pi(1)\pi(n)} \\ a_{\pi(2)\pi(1)} & a_{\pi(2)\pi(2)} & \cdots & a_{\pi(2)\pi(n)} \\ \cdots & \cdots & \cdots & \cdots \\ a_{\pi(n)\pi(1)} & a_{\pi(n)\pi(2)} & \cdots & a_{\pi(n)\pi(n)} \end{pmatrix}.$$
(12)

**Proposition 14.** *[9] Let $A \in RM(3)$ and $(\pi(1), \pi(2), \pi(3))$ a permutation of $(1, 2, 3)$, then:*

$$d_{\mathcal{G}}(a_{\pi(1)\pi(3)}, a_{\pi(1)\pi(2)} \odot a_{\pi(2)\pi(3)}) = d_{\mathcal{G}}(a_{13}, a_{12} \odot a_{23}).$$

By Proposition 15 the $\odot$-consistency index $I_{\mathcal{G}}(A)$ is independent from the order in which the alternatives are presented.

**Proposition 15.** *Let $A \in RM(n)$ and $\Pi$ the function in (12), then the following equality holds:*

$$I_{\mathcal{G}}(\Pi(A)) = I_{\mathcal{G}}(A).$$

*Proof.* If $n = 3$ then, by Definition 14 and Proposition 14, we have:

$$I_{\mathcal{G}}(\Pi(A)) = d_{\mathcal{G}}(a_{\pi(1)\pi(3)}, a_{\pi(1)\pi(2)} \odot a_{\pi(2)\pi(3)}) = d_{\mathcal{G}}(a_{13}, a_{12} \odot a_{23}) = I_{\mathcal{G}}(A).$$
(13)

If $n > 3$, by (11), then:

$$I_{\mathcal{G}}(\Pi(A)) = \Big( \bigodot_{(i,j,k)\in T} I_{\mathcal{G}}((\Pi(A))_{ijk}) \Big)^{(\frac{1}{n_T})} = \Big( \bigodot_{(i,j,k)\in T} I_{\mathcal{G}}(A_{(\pi(i)\pi(j)\pi(k))}) \Big)^{(\frac{1}{n_T})}.$$

Thus, by (13), the following equality holds:

$$I_{\mathcal{G}}(\Pi(A)) = \Big( \bigodot_{(r,s,t)\in T} I_{\mathcal{G}}(A_{rst}) \Big)^{(\frac{1}{n_T})} = I_{\mathcal{G}}(A),$$

where $(r, s, t)$ is a permutation of $(\pi(i), \pi(j), \pi(k))$ such that $r < s < t$.

### 4.2   Link between $I_{\mathcal{G}}(A)$ and $\underline{w}_{m_\odot}(A)$

In [13], we focus on properties of the $\odot$-mean vector $\underline{w}_{m_\odot}(A)$ and choose it as a weighting vector for the alternatives. In [12], we provide the following:

**Theorem 1.** *[12] Let $\underline{w}_{m_\odot}(A) = (m_\odot(\underline{a}_1), \ldots, m_\odot(\underline{a}_n))$ be the $\odot$-mean vector associated to $A = (a_{ij})$. Then, for $i, j = 1, \ldots, n$, we have:*

$$d_{\mathcal{G}}((m_\odot(\underline{a}_i) \div m_\odot(\underline{a}_j)), a_{ij}) \begin{cases} = I_{\mathcal{G}}(A)^{(\frac{1}{3})}, & \text{if } n = 3, \\ \leq I_{\mathcal{G}}(A)^{(\frac{(n-2)(n-1)}{6})}, & \text{if } n > 3 . \end{cases}$$

Theorem 1 gives more validity to $I_\mathcal{G}(A)$ as $\odot$-consistency measure and more meaning to $\underline{w}_{m_\odot}(A)$; in fact, it ensures that if $I_\mathcal{G}(A)$ is close to the identity element then, from a side $A$ is close to be a $\odot$-consistent PCM and from the other side $\underline{w}_{m_\odot}(A)$ is close to be a $\odot$-consistent vector; thus, it can be chosen as a weighting vector for the alternatives.

### 4.3  Monotonicity under Reciprocity Preserving Mapping

Let $A \in RM(n)$ and $r \in \mathbb{R}$, by Proposition 8, we have:

$$r > 1 \Rightarrow \begin{cases} a_{ij} > e \Rightarrow & e < a_{ij} < a_{ij}^{(r)}, \\ a_{ij} < e \Rightarrow & a_{ij}^{(r)} < a_{ij} < e; \end{cases}$$

$$0 < r < 1 \Rightarrow \begin{cases} a_{ij} > e \Rightarrow & e < a_{ij}^{(r)} < a_{ij}, \\ a_{ij} < e \Rightarrow & a_{ij} < a_{ij}^{(r)} < e; \end{cases} \tag{14}$$

$$r < 0 \Rightarrow \begin{cases} a_{ij} > e \Rightarrow & a_{ij}^{(r)} < e < a_{ij}, \\ a_{ij} < e \Rightarrow & a_{ij} < e < a_{ij}^{(r)}. \end{cases}$$

Thus, if $r > 1$ then $a_{ij}^{(r)}$ represents an intensification of the preference $a_{ij}$, if $0 < r < 1$ a weakening of the preference and if $r < 0$ a preference reversal.

**Proposition 16.** *Let $r \in \mathbb{R}$, then the function:*

$$F_{(r)} : A \in RM(n) \mapsto A^{(r)} \in RM(n) \tag{15}$$

*is $\odot$-consistency preserving and, if $r \in \mathbb{R} \backslash \{0\}$, it is a bijection.*

*Proof.* The proof is given in the working paper version of this paper.

We study how $I_\mathcal{G}(A)$ changes its value, when the function $F_{(r)}$ is applied to $A$.

**Proposition 17.** *Let $A \in RM(n)$ and $r \in \mathbb{R}$, then:*

$$I_\mathcal{G}(A^{(r)}) = (I_\mathcal{G}(A))^{(|r|)} = \begin{cases} (I_\mathcal{G}(A))^{(r)} & \text{if } r \geq 0, \\ (I_\mathcal{G}(A))^{(-r)} & \text{if } r < 0. \end{cases}$$

*Proof.* By (11), for $n > 3$, $I_\mathcal{G}(A^{(r)}) = \left( \bigodot_{(i,j,k) \in T} (I_\mathcal{G}(A_{ijk}^{(r)})) \right)^{(\frac{1}{n_T})}$, thus it is enough to prove the assertion for $n = 3$. Let $A \in RM(3)$, then:

$$I_\mathcal{G}(A^{(r)}) = d_\mathcal{G}(a_{13}^{(r)}, a_{12}^{(r)} \odot a_{23}^{(r)}) = (a_{13}^{(r)} \div (a_{12}^{(r)} \odot a_{23}^{(r)})) \vee ((a_{12}^{(r)} \odot a_{23}^{(r)}) \div a_{13}^{(r)}) =$$
$$= ((a_{13} \div (a_{12} \odot a_{23}))^{(r)}) \vee (((a_{12} \odot a_{23}) \div a_{13})^{(r)}).$$

By Proposition 7 and the first property in Proposition 6, the assertion is achieved.

**Corollary 1.** *Let $A \in RM(n) \backslash CM(n)$. Then:*

$$I_{\mathcal{G}}(A^{(r)}) \begin{cases} > (I_{\mathcal{G}}(A)) & if \ |r| > 1, \\ < (I_{\mathcal{G}}(A)) & if \ |r| < 1. \end{cases}$$

*Proof.* By Proposition 13, $I_{\mathcal{G}}(A) > e$. Then, the assertion follows by Proposition 17 and Proposition 8.

By Corollary 1, Proposition 16 and Proposition 13, if $A \in RM(n)$, then the following inequality holds:

$$I_{\mathcal{G}}(A^{(r)}) \geq I_{\mathcal{G}}(A) \quad \forall r > 1. \tag{16}$$

Inequality (16) corresponds to the third characterizing property in [7].

**Proposition 18.** *Let $A \in RM(n)$. Then the function:*

$$m : r \in \mathbb{R} \to I_{\mathcal{G}}(A^{(r)}) \in G$$

*satisfies the following properties:*

- *if $A \in CM(n)$ then $m$ is the constant function $m : r \in \mathbb{R} \to e \in G$;*
- *if $A \notin CM(n)$ then $m$ is strictly increasing in $[0, +\infty[$ and strictly decreasing in $] - \infty, 0]$.*

*Proof.* The proof is given in the working paper version of this paper.

For multiplicative, additive and fuzzy cases, for some value of $I_{\mathcal{G}}(A)$, the graphics of $I_{\mathcal{G}}(A^{(r)})$ are shown in Figure 1, Figure 2 and Figure 3, respectively.

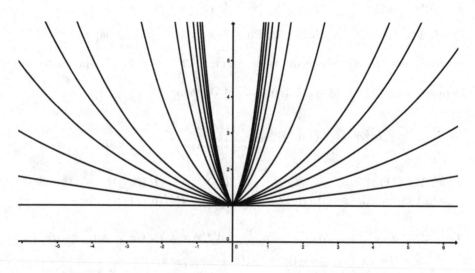

**Fig. 1.** Multiplicative case: $m : r \in \mathbb{R} \to I_{\mathcal{G}}(A^{(r)}) = I_{\mathcal{G}}((a_{ij}^r)) = (I_{\mathcal{G}}(A))^{|r|} \in [1, +\infty[$

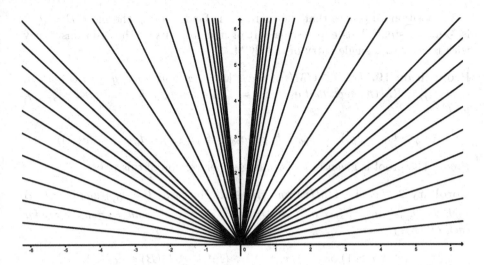

**Fig. 2.** Additive case: $m : r \in \mathbb{R} \rightarrow I_{\mathcal{G}}(A^{(r)}) = I_{\mathcal{G}}((r \cdot a_{ij})) = |r| \cdot I_{\mathcal{G}}(A) \in [0, +\infty[$

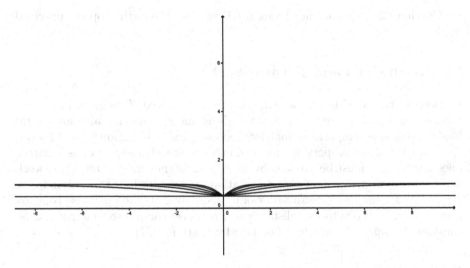

**Fig. 3.** Fuzzy case: $m : r \in \mathbb{R} \rightarrow I_{\mathcal{G}}(A^{(r)}) = I_{\mathcal{G}}((\frac{(a_{ij}^r)}{(a_{ij}^r)+(1-a_{ij}^r)})) = \frac{(I_{\mathcal{G}}(A))^r}{(I_{\mathcal{G}}(A))^r+(1-I_{\mathcal{G}}(A))^r} \in [0.5, 1[$

### 4.4 Strict Monotonicity on Single Entries

Let us consider $A = (a_{ij})$, a $\odot$-consistent PCM, and choose one of its non-diagonal entries $a_{pq}$. If we change $a_{pq}$ in $b_{pq}$, by increasing or decreasing its value, and modify its reciprocal $a_{qp}$ accordingly, while all the other entries remain unchanged, then the resulting PCM, $B = (b_{ij})$, is not anymore $\odot$-consistent and, by Proposition 13, $I_{\mathcal{G}}(B) > e$.

Proposition 19 proves that the more $b_{pq}$ is far from $a_{pq}$, the more $B = (b_{ij})$ is $\odot$-inconsistent. This expresses a sort of monotonicity of the $\odot$-inconsistency with respect to a single entry of the PCM.

**Proposition 19.** *Let $A \in CM(n)$, $p, q \in \{1, \ldots, n\}$, with $p \neq q$, and $B = (b_{ij})$, $C = (c_{ij}) \in RM(n)$ such that $a_{ij} = b_{ij} = c_{ij}$ for $i \neq p$, $j \neq q$ and for $i \neq q$, $j \neq p$. Then:*

$$((c_{pq} > b_{pq} > a_{pq}) \text{ or } (a_{pq} > b_{pq} > c_{pq})) \Rightarrow (I_{\mathcal{G}}(A) < I_{\mathcal{G}}(B) < I_{\mathcal{G}}(C)).$$

*Proof.* The proof is given in the working paper version of this paper.

**Corollary 2.** *Let $A \in CM(n)$ and $r, r' \in \mathbb{R}$. For each $B = (b_{ij})$ and $C = (c_{ij})$ such that $b_{pq} = a_{pq}^{(r)}$, $c_{pq} = a_{pq}^{(r')}$, $b_{qp} = b_{pq}^{(-1)}$, $c_{qp} = c_{pq}^{(-1)}$ and $a_{ij} = b_{ij} = c_{ij}$ for each other $i, j$, then:*

$$((r' > r > 1) \text{ or } (r' < r < 1)) \Rightarrow (I_{\mathcal{G}}(A) \leq I_{\mathcal{G}}(B) \leq I_{\mathcal{G}}(C)).$$

*Proof.* By property 5 of Proposition 6, Proposition 8 and Proposition 19.

By Corollary 2, $\odot$-consistency index $I_{\mathcal{G}}(A)$ satisfies the forth property provided in [7].

# 5    Conclusions and Future Work

Properties of $\odot$-consistency index $I_{\mathcal{G}}(A)$ are investigated. This index has an intuitive meaning, because is a $\odot$-mean of $\mathcal{G}$-distances, and is suitable for several kinds of pairwise comparisons matrices (e.g. multiplicative, additive and fuzzy). $I_{\mathcal{G}}(A)$ satisfies some properties, proposed in literature, that are very basic, hardly questionable and must be satisfied by an (in)consistency index. Our future work will be direct to perform an experimentation for establishing the random index $RI_{\odot}$, representing the $\odot$-consistency of a randomly generated pairwise comparison matrix, in order to establish when a pairwise comparison matrix can be considered enough $\odot$-consistent (as done by Saaty for $CI$).

# References

1. Aguarón, J., Moreno-Jiménez, J.M.: The geometric consistency index: Approximated thresholds. European Journal of Operational Research 147(1), 137–145 (2003)
2. Barzilai, J.: Consistency measures for pairwise comparison matrices. Journal of Multi-Criteria Decision Analysis 7(3), 123–132 (1998)
3. Basile, L., D'Apuzzo, L.: Ranking and weak consistency in the a.h.p. context. Rivista di Matematica per le Scienze Economiche e Sociali 20(1), 99–110 (1997)
4. Basile, L., D'Apuzzo, L.: Weak consistency and quasi-linear means imply the actual ranking. International Journal of Uncertainty, Fuzziness and Knowledge-Based Systems 10(3), 227–239 (2002)

5. Basile, L., D'Apuzzo, L.: Transitive matrices, strict preference and intensity operators. Mathematical Methods in Economics and Finance 1, 21–36 (2006)
6. Basile, L., D'Apuzzo, L.: Transitive matrices, strict preference and ordinal evaluation operators. Soft Computing 10(10), 933–940 (2006)
7. Brunelli, M., Fedrizzi, M.: Characterizing properties for inconsistency indices in the ahp. In: ISAHP (2011)
8. Brunelli, M.: A note on the article inconsistency of pair-wise comparison matrix with fuzzy elements based on geometric mean. Fuzzy Sets and Systems 161, 1604–1613 (2010); Fuzzy Sets and Systems 176(1), 76–78 (2011)
9. Cavallo, B., D'Apuzzo, L.: A general unified framework for pairwise comparison matrices in multicriterial methods. International Journal of Intelligent Systems 24(4), 377–398 (2009)
10. Cavallo, B., D'Apuzzo, L.: Characterizations of consistent pairwise comparison matrices over abelian linearly ordered groups. International Journal of Intelligent Systems 25(10), 1035–1059 (2010)
11. Cavallo, B., D'Apuzzo, L., Squillante, M.: Building Consistent Pairwise Comparison Matrices over Abelian Linearly Ordered Groups. In: Rossi, F., Tsoukias, A. (eds.) ADT 2009. LNCS (LNAI), vol. 5783, pp. 237–248. Springer, Heidelberg (2009)
12. Cavallo, B., D'Apuzzo, L., Squillante, M.: About a consistency index for pairwise comparison matrices over a divisible alo-group. International Journal of Intelligent Systems 27(2), 153–175 (2012)
13. Cavallo, B., D'Apuzzo, L.: Deriving weights from a pairwise comparison matrix over an alo-group. Soft Computing - A Fusion of Foundations, Methodologies and Applications 16(2), 353–366 (2012)
14. Crawford, G., Williams, C.: A note on the analysis of subjective judgment matrices. Journal of Mathematical Psychology 29(4), 387–405 (1985)
15. D'Apuzzo, L., Marcarelli, G., Squillante, M.: Generalized consistency and intensity vectors for comparison matrices. International Journal of Intelligent Systems 22(12), 1287–1300 (2007)
16. Golden, B.L., Wang, Q.: An alternate measure of consistency. In: Golden, B.L., Wasil, E.A., Harker, P.T. (eds.) The Analythic Hierarchy Process, Applications and Studies, pp. 68–81. Springer, Heidelberg (1989)
17. Herrera-Viedma, E., Herrera, F., Chiclana, F., Luque, M.: Some issue on consistency of fuzzy preferences relations. European Journal of Operational Research 154, 98–109 (2004)
18. Peláez, J.I., Lamata, M.T.: A new measure of consistency for positive reciprocal matrices. Computers & Mathematics with Applications 46(12), 1839–1845 (2003)
19. Ramík, J., Korviny, P.: Inconsistency of pair-wise comparison matrix with fuzzy elements based on geometric mean. Fuzzy Sets Syst. 161, 1604–1613 (2010)
20. Saaty, T.L.: A scaling method for priorities in hierarchical structures. J. Math. Psychology 15, 234–281 (1977)
21. Saaty, T.L.: The Analytic Hierarchy Process. McGraw-Hill, New York (1980)
22. Saaty, T.L.: Axiomatic foundation of the analytic hierarchy process. Management Science 32(7), 841–855 (1986)

# Finding Optimal Presentation Sequences for a Conversational Recommender System

Núria Bertomeu Castelló*

Zentrum für Allgemeine Sprachwissenschaft
Schützenstr. 18 10117 Berlin, Germany
bertomeu@zas.gwz-berlin.de
http://www.zas.gwz-berlin.de

**Abstract.** This paper presents an approach for finding optimal presentation sequences in conversational Recommender Systems. The strategies simultaneously pursuit the goals of acquainting the user with the different possibilities, successfully accomplishing the task in the shortest possible time, and obtaining an accurate user model. The approach is modeled as an MDP where the states include belief states about the acceptability of the different alternatives, modeled as Bayesian networks.

**Keywords:** presentation strategy, Recommender System, predictive user model, Active Learning, Markov Decision Process, Bayesian network.

## 1 Introduction

The task of a Recommender System is to propose items from a catalog, based on the preferences provided by the user. Often the amount of potentially interesting items is too large and the system has to decide how many and which items to present, as well as how and when to present them. In this paper we present an approach to finding optimal long-term presentation sequences within a conversational Recommender System in a virtual world furniture-sales scenario (see [1]). Typically, the user provides certain constraints and the system shows him items fulfilling these constraints. However, often there is no object in the catalog fulfilling the user's requirements. In such cases, the system retrieves a set of optimal candidates based on their similarity to the user's query (see [3]). The procedure presented in this paper takes as input the retrieved set of optimal candidates and generates a strategy for their presentation.

There are two presentation modalities in our scenario. Since the Recommender System is a conversational agent, it can present options to the user by verbalizing them with a natural language utterance. Alternatively, it can display items, by placing them in the virtual room. Although in the verbal modality the agent can present up to three options, the options presented are property-value combinations representative of more or less large sets of items and, therefore, the

---

* I acknowledge support by the Investitionsbank Berlin (ProFIT program) and by the Bundesministerium für Bildung und Forschung (BMBF), grant 01UG0711.

S. Greco et al. (Eds.): IPMU 2012, Part IV, CCIS 300, pp. 328–337, 2012.

judgements elicited cannot be totally transferred to the items exhibiting the property-value combinations. On the other hand, in the visual modality only one item can be shown at a time, since the item is placed on a particular spot in the room where the user can visually judge it in its environment, however, presentation in this modality elicits more exact judgments from the user.

All agent actions have two kinds of effects: a) material effects, i.e. the user becomes acquainted with available alternatives; and b) informational effects, i.e. by eliciting user feedback the actions provide information about the user preferences. On the material side, a strategy must pursue two goals: provide the user with a good overview of the available options and, once the user has focused on some option, recommend items within it. On the informational side, the strategy's goal is to acquire a model of the user preferences as accurate as possible.

Learning about the user preferences in a sequential setting allows the agent to dynamically adapt his strategy based on the user feedback. A desired feature of a conversational Recommender System is, thus, the ability to perform Active Learning (see [9] for an introduction to Active Learning). A system performs Active Learning in the standard sense if it selects the alternatives to present based on the informational effects of the user's feedback about them, i.e. those alternatives that allow to obtain an overall more accurate predictive model of the user preferences are selected for presentation. The presentation of a certain alternative is informative if the alternative is a representative of a dense area in the search space and the area is not represented by an already presented alternative. The later means that by presenting alternatives as intrinsically different as possible, not only the user will be able to make a more informative choice, but more information is obtained about the user preferences. Therefore, much research in the Recommender System's community has been devoted to ensure diversity in the recommendation set, e.g. [6].

As discussed by [9], conversational Recommender Systems do perform Active Learning, but not in the standard way. Their goal is rather to elicit feedback from the user that enables them to successively narrow down the set of interesting options. In addition to this type of Active Learning, our system also performs standard Active Learning on the subset of optimal candidates. This is useful in situations in which preferred exploration paths are exhausted and the system has to figure out what to present next.

The presentation strategies generated by our approach perform non-intrusive Active Learning during the course of the interaction, that is, items with higher probabilities of being liked will be presented first, since we assume that the user does not want to waste time only to enable the system to get a more accurate user model. Everything else being equal, however, alternatives to be presented are chosen according to diversity and representativeness. The Active Learning performed by our strategies is similar in spirit to the Output Estimates Change approach [10]. In addition, our approach exploits similarity between alternatives for Active Learning, by partially inferring how the user stands to not presented alternatives, based on his feedback about presented alternatives belonging to related categories. Therefore the amount of connections to related alternatives also plays a role when deciding about the degree of informativeness that involves presenting a certain alternative.

## 1.1 Methodology

The approach presented here models the search for an optimal presentation policy as a Markov Decision Process (MDP) and analyzes it with the techniques of Decision Theory (see [4] for an overview about this methodology). An MDP consists of a set of possible states, a set of possible events, a set of time points, and transitions from a particular state at time $t$ to a particular state at time $t+1$. States contain all information that the agent needs to consider when making a decision. Events can be of two types: agent actions and exogenous events. Events bring the system from a state at time $t$ to a different state at time $t+1$. If the system is stochastic, there are different possible transitions from a state at time $t$ to different states at $t+1$. Such transitions are determined by exogenous events, which are associated with a probability of occurrence. The agent may receive perfect, partial or no feedback from the results of his actions and the effects of the exogenous events. The performance of the agent is evaluated by a value function V(.), that judges the quality of an action at a certain stage on the basis of the state to which this action leads. The system computes the expected value of each candidate course of action and chooses to perform the one maximizing that quantity.

The selection of optimal behavior policies in dialogue systems has already been modeled with these techniques and learned with Reinforcement Learning by e.g. [8]. Those approaches, having spoken dialogue in mind and the uncertainty associated with speech recognition predictions, model the sequential decision problem as a partially observable MDP (POMPD), i.e. an MDP where the user's feedback (an exogenous event) cannot be fully observed and the agent entertains a probability distribution about the different possible states he may be in.

Since in our system interaction takes place through typed written language, we assume that the agent can fully observe the consequences of his actions and the exogenous events. However, in our model states are since the beginning until all objects have been shown only partially observable. They contain information about: 1) the knowledge already transferred to the user about the available alternatives, and 2) the agent's beliefs about the acceptability of the different alternatives for the user. Our states are, thus, predictive user models that become increasingly accurate thanks to the informational effects of the actions.

Cassandra [5] proposes to model states in POMPDs as belief states, consisting of a probability distribution over the different states the system may be in. All possible states must be, thus, explicitly enumerated. As we will see in brief, by having as states probability distributions over the acceptability of the different alternatives represented in a *Bayesian Network* [7], we implicitly represent belief states about the state , without the need of explicitly enumerating all possible states.

But the agent's beliefs about the acceptability of the different alternatives do not consist only of the information explicitly provided by the user. As we already mentioned, the agent partially transfers what he has learnt about a particular alternative to related alternatives. By representing the agent's beliefs in a *Bayesian Network* such inferences can also be efficiently modeled. First, the network structure allows to represent connections between the different alternatives, and, second, belief propagation techniques allow to update the beliefs associated with the different alternatives, each time the user provides some feedback.

In MDP models of sequential decision-making in dialogue, user responses are treated as exogenous events. They are typically associated with a probability of occurrence based on the agent's previous action, as in e.g. [8]. Such probabilities are normally obtained from corpora. In our system, since the agent entertains beliefs about the acceptability of the different alternatives, he can also predict whether the user's response will be an acceptance or a rejection of the proposed alternative. So, by having in the states information about the agent's beliefs regarding the acceptability of the different alternatives, we also have information about the probability of occurrence of the different user responses and, thus, of the probability of the different state transitions. In contrast to other systems, the probability of occurrence of the exogenous events are not statically coded in advance, but they change dynamically, as the agent's beliefs about the acceptability of the alternatives change. Rewards are neither statically associated with states, but are computed with a function. Since there is no need for specifying probabilities for the state transitions or reward-state associations, the state space does not need to be statically declared at all. States are dynamically computed after each transition, avoiding, thus, the problem of representing large action-state and state-reward spaces.

Our main contributions is, thus, a procedure for finding recommendation strategies that simultaneously present interesting alternatives to the user and perform unobtrusive Active Learning, exploiting the relatedness of the different alternatives. A further interesting aspect of this work is the implicit representation of state transition probabilities and associated rewards within the states, obviating the need for a static representation of the state space.

The paper is structured as follows: next section describes the MDP model for finding an optimal presentation sequence, section 3 discusses the implementation and the behavior exhibited by the agent. Finally, section 4 summarizes and concludes.

# 2   A Model for Finding Optimal Presentation Sequences

In the following subsections we describe the states, the events and the evaluation function in our MDP model for finding an optimal presentation strategy.

## 2.1   States

In our MDP model the states contain two types of information: 1) belief states about the user's acceptance of the different items, property-value combinations and trade-offs, and 2) the user's degree of awareness about the existence and characteristics of the different alternatives. The belief states are represented in a *Bayesian network* [7]. A Bayesian network is a directed acyclic graph (DAG). The nodes in the network are the random variables in the domain and the edges represent the direct influence of one node on another. Each variable X is associated with a conditional probability distribution (CPD) over the values of X for each possible joint assignment of values to its parents in the model. For a node with no parents the CPD is a marginal distribution, such as P(X). When a new evidence is obtained probabilistic inference takes place via belief propagation, a message passing process among related nodes.

As mentioned in the introduction, in the situation of a retrieval failure, the system selects a set of optimal candidate items. These items are clustered according to the property-value combination (PVC) they exhibit and PVCs are clustered according to the trade-off (TO) they involve. A Bayesian network is constructed, in which for each TO, PVC and item there is a binary variable node representing its *acceptance* by the user. TO variables are parent less in the network and have as children the variables of the corresponding PVCs. PVC variables in turn have as children the variables of the items exhibiting the given PVCs. Variables corresponding to TOs and PVCs represent the agent's belief about whether the user will/will not express preference for the TO/PVC in question. Variables corresponding to items represent the agent's belief about whether the user will accept/reject the item in question. Marginal probability distributions for the TOs and CPDs are obtained from a corpus of dialogues in the furniture sales scenario [2].

Figure 1 shows the Bayesian network representing the agent's beliefs about the alternatives retrieved for the unfulfillable preferences: "sofa, leather, orange, antique". At the top level we find three different TOs. TOs are represented as coordinates in a scale from 0 to 1 with respect to the original preferences (the target), 0, in a geometrical search-space (see [3]). All TOs have the same marginal probability. At the following levels we find the PVCs and the items. The tables represent the CPDs connecting TOs with PCVs and PCVs with items (I).

When the agent learns that the user has a preference for a particular PVC or that he accepts or rejects a particular item belief propagation takes places. If a PVC or an item are accepted the beliefs about the acceptance of the related alternatives increase. If, on the contrary, an item is rejected by the user, the beliefs about the acceptance of the related alternatives decrease. See [7] for the details about how belief is computed and propagated.

The level of knowledge of the user about the existence and characteristics of the different alternatives is represented by a feature called *status* that takes as possible values: *unknown, trade-off presented, presented* or *shown*. All TOs, PVCs and items are specified for this feature, whose default value is *unknown*. When a PVC is presented or an item is shown, its *status* value and those of the alternatives related to it are altered. Concretely, when an item is shown it gets the status *shown* and the PVC exhibited by it gets the status *presented* (if it was not already). When a PVC is presented it gets the status *presented*

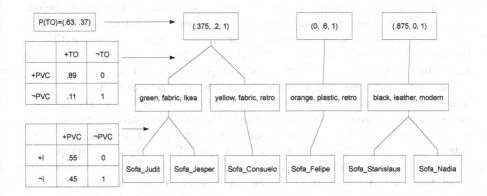

**Fig. 1.** Optimal alternatives represented in a Bayesian network

and the items exhibiting it get the status *presented* as well. In both cases the corresponding TO also gets the status *presented*, while other PVCs involving this TO and the items that exhibit those PVCs become *trade-off presented* (if they have not been themselves presented or shown).

## 2.2   Events

Events in our model are of two types: agent actions and user responses. The agent can handle in two ways: he can either 1) propose two or three PVCs to the user, or 2) show him an item. Possible user responses to agent actions of the first type can be: a) choose one of the proposed PVCs (CHOOSE), or b) request a different PVC (REQUEST). Possible responses to the act of showing an item are of the type: a) accept the item (ACCEPT), b) accept the item, but request a different PVC (ACCEPT-REQUEST), c) reject the item and request a different PVC (ACCEPT-REJECT), or d) simply reject the item (REJECT).

Requests for a different PVC and acceptances bring the current recommendation strategy to an end. When the user requests a different PVC, the database has to be searched again, resulting in a new and eventually different set of candidate items to be presented. If the user accepts an item, we assume that the recommendation task is successfully accomplished. These user responses bring, thus, the MDP to a final stage. If the agent has already shown all alternatives the process comes also to an end.

User responses are associated with probabilities of occurrence. As we announced in the introduction, these probabilities are basically extracted from the agent's beliefs about the acceptability of the different alternatives. In addition, information from the corpus of furniture-sales dialogues about the frequency of actions that are not simple rejections or acceptances is also used to determine the probabilities. To illustrate this let us calculate the probability that the user responds with the actions REJECT and REJECT-REQUEST to the agent's act of showing an item $x$ with the following associated beliefs $B(x) = (.3, .7)$.

The probability that the user rejects the item is according to the agent's beliefs .7. According to the corpus data, in 47% of the cases when the user rejects an item, he makes an additional request. Therefore, we compute the probabilities of the two user responses as follows: $P(\text{REJECT-REQUEST}(x)) = .47B(\neg x)) = .329$ and $P(\text{REJECT}(x)) = B(\neg x) - P(\text{REJECT-REQUEST}(x)) = .371$.

The agent's actions and user's responses have effects over the state. The agent's actions have a material effect by changing the *status* of the shown or presented alternatives, as explained in 2.1. The user's responses have an informational effect by eliminating uncertainty about the value of the *acceptance* variable for the alternative chosen or seen by the user. Concretely, if a user chooses a PVC $a$ the corresponding node in the network is associated with the following belief $B(a) = (1, 0)$, meaning that the agent is now certain that the user has a preference for this PVC. Similarly, if the user rejects an item $i$ the agent updates its beliefs as follows: $B(x) = (0, 1)$. Once the new evidence is integrated in the network, belief propagation takes place. The following table summarizes the probabilities and immediate effects of the different user responses and specifies whether they bring the process to an end.

**Table 1.** User responses

| agent's action type | user's response | end | effect | probability |
|---|---|---|---|---|
| present($A$), where $\{a \in A : a \text{ is a PVC}\}$ | choose($a_i$) from $A = \{a_1, ...a_n\}$ | no | $B(a_i) = (1, 0)$ | $\dfrac{.9(1 - (\prod_{a \in A} B(\neg a)))}{|A|}$ |
| | request | yes | — | $1-(.9(1 - (\prod_{a \in A} B(\neg a))))$ |
| show($x$), where $x$ is an item | accept($x$) | yes | $B(x) = (1, 0)$ | $.86(B(+x))$ |
| | accept-request($x$) | yes | $B(x) = (1, 0)$ | $.14(B(+x))$ |
| | reject($x$) | if all items shown | $B(x) = (0, 1)$ | $.53(B(\neg x))$ |
| | reject-request($x$) | yes | $B(x) = (0, 1)$ | $.47(B(\neg x))$ |

## 2.3   The Evaluation Function

We are interested at how well the agent accomplished its task at the time point when the task ends. Therefore we have chosen a *goal only* evaluation function, instead of a *time-separable additive* one. *Goal only* evaluation functions evaluate the performance of the agent based on the final state that his course of action reaches, instead of evaluating his performance after every action. Note that in our system the task can be ended at any stage. The horizon is, thus, finite but uncertain. Therefore the evaluation function has to guarantee that whenever the user chooses to end the task the value is as high as it possibly can be at that stage of the task. Consequently, the same value should count more at an early stage than at a later stage. A discount factor makes this possible.

The task is to find the action policy $\pi$ with the maximal expected value (EV). To compute EV for a policy we need to consider the discounted reward that can be obtained at any final state with a positive probability of being reached by performing the policy, as shown by the following equation:

$$EV(\pi) = \sum_{s^T \in S} \gamma^T R(s^T) P(s^T|\pi) \tag{1}$$

$s^T$ is any final state, where $T$ can be any (final) stage. We assume that there are no costs. The reward is discounted according to the number of stages gone (or duration of the task). $\gamma^T$ is the value of the discount factor at stage $T$, $R(s^T)$ is the reward associated with state $s^T$ and $P(s^T|\pi)$ is the probability of reaching $s^T$ when performing $\pi$. $R(s^T)$ is calculated as follows:

$$R(s^T) = \sum_{k \in K} \delta_{k_{s^T}} B(+k)_{s^T} \tag{2}$$

$k$ is an item from the set $K$ of retrieved optimal items, $\delta_{k_s}$ is a penalty factor associated with the *status* value of $k$ in $s^T$, and $B(+k)_{s^T}$ is the belief/knowledge of the system as represented by $s^T$ about the *acceptance* of $k$ by the user. The different values of $\delta$ for the different values of the feature *status* are the following: *unknown*=0.1, *trade-off presented*=0.6, *presented*=0.8 and *shown*=1. The value of the discount factor $\gamma$ is set to 0.7.

The reward function, thus, strongly penalizes that items remain completely unknown to the user. The more aware the user becomes about the different alternative items the better. The reward function also disfavors states containing rejected items, causing the agent to show those items with the highest probability of being accepted first. The interaction of the discount factor, the positive beliefs and the network structure leads the agent to prefer those alternatives in more populated and interconnected search-space areas.

## 3   Implementation and Behavior of the Selected Policy

When the user's preferences cannot be fulfilled or the user has already seen all the objects fulfilling them, the system selects an optimal policy for the presentation of the best alternatives and performs it. At first a Bayesian network is constructed from the set of retrieved optimal candidates. For each intrinsically different[1] initial action the system constructs a decision tree. Decision trees are evaluated after construction by a *rollback procedure* (see [4]). At each decision point, the EVs of the different possible agent moves are computed and compared. Sub-optimal moves and their descendants are pruned out. A the end of the evaluation the decision trees are policies, since for every possible non-final user move there is a single agent move as a response to it. The policy with the highest EV is selected for performance.

---

[1] At each stage available agent actions are clustered according to the quality of their effects over the state. Only one action from each cluster is considered for performance.

Optimal candidate sets typically contain between two and ten optimal candidate items. The resulting Bayesian networks can have a more or less complex structure, i.e. more or less TOs, more or less PVCs within a TO, more or less items within a PVC. Networks can also vary with respect to homogeneity, e.g. PVCs may be exhibited by the same or a different amount of items. Both the degrees of complexity and homogeneity have an influence on the complexity and length of decision trees. For example, if there are few PVCs, there are not so many options as to which of them to present. Networks with an heterogeneous structure result in more complex and longer decision-trees, since most agent actions are intrinsically different and have all to be considered. We have tested our algorithm with 35 different preference statements and found 15 intrinsically different network configurations, ranging from very simple (e.g. one TO, two PVCs with one item each) to quite heterogeneous and complex (e.g. four TOs, one PVC each, with four, two, one and one children, respectively). Towards the end of our testing we always encountered networks with degrees of complexity/heterogeneity already seen. We can assume, thus, that we are aware of the different degrees of complexity/heterogeneity that occur in our scenario. For all of these our approach finds a presentation strategy in real-time.

The value function seems to model the desired behavior. Usually, a question presenting the three PVCs most representative of the different options will be asked first. Then, the agent will show the objects exhibiting the chosen PVC. Next, if there are other TOs still unknown to the user, the agent will attempt their presentation by showing some item or presenting the corresponding PVCs. The agent will go on showing items with the highest chances of being accepted and in case of ties, items with the most relatives.

Figure 2 shows the behavior policy generated for the optimal candidates set represented in the mid-high-complexity Bayesian network in Figure 1. Note that

```
S: [[green, fabric, Ikea] [orange, plastic, retro], [black, leather, modern classic]]

U: choose one [green, fabric, Ikea]    U: choose one [orange, plastic, retro]  U: choose one [black, leather, modern classic]
S:[Sofa_Judit]                         S:  [Sofa_Felipe]                        S:   [Sofa_Stan]
U: reject [Sofa_Judit]                 U: reject [Sofa_Felipe]                  U: reject [Sofa_Stan]
S: [Sofa_Jesper]                       S: [Sofa_Judit]                          S:  [Sofa_Nadia]
U: reject [Sofa_Jesper]                U: reject [Sofa_Judit]                   U: reject [Sofa_Nadia]
S: [Sofa_Consuelo]                     S: [Sofa_Stan]                           S: [Sofa_Judit]
U: reject [Sofa_Consuelo]              U: reject [Sofa_Stan]                    U: reject [Sofa_Judit]
S: [Sofa_Stan]                         S: [Sofa_Consuelo]                       S: [Sofa_Felipe]
U: reject [Sofa_Stan]                  U: reject [Sofa_Consuelo]                U: reject [Sofa_Felipe]
S: [Sofa_Felipe]                       S: [Sofa_Nadia]                          S: [Sofa_Consuelo]
U: reject [Sofa_Felipe]                U: reject [Sofa_Nadia]                   U: reject [Sofa_Consuelo]
S: [Sofa_Nadia]                        S: [Sofa_Jesper]                         S: [Sofa_Jesper]
```

**Fig. 2.** Optimal presentation policy

the PVC "yellow fabric retro" is not selected for presentation in the first question because a PVC exhibiting the same TO and exhibited by more items is selected instead, namely "green, fabric, Ikea". Note also that in the path in which the user has chosen "green, fabric, Ikea", when all the items exhibiting this PVC have been rejected, the agent shows an item exhibiting the PVC "yellow, fabric, retro", since this is similar to the chosen option. Finally, note that if this item is also rejected the agent presents an item from a more populated area, namely "Sofa_Stan", since he can partially transfer the obtained user feedback to his brother item "Sofa_Nadia".

## 4    Summary and Conclusion

We have presented an approach for finding optimal presentation strategies for retrieval sets in conversational Recommender Systems. The generated strategies simultaneously pursuit the goals of providing the user with a good overview of the available options, successfully accomplishing the task as early as possible, and obtaining an accurate user model through Active Learning, all of these in a scenario in which the presentation modalities only allow to present few alternatives at a time. Future work will include evaluation with respect to task success, user satisfaction and scalability.

## References

1. Adolphs, P., Benz, A., Bertomeu, N., Cheng, X., Klüwer, T., Krifka, M., Strekalova, A., Uszkoreit, H., Xu, F.: Conversational Agents in a Virtual World. In: Bach, J., Edelkamp, S. (eds.) KI 2011. LNCS, vol. 7006, pp. 38–49. Springer, Heidelberg (2011)
2. Bertomeu, N., Benz, A.: Annotation of joint projects and information states in human-NPC dialogue. In: Proc. of the 1st International Conference on Corpus Linguistics, CILC 2009, Murcia, pp. 723–740 (2009)
3. Benz, A., Bertomeu, N., Strekalova, A.: A decision-theoretic approach to finding optimal responses to over-constrained queries in a conceptual search space. In: Proc. of the 15th Workshop on the Semantics and Pragmatics of Dialogue, Los Angeles, pp. 37–46 (2011)
4. Boutilier, C., Dean, T., Hanks, S.: Decision-Theoretic Planning: Structural Assumptions and Computational Leverage. Journal of Artificial Intelligence 11, 1–94 (1999)
5. Cassandra, A.R., Littman, M.L., Zhang, N.L.: Acting Optimally in Partially Observable Stochastic Domains. In: Proc. of the 12th National Conference on Artificial Intelligence, Seattle (1994)
6. McSherry, D.: Similarity and Compromise. In: Ashley, K.D., Bridge, D.G. (eds.) ICCBR 2003. LNCS, vol. 2689, pp. 29–305. Springer, Heidelberg (2003)
7. Pearl, J.: Probabilistic reasoning in intelligent systems: networks of plausible inference. Morgan Kaufmann, San Francisco (1988)
8. Rieser, V., Lemon, O.: Learning Effective Multimodal Dialogue Strategies from Wizard-of-Oz data: Bootstrapping and Evaluation. In: Proc. of the 46th Annual Meeting of the Association for Computational Linguistics, Columbus (2008)
9. Rubens, N., Kaplan, D., Sugiyama, M.: Active Learning in Recommender Systems. In: Richi, F., Rokach, L., Shapira, B., Kantor, P.B. (eds.) Handbook of Recommender Systems. Springer, New York (2011)
10. Rubens, N., Tomioka, R., Sugiyama, M.: Output divergence criterion for active learning in collaborative settings. IPSJ Transactions on Mathematical Modeling and Its Applications 2(3), 87–96 (2009)

# Rank Reversal as a Source of Uncertainty and Manipulation in the PROMETHEE II Ranking: A First Investigation

Julien Roland, Yves De Smet, and Céline Verly

Computer & Decision Engineering (CoDE) Department
Ecole Polytechnique de Bruxelles
Université Libre de Bruxelles, Belgium
{julien.roland,yves.de.smet,ceverly}@ulb.ac.be

**Abstract.** PROMETHEE II is an aggregating procedure based on pairwise comparisons for ranking alternatives evaluated on multiple criteria. As other outranking methods, PROMETHEE II does not satisfy the assumption of independence to third alternatives. In other words, the ranks of two given alternatives may be influenced by the presence of a third one. This phenomenon, also called rank reversal, can be viewed as a source of uncertainty on the final ranking. Additionally, it raises the natural question of possible rank manipulations by adding "well-chosen" alternatives. This problem is studied in the context of a simplified version of the PROMETHEE II method also known as the Copland score. A linear program is proposed to test whether there is a way to rank a given alternative at the first position by adding artificial ones. Simulations are used to quantify the likelihood of this possibility and to test if it can be avoided.

## 1 Introduction

We consider the problem of ranking a finite set of alternatives evaluated on several conflicting criteria. Many aggregating methods are available in the literature to address this question. Among them, we may cite AHP, ELECTRE or PROMETHEE.

It is of common knowledge that these methods do not respect the assumption of independence to third alternatives. In other words, the relative ranks of two given alternatives may be influenced by the presence of a third one. This phenomena is also known as *rank reversal* (even if different definitions of this concept seems to co-exist[1]). We refer the interested reader to [2], [1], [6], [8], [9], [10] and [12] for AHP, to [5] and [7] for PROMETHEE and to [13] for ELECTRE. Of course, this effect may be viewed as a source of uncertainty and manipulation in the final ranking.

---

[1] Some authors consider the dependance to any kind of third alternatives, to an alternative that is dominated by all the others, to a copy of a given alternative or even the influence of a non-discriminating criterion.

S. Greco et al. (Eds.): IPMU 2012, Part IV, CCIS 300, pp. 338–346, 2012.
© Springer-Verlag Berlin Heidelberg 2012

A first natural question is to investigate if the rank of a given alternative is robust or not with respect to the other alternatives. A second question is to wonder if a given alternative could eventually become first by introducing artificial ones. Naturally, those alternatives should be well-chosen with respect to the initial set of alternatives (and not randomly). In this paper, the uncertainty of the final ranking is studied by means of the number of new alternatives needed to make first any given alternative. A low number of artificial alternatives meaning a higher uncertainty of the alternative rank. Of course, this question is strongly related to the possibility of manipulation in MCDA ranking methods which is of crucial importance.

In this paper, we restrict ourselves to a simplified version of the PROMETHEE II method (usual preference functions and equally weighted criteria). This method is described in Section 2. A linear program is then developed to test whether it is possible to bring an alternative ranked at the j-th place to the first place by adding a precise number of artificial alternatives. This linear program is presented in Section 3. Finally, we proceed by simulations to quantify the likelihood of manipulation. The design of the experiments and results are discussed in Section 4.

## 2   Concepts and Notations

Let us consider a set of alternatives $A = \{a_1, a_2, \ldots, a_i, \ldots, a_n\}$ and a family of criteria $g_k$ with $k \in K = \{1, 2, \ldots, k, \ldots, q\}$. Without loss of generality, we assume that all the criteria are positive and have to be maximized. Let $g_k(a_i)$ be the evaluation of alternative $a_i$ with respect to criterion $g_k$. Each pair of alternatives $a_i, a_j \in A$ are compared by computing the preference index $\pi(a_i, a_j)$ in the following way:

$$\pi(a_i, a_j) = \frac{1}{q} \sum_{k \in K} 1_{B(a_i, a_j)}(k), \tag{1}$$

where $B(a_i, a_j) = \{l \in K : g_l(a_i) > g_l(a_j)\}$ and $1_{B(a_i, a_j)} : K \to \{0, 1\}$ is an indicator function.

Based on this index, the PROMETHEE net flow gives a score for each alternative $a_i \in A$:

$$\phi_A(a_i) = \frac{1}{n-1} \sum_{j=1, j \neq i}^{n} (\pi(a_i, a_j) - \pi(a_j, a_i)). \tag{2}$$

This flow is related to the Copland score [4] and can be viewed as an extremely simplified version of the PROMETHEE II method because the preference function used to compute the flow is the usual one and the weights are supposed to be equal. The interested reader may refer to [3] and [11] for more details about PROMETHEE methods.

Based on this score, the PROMETHEE II ranking is computed as follows :

1. $a_i$ is ranked before $a_j$ if $\phi(a_i) > \phi(a_j)$;
2. $a_i$ has the same rank as $a_j$ if $\phi(a_i) = \phi(a_j)$.

As explained in the introduction, the PROMETHEE II method does not satisfy the assumption of independance to third alternatives and therefore is subject to rank reversal. More formally, let us consider a set of alternatives $A$ and let us denote $\phi_A$ the net flow score computed with respect to this set. We say that a rank reversal occurs between $a_i$ and $a_j$ if there exists a non-empty set of alternatives, denoted $C$, such that $\phi_A(a_i) > \phi_A(a_j)$ and $\phi_{A\cup C}(a_i) < \phi_{A\cup C}(a_j)$.

At this point, it is worth noting that Bertrand Mareschal and al. [7] have already shown some interesting results about the conditions of potential rank reversal occurences; if we consider a set $C$ composed of $m$ alternatives, rank reversal never happen between two alternatives $a_i, a_j \in A$ as soon as $|\phi_A(a_i) - \phi_A(a_j)| > \frac{2m}{n-1}$. If we restrict this result to $m = 1$, we may conclude that the addition of a single alternative may only have an impact between pairs of alternatives that had initially close net flow scores (in other words, such that the difference is lower than $\frac{2}{n-1}$).

# 3    Evaluation of Rank Reversal through Linear Programming

Let us consider an alternative $a_s \in A$ ranked at the j-th place by the procedure as described previously. In this section, a linear program is proposed in order to determine whether or not it is possible to bring this alternative to the first place by introducing a set of exactly $m$ well-chosen artificial alternatives. This set is denoted by $C = \{a_{n+1}, a_{n+2}, \ldots, a_{n+m}\}$.

In order to build this linear program, let us first define the set of variables and their respective constraints. The binary variables $P_k(a_i, a_j)$ are defined for all $k \in K$ and pair of alternatives $a_i, a_j \in A \cup C$ as follows:

$$P_k(a_i, a_j) = \begin{cases} 1, \text{ if } g_k(a_i) > g_k(a_j), \\ \\ 0, \text{ otherwise.} \end{cases} \tag{3}$$

It is easy to check that the following set of constraints converts this definition. For all $k \in K$ and pair of alternatives $a_i, a_j \in A \cup C$:

$$\begin{cases} P_k(a_i, a_j)\overline{g_k} \geqslant g_k(a_i) - g_k(a_j), \\ \\ (P_k(a_i, a_j) - 1)\overline{g_k} < g_k(a_i) - g_k(a_j). \end{cases} \tag{4}$$

where $\overline{g_k} = \max\{g_k(a) : k \in K, a \in A\}$.

As defined in the PROMETHEE procedure, for all pair of alternatives $a_i, a_j \in A \cup C$, the value of $\pi(a_i, a_j)$ is given by:

$$\pi(a_i, a_j) = \frac{1}{q} \sum_{k \in K} P_k(a_i, a_j) \tag{5}$$

The PROMETHEE II net flow is easily defined for all $a \in A \cup C$[2]:

$$\phi(a) = \frac{1}{n + m - 1} \sum_{x \in A \cup C} \pi(a, x) - \pi(x, a) \tag{6}$$

Finally, a binary variable testing whether or not $a_s$ is ranked at a place at least as good than another alternative $a \in A \cup C$ is introduced as follows:

$$y(a_s, a) = \begin{cases} 1, \text{ if } \phi(a_s) \geqslant \phi(a), \\ \\ 0, \text{ otherwise.} \end{cases} \tag{7}$$

This is expressed by the two following constraints, for all $a \in A$:

$$\begin{cases} 2(y(a_s, a) - 1) \leqslant \phi(a_s) - \phi(a), \\ \\ 2y(a_s, a) > \phi(a_s) - \phi(a). \end{cases} \tag{8}$$

The correctness of these constraints is easy to check since $-1 \leqslant \phi(a) \leqslant 1$.

When maximizing the objective function $\sum_{a \in A \cup C} y(a_s, a)$ over this set of constraints one can determine whether or not there is a way to make $a_s$ first. Indeed, when $\sum_{a \in A \cup C} y(a_s, a)$ equals $|A \cup C|$ it implies from definition of $y(a_s, a)$ that for all $a \in A : \phi(a_s) \geqslant \phi(a)$ which occurs when $a_s$ is ranked first.

The resulting linear program can be stated as follows:

$$\max \sum_{a \in A \cup C} y(a_s, a)$$

subject to: $(P_j(a_i, a_j) - 1)\overline{g_k} < g_k(a_i) - g_k(a_j), \forall a_i, a_j \in A \cup C, \ \forall k \in K$

$P_k(a_i, a_j)\overline{g_k} \geqslant g_k(a_i) - g_k(a_j), \forall a_i, a_j \in A \cup C, \ \forall k \in K$

$\pi(a_i, a_j) = \frac{1}{q} \sum_{k \in K} P_k(a_i, a_j), \forall a_i, a_j \in A \cup C$

$\phi(a) = \frac{1}{n + m - 1} \sum_{x \in A \cup C} \pi(a, x) - \pi(x, a), \forall a \in A \cup C$

$g_k(a) \leqslant \overline{g_k}, \forall a \in C$

$g_k(a) \geqslant 0, \forall a \in C$

$2(y(a_s, a) - 1) \leqslant \phi(a_s) - \phi(a), \forall a \in A \cup C$

$2y(a_s, a) > \phi(a_s) - \phi(a), \forall a \in A \cup C$

---

[2] For the sake of simplicity we will denote $\phi = \phi_{A \cup C}$.

# 4  Experiments

In order to test the linear program described in the previous section, we have generated artificial data sets constituted by non-dominated alternatives (dominated alternatives are not generated, because they are considered as irrelevant). For a given number of alternatives $n$ and criteria $q$, Algorithm 1 is used to generate 30 instances. An instance is represented by a matrix $M$ where the element $M_{ik}$ corresponds to $g_k(a_i)$. It is obvious that this algorithm is elementary and could be improved. However, it is out of the scope of this paper.

---

**Algorithm 1.** Algorithm to generate a multi-criteria evaluation table composed of non-dominated alternatives.

---

1: **Inputs:** n,q
2: for all $k = 1, 2, \ldots, q : M_{1,k} \sim U[0; 1]$
3: $i = 2$
4: **while** $i \leqslant n$ **do**
5:    for all $k = 1, 2, \ldots, q : M_{i,k} \sim U[0; 1]$
6:    **if** alternative $i$ is not dominated by alternatives $1, \ldots, i - 1$ **then**
7:      $i = i + 1$
8:    **end if**
9: **end while**

---

Once an instance has been built, the procedure described in section 2 is ran in order to obtain the initial ranking. Then, for every alternative ranked from the second position to the last ($j = 2, \ldots, n$), the linear program is solved by using the CPLEX solver for a given value of m.

Only problems with 10 alternatives and 3 or 4 criteria are considered here due to the high computation time needed to solve the linear program (see tables 1 and 2, respectively). Results presented in these tables are such that the element at the j-th line and the m-th column represents the percentage of instances where it was not possible to bring the alternative ranked at the j-th place to the first place when introducing $m$ well-chosen artificial alternatives.

**Table 1.** Percentage of instances (with 10 alternatives and 3 criteria) where it was not possible to bring the alternative ranked at the j-th place to the top when adding $m$ well-chosen artificial alternatives

| $j\backslash m$ | 1 | 2 | 3 | 4 | 5 | 6 | 7 | 8 | 9 |
|---|---|---|---|---|---|---|---|---|---|
| 2 | 7 | 3 | 0 | 0 | 0 | 0 | 0 | 0 | 0 |
| 3 | 37 | 13 | 7 | 0 | 0 | 0 | 0 | 0 | 0 |
| 4 | 57 | 33 | 17 | 3 | 0 | 0 | 0 | 0 | 0 |
| 5 | 83 | 63 | 40 | 13 | 0 | 0 | 0 | 0 | 0 |
| 6 | 90 | 83 | 60 | 23 | 0 | 0 | 0 | 0 | 0 |
| 7 | 90 | 90 | 77 | 43 | 10 | 0 | 0 | 0 | 0 |
| 8 | 100 | 100 | 87 | 70 | 37 | 7 | 0 | 0 | 0 |
| 9 | 100 | 100 | 97 | 83 | 63 | 33 | 3 | 0 | 0 |
| 10 | 100 | 100 | 97 | 93 | 83 | 63 | 33 | 3 | 0 |

When considering instances with 3 criteria, in 93% of instances, it was possible to put the second alternative first when adding only one alternative. This implies an high uncertainty on the rank of the first alternatives. However, it was never possible to put the 8-th, 9-th and 10-th alternatives first if we add only one alternative and we have to add more than 3 alternatives to succeed (let us note that for 3 alternatives, the percentages remain high). More generally, these results show that an important number of alternatives has to be added in order to manipulate alternatives that have high ranks (typically 50% of new alternatives have to be added to the initial data set).

**Table 2.** Percentage of instances (with 10 alternatives and 4 criteria) where it was not possible to bring the alternative ranked at the j-th place to the top when adding $m$ well-chosen artificial alternatives

| $j\backslash m$ | 1 | 2 | 3 | 4 | 5 | 6 | 7 | 8 | 9 | 10 | 11 | 12 | 13 | 14 |
|---|---|---|---|---|---|---|---|---|---|---|---|---|---|---|
| 2 | 30 | 17 | 13 | 3 | 0 | 0 | 0 | 0 | 0 | 0 | 0 | 0 | 0 | 0 |
| 3 | 70 | 43 | 33 | 10 | 10 | 3 | 0 | 0 | 0 | 0 | 0 | 0 | 0 | 0 |
| 4 | 83 | 70 | 50 | 17 | 10 | 10 | 3 | 0 | 0 | 0 | 0 | 0 | 0 | 0 |
| 5 | 100 | 90 | 70 | 30 | 23 | 10 | 10 | 0 | 0 | 0 | 0 | 0 | 0 | 0 |
| 6 | 100 | 97 | 80 | 67 | 57 | 40 | 23 | 7 | 0 | 0 | 0 | 0 | 0 | 0 |
| 7 | 100 | 100 | 93 | 83 | 77 | 57 | 43 | 27 | 7 | 0 | 0 | 0 | 0 | 0 |
| 8 | 100 | 100 | 100 | 87 | 87 | 73 | 73 | 53 | 20 | 10 | 0 | 0 | 0 | 0 |
| 9 | 100 | 100 | 100 | 97 | 80 | 77 | 77 | 73 | 50 | 33 | 13 | 7 | 0 | 0 |
| 10 | 100 | 100 | 100 | 100 | 100 | 97 | 93 | 87 | 83 | 53 | 40 | 30 | 10 | 0 |

When considering instances with 4 criteria, it is not surprising to notice that it is more difficult to make an alternative first. For instance, we have to add more than 50% of alternatives to put the 10-th alternative first.

As already stressed, Bertrand Mareschal and al. [7] have shown that rank reversal never happens between two alternatives $a_i, a_j \in A$ if $|\phi(a_i) - \phi(a_j)| > \frac{2m}{n-1}$. Then, in some cases, it is known (without solving the linear program) that it is not possible to make some alternatives first. However, when $|\phi(a_i) - \phi(a_j)| \leqslant \frac{2m}{n-1}$ is satisfied, a rank reversal could potentially occur. The linear program allows to answer this question. Tables 3 and 4 represent the percentage of instances where it was not possible to bring the alternative ranked at the j-th place to the top when adding $m$ artificial alternatives while the Mareschal's bound is not reached (in other words, such that $\phi(a_{(1)}) - \phi(a_{(i)}) \leqslant \frac{2m}{n-1}$).

When considering generated instances with 3 criteria, the Mareschal's bound is not reached for all pairs of alternatives if $m \geqslant 3$. Therefore, only the two first columns of table 3 are interesting, the next ones are exactly the same as table 1. For the same reason, in the case of 4 criteria, the 3 first columns are different from table 2.

Let us consider instances with 3 criteria. As listed in table 1, in 57% of the cases it was not possible to put the 4th alternative at the first place by adding one artificial alternative. In table 3, 27% of the cases correspond to situations

**Table 3.** Percentage of instances (with 10 alternatives and 3 criteria) where it was not possible to bring the alternative ranked at the j-th place to the top when adding $m$ well-chosen artificial alternatives while the Mareschal's bound is not reached

| $j\backslash m$ | 1 | 2 |
|---|---|---|
| 2 | 7 | 3 |
| 3 | 30 | 13 |
| 4 | 27 | 33 |
| 5 | 17 | 63 |
| 6 | 7 | 83 |
| 7 | 0 | 90 |
| 8 | 7 | 73 |
| 9 | 3 | 40 |
| 10 | 0 | 20 |

where the Mareschal's bound was not reached and, as a consequence, 30% correspond to situations where the bound was reached. Therefore, it appears that in a significative amount of instances there is no way to make the alternative first while the Mareschal's bound is not reached. This implies that the use of this bound does not allow to detect all the cases for which manipulation is not possible (in the considered case, only 27% among 57% could have been detected thanks to this bound). These results suggest that it could be improved. Similar conclusions can be drawn from table 4.

**Table 4.** Percentage of instances (with 10 actions and 4 criteria) where it was not possible to bring the alternative ranked at the j-th place to the top when adding $m$ well-chosen artificial alternatives while the Mareschal's bound is not reached

| $j\backslash m$ | 1 | 2 | 3 |
|---|---|---|---|
| 2 | 23 | 17 | 13 |
| 3 | 43 | 43 | 33 |
| 4 | 30 | 67 | 50 |
| 5 | 23 | 80 | 70 |
| 6 | 20 | 60 | 80 |
| 7 | 3 | 57 | 93 |
| 8 | 3 | 23 | 93 |
| 9 | 0 | 20 | 77 |
| 10 | 0 | 3 | 53 |

# 5  Conclusion

In this paper, we have investigated rank reversal as a source of uncertainty and manipulation in a simplified version of the PROMETHEE II method. Therefore, a linear program has been developed and experiments have been ran on artificial data sets. One main result of this study show that, on average, a significative number of alternatives have to be added to the initial data set in order to make a given alternative first. Additionally, it is clear that there is a link between the rank of the alternative and the number of alternatives to add (alternatives with a high rank could never become first except by adding a lot of new alternatives and so by modifying completely the initial problem). It is important to notice that even when manipulation is possible, perfect information on alternatives evaluation is needed to produce such kinds of effects. Therefore, in practice, these conclusions are expected to be stronger.

Different extensions of this work are straightforward. The current work is based on an extremely simplified version of the PROMETHEE II method. Therefore, attention should be paid to the influence of other preference functions, intra-criterion parameters and weights. Some constraints may be imposed on the artificial alternatives (for instance it could be emphasized that adding dominated alternatives is not meaningful). Finally, by taking into account these results, theoretical properties could be obtained to improve the bound proposed by Bertrand Mareschal and al. [7].

**Acknowledgments.** Julien Roland acknowledges support from the META-X Arc project, funded by the Scientific Research Directorate of the French Community of Belgium.

# References

1. Barzilai, J., Golany, B.: AHP rank reversal, normalization and aggregation rules. INFOR 32, 57–63 (1994)
2. Belton, V., Gear, T.: On a Short-comming of Saaty's method of Analytic Hierarchies. Omega 11, 228–230 (1983)
3. Brans, J.P., Mareschal, B.: PROMETHEE Methods. In: Figueira, J., Greco, S., Ehrgott, M. (eds.) Multiple Criteria Decision Analysis: State of the Art Surveys, pp. 163–196. Springer, Heidelberg (2005)
4. Copeland, A.: A "reasonable" social welfare function. Mimeographed notes from a Seminar on Applications of Mathematics to the Scoial Sciences. University of Michigan (1951)
5. De Keyser, W., Peeters, P.: A note on the use of PROMETHHE multicriteria methods. European Journal of Operational Research 89, 457–461 (1996)
6. Harker, P.T., Vargas, L.G.: The theory of ratio scale estimation: Saaty's analytic hierarchy process. Management Science 33, 1383–1403 (1987)
7. Mareschal, B., De Smet, Y., Nemery, P.: Rank reversal in the PROMETHEE II method: Some new results. In: Proceedings of the IEEE 2008 International Conference on Industrial Engineering and Engineering Management, pp. 959–963 (2008)
8. Saaty, T.L., Vargas, L.G.: The legitimacy of rank reversal. Omega 12, 513–516 (1984)
9. Saaty, T.L.: Decision making, new information, ranking and structure. Mathematical Modelling 8, 125–132 (1987)

10. Triantaphyllou, E.: Two New Cases of Rank Reversal when the AHP and Some of its Additive Variants are Used that do not Occur with the Multiplicative AHP. Journal of Multi-Criteria Decision Analysis 10, 11–25 (2001)
11. Vincke, P.: L'aide Multicritère à la décision. Editions de l'Université de Bruxelles-Ellipses (1989)
12. Wang, Y.-M., Elhag, T.M.S.: An approach to avoiding rank reversal in AHP. Decision Support Systems 42, 1474–1480 (2006)
13. Wang, X., Triantaphyllou, E.: Ranking irregularities when evaluating alternatives by using some ELECTRE methods. Omega 36, 45–63 (2008)

# Environmental Aspects Selection for EEE Using ANP Method[*]

İlke Bereketli[**] and Mujde Erol Genevois

Galatasaray University, Industrial Engineering Department,
Ciragan Cad, No:36, Besiktas, Istanbul, TURKEY
{ibereketli,merol}@gsu.edu.tr

**Abstract.** Life Cycle Assessment (LCA) is a tool to assess the environmental aspects, impacts and resources used throughout a product's life cycle. It is widely accepted and considered as one of the most powerful tools to support decision making processes used in ecodesign. However, since LCA is a cost and time intensive method, the companies do not intend to carry out a full LCA, except for large corporate ones. Especially for small and medium sized enterprises (SMEs), which do not have enough budget for and knowledge on ecodesign approaches, focusing only on the most important possible environmental aspect is unavoidable. In this direction, finding the right environmental aspect to work on is crucial. In this study, a multi-criteria decision making (MCDM) methodology to select environmental aspects for Electrical and Electronic Equipment (EEE) by using Analytic Network Process (ANP) is proposed. The evaluation is made by ANP in order to create a realistic approach to inter-dependencies among the criteria.

**Keywords:** ANP, Environmental aspect selection, Environmental impacts, LCA, Electrical and Electronic Equipment, Small and Medium Sized Enterprises (SMEs).

## 1 Introduction

Since the last twenty years, the environmental concepts (such as sustainable production, environmental assessment, ecodesign, etc.) are getting more and more attention both in the literature and in mass media due to the alarming situation of the nature and significant damages provoked by human actions [1]. Although there is legislation [2-4], which forces the manufacturers to take the responsibility of their products; environmental methods and tools are not commonly used among the companies yet [5-6]. Many methods, tools and indicators for assessing and benchmarking environmental impacts have been developed to improve the environmental performance of different systems and products. Examples include Life Cycle Assessment (LCA), Strategic Environmental Assessment (SEA), Environmental Impact Assessment (EIA),

---

[*] This research has been financially supported by Galatasaray University Research Fund.
[**] Corresponding author.

S. Greco et al. (Eds.): IPMU 2012, Part IV, CCIS 300, pp. 347–353, 2012.
© Springer-Verlag Berlin Heidelberg 2012

Environmental Risk Assessment (ERA), Cost Benefit Analysis (CBA), Material Flow Analysis (MFA), Ecological Footprint, etc. [7-10].

Life Cycle Assessment is one of the most powerful methods which models and environmentally assesses all life cycle stages of a product from cradle to grave for the implementation of ecodesign [10-11]. However conducting a full LCA poses an additional workload and cost on manufacturers' shoulders [6]. The aim of this study is to develop a framework for helping SMEs and/or beginners in environmental assessment, who cannot afford a complete LCA in their business. The proposed methodology will provide a simplified LCA in the evaluation and selection of environmental aspects for Electrical and Electronic Equipment (EEE) family EEE's fast expansion driven by technological developments and consumerism generates an increased amount of e-wastes and their accumulation comes along with significant negative impact on the environment and the human health [12-13]. Along with the resource depletion, the negative aspects of EEE lead us to choose them as the main application field for this study. An Analytic Network Process (ANP) [14] technique is proposed in this paper to evaluate and select the most important environmental aspect of EEE. ANP is well suited to deal with decision problems, which has interdependencies between its alternatives and criteria.

The outline of the paper is as following: Life Cycle Assessment is briefly defined, environmental aspects and impacts, and the challenge for SMEs and beginners, which is the main motivation of this study are stated in Section 2. In Section 3, the selection problem, methodology and the results are presented. Conclusions driven from the research are finally provided in Section 4.


## 2    Life Cycle Assessment

In ISO 14040 (2006) LCA is defined as the "compilation and evaluation of the inputs, outputs and potential environmental impacts of a product system throughout its life cycle". Thus, LCA is a tool for the analysis of the environmental burden of products at all stages of their life cycle – from the extraction of resources, through the production of materials, product parts and the product itself, and the use of the product to the management after it is discarded, either by reuse, recycling or final disposal (in effect, therefore, "from the cradle to the grave"). Hence it can be named five different phases at LCA: raw material phase, manufacturing phase, distribution phase, use phase, and end-of-life phase [15-16]. In this paper, a new methodology will be proposed to reduce the complexity LCA by finding out the most important environmental aspect causing the most significant environmental impacts and thus eliminating the less significant ones from the assessment study.

An environmental aspect is defined as an element of a facility's activities, products, or services that can or does interact with the environment, while an environmental impact is defined as any change to the environment, whether adverse or beneficial, resulting from a facility's activities, products, or services [17]. Confusing environmental aspects and impacts with each other is a common mistake in daily use. However the relation between these two terms is based on the fact that the aspects are the causes of impacts. The previous studies in the literature show that conducting a complete LCA is mostly time and cost consuming for the companies [18-19]. Especially for SMEs, any kind of environmental assessment is accepted to be a significant additional load on the company's shoulders since they have limited resources. Therefore they tend to ignore environmental concerns in their product development management except for some obligatory requirements of regulations [16].

There exist in the literature some studies concentrating on multi criteria decision making for a simplified environmental assessment by fuzzy logic methods [20], for ranking the impact categories by using AHP with the regional scale point of view [21], and for weighting them by using a panel approach and a Multi-Criteria Decision Aid (MCDA) [22]. Amongst these efforts already made, the originality of this paper lies on the method used and the focus point. Analytic Network Process is chosen as a suitable method thanks to its ability to consider interdependencies between different levels, interdependencies between environmental aspects and impacts in our case. Environmental aspects, instead of impacts, are on the main focus since they are not the consequences but the main reasons of the environmental problems that we encounter. The proposed methodology in this paper is to select the most significant environmental aspect by using ANP. It will lead SMEs and environmentally less experienced companies to decide where to focus in order to assess their products in a simpler way.

## 3    Environmental Aspect Selection Problem

Analytic Network Process (ANP) is a Multi Criteria Decision Making tool considered to be an extension of Analytic Hierarchy Process (AHP) [23]. Whereas AHP models a decision making framework using a unidirectional hierarchical relationship among decision levels, ANP allows for more complex interrelationships among the decision levels and components, like a network [24]. ANP's algorithm for the selection problem is built in 8 steps.

*Step 1*: The first step is to define the decision problem, then the model to be evaluated is constructed. The main objective of the problem is to evaluate the environmental aspects of an electrical and electronic product. The *environmental aspects* to be selected are the alternatives of this evaluation model and as follows: *Energy consumption, water consumption, raw material consumption, hazardous waste generation, radioactive waste generation, emissions to air, release to water, land use* [15], [25]. For the proposed environmental aspect evaluation model, 5 main *impact categories* are determined as criteria: *impact on human beings, impact on ecology, resource depletion, pollution/contamination/wastes,* and *impacts on landscape and cultural heritage*. These 5 main categories, representing the clusters in the model, can be divided into sub-criteria which are formed by detailed environmental impact categories: *global warming, carcinogenicity, ozone layer depletion, acidification, eutrophication, eco-toxicity, human toxicity, radiation, fossil fuels depletion, resource depletion, and photochemical smog* [15], [26-27], *depletion of forests, depletion of coral reefs, and decrease in agricultural fields*.

*Step 2 & 3*: Given this model, the relevant criteria and alternatives are structured in the form of a simple network by the decision makers (see Fig. 1). Interdependencies are represented by the arrows among the clusters (outer dependence) and a looped arc within the same cluster (inner dependence).

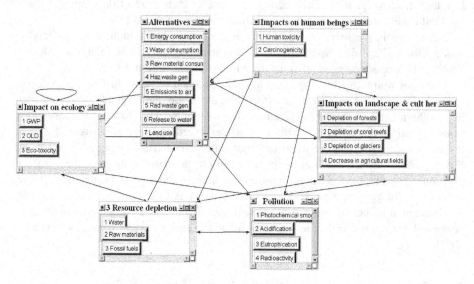

**Fig. 1.** The ANP network scheme of the decision problem

*Step 4, 5 & 6*: In this study, in order to reflect the priorities of EEE, comparison matrices are completed by experts who have experience in the EEE field. The experts' opinions are used to fill in the pairwise comparison matrices for both criteria and alternatives and then the supermatrix is built according to these pairwise comparison matrices by using the Super Decisions software. As for the evaluation of the alternatives and criteria, the fundamental comparison scale "1 to 9" (equally important to extremely more important) is used [14]. Among the several comparison matrices completed by decision makers, a representative one for the comparison between sub-criteria elements (Table 1) is given as example. Table 1 shows the pairwise comparison matrix for the *Impact on Ecology* cluster with respect to the *"Human Toxicity"* criterion.

**Table 1.** Pairwise comparison matrix for Human Toxicity

| Human toxicity | OLD | Eco toxicity | Weights |
|---|---|---|---|
| **OLD** | 1 | 1/5 | 0,167 |
| **Eco toxicity** | 5 | 1 | 0,883 |

*Step 7*: Given the comparison matrices, the Super Decisions software computed the unweighted, weighted and limit supermatrices and provided the synthesized results and the priorities.

*Step 8*: Finally, the overall results in the environmental aspect selection model of ANP are synthesized and shown in Table 2.

**Table 2.** Results for Alternatives

| Name | Ideals | Normals |
|------|--------|---------|
| **Energy consumption** | **1.000.000** | **0.516441** |
| Water consumption | 0.281170 | 0.145208 |
| Raw material consumption | 0.009886 | 0.005106 |
| Hazardous waste gen. | 0.044313 | 0.022885 |
| Emissions to air | 0.382636 | 0.197609 |
| Radioactive waste gen. | 0.069289 | 0.035784 |
| Release to water | 0.118016 | 0.060948 |
| Land use | 0.031020 | 0.016020 |

The overall results given in Table 7 show that the best alternative as the most significant environmental aspect for the EEE family is "energy consumption". According to this result, assessing only the impacts related to the energy consumption, i.e. global warming potential, fossil fuel depletion, photochemical smog, depletion of glaciers, would be enough to have a rough overview about the product's environmental performance. EEE manufacturers should find solutions to decrease the energy consumption levels for the whole life cycle, especially for the use phase, in order to reduce or eliminate its impacts, hence to improve the environmental performance.

# 4    Conclusion

Life Cycle Assessment is one of the most important methodologies used in ecodesign and sustainable production. However, except large corporate companies, the manufacturers tend not to carry out an LCA since it is time and cost intensive, generates additional workload and requires a full data set about the product and knowledge in environmental assessment. Therefore the manufacturers, especially SMEs and the ones who lack experience in fulfilling the environmental regulations, require a simplified LCA approach rather than a full methodology which analyses the whole of life cycle by considering every type of environmental impacts. They first need to have a general overview of the environmental performance of their product and to focus on the right environmental aspect causing most of the impacts. Electrical and Electronic Equipment is one of the product families having the highest impacts on the environment and human health. Therefore it's crucial to assess deeply their performance and to find out the most significant environmental aspect. This paper presented a methodology for applying the Analytic Network Process in environmental aspects decision-making. The selected problem for EEE was modeled by setting all the network relationships with their dependence and feedback. Using the Super Decisions software the results were computed and the best alternative, i.e. the most significant environmental aspect was found to be "energy consumption". Thus, it can be recommended to the EEE manufacturers to focus first on energy consumption to have a general perspective about the environmental performance of their products and to generate improvement strategies related to this aspect.

Considering future work, the ANP based decision making methodology for the selection of environmental aspects can be applied to one of the ten EEE categories defined in EU's WEEE Directive or to a specific electrical and electronic product. Hence the priorities for each sub-category or the single product can be computed with a more detailed evaluation. As another future work direction, a fuzzy approach can be applied to the proposed methodology.

# References

[1] Byggeth, S., Hochschorner, E.: Handling trade-offs in ecodesign tools for sustainable product development and procurement. Journal of Cleaner Production 14(15-16), 1420–1430 (2006)

[2] Directive 2002/95/EC of the European Parliament and of the Council of 27 January 2003 on the restriction of the use of certain hazardous substances in electrical and electronic equipment, RoHS (2003)

[3] Directive 2002/96/EC of the European Parliament and of the Council of 27 January 2003 on waste electrical and electronic equipment (WEEE). Official Journal of the European Union, L 37(24-38) (2003)

[4] Directive 2009/125/EC of The European Parliament and of The Council of 21 October 2009 establishing a framework for the setting of ecodesign requirements for energy-related products (2009)

[5] Ernzer, M., Lindahl, M., Masui, K., Sakao, T.: An International Study on Utilizing of Design Environmental Methods (DfE)–a pre-study. In: Proc. of Third International Symposium on Environmentally Conscious Design and Inverse Manufacturing, pp. 124–131. IEEE Computer Society (2003)

[6] Knight, P., Jenkins, J.O.: Adopting and applying eco-design techniques: a practitioners perspective. Journal of Cleaner Production 17, 549–558 (2009)

[7] Wanyama, W., Ertas, A., Zhang, H.-C., Ekwaro-Osire, S.: Life-cycle engineering: issues, tools and research. Journal of Computer Integrated Manufacturing 16(4-5), 307–316 (2003)

[8] Karlsson, R., Luttropp, C.: EcoDesign: what's happening? An overview of the subject area of EcoDesign and of the papers in this special issue. Journal of Cleaner Production 14, 1291–1298 (2006)

[9] Finnveden, G., Hauschild, M.Z., Ekvall, T., Guinee, J., Heijungs, R., Hellweg, S., Koehler, A., Pennington, D., Suh, S.: Recent developments in Life Cycle Assessment. Journal of Environmental Management 91, 1–21 (2009)

[10] Pigosso, D.C.A., Zanette, E.T., Filho, A.G., Ometto, A.R., Rozenfeld, H.: Ecodesign methods focused on remanufacturing. Journal of Cleaner Production 18, 21–31 (2010)

[11] ISO 14040, Environmental management: Life cycle assessment, Principles and guidelines. ISO 14040:2006 (E) (2006)

[12] Widmer, R., Oswald-Krapf, H., Sinha-Khetriwal, D., Schnellmann, M., Böni, H.: Global perspectives on e-waste. Environmental Impact Assessment Review 25, 436–458 (2005)

[13] Tsydenova, O., Bengtsson, M.: Chemical hazards associated with treatment of waste electrical and electronic equipment. Waste Management 31, 45–58 (2011)

[14] Saaty, T.L.: Decision Making with Dependence and Feedback: The Analytic Network Process, 2nd edn. RWS Publications, Pittsburgh (2001)

[15] Guinee, J.B.: Handbook on Life Cycle Assessment: Operational Guide to the ISO Standards. Kluwer Academic Publishers, Netherlands (2002)

[16] Hauschild, M., Jeswiet, J., Alting, L.: From life cycle as-sessment to sustainable production: Status and perspectives. CIRP Annals-Manufacturing Technology 54(2), 1–21 (2005)

[17] Environmental Protection Agency; EMS Implementation Guide for the Shipbuilding and Ship Repair Industry; Module 5 (2003), http://www.epa.gov/sectors/sectorinfo/sectorprofiles/shipbuilding/module_05.pdf

[18] Rebitzer, G., Ekvall, T., Frischknecht, R., Hunkeler, D., Norris, G., Rydberg, T., Schmidt, W.-P., Suh, S., Weidema, B.P., Pennington, D.W.: Life cycle assessment Part 1: Framework, goal and scope definition, inventory analysis, and applications. Environment International 30, 701–720 (2004)

[19] Collado-Ruiz, D., Ostad-Ahmad-Ghorabi, H.: Fuon theory: Standardizing functional units for product design. Resources, Conservation and Recycling 54(10), 683–691 (2010)

[20] Gonzalez, B., Adenso-Diaz, B., Gonzalez-Torre, P.L.: A fuzzy logic approach for the impact assessment in LCA. Resources, Conservation and Recycling 37, 61–79 (2002)

[21] Hermann, B.G., Kroeze, C., Jawjit, W.: Assessing environmental performance by combining life cycle assessment, multi-criteria analysis and environmental performance indicators. Journal of Cleaner Production 15, 1787–1796 (2007)

[22] Soares, S.R., Toffoletto, L., Deschenes, L.: Development of weighting factors in the context of LCIA. Journal of Cleaner Production 14, 649–660 (2006)

[23] Saaty, T.L.: The Analytical Hierarchy Process. McGraw Hill, New York (1981)

[24] Sarkis, J.: Evaluating environmentally conscious business practices. European Journal of Operational Research 107(1), 159–174 (1998)

[25] ISO 14001, Environmental management systems - Requirements with guidance for use. International Organization for Standardization, Geneva. EN ISO 14001:2004 (2004)

[26] Environmental Protection Agency, Life Cycle Assessment: Principles and Practice, EPA/600/R-92/245, Cincinnati, Ohio (May 2006)

[27] Roy, P., Nei, D., Orikasa, T., Xu, Q., Okadome, H., Nakamura, N., Shiina, T.: A review of life cycle assessment (LCA) on some food products. Journal of Food Engineering 90, 1–10 (2009)

# A Hybrid Weighting Methodology
# for Performance Assessment in Turkish Municipalities

Hüseyin Selçuk Kılıç[1] and Emre Çevikcan[2]

[1] Marmara University, Industrial Engineering Department
34722/ Kadıköy Istanbul, Turkey
huseyin.kilic@marmara.edu.tr
[2] Istanbul Technical University, Industrial Engineering Department
34367/Beşiktaş Istanbul, Turkey
cevikcan@itu.edu.tr

**Abstract.** Performance assessment systems play an important role for controlling and improving a system. In case a robust performance assessment system is established, it will be easier and more trustable to make decisions. Although performance assessment systems have been applied in private sector for a long time, it can be regarded as new for the municipalities in Turkey. As a result of the legal compulsories, every municipality satisfying the conditions has to prepare a strategic plan and a performance program related with it. Performance assessment is carried out by considering the performance program of the municipalities. With this study, after the observations of performance assessment studies in some of the municipalities, a hybrid weighting methodology depending on ranking and fuzzy pairwise comparison is proposed. After giving the related literature about the performance assessment systems in municipalities, existing and proposed methodologies are explained and differences are indicated. For showing the applicability of the proposed model, a numerical example inspired by the real applications is developed and the proposed methodology is executed.

**Keywords:** Decision making, fuzzy AHP, weighting, performance assessment system.

## 1 Introduction

It is difficult to manage a system without measuring the performance of it. Depending on the quality of the performance assessment system, right decisions providing the improvement can be taken. Unlike the OECD countries which performance measurement system is regarded as the essential part of the public sector improvements for the past twenty years (Greiling, 2006), Turkish municipalities started performance assessment studies approximately six years ago as a result of the legal obligations including the municipalities having a population greater than 50000 (Financial Management and Control Law numbered 5018).

S. Greco et al. (Eds.): IPMU 2012, Part IV, CCIS 300, pp. 354–363, 2012.
© Springer-Verlag Berlin Heidelberg 2012

Strategic plans for five year periods are prepared by the municipalities. Every strategic plan has a performance program including the activities to be accomplished by each unit within the following year. Different from the strategic plans which are revised when required, performance programs are prepared every year for each unit in the municipality. SMART (Specific, Measurable, Attainable, Relevant, Timely) goals satisfying the strategies in the strategic plan are defined and they are evaluated within the year. For the success of the performance program, both determining the goals and evaluating them are very important. However, in this study, the scope is limited with only performance assessment.

Since performance measurement affects the organizational performance, performance measurement has great importance in public sector (Mimba et al., 2007). There are so many studies about the performance assessment in the public sector but few contain a quantitative approach.

The reasons why performance measurement was important in local government and the properties of an effective performance measurement system were explained by Ghobadian (1994). Black et al. (2001) explained the similarities and differences of performance measurement systems in public and private sectors by performing an analysis on a comparative basis. The potential negative results of the performance measurement system in public sector are stated by Bruijn (2002). For minimizing the effect of negative results, strategies such as "tolerating competing product definitions", "banning a monopoly on interpreting production figures", "limiting the functions of and forums for performance measurement", "strategically limiting the products that can be subjected to performance measurement" and "using a process perspective of performance in addition to a product perspective" are also presented. A research was made by Pollanen (2005) in Canadian municipalities by examining the real and aimed use of performance measures for management and external reporting. It is seen that although the legal obligations started in Canada later than some countries like UK, USA and Australia, an important level of usage occurred in Canadian municipalities. Greiling (2005) made a study of performance measurement systems in German municipalities. For a better measurement system, recommendations were presented. A similar study was made by Sotirakou and Zeppou (2006) for Greek public administration. They tried to determine the factors which make the performance measurement systems more effective by carrying out a qualitative approach. The problems occurring during the design and implementation of performance measurement systems in Finnish public sector were investigated and three case studies were considered for this aim (Rantanen et al., 2007). The characteristics of the public sector which affect the performance measurement in developing countries were analyzed by Mimba et al. (2007). The impact of balanced scorecards on the performance of the public sector was investigated by analyzing a case study (Greatbanks and Tapp, 2007).

In addition to the qualitative and conceptual studies which are mostly seen in literature, this study makes a contribution to the literature by presenting a quantitative approach including a novel hybrid weighting method. The rest of the paper is organized as follows: The weighting methods are given in Section 2. The existing and proposed weighting methodologies are explained in section 3. Section 4 includes a numerical example and finally, conclusions are provided in section 5.

## 2    Weighting Methods

To assign the proper importance values to the criteria is very important while making a decision with multiple criteria. Various weighting methodologies are developed for this aim. Although there can be defined a lot of methods as seen in some classification schemes including subjective methods (SMART, SWING, SIMOS, pair-wise comparison, AHP), objective methods (Entropy method, TOPSIS, vertical and horizontal method) and combination weighting methods (Wang et al., 2009), main methods seen in literature are ranking, rating, pair-wise comparison and trade-off analysis. These methods vary from each other with respect to ease of use, applicability, trustworthiness and theoretical structure (Malczewski, 1999).

In both prescriptive and descriptive studies of multi-attribute decision making, there can widely be seen additive value and utility models. Since additive models are simple and present good approximations to a huge number of preference structure types, they can be regarded as a very useful decision tool. Direct tradeoff methods, direct judgments of swing weights, and lottery-based utility assessments (von Winterfeldt and Edwards, 1986) are some of the many approaches developed to provide numerical weights. Regardless of the method used, making judgments providing ratio-scale information considering the attribute's relative importance are expected from the decision maker. Regarding the decision maker's tradeoffs, some trials have been performed to rely on weighting methods requiring less precise information. Moreover, there exist several arguments favoring rank order methods (Barron and Barrett, 1996; Stillwell et al., 1981). One of them is about the easiness and reliability of the ranking method (Eckenrode, 1965). Another one is about the unwillingness of the respondents to provide more than ordinal information (Kirkwood and Sarin, 1985) and finally, there is more correlation between the evaluations produced by rank order methods and those produced by more precise numerical methods than the evaluations produced by the equal weights method (Barron and Barrett, 1996; Stillwell et al. 1981). Recently, an increasing number of clustering oriented attribute weighting methods have been proposed (Özşen and Güneş, 2009; Bai et al, 2011).

## 3    The Existing And Proposed Performance Assessment Systems

Based on the observations in some of the municipalities in İstanbul, the existing performance assessment system used in the municipalities is explained. Then, the proposed methodology is presented.

### 3.1    Existing Methodology

Municipalities consist of units and units include activities that must be accomplished. Each activity in the units is determined in parallel to the strategic plan's requirements. Performance indicators are determined for each of the activities and on a monthly basis, they are measured. The performance of a unit is simply the average of the performance values of all the activities included. All the activities in a unit are considered as equal and no weight showing the importance is attributed. Similarly, while calculating the performance of the municipality, the average of the units' performances is obtained. The performance assessment system is shown in Figure 1.

| UNIT 1 | | UNIT 2 | | UNIT N | |
|---|---|---|---|---|---|
| Activity No | Activity Per. | Activity No | Activity Per. | Activity No | Activity Per. |
| 1 | x1% | 1 | x2% | 1 | xn% |
| 2 | y1% | 2 | y2% | 2 | yn% |
| ... | ... | ... | ... | ... | ... |
| Unit Per. | z1% | Unit Per. | z2% | Unit Per. | zn% |

| MUNICIPALITY | |
|---|---|
| Unit No | Unit Per. |
| 1 | z1% |
| 2 | z2% |
| ... | ... |
| n | zn% |
| Unit Per. Avg. | M% |

**Fig. 1.** General performance assessment scheme of the existing system

## 3.2    Proposed Hybrid Weighting Approach

It would be meaningful to give explanatory information about Fuzzy Analytical Hierarchy Process (FAHP), since the proposed weighting approach includes this technique.

**Fuzzy Analytical Hierarchy Process**
The Analytical Hierarchy Process (AHP) is a widely used approach for multiple criteria decision-making. The aim of AHP is to capture the human's knowledge when multi-person and multi-attribute decision making problems are regarded. However, the traditional AHP may not fully represent a style of human judgment and preferences because of several drawbacks related with the technique. In real world, decision makers usually feel more confident to express their judgments in the form of natural language expressions instead of assigning exact numerical values to the comparison judgments. As a result, fuzzy AHP (FAHP), a fuzzy extension of AHP, was developed to solve the hierarchical fuzzy problems.

In this study, a fuzzy multiple criteria decision making procedure based on AHP approach combined with fuzzy extent analysis method (Buckley, 1985) is used.

Steps of the FAHP are as follows:

*Step 1:* Decision makers are asked to express relative importance of two decision elements in the same level by the linguistic scale; equally important (E) (1,1,1), weakly important (W) (1,3,5), fairly important (F) (3,5,7), very strongly important (VS) (5,7,9), absolutely important (A) (7,9,9). Let $\tilde{d}_{ij}^{k}$ be a set of the kth decision maker's preference of one attribute over another then; construct the pair-wise comparison matrices such as

$$
\tilde{A}^{k} = \begin{bmatrix} \tilde{d}_{11}^{k} & \tilde{d}_{12}^{k} & \cdots & \tilde{d}_{1n}^{k} \\ \tilde{d}_{21}^{k} & \cdots & \cdots & \tilde{d}_{2n}^{k} \\ \cdots & \cdots & \cdots & \cdots \\ \tilde{d}_{n1}^{k} & \tilde{d}_{n2}^{k} & \cdots & \tilde{d}_{nn}^{k} \end{bmatrix}
$$

(1)

where n is the number of the related elements at this level and $\tilde{d}_{ij}^{k} = 1 / \tilde{d}_{ji}^{k}$. Also, for $i=j$ $\tilde{d}_{ij}^{k} = (1,1,1)$.

*Step 2:* The fuzzy judgment values of K decision makers are integrated by using the arithmetic mean method, that is;

$$
\tilde{d}_{ij} = \frac{\sum_{k=1}^{K} \tilde{d}_{ij}^{k}}{K}
$$

(2)

$\tilde{d}_{ij}$ denotes the average value of the preferences of the decision makers and can be indicated by a triangular fuzzy number.

*Step 3:* Obtain the fuzzy weights of each criterion of synthetic pair-wise comparison matrix by using the geometric mean method suggested by Buckley (1985):

First, find the geometric mean of fuzzy comparison value of criterion $i$ to each criterion.

$$
\tilde{r}_{i} = \left( \prod_{j=1}^{n} \tilde{d}_{ij} \right)^{1/n} , \quad i=1, 2, \ldots, n
$$

(3)

Then, obtain the fuzzy weight of the $i$th criterion indicated by a triangular fuzzy number.

$$
\begin{aligned}
\tilde{w}_{i} &= \tilde{r}_{i} \otimes (\tilde{r}_{1} \oplus \tilde{r}_{2} \oplus \cdots \oplus \tilde{r}_{n})^{-1} \\
&= (lw_{i}, mw_{i}, uw_{i})
\end{aligned}
$$

(4)

*Step 4:* Rank the fuzzy numbers denotes the weights of each criterion by an appropriate defuzzification method. Methods of such defuzzified fuzzy ranking generally include Mean of Maximal (MOM), Centre of Area (COA), $\alpha$-cut and signed distance method. The COA method is a simple and practical method, and there is no need to bring in the preferences of any decision makers (Chou et al, 2008), so it is used in this study. The nonfuzzy value $M_i$ of the fuzzy number $\widetilde{w}_i$ can be found by the following equation:

$$M_i = \frac{lw_i + mw_i + uw_i}{3} \tag{5}$$

where $M_i$ is a nonfuzzy number., we get the normalized weights $N_i$.via normalization.

*Step 5:* After obtaining the normalized local values of each $M_i$, calculate the global weights of all criteria $W_i$ by multiplying the local normalized weights of criteria by the normalized weights of the related dimension.

### 3.3    Framework of the Approach

Since all the activities in the unit have different importance, a weighting system is needed for differentiating the importance of the activities. Different from the existing methodology, a hybrid weighting methodology is used. In the hybrid weighting methodology, ranking and pair-wise comparison techniques are used together. These two methods are commonly used and have advantages and disadvantages. Ranking is easy but not trustworthy, because after ranking, the differences between the superiority levels are not determined clearly. For instance, suppose that the ranking is A, B and C. And A is slightly better than B, but it could also be much better than B. But this difference is not shown in the calculation of the weights in ranking method. On the other hand, different from the ranking, pair-wise technique provides the levels of importance by making pair-wise comparisons. But the disadvantage observed in this method is the difficulty of providing the consistency when the number of criteria increases. To increase the consistency, firstly the decision maker is asked to rank the criteria, and then in a matrix consisting of ranked criteria, he makes pair-wise comparisons. Different from the classical pair-wise comparison, at the beginning he ranks the criteria and performs the pair-wise comparison regarding this ranking. Finally the importance weights are obtained by performing the required fuzzy AHP based on pair-wise comparison steps.

Firstly, the factors which will be used for evaluating the activities are determined. All of the activities are evaluated according to these factors. Factors can change according to the properties of the municipality. Proposed hybrid weighting methodology is used for obtaining the importance weights of the factors. Then each activity is rated over 100 with respect to each factor. By the multiplication of the rated scores and importance weights of the factors, the importance weights of the activities are determined as shown in Figure 2.

Each activity is then evaluated according to performed and targeted value. The unit performance is obtained by the weighted average of the performed value and the activity weights. The whole system including municipality performance can be shown as in Figure 3.

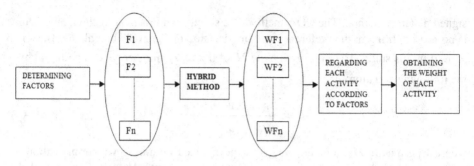

**Fig. 2.** The steps for obtaining the weight of each activity

| UNIT 1 | | |
|---|---|---|
| **Act. No** | **Act. Per.** | **Weight** |
| 1 | x1% | W11 |
| 2 | y1% | W12 |
| ... | ... | ... |
| Un. Per. | z1% | W2 (∑) |

| UNIT N | | |
|---|---|---|
| **Act. No** | **Act. Per.** | **Weight** |
| 1 | xn% | Wn1 |
| 2 | yn% | Wn2 |
| ... | ... | ... |
| Un. Per. | zn% | Wn (∑) |

| MUNICIPALITY | | |
|---|---|---|
| **Unit No** | **Unit Per.** | **Weight** |
| 1 | z1% | W1 |
| 2 | z2% | W2 |
| ... | ... | |
| n | zn% | Wn |
| Weighted avg. perf. | M% | |

**Fig. 3.** General performance assessment scheme of the proposed system

For the municipality performance, a weighted average performance assessment system regarding the weights of the units as the sum of the activity weights is used.

## 4    Numerical Example

Proposed hybrid weighting methodology is illustrated in a numerical example to show how it can be applied to the municipalities. For showing the applicability of the hybrid weighting methodology, it will only be applied for calculating the performance of one unit. Similar steps can be accomplished for the other units. The steps of the methodology can be shown as below:

Main step 1 (Determining the factors)

The factors which will be used while calculating the weights of the units are determined as:

Factor1: Economical dimension of the activities
Factor2: Social dimension of the activities
Factor3: Cultural dimension of the activities
Factor4: Effect to internal process development
Factor5: Effect to customer satisfaction
Main step 2 (Applying the hybrid method)

As the first step of the hybrid methodology, the five factors are ranked according to their importance. Supposing that the ranking is; F5, F1, F2, F3 and F4.

As the second step of the methodology, fuzzy pair-wise comparison is applied as shown in Table 1. The difference from the classical pair-wise comparison is that all the expressions used in the pair-wise comparison will be at least "equal". However, during performing the required steps of the fuzzy pair-wise comparison, the reciprocals of the evaluation expressions will be used. The comparisons will be represented by five degrees as mentioned in the first step of the FAHP method.

Table 1. Fuzzy pair-wise comparison of the factors

| Fuzzy pair-wise | F5 | F1 | F2 | F3 | F4 |
|---|---|---|---|---|---|
| F5 | (1,1,1) | Fairly | Very strongly | Absolutely | Absolutely |
| F1 | | (1,1,1) | Weakly | Fairly | Very strongly |
| F2 | | | (1,1,1) | Weakly | Fairly |
| F3 | | | | (1,1,1) | Weakly |
| F4 | | | | | (1,1,1) |

When the required operations of fuzzy pair-wise comparison are performed. The following weights in Table 2 are obtained for the factors.

Table 2. Weights of the factors

| Factors | F5 | F1 | F2 | F3 | F4 |
|---|---|---|---|---|---|
| Weights | 0.56 | 0.23 | 0.12 | 0.06 | 0.03 |

Main Step 3 (Regarding each activity according to factors)
After finding the weights of the factors, each activity is rated over 100 with respect to these factors to determine the importance weights of the unit activities. Two of the ten activities and the scores given to the activities are shown in Table 3.

**Table 3.** Rating of activities with respect to factors

| Act. No | F1 (W*=0.56 ) | F2 (W*=0.23) | F3 (W*=0.12 ) | F4 (W*=0.06 ) | F5 (W*=0.03) | W. Avg. |
|---------|---------------|--------------|---------------|---------------|--------------|---------|
| 1 | 90 | 80 | 75 | 60 | 90 | 84,1 |
| ... | ... | ... | ... | ... | ... | ... |
| 10 | 85 | 45 | 35 | 40 | 30 | 65,45 |

\* The importance weight of the factor found as a result of the hybrid methodology.

Main Step 4 (Obtaining the weight of each activity)
The weighted average of factors and scores are calculated to find the importance weight of each activity. As shown in the last column of the table 3, all the importance weights of activities are obtained.

After obtaining the weights of activities, the weighted performance 'value of the unit is calculated and similar operations are done for the other units. Finally, the municipality performance value is gathered as shown in Figure 3 by calculating the weighted average of the unit performances where the unit weights consist of the sum of activity weights.

# 5     Conclusion

In parallel with its importance in private sector, performance measurement system has become an important issue in the municipalities as a result of the legal compulsories. A robust performance system is very important to obtain accurate performance scores. With this study, the existing performance assessment system regarding each unit activity as equally weighted is explained. Different from it, a new performance assessment system proposal based on activity weighting is made. In the new proposed system, each unit activity is given an importance weight by using a hybrid weighting method. In the method, ranking and fuzzy pair-wise comparison are accomplished respectively. Inspired by the potential need for municipalities, the method is reflected to a numerical example to show the applicability of the proposed method. For further studies, the proposed hybrid method can be applied in different fields. Moreover, different decision making techniques or quantitative methods can be developed for constructing a stable performance assessment system in Turkish municipalities.

# References

1. Bai, L., Liang, J., Dang, C., Caov, F.: A novel attribute weighting algorithm for clustering high-dimensional categorical data. Pattern Recognition 44(12), 2483–2861 (2011)
2. Barron, F.H., Barrett, B.E.: Decision quality using ranked attribute weights. Management Science 42, 1515–1525 (1996)
3. Black, S., Briggs, S., Keogh, W.: Service quality performance measurement in public/private sectors. Managerial Auditing Journal 16(7), 400–405 (2001)

4. Bruijn, H.: Performance measurement in the public sector: strategies to cope with the risks of performance measurement. The International Journal of Public Sector Management 15(7), 578–594 (2002)
5. Buckley, J.J.: Fuzzy hierarchical analysis. Fuzzy Sets Systems 17(1), 233–247 (1985)
6. Chou, S., Chang, Y., Shen, C.: A fuzzy simple additive weighting system under group decision-making for facility location selection with objective/subjective attributes. European Journal of Operational Research 189(1), 132–145 (2008)
7. Eckenrode, R.T.: Weighting multiple criteria. Management Science 12, 180–192 (1965)
8. Ghobadian, A.: Performance measurement in local government-Concept and practice. International Journal of Operations & Production Management 14(5), 35–51 (1994)
9. Greatbanks, R., Tapp, D.: The impact of balanced scorecards in a public sector environment. International Journal of Operations & Production Management 27(8), 846–873 (2007)
10. Greiling, D.: Performance measurement in the public sector: The German experience. International Journal of Productivity and Performance Management 54(7), 551–567 (2005)
11. Greiling, D.: Performance measurement: a remedy for increasing the efficiency of public services? International Journal of Productivity and Performance Management 55(6), 448–465 (2006)
12. Kirkwood, C., Sarin, R.: Ranking with partial information: a method and an application. Operations Research 33, 38–48 (1985)
13. Malczewski, J.: GIS and Multicriteria Decision Analysis. John Wiley and Sons, New York (1999)
14. Mimba, N.P.S.H., Helden, G.J., Tillema, S.: Public sector performance measurement in developing countries, A literature review and research agenda. Journal of Accounting & Organizational Change 3(3), 192–208 (2007)
15. Özşen, S., Güneş, S.: Attribute weighting via genetic algorithms for attribute weighted artificial immune system (AWAIS) and its application to heart disease and liver disorders problems. Expert Systems with Applications 36(1), 386–392 (2009)
16. Pollanen, R.M.: Performance measurement in municipalities: Empirical evidence in Canadian context. International Journal of Public Sector Management 18(1), 4–24 (2005)
17. Rantanen, H., Kulmala, H.I., Lönnqvist, A., Kujansivu, P.: Performance measurement systems in the Finnish public sector. International Journal of Public Sector Management 20(5), 415–433 (2007)
18. Sotirakou, T., Zeppou, M.: Utilizing performance measurement to modernize the Greek public sector. Management Decision 44(9), 1277–1304 (2006)
19. Stillwell, W.G., Seaver, D.A., Edwards, W.: A comparison of weight approximation techniques in multi-attribute utility decision making. Organizational Behavior and Human Performance 28, 62–77 (1981)
20. von Winterfeldt, D., Edwards, W.: Decision Analysis and Behavioral Research. Cambridge University Press, Cambridge (1986)
21. Wang, J.-J., Jing, Y.-J., Zhang, C.-F., Zhao, J.-H.: Review on multi-criteria decision analysis aid in sustainable energy decision-making. Renewable and Sustainable Energy Reviews 13, 2263–2278 (2009)

# Approximation and Optimization of Polyhedral Discrete and Differential Inclusions

Elimhan N. Mahmudov

Industrial Engineering Department Faculty of Management, Istanbul Technical University
34367 Maçka Istanbul, Turkey

**Abstract.** In the first part of the paper optimization of polyhedral discrete and differential inclusions is considered, the problem is reduced to convex minimization problem and the necessary and sufficient condition for optimality is derived. The optimality conditions for polyhedral differential inclusions based on discrete-approximation problem according to continuous problems are formulated. In particular, boundedness of the set of adjoint discrete solutions and upper semicontinuity of the locally adjoint mapping are proved. In the second part of paper an optimization problem described by convex inequality constraint is studied. By using the equivalence theorem concerning the subdifferential calculus and approximating method necessary and sufficient condition for discrete-approximation problem with inequality constraint is established.

**Keywords:** Set-valued, polyhedral, inequality constraint, dual cone, subdifferential, discrete-approximation, uniformly bounded, upper semicontinuous.

## 1 Introduction

Suppose we have the following problem for polyhedral discrete inclusions

$$\text{minimize} \sum_{t=0}^{T} g(x_t, t), \tag{1}$$

(P_D)

subject to

$$x_{t+1} \in F(x_t), \ t = 0, ..., T-1,$$
$$x_0 \in N_0, \ x_T \in M_T; \tag{2}$$

where

$$F(x) = \{ y : Px - Qy \leq d \} \tag{3}$$

is a polyhedral multivalued [2] mapping; $F : \mathbb{R}^n \rightarrow P(\mathbb{R}^n)$ ($P(\mathbb{R}^n)$ is a set of all subsets of $\mathbb{R}^n$), $P, Q$ are $m \times n$ dimensional matrices with rows $P_i, Q_i, i = 1, ..., m$,

S. Greco et al. (Eds.): IPMU 2012, Part IV, CCIS 300, pp. 364–372, 2012.

respectively, $d$-$m$ dimensional vector-column with components $d_i, i = 1, ..., m$; $N_0, M_T \subset \mathbb{R}^n$ are polyhedral sets. Moreover, $g(\cdot, t) : \mathbb{R}^n \to \mathbb{R}$ is a polyhedral function that is its epigraph epi $g(\cdot, t)$ is a polyhedral set in $\mathbb{R}^{n+1}$. It is required to find a sequence of points $\{\tilde{x}_0, \tilde{x}_1, ..., \tilde{x}_T\} \equiv \{\tilde{x}_t\}_{t=0}^{T}$ of the problem (1)- (3) that minimizes the sum of functions $\sum_{t=0}^{T} g(x_t, t)$. We label this problem as (P$_D$). In Section 2, the problem (P$_D$) is converted to a problem with geometric constraints and is formulated necessary and sufficient conditions for optimality for it.

In Section 3 the next subject of our study is a problem for polyhedral differential inclusions:

$$\text{Minimize } J[x(\cdot)] = \int_0^1 g(x(t), t)dt + \varphi_0(x(1)), \tag{4}$$

(P$_C$)    subject to

$$\dot{x}(t) \in F(x(t)), \quad t \in [0,1],$$
$$x(0) \in N, \ x(1) \in M; \ F(x) = \{y : Px - Qy \leq d\} \tag{5}$$

where the sets, functions and multivalued mapping encountered in Problem (4),(5) are polyhedral. A feasible solution $x(\cdot)$ is an absolutely continuous function satisfying the polyhedral differential inclusion in (5) almost everywhere (a.e.). It is required to find an absolutely continuous function $\tilde{x}(\cdot)$ of the problem (4),(5) that minimizes a functional (4). We label this problem as (P$_C$). The problems (P$_D$) and (P$_C$) have a wider class of applications. For example, they can be applied in investigations of the so-called von Neumann economic dynamics models [8] the graph of which is a polyhedral cone $K = \{(x, y) : \ x \geq B\lambda, \ y = A\lambda, \ \lambda \geq 0, \ \lambda \in \mathbb{R}^m\}$, where $A, B$ are $n \times m$ matrices with non-negative elements and $\lambda$ is a vector with components $\lambda_j, j = 1, ..., m$. Moreover, the problems (P$_D$) and (P$_C$) can be applied in the linear discrete

$(x_{t+1} = Ax_t + Bu_t, u_t \in U \subset \mathbb{R}^r, \quad t = 0, ..., T-1, A, B$ - $n \times n$   and   $n \times r$ matrices, respectively) or linear differential optimal control problem $\dot{x} = Ax + Bu, u = u(t) \in U, \quad t \in [0,1]$, where a control domain $U$ is a polyhedral set. The key problem for investigation of the problem (P$_C$) is discrete-approximation problem. Note that in [2] some properties of non-degenerate polyhedral mappings(the number of constraints defining every vertex of polytope $F(x)$ is $n$) are studied. Although the given problems (P$_D$), (P$_C$) in Sections 2 and 3 are governed by multi-valued mappings, we do not use the locally adjoint mapping notion in formulation of any optimality conditions. It should be pointed out that for a problem (P$_C$), this occurs due to skillfully application of approximation method. An important role of this method both from the theoretical and practical points of view are demonstrated in [3]-[7], [10].

Section 4 is devoted to a problem with discrete and continuous time described by multivalued   mapping   $F(x) = \{ y : \varphi(x, y) \leq 0 \}$, where   $\varphi(z)$, $z = (x, y)$ is continuous convex function ; $\varphi : \mathbb{R}^n \times \mathbb{R}^n \to \mathbb{R}$. In order to formulate necessary and sufficient conditions for such problems, Theorem 6.1 plays a significant role in equivalency of subdifferential relationships.

Note that for different problems described by ordinary and partial differential inclusions the reader can consult Aubin and Cellina [1], Mordukhovich [9] and the bibliography therein.

## 2     Optimization of Polyhedral Discrete Inclusions

We reduce the problem (P$_D$) to a convex mathematical programming problem with constraints consisting of linear inequalities. Let us denote

$$
A = \begin{pmatrix} P & -Q & 0\cdots & 0 & 0 \\ 0 & P & -Q\cdots & 0 & 0 \\ \cdots & \cdots & \cdots & \cdots & \cdots \\ 0 & 0 & 0\cdots & P & -Q \end{pmatrix}, D = \begin{pmatrix} d \\ \vdots \\ \vdots \\ d \end{pmatrix} \tag{6}
$$

where $A$ is the partitioned into submatrices $P, -Q$ and $m \times n$ zero matrices $0, D$ is $m(T+1)$ dimensional vector-column. Obviously $A$ is a matrix with sizes $m(T+1) \times n(T+1)$ ; the number of rows and the number of columns are equal to $T+1$. If we introduce a vector $w = (x_0, x_1, ..., x_T) \in \mathbb{R}^{n(T+1)}$, then the problem can be reduced to the problem with geometric constraints and an objective function $f(w) = \sum_{t=0}^{T} g(x_t, t)$; the problem (P$_D$) can be replaced by the following equivalent problem in Euclidean space $\mathbb{R}^{n(T+1)}$ :

  minimize $f(w)$, subject to $w \in \widetilde{A} \cap \widetilde{N}_0 \cap \widetilde{M}_T$, $w \in \mathbb{R}^{n(T+1)}$,      (7)
where

$$
\widetilde{A} = \{ w : Aw \leq D \},
$$

$\widetilde{N}_0 = \{ w : x_0 \in N_0 \}$, $\widetilde{M}_T = \{ w : x_T \in M_T \}$. Thus, if $\{ \tilde{x}_t \}_{t=0}^{T}$ is a solution of problem (1)-(4), then $w = (\tilde{x}_0, \tilde{x}_1, ..., \tilde{x}_T)$ is a solution of problem (7) and vice versa.

Obviously, $\tilde{A} = \bigcap_{t=0}^{T-1} \tilde{A}_t$ , where $\tilde{A}_t = \{w : Px_t - Qx_{t+1} \le d\}$, $t = 0, ..., T-1$. Let

$K_{\tilde{A}}(\tilde{w}), \tilde{w} \in \tilde{A}$; $K_{\tilde{N}_0}(\tilde{w}), \tilde{w} \in \tilde{N}_0$ and $K_{\tilde{M}_T}(\tilde{w}), \tilde{w} \in \tilde{M}_T$ be cone of tangent

directions [2],[7], [10] . By Theorem 2.4 [10,p.144] there exist a vector

$w_f^* \in \partial_w f(\tilde{w})$ and vectors $w_{\tilde{A}}^* \in K_{\tilde{A}}^*(\tilde{w})$, $w_0^* \in K_{\tilde{N}_0}^*(\tilde{w})$, $w_T^* \in K_{\tilde{M}_T}^*(\tilde{w})$ such

that $w_f^* = w_0^* + w_{\tilde{A}}^* + w_T^*$. On the other hand the cone of tangent directions

$K_{\tilde{A}_t}(\tilde{w})$, $t = 0, ..., T-1$ are polyhedral cones and so by Theorem4.14 [10,p.48]

$K_{\tilde{A}}^*(\tilde{w}) = \sum_{t=0}^{T-1} K_{\tilde{A}_t}^*(\tilde{w})$ . Thus we have

$$w_f^* = w_0^* + \sum_{t=0}^{T-1} w_{\tilde{A}_t}^* + w_T^*, \quad w_{\tilde{A}_t}^* \in K_{\tilde{A}_t}^*(\tilde{w}). \tag{8}$$

In fact, in order for $\tilde{w}$ to be a point minimizing $f$ over $\tilde{A} \cap \tilde{N}_0 \cap \tilde{M}_T$ in problem (7)

it is necessary and sufficient that the condition (8) is fulfilled. Clearly, $w_f^* \in \partial_w f(\tilde{w})$

implies that $w_f^* = (x_{f0}^*, x_{f1}^*, ..., x_{fT}^*)$, $x_{ft}^* \in \partial_x g(\tilde{x}_t, t), t = 0, ..., T$ .

**Lemma 2.1.** For a polyhedral set $\tilde{A}_t$ one has

$$K_{\tilde{A}_t}^*(\tilde{w}) = \{w^*(t) : x_t^*(t) = -P^*\lambda_t, \ x_{t+1}^*(t) = Q^*\lambda_t, x_k^* = 0, k \ne t, t+1,$$

$$\lambda_t \ge 0, \langle P\tilde{x}_t - Q\tilde{x}_{t+1} - d, \lambda_t \rangle = 0 \}, \ \lambda_t \in \mathbb{R}^m, \ t = 0, ..., T-1.$$

*Proof.* Let us compute the dual cones $K_{\tilde{A}}^*(\tilde{w})$, $K_{\tilde{M}_0}^*(\tilde{w})$ and $K_{\tilde{M}_T}^*(\tilde{w})$. By the

definition of the cone of tangent directions

$$K_{\tilde{A}_t}(\tilde{w}) = \{\overline{w} : P_i(\tilde{x}_t + \lambda\overline{x}_t) - Q_i(\tilde{x}_{t+1} + \lambda\overline{x}_{t+1}) \le d \text{ for a small } \lambda > 0\},$$

$$t = 0, ..., T-1 \tag{9}$$

Let $I(\tilde{w})$ denote $I(\tilde{w}) = \{i : P_i\tilde{x}_t - Q_i\tilde{x}_{t+1} = d_i, \ i = 1, 2, ..., m\}$. By the definition

(9) if $i \in I(\tilde{w})$ ,then the equality $P_i(\tilde{x}_t + \lambda\overline{x}_t) - Q_i(\tilde{x}_{t+1} + \lambda\overline{x}_{t+1}) \le d_i$ holds, if

$$P_i\overline{x}_t - Q_i\overline{x}_{t+1} \le 0, \ i \in I(\tilde{w}). \tag{10}$$

Then if $i \notin I(\tilde{w})$ ,then $P_i(\tilde{x}_t + \lambda\overline{x}_t) - Q_i(\tilde{x}_{t+1} + \lambda\overline{x}_{t+1}) < d_i$ holds for a small $\lambda$,

regardless choosing of $(\overline{x}_t, \overline{x}_{t+1})$. Thus, a cone $K_{\tilde{A}_t}^*(\tilde{w})$ completely is defined by system of inequalities (10). Apply Theorem 4.9 (Farkas) [10,p.47] to system (10) and rewrite it in the form: $\langle \overline{x}_t, -A_t \rangle + \langle \overline{x}_{t+1}, -Q_i \rangle \geq 0$, $i \in I(\tilde{w})$. Since, $\overline{x}_k, k \neq t, t+1$ are arbitrary, it follows that $w^* = (x_0^*, x_1^*, ..., x_T^*) \in K_{\tilde{A}_t}^*(\tilde{w})$ if and only if

$$x_t^* = -\sum_{i \in I(\tilde{w})} P_i^* \lambda_i^t, \; x_{t+1}^* = \sum_{i \in I(\tilde{w})} Q_i^* \lambda_i^t, \; \lambda_i^t \geq 0, \tag{11}$$

where $P_i^*, Q_i^*$ are transposed vectors of $P_i, Q_i$. Now taking $\lambda_i^t = 0, i \notin I(\tilde{w})$ and denoting $\lambda_t$ a vector with the components $\lambda_i^t$, the formula (11) can be rewritten in the equivalent form

$$
\begin{aligned}
K_{\tilde{A}_t}^*(\tilde{w}) = &\left\{ w^*(t) = \left( 0, ..., 0, x_t^*(t), x_{t+1}^*(t), 0, ..., 0 \right) : x_t^*(t) = -P^* \lambda_t, \right. \\
&\left. x_{t+1}^*(t) = Q^* \lambda_t, \lambda_t \geq 0, \langle P\tilde{x}_t - Q\tilde{x}_{t+1} - d, \lambda_t \rangle = 0 \right\}, \lambda_t \in \mathbb{R}^m, t = 0, ..., T-1.
\end{aligned}
\tag{12}
$$

The proof of lemma is completed. Now we can formulate necessary and sufficient conditions for optimality of the polyhedral optimization problem (P$_D$).

**Theorem 2.1.** In order for $\{\tilde{x}_t\}_{t=0}^T$ to be an optimal solution of the polyhedral optimization problem (P$_D$), it is necessary and sufficient that there exist vectors $x_0^*, x_e^*$ and finite sequence $\{x_t^*\}_{t=0}^T$ of the adjoint discrete inclusions, such that

$$x_t^* \in P^* \lambda_t + \partial g(\tilde{x}_t, t), \; t = 0, ..., T-1,$$
$$x_{t+1}^* = Q^* \lambda_t, \; \lambda_t \geq 0, \; \langle P\tilde{x}_t - Q\tilde{x}_{t+1} - d, \lambda_t \rangle = 0,$$
$$x_T^* + x_e^* \in \partial g(\tilde{x}_T, T), \; x_e^* \in K_{M_T}^*(\tilde{x}_T), \; x_0^* \in K_{N_0}^*(\tilde{x}_0).$$

*Proof.* It is easy to compute that

$$
\begin{aligned}
K_{\tilde{N}_0}^*(\tilde{w}) &= \left\{ w^* : x_0^* \in K_{N_0}^*(\tilde{x}_0), t \neq 0 \right\}, \\
K_{\tilde{M}_T}^*(\tilde{w}) &= \left\{ w^* : x_T^* \in K_{M_T}^*(\tilde{x}_T), x_t^* = 0, t \neq T \right\}.
\end{aligned}
\tag{13}
$$

Thus, in accordance with Lemma 2.1 and formulas (13), it is obvious that

$$w_0^* = (x_{00}^*, 0..., 0), \; x_{00}^* \in K_{N_0}^*(\tilde{x}_0), \; w_T^* = (0..., 0, x_e^*),$$
$$x_e^* \in K_{M_T}^*(\tilde{x}_T), w^*(t) = (0, ..., 0, x_t^*(t), x_{t+1}^*(t), 0, ..., 0),$$

$t = 0, ..., T-1$. Then, the componentwise representation of (8) means that

$$x_{f0}^* = x_{00}^* + x_0^*(0), \; x_{00}^* \in K_{N_0}^*(\tilde{x}_0), \tag{14}$$

$$x_{ft}^* = x_t^*(t-1) + x_t^*(t),\ t = 1,...,T-1, \tag{15}$$

$$x_{fT}^* = x_T^*(T-1) + x_e^*. \tag{16}$$

Moreover, by Lemma 2. $x_{ft}^* - x_t^*(t-1) = -P^*\lambda_t$, $x_{t+1}^* = Q^*\lambda_t$, $\lambda_t \geq 0$. Denoting $x_{t+1}^* \equiv x_{t+1}^*(t)$, $t = 0,...,T-1, x_{ft}^* \equiv u_t^*, x_{00}^* \equiv x_0^*$ in view of (14) we obtain $x_t^* = P^*\lambda_t + u_t^*$, $\lambda_t \geq 0$, $u_t^* \in \partial g(\tilde{x}_t, t)$, $t = 0,...,T-1$. Besides, taking into account (16), we have $x_T^* + x_e^* \in \partial g(\tilde{x}_T, T)$, $x_e^* \in K_{M_T}^*(\tilde{x}_T)$, $x_0^* \in K_{N_0}^*(\tilde{x}_0)$. The proof of theorem is ended.

# 3    Optimization of Polyhedral Discrete-Approximation Problem

According to continuous problem (5) we associate the following discrete-approximation problem

$$\text{minimize } \sum_{t=0}^{1-h} hg(x_h(t),t) + \varphi_0(x_h(1)),$$

$$\text{subject to } \begin{array}{l} Px_h(t) - Q\Delta_h x_h(t) \leq d, \\ x_h(0) \in N,\ x_h(1) \in M,\ t = 0,h,2h,...,1-h \end{array};$$

$$\Delta_h x_h(t) = \frac{x_h(t+h) - x_h(t)}{h} \tag{17}$$

where $h$ is a discrete step.

In the next theorem are formulated the necessary and sufficient conditions for problem (17).

**Theorem 3.1.** In order that $\{x_h(t)\}_{t=0}^1$ be a solution of the discrete-approximation problem (17), it is necessary and sufficient that there exist an adjoint trajectory $\{x_h^*(t)\}_{t=0}^1$ and vector $x_{eh}^*$, satisfying the adjoint discrete inclusions and boundary condition, respectively

$$-\Delta_h x_h^*(t) \in P^*\lambda_h(t) + \partial g(\tilde{x}_h(t),t),$$

$$\langle P\tilde{x}_h(t) - Q\Delta_h \tilde{x}_h(t) - d, \lambda_h(t)\rangle = 0,\ t = 0,...,1-h,$$

$$x_h^*(1) + x_{eh}^* \in \partial\varphi_0(\tilde{x}_h(1)),\ x_{eh}^* \in K_{M_h}^*(\tilde{x}_h(1)),\ x_h^*(0) \in K_{N_h}^*(\tilde{x}_h(0)).$$

The proof of theorem is over.

By passing to the formally limit here as $h \to 0$, we have the adjoint polyhedral inclusion with some boundary condition. It occurs that these conditions are necessary and sufficient for optimality of $\tilde{x}(t), t \in [0,1]$ in the problem for polyhedral differential inclusions ($P_C$).

**Theorem 3.2.** Let $g(\cdot, t)$ and $\varphi_0(\cdot)$ be polyhedral functions. Moreover, let $N$ and $M$ be polyhedral sets in $\mathbb{R}^n$. Then, in order for the trajectory $\tilde{x}(t), t \in [0,1]$, lying interior to dom $F$ be optimal in continuous problem ($P_C$), it is sufficient, that there exist a vector $x_e^*$ and absolutely continuous function $x^*(t)$, such that

(a)  $x^*(1) + x_e^* \in \partial \varphi_0(\tilde{x}(1))$, $x_e^* \in K_M^*(\tilde{x}(1))$, $x^*(0) \in K_N^*(\tilde{x}(0))$,

(b)  $-\dot{x}^*(t) \in P^* \lambda(t) + \partial g(\tilde{x}(t), t)$, a.e. $t \in [0,1]$,

$\left\langle P\tilde{x}(t) - Q\dot{\tilde{x}}(t) - d, \lambda(t) \right\rangle = 0$, a.e. $t \in [0,1]$.

# 4     Approximation and Optimization of Inequality Constraints

In the second part of the presented paper, we have considered a problem with discrete and continuous time described by another type of inequality constraints; first we consider the following discrete problem:

$$\text{minimize} \sum_{t=0}^{T} g(x_t, t)$$

$$(\varphi_D) \text{ subject to} \quad \begin{aligned} x_{t+1} &\in F(x_t), \ t = 0, \ldots, T-1, \\ x_0 &\in N_0, \ x_T \in M_T, \ F(x) = \{y : \varphi(x, y) \le 0\} \end{aligned}$$

and $\varphi(z)$, $z = (x, y)$ is continuous convex function and there is a point $z_0$, such that $\varphi(z_0) < 0$. Here $N_0, M_T \subset \mathbb{R}^n$ are an arbitrary convex sets and $g(\cdot, t) : \mathbb{R}^n \to \mathbb{R}$ is a convex function. Thus using the same notations in the proof of Theorem 2.1 we can formulate necessary and sufficient conditions for optimality of the trajectory $\{\tilde{x}_t\}_{t=0}^{T}$ as follows

$$(x_t^* - \lambda u_t^*, -x_{t+1}^*) \in \mu_t \partial_z \varphi(\tilde{x}_t, \tilde{x}_{t+1}), \quad \mu_t \varphi(\tilde{x}_t, \tilde{x}_{t+1}) = 0,$$

$$u_t^* \in \partial g(\tilde{x}_t, t), \quad x_T^* + x_e^* \in \lambda \partial g(\tilde{x}_T, T), \quad x_e^* \in K_{M_T}^*(\tilde{x}_T), \tag{18}$$

$$x_0^* \in K_{N_0}^*(\tilde{x}_0), \quad \mu_t \ge 0, \ t = 0, \ldots, T-1.$$

Now by approximating method, we shall formulate the sufficient condition for the continuous problem, consisting of the following

$$\text{minimize } J\left[x(\cdot)\right] = \int_0^1 g(x(t),t)dt + p(x(1)),$$

$(\varphi_C)$ subject to
$$\dot{x}(t) \in F(x(t)), \quad t \in [0,1],$$
$$x(0) \in N, \; x(1) \in M; \; F(x) = \left\{y : \varphi(x,y) \le 0\right\}$$

where the functions $g(\cdot,t), p(\cdot), \varphi(\cdot,\cdot)$ are convex. It is required to find an absolutely continuous function $\tilde{x}(t), t \in [0,1]$ of problem $(\varphi_C)$, minimizing $J\left[x(\cdot)\right]$. We label this problem as $(\varphi_C)$.

**Theorem 4.2.** Assume that $g(\cdot,t)$ and $p(\cdot)$ are convex and continuous at the points of some feasible solution of discrete- approximation problem $(\varphi_D)$.Then, for the optimality of a feasible solution $\left\{\tilde{x}_h(t)\right\}_{t=0}^1$ in the convex problem $(\varphi_D)$, it is necessary that there exist a number $\lambda = \lambda_h \in \{0,1\}$ and grid functions $\left\{x_h^*(t)\right\}_{t=0}^1$, not all equal to zero satisfying the conditions18). If $\lambda_h = 1$,these conditions are sufficient for optimality of $\left\{\tilde{x}_h(t)\right\}_{t=0}^1$.

Thus, we can formulate the following result.

**Theorem 4.3.** Let $\varphi(\cdot,\cdot)$ be continuous convex function and $F$ be bounded at least for one point. Moreover, let $(x_0, y_0)$ be a point such that $\varphi(x_0, y_0) < 0$. Then, in order for a trajectory $\tilde{x}(\cdot)$ ($\tilde{x}(t) \in \text{int dom} F$) to be an optimal solution of continuous problem
$(\varphi_C)$, it is sufficient that there exist not all equal to zero an absolutely continuous function $x^*(\cdot)$, function $\lambda(\cdot)$ and number $\lambda_0 > 0$ satisfying the conditions

$$-\left(\dot{x}^*(t) + \lambda_0 v^*(t), \; x^*(t)\right) \in \lambda(t)\partial\varphi\left(\tilde{x}(t),\dot{\tilde{x}}(t)\right),$$

$$\lambda(t)\varphi\left(\tilde{x}(t),\dot{\tilde{x}}(t)\right) = 0, \lambda(t) \ge 0, \text{ a.e. } t \in [0,1],$$

$$v^*(t) \in \partial g(\tilde{x}(t),t), \; x^*(1) + x_e^* \in \lambda_0\partial p(\tilde{x}(1)), \; x_e^* \in K_M^*\left(\tilde{x}(1)\right),$$

$$x^*(0) \in K_N^*\left(\tilde{x}(0)\right), \; \lambda_0 \ge 0.$$

# References

[1]  Aubin, J.P., Cellina, A.: Differential inclusions. Grudlehnen der Math. Springer, Wiss. (1984)

[2]  Mahmudov, E.N., Pshenichnyi, B.N.: Necessary condition of extremum and evasion problem, pp. 3–22. Preprint, Institute Cybernetcis of Ukraine SSR, Kiev (1978)

[3]  Mahmudov, E.N.: On duality in problems of optimal control described by convex differential inclusions of Goursat-Darboux type. J. Math. Anal. Appl. 307, 628–640 (2005)

[4]  Mahmudov, E.N.: The optimality principle for discrete and the first order partial differential inclusions. J. Math. Anal. Appl. 308, 605–619 (2005)

[5]  Mahmudov, E.N.: Necessary and sufficient conditions for discrete and differential inclusions of elliptic type. J. Math. Anal. Appl. 323(2), 768–789 (2006)

[6]  Mahmudov, E.N.: Optimal control of higher order differential in clusions of Bolza type with varying time interval. Nonlinear Analysis-Theory, Method & Applications 69(5-6), 1699–1709 (2008)

[7]  Mahmudov, E.N.: Duality in the problems of optimal control described by first order partial differential inclusions. Optimization a J. of Math. Program. and Oper. Research 59(4), 589–599 (2010)

[8]  Makarov, V.L., Rubinov, A.M.: The Mathematical Theory of Economic Dynamics and Equilibrium, Nauka, Moscow (1977); English transl., Springer, Berlin (1973)

[9]  Mordukhovich, B.S.: Variational Analysis and Generalized Differentiation, I: Basic Theory; II: Applications, Grundlehren Series. Fundamental Principles of Mathematical Sciences, vol. 330, 331. Springer (2006)

[10] Pshenichnyi, B.N.: Convex analysis and extremal problems, Nauka, Moscow (1980)

# Reasoning under Uncertainty in the AHP Method Using the Belief Function Theory

Amel Ennaceur[1], Zied Elouedi[1], and Eric Lefevre[2]

[1] LARODEC, University of Tunis, Institut Supérieur de Gestion, Tunisia
amel_naceur@yahoo.fr, zied.elouedi@gmx.fr
[2] Univ. Lille Nord of France, UArtois EA 3926 LGI2A, France
eric.lefevre@univ-artois.fr

**Abstract.** The Analytic Hierarchy Process (AHP) method was introduced to help the decision maker to express judgments on alternatives over a number of criteria. In this paper, our proposal extends the AHP method to an uncertain environment, where the uncertainty is represented through the Transferable Belief Model (TBM), one interpretation of the belief function theory. In fact, we suggest a novel framework that tackles the challenge of introducing uncertainty in both the criterion and the alternative levels, where the objective is to represent imperfection that may appear in the pair-wise comparisons and to model the relationship between these alternatives and criteria through conditional beliefs.

## 1 Introduction

Within the framework of Multi-Criteria Decision Making (MCDM) problems, many methods have been proposed and each one has its own characteristics [17]. We have then two major families. On the one hand, the outranking approach introduced by Roy where some methods like Electre and Promethee are developed [2], [5]. On the other hand, the value and utility theory approaches mainly started by Keeney and Raiffa [6], and then implemented in a number of methods [15]. Amongst the most well known ones is the Analytic Hierarchy Process (AHP) [8], [9], introduced by Saaty (1980) and based on preference judgments. In fact, in the AHP method, the problem is structured hierarchically at different levels. Within the same context, the purpose of constructing this hierarchy is to evaluate the influence of the criteria on the alternatives to attain objectives. In other words, the decision maker is required to provide his preferences by comparing all criteria, sub-criteria and alternatives with respect to upper level decision elements. This is accomplished through pair-wise comparisons.

The capability to deal with uncertainty and imprecision is the common problem of decision making. In fact, this imperfection can arise due to different situations: incomplete data for making decisions, imprecise judgments, etc.

However, standard AHP method was criticized because it does not well perform their task in such environment. Sometimes, the decision maker cannot ensure pair-wise comparisons between all the criteria and alternatives because

S. Greco et al. (Eds.): IPMU 2012, Part IV, CCIS 300, pp. 373–382, 2012.
© Springer-Verlag Berlin Heidelberg 2012

the information about them may be incomplete due to the time pressure and the lack of data. In order to overcome this limitation, several extensions were developed such as referenced AHP [10], fuzzy AHP [7], etc.

In our work, we will focus on belief function framework. It is considered as a useful theory for representing and managing uncertain knowledge [11]. This theory provides a convenient framework for dealing with incomplete and uncertain information, notably those given by experts. So, a first work has been tackled by Beynon et al. have proposed a method called the DS/AHP method [1] comparing not only single alternatives but also groups of them. Besides, belief AHP approach was introduced by [4] which evaluates sets of alternatives according to sets of criteria. Also, several works has been proposed by Utkin [16], etc. Despite all the advantages of these two approaches, allowing different comparisons to be made for groups of alternatives and/or criteria, they do not take into account the conditional relationships between alternatives and criteria. In fact, alternatives do not always have a unique priority relationship between them. For instance, in a problem of buying a car, the expert might consider that "Peugeot" is evaluated to be more important than "Renault" regarding comfort criterion, but "Renault" is more important than "Peugeot" with respect to style criterion. As we can see, the alternative priorities are dependent on each specific criterion.

To solve the problem presented above, this paper presents a new AHP approach under uncertainty, a MCDM method adapted to incomplete and uncertain preferences but also it models conditional relationships between alternatives and criteria, where the uncertainty is represented by belief functions as defined in the Transferable Belief Model (TBM). The choice of the TBM seems appropriate as it allows experts that represent sources of information to express their believes about the cause-effect relationship degree not only in terms of elementary events but also in terms of subsets. Besides, belief function theory offers interesting tools to model the partial and total ignorance and to combine several pieces of evidence as the conjunctive and the disjunctive rules of combination and for conditioning. Our aim through this work is then to represent uncertainty and to more imitate the expert reasoning since he tries to express his preferences over the sets of alternatives regarding each criterion and not regardless of the criteria. Consequently, we try to represent the influences of the criteria on the evaluation of alternatives.

The remainder of this paper is organized as follows. In section 2, we focus on AHP method. Next, we present some useful definitions needed for belief function context. Section 4 represents our new AHP method based on conditional belief functions, and gives an example to show its application. Finally, section 5 concludes the paper.

## 2    Analytic Hierarchy Process

The AHP approach is a decision-making technique developed by Saaty [8], [9] to solve complex problems of choice and prioritization. The basic idea of the approach is to convert subjective assessments of relative importance to a set of overall scores or weights. The AHP decision problem is structured hierarchically at different levels. The purpose of constructing this hierarchy is to evaluate the influence of the criteria on the alternatives to attain objectives. So, an AHP hierarchy has at least three levels: The highest level consists of a unique element that is the overall objective. Then, each level of the hierarchy contains criteria or sub-criteria that influence the decision. Alternative elements are put at the lowest level.

Once the hierarchy is built, the decision maker starts the prioritization procedure to determine the relative importance of the elements on each level of the hierarchy (criteria and alternatives). Elements of a problem on each level are paired (with respect to their upper level decision elements) and then compared. This method elicits preferences through pair-wise comparisons which are constructed from decision maker's answers. Indeed, the decision maker can use both objective information about the elements as well as subjective opinions about the elements relative meaning and importance. The responses to the pair-wise comparison question use a nine-point scale [8], which translates the preferences of a decision maker into crisp numbers.

Next, the comparison matrix is formed by repeating the process for each level of the hierarchy. After filling all the pair-wise comparison matrices, the local priority weights are determined by using the eigenvalue method. The objective is then to find the weight of each criterion, or the score of each alternative by calculating the eigenvalue vector. With these values, the AHP method permits to compute a consistency ration to check if the matrix is consistent or not. When the matrix is considered inconsistent, the entries that are given by the decision maker have to be revised until a satisfactory consistency ratio is obtained. The last step of the AHP aggregates all local priorities from the decision table by a simple weighted sum. The global priorities thus obtained are used for final ranking of the alternatives and selection of the best one.

## 3 Belief Function Theory

In this section, we briefly review the main concepts underlying the Transferable Belief Model (TBM), one interpretation of the belief function theory [14].

### 3.1 Basic Concepts

The TBM is a model to represent quantified belief functions [14]. Let $\Theta$ be the frame of discernment representing a finite set of elementary hypotheses related to a problem domain. We denote by $2^{\Theta}$ the set of all the subsets of $\Theta$ [11].

The impact of a piece of evidence on the different subsets of the frame of discernment $\Theta$ is represented by the so-called basic belief assignment (bba), called initially by Shafer basic probability assignment [11].

A bba is a function denoted by $m$ that assigns a value in $[0, 1]$ to every subset $A$ of $\Theta$ such that:

$$\sum_{A \subseteq \Theta} m(A) = 1 \ . \tag{1}$$

The value $m(A)$, named a basic belief mass (bbm), represents the portion of belief committed exactly to the event $A$.

The belief function theory offers many interesting tools. For instance, to combine beliefs induced by distinct pieces of evidence, we can use the conjunctive rule of combination [13]. Also, to select the most likely hypothesis, one of the most used solutions is the pignistic probability [14].

## 3.2   Operations on the Product Space

Let $U = \{X, Y, Z, \ldots\}$ be a set of variables, where each variable has its frame of discernment. Let $X$ and $Y$ be two disjoint subsets of $U$. Their frames are the product space of the frames of the variables they include.

**Vacuous Extension.** Given a bba defined on $X$, its vacuous extension on $X \times Y$ denoted $m^{X \uparrow X \times Y}$ is given by [12]:

$$m^{X \uparrow X \times Y}(B) = \begin{cases} m^X(A) & \text{if } B = A \times Y, A \subseteq X, \\ 0 \text{ otherwise .} \end{cases} \tag{2}$$

**Marginalization.** A bba defined on a product space $X \times Y$ may be marginalized on $X$ by transferring each mass $m^{X \times Y}(B)$ for $B \subseteq X \times Y$ to its projection on $X$ [12]:

$$m^{X \times Y \downarrow X}(A) = \sum_{\{B \subseteq X \times Y | Proj(B \downarrow X) = A)\}} m^{X \times Y}(B), \forall A \subseteq X . \tag{3}$$

where $Proj(B \downarrow X)$ denotes the projection of $B$ onto $X$.

**Ballooning Extension.** Let $m^X[y_i]$ represents your beliefs on $X$ conditionnally on $y_i$ a subset of $Y$, i.e., in a context where $y_i$ holds. The ballooning extension is defined as:

$$m^X[y_i]^{\uparrow X \times Y}(A \times y_i \cup X \times \bar{y}_i) = m^X[y_i](A), \forall A \subseteq X . \tag{4}$$

# 4   AHP Method in an Uncertain Environment

In this section, we introduce the concept of the AHP method within the belief function framework. We start by explaining how this method works, and then an example will be traced to further understand and illustrate our approach.

## 4.1   AHP Method in the Belief Function Context

Since impression and uncertainty are common characteristics in many decision-making problems, our new AHP method should be able to deal with this uncertainty. Within this context, a first work has been introduced by Beynon et al. [1].

They developed a method, called DS/AHP which compares not only one alternative but also groups of alternatives. With the comparison matrix, the eigenvector is computed and transformed into a bba. Then a combination rule is used to aggregate these bba's, and the belief and plausibility measures are used to choose the best alternatives. In addition, Ennaceur et al. [4] have proposed a method named belief AHP, a combination between the AHP method and the belief function theory as understood in the transferable belief model, that evaluates sets of alternatives according to sets of criteria. To choose the best alternative, this approach proposes to use the pignistic probabilities. From another perspective, Dezert et al. [3] have proposed to follow Beynon's approach, but instead of using the belief function theory, they investigate the possibility to use the Dezert-Smarandache theory. The DSmT/AHP method uses the PCR5 rule to combine the priorities vectors whereas the DS/AHP applies the Dempster's rule.

In spite of all the advantages of the proposed methods, they do not take into account the conditional relationships between alternatives and criteria. For instance, in the alternative level, the expert tries to estimate his opinions-beliefs about alternatives according to each criterion. That is why; representing uncertainty by bba's seems to be inconsistent with the expert reasoning because he tries to express his preferences regarding each criterion and not regardless of the criteria. As a result, in this work, we want to more imitate the human reasoning. Therefore, we suggest a new approach based on AHP method. Unlike belief AHP where the evaluation of each alternative with respect to each criterion is given by a bba, we try to model the evaluation of each subset of alternatives with respect to each criterion by conditional beliefs. Additionally, after eliciting the expert's preferences at the criterion level, we suppose that criteria weights are also expressed by means of a bba in order to represent the imperfect evaluation.

## 4.2    Uncertain AHP Approach

**Identification of the Candidate Alternatives and Criteria.** One of the key questions being issued over the implementation of any MCDM problem is the identification of the candidate alternatives and criteria. As in [4], the main aim of our proposed approach is the allowance for incompleteness in the judgments made by expert. Besides, in many complex problems decision makers are able to compare only subsets of criteria and cannot evaluate separate ones. To solve this problem, that means to reduce the number of criteria which decreases the number of comparisons, our method suggests to allow the expert to express his opinions on groups of criteria instead of single one. So, he chooses these subsets by assuming that criteria having the same degree of preference are grouped together. For instance, if an expert identifies a group of criteria, then we could suppose that all of them have the same importance.

Let $\Omega = \{c_1, \ldots, c_m\}$ be a set of criteria, we denote the set of all subsets of $\Omega$ by $2^\Omega$, and let $C_k$ be the short notation of a subset of $\Omega$. By generalization, these groups of criteria can be defined as:

$$C_k \succ C_j, \forall\, k, j | C_k, C_j \in 2^\Omega, C_k \cap C_j = \emptyset\ . \tag{5}$$

On the other hand and similarly to the criterion level, our method proposes not to consider all the alternatives but just to choose groups of them. So, we assume that $\Theta = \{a_1, \ldots, a_n\}$ is a set of alternatives, and we denote the set of all subsets of $\Theta$ by $2^\Theta$. In other terms and as explained in [4], the decision maker compares not only a single one but also sets of alternatives between each other.

By comparing subsets between each other, we provide a major benefit to the decision maker. In fact, our proposed approach has reduced the number of comparisons, because instead of using single elements, we have used subsets.

**Pair-Wise Comparisons and Preference Elicitation.** Once the sets of criteria and alternatives are defined, the expert tries to specify his preferences in order to obtain the criterion weights and the alternative scores in terms of each criterion. In this study, we have adopted the Saaty's scale to evaluate the importance of pairs of grouped elements in terms of their contribution. Thus, the priority vectors are then generated using the eigenvector method and we have chosen the standard consistency index in order to ensure that uncertain AHP's pair-wise comparison matrix is consistent.

**Updating the Alternatives Priorities.** Having made all the pair-wise comparisons, we will be interested in this step by showing how to combine the obtained alternatives priorities with the importance of their corresponding criteria. In the first step of the approach, the uncertainty is introduced on the decision maker preferences. Besides, we propose to represent the imperfection over the sets of criteria. Within our framework, we have $C_i \subseteq 2^\Omega$ and we have the priority values of each $C_i$ representing the opinions-beliefs of the expert about his preferences. We also notice that this priority vector sums to one which can be regarded as a bba. As a result, this bba can be denoted by $m^\Omega$.

Furthermore, we propose to represent the uncertainty at the alternative level. Unlike the criterion level, the expert tries to express his preferences over the sets of alternatives regarding each criterion and not regardless of the criteria. Accordingly, and to more imitate the expert reasoning, we indicate that to define the influences of the criteria on the evaluation of alternatives, we might use a conditional belief. Given a pair-wise comparison matrix which compares the sets of alternatives according to a specific criterion, a conditional bba can be represented by:

$$m^\Theta[c_j](A_k) = w_k, \quad \forall A_k \subseteq 2^\Theta \text{ and } c_j \in \Omega . \quad (6)$$

where $A_k$ represents a subset of $2^\Theta$, $w_k$ is the eigen value of the $k^{th}$ sets of alternatives regarding the criterion $c_j$. $m^\Theta[c_j](A_k)$ means that we know the belief about $A_k$ regarding $c_j$.

As indicated above, our objective through this step is to combine the obtained conditional belief with the importance of their respective criteria to measure their contribution. In this context, our major problem here is that we have priorities concerning criteria and groups of criteria that are defined on the frame of discernment $\Omega$, whereas the sets of decision alternatives are generally defined on another frame $\Theta$. In order to solve this problem, we propose to standardize our frame of discernment. First, at the criterion level, our objective is then to redefine the bba that represents criteria weights. Indeed, we propose to extend this bba from $\Omega$ to $\Theta \times \Omega$:

$$m^{\Omega \uparrow \Theta \times \Omega}(B) = m^{\Omega}(C_i) \quad B = \Theta \times C_i, C_i \subseteq \Omega \ . \tag{7}$$

Second, at the alternative level, the idea was to use the deconditionalization process in order to transform the conditional belief into a new belief function. In this case, the ballooning extension technique is applied:

$$m^{\Theta}[c_j]^{\Uparrow \Theta \times \Omega}(A_k \times c_j \cup \Theta \times \bar{c}_j) = m^{\Theta}[c_j](A_k), \forall A_k \subseteq \Theta \ . \tag{8}$$

Once the frame of discernment $\Theta \times \Omega$ is formalized, our approach proposes to combine the alternative priorities. In fact, we assume that each pair-wise comparison matrix is considered as a distinct source of evidence, which provides opinions towards the preferences of particular decision alternatives. Then, based on the belief function framework, we can apply the conjunctive rule of combination. The obtained bba represents the belief in groups of alternatives based on the combined evidence from the decisions matrices.

Finally, we might combine the obtained bba with the importance of their respective criteria to measure their contribution. That is, we will apply the conjunctive rule of combination and we get:

$$m^{\Theta \times \Omega} = \left[ \bigcirc_{j=1,\ldots,m} m^{\Theta}[c_j]^{\Uparrow \Theta \times \Omega} \right] \bigcirc m^{\Omega \uparrow \Theta \times \Omega} \ . \tag{9}$$

So, we obtain $m^{\Theta \times \Omega}$ reflecting the importance of alternatives to the given criteria.

**Decision Making.** To this end and after combining the resulting ballooning extension, a decision under uncertainty must be defined. In the sequel, the pignistic probabilities is used. However, our obtained beliefs are defined on the product space $\Theta \times \Omega$. To solve this problem, we propose to marginalize this bba on $\Theta$ (frame of alternatives) by transferring each mass $m^{\Theta \times \Omega}$ to its projection on $\Theta$:

$$m^{\Theta \times \Omega \downarrow \Theta}(A_j) = \sum_{\{B \subseteq \Theta \times \Omega | Proj(B \downarrow \Theta) = A_j\}} m^{\Theta \times \Omega}(B), \forall A_j \subseteq \Theta \ . \tag{10}$$

Finally, we can compute the pignistic probabilities to choose the best alternatives:

$$BetP(a_j) = \sum_{A_i \subseteq \Theta} \frac{|a_j \cap A_i|}{|A_i|} \frac{m^{\Theta \times \Omega \downarrow \Theta}(A_i)}{(1 - m^{\Theta \times \Omega \downarrow \Theta}(\emptyset))}, \forall a_j \in \Theta \ . \tag{11}$$

### 4.3   Example

To describe this approach, we consider the problem of purchasing a car. Suppose that this problem involves four criteria: $\Omega = \{$Comfort (c1), Style (c2), Fuel (c3),

Quietness (c4)}, and three selected alternatives: $\Theta = \{\text{Peugeot}(p), \text{Renault}(r), \text{Ford}(f)\}$.

The first stage is the identification of the groups of criteria and alternatives. Then, the expert can express his preferences over these subsets. At the criterion level, the following pair-wise matrix can be obtained (see Table 1). As indicated above, the criterion weights are expressed by a basic belief assessment (bba). In fact, after eliciting the expert's preferences, we get: $m^{\Omega}(\{c1\}) = 0.58$, $m^{\Omega}(\{c4\}) = 0.32$ and $m^{\Omega}(\{c2, c3\}) = 0.1$.

**Table 1.** The weights assigned to the criteria according to the expert's opinion

| Criteria | $\{c1\}$ | $\{c4\}$ | $\{c2, c3\}$ | Priority |
|----------|----------|----------|--------------|----------|
| $\{c1\}$ | 1 | 2 | 6 | 0.58 |
| $\{c4\}$ | $\frac{1}{2}$ | 1 | 4 | 0.32 |
| $\{c2, c3\}$ | $\frac{1}{6}$ | $\frac{1}{4}$ | 1 | 0.1 |

Next, we propose to model the alternative score by means of conditional bba. After constructing the pair-wise comparison matrices, the priorities vectors regarding each criterion are shown in Table reftab1. For example, the alternative $\{p\}$ given $c1$ can be represented by $m^{\Theta}[c1](\{p\}) = 0.806$, which means that we know the belief about $\{p\}$ regarding the criterion $c1$.

**Table 2.** Priorities values

| $c1$ | Priority | $c2$ | Priority | $c3$ | Priority | $c4$ | Priority |
|------|----------|------|----------|------|----------|------|----------|
| $\{p\}$ | 0.806 | $\{p\}$ | 0.4 | $\{r\}$ | 0.889 | $\{f\}$ | 0.606 |
| $\{p, r, f\}$ | 0.194 | $\{r, f\}$ | 0.405 | $\{p, r, f\}$ | 0.111 | $\{p, r, f\}$ | 0.394 |
| | | $\{p, r, f\}$ | 0.191 | | | | |

According to our approach, the next step is to standardize the criterion and the alternative frames of discernment. For the criterion level, we suggest to apply the extension procedure. Hence, Equation 7 is used and the resulting bba's is summarized in Table 3.

**Table 3.** Vacuous extension of bba

| bbm | Vacuous extension | Values |
|-----|-------------------|--------|
| $m^{\Omega}(\{c1\})$ | $\{(p, c1), (r, c1), (f, c1)\}$ | 0.58 |
| $m^{\Omega}(\{c4\})$ | $\{(p, c4), (r, c4), (f, c4)\}$ | 0.32 |
| $m^{\Omega}(\{c2, c3\})$ | $\{(p, c2), (r, c2), (f, c2), (p, c3), (r, c3), (f, c3)\}$ | 0.1 |

After normalizing the criteria's bba, the next step is to transform the conditional belief into joint distribution. Indeed, we suggest to compute the ballooning extension using Equation 8 (see Table 4).

**Table 4.** Ballooning extension of conditional bba

| conditional bbm | Ballooning extension | Values |
|---|---|---|
| $m^{\Theta}[c1](\{p\})$ | $\{(p,c1),(p,c2),(p,c3),(p,c4),(r,c2),$ $(r,c3),(r,c4),(f,c2),(f,c3),(f,c4)\}$ | 0.806 |
| $m^{\Theta}[c1](\{p,r,f\})$ | $\{(p,c1),(p,c2),(p,c3),(p,c4),$ $(r,c1),(r,c2),(r,c3),(r,c4),(f,c1),(f,c2),(f,c3),(f,c4)\}$ | 0.194 |

As explained before, once the ballooning extensions are obtained, we can apply the conjunctive rule. The result of this combination will be a unique bba representing the belief in groups of alternatives based on the combined evidence from the decisions matrices.

Then, we propose to apply Equation 9, to combine the obtained bba with the criterion weights (bba) as exposed in Table 5.

**Table 5.** The obtained bba: $m^{\Theta \times \Omega}$

| | |
|---|---|
| $\{(p,c1),(f,c1),(r,c1)\}$ | 0.362 |
| $\{(p,c1)\}$ | 0.315 |
| $\{(p,c4),(f,c4),(r,c4)\}$ | 0.1302 |
| $\{(f,c1)\}$ | 0.0064 |
| $\{(p,c2),(f,c2),(r,c2),(p,c3),(f,c3),(r,c3)\}$ | 0.008 |
| $\{(r,c2),(r,c3),(f,c2),(p,c2)\}$ | 0.0664 |
| $\emptyset$ | 0.112 |

Next, to choose the best alternatives, we must define our beliefs over the frame of alternatives. The solution is then to marginalize on $\Theta$ using the Equation 10, and we obtain the following distribution: $m^{\Theta \times \Omega \downarrow \Theta}(\{p,r,f\}) = 0.5666$, $m^{\Theta \times \Omega \downarrow \Theta}(\{p\}) = 0.315$, $m^{\Theta \times \Omega \downarrow \Theta}(\{f\}) = 0.0064$ and $m^{\Theta \times \Omega \downarrow \Theta}(\emptyset) = 0.112$.

Finally, the pignistic probabilities can be computed, and we get: $BetP(p) = 0.567$, $BetP(r) = 0.220$ and $BetP(f) = 0.213$.

As a consequence, the alternative "Peugeot" is the recommended car since it has the highest values.

## 5   Conclusion

This paper provides a new MCDM method that combines the analytic hierarchy process with the belief function theory. We have first introduced imperfection in the criterion and alternative levels, in order to allow the decision maker to easily express his assessments and also to correctly represent his preferences. In addition, we have shown that to correctly represent the expert's opinion, our approach investigates some ways to define the influences of the criteria on the evaluation of alternatives. Moreover, we have noticed that when applying our proposed approach, the number of comparisons is usually inferior to standard AHP because instead of using single elements we have used subsets.

As future works, we plan to apply our approach on a real application problem and we propose to do a sensibility analysis. A comparison between our presented solution and other methods like Fuzzy AHP will be also interesting to make.

# References

1. Beynon, M., Curry, B., Morgan, P.: The Dempster-Shafer theory of evidence: An alternative approach to multicriteria decision modelling. Omega 28(1), 37–50 (2000)
2. Brans, J.P., Vincke, P., Marechal, B.: How to select and how to rank projects: The PROMOTEE method. European Journal of Operational Research 24, 228–238 (1986)
3. Dezert, J., Tacnet, J.M., Batton-Hubert, M., Smarandache, F.: Multi-Criteria Decision Making based on DSmT-AHP. In: Workshop on the Theory of Belief Functions (2010)
4. Ennaceur, A., Elouedi, Z., Lefevre, E.: Handling Partial Preferences in the Belief AHP Method: Application to Life Cycle Assessment. In: Pirrone, R., Sorbello, F. (eds.) AI*IA 2011. LNCS (LNAI), vol. 6934, pp. 395–400. Springer, Heidelberg (2011)
5. Figueira, J., Greco, S., Ehrgott, M.: Multiple Criteria Decision Analysis: state of the art surveys. Springers International Series in Operations Research and Management Science, vol. 4 (2005)
6. Keeney, R.L., Raiffa, H.: Decisions with multiple objectives: Preferences and value tradeoffs. Cambridge University Press (1976)
7. Laarhoven, P.V., Pedrycz, W.: A fuzzy extension of Saaty's priority theory. Fuzzy Sets and Systems 11, 199–227 (1983)
8. Saaty, T.: A scaling method for priorities in hierarchical structures. Journal of Mathematical Psychology 15, 234–281 (1977)
9. Saaty, T.: The Analytic Hierarchy Process. McGraw-Hill, New-York (1980)
10. Schoner, B., Wedley, W.C.: Ambiguous criteria weights in AHP: consequences and solutions. Decision Sciences 20, 462–475 (1989)
11. Shafer, G.: A Mathematical Theory of Evidence. Princeton University Press (1976)
12. Smets, P.: Belief functions: the disjunctive rule of combination and the generalized bayesian theorem. International Journal of Approximate Reasoning 9, 1–35 (1993)
13. Smets, P.: The combination of evidence in the Transferable Belief Model. IEEE Pattern Analysis and Machine Intelligence, 447–458 (1990)
14. Smets, P., Kennes, R.: The Transferable Belief Model. Artificial Intelligence 66, 191–234 (1994)
15. Triantaphyllou, E.: Multi-Criteria Decision Making methods: a comparative study. Kluwer Academic Publishers (2000)
16. Utkin, L.V.: A new ranking procedure by incomplete pairwise comparisons using preference subsets. Intelligent Data Analysis 13(2), 229–241 (2009)
17. Zeleny, M.: Multiple Criteria Decision Making. McGraw-Hill Book Company (1982)

# Studying the Impact of Information Structure in the PROMETHEE II Preference Elicitation Process: A Simulation Based Approach

Stefan Eppe and Yves De Smet

Computer & Decision Engineering (CoDE) Department
Polytechnic School of Brussels, Université Libre de Bruxelles, Belgium (ULB)
{stefan.eppe,yves.de.smet}@ulb.ac.be

**Abstract.** In the context of a Multi-criteria Decision Aiding process, eliciting a decision maker's (DM) preferences is a crucial preliminary step. In this paper, we consider the PROMETHEE II outranking method and a aggregation-disaggregation elicitation approach. The DM is asked to provide a set of partial yet rather holistic information about, for instance, his preference of one action over another. The goal is to discover the parameter values of PROMETHEE II that best represents the DM's preferences. However, the partial information that is provided can take many forms and the goal of this work is to investigate what impact both the nature and the quantity of information – which we will globally call the *information structure* – has on the quality of the elicitation process' result. We adopt an empirical approach that aims at providing some insights to guide a future, deeper exploration. However, the results so far already suggest some interesting preliminary conclusions.

## 1  Introduction

Most Multi-criteria Decision Aiding (MCDA) methods such as Multi-Attribute Utility Theory (MAUT), or outranking methods are aimed at helping a decision maker (DM) in the non trivial task of aggregating the evaluations of a set of alternatives on several conflicting criteria. These methods require the DM to provide a set of parameters that describe his preferences and allow the chosen method to compute a consistent result. In order to ease this process of determining the preference parameters, so-called elicitation methods are used. Their goal is to extract the DM's knowledge in an indirect manner, without requiring him to state his preferences explicitly and quantitatively in terms of preference parameters. In this paper we will focus on the PROMETHEE II ranking method (described in Sec. 2). Indeed, elicitation methods specifically designed for that method have only received little attention by the community yet [3,4,6]. We assume that the preferences of the DM are expressed as a ranking on the set of alternatives. We also assume that the DM *knows* his preferences, but that he is unable to express them in a quantitatively formalized way. We consider a aggregation-disaggregation method [8] for eliciting the preference parameters,

S. Greco et al. (Eds.): IPMU 2012, Part IV, CCIS 300, pp. 383–392, 2012.

asking the DM to give partial information about his preferences. This information can be provided in different ways: pairwise comparisons of alternatives, partial rankings of alternatives, rankings of weights, etc. The quantity of preference information is given by the number of comparisons, partial rankings, etc. In this preliminary work, we limit the *preference parameters* we study to the weight parameters of the PROMETHEE II method. The indifference and preference thresholds $q_h$ and $p_h$, where $h \in \{1, \dots, m\}$, will be considered as given.

When only little preferential information is given by the DM it is hard to determine which particular set of compatible preference parameters will best represent the DM's *implicit* preferences, yielding a high uncertainty on the chosen preference parameters. This uncertainty decreases with increasing amount of information. Practically, our aim is to be able to provide the decision maker with information of the type: *"Given 10 actions evaluated on 3 criteria, it is sufficient to provide 6 pairwise comparisons of actions to determine a satisfying set of preference parameters."* [1]

The simulation process we propose is using a fictitious DM who provides partial information about his *"preferences"*. Practically, the DM's preferences are represented by a randomly generated set of preference parameters $w^\star$. Pieces of partial preferential information (e.g. pairwise comparisons of actions, partial rankings of sub-sets of actions or weights, etc.) that are compatible with $w^\star$ are then randomly generated and transformed into constraints. In turn, these constraints are used to determine the set of preference parameters $\mathcal{W}$ that are compatible with all constraints. We finally compare $w^\star$ with all preference parameter sets of $\mathcal{W}$ to compute the quality that can be reached with the amount of provided information (Sec. 3). The quality measure is computed by adopting a pessimistic point of view: We assess the quality that can be reached by a set of partial preference information with respect to the hidden preference parameters by taking the worst possible ranking, i.e. the most distant ranking induced by $w_{\text{worst}} \in \mathcal{W}$ from $w^\star$. We choose to use Kendall's $\tau$ rank correlation measure.

One of the main questions we wish to answer in this work is: *"For a given MCDA problem (n actions evaluated on m conflicting criteria), how much information does a decision maker have to provide on average in order to reach a satisfying quality of preference parameters of the PROMETHEE II method?"*

Since the answer to this question also depends on the method chosen for querying a DM's preferences, we use a very simple approach (random generation) to select the pairs of actions the DM has to make a preference statement on. Rather than proposing a novel preference elicitation method, inspired by other existing approaches [5,7] and adapted to PROMETHEE II, our focus lays on investigating a more general quality assessment methodology for elicitation procedures.

The structure of the present contribution is directly derived from the above outlined approach: After briefly introducing the PROMETHEE II method (Sec. 2), we formally present the experimental setup of our simulation (Sec. 3). Results are discussed in Sec. 4.

---

[1] The required satisfaction level has to be provided by the decision maker.

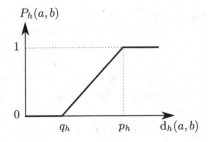

**Fig. 1.** Shape of a PROMETHEE preference function type V, with, for each objective $h$, an indifference threshold $q_h$, and a preference threshold $p_h$. For $d_h(a,b) \in [0, q_h]$, both solutions $a$ and $b$ are considered indifferently on criterion $h$; for a relative difference greater than $p_h$, a strict preference (with value 1) of $a$ over $b$ is stated. Between the two thresholds, the preference evolves linearly with increasing evaluation difference.

## 2    The PROMETHEE II Method

We consider a set $A = \{a_1 \ldots a_n\}$ of $n$ actions that are evaluated over $m$ criteria: $f_h : A \to \mathbb{R} : a \to f_h(a)$, $\forall h \in \{1 \ldots m\}$.

PROMETHEE II is a widely used method [1,2], which provides the DM with a complete ranking over the set $A$. . The net flow $\Phi(a)$ associated with an action $a \in A$ is defined by: $\Phi(a) = \frac{1}{n-1} \sum_{b \in A \backslash a} \sum_{h=1}^{m} w_h \left( P_h(a,b) - P_h(b,a) \right)$, where $w_h$ and $P_h(a,b)$ are respectively the relative weight and the preference function (Fig. 1) for criteria $h \in \{1 \ldots m\}$. The net flow value induces a ranking over $A$.

For our study, we solely consider the "*V-shape*" preference function $P : A \times A \to \mathbb{R}_{[0,1]}$ (Fig. 1).

In the following, we will focus on the (elicitation of) parameters that express a decision maker's preferences into a set of quantified parameters. The nature, meaning, and amount of such parameters depend on the problem size and the chosen preference model. As already mentioned, PROMETHEE II requires several types of preference parameters. In this paper, we only consider the elicitation of the criteria relative weights and assume that the indifference and preferences thresholds are given by the decision maker.

## 3    Experimental Setup

Our goal of determining the information structure required for reaching a satisfying quality of the preference parameters raises some preliminary questions:

1. We have to explain in more detail what we mean by ***information structure*** in the context of a aggregation-disaggregation method: When eliciting a DM's preferences by this approach, he is asked to provide (partial) information about his preferences. Based on these, the parameters of the chosen preference model, i.e., the weights of PROMETHEE II in our case, will be approximated. However, the information can take several *forms*: pairwise

comparisons of actions, rankings of sub-sets of actions and/or weights, etc. On the other hand, the quality of the elicitation process is also influenced by the *quantity* of information provided (e.g. the number of pairwise comparisons). Since both aspects — *form* and *quantity* — are closely related, we call this the *information structure*. It describes *how* the DM has to provide the information. Let us consider for instance a set of actions $A$ and two information structures:

(a) we provide $K_{\mathrm{PAC}}^a$ comparisons of pairs of actions;
(b) we provide a ranking on a subset of $K_{\mathrm{ASR}}^a$ actions of $A$: $\left(a_{i_1} \ldots a_{i_{k'}}\right)$.

2. We also need to specify our definition of **how to measure the quality** of a set of preference parameters. As already mentioned, the main assumption that underlies our experimental approach is that a DM *knows* his preferred ranking, but is unable to express the parameter values in a formalized way. Since our aim is to study the relation between the information structure and the minimum reachable quality of an elicitation procedure, we have to define some measure for that quality. As we are handling and comparing *rankings*, we have decided to use Kendall's $\tau$ rank correlation. Practically, we compare a ranking $R$ (induced by a given weight vector $w$) with a reference ranking $R^\star$ that simulates the unformulated preferences of the DM. In the following we will use the notation $\tau_w$ as Kendall's $\tau$ between rankings $R$ and $R^\star$, respectively induced by $w$ and $w^\star$. We assume that the reference ranking is clear from the context. As already mentioned, we take a pessimistic point of view: indeed, we consider the worst possible value of Kendall's $\tau$ for the set of possible rankings $R$ with respect to $R^\star$.

We are now able to describe the actual experimental work-flow we follow in this work (Algo. 1).

Let us, for the sake of ease and representability (Fig. 2), consider a 3-criteria action set $A$. The evaluations for each criterion are generated based on a uniform random distribution. Let us also consider a set of constraints $\mathcal{C} = \{c_1 \ldots c_{K_{\mathrm{PAC}}^a}\}$. Each constraint $c_q = (i_q, j_q)$, with $q \in \{1 \ldots K_{\mathrm{PAC}}^a\}$, expresses that $a_{i_q} \succ a_{j_q}$. We will extend the approach to other forms of constraints below.

Each piece of information adds a linear constraint on the set of weights (Fig. 2(b)), which may reduce the domain of *compatible weight vectors*, i.e. where no constraint is violated. This area is denoted $\Omega_\mathcal{C}$ in the following; it is the area of the white polytope of Fig. 2(b) and it will be at the heart of our study.

For a first approach, we have chosen ($i$) to limit ourselves to problems with three criteria, and ($ii$) to work on a representative sample of weight vectors from $\Omega_\mathcal{C}$ instead of considering the whole continuous domain.

We now have a sampled set $\mathcal{W}_\mathcal{C}$ of weight vectors that satisfy all constraints. As already mentioned briefly in the introduction, we follow a pessimistic approach: we use the one weight vector associated with the most distant ranking from the reference ranking, i.e., with the smallest value of Kendall's $\tau$:

$$\underline{w} = \operatorname*{argmin}_{w \in \mathcal{W}_\mathcal{C}} \tau_w$$

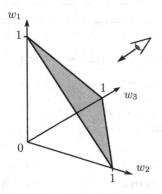
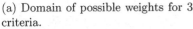
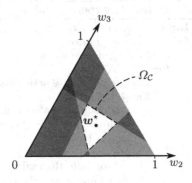

(a) Domain of possible weights for 3 criteria.

(b) Example of constraint statisfaction areas for 4 constraints.

**Fig. 2.** Representation with 3 criteria. The dot on the right plot represents the reference weight $w^\star$. The surrounding white polytope represents the domain of weight vectors $\Omega_C$ that satisfy all constraints. The darker an area, the more constraints are violated inside that area.

Since we use a stochastic approach to determine $\underline{w}$, we repeat the process a given number *trials* of times to describe the distribution of reachable quality as a function of information structure (type and quantity). For each trial, the set of actions as well as the constraints are randomly generated (Algo. 1).

For our tests, we consider two types of partial preference information:

**Pairwise Action Comparisons (PAC).** Each constraint $c_q = (i_q, j_q)$, with $q \in \{1 \ldots K_{PAC}^a\}$, expresses that $a_{i_q} \succ a_{j_q}$. This is a very basic and one of the most common ways of providing partial preference information. In our experimental approach, PAC-constraints are generated by randomly selecting $K_{PAC}^a$ different pairs of actions and reordering each pair $(a_{i_q}, a_{j_q})$ to be compatible with their relative order in the reference ranking $R^\star$;

**Action Sub-rankings (ASR).** We consider a sub-ranking $c = (i_1 \ldots i_{K_{ASR}^a})$ that expresses that $a_{i_1} \succ a_{i_2} \succ \ldots \succ a_{i_{K_{ASR}^a}}$. Practically, we generate a random permutation of $K_{ASR}^a$ randomly selected elements of $A$ (based on a uniform distribution) and reorder them so that the actions appear in the same order as in the reference ranking $R^\star$.

The information contained in the $ASR$ information structure can be converted into $PAC$. For instance, having a sub-ranking of three actions $a \succ b \succ c$, we can convert it into the transitive closure of all contained pairwise comparisons: $a \succ b, a \succ c, b \succ c$. This allows us, further in the results sections, to use a common scale for the quantity of information, by transforming the size of a sub-ranking into a number of pairwise comparisons: $K_{ASR}^a = \frac{1}{2} K_{PAC}^a (K_{PAC}^a - 1)$.

---

**Algorithm 1.** Experimental process

**Input**: $n$, $m$, $trials$, $\boldsymbol{K}^a$, $\boldsymbol{K}^w$
**for** $i = 1 \ldots trials$ **do**
    randomly generate set of actions $A_i$ and a reference weight vector $\boldsymbol{w}_i^\star$;
    **for** $k^a \in \boldsymbol{K}^a$ **do**
        randomly generate action constraints $aConst$;
        **for** $k^w \in \boldsymbol{K}^w$ **do**
            randomly generate weight constraints $wConst$;
            compute a set $\mathcal{W}_C$ of compatible weight vectors $\{\boldsymbol{w}_1 \ldots \boldsymbol{w}_{samples}\}$;
            $\tau_{\min} = 1$;
            **for** $s = 1 \ldots |\mathcal{W}_C|$ **do**
                compute the ranking $R_s$ based on $\boldsymbol{w}_s$;
                compute $\tau_{\boldsymbol{w}_s}$, the Kendall $\tau$ rank correlation between $R_s$ and $R^\star$;
                $\tau_{\min} = \min\left(\tau_{\min}, \tau_{\boldsymbol{w}_s}\right)$;
            **end**
            add $\tau_{\min}$ to statistics for action-weight constraint pair $(k^a, k^w)$;
        **end**
    **end**
**end**

---

Additionally to these two types of preference information, we also use partial information on the ranking of criteria. This information is to be provided as sub-ranking of $\boldsymbol{K}^w$ criteria, expressing, for instance, that criterion 1 is more important than criterion 3, which in turn is more important than criterion 2. This is formally stated as $w_1 \geq w_3 \geq w_2$. We want to study the possible impact of this additional parameter on the results. In our tests, we thus run the procedure with sub-rankings of criteria from zero to $m$ elements.

For the experiments we have used the following parameters: (1) randomly generated instances of $n = 10$ actions evaluated on $m = 3$ criteria, (2) $K^a_{\text{PAC}} \in \{1 \ldots \frac{n(n-1)}{2}\}$ (resp. $K^a_{\text{ASR}} \in \{2 \ldots n\}$) action constraints, (3) $\boldsymbol{K}^w \in \{0, 2, 3\}$ weight constraints, and (4) $trials = 500$ trials.

## 4 Results

As described in the previous section, we study the relationship between the information structure and the quality that can be reached in terms of ranking. Several aspects are taken into consideration in this section:
1) *"How can the relationship between the number of constraints and the size of the compatible polytope be characterized?"*

By determining the ratio of the polytope's area of constraint compatible weights over the area of all possible weight vectors $\frac{\Omega_C}{\Omega}$, we get an indication of how restrictive the constraints actually are. Although that computation is exact (for three criteria), it still depends on both the set of actions and the set of constraints, and, thus, we use a stochastic approach for this indicator. The average evolution of the ratio of compatible weights (for a given number of weight

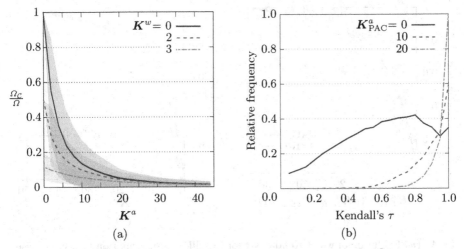

(a)                                                            (b)

**Fig. 3.** (a) Evolution of the ratio of compatible weight domain area $\frac{\Omega_C}{\Omega}$ with respect to the whole domain of possible weights $\Omega$, depending on the number of action constraints $K^a$, for different numbers of weight constraints $K^w$. Results are shown for 1000 randomly generated action sets ($n = 10$, $m = 3$) and PAC constraint sets. — (b) Distribution of all values of Kendall's $\tau$ in the compatible weights domain $\Omega_C$, for respectively $K^a_{\text{PAC}} = 0$, 10, and 20 pairwise action comparisons. No constraints on the weights relative importance are given here ($K^w = 0$).

constraints $K^w$) with an increasing number of action constraints $K^a$ (Fig. 3(a)) shows that: ($i$) the domain of compatible weights is rapidly decreasing for the first added action constraints; ($ii$) providing some constraints on the weights has a high impact on the compatible domain when only few action constraints are given.

**2)** *"Since we use the worst Kendall's $\tau$ to evaluate an information structure, what is the distribution of Kendall's $\tau$ values for a set of compatible weights?"*

We present the distribution of Kendall's $\tau$ for compatible weight parameters in the case of 0, 10, and 20 pairwise action comparisons (Fig. 3(b)). As expected, the distribution tends to be concentrated more closely at the maximum value ($\tau_{\max} = 1$) when the number of constraints is increasing. The plots show that we are considering a very pessimistic case for our quality measure, as we take the worse value of Kendall's $\tau$, the probabiliy of occurence of which is marginal.

**3)** *"What is the influence of the preference information **type** on the quality?"*

We compare (Fig. 4(a)) the evolution for two different types of information structures: pairwise action comparisons (PAC) and action sub-ranking (ASR). For the latter, as previously described, the number of constraints $K^a_{\text{ASR}}$ (size of the provided sub-rank) has been transformed into an equivalent number of pairwise comparisons. The very similar results could suggest that, at least for the studied information structures, the type of preferential information does not influence the quality of the results. Another aspect, although intuitively foreseeable (based, for instance, on the observations on the ratio of compatible

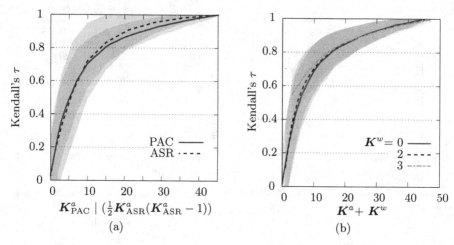

**Fig. 4.** (a) Evolution of worst Kendall's $\tau$ for two different information types: pairwise action comparisons (PAC) and action sub-ranking (ASR). — (b) Impact of "weight constraints" on the reachable quality for pairwise action comparisons (PAC). Note that the $x$-axis represents the sum of action *and* weight constraints, i.e. $K^a + K^w$.

weights), is that the first few provided constraints contribute much more to improving the result's quality than the last one: the "marginal usefulness" of the last possible pairwise comparisons tend to zero. Let us note that the relatively high value of Kendall's $\tau$ for one constraint could question the use of our measure. Another metric could be looked for in a future work.

**4)** *"What is the influence of imposing a partial ranking on the criteria's weights?"*

If we account for the quantity of preferential information on weight sub-ranks in the same way as for action comparisons (either pairwise or sub-ranks), the impact of using sub-ranks of criteria weights on the quality seems only noticeable (Fig. 4(b)) if the DM provides a ranking on three weights, and only as long as the number of action constraints is less than approximatively 10 pairwise comparisons. This suggests that a maximum amount of information on the weights relative ranking should be given first, then gradually adding action based comparisons. Further experiments should be run with different settings to confirm if this observation can be generalized.

**5)** *"Does increasing the number of constraints always yield better results?"*

We have performed some statistical tests to evaluate, for a given number of constraints, if adding a further constraint provides a significantly better result. Practically, we have used one-tailed, two-sample $t$-tests to compare the results for $k$ constraints, with those for $(k + 1)$ constraints (Fig. 5). The generally low p-values (maximum being at 14%) suggest that providing one additional action constraint increases the quality of the elicitation process almost at every stage of the process.

**6)** *"Is it possible to determine the amount of information the DM should provide in order to reach a chosen level of quality for the elicitation process?"*

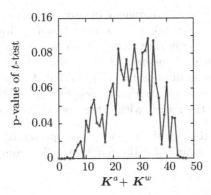

**Fig. 5.** p-values of one-tailed, two-sample $t$-tests to see if the results for $(k + 1)$ constraints are significantly better than for $k$ constraints. Plots are shown for $K^w = 3$.

**Table 1.** Number of pairwise action comparisons that have to be given by a DM to reach the desired level of quality $\underline{w}$, assuming that $K^w$ weight constraints have already been provided. The results are shown for randomly generated 3-criteria action sets with a uniform distribution.

| $K^w$ | $w$ | | | | | | |
|---|---|---|---|---|---|---|---|
| | 0.50 | 0.60 | 0.70 | 0.80 | 0.90 | 0.95 | 0.99 |
| 0 | 6 | 8 | 10 | 15 | 25 | 34 | 43 |
| 2 | 4 | 6 | 9 | 14 | 24 | 33 | 43 |
| 3 | 0 | 1 | 5 | 11 | 22 | 32 | 42 |

This is the main question the present paper intends to answer. From our observations so far, it seems that we could provide the DM with this kind of information for a given type of action sets. This can be graphically deduced, for instance, from Fig. 4(b), or alternatively be given as a table (e.g., Table 1).

## 5 Conclusion

When using a aggregation-disaggregation method for eliciting a decision makers preferences, there is a certain amount of uncertainty that inevitably comes with the process and its results. In particular, our aim has been to investigate, for the PROMETHEE II method, how the *quality* of such an elicitation result could be assessed. This has led us to also look at the structure of the domain of weights that are compatible with all partial preferential information provided so far by the decision maker. As outcome, we propose an approach that gives the DM prescriptive indications about how much partial preferential information he has to provide in order to reach a chosen quality for the preference parameters. The first approach described in this paper opens questions and offers opportunities for further investigations. To mention only a few:

- We could explore alternative quality measures to Kendall's $\tau$;
- Other distributions of action evaluations should be investigated: we so far have only considered uniformly distributed evaluations. What would happen if the evaluations were "clustered" (on one ore more criteria)? We also only consider continuous evaluation functions. What if some or all were discrete?
- Alternative preference information structures could be considered;
- We could compare the results with other preference models (weighted sum).

We are currently investigating the impact on the presented results when using a guided query selection scheme for the pairwise action comparisons rather than a random one.

**Acknowledgments.** Stefan Eppe acknowledges support from the META-X Arc project, funded by the Scientific Research Directorate of the French Community of Belgium.

# References

1. Behzadian, M., Kazemzadeh, R.B., Albadvi, A., Aghdasi, M.: PROMETHEE: A comprehensive literature review on methodologies and applications. European Journal of Operational Research 200(1), 198–215 (2010)
2. Brans, J.-P., Mareschal, B.: PROMETHEE methods. In: Figueira, J.R., Greco, S., Ehrgott, M. (eds.) Multiple Criteria Decision Analysis, State of the Art Surveys, ch. 5, pp. 163–195. Springer (2005)
3. Eppe, S., De Smet, Y., Stützle, T.: A Bi-objective Optimization Model to Eliciting Decision Maker's Preferences for the PROMETHEE II Method. In: Brafman, R.I., Roberts, F., Tsoukiás, A. (eds.) ADT 2011. LNCS, vol. 6992, pp. 56–66. Springer, Heidelberg (2011)
4. Frikha, H., Chabchoub, H., Martel, J.-M.: Inferring criteria's relative importance coefficients in PROMETHEE II. International Journal of Operational Research 7(2), 257–275 (2010)
5. Greco, S., Kadziński, M., Mousseau, V., Słowiński, R.: ELECTRE$^{GKMS}$: Robust ordinal regression for outranking methods. European Journal of Operational Research 214(1), 118–135 (2011)
6. Kadziński, M., Greco, S., Słowiński, R.: Extreme ranking analysis in robust ordinal regression. Omega 40(4), 488–501 (2012)
7. Lahdelma, R., Hokkanen, J., Salminen, P.: SMAA - Stochastic multiobjective acceptability analysis. European Journal of Operational Research (1998)
8. Mousseau, V.: Elicitation des préférences pour l'aide multicritère à la décision. PhD thesis, Université Paris-Dauphine, Paris, France (2003)

# Fuzzy IRR with Fuzzy WACC and Fuzzy MARR

Esra Bas

Istanbul Technical University, Department of Industrial Engineering, Macka,
Istanbul, Turkey
atace@itu.edu.tr

**Abstract.** In this paper, several uncertainties are considered for investment acceptability decision by IRR method. First, some parameters in weighted average cost of capital (WACC) equation are assumed to be fuzzy numbers, a fuzzy WACC is obtained, and defuzzified by t-norm and t-conorm fuzzy relations. Assuming that WACC is a minimum threshold for minimum attractive rate of return (MARR), fuzzy MARR is determined to be greater than or equals to fuzzy WACC. Finally, by assuming the net cash flows to be fuzzy numbers, a fuzzy IRR formula is obtained, defuzzified by t-norm and t-conorm fuzzy relations, and the results are compared to fuzzy MARR to evaluate the acceptability of a pure and simple investment. This study is an extension of Bas (2008) where t-norm and t-conorm fuzzy relations are considered for the defuzzification of fuzzy IRR formula.

**Keywords:** Fuzzy WACC, fuzzy MARR, fuzzy IRR, t-norm/t-conorm fuzzy relations.

## 1   Introduction

Weighted average cost of capital (WACC) is a method of calculating cost of capital for a firm by assigning weights to two components of cost of capital: Cost of debt and cost of equity (White et al., 2010). Minimum attractive rate of return (MARR) is a threshold rate of return for evaluating a project's acceptability, and WACC is generally accepted as the lower limit of the MARR (White et al., 2010). Internal rate of return (IRR) is a popular method for project evaluation, and defined as the rate of return at which the total discounted positive net cash flows are equal to the total discounted negative net cash flows. As a general rule, if the IRR of a project is higher than MARR, then the project is accepted, otherwise it is rejected or the investor stays indifferent.

Although IRR is a popular practical approach for simple investment analysis, some shortcomings hinder its benefits. Two examples are multiple rates of return and high sensitivity of the results to the changes in net cash flows, WACC, and MARR. The concern of this paper is an integrated uncertainty consideration with respect to investment evaluation by IRR approach. In this approach, not only the uncertainty in positive and negative cash flows of IRR formula, but also uncertainty in calculating WACC, and determining a MARR value are covered. The literature in uncertainty consideration with respect to IRR formula is relatively rich: Buckley et al. (2002)

S. Greco et al. (Eds.): IPMU 2012, Part IV, CCIS 300, pp. 393–402, 2012.
© Springer-Verlag Berlin Heidelberg 2012

proposed a fuzzy IRR for a simple project with fuzzy net cash flows, and proposed to solve the problem by α-cut of fuzzy net cash flows. Bas (2008) proposed fuzzy t-norm and t-conorm relations for the defuzzification of IRR formula with net cash flows as fuzzy numbers. Sarper et al. (2010) considered net cash flows as random variables, and calculated probability density function of IRR for pure and simple investment with single period and two periods of project life. Carmichael (2011) proposed markov chain theory to present value method by considering discount rate, cash flows and project life as uncertain, and extended it to IRR calculation. However, to the best of our knowledge, an integrated uncertainty consideration from WACC formula to IRR formula has been neglected. Specifically, uncertainty consideration in WACC formula has even been relatively scarce, and one application of fuzzy set theory to WACC has been by Wang and Hwang (2010). This paper is basically an extension of Bas (2008). In Bas (2008), t-norm and t-conorm fuzzy relations were considered for defuzzification of present-value formulation with fuzzy net cash flows, and the IRR was compared with fuzzy MARR by proposed decision rules. However, in this paper, possible fuzziness in WACC is also considered to be set as a lower limit of fuzzy MARR for a whole uncertainty consideration in finding the IRR of a simple and pure project.

In this paper, fuzzy approach is used for uncertainty consideration in WACC formula, MARR value, IRR formula, and t-norm and t-conorm fuzzy relations are used for the defuzzification. The structure of the paper is as follows: In Section 2, t-norm and t-conorm fuzzy relations are briefly reviewed. In Section 3, the structure of the proposed methodology and the details are given. In Section 4, the proposed methodology is illustrated with a numerical example. Finally, in Section 5, results are discussed.

## 2    T-Norm and T-Conorm Fuzzy Relations

It is not the scope of this study to provide a comprehensive review of fuzzy logic and t-norm and t-conorm fuzzy relations, and the reader is referred to the literature specifically designed for their theory (for example see Ross, 1995; Inuiguchi et al., 2003). Some basics of fuzzy theory and basic formulations of t-norm and t-conorm fuzzy relations relevant to the paper are provided as follows:

An α-cut of fuzzy set $\tilde{A}$ is defined as $\left[\tilde{A}\right]_\alpha = \left\{x \in X \big| \mu_{\tilde{A}}(x) \geq \alpha\right\}$ and strict α-cut of fuzzy set $\tilde{A}$ is defined as $(\tilde{A})_\alpha = \left\{x \in X \big| \mu_{\tilde{A}}(x) > \alpha\right\}$, where $\mu_{\tilde{A}}(x)$ is the membership function of fuzzy set $\tilde{A}$ (Inuiguchi et al., 2003; Bas and Kahraman, 2009; Bas, 2011).

If T=min is a t-norm, and S=max is a t-conorm, then the following identities hold (Inuiguchi et al., 2003; Bas and Kahraman, 2009; Bas, 2011):

$$\mu_{\tilde{\leq}_T}(\tilde{A},\tilde{B}) \geq \alpha \quad \text{iff} \quad \inf\left[\tilde{A}\right]_\alpha \leq \sup\left[\tilde{B}\right]_\alpha \tag{1}$$

$$\mu_{\tilde{\leq}_S}(\tilde{A},\tilde{B}) \geq \alpha \quad \text{iff} \quad \sup(\tilde{A})_{1-\alpha} \leq \inf(\tilde{B})_{1-\alpha} \tag{2}$$

# 3     Structure of the Proposed Methodology

The general structure of the paper is illustrated in Fig.1. A fuzzy WACC is proposed, and a fuzzy MARR is assigned based on fuzzy WACC. The net cash flows are assumed to be fuzzy in IRR equation, and the fuzzy IRR is compared to fuzzy MARR to evaluate the acceptability of the project.

Fig. 1. The general structure of the study

## 3.1     Fuzzy WACC

Although several WACC formulations are possible in crisp case, the following WACC equation will be considered for the study (White et al., 2010):

$$WACC = (E/V)i_e + (D/V)i_d(1-t) \tag{3}$$

In eq.(1), $E$ is total equity, $D$ is total debt and leases, $V=E+D$ is total invested capital, $i_e$ is cost of equity in percent, $i_d$ is cost of debt and leases in percent, and t is corporate tax rate (White et al., 2010). It is assumed that only some selected parameters in eq.(3) are fuzzy numbers as in Wang and Hwang (2010):

$$WA\tilde{C}C = (E/V)\tilde{i}_e + (D/V)\tilde{i}_d(1-\tilde{t}) \tag{4}$$

As in Wang and Hwang (2010), any fuzzy number in eq.(4) is assumed to be trapezoidal fuzzy number such that $\tilde{i}_e = (i_{e1}, i_{e2}, i_{e3}, i_{e4})$, $\tilde{i}_d = (i_{d1}, i_{d2}, i_{d3}, i_{d4})$, and $\tilde{t} = (t_1, t_2, t_3, t_4)$. Note that any trapezoidal fuzzy number $\tilde{F}$ can be reduced to triangular fuzzy number by $i_{e2} = i_{e3}$, $i_{d2} = i_{d3}$, and $t_2 = t_3$.

**Defuzzification by t-Norm Fuzzy Relation**

$$\inf[WA\tilde{C}C]_\alpha = (E/V)\inf[\tilde{i}_e]_\alpha + (D/V)\inf[\tilde{i}_d]_\alpha(1-\sup[\tilde{t}]_\alpha) \tag{5}$$

**Defuzzification by t-conorm Fuzzy Relation**

$$\sup(WA\tilde{C}C)_{1-\alpha} = (E/V)\sup(\tilde{i}_e)_{1-\alpha} + (D/V)\sup(\tilde{i}_d)_{1-\alpha}(1-\inf(\tilde{t})_{1-\alpha}) \tag{6}$$

and finally

$$[WA\tilde{C}C]_\alpha = [\inf[WA\tilde{C}C]_\alpha, \sup(WA\tilde{C}C)_{\alpha'}] \tag{7}$$

where $\alpha' = 1 - \alpha$, and is set to be such that $\alpha' = \alpha$ for each $\left[WA\widetilde{C}C\right]_\alpha$. It should be noted that, although $\alpha' = 1 - \alpha$ is by definition, the values for $\alpha'$ and $\alpha$ such that $\alpha' = \alpha$ are used for $\alpha$-cut of fuzzy set $\left[WA\widetilde{C}C\right]_\alpha$.

## 3.2    Fuzzy MARR

Although several criteria are possible to determine the MARR value of a firm, in this paper, it is assumed that the only criterion of MARR is to be at least as high as WACC as follows:

$$MA\widetilde{R}R \gtrsim WA\widetilde{C}C \tag{8}$$

**Defuzzification by t-Norm Fuzzy Relation**

$$\sup \left[MA\widetilde{R}R\right]_\alpha \gtrsim \inf \left[WA\widetilde{C}C\right]_\alpha \tag{9}$$

**Defuzzification by t-Conorm Fuzzy Relation**

$$\inf (MA\widetilde{R}R)_{1-\alpha} \gtrsim \sup (WA\widetilde{C}C)_{1-\alpha} \tag{10}$$

and finally

$$\left[MA\widetilde{R}R\right]_\alpha = \left[\sup \left[MA\widetilde{R}R\right]_\alpha, \inf (MA\widetilde{R}R)_{\alpha'}\right] \tag{11}$$

where $\alpha' = 1 - \alpha$, and is set to be such that $\alpha' = \alpha$ for each $\left[MA\widetilde{R}R\right]_\alpha$. It should be noted that, although $\alpha' = 1 - \alpha$ is by definition, the values for $\alpha'$ and $\alpha$ such that $\alpha' = \alpha$ are used for $\alpha$-cut of fuzzy set $\left[MA\widetilde{R}R\right]_\alpha$.

## 3.3    Fuzzy IRR

In this paper, a pure and simple project is considered to avoid the problem of possible multiple rates of return. A simple project is defined with a single sign change of net cash flows, while a pure project is defined as a project with non-positive project balances at its IRR for each time period during its project life (Park and Sharp-Bette, 1990). It is sufficient that a project is simple to ensure that there is at most one positive IRR value, and this property stays valid if the net cash flows are converted to fuzzy numbers. The solution of the following net present value (NPV) equation provides internal rate of return in crisp case (Park and Sharp-Bette, 1990):

$$NPV\,(i^*) = \sum_{n=0}^{N} \frac{F_n}{(1+i^*)^n} = 0 \tag{12}$$

In eq.(12), $F_n$ is net cash flow at time $n$, $N$ is project life, and $i^*$ is internal rate of return. The fuzzy version of eq. (12) with all net cash flows as fuzzy numbers is given as follows:

$$NPV(i^*) = \sum_{n=0}^{N} \frac{\tilde{F}_n}{(1+i^*)^n} = 0 \qquad (13)$$

Bas (2008) proposed the net cash flows in IRR equation to be symmetric and strictly convex triangular fuzzy numbers. However, in this paper, net cash flows are assumed to be trapezoidal fuzzy numbers such that $\tilde{F}_n = (F_{n1}, F_{n2}, F_{n3}, F_{n4})$ for $n = 0,1,2,\ldots\ldots, N$.

**Defuzzification by t-Norm Fuzzy Relation**

$$NPV\left(\left[\tilde{i}_1^*\right]_\alpha\right) = \sum_{n=0}^{N} \frac{\inf\left[\tilde{F}_n\right]_\alpha}{(1+\left[\tilde{i}_1^*\right]_\alpha)^n} = 0 \qquad (14)$$

**Defuzzification by t-Conorm Fuzzy Relation.**

$$NPV\left(\left(\tilde{i}_2^*\right)_{\alpha'}\right) = \sum_{n=0}^{N} \frac{\sup\left(\tilde{F}_n\right)_{1-\alpha}}{(1+\left(\tilde{i}_2^*\right)_{\alpha'})^n} = 0 \qquad (15)$$

and finally,

$$\left[\tilde{i}^*\right]_\alpha = \left[\left[\tilde{i}_1^*\right]_\alpha, \left(\tilde{i}_2^*\right)_{\alpha'}\right] \qquad (16)$$

where $\alpha' = 1 - \alpha$, and is set to be such that $\alpha' = \alpha$ for each $\left[\tilde{i}^*\right]_\alpha$. It should be noted that, although $\alpha' = 1 - \alpha$ is by definition, the values for $\alpha'$ and $\alpha$ such that $\alpha' = \alpha$ are used for $\alpha$-cut of fuzzy set $\left[\tilde{i}^*\right]_\alpha$. It should also be noted that infimum and supremum properties are defined for all fuzzy net cash flows with positive or negative sign to ensure that $\left[\tilde{i}_1^*\right]_\alpha < \left(\tilde{i}_2^*\right)_{\alpha'}$ for each $\tilde{i}^*$.

### 3.4    Decision Rules

In this paper, the following acceptability rule for a project is assumed:

If $\tilde{i}^* \geq M\tilde{A}RR$, accept the project.

**Defuzzification by t-Norm Fuzzy Relation**
If the following condition holds, then accept the project:

$$\left(\tilde{i}_2^*\right)_{\alpha'} \geq \sup\left[M\tilde{A}RR\right]_\alpha \qquad (17)$$

**Defuzzification by t-Conorm Fuzzy Relation**

If the following condition holds, then accept the project:

$$\left[\tilde{i}_1^{\,*}\right]_\alpha \geq \inf(\widetilde{MARR})_{\alpha'} \tag{18}$$

## 4    Numerical Example

The cost of debt is \$100.000 and the cost of equity is \$200.000 in the firm. The fuzzy values are assumed to be $\tilde{i}_d = (0.085, 0.09, 0.095, 0.10)$, $\tilde{i}_e = (0.15, 0.16, 0.165, 0.17)$ and $\tilde{t} = (0.45, 0.47, 0.49, 0.51)$ for WACC formula. The cash flow stream of a project with 4 year project life is assumed to be as follows: $\tilde{F}_0 = (-110, -100, -95, -90)$, $\tilde{F}_1 = (15, 20, 25, 30)$, $\tilde{F}_2 = (35, 40, 45, 50)$, $\tilde{F}_3 = (30, 35, 40, 45)$ and $\tilde{F}_4 = (35, 40, 45, 50)$.

### 4.1    Fuzzy WACC

$$(WA\tilde{C}C)_\alpha = \left[\inf\,\left[WA\tilde{C}C\right]_\alpha, \sup\,(WA\tilde{C}C)_{\alpha'}\right]$$

is calculated for the numerical example with

$\inf\left[WA\tilde{C}C\right]_\alpha = (200000\,/(200000 + 100000\,)) \inf\left[\tilde{i}_e\right]_\alpha + (100000\,/(200000 + 100000\,)) \inf\left[\tilde{i}_d\right]_\alpha (1 - \sup\left[\tilde{t}\right]_\alpha)$

$\qquad = (200000\,/(200000 + 100000\,))(0.01\alpha + 0.15) +$

$\qquad\qquad (100000\,/(200000 + 100000\,))(0.085 + 0.005\alpha)(1 - (0.51 - 0.02\alpha))$

$\qquad = 0.667(0.01\alpha + 0.15) + 0.333(0.085 + 0.005\alpha)(1 - (0.51 - 0.02\alpha)) =$

$\qquad = 0.0000333\,\alpha^2 + 0.00805\,\alpha + 0.113$

$\sup\,(WA\tilde{C}C)_{1-\alpha} = ((200000\,/(200000 + 100000\,)) \sup\,(\tilde{i}_e)_{1-\alpha} +$

$\qquad\qquad ((100000\,/(200000 + 100000\,)) \sup\,(\tilde{i}_d)_{1-\alpha}(1 - \inf\,(\tilde{t})_{1-\alpha})$

$\qquad = (200000\,/(200000 + 100000\,))(0.17 - 0.005(1-\alpha)) +$

$\qquad\qquad (100000\,/(200000 + 100000\,))(0.10 - 0.005(1-\alpha))(1 - (0.45 + 0.02(1-\alpha))$

$\qquad = 0.000633\,\alpha^2 + 0.02015\,\alpha + 0.111$

The results of fuzzy WACC for selected α-cut values are given in Table 1.

**Table 1.** Fuzzy WACC

| α - cut | $\inf\left[WA\tilde{C}C\right]_\alpha$ | $\sup(WA\tilde{C}C)_{\alpha'}$ |
|---------|------------------|-----------------|
| 0.0 | 11.39% | 13.18% |
| 0.1 | 11.47% | 12.96% |
| 0.2 | 11.55% | 12.75% |
| 0.3 | 11.63% | 12.54% |
| 0.4 | 11.71% | 12.33% |
| 0.5 | 11.79% | 12.12% |
| 0.6 | 11.87% | 11.92% |
| 0.7 | 11.95% | 11.71% |
| 0.8 | 12.03% | 11.51% |
| 0.9 | 12.12% | 11.30% |
| 1.0 | 12.20% | 11.10% |

**Remark 1.** Note that $WA\tilde{C}C$ is not a fuzzy number. It can also be interpreted as a subnormal triangular fuzzy number with a height of 0.6.

## 4.2  Fuzzy MARR

$$\left[MA\tilde{R}R\right]_\alpha = \left[\sup \left[MA\tilde{R}R\right]_\alpha, \inf \left(MA\tilde{R}R\right)_{\alpha'}\right]$$

is calculated for the numerical example with

$$\inf (MA\tilde{R}R)_{1-\alpha} \gtrsim \sup (WA\tilde{C}C)_{1-\alpha}$$

$$\inf (MA\tilde{R}R)_{1-\alpha} \geq 0.000633\alpha^2 + 0.02015\alpha + 0.111$$

and

$$\sup \left[MA\tilde{R}R\right]_\alpha \gtrsim \inf \left[WA\tilde{C}C\right]_\alpha$$

$$\sup \left[MA\tilde{R}R\right]_\alpha \geq 0.0000333\alpha^2 + 0.00805\alpha + 0.113$$

If a 50% percent of increase over WACC value is assumed, then

$$\inf \left[MA\tilde{R}R\right]_{1-\alpha} = (0.000633\,\alpha^2 + 0.02015\,\alpha + 0.111) + 0.5(0.000633\,\alpha^2 + 0.02015\,\alpha + 0.111)$$
$$= 0.00095\,\alpha^2 + 0.03\,\alpha + 0.166$$

$$\sup \left[MA\tilde{R}R\right]_\alpha = (0.0000333\,\alpha^2 + 0.00805\,\alpha + 0.113) + 0.5(0.0000333\,\alpha^2 + 0.00805\,\alpha + 0.113)$$
$$= 0.00005\,\alpha^2 + 0.012075\,\alpha + 0.1695$$

The results of fuzzy MARR for some selected $\alpha$-cut values are given in Table 2.

**Table 2.** Fuzzy MARR

| $\alpha$-cut | $\sup \left[MA\tilde{R}R\right]_\alpha$ | $\inf(MA\tilde{R}R)_{\alpha'}$ |
|:---:|:---:|:---:|
| 0.0 | 16.95% | 19.75% |
| 0.1 | 17.07% | 19.43% |
| 0.2 | 17.19% | 19.11% |
| 0.3 | 17.31% | 18.79% |
| 0.4 | 17.43% | 18.48% |
| 0.5 | 17.56% | 18.17% |
| 0.6 | 17.68% | 17.86% |
| 0.7 | 17.80% | 17.55% |
| 0.8 | 17.92% | 17.24% |
| 0.9 | 18.04% | 16.94% |
| 1.0 | 18.16% | 16.63% |

Remark 2. Note that $M\widetilde{ARR}$ is also not a fuzzy number. It can also be interpreted as a subnormal triangular fuzzy number with a height of 0.6.

### 4.3    Fuzzy IRR

$$\left[\tilde{i}^*\right]_\alpha = \left[\left[\tilde{i}_1^*\right]_\alpha, \left(\tilde{i}_2^*\right)_{\alpha'}\right]$$

is calculated for the numerical example with selected α-cut values as given in Table 3 and Table 4.

**Table 3.** Fuzzy IRR

| α-cut | $\inf\left[\widetilde{F}_n\right]_\alpha$ | | | | | $\left[\tilde{i}_1^*\right]_\alpha$ |
|---|---|---|---|---|---|---|
| | $n=0$ | $n=1$ | $n=2$ | $n=3$ | $n=4$ | |
| 0.0 | -110 | 15 | 35 | 30 | 35 | 2% |
| 0.1 | -109 | 16 | 36 | 31 | 36 | 3% |
| 0.2 | -108 | 16 | 36 | 31 | 36 | 4% |
| 0.3 | -107 | 17 | 37 | 32 | 37 | 5% |
| 0.4 | -106 | 17 | 37 | 32 | 37 | 6% |
| 0.5 | -105 | 18 | 38 | 33 | 38 | 7% |
| 0.6 | -104 | 18 | 38 | 33 | 38 | 8% |
| 0.7 | -103 | 19 | 39 | 34 | 39 | 9% |
| 0.8 | -102 | 19 | 39 | 34 | 39 | 10% |
| 0.9 | -101 | 20 | 40 | 35 | 40 | 11% |
| 1.0 | -100 | 20 | 40 | 35 | 40 | 12% |

**Table 4.** Fuzzy IRR *(cont.)*

| α | $\sup(\widetilde{F}_n)_{1-\alpha}$ | | | | | $\left(\tilde{i}_2^*\right)_{\alpha'}$ |
|---|---|---|---|---|---|---|
| | $n=0$ | $n=1$ | $n=2$ | $n=3$ | $n=4$ | |
| 0.0 | -95 | 25 | 45 | 40 | 45 | 30% |
| 0.1 | -95 | 26 | 46 | 41 | 46 | 29% |
| 0.2 | -94 | 26 | 46 | 41 | 46 | 28% |
| 0.3 | -94 | 27 | 47 | 42 | 47 | 28% |
| 0.4 | -93 | 27 | 47 | 42 | 47 | 27% |
| 0.5 | -93 | 28 | 48 | 43 | 48 | 26% |
| 0.6 | -92 | 28 | 48 | 43 | 48 | 25% |
| 0.7 | -92 | 29 | 49 | 44 | 49 | 24% |
| 0.8 | -91 | 29 | 49 | 44 | 49 | 23% |
| 0.9 | -91 | 30 | 50 | 45 | 50 | 22% |
| 1.0 | -90 | 30 | 50 | 45 | 50 | 21% |

**4.4    Decision Rules**

According to the decision rules, results of comparison of fuzzy IRR to fuzzy MARR for selected α-cut values are summarized in Table 5.

**Table 5.** Results of comparison of fuzzy IRR to fuzzy MARR

| α | $\left[\tilde{i}_1^*\right]_\alpha$ | $\inf(M\tilde{A}\tilde{R}R)_{\alpha'}$ | $\left(\tilde{i}_2^*\right)_{\alpha'}$ | $\sup\left[M A\tilde{R}R\right]_\alpha$ |
|---|---|---|---|---|
| 0.0 | 2% | 19.75% | 30% | 16.95% |
| 0.1 | 3% | 19.43% | 29% | 17.07% |
| 0.2 | 4% | 19.11% | 28% | 17.19% |
| 0.3 | 5% | 18.79% | 28% | 17.31% |
| 0.4 | 6% | 18.48% | 27% | 17.43% |
| 0.5 | 7% | 18.17% | 26% | 17.56% |
| 0.6 | 8% | 17.86% | 25% | 17.68% |
| 0.7 | 9% | 17.55% | 24% | 17.80% |
| 0.8 | 10% | 17.24% | 23% | 17.92% |
| 0.9 | 11% | 16.94% | 22% | 18.04% |
| 1.0 | 12% | 16.63% | 21% | 18.16% |

According to the results in Table 5, project is not accepted for any α-cut value when using defuzzification by t-conorm fuzzy relation, while it is accepted for any α-cut value when using defuzzification by t-norm fuzzy relation. Fig.2 also illustrates the comparison of fuzzy numbers for MARR and IRR.

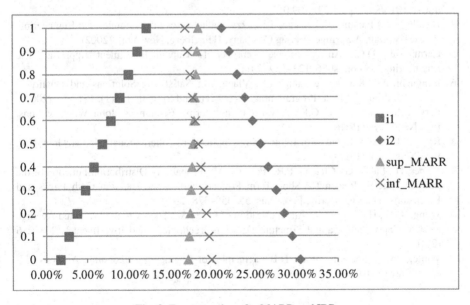

**Fig. 2.** Fuzzy numbers for MARR and IRR

Remark 3. Note that $\tilde{i}^*$ is a trapezoidal normal fuzzy number.

# 5    Conclusions

In this paper, an integrated uncertainty consideration from WACC formula to IRR formula is proposed for evaluating a pure and simple project. Not only uncertainty in cash flows of IRR formula, but also uncertainty in cost of equity, cost of debt and leases, and corporate tax rate in WACC formula are considered. Since an IRR is compared to MARR, which is selected to be at least equal to WACC, lack of uncertainty consideration in WACC and MARR may also give non-robust results, although uncertainty in IRR is considered. Although the methodology proposed is applicable, most investors are not likely to be in a purely optimistic position or purely pessimistic position. A methodology is proposed as a next research including consideration of adjustable flexibility in uncertainty of parameters.

# References

1. Bas, E.: Internal Rate of Return of Fuzzy Cash Flows Based on Pessimistic and Optimistic Fuzzy-Relation Approach. In: Proceedings of the 8th International FLINS Conference, Madrid, Spain, September 21-24. Proceedings Series on Computer Engineering and Information Science. World Scientific, New Jersey (2008)
2. Bas, E., Kahraman, C.: Fuzzy Capital Rationing Model. Journal of Computational and Applied Mathematics 224, 628–645 (2009)
3. Bas, E.: Surrogate Relaxation of a Fuzzy Multidimensional 0–1 Knapsack Model by Surrogate Constraint Normalization Rules and a Methodology for Multi-Attribute Project Portfolio Selection. Engineering Applications of Artificial Intelligence (2011), doi:10.1016/j.engappai.2011.09.015
4. Buckley, J.J., Eslami, E., Feuring, T.: Fuzzy Mathematics in Economics and Engineering. Physica-Verlag, A Springer-Verlag Company, Heidelberg, New York (2002)
5. Carmichael, D.G.: An Alternative Approach to Capital Investment Appraisal. The Engineering Economist 56, 123–139 (2011)
6. Inuiguchi, M., Ramik, J., Tanino, T., Vlach, M.: Satisficing Solutions and Duality in Interval and Fuzzy Linear Programming. Fuzzy Sets and Systems 135(1), 151–177 (2003)
7. Park, C.S., Sharp-Bette, G.P.: Advanced Engineering Economics. John Wiley & Sons, Inc., New York (1990)
8. Ross, T.J.: Fuzzy Logic with Engineering Applications, International edn. McGraw-Hill, Inc., New York (1995)
9. Sarper, H., Palak, G., Chacon, P.R., Fraser, J.M.: Probability Distribution Function of the Internal Rate of Return for Short-Term Projects with Some Random Cash Flows and Extensions. The Engineering Economist 55, 350–378 (2010)
10. Wang, S.-Y., Hwang, C.-C.: An Application of Fuzzy Set Theory to the Weighted Average Cost of Capital and Capital Structure Decision. Technology and Investment 1, 248–256 (2010)
11. White, J.A., Case, K.E., Pratt, D.B.: Principles of Engineering Economic Analysis, 5th edn. Wiley (2010)

# Risk Evaluation of Warehouse Operations Using Fuzzy FMEA

Alp Ustundag

Istanbul Technical University, Industrial Engineering Department
34367 Macka Istanbul, Turkey
ustundaga@itu.edu.tr

**Abstract.** Warehouse processes in supply chain operations contain risks which lead to a poor supply chain performance. Therefore, risk analysis in warehouse operations is a critical issue to increase both the supply chain efficiency and the customer service level. In this study, fuzzy FMEA method is used to evaluate the risks of warehouse operations. Ten failure factors are determined for warehouse operations of a food retail distributor. As the first five cause permanent shrinkage of products, the second five are related to the processes. According to the evaluations of the FMEA team members, fuzzy and crisp risk priority numbers (RPN) of ten failure factors are determined.

**Keywords:** risk evaluation, fuzzy FMEA, risk priority number (RPN), warehouse operations.

## 1 Introduction

Uncertainty about a situation can often indicate risk, which is possibility of loss, damage, or any other undesirable event. According to the Association of the Project Managers, risk is defined as an uncertain event or set of circumstances which, should it occur, will have an effect on achievement of one or more objectives. In this definition, the concepts namely the objectives, the occurrences and the impact are emphasized (Tuncel and Alpan, 2011). In supply chain point of view, risk sometimes interpreted as unreliable and uncertain resources creating supply chain interruption, where as uncertainty can be explained as matching risk between supply and demand in supply chain processes (Tang and Musa, 2011). Warehouse processes in supply chain operations contain risks which deteriorate supply chain performance.

Delanuay et al. (2007) identify four types of errors in warehouse operations: The first is permanent shrinkage in the physical stock due to theft, obsolescence, or damage. The second is misplacement, which is temporary shrinkage in the physical stock that can be replaced after every counting or after every period. The third is randomness of the supplier yield which is the permanent loss or surplus in the physical inventory due to supplier errors. And finally the fourth one is the transaction type error that affects the information system differently than the first three errors, which modify the physical inventory. Normally, due to these errors, the accuracy rate

S. Greco et al. (Eds.): IPMU 2012, Part IV, CCIS 300, pp. 403–412, 2012.

in inventory decreases and a gap occurs between the actual and system inventory of the company. So, the supply chain performance and thereby the customer service level decrease. Therefore, the companies have to calculate the risks of warehouse operations to reach the required customer service level and increase the supply chain performance.

A typical process of risk management contains four basic steps (Hallikas et al., 2004): Risk identification, risk assessment, risk management and risk monitoring. The most known method for risk assessment, Failure Mode and Effects Analysis (FMEA) is an analysis method of reliability which can identify potential failure modes and its effect. FMEA has been extensively used for examining potential failures in products, processes, designs and services. In FMEA method, risk rating of failure modes is estimated by risk priority numbers (RPN) and correction measure is decided in order to increase the reliability. Traditional FMEA determines the risk priorities which require the risk factors like the occurrence (O), severity (S) and detection (D) of each failure mode to be precisely evaluated (Wang et al. 2009). The traditional FMEA has some drawbacks so that affect the risk evaluation and correction action. It is very difficult for three risk factors to be evaluated precisely. Additionally, traditional FMEA doesn't consider the relative importance of three risk factors. The critical problem is that same RPN can be obtained by different combination of three risk factors (Huadong and Zhigang, 2009). Therefore, fuzzy logic is introduced to overcome all the problems in traditional FMEA (Wang et al, 2009).

In this study, the fuzzy FMEA is used to analyze and assess the risks of warehouse operations. Ten risk factors are determined for warehouse operations of a food retail distributor. As the first five cause permanent shrinkage of products, the second five are related to the processes. When considering the literature, it is noticed that there has not been any published study which considers risk factors under fuzzy environment for warehouse operations. In this context, this paper has the originality of applying the fuzzy FMEA method that evaluates risk factors for warehouse operations to address this research gap. The rest of the paper is organized as follows: The brief summary of fuzzy numbers is given in Section 2. The fuzzy FMEA method is explained in Section 3. Section 4 introduces the risks in warehouse operations and Section 5 presents the numerical example. Finally, conclusions are provided in section 6.

## 2    Fuzzy Numbers

Fuzzy set theory, first introduced by Zadeh in 1965, is based on the idea of representing human's natural language expressions by mathematical operators. A fuzzy number $\tilde{x}$ is a fuzzy subset of real numbers, expresses the meaning "about x". In the literature, triangular and trapezoidal fuzzy numbers are very popular for fuzzy applications. In this paper, triangular fuzzy numbers are used to consider the fuzziness of the decision elements. A triangular fuzzy number $\tilde{A}$ is represented by (p,r,s), as shown in Figure 1.

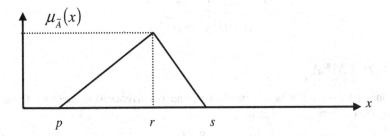

**Fig. 1.** The membership function of the triangular fuzzy number $\tilde{A}$

The parameters $p$; $r$; and $s$; respectively, denote the lower bound, the modal value and the upper bound that describe a fuzzy event. The membership function of triangular fuzzy numbers can be described as:

$$\mu_{\tilde{A}}(x) = \begin{cases} \dfrac{x-p}{r-p}, & p < x \le r \\ \dfrac{s-x}{s-r}, & r \le x < s \\ 0, & \text{otherwise} \end{cases} \qquad (1)$$

Let $\tilde{A} = (p_1, r_1, s_1)$ and $\tilde{B} = (p_2, r_2, s_2)$ be two triangular fuzzy numbers and the main arithmetic operations on these triangular fuzzy numbers are as shown;
Addition operation in fuzzy numbers via $\oplus$ symbol:

$$\tilde{A} \oplus \tilde{B} \cong (p_1, r_1, s_1) + (p_2, r_2, s_2) \cong (p_1 + p_2, r_1 + r_2, s_1 + s_2) \qquad (2)$$

Multiplication operation in fuzzy numbers via $\otimes$ symbol:

$$\tilde{A} \otimes \tilde{B} \cong (p_1, r_1, s_1) \times (p_2, r_2, s_2) \cong (p_1 p_2, r_1 r_2, s_1 s_2) \qquad (3)$$

Exponentiation operation in fuzzy numbers:

$$\tilde{A}^m \cong (p_1^m, r_1^m, s_1^m) \qquad (4)$$

The cut of the fuzzy number can be denoted by $\tilde{A}_\alpha = [\tilde{A}_\alpha^l, \tilde{A}_\alpha^u]$. The index $\beta$ is used as the degree of satisfactory index.

$$\tilde{A}_\alpha^l = (p_1 - r_1)\alpha + p_1 \qquad (5)$$

$$\tilde{A}_\alpha^u = s_1 - (s_1 - r_1)\alpha \tag{6}$$

$$\tilde{A}_\alpha^\beta = (1 - \beta)\tilde{A}_\alpha^l + \beta\tilde{A}_\alpha^u \tag{7}$$

# 3    Fuzzy FMEA

In traditional FMEA, RPN is the product of the occurrence (O), severity (S) and detection (D) of failure mode, that is:

$$RPN = O \times S \times D \tag{8}$$

where O and S are frequency and seriousness of failure and D is the ability to detect failure before it reaches customer. In this study, fuzzy numbers are used since three risk factors are difficult to evaluate precisely. The rating of three factors is expressed as triangular fuzzy number and the relative importance among O (occurrence), S (severity) and D (detection) is also considered as triangular number (Huadong and Zhigang, 2009). In calculating the risk priority of failure modes, $\alpha$-cut and satisfactory index $\beta$ are used to obtain crisp number by defuzzification. The linguistic terms and and fuzzy numbers of the factors are given in Table 1-3 (Wang et al., 2009).

**Table 1.** Fuzzy ratings for occurrence of a failure

| Rating | Probability of Occurrence | Fuzzy Number |
|---|---|---|
| Very High | Failure is almost inevitable | (8,9,10) |
| High | Repeated failures | (7,8,9) |
| Medium | Occasional failures | (4,5,6) |
| Low | Relatively few failures | (3,4,5) |
| Very Low | Failure is unlikely | (1,2,3) |

**Table 2.** Fuzzy ratings for severity of a failure

| Rating | Severity | Fuzzy Number |
|---|---|---|
| Very high (VH) | System with destructive failure | (8,9,10) |
| High(H) | System with equipment damage | (6,7,8) |
| Moderate(M) | System with minor damage | (4,5,6) |
| Low(L) | System without damage | (3,4,5) |
| Very low(VL) | System with significant degradation | (2,3,4) |
| Minor | System with minor degradation | (1,2,2) |
| None | No effect | (1,1,2) |

Table 3. Fuzzy ratings for detection of a failure

Table 3. Fuzzy ratings for detection of a failure

| Rating | Likelihood of detection | Fuzzy Number |
|---|---|---|
| Absolute uncertainty(AU) | No chance | (8,9,10) |
| Minor(MR) | Minor chance | (7,8,9) |
| Very low(VL) | Very low chance | (6,7,8) |
| Low(L) | Low chance | (5,6,7) |
| Moderate (M) | Moderate chance | (3,4,5) |
| High (H) | High chance | (2,3,4) |
| Very high (VH) | Very high chance | (1,2,3) |
| Certainty (C) | Almost certainty | (1,1,2) |

Since three risk factors are not assumed to be equally important, the fuzzy ratings of relative importance among these three factors are given in Table 4.

Table 4. Fuzzy ratings for detection of a failure

| Rating | Fuzzy Number |
|---|---|
| Very high(VH) | (3/5,1,1) |
| High(H) | (1/2,3/5,1) |
| Moderate(M) | (1/4,1/2,3/5) |
| Low(L) | (0,1/4,1/4) |
| Very low(VL) | (0,0,1/4) |

The fuzzy FMEA method can be through the following steps (Huadong and Zhigang, 2009):

*Step 1:* Determine the FMEA team members' opinions quantitatively. Failure modes are expressed as $F_i(i=1,....,n)$ and FMEA team members are expressed as $T\ (j=1,....,m)$. The occurrence, severity and detection rating of $F_i$ are expressed as:

$$\tilde{A}_{ij}^{O} = \left(\tilde{A}_{ijL}^{O}, \tilde{A}_{ijM}^{O}, \tilde{A}_{ijU}^{O}\right) \qquad \tilde{A}_{ij}^{S} = \left(\tilde{A}_{ijL}^{S}, \tilde{A}_{ijM}^{S}, \tilde{A}_{ijU}^{S}\right) \qquad \tilde{A}_{ij}^{D} = \left(\tilde{A}_{ijL}^{D}, \tilde{A}_{ijM}^{D}, \tilde{A}_{ijU}^{D}\right)$$

$$\tilde{A}_{i}^{O} = \begin{bmatrix} \tilde{A}_{i1L}^{O} & \tilde{A}_{i1M}^{O} & \tilde{A}_{i1U}^{O} \\ \tilde{A}_{i2L}^{O} & \tilde{A}_{i2M}^{O} & \tilde{A}_{i2U}^{O} \\ ... \\ \tilde{A}_{imL}^{O} & \tilde{A}_{imM}^{O} & \tilde{A}_{imU}^{O} \end{bmatrix} \quad \tilde{A}_{i}^{S} = \begin{bmatrix} \tilde{A}_{i1L}^{S} & \tilde{A}_{i1M}^{S} & \tilde{A}_{i1U}^{S} \\ \tilde{A}_{i2L}^{S} & \tilde{A}_{i2M}^{S} & \tilde{A}_{i2U}^{S} \\ ... \\ \tilde{A}_{imL}^{S} & \tilde{A}_{imM}^{S} & \tilde{A}_{imU}^{S} \end{bmatrix} \quad \tilde{A}_{i}^{D} = \begin{bmatrix} \tilde{A}_{i1L}^{D} & \tilde{A}_{i1M}^{D} & \tilde{A}_{i1U}^{D} \\ \tilde{A}_{i2L}^{D} & \tilde{A}_{i2M}^{D} & \tilde{A}_{i2U}^{D} \\ ... \\ \tilde{A}_{imL}^{D} & \tilde{A}_{imM}^{D} & \tilde{A}_{imU}^{D} \end{bmatrix}$$

*Step 2:* Calculate the relative importance among O, S and D as follows:

$$\tilde{W}_j^O = \left(\tilde{W}_{jL}^O, \tilde{W}_{jM}^O, \tilde{W}_{jU}^O\right) \qquad \tilde{W}_j^S = \left(\tilde{W}_{jL}^S, \tilde{W}_{jM}^S, \tilde{W}_{jU}^S\right) \qquad \tilde{W}_j^D = \left(\tilde{W}_{jL}^D, \tilde{W}_{jM}^D, \tilde{W}_{jU}^D\right)$$

$$\tilde{W}^O = \begin{bmatrix} \tilde{W}_{1L}^O & \tilde{W}_{1M}^O & \tilde{W}_{1U}^O \\ \tilde{W}_{2L}^O & \tilde{W}_{2M}^O & \tilde{W}_{2U}^O \\ \cdots & & \\ \tilde{W}_{mL}^O & \tilde{W}_{mM}^O & \tilde{W}_{mU}^O \end{bmatrix} \qquad \tilde{W}^S = \begin{bmatrix} \tilde{W}_{1L}^S & \tilde{W}_{1M}^S & \tilde{W}_{1U}^S \\ \tilde{W}_{2L}^S & \tilde{W}_{2M}^S & \tilde{W}_{2U}^S \\ \cdots & & \\ \tilde{W}_{mL}^S & \tilde{W}_{mM}^S & \tilde{W}_{mU}^S \end{bmatrix} \qquad \tilde{W}^D = \begin{bmatrix} \tilde{W}_{1L}^D & \tilde{W}_{1M}^D & \tilde{W}_{1U}^D \\ \tilde{W}_{2L}^D & \tilde{W}_{2M}^D & \tilde{W}_{2U}^D \\ \cdots & & \\ \tilde{W}_{mL}^D & \tilde{W}_{mM}^D & \tilde{W}_{mU}^D \end{bmatrix}$$

The *α-cut* of fuzzy numbers can be calculated as follows:

$$W_\alpha^O = \begin{bmatrix} \tilde{W}_{1\alpha}^{Ol} & \tilde{W}_{1\alpha}^{Ou} \\ \tilde{W}_{2\alpha}^{Ol} & \tilde{W}_{2\alpha}^{Ou} \\ \cdots & \\ \tilde{W}_{m\alpha}^{Ol} & \tilde{W}_{m\alpha}^{Ou} \end{bmatrix} \qquad W_\alpha^S = \begin{bmatrix} \tilde{W}_{1\alpha}^{Sl} & \tilde{W}_{1\alpha}^{Su} \\ \tilde{W}_{2\alpha}^{Sl} & \tilde{W}_{2\alpha}^{Su} \\ \cdots & \\ \tilde{W}_{m\alpha}^{Sl} & \tilde{W}_{m\alpha}^{Su} \end{bmatrix} \qquad W_\alpha^D = \begin{bmatrix} \tilde{W}_{1\alpha}^{Dl} & \tilde{W}_{1\alpha}^{Du} \\ \tilde{W}_{2\alpha}^{Dl} & \tilde{W}_{2\alpha}^{Du} \\ \cdots & \\ \tilde{W}_{m\alpha}^{Dl} & \tilde{W}_{m\alpha}^{Du} \end{bmatrix}$$

*Step 3:* Determine the crisp number of the relative importance among O, S and D using *α-cut* and satisfactory degree of *β* as follows:

$$W_\alpha^{O\beta} = \begin{bmatrix} \tilde{W}_{1\alpha}^{O\beta} \\ \tilde{W}_{2\alpha}^{O\beta} \\ \cdots \\ \tilde{W}_{m\alpha}^{O\beta} \end{bmatrix} \qquad W_\alpha^{O\beta} = \begin{bmatrix} \tilde{W}_{1\alpha}^{O\beta} \\ \tilde{W}_{2\alpha}^{O\beta} \\ \cdots \\ \tilde{W}_{m\alpha}^{O\beta} \end{bmatrix} \qquad W_\alpha^{O\beta} = \begin{bmatrix} \tilde{W}_{1\alpha}^{O\beta} \\ \tilde{W}_{2\alpha}^{O\beta} \\ \cdots \\ \tilde{W}_{m\alpha}^{O\beta} \end{bmatrix}$$

Where $W_{i\alpha}^{O\beta} = (1-\beta)W_{i\alpha}^{Ol} + \beta W_{i\alpha}^{Ou}$ ; $W_{i\alpha}^{S\beta} = (1-\beta)W_{i\alpha}^{Sl} + \beta W_{i\alpha}^{Su}$ ; $W_{i\alpha}^{D\beta} = (1-\beta)W_{i\alpha}^{Dl} + \beta W_{i\alpha}^{Du}$ ;

The normalization process is conducted as follows:

$$W^O = \frac{\sum_{j=1}^m W_{j\alpha}^{O\beta}}{m} \; ; \; W^S = \frac{\sum_{j=1}^m W_{j\alpha}^{S\beta}}{m} \; ; W^D = \frac{\sum_{j=1}^m W_{j\alpha}^{D\beta}}{m} \qquad (9)$$

The relative importance among O, S and D is determined as:

$$RW^O = \frac{W^O}{W^O + W^S + W^D};$$

$$RW^S = \frac{W^S}{W^O + W^S + W^D}; \tag{10}$$

$$RW^D = \frac{W^D}{W^O + W^S + W^D};$$

*Step 4:* Determine the fuzzy Risk Priority Number (FRPN) using the following equation:

$$FRPN = \left(\tilde{A}_i^O\right)^{RW^O} \times \left(\tilde{A}_i^S\right)^{RW^S} \times \left(\tilde{A}_i^D\right)^{RW^D} \tag{11}$$

*Step 5:* Determine the priority of failure modes by *α-cut* and satisfactory degree of *β*.

# 4 The Failure Modes of Warehouse Operations

In this study, a risk analysis is conducted for a warehouse of a food retail distributor. Ten failure modes are determined for warehouse operations. The first five cause permanent shrinkage of products. The second five are related to the processes. However, the last risk factor called transaction type error differs from others since it is related with the information system not the physical inventory. All the risk factors should be considered and calculated by the distributor company to increase the supply chain performance and the customer satisfaction. The warehouse risk factors are described below:

- Risks causing permanent shrinkage of products
  - Theft risk (F1): The products may be stolen.
  - Expiration risk (F2): The products can pass the expiration date.
  - Damage risk (F3): The products may be damaged due to the careless physical movement in warehouse.
  - Fire risk (F4): Fire may break out in warehouse.
  - Chemical/Biological risk (F5): The products may spoil due to biological or chemical factors.
- Process risks
  - Receiving errors (F6): Orders coming from supplier may contain wrong or missing items.
  - Put-away errors (F7): The products may be misplaced by the warehouse personnel, so there is a temporary shrinkage in the physical stock.
  - Pick-up errors (F8): The warehouse personnel may pick up wrong items or miss some products.
  - Shipment errors (F9): The personnel could deliver the products to wrong customer address or they could miss some products to deliver.

— Transaction type errors (F10): The personnel may input wrong data into the warehouse information system. Transaction type errors affect the information system differently than the first two types of errors, which modify the physical inventory.

# 5    Risk Evaluation of Warehouse Operations

FMEA team consisting of three experts prioritizes ten failure modes according the three risk factors. The main objective is here to identify the highest risky failure mode. The evaluation results of FMEA team using linguistic terms are presented in Table 5-6. Table 7 shows the fuzzy RPN of 10 failure modes and crisp priority numbers for $\alpha=0.6$ and $\beta=0.5$. In Table 7, it is noticed that the risk priority number of failure mode 8 is the highest, followed by 9,4,10,5,1,6,2,3 and 7. Therefore , the pick up and shipment errors should be considered seriously as well as the fire risks in warehouse operations.

Table 5. Relative importance for three factors

| Risk Factors | Team Member | | |
|---|---|---|---|
| | 1 | 2 | 3 |
| Occurence | H | H | M |
| Severity | VH | H | M |
| Detection | M | L | M |

Table 6. Evaluation results in linguistic terms

| Team Member | Failure Modes - Occurence | | | | | | | | | |
|---|---|---|---|---|---|---|---|---|---|---|
| | 1 | 2 | 3 | 4 | 5 | 6 | 7 | 8 | 9 | 10 |
| 1 | L | L | M | VL | VL | M | L | L | M | H |
| 2 | L | M | L | VL | VL | L | L | L | L | H |
| 3 | VL | L | L | L | VL | L | VL | M | L | M |
| | Failure Modes – Severity | | | | | | | | | |
| 1 | M | L | L | VH | H | L | L | M | M | L |
| 2 | M | L | L | VH | H | L | M | M | M | L |
| 3 | L | VL | VL | VH | VH | VL | L | H | H | VL |
| | Failure Modes – Detection | | | | | | | | | |
| 1 | MR | M | M | AU | AU | L | L | L | VL | L |
| 2 | VL | M | M | AU | AU | L | M | L | L | L |
| 3 | L | L | L | MR | MR | M | M | M | L | VL |

**Table 7.** Fuzzy and crisp risk priority numbers (RPN)

| Failure Modes | Fuzzy RPN | Crisp RPN $\alpha=0.6; \beta=0.5$ |
|---|---|---|
| Theft risk (F1) | (3.46, 4.53, 5.57) | 4.05 |
| Expiration risk (F2) | (3.05, 4.07, 5.08) | 3.61 |
| Damage risk (F3) | (3.05, 4.07, 5.08) | 3.61 |
| Fire risk (F4) | (4.11, 5.38, 6.53) | 4.78 |
| Chemical/Biological risk (F5) | (3.52, 4.91, 6.11) | 4.26 |
| Receiving errors (F6) | (3.21, 4.23, 5.24) | 3.84 |
| Put-away errors (F7) | (2.93, 3.97, 4.99) | 3.56 |
| Pick-up errors (F8) | (4.25, 5.27, 6.28) | 4.87 |
| Shipment errors (F9) | (4.24, 5.26, 6.27) | 4.85 |
| Transaction type errors (F10) | (3.96, 5.01, 6.04) | 4.59 |

# 6    Conclusion

Warehouse processes in supply chain operations contain risks which lead to a poor supply chain performance. Hence, risk analysis in warehouse operations is a very critical issue to increase the performance in supply chain. In this study, fuzzy FMEA method is used to evaluate the risks of warehouse operations. In fuzzy FMEA, the relative importance among the risk factors O, S and D is taken into consideration in the process of prioritization of failure modes. Additionally, risk factors and their relative importance weights are evaluated in a linguistic manner rather than in precise numerical values. Therefore, fuzzy FMEA is more realistic than traditional FMEA. In this paper, this method is applied to a warehouse of a food retail store. According to the results, the pick-up and shipment processes have critical risk values. In addition to this, fire risk should also be considered as a critical risk factor. For further studies, the fuzzy FMEA method can be applied in different processes in supply chains. Moreover, different quantitative methods can be developed for evaluating the risks in supply chains.

# References

1. Tuncel, G., Alpan, G.: Risk Assessment and Management for Supply Chain Networks: A Case Study. Computers in Industry 61, 250–259 (2010)
2. Tang, O., Musa, N.S.: Identifying Risk Issues and Research Advancements in Supply Chain Risk Management. Int. J. of Prod. Econ. 133, 25–34 (2011)
3. Delanuay, C., Sahin, E., Dallery, Y.: A Literature Review on Investigations Dealing with Inventory Management with Data Inaccuracies. In: 1st RFID Eurasia Conference, pp. 20–26. Cenkler Press, Istanbul (2007)

4. Hallikas, J., Karvonen, I., Pulkkinen, U., Virolainen, V.M., Tuominen, M.: Risk management processes in supplier networks. Int. J. of Prod. Econ. 90, 47–58 (2004)
5. Huadong, Y., Zhigang, B.: Risk Evaluation of Boiler Tube using FMEA. In: International Conference on Fuzzy Systems and Knowledge Discovery, pp. 81–85. IEEE Press, Tianjin (2009)
6. Wang, Y.M., Chin, K.S., Poon, G.K.K., Yang, J.B.: Risk evaluation in failure mode and effects analysis using fuzzy weighted geometric mean. Exp. Sys. with App. 36, 1195–1207 (2009)
7. Zadeh, L.A.: Fuzzy sets. Inf. and Control 8, 338–353 (1965)

# End-of-Life Tyres Recovery Method Selection in Turkey by Using Fuzzy Extended AHP

Yesim Kop, Mujde Erol Genevois, and H. Ziya Ulukan

Galatasaray University, Industrial Engineering Department, Istanbul, Turkey
{ykop,merol,zulukan}@gsu.edu.tr

**Abstract.** This study focuses on 'Tyres and Tyre related wastes'. End of Life Tyres (ELT) are detected according to waste and waste disposal regulations. Many studies have been conducted in different countries in order to determine the most suitable ELT recovery method. The results vary depending on economical, social and legislative conditions of the country. This research includes a survey on global ELT engendering, ELT disposal methods then focuses on the situation in Turkey. Its aim is to make an ELT disposal method selection for Turkey, considering current conditions. Considering the lack of quantitative data and the presence of qualitative perspectives, the selection has been made using a Multi Criteria Decision Making (MCDM) tool named Analytic Hierarchy Process (AHP). To handle the imprecise nature of the expert judgments, this study proposes the fuzzy extended AHP as selection method.

**Keywords:** End-of-Life Tyres (ELT), Mechanical Pulverization, Waste to Energy Process, Pyrolysis, Fuzzy Triangular Numbers, Fuzzy Extended AHP.

## 1 Introduction

In today's world where natural resources are exhausting with an exponentially growing speed, the concept of sustainability becomes the main concern. Material recycling will be the most significant behaviour to provide the sustainability. It is considered as one of the most important four pillars of effective resource utilization and comprises the management, the prevention and the reduction of waste [1].

The Basel Convention created in 1989 provided a common framework for the classification, management and disposal of wastes. Basel Convention and OECD (Organization for Economic Cooperation and Development) prepared independently lists of materials qualified as waste and classify them as hazardous and non-hazardous [1].

This study focuses on 'Tyres and Tyre related wastes' categorized as B3140-Waste pneumatic tyres and B3080-Waste parings and scrap of rubber. With respect to waste regulations of Turkish Ministry of Environment and Forestry, tyres dating over eight years, tyres with more than three tears on the wheel rim, requiring repair, tyres with metals or textiles protruding, tyres with fissures or tyres contaminated with petroleum or chemicals, tyres with tread depth less than 1.6mm are ELTs [2].

S. Greco et al. (Eds.): IPMU 2012, Part IV, CCIS 300, pp. 413–422, 2012.

Many studies have been conducted in different countries in order to determine the most suitable ELT recovery method. According to Sharma et al., incinerators with energy recovery systems are most advantageous technically and economically compared to the tyre pulverisation or the pyrolysis process, having higher energy recovery and being attractive environmentally [3]. Amari et al. examine the technologies used to recover the ELT for energy or as rubber in USA [4]. In their study Corti and Lombardi compare different processes for the end life treatment of exhausted tyres, using life cycle assessment [5]. Mergias et al. used PROMETHEE, a MCDM method for selecting the best compromise scheme for the management of ELV [6].

In this study, ELT recovery method selection has been made considering different conflicting quantitative and qualitative perspectives as environmental protection, energy saving, user friendliness, application risks and costs. To handle the imprecise nature of the expert judgments, this study proposes the fuzzy extended AHP as selection method.

# 2    Tyre

All kind of tyres consists of four essential material groups: rubber, carbon black (CB), reinforcing materials and facilitators. Table.1 shows material weight percentages and of car and truck tyres [7].

**Table 1.** Material Weight Percentages

| Material | Car Tyres (%) | Truck Tyres (%) |
|---|---|---|
| Rubber/Elastomers | ±48 | ±45 |
| Carbon Black and silica | ±22 | ±22 |
| Metals | ±15 | ±25 |
| Textiles | ±5 | - |
| Sulphur, stearic acid, zinc oxide | ±2 | ±3 |
| Additives | ±8 | ±5 |

Among all of the materials composing a tyre, natural rubber extracted from the Hevea tree or synthetic rubber which is a petroleum product are in the first rank with a weight percentage of 40-45%. In truck tyres, the ratio of natural rubber to synthetic rubber is 2/1 whereas in car tyres it becomes 4/3. Carbon Black (CB) is in the second rank with a weight percentage of 22-27%. Various types and shapes of CB are used in different parts of tyre. Recently, CB is replaced by silica, especially in green tyres. The third group is constituted of reinforcing materials: metals or textiles. Additives as fourth group are comprised of oils, waxes, anti-oxidants, anti-ozonants and many other materials added to tyre. They are increasing the tyre performance and also the manufacturing efficiency by facilitating the curing process. Other materials as sulphur, stearic acid and zinc oxide facilitate the vulcanisation [1].

# 3    Tyre and ELT Statistics

The table (Table.2) below includes the cost analysis of the European tyre production in 1992 [8].

**Table 2.** Cost Analysis

|                   | Kg/Tyre | $/kg   | Cost/Tyre |
|-------------------|---------|--------|-----------|
| Rubber            | 6.3     | $1.41  | $8.87     |
| Steel cord        | 1.0     | $3.60  | $3.60     |
| Bead wire         | 0.3     | $2.00  | $0.60     |
| Rayon cord        | 0.4     | $7.00  | $2.80     |
| Solvents/Additives| -       | -      | $0.50     |
| Energy            | -       | -      | $1.00     |
| **Total**         | **8.0** |        | **$17.37**|

As of 2004, natural and synthetic rubber production has reached 20,000,000 tonnes in whole world. 20% of this amount i.e. 4,000,000 tonnes are consumed in Europe. In addition, European Union imports 1,000,000 tonnes of rubber each year [8]. By the way, 75% of tyre resources are used in different sectors of automotive industry in whole world and 60% of this amount are used primarily in cars, trucks but further applications areas include airplanes, motorcycles, bikes etc. 15% of rubber are used in safety belts, hoses, housings, mouldings, rings and seals. The remaining 25% are consumed by other industrial sectors [1]. In Turkey, 210,000 tonnes of new tyre are sold in 2010. As each sale means changing the used one by a new tyre, the ETL amount in 2011 is estimated to be approximately 246,000 tonnes. As used tyres are worn off, ELT amount would be less than new tyres amount.

# 4    Tyre Recovery

LASDER (Tyre Manufacturers Association) is the Turkish institution partly responsible of ELT collection and distribution to different recovery facilities. It was founded in April 2007 by the cooperation of BRISA, CONTINENTAL, GOODYEAR, MICHELIN and PIRELLI. The first and essential aim of the association is to "adopt the management of ELT in Turkey in order to decrease the hazardous effects of ELT to the environment". In 2010, 62,500 tonnes of ELT is collected and the half of this amount is distributed to recovery facilities and the other half is sent to cement factories. In 2011, 172,200 tonnes of ELT is collected in the aggregate. 87,000tonnes is collected by LASDER and 52% of this amount is distributed to recovery facilities, the rest to cement factories [9]. In Turkey, ELT is evaluated currently by three different methods: Mechanical pulverisation, Waste to energy process in cement factories and Fuel/Raw material extraction by pyrolysis. Turkey is one of the ten countries in Europe that adopts the consumer responsibility principle and applies the same tax in the name of eco fee [9].

**Table 3.** ELT usage areas and amounts in USA and in EU, in 1999 [10]

| Usage Area | EU | | USA | |
|---|---|---|---|---|
| | Weight (tonne) | Percentage | Weight (tonne) | Percentage |
| Fuel | 508,500 | 22% | 950,000 | 40% |
| Filling Material | 1,017,100 | 46% | 920,000 | 38% |
| Construction | 228,900 | 10% | 225,000 | 9% |
| Rubber recycling | 228,800 | 10% | 180,000 | 7% |
| Export | 279,700 | 12% | 135,000 | 6% |
| **TOTAL** | **2,263,000** | | **2,140,000** | |

## 4.1    Mechanical Pulverization

Mechanical pulverization is the granulation of rubber under normal temperature conditions. It consists of three main phases [5]. In the initial grinding phase, the tyre parts are fed to a grinder with oil and water, as a result smaller parts of 7 to 10 cm are formed. In the crushing phase, the tyre parts are fed between cylinders with cutting knives. As a result the sizes of the parts are further reduced to 2cm. In the pulverization phase, cylinders with finer knives are utilized to further reduce the particle size to 1mm. The pulverized particles are transported by a hose and fan system [5].

**Table 4.** Energy Usage for Mechanical Pulverization

| Mechanical Pulverization | Power Consumption |
|---|---|
| 1. Grinding | 170 MJ |
| 2. Crushing | 573 MJ |
| 3. Pulverisation | 513 MJ |

This process requires 1,256 MJ of electrical energy, 150 l. of water, 0.23 kg of steel and 0.011kg of oil are utilized for the pulverization of 1 tonne of ELT.

## 4.2    Waste to Energy Process in Cement Factory

ELT's are utilized in cement factories as coal or petrol replacement. Their use provides 5000-7000 kcal of thermal energy resulting in cost savings of 160-180 $. ELT's are also preferred because of their lower $CO_2$ emissions compared to coal and petrol. ELT's provide about %20 of the thermal energy requirements in the cement furnaces. Many European cement factories are utilizing ELT's since 1970. Heidelberg Zement AG, Germany, utilizes 50,000 tonnes of ELT's to supply 20% of its fuel needs. Use of ELT's is also common among certain cement factories in the USA, Genstar Cement utilizes 20,000 tonnes to supply 25% of its thermal energy needs [8].

Ferrer proposes the following equation to calculate the profit from the use of ELT's:

Profit = Garbage Cleanout Cost + Revenue - Process Cost – Transportation Cost – Disposal Cost.

When compared to coal, the energy value of a single tire is 0.38$. In cement factories the tires are usually grinded before they are used as fuel; this constitutes the process cost. For a passenger car this is between 0.12-0.16$. Garbage Cleanout cost and transportation costs may be neglected here because different tariffs apply to different countries. ELT's can be supplied to cement factories free of charge without transportation cost [8].

$$Profit = 0+0.95-0.33-0-0=0.62\$/tire.$$

### 4.3    Pyrolysis

Pyrolysis is the process of decomposing organic materials in an elevated temperature and anoxic environment. Oil gas and carbon are the products of pyrolysis; the temperature of the pyrolysis reactor determines the ratios of the products obtained from the process. 450-500 L pyrolysis oil, 100-120 kg of hydrocarbon gas and 300-350 kg of carbon black are obtained from the pyrolysis of 1 tonne of ELT.

**Table 5.** Pyrolysis products

| PYROLYSIS | |
|---|---|
| INPUT | OUTPUT |
| 1 tonne Tyre | 450-500 L pyrolysis oil |
| | 100-120 kg of hydrocarbon gas |
| | 300-350 kg of carbon black |

Pyrolysis technology from SIMEKEN Inc. is utilized in Mexico to process 75 tonnes of waste wood. Total annual investment and operating cost of this facility is 1,940,200 $US (2005) where the annual cost per tonne is 77.04 $US (2005) [11]. The annual income is calculated as 4,166,946 $US (2005).

## 5    Methodology-Fuzzy Extended AHP

In their research, Tüysüz and Kahraman reviewed a number of fuzzy AHP approaches [12]. The first study of FAHP is presented by Van Laarhoven and Pedrycz [13]. Buckly determines fuzzy priorities of comparison ratios whose membership functions are trapezoidal [14]. Chang introduces a new approach for FAHP, with the use of the extent analysis method [15]. Chang's [15] extent analysis method will be used in our study. In FAHP proposed by Chang [15], the steps of Saaty's [16] crisp AHP can be followed. Let X={x1, x2,..., xn} be an object set, and U={u1,u2,..., um} be a goal set. According to the method of Chang's extent analysis [15], we now take each object and perform extent analysis for each goal respectively. Therefore, we can get m extent analysis values for each object, with the following signs:

$$M_{g_i}^1, M_{g_i}^2, \ldots, M_{g_i}^m, \quad i=1,2,\ldots,n \tag{1}$$

where all the M jgi (j=1,2,…,m) are triangular fuzzy numbers.

Step 1: The value of fuzzy synthetic extent with respect to the i th object is defined as

$$S_i = \sum_{j=1}^m M_{g_i}^j \otimes \left[ \sum_{i=1}^n \sum_{j=1}^m M_{g_i}^j \right]^{-1} \tag{2}$$

Step 2: The degree of possibility of M1≥M2 is defined as

$$V(M_1 \geq M_2) = \sup_{x \geq y} \left[ \min\left( \mu_{M_1}(x), \mu_{M_2}(y) \right) \right] \tag{3}$$

When a pair (x,y) exists such that x≥y and $\mu M1(x)=\mu M2(y)=1$, then we have V(M1≥M2)=1. Since M1 and M2 are convex fuzzy numbers;

$V(M_1 \geq M_2)=1$ iff $m_1 \geq m_2$,

$$V(M_2 \geq M_1) = hgt(M_1 \cap M_2) = \mu_{M_1}(d), \tag{4}$$

where d is the ordinate of the highest (hgt) intersection point D between $\mu M1$ and $\mu M2$. When M1 = (l1,m1,u1) and M2 = (l2,m2,u2), the ordinate of D is given by

$$V(M_2 \geq M_1) = hgt(M_1 \cap M_2)$$
$$= \frac{(l_1 - u_2)}{\left[ (m_2 - u_2) - (m_1 - l_1) \right]} \tag{5}$$

To compare M1 and M2, we need both the values of V(M1≥M2) and V(M2≥M1).

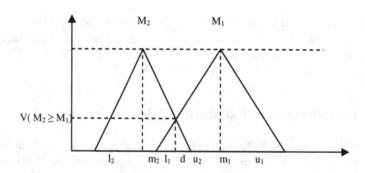

**Fig. 1.** The intersection between $M_1$ and $M_2$

Step 3: The degree possibility for a convex fuzzy number to be greater than k convex fuzzy numbers Mi(i = 1, 2, ..., k) can be defined by

$$V(M \geq M_1, M_2, ..., M_k) = V\left[ (M \geq M_1) \text{ and } (M \geq M_2) \text{ and...and}(M \geq M_k) \right]$$

$$= \min V(M \geq M_i), \quad i = 1, 2, ..., k$$

Assume that

$$d'(A_i) = \min V(S_i \geq S_k)$$

For k=1,2,...,n; k ≠ i. Then the weight vector is given by

$$W' = (d'(A_1), d'(A_2), ..., d'(A_n))^T$$

where Ai(i=1,2,...,n) are n elements.
Step 4: Via normalization, the normalized weight vectors are

$$W = (d(A_1), d(A_2), ..., d(A_n))^T$$

where W is a non fuzzy number.

# 6    Application

In this evaluation there are five main criteria:

C1: Environmental Impact: the releases, the damages and the profits of the method. It includes three sub-criteria as Environment, Human Health and Resource Depletion. Each sub-criterion has his own fourth level sub-criteria as indicated in Table.6. Figure.2 shows the hierarchy of this selection.
C2: Energy Saving; the energy consumed and saved by the recovery method.
C3: User Friendliness; the commonness and the ease-of-use of the method.
C4: Risks; the operating risks of the method
C5: Costs; the operating costs and initial costs.

The Eco-indicator95 environmental impact categories are presented in the following table [5]:

**Table 6.** Environmental impact criteria [5]

| Category | Environmental Effect | | Units |
|---|---|---|---|
| Environment Protec. | Greenhouse Effect | 1 | kg $CO_2$ |
| | Ozone Layer Depl. | 2 | g CFC11 |
| | Acidification | 3 | kg $SO_2$ |
| | Eutrophication | 4 | g $PO_4$ |
| Human Health | Heavy Metals | 5 | g Pb |
| | Carcinogens | 6 | g Benzo(a)pyrene |
| | Winter smog | 7 | kg SPM |
| | Summer Smog | 8 | g $S_2H_4$ |
| Resources Depletion | Water Consumption | 9 | Kg |
| | Energy | 10 | MJ |
| | Solid Waste | 11 | Kg |

Green House Gases: The primary contributors to greenhouse gases are 36-70% water vapour, 9-26% carbon dioxide, 4-9% methane and 3-7% ozone.

Acidification: Ocean acidification is the phenomenon of $CO_2$ dissolving in oceans and increasing its acidity. $CO_2$ is a primarily a result of combustion of fossil fuels.

Eutrophication: Eutrophication is the process of over accumulation of plant nutrients in large water ecosystems such as lakes. The accumulation of nutrients causes the vegetation to over grow and consume the oxygen in the environment.

The alternatives are three ELT recovery methods existing in Turkey:

A1: Mechanical Pulverization
A2: Waste to Energy Process in a cement factory
A3: Pyrolysis

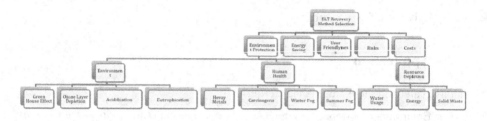

**Fig. 2.** Hierarchy

A meeting was organized with general secretary, logistic manager and chief of LASDER for determining expert evaluations. Experts made their evaluation according to triangular fuzzy numbers. Table.7 and Table.8 contain triangular fuzzy scale for evaluating criteria and fuzzy scale for evaluating alternatives. The consistency of each pair-wise comparison matrices is acceptable. In other words, expert evaluations are consistent.

**Table 7.** FAHP criteria evaluation scale

| Definition | Equal | Slightly Strong | Fairly Strong | Very Strong | Absolutely Strong |
|---|---|---|---|---|---|
| Fuzzy s | (1, 1, 1) | (1, 1, 3/2) | (1,3/2,2) | (3/2,2, /2) | (2, 5/2, 3) |

**Table 8.** FAHP alternative evaluation scale

| Definition | Fair | Medium Good | Good | Very Good |
|---|---|---|---|---|
| Fuzzy scale | (1, 1, 1) | (1, 1, 3/2) | (1, 3/2, 2) | (3/2,2, 5/2) |

**Table 9.** Fuzzy extended AHP results

|     | C1 | C2 | C3 | C4 | C5 | Priority Weight |
|-----|------|------|------|------|------|------|
|     | 0.2479 | 0.2479 | 0.1051 | 0.1512 | 0.2479 |      |
| A1  | 0.2438 | 0 | 0.4099 | 0.5584 | 0.3140 | **0.2658** |
| A2  | 0.4301 | 0.5 | 0.5181 | 0.3446 | 0.4161 | **0.4403** |
| A3  | 0.3262 | 0.5 | 0.0719 | 0.0970 | 0.2698 | **0.2939** |

# 7    Conclusion

In this study, ELT recovery method selection has been made considering different conflicting quantitative and qualitative perspectives as environmental protection, energy saving, user friendliness, application risks and costs. In Turkey, ELT is evaluated currently by three different methods: Mechanical pulverisation, Waste to energy process in cement factories and Fuel/Raw material extraction by pyrolysis. Expert opinions have been evaluated through fuzzy extended AHP and the results indicate that Waste to Energy process in cement factories is the best-suited ELT recovery method in Turkey. The other alternatives have approximately the same weight for current applications. However, with advances in technology resulting in cost reductions, it is believed that pyrolysis will be a promising candidate. A detailed research and analysis of pyrolysis system integrability in Turkish ELT recovery process will be subject to further researches.

**Acknowledgements.** This research has been financially supported by Galatasaray University Research Fund.

# References

1. Shulman, V.L.: Tyre Recycling, Shrewsbury, Rapra Technology, UK (2004)
2. Republic of Turkey Ministry of Environment and Forestry: ELT Safe Disposal Regulations (2006)
3. Sharma, V.K., Mincarini, M., Fortuna, F., Cognini, F., Cornacchia, G.: Disposal of waste tyres for energy recovery and safe environment-review. Energy Convers 39(3/4), 511–528 (1997)
4. Amari, T., Themelis, N.J., Wernick, I.K.: Resource recovery from used rubber tires. Resources Policy 25, 179–188 (1999)
5. Corti, A., Lombardi, L.: End life tyres: Alternative final disposal processes compared by LCA. Energy 29, 2089–2108 (2004)
6. Mergias, I., Moustakas, K., Papadopoulos, A., Loizidou, M.: Multi-criteria decision aid approach for the selection of the best compromise management scheme for ELVs: The case of Cyprus. Journal of Hazardous Materials 147, 706–717 (2007)
7. European Tyre Recycling association (2011), http://www.etra-eu.org/
index.php?option=com_content&view=article&id=76&Itemid=61

8. Ferrer, G.: The economics of tire remanufacturing, resources, conservation and recycling, vol. 19, pp. 221–255 (1997)
9. Tyre Manufacturers Association, LASDER (2011), http://www.lasder.org.tr/anasayfa.aspx?MenuID=1
10. European Tyre Recycling association (1999), http://www.etra-eu.org
11. Snow, M., Lopez, K.: Pyrolysis transformation of organic wastes-Result of full-scale trial demonstrations, the Governement of Canada, The Government of Mexico. SIMEKEN Inc. (2004)
12. Tüysüz, F., Kahraman, C.: Project Risk Evaluation Using a Fuzzy Analytic Hierarchy Process: An Application to Information Technology Projects. International Journal of Intelligence Systems 21, 559–584 (2006)
13. Van Laarhoven,.P.J.M., Pedrycz, W.: A Fuzzy Extension of Saaty's Priority Theory. Fuzzy Sets and Systems 11, 229–241 (1983)
14. Buckley, J.J.: Fuzzy Hierarchical Analysis. Fuzzy Sets and Systems 17, 233–247 (1985)
15. Chang, D.Y.: Applications of the Extent Analysis Method. European Journal of Operations Research 95, 649–655 (1996)
16. Saaty, T.L.: The analytic hierarchy process. Mc Graw-Hill, New York (1980)

# Multi-criteria Evaluation of Target Market Policies Using Choquet Integral

Nihan Çetin Demirel and Betül Özkan

Yildiz Technical University, Department of Industrial Engineering,
Yildiz Technical University, Besiktas, 34349 Istanbul, Turkey
{nihan,bozkan}@yildiz.edu.tr

**Abstract.** Determining on the target market policy is one of the important strategic decisions for companies. In this study we determine 4 different target market policies for a distributor company. The problem is dealt as a multi criteria decision making problem and it is solved using Choquet Integral which is one of the multi criteria decision making methods. In this study according to the firm's characteristics; financial factors, risk, demand and environmental and social factors are determined as main criteria and under these main criteria 11 sub-criteria are identified.

**Keywords:** Choquet integral, Target market policies, Fuzzy sets, Multi-criteria.

## 1 Introduction

In globalization world companies can survive when they open to new markets and improve their investments. Determining on the target market, marketing strategies and investment decisions are important strategic decisions in business. There are many factors that affects the target market policies. In the literature, there are some studies about target market and market area selection. Doherty explains a case study about the market and partner selection processes of retailers which operate internationally via franchising [6]. Mobley et al. prepared a report about market area selection and data development for medicare fee-for-service reform. Firstly they performed economic assessment of market conditions and then they identified which commonly used geographic market definition methodology is most appropriate. And finally they used a query-based approach to determine the feasible market areas [7]. Robertson and Wood shows an empirical study that investigates export decision making. International managers evaluated the relative importance of foreign market information while choosing the export markets [8]. Papadopoulos et al. proposed a tradeoff model for International Market Selection problem. The model was tested in real market conditions for 17 target countries [9]. Brouthers et al. developed a model based on Dunning's Eclectic Framework of international market selection that adds firms advantages. They used neural network analysis and they found their model has strong predictive power for international market selection [10].

The aim in this study is to choose the most appropriate target market policies for a distributor company. We have 4 potential strategy and there are different criteria that

S. Greco et al. (Eds.): IPMU 2012, Part IV, CCIS 300, pp. 423–431, 2012.
© Springer-Verlag Berlin Heidelberg 2012

affects the target market policies. So we used Choquet integral one of the multi-criteria decision making techniques to choose the best market area.

The remainder of this paper is organized as follows. Section 2 goes over description of selection criteria for target market policies. Section 3 explains Choquet integral and steps of methodology. Section 4 contains the proposed model and applications of the Choquet integral in a multi criteria decision making for the best target market policy. Some conclusion remarks are made in the last section.

## 2    Selection Criteria for Target Market Policies

The company has four alternatives as marketing strategy. The first one is to extend market area by selling the machines to outside market with no investment. Outside market means for the company the Turkic Republics. The second alternative is to extend market area in Turkey with investment. In this alternative, the company will produce its own machines while continuing buying from abroad. The third alternative is to extend market area by selling the machines to outside market with investment. In this alternative, the company will produce its own machines and continue buy from abroad and start to sell them to outside market (Turkic Republics). And the last alternative for the company is to continue with its current situation. The company won't have a new investment and want to keep its old customers.

To decide on the marketing strategy there are main and sub-criteria. In this study there are 4 main and 11 sub-criteria. The main and sub-criteria are determined considering the firm's characteristics and the market structure. The hierarchy of the selection criteria, sub-criteria and decision alternatives can be seen in Figure 1.

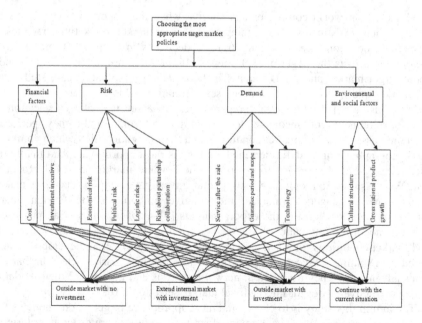

**Fig. 1.** The hierarchy of the selection problem

## 2.1    Financial Factors $(F)$

- Cost $(F_1)$: The cost of the alternatives affects while choosing the new strategy. The financial situation of the company is important. The amount of bank credits that the company can get affects the new target market policy.
- Investment incentive $(F_2)$: The places that the new investments will be built affect the amount of the investment incentive.

## 2.2    Risk $(R)$

- Economical risk $(R_1)$: This sub-criterion includes the global economic crisis and its effects.
- Political risk $(R_2)$: The potential areas are very important for the new strategy. Political inconsistency in the potential areas affects the complete target market policy.
- Logistic risks $(R_3)$: This sub-criterion includes the delivery time to customers. There can be accidents on the way to customers and the machines can be damaged.
- Risk about partnership collaboration $(R_4)$: There is a risk that the partner does not abide the contract rules or does not act ethical. There can be conflict of interests between the partners. All of the factors are about risks.

## 2.3    Demand $(D)$

- Service after the sale $(D_1)$: The behavior and the service quality of the company after the sale affects the demand to the machines.
- Guarantee period and scope $(D_2)$: The guarantee period length and the activities included in the guarantee certificate are important for the customers. The customer tend to prefer the company with better conditions.
- Technology $(D_3)$: The technological condition of the machines is also very important. The customers will prefer mostly the machines with the new and high technology.

## 2.4    Environmental and Social Factors $(ES)$

- Cultural structure $(ES_1)$: To have similar cultural structure is a positive effect on the potential customers. It could be better for the company to make new investment on an area with similar culture.
- Gross national product growth $(ES_2)$: Because the company sells machines, gross national product growth is important. The income level should be high for potential areas.

# 3    Choquet Integral And Steps Of Methodology

The Choquet integral generalizes the weighted arithmetic mean in the sense that, as soon as the capacity is additive, which intuitively coincides with the independence of the criteria, it collapses into a weighted arithmetic mean [12].

In the following, some definitions are given to explain the basics of Choquet integral [11]: Let I be the set of attributes (or any set in a general setting). A set function $\mu : P(I) \rightarrow [0, 1]$ is called a fuzzy measure if it satisfies the three following axioms: (1) $\mu(\emptyset) = 0$ : an empty set has no importance, (2) $\mu(I) = 1$ : the maximal set has a maximal importance, (3) $\mu(B) \leq \mu(C)$ if B, C $\subseteq$ I and B $\subseteq$ C: a new added criterion cannot make the importance of a coalition (a set of criteria) diminish.

Yang and Chen (2012), Ashayeri et al. (2012), Cao (2012), Jang (2012), Tsai and Lu (2006), Auephanwiriyakul et al. (2002) used Choquet integral for the solution of their multiple criteria decision making problems in the literature [1, 2, 4, 5, 13, 17]. The methodology is composed of eight steps [13, 3]:

Step 1: Given criterion i, respondents' linguistic preferences for the degree of importance, perceived performance levels of alternative target market policies, and tolerance zone are surveyed.

Step 2: In view of the compatibility between perceived performance levels and the tolerance zone, trapezoidal fuzzy numbers are used to quantify all linguistic terms in this study. Given respondent t and criteria i, linguistic terms for the degree of importance is parameterized by $\tilde{A}_i^t = \left(a_{i1}^t, a_{i2}^t, a_{i3}^t, a_{i4}^t\right)$, perceived performance levels by $\tilde{p}_i^t = \left(p_{i1}^t, p_{i2}^t, p_{i3}^t, p_{i4}^t\right)$, and the tolerance zone by $\tilde{e}_i^t = \left(e_{i1L}^t, e_{i2L}^t, e_{i3U}^t, e_{i4U}^t\right)$.

Step 3. Average $\tilde{A}_i^t$, $\tilde{p}_i^t$ and $\tilde{e}_i^t$ into $\tilde{A}_i$, $\tilde{p}_i$, and $\tilde{e}_i$, respectively using Eq. (1).

$$\tilde{A}_i = \frac{\sum_{t=1}^{k} \tilde{A}_i^t}{k} = \left(\frac{\sum_{t=1}^{k} a_{i1}^t}{k}, \frac{\sum_{t=1}^{k} a_{i2}^t}{k}, \frac{\sum_{t=1}^{k} a_{i3}^t}{k}, \frac{\sum_{t=1}^{k} a_{i4}^t}{k}\right) \tag{1}$$

Step 4. Normalize the target market policy score of each criterion using Eq. (2).

$$\tilde{f}_i = \left\|_{\alpha \in [0,1]} \tilde{f}_i^\alpha = \right\|_{\alpha \in [0,1]} [f_{i,\alpha}^-, f_{i,\alpha}^+] \tag{2}$$

where $f_i \in F(S)$ is a fuzzy-valued function. $\tilde{F}(S)$ is the set of all fuzzy-valued functions $f, f_i^\alpha = [f_{i,\alpha}^-, f_{i,\alpha}^+] = \frac{\overline{p}_i^\alpha - \overline{e}_i^\alpha + [1,1]}{2}$, $\overline{p}_i^\alpha$ and $\overline{e}_i^\alpha$ are $\alpha$-level cuts of $\tilde{p}_i$ and $\tilde{e}_i$ for all $\alpha = [0,1]$.

Step 5. Find the target market policy score of dimension j using Eq.(3).

$$(C) \int \tilde{f} d\tilde{g} = \left\|_{\alpha=[0,1]} \left[ (C) \int f_\alpha^- dg_\alpha^-, (C) \int f_\alpha^+ dg_\alpha^+, \right] \tag{3}$$

where $\overline{g}_i : P(S) \rightarrow I(R^+), \overline{g}_i = [g_i^-, g_i^+]$, $\overline{g}_i^\alpha = [g_{i,\alpha}^-, g_{i,\alpha}^+]$, $\overline{f}_i : S \rightarrow I(R^+)$, and $f_i = [f_i^-, f_i^+]$ for i=1, 2, 3, ..., nj.

To be able to calculate this score, a $\lambda$ value and the fuzzy measures g(A(i)), i=1,2,...,n, are needed. These are obtained from the following Eqs. (4), (5), and (6) [15], [16]:

$$g\left(A_{(n)}\right)= g\left(\left\{s_{(n)}\right\}\right)= g_n \tag{4}$$

$$g\left(A_{(i)}\right)= g_i + g\left(A_{(i+1)}\right)+ \lambda g_i\, g\left(A_{(i+1)}\right), \qquad \text{where } 1\le i < n \tag{5}$$

$$1= g(S)= \begin{cases} \dfrac{1}{\lambda}\left\{\displaystyle\prod_{i=1}^{n}[1+ \lambda g(A_i)]-1\right\} & \text{if } \lambda \ne 0 \\[2mm] \displaystyle\sum_{i=1}^{n} g(A_i) & \text{if } \lambda =0 \end{cases} \tag{6}$$

where, $A_i \cap A_j = \phi$ for all i, j = 1,2,3,...,n and $i \ne j$, and $\lambda \in (-1,\infty]$.

Let $\mu$ be a fuzzy measure on (I,P(I)) and an application $f : I \to \Re^+$. The Choquet integral of f with respect to $\mu$ is defined by:

$$(C) \int_I f d\mu = \sum_{i=1}^{n}(f(\sigma(i))- f(\sigma(i-1)))\mu\left(A_{(i)}\right) \tag{7}$$

where $\sigma$ is a permutation of the indices in order to have

$f(\sigma(1)) \le ... \le f(\sigma(n))$, $A_{(i)} = \{\sigma(i),...,\sigma(n)\}$ and $f(\sigma(0))= 0$, by convention.

It is easy to see that the Choquet integral is a Lebesgue integral up to a reordering of the indices. Actually, if the fuzzy measure $\mu$ is additive, then the Choquet integral reduces to a Lebesgue integral. It is shown in Modave and Grabisch ([11]) that under rather general assumptions over the set of alternatives X, and over the weak orders $\succeq_i$, there exists a unique fuzzy measure $\mu$ over I such that:

$$\forall x, y \in X, x \succeq y \Leftrightarrow u(x) \ge u(y) \tag{8}$$

where

$$u(x)= \sum_{i=1}^{n}\left[u_{(i)}\left(x_{(i)}\right)- u_{(i-1)}\left(x_{(i-1)}\right)\right]\mu\left(A_{(i)}\right) \tag{9}$$

which is simply the aggregation of the monodimensional utility functions using the Choquet integral with respect to $\mu$.

Step 6. Aggregate all dimensional performance levels of the policy alternatives into overall performance levels, using a hierarchical process applying the two-stage aggregation process of the generalized Choquet integral. This is represented in Eq. (10). The overall performance levels yields a fuzzy number, $\widetilde{V}$.

$$main\ criterion_{(1)} = (C)\int fdg$$
$$\vdots$$
$$main\ criterion_{(m)} = (C)\int fdg$$
$$\rangle\ V = (C)\int main\ criterion\ dg \tag{10}$$

Step 7. Assume that the membership of $\tilde{V}$ is $\mu_{\tilde{V}}(x)$; defuzzify the fuzzy number $\tilde{V}$ into a crisp value v using Eq. (11) and make a comparison of the overall performance levels of alternative policies.

$$F(\tilde{A}) = \frac{a_1 + a_2 + a_3 + a_4}{4} \tag{11}$$

Step 8. Compare weak and advantageous criteria among the policies alternatives using Eq. (1).

# 4    Application to Target Market Policies Evaluation in a Distributor Firm

A distribution company in Turkey that buys machines from abroad and sells them to its customers in Turkey wants to decide on the most appropriate target market policy. Our hierarchy were evaluated by 3 experts who were from the department of marketing (1 expert), strategic planning (1 expert), and financial (1 expert). These three experts confirmed the main criteria and sub-criteria and decided on using the evaluation scale in Table 1.

Table 2 and Table 3 give the evaluation results by the generalized Choquet Integral for α=0 and α=1 . For the sub-criteria, Eq.(2) is used while Eq.(3) is for the main criteria.

**Table 1.** The relationship between trapezoidal fuzzy numbers and degrees of linguistic importances in a nine-linguistic-term scale (Delgado et al., 1998)

| Low/High Levels | | The degrees of importance | | Trapezoidal |
|---|---|---|---|---|
| Label | Linguistic terms | Label | Linguistic terms | fuzzy numbers |
| EL | Extra Low | EU | Extra Unimportant | (0,0,0,0) |
| VL | Very Low | VU | Very Unimportant | (0,0.01,0.02,0.07) |
| L | Low | U | Unimportant | (0.04,0.1,0.18,0.23) |
| SL | Slightly Low | SU | Slightly Unimportant | (0.17,0.22,0.36,0.42) |
| M | Middle | M | Middle | (0.32,0.41,0.58,0.65) |
| SH | Slightly High | SI | Slightly Important | (0.58,0.63,0.8,0.86) |
| H | High | HI | High Important | (0.72,0.78,0.92,0.97) |
| VH | Very High | VI | Very Important | (0.93,0.98,0.98,1.0) |
| EH | Extra | EI | Extra Important | (1,1,1,1) |

**Table 2.** Evaluation results by generalized of Choquet integal for $\alpha = 0$

| Criteria | Individual importance of criteria $\bar{g}_i = [g_i^-, g_i^+]$ | The normalized dicrepancy $\bar{f}_i = [f_i^-, f_i^+]$ and policy performance value $[(C)\int f^-dg^-, (C)\int f^+dg^+]$ | | | | Fuzzy Measures $\lambda$ |
|---|---|---|---|---|---|---|
| | | Policy 1 | Policy 2 | Policy 3 | Policy 4 | |
| F | | [0.3501, 0.7168] | [0.4932, 0.7915] | [0.4072, 0.7622] | [0.1805, 0.523] | 0,1297; |
| $F_1$ | [0,42,0,55] | [0.44,0.8] | [0.485,0.805] | [0.5,0.805] | [0.195,0.55] | -0,5786 |
| $F_2$ | [0,55,0,66] | [0.285,0.615] | [0.5,0.775] | [0.34,0.71] | [0.17,0.49] | |
| R | | [0.3873, 0.7223] | [0.3441, 0.7053] | [0.4472, 0.7787] | [0.2591, 0.6043] | |
| $R_1$ | [0,57,0,66] | [0.32,0.7] | [0.38,0.745] | [0.455,0.8] | [0.2,0.54] | -0,7063; |
| $R_2$ | [0,42,0,55] | [0.435,0.695] | [0.33,0.635] | [0.435,0.695] | [0.305,0.6] | -0,9274 |
| $R_3$ | [0,16,0,36] | [0.445,0.75] | [0.25,0.6] | [0.38,0.695] | [0.25,0.6] | |
| $R_4$ | [0,3,0,46] | [0.345,0.715] | [0.25,0.625] | [0.455,0.775] | [0.25,0.625] | |
| D | | [0.4506, 0.7166] | [0.3867, 0.6948] | [0.4566, 0.7188] | [0.2979, 0.6083] | |
| $D_1$ | [0,35,0,54] | [0.405,0.72] | [0.315,0.645] | [0.475,0.73] | [0.27,0.61] | -0,4472; |
| $D_2$ | [0,48,0,65] | [0.445,0.725] | [0.41,0.72] | [0.41,0.72] | [0.275,0.61] | -0,8587 |
| $D_3$ | [0,37,0,47] | [0.485,0.66] | [0.405,0.65] | [0.485,0.66] | [0.34,0.595] | |
| ES | | [0.4106, 0.7398] | [0.3146, 0.6704] | [0.475, 0.748] | [0.2558, 0.6154] | |
| $ES_1$ | [0,16,0,36] | [0.44,0.775] | [0.22,0.585] | [0.475,0.78] | [0.245,0.625] | 5,9586; |
| $ES_2$ | [0,43,0,61] | [0.405,0.72] | [0.44,0.725] | [0.475,0.73] | [0.27,0.61] | 0,1364 |

**Table 3.** Evaluation results by generalized of Choquet integal for $\alpha = 1$

| Criteria | Individual importance of criteria $\bar{g}_i = [g_i^-, g_i^+]$ | The normalized dicrepancy $\bar{f}_i = [f_i^-, f_i^+]$ and policy performance value $[(C)\int f^-dg^-, (C)\int f^+dg^+]$ | | | | Fuzzy Measures $\lambda$ |
|---|---|---|---|---|---|---|
| | | Policy 1 | Policy 2 | Policy 3 | Policy 4 | |
| F | | [0.3732, 0.6766] | [0.5, 0.7708] | [0.4294, 0.7326] | [0.1965, 0.489] | -0,1844; |
| $F_1$ | [0,46,0,52] | [0.465,0.775] | [0.5,0.79] | [0.505,0.795] | [0.21,0.525] | -0,458 |
| $F_2$ | [0,59,0,63] | [0.295,0.57] | [0.5,0.75] | [0.365,0.665] | [0.185,0.45] | |
| R | | [0.4272, 0.6862] | [0.3816, 0.6738] | [0.4711, 0.7544] | [0.2971, 0.5591] | |
| $R_1$ | [0,59,0,64] | [0.345,0.68] | [0.41,0.725] | [0.475,0.785] | [0.215,0.525] | -0,7909; |
| $R_2$ | [0,46,0,52] | [0.47,0.655] | [0.375,0.59] | [0.47,0.655] | [0.345,0.55] | -0,9005 |
| $R_3$ | [0,21,0,31] | [0.48,0.71] | [0.29,0.55] | [0.415,0.655] | [0.29,0.55] | |
| $R_4$ | [0,33,0,43] | [0.38,0.675] | [0.285,0.58] | [0.475,0.745] | [0.285,0.58] | |
| D | | [0.4766, 0.6705] | [0.4196, 0.643] | [0.482, 0.6744] | [0.3359, 0.5586] | |
| $D_1$ | [0,4,0,5] | [0.435,0.67] | [0.35,0.595] | [0.5,0.69] | [0.31,0.56] | -0,6092; |
| $D_2$ | [0,52,0,61] | [0.48,0.68] | [0.445,0.67] | [0.445,0.67] | [0.32,0.56] | -0,8073 |
| $D_3$ | [0,4,0,45] | [0.495,0.63] | [0.425,0.605] | [0.495,0.63] | [0.365,0.55] | |
| ES | | [0.4424, 0.6917] | [0.3534, 0.622] | [0.5, 0.7086] | [0.2941, 0.5662] | |
| $ES_1$ | [0,21,0,31] | [0.47,0.74] | [0.25,0.545] | [0.5,0.75] | [0.28,0.58] | 3,2417; |
| $ES_2$ | [0,47,0,57] | [0.435,0.67] | [0.47,0.68] | [0.5,0.69] | [0.31,0.56] | 0,6789 |

In Table 4, using the calculation for Choquet integral just above, the overall target market policies performance values are obtained.

**Table 4.** Defuzzified overall values of alternative policies using Choquet integral

| $(C)\int \tilde{f} d\tilde{g}$ | | | |
|---|---|---|---|
| Policy 1 | Policy 2 | Policy 3 | Policy 4 |
| (0.4218, 0.4506, 0.6838, 0.7297) | (0.4363, 0.4557, 0.6411, 0.6875) | (0.4557, 0.4804, 0.7038, 0.7427) | (0.2706, 0.306, 0.5593, 0.6075) |

Overall location value

| **Defuzzified** $(C)\int \tilde{f} d\tilde{g}$ | | | |
|---|---|---|---|
| 0,5715 | | 0,5552 | 0,5956 | 0,4358 |

The analysis results indicate that the best policy is "outside market with investment" (Policy 3) with overall value of 0.5956. "Outside market with no investment" (Policy 1) with overall value of 0.5715 and "extend internal market with investment" (Policy 2) with overall value of 0.5552 follow the best policy. "Continue with the current situation" (Policy 4) with overall value of 0.4358 is the worst policy according to the multi-criteria evaluation.

# 5    Conclusion

In this study we choose the most appropriate target market policies from 4 different policies using Choquet Integral. "Outside market with investment" is get as a best policy. In future research it can be investigated which country is the best to start the investment. New criteria and policies may be proposed and added to the multi-criteria evaluation for strategies or policies. For further research, the case in this paper may be solved by other multi-criteria decision making methods.

# References

1. Yang, W., Chen, Z.: New aggregation operators based on the Choquet integral and 2-tuple linguistic information. Expert Systems with Applications 39, 2662–2668 (2012)
2. Ashayeri, J., Tuzkaya, G., Tuzkaya, U.R.: Supply chain partners and configuration selection: An intuitionistic fuzzy Choquet integral operator based approach. Expert Systems with Applications 39, 3642–3649 (2012)
3. Demirel, T., Çetin Demirel, N., Kahraman, C.: Multi-criteria warehouse location selection using Choquet integral. Expert Systems with Applications 37, 3943–3953 (2010)
4. Cao, Y.: Aggregating multiple classification results using Choquet integral for financial distress early warning. Expert Systems with Applications 39, 1830–1836 (2012)

5. Jang, L.C.: A note on convergence properties of interval-valued capacity functionals and Choquet integrals. Information Sciences 183, 151–158 (2012)
6. Doherty, A.M.: Market and Partner Selection Processes in International Retail Franchising. Journal of Business Research 62, 528–534 (2009)
7. Mobley, L.R., Hoerger, T.J., Greenwald, L.M., Andrews, L., Bruhn, M., Tate, K.C.: Market Area Selection and Data Development for Medicare Fee-for-Service Reform. Final Report for Centers for Medicare & Medicaid Services (December 2002)
8. Robertson, K.R., Wood, V.R.: The Relative Importance of Types of Information in the Foreign Market Selection Process. International Business Review 10, 363–379 (2001)
9. Papadopoulos, N., Chen, H., Thomas, D.R.: Toward a Tradeoff Model for International Market Selection. International Business Review 11, 165–192 (2002)
10. Brouthers, L.E., Mukhopadyay, S., Wilkinson, T.J., Brouthers, K.D.: International Market Selection and Subsidiary Performance: A neural Network Approach. Journal of World Business 44, 262–273 (2009)
11. Modave, F., Grabisch, M.: Preference representation by the Choquet integral: The commensurability hypothesis. In: Proceedings 7th International Conference on Information Processing and Management of Uncertainty in Knowledge-Based Systems (IPMU), Paris, France (1998)
12. Grabisch, M., Kojadinovic, I., Meyer, P.: A review of methods for capacity identification in Choquet integral based multi-attribute utility theory: Applications of the Kappalab R package 186, 766–785 (2008)
13. Tsai, H.H., Lu, I.Y.: The evaluation of service quality using generalized Choquet integral. Information Sciences 176(6), 640–663 (2006)
14. Delgado, M., Herrera, F., Herrera-Viedma, E., Martnez, L.: Combining numerical and linguistic information in group decision making. Information Sciences 107, 177–194 (1998)
15. Sugeno, M.: Theory of fuzzy integrals and its applications, PhD thesis.Tokyo Institute of Technology, Tokyo (1974)
16. Ishii, K., Sugeno, M.: A Model of Human Evaluation Process Using Fuzzy Integral. International Journal of Man-Machine Studies 22(1), 19–38 (1985)
17. Auephanwiriyakul, S., Keller, M.J., Gader, P.D.: Generalized Choquet fuzzy integral fusion. Information Fusion 3, 69–85 (2002)

# Multi-criteria Evaluation to Prioritize the Organic Farm Site Using Extended Vikor Method

Tufan Demirel, Serhat Tüzün, and Vildan Özkır

Yildiz Technical University, Department of Industrial Engineering,
Yildiz Technical University, Besiktas, 34349 Istanbul, Turkey
{tdemirel,serhat,vozkir}@yildiz.edu.tr

**Abstract.** The aim of the present study is to prioritize the sites in Turkey that organic farming is being practiced through extended VIKOR. The problem was considered as a multi-criteria decision making problem. Among the main criteria taken into account in this paper, some are ecological, technological, economic, and risk factors with the impacts of infrastructure and local community. Then, the problem was solved by using extended VIKOR method and the prioritization of the organic farming sites was determined.

## 1 Introduction

Organic farming is the process of producing food and fibers naturally, intended to overcome the negative impacts of the Green Revolution on soil, air, water, produce, landscape, and humans worldwide [1]. It relies on techniques such as crop rotation, green manure, compost and biological pest control. Fertilizers and pesticides can be used but the usage of synthetic fertilizers, genetically modified organisms, and etc. are prohibited [2].

It has been claimed that organic agriculture is the fastest growing agriculture based industry in the world [3]. Global data for organic agriculture have been published annually since 2000 [4], with the most recent account being Willer and Kilcher [5]. Between 2001 and 2011, the total worldwide organic agricultural hectares have grown by 135%, which equates to an 8.9% per annum compound growth over the decade [6]. The 2011 figures report organic agriculture data from 160 countries and a total of 37,232,127 organic agricultural hectares [5]. As a result, the market for organic products has grown from nothing, reaching $60 billion in 2010 [7].

This paper develops a framework for multiple criteria decision making that includes ecological, technological, economic, and risk factors with the impacts of infrastructure and local community; and the views of experts in the context of improving organic farming in Turkey for a more sustainable agriculture using Extended VIKOR Method.

## 2 Organic Agriculture in Turkey

Organic agriculture in Turkey has started in 1986, to meet the requirements of importing countries. Since 1991, the production and export of organic goods are supported with the regulations of EU [8]. The ministry of agriculture is publishing reports and statistics of the organic farming in Turkey annually since 2002 [9]:

S. Greco et al. (Eds.): IPMU 2012, Part IV, CCIS 300, pp. 432–440, 2012.
© Springer-Verlag Berlin Heidelberg 2012

**Table 1.** Organic Farming Production Statistics of Turkey

| Year | # of Products | # of Farmers | Cultivation Area (ha) | Total Production Area (ha) | Amount of Production (tones) |
|---|---|---|---|---|---|
| 2002 | 150 | 12.428 | 57.365 | 89.827 | 310.125 |
| 2003 | 179 | 14.798 | 73.368 | 113.621 | 323.981 |
| 2004 | 174 | 12.806 | 108.598 | 209.573 | 378.803 |
| 2005 | 205 | 14.401 | 93.134 | 203.811 | 421.934 |
| 2006 | 203 | 14.256 | 100.275 | 192.789 | 458.095 |
| 2007 | 201 | 16.276 | 124.263 | 174.283 | 568.128 |
| 2008 | 247 | 14.926 | 109.387 | 166.883 | 530.225 |
| 2009 | 212 | 35.565 | 325.831 | 501.641 | 983.715 |
| 2010 | 216 | 42.097 | 383.782 | 510.033 | 1.343.737 |

Since organic farming in Turkey has started to meet the requirements of importing countries, primarily exported products such as raisins and dried figs were produced organically in the Aegean region [10]. In 2000s, between the organic products produced in Turkey, the biggest product group is fruits (%66), which is followed by field crops (%16) and vegetables (%9) [11].

Today, organic agriculture is practiced in every region of Turkey. City with the most production of organic goods is İzmir with 28,669.00 tones. It is followed by Niğde, Manisa, Aydın, Erzurum, Malatya, Ağrı, respectively [9].

## 3    Extended VIKOR Method

Selecting or prioritizing alternatives from a set of available alternatives with respect to multiple criteria is often referred to as Multi-Criteria Decision Making (MCDM). Academics have developed and used various MCDM methods to solve different problems [12–15].

VIKOR was first presented by Opricovic in 1998 and Opricovic and Tzeng in 2002 with the Serbian name: VlseKriterijumska Optimizacija I Kompromisno Resenje [16]. In the literature, VIKOR has been used to solve various multi-criteria decision making problems [16–19].

In this paper the problem is evaluated under fuzzy environment with fuzzy sets. The main steps of the algorithm are taken from Sanayei et al.'s [17] study:

*Step 1:* Identifying the objectives of the decision making process and define the problem scope.

*Step 2:* Arranging the decision making group and define and describe a finite set of relevant attributes.

*Step 3:* Identifying the appropriate linguistic variables, as in Figure 1 and Figure 2 must be defined.

*Step 4:* Pull the decision makers' opinions to get the aggregated fuzzy weight of criteria, and aggregated fuzzy rating of alternatives and construct a fuzzy decision matrix: Let the fuzzy rating and importance weight of the $k^{th}$ dm be $\tilde{x}_{ijk} = \left(x_{ijk1}, x_{ijk2}, x_{ijk3}, x_{ijk4}\right)$ and $\tilde{w}_{jk} = \left(w_{jk1}, w_{jk2}, w_{jk3}, w_{jk4}\right)$; $i = 1, 2, \ldots,$ m and $j = 1, 2, \ldots,$ n respectively. Hence, the aggregated fuzzy ratings ($\tilde{x}_{ij}$) of alternatives with respect to each criterion can be calculated as:

$$\tilde{x}_{ij} = \left(x_{ij1}, x_{ij2}, x_{ij3}, x_{ij4}\right) \tag{1}$$

where $x_{ij1} = \min_k\{x_{ijk1}\}$ , $x_{ij2} = \frac{1}{K}\sum_{k=1}^{K} x_{ijk2}$ , $x_{ij3} = \frac{1}{K}\sum_{k=1}^{K} x_{ijk3}$ , $x_{ij4} = \max_k\{x_{ijk4}\}$.

The aggregated fuzzy weights ($\tilde{w}_j$) of each criterion can be calculated as:

$$\tilde{w}_j = \left(w_{j1}, w_{j2}, w_{j3}, w_{j4}\right) \tag{2}$$

where $w_{j1} = \min_k\{w_{jk1}\}, w_{j2} = \frac{1}{K}\sum_{k=1}^{K} w_{jk2}$, $w_{j3} = \frac{1}{K}\sum_{k=1}^{K} w_{jk3}$, $w_{j4} = \max_k\{w_{jk4}\}$.

A selection problem can be concisely expressed in matrix format as follows:

$$\tilde{D} = \begin{bmatrix} \tilde{x}_{11} & \tilde{x}_{12} & \cdots & \tilde{x}_{1n} \\ \tilde{x}_{12} & \tilde{x}_{22} & \cdots & \tilde{x}_{2n} \\ \vdots & \vdots & \cdots & \vdots \\ \tilde{x}_{m1} & \tilde{x}_{m2} & \cdots & \tilde{x}_{mn} \end{bmatrix}, \quad \tilde{W} = \left[\tilde{w}_1, \tilde{w}_2, \ldots, \tilde{w}_n\right],$$

where $\tilde{x}_{ij}$ the rating of alternative $A_i$ with respect to $C_j$, $\tilde{w}_j$ the importance weight of the $j^{th}$ criterion holds, $\tilde{x}_{ij} = \left(x_{ij1}, x_{ij2}, x_{ij3}, x_{ij4}\right)$ and $\tilde{w}_j = \left(w_{j1}, w_{j2}, w_{j3}, w_{j4}\right)$; $i = 1, 2, \ldots,$ m and $j = 1, 2, \ldots,$ n are linguistic variables can be approximated by positive trapezoidal fuzzy numbers.

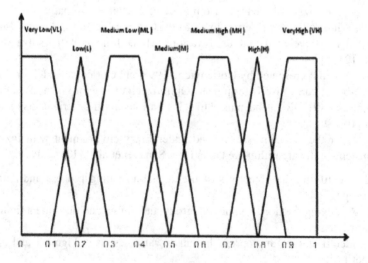

**Fig. 1.** Linguistic variables for importance weight of each criteria [17]

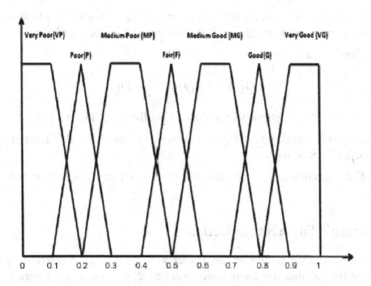

**Fig. 2.** Linguistic variables for ratings [17]

*Step 5:* Defuzzify the fuzzy decision matrix and fuzzy weight of each criterion into crisp values: This calculation is done by using center of area defuzzification method.

*Step 6:* Determine the best $f_j^*$ and the worst $f_j^-$ values of all criterion ratings, j = 1, 2, …, n.

$$f_j^* = \max_i x_{ij} \tag{3}$$

$$f_j^- = \min_i x_{ij} \tag{4}$$

*Step 7:* Compute the values $S_i$ and $R_i$ by the relations.

$$S_i = \sum_{j=1}^{n} w_j \left( f_j^* - f_{ij} \right) / \left( f_i^* - f_i^- \right) \tag{5}$$

$$R_i = \max_j w_j \left( f_j^* - f_{ij} \right) / \left( f_i^* - f_i^- \right) \tag{6}$$

*Step 8:* Compute the values $Q_i$ by the relations.

$$Q_i = v \left( S_i - S^* \right) / \left( S^- - S^* \right) + (1-v)\left( R_i - R^* \right) / \left( R^- - R^* \right) \tag{7}$$

where $S^* = \min_i S^i$ , $S^- = \max_i S^i$ , $R^* = \min_i R^i$ , $R^- = \max_i R^i$ and v is introduced as a weight for the strategy of maximum group utility, whereas 1-v is the weight of the individual regret.

*Step 9:* Rank the alternatives, sorting by the values S, R and Q in ascending order.

*Step 10:* Propose as a compromise solution the alternative $(A^{(1)})$ which is the best ranked by the measure Q (minimum) if the two conditions are satisfied:

- C1. Acceptable advantage:

$$Q\left(A^{(2)}\right) - Q\left(A^{(1)}\right) \geq DQ \tag{8}$$

where $A^{(2)}$ is the $2^{nd}$ best alternative in the ranking list by Q; $DQ = 1 / (J - 1)$.

- C2. Acceptable stability in decision making: The alternative $A^{(1)}$ must also be the best ranked by S or/and R.

If one of the conditions is not satisfied, then a set of compromise solutions is proposed.

# 4    Organic Farm Site Selection

Experts' views and the studies on this matter were referenced in determining criteria for locating the suitable site for organic farm [20–23]. These criteria were explained in detail as the following:

**Ecological Factors:** Ecology is the main factor for agriculture. Since no chemical or genetically modified organisms can be used in organic farming, ecologic factors in the farming site should be in the desired level. These factors can be detailed as; water quality and availability, soil quality, biodiversity and climate effects.

**Technological Factors:** In organic farming, the production has to be taken care of carefully. Since it is all natural, the process is highly fragile. So the use of technology gains importance in controlling it. Feasibility, reliability and ease of access are the factors that have to be taken into consideration in the use of technology.

**Economic Factors:** Today's capitalist world checks one main output above all in any business: Profitability. Knowledge of costs and the available demand are essential to determine whether a business is profitable or not. So, before building an organic farm site, the area should be investigated in terms of economic factors. Cost of ownership, fund availability, consumer behavior and profitability are the main economic factors for determining location for organic farm sites.

**Risk Factors:** Organic agriculture is not apart from its external environment and is affected from it. Natural disasters, economic crisis, etc. are risks for organic farming. So locating organic farm site in a risk-free environment is better. These risks can be divided into 3: Ecological risks, economic risks and societal risks.

**Infrastructure:** The site has necessities to practice organic farming efficiently. Without enough raw materials, energy or transportation, the output will not be on desired level. Distance to highway, distance to industrial, distance to local market and distance to energy are highly important for an efficient practice of organic farming.

**Local Community:** Farming cannot be done without humans, at least for now. Also the output of organic farming is offered to the benefit of humans. So; humans, especially the local community are important for organic farming. In determining the location of organic farming site; local know-how, labor availability and contribution to local develop are the important factors in terms of local community.

# 5    The Case of Turkey

The problem discussed here is about prioritization of the organic farming sites in Turkey. As step 1, criteria in section 4 are determined from the effecting factors of organic farming. After that, a decision making group of 4 DM's is arranged; followed by identification of the appropriate linguistic variables. Application of the rest of the method can be seen in below.

Step 4: Pull the DM's opinions to get the aggregated fuzzy weight of criteria and fuzzy rating of alternatives and construct a fuzzy decision matrix. The opinions of DM's and combined fuzzy values are given in table 3, 4, 5 and 6:

Table 2. Importance weight of criteria from four decision makers

| Criteria | Decision makers | | | |
|---|---|---|---|---|
| | D1 | D2 | D3 | D4 |
| Ecological Factors | M | H | MH | M |
| Technological Factors | MH | ML | M | H |
| Economic Factors | H | ML | VH | H |
| Risk Factors | L | VH | MH | L |
| Infrastructure | M | M | M | VH |
| Local Community | H | M | MH | M |

Table 3. Ratings of the alternative cities by the decision makers under the various criteria

| | | Criteria | | | | | |
|---|---|---|---|---|---|---|---|
| | Alternatives | Ecological Factors | Technological factors | Economic Factors | Risk Factors | Infrastructure | Local Community |
| D1 | Ağrı | F | P | P | VP | P | F |
| | Erzurum | G | MP | MP | F | G | G |
| | İzmir | G | G | VG | F | G | G |
| | Niğde | MP | MG | F | VG | G | MG |
| D2 | Ağrı | MG | MP | P | P | MP | MG |
| | Erzurum | VG | F | F | MG | MG | F |
| | İzmir | MG | F | G | MG | MG | MG |
| | Niğde | F | F | MP | VG | G | VG |
| D3 | Ağrı | MG | MP | VP | P | MP | F |
| | Erzurum | MG | F | MP | MP | MG | MG |
| | İzmir | F | MG | VG | MP | G | F |
| | Niğde | F | MG | F | G | F | G |
| D4 | Ağrı | MG | P | P | MP | P | G |
| | Erzurum | MG | MG | MG | F | G | F |
| | İzmir | G | VG | VG | F | VG | MG |
| | Niğde | MG | MG | F | G | G | G |

**Table 4.** Aggregated fuzzy weight of criteria and aggregated fuzzy rating of alternatives

| | Criteria | | |
|---|---|---|---|
| | Ecological Factors | Technological factors | Economic Factors |
| **Weight** | **(0.4, 0.6, 0.625, 0.9)** | **(0.2, 0.55, 0.6, 0.9)** | **(0.2, 0.7, 0.75, 1)** |
| Ağrı | (0.4, 0.575, 0.65, 0.8) | (0.1, 0.25, 0.3, 0.5) | (0, 0.15, 0.175, 0.3) |
| Erzurum | (0.5, 0.725, 0.8, 1) | (0.2, 0.475, 0.525, 0.8) | (0.2, 0.425, 0.5, 0.8) |
| İzmir | (0.4, 0.675, 0.7, 0.9) | (0.4, 0.7, 0.75, 1) | (0.7, 0.875, 0.95, 1) |
| Niğde | (0.2, 0.475, 0.525, 0.8) | (0.4, 0.575, 0.65, 0.8) | (0.2, 0.45, 0.475, 0.6) |

**Table 5.** Aggregated fuzzy weight of criteria and aggregated fuzzy rating of alternatives (continued)

| | Criteria | | |
|---|---|---|---|
| | Risk Factors | Infrastructure | Local Community |
| **Weight** | **(0.1, 0.475, 0.525, 1)** | **(0.4, 0.6, 0.625, 1)** | **(0.4, 0.6, 0.625, 0.9)** |
| Ağrı | (0, 0.175, 0.225, 0.5) | (0.1, 0.25, 0.3, 0.5) | (0.4, 0.6, 0.625, 0.9) |
| Erzurum | (0.2, 0.475, 0.525, 0.8) | (0.5, 0.7, 0.75, 0.9) | (0.4, 0.6, 0.625, 0.9) |
| İzmir | (0.2, 0.475, 0.525, 0.8) | (0.5, 0.775, 0.825, 1) | (0.4, 0.625, 0.675, 0.9) |
| Niğde | (0.7, 0.85, 0.9, 1) | (0.4, 0.725, 0.725, 0.9) | (0.5, 0.775, 0.825, 1) |

*Step 5:* The crisp values for decision matrix and weight of each criterion are computed as shown in Table 6.

**Table 6.** Crisp values for decision matrix and weight of each criterion

| | Criteria | | | | | |
|---|---|---|---|---|---|---|
| | Ecological Factors | Technological factors | Economic Factors | Risk Factors | Infrastructure | Local Community |
| **Weight** | **0.64** | **0.56** | **0.64** | **0.53** | **0.67** | **0.64** |
| Ağrı | 0.60 | 0.29 | 0.15 | 0.23 | 0.29 | 0.64 |
| Erzurum | 0.75 | 0.50 | 0.49 | 0.50 | 0.71 | 0.64 |
| İzmir | 0.66 | 0.71 | 0.88 | 0.50 | 0.77 | 0.65 |
| Niğde | 0.50 | 0.60 | 0.42 | 0.86 | 0.68 | 0.77 |

*Step 6:* The best and the worst values of all criterion ratings are determined as follows:

$f_1^* = 0.75$     $f_2^* = 0.71$     $f_3^* = 0.88$     $f_4^* = 0.86$     $f_5^* = 0.77$     $f_6^* = 0.77$

$f_1^- = 0.50$     $f_2^- = 0.29$     $f_3^- = 0.15$     $f_4^- = 0.23$     $f_5^- = 0.29$     $f_6^- = 0.64$

In step 7 and 8, the values of S, R and Q (for different values of v) are calculated for all alternative firms as Table 7.

**Table 7.** The values of S and R for all alternatives

|           | Alternatives | | | |
| --- | --- | --- | --- | --- |
|           | Ağrı | Erzurum | İzmir | Niğde |
| S         | 3.42 | 1.65 | 1.11 | 1.31 |
| R         | 0.67 | 0.64 | 0.57 | 0.64 |
| Q (v = 0) | 1.00 | 0.66 | 0.00 | 0.66 |
| Q (v = 0.5) | 1.00 | 0.45 | 0.00 | 0.37 |
| Q (v = 1) | 1.00 | 0.24 | 0.00 | 0.09 |

*Step 9:* The alternatives are ranked, sorting by the values S, R and Q in ascending order:

**Table 8.** The ranking of the alternative insurance firms by S, R and Q in decreasing order

|  | Ranking alternatives | | | |
| --- | --- | --- | --- | --- |
|  | 1 | 2 | 3 | 4 |
| By S | İzmir | Niğde | Erzurum | Ağrı |
| By R | İzmir | Niğde = | Erzurum | Ağrı |
| By Q (v = 0) | İzmir | Niğde = | Erzurum | Ağrı |
| By Q (v = 0.5) | İzmir | Niğde | Erzurum | Ağrı |
| By Q (v = 1) | İzmir | Niğde | Erzurum | Ağrı |

# 6 Conclusion

In Turkey, organic farming is being applied only in %0.14 of the agricultural lands [22]. Since the demand in organic products have an increasing growth rate [7], Turkey should use its great potential. This can be achieved with regulations, incentives and inspections. This study was aimed to show the lawmakers the organic farming sites that they should give weight to.

In the present study, after criteria were determined, the prioritization of the organic farm sites in Turkey was determined by using extended VIKOR method. In this methodology, distances of alternatives to the ideal solution are calculated and ranked from best to worst.

The results show us that; İzmir is by far the most important organic farming site for Turkey. So for the future research, necessities of Turkey's main organic farming sites should be investigated in detail and effects of the developments on them should be evaluated.

# References

1. Paull, J., Hennig, B.: A World Map of Organic Agriculture. European Journal of Social Sciences 24(3), 360–369 (2011)
2. What is organic farming, http://ec.europa.eu/agriculture/organic/organic-farming/what-organic_en

3. Organic-The fastest growing agricultural based industry in the world. OFA Organic Update (August 2011)
4. Willer, H., Yussefi, M.: Organic Agriculture World-Wide: Statistics and Perspectives. Stiftung Ökologie & Landbau, Bad Durkheim (2000)
5. Willer, H., Kilcher, L.: The World of Organic Agriculture: Statistics and Emerging Trends 2011. In: Research Institute of Organic Agriculture, IFOAM, Frick, Switzerland (2011)
6. Paull, J.: The Uptake of Organic Agriculture: A Decade of Worldwide Development. Journal of Social and Development Sciences 2(3), 111–120 (2011)
7. Global Organic Food & Drink Sales Approach $60 Billion, http://www.triplepundit.com/2010/12/global-organic-food-drink-sales-approach-60-billion/
8. Organic farming (in Turkish), http://www.tarim.gov.tr/uretim/Organik_Tarim.html
9. Organic Farming Production Statistics (in Turkish), http://www.tarim.gov.tr/Files/Images/organik_Tarim/2010genelorganik_tarimsaluretimve rileri.doc
10. Aksoy, U., Altındişli, A.: Production, export and development opportunuties of ecological agricultural products in the world and in Turkey. İTO Yayınları, İstanbul (1999)
11. Taşbaşlı, H., Zeytin, B.: Principicals of Organic farming. TKB Yayınları, Ankara (2003)
12. Chang, D.Y.: Applications of the extent analysis method on fuzzy AHP. European Journal of Operational Research 95, 649–655 (1996)
13. Demirel, T., Demirel, N.Ç., Kahraman, C.: Multi-Criteria Warehouse Location Selection Using Choquet Integral. Expert Systems with Applications 5(37), 3943–3952 (2010)
14. Dağdeviren, M., Yüksel, İ., Kurt, M.: A fuzzy analytic network process (ANP) model to identify faulty behavior risk (FBR) in work system. Safety Science (2007) 10.1016
15. Mikhailov, L.: Fuzzy analytical approach to partnership selection in formation of virtual enterprises. Omega 30, 393–401 (2002)
16. Opricovic, S., Tzeng, G.-H.: Extended VIKOR method in comparison with outranking methods. European Journal of Operational Research 178, 514–529 (2007)
17. Sanayei, A., Mousavi, S.F., Yazdankhah, A.: Group decision making process for supplier selection with VIKOR under fuzzy environment. Expert Systems with App. 37, 24–30 (2010)
18. Liou, J.J.H., Tsai, C.-Y., Lin, R.-H., Tzeng, G.-H.: A modified VIKOR multiple-criteria decision method for improving domestic airlines service quality. J. of Air Trans. Man., 1–5 (2010)
19. Demirel, N.Ç., Yücenur, G.N.: The Cruise Port Place Selection Problem with Extended VIKOR and ANP Methodologies under Fuzzy Environment. In: Proceedings of the World Congress on Engineering 2011, pp. 1128–1133 (2011)
20. Asami, D.K.: Comparison of the Total Phenolic and Ascorbic Acid Content of Freeze-Dried and Air-Dried Marionberry, Strawberry, and Corn Grown Using Conventional, Organic, and Sustainable Agricultural Practices. J. of Agr. and Food Chem. 51, 1237–1241 (2003)
21. Stolze, M., Piorr, A., Häring, A., Dabbert, S.: The Environmental Impacts of Organic Farming in Europe. Organic Farming in Europe: Economics and Policy 6 (2000)
22. Yussefi, M.: Development and state of organic agriculture world-wide. In: Yussefi, M., Willer, H. (eds.) The World of Organic Agriculture: Statistics and Future Prospects, 5th revised edn., pp. S.7–S.25. IFOAM, Tholey-Theley (2003)
23. Darnhofer, I., Schneeberger, W., Freyer, B.: Converting or not converting to organic farming in Austria: Farmer types and their rationale. Agr. and Human Val. 22(1), 39–52 (2005)

# New Product Selection Using Fuzzy Linear Programming and Fuzzy Monte Carlo Simulation

İrem Uçal Sarı and Cengiz Kahraman

İstanbul Technical University, Industrial Engineering Department, Maçka, 34367,
İstanbul, Turkey
{ucal,kahramanc}@itu.edu.tr

**Abstract.** Investment decisions are important due to their critical role in organizations' success. Sometimes, especially in uncertain conditions the results obtained from traditional analysis techniques can be different from the real world results. Due to this fact the techniques that take uncertainty into account are preferred in investment analysis to aware of the effect of an uncertain environment. In this paper, fuzzy Monte Carlo simulation method is used to determine the best investment strategy on new product selection for an organization in the condition when the fuzzy net present value is not the only point of concern for decision making.

**Keywords:** Fuzzy Monte Carlo Simulation Method, Capital Budgeting, Linear Programming.

## 1 Introduction

New product selection is a critical issue for companies due to their direct effect on profit and compatibility. Since the position of the company in the market due to the competitive structure is an important issue, the selection of new product attracts a lot attention of not only practitioners but also researches. It is a complex process, which include technological requirements and their accessibility, consumer behavior analysis and economic analysis. Economic analysis of a new product selection is a critical parameter that can satisfy the profitability goal of a company.

The best known investment valuation methods are discounted cash flows methods in which the investment valuation can be determined by different terms such as net present value, net future value, internal rate of return, discounted payback period and equivalent uniform annual value. Moreover, linear programming is used in capital budgeting when the project alternatives have to satisfy some constraints. The objective function of the linear programming model is a maximization problem when the project is profitable, and when it is non-profitable project, the objective function is constructed as a minimization problem.

Occasionally, especially under uncertain conditions the results obtained from traditional analysis techniques can be different from the real world results. Due to this fact, the techniques which take uncertainty into account are preferred. However, the representation of the uncertainty by one estimation causes lack of information, in

S. Greco et al. (Eds.): IPMU 2012, Part IV, CCIS 300, pp. 441–448, 2012.
© Springer-Verlag Berlin Heidelberg 2012

deterministic techniques, just one of the estimations of a parameter is considered. On the other hand, in probabilistic approaches which are widely used on analyzing investments, the models can be inadequate if the collection of the previous data is unavailable. Henceforth, the utilization of fuzzy logic to count the uncertainty in the mathematical models has recently become widespread.

The purpose of the study is to determine the best investment strategy for new product selection by using fuzzy Monte Carlo simulation method when the fuzzy net present value is not the only criteria for decision making.

The rest of the paper is organized as follows. In Section 2, literature review on new product development and fuzzy Monte Carlo simulation method. In Sections 3 and 4, mathematical programming for capital budgeting and fuzzy Monte Carlo simulation method are given. In Section 5, there is an application on project investment. Finally in Section 6, the paper is concluded with the obtained results.

## 2    Literature Review

There are many works on new product development in literature. Liao (2011) proposed a model based on fuzzy analytical hierarchy process and multi-segment goal programming to select the best pricing strategy for new product development. Wei and Chang (2011), proposed a new approach which combines fuzzy set theory and multi criteria group decision making method into a new product development project selection model. Wang and Chin (2008) proposed a linear goal programming model priority method and tested the proposed method with new product development project screening decision making examples. Ngan (2011) proposed an alternative formulation based on sampling distribution and applied the proposed methodology on evaluating new product development ideas and on survey analysis.

There are different applications of fuzzy Monte Carlo simulation in the literature. Prasad et. al (2011) and Park et.al (2011) are used fuzzy Monte Carlo simulation for failure probability evaluation. Wu (2011) used fuzzy Monte Carlo simulation to evaluate fuzzy Riemann integrals. Ng et. al (2007)proposed a fuzzy simulation model to assist a public partner to identify the concession period based on the expected investment. Bai and Asgarpoor (2004) described a fuzzy-based analytical method and a fuzzy-based Monte Carlo simulation technique to obtain a possibility distribution of reliability indices for substations.

## 3    Mathematical Programming for Fuzzy Capital Budgeting

In this section definition of fuzzy set theory and algebraic operations on fuzzy numbers are given. After definitions, the linear programs of investment opportunities are analyzed with respect to their dependency in fuzzy case.

### 3.1    Fuzzy Set Theory

Zadeh first found the fuzzy set theory in 1965. A fuzzy set is defined as a class of objects with a continuum of grades of membership, which is characterized by a membership function that assigns to each object a grade of membership ranging between zero and one. A fuzzy set $\tilde{A}$ in U is characterized by a membership function $\mu_{\tilde{A}}(x)$ which associates with each point in U a real number in interval $[0,1]$, with the value of $\mu_{\tilde{A}}(x)$ at x representing "the grade of membership" of x in $\tilde{A}$ (Zadeh, 1965).

A formula for a membership function $\mu_{\tilde{A}}(x)$ of fuzzy number $\tilde{A}$ is given in Eq. 1, where $a$, $b$ and c denotes real numbers (Ross, 1995):

$$\mu_{\tilde{A}}(x) = \mu_{\tilde{A}}(x; a, b, c) = \begin{cases} \frac{x-a}{b-a} & ; \quad a \leq x \leq b \\ \frac{c-x}{c-b} & ; \quad b \leq x \leq c \\ 0 & ; \quad x \geq c \ or \ x \leq a \end{cases} \tag{1}$$

Dubois and Prade (1978) proposed the LR representation of fuzzy numbers. A function, usually denoted L or R is a reference function of fuzzy numbers iff $L(x) = L(-x)$, $L(0) = 1$, and L is nonincreasing on $[0, +\infty)$. A fuzzy number $\tilde{A}$ is said to be an LR type fuzzy number iff it provides Eq.2.

$$\mu_{\tilde{A}}(x) = \begin{cases} \frac{L(m-x)}{\alpha} & ; \quad x \leq m, \alpha > 0 \\ \frac{L(x-m)}{\beta} & ; \quad x \geq m, \beta > 0 \end{cases} \tag{2}$$

In Eq. 2, L represents left reference and R represents right reference, m is the mean value of $\tilde{A}$, $\alpha$ and $\beta$ are called left and right spreads, respectively.

A triangular fuzzy number (TFN) is a special type of LR fuzzy numbers which has linear reference functions on both sides. TFN is one of the most frequently used fuzzy numbers because of its simple membership function. Hanns (2005) defined the membership function for a TFN $\tilde{A} = (a_l, a_m, a_r)$ in Eq. 3:

$$\mu_{\tilde{A}}(x) = \begin{cases} 1 + \frac{x-a_m}{a_m-a_l} & ; \quad a_l < x \leq a_m \\ 1 - \frac{x-a_m}{a_r-a_m} & ; \quad a_m \leq x < a_r \\ 0 & ; \quad x \geq a_r \ or \ x \leq a_l \end{cases} \tag{3}$$

## 3.2 Fuzzy Operations

Algebraic operations for TFNs $\tilde{M} = (m_l, m_m, m_r)$ and $\tilde{N} = (n_l, n_m, n_r)$ are given by following equations with the order of summation, subtraction, multiplication, division and multiplication by a scalar (Chen et al., 1992):

$$\tilde{M} \oplus \tilde{N} = (m_l + n_l, m_m + n_m, m_r + n_r) \tag{4}$$

$$\tilde{M} \ominus \tilde{N} = (m_l - n_r, m_m - n_m, m_r - n_l) \tag{5}$$

$$\tilde{M} \otimes \tilde{N} \cong \begin{cases} (m_l n_l, m_m n_m, m_r n_r) & (m_l, m_m, m_r) \geq 0, (n_l, n_m, n_r) \geq 0 \\ (m_l n_r, m_m n_m, m_r n_l) & if \quad (m_l, m_m, m_r) \leq 0, (n_l, n_m, n_r) \geq 0 \\ (m_r n_r, m_m n_m, m_l n_l) & (m_l, m_m, m_r) \leq 0, (n_l, n_m, n_r) \leq 0 \end{cases} \tag{6}$$

$$\widetilde{M} \oslash \widetilde{N} \cong \begin{cases} \left(\frac{m_l}{n_r}, \frac{m_m}{n_m}, \frac{m_r}{n_l}\right) & (m_l, m_m, m_r) \geq 0, (n_l, n_m, n_r) \geq 0 \\ \left(\frac{m_r}{n_r}, \frac{m_m}{n_m}, \frac{m_l}{n_l}\right) & if \quad (m_l, m_m, m_r) \leq 0, (n_l, n_m, n_r) \geq 0 \\ \left(\frac{m_r}{n_l}, \frac{m_m}{n_m}, \frac{m_l}{n_r}\right) & (m_l, m_m, m_r) \leq 0, (n_l, n_m, n_r) \leq 0 \end{cases} \quad (7)$$

$$\widetilde{M} \otimes \lambda = \begin{cases} (\lambda m_l, \lambda m_m, \lambda m_r) \\ (\lambda m_r, \lambda m_m, \lambda m_l) \end{cases} if \begin{matrix} \lambda \geq \\ \lambda \leq \end{matrix}, \forall \lambda \in \mathcal{R} \quad (8)$$

An $\gamma$ cut of a fuzzy number $\tilde{A}$ which is one of the most important concepts of fuzzy sets, is symbolized as $A^\gamma$ and determined as a crisp set that contains all the elements of the universal set U whose membership grades in $\tilde{A}$ are greater than or equal to the specific value of $\gamma$. The formula of $A^\gamma$ is given in Eq. 9 (Klir & Yuan, 1995):

$$A^\gamma = \{x | A(x) \geq \gamma\} \quad (9)$$

### 3.3    Ranking Fuzzy Numbers

In the literature there are lots of methods for ranking fuzzy numbers. These can be classified as (1) ranking using degree of optimality, (2) ranking using Hamming distance, (3) ranking using α-cuts, (4) ranking using comparison function, (5) ranking using fuzzy mean and spread, (6) ranking using proportion to the ideal, (7) ranking using left and right scores, (8) ranking using centroid index, (9) ranking using area measurement, (10) linguistic ranking methods and (11) others (Chen et al.,1992). As an example, Yager (1980) developed a centroid index to rank fuzzy numbers. This index is given by Eq. 10.

$$x_{\tilde{A}}^* = \frac{\int_0^1 x f_{\tilde{A}}(x) dx}{\int_0^1 f_{\tilde{A}}(x) dx} \quad (10)$$

In this study we will use Chiu and Park's (1994) weighted method to rank fuzzy numbers. The weighted method compares the fuzzy numbers by assigning relative weights to determine the preference of fuzzy numbers. The preference of a TFN $\tilde{A}$ is given in Eq. 11 where $w$ is the relative weight determined by the nature and magnitude of the most promising value:

$$A_{CP} = \frac{A_l + A_m + A_r}{3} + w A_m \quad (11)$$

The importance of the most promising value is increased by a larger weight.

### 3.4    Capital Budgeting Using Fuzzy Linear Programming

The investment opportunities can be analyzed due to their dependency and divisibility. The objective functions and constraints of fuzzy linear programs for the possible cases of indivisible investment opportunities are given below:

### 3.4.1  Independent Investment Opportunities

In this case, we have $m$ new independent indivisible investment opportunities available. Investment opportunity $i$ has a present worth of $\tilde{p}_i$ an initial investment of $\tilde{c}_i$, and annual operating and maintenance costs of $\tilde{a}_i$. There exists a capital budget limitation of $\$\tilde{C}$ for new investments. A limitation of $\$\tilde{A}$ exists on total annual operating and maintenance costs for new investments. It is desired to select the set of investment opportunities which maximizes present worth subject to the budgetary limitations.

Let $x_i$ is defined to be 0 if opportunity $i$ is not selected for investment and it is defined to be 1 if opportunity $i$ is selected for investment. The following mathematical programming formulation of the investment decision problem is obtained:

$$
\begin{aligned}
\text{Maximize} \quad & \tilde{p}_1 x_1 + \tilde{p}_2 x_2 + \cdots + \tilde{p}_m x_m \\
\text{Subject to} \quad & \tilde{c}_1 x_1 + \tilde{c}_2 x_2 + \cdots + \tilde{c}_m x_m \leq \tilde{C} \\
& \tilde{a}_1 x_1 + \tilde{a}_2 x_2 + \cdots + \tilde{a}_m x_m \leq \tilde{A} \\
& x_i = (0,1) \quad i = 1, \dots, m
\end{aligned}
$$

### 3.4.2  Dependent Investment Opportunities

If opportunities $j$ and $k$ are mutually exclusive, then the following constraint can be added to the mathematical programming formulation: $x_j + x_k \leq 1$. Similarly if the selection of opportunity $e$ is contingent upon the selection of either opportunity $f$ or $g$, then the following constraint applies: $x_e \leq x_f + x_g$ or $x_e - x_f - x_g \leq 0$.

### 3.4.3  Independent Collections of Mutually Exclusive Opportunities

In this subsection a capital budgeting problem involving indivisible investment opportunities consisting of independent collections of mutually exclusive investment opportunities is considered. A firm that has m sources of investment opportunities, with source $i$ providing $n_i$ mutually exclusive investment opportunities for consideration. A single budgetary constraint limits the total amount invested. The budget allocation problem is formulated as follows:

$$
\begin{aligned}
\text{Maximize} \quad & \sum_{i=1}^{m} \sum_{j=1}^{n_i} \tilde{p}_{ij} x_{ij} \\
\text{Subject to} \quad & \sum_{i=1}^{m} \sum_{j=1}^{n_i} \tilde{c}_{ij} x_{ij} \leq \tilde{C} \\
& \sum_{j=1}^{n_i} x_{ij} \leq 1, \quad i = 1, \dots, m \\
& x_{ij} = (0,1) \text{ for all } i, j
\end{aligned}
$$

where $m$ is the number of sources of investment opportunities, $n_i$ is the number of mutually exclusive investment opportunities available from source $i$, $\tilde{p}_{ij}$ is the fuzzy present worth of investment opportunity $j$ from source $i$, $\tilde{c}_{ij}$ is the initial investment required for investment opportunity $j$ from source $i$, $x_{ij}$ is defined to be 0 if opportunity $j$ from source $i$ is not selected for investment and it is defined to be 1 if opportunity $j$ from source $i$ is selected for investment and $\tilde{C}$ is the budget limit.

# 4    Fuzzy Monte Carlo Simulation Method

The Monte Carlo simulation technique is an especially useful means of analyzing situations involving risk to obtain approximate answers when a physical experiment or the use of analytical approaches is either too burdensome or not feasible. The technique is sometimes descriptively called the method of statistical trials. It involves, first, the random selection of an outcome for each variable of interest, the combining of these outcomes with any fixed amounts, and calculation if necessary to obtain one trial outcome in terms of the desired answer. This done repeatedly will result in enough trial outcomes to obtain a sufficiently close approximation of the mean, variance, distribution shape, or other characteristic of the desired answer (Canada and White, 1980).

If the probability distributions of decision parameters are not known, fuzzy simulation is still a way of producing outcomes. Monte Carlo simulation methods in fuzzy optimization are defined in detail by Buckley and Lowers (2008). There are four steps in this method which are determined as follows:

*Step 1.* Formulation of objective function and the constraints

*Step 2.* Determination of vector intervals: There is no special upper bound for the intervals, and mostly the experts chose the upper bound. It is important to determine the interval not too big also not too small to reach the optimal solution in an early stage of the iterations.

*Step 3.* Generation random fuzzy vectors: Fuzzy TFN vectors are generated randomly using a random number generator by ordering three random numbers.

*Step 4.* Comparison of the fuzzy vectors and constraints: If the fuzzy vectors satisfy the constraints and that fuzzy vector is feasible, calculate $\tilde{Z}^*$. Defuzzification is here necessary to compare fuzzy outcomes of simulation.

*Step 5.* If $\tilde{Z}^* > \tilde{Z}$ set $\tilde{Z}$ as $\tilde{Z}^*$ ,then turn Step 2 for the next iteration.

When the number of the iterations increases, the closer values of $\tilde{Z}$ to the best solution are calculated.

# 5    An Application: New Product Selection

A manufacturer wants to invest on projects to produce new products. Each project has a different new product. The budget of the firm is approximately 1000000\$ which is fuzzified as $\tilde{I} = (900000, 1000000, 1100000)$. There are 5 different project alternatives. Project A, B and E are independent. Project D is feasible if only if the manufacturer invests on project C and they are indivisible. Project A and Project D are mutually exclusive. The capacity of each project is 100.000 products. The fuzzy net present values of the projects are given in Table 1.

The linear program of the problem is as follows:

```
Maximize    p̃_A a_A x̃_A + p̃_B a_B x̃_B + p̃_C a_C x̃_C + p̃_D a_D x̃_D + p̃_E a_E x̃_E
Subject to  Ĩ_A a_A + Ĩ_B a_B + Ĩ_C a_C + Ĩ_D a_D + Ĩ_E a_E ≤ Ĩ
```

$$\tilde{x}_{A,B,C,D,E} \leq \tilde{C}$$
$$a_D \leq a_C$$
$$a_A + a_D \leq 1$$
$$\tilde{x}_{A,B,C,D,E} \geq 0$$
$$a_{A,B,C,D,E} = \{0,1\}$$

**Table 1.** The Fuzzy Cash Flows of the Project

| | Project A (x1000) | Project B (x1000) | Project C (x1000) | Project D (x1000) | Project E (x1000) |
|---|---|---|---|---|---|
| Initial Investments ($I$) | (120,150,200) | (150,175,190) | (115,130,160) | (50,90,125) | (250,290,350) |
| Fuzzy profits of the projects ($\tilde{p}$) | (5.6,5.9,6.1) | (5.5,5.7,5.9) | (4.9,5.1,5.2) | (1.8,2.2,2.5) | (6.8,7.5,8.2) |

where $a_i$ is a binary variable which denotes whether the project $i$ is invested or not, $\tilde{x}_i$ denotes the capacity usage of project $i$, $\tilde{p}_A$ denotes the fuzzy profits of the project $i$, $\tilde{I}_i$ denotes initial investment of project $i$, $\tilde{I}$ denotes the budget of the firm and $\tilde{C}$ denotes the capacity limit of project $i$.

Maximize $\quad (5.6,5.9,6.1)a_A x_A + (5.5,5.7,5.9)a_B x_B + (4.9,5.1,5.2)a_C x_C + (1.8,2.2,2.5)a_D x_D + (6.8,7.5,8.2)a_E x_E$

Subject to $\quad (120,150,200)a_A + (150,175,190)a_B + (115,130,160)a_C + (50,90,125)a_D + (250,290,350)a_E \leq (900,1000,1100)$

$$x_{A,B,C,D,E} \leq (100000)$$
$$a_D \leq a_C$$
$$a_A + a_D \leq 1$$
$$x_{A,B,C,D,E} \geq 0$$
$$a_{A,B,C,D,E} = \{0,1\}$$

The vector intervals for number of production variable are chosen as $\tilde{V}_{x_i} = [0,1000]$ due to the capacity constraint. 7500 random numbers are generated for 2500 fuzzy vectors to make 500 iterations. Vector intervals for investment constraint are chosen as $V_{a_i} = [0,1]$. 313 of the iterations are feasible and 187 of them are infeasible. The maximum fuzzy net present value is found as (1894566, 2294877,2536347)\$ by investing on Projects A, B, C and E. The optimum solution is found with the fuzzy random vectors $\tilde{V}_{x_A} = (87308,93122,99948)$, $\tilde{V}_{x_B} = (83414,96832,99834)$, $\tilde{V}_{x_C} = (61609,92618,99867)$, $\tilde{V}_{x_D} = (89112,96550,99865)$, and $\tilde{V}_{x_E} = (94850,96155,99797)$. With maximum capacity usage the fuzzy net present value is calculated as (2280000, 2420000, 2540000)\$.

# 6    Conclusions

New product development is critical for organizations to be compatible and successful in the market. New product development is a complex process and one of the most important criteria on new product development is profit maximization. In uncertain conditions such as; predicting new product's possible profits, traditional investment analysis methods cannot give the exact solutions. Fuzzy logic becomes necessary to be used when the parameters cannot be determined in crisp numbers and/or the decision makers require taking uncertainty into account.

In this paper, fuzzy linear programming is used to determine the most profitable project for new product inception. Fuzzy Monte Carlo simulation method is used to solve that fuzzy maximization problem and to determine the best investment strategy on new product selection for an organization.

For further research, the fuzzy Monte Carlo simulation method could be applied on valuation of a project such as fuzzy discounted cash flow analysis methods.

# References

1. Chiu, C.Y., Park, C.S.: Fuzzy cash flow analysis using present worth criterion. The Engineering Economist 39(2), 113–138 (1994)
2. Chen, S.J., Hwang, C.L., Hwang, F.P.: Fuzzy multiple attribute decision making: Methods and applications. Springer, Berlin (1992)
3. Dubois, D., Prade, H.: Operations on fuzzy numbers. International Journal of Systems Science 9, 613–626 (1978)
4. Klir, G.J., Yuan, B.: Fuzzy Sets and Fuzzy Logic_Theory and Applications. Prentice Hall PTR (1995)
5. Hanns, M.: Applied Fuzzy Arithmetics_An Introduction with Engineering Applications. Springer, Netherlands (2005)
6. Buckley, J.J., Lowers, L.J.: Monte Carlo Methods in Fuzzy Optimization. Springer, Berlin (2008)
7. Canada, J.R., White, J.A.: Capital investment decision analysis for management and engineering. Prentice-Hall, USA (1980)
8. Ross, T.J.: Fuzzy Logic With Engineering Applications. Mc-Graw Hill, USA (1995)
9. Zadeh, L.A.: Fuzzy Sets. Information and Control 8, 338–353 (1965)
10. Liao, C.N.: Fuzzy analytical hierarchy process and multi-segment goal programming applied to new product segmented under price strategy. Computers & Industrial Engineering 6, 831–841 (2011)
11. Wei, C.C., Chang, H.W.: A new approach for selecting portfolio of new product development projects. Expert Systems with Applications 38, 429–434 (2011)
12. Wang, Y.M., Chin, K.S.: A linear goal programming priority method for fuzzy analytic hierarchy process and its applications in new product screening. International Journal of Approximate Reasoning 49, 451–465 (2008)
13. Ngan, S.C.: Decision making with extended fuzzy linguistic computing, with applications to new product development and survey analysis. Expert Systems with Applications 38, 14052–14059 (2011)
14. Ng, S.T., Xie, J., Skitmore, M., Cheung, Y.K.: A fuzzy simulation model for evaluating the concession items of public–private partnership schemes. Automation in Construction 17, 22–29 (2007)
15. Prasad, M.H., Gaikwad, A.J., Srividya, A., Verma, A.K.: Failure probability evaluation of passive system using fuzzy Monte Carlo simulation. Nuclear Engineering and Design 241, 1864–1872 (2011)
16. Wu, H.C.: Evaluate Fuzzy Riemann Integrals Using the Monte Carlo Method. Journal of Mathematical Analysis and Applications 264, 324–343 (2001)
17. Park, H.J., Um, J.G., Woo, I., Kim, J.W.: Application of fuzzy set theory to evaluate the probability of failure in rock slopes. Engineering Geology (2011) (in press)
18. Bai, X., Asgarpoor, S.: Fuzzy-based approaches to substation reliability evaluation. Electric Power Systems Research 69, 197–204 (2004)

# Multicriteria Environmental Risk Evaluation Using Type II Fuzzy Sets

Cengiz Kahraman and İrem Uçal Sarı

Istanbul Technical University Department of Industrial Engineering, 34367 Macka Istanbul Turkey
{kahramanc,ucal}@itu.edu.tr

**Abstract.** In this paper, interval type-2 fuzzy TOPSIS is used for environmental risk evaluation. By type-2 fuzzy sets we can consider the footprint of uncertainty in the membership functions. A multicriteria selection among the treatment alternatives of hazardous waste management is made. An application is presented.

**Keywords:** Type-II fuzzy sets, TOPSIS, waste management, risk evaluation, multicriteria.

## 1 Introduction

Environmental risk is an actual or potential threat of adverse effects on living organisms and environment by effluents, emissions, wastes, resource depletion, etc., arising out of an organization's activities. Environmental risk deals with the probability of an event causing a potentially undesirable effect. It has long been applied to evaluate the risks to human health arising from radionuclides and chemicals in the environment. Hazard assessment has been used to study natural hazards and assist in preparing for them. The recent application of risk assessment techniques to flora and fauna is being called ecological risk analysis. The means by which risk is managed, the means by which risk is communicated to the public and the consequences of failing to undertake adequate risk assessment or undertaking incorrect risk assessments need to be known and appreciated by environmental practitioners. These issues are seen as an integral part of a quality assured environmental management system.

In this paper, we aim to apply a type-II fuzzy TOPSIS method to make a multicriteria selection among the treatment alternatives of hazardous waste management. The proposed methodology is applied to a problem case of Istanbul to demonstrate the potential of the methodology.

The rest of this paper is organized as follows. Section 2 explains environmental risk evaluation. Section 3 presents type-II fuzzy sets. Section 4 gives the steps of type-II fuzzy TOPSIS. Section 5 gives an application of type-II fuzzy TOPSIS to environmental risk evaluation. Finally Section 6 includes the conclusions.

S. Greco et al. (Eds.): IPMU 2012, Part IV, CCIS 300, pp. 449–457, 2012.

# 2     Environmental Risk Evaluation: Alternatives and Criteria

Hazardous waste has a chemical composition or other properties that have to be managed in order to prevent its release into the environment that can result in illness, death or other harm to living organisms including humans. A hazardous waste management scheme must be justified in terms of scientific evidence, engineering designs and processes, technologic practicality, economic realities, ethical considerations, and local, state, and national regulations (Vallero and Peirce, 2003). Hazardous waste risk range from toxic risks which the probability that a certain population will have an incidence of a particular illness to other risks such as ecosystem stress, loss of important habitats, decreases in the size of the population of sensitive species, public safety and public welfare hazards. The wide range of risks encountered requires specific solutions often at high costs. Facilities that generate, transport, transfer, treat or dispose of hazardous wastes require substantial construction, operating costs and have become extremely expensive and complex. There are usually a range of treatment alternatives for various types of hazardous wastes and their components dependent upon physical and/or chemical properties (Cheremisinoff and Cheremisinoff, 1995). A challenge of hazardous waste management is the selection of treatment alternative considering the technical, economical and risk associated aspects. The aspects of the problem are usually represented in the form of multiple criteria which often express tradeoffs between the management objectives.

It is essential to identify the decision objectives and the set of comprehensive and non-redundant criteria corresponding to the objectives in decision analysis. The immediate objectives in hazardous waste management typically include reducing the risks and minimizing the costs. Technical efficiency may also be included in the objectives with an attention on the hazardous waste treatments.

After a wide literature review, the criteria corresponding to the objectives have been specified as the capital costs, operations and maintenance costs, land costs, waste-treatment technology compatibility, efficiency of offsetting hazard potential, pollutant removal efficiency, human health risks, ecological risks and transportation risks (Ugurlu and Kahraman, 2011). We tried to include all criteria affecting the environmental risk evaluation.

*Capital Costs:* This criterion includes the economical amount of the first investment for the facility and the technology.

*Operation and Maintenance Costs:* This criterion represents the total operation and annual costs per treated waste.

*Land Costs:* This criterion takes into account the economic value of the land needed for the hazardous waste management system based on the size of the area and the placement of the land with respect to its distance to the city center.

*Waste-Treatment Technology Compatibility:* This criterion refers to the consideration of compatibility between the technology and different waste types.

*Efficiency of Offsetting Hazard Potential:* This criterion includes the degree waste management system eliminates the hazardousness of the waste.

*Waste residue:* This criterion represents the amount of waste generated as a result of the waste treatment.

*Resource recovery:* This criterion stands for the amount of value (e.g. output energy, recovered waste, etc.) that can be recovered from the waste.

*Capacity:* This criterion refers to amount of waste which the hazardous waste management system is able to treat.

*Human health risks:* This criterion consists of risks associated with the hazardous substances such as emission levels and heavy metal released to air, water or land affecting human health.

*Ecological risks:* This criterion infers to the risks associated with the hazardous substances such as emission levels and heavy metal released to air, water or land affecting the ecosystem and causing loss of important habitats, decreases in the size of the population of sensitive species.

*Transportation risk:* This criterion covers the total transport risk imposed on the public and the environment by the movement of the hazardous waste between locations such as generation, collection, storage, treatment and disposal locations.

The considered treatment alternatives for hazardous waste are *Landfilling*: Landfill incorporates an engineered method of disposal of solid waste on land in a manner that minimizes environmental hazards by spreading the solid waste in thin layers, compacting the solid waste to the smallest practical volume and applying a cover at the end of the operating day (Sumathi et al., 2008). *Composting:* Composting is defined as the biological decomposition of organic matter under controlled aerobic conditions to form a stable, humus- like end product (Farrell and Jones, 2009). *Conventional incineration:* Another solid waste disposal method is conventional incineration which has been practiced as a waste management and volume reduction technique since the 1890s. It is an extremely effective bulk waste reduction technology, typically reducing waste volume by around 90% and mass by around 70%. In terms of waste processing, conventional incineration is a relatively simple option, with unsorted waste being fed into a furnace and, by burning, reduced to one-tenth of its original volume (Eduljee and Arthur, 2001).

# 3    Type II Fuzzy Sets

The concept of a type-II fuzzy set was introduced first by Zadeh (1975) as an extension of the concept of an ordinary fuzzy set, i.e. a type-I fuzzy set. Type-II fuzzy sets have grades of membership that are themselves fuzzy. At each value of the primary variable, the membership is a function (and not just a point value) –the secondary membership function (MF)-, whose domain -the primary membership- is in the interval [0,1], and whose range -secondary grades- may also be in [0,1]. Hence, the MF of a type-II fuzzy set is three-dimensional, and it is the new third dimension that provides new design degrees of freedom for handling uncertainties. Such sets are useful in circumstances where it is difficult to determine the exact MF for a fuzzy set

(FS), as in modeling a word by a FS. . Interval type-II fuzzy sets, each of which is characterized by the footprint of uncertainty, are a very useful means to depict the decision information in the process of decision making. Type-II fuzzy sets are handled in two ways: interval type-II fuzzy sets and generalized type-II fuzzy sets. A triangular interval type-II fuzzy set is illustrated in Figure 1.

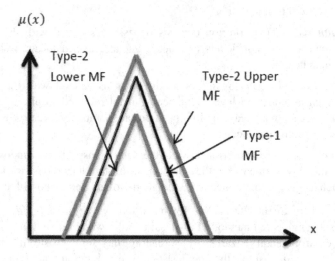

**Fig. 1.** Triangular Interval Type-II Fuzzy Set

A trapezoidal type-II fuzzy number is illustrated in Figure 2. The nine points to determine a footprint of uncertainty. (a, b, c, d) determines a normal trapezoidal upper membership function and (e, f, g, i, h) determines a trapezoidal lower membership function with height h.

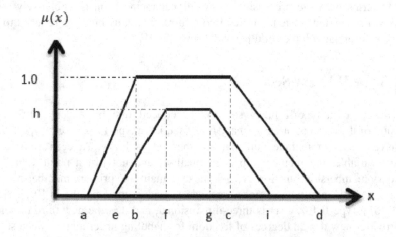

**Fig. 2.** Trapezoidal Interval Type-II Fuzzy Set

In continuous case, type-II fuzzy sets can be defined as follows:

$\tilde{A}$ is defined as a type-II fuzzy set on a universe of discourse X, where $\tilde{A} \subseteq X$. The type-II fuzzy set $\tilde{A}$ is a set of pairs $\{x, \mu_{\tilde{A}}(x)\}$, and it is notated as folllows:

$$\tilde{A} = \int_{x \in X} \mu_{\tilde{A}}(x)/x = \int_{x \in X} \left[ \int_{u \in J_x} f_x(u)/u \right]/x, \tag{1}$$

where x is an element of this type-II fuzzy set, $\mu\tilde{A}$ (x) is the grade of membership and it is defined in the interval [0,1] as

$$\mu_{\tilde{A}}(x) = \int_{u \in J_x} f_x(u)/u, \tag{2}$$

where $f_x$ is named as the secondary membership function, and the value of $f_x(u)$ is named as the secondary grade or secondary membership function. In addition, u is an argument of the secondary membership function, and $J_x$ is named as the primary membership of $x$. Arithmetic operations with type-2 fuzzy sets can be found in (Chen and Lee, 2010).

# 4    Fuzzy TOPSIS with Type-II Fuzzy Sets

In this paper, we use the fuzzy TOPSIS method developed by Lee and Chen (2008). Assume that there is a set X of alternatives and assume that there is a set F of attributes. Assume that there are k decision-makers. The set F of attributes can be divided into two sets F1 and F2, where F1 denotes the set of benefit attributes, F2 denotes cost attributes. Chen and Lee's method is given in the following:

**Step 1.** Construct the decision matrix of each decision-maker and then calculate the average decision matrix given as follows:

$$A = \begin{array}{c} f_1 \\ f_2 \\ \vdots \\ f_m \end{array} \begin{bmatrix} \overset{\approx}{f}_{11} & \overset{\approx}{f}_{12} & \cdots & \overset{\approx}{f}_{1n} \\ \overset{\approx}{f}_{21} & \overset{\approx}{f}_{22} & \cdots & \overset{\approx}{f}_{2n} \\ \vdots & \vdots & \vdots & \vdots \\ \overset{\approx}{f}_{m1} & \overset{\approx}{f}_{m2} & \cdots & \overset{\approx}{f}_{mn} \end{bmatrix} \begin{array}{c} X_1 \quad X_2 \quad \cdots \quad X_n \end{array} \tag{3}$$

**Step 2.** Construct the weighting matrix W of the attributes of each decision-maker and construct the average weighting matrix $\overline{W}$.

**Step 3.** Construct the weighted decision matrix $\overline{Y}_w$

$$\overline{Y}_w = \begin{array}{c} f_1 \\ f_2 \\ \vdots \\ f_m \end{array} \begin{bmatrix} \tilde{\tilde{v}}_{11} & \tilde{\tilde{v}}_{12} & \cdots & \tilde{\tilde{v}}_{1n} \\ \tilde{\tilde{v}}_{21} & \tilde{\tilde{v}}_{22} & \cdots & \tilde{\tilde{v}}_{2n} \\ \vdots & \vdots & \vdots & \vdots \\ \tilde{\tilde{v}}_{m1} & \tilde{\tilde{v}}_{m2} & \cdots & \tilde{\tilde{v}}_{mn} \end{bmatrix} \begin{array}{c} X_1 \quad X_2 \quad \cdots \quad X_n \end{array} \tag{4}$$

where $\tilde{\tilde{v}}_{ij} = \tilde{\tilde{w}}_i \otimes \tilde{\tilde{f}}_{ij}$

**Step 4.** Calculate the ranking value of the interval type-2 fuzzy set $\tilde{\tilde{v}}_{ij}$. Then construct the ranking weighted decision matrix:

$$\bar{Y}_w^* = \left(Rank(\tilde{\tilde{v}}_{ij})\right)_{m \times n} \tag{5}$$

**Step 5.** Determine the positive ideal solution $(v_1^+, v_2^+, ..., v_m^+)$ and the negative ideal solution $(v_1^-, v_2^-, ..., v_m^-)$ where

$$v_i^+ = \begin{cases} \max_{1 \leq j \leq n}\{Rank(\tilde{\tilde{v}}_{ij})\}, & if \ f_i \epsilon F_1 \\ \min_{1 \leq j \leq n}\{Rank(\tilde{\tilde{v}}_{ij})\}, & if \ f_i \epsilon F_2 \end{cases} \tag{6}$$

and

$$v_i^- = \begin{cases} \min_{1 \leq j \leq n}\{Rank(\tilde{\tilde{v}}_{ij})\}, & if \ f_i \epsilon F_1 \\ \max_{1 \leq j \leq n}\{Rank(\tilde{\tilde{v}}_{ij})\}, & if \ f_i \epsilon F_2 \end{cases} \tag{7}$$

**Step 6.** Calculate the distance from each alternative to the positive ideal solution and the negative ideal solution, respectively as follows:

$$d^+(x_j) = \sqrt{\sum_{i=1}^{m}\left(Rank(\tilde{\tilde{v}}_{ij}) - v_i^+\right)^2} \tag{8}$$

$$d^-(x_j) = \sqrt{\sum_{i=1}^{m}\left(Rank(\tilde{\tilde{v}}_{ij}) - v_i^-\right)^2} \tag{9}$$

**Step 7.** Calculate the relative degree of closeness with respect to the positive ideal solution.

$$C(x_j) = \frac{d^-(x_j)}{d^+(x_j) + d^-(x_j)} \tag{10}$$

**Step 8.** Sort the relative degree of closeness values in a descending order. Select the alternative with the highest value.

## 5     Application

There are three decision makers who evaluate three possible hazardous solid waste treatment alternatives. These are *Landfilling, Composting,* and *Con. Incineration.*

The considered criteria are capital costs, operation and maintenance costs, land costs, transportation risks, ecological risks, and human health risks.We use Tables 1 and 2 to assign scores for weighting criteria and evaluating alternatives. They fill in Tables 3 and 4 as below.

**Table 1.** Linguistic terms for assigning weights (Type-II Fuzzy sets) (Chen and Lee, 2000)

| Very low (VL) | ((0, 0, 0, 0.1; 1, 1), (0, 0, 0, 0.05; 0.9, 0.9)) |
|---|---|
| Low (L) | ((0, 0.1, 0.1, 0.3; 1, 1), (0.05, 0.1, 0.1, 0.2;0.9, 0.9)) |
| Medium Low (ML) | ((0.1, 0.3, 0.3, 0.5; 1, 1), (0.2, 0.3, 0.3, 0.4; 0.9, 0.9)) |
| Medium (M) | ((0.3, 0.5, 0.5, 0.7; 1, 1), (0.4, 0.5, 0.5, 0.6; 0.9, 0.9)) |
| Medium High (MH) | ((0.5, 0.7, 0.7, 0.9; 1, 1), (0.6, 0.7, 0.7, 0.8; 0.9, 0.9)) |
| High (H) | ((0.7, 0.9, 0.9, 1; 1, 1), (0.8, 0.9, 0.9, 0.95; 0.9, 0.9)) |
| Very High (VH) | ((0.9, 1, 1, 1; 1, 1), (0.95, 1, 1, 1; 0.9, 0.9)) |

**Table 2.** Linguistic terms for evaluating alternatives (Type-II Fuzzy sets)

| Very Poor (VP) | ((0, 0, 0, 1; 1, 1), (0, 0, 0, 0.5; 0.9, 0.9)) |
|---|---|
| Poor (P) | ((0, 1, 1, 3; 1, 1), (0.5, 1, 1, 2; 0.9, 0.9)) |
| Medium Poor (MP) | ((1, 3, 3, 5; 1, 1), (4, 5, 5, 6; 0.9, 0.9)) |
| Medium (M) | ((3, 5, 5, 7; 1, 1), (6, 7, 7, 8; 0.9, 0.9)) |
| Medium Good (MG) | ((5, 7, 7, 9; 1, 1), (6, 7, 7, 8; 0.9, 0.9)) |
| Good (G) | ((7, 9, 9, 10; 1, 1), (8, 9, 9, 9.5; 0.9, 0.9)) |
| Very Good (VG) | ((9, 10, 10, 10; 1, 1), (9.5, 10, 10, 10; 0.9, 0.9)) |

**Table 3.** Evaluation of Attributes by the Decision-Makers

| Attributes | Decision-Makers | | |
|---|---|---|---|
| | DM1 | DM2 | DM3 |
| Capital costs | H | H | VH |
| Operation and maintenance costs | M | L | M |
| Land costs | V H | H | H |
| Transportation risks | VH | V H | H |
| Ecological risks | VH | H | VH |
| Human health risks | H | VH | VH |

Applying the type-II fuzzy TOPSIS method the ranking order is determined as Composting > Landfilling > Conventional incineration.

Table 4. Evaluation of Alternatives by Decision-Makers

| Attributes | Alternatives | Decision-Makers | | |
|---|---|---|---|---|
| | | DM1 | DM2 | DM3 |
| Capital costs | *Landfilling* | VG | G | VG |
| | *Composting* | P | P | VP |
| | *Con. incineration* | G | VG | G |
| Operation and maintenance costs | *Landfilling* | VG | VG | VG |
| | *Composting* | G | G | G |
| | *Con. incineration* | G | G | VG |
| Land costs | *Landfilling* | P | VP | P |
| | *Composting* | VG | VG | G |
| | *Con. incineration* | G | G | MG |
| Transportation risk | *Landfilling* | P | P | P |
| | *Composting* | VG | G | G |
| | *Con. Incineration* | G | MG | MG |
| Ecological risks | *Landfilling* | VP | VP | VP |
| | *Composting* | G | VG | VG |
| | *Con. incineration* | VG | G | G |
| Human health risks | *Landfilling* | P | P | VP |
| | *Composting* | VG | G | G |
| | *Con. incineration* | G | MG | G |

# 6    Conclusion

Indeed, type-II fuzzy sets have more parameters with higher computational complexity than their counterparts. Type-2 fuzzy sets have grades of membership that are themselves fuzzy. Type-II fuzzy sets are especially used  when knowledge is mined from a group of experts using questionnaires that involve uncertain words and linguistic terms are used that have a nonmeasurable domain. We used type-II fuzzy sets in TOPSIS method. Thus we could consider the footprint of uncertainty.  Using this method, the environmental risk for solid waste treatments was reduced. The best solution was obtained as Composting. The other treatment alternatives may be incorporated to this analysis. For further research other fuzzy multicriteria decision making methods based on type-1 fuzzy sets can be converted to apply type-II fuzzy sets such as fuzzy AHP  with  type-II fuzzy sets or fuzzy VIKOR with type-II fuzzy sets.

# References

1.  Chen, C.T.: Extensions of the TOPSIS for group decision-making under fuzzy environment. Fuzzy Sets and Systems 114(1), 1–9 (2000)
2.  Cheremisinoff, N.P., Cheremisinoff, P.N.: Hazardous Materials And Waste Management: A Guide for the Professional Hazards Manager. Noyes Publications, New Jersey (1995)

3. Eduljee, G., Arthur, D.: Solid waste management. In: Harrison, R.M. (ed.) Pollution: Causes Effects and Control, pp. 378–410. Royal Society of Chemistry, Cambridge (2001)
4. Farrell, M., Jones, D.L.: Critical evaluation of municipal solid waste composting and potential compost markets. Bioresource Technology 100, 4301–4310 (2009)
5. Lee, L.W., Chen, S.M.: Fuzzy multiple attributes group decision-making based on the extension of TOPSIS method and interval type-2 fuzzy sets. In: Proceedings of the 2008 International Conference on Machine Learning and Cybernetic, Kunming, China, pp. 3260–3265 (2008)
6. Uğurlu, S., Kahraman, C.: Fuzzy Multicriteria Risk Assessment for Hazardous Waste Management: The Case of Istanbul. Journal of Risk analysis and Crisis Response 1(1), 29–41 (2011)
7. Chen, S.-M., Lee, L.-W.: Fuzzy multiple attributes group decision-making based on the interval type-2 TOPSIS method. Expert Systems with Applications 37, 2790–2798 (2010)
8. Sumathi, V.R., Natesan, U., Sarkar, C.: GIS-based approach for optimized siting of municipal solid waste landfill. Waste Management 28, 2146–2160 (2008)
9. Vallero, D.A., Peirce, J.J.: Engineering the Risks of Hazardous Wastes. Butterworth–Heinemann Publications, Elsevier Science, MA (2003)

# Fuzzy Multiobjective Linear Programming: A Bipolar View

Dipti Dubey and Aparna Mehra

Department of Mathematics, Indian Institute of Technology,
Hauz Khas, New Delhi-110016, India
diptidubey@gmail.com, apmehra@maths.iitd.ac.in

**Abstract.** The traditional frameworks for fuzzy linear optimization problems are inspired by the max-min model proposed by Zimmermann using the Bellman-Zadeh extension principle. This paper attempts to view fuzzy multiobjective linear programming problem (FMOLPP) from a perspective of preference modeling. The fuzzy constraints are viewed as negative preferences for rejecting what is unacceptable while the objective functions are viewed as positive preferences for depicting satisfaction to what is desired. This bipolar view enable us to handle fuzzy constraints and objectives separately and help to combine them in distinct ways. The optimal solution of FMOLPP is the one which maximizes the disjunctive combination of the weighted positive preferences provided it satisfy the negative preferences combined in conjunctive way.

**Keywords:** Fuzzy multiobjective linear program, bipolarity, OWA operator.

## 1 Introduction

We aim to take a closer look at the multiobjective linear programming formulation in fuzzy framework. Probably one of the earliest model of fuzzy linear programming was proposed by Zimmermann [17]. In the model he studied, an aspiration level for objective function is given along with certain tolerances and inequalities in linear constraints are made flexible or soft (in an appropriate sense). Thereafter the fuzzy objective function and the fuzzy constraints received the same treatment leading to a symmetric model. The classic Bellman-Zadeh principle [2] is used to define a fuzzy decision set of solutions by aggregating all fuzzy inequalities using 'min' aggregation. An optimal solution of the linear program is the one for which this minimum (aggregated function) is maximal. The core ideas of Zimmerman and Bellman-Zadeh paradigms have been adopted in the years to follow so much so that several other fuzzy optimization models ultimately come down to max-min optimization models. In [4,9,17] to name a few, researchers used similar approach to model fuzzy multiobjective linear programming problems (FMOLPPs). The main advantage of the max-min framework is that it enables a better discrimination between good and less good solutions to a set of inequalities represented by both the fuzzy objective function and the fuzzy (flexible/soft) constraints.

S. Greco et al. (Eds.): IPMU 2012, Part IV, CCIS 300, pp. 458–468, 2012.

However, the major disadvantage of using the aforementioned approach is that it tends to somewhat abolish the distinction between the objective aspiration and the constraints by combining all fuzzy sets representing them together. This is indeed a subject of debate. A constraint is something which should be satisfied, at least to some extent for a flexible constraint, or as far as it does not lead to an empty set of feasible solutions for a constraint whose priority is not maximal. In other words, constraints are something to be respected. On the other hand, there is no idea of requirement associated with an objective criteria. Particularly in case of FMOLPPs, the objective functions aspiration levels only depicts the desire or wish of the decision maker (DM) and hence non compulsory. Even if not all but some objective aspirations are met, the corresponding solution (provided it also satisfy the constraints) should give a reason for satisfaction of the DM. This is somehow completely missing in all studies based on Bellman-Zadeh principle where all objective aspirations are to be met to give some positive satisfaction to DM. At this point we would like to cite Benferhat et al. [3] and Dubois [6], who advocated to use negative preferences and positive preferences to discriminate between what is unacceptable and what is really satisfactory for DM. The negative preferences act as a constraints discarding unacceptable solutions and positive preferences lead to support appealing solutions. Thus, the problem can be modeled for computing the best solutions after merging the negative and the positive preferences separately. These ideas obviously provide a bipolar views of preferences. Motivated by these thoughts, in this paper, we attempt to study FMOLPPs with a bipolar view. We shall be using a different aggregation schemes for aggregating the fuzzy (flexible/soft) constraints with predefined tolerances and the objective functions with preset desired aspiration levels by the DM.

The paper is structured as follows. In Section 2, we present a set of concepts from bipolarity and ordered weighted averaging (OWA) operator which facilitate the discussion. In Section 3, a general frame work for FMOLPPs in a bipolar setting is explained. Section 4 presents an illustration while the paper concludes with some future directions in Section 5.

## 2   Preliminaries

### 2.1   Bipolarity

There are mainly three forms of bipolarity described in literature. For details, please refer to [6] and [3].

Type I : **Symmetric Bipolarity.** It relies on the use of single bipolar scale $[0, 1]$ whose top value 1 means totally sure and bottom value 0 denotes impossible. The neutral value is taken as 0.5 and it refers to the total uncertainty about whether an event or its contrary occurs. Probability measure is one such well known example. Tversky-Kahneman's [12] cumulative prospect theory uses the entire real line as a bipolar scale. Note that homogeneity in the information semantic is subsumed in this kind of bipolarity.

Type II : **Homogeneous Bivariate Bipolarity.** It works with two separate positive and negative scales related via a duality relation. Here, an item is judged according to two independent evaluations : a positive scale and a negative scale. A positive scale (in favor) is denoted by $L^+ = (0,1]$ where its top represents maximal possible satisfaction and its bottom is neutral denoting mere tolerance. A negative scale (in disfavor) is denoted by $L^- = (0,1]$ in which the top represents full rejection while its bottom is neutral and represents feasibility. The point is that the positive and the negative sides do not exhaust all possibilities. The possibility/necessity measures [5] and the Atanassov's intuitionistic FS [1] are in the spirit of type II bipolarity.

Type III : **Heterogeneous Bipolarity.** In this form of bipolarity, the negative part of the information does not refer to the same kind of source as the positive part. In other words, positive and negative information are from different sources and perhaps having different meanings attached. In merging the information, negative and positive information will not be aggregated using the same principles. It is immediate that in decision making, this kind of bipolarity is natural between the constraints that state which solutions to a problem are unfeasible, and objectives or goals that state which solutions are to be preferred.

In this paper we shall be modeling our decision making problem, viz. FMOLPP, with a heterogeneous bipolarity view.

## 2.2    OWA Operator

From above discussion it is clear that we shall be using different aggregation functions for merging two distinct types of information expressed as fuzzy sets.

In this context we look at the basics of ordered weighted averaging (OWA) operators introduced by Yager [14].

**Definition 1.** *A mapping $F : I^n \to I$, where $I = [0,1]$, is called an OWA operator of dimension $n$ if associated with $F$ is a weighting vector $W$, $W^T = (w_1, \ldots, w_n)$, such that $w_i \in (0,1)$, $i = 1, \ldots, n$, and $\sum_{i=1}^{n} w_i = 1$ and*

$$F(a_1, \ldots, a_n) = \sum_{i=1}^{n} w_i b_i,$$

*where $b_i$ is the $i^{th}$ largest element in the collection $a_1, \ldots, a_n$.*

The most noteworthy aspect of these operators is that the weight $w_i$ is associated with an ordered position rather than a specific argument $a_i$. That is, $w_i$ is the weight associated with the $i^{th}$ largest element whichever component it is. The vector $W$, characterizing the OWA operator, is called the OWA weighting vector. A large class of aggregation operators can be described by an appropriate selection of $W$ in the OWA operator.

An OWA operator $F$ always lies between the *and* and the *or* aggregation; hence it can be thought of some kind of *orand* operator. It is this feature of OWA operators that allow them to use in soft aggregations where one is not looking for merging all-or nothing but linguistically expressed imperatives like *most* or *few.* To know more about the properties and applications of OWA operators, refer [14,15].

In the sequel we shall be using a particular OWA operator to aggregate the information in the fuzzy sets describing the achievement of the aspiration levels by the objective functions. The main issue is to find OWA weights. For this, two important measures, called the dispersion (or entropy) and the orness, are defined in [14] by the following formulae.

$$\text{Disp}(W) = -\sum_{i=1}^{n} w_i \ln w_i, \quad \text{Orness}(W) = \frac{1}{n}\sum_{i=1}^{n}(n-i)\,w_i.$$

The dispersion measures the degree to which all the aggregates are equally used. The orness is a value that lies in the unit interval $[0,1]$. It measures the degree to which the aggregation is like an *or* operation, and can be viewed as a measure of optimism of a DM. One of the first approaches, suggested by O' Hagan [8], determines a special class of OWA operators having maximal entropy of the OWA weights for a given level of orness. Algorithmically it is based on the solution of the following constrained optimization problem.

$$(\text{NLP}) \qquad \max \quad -\sum_{i=1}^{n} w_i \ln w_i$$

$$\text{subject to} \quad \frac{1}{n-1}\sum_{i=1}^{n}(n-i)w_i = \rho$$

$$\sum_{i=1}^{n} w_i = 1, \quad 0 \le w_i \le 1 \quad i = 1,\dots,n,$$

where $\rho$ is desired degree of orness. Liu [7] proved an equivalence of maximal entropy OWA operator and geometric OWA operator for a given degree of orness. In fact a geometric OWA operator is defined as

$$w_i = aq^{i-1}, \quad a > 0, \quad q \ge 0.$$

For $\sum_{i=1}^{n} w_i = 1$, we must have,

$$a = \begin{cases} \dfrac{1}{n} & q = 1 \\[2mm] \dfrac{q-1}{q^n-1} & q \ne 1. \end{cases}$$

One can easily get the maximal entropy OWA weights by solving the following equation for $q$.

$$(n-1)\rho q^{n-1} + \sum_{i=2}^{n}((n-1)\rho - i + 1)q^{n-i} = 0, \tag{1}$$

where $\rho = \text{Orness}(W)$.

# 3 Fuzzy Multiobjective Linear Programming

A fuzzy decision making problem is characterized by a set $X$ in $\mathbb{R}^n$ of decision vectors $x$, and a set of goals $G_k$ $(k = 1,\dots,p)$, along with a set of constraints

$R_i$ $(i = 1, \ldots, m)$, each of which is expressed by a FS on $X$. For such a decision problem, Bellman and Zadeh [2] proposed that the decision $D$ is a FS given by $D = \{\langle x, \mu_D(x) \rangle \mid x \in X\}$, where

$$\mu_D(x) = \min_{k,\, i} \left(\mu_{G_k}(x), \mu_{R_i}(x)\right).$$

We have already pointed out the difficulties in this approach. The constraints and the objectives are treated together despite the very fact that they convey different meanings. Moreover, the goals or desirable objectives to achieve generally came from a source which is at a primary hierarchy in the decision making while the constraints are framed at the implementation levels of the decision by a secondary hierarchy in the same problem. For example, a curriculum revision committee of the institute may come up with the desired set of recommendations after series of thought processing and taking into consideration the desires of various stake-holders including students, faculty, management, and companies that regularly employee the institute students, besides few others. However, some of these recommendations are not feasible to implement due to logistics and administrative constraints. Here, the desired set of goals are framed by a committee of few members and the implementation constraints are provided by the institute administration. The two different sources view their problems in different perspectives leading to a heterogenous bipolarity. The committee recommendations can be viewed as positive preferences while the logistic constraints can be seen as the negative preferences. Note that there is no symmetry between positive and negative preferences. Moreover, all what is desired by the committee (in turn the stake-holders) may not be fully achievable but the logistic constraints simply can not be ignored. In such a scenario, the ideal way is to treat the two information differently. Our aim should be to identify the set of *potential solutions* which do not violate the mandatory constraints and achieve as many as possible objectives. We shall be viewing the decision problem in the heterogenous bipolarity framework. The constraints will be treated as negative preferences, that is, if a vector $x$ fails to satisfy them, it should be unacceptable or unfeasible. On the other hand the objectives will be treated as something that the DM wishes to achieve and so positive preferences. The optimal solution is the one which maximizes the weighted fusion of positive preferences provided it satisfy the negative preferences.

The general model of FMOLPP can be stated as follows.

$$\text{(FMOLP)} \qquad \max \quad (c_1^T x, c_2^T x, \ldots, c_p^T x)$$
$$\text{subject to} \quad A_i^T x \preceq b_i \qquad i = 1, \ldots, m$$
$$x \in S,$$

where $A_i \in \mathbb{R}^n$, $b_i \in \mathbb{R}$, $i = 1, \ldots, m$, $C \in \mathbb{R}^{p \times n}$ with $c_k^T$ denoting the $k^{th}$ row of $C$, $k = 1, \ldots, p$, and $S \subseteq \mathbb{R}^n$ comprises of all crisp inequalities (or hard linear constraints, if any).

The constraints $A_i x \preceq b_i$ are fuzzy (flexible/soft) resource constraints in which the resource availability $b_i$ can be relaxed to the positive tolerance $r_i$. Here the symbol " $\preceq$ " is *essentially less than or equal to* and to be understood in the sense of chosen membership functions for the FS corresponding to each soft constraint. The objective function m̄ax is to be understood in the fuzzy sense of satisfaction of aspiration levels $Z_k$ assigned by the DM to the $k^{th}$ objective $c_k^T x$, $k = 1, \ldots, p$. Actually problem (FMOLP) is equivalent to finding $x \in \mathbb{R}^n$ such that the following hold

$$c_k^T x \succeq Z_k \quad k = 1, \ldots, p,$$
$$A_i^T x \preceq b_i \quad i = 1, \ldots, m,$$
$$x \in S.$$

The membership functions of the fuzzy objectives (goals) and fuzzy constraints are respectively defined as follows. For $k = 1, \ldots, p$, and $i = 1, \ldots, m$,

$$\mu_{G_k}(c_k^T x) = \begin{cases} 0 & c_k^T x < Z_k - g_k \\ 1 - \dfrac{Z_k - c_k^T x}{g_k} & Z_k - g_k \leq c_k^T x < Z_k \\ 1 & c_k^T x \geq Z_k \end{cases}$$

$$\mu_{R_i}(A_i^T x) = \begin{cases} 0 & A_i^T x > b_i + r_i \\ 1 - \dfrac{A_i^T x - b_i}{r_i} & b_i < A_i^T x \leq b_i + r_i \\ 1 & A_i^T x \leq b_i \end{cases}$$

where we take $g_k$ is a positive tolerance in the aspiration level of objective (goal) $G_k$, and $r_i$ is a positive tolerance in the fuzzy constraints (restrictions) $R_i$.

The optimal solution of (FMOLP) is the one which maximizes the disjunctive combination of the weighted positive preferences provided it satisfy the negative preferences combined in conjunctive way.

In this paper we aggregate the negative preferences or fuzzy constraints by conjunctive operator *min*. This will ensure that any $x$ which fails to satisfy them is unacceptable or unfeasible. On the other hand, the positive preferences represented by objectives are aggregated using an OWA operator $F$. The $p$ objectives are first ordered in priority of their achievement and thereafter the OWA weight vector is used to aggregate the objective vector. In this way, the decision set $D$ is a bipolar fuzzy set as a triple $\{X, D_P, D_N\}$, where $D_P$ and $D_N$ respectively are fuzzy sets representing the positive and the negative preferences aggregations.

$$\mu_{D_P}(x) = F(\mu_{G_1}(c_1^T x), \mu_{G_2}(c_2^T x), \ldots, \mu_{G_p}(c_p^T x)),$$

and

$$\mu_{D_N}(x) = \min(\mu_{R_1}(A_1^T x), \mu_{R_2}(A_2^T x), \ldots, \mu_{R_m}(A_m^T x)).$$

Problem (FMOLP) can be re-casted as follows.

$$\max_{x \in X} \left( F(\mu_{G_1}(c_1^T x), \mu_{G_2}(c_2^T x), \ldots, \mu_{G_p}(c_p^T x)) - \max_i (1 - \mu_{R_i}(A_i^T x)) \right),$$

which is equivalent to the following constrained OWA aggregation problem

$$\text{(COAP)} \quad \max \quad F(\mu_{G_1}(c_1^T x), \mu_{G_2}(c_2^T x), \ldots, \mu_{G_p}(c_p^T x)) - \beta$$
$$\text{subject to} \quad \mu_{R_i}(A_i^T x) \geq 1 - \beta \quad i = 1, \ldots, m$$
$$0 \leq \beta \leq 1, \quad x \in S.$$

All solutions $x \in S$ satisfying $\mu_{R_i}(A_i^T x) \geq 1 - \beta$, $i = 1, \ldots, m$, are tolerated at most to a degree $\beta$. Note that if $\beta = 1$ then all $x \in S$ are tolerated or acceptable as feasible solutions while if $\beta = 0$ then only those $x \in S$ qualifies to be tolerated or feasible for which $A_i^T x \leq b_i$, for all $i$. Although we have associated the same degree $\beta$ of tolerance with each fuzzy (flexible/soft) constraint but the same could have been varied over constraints. However the latter will not affect our discussion.

We want that the structure of $F$ be such that if satisfaction in individual objective aspiration achievement increases, then the overall satisfaction of the DM in solution should increase. As suggested by Yager [14] we take $F$ to be an OWA operator. Thus,

$$\mu_{D_P}(x) = w_1 y_1 + w_2 y_2 + \ldots + w_p y_p$$

where $y_k$ is the $k^{th}$ largest element in the collection $\mu_{G_1}(c_1^T x), \ldots, \mu_{G_p}(c_p^T x)$. And $W^T = (w_1, \ldots, w_p)$ is the OWA weight vector.

Using the method given by Yager to solve constrained OWA aggregation in [16], problem (COAP) reduces to the following model, for $w_k \in (0,1)$, $i = k, \ldots, p$, and $\sum_{k=1}^{p} w_k = 1$.

$$
\begin{aligned}
\text{(COAP)} \qquad \max \quad & w_1 y_1 + \ldots + w_p y_p - \beta \\
\text{subject to} \quad & \mu_{R_i}(A_i^T x) \geq 1 - \beta \qquad i = 1, \ldots, m \\
& GY \leq 0 \\
& y_j I - O - K Z_j \leq 0 \quad j = 1, \ldots, p \\
& I^T Z_j \leq n - j \quad j = 1, \ldots, p \\
& z_{j,k} \in \{0,1\} \quad j = 1, \ldots, p, \quad k = 1, \ldots, p \\
& 0 \leq \beta \leq 1, \quad x \in S
\end{aligned}
$$

where $G = \begin{bmatrix} -1 & 1 & 0 & \ldots & 0 & 0 \\ 0 & -1 & 1 & \ldots & 0 & 0 \\ \vdots & \vdots & \vdots & & \vdots & \vdots \\ 0 & 0 & 0 & \ldots & -1 & 1 \end{bmatrix}$ is the $(p-1) \times p$ matrix, $Y$ is the $p$ column vector whose components are $y_j$, $I$ is the $p$ column vector with all elements equal to 1, $O$ is the $p$ column vector whose components are $\mu_{G_j}(c_j^T x)$, $Z_j$ is an $p$ column vector whose componets are $z_{j,k}$ and $K$ is a large positive real number.

# 4    Illustration

A company produces three products A, B, C. To produce these, it requires three types of raw material namely X, Y, Z. The amount (in kg) of raw material required to produce one unit of the products A, B, C, is given in the table 1.

There are three goals set by the heads (top hierarchy) of the company.

1. **To maximize the revenue:** The first priority set is to maximize the total revenue from sale. The heads aim a revenue of Rs 150 thousand but a revenue up to Rs 130 thousand is tolerable. The selling price of the one unit of products A, B, C are given in the following table.

Table 1. Requirement/per unit production

|   | X | Y | Z |
|---|---|---|---|
| A | 2 | 8 | 4 |
| B | 10 | 1 | 0 |
| C | 4 | 4 | 2 |

Table 2. Sales data

|   | A | B | C |
|---|---|---|---|
| selling price (in thousands)/unit | 10 | 22 | 12 |

2. **To minimize the production of a harmful pollutant:** During the production process, certain harmful pollutant is produced. The second objective aims to reduce production of harmful pollutant preferably 30 kg but must not exceed 35 kg. The amount of harmful pollutant generated per unit production is given in the following table.

Table 3. Harmful pollutant production data

|   | A | B | C |
|---|---|---|---|
| Pollutant generated (in kg)/unit product | 1 | 1 | 3 |

3. **To minimize the production cost:** The third goal is set to minimize the cost of production to be interpreted as inclusive of all kind of costs incurred in the production of three products. The cost of production of per unit of A, B, C is specified in the following table. It is desired that production cost should not exceed Rs 70 thousands but the heads of the company have a flexible views on it and can tolerate a cost up to Rs 80 thousand.

Table 4. Production cost data

|   | A | B | C |
|---|---|---|---|
| Production cost (in thousand) /unit product | 1 | 3 | 3 |

On the other hand, people involved in actual implementation phase of production of three products (lower hierarchy in the company) have tough time and certain logistic constraints to face. These are listed as follows on weekly basis.

I.  **Constraint 1.** The market cost of procuring material $X$ is very high; hence it is unacceptable to ask for more than 110 kg of $X$ but procurement of 100 kg or less is indeed acceptable.

II. **Constraint 2.** The supply of material $Y$ is not sufficient and often shortages are encountered. In no circumstances, the requirement of $Y$ above 55 kg could be met. It is though advisable to use 50 kg of $Y$ only.

The above two constraints on usage of materials $X$ and $Y$ are soft; the constraint on material $Z$ is hard.

III.  **Constraint 3.** The use of material $Z$ above 50 kg is unacceptable.

IV.  **Constraint 4.** With the information regarding demand of product A and C in the market, it was decided to produce at least 3 units of A; and at least 5 units of C, per week.

The problem is to find the optimal production quantities (in kg) per week of products A, B, C. The problem is modeled as follows.

$$\text{max } z_1 = 10x_1 + 22x_2 + 12x_3 \succeq 150 \text{ with tolerance } g_1 = 20.$$
$$\text{min } z_2 = x_1 + x_2 + 3x_3 \preceq 30 \text{ with tolerance } g_2 = 5$$
$$\text{min } z_3 = x_1 + 3x_3 + 3x_3 \preceq 70 \text{ with tolerance } g_1 = 10$$

subject to

$$2x_1 + 10x_2 + 4x_3 \preceq 100 \text{ with tolerance } r_1 = 10$$
$$8x_1 + x_2 + 4x_3 \preceq 50 \text{ with tolerance } r_2 = 10$$
$$4x_1 + 2x_3 \leq 50$$
$$x_1 \geq 3$$
$$x_3 \geq 5$$
$$x_1, \ x_2, \ x_3 \geq 0.$$

To apply the above method we require the weights of OWA operator. Suppose the the degree of orness is $\frac{3}{4}$ then we get $w_1 = 0.6162$, $w_2 = 0.2676$ and $w_3 = 0.1162$ from (1). The equivalent crisp model is given by

$$\text{max } 0.6162y_1 + 0.2676y_2 + 0.1162y_3 - \beta$$

subject to
$$0.2x_1 + x_2 + 0.4x_3 - \beta \leq 10$$
$$1.6x_1 + 0.2x_2 + 0.8x_3 - \beta \leq 10$$
$$4x_1 + 2x_3 \leq 50$$
$$x_1 \geq 3$$
$$x_3 \geq 5$$
$$y_2 - y_1 \leq 0$$
$$y_3 - y_2 \leq 0$$
$$y_3 - 0.25x_1 - 0.5x_2 - 0.6x_3 \leq -6.5$$
$$y_3 + 0.2x_1 + 0.4x_2 + 0.2x_3 \leq 7$$
$$y_3 + 0.1x_1 + 0.3x_2 + 0.4x_3 \leq 8$$
$$y_2 - 0.25x_1 - 0.5x_2 - 0.6x_3 - Kz_{11} \leq -6.5$$
$$y_2 + 0.2x_1 + 0.4x_2 + 0.2x_3 - Kz_{12} \leq 7$$
$$y_2 + 0.1x_1 + 0.3x_2 + 0.4x_3 - Kz_{13} \leq 8$$
$$z_{11} + z_{12} + z_{13} \leq 1$$
$$y_1 - 0.25x_1 - 0.5x_2 - 0.6x_3 - Kz_{21} \leq -6.5$$
$$y_1 + 0.2x_1 + 0.4x_2 + 0.2x_3 - Kz_{22} \leq 7$$
$$y_1 + 0.1x_1 + 0.3x_2 + 0.4x_3 - Kz_{23} \leq 8$$
$$z_{21} + z_{22} + z_{23} \leq 2$$
$$y_j \leq 1 \quad j = 1, 2, 3.$$
$$z_i \in \{0, 1\} \quad i = 1, \dots, 6$$
$$\beta \leq 1$$
$$x_1, \ x_2, \ x_3, \ \beta \geq 0.$$

The optimal solution is $x_1^* = 3$, $x_2^* = 6$, $x_3^* = 5$ and $\beta = 0$. The values of the three objectives are respectively, 135, 20, and 42 and the overall satisfaction degree of DM is 0.9128.

On the other hand, if we use the Bellman-Zadeh principle and Zimmermann's approach to aggregate the the fuzzy objectives and the fuzzy constraints, it can be seen that equivalent crisp model is infeasible. This example indicates an advantage of our proposed modeling over the classic Zimmermann's modeling for FMOLPPs; something to be excited about.

## 5   Concluding Remarks

In this paper, we have attempted to handle a FMOLPP with a heterogeneous bipolar view which refers to opposition between constraints and objectives. The representation framework is to distinguish between two fundamental concepts involved in LP formulation: one representing constraints whose violation is unacceptable, and the other is objectives whose achievement generate satisfaction. We have used an OWA operator to aggregate the fuzzy objectives and *min* operator to aggregate the constraints. The solution methodology given by Yager to solve constrained OWA aggregation has been used to solve the problem COAP.

Our approach differs, both in viewpoint and modeling, from the other studies inspired by the Bellman-Zadeh extension principle and Zimmermann modeling ideas on similar class of problems. We highlighted few important differences. It is clear from our model formulation that the form of the overall decision function based upon weighted summing the individual objectives most nearly corresponds to the situation in which we aim to get as much satisfaction to objectives as possible unlike the other studies where the aim is to achieve *all* objectives aspirations.

The use of other aggregation operators [10,11,13,18], as suggested by anonymous referee, to the present study and their corresponding analysis in our problem seems worth exploring. We would indeed looked into them in updating this work.

**Acknowledgements.** The first author would like to thank the National Board of Higher Mathematics (NBHM), India, for financial support for research.

## References

1. Atanassov, K.: Intuitionistic Fuzzy Sets. Physica-Verlag, Heidelberg (1999)
2. Bellman, R.E., Zadeh, L.A.: Decision making in fuzzy environment. Management Sciences 17, B-141–B-164 (1970)
3. Benferhat, S., Dubois, D., Kaci, S., Prade, H.: Bipolar possibility theory in preference modeling: Representation, fusion and optimal solutions. Information Fusion 7, 135–150 (2006)
4. Cadenes, J.M., Jimènez, F.: Interactive decision making in multiobjective fuzzy programming. Mathware and Soft Computing 3, 210–230 (1994)

5. Dubois, D., Prade, H.: Possibility theory, probability theory and multiple-valued logics: a clarification. Annals Math. and Artificial Intelligence 32, 35–66 (2001)
6. Dubois, D., Prade, H.: Bipolar Representations in Reasoning, Knowledge Extraction and Decision Processes. In: Greco, S., Hata, Y., Hirano, S., Inuiguchi, M., Miyamoto, S., Nguyen, H.S., Słowiński, R. (eds.) RSCTC 2006. LNCS (LNAI), vol. 4259, pp. 15–26. Springer, Heidelberg (2006)
7. Liu, X.-W., Chen, L.H.: The equivalence of maximal entropy OWA operator and geometric OWA operator. In: Proceeding of the Second International Conference of Machine Learning and Cybernetics, Xi'an, pp. 2673–2676 (2003)
8. O'Hagan, M.: Aggregating template or rule antecedents in real time expert systems with fuzzy set logic. In: Proceeding of 22nd Annual IEEE Asilomar Conf. Signals, Systems, Computers, Pacific Grove, pp. 681–689 (1988)
9. Sakawa, M., Inuiguchi, M.: A fuzzy satificing method for large- scale multiobjective linear programming problems with block angular structure. Fuzzy Sets and Systems 78, 279–288 (1996)
10. Sommer, G., Pollatschek, M.A.: A fuzzy programming approach to an air pollution regulation problem. Progress of Cybernetics and Systems Research III, 303–313 (1978)
11. Tsai, C.C., Chu, C.H., Barta, T.A.: Modelling and analysis of a manufacturing cell formation problem with fuzzy mixed integer programming. IIE Transactions 29, 533–547 (1997)
12. Tversky, A., Kahneman, D.: Advances in prospect theory: cumulative representation of uncertainty. Journal of Risk and Uncertainty 5, 297–323 (1992)
13. Werner, B.M.: Aggregation models in mathematical programming. In: Mitra, G. (ed.) Mathematical Models for Decision Support, pp. 295–305. Springer, Berlin (1988)
14. Yager, R.R.: On ordered weighted averaging aggregation operators in multicriteria decision making. IEEE Transaction on System, Man and Cybernetics 18, 183–190 (1988)
15. Yager, R.R.: Quantifier guided aggregation using OWA operators. Int. J. Intelligent Systems 11, 49–73 (1996)
16. Yager, R.R.: Constrained OWA aggregation. Fuzzy Sets and Systems 81, 89–101 (1996)
17. Zimmerman, H.-J.: Fuzzy programming and linear programming with several objective functions. Fuzzy Sets and Systems 1, 45–55 (1978)
18. Zimmerman, H.-J., Zysno, P.: Latent connectives in human decision making. Fuzzy Sets and Systems 4, 37–51 (1980)

# Interaction of Criteria and Robust Ordinal Regression in Bi-polar PROMETHEE Methods

Salvatore Corrente[1], José Rui Figueira[2], and Salvatore Greco[1]

[1] Department of Economics and Business, University of Catania, Italy
{salvatore.corrente,salgreco}@unict.it
[2] CEG-IST, Instituto Superior Técnico, Av. Rovisco Pair, 1049-001 Lisboa, Portugal
figueira@ist.utl.pt

**Abstract.** In this paper we consider the bipolar approach to Multiple Criteria Decision Analysis (MCDA). In particular we aggregate positive and negative preferences by means of the bipolar PROMETHEE method. To elicit preferences we consider Robust Ordinal Regression (ROR) that has been recently proposed to derive robust conclusions through the use of the concepts of possible and necessary preferences. It permits to take into account the whole set of preference parameters compatible with the preference information given by the Decision Maker (DM).

**Keywords:** Multiple criteria outranking methods, Interaction between criteria, Bi-polar Choquet integral.

## 1 Introduction

Multiple Criteria Decision Analysis (MCDA) (for state-of-the-art surveys on MCDA see [5]) dealing with the comparison of the reasons in favor and against a preference of an alternative $a$ over an alternative $b$ is of the utmost importance. This kind of comparison is important, but it is only a part of the question. Indeed, after *recognizing the criteria in favor and the criteria against* of the preference of $a$ over $b$, there is the very tricky question of comparing them (for a general discussion about bipolar aggregations of pros and cons in MCDA see [14]). In this second step, some important observations must be taken into account.

One element that should be considered is the *synergy* or the *redundancy* of criteria in favor of a preference of an action $a$ against an action $b$. Of course there could be similar effects of synergy and redundancy regarding the criteria against the comprehensive preference of $a$ over $b$. We have also to take into account the antagonism effects related to the fact that *the importance of criteria may also depend on the criteria which are opposed* to them. Those types of interactions between criteria have been already taken into consideration in the ELECTRE methods [13]. In this paper, we deal with the same problem using the bipolar Choquet integral [7,8] (for the original Choquet integral see [4]) applied to the PROMETHEE method [3].

The paper is organized as follows. In the next section we introduce the application of the bipolar Choquet integral to PROMETHEE method. In the third section, we discuss elicitation of preference information permitting to fix the

S. Greco et al. (Eds.): IPMU 2012, Part IV, CCIS 300, pp. 469–479, 2012.
© Springer-Verlag Berlin Heidelberg 2012

value of the preference parameter of the model (essentially the bicapacity of the bipolar Choquet integral). To take into account that there may be not only one, but a plurality of bicapacities representing the preference information, we propose also to adopt Robust Ordinal Regression (ROR) [11,6,1,10,9], in order to take into account the whole set of bicapacities compatible with the Decision Maker (DM) preferences. Within ROR we distinguish between necessary preference, in case an alternative $a$ is at least as good as an alternative $b$ for all the compatible bicapacities, and the possible preference, in case an alternative $a$ is at least as good as an alternative $b$ for at least one of the compatible bicapacities. The last section contains conclusions.

## 2   The Bipolar PROMETHEE

Let us consider a set of actions or alternatives $A = \{a, b, c, \ldots\}$ evaluated with respect to a set of criteria $G = \{g_1, \ldots, g_n\}$, where $g_j : A \to \mathbb{R}$, $j \in \mathcal{J} = \{1, \ldots, n\}$ and $|A| = m$. PROMETHEE [2,3] is a well known MCDA method that aggregates preference information of a DM using an outranking relation. Considering a weight $w_j$ representing the importance of criterion $g_j$ within the family of criteria $G$, an indifference threshold $q_j$, and a preference threshold $p_j$, for each criterion $g_j$, PROMETHEE builds a non decreasing function $P_j(a, b)$ with respect to the difference $d_j(a, b) = g_j(a) - g_j(b)$, whose formulation (see [2] for other formulations) could be the following

$$P_j(a,b) = \begin{cases} 0 & \text{if } d_j(a,b) \leq q_j \\ \frac{d_j(a,b)-q_j}{p_j-q_j} & \text{if } q_j < d_j(a,b) < p_j \\ 1 & \text{if } d_j(a,b) \geq p_j \end{cases}$$

It represents the degree of preferability of $a$ over $b$ on criterion $g_j$.
For each ordered pair of alternatives $(a, b) \in A$, PROMETHEE method computes the value

$$\pi(a,b) = \sum_{j \in \mathcal{J}} w_j P_j(a,b)$$

representing how much alternative $a$ is preferred to alternative $b$. It can assume values between 0 and 1 and obviously the greater the value of $\pi(a, b)$, the greater the preference of $a$ over $b$ is.

In order to compare an alternative $a$ against all the other alternatives of the set $A$, PROMETHEE computes the positive and the negative net flow of $a$ in the following way:

$$\phi^-(a) = \frac{1}{m-1} \sum_{c \in A \setminus \{a\}} \pi(c,a) \quad \text{and} \quad \phi^+(a) = \frac{1}{m-1} \sum_{c \in A \setminus \{a\}} \pi(a,c).$$

These net flows represent, respectively, how much the alternatives in $A \setminus \{a\}$ are preferred to $a$ and how much $a$ is preferred to the alternatives in $A \setminus \{a\}$. Besides the negative and the positive flows, PROMETHEE computes also the net flow $\phi(a) = \phi^+(a) - \phi^-(a)$. Taking into account these net flows, three relations can be built: preference ($\mathcal{P}$), indifference ($\mathcal{I}$), and incomparability ($\mathcal{R}$). In order to see how alternatives $a$ and $b$ are compared in PROMETHEE I method, see [2]; in case of PROMETHEE II, the comparison between alternatives $a$ and $b$ is done considering their net flows $\phi(a)$ and $\phi(b)$. In particular, we have that $a$ is preferred to $b$ if $\phi(a) > \phi(b)$, while $a$ and $b$ are indifferent if $\phi(a) = \phi(b)$.

Within the bipolar framework, the bipolar preference functions $P_j^B : A \times A \to [-1, 1], j \in \mathcal{J}$ are aggregated as follows

$$P_j^B(a,b) = P_j(a,b) - P_j(b,a) = \begin{cases} P_j(a,b) & \text{if } P_j(a,b) > 0 \\ \\ -P_j(b,a) & \text{if } P_j(a,b) = 0 \end{cases}$$

## 2.1  Determining Comprehensive Preferences

The aggregation of bipolar preference functions $P_j^B$ through the bipolar Choquet integral is based on a bicapacity [7,8], being a function $\hat{\mu} : P(\mathcal{J}) \to [-1, 1]$, where $P(\mathcal{J}) = \{(A, B) : A, B \subseteq \mathcal{J} \text{ and } A \cap B = \emptyset\}$, such that

- $\hat{\mu}(\emptyset, \mathcal{J}) = -1, \hat{\mu}(\mathcal{J}, \emptyset) = 1, \hat{\mu}(\emptyset, \emptyset) = 0,$
- for all $(A, B), (C, D) \in P(\mathcal{J})$, if $A \subseteq C$ and $B \supseteq D$, then $\hat{\mu}(A, B) \leq \hat{\mu}(C, D)$.

The interpretation of the bicapacity is the following: for $(A, B) \in P(\mathcal{J})$, and considering a pair of alternatives $(a, b) \in A \times A$, $\hat{\mu}(A, B)$ gives the net weight for the preference of $a$ over $b$ of criteria from $A$ in favor of $a$ and criteria from $B$ in favor of $b$.

Given $(a, b) \in A \times A$, the bipolar Choquet integral of preference functions $P_j^B(a, b)$ representing the comprehensive preference of $a$ over $b$ with respect to the bicapacity $\hat{\mu}$ can be written as follows

$$Ch^B(P^B(a,b), \hat{\mu}) = \int_0^1 \hat{\mu}(\{j \in \mathcal{J} : P_j^B(a,b) > t\}, \{j \in \mathcal{J} : P_j^B(a,b) < -t\})dt.$$

Operationally, the bi-polar aggregation function $P_j^B(a, b)$ can be computed as follows. For all the criteria $j \in \mathcal{J}$, the absolute values of this function should be re-ordered in a non-decreasing way,

$$|P_{(1)}^B(a,b)| \leq |P_{(2)}^B(a,b)| \leq \ldots \leq |P_{(j)}^B(a,b)| \leq \ldots \leq |P_{(n)}^B(a,b)|$$

The comprehensive bi-polar Choquet integral with respect to the bicapacity $\hat{\mu}$ for the pair $(a, b) \in A \times A$ can now be determined as follows:

$$Ch^B(P^B(a,b),\hat{\mu}) = \sum_{j \in \mathcal{J}^>} |P_{(j)}^B(a,b)| \Big[ \hat{\mu}(C_{(j-1)}, D_{(j-1)}) - \hat{\mu}(C_{(j)}, D_{(j)}) \Big]$$

where:
$\hat{\mu}$ is a bi-capacity, $P^B(a,b) = \Big[ P_j^B(a,b), \ j \in \mathcal{J} \Big]$, $C_{(0)} = \{ j \in J : P_j^B(a,b) > 0 \}$, $D_{(0)} = \{ j \in J : P_j^B(a,b) < 0 \}$, $\mathcal{J}^> = \{ j \in \mathcal{J} \ : \ |P_{(j)}^B(a,b)| > 0 \}$, $C_{(j)} = \{ i \in \mathcal{J}^> \ : \ P_i^B(a,b) \geq |P_{(j)}^B(a,b)| \}$, and $D_{(j)} = \{ i \in \mathcal{J}^> \ : \ -P_i^B(a,b) \geq |P_{(j)}^B(a,b)| \}$.

The value $Ch^B(P^B(a,b),\hat{\mu})$ gives the comprehensive preference of $a$ over $b$ and it is equivalent to $\pi(a,b) - \pi(b,a) = P^C(a,b)$ in the classical PROMETHEE method. Let us remark that it is reasonable to expect that $P^C(a,b) = -P^C(b,a)$. This leads to the following *symmetry condition*,

$$Ch^B(P^B(a,b),\hat{\mu}) = -Ch^B(P^B(b,a),\hat{\mu}).$$

**Proposition 2.1** $Ch^B(P^B(a,b),\hat{\mu}) = -Ch^B(P^B(b,a),\hat{\mu})$, *for all possible* $a, b$, *iff* $\hat{\mu}(C,D) = -\hat{\mu}(D,C)$ *for each* $(C,D) \in P(\mathcal{J})$.

The above redefinition of $\pi(a,b) - \pi(b,a)$ in bi-polar terms leads to the following bi-polar definition of the net flows,

$$\phi^B(a) = \frac{1}{m-1} \sum_{c \in A \setminus \{a\}} Ch^B(P^B(a,c),\hat{\mu})$$

## 2.2    Determining the Importance, the Interaction, and the Power of the Opposing Criteria

Several studies dealing with the determination of the relative importance of criteria were proposed in MCDA (see e.g. [17]). The question of the interaction between criteria was also studied in the context of MAUT methods [15]. In this section we present a quite similar methodology for outranking methods, which takes into account also the power of the opposing criteria.

## 2.3    The Case of PROMETHEE Method

The use of the bi-polar Choquet integral is based on a bi-polar capacity which assigns numerical values to each element $P(\mathcal{J})$. Let us remark that the number of elements of $P(\mathcal{J})$ is $3^n$. This means that the definition of a bi-polar capacity requires a rather huge and unpractical number of parameters. Moreover, the interpretation of these parameters is not always simple for the DM. Therefore, the use of the bi-polar Choquet integral in real-world decision making problems requires some methodology to assist the DM in assessing the preference parameters (bi-polar capacities). In the following we consider only the 2−order decomposable capacities, a particular class of bi-polar capacity.

## 2.4 Defining a Manageable and Meaningful Bi-polar Capacity Measure

We define a 2−order decomposable bi-capacity [12] such that for all $(C, D) \in P(\mathcal{J})$

$$\hat{\mu}(C, D) = \mu^+(C, D) - \mu^-(C, D)$$

where

$$- \mu^+(C, D) = \sum_{j \in C} a^+(\{j\}, \emptyset) + \sum_{\{j,k\} \subseteq C} a^+(\{j, k\}, \emptyset) + \sum_{j \in C,\, k \in D} a^+(\{j\}, \{k\})$$

$$- \mu^-(C, D) = \sum_{j \in D} a^-(\emptyset, \{j\}) + \sum_{\{j,k\} \subseteq D} a^-(\emptyset, \{j, k\}) + \sum_{j \in D,\, k \in C} a^-(\{k\}, \{j\})$$

The interpretation of each $a^\pm(.)$ is the following:

- $a^+(\{j\}, \emptyset)$, represents the power of criterion $g_j$ by itself; this value is always positive.
- $a^+(\{j, k\}, \emptyset)$, represents the interaction between $g_j$ and $g_k$, when they are in favor of the preference of $a$ over $b$; when its value is zero there is no interaction; on the contrary, when the value is positive there is a synergy effect when putting together $g_j$ and $g_k$; a negative value means that the two criteria are redundant.
- $a^+(\{j\}, \{k\})$, represents the power of criterion $g_k$ against criterion $g_j$, when criterion $g_j$ is in favor of $a$ over $b$ and $g_k$ is against to the preference of $a$ over $b$; this leads always to a reduction or no effect on the value of $\mu^+$ since this value is always non-positive.

An analogous interpretation can be applied to the values $a^-(\emptyset, \{j\})$, $a^-(\emptyset, \{j, k\})$, and $a^-(\{k\}, \{j\})$.

In what follows, for the sake of simplicity, we will use $a_j^+$, $a_{jk}^+$, $a_{j|k}^+$, instead of $a^+(\{j\}, \emptyset)$, $a^+(\{j, k\}, \emptyset)$, and, $a^+(\{j\}, \{k\})$, respectively; and $a_j^-$, $a_{jk}^-$, $a_{j|k}^-$, instead of $a^-(\emptyset, \{j\})$, $a^-(\emptyset, \{j, k\})$, and $a^-(\{k\}, \{j\})$, respectively, obtaining

$$\hat{\mu}(C, D) = \mu^+(C, D) - \mu^-(C, D) = \sum_{j \in C} a_j^+ - \sum_{j \in D} a_j^- + \sum_{\{j,k\} \subseteq C} a_{jk}^+ - \sum_{\{j,k\} \subseteq D} a_{jk}^- + \sum_{j \in C,\, k \in D} a_{j|k}$$

where, $a_{j|k} = a_{j|k}^+ - a_{j|k}^-$.

The following conditions should be fulfilled.

### Monotonicity Conditions

1) $\mu^+(C, D) \leq \mu^+(C \cup \{j\}, D)$, $\forall j \in \mathcal{J}, \forall (C \cup \{j\}, D) \in P(\mathcal{J})$

$$\sum_{h \in C} a_h^+ + \sum_{\{h,k\} \subseteq C} a_{hk}^+ + \sum_{h \in C,\, k \in D} a_{h|k}^+ \leq \sum_{h \in C \cup \{j\}} a_h^+ + \sum_{\{h,k\} \subseteq C \cup \{j\}} a_{hk}^+ + \sum_{h \in C \cup \{j\},\, k \in D} a_{h|k}^+ \Leftrightarrow$$

$$\Leftrightarrow a_j^+ + \sum_{k \in C} a_{jk}^+ + \sum_{k \in D} a_{j|k}^+ \geq 0, \ \forall j \in \mathcal{J}, \forall (C \cup \{j\}, D) \in P(\mathcal{J})$$

2) $\mu^+(C,D) \geq \mu^+(C,D \cup \{j\})$, $\forall j \in \mathcal{J}$, $\forall (C,D \cup \{j\}) \in P(\mathcal{J})$

$$\sum_{h \in C} a_h^+ + \sum_{\{h,k\} \subseteq C} a_{hk}^+ + \sum_{h \in C, k \in D} a_{h|k}^+ \geq \sum_{h \in C} a_h^+ + \sum_{\{h,k\} \subseteq C} a_{hk}^+ + \sum_{h \in C, k \in D \cup \{j\}} a_{h|k}^+ \Leftrightarrow$$

$$\Leftrightarrow \sum_{h \in C} a_{h|j}^+ \leq 0, \ \forall j \in \mathcal{J}, \ \forall (C, D \cup \{j\}) \in P(\mathcal{J})$$

The same kind of monotonicity should be satisfied for $\mu^-$. Let us call them Conditions 3) and 4). They are equivalent to the general monotonicity for $\mu^-$, i.e.,

$\forall (C,D), (E,F) \in P(\mathcal{J})$ such that $C \supseteq E$, $D \subseteq F$, $\mu^-(C,D) \leq \mu^-(E,F)$.

Conditions 1), 2), 3) and 4) together ensure the monotonicity of the bi-capacity, $\hat{\mu}$, on $\mathcal{J}$, obtained as the difference of $\mu^+$ and $\mu^-$, that is,

$\forall (C,D), (E,F) \in P(\mathcal{J})$ such that $C \supseteq E$, $D \subseteq F$, $\hat{\mu}(C,D) \geq \hat{\mu}(E,F)$.

**Boundary Conditions**

1. $\mu^+(\mathcal{J}, \emptyset) = 1$, i.e., $\displaystyle\sum_{j \in \mathcal{J}} a_j^+ + \sum_{\{j,k\} \subseteq \mathcal{J}} a_{jk}^+ = 1$

2. $\mu^-(\emptyset, \mathcal{J}) = 1$, i.e., $\displaystyle\sum_{j \in \mathcal{J}} a_j^- + \sum_{\{j,k\} \subseteq \mathcal{J}} a_{jk}^- = 1$

## 2.5   The 2-Order Bi-polar Choquet Integral

The following theorem gives a definition of the bi-polar Choquet integral in terms of the above 2-order decomposition.

**Theorem 2.5** *If the bi-capacity $\hat{\mu}$ is $2-order$ decomposable, then for all $x \in \mathbb{R}^n$*

$$Ch^B(x, \hat{\mu}) = \sum_{j \in \mathcal{J}, x_j > 0} a_j^+ x_j + \sum_{j \in \mathcal{J}, x_j < 0} a_j^- x_j +$$

$$+ \sum_{j,k \in \mathcal{J}, j \neq k, x_j, x_k > 0} a_{jk}^+ \min\{x_k, x_j\} + \sum_{j,k \in \mathcal{J}, j \neq k, x_j, x_k < 0} a_{jk}^- \max\{x_k, x_j\} +$$

$$\sum_{j,k \in \mathcal{J}, x_j > 0, x_k < 0} a_{j|k}^+ \min\{x_j, -x_k\} + \sum_{j,k \in \mathcal{J}, x_j > 0, x_k < 0} a_{j|k}^- \max\{-x_j, x_k\}$$

**Proposition 2.5** *If $\hat{\mu}$ is 2-order decomposable then $\hat{\mu}(C,D) = -\hat{\mu}(D,C)$ for each $(C,D) \in P(\mathcal{J})$ iff*

1. *for each $j \in \mathcal{J}$, $a_j^+ = a_j^- = a_j$,*
2. *for each $\{j,k\} \subseteq \mathcal{J}$, $a_{jk}^+ = a_{jk}^- = a_{jk}$,*
3. *for each $j,k \in \mathcal{J}$, $j \neq k$, $a_{j|k}^+ = a_{k|j}^-$.*

## 2.6    Assessing the Preference Information

On the basis of the above 2−order decomposition and holding the symmetry condition in Proposition 2.5, we propose the following methodology which simplifies the assessment of the preference information. We consider the following information given by the DM and their representation in terms of linear constraints:

1. *Comparing pairs of actions.* The constraints represent some pairwise comparisons on a set of training actions. Given two actions $a$ and $b$, the DM may prefer $a$ to $b$, $b$ to $a$ or be indifferent to both:
   (a) the linear constraint associated with $a\mathcal{P}b$ is $Ch^B(P^B(a,b),\hat{\mu}) > 0$;
   (b) the linear constraint associated with $a\mathcal{I}b$ is $Ch^B(P^B(a,b),\hat{\mu}) = 0$.
2. *Comparison of the intensity of preferences between pairs of actions.* This comparison can be stated as follows:

$$Ch^B(P^B(a,b),\hat{\mu}) > Ch^B(P^B(c,d),\hat{\mu}) \quad \text{if} \quad (a,b)\mathcal{P}(c,d)$$

   where, $(a,b)\mathcal{P}(c,d)$ means that the comprehensive preference of $a$ over $b$ is larger than the comprehensive preference of $c$ over $d$. ·
3. *Importance of criteria.* A partial ranking over the set of criteria $\mathcal{J}$ may be provided by the DM:
   (a) criterion $g_j$ is more important than criterion $g_k$, which leads to the constraint $a_j > a_k$;
   (b) criterion $g_j$ is equally important to criterion $g_k$, which leads to the constraint $a_j = a_k$.
4. *Interaction between pairs of criteria.* The DM can provide some information about interaction between criteria:
   (a) if the DM feels that interaction between $g_j$ and $g_k$ is more important than the interaction between $g_p$ and $g_q$, the constraint should be defined as follows: $a_{jk} > a_{pq}$;
   (b) if the DM feels that interaction between $g_j$ and $g_k$ is the same of the interaction between $g_p$ and $g_q$, the constraint will be the following: $a_{jk} = a_{pq}$.
5. *The sign of interactions.* The DM may be able, for certain cases, to provide the sign of some interactions. For example, if there is a synergy effect when criterion $g_j$ interacts with criterion $g_k$, the following constraint should be added to the model: $a_{jk} > 0$.
6. *The power of the opposing criteria.* Concerning the power of the opposing criteria several situations may occur. For example:
   (a) when the opposing power of $g_k$ is larger than the opposing power of $g_h$, with respect to $g_j$, which expresses a positive preference, we can define the following constraint: $a^+_{j|k} > a^+_{j|h}$;
   (b) if the opposing power of $g_k$, expressing negative preferences, is larger with $g_j$ rather than with $g_h$, the constraint will be $a^+_{j|k} > a^+_{h|k}$.

## 2.7   A Linear Programming Model

All the constraints presented in the previous section along with the symmetry, boundary and monotonicity conditions can now be put together and form a system of linear constraints. Strict inequalities can be converted into weak inequalities adding a variable $\varepsilon$. It is well-know that such a system has a feasible solution if and only if when maximizing $\varepsilon$, its value is strictly positive [15]. Considering constraints of Proposition 2.5, the linear programming model can be stated as follows (where $jPk$ means that criterion $g_j$ is more important than criterion $g_k$; the remaining relations have similar interpretation):

Max $\varepsilon$

$Ch^B(P^B(a,b)) \geq \varepsilon$ if $aPb$,

$Ch^B(P^B(a,b)) \geq Ch^B(P^B(c,d)) + \varepsilon$ if $(a,b)\mathcal{P}(c,d)$,

$a_j - a_k \geq \varepsilon$ if $j\mathcal{P}k$,

$a_{jk} - a_{pq} \geq \varepsilon$ if $\{j,k\}\mathcal{P}\{p,q\}$,

$a_{jk} \geq \varepsilon$ if there is synergy between criteria $j$ and $k$,

$a_{jk} \leq -\varepsilon$ if there is redundancy between criteria $j$ and $k$,

$a_{jk} = 0$ if criteria $j$ and $k$ are not interacting,

Power of the opposing criteria of the type 6:

$a^+_{j|k} - a^+_{j|p} \geq \varepsilon$,

$a^+_{j|k} - a^+_{p|k} \geq \varepsilon$,

$a^+_{j|k} - a^-_{j|p} \geq \varepsilon$,

Symmetry condition (point 3. of Proposition 2.5):

$a^+_{j|k} = a^-_{k|j}, \; \forall j,k \in \mathcal{J}$,

Boundary and monotonicity constraints:

$\sum_{j \in \mathcal{J}} a_j + \sum_{\{j,k\} \subseteq \mathcal{J}} a_{jk} = 1$,

$a_j \geq 0 \; \forall j \in \mathcal{J}$,

$a_j + \sum_{k \in C} a_{jk} + \sum_{k \in D} a^+_{j|k} \geq 0, \; \forall j \in \mathcal{J}, \forall (C \cup \{j\}, D) \in P(\mathcal{J})$,

$a_j + \sum_{k \in D} a_{jk} + \sum_{k \in C} a^-_{k|j} \geq 0, \; \forall j \in \mathcal{J}, \forall (C, D \cup \{j\}) \in P(\mathcal{J})$.

$Ch^B(P^B(a,b)) = 0$ if $aIb$,

$Ch^B(P^B(a,b)) = Ch^B(P^B(c,d))$ if $(a,b)\mathcal{I}(c,d)$,

$a_j = a_k$ if $j\mathcal{I}k$,

$a_{jk} = a_{pq}$ if $\{j,k\}\mathcal{I}\{p,q\}$,

$a^-_{j|k} - a^-_{j|p} \geq \varepsilon$,

$a^-_{j|k} - a^-_{p|k} \geq \varepsilon$,

$a^+_{j|k}, a^-_{j|k} \leq 0 \; \forall j,k \in \mathcal{J}$,

$\left.\right\} E^{AR}$

## 2.8   Restoring PROMETHEE

The condition which allows to restore PROMETHEE is the following:

1. $\forall j,k \in \mathcal{J}, \; a_{jk} = a^+_{j|k} = a^-_{j|k} = 0$.

If condition 1 is not satisfied and holds

2. $\forall j,k \in \mathcal{J}, a^+_{j|k} = a^-_{j|k} = 0$,

then the comprehensive preference of $a$ over $b$ is calculated as the difference between the Choquet integral of the positive preference and the Choquet integral of the negative preference, with a common capacity for the positive and the negative preferences, i.e. there exist a capacity $\mu : 2^{\mathcal{J}} \to [0,1]$, with $\mu(\emptyset) = 0$, $\mu(\mathcal{J}) = 1$, and $\mu(A) \leq \mu(B)$ for all $A \subseteq B \subseteq \mathcal{J}$, such that

$$Ch^B(P^B(a,b),\hat{\mu}) = \int_0^1 \mu(\{j \in \mathcal{J} : P^B_j(a,b) > t\})dt - \int_0^1 \mu(\{j \in \mathcal{J} : P^B_j(a,b) < -t\})dt.$$

We shall call this type of aggregation of preferences, the Choquet integral PROMETHEE method.

If neither 1. nor 2. are satisfied, then we have the Bipolar Choquet integral.

## 2.9    A Constructive Learning Preference Information Elicitation Process

The previous Conditions 1-2 suggest a proper way to deal with the linear programming model in order to assess the interactive bi-polar criteria coefficients. Indeed, it is very wise to try before to elicit weights concordant with the classic PROMETHEE method. If this is not possible, one can consider a PROMETHEE method which aggregates positive and negative preferences using the Choquet integral. If, by proceeding in this way, we are not able to represent the DM's preferences, we can take into account a more sophisticated aggregation procedure by using the bi-polar Choquet integral. This way to progress from the simplest to the most sophisticated models can be outlined in a four step procedure as follows,

1. Solve the linear programming model adding the constraint related to the previous Condition 1. If the model has a feasible solution with $\varepsilon > 0$, the obtained preferential parameters are concordant with the classical PROMETHEE method. Otherwise,
2. Solve the linear programming model adding Condition 2. If there is a solution with $\varepsilon > 0$, the information is concordant with the Choquet integral PROMETHEE method. Otherwise,
3. Solve the problem without any of the Conditions 1-2. A solution with $\varepsilon > 0$ means that the preferential information is concordant with the bi-polar Choquet integral PROMETHEE method. Otherwise,
4. We can try to help the DM by providing some information about inconsistent judgments, when it is the case, by using a similar constructive learning procedure proposed in [16].

In fact, in the linear programming model some of the constraints cannot be relaxed, that is, the basic properties of the model (symmetry, boundary and monotonicity constraints). The remaining constraints can lead to an unfeasible linear system which means that the DM provided inconsistent information about her/his preferences. The methods proposed in [16] can then be used in this context, providing to the DM some useful information about inconsistent judgements.

## 3    ROR Applied to Bipolar PROMETHEE Method

In above sections we dealt with the problem of finding a set of measures restoring preference information provided by the DM in case where multiple criteria evaluations are aggregated by Bipolar PROMETHEE outranking method. In this context it is meaningful to take into account the Robust Ordinal Regression (ROR) [11,6,1,10,9]. ROR is a family of MCDA methodologies recently developed, taking into account not only one model compatible with preference information provided by the DM, but the whole set of models compatible with preference information provided by the DM considering two preference relations: the weak *necessary* preference relation, for which alternative $a$ is necessarily weakly preferred to alternative $b$ if $a$ is at least as good as $b$ for all compatible models, and the weak *possible* preference relation, for which alternative $a$ is possibly weakly preferred to alternative $b$ if $a$ is at least as good as $b$ for at least one compatible model. In case of bi-polar PROMETHEE method, we can consider the necessary and the possible preference relations as follows:

- $a$ is weakly possibly preferred to $b$, and we shall write $a \succsim^P b$, if $Ch^B(P^B(a,b), \hat{\mu}) \geq 0$ for at least one bi-capacity $\hat{\mu}$ compatible with the preference information given by the DM,
- $a$ is weakly necessarily preferred to $b$, and we shall write $a \succsim^N b$, if $Ch^B(P^B(a,b), \hat{\mu}) \geq 0$ for all bi-capacity $\hat{\mu}$ compatible with the preference information given by the DM.

Given two alternatives $a, b \in A$, the set of constraints $E^{A^R}$, and considering the following sets of constraints,

$$\left. \begin{array}{l} Ch^B(P^B(a,b), \hat{\mu}) \geq 0 \\ E^{A^R} \end{array} \right\} E^P(a,b), \qquad \left. \begin{array}{l} Ch^B(P^B(b,a), \hat{\mu}) \geq \varepsilon \\ E^{A^R} \end{array} \right\} E^N(a,b),$$

the necessary and possible preference relations for the couple $(a, b) \in A \times A$, can be computed as follows:

- $a$ is weakly possibly preferred to $b$ iff $E^P(a,b)$ is feasible and $\varepsilon^* > 0$ where $\varepsilon^* = \max \varepsilon$ s.t. $E^P(a,b)$,
- $a$ is weakly necessarily preferred to $b$ iff $E^N(a,b)$ is infeasible or $\varepsilon^* \leq 0$ where $\varepsilon^* = \max \varepsilon$ s.t. $E^N(a,b)$.

## 4   Conclusions

The paper dealt with the aggregation of positive and negative preferences by means of the bipolar PROMETHEE method. ROR methodology has been proposed to derive robust conclusions through the use of the concepts of possible and necessary preferences. It permits to take into account the whole set of preference parameters compatible with the preference information given by the DM.

## References

1. Angilella, S., Greco, S., Matarazzo, B.: Non-additive robust ordinal regression: A multiple criteria decision model based on the choquet integral. European Journal of Operational Research 201(1), 277–288 (2010)
2. Brans, J., Maréchal, B.: PROMETHEE Methods. In: Figueira, J., Greco, S., Ehrgott, M. (eds.) Multiple Criteria Decision Analysis: State of the Art Surveys. Springer, Berlin (2005)
3. Brans, J., Vincke, P.: A preference ranking organisation method: The PROMETHEE method for MCDM. Management Science 31(6), 647–656 (1985)

4. Choquet, G.: Theory of Capacities. Annales de l'Institute Fourier 5, 131–295 (1953/1954)
5. Figueira, J., Greco, S., Ehrgott, M.: Multiple Criteria Decision Analysis: State of the Art Surveys. Springer, Berlin (2005)
6. Figueira, J.R., Greco, S., Słowiński, R.: Building a set of additive value functions representing a reference preorder and intensities of preference: GRIP method. European Journal of Operational Research 195(2), 460–486 (2009)
7. Grabisch, M., Labreuche, C.: Bi-capacities-I: definition, Möbius transform and interaction. Fuzzy Sets and Systems 151(2), 211–236 (2005)
8. Grabisch, M., Labreuche, C.: Bi-capacities-II: the Choquet integral. Fuzzy Sets and Systems 151(2), 237–259 (2005)
9. Greco, S., Kadzinski, M., Słowiński, R.: Extreme ranking analysis in Robust Ordinal Regression. Omega 40(4), 488–501 (2012)
10. Greco, S., Kadziński, M., Mousseau, V., Słowiński, R.: ELECTRE$^{GKMS}$: Robust Ordinal Regression for outranking methods. European Journal of Operational Research 214(1), 118–135 (2011)
11. Greco, S., Mousseau, V., Słowiński, R.: Ordinal regression revisited: multiple criteria ranking using a set of additive value functions. European Journal of Operational Research 191(2), 416–436 (2008)
12. Greco, S., Figueira, J.R.: Dealing with interaction between bi-polar multiple criteria preferences in outranking methods. Research Report 11-2003, INESC-Coimbra, Portugal (2003)
13. Greco, S., Figueira, J.R., Roy, B.: Electre methods with interaction between criteria: An extension of the concordance index. European Journal of Operational Research 199(2), 478–495 (2009)
14. Greco, S., Grabish, M., Pirlot, M.: Bipolar and bivariate models in multicriteria decision analysis: Descriptive and constructive approaches. International Journal of Intelligent Systems 23(9), 930–969 (2008)
15. Marichal, J., Roubens, M.: Determination of weights of interacting criteria from a reference set. European Journal of Operational Research 124(3), 641–650 (2000)
16. Mousseau, V., Figueira, J., Dias, L., Gomes da Silva, C., Clímaco, J.: Resolving inconsistencies among constraints on the parameters of an MCDA model. European Journal of Operational Research 147, 72–93 (2003)
17. Roy, B., Mousseaui, V.: A theoretical framework for analysing the notion of relative importance of criteria. Journal of Multi-Criteria Decision Analysis 5, 145–159 (1996)

# On the Use of Argumentation
# for Multiple Criteria Decision Making

Leila Amgoud and Srdjan Vesic

IRIT – CNRS

**Abstract.** This paper studies the possibilities and limits of applying a Dung-style argumentation framework in a decision making problem. This study is motivated by the fact that many examples in the literature use this setting for illustrating advantages or drawbacks of Dung's argumentation framework or one of its enhancements (such as PAFs, VAFs, ADFs, AFRAs). We claim that it is important to clarify the concept of argumentation-based decision making, i.e., to precisely define and consider all its components (e.g. options, arguments, goals). We show that a Dung-style argumentation framework cannot be simply "attached" to a set of options. Indeed, such a construct does not provide a sophisticated decision-making environment. Finally, we discuss the points that must be taken into account if argumentative-based decision making is to reach its full potential.

## 1 Introduction

A multiple criteria decision problem amounts to selecting the 'best' or sufficiently 'good' option(s) among different alternatives. The goodness of an option is judged by estimating by means of several criteria how much its possible consequences fit the preferences of the decision maker. Fargier and Dubois ([6]) proposed an abstract framework for qualitative bipolar multiple criteria decision. It assumes that each option may have positive and negative features. Various efficient *decision rules* that compare pairs of options were proposed and axiomatized in the same paper.

Besides, several attempts have recently been made for explaining and suggesting choices in decision making problems on the basis of arguments [3,8,2]. Moreover, it is very common in argumentation literature that an argumentation process is illustrated by informal examples of decision problems. However, it is not clear which decision rule is used for comparing options in those argument-based decision frameworks. Thus, it is difficult to formally evaluate the quality of those works and to compare them with existing works on non-argumentative decision theory.

Starting from the decision problem studied in [6], the aim of this paper is to investigate the kind of decision rules that may be encoded within Dung's argumentation framework [7]. We study three argumentation frameworks: The first and second frameworks assume that the options are evaluated and compared on the basis only of arguments pros (respectively arguments cons). In the third framework, both types of arguments are involved in the comparison process. For each framework we study two cases: the case where all the criteria in the decision problem have the same importance and the case where some of them may be more important than others. The results show that in this

S. Greco et al. (Eds.): IPMU 2012, Part IV, CCIS 300, pp. 480–489, 2012.

setting (i.e. when a Dung-style argumentation framework is attached to a set of options) there is no added value of argumentation. Furthermore, the framework proposed in [6] performs better than its simple argumentative counterpart.

The paper is organized as follows: We start by recalling the fundamentals of argumentation theory, then we describe the formal framework for qualitative bipolar multi-criteria decision that was proposed in [6]. In a next section, we study the different argumentation frameworks that may encode the decision problem discussed in [6]. The last section is devoted to some concluding remarks and some ideas of future work.

## 2  Basics of Argumentation

Dung has developed the most abstract argumentation framework in the literature [7]. It consists of a set of arguments and an attack relation between them.

**Definition 1 (Argumentation framework).** *An* argumentation framework *(AF) is a pair* $\mathcal{F} = (\mathcal{A}, \mathcal{R})$ *where* $\mathcal{A}$ *is a set of* arguments *and* $\mathcal{R}$ *is an* attack relation *(*$\mathcal{R} \subseteq \mathcal{A} \times \mathcal{A}$*). The notation* $\alpha \mathcal{R} \beta$ *means that argument* $\alpha$ attacks *argument* $\beta$.

Different *acceptability semantics* for evaluating arguments are proposed in the same paper [7]. Each semantics amounts to define sets of acceptable arguments, called *extensions*. Before recalling those semantics, let us first introduce the two basic properties underlying them, namely *conflict-freeness* and *defence*.

**Definition 2 (Conflict-free, Defence).** *Let* $\mathcal{F} = (\mathcal{A}, \mathcal{R})$ *be an AF and* $\mathcal{E} \subseteq \mathcal{A}$. $\mathcal{E}$ *is* conflict-free *iff* $\nexists \, \alpha, \, \beta \in \mathcal{E}$ *s.t.* $\alpha \mathcal{R} \beta$. $\mathcal{E}$ *defends* an argument $\alpha$ *iff for all* $\beta \in \mathcal{A}$ *s.t.* $\beta \mathcal{R} \alpha$, *there exists* $\delta \in \mathcal{E}$ *s.t.* $\delta \mathcal{R} \beta$.

The following definition recalls some acceptability semantics proposed in [7]. Note that other semantics refining them are proposed in the literature. However, we do not need to recall them for the purpose of our paper.

**Definition 3 (Acceptability semantics).** *Let* $\mathcal{F} = (\mathcal{A}, \mathcal{R})$ *be an AF and* $\mathcal{E} \subseteq \mathcal{A}$. $\mathcal{E}$ *is an* admissible *set iff it is conflict-free and defends its elements.* $\mathcal{E}$ *is a* preferred extension *iff it is a maximal (for set* $\subseteq$*) admissible set.* $\mathcal{E}$ *is a* stable *extension iff it is conflict-free and attacks any argument in* $\mathcal{A} \setminus \mathcal{E}$.

A status is assigned for each argument as follows.

**Definition 4 (Status of arguments).** *Let* $\mathcal{F} = (\mathcal{A}, \mathcal{R})$ *be an AF and* $\mathcal{E}_1, \ldots, \mathcal{E}_n$ *its extensions (under a given semantics). An argument* $\alpha \in \mathcal{A}$ *is* skeptically accepted *iff* $\alpha \in \mathcal{E}_i, \forall i \in \{1, \ldots, n\}$. *It is* credulously accepted *iff* $\exists i \in \{1, \ldots, n\}$ *s.t.* $\alpha \in \mathcal{E}_i$. *It is* rejected *iff* $\forall i \in \{1, \ldots, n\}, \alpha \notin \mathcal{E}_i$.

**Example 1.** *Assume a framework* $\mathcal{F}_1 = (\mathcal{A}, \mathcal{R})$ *where* $\mathcal{A} = \{\alpha, \beta, \delta, \gamma\}$ *and* $\alpha \mathcal{R} \beta$, $\beta \mathcal{R} \gamma$, $\gamma \mathcal{R} \delta$ *and* $\delta \mathcal{R} \alpha$. $\mathcal{F}_1$ *has two preferred and stable extensions:* $\{\alpha, \gamma\}$ *and* $\{\beta, \delta\}$. *The four arguments are credulously accepted under stable and preferred semantics.*

When the attack relation is symmetric, the corresponding argumentation framework is called *symmetric*. It has been shown [4] that such a framework is *coherent* (i.e. its stable extensions coincide with the preferred ones). These extensions are exactly the maximal (for set inclusion) sets of arguments that are conflict-free. Moreover, each argument belongs to at least one extension which means that it cannot be rejected.

It was argued in [1] that arguments may not have the same intrinsic strength. *Preference-based argumentation frameworks* (PAF) have thus been defined. They evaluate arguments on the basis of their strengths and interactions with other arguments.

**Definition 5 (PAF).** *A PAF is a tuple* $\mathcal{T} = (\mathcal{A}, \mathcal{R}, \geq)$ *where* $\mathcal{A}$ *is a set of arguments,* $\mathcal{R}$ *is an attack relation and* $\geq \subseteq \mathcal{A} \times \mathcal{A}$ *is a (partial or total) preorder (i.e. reflexive and transitive). The notation* $\alpha \geq \beta$ *means that* $\alpha$ *is at least as strong as* $\beta$. *The extensions of* $\mathcal{T}$ *under a given semantics are the extensions of the AF* $(\mathcal{A}, \text{Def})$ *where for* $\alpha, \beta \in \mathcal{A}$, $\alpha \text{Def} \beta$ *iff* $\alpha \mathcal{R} \beta$ *and not* $(\beta > \alpha)$[1].

# 3  Qualitative Bipolar Multiple Criteria Decisions

In [6], an abstract framework for *qualitative bipolar multiple criteria decision* consists of a finite set $\mathcal{D}$ of *potential decisions* (or *options*) $d_1, \ldots, d_n$; a finite set $\mathcal{C}$ of *criteria* $c_1, \ldots, c_m$, viewed as attributes ranging on a bipolar scale $\mathcal{S} = \{-, 0, +\}$. With this scale, a criterion is either completely against $(-)$, totally irrelevant $(0)$, or totally in favor of each decision in $\mathcal{D}$. The set $\mathcal{C}$ of criteria is ordered using a totally ordered scale $\mathcal{L}$ expressing the relative importance of each criterion or of a group of criteria. This scale has a top element $1_{\mathcal{L}}$ (full importance) and a bottom one $0_{\mathcal{L}}$ (no importance). Let $\pi : 2^{\mathcal{C}} \mapsto \mathcal{L}$ be a function that returns the importance value of a group of criteria. We assume that $\pi(\emptyset) = 0_{\mathcal{L}}$. In addition to the two sets $\mathcal{D}$ and $\mathcal{C}$, a base $\mathcal{K}$ is available. It contains information of the form $c^+(d)$ or $c^-(d)$ about the behavior of a decision $d$ towards a criterion $c$. In fact, $c^+(d)$ means that decision $d$ satisfies criterion $c$ while $c^-(d)$ means that $d$ violates $c$. Two functions $\mathcal{F}^+$ and $\mathcal{F}^-$ that return respectively the criteria that are satisfied (violated) by each decision are assumed. Formally: $\mathcal{F}^+ : \mathcal{D} \mapsto 2^{\mathcal{C}}$ s.t. $\mathcal{F}^+(d) = \{c \in \mathcal{C} \mid c^+(d) \in \mathcal{K}\}$ and $\mathcal{F}^- : \mathcal{D} \mapsto 2^{\mathcal{C}}$ s.t. $\mathcal{F}^-(d) = \{c \in \mathcal{C} \mid c^-(d) \in \mathcal{K}\}$. A multiple criteria decision problem consists of defining a *decision rule* for rank-ordering the options. The authors in [6] proposed and investigated different rules. According to those rules, comparing two decisions $d_i$ and $d_j$ amounts to comparing the pairs $(\mathcal{F}^+(d_i), \mathcal{F}^-(d_i))$ and $(\mathcal{F}^+(d_j), \mathcal{F}^-(d_j))$. The criteria that got value 0 by a decision are not taken into account in the comparison process since they are neutral.

**Definition 6 (Decision problem).** *A decision problem is a tuple* $(\mathcal{D}, \mathcal{C}, \pi, \mathcal{K}, \mathcal{F}^+, \mathcal{F}^-)$.

Let us illustrate the above concepts on the following example borrowed from [6].

**Example 2.** *Luc hesitates between two destinations for his next holidays:* $\mathcal{D} = \{d_1, d_2\}$. *Assume that* $\mathcal{C} = \{landscape, price, airline reputation, governance, tennis, pool, disco\}$ *such that* $\pi(\{landscape\}) = \pi(\{price\}) = \pi(\{airline\}) = \pi(\{governance\}) = \lambda$ *and*

---

[1] The relation $>$ is the strict version of $\geq$. Indeed, for $\alpha, \beta \in \mathcal{A}$, $\alpha > \beta$ iff $\alpha \geq \beta$ and not $(\beta \geq \alpha)$.

$\pi(\{tennis\}) = \pi(\{pool\}) = \pi(\{disco\}) = \delta$ *with* $\lambda > \delta > 0_{\mathcal{L}}$. *Assume also that option* $d_1$ *has landscape, but it is very expensive and the local airline has a terrible reputation. Option* $d_2$ *is in a non-democratic region. On the other hand, this region has a tennis court, a disco, and a swimming pool. Thus,* $\mathcal{F}^+(d_1) = \{landscape\}$, $\mathcal{F}^-(d_1) = \{airline, price\}$, $\mathcal{F}^+(d_2) = \{tennis, pool, disco\}$ *and* $\mathcal{F}^-(d_2) = \{governance\}$. *An example of a relation that compares the two destinations is* Pareto Dominance *rule defined as follows:* $d_i \succeq d_j$ *iff* $max_{x \in \mathcal{F}^+(d_i)}\pi(\{x\}) \geq max_{x \in \mathcal{F}^+(d_j)}\pi(\{x\})$ *and* $max_{x \in \mathcal{F}^-(d_i)}\pi(\{x\}) \leq max_{x \in \mathcal{F}^-(d_j)}\pi(\{x\})$. *(PDR) According to this rule, Luc will choose option* $d_1$ *since* $\pi(\{landscape\}) > \pi(\{tennis\})$, $\pi(\{pool\})$, $\pi(\{disco\})$ *and* $max(\pi(\{airline\}), \pi(\{price\})) = \pi(\{governance\})$.

## 4    Argument-Based Decisions

The backbone of an argumentation framework is the notion of argument. In a multiple criteria decision context, it can be defined in two ways: an *atomic* way and a *cumulative* one. In the former case, an argument *pro* an option $d$ is any information $c^+(d)$. We say that there is a reason to select $d$ since it satisfies criterion $c$. Similarly, an argument *cons* $d$ is any information $c^-(d)$, i.e. the fact that $d$ violates criterion $c$. Hence, an option may have several arguments pros and several arguments cons. The total number of arguments would not exceed the total number of available criteria (i.e. $|\mathcal{C}|$). The cumulative way of defining an argument consists of accruing all the atomic arguments into a single one. Thus, an argument pro an option $d$ would be the set of all criteria satisfied by that option (i.e. $\{c^+(d) \mid c^+(d) \in \mathcal{K}\}$), and an argument cons is the set of all criteria violated by that option (i.e. $\{c^-(d) \mid c^-(d) \in \mathcal{K}\}$). With this definition, an argument may have at most one argument pro and at most one argument cons.

**Notation:** Whatever the definition of an argument is, the function Conc returns for a given argument, the option that is supported or attacked by this argument.

Next, we will show that if we attach a Dung's abstract framework to a set of options, we can encode some decision rules that are proposed in [6]. We will discuss three cases: In the first case, we assume that only arguments pros are considered for comparing options. In the second case, we assume that options are compared on the basis of their arguments cons. In the third case, both types of arguments are taken into account.

### 4.1    Handling Arguments Pros

Let $(\mathcal{D}, \mathcal{C}, \pi, \mathcal{K}, \mathcal{F}^+, \mathcal{F}^-)$ be a decision problem such that for all $d \in \mathcal{D}$, $\mathcal{F}^-(d) = \emptyset$. Thus, options in $\mathcal{D}$ may only have arguments pros. In what follows, we will discuss two cases: the case where all the criteria have the same importance (called flat case) and the case where they may have different degrees of importance (prioritized case).

**Flat Case.** We assume that criteria in $\mathcal{C}$ have the same importance (i.e., $\pi(\{c_1\}) = \ldots = \pi(\{c_m\})$). The argumentation framework corresponding to this decision problem is a pair of the set of all arguments pros, and an attack relation which expresses that two arguments support distinct options. Note that this is the only meaningful definition of an attack relation in this case. Let us first consider the atomic definition of arguments.

**Definition 7.** *Let* $(\mathcal{D}, \mathcal{C}, \pi, \mathcal{K}, \mathcal{F}^+, \mathcal{F}^-)$ *be a decision problem s.t.* $\forall d \in \mathcal{D},\ \mathcal{F}^-(d) = \emptyset$, *and* $\pi(\{c_1\}) = \ldots = \pi(\{c_m\})$ *with* $m = |\mathcal{C}|$. *The corresponding AF is a pair* $\mathcal{F}_p = (\mathcal{A}_p, \mathcal{R}_p)$ *where:* $\mathcal{A}_p = \bigcup_{d \in \mathcal{D}} c^+(d)$ *where* $c^+(d) \in \mathcal{K}$ *and* $\mathcal{R}_p = \{(\alpha, \beta) \mid \alpha, \beta \in \mathcal{A}_p$ *and* $\mathrm{Conc}(\alpha) \neq \mathrm{Conc}(\beta)\}$.

It is clear from the above definition that the attack relation is *symmetric*. Moreover, it does not contain self-attacking arguments.

*Property 1.* $\mathcal{R}_p$ is symmetric and does not contain self-attacking arguments.

The argumentation framework $\mathcal{F}_p = (\mathcal{A}_p, \mathcal{R}_p)$ is thus coherent. We show that it has as many extensions as decisions that are supported by at least one argument. Moreover, each extension contains the arguments of the same option.

**Proposition 1.** *Let* $\mathcal{F}_p = (\mathcal{A}_p, \mathcal{R}_p)$ *be the AF corresponding to a decision problem* $(\mathcal{D}, \mathcal{C}, \pi, \mathcal{K}, \mathcal{F}^+, \mathcal{F}^-)$.

- $\mathcal{F}_p$ *has* $n$ *extensions where* $n = |\{d \in \mathcal{D}$ *s.t.* $\mathcal{F}^+(d) \neq \emptyset\}|$.
- *For each extension* $\mathcal{E}$, $\mathcal{E} = \{\alpha_1, \ldots, \alpha_m\}$ *with* $\mathrm{Conc}(\alpha_1) = \ldots = \mathrm{Conc}(\alpha_m)$ *and* $m = |\mathcal{F}^+(\mathrm{Conc}(\alpha_1))|$.
- *For all* $\alpha \in \mathcal{A}_p$, $\alpha$ *is credulously accepted in* $\mathcal{F}_p$.

Since all arguments are credulously accepted, all options that are supported by at least one argument pro are equally preferred, and they are preferred to the decisions that are supported only by neutral arguments. This shows that $\mathcal{F}_p$ does not allow any efficient comparison between decisions.

**Example 2 (Cont):** Let us re-consider the decision problem of Luc. There are four arguments: $\alpha = landscape^+(d_1)$, $\alpha_1 = tennis^+(d_2)$, $\alpha_2 = pool^+(d_2)$ and $\alpha_3 = disco^+(d_2)$. Moreover, the attack relation is as depicted in the figure below.

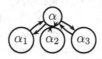

This framework has two extensions: $\mathcal{E}_1 = \{\alpha\}$ and $\mathcal{E}_2 = \{\alpha_1, \alpha_2, \alpha_3\}$. The two destinations are equally preferred which is certainly not realistic. Even if the four criteria are equally preferred, Luc still can select the option that satisfies *more* criteria, i.e. $d_2$.

The above result is not due to the atomic definition of an argument. The result is obtained by the next framework which defines arguments pros in a cumulative way.

**Definition 8.** *Let* $(\mathcal{D}, \mathcal{C}, \pi, \mathcal{K}, \mathcal{F}^+, \mathcal{F}^-)$ *be a decision problem s.t.* $\forall d \in \mathcal{D},\ \mathcal{F}^-(d) = \emptyset$, *and* $\pi(\{c_1\}) = \ldots = \pi(\{c_m\})$ *with* $m = |\mathcal{C}|$. *The corresponding AF is a pair* $\mathcal{F}'_p = (\mathcal{A}'_p, \mathcal{R}'_p)$ *where:* $\mathcal{A}'_p = \{\{c_i^+(d) \mid c_i^+(d) \in \mathcal{K}\}$ *s.t.* $d \in \mathcal{D}\}$ *and* $\mathcal{R}'_p = \{(\alpha, \beta) \mid \alpha, \beta \in \mathcal{A}'_p$ *and* $\mathrm{Conc}(\alpha) \neq \mathrm{Conc}(\beta)\}$.

It is worth noticing that each option is supported by exactly one argument which may be the empty set in case the option does not satisfy any criterion. Thus, $|\mathcal{A}'_p| = |\mathcal{D}|$.

**Proposition 2.** *Let* $\mathcal{F}'_p = (\mathcal{A}'_p, \mathcal{R}'_p)$ *be the AF corresponding to a decision problem* $(\mathcal{D},$ $\mathcal{C}, \pi, \mathcal{K}, \mathcal{F}^+, \mathcal{F}^-)$.

- $\mathcal{F}'_p$ *has* $n$ *extensions where* $n = |\mathcal{D}|$.
- *For each extension* $\mathcal{E}$, $|\mathcal{E}| = 1$.
- *All arguments of* $\mathcal{A}'_p$ *are credulously accepted.*

The fact that $\mathcal{F}_p$ and $\mathcal{F}'_p$ do not capture correctly Example 2 does not mean that there is no instantiation of Dung's framework which computes the expected result. We propose a PAF which prefers the option(s) satisfying the highest number of criteria. This PAF considers cumulative arguments and assumes that arguments do not necessarily have the same strength. The strongest arguments are those referring to more criteria.

**Definition 9.** *Let* $(\mathcal{D}, \mathcal{C}, \pi, \mathcal{K}, \mathcal{F}^+, \mathcal{F}^-)$ *be a decision problem s.t.* $\forall d \in \mathcal{D},$ $\mathcal{F}^-(d) =$ $\emptyset$. *The corresponding PAF is* $(\mathcal{A}'_p, \mathcal{R}'_p, \geq'_p)$ *where* $\geq'_p \subseteq \mathcal{A}'_p \times \mathcal{A}'_p$ *and for* $\alpha, \beta \in \mathcal{A}'_p,$ $\alpha \geq'_p \beta$ *iff* $|\alpha| \geq |\beta|$.

Note that the relation $\geq'_p$ is a total preorder. Moreover, this PAF is coherent and it has non-empty extensions. Let us now recall the decision rule which privileges the options which satisfy more criteria: $d_i \succeq d_j$ iff $|\mathcal{F}^+(d_i)| \geq |\mathcal{F}^+(d_j)|$.

**Notation:** We denote by $\text{Max}(\mathcal{D}, \succeq)$ the top elements of $\mathcal{D}$ according to a preference relation $\succeq$, i.e. $\text{Max}(\mathcal{D}, \succeq) = \{d \in \mathcal{D} \text{ s.t. } \forall d' \in \mathcal{D}, d \succeq d'\}$.

**Proposition 3.** *Let* $(\mathcal{D}, \mathcal{C}, \pi, \mathcal{K}, \mathcal{F}^+, \mathcal{F}^-)$ *be a decision problem s.t.* $\forall d \in \mathcal{D},$ $\mathcal{F}^-(d) =$ $\emptyset$ *and* $\mathcal{T}' = (\mathcal{A}'_p, \mathcal{R}'_p, \geq'_p)$ *its corresponding PAF.* $d \in \text{Max}(\mathcal{D}, \succeq)$ *iff there exists a stable extension* $\mathcal{E}$ *of* $\mathcal{T}'$ *s.t.* $\mathcal{E} = \{\alpha \text{ s.t. } \alpha \in \mathcal{A}'_p \text{ and } \text{Conc}(\alpha) = d\}$.

**Example 2 (Cont):** The PAF corresponding to the decision problem of Luc has $\mathcal{A}'_p =$ $\{\delta, \gamma\}$, $\delta = \{landscape^+(d_1)\}$, $\gamma = \{tennis^+(d_2), pool^+(d_2), disco^+(d_2)\}$, $\mathcal{R}'_p =$ $\{(\delta, \gamma), (\gamma, \delta)\}$, and $\gamma \geq'_p \delta$ since $|\gamma| = 3$ and $|\delta| = 1$. This PAF has one extension: $\mathcal{E} = \{\gamma\}$, thus Luc would choose destination $d_2$.

Note that the previous PAF returns only the best options and says nothing on the remaining ones. In this sense, a non argumentative-approach is richer since it compares any pair of options. This latter is also simpler since it does not need to pass through different concepts (like attacks and extensions) in order to get the solution.

**Prioritized Case.** Let us now assume that the criteria are not equally important. It is clear that in this case arguments may not have the same *strength*. We propose a simple preference-based argumentation framework which encodes the well-known Wald's *optimistic* ordering [11]. This PAF considers an atomic definition of arguments, and compares arguments wrt the importance of the criteria to which they refer.

**Definition 10.** *Let* $(\mathcal{D}, \mathcal{C}, \pi, \mathcal{K}, \mathcal{F}^+, \mathcal{F}^-)$ *be a decision problem s.t.* $\forall d \in \mathcal{D}$ *and* $\mathcal{F}^-(d) = \emptyset$. *The corresponding PAF is* $\mathcal{T}_p = (\mathcal{A}_p, \mathcal{R}_p, \geq_p)$ *where for two arguments* $c_i^+(d)$ *and* $c_j^+(d')$, $c_i^+(d) \geq_p c_j^+(d')$ *iff* $\pi(\{c_i\}) \geq \pi(\{c_j\})$.

It is easy to check that the preference relation $\geq_p$ is a complete preorder. Besides, we show that the number of extensions of the PAF $(\mathcal{A}_p, \mathcal{R}_p, \geq_p)$ is the number of options that satisfy the most important criteria. Moreover, each extension contains *all* the arguments in favor of the same option.

**Proposition 4.** *Let $(\mathcal{D}, \mathcal{C}, \pi, \mathcal{K}, \mathcal{F}^+, \mathcal{F}^-)$ be a decision problem s.t. $\forall d \in \mathcal{D}, \mathcal{F}^-(d) = \emptyset$ and $\mathcal{T}_p = (\mathcal{A}_p, \mathcal{R}_p, \geq_p)$ its corresponding PAF.*

- *$\mathcal{T}_p$ has exactly $n$ stable extensions s.t. $n = |\{d \in \mathcal{D} \text{ s.t. } \exists c \in \mathcal{F}^+(d) \text{ and } \forall c' \in \mathcal{C}, \pi(\{c\}) \geq \pi(\{c'\})\}|$.*
- *For each stable extension $\mathcal{E}$ of $\mathcal{T}_p$, $\exists c^+(d) \in \mathcal{E}$ s.t. $\forall c' \in \mathcal{C}, \pi(\{c\}) \geq \pi(\{c'\})$.*
- *For each stable extension $\mathcal{E}$ of $\mathcal{T}_p$, $\exists d \in \mathcal{D}$ s.t. $\mathcal{E} = \{c^+(d) \mid c^+(d) \in \mathcal{K}\}$.*

The following result shows that this PAF privileges the decisions that are supported by at least one strong argument. This relation is a simplified version of the Pareto Dominance Rule (PDR) when arguments cons are not available. It collapses to Wald's *optimistic* ordering [11]. $d_i \succeq_o d_j$ iff $max_{x \in \mathcal{F}^+(d_i)} \pi(\{x\}) \geq max_{x \in \mathcal{F}^+(d_j)} \pi(\{x\})$.

**Proposition 5.** *Let $\mathcal{T}_p = (\mathcal{A}_p, \mathcal{R}_p, \geq_p)$ be the PAF corresponding to a decision problem $(\mathcal{D}, \mathcal{C}, \pi, \mathcal{K}, \mathcal{F}^+, \mathcal{F}^-)$ s.t. $\forall d \in \mathcal{D}, \mathcal{F}^-(d) = \emptyset$ and $\mathcal{A}_p \neq \emptyset$. Let $d \in \mathcal{D}$. $d \in \text{Max}(\mathcal{D}, \succeq_o)$ iff there exists a stable extension $\mathcal{E}$ of $\mathcal{T}_p$ s.t. $\exists c^+(d) \in \mathcal{E}$.*

**Example 2 (Cont):** The PAF corresponding to the decision problem of Luc is $\mathcal{T}_p = (\mathcal{A}_p, \mathcal{R}_p, \geq_p)$ where $\mathcal{A}_p = \{\alpha, \alpha_1, \alpha_2, \alpha_3\}$, $\alpha \mathcal{R}_p \alpha_1, \alpha_1 \mathcal{R}_p \alpha, \alpha \mathcal{R}_p \alpha_2, \alpha_2 \mathcal{R}_p \alpha, \alpha \mathcal{R}_p \alpha_3$, $\alpha_3 \mathcal{R}_p \alpha$, and $\alpha >_p \alpha_1, \alpha >_p \alpha_2, \alpha >_p \alpha_3$. This PAF has one stable extension: $\mathcal{E} = \{\alpha\}$, thus Luc would choose destination $d_1$.

The PAF $\mathcal{T}_p$ returns only the best options wrt $\succeq_o$. However, the qualitative approach of [6] compares any pair of options. This is suitable in negotiation dialogs where agents are sometimes constrained to make concessions, i.e. to propose/accept less preferred options in order to reach an agreement.

## 4.2 Handling Arguments Cons

In the previous section, we have investigated the case where only arguments pros are taken into account for comparing options. In what follows, we assume that options are compared on the basis of their arguments cons. Let $(\mathcal{D}, \mathcal{C}, \pi, \mathcal{K}, \mathcal{F}^+, \mathcal{F}^-)$ be a decision problem such that for all $d \in \mathcal{D}, \mathcal{F}^+(d) = \emptyset$. This means that the different decisions may only have arguments cons. Note that this case is dual to the previous case where only arguments pro are considered. Thus, it is easy to check that the framework $\mathcal{F}_c$ (dual version of $\mathcal{F}_p$) does not say anything about options that do not have arguments cons. Moreover, it considers options having at least one argument cons as equally preferred. This framework is thus not decisive since an option that has no argument cons is certainly better than one that has at least one argument cons, and in case two options have both arguments cons, it is more natural to choose the one that has less arguments. For instance, it is more natural for Luc to choose the option that violates less criteria, i.e. $d_2$.

Contrarily to the PAF $\mathcal{T}_p$ which returns the best options, its dual $\mathcal{T}_c$ returns the worst ones. Indeed, it computes the decisions that violate the most important criteria. The following result shows that these decisions are the worse elements of the Wald's *pessimistic* ordering defined as follows [11]: $d_i \succeq_p d_j$ iff $max_{x \in \mathcal{F}^-(d_i)} \pi(\{x\}) \leq max_{x \in \mathcal{F}^-(d_j)} \pi(\{x\})$. It is worth noticing that this relation is a complete preorder. In what follows, we denote by $\text{Min}(\mathcal{D}, \succeq_p)$, the bottom elements of $\mathcal{D}$ according to the preference relation $\succeq_p$. $\text{Min}(\mathcal{D}, \succeq_p) = \{d \in \mathcal{D} \text{ s.t. } \forall d' \in \mathcal{D}, d' \succeq_p d\}$.

**Proposition 6.** *Let $\mathcal{T}_c = (\mathcal{A}_c, \mathcal{R}_c, \geq_c)$ be the PAF corresponding to a decision problem $(\mathcal{D}, \mathcal{C}, \pi, \mathcal{K}, \mathcal{F}^+, \mathcal{F}^-)$ s.t. $\forall d \in \mathcal{D}, \mathcal{F}^+(d) = \emptyset$, and $\mathcal{A}_c \neq \emptyset$. Let $d \in \mathcal{D}$. $d \in \text{Min}(\mathcal{D}, \succeq_p)$ iff there exists an extension $\mathcal{E}$ of $\mathcal{T}_c$ s.t. $\exists c^-(d) \in \mathcal{E}$.*

This result shows that the framework $\mathcal{T}_c$ is poor compared to the qualitative model of [6]. Indeed, not only it does not compare all the options but it does not even return the best ones. Note that if the preference relation $\geq_c$ is defined in such a way to prefer the argument violating the less important criterion, then the corresponding PAF will return the best option(s). However, such a preference relation would not be intuitive since it is intended to reflect the strengths of arguments.

### 4.3 Bipolar Argumentation Frameworks

Previously, we have considered only pros arguments for comparing decisions in $\mathcal{D}$. In what follows, the comparison is made on the basis of both types of arguments. We start with the case where all criteria in $\mathcal{C}$ have the same importance level.

The argumentation framework corresponding to a decision problem is a pair $(\mathcal{A}_b, \mathcal{R}_b)$ consisting of the sets of arguments pros and cons each decision. The definition of the attack relation $\mathcal{R}_b$ is not obvious. While it is natural to assume that arguments pros or cons distinct options are conflicting, it is not always natural to assume that an argument pro an option conflicts with an argument con the same option. Let us consider the case of Luc who wants to choose his future destination. The fact that destination $d_1$ has beautiful landscape does not necessarily attack the fact that the airline company that deserves that destination has a bad reputation. In what follows, we will study two cases: the case where arguments pros and cons conflict, and the case where they do not.

**Definition 11 (Bipolar AF).** *Let $(\mathcal{D}, \mathcal{C}, \pi, \mathcal{K}, \mathcal{F}^+, \mathcal{F}^-)$ be a decision problem s.t. $\pi(\{c_1\}) = \ldots = \pi(\{c_m\})$ with $m = |\mathcal{C}|$. The corresponding AF is a pair $\mathcal{F}_b = (\mathcal{A}_b, \mathcal{R}_b)$ where:*

- $\mathcal{A}_b = \{c^+(d) \mid c^+(d) \in \mathcal{K}\} \cup \{c^-(d) \mid c^-(d) \in \mathcal{K}\}$.
- $\mathcal{R}_b = \{(a, b) \mid Conc(a) \neq Conc(b)\} \cup \{(a, b), (b, a) \mid a = c_i^+(d), b = c_j^-(d') \text{ and } d = d'\}$.

The framework $\mathcal{F}_b$ is symmetric. Consequently, its stable and preferred extensions are exactly the maximal conflict-free subsets of $\mathcal{A}_b$. Moreover, each decision is supported at most by two extensions: one containing its arguments pros and another containing its arguments cons.

**Proposition 7.** *Let $\mathcal{F}_b = (\mathcal{A}_b, \mathcal{R}_b)$ be the AF corresponding to a decision problem $(\mathcal{D}, \mathcal{C}, \pi, \mathcal{K}, \mathcal{F}^+, \mathcal{F}^-)$.*

- For all $d \in \mathcal{D}$, if $\mathcal{F}^+(d) \neq \emptyset$ (resp. $\mathcal{F}^-(d) \neq \emptyset$), then $\mathcal{F}_b$ has an extension $\mathcal{E} = \{c^+(d) \mid c^+(d) \in \mathcal{K}\}$ (resp. an extension $\mathcal{E} = \{c^-(d) \mid c^-(d) \in \mathcal{K}\}$).
- The number of extensions of $\mathcal{F}_b$ is $n$ where $n = |\{d \in \mathcal{D} \ s.t. \ \mathcal{F}^+(d) \neq \emptyset\}| + |\{d \in \mathcal{D} \ s.t. \ \mathcal{F}^-(d) \neq \emptyset\}|$.

**Example 2 (Cont):** The bipolar framework corresponding to Luc's decision problem has four extensions: $\mathcal{E}_1 = \{\alpha\}$, $\mathcal{E}_2 = \{\beta_1, \beta_2\}$, $\mathcal{E}_3 = \{\alpha_1, \alpha_2, \alpha_3\}$ and $\mathcal{E}_4 = \{\beta\}$.

With such a framework, all the arguments are credulously accepted. Consequently, the different options supported at least by one argument (either pros or cons) are equally preferred. This means that $\mathcal{F}_b$ is not decisive and even useless. Moreover, this result is *not intuitive* as illustrated by the following example.

**Example 3.** *Carla wants to buy a mobile phone. The seller proposes two options, say* $d_1$ *and* $d_2$*. The first option has a large screen while the second has 2 bands only. Thus,* $\mathcal{K} = \{screen^+(d_1), bands^-(d_2)\}$*. According to the above framework, there are two extensions:* $\mathcal{E}_1 = \{screen^+(d_1)\}$ *and* $\mathcal{E}_2 = \{bands^-(d_2)\}$*. Consequently, the two options are equally preferred. However, it is more rational for Carla to choose option* $d_1$ *which has only arguments pros rather than* $d_2$ *which has only arguments cons.*

Let us now study the more interesting case, namely when criteria have different levels of importance.

**Definition 12 (Bipolar PAF).** *Let* $(\mathcal{D}, \mathcal{C}, \pi, \mathcal{K}, \mathcal{F}^+, \mathcal{F}^-)$ *be a decision problem. The corresponding PAF is* $\mathcal{T}_b = (\mathcal{A}_b, \mathcal{R}_b, \geq_p)$ *where* $\geq_p \subseteq \mathcal{A}_b \times \mathcal{A}_b$*.*

According to [5], the PAF $\mathcal{F}_b$ is coherent. Moreover, it has as many extensions as strong criteria that are satisfied or violated by decisions. Moreover, each extension contains all the arguments pros (or cons) the same decision.

**Proposition 8.** *Let* $(\mathcal{D}, \mathcal{C}, \pi, \mathcal{K}, \mathcal{F}^+, \mathcal{F}^-)$ *be a decision problem and* $\mathcal{T}_b = (\mathcal{A}_b, \mathcal{R}_b, \geq_p)$ *its corresponding PAF.*

- *For each stable extension* $\mathcal{E}$ *of* $\mathcal{T}_b$*,* $\exists c^x(d) \in \mathcal{E} \ s.t. \ \forall c' \in \mathcal{C}, \ \pi(\{c\}) \geq \pi(\{c'\})$
- *For each stable extension* $\mathcal{E}$ *of* $\mathcal{T}_b$*,* $\exists d \in \mathcal{D} \ s.t. \ \mathcal{E} = \{c^+(d)|c^+(d) \in \mathcal{K}\}$ *or* $\mathcal{E} = \{c^-(d)|c^-(d) \in \mathcal{K}\}$
- $\mathcal{T}_b$ *has* $n$ *stable extensions s.t.* $n = |d \in \mathcal{D} \ s.t. \ \exists c \in \mathcal{F}^+(d) s.t. \forall c' \in \mathcal{C}, \pi(\{c\}) \geq \pi(\{c'\})| + |d \in \mathcal{D} \ s.t. \ \exists c \in \mathcal{F}^-(d) s.t. \forall c' \in \mathcal{C}, \pi(\{c\}) \geq \pi(\{c'\})|$.

From the previous result, it follows that Dung's framework cannot be used for decision making since it simply selects groups of arguments containing at least one of the strongest (positive or negative) arguments of the corresponding PAF. It does not encode any meaningful decision relation, and it does not capture the Pareto Dominance rule as shown by the following example.

**Example 2 (Cont):** The bipolar PAF has three stable extensions: $\mathcal{E}_1 = \{\alpha\}$, $\mathcal{E}_2 = \{\beta\}$ and $\mathcal{E}_3 = \{\beta_1, \beta_2\}$. $\mathcal{E}_1$ and $\mathcal{E}_3$ concern option $d_1$ and $\mathcal{E}_2$ concerns $d_2$. Thus, it is impossible to compare the two options.

Note that this negative result holds also when arguments pros and cons the same option are not conflicting. In this case, the corresponding argumentation framework has as many extensions as decisions that satisfy or violate at least one criterion (in the flat case). In the prioritized case, the corresponding PAF has as many extensions as decisions that satisfy at least one of the most important criteria plus the ones that violate at least one of such criteria.

# 5 Discussion

It is very common that Dung's abstract framework is illustrated with an example of multiple criteria decision problem, where arguments pros an option are advanced and then attacked by arguments cons that option. Our aim in this paper is to show that things are not so simple. We have shown that simply attaching a Dung-style argumentation system and using its extensions for decision making, in the best case leads to encoding a particular decision rule while in the worst case the system equally prefers all options, thus it is not decisive. It is worth noticing that in the best case, only the best option(s) are returned and nothing is said about the remaining ones. We have also shown that the qualitative model proposed in [6] performs better than the argumentative approach since it returns more results (an ordering on the whole set of options). Moreover, that approach is simpler since it does not need to compute extensions as in Dung's system.

A possible extension of this work consists of studying whether it is possible (and how) to encode in argumentation the efficient decision rule based on Choquet Integral [9] and that based on Sugeno Integral [10].

# References

1. Amgoud, L., Cayrol, C.: A reasoning model based on the production of acceptable arguments. Annals of Mathematics and Artificial Intelligence 34, 197–216 (2002)
2. Amgoud, L., Prade, H.: Using arguments for making and explaining decisions. AIJ 173, 413–436 (2009)
3. Bonet, B., Geffner, H.: Arguing for decisions: A qualitative model of decision making. In: UAI 1996, pp. 98–105 (1996)
4. Coste-Marquis, S., Devred, C., Marquis, P.: Symmetric Argumentation Frameworks. In: Godo, L. (ed.) ECSQARU 2005. LNCS (LNAI), vol. 3571, pp. 317–328. Springer, Heidelberg (2005)
5. Dimopoulos, Y., Moraitis, P., Amgoud, L.: Theoretical and computational properties of preference-based argumentation. In: ECAI 2008, pp. 463–467 (2008)
6. Dubois, D., Fargier, H., Bonnefon, J.: On the qualitative comparison of decisions having positive and negative features. J. Artif. Intell. Res. (JAIR) 32, 385–417 (2008)
7. Dung, P.M.: On the acceptability of arguments and its fundamental role in nonmonotonic reasoning, logic programming and $n$-person games. AIJ 77, 321–357 (1995)
8. Fox, J., Das, S.: Safe and Sound. Artificial Intelligence in Hazardous Applications. AAAI Press, The MIT Press (2000)
9. Grabisch, M., Kojadinovic, I., Meyer, P.: Using the kappalab r package for choquet integral based multi-attribute utility theory. In: IPMU 2006, pp. 1702–1709 (2006)
10. Sugeno, M.: Theory of fuzzy integrals and its applications. Ph.D. Thesis, Tokyo Institute of Technology (1974)
11. Wald, A.: Statistical decision functions. Wiley, New York (1971)

# Privacy-Aware Database System
# for Retrieving Facial Images

Tomohiko Fujita, Takuya Funatomi, Yoshitaka Morimura,
and Michihiko Minoh

Kyoto University, Yoshidahonmachi, Sakyo-ku, Kyoto-shi, Kyoto, 606-8501 Japan
tfujita@mm.media.kyoto-u.ac.jp

**Abstract.** To achieve privacy protection on facial image retrieval systems, we propose a method of encrypting facial images with a key produced from facial features. Because facial features vary even for the same person, it is not recommended to use facial features as the cryptographic key. Therefore, we propose a method for generating a key by quantizing the facial features based on entropy. In our experiment, we applied the proposed method to a public facial image database, and evaluated the system performance and integrity by calculating the false acceptance rate and the false rejection rate.

## 1 Introduction

Surveillance cameras have been widely used to assist with criminal investigations. It is therefore useful to build a retrieval system for finding suspects from recorded videos (Fig. 1). Instead of using texts such as dates and locations, it is preferred to use facial images as queries for retrieval, because images provide more information than offered by texts and enable direct comparisons to be made between the query images and the facial images in the recorded videos.

Because surveillance cameras capture images of people in public places, the faces of not only suspects but also innocent citizens get captured. In order to protect the privacy of innocent citizens, only authorized persons (e.g., detectives) should be able to use the system. Even if an authorization mechanism is introduced in the system, the recorded videos may be inadvertently leaked owing to information security crises, thereby compromising the privacy of these people. To prevent this occurrence, encryption techniques should be incorporated into the system. In this study, we aim to realize a privacy protection framework for the system. In section 2, we explain the encryption method using facial features that generate the encryption key. Moreover, we highlight the problem associated with the application of conventional encryption methods to this system. In section 3, we propose a suitable quantization method, and in section 4, we explain the results of the experiment. In section 5, we give our conclusions.

S. Greco et al. (Eds.): IPMU 2012, Part IV, CCIS 300, pp. 490–498, 2012.

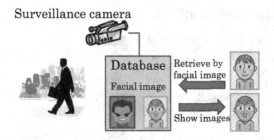

**Fig. 1.** The facial retrieval system

# 2 Privacy Protection for Facial Image Retrieval System

## 2.1 Encryption of Facial Images Using a Cryptographic Key

Encryption prevents non-authorized users from freely browsing specific data. To decrypt an encrypted data, a cryptographic key is required, which must be possessed by authorized users only. In this study, we propose a method for encrypting facial images using facial features extracted from the image to generate the cryptographic key.

Facial features used for personal identification are different for each person. Using these features, we can produce a key corresponding to each individual. This therefore requires both privacy protection and secure encryption. Because we can produce the key from the facial image of each person, we can also produce the key from the query image in order to decrypt the image of the same person in the database. Therefore, it is not necessary to store the cryptographic keys after encryption. This helps to reduce the risks of the keys being compromised. On the other hand, a key generated from a query image cannot be used to decrypt images of other persons. This makes it possible to prevent a user from browsing collected images that are not included in the query results. Although the system disposes the cryptographic encryption keys, it will maintain the hash value of the key as an index for efficient future retrieval.

We therefore propose an enrollment and reference (retrieving and decrypting) framework as follows (Fig. 2):

*Data Collection*

1. Extract facial features from a facial image
2. Generate a cryptographic key from the facial features
3. Encrypt the facial image using the key
4. Calculate a hash value of the key and register it to the encrypted image

*Retrieval*

1. Extract facial features from a query image
2. Generate a cryptographic key from the facial features

# Data collection

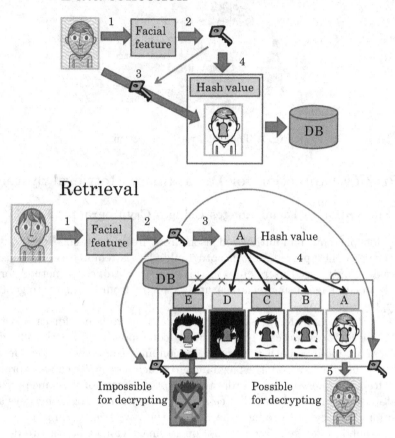

## Retrieval

**Fig. 2.** The scheme of privacy-aware system for retrieving facial images

3. Calculate a hash value of the key
4. Retrieve images that have the same hash value
5. Decrypt the retrieved images using the key

## 2.2 Problem Associated with Previously Developed Methods

Several methods have been proposed for producing the cryptographic key from facial features [1][2][3]. Facial features usually vary under the influence of illumination and variations in expressions. This would result in different keys being generated from the facial features of the same person, or the same key being generated from facial features of different persons. To solve this problem, previous methods generated a stable key from facial features of each person. Of these previous methods, we focus on the methods that quantize the facial features to generate a stable key [2][3].

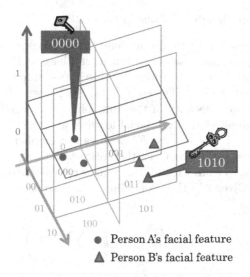

Person A's facial feature

Person B's facial feature

**Fig. 3.** Producing cryptographic key by quantizing facial feature

These methods generate a binary string from the facial features and use it as a key. This binary string is generated by quantizing and coding a facial feature independent of each dimension based on bins. The bins are determined by analyzing the distributions within the facial features. These methods enable the same key to be generated from facial features that vary within the same bins.

We apply the idea of quantizing facial features to generate a key. If an adequate quantization is performed, the same key can be obtained from the facial images of the same person and different keys can be obtained from the features of different persons (Fig. 3). However, an inadequate quantization will lead to degradation of the retrieval performance. Thus, it is important to perform an adequate quantization and several methods have been proposed for this so far. In [2], the authors separated the mean of the background distribution in each dimension of the feature space. However, this method can significantly degrade the retrieval performance because it does not consider the feature distribution of each person. Chen et al. [3] proposed a quantization method in which each bin is determined on the basis of the likelihood ratio between each personfs feature distribution and the background distribution. This method prepares different bins for each user of the system by learning facial features of all users. Although this user-specific quantization approach achieves a higher retrieval performance, it cannot prepare an adequate quantization for unspecified persons. It is therefore not ideal to apply this method to our system. We therefore need another quantization method that is applicable to unspecified persons.

## 3    Facial Feature Quantization for Encryption

As described above, it is preferable to consider the feature distributions of each person when setting bins in order to achieve high retrieval performance. Moreover, it is preferable to set common bins for use by unspecified persons.

## 3.1    Quantization Based on Entropy

We propose a quantization method that determines the common bins applicable to unspecified persons using the facial image database as the prior knowledge of the distributions of facial features. We use the entropy as the evaluation value that determines the bins. The entropy takes a higher value when the facial features of different persons vary in the same bin. We calculate the entropy as follows. In the $i$th dimension of the facial feature, we define $t_k^i(k = 1,\ldots,K^i - 1)$ as the $k$th threshold to the bins. $K^i$ denotes the number of bins in the $i$th dimension. Moreover, we define $C$ as the entire facial image set, and $C_k^i(k = 1,\ldots,K^i)$ as the group from which facial images are classified into bins by $t_k^i$ in the $i$th dimension. Given $C_k^i$, the probability of occurrence of person $x$ in $C_k^i$ is defined as follows.

$$p(x; C_k^i) = \frac{n_k^i(x)}{N_k^i} \quad \left(N_k^i = \sum_x n_k^i(x)\right) \tag{1}$$

where, $n_k^i(x)$ denotes the number of facial images of person $x$ in $C_k^i$ and $N_k^i$ denotes the total number of facial images in $C_k^i$. Thus, the entropy of $C_k^i$ is defined as

$$H(C_k^i) = -\sum_{x \in I} p(x; C_k^i) \log p(x; C_k^i) \quad (k = 1,\ldots,K^i) \tag{2}$$

where $I$ denotes the set of persons in $C$. The value of the entropy $p(x; C_k^i) \log p(x; C_k^i)$ is high when $C_k^i$ includes the facial features of many persons, and is low when $C_k^i$ includes the facial features of fewer people. Using (2), the expected value of entropy in the $i$th dimension is calculated as follows:

$$\sum_{k=1}^{K^i} H(C_k^i) \frac{N_k^i}{\sum_k N_k^i} \tag{3}$$

The term $\frac{N_k^i}{\sum_k N_k^i}$ refers to the probability of obtaining a specific number of facial images for each person.

According to the entropy, we incrementally determine the threshold of bins as follows:

1. Start from the empty set of thresholds.
2. The new threshold for bins is defined as $t$. Let $K^i$ be the number of bins that divide $C$ into $\hat{C}_k^i(k = 1,\ldots,K^i + 1)$ by adding $t$. First, we calculate the expected value of the entropy after adding $t$ as follows:

$$\sum_{k=1}^{K^i+1} H(\hat{C}_k^i) * \frac{\hat{N}_k^i}{\sum_k \hat{N}_k^i} \tag{4}$$

where $\hat{N}_k^i$ denotes the total number of facial images in $\hat{C}_k^i$. Using (3) and (4), we calculate the entropy gain $Gain^i$ as follows.

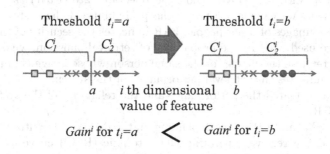

Fig. 4. Deciding threshold of bins based on entropy

$$Gain^i = \sum_{k=1}^{K^i+1} H(\hat{C}_k^i) * \frac{\hat{N}_k^i}{\sum_k \hat{N}_k^i} - \sum_{k=1}^{K^i} H(C_k^i) * \frac{N_k^i}{\sum_k N_k^i} \tag{5}$$

When there is a large difference in the number of facial images between groups (that is, most of the facial images belong to a single bin), $Gain^i$ becomes small. We calculate $t$ that maximizes $Gain^i$, and adopt it as a candidate for a new threshold of bins $\widehat{t^i_{K^i+1}}$.

3. We calculate $\widehat{t^i_{K^i+1}}$ in each dimension $i$, and select the $\widehat{t^i_{K^i+1}}$ that maximizes $Gain^i$ as a new threshold of bins. At this time, $K^i$ is updated to $K^i + 1$.

We select the threshold of bins for quantization so that the entropy gain is maximized.

## 4 Experiment

### 4.1 System Implementation

We implemented the cryptographic system for registering and referring to the facial image database. To obtain a hash value from the cryptographic key, we adopted the cryptographic hash function SHA-1 [4]. We also adopted password-protected zip compression with advanced encryption standard (AES) encryption [5], and used the cryptographic key as the password.

### 4.2 Experiment and Evaluation

We examined the performance and reliability of the proposed method. For the experiment, we used a public facial image database CAS_PEAL [6]. First, we select one facial image from the database and register other images to our system. Then, we query the system for the selected image, and evaluate whether the images of the same person are retrieved. For evaluation purposes, we used the false acceptance rate (FAR) and false rejection rate (FRR) as criteria. In this experiment, we calculate FAR as the probability of the system to incorrectly retrieve images of other people. FAR indicates the security of the system. Moreover, we used FRR as the probability of retrieval omission, where the system fails to retrieve the images of the same person whose image is in the query. Thus, FRR indicates the retrieval performance of the system.

Hence, we evaluated the performance and the reliability of the system using FAR and FRR.

However, FAR and FRR vary depending on the degree of quantization. Thus, we calculated the receiver operating characteristic (ROC) curve of FAR and FRR for various degrees of quantization. The ROC curve is the criterion usually used in studies of personal authentication. In general, the closer the ROC curve is to zero, the higher will be the performance and reliability of the method.

We conducted two experiments as follows. In the first experiment, we used 714 images (100 persons, about seven variations in expressions of each person) in the database for both determining the thresholds of the bins and evaluation. In the second experiment, we used the same dataset for determining the thresholds of the bins and used another 5,194 images (1,024 persons, about five variations in ornaments of each person) for evaluation. We evaluated the reliability and performance of the system in the first experiment, and the versatility in the second experiment.

### 4.3    Results and Discussion

The results of the first experiment are shown in Table 1 (FAR and FRR) and Fig. 1 (ROC curve).

In general, when the length of the binary code is more than 64 bits, the key is computationally secure. Thus, we selected the quantization in which the length of the binary code $b(m) = \log_2 m$ generated from the facial features is more than 64, where $m$ denotes the number of divisions $\prod_i K^i$. The FAR obtained in all quantizations satisfied the above constraint condition; the FAR was 0%. We therefore selected the quantization for which FRR was the lowest. We present these experiment results in Table 2.

From FRR in Table 2, we can retrieve 35% of the images of the same person shown in the query image. Because the proposed system collects images captured by surveillance cameras, it is expected that there will be multiple images of the same person within the database. Therefore, even if the FRR is about 35%, it can achieve satisfactory performance. Moreover, 0% of FAR implies that the system rarely retrieves the images of other persons. Therefore, the reliability of the system is sufficiently high against the spillage of the database. Table 2 shows that the FRR for $b(m) = 64$ increases by about 11% in the second experiment when compared to the first experiment. This implies that the retrieval performance

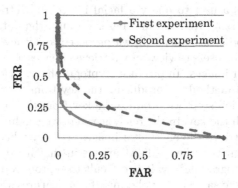

**Fig. 5.** Result of the experiments(ROC curve)

**Table 1.** Result of the experiments(FAREFRR)

| m | First experiment | | Second experiment | |
|---|---|---|---|---|
| | FAR(%) | FRR(%) | FAR(%) | FRR(%) |
| 288 | 24.68 | 10.24 | 32.98 | 25.87 |
| $8.3 \times 10^4$ | 9.38 | 20.70 | 15.08 | 34.45 |
| $4.0 \times 10^6$ | 2.22 | 29.28 | 9.99 | 41.29 |
| $2.9 \times 10^8$ | 0.93 | 39.19 | 5.27 | 47.07 |
| $1.8 \times 10^{12}$ | 0.08 | 43.16 | 4.02 | 54.65 |
| $4.1 \times 10^{15}$ | 0 | 53.08 | 0.1 | 65.75 |
| $6.2 \times 10^{18}$ | 0 | 62.35 | 0 | 74.39 |
| $1.2 \times 10^{19}$ | 0 | 64.59 | 0 | 76.23 |

**Table 2.** evaluate value of our method

| | m | b(m) | FAR(m) | FRR(m) |
|---|---|---|---|---|
| First experiment | $1.2 \times 10^{19}$ | 64 | 0 | 64.59 |
| Second experiment | $1.2 \times 10^{19}$ | 64 | 0 | 76.23 |

is degraded for unknown datasets, but it maintains a certain minimum retrieval performance.

Experimental results show that there is a trade-off between FAR and FRR. When $b(m)$ is large and FRR is high, FAR is low. Therefore, if we need to enhance privacy protection, we should increase $b(m)$. In contrast, when $b(m)$ is small and FRR is low, FAR is high. This suggested that if we want to retrieve all the possible images of criminals, we should reduce $b(m)$. Thus we can appropriately choose the parameter $b(m)$ based on the requests made for the system.

## 5  Conclusion

To increase the efficiency of criminal investigations and to enhance privacy protection, we proposed a method for encrypting facial images in a retrieval system.

This system enables a user to query a facial image and retrieve the facial images of the same person from the database. Because the database will include facial images of good citizens as well, we proposed a privacy protection framework that restricts the users to view only retrieved images, preventing them from freely browsing other images. To produce cryptographic keys for unspecified persons, we proposed a method for producing the key from the facial image itself. During the registration step, we produce the key from the facial image and encrypt the image with the key. In the reference step, we produce the key from the query image and retrieve the encrypted images that have been encrypted with the same key. This method has a disadvantage in that if we use facial features directly as the cryptographic key, it is difficult to reproduce the same key even for facial images of the same person, because facial features are not stable owing to illumination and variations in expression. To increase the stability of the key that is produced, we proposed a quantization method that is based on entropy. This method determines the bin that maximizes entropy for each dimension of the feature space. In the experiments, we examined the performance and reliability of the system using a public facial image database. We used FAR and FRR as the criteria. The results of the experiment showed that FRR was about 35% and FAR was 0% with a higher reliability.

**Acknowledgements.** This research was partly supported by OMRON Co. Ltd and Strategic Funds for the Promotion of Science and Technology, MEXT, Japan. In our research, we used the CAS-PEAL-R1 face database collected under the sponsorship of the Chinese National Hi-Tech Program and ISVISION Tech. Co. Ltd.

# References

1. Juels, A., Sudan, M.: A fuzzy vault scheme. Des. Codes Cryptography 38(2), 237–257 (2006)
2. Tuyls, P., Akkermans, A.H.M., Kevenaar, T.A.M., Schrijen, G.-J., Bazen, A.M., Veldhuis, R.N.J.: Practical Biometric Authentication with Template Protection. In: Kanade, T., Jain, A., Ratha, N.K. (eds.) AVBPA 2005. LNCS, vol. 3546, pp. 436–446. Springer, Heidelberg (2005)
3. Chen, C., Veldhuis, R.N.J.: Multi-Bits Biometric String Generation based on the Likelihood Ratio. In: IEEE Conference on Biometrics: Theory, Applications and Systems, pp. 27–29 (September 2007)
4. Eastlake, D., Jones, P.: US Secure Hash Algorithm 1 (SHA1) RFC3174 Cisco Systems (September 2008)
5. Announcing the Advanced Encryption Standard Federal Information Processing Standards Publication 197 (November 26, 2001)
6. Gao, W., Cao, B., Shan, S., Chen, X., Zhou, D., Zhang, X., Zhao, D.: The CAS-PEAL Large-Scale Chinese Face Database and Baseline Evaluations. IEEE Trans. on System Man, and Cybernetics (Part A) 38(1), 149–161 (2008)

# A Model for Assessing the Risk of Revealing Shared Secrets in Social Networks

Luigi Troiano[1], Irene Díaz[2], and Luis J. Rodríguez-Muñiz[3]

[1] University of Sannio, Dept. of Engineering
I-82100 Benevento, Italy
troiano@unisannio.it
[2] University of Oviedo, Dept. of Computer Science
E-33204 Oviedo, Spain
sirene@uniovi.es
[3] University of Oviedo, Dept. of Statistics and O.R
E-33204 Oviedo, Spain
luisj@uniovi.es

**Abstract.** We introduce the problem of information which become sensitive when combined, named shared secrets, and we propose a model based on Choquet integral to assess the risk that an actor in a social network is able to combine all information available. Some examples are presented and discussed and future directions are outlined.

**Keywords:** Privacy, social networks, fuzzy measure, choquet integral.

## 1 Introduction

The issue of preventing privacy leakage in social networks has became prominent due the diffusion of social software, also in business environments. Problems in this contexts go beyond those related to the release of tabular micro-data, as generally faced by researchers and practitioners with paradigms, techniques and methods aimed at masking data in such a way sensitive information are protected. In social network, collaboration among users and the related exchange of information play a relevant role to take into account in preventing the disclosure of sensitive information [1].

A Social Network can be formally defined as a graph $G = (V, E)$, with vertices $V = \{v_1, \ldots, v_n\}$ corresponding to individuals or other entities and edges $E = \{(v_i, v_j)/v_i, v_j \in V, i \neq j, 1 \leq i, j \leq n\}$ that model the social relationships between vertices [6].

Different problems can be identified and addressed by specific tools. One of the most important challenges for research community in Social Networks is the privacy issue. Research in anonymizing data sets to prevent disclosure of sensitive information has focused the efforts of both database and data mining communities (see [19], [17]).

In this paper we consider one specific problem related to the privacy issue, which we call *disclosure of shared secrets*. We assume that sensitive information

S. Greco et al. (Eds.): IPMU 2012, Part IV, CCIS 300, pp. 499–508, 2012.

can be given split to different actors. Split information is not problematic as sensitiveness resides in completeness of information, instead of information fragments. So that giving releasing pieces of information is not a threat to privacy by itself. But, if we assume actors able to access and compose different pieces of information, privacy could be broken at some point. Therefore quantifying and assessing this risk would make possible to prevent and manage the possibility that sensitive information can be re-composed and revealed to some actors.

The reminder of this paper is organized as follows: Section 2 provides an overview of related literature; Section 3 is aimed at providing preliminary definition and properties of mathematical tools we use; Section 4 is devoted to problem formulation and model; Section 5 shows an illustrative example; Section 6 outlines conclusions and future directions.

## 2   Related Work

The Sharing Secret problem has been deeply studied in different areas along time. Shamir [10] studied how to divide data into n pieces in such a way that the data is easily reconstructable from any $k$ pieces, but even complete knowledge of $k-1$ pieces does not reveal information. This hypothesis enables the construction of robust key management schemes for cryptographic systems (the well-known Shamir algorithm) that can function securely. Some years later Simmons [11] studied two types of partitioning of secret information and combined them to form hybrid control schemes. From this initial work to nowadays, much work has been done. For example Youna et al. presents in [4] a survey regarding security issues in multi-agent systems. multi-agent systems provide services in areas such as banking, transportation, e-business, and healthcare where the security must be guaranteed.

Protecting sensitive information is an important issue when data are publicly released. Different techniques have been investigated and proposed in order to measure the risk of linking sensitive information to individuals and/or organization. Samarati and Sweeney [9,13] define $k$-anonymity as the property that makes each record indistinguishable with at least $k - 1$ other records with respect to the quasi-identifier (i. e. a set of nonsensitive attributes). Although $k$-anonymity is able to quantify the risk of identity disclosure, it is not able to assess the risk of attribute disclosure. Machanavajjhala et al. [7] propose $l$-diversity as means to overcome $k$-anonymity limitations. $l$-diversity requires that the distribution of a sensitive attribute in each equivalence class has at least $l$ values. Li et al. [5] attempt to solve leaks of $k$-anonymity and $l$-diversity by proposing a definition of privacy based on semantic distance between sensitive attributes, known as $t$-closeness. This metric requires that the distribution of a sensitive attribute in any equivalence class is close to the distribution of the attribute in the overall table.

The previous techniques have been adapted to study privacy issues in Social Network environments. See, for example [19] , [16] or [2]. At the same time, some other methods have been studied to cope with privacy and revealing secrets concern in Social Networks. For example, Ying and Wu in [18] show that similarity measures can be exploited by attackers to significantly improve their confidence and accuracy about sensitive links between nodes with high similarity values, allowing them revealing secrets. This work presents a new framework to study privacy concerns in Social Networks based on the statistical concept of Entropy, that is used to measure the risk of recombining sensitive information, Entropy has been used in data privacy, for example, in [14], although their use is quite different as it was used for information loss.

## 3 Preliminaries

In this section we provide some preliminary definitions in order to fix notation and to share a common understanding with the reader unfamiliar with the concepts expressed in this paper.

**Definition 1 (Fuzzy measure (capacity)[8], [12]).** *Given a finite set $N \equiv \{1, \ldots, n\}$, a fuzzy measure (or capacity) on $N$ is any set function $\mu : \mathcal{P}(\mathcal{N}) \to \mathbb{R}^+$, such that*

1. $\mu(\emptyset) = 0$
2. $\mu(X) \leq \mu(Y)$, *if* $X \subset Y \subseteq N$ $\qquad\qquad\square$

The main properties of a fuzzy measure are listed below. Given $X, Y \subseteq N$ a fuzzy measure is said to be

- *additive* iff $\mu(X \cup Y) = \mu(X) + \mu(Y)$ $(X \cap Y = \emptyset)$
- *superadditive* iff $\mu(X \cup Y) \geq \mu(X) + \mu(Y)$ $(X \cap Y = \emptyset)$
- *subadditive* iff $\mu(X \cup Y) \leq \mu(X) + \mu(Y)$ $(X \cap Y = \emptyset)$

Additive capacities are also *modular*, that is $\mu(X \cup Y) + \mu(X \cap Y) = \mu(X) + \mu(Y)$,

- *supermodular* iff $\mu(X \cup Y) + \mu(X \cap Y) \geq \mu(X) + \mu(Y)$,
- *submodular* iff $\mu(X \cup Y) + \mu(X \cap Y) \leq \mu(X) + \mu(Y)$.

We observe that submodular (supermodular) measures are also subadditive (superadditive) but not vice versa. We also note that submodularity is equivalent to the following conditions

$$\mu(X \cup \{z\}) - \mu(X) \geq \mu(Y \cup \{z\}) - \mu(Y) \ \forall X \subseteq Y \subseteq N, z \in N \setminus Y \quad (1)$$

$$\mu(X \cup \{z_1\}) + \mu(X \cup \{z_2\}) \geq \mu(X \cup \{z_1, z_2\}) + \mu(X) \ \forall X \subseteq N, z_1, z_2 \in N \setminus X \quad (2)$$

Similar equivalence can be stated for supermodular measures

**Definition 2 ((Discrete) Choquet integral([3])).** *Let $x : N \to \mathbb{R}^+$ a discrete function, i.e. $x_1, \ldots x_n$ a collection of non-negative reals. The Choquet integral of $x$ w.r.t. $\mu$ is defined as*

$$\mathcal{C}_\mu(x) = \sum_{i=1..n} x_{(i)} [\mu(X_{(i)}) - \mu(X_{(i+1)})] \quad (3)$$

*where $(\cdot)$ is a decreasing permutation of $x$, so that $x_{(i)} \geq x_{(i+1)}$, and $X_{(i)} = \{(i), (i+1), \ldots, (n)\}$, assuming $X_{(n+1)} = \emptyset$.* $\qquad\qquad\square$

Definition of Choquet integral depends on the original aim of using it in the context of utility theory. For this reason, variable $x$ is arranged in decreasing order, so that better values come first. We can easily generalize this condition, by considering a permutation of values so that $x_{(i)} \succeq x_{(i+1)}$, meaning that the former is preferable to the latter.

Properties of fuzzy measures are able to better characterize Choquet integrals. In particular, subadditive (superadditive) fuzzy measures result into convex (concave) Choquet integrals.

## 4    Problem Definition and Model

Let $K \equiv \{a_1, \ldots, a_n\}$ be the set of actors, organized in a social network $N(t) \equiv\ <K, E>$, that we assume being an undirected graph whose vertices are actors in $K$ and edges $E = \{e_1, \ldots, e_m\}$ are pairwise relations between actors. We also assume that the social network $N$ is time variant, so that although actors will not change over the time, new connections can be established among them.

Let $S$ be the sensitive information to protect, and $\mathcal{S}^* = \{S_1, \ldots, S_m\}$ a partition of $S$, i.e. $S = \bigcup_{i=1..m} S_i$ and $S_i \bigcap S_j = \emptyset \ \forall i \neq j$. Each $S_i \in \mathcal{S}^*$ can is associated to a subset of actors. Let $\mathcal{P}(K)$ be the set of the subsets of $K$, we assume an injective mapping

$$A : \mathcal{S}^* \to \mathcal{P}(K) \qquad (4)$$

between parts of a secret and actors, i.e. $A(S_i) = \{a_{S_i(1)}, \ldots, a_{S_i(h)}\}$ the actor subset associated to $S_i$. Without any loss of generality we can split information $S$ in a partition such that mapping $A$ is also surjective, thus bijective, i.e. $\forall i \neq j$ we have $A(S_i) \neq A(S_j)$. An example of network is depicted in Fig.1.

**Definition 3 ($k$-accessible set of an actor $a_i$)**

$$acc_k(a_i) = \{a_i\} \cup \{a_j/c = a_i, \ldots, a_j\}$$

with $c$ a simple and elemental path from $a_i$ to $a_j$ with length at most $k$

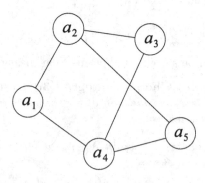

**Fig. 1.** A set of actors connected in a social network

This definition is strongly related to the definition of accessibility in graph theory. It defines the possible actors (nodes) related directly or indirectly (by means of other actors) to a given one. For instance, with respect to graph outlined in Fig.1, $acc_1(a_1) = \{a_1, a_2, a_4\}$. Coverage definition can be extended to a subset $K' \subseteq K$ as the set $K'$ and all vertices covered by actors in $K'$. For instance, $acc_1(a_1) \cup acc_1(a_4) = \{a_1, a_2, a_3, a_4, a_5\}$.

**Definition 4** (*k*-coverage). *We define* $k - coverage$ *of* $K' \subseteq K$, *denoted as* $cov_k(K')$, *the set actors*

$$cov_k(K') = \cup_{a_i \in K'} acc_k(a_i) \tag{5}$$

**Definition 5** (*k*-coverage ratio). *We define* $k$*-coverage ratio of subset* $K' \subseteq K$ *as*

$$\mu_k(K') = \frac{|cov_k(K')|}{|K|} \tag{6}$$

*that is the ratio of actors* $k$*-covered by* $K'$ *and the overall number of actors.*

**Proposition 1.** *The* $k$*-coverage ratio is a submodular fuzzy measure for any choice of* $k$. *In particular* $\mu_0$ *is additive.*

*Proof.* We can prove that $\mu_k$ is a fuzzy measure straightforward. Indeed,

1. $\mu_k(\emptyset) = 0$
2. $\mu_k(K) = 1$
3. $\mu_k(X) \le \mu_k(Y) \ \forall X \subset Y \subseteq K$.

Submodularity of $\mu_k$ can be proven using condition expressed by Eq.(1) or Eq.(2). Indeed, with respect to the latter, denoted for the sake of simplicity $cov_k(K')$ as $\overline{K'}$ and $cov_k(\{z\})$ as $\overline{z}$. Taking into account that $\overline{X \cup \{z_1\}} \supseteq \overline{X}$, then

$$|\overline{X \cup \{z_2\}}| \ge |\overline{X}| + |\overline{z_2}| - |\overline{X \cup \{z_1\}} \cap \overline{z_2}|$$

Since,

$$\overline{X \cup \{z_1, z_2\}}| = |\overline{X \cup \{z_1\}}| + |\overline{z_2}| - |\overline{X \cup \{z_1\}} \cap \overline{z_2}|$$

we have

$$|\overline{X \cup \{z_1\}}| + |\overline{X \cup \{z_2\}}| \ge |\overline{X \cup \{z_1, z_2\}}| + |\overline{X}|$$

Therefore, dividing each term by $|K|$, we have

$$\mu_k(X \cup \{z_1\}) + \mu_k(X \cup \{z_2\}) \ge \mu_k(X \cup \{z_1, z_2\}) + \mu_k(X).$$

When $k = 0$ we have $cov_k(K') = K'$ for any $K' \subseteq K$. Therefore, for any pair $X, Y \subset K$ such that $X \cap Y = \emptyset$, we have $|\overline{X \cup Y}| = |X| + |Y|$, which entails

$$\mu_0(X \cup Y) = \mu_0(X) + \mu_0(Y) \qquad \square$$

Coverage ratio provides a measure of how many vertices in the social network can be accessed through a specific subset of actors. Therefore it is a measure of the number of pieces of sensitive information that can be potentially made available by the actor subset. Which information is exactly accessed is given by mapping

$$I : \mathcal{P}(\mathcal{K}) \to \mathcal{P}(\mathcal{S}^*) \tag{7}$$

defined as $I(K') = \bigcup_{a \in K'} A^{-1}(a)$, where $K' \subseteq K$. We note that Eq.(7) also stands for non-bijective $A$.

The risk of disclosure is related to information *reconstructability*, that is the degree by which the whole information can be reconstructed from a partial knowledge of it. This depends on the set $D(S)$ of sensitive information known to a potential attacker. An example is given by Tab.1. In general, the wider $D(S)$ is, the lower the risk is. However, probability of reconstruction depends on which information has been accessed so far. We can approximate this probability as likelihood given by conditional data frequencies, that is

$$Pr(S = t) = \frac{|S = t|}{|D(S)|} = p_t \tag{8}$$

where $t \in D(S)$ is one of the possible states assumed by the sensitive information.

The more distributed the values are, the lower the risk is. A measure of value dispersion is (Shannon's) Entropy, that is

$$H(S) = - \sum_{t \in D(S)} p_t ln(p_t) \tag{9}$$

Each value assumed by $S' \subseteq S$ selects a different group of tuples, entailing a different distribution of values, therefore a different entropy. We define *conditional entropy* as

$$H(S|S') = \sum_{t' \in D(S')} p_{t'} H(S|S' = t') \tag{10}$$

**Table 1.** An example of (tabular) sensitive information

| Who | Day | Month | Year | Place |
|-----|-----|-------|------|-------|
| Mike | 2 | Jan | 2010 | NY |
| Mike | 14 | Mar | 2011 | LA |
| Tom | 2 | Mar | 2010 | LA |
| Linda | 18 | Oct | 2011 | SF |
| Angela | 18 | Jan | 2011 | LA |
| Tom | 18 | Sep | 2011 | LA |
| Alice | 23 | Aug | 2010 | NY |
| Linda | 14 | Sep | 2011 | SF |
| Tom | 2 | Oct | 2011 | NY |
| Angela | 5 | Aug | 2010 | LA |

An aggregated measure can be provided by Choquet integral of conditional entropy. More specifically, we have

$$\mathcal{C}_{\mu_k}(H) = \sum_{i=1..n} H_S(a_{(i)})[\mu_k(K_{(i)}) - \mu_k(K_{(i+1)})] \tag{11}$$

where $H_S(a_{(i)}) = H(S|I(a_{(i)}))$ and they are ordered by increasing values as we focus attention on disclosure risk.

**Proposition 2.** *The aggregated information gain measure provided by Eq.(11) is concave.*

*Proof.* An immediate consequence of submodularity of fuzzy measure $\mu_k(\cdot)$. $\square$

According to [15] Eq.(11) can be rewritten as

$$\mathcal{C}_{\mu_k}(H) = \sum_{i=1..n} [H_S(a_{(i)}) - H_S(a_{(i-1)})]\mu_k(K_{(i)}) \tag{12}$$

where we assume $H_S(a_{(0)}) = 0$ by convention.

Therefore, coverage ratio used in Eq.(11) (and Eq.(12)) can be regarded as a weighting operator which defines at which extent a variation of entropy given by partial knowledge can perturb the natural entropy of data.

*Information gain* provides the difference between entropy of initial distribution and expected value of entropy after information $S'$ is made available.

$$IG(S|S') = H(S) - H(S|S') \tag{13}$$

In particular, with respect to information that can be potentially accessed through actor $a_i$, we have

$$IG(S|I(a_i)) = H(S) - H(S|I(a_i)) \tag{14}$$

Also for information gain, we can compute an aggregated value as

$$\mathcal{C}_{\mu_k}(IG) = \sum_{i=1..n} IG_S(a_{(i)})[\mu_k(K_{(i)}) - \mu_k(K_{(i+1)})] \tag{15}$$

where $IG_S(a_{(i)}) = IG(S|I(a_{(i)}))$.

The higher the information gain is, the higher the risk of recombining sensitive information is. In order to catch the relationship between Eq.(11) and Eq.(15), we should rewrite it as

$$\mathcal{C}_{\mu_k}(H) = \sum_{i=1..n} [IG_S(a_{(i)}) - IG_S(a_{(i-1)})]\mu_k(K_{(i)}) \tag{16}$$

assuming again $IG_S(a_{(0)}) = 0$ by convention. But,

$$IG_S(a_{(i)}) - H_S(a_{(i-1)}) = H(S|I(a_{(i-1)})) - H(S|I(a_{(i)}))  \qquad (17)$$

so that Eq.(16) becomes

$$\mathcal{C}_{\mu_k}(IG_S) = \sum_{i=1..n} [H(S|I(a_{(i-1)})) - H(S|I(a_{(i)}))]\mu_k(K_{(i)}) = H(S) - \mathcal{C}_{\mu_k}(H)  \quad (18)$$

being $IG(S|I(a_{(0)})) = 0$.

We note that, if $k = 0$ we have

$$\mathcal{C}_{\mu_0}(IG_S) = H(S) - \frac{1}{n} \sum_{i=1..n} H(S|I(a_i))  \qquad (19)$$

and, if $k = \infty$ we get

$$\mathcal{C}_{\mu_\infty}(IG_S) = H(S) - \min_{i=1..n} H(S|I(a_i))$$
$$= \max_{i=1..n}[H(S) - H(S|I(a_i))] = \max_{i=1..n} IG_S(a_i)  \qquad (20)$$

## 5  An Illustrative Example

With respect to network depicted in Fig.1, we consider sensitive information of Tab.1. In particular, we assume that each actor $a_i$ has granted access to one column of Tab.1. Association between actors and information is given in Tab.2. Initial distribution of values are summarized in Tab.3. Since all tuples in Tab.1

Table 2. Actor-Information association

| Column | Who | Day | Month | Year | Place |
|--------|-----|-----|-------|------|-------|
| Actor | $a_1$ | $a_2$ | $a_3$ | $a_4$ | $a_5$ |

are different, we have $H(S) = 2.3026$ is maximal. This leads to consider the conditional entropy as outlined by Tab.4. Therefore, sorted actors by decreasing information gain, we get Aggregated values are reported and compared in Tab.6, where we can see how aggregated value of entropy and information gain are depending on accessibility of network actors.

Table 3. A priori distributions

| Column | Who | Day | Month | Year | Place |
|--------|-----|-----|-------|------|-------|
| Values | 5 | 5 | 5 | 2 | 3 |
| Entropy $H$ | 1.5571 | 1.5048 | 1.6094 | 0.6730 | 1.0297 |
| Norm.ed $H$ | 0.9675 | 0,4957 | 1.0000 | 0.9710 | 0.9372 |

**Table 4.** Conditional entropy and information gain

| Actor | $a_1$ | $a_2$ | $a_3$ | $a_4$ | $a_5$ |
|---|---|---|---|---|---|
| $H(S|I(a_i))$ | 0.7455 | 0.7978 | 0.6931 | 1.6296 | 1.2729 |
| $IG(S|I(a_i))$ | 1.5571 | 1.5048 | 1.6094 | 0.6730 | 1.0297 |

**Table 5.** Example terms to integrate

| Actor | $a_4$ | $a_5$ | $a_2$ | $a_1$ | $a_3$ |
|---|---|---|---|---|---|
| $IG(S|I(a_i))$ | 0.6730 | 1.0297 | 1.5048 | 1.5571 | 1.6094 |
| Subset | 1,2,3,4,5 | 1,2,3,5 | 1,2,3 | 1,3 | 3 |
| 1-Coverage | 1,2,3,4,5 | 1,2,3,4,5 | 1,2,3,4,5 | 1,2,3,4 | 2,3,4 |
| ratio | 1.0 | 1.0 | 1.0 | 0.8 | 0.6 |

**Table 6.** Aggregated measure

| k | $\mathcal{C}_{\mu_k}(H)$ | $\mathcal{C}_{\mu_k}(IG)$ |
|---|---|---|
| 0 | 1.0277 | 1.2748 |
| 1 | 0.7245 | 1.5780 |
| $\infty$ | 0.6931 | 1.6094 |

# 6   Conclusions and Future Directions

We outlined a metric based on Choquet integral aimed at assessing the risk that sensitive information is released when pieces of partial information are exchanged within a social network. This information can be used for different purposes. For example it can be adopted as a metric of how risky a network is with respect to aggregation of sensitive information, or to compare two networks, or even to focus on new nodes in evolving social networks. Many open questions arise. Among them, how to determine the value of $k$. Indeed, although increasing this parameter would lead to more conservative cases, as we assume that farther actors will gain access to pieces of information, it is not realistic in many circumstances of practical interest. A second step in this research is to develop efficient algorithms to compute the coverage in real-sized networks.

**Acknowledgements.** Authors acknowledge financial support by Grant MTM2008-01519 from Ministry of Science and Innovation and Grant TIN2010-14971 from Ministry of Education and Science, Government of Spain.

# References

1. Beach, A., Gartrell, M., Han, R.: Social-K: Real-time K-anonymity guarantees for social network applications. In: 2010 8th IEEE International Conference on Pervasive Computing and Communications Workshops (PERCOM Workshops), pp. 600–606. IEEE (March 2010)

2. Campan, A., Truta, T.M.: Data and Structural k-Anonymity in Social Networks. In: Bonchi, F., Ferrari, E., Jiang, W., Malin, B. (eds.) PinKDD 2008. LNCS, vol. 5456, pp. 33–54. Springer, Heidelberg (2009)
3. Faigle, U., Grabisch, M.: A discrete choquet integral for ordered systems. CoRR, abs/1102.1340 (2011)
4. Jung, Y., Kim, M., Masoumzadeh, A., Joshi, J.: A survey of security issue in multi-agent systems. Artificial Intelligence Review, 1–22 (2011), doi:10.1007/s10462-011-9228-8
5. Li, N., Li, T., Venkatasubramanian, S.: t-closeness: Privacy beyond k-anonymity and l-diversity. In: Proceedings of IEEE International Conference on Data Engineering, pp. 106–115 (2007)
6. Liu, K., Das, K., Grandison, T., Kargupta, H.: Privacy-preserving data analysis on graphs and social networks
7. Machanavajjhala, A., Gehrke, J., Kifer, D., Venkitasubramaniam, M.: l-diversity: Privacy beyond k-anonymity. In: 22nd IEEE International Conference on Data Engineering (2006)
8. Mesiar, R.: Fuzzy measures and integrals. Fuzzy Sets and Systems 156(3), 365–370 (2005)
9. Samarati, P.: Protecting respondents' identities in microdata release. IEEE Transactions on Knowledge and Data Engineering 13, 1010–1027 (2001)
10. Shamir, A.: How to share a secret. Commun. ACM 22(11), 612–613 (1979)
11. Simmons, G.J.: How to (Really) Share a Secret. In: Goldwasser, S. (ed.) CRYPTO 1988. LNCS, vol. 403, pp. 390–448. Springer, Heidelberg (1990)
12. Sugeno, M.: Theory of fuzzy integrals and its applications. PhD thesis, Tokyo Institute of Technology (1974)
13. Sweeney, L.: Achieving k-anonymity privacy protection using generalization and suppression. International Journal of Uncertainty, Fuzziness and Knowledge-Based Systems 10(5), 571–588 (2002)
14. Torra, V., Domingo-Ferrer, J.: Disclosure control methods and information loss for microdata, pp. 91–110. Elsevier (2001)
15. Torra, V., Narukawa, Y.: Modeling decisions - information fusion and aggregation operators. Springer (2007)
16. Wong, R.C., Li, J., Fu, A.W., Wang, K.: (α,k) Anonymity: An Enhanced k - Anonymity Model for Privacy-Preserving Data Publishing, pp. 754–759. ACM (2006)
17. Ying, X., Wu, X.: On Link Privacy in Randomizing Social Networks. In: Theeramunkong, T., Kijsirikul, B., Cercone, N., Ho, T.-B. (eds.) PAKDD 2009. LNCS, vol. 5476, pp. 28–39. Springer, Heidelberg (2009)
18. Ying, X., Wu, X.: On link privacy in randomizing social networks. Knowl. Inf. Syst. 28(3), 645–663 (2011)
19. Zhou, B., Pei, J.: The k-anonymity and l-diversity approaches for privacy preservation in social networks against neighborhood attacks. Knowledge and Information Systems 28(1), 1–38 (2010)

# Privacy Issues in Social Networks:
# A Brief Survey

Irene Díaz[1] and Anca Ralescu[2]

[1] University of Oviedo
Department of Computer Science
E-33204, Spain
sirene@uniovi.es
[2] University of Cincinnati
School of Computing Sciences & Informatics
Machine Learning & Computational Intelligence Lab
Cincinnati, Ohio 45221-0008, USA
anca.ralescu@uc.edu

**Abstract.** Most social networks allow individuals to share their information with friends but also with unknown people. Therefore, in order to prevent unauthorized access to sensitive, private information, the study of privacy issues in social networks has become an important task. This paper provides a brief overview of the emerging research in privacy issues in social networks.

**Keywords:** Link Privacy, data mining, social networks.

## 1 Introduction

Nowadays more and more data are being publicly available in different ways. Large amounts of private information is delivered in different fields as for example medical information, taxes or social networks. The case of *online* social networks (SNs) is especially important because they expand rapidly, providing, sometimes, more information than we could ever expect. A social network is defined as a social structure of individuals related to each other based on a common relation of interest. The online proliferation of social networks and other communities, peer-to-peer file sharing, and telecommunication systems, has created large and very complex representations.

When joining social networking sites, people create a profile and make connections to entities/individuals already on these sites. These connections are often suggested by the site upon its being given access to a list of people who are already known to the new member (e.g. his/her address book). Alternatively, since individual members share personal information, name, photographs, birthday, personal interests and so on, this information is mined and suggestions for connections are presented. Members use these sites for communication, maintaining relationships, sharing photos and archiving events, etc. [13].

S. Greco et al. (Eds.): IPMU 2012, Part IV, CCIS 300, pp. 509–518, 2012.

The rise of online SNs usage is very strong. For example, currently, Facebook[1] has more than 800 million active users of which more than 50% log on in any given day. A Facebook user has, on average, 130 friends. In addition, on average, more than 900 million objects that people interact with, and more than 250 million photos are uploaded per day [33].

The privacy issue within the context of SNs has became a challenge for research community. Research in anonymizing data sets to prevent disclosure of sensitive information has focused the efforts of both database and data mining communities. The difference between the priavcy issues in such data and in social networks arises especially from the way they are created, maintained, and their intended uses.

Databases are created by an entity with the objective of keeping track of individuals according to various criteria and with a definite purpose (e.g. in a hospital data base individual patients are recorded, with the purpose to give access to health professionals to the patients' history and medical needs). The privacy issue arises when the owner of the database is requested for some information and needs to transfer some of the data to fulfill this query. An important aspect of databases is that *individuals whose information is stored in the database have no access to each other's records.*

By contrast, in online SNs individuals join voluntarily, and different types of information, most of which accessible to many other members of the network, is stored. In fact, it can be said that the main purpose of online SNs is that of sharing – news, personal information, etc. Thus, online SNs enable individuals to access other network member's information. An attack on a node privacy may come from another node in the network as it is conceivable that would be attackers will join the network mascarading as valid network members. Link lookahead procedures can be used in order glean information on various network members which can then be used to damage them (e.g. steal their identities) [20]. It follows that *the type of anonymity needed in social networks is different from that in databases.* Yet, it is to be expected that, as different as online SNs and databases are, the definition and treatment of privacy in these networks are inspired by the corresponding concepts and ideas in databases.

Many traditional approaches to maintain privacy in micro-data are based on anonymizing data by masking or generalizing them. However, although interesting, for the reasons discussed above, this approach is not currently an option in the online SNs context where data is not anonymized and where there are no plans to do that [3]. Therefore, assuring SNs privacy has become a much more difficult task due to the structure of the networks, and the nature of the problem itself. As already discussed above, just the collaboration among users and the related exchange of information, operations for which social networks evolved in the first place, make the issue of privacy in social networks much more complicated.

The reminder of this paper is organized as follows: Section 2 provides a succint overview of the main concepts in online SNs; Section 3 describes the issue of

---

[1] www.facebook.com

privacy preserving in SNs; Section 4 illustrates the difficulty of the privacy issue by a somewhat deeper discussion of two particular approaches, both of which rely on some form of randomization; The paper closes with a short conclusion section and future direction.

## 2  Basic Concepts in Social Networks

A common representation of a SN is as a graph $G = (V, E)$, with vertices $V = \{v_1, \ldots, v_n\}$ corresponding to individuals or other entities (e.g. radio stations, retailers on Facebook, or Twitter) and edges $E = \{(v_i, v_j)/v_i, v_j \in V, i \neq j, 1 \leq i, j \leq n\}$ that model the social relationships between vertices [27]. Both directed and undirected graphs may be used. For instance, Facebook is an example of a social network modeled mainly as an undirected graph[2], where each node posts information accessible to all the nodes in the community of *friends*. By contrast, Twitter[3] is modeled by a directed graph where nodes correspond to users who provide information, *followees*, and users who consume information *followers*. A link between two nodes models the *followee-follower* relationship.

The graph-based representation of SNs makes possible compact mathematical representations [18], as for example, (adjacency) matrices, or, in the case of large sparse matrices, as adjacency lists. In turn, such representations make possible defining and capturing various characteristics such as size, density, degree, reachability, distance, diameter or geodesic distance, which can then be used to study network structure and behavior [15]. An important task in SN analysis is the study of the dynamics of the network, i.e. the study of the *relationships* between the network members which can give them useful information. However, when exactly the same information is obtained by an intruder, it can harm the network members (for example, by disclosing non public information). The variety of approaches to privacy issues in SN makes necessary a critical discussion of this subject. This paper, necessarily incomplete due to space constraints, serves as an entry point to such a discussion.

It is worth noting at this point that social networks as research topic are not new. Indeed, one can find research on this topic going back to the early and mid 20th century, often in relation to social psychology [6], [5], [16], social sciences [7], and economics [23]. What is new in the context of *online* SNs is their sheer size, the basic model where node-to-node interaction is possible, and the computational issues these features entail.

## 3  Privacy Attacks on Social Networks

In common understanding, *privacy* refers to *"the ability of individual or group to seclude themselves or information about themselves and thereby reveal themselves selectively"*[4]. One way to achieve privacy is to ensure anonymity. By analogy

---

[2] The Facebook concept of *close friends*. is better modeled as a directed graph.

[3] www.twitter.com

[4] http://en.wikipedia.org/wiki/Privacy

with a physical model of a city and its inhabitants, the larger a city, the more anaonymous its inhbitants are, and therefore more private. Likewise, privacy in SNs is also related to *annonymity* and *security*, and in this regard it is very important in SNs.

Data anonymization, successfully used in privacy preserving in relational databases, is much more complex in SNs [37] due to several factors. As already discussed, in the relational model, the information is much more controlled. In particular relations between various data points (individual records) is not explicitly represented, rather, each individual record, a user and his/hers properties, are represented and accessible only to a central entity, the curator of the database. In this model it is then quite easy to measure information loss and to model background knowledge of adversaries and attacks.

By contrast, information loss for graphs, while perhaps not difficult to define *conceptually*, is much more difficult to implement due to computational aspects entailed by its distributed model which supports node-to-node communication and information sharing. Moreover to identify privacy attacks in SNs, one needs to identify the information of remarkable, private nature [38]. The graph structure of SNs makes the task of indentifying background knowledge much more difficult than in the relational model. Different ways to accomplish this are adopted, including:

(1) neighborhoods and
(2) embedded subgraphs.

In (1) an adversary has the background knowledge about the neighborhood of some target individuals. This includes knowledge of some of the target's links and neighbors. Access to these enables access to the target node. In (2) an adversary embeds certain subgraphs into a SN before the network is released [38].

## 4   Metrics for Privacy Study in SNs

Variability is an important dimension of the notion of privacy, leading to the concept of *level of privacy*. Accordingly, rather than ensuring that an individual private information cannot be distinguished in a database, the probability of its being distinguishable from a subset of other individual is produced.

Different metrics for measuring the level of privacy guaranteed by Statistical Disclosure Control (SDC) have been proposed over the time. Among them, [31] and [34] define $k$-anonymity with respect to a *quasi-identifier* (a subset of the released information) as the property that makes each record of a released table indistinguishable from at least $k - 1$ other records. Further, to address some of the limitations of $k$-anonymity, when the the knowlegde possesed by an attacker is not known, Machanavajjhala *et al.* propose $l$-diversity [30], and yet another model, $t$-closeness [25], formalizes the idea of *global background knowledge*. It requires that the distribution of a sensitive attribute in any equivalence class be close to the distribution of the attribute in the overall table.

Other approaches aim to prevent *range disclosure*, which would happen when an attacker is able to link an individual not to a specific sensitive value, but to a set of values that collectively disclose some sensitive information [28], [9], [8].

Although none of the approaches mentioned above can be adopted directly with SN data, extensions have been developed. For instance, in [37] $k$-anonymity and $l$-diversity approaches were developed with the objective of avoiding neighborhood attacks in SNs. According to [37], an anonymized SN is defined as follows:

**Definition 1.** *Given the graph $G$, representing a social network, the graph $G'$ sassociated to $G$, satisfies $k$-anonymity if no vertex in $G$ can be re-identified in $G'$ with confidence larger than $\frac{1}{k}$.*

The anonymized version, $G'$, of $G$ is usually obtained by altering in some manner $G$, in particular by generating *false* nodes in $G'$ that is nodes which are not in $G$. More precisely $G'$ is computed as follows [37]:

1. Each vertex in $G$ is anonymized to a vertex in $G'$ and $G$ does not contain any false vertex;
2. Every edge in $G$ is retained in $G'$;
3. The number of additional edges is minimized.

Similarly, the concept of $l$-diversity extended to SN in [37] is defined as follows:

**Definition 2.** *Given the graph $G = (V, E)$ associated to a social network, with $|V| = n$ and where each vertex carries a sensitive label, there exists an $l$-diverse partition of the $n$ vertices if and only if there are at most $\frac{n}{l}$ vertices associated with a sensitive label.*

A different approach is proposed by Beach et al. in [3] according to which SN data should be *assumed public but treated private*. They introduce the concept of $q$-Anon, which measures the probability of an attacker logically deducing previously unknown information from a social network API under the assumption that the data being protected may already be public information. The same authors introduce in [4] a new formulation of $k$-anonymity in which SNs could provide privacy guarantees to users of their API. This approach assumes that all SN data may be a quasi-identifier and does not assume that data may be generalized and still be useful. The nodes of the graph $G$ represent the individuals who interact in the network while the ties represent some kinf of collaboration between each pair of individuals (friendship at Facebook, a photo in Flickr, etc).

### 4.1    Data Mining Approaches to Privacy Preserving in Social Networks

The relationship between data mining (DM) and privacy preserving has been first outlined in [10]. Data Mining [17] searches for the relationships that exist in large databases, but hidden due to the large amount of data. Data Mining models the behavior of a given variable/attribute in terms of the others, finding non-trivial relationships among the attributes involved [21]. These relationships may provide valuable knowledge regarding the individuals the data are related to.

If in data mining it is enough to infer models from training data sets in order to overcome data distortion, privacy preserving is interested in models able to not reveal and explain relationships in presence of data distortion, as generally introduced by the anonymization process. Indeed some information, although hidden or even removed, could be still linked to identities at some extent considering a lower level of data granularity, at which different point-wise information are assimilated. This problem has been raised in [24] and [2] analyzed several data mining approaches to preserve privacy.

## 4.2 Link Privacy

Link privacy is important as knowledge of links enables access to node information, where node ID and private data is stored. However, link privacy is also important in its own right, due to the "sensitive, stigmatizing, or confidential nature of the relationship" [35]. In other words, some SN members may not like some of their relations to be known. Furthermore, node-anonymization does not guarantee immunity to link attacks as structural information extracted from a graph representing the network, such as node degrees, may provide sufficient information to distinguish an individual in the network. Similar to node anonymization, link anonymization can be implemented by edge randomization, and work has been done [35] which investigates how well edge randomization can protect link privacy. There is an intimate connection between link/edge prediction and link privacy, for, an attack on links which uses an effective link prediction scheme, will jeopardize the links in the network. Although there are valid reasons for link prediction, for example, to study the evolution in time of a network, the type of link prediction in those applications is quite different from the problem of link prediction when the network has changed via a randomization procedure.

A substantial body of work on link prediction uses low rank approximation methods (see [14] and references therein). An alternative to that approach is the work described in [35] which uses proximity/similarity measures between node pairs. Four similarity measures (evaluated with respect to how well they related to the proportion of true edges in a specific graph, the US political books network) were considered in [35], including

1. the number of common neighbors [22];
2. the weighted number of common neighbors [1], with weights based on an information theoretical approach;
3. the weighted sum of the number of paths that connect two nodes [19], and
4. the commute time (a dissimilarity measure), computed using spectral methods [29].

The impact of node similarity must not be underestimated. Indeed, intuitively, node similarity *may determine link formation*. This intuition is borne by the actual analysis in [26] where it was shown that the probability of a link forming between two nodes depends directly on their similarity. The same was observed in [35] although the framework in which they address the problem of link prediction is quite different from that in [26].

The result reported in [35] is also probabilistic in nature where edge randomization of the graph $G$ to obtain $\widetilde{G}$ the randomized version of the graph $G$, is accomplished by (1) adding randomly $k$ false edges and then (2) deleting randomly $k$ true edges. The only information obtainable from $\widetilde{G}$ is, for each node pair $(i, j)$, whether there is or not an edge connecting these nodes. Because of the procedure of constructing $\widetilde{G}$, it is possible that a true edge exists between the node pair $(i, j)$ both when such an edge exists in $\widetilde{G}$ and when it does not. Indeed, the authors compute, for a node pair in $\widetilde{G}$ with fixed node similarity, the posterior probability of a true edge, in both cases, when an edge exists in $\widetilde{G}$ and when it does not. Intuitively, one would like the existence of such an edge in $\widetilde{G}$ to be a strong evidence for the existence of a true edge. However, as shown in [35] when $k$, the number of false edges randomly added in (and true edges randomly deleted from) $G$, satisfies the inequality

$$k \leq m(1 - \frac{m}{A})  \tag{1}$$

where $m = |E|$ and $n = |V|$, and $A = \binom{n}{2}$, the existence of an edge in $\widetilde{G}$ is indeed a stronger evidence for the existence of a true edge, than lack of such an edge in $\widetilde{G}$. But what does equation (1) really mean? It can be trivially verified that for values of $m \geq \frac{A}{2}$ the bound on $k$ (right hand side of equation (1)) decreases from $\frac{A}{4}$ to 0 (when the graph $G$ is fully connected). At this moment the importance of the order of the two steps which produce $\widetilde{G}$ can be gleaned. Since the first step is to add $k$ false edges, the number of such edges is limited by the number of node pairs which are not connected. Thus the more $G$ is connected, the fewer false edges can be added, and therefore, the larger the ratio of true edges to the total number of edges in $\widetilde{G}$. Hence, it is more likely that an edge in $\widetilde{G}$ corresponds to a true edge in $G$. This means that when the graph $G$ is more connected, the graph $\widetilde{G}$ is actually less random.

### 4.3 Differential Privacy

Concern over privacy issues, may cause some individuals to opt out of belonging to an online SN [36], although such an option is not available for many data bases (e.g. insurance databases). An approach to privacy which has recently received a lot of attention, and which addresses the concerns of the type indicated above, is *differential privacy* introduced in [11] and further studied in [12]. Differential privacy addresses the privacy issue in statistical databases or networks where the goal is to reveal properties of the data, as a whole (database, or network) without compromising individual aspects (e.g. without revealing information on nodes and/or edges). This approach relies on some form of data pertubation with the objective of ensuring that even when an intruder knows all but one record/observation of the data, the intruder should not be able to distinguish, on the basis of the result returned to his/her query, between the presence or absence of an individual. Differenttial privacy aims to protect not only individuals present in the databse, but also those in the universe from which this database records come[32]. This way, belonging to the data base does not increase the risk of breach of privacy. In differential privacy the perturbation of the data is achieved via a randomization procedure, $\mathcal{K}$ [12], which is defined as a probability distribution over the collection of the data of interest (e.g. database, or network). That is, $\mathcal{K}$ is defined by a probability distribution on $\mathcal{K}(\mathcal{D})$, specified as $P[\mathcal{K}(\mathcal{D})] \in S \subseteq Range(\mathcal{K})$. Differential privacy is then defined with respect to $0 < \epsilon < 1$, for two data sets $D_1$ and $D_2$ which differ on at most one element, as

$$P[\mathcal{K}(D_1) \in S] \leq e^{\epsilon} P[\mathcal{K}(D_2) \in S] \tag{2}$$

Thus, the probability of same possible outputs for $D_1$ and $D_2$ remains approximately the same. Rather than to quantify the level of privacy it affords (in fact according to [12] it is impossible to guarantee absolute immunity to attacks) differential privacy is more concerned with *privacy preserving data analysis*. When stated in the context of networks rather than databases, statistical properties of the network are affected by the deletion of a node from the network, *according to the status of the node in the network*: deleting a node with a larger degree will affect more of the network than deleting a node with a low degree.

An interesting point on the limitations or drawback of differential privacy is made in [32] where it is shown that the application of Laplacian noise, crucial for the result of differential privacy, achieves its intended result only when it is applied in "large quantities even for relatively large subsets".

## 5    Conclusions and Future Directions

A brief review of various approaches to privacy issues in social networks reveals that to some extent, some of the existent procedures already used in (relational) databases can be adopted and adapted to the social network setting. However, the structural complexity of social networks means that the privacy issue is also more difficult and complex. The basic idea is to alter/perturb the original network in a suitable way, usually by a randomization procedure. The question that arises is whether other approaches than randomization can be devised to perturb the data in a way that it is useful to prevent privacy breaches.

**Acknowledgements.** Partial support for this work was provided by the Grant TIN2010-14971 from Ministry of Education and Science, Government of Spain, and a Fellowship from CajAstur. Comments made by the reviewers have grately assisted in improving the contents of the paper.

# References

1. Adamic, L.A., Adar, E.: Friends and neighbors on the web. Social networks 25(3), 211–230 (2003)
2. Aggarwal, C.C., Yu, P.S.: An introduction to privacy-preserving data mining. In: Privacy-Preserving Data Mining, pp. 1–9 (2008)
3. Beach, A., Gartrell, M., Han, R.: q-anon: Rethinking anonymity for social networks. In: Elmagarmid, A.K., Agrawal, D. (eds.) SocialCom/PASSAT, pp. 185–192. IEEE Computer Society (2010)
4. Beach, A., Gartrell, M., Han, R.: Social-K: Real-time K-anonymity guarantees for social network applications. In: 2010 8th IEEE International Conference on Pervasive Computing and Communications Workshops (PERCOM Workshops), pp. 600–606. IEEE ( March 2010)
5. Cartwright, D.: Achieving change in people: Some applications of group dynamics theory. Human Relations 4(4), 381–392 (1951)
6. Cartwright, D., Harary, F.: Structural balance: a generalization of heider's theory. Psychological Review 63(5), 277 (1956)
7. Deutsch, K.W.: On communication models in the social sciences. Public Opinion Quarterly 16(3), 356–380 (1952)
8. Díaz, I., Ranilla, J., Rodríguez-Muniz, L.J., Troiano, L.: Identifying the Risk of Attribute Disclosure by Mining Fuzzy Rules. In: Hüllermeier, E., Kruse, R., Hoffmann, F. (eds.) IPMU 2010. CCIS, vol. 80, pp. 455–464. Springer, Heidelberg (2010)
9. Díaz, I., Rodríguez-Muñiz, L.J., Troiano, L.: Fuzzy sets in data protection: strategies and cardinalities. Logic Journal of IGPL (2011)
10. Domingo-Ferrer, J., Torra, V.: On the connections between statistical disclosure control for microdata and some artificial intelligence tools. Inf. Sci. Inf. Comput. Sci. 151, 153–170 (2003)
11. Dwork, C.: Differential Privacy. In: Bugliesi, M., Preneel, B., Sassone, V., Wegener, I. (eds.) ICALP 2006. LNCS, vol. 4052, pp. 1–12. Springer, Heidelberg (2006)
12. Dwork, C.: Differential Privacy: A Survey of Results. In: Agrawal, M., Du, D.-Z., Duan, Z., Li, A. (eds.) TAMC 2008. LNCS, vol. 4978, pp. 1–19. Springer, Heidelberg (2008)
13. Dwyer, C., Hiltz, S.R., Passerini, K.: Trust and privacy concern within social networking sites: A comparison of facebook and myspace. In: Proceedings of the Thirteenth Americas Conference on Information Systems (AMCIS 2007) (2007) Paper 339
14. Fang, C., Kohram, M., Ralescu, A.: Towards a spectral regression with low-rank approximation approach for link prediction in dynamic graphs. IEEE Intelligent Systems 99, 1
15. Hanneman, R.A., Riddle, M.: Introduction to social network methods. University of California, Riverside (2005)
16. Heider, F.: Attitudes and cognitive organization. The Journal of Psychology 21(1), 107–112 (1946)
17. Holsheimer, M., Siebes, A.P.J.M.: Data mining: the search for knowledge in databases. Technical report, Amsterdam, The Netherlands, The Netherlands (1994)
18. Jamali, M., Abolhassani, H.: Different aspects of social network analysis. In: IEEE/WIC/ACM International Conference on Web Intelligence, WI 2006, pp. 66–72 (December 2006)

19. Katz, L.: A new status index derived from sociometric analysis. Psychometrika 18(1), 39–43 (1953)
20. Korolova, A., Motwani, R., Nabar, S.U., Xu, Y.: Link privacy in social networks. In: Proceeding of the 17th ACM Conference on Information and Knowledge Management, pp. 289–298. ACM (2008)
21. Laird, P.D.: Learning from good and bad data. Kluwer Academic Publishers, Norwell (1988)
22. Leicht, E.A., Holme, P., Newman, M.E.J.: Vertex similarity in networks. Physical Review E 73(2), 26120 (2006)
23. Leontief, W.W.: The structure of American economy, 1919-1939: An empirical application of equilibrium analysis. Oxford University Press, New York (1951)
24. Li, N., Li, T.: t-closeness: Privacy beyond k-anonymity and?-diversity. In: Proceedings of IEEE International Conference on Data Engineering (2007)
25. Li, N., Li, T., Venkatasubramanian, S.: t-closeness: Privacy beyond k-anonymity and l-diversity. In: ICDE, pp. 106–115 (2007)
26. Liben-Nowell, D., Kleinberg, J.: The link-prediction problem for social networks. Journal of the American society for information science and technology 58(7), 1019–1031 (2007)
27. Liu, K., Das, K., Grandison, T., Kargupta, H.: Privacy-preserving data analysis on graphs and social networks
28. Loukides, G., Shao, J.: Preventing range disclosure in k-anonymised data. Expert Syst. Appl. 38(4), 4559–4574 (2011)
29. Lovász, L.: Random walks on graphs: A survey. Combinatorics, Paul Erdos is Eighty 2(1), 1–46 (1993)
30. Machanavajjhala, A., Gehrke, J., Kifer, D., Venkitasubramaniam, M.: l-diversity: Privacy beyond k-anonymity. In: 22nd IEEE International Conference on Data Engineering (2006)
31. Samarati, P.: Protecting respondents' identities in microdata release. IEEE Transactions on Knowledge and Data Engineering 13, 1010–1027 (2001)
32. Sarathy, R., Muralidhar, K.: Evaluating laplace noise addition to satisfy differential privacy for numeric data. Transactions on Data Privacy 4(1), 1–17 (2011)
33. Facebook Statistics, www.facebook.com/press/info.php?statistics
34. Sweeney, L.: k-anonymity: a model for protecting privacy. International Journal on Uncertainty, Fuzziness and Knowledge-based Systems 10(5), 557–570 (2002)
35. Ying, X., Wu, X.: On Link Privacy in Randomizing Social Networks. In: Theeramunkong, T., Kijsirikul, B., Cercone, N., Ho, T.-B. (eds.) PAKDD 2009. LNCS, vol. 5476, pp. 28–39. Springer, Heidelberg (2009)
36. Zheleva, E., Getoor, L.: To join or not to join: the illusion of privacy in social networks with mixed public and private user profiles. In: Proceedings of the 18th International Conference on World Wide Web, pp. 531–540. ACM (2009)
37. Zhou, B., Pei, J.: The k-anonymity and l-diversity approaches for privacy preservation in social networks against neighborhood attacks. Knowledge and Information Systems 28(1), 1–38 (2010)
38. Zhou, B., Pei, J., Luk, W.: A brief survey on anonymization techniques for privacy preserving publishing of social network data. SIGKDD Explor. Newsl. 10, 12–22 (2008)

# Towards k-Anonymous Non-numerical Data via Semantic Resampling

Sergio Martínez, David Sánchez, and Aïda Valls

Department of Computer Science and Mathematics, Universitat Rovira i Virgili
Av. Països Catalans, 26, 43007, Tarragona, Catalonia, Spain
{sergio.martinez,david.sanchez,aida.valls}@urv.cat

**Abstract.** Privacy should be carefully considered during the publication of data (e.g. database records) collected from individuals to avoid disclosing identities or revealing confidential information. Anonymisation methods aim at achieving a certain degree of privacy by performing transformations over non-anonymous data while minimising, as much as possible, the distortion (i.e. information loss) derived from these transformations. *k*-anonymity is a property typically considered when masking data, stating that each record (corresponding to an individual) is indistinguishable from at least *k-1* other records in the anonymised dataset. Many methods have been developed to anonymise data, but most of them are focused solely on numerical attributes. Non-numerical values (e.g. categorical attributes like job or country-of-birth or unbounded textual ones like user preferences) are more challenging because arithmetic operations cannot be applied. To properly manage and interpret this kind of data, it is required to have operators that are able to deal with data semantics. In this paper, we propose an anonymisation method based on a classic data re-sampling algorithm that guarantees the fulfilment of the *k*-anonymity property and is able to deal with non-numerical data from a semantic perspective. Our method has been applied to anonymise the well-known Adult Census dataset, showing that a semantic interpretation of non-numerical values better minimises the information loss of the masked data file.

**Keywords:** Privacy protection, anonymity, resampling, semantics.

## 1 Introduction

Privacy protection in published data (e.g. polls, usage logs, questionnaires, etc.) is crucial to avoid revealing individual's identities and/or linking those to confidential attributes (e.g. salary, medical conditions, etc.). Several methods have been proposed in the literature aiming at generating an anonymised version of the original data so that it can be published with low disclosure risk. These methods mask the set of records in the original dataset by introducing some distortion on the original values, making difficult the re-identification of individuals while, at the same time, trying to retain the utility of data (i.e. the fact that equal or similar conclusions can be extracted

S. Greco et al. (Eds.): IPMU 2012, Part IV, CCIS 300, pp. 519–528, 2012.

from both the original and anonymised version of a dataset). To generate an anonymised version of a dataset, the $k$-anonymity property is commonly considered. A masked dataset is considered $k$-anonymous if each record is indistinguishable from, at least, $k$-1 other records [1]. To retain data utility, authors select the data transformation that minimizes the information loss.

Several techniques introducing distortions to mask data can be found, such as: Additive Noise, Microaggregation, Rank Swapping or Resampling [2]. These have been widely used for statistical disclosure control on numerical data [2].

In this paper we focus on Resampling [3], a method that, even though has not gained as much research attention as other algorithms like Microaggregation [4], it has demonstrated to retain a high utility of data with respect to other methods [5, 6]. In a nutshell, Resampling is based on taking $t$ independent samples from the original attributes, sorting them and finally building a new masked record as the average of the ranked values of the $t$ samples. Even though this method reduces the disclosure risk, it does not ensure the $k$-anonymity property on the masked dataset.

The application of this method to numerical attributes (e.g. salaries, outcomes) is straightforward by using some ordering criterion on numbers and then calculating the arithmetic average of the ranked values of the different samples. However, nowadays, thanks to the growth of the Information Society, non-numerical data (e.g. categorical attributes such as country-of-birth or even textual values like user preferences, medical visit outcomes) are commonly collected and published. The management of this kind of data for masking purposes (i.e. resampling) is challenging due to the lack of appropriate aggregation and sorting operators. A proper interpretation of non-numerical data necessarily requires a semantic interpretation of their meaning (e.g. sports like *swimming* or *sailing* are more similar than *swimming* and *trekking*). In fact, as stated by several authors [7, 8], the preservation of the semantics of non-numerical data during the masking process is crucial to maintain their utility. Because semantics is an inherently human feature that can be hardly modelled in a mathematical way, semantically-grounded masking methods have to deal with a degree of uncertainty to assess the meaning of the textual values.

This paper focuses on this kind of data, presenting a resampling method that is able to deal with non-numerical attributes from a semantic perspective, proposing appropriate sorting and averaging operators. These will exploit structured knowledge bases (i.e. taxonomies or more general ontologies) and the theory of semantic similarity [9] as the basis to semantically interpret data. As far as we know, no other semantically-grounded masking resampling methods have been proposed in the literature. Moreover, to guarantee a theoretical level of privacy, the resampling method will be designed so that it fulfils the well-known $k$-anonymity property (on the contrary to classic resampling methods [5, 10]).

The rest of the paper is organized as follows. Section 2 introduces preliminary concepts, discussing classical resampling methods and reviewing the principles that enable a semantic interpretation of data. In section 3, our semantically-grounded $k$-anonymous resampling method is presented. Section 4 is devoted to evaluate our method proposed. The final section contains the conclusions and future work.

# 2    Preliminaries

In this section we introduce the main elements that constitute the basis of our proposal. First we present the original resampling method. Then, we discuss how semantics modelled in knowledge bases can be exploited to interpret and compare terms.

## 2.1    The Resampling Method

Resampling was defined in [11] as a method for perturbation of output data that consists on modifying only the answers to some queries while leaving the original data unchanged. Later, in Heer [3] resampling was applied to anonymise contingency tables based on bootstrapping. A cell-oriented version resampling procedure was proposed later in [10]. However, in this case the masked data file generated does not rely on resampling the original data, but on generating binomial random perturbations that preserve some statistics (obtaining an asymptotically unbiased estimate of the original data). Resampling has been also applied to anonymise input data (i.e. original records of the published dataset). In [5] a distributed version of the resampling method is proposed for dealing with the case where the original data is partitioned among several providers. All these methods focus on numerical data.

In this paper, as done in related works [5, 10], we base our method in the Heer's resampling approach (detailed in Algorithm 1). Briefly, being $n$ the number of records in the dataset, the method take $t$ samples with replacement (i.e. values can be taken more than once). Each sample is sorted in increasing order. Then, the masked dataset is obtained by taking, as first value, the average of the first values of all samples, as second value, the average of the second values of all samples, and so on.

```
Algorithm 1. Resampling
Inputs: D (dataset), t (number of samples)
Output: Dᴬ (a masked version of D)
1 Take t samples S₁,...,Sₜ of n records of D (with replacement)
2 Sort each sample Sᵢ in S₁,...,Sₜ
3 Make a set Pᵢ with t elements with the records at the i-th
  position of the sorted samples
4 Add the average of each Pᵢ to Dᴬ
5 Output Dᴬ
```

Comparison studies [5, 6] show that Heer's resampling achieves a high utility score with respect to other masking techniques, but with a slightly higher disclosure risk. This is related to the fact that, unlike other masking methods [4, 12, 13], the Heer's approach was designed without considering the $k$-anonymity property (formalized years later in [1]). Hence, resampled results cannot guarantee a – theoretical- level of privacy.

Our method will tackle this issue proposing a resampling method that fulfils the $k$-anonymity property while it is also able to deal with non-numerical data from a semantic perspective. Two issues that were not considered in previous works [5, 10].

## 2.2    Ontology-Based Semantic Similarity

When dealing with non-numerical data, the preservation of semantics plays a crucial role to ensure the utility of the anonymised datasets [7, 8, 14, 15]. Hence, considering the semantics to compare two concepts (in the sorting or averaging processes) may improve the utility of the masked data file. To make a semantic interpretation of textual values, algorithms require some sort of structured knowledge source that represents the relations between words at a conceptual level, such as taxonomies or ontologies. Ontologies are formal and machine-readable structures of shared conceptualisations of knowledge domains expressed by means of semantic relationships. These allow mapping words to concepts, so that terms can be interpreted according to their semantic relations. As a result, semantic similarity measures can be defined [9].

In previous works on data privacy for non-numerical data [12], the distance between records was measured with the Wu & Palmer similarity measure [9] using WordNet [16] as ontology. The Wu & Palmer measure, which will also applied be in this work, evaluates the distance taking as reference the Least Common Subsumer (LCS, i.e. the most specific ancestor that generalizes the two concepts). It evaluates the number of taxonomical links from $x_1$ to the LCS (N1) and from $x_2$ to the LCS (N2), as well as the number of taxonomical links from the LCS to the root of the ontology ($N_3$), as shown in (Eq.1). The result ranges from 1 (for identical concepts) to 0.

$$dis_{w\&p}(x_1, x_2) = 1 - \frac{2 \times N_3}{N_1 + N_2 + 2 \times N_3} \tag{1}$$

Several ontologies are being developed in many different domains, and specific search engines may help to find the appropriate ontology for each particular dataset [17]. In addition, general-purpose ontologies are also available, such as the Wordnet thesaurus [16], which includes more than 100,000 English terms.

# 3    Semantic *k*-Anonymous Resampling for Non-numerical Data

This section proposes a new resampling method (named S*k*Resampling) focused on minimizing the information loss when masking non-numerical data while ensuring the fulfilment of the k-anonymity property. It is based on the Heer's resampling method [3] with the following modifications:

- *K-anonymous resampling*: the original sampling method has been modified (as detailed in section 3.1) so that masked records fulfil the k-anonymity property.
- *Semantic resampling of non-numerical data*: in order to semantically interpret non-numerical data during the resampling process, new semantically-grounded ontology-based *comparison*, *sorting* and *averaging* operators are proposed in section 3.2.

## 3.1    *k*-Anonymous Resampling

To guarantee the k-anonymity on the masked dataset we modified Heer's method (detailed in Algorithm 1) as detailed in Algorithm 2. Let $D$ be the input dataset, $k$ is the desired level of $k$-anonymity and $n$ is the number of records in $D$.

**Algorithm 2. *k*-anonymous Resampling**
```
Inputs: D (dataset), k (level of anonymity)
Output: Dᴬ (a new version of D that fulfils k-anonymity)
1   Take k samples S₁,…,Sₖ of n/k records of D (no replacement)
2   Take the (n mod k) remaining records as sample Sᵣ
3   Sort each sample Sᵢ in S₁,…,Sₖ
4   Make a set Pᵢ with k elements with the records at the i-th
    position of the sorted samples
5   Generate the average of each Pᵢ denoted as cᵢ.
6   For each record rₜ in Sᵣ do
7     Add rₜ to the set Pᵢ with the closest average cᵢ
8     Recalculate the average cᵢ of the modified set
9   For each Pᵢ do
10    Replace each record in Pᵢ by the average cᵢ
11    Add the new version of the record to Dᴬ
12  Output Dᴬ
```

The algorithm proceeds as follows. First, to guarantee the *k*-anonymity property, it is required to create *k* samples, so that *k* records can be replaced by their average in a later stage and become *k*-indistinguishable. To do so, *k* samples of *n/k* records are created (line 1), without replacement (i.e. each record is taken only once). It is important to avoid record repetitions to ensure that all records fulfil the k-anonymity. Then these samples are sorted (line 3) and sets $P_i$ are created with the $i^{th}$ records of all samples (line 4). Then, the masked dataset $D^A$ is created by replacing, for each $P_i$, all records in $P_i$ by the average $c_i$ (lines 10-11). Because by definition $P_i$ contains *k* records without repetition, this replacement generates a set that fulfils the *k*-anonymity.

Note that, when taking *n/k* records for sample, the remaining *n mod k* records ($S_r$) should be also treated. These records are added to the set with the closest average (line 7), recalculating its average (line 8) before the replacement (lines 9 and 10).

## 3.2    Semantic Operators for Non-numerical Data

To consider the semantics of non-numerical data, semantically-grounded *comparison*, *sorting* and *averaging* operators for computing with words are needed.

As introduced in section 2, to semantically compare term pairs, an ontology-based measure like the Wu and Palmer distance (Eq 1) can be used. In Algorithm 2, this measure is used to discover the closest records (line 7), to sort sets of records (line 3) and to calculate averages (lines 5 and 8), as detailed below. Note that to apply this distance to multi-attributed records ($\{x_{11},…,x_{1m}\}$, $\{x_{21},…x_{2m}\}$, where $x_{ij}$ is the $j^{th}$ attribute value of the $i^{th}$ record and *m* is the number of attributes), we can calculate the average of the distances between the values attribute by attribute, as follows:

$$semantic\_distance(\{x_{11},…,x_{1m}\},\{x_{21},…,x_{2m}\}) = \frac{\sum\limits_{j=1}^{m} dis_{w\&p}(x_{1j},x_{2j})}{m} \qquad (2)$$

When dealing with non-numerical attributes, the definition of a sorting operator (line 3) is not straightforward. To sort a set of elements, it is needed to have an initial point from which starting sorting according to the similarity of the rest of values to that initial value. Numerically, this is done by taking the max (or min) value in the set. From a semantic perspective we follow a similar principle as propose Algorithm 3:

**Algorithm 3. Sorting procedure**
```
Inputs: P (dataset)
Output: P' (P sorted)
1 c = average(P)
2 f = argMax_vᵢ(semantic_distance(c,vᵢ)) ∀ vᵢ ∈ P
3 Add f to P' and remove it from P
4 while (|P| > 0) do
5     r = argMin_vᵢ(semantic_distance(f,vᵢ)) ∀ vᵢ ∈ P
6     Add r to P' and remove it from P
7     f = r
8 Output P'
```

Similarly to numbers, we begin by taking the initial point from which start sorting as the farthest record to the average of the dataset (lines 1-2). By using the semantic distance (Eq. 2) we sort the rest of the records by comparison (lines 2-5).

The sorting procedure and also the resampling method rely on the calculation of averages of non-numerical values to sort and replace values. Hence, the selection of an accurate average is crucial to minimise the information loss resulting from the masking process. Intuitively, the average of a dataset can be seen as the "centre". Based on this, we propose calculating the average as the semantic centroid of the dataset, exploiting the knowledge structure provided by a background ontology.

The usual approach to centroid construction for non-numerical data is based on the data distribution, mainly using the mode operator [4, 13]. This approach omits the semantics of data and, hence, a crucial dimension of data utility. Moreover, centroids are constrained to the values appearing in the input dataset. Otherwise, semantic centroids are constructed using the concept in the ontology that subsumes all the values in the cluster (i.e. the LCS [12]). This approach is affected by outliers and thus, it commonly results too abstract generalisations, causing a high information loss.

In our centroid construction method, a background ontology is exploited not only to assess the semantic distance between terms, but also to retrieve the centroid candidates. To calculate the centroid, we assume the classical centroid definition as the record that minimises the distance (in our case, *semantic distance*) against all the elements in a set. Formally, given a the semantic distance of Eq. 2, the centroid of a set of records $\{r_1, r_2, \ldots, r_n\}$ is defined as:

$$centroid\left(r_1, r_2, \ldots, r_n\right) = \arg\min_c \left( \sum_{i=1}^{n} semantic\_distance\left(c, r_i\right) \right) \quad (3)$$

where $c$ is a centroid candidate for the set of arguments.

The search space of centroid candidates $c$ has a great importance. When selecting the centroid according to the frequency of values (i.e. mode) the number of centroid candidates is limited to the set of different values that appear in the cluster. On the contrary, using a background ontology such as WordNet, we potentially extend the search space to all concepts modelled in the ontology and, hence, we can construct the centroid from a finer grained set of candidates. For semantic coherency and efficiency, we limit the search space to the hierarchical trees to which input values belong, taking as centroid candidates the set of taxonomical ancestors.

Formally, let us take $V=\{v_1,\ldots,v_n\}$ as the set of possible values for a non-numerical attribute $A_i$. Let us take ontology $O$ containing and semantically modelling all $v_i$ in $V$.

The first step of our method consists of mapping the values in $V$ to concepts in $O$, so that semantically related concepts can be extracted from $O$ following the semantic relationships. We assume that taxonomical subsumers of a term (including itself) are valid centroid candidates. The set of candidates is then given in the *minimum subsumer hierarchy* $(H_O(V))$ that goes from the concepts corresponding to the values in $V$ to the Least Common Subsummer of all these values. The *Least Common Subsumer* (LCS) of a set of categorical values $V$ $(LCS_O(V))$ is the deepest taxonomical ancestor that all the terms in $V$ have in common in the ontology $O$. We omitted taxonomical ancestors of the LCS because those will always be more general (i.e. more semantically distant) than the LCS and, hence, worse centroid candidates. Then, all the concepts $c$ in $H_O(V)$ are the centroid candidates of the set $V$.

The centroid of a set of values $V$ in ontology $O$ is defined as the concept $c_j$ in $H_O(V)$ that minimises the semantic distance $dis_{w\&p}$ with respect to all the values in $V$.

$$centroid_O(V) = \left\{ \arg Min\left( \sum_1^n dis_{w\&p}(c_j, v_i) \right) \right\}, \forall c_j \in H_O(V), \forall v_i in V \qquad (4)$$

When more than one candidate minimises the distance, all of them would be equally representative, so any of them can be selected as the final centroid. When dealing with multi-attributed data, we assume that attributes are independent, so that, the centroid of each attribute can be calculated separately, and the final centroid is the tuple of individual ones. This assumption is usual for numerical data, where the average of attributes is calculated independently.

Hence, the centroid of a multivariate dataset $MV$ in the ontology $O$ is defined as:

$$centroid_O(MV) = \{ centroid_O(A_1), centroid_O(A_2), ..., centroid_O(A_m) \} \qquad (5)$$

, where $A_j$ is the set of values for the $j^{th}$ attribute in $MV$ and $m$ is the number of attributes in $MV$.

# 4    Evaluation

In this section, the evaluation of the proposed S*k*Resampling method is detailed. As evaluation data, we used the well-known *Adult Census* dataset [18]. Two non-numerical attributes have been taken, corresponding to "occupation" (14 distinct modalities) and "native-country" (41 modalities). This result in 30,162 records (after removing rows with missing values) distributed into 388 different responses, 83 of them being unique. Attribute values have been mapped to WordNet [16], which has been used as the knowledge base that enables the semantic interpretation of data.

Because the theoretical level of privacy is guaranteed by the fulfilment of the *k*-anonymity property, the evaluation has been focused on the quantification of the information loss. To do so, we have employed the *sum of square errors* (SSE), which has been extensively used to evaluate anonymisation methods [4, 12]. It is defined as the sum square of distances between each original record and their corresponding masked version (Eq. 6). Hence, the higher the SSE is, the higher the information loss.

$$SSE = \sum_{i=1}^{n} (semantic\_distance(x_i, x^A{}_i))^2 \qquad (6)$$

,where $n$ is the number of records in the dataset, $x_i$ is the $i^{th}$ record and $x^A_i$ denotes the masked version of $x_i$. As a distance measure, we employ again the *semantic_distance* defined in Eq. 2 to quantify the loss in semantics.

To evaluate the benefits that the semantic S*k*Resampling approach brings with regards to the preservation of the data utility in comparison with non-semantic methods, we configured four settings that, while based on the same resampling algorithm (Alg. 2), they vary the criteria used to compare, sort and replace the original values:

- Setting 1: no semantics are considered when masking the dataset. On one hand, values are compared using the equality predicate (0 if identical, 1 otherwise). On the other hand, the centroid is selected as the mode (i.e., the most frequently occurring value in the set). This mimics the behavior of anonymising approaches dealing with non-numerical data in a categorical fashion [4, 13].

- Setting 2: semantics are considered when comparing values. The Wu & Palmer measure (Eq. 2) applied to WordNet as knowledge structure are used. The centroid is kept the same as in setting 1. Comparing this to setting 1, one can quantify the influence in information loss of the distance calculation method.

- Setting 3: the same as setting 2, but taking as centroid the concept in WordNet that taxonomically subsumes all elements in the set (i.e. the Least Common Subsumer, as done in [12]). This approach considers the semantics of data in the centroid calculation but neglect their distribution in the taxonomical tree.

- Setting 4 (S*k*Resampling): the method presented in section 3 is applied. It shows the contribution of our proposal on the information loss.

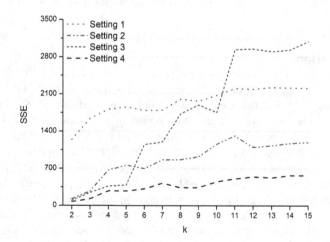

**Fig. 1.** Comparison of Information Loss (SSE) values for the evaluated settings

The information loss values (i.e. *SEE*) obtained for the four settings while varying the $k$-anonymity level from 2 to 15 are shown in Fig. 1.

First of all we can see that our approach (*setting 4*) achieves the lowest information loss for all the $k$-anonymity values. Compared to other settings, we observe that a non-semantic method (*setting 1*) results in the highest information loss for most $k$-values. This shows that managing and transforming non-numerical data only by means of their distribution features (i.e. repetitions, mode) hardly preserves the meaning of masked data and hence their utility. By considering semantics in distance calculations (*setting 2*), information loss is significantly reduced showing the limitations of comparing attribute values according to the equality/inequality of their textual labels. Regarding the results obtained by *setting 3* (i.e. centroid computed as the LCS), we observe that, even though it is able to retain more information than non-sematic centroid calculation methods (i.e. mode) for low $k$-values, it produces severely worse results when a higher anonymity degree is required. The fact that the LCS is used as the centroid causes that very general abstraction are picked when a larger and more heterogeneous set of values should be generalized (i.e. higher $k$-anonymity). In comparison, our method (*setting 4*) produces more accurate centroids, by considering both the semantics and the data distribution.

# 5    Conclusions

In recent years, the interest in data semantics has grown in the privacy-preserving community due to the increasing availability of non-numerical data [8, 12]. Several authors have shown the benefits that a semantic treatment of data can bring with regards to the preservation of the utility of masked data [7, 8].

In this paper, we have adapted a classic resampling method to always fulfil the $k$-anonymity property, in order to guarantee a certain level of privacy. While considering the semantics of the data by means of the definition of semantically-grounded comparison, sorting and averaging operators, we obtain an effective method for anonymising non-numerical data. The evaluation results sustain our hypothesis, being able to minimise the information loss in comparison with non-semantic approaches.

As future work, the effect of different semantic similarity measures on the quality of the masked data should be studied. A deeper analysis of the performance of the anonymised data over other types of security attacks (*e.g.* re-identification by record linkage) could be also interesting. Finally, we plan to compare our S$k$Resampling method with other anonymisation approaches that also consider data semantics up to a degree, like those based on generalizing attribute values [1], substituting values with similar ones [8] or aggregating semantically similar records [12].

**Acknowledgements.** This work was partly funded by the Spanish Government through the projects CONSOLIDER INGENIO 2010 CSD2007-0004 "ARES" and eAEGIS TSI2007-65406-C03-02, and by the Government of Catalonia under grant 2009 SGR 1135 and 2009 SGR-01523. Sergio Martínez Lluís is supported by a research grant of the Ministerio de Educación y Ciencia (Spain).

# References

1. Samarati, P., Sweeney, L.: Protecting Privacy when Disclosing Information: k-Anonymity and Its Enforcement through Generalization and Suppression. Technical Report SRI-CSL-98-04, SRI Computer Science Laboratory (1998)
2. Domingo-Ferrer, J.: A Survey of Inference Control Methods for Privacy-Preserving Data Mining. In: Aggarwal, C.C., Yu, P.S. (eds.) Privacy-Preserving Data Mining, vol. 34, pp. 53–80. Springer US (2008)
3. Heer, G.R.: A bootstrap procedure to preserve statistical confidentiality in contingency tables. In: Int. Seminar on Statistical Confidentiality, Eurostat, pp. 261–271 (1993)
4. Domingo-Ferrer, J., Mateo-Sanz, J.M.: Practical Data-Oriented Microaggregation for Statistical Disclosure Control. IEEE Trans. on Knowl. and Data Eng. 14, 189–201 (2002)
5. Herranz, J., Nin, J., Torra, V.: Distributed Privacy-Preserving Methods for Statistical Disclosure Control. In: Garcia-Alfaro, J., Navarro-Arribas, G., Cuppens-Boulahia, N., Roudier, Y. (eds.) DPM 2009. LNCS, vol. 5939, pp. 33–47. Springer, Heidelberg (2010)
6. Karr, A.F., Kohnen, C.N., Oganian, A., Reiter, J.P., Sanil, A.P.: A Framework for Evaluating the Utility of Data Altered to Protect Confidentiality. The American Statistician 60, 224–232 (2006)
7. Torra, V.: Towards knowledge intensive data privacy. In: Proceedings of the 5th International Workshop on Data Privacy Management, and 3rd International Conference on Autonomous Spontaneous Security, pp. 1–7. Springer, Athens (2011)
8. Martínez, S., Sánchez, D., Valls, A., Batet, M.: Privacy protection of textual attributes through a semantic-based masking method. Information Fusion. Special Issue on Privacy and Security 13, 304–314 (2012)
9. Wu, Z., Palmer, M.: Verbs semantics and lexical selection. In: The 32nd Annual Meeting on Association for Computational Linguistics, pp. 133–138. Association for Computational Linguistics, Las Cruces (1994)
10. Domingo-Ferrer, J., Mateo-Sanz, J.M.: Resampling for statistical confidentiality in contingency tables. Computers & Mathematics with Applications 38, 13–32 (1999)
11. Jones, D.H., Adam, N.R.: Disclosure avoidance using the bootstrap and other resampling schemes. In: Proceedings of the Fifth Annual Research Conference, U.S. Bureau of the Census, pp. 446–455 (1989)
12. Abril, D., Navarro-Arribas, G., Torra, V.: Towards Semantic Microaggregation of Categorical Data for Confidential Documents. In: Torra, V., Narukawa, Y., Daumas, M. (eds.) MDAI 2010. LNCS, vol. 6408, pp. 266–276. Springer, Heidelberg (2010)
13. Torra, V.: Microaggregation for Categorical Variables: A Median Based Approach. In: Domingo-Ferrer, J., Torra, V. (eds.) PSD 2004. LNCS, vol. 3050, pp. 162–174. Springer, Heidelberg (2004)
14. Martínez, S., Sánchez, D., Valls, A.: Ontology-Based Anonymization of Categorical Values. In: Torra, V., Narukawa, Y., Daumas, M. (eds.) MDAI 2010. LNCS, vol. 6408, pp. 243–254. Springer, Heidelberg (2010)
15. Martínez, S., Sánchez, D., Valls, A., Batet, M.: The Role of Ontologies in the Anonymization of Textual Variables. In: Proceeding of the 2010 conference on Artificial Intelligence Research and Development: Proceedings of the 13th International Conference of the Catalan Association for Artificial Intelligence, pp. 153–162. IOS Press (2010)
16. Fellbaum, C.: WordNet: An Electronic Lexical Database (Language, Speech, and Communication). The MIT Press (1998)
17. Ding, L., Finin, T., Joshi, A., Pan, R., Cost, R.S., Peng, Y., Reddivari, P., Doshi, V., Sachs, J.: Swoogle: a search and metadata engine for the semantic web. In: Proceedings of the Thirteenth ACM International Conference on Information and Knowledge Management, pp. 652–659. ACM, Washington, D.C. (2004)
18. Hettich, S., Bay, S.D.: The UCI KDD Archive (1999)

# Exploiting Adversarial Uncertainty in Robotic Patrolling: A Simulation-Based Analysis

Pablo J. Villacorta and David A. Pelta

Models of Decision and Optimization Research Group,
Dept. of Computer Science and AI, CITIC,
University of Granada, 18071 Granada, Spain
{pjvi,dpelta}@decsai.ugr.es

**Abstract.** Recently, several models for autonomous robotic patrolling have been proposed and analysed on a game-theoretic basis. The common drawback of such models are the assumptions required to apply game theory analysis. Such assumptions do not usually hold in practice, especially perfect knowledge of the adversary's strategy, and the belief that we are facing always a best-responser. However, the agents in the patrolling scenario may take advantage of that fact. In this work, we try to analyse from an empirical perspective a patrolling model with an explicit topology, and take advantage of the adversarial uncertainty caused by the limited, imperfect knowledge an agent can acquire through simple observation. The first results we report are encouraging.

**Keywords:** Adversarial decision making, Robotic patrolling, Stackelberg games, Empirical study.

## 1 Introduction

The problem of patrolling an area with autonomous mobile robots has been studied more and more in the last years, especially nowadays due to the terrorism threat, and is still open. A patrolling scenario can be described as follows. There is one patroller that must defend an area against one or more robbers, assuming the whole area cannot be protected aginst attacks simultaneously so he must move from one location to another within the area all the time.

This means that the patroller has to move within the area to patrol the locations and get sure nobody is trying to steal them. The locations can represent houses or any other good that is valuable for a possible robber. In principle, not all the locations are equally valuable: both the patroller and the robber have their own preferences. The former knows which locations are more important to keep safe, and the robber knows or can intuit in which locations the most valuable goods are. Robbers may have different preferences over the same set of locations according to the kind of criminal he is and the type of product he is interested in: art works in a museum, cars in a factory, jewellery, money from a house, etc.

This situation admits different models and solution techniques. It is clear that the patroller will visit the locations sequentially, although in a sophisticated

S. Greco et al. (Eds.): IPMU 2012, Part IV, CCIS 300, pp. 529–538, 2012.

model we could think of a technologically-advanced patroller that senses several locations at a time, or even think of a team of coordinated patrollers [1,2]. The patroller can make a decision over the next location to visit [2] or over a whole route of several locations that will be patrolled sequentially before deciding again a new route [6]. Finally, the model may consider a spatial topology describing the relative positions of the locations [2] or not [6].

Although deterministic algorithms were initially proposed for situations where the patroller cannot defend the whole area at a time, they sometimes show an important drawback: they give to the robber the possibility to rob certain locations when the patroller is far enough, provided that the robber was patient enough to observe and learn the deterministic strategy of the patroller before the attack. To make this learning more difficult, randomized patrolling strategies have been proposed in a lot of models. This idea has been also suggested in other non-patrolling adversarial models as it allows a better equilibrium between the confusion induced in the observer agent and the payoff obtained by the patroller, in terms of the routes chosen [7,6].

This work is aimed at analysing the so-called BGA model [2], proposed to capture a patrolling situation, from a strictly empirical point of view in order to show deviations from the expected behaviour when applied to a real scenario. Insights are provided on the causes of this, along with a brief discussion on how to take advantage of them. The main reasons are the wrong assumptions made by the model, which hold only partially in real life. Similar attempts were made in [3,4] but the former does not go in enough detail and the latter still abides by a slightly extended game-theoretical model like [2].

This paper is structured as follows. Section 2 briefly reviews the model we will focus on. A numerical perspective with practical results when applying and simulating the model is given in Section 3, which contains the hypothesis together with the experiments that support them, as they are impossible to separate. Section 3.2 suggests an improvement based on the previous numerical results and shows the effectiveness of the proposal. Finally, section 4 contains a brief discussion and further work.

## 2    Review of the BGA Model

Maybe the most general model was first proposed in [2] and extended in [4]. It allows for a topological representation of the area being patrolled, which does not need to be a perimeter but admits any arbitrary bi-dimensional disposition of the locations. The environment is divided into a set of $C = \{c_1, ..., c_n\}$ cells, with a directed graph $G$ that specifies how they are connected. $G$ can be represented with its adjacency matrix $A(n \times n)$ so $A(i, j) = 1$ if cells $c_i$ and $c_j$ are connected. In the enviroments of our examples we will take $G$ as non-directed but it could also be directed. A subset $T$ of $C$ contains the cells that have some value for both patroller and intruder. The rest of the cells can be seen merely as a link between the interesting locations.

At one turn, the patroller can move from one cell to any of the adjacents and patrol the destination cell. Every cell $c_i$ has associated an integer $d_i$ indicating the number of turns needed to rob it. To rob that cell, the intruder directly enters the cell at once (i.e. the model does not initially consider doors or paths through the environment, although an extension does [4]) and must stay in it for $d_i$ turns from the entering turn. If the patroller reaches the cell during that period, then the intruder will have been caught.

It is assumed that the intruder first observes the patroller without being detected and perfectly learns the patrolling strategy. It is a so-called leader-follower situation, because the patroller can impose the strategy he wants and the intruder will try his best to respond to that strategy. In game-theoretic terms, this can be modeled as a strategic-form game, i.e. a game in which both players, the patroller and the intruder, only play once and act simultaneously. To achieve this, the temporal component has to be eliminated. This can be done by defining the possible actions available to the intruder as $enter\text{-}when(c_i, c_j)$, meaning that the intruder enters cell $c_i$ the turn after the patroller was in $c_j$. The randomized strategy of the patroller are the set of probabilities $\{\alpha_{ij}\}$ that indicate the probability that the patroller moves to cell $c_j$ when it is in cell $c_i$. The intruder is assumed to perfectly know these probabilites because it has been observing the patroller for long enough before choosing a location to rob.

The possible outcomes of this strategic-form game are $penetration\text{-}c_i$, $intruder\text{-}capture$ and $no\text{-}attack$ if the best choice for the intruder is not to attack any cell ever. The payoffs attained respectively by the patroller and the intruder for each of these outcomes are $(X_i, Y_i)$, $(X_0, 0)$ and $(X_0, Y_0)$, with the restrictions: $X_i < X_0$ (capturing the intruder or persuading it not to attack always reports a higher payoff for the patroller) and $Y_0 \leq 0 < Y_i$ for all $c_i$ (being captured is worse for the intruder than successfully robbing any cell).

According to game theory, the solution of this game is the *leader-follower equilibrium*, which gives the leader (patroller) the maximum expected utility when the follower acts as a best responser to the strategy imposed by the leader, i.e. the follower tries to maximize its own payoff according to the strategy (probabilities) imposed by the leader [5,2]. This constitutes a bi-level optimization problem whose solution is computed using mathematical programming techniques. It can be proved that, when the leader imposes a randomized strategy, the best response of the follower is always a deterministic action and not another randomization over its actions. In other words, there always exists an action $enter\text{-}when(c_i, c_j)$ that reports the follower a higher payoff than any randomization over all the $enter\text{-}when(\cdot,\cdot)$ actions available.

## 3   An Experimental Approach

The authors of the model state in [3] that some of the assumptions are not realistic and prevent the model to be applied in real situations. A 3D simulator is used to evaluate the impact of the violation of some assumptions. Here we try to provide insights on the causes of the deviations from the expected behaviour.

## 3.1    Discrete Perception of Probabilities

The hypothesis of perfect knowledge of the patrolling strategy by the intruder will be relaxed and modeled in a more realistic manner. We will now consider an intruder which does not know precisely the strategy of the patroller, but only knows what it observes turn after turn, in a discrete way. Suppose the intruder has an *observation matrix* $O$ with dimensions $n \times n$. $O_{ij}$ is the number of times that, in the past, the patroller has moved to $c_j$ from $c_i$. This number can be expressed as a probability: $\hat{\alpha}_{ij} = O_{ij}/\sum_{j=1}^{n} O_{ij}$, where $\hat{\ }$ indicates that it is a discrete estimation of the true probability $\alpha_{ij}$. Notice that $\sum_{j=1}^{n} O_{ij}$ is the number of times that the patroller has passed over $c_i$. This means that the probabilites are perceived as a relative frequency over the number of observations made, so the observed probabilites will approach the true ones only after a long time. Probably, in a real scenario the intruder does not have so much time to observe and learn but it will attack much earlier. As a result, the most interesting part is not the asymptotically stable behaviour predicted by the leader-follower equilibrium, but a *transient*, difficult-to-predict behaviour in early stages of the patrolling situation. This is why empirical simulations are required.

Note that limiting the knowledge of the intruder about the patroller strictly to *what it has observed* has important implications. The most important is that it allows strategic manipulation. At the same time, it causes more complicated strategies for the patroller to be very difficult to perceive. The observation matrix we have introduced above is the simplest way to model the observations, but an agent with this kind of memory is unable to detect complex behaviours, such as non-Markovian, or partially deterministic routes. Such behaviours will be wrongly perceived just as probabilities, which can induce the intruder not to act as a *true* best-responser but just as a best-responser regarding its own perceptions about the patroller. This represents a subtle form of manipulation and has been analysed on a more abstract model in [9,8].

## 3.2    Experimental Settings and Results

We have used the map proposed in [2], with its corresponding optimal strategy as given by the authors. Both are reproduced in Fig. 1. We implemented the BGA model in a general-purpose language and simulated a patrolling situation in that map. Three different experiments were conducted. The first one is aimed at determining how important it is for the intruder to follow the prescribed best-response action. The second one shows the empirical perception that the intruder has of the patroller's randomized movement, and how the deviation from the true probabilities affect the best-response the intruder would choose at every moment. Finally, the third one is aimed at evaluating the impact of including occasional deterministic movements in the patroller's strategy to anticipate the intruder's attacks and increase the capture chance.

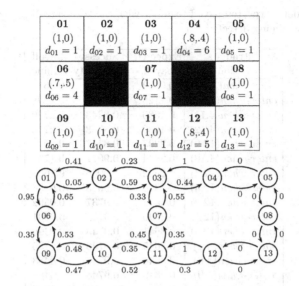

**Fig. 1.** A simple map used in the experiments and the optimal strategy for the patroller prescribed by the leader-follower equilibrium. Figure reproduced from [2].

**Expected Payoff for a Best Responser.** In the first experiment, we did not use the implementation of the model but only tried to gain a clearer idea on how important it is to follow the strategy prescribed by the leader-follower equilibrium. According to the optimal probabilities of Fig. 1, the expected payoffs attained by the intruder for every *enter-when*($\cdot$,$\cdot$) action are shown in Table 1. Only the actions whose expected payoff is greater than 0 are listed. The *success probability*, or probability of not being detected, is given for informational purposes. For a given action *enter-when*($q$, $s$), such probability is the value $\alpha$ = $\sum_{i \in C \setminus q} \gamma_{s,i}^{d_q,i}$ mentioned in [2], which stands for the sum of the probabilities of all the paths that the patroller can follow in $d_q$ turns, starting in cell $s$ and not passing through cell $q$. We can see the payoff for that action as a random variable that takes value $Y_0$ with probability $(1 - \alpha)$ and $Y_q$ with probability $\alpha$. The variance of such variable can be very informative so it has been added to the table. An enumeration like Table 1 is exactly what a best-responser is expected to do to make a decision. With those results, the intruder would choose *enter-when*(6, 12). It gives him the highest expected payoff, and it is preferable to *enter-when*(6,11) because, despite having the same expected payoff, cell 11 is nearer target cell 6 than cell 12. However, notice both actions have a high variance in relation to the payoff. On the contrary, actions *enter-when*(4,1), *enter-when*(4,6) and *enter-when*(4,9) yield a slightly smaller payoff but their probability of success is 6 % higher and their variance is smaller. In simple words, what we see is that a cell with a high payoff is worth running a risk to rob it because of the expected payoff, although such expectation has a high

**Table 1.** Intruder's expected payoff together with the corresponding variance and the probability of not being detected

| Intruder's action | Expected payoff | Sucess probability | Payoff variance |
|---|---|---|---|
| enter-when(12,10) | 0.0582 | 0.7558 | 0.3617 |
| enter-when(12,7) | 0.1125 | 0.7947 | 0.3198 |
| enter-when(4,11) | 0.1680 | 0.8343 | 0.2710 |
| enter-when(4,12) | 0.1680 | 0.8343 | 0.2710 |
| enter-when(12,9) | 0.2203 | 0.8716 | 0.2193 |
| enter-when(4,10) | 0.2624 | 0.9017 | 0.1737 |
| enter-when(12,3) | 0.2692 | 0.9066 | 0.1660 |
| enter-when(12,4) | 0.3376 | 0.9555 | 0.0834 |
| enter-when(12,2) | 0.3632 | 0.9737 | 0.0502 |
| enter-when(12,1) | 0.3640 | 0.9743 | 0.0491 |
| enter-when(12,6) | 0.3641 | 0.9743 | 0.0490 |
| enter-when(4,1) | 0.3645 | 0.9746 | 0.0485 |
| enter-when(4,6) | 0.3646 | 0.9747 | 0.0483 |
| enter-when(4,9) | 0.3648 | 0.9748 | 0.0481 |
| enter-when(6,3) | 0.3656 | 0.9104 | 0.1835 |
| enter-when(6,4) | 0.3656 | 0.9104 | 0.1835 |
| enter-when(6,7) | 0.3660 | 0.9107 | 0.1831 |
| enter-when(6,11) | 0.3664 | 0.9110 | 0.1825 |
| enter-when(6,12) | 0.3664 | 0.9110 | 0.1825 |

variance (risk) associated. However, if two cells are very similar in payoff, maybe the one with a slightly smaller payoff but smaller variance and higher success probability is a better choice because the risk of being detected is smaller. This is another practical issue an intruder could consider but is not taken into account by strict game-theoretic models.

**Intruder's Deviation from the Predicted Action.** The second experiment required running simulations of the model. The intruder was provided with an observation matrix as explained in the previous section. The patroller moved all the time along the map following the strategy described in Fig. 1, starting at cell 1[1]. The intruder was observing the patroller all the time and recording the observations in the observation matrix. We wanted to check how his observations matched the true probabilities of the patroller, and if the differences changed his decision regarding what we could predict about the intruder as a best-responser. Every 100 turns, the intruder evaluated the expected payoff it could attain for each enter-when($q$, $s$) combination, based on the empirical probabilities he had observed up to that turn. The results after two independent runs (in the same conditions and with the same map) are shown in Fig. 2.

Each plot shows two lines. Every change in the action chosen by a best-responser is shown so that every action is at a different height in the graph. The

---

[1] Since the experiments are long enough, the starting point is not important.

height of an *enter-when* action does not have a meaning nor is it related to its payoff; its purpose is just to clearly show changes in the action preferred by the intruder along the time. The continuous, thick line measures the distance between the observed probability distribution, built with the discrete observations recorded in the intruder's observation matrix, and the true probability distribution used by the patroller, namely the leader-follower equilibrium strategy. There are many ways to measure the distance between two discrete probability distributions; a very simple one is the *maximum norm* between two vectors. Let $\mathbf{x}$ and $\mathbf{y}$ be two vectors of $R^n$. The distance between them, according to the maximum norm, is

$$||\mathbf{x} - \mathbf{y}||_\infty = \max(|x_1 - y_1|, ..., |x_n - y_n|) \qquad (1)$$

This distance gives an idea of how well the relative frequency of the observations matches the true probabilities used by the patroller during the simulation. As could be expected, it becomes smaller as the simulation goes on, because a lot of samples can approximate a probability distribution better than just a few.

The figures confirm that it is not possible to predict exactly the action of the intruder in a real scenario, because its perceptions do not exactly match the probabilities of the patroller, and the deviation can change the decision. This happens even more if the payoff of two actions is very similar or if the map contains zones with symmetric access paths like in our case. The fact that after a long time the best action for the intruder continues unstabilized like in Fig.2 can be explained by those reasons, and actually the target cell is the same; only the entering moment (the cell where the patroller should be) varies. What is more surprising is that we can still find some changes in the target cell in the long run. The expected payoff between target cells 4 and 6 (see Table 1) is so similar and may lead the intruder to prefer any of them. However, recall that they do have very different success probabilities as can be seen in the table, but the intruder did not take this into account.

**Occasional Deterministic Paths.** As stated in Section 3.1, the limited perception of the patroller's behaviour as a set of probabilities opens the door to the possibility of manipulating the observer with a behaviour that cannot be described in terms of probabilities. This form of manipulation may improve the results of the patroller.

Assume the patroller can take into account his own actions just as the intruder is doing, by recording his own movements in an observation matrix identical to that used by the intruder. That way the patroller is able to know exactly what is being perceived about his strategy for an external observer, and which seems to be the best-response cell at each moment, disregarding the true best-response. It is a way to anticipate the most feasible enter cell for the intruder. But in order for this to be effective, it is necessary to have a mechanism to increase vigilance over the cell that is a best-response at every moment, no matter if this violates the movement probabilities used by the patroller. To achieve that, occasional deterministic paths arriving to such probable target cell have been added to the

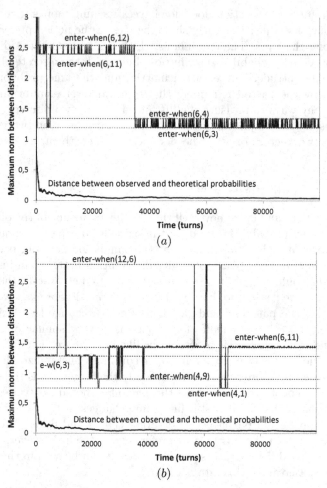

**Fig. 2.** Intruder's best choice every 100 turns according to the observed probabilities in two independent runs (a) and (b)

patroller's normal behaviour. Since they are still perceived as samples of the probabilistic movement, they should not be too frequent because otherwise they would influence and change the observed relative frequencies very quickly and as a result, that cell would not be the best response anymore for the intruder.

In order to test this, the following experiment was done. The patroller and the intruder engage in a simulation so that every 100 turns, both update their observation matrices (which are identical) and consequently, both update the current best-response for the intruder, according to the observed probabilities, i.e. the relative frequencies of the patroller's past actions. Now, as the patroller also has this information, it decides to occasionally move straightforward to that best-response cell in order to increase the probability of capturing it. This movement is a deterministic path from cell $s$ to cell $q$, since the intruder will only enter cell $q$ the turn after the patroller is in cell $s$ according to the best-response

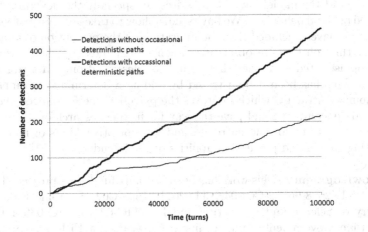

**Fig. 3.** Accumulated number of times the intruder was detected when trying to rob the cell prescribed by the optimal *enter-when* action according to observed probabilities

*enter-when*$(q,s)$ action. In our simulation, every time the patroller reaches cell $s$, it takes a probabilistic decision: it will go straight to cell $q$ with a probability $u$, following the shortest path through the environment[2]. Once the patroller arrives at cell $q$, it returns to normal probabilistic movement. In the experiments, $u$ was set to 0.1. Independently, at every turn, the intruder decides probabilistically whether to execute the best-response action *enter-when*$(q,s)$ with probability $r$, or not to attack. In the experiments, $r$ was set to 0.1. If it decides to attack, it waits until the patroller reaches cell $s$ and then enters the cell. The model prescribes that the game is one-shot so the simulation should end after an attack, be it successful or not. In our experiments, we annotated the result after every attack but did not inform any of the agents of the result of the attack, so for them the simulation continues as if nothing had happened.

Results are depicted in Fig.3 and confirm the hypothesis. Two independent runs were made, one using with occasional deterministic paths with probability $u = 0.1$ and the other without such paths. The attack probability $r$ remained the same in both cases, $r = 0.1$ so approximately the same number of attacks are expected to arise in both simulations. The graph shows the accumulated number of times the patroller detected the intruder during the simulation. As can be seen, the patroller performed better with occasional deterministic paths, and they were not perceived very clearly by the intruder because otherwise the prescribed best-response would have changed the target cell to avoid being captured.

## 4   Conclusions and Further Work

A patrolling model for topologically-represented environments has been anal-ysed following a strictly empirical approach. Practical issues concerning the

---

[2] We assume the patroller can compute itself the shortest path or it is provided in the control software.

application of the model have been addressed, specially the deviation from the expected optimal behaviour. We have studied how to take advantage of such deviations, and have concluded that the limitation on the perception of a movement strategy through discrete observations can be exploited by the patroller with more sophisticated strategies that cannot be described only in terms of probabilities. This has been demonstrated by adding a deterministic component to a randomized strategy, which improves the patroller's performance. These early results are encouraging and pave the way for further research on more complex movement patterns for the patroller, and also for other kinds of manipulation exploiting the limited perception abilities of the intruder.

**Acknowledgments.** This work has been partially funded by projects TIN2008-01948, TIN2008-06872-C04-04, TIN2011-27696-C02-01 from the Spanish Ministry of Science and Innovation and P07-TIC-02970, TIC 08001 from the Andalusian Government. First author acknowledges a FPU scholarship from Spanish Ministry of Education.

# References

1. Agmon, N., Kraus, S., Kaminka, G.: Multi-robot perimeter patrol in adversarial settings. In: Proc. of the IEEE Conf. on Robotics and Automation, pp. 2339–2345 (2008)
2. Amigoni, F., Basilico, N., Gatti, N.: Finding the optimal strategies for robotic patrolling with adversaries in topologically-represented environments. In: Proc. of the IEEE Conf. on Robotics and Automation, pp. 819–824 (2009)
3. Amigoni, F., Basilico, N., Gatti, N., Saporiti, A., Troiani, S.: Moving Game Theoretical Patrolling Strategies from Theory to Practice: an USARSim Simulation. In: Proc. of the IEEE Conf. on Robotics and Automation, pp. 426–431 (2010)
4. Basilico, N., Gatti, N., Rossi, T.: Capturing augmented sensing capabilities and intrusion delay in patrolling-intrusion games. In: Proc. of the 5th Int. Conf. on Computational Intelligence and Games, pp. 186–193 (2009)
5. Osborne, M., Rubinstein, A.: A Course in Game Theory. MIT Press, Cambridge (1994)
6. Paruchuri, P., Pearce, J., Tambe, M., Ordonez, F., Kraus, S.: An efficient heuristic approach for security against multiple adversaries. In: Proc. of the 6th Int. Conf. on Autonomous Agents and Multiagent Systems, pp. 311–318 (2007)
7. Pelta, D., Yager, R.: On the conflict between inducing confusion and attaining payoff in adversarial decision making. Information Sciences 179, 33–40 (2009)
8. Villacorta, P.J., Pelta, D.A.: Theoretical analysis of expected payoff in an adversarial domain. Information Sciences 186(1), 93–104 (2012)
9. Villacorta, P., Pelta, D.: Expected payoff analysis of dynamic mixed strategies in an adversarial domain. In: Proc. of the IEEE Symposium on Intelligent Agents (IA 2011). IEEE Symposium Series on Computational Intelligence, pp. 116–122 (2011)

# General Information for the Union
# of Not Disjoint Fuzzy Sets

Doretta Vivona[1] and Maria Divari[2]

[1] Sapienza Universitá di Roma, Dip.SBAI, v.A.Scarpa n.16, 00161 Roma, Italy
doretta.vivona@uniroma1.it
[2] Sapienza Universitá, v.Borgorose, 00189 Roma, Italy
maria.divari@alice.it

*Dedicated to the memory of Prof.P.Benvenuti*

**Abstract.** The aim of this paper is to propose a class of general information for the union of not disjoint sets.

## 1 Introduction

In 1990 P.Benvenuti and ourselves introduced the general information for fuzzy sets [2]. We applied this information to many problems [3, 4]. After Benvenuti's death, we continued these researches also in different cases [8, 10, 11]. We call *compositive* those sets which are disjoint [9, 12].

We turn to consider fuzzy sets which are not disjoint. For the union of these sets, we shall propose a general information, solving a system of functional equations [1].

In the Sect. 2 and 3 we shall give some preliminaires and we shall present the statement of the problem and its solution, respectively. Section 4 is devoted to the conclusion.

## 2 Preliminaires

Let $\Omega$ be an abstract space, a $\sigma$-algebra $\mathcal{F}$ of not empty fuzzy sets $F$ [13], such that $(X, \mathcal{F})$ is measurable.

In [2] we considered the *measure of general information* as a map

$$J(\cdot) : \mathcal{F} \to [0, +\infty]$$

such that:
(i) $\quad F \supset F' \Rightarrow J(F) \leq J(F')$ ,
(ii) $\quad J(\emptyset) = +\infty$ , $\quad J(\Omega) = 0$ .

For fixed $J$, we have proposed [2] that two fuzzy sets are $J-independent$ if, being $F_1 \cap F_2 \neq \emptyset$,
$$J(F_1 \cap F_2) = J(F_1) + J(F_2) .$$

S. Greco et al. (Eds.): IPMU 2012, Part IV, CCIS 300, pp. 539–541, 2012.

# 3    Statement of the Problem and Its Solution

Now we recall the properties of information of the union among not disjoint fuzzy sets $(F \neq \Omega)$.

$(I)\ J(F_1 \cup F_2) = J(F_2 \cup F_1)$ ,
$(II)\ J((F_1 \cup F_2) \cup F_3)) = J(F_1 \cup (F_2 \cup F_3)) = J(F_1 \cup F_3) \cup F_2), F_1 \cap F_2 \neq \emptyset, F_2 \cap F_3 \neq \emptyset, F_3 \cap F_1 \neq \emptyset, F_1 \cap F_2 \cap F_3 \neq \emptyset$ ,
$(III)\ F_1' \supset F_1 \Rightarrow J(F_1' \cup F_2) \leq J(F_1 \cup F_2)$ ,
$(IV)\ J(F_1 \cup F_2) \leq J(F_1) \wedge J(F_2)$ .

We suppose that $J(F_1 \cap F_2)$ influences $J(F_1 \cup F_2)$, for this reason we are looking for a function $\Phi : D \to [0, +\infty]$ such that

$$J(F_1 \cup F_2) = \Phi \Big( J(F_1), J(F_2), J(F_1 \cap F_2) \Big) .$$

Now we specificate $D$.

Putting: $J(F_1) = x, J(F_2) = y, J(F_3) = z, J(F_1') = x', J(F_1 \cap F_2) = u, J(F_2 \cup F_3) = v, J(F_3 \cap F_1) = w, J(F_1' \cap F_2) = u', J(F_1 \cap F_2 \cap F_3) = t, x, y, z, x', u, v, w, u't \in [0, +\infty], x \leq u, y \leq u, y \leq v, z \leq v, x \leq w, z \leq w, x' \leq u', y \leq u', u \leq t, v \leq t, w \leq t$, we get that

$$D = \{(x, y, u) \in [0, +\infty] : x \leq u, y \leq u\} .$$

Now, we shall looking for the solutions of the following system of functional equations:

$$\begin{cases} (I')\ \Phi(x, y, u) = \Phi(y, x, u) \ , \\ (II')\ \Phi \Big( \Phi(x, y, u), z, \Phi(v, w, t) \Big) = \Phi \Big( x, \Phi(y, z, v), \Phi(u, w, t) \Big) \ , \\ (III')\ \Phi(x', y, u') \leq \Phi(x, y, u), \quad x' \leq x, x \leq u, x' \leq u', u' \leq u \ , \\ (IV')\ \Phi(x, y, u) \leq x \wedge y \leq u \ . \end{cases}$$

First of all, it is easy to prove that

**Proposition 1.** *A solution of the system is*

$$\Phi(x, y, u) = x \wedge y \wedge u = x \wedge y . \tag{1}$$

Second, we get the following:

**Proposition 2.** *A class of solutions of the system* $[(I') - (IV')]$ *is*

$$\Phi_h(x, y, u) = h^{-1} \Big( h(x) + h(y) + h(u) \Big) , \tag{2}$$

*where* $h : (0, +\infty] \to [0, +\infty)$ *is any decreasing function with* $h(+\infty) = 0$.

*Proof.* The properties $[(I') - (III')]$ are satisfied easily. Moreover, if $x \leq y$, it is $x \wedge y = x$, then $h(x) + h(y) + h(z) \geq h(x)$ and $(IV')$, is verified. □

*Remark 1.* In both cases we have obtained a generalization of the result given by Kampé De Feriét, Forte and Benvenuti in crisp setting [6, 7, 5] and by ourselves in fuzzy setting [2], when the (crisp or fuzzy) sets are disjoint.

## 4 Conclusion

In this paper, we have given some forms for the union of fuzzy sets when their intersection is not empty. These forms generalize classical results for the union of disjoint sets.

## References

[1] Aczél, J.: Functional equations and their applications. Academic Press (1966)
[2] Benvenuti, P., Vivona, D., Divari, M.: A General Information for Fuzzy Sets. In: Bouchon-Meunier, B., Zadeh, L.A., Yager, R.R. (eds.) IPMU 1990. LNCS, vol. 521, pp. 307–316. Springer, Heidelberg (1991)
[3] Benvenuti, P., Vivona, D.: Comonotone aggregation operators. Rend. Mat. VII, 323–336 (2000)
[4] Benvenuti, P., Vivona, D., Divari, M.: Aggregation operators and associated fuzzy measures. Int. Journal of Uncertainty, Fuzziness and Knowledge-Based Systems 2, 197–204 (2001)
[5] Forte, B.: Measures of information: the general axiomatic theory. R.A.I.R.O, 63–90 (1969)
[6] Kampé De Fériet, J., Benvenuti, P.: Sur une classe d'informations. C. R. Acad. Sc. Paris 269A, 97–101 (1969)
[7] Kampé De Fériet, J., Forte, B.: Information et Probabilité. C. R. Acad. Sc. Paris 265, 110–114, 142–146, 350–353 (1967)
[8] Vivona, D., Divari, M.: A collector for information without probability in a fuzzy setting. Kybernetika 41, 389–396 (2005)
[9] Vivona, D., Divari, M.: Entropies of fuzzy compositive partitions. In: Proc. IPMU 2006 Congress, pp. 1811–1815 (2005)
[10] Vivona, D., Divari, M.: Fuzzy Measures: Collectors of Entropies. In: Masulli, F., Mitra, S., Pasi, G. (eds.) WILF 2007. LNCS (LNAI), vol. 4578, pp. 285–290. Springer, Heidelberg (2007)
[11] Vivona, D., Divari, M.: Conditional entropy for the union of fuzzy and crisp partitions. In: Proc. EUSFLAT 2007, pp. 169–173 (2007)
[12] Vivona, D., Divari, M.: Measures of local entropies for compositive fuzzy partitions. Int. Journal of Uncertainty, Fuzziness and Knowledge-Based Systems 19(4), 717–728 (2011)
[13] Zadeh, L.A.: Fuzzy sets. Inf. and Control 8, 338–353 (1965)

# A Note on Decomposition Integrals

Andrea Stupňanová

Department of Mathematics, Slovak University of Technology, Radlinského 11,
813 68 Bratislava, Slovak Republic
andrea.stupnanova@stuba.sk

**Abstract.** Based on the idea of the decomposition integral proposed by Event and Lehrer, we introduce a new type of integrals. Moreover, we study the classes of measures turning inequalities (or incomparability) between special integrals such as Shilkret, Choquet, concave etc. integrals, into equalities.

**Keywords:** Choquet integral, concave integral, decomposition integral, supermodular measure, unanimity game.

## 1 Introduction

Among several kinds of integrals introduced to deal with monotone measures (i.e., not necessarily additive measures), we focus on those which are related to the basic arithmetic operations of summation $+$ and multiplication $\cdot$. Obviously, these two operations are the background of the classical Riemann and Lebesgue integrals, as well, and thus the discussed integrals can be seen as a generalization of those two classical integrals. All discussed integrals belong to the decomposition integrals recently proposed by Event and Lehrer [2], and some of them go beyond the framework of universal integrals introduced by Klement at al. in [4]. Note that we can introduce a structure of a lattice on the class of decomposition integrals, with the bottom being the Shilkret integral [7] and the top being the concave integral introduced by Lehrer [5]. Up to integrals well known from the literature, we introduce a new type of integral, the PC integral $I_{PC}$, which in the above mentioned lattice structure can be seen as an upper boundary of the PAN integral and the Choquet integral. Moreover, we study the conditions on monotone measures turning the inequality (incomparability) between single discussed integrals into equality.

The paper is organized as follows. In Section 2, four integrals well known from the literature are recalled. Section 3 recalls the decomposition integral introduced in [2] and brings a proposal of PC integral. In Section 4, we study the conditions on measures ensuring the equality of single integrals discussed in Section 3. Finally, some concluding remarks are added.

## 2 Well-Known Integrals

Let $(X, \mathcal{A})$ be a measurable space, i.e. $X$ is non-empty set and $\mathcal{A}$ is a $\sigma$ - algebra of subsets of $X$. A *measure* $m$ is a non-decreasing set function $m : \mathcal{A} \to [0, 1]$

S. Greco et al. (Eds.): IPMU 2012, Part IV, CCIS 300, pp. 542–548, 2012.
© Springer-Verlag Berlin Heidelberg 2012

satisfying $m(\emptyset) = 0$ and $m(X) = 1$. Each set and function $f : X \to [0, \infty[$ considered in the subsequent text is considered to be measurable. The next four integrals are well known from the literature, so far.

1. SHILKRET 1971 [7]

$$I_{Sh}(m, f) = \sup_{a \in [0, \infty[} \{a \cdot m(f \geqslant a)\}$$

2. YANG 1983 (PAN integral) [8]

$$I_{PAN}(m, f) = \sup \left\{ \sum_{i \in J} a_i \cdot m(A_i) \, \middle| \, J \text{ finite}, \sum_{i \in J} a_i \cdot 1_{A_i} \leqslant f, (A_i)_{i \in J} \text{ a disjunctive system} \right\},$$

if $m$ is a $\sigma$- additive measure we get the LEBESGUE integral (1902).

3. CHOQUET 1953 [1]

$$I_{Ch}(m, f) = \int_0^\infty m(f \geqslant a) da$$

4. LEHRER 2009 (the concave integral) [5]

$$I_L(m, f) = \sup \left\{ \sum_{i \in J} a_i \cdot m(A_i) \, \middle| \, J \text{ finite}, \sum_{i \in J} a_i \cdot 1_{A_i} \leqslant f \right\}$$

## 3    The PC Integral

Our paper is based on the idea of the decomposition integral introduced in [2]. Consider *a basic function* $b(a, A) : X \to [0, \infty[$ given by

$$b(a, A)(x) = \begin{cases} a, & \text{if } x \in A \\ 0, & \text{elsewhere} \end{cases} = a \cdot 1_A.$$

Let $\mathcal{H}$ be a system of some finite set systems H (we always assume the measurability of considered sets).

**Definition 1.** *Consider a measurable function* $f : X \to [0, \infty[$. *Each simple function* $s = \sum b(a_i, A_i)$ *(a finite sum of basic functions) such that* $(A_1, \ldots, A_n) \in \mathcal{H}$ *and* $s \leqslant f$ *will be called an $\mathcal{H}$-sub-decomposition of* $f$.

**Definition 2.** *Let* $(X, \mathcal{A})$ *be a measurable space and* $m$ *be a measure. Consider a measurable function* $f : X \to [0, \infty[$, *then the integral* $I_{\mathcal{H}}$ *with respect to the system* $\mathcal{H}$ *of some finite set systems is defined by*

$$I_{\mathcal{H}}(m, f) = \sup \left\{ \sum a_i \cdot m(A_i) \, \middle| \, \sum b(a_i, A_i) = s, s \text{ is an $\mathcal{H}$-sub-decomposition of } f \right\}.$$

*This integral is called an $\mathcal{H}$- integral.*

**Definition 3.** *Special types of systems $\mathcal{H}$ will be denoted as follows:*

*i)* $\mathcal{H}_1$: $H = (A)$, $\forall A \in \mathcal{A}$.

*ii)* $\mathcal{H}_2$: $H = (A_1, \ldots, A_n)$, $n \in \mathbb{N}, A_i \in \mathcal{A}$, $i = 1, \ldots n$ *such that* $A_i \cap A_j = \emptyset$ *if* $i \neq j$.

*iii)* $\mathcal{H}_3$: $H = (A_1, \ldots, A_n)$, $n \in \mathbb{N}, A_i \in \mathcal{A}$, $i = 1, \ldots n$ *such that* $A_1 \supset A_2 \supset \cdots \supset A_n$.

*iv)* $\mathcal{H}_4$: $H = (A_1, \ldots, A_n)$, $n \in \mathbb{N}, A_i \in \mathcal{A}$, $i = 1, \ldots n$ *such that* $A_i \cap A_j \in \{\emptyset, A_i, A_j\}$.

*v)* $\mathcal{H}_5$: $H = (A_1, \ldots, A_n)$, $n \in \mathbb{N}, A_i \in \mathcal{A}$, $i = 1, \ldots n$.

Observe that the class $\mathbb{H}$ of all systems $\mathcal{H}$ (for a fixed measurable space $(X, \mathcal{A})$), such that each $A \in \mathcal{A}$ is contained in some $H \in \mathcal{H}$, forms a lattice equipped with the standard ordering. Then $\mathcal{H}_1$ is the bottom element and $\mathcal{H}_5$ is the top element of $\mathbb{H}$. The next relations are obvious:

$$\mathcal{H}_1 \subset \mathcal{H}_2, \mathcal{H}_1 \subset \mathcal{H}_3, \mathcal{H}_2 \cup \mathcal{H}_3 \subseteq \mathcal{H}_4 \subset \mathcal{H}_5 \tag{1}$$

**Proposition 1.** *For single systems $\mathcal{H}_i$ introduced in Definition 3 we obtain the subsequent $\mathcal{H}_i$ - integrals:*

$\diamond$ $I_{\mathcal{H}_1}(m, f) = \sup\{a \cdot m(A) | a \cdot 1_A \leqslant f\} = I_{Sh}(m, f)$    SHILKRET INTEGRAL

$\diamond$ $I_{\mathcal{H}_2} = I_{PAN}$    PAN INTEGRAL

$\diamond$ $I_{\mathcal{H}_3}(m, f) = \sup\left\{\sum a_i \cdot m(A_i) \mid \sum a_i \cdot 1_{A_i} \leqslant f, (A_i) \text{ a chain}\right\} = I_{Ch}(m, f)$    CHOQUET INTEGRAL

$\diamond$ $I_{\mathcal{H}_5} = I_L$    LEHRER INTEGRAL

**Definition 4.** *Let $(X, \mathcal{A})$ be a measurable space and $m$ be a measure. Consider a measurable function $f : X \to [0, \infty[$, then the integral $I_{PC}$ with respect to the system $\mathcal{H}_4$ is defined by*

$$I_{PC}(m, f) = \sup\left\{\sum a_i \cdot m(A_i) \middle| \sum b(a_i, A_i) = s, s \text{ is an } \mathcal{H}_4\text{-sub-decomposition of } f\right\}. \tag{2}$$

*This integral is called a PC integral.*

From (1) we get the following inequalities (see Fig. 1)

$$I_{Sh} \leqslant I_{PAN}, I_{Sh} \leqslant I_{Ch}, \quad I_{Ch} \vee I_{PAN} \leqslant I_{PC} \leqslant I_L. \tag{3}$$

*Example 1.* Let X = {1,2,3}, $f(1) = 8$, $f(2) = 3$, $f(3) = 6$. Let

| A | $\emptyset$ | {1} | {2} | {3} | {1,2} | {2,3} | {1,3} | {1,2,3} |
|---|---|---|---|---|---|---|---|---|
| m | 0 | 0,2 | 0,3 | 0,4 | 1 | 1 | 1 | 1 |

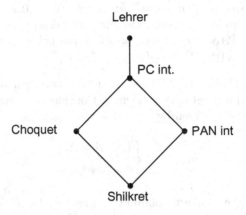

**Fig. 1.**

1. (SHILKRET INTEGRAL)
   $I_{Sh}(m, f) = (3 \cdot m(\{1, 2, 3\})) \bigvee (6 \cdot m(\{1, 3\})) \bigvee (8 \cdot m(\{1\})) = 6$
2. (PAN INTEGRAL)
   $I_{PAN}(m, f) = (8 \cdot m(\{1\}) + 3 \cdot m(\{2\}) + 6 \cdot m(\{3\})) \bigvee (8 \cdot m(\{1\}) + 3 \cdot m(\{2, 3\})) \bigvee$
   $\bigvee (3 \cdot m(\{2\}) + 6 \cdot m(\{1, 3\})) \bigvee (6 \cdot m(\{3\}) + 3 \cdot m(\{1, 2\})) \bigvee (3 \cdot m(\{1, 2, 3\})) =$
   $0, 9 + 6 = 6, 9$
3. (CHOQUET INTEGRAL)
   $I_{Ch}(m, f) = 3 \cdot m(\{1, 2, 3\}) + (6 - 3) \cdot m(\{1, 3\}) + (8 - 6) \cdot m(\{1\}) = 3 + 3 +$
   $+ 0, 4 = 6, 4$
4. (PC INTEGRAL)
   $I_{PC}(m, f) = 6 \cdot m(\{1, 3\}) + 3 \cdot m(\{2\}) + (8 - 6) \cdot m(\{1\}) = 6 + 0, 9 + 0, 4 = 7, 3$
5. (LEHRER INTEGRAL)
   $I_L(m, f) = 3 \cdot m(\{1, 2\}) + (8 - 3) \cdot m(\{1, 3\}) + (6 - 5) \cdot m(\{3\}) = 3 + 5 +$
   $+ 0, 4 = 8, 4$

# 4   Conditions for Equality of Integrals

For the sake of transparency, in this section we assume that the considered space $X$ is finite.

**Theorem 1 (Lehrer [5]).** *Consider a measurable function $f : X \to [0, \infty[$ and a fixed measure $m$. Then the following claims are equivalent:*

*i) The measure $m$ is supermodular, i.e., $m(A \cup B) + m(A \cap B) \geqslant m(A) + m(B)$ for all $A, B \in \mathcal{A}$.*

*ii) The Choquet integral coincides with the Lehrer integral for arbitrary function $f$, i.e., $I_{Ch}(m, f) = I_{PC}(m, f) = I_L(m, f)$.*

In what follows we focus our attention to the study of equalities (for a fixed measure $m$) of some of introduced integrals.

**Theorem 2.** *Consider a measurable function* $f : X \to [0, \infty[$ *and a fixed measure* $m$. *If the measure* $m$ *is subadditive, (i.e.,* $m(A \cup B) \leqslant m(A) + m(B)$ *for all* $A, B \in \mathcal{A}$) *then the PAN integral coincides with the Lehrer integral for arbitrary function* $f$, *i.e.,* $I_{PAN}(m, f) = I_{PC}(m, f) = I_L(m, f)$.

Observe that the subadditivity of the measure $m$ is only a sufficient condition ensuring $I_{PAN}(m, .) = I_{PC}(m, .) = I_L(m, .)$. Consider, for example, the weakest measure $m_* : 2^X \to [0, 1]$ given by

$$m_*(A) = \begin{cases} 1, & \text{if } A = X \\ 0, & \text{elsewhere,} \end{cases}$$

i.e., $m_* = m_X$ is the weakest unanimity game (see Definition 5). Obviously, if card $X > 1$ then $m_*$ is not subadditive. However, for each $f$ we have $I_{PAN}(m_*, f) = I_{H_4}(m_*, f) = I_L(m_*, f) = \min f$ (compare also Theorem 4 ).

*Example 2.* Let X $= \{1,2,3\}$, $f(1) = 8$, $f(2) = 10$, $f(3) = 3$. Consider a subadditive measure $m$:

| A | $\emptyset$ | {1} | {2} | {3} | {1,2} | {2,3} | {1,3} | {1,2,3} |
|---|---|---|---|---|---|---|---|---|
| m | 0 | 0,2 | 0,8 | 0,6 | 0,8 | 0,9 | 0,7 | 1 |

1. (SHILKRET INTEGRAL)
   $I_{Sh}(m, f) = 10 \cdot m(\{2\}) = 8$
2. (PAN INTEGRAL)
   $I_{PAN}(m, f) = 8 \cdot m(\{1\}) + 10 \cdot m(\{2\}) + 3 \cdot m(\{3\}) = 1,6 + 8 + 1,8 = 11,4$
3. (CHOQUET INTEGRAL)
   $I_{Ch}(m, f) = 3 \cdot m(\{1, 2, 3\}) + 5 \cdot m(\{1, 2\}) + 2 \cdot m(\{2\}) = 3 + 4 + + 1,6 = 8,6$
4. (PC INTEGRAL)
   $I_{PC}(m, f) = 8 \cdot m(\{1\}) + 10 \cdot m(\{2\}) + 3 \cdot m(\{3\}) = 1,6 + 8 + 1,8 = 11,4$
5. (LEHRER INTEGRAL)
   $I_L(m, f) = 8 \cdot m(\{1\}) + 10 \cdot m(\{2\}) + 3 \cdot m(\{3\}) = 1,6 + 8 + 1,8 = 11,4$

Based on the results from [4], observing that both Choquet and Shilkret integrals are universal integrals on $[0, 1]$, we have the next result.

**Theorem 3.** *Consider a measurable function* $f : X \to [0, \infty[$ *and a fixed measure* $m$.
*Then the following claims are equivalent:*

i) *The measure* $m$ *takes only the values zero and one, i.e., range* $m = \{0, 1\}$.
ii) *The Shilkret integral coincides with the Choquet integral for arbitrary function* $f$, *i.e.,* $I_{Sh}(m, f) = I_{Ch}(m, f) = \max\limits_{m(A)=1} \left( \min\limits_{x \in A} f(x) \right)$.

We recalled the next special measure.

**Definition 5 ([3]).** *Let $(X, \mathcal{A})$ be a measurable space and $A \in \mathcal{A}$. Then a measure $m_A : \mathcal{A} \to [0, 1]$ defined by*

$$m_A(B) = \begin{cases} 1, & \text{if } B \supseteq A \\ 0, & \text{elsewhere} \end{cases} \tag{4}$$

*is called an* unanimity game.

**Theorem 4.** *Consider a measurable function $f : X \to [0, \infty[$ and a fixed measure $m$. Then the following claims are equivalent:*

*i) The measure $m = m_A$ is the unanimity game.*
*ii) The Shilkret integral coincides with the Lehrer integral for arbitrary function $f$, i.e., $I_{Sh}(m, f) = \cdots = I_L(m, f) = \min_{x \in A} f(x)$.*

*Example 3.* Let $X = \{1,2,3\}$, $f(1) = 8$, $f(2) = 3$, $f(3) = 6$. Let

| $A$ | $\emptyset$ | $\{1\}$ | $\{2\}$ | $\{3\}$ | $\{1,2\}$ | $\{2,3\}$ | $\{1,3\}$ | $\{1,2,3\}$ |
|---|---|---|---|---|---|---|---|---|
| $m$ | 0 | 0 | 1 | 0 | 1 | 1 | 0 | 1 |

This measure is the unanimity game $m_{\{2\}}$. In this case

$$I_{Sh}(m, f) = I_{PAN}(m, f) = I_{Ch}(m, f) = I_{PC}(m, f) = I_L(m, f) = 3.$$

**Theorem 5.** *Consider a measurable function $f : X \to [0, \infty[$ and a fixed measure $m$. Then the following claims are equivalent:*

*i) The measure $m$ is an inner probability [6].*
*ii) The PAN integral coincides with the Choquet and the Lehrer integral for arbitrary function $f$, i.e., $I_{PAN}(m, f) = I_{Ch}(m, f) = I_{PC}(m, f) = I_L(m, f)$.*

Observe that $m : 2^X \to [0, 1]$ is inner probability whenever there is a disjoint system $(A_1 \ldots A_k)$ in $2^X$ such that $\sum_{B \subseteq A} (-1)^{\text{card}(A \smallsetminus B)} m(B) \neq 0$ if and only if $A = A_i$ for some $i = 1, \ldots, k$. Then

$$I_{PAN}(m, f) = I_{Ch}(m, f) = I_{PC}(m, f) = I_L(m, f) = \sum_{i=1}^{k} m(A_i) \cdot \min_{x \in A_i} f(x).$$

Note that additive measures and unanimity games are special instances of inner probabilities.

*Example 4.* Let an inner measure $m$ on $X = \{1,2,3\}$ has two focal element $A_1 = \{1, 2\}$ and $A_2 = \{3\}$ such that $m(A_1) = m(A_2) = \frac{1}{2}$. Then

$$I_{Sh}(m, f) = \max \left( \min \left( f(1), f(2), f(3) \right), \frac{1}{2} \cdot f(3), \frac{1}{2} \cdot \min \left( f(1), f(2) \right) \right),$$

while

$$I_{PAN}(m, f) = I_{Ch}(m, f) = I_{PC}(m, f) = I_L(m, f) = \frac{1}{2} \cdot \left( f(3) + \min \left( f(2), f(3) \right) \right).$$

# 5  Conclusion

We have introduced a new type of integral unifying both PAN integral and Choquet integral and we have studied conditions on measures assuring the equality of some of discussed integrals. For distinguished measures, closed formulas for single considered integrals were given, too. All discussed integrals have some interpretation in the real world problems. More detailed discussion and examination of properties and relationships of there integrals will be the topic our subsequent research.

**Acknowledgments.** The support of the grants VEGA 1/0171/12 and APVV–0073–10 is kindly announced.

# References

1. Choquet, G.: Theory of capacities. Ann. Inst. Fourier 5, 131–295 (1955)
2. Event, Y., Lehrer, E.: Decomposition-Integral: Unifying Choquet and the Concave Integrals, working paper
3. Grabisch, M., Marichal, J.-L., Mesiar, R., Pap, E.: Aggregation functions. Cambridge University Press, Cambridge (2009)
4. Klement, E.P., Mesiar, R., Pap, E.: A universal integral as common frame for Choquet and Sugeno integral. IEEE Transactions on Fuzzy Systems 18, 178–187 (2010)
5. Lehrer, E.: A new integral for capacities. Economic Theory 39, 157–176 (2009)
6. Lin, T.Y.: Belief functions and probability for general spaces. In: 2011 IEEE Int. Conference on Granular Computing, pp. 314–319 (2010)
7. Shilkret, N.: Maxitive measure and integration. Indag. Math. 33, 109–116 (1971)
8. Yang, Q.: The Pan-integral on the Fuzzy Measure Space. Fuzzy Mathematics 3, 107–114 (1985)

# Measures of Disagreement and Aggregation of Preferences Based on Multidistances

Tomasa Calvo[1], Javier Martín[2], and Gaspar Mayor[2]

[1] University of Alcalá,
Pza. San Diego, 28801 Alcalá de Henares (Madrid), Spain
tomasa.calvo@uib.es
[2] University of the Balearic Islands,
Cra. Valldemossa km 7.5, 07122 Palma, Spain
{javier.martin,gmayor}@uib.es

**Abstract.** This paper deals with measures of disagreement and aggregation of preferences. Multidistances are used as measures of disagreement and also as a key element in the definition of aggregation of preferences. After introducing contractive multidistances, they are shown to be particularly suitable for our purpose. Two families of multidistances are studied, and, in particular, those satisfying contractivity, homogeneity and generalized maximum dissension properties.

**Keywords:** distance, Kemeny distance, multidistance, contractivity, aggregation of preferences, measures of disagreement, Fermat preferences.

## 1 Introduction

Social choice theory, as William H. Riker points out, is the description and the analysis of the way that preferences of individual members of a group are amalgamated into a decision of the group as a whole. The problem of aggregating individual preferences into a collective choice was already made explicit by Condorcet in 1785 [3], but it is the seminal work of Arrow of 1950 [1] that is usually considered the starting point of modern reflection on collective choice. Recently, the problems raised by social choice theory have been also investigated from the point of view of logic and computation (computational social choice).

In the same field, consensus is related to the degree of agreement in a group. The problem of measuring the concordance or discordance between two preferences (modeled by linear orders) has been widely explored in the literature. In this way different rank correlation indices have been considered for assigning grades of agreement between two preferences. Recently, some natural extensions of that approach have been introduced for measuring the concordance or discordance among more than two linear orders. In 2005, Bosch [2] introduced the notion of consensus measure as a mapping that assigns a number between 0 an 1 to every profile of linear orders, satisfying three properties: unanimity, anonymity and neutrality. In this way, García-Lapresta et al [4] extend Bosch's notion of consensus measure to the context of preferences modelled by weak

S. Greco et al. (Eds.): IPMU 2012, Part IV, CCIS 300, pp. 549–558, 2012.

orders (indifference among different alternatives is allowed), and they consider some additional properties that such measures could fulfill: maximum dissension, reciprocity and homogeneity. They also introduce a class of consensus measures based on distances among weak orders induced by ordinary distances on $\mathbb{R}^n$.

In this paper, multidistances [6] are used as measures of disagreement and also as basic elements in the definition of aggregation of preferences. After the preliminaries, Section 3 is devoted to the introduction and study of the class of contractive multidistances, which are shown to be particularly suitable for our purpose. Measures of disagreement based on multidistances are introduced in Section 4, and, in Section 5, the treatment of aggregation of preferences based on multidistances is carried on. Finally, in Section 6 we illustrate some contents with an example.

## 2    Preliminaries

We recall here some definitions, properties and examples related to multidistances. For more details see [5,6].

**Definition 1.** *A function* $D : \bigcup_{n \geqslant 1} X^n \to [0, \infty)$ *is a* multidistance *on a non empty set* $X$ *when the following properties hold, for all $n$ and $x_1, \ldots, x_n, y \in X$:*

*(1)* $D(x_1, \ldots, x_n) = 0$ *if and only if* $x_i = x_j$ *for all* $i, j = 1, \ldots n$.
*(2)* $D(x_1, \ldots, x_n) = D(x_{\pi(1)}, \ldots, x_{\pi(n)})$ *for any permutation $\pi$ of* $1, \ldots, n$,
*(3)* $D(x_1, \ldots, x_n) \leqslant D(x_1, y) + \ldots + D(x_n, y)$,

*We say that $D$ is a* strong *multidistance if it fulfills (1), (2) and:*

*(3')* $D(x_1, \ldots, x_n) \leqslant D(x_1, \ldots, x_i, y) + D(x_{i+1}, \ldots, x_n, y)$, *for any* $i = 1, \ldots, n$.

*Remark 1.* If $D$ is a multidistance on $X$, then the restriction of $D$ to $X^2$, $D|_{X^2}$, is an ordinary distance on $X$. On the other hand, ordinary distances $d$ on $X$ can be extended in order to obtain multidistances.

These are two properties that multidistances may satisfy [5]:

– Regularity: $D(x_1, \ldots, x_n, y) \geqslant D(x_1, \ldots, x_n)$, for any $(x_1, \ldots, x_n) \in \bigcup_{n \geqslant 1} X^n$, $y \in X$. That is, the multidistance of a list cannot decrease when adding a new element.
– Stability: $D(x_1, \ldots, x_n) = D(x_1, \ldots, x_n, x_i)$, for any list $(x_1, \ldots, x_n)$ and any element $x_i$ of the list. In other words, repeated elements are superfluous regarding the value of the multidistance of a list.

Strong multidistances are regular and stable too.

**Definition 2.** *[7] Let $D$ be a multidistance on a set $X$. We will say that $D$ is* functionally expressible *if there exist a function* $F : \bigcup_{m \geqslant 1} (\mathbb{R}^+)^m \to \mathbb{R}^+$ *such that for all* $n \geqslant 2$,

$$D(x_1, \ldots, x_n) = F(x_1 x_2, \ldots, x_i x_j, \ldots, x_{n-1} x_n), \tag{1}$$

*where $x_i x_j$ stands for the distance $D(x_i, x_j)$, for all $1 \leqslant i < j \leqslant n$.*

*Example 1.* The following are multidistances which can be defined on any metric space $(X, d)$. Observe that all of them extend the ordinary distance $d$ and are functionally expressible.

– The *maximum* multidistance:

$$D_M(x_1, \ldots, x_n) = \max_{i,j:1,\ldots,n} \{d(x_i, x_j)\}. \tag{2}$$

It is a strong multidistance, hence regular and stable.

– The *Fermat* multidistance:

$$D_F(x_1, \ldots, x_n) = \inf_{x \in X} \left\{ \sum_{i=1}^{n} d(x_i, x) \right\}. \tag{3}$$

$D_F$ is a regular, non strong multidistance, and is maximum in the sense that any other multidistance $D$ such that $D|_{X^2} = d$ takes values not greater than $D_F$, i.e. $D(x_1, \ldots, x_n) \leqslant D_F(x_1, \ldots, x_n)$, for all $(x_1, \ldots, x_n) \in X^n$.
If $X$ is a *proper* metric space, that is, a metric space where closed balls are compact, then the infimum converts into a minimum. The points where it is reached are called *Fermat points* and the set of this points is the *Fermat set* of a list.

– The *sum–based* multidistances:

$$D_\Sigma^\lambda(x_1, \ldots, x_n) = \begin{cases} 0 & \text{if } n = 1, \\ \lambda(n) \sum_{i<j} d(x_i, x_j), & \text{if } n \geqslant 2, \end{cases} \tag{4}$$

where $\lambda(1) = \lambda(2) = 1$ and $0 < \lambda(n) \leqslant \frac{1}{n-1}$ for any $n > 2$. The multidistances of this family are not strong neither stable, and only $\lambda(n) = \frac{1}{n-1}$ gives a regular multidistance.

Balls centered at a list can be defined with multidistances.

**Definition 3.** *Given a multidistance $D$ and a list $(x_1, \ldots, x_n) \in \bigcup_{n \geqslant 1} X^n$, the closed ball with center $(x_1, \ldots, x_n)$ and radius $r \in \mathbb{R}$ is the set:*

$$B((x_1, \ldots, x_n), r) = \{y \in X : D(x_1, \ldots, x_n, y) \leqslant D(x_1, \ldots, x_n) + r\}. \tag{5}$$

*Remark 2*

1) If $n = 1$ and $r \geqslant 0$, the list reduces to a point $x$, and the ball is $B(x, r) = \{y \in X : D(x, y) \leqslant D(x) + r\}$. As $D(x) = 0$, $B(x, r)$ is an ordinary ball of the metric space $X$.
2) The closed ball centered at a list $(x_1, \ldots, x_n)$ and radius 0 is the set of points $x \in X$ such that $D(x_1, \ldots, x_n, x) = D(x_1, \ldots, x_n)$.
3) There exist non empty balls with negative radius if and only if $D$ is not regular.

## 3    Contractive Multidistances

Let $(X, d)$ be a non trivial $(|X| \geqslant 2)$ proper metric space.

**Definition 4.** *A multidistance* $D \colon \bigcup_{n \geqslant 1} X^n \to \mathbb{R}^+$ *is said to be* contractive *if for any $n$ and $(x_1, \ldots, x_n) \in X^n$ with $D(x_1, \ldots, x_n) > 0$ there exist $x \in X$ such that $D(x_1, \ldots, x_n, x) < D(x_1, \ldots, x_n)$.*

Let us observe that if $D$ is contractive then is not regular. Obviously the converse is not true. Fermat and Maximum multidistances are not contractive because they are regular.

The next proposition presents a characterization of the contractivity in terms of balls with negative radius.

**Proposition 1.** *A multidistance is contractive if and only if, for any $n$ and $(x_1, \ldots, x_n) \in X^n$ with $D(x_1, \ldots, x_n) > 0$, there exist a non empty ball centered at $(x_1, \ldots, x_n)$ with negative radius.*

*Example 2.* The arithmetic mean multidistance:

$$D_{AM}(x_1, \ldots, x_n) = \begin{cases} 0 & \text{if } n = 1, \\ \frac{2}{n(n-1)} \sum_{i<j} d(x_i, x_j), & \text{if } n \geqslant 2, \end{cases} \tag{6}$$

is contractive if and only if the following inequation has solution for any $x \in X$ (for all $(x_1, \ldots, x_n) \in \bigcup_{n \geqslant 1} X^n$ with $D(x_1, \ldots, x_n) > 0$):

$$\sum_{r=1}^{n} d(x_r, x) < \frac{2}{n-1} \sum_{i<j} d(x_i, x_j). \tag{7}$$

And it can be proved that if $f$ is a Fermat point of $(x_1, \ldots, x_n)$ then (7) holds for $x = f$.

As said before, Fermat multidistance $D_F$ is not contractive, but it can be multiplied by a convenient factor $\lambda(n)$, depending on the length of the list, in order to obtain contractive multidistances.

**Proposition 2.** *Let* $\lambda \colon \mathbb{N} \to (0, 1]$ *with* $\lambda(1) = \lambda(2) = 1$. *The function*

$$D_F^\lambda \colon \bigcup_{n \geqslant 1} X^n \to \mathbb{R}^+,$$

*defined by*

$$D_F^\lambda(x_1, \ldots, x_n) = \lambda(n) D_F(x_1, \ldots, x_n), \tag{8}$$

*is a multidistance extending $d$.*

We will say that $D_F^\lambda$ is a $\lambda$–*multidistance of Fermat*.

**Proposition 3.** *A $\lambda$-multidistance of Fermat $D_F^\lambda$ is contractive if and only if $\lambda(n+1) < \lambda(n)$ for all $n > 1$.*

An equivalent statement is the following.

**Proposition 4.** *A $\lambda$–multidistance of Fermat $D_F^\lambda$ is contractive if and only if for any non–constant list $(x_1, \ldots, x_n)$ the inequality*

$$D_F^\lambda(x_1, \ldots, x_n, f) < D_F^\lambda(x_1, \ldots, x_n)$$

*holds, $f$ being a Fermat point of $(x_1, \ldots, x_n)$.*

Contractive multidistances can be constructed from sum–based multidistances in a similar way.

We know that the function $D_\Sigma^\lambda \colon \bigcup_{n \geqslant 1} X^n \to \mathbb{R}^+$ defined by $D_\Sigma^\lambda(x_1, \ldots, x_n)$ $= \lambda(n) D_F \sum_{i<j} d(x_i, x_j)$, $\lambda \colon \mathbb{N} \to \mathbb{R}^+$ being a sequence with $\lambda(1) = \lambda(2) = 1$ and $\lambda(n) \leqslant \frac{1}{n-1}$ for all $n > 1$, is a multidistance extending $d$.

**Proposition 5.** *For a sum–based $\lambda$–multidistance $D_\Sigma^\lambda$, the following are equivalent.*

*i) $D_\Sigma^\lambda$ is contractive.*

*ii) $D_\Sigma^\lambda(x_1, \ldots, x_n, f) < D_\Sigma^\lambda(x_1, \ldots, x_n)$ for all $(x_1, \ldots, x_n)$ with $D_\Sigma^\lambda(x_1, \ldots, x_n)$ $> 0$, where $f$ is a Fermat point of $(x_1, \ldots, x_n)$.*

*iii) $\left( \frac{1}{\lambda(n+1)} - \frac{1}{\lambda(n)} \right) D_\Sigma^\lambda(x_1, \ldots, x_n) > D_F(x_1, \ldots, x_n)$.*

*Remark 3.* From the proof of the above proposition it can be deduced that if $D_\Sigma^\lambda$ is contractive, then the sequence $\lambda$ is strictly decreasing. But the converse is not true: the multidistance $D_\Sigma^\lambda$ with $\lambda(n) = \frac{1}{n-1}$ is not contractive.

The following result establishes a relation between $D_F^\lambda$ and $D_\Sigma^\lambda$.

**Proposition 6.** *The following inequalities hold, for a non constant list $(x_1, \ldots, x_n)$:*

$$\frac{n}{2} \leqslant \frac{D_\Sigma^\lambda(x_1, \ldots, x_n)}{D_F^\lambda(x_1, \ldots, x_n)} \leqslant n - 1 \tag{9}$$

**Proposition 7**

*i) A necessary but not sufficient condition for a multidistance $D_\Sigma^\lambda$ to be contractive is that the following holds, for any $n > 1$:*

$$\lambda(n+1) = \begin{cases} \frac{n}{n+2}\lambda(n) & \text{if } n \text{ is even,} \\ \frac{n+1}{n+3}\lambda(n) & \text{if } n \text{ is odd.} \end{cases} \tag{10}$$

*ii) A sufficient condition for a multidistance $D_\Sigma^\lambda$ to be contractive is that the sequence $\lambda$ verifies, for any $n > 1$:*

$$\lambda(n+1) < \frac{n}{n+2}\lambda(n). \tag{11}$$

*Example 3.* The following sequences satisfy (11):

i) The geometric progressions $\lambda = k^{n-2}$, $\lambda(1) = 1$, with $0 < k < \frac{1}{2}$.
ii) $\lambda(n) = \frac{4}{n^2}$.

# 4    Measures of Disagreement

Let us consider now a set of alternatives $A = \{1, \dots, m\}$, $m \geqslant 2$, and a set of voters $V = \{v_1, \dots, v_n\}$, $n \geqslant 1$. Each voter $v_i$ expresses his preference giving an ordered partition $P = (A_1, \dots, A_k)$ of the set of alternatives.

Let $\mathbb{P}$ be the set of the preferences. A preference $P \in \mathbb{P}$ can be represented as a matrix, the element $a_{ij}$, $i, j \in A$, being 1 if the voter prefers $i$ to $j$, 0 if $i, j$ are indifferent, or $-1$ if $j$ is preferred to $i$. With this representation the *Kemeny distance* between two preferences $P, P'$ is:

$$d_k(P, P') = \sum_{i<j} |a_{ij} - a'_{ij}|. \tag{12}$$

For a given preference $P$, its reverse ordered partition is the *inverse* preference, $P^{-1}$.

*Example 4.* The preferences

$$P_1 = (1, 234), \quad P_2 = (1, 4, 3, 2), \quad P_3 = (3, 1, 24),$$

ver the set of four alternatives $A = \{1, 2, 3, 4\}$, are expressed as ordered partitions. Their matrix and lattice representations can be seen in Fig. 1.

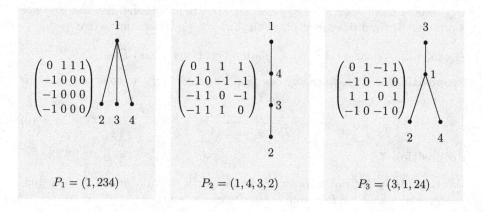

$P_1 = (1, 234)$        $P_2 = (1, 4, 3, 2)$        $P_3 = (3, 1, 24)$

**Fig. 1.** Preferences $P_1$, $P_2$ and $P_3$

The Kemeny distances are $d_k(P_1, P_2) = 3$, $d_k(P_1, P_3) = 4$ and $d_k(P_2, P_3) = 5$. Finally, the inverse preferences are:

$$P_1^{-1} = (234, 1), \quad P_2^{-1} = (2, 3, 4, 1), \quad P_3^{-1} = (24, 1, 3).$$

A profile is a vector of preferences $(P_1, \dots, P_n) \in \mathbb{P}^n$, where $P_i$ is the preference of the voter $v_i$. Over the set of profiles of any length $\bigcup_{n \geqslant 1} \mathbb{P}^n$, measures of disagreement can be defined in a similar way as the definition of measures of consensus given by Bosch [2].

**Definition 5.** *A function* $\mu\colon \bigcup_{n\geqslant 1} \mathbb{P}^n \to [0,\infty)$ *is a measure of disagreement if fulfills these three properties:*

*i)* $\mu(P_1,\ldots,P_n) = 0$ *if and only if* $P_1 = \ldots = P_n$ *(unanimity).*
*ii)* *A permutation* $\pi$ *of the voters does not change the measure of disagreement:*
$\mu(P_{\pi(1)},\ldots,P_{\pi(n)}) = \mu(P_1,\ldots,P_n)$ *(anonymity).*
*iii)* *A permutation* $\alpha$ *of the alternatives does not change the measure of disagreement:* $\mu(P_1^\alpha,\ldots,P_n^\alpha) = \mu(P_1,\ldots,P_n)$ *(neutrality), where for a given* $P = (A_1,\ldots,A_k)$, $P^\alpha = (\alpha(A_1),\ldots,\alpha(A_k))$.

*Example 5.* The permutation $\alpha(1) = 3$, $\alpha(2) = 1$, $\alpha(3) = 4$, $\alpha(4) = 2$ of the alternatives, applied to the preferences of Ex. 4, gives the preferences

$$P_1^\alpha = (3,124), \quad P_2^\alpha = (3,2,4,1), \quad P_3^\alpha = (4,3,12).$$

From now on, multidistances on $\mathbb{P}$ are supposed to be extensions of the Kemeny distance $d_k$.

**Proposition 8.** *Let $D$ be a multidistance defined on $\mathbb{P}$.*

*i)* *$D$ fulfills the properties of unanimity and anonymity.*
*ii)* *If $D$ is functionally expressible, then is neutral.*

So, functionally expressible multidistances can be used as measures of disagreement.
Other properties that measures of desagreement may satisfy are the following.

– Maximum dissension [4]: $D(P_1,P_2) \leqslant D(P,P^{-1})$, where $P$ is a linear preference and $P^{-1}$ its inverse.
– Generalized maximum dissension (*gmd* in short): $D(P_1,\ldots,P_n) \leqslant D(P,P^{-1})$.
– Homogeneity [4]: $D(P_1,\ldots,P_n,\ldots,P_1,\ldots,P_n) = D(P_1,\ldots,P_n)$. That is, the disagreement does not change if the profile is replicated.

*Remark 4.*

As we are applying multidistances $D$ extending the Kemeny distance, the maximum dissension property is $D(P_1,P_2) \leqslant d_k(P,P^{-1}) = m(m-1)$. It is fulfilled for any $D$.
ii) A *gmd* multidistance can be normalized: if we divided it by $m(m-1)$, we obtain a multidistance $D'$ which takes values in $[0,1]$.

We are going to focus on the two families of multidistances considered in Section 3, and how they fulfill the *gmd* and homogeneity properties.
With respect to the family of $\lambda$–multidistances of Fermat, the following can be established.

**Proposition 9.** *Let $D_F^\lambda$ be a $\lambda$–multidistance of Fermat.*

*i)* *$D_F^\lambda$ is gmd if and only if $\lambda(n) \leqslant \frac{2}{n}$ for all $n$.*
*ii)* *$D_F^\lambda$ is homogeneous if and only if $\lambda(n) = \frac{2}{n}$ for all $n$.*

The following result refers to the other family of multidistances considered in Section 3.

**Proposition 10.** *Let $D_\Sigma^\lambda$ be a sum–based multidistance.*

*i) If $\lambda(n) \leqslant \frac{2}{n(n-1)}$ then $D_\Sigma^\lambda$ is gmd. On the other hand, if $D_\Sigma^\lambda$ is gmd then:*

$$\lambda(n) \leqslant \begin{cases} \frac{4}{n^2} & \text{if } n \text{ is even}, \\ \frac{4}{n^2-1} & \text{if } n \text{ is odd}. \end{cases} \tag{13}$$

*ii) $D_\Sigma^\lambda$ is homogeneous if and only if $\lambda(n) = \frac{4}{n^2}$.*

# 5   Aggregation of Preferences Based on Multidistances

In this section it is shown how multidistances can be applied to the problem of choosing collective preferences which better fit the individual preferences of the voters.

**Definition 6.** *Let $D$ be a multidistance defined on $\mathbb{P}$, extending $d_k$. A function $\mathrm{agg}_D \colon \bigcup_{n \geqslant 1} \mathbb{P}^n \to \mathcal{P}(\mathbb{P})$, defined by:*

$$\mathrm{agg}_D(P_1, \ldots, P_n) = \{\overline{P} \in \mathbb{P}; D(P_1, \ldots, P_n, \overline{P}) \leqslant D(P_1, \ldots, P_n, P) \ \forall P\} \tag{14}$$

*will be called* aggregation of preferences *based on $D$.*

A useful notation is $\mathrm{agg}_D(P_1, \ldots, P_n) = \arg_{P \in \mathbb{P}} \min\{D(P_1, \ldots, P_n, P)\}$.

*Example 6.* Let $A = \{1, 2, 3\}$ be the set of alternatives. The set of preferences is

$$\mathbb{P} = \{ \ (1,2,3), (1,3,2), (2,1,3), (2,3,1), (3,1,2), (3,2,1),$$
$$(12,3), (13,2), (23,1), (1,23), (2,13), (3,12),$$
$$(123)\}.$$

Let us compute the aggregation of the preferences $P_1 = (1, 23)$ and $P_2 = (13, 2)$ using the multidistance based on the maximum.

$$\mathrm{agg}_D(P_1, P_2) = \{\overline{P} \in \mathbb{P}; D(P_1, P_2, \overline{P}) \leqslant D(P_1, P_2, P) \ \forall P \in \mathbb{P}\},$$

where $D = D_M$. We can observe that $P = (123)$ verifies $D(P_1, P_2, P) = 2 = D(P_1, P_2)$ and, as $D(P_1, P_2, P) \geqslant D(P_1, P_2)$ for all $P \in \mathbb{P}$ ($D$ is regular), we can say that $\overline{P} \in \mathrm{agg}_D(P_1, P_2)$ if and only if $D(P_1, P_2, \overline{P}) = 2$. That is, $\mathrm{agg}_D(P_1, P_2) = \{(12,3), (13,2), (123), (1,3,2)\}$.

*Remark 5*

i) If $D$ is regular and there exists $P_0 \in \mathbb{P}$ such that $D(P_1, \ldots, P_n, P_0) = D(P_1, \ldots, P_n)$ (for example if $D$ is stable), then $\overline{P} \in \mathrm{agg}_D(P_1, \ldots, P_n)$ if and only if $D(P_1, \ldots, P_n, \overline{P}) = D(P_1, \ldots, P_n)$. See Ex. 6.

ii) In this context of aggregation of preferences, contractive multidistances are desirable; that is, multidistances such that, for any non constant profile $(P_1, \ldots, P_n)$, there exists $P' \in \mathbb{P}$ with $D(P_1, \ldots, P_n, P') < D(P_1, \ldots, P_n)$. In this case, if $\overline{P} \in \text{agg}_D(P_1, \ldots, P_n)$, then

$$D(P_1, \ldots, P_n, \overline{P}) \leqslant D(P_1, \ldots, P_n, P') < D(P),$$

and so the preferences resulting from the aggregation of $(P_1, \ldots, P_n)$ strictly decrease the degree of disagreement among the voters.

General properties of the function $\text{agg}_D$ are the following.

**Proposition 11.** *the function* $\text{agg}_D$ *defined by (14) satisfies the following properties, for any multidistance D:*

*1)* $\text{agg}_D(P_1, \ldots, P_n) \neq \emptyset$.

*2)* $\text{agg}_D(\overset{n}{\overbrace{P, \ldots, P}}) = \{P\}$ *for any* $P \in \mathbb{P}$ *and* $n \geqslant 1$ *(unanimity).*
*3)* $\text{agg}_D(P_1, \ldots, P_n) = \text{agg}_D(P_{\sigma(1)}, \ldots, P_{\sigma(n)})$ *for any permutation* $\sigma$ *of* $1, \ldots, n$ *(anonymity).*

**Proposition 12.** *Let D be a contractive multidistance belonging to one of the families* $D_\Sigma^\lambda$ *or* $D_F^\lambda$, *and* $(P_1, \ldots, P_n)$ *a profile of preferences. A preference* $\overline{P}$ *belongs to* $\text{agg}_D(P_1, \ldots, P_n)$ *if and only if* $\overline{P}$ *is a Fermat preference of* $(P_1, \ldots, P_n)$.

# 6   An Example

Let us consider the set of alternatives $A = \{1, 2, 3, 4\}$ and five voters with preferences $P_1 = (1, 234)$, $P_2 = (1, 4, 3, 2)$, $P_3 = (3, 1, 24)$, $P_4 = (3, 14, 2)$ and $P_5 = (14, 23)$ (see Fig. 2).

To measure the degree of disagreement between the voters, two multidistances are applied. They are the homogeneous, *gmd*, contractive multidistances, belonging to each one of the families (4) and (8):

$$- D_1(P_1, \ldots, P_n) = \begin{cases} 0 & \text{if } n = 1, \\ \frac{4}{n^2} \sum_{i<j} d_k(P_i, P_j) & \text{if } n \geqslant 2; \end{cases}$$
$$- D_2(P_1, \ldots, P_n) = \begin{cases} 0 & \text{if } n = 1, \\ \frac{2}{n} \sum_{i<j} D_F(P_1, \ldots, P_n) & \text{if } n \geqslant 2. \end{cases}$$

Denoting by $d_{ij}$ the distance $d_k(P_i, P_j)$, we have $d_{25} = d_{34} = 2$, $d_{12} = d_{15} = 3$, $d_{13} = 4$, $d_{24} = d_{45} = d_{23} = 5$, $d_{14} = 6$ and $d_{35} = 7$. Hence, $\sum_{1 \leqslant i < j \leqslant 5} d_k(P_i, P_j) = 42$ and $D_1(P_1, P_2, P_3, P_4, P_5) = \frac{4}{5^2} 42 = 6.72$.

On the other hand, the Fermat multidistance is $D_F(P_1, P_2, P_3, P_4, P_5) = 14$ and so, $D_2(P_1, P_2, P_3, P_4, P_5) = \frac{2}{5} 14 = 5.6$.

If these values are divided by $m(m-1) = 12$, as explained in Remark 4, the corresponding *normalized* multidistances are $D_1' = 0.56$ and $D_2' = 0.47$.

The result of the aggregation is the same in both cases: the set of the Fermat preferences (see Prop. 12). In this case it reduces to the preference $(1, 34, 2)$:

$$\text{agg}_{D_1}(P_1, P_2, P_3, P_4, P_5) = \text{agg}_{D_2}(P_1, P_2, P_3, P_4, P_5) = \{(1, 34, 2)\}.$$

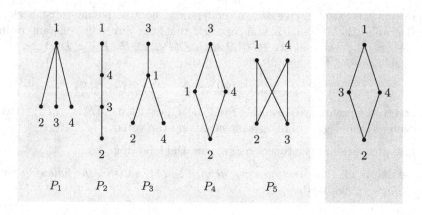

**Fig. 2.** The five preferences and the result of the aggregation

**Acknowledgments.** The authors acknowledge the support of the Spanish DGI grants MTM2009-10962 and TIN2009-07901.

# References

1. Arrow, K.J.: A Difficulty in the Concept of Social Welfare. The Journal of Political Economy 58, 328–346 (1950)
2. Bosch, R.: Characterizations of Voting Rules and Consensus measures. Ph. D. Dissertation, Tilburg University (2005)
3. de Condorcet, M.J.A.: Essai sur l'application de l'analyse à la probabilité des décisions rendues à la pluralité des voix. L'Imprimerie Royale, Paris (1785)
4. García-Lapresta, J.L., Pérez-Román, D.: Measuring Consensus in Weak Orders. In: Herrera-Viedma, E., García-Lapresta, J.L., Kacprzyk, J., Fedrizzi, M., Nurmi, H., Zadrożny, S. (eds.) Consensual Processes. STUDFUZZ, vol. 267, pp. 213–234. Springer, Heidelberg (2011)
5. Martín, J., Mayor, G.: Some Properties of Multi–argument Distances and Fermat Multidistance. In: Hüllermeier, E., Kruse, R., Hoffmann, F. (eds.) IPMU 2010. CCIS, vol. 80, pp. 703–711. Springer, Heidelberg (2010)
6. Martín, J., Mayor, G.: Multi–argument Distances. Fuzzy Sets and Systems 167, 92–100 (2011)
7. Martín, J., Mayor, G., Valero, O.: Functionally Expressible Multidistances. In: Proceedings of EUSFLAT–LFA 2011 (2011)

# Copula-Based Integration of Vector-Valued Functions

Erich Peter Klement[1] and Radko Mesiar[2]

[1] Department of Knowledge-Based Mathematical Systems
Johannes Kepler University, Linz, Austria
ep.klement@jku.at
[2] Department of Mathematics and Descriptive Geometry, Faculty of Civil Engineering
Slovak University of Technology, Bratislava, Slovakia,
and Institute of Theory of Information and Automation
Czech Academy of Sciences, Prague, Czech Republic
radko.mesiar@stuba.sk

**Abstract.** A copula-based method to integrate a real vector-valued function, obtaining a single real number, is discussed. Special attention is paid to the case when the underlying universe is finite. The integral considered here is shown to be an extension of $[0, 1]$-valued copula-based universal integrals.

**Keywords:** Capacity, Copula, Universal integral, Vector-valued function.

## 1 Introduction

The concept of universal integrals was proposed in [4]. As a particular case, $[0, 1]$-valued universal integrals were considered: these integrals assign to a measurable function $f\colon X \to [0, 1]$ a value from $[0, 1]$, and the measure under consideration is a capacity on the measurable space $(X, \mathcal{A})$. The case of $[0, 1]$-valued universal integrals based on some special(two-dimensional) copulas was proposed first in [2] in an attempt to find a natural link between Choquet and Sugeno integral. General (two-dimensional) copulas were considered in [3] (see also [4]).

We propose a copula-based integral for measurable functions with values in $[0, 1]^n$, i.e., for real vector-valued functions, with respect to some capacity, considering particularly the case of a finite universe.

## 2 Copulas and $[0, 1]$-Valued Integrals

Copulas were introduced in [6] in an attempt to describe the stochastic dependence within random vectors. Recall that, for a fixed $n \geq 2$, an $n$-dimensional copula $C\colon [0, 1]^n \to [0, 1]$ provides a link between the joint probability distribution $F_Z\colon \mathbb{R}^n \to [0, 1]$ of a random vector $Z = (X_1, X_2, \ldots, X_n)$ and the marginal probability distributions $F_{X_1}, F_{X_2}, \ldots, F_{X_n}\colon \mathbb{R} \to [0, 1]$ of the random variables $X_1, X_2, \ldots, X_n$ via

$$F_Z(x_1, x_2, \ldots, x_n) = C\left(F_{X_1}(x_1), F_{X_2}(x_2), \ldots, F_{X_n}(x_n)\right).$$

S. Greco et al. (Eds.): IPMU 2012, Part IV, CCIS 300, pp. 559–564, 2012.

**Definition 1.** An (*n-dimensional*) *copula* is a function $C \colon [0,1]^n \to [0,1]$ which is $n$-increasing, i.e., for each $n$-dimensional interval $[\mathbf{u}, \mathbf{v}] \subseteq [0,1]^n$ we have

$$V_C([\mathbf{u}, \mathbf{v}]) = \sum_{\mathbf{a} \in \{0,1\}^n} (-1)^{\sum\limits_{i=1}^{n} a_i} \cdot C(\mathbf{w_a}) \geq 0,$$

where

$$(\mathbf{w_a})_i = \begin{cases} v_i & \text{if } a_i = 0, \\ u_i & \text{if } a_i = 1, \end{cases}$$

and which satisfies the following two boundary conditions:

(i) 1 is a neutral element of $C$ in the sense that $C(u_1, u_2, \ldots, u_n) = u_i$ whenever $u_j = 1$ for all $j \neq i$,
(ii) 0 is an annihilator of $C$ in the sense that $C(u_1, u_2, \ldots, u_n) = 0$ whenever $0 \in \{u_1, u_2, \ldots, u_n\}$.

As a consequence, each copula is non-decreasing in each coordinate and 1-Lipschitz (with respect to the $L_1$-norm). The set of $n$-dimensional copulas is convex.

Prototypical examples are the greatest copula $M$ given by $M(u_1, \ldots, u_n) = \min(u_1, \ldots, u_n)$ describing comonotone dependence, and the copula $\Pi$ given by $\Pi(u_1, \ldots, u_n) = \prod_{i=1}^{n} u_i$ describing independence. Note that, in the case $n = 2$, the function $W \colon [0,1]^2 \to [0,1]$ given by $W(u_1, u_2) = \max(u_1 + u_2 - 1, 0)$ is the smallest copula, describing countermonotone dependence, i.e., for each two-dimensional copula $C$ we have $W \leq C \leq M$. If $n > 2$, no smallest copula exists, but still the $n$-ary extension of the associative copula $W$ provides a greatest lower bound for the set of all $n$-dimensional copulas.

Note that $n$-dimensional copulas are in a one-to-one correspondence with probability measures on the Borel subsets of $[0,1]^n$ with uniform margins. This correspondence is fully described by

$$P_C([0, u_1] \times [0, u_2] \times \cdots \times [0, u_n]) = C(u_1, u_2, \ldots, u_n).$$

For more details about copulas see [5].

Denote by $\mathcal{S}$ the class of all measurable spaces $(X, \mathcal{A})$. For a given measurable space $(X, \mathcal{A})$, let $\mathcal{F}_{(X,\mathcal{A})}$ be the set of all $\mathcal{A}$-measurable functions from $X$ to $[0,1]$, and $\mathcal{M}_{(X,\mathcal{A})}$ the set of all capacities $m \colon \mathcal{A} \to [0,1]$, i.e., the set of all monotone set functions $m$ satisfying the boundary conditions $m(\emptyset) = 0$ and $m(X) = 1$. Following [4], we can define $[0,1]$-valued universal integrals.

**Definition 2.** A function $\mathbf{I} \colon \bigcup_{(X,\mathcal{A}) \in \mathcal{S}} (\mathcal{M}_{(X,\mathcal{A})} \times \mathcal{F}_{(X,\mathcal{A})}) \to [0,1]$ is called a $[0,1]$-*valued universal integral* if it satisfies the following axioms:

(I1) $\mathbf{I}$ is non-decreasing in each component;
(I2) $\mathbf{I}(m, 1_E) = m(E)$    for each $(X, \mathcal{A}) \in \mathcal{S}$, $m \in \mathcal{M}_{(X,\mathcal{A})}$ and $E \in \mathcal{A}$;

(I3) $\mathbf{I}(m, c \cdot \mathbf{1}_X) = c$    for each $(X, \mathcal{A}) \in \mathcal{S}$, $m \in \mathcal{M}_{(X,\mathcal{A})}$ and $c \in [0, 1]$;

(I4) $\mathbf{I}(m_1, f_1) = \mathbf{I}(m_2, f_2)$    whenever $(m_1, f_1) \in \mathcal{M}_{(X_1,\mathcal{A}_1)} \times \mathcal{F}_{(X_1,\mathcal{A}_1)}$ and $(m_2, f_2) \in \mathcal{M}_{(X_2,\mathcal{A}_2)} \times \mathcal{F}_{(X_2,\mathcal{A}_2)}$ satisfy $m_1(\{f_1 \geq t\}) = m_2(\{f_2 \geq t\})$ for all $t \in [0, 1]$.

The special class of *copula-based* $[0, 1]$-*valued universal integrals* was proposed in [3] (see also [4]).

**Proposition 1.** *Let* $C \colon [0, 1]^2 \to [0, 1]$ *be a two-dimensional copula. Then the function* $\mathbf{I}_C \colon \bigcup_{(X,\mathcal{A}) \in \mathcal{S}} (\mathcal{M}_{(X,\mathcal{A})} \times \mathcal{F}_{(X,\mathcal{A})}) \to [0, 1]$ *given by*

$$\mathbf{I}_C(m, f) = P_C(\{(u_1, u_2) \in [0, 1]^2 \mid u_2 \leq m(\{f \geq u_1\})\})$$

*is a* $[0, 1]$-*valued universal integral.*

Observe that $\mathbf{I}_\Pi$ coincides with the *Choquet integral* [1], and that $\mathbf{I}_M$ is the *Sugeno integral* [7].

# 3  Vector-Valued Functions and Copula-Based $[0, 1]$-Valued Universal Integrals

For fixed $n \in \mathbb{N}$ and $(X, \mathcal{A}) \in \mathcal{S}$, let $\mathcal{F}_{(X,\mathcal{A})}^{(n)}$ be the set of all $\mathcal{A}$-measurable functions from $X$ to $[0, 1]^n$.

**Definition 3.** A function $\mathbf{I}^{(n)} \colon \bigcup_{(X,\mathcal{A}) \in \mathcal{S}} \left( \mathcal{M}_{(X,\mathcal{A})} \times \mathcal{F}_{(X,\mathcal{A})}^{(n)} \right) \to [0, 1]$ is called a $[0, 1]$-*valued n-universal integral* if it satisfies the following axioms:

(In1) $\mathbf{I}^{(n)}$ is non-decreasing in each component;

(In2) $\mathbf{I}^{(n)}(m, \mathbf{1}_E^{(n)}) = m(E)$    for each $(X, \mathcal{A}) \in \mathcal{S}$, $m \in \mathcal{M}_{(X,\mathcal{A})}$ and $E \in \mathcal{A}$, where $\mathbf{1}_E^{(n)} \colon X \to [0, 1]^n$ is given by

$$\mathbf{1}_E^{(n)}(x) = \begin{cases} (1, 1, \ldots, 1) & \text{if } x \in E, \\ (0, 0, \ldots, 0) & \text{otherwise}; \end{cases}$$

(In3) $\mathbf{I}^{(n)}(m, c^{(i,n)}) = c$    for each $(X, \mathcal{A}) \in \mathcal{S}$, $m \in \mathcal{M}_{(X,\mathcal{A})}$, $i \in \{1, 2, \ldots, n\}$ and $c \in [0, 1]$, where $c^{(i,n)} \in \mathcal{F}_{(X,\mathcal{A})}^{(n)}$ is given by $c^{(i,n)}(x) = (c_{1,i}, \ldots, c_{n,i})$ with $c_{i,i} = c$ and $c_{j,i} = 1$ whenever $j \neq i$;

(In4) $\mathbf{I}^{(n)}(m_1, f_1) = \mathbf{I}^{(n)}(m_2, f_2)$    whenever $(m_1, f_1) \in \mathcal{M}_{(X_1,\mathcal{A}_1)} \times \mathcal{F}_{(X_1,\mathcal{A}_1)}^{(n)}$ and $(m_2, f_2) \in \mathcal{M}_{(X_2,\mathcal{A}_2)} \times \mathcal{F}_{(X_2,\mathcal{A}_2)}^{(n)}$ satisfy $m_1(\{f_1 \geq \mathbf{u}\}) = m_2(\{f_2 \geq \mathbf{u}\})$ for all $\mathbf{u} \in [0, 1]^n$.

Evidently, this generalizes the concept of $[0, 1]$-valued universal integrals given in Definition 2 which are obtained here if $n = 1$.

**Theorem 1.** *For each $n \in \mathbb{N}$ and each $(n+1)$-dimensional copula $C$ the function* $\mathbf{I}_C^{(n)} \colon \bigcup_{(X,\mathcal{A}) \in \mathcal{S}} \left( \mathcal{M}_{(X,\mathcal{A})} \times \mathcal{F}_{(X,\mathcal{A})}^{(n)} \right) \to [0,1]$ *given by*

$$\mathbf{I}_C^{(n)}(m,f)$$
$$= P_C(\{((u_1,\ldots,u_n,v) \in [0,1]^{n+1} \mid v \le m(\{f \ge (u_1,\ldots,u_n)\})\})  \quad (1)$$

*is a $[0,1]$-valued $n$-universal integral.*

Observe that, because of the $\mathcal{A}$-measurability of $f$, the set

$$\{(u_1,\ldots,u_n,v) \in [0,1]^{n+1} \mid v \le m(\{f \ge (u_1,\ldots,u_n)\})\}$$

is a Borel subset of $[0,1]^{n+1}$, implying that $\mathbf{I}_C^{(n)}$ is well-defined.

**Proposition 2.** *Assume that for $f = (f_1, f_2, \ldots, f_n) \in \mathcal{F}_{(X,\mathcal{A})}^{(n)}$ the set*

$$\{\{f_i \ge t\} \mid i \in \{1, 2, \ldots, n\}, t \in [0,1]\}$$

*forms a chain. Then for each $m \in \mathcal{M}_{(X,\mathcal{A})}$ we have*

$$\mathbf{I}_\Pi^{(n)}(m,f) = \mathbf{I}_\Pi \left( m, \prod_{i=1}^n f_i \right),$$

$$\mathbf{I}_M^{(n)}(m,f) = \mathbf{I}_M \left( m, \bigwedge_{i=1}^n f_i \right).$$

# 4    Discrete Copula-Based $[0,1]$-Valued $n$-Universal Integrals

Given an $(n+1)$-dimensional copula $C$, the function $\mathbf{I}_C^{(n)}$ in (1) is a copula-based $[0,1]$-valued $n$-universal integral and, therefore, can be defined on arbitrary measurable spaces $(X, \mathcal{A}) \in \mathcal{S}$. In this section we consider finite sets $X = \{1, 2, \ldots, k\}$ only, and $\mathcal{A} = 2^X$. Then the function $h_{m,f} \colon [0,1]^n \to [0,1]$ given by $h_{m,f}(\mathbf{u}) = m(\{f \ge \mathbf{u}\})$ is a piecewise constant function, with constant values on some $n$-dimensional intervals determined by the function $f \colon X \to [0,1]^n$. The additivity of the probability measure $P_C$ allows us to obtain the following simplification of (1) in this discrete situation.

**Theorem 2.** *For each $n \in \mathbb{N}$, for each $X = \{1, 2, \ldots, k\}$, for each capacity $m \colon 2^X \to [0,1]$, for each $(n+1)$-dimensional copula $C \colon [0,1]^{n+1} \to [0,1]$, and for each $f = (f_1, f_2, \ldots, f_n) \in \mathcal{F}_{(X,\mathcal{A})}^{(n)}$ we have*

$$\mathbf{I}_C^{(n)}(m,f) = \sum_{i \in X^n} V_{D_i^{(m,f)}}([f_1(\sigma_1(i_1 - 1)), \ldots, f_n(\sigma_n(i_n - 1))]$$

$$\times [f_1(\sigma_1(i_1)), \ldots, f_n(\sigma_n(i_n))]),$$

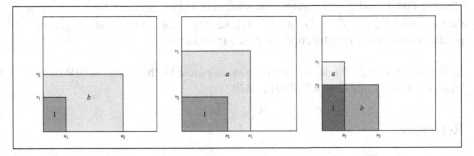

**Fig. 1.** The three cases in Example1: $f(1) \leq f(2)$ (left), $f(2) \leq f(1)$ (center), and $f(1), f(2)$ incomparable

*where the function $D_{\mathbf{i}}^{(m,f)} : [0,1]^n \to [0,1]$ is given by*

$$D_{\mathbf{i}}^{(m,f)}(\mathbf{u}) = C(u_1, \ldots, u_n, h_{m,f}(f_1(\sigma_1(i_1)), \ldots, f_n(\sigma_n(i_n)))),$$

*and, for each $j \in \{1, 2, \ldots, n\}$, $\sigma_j : X \to X$ is a permutation satisfying*

$$f_j(\sigma_j(1)) \leq f_j(\sigma_j(2)) \leq \cdots \leq f_j(\sigma_j(n)),$$

*using the convention $\sigma_j(0) = 0$.*

Observe that, in the case $n = 1$, the "vector" $\mathbf{i} = (i)$ has one column only, i.e., $D_i^{(m,f)}(u) = C(u, h_{m,f}(f(\sigma(i))))$. Subsequently, we get

$$\mathbf{I}_C^{(n)}(m, f)$$
$$= \sum_{i \in X} (C(f(\sigma(i)), h_{m,f}(f(\sigma(i)))) - C(f(\sigma(i-1)), h_{m,f}(f(\sigma(i))))),$$

which is exactly the formula for a discrete copula-based $[0,1]$-valued universal integral as discussed in [4].

*Example 1.* Consider $n = k = 2$, i.e., $X = \{1, 2\}$, a capacity $m : 2^X \to [0,1]$ determined by $m(\{1\}) = a$ and $m(\{2\}) = b$, and the product copula $\Pi : [0,1]^2 \to [0,1]$. For an $f = (f_1, f_2) \in \mathcal{F}_{(X, \mathcal{A})}^{(2)}$ the two values $f(1) = (u_1, v_1)$ and $f(2) = (u_2, v_2)$ can be either comparable or incomparable. In Figure 1 all three cases ($f(1) \leq f(2)$, $f(2) \leq f(1)$, and $f(1), f(2)$ incomparable) are visualized, the values inside the areas indicating the value of the corresponding function.

For the $\Pi$-based $[0,1]$-valued 2-universal integral $\mathbf{I}_\Pi^{(2)}$ we obtain

$$\mathbf{I}_\Pi^{(2)}(m, f)$$
$$= \begin{cases} u_1 v_1 + b(u_2 v_2 - u_1 v_1) & \text{if } f(1) \leq f(2), \\ u_2 v_2 + a(u_1 v_1 - u_2 v_2) & \text{if } f(2) \leq f(1), \\ a u_1 v_1 + b u_2 v_2 + (1 - a - b)(u_1 \wedge u_2)(v_1 \wedge v_2) & \text{otherwise.} \end{cases}$$

Observe that $f_1$ and $f_2$ are comonotone whenever $f(1) \leq f(2)$ or $f(2) \leq f(1)$, and then we have $\mathbf{I}_\Pi^{(2)}(m, f) = \mathbf{I}_\Pi(m, f_1 \cdot f_2)$, i.e., the standard Choquet integral of the product of the component functions of $f$ (see Proposition 2).

**Acknowledgments.** The second author was supported by the Grants APVV-0073-10, VEGA 1/0171/12 and GACR P 402/11/0378.

# References

1. Choquet, G.: Theory of capacities. Ann. Inst. Fourier (Grenoble) 5, 131–295 (1954)
2. Imaoka, H.: On a subjective evaluation model by a generalized fuzzy integral. Internat. J. Uncertain. Fuzziness Knowledge-Based Systems 5, 517–529 (1997)
3. Klement, E.P., Mesiar, R., Pap, E.: Measure-based aggregation operators. Fuzzy Sets and Systems 142, 3–14 (2004)
4. Klement, E.P., Mesiar, R., Pap, E.: A universal integral as common frame for Choquet and Sugeno integral. IEEE Trans. Fuzzy Systems 18, 178–187 (2010)
5. Nelsen, R.B.: An Introduction to Copulas, 2nd edn. Lecture Notes in Statistics, vol. 139. Springer, New York (2006)
6. Sklar, A.: Fonctions de répartition à $n$ dimensions et leurs marges. Publ. Inst. Statist. Univ. Paris 8, 229–231 (1959)
7. Sugeno, M.: Theory of fuzzy integrals and its applications. PhD thesis, Tokyo Institute of Technology (1974)

# Pseudo-concave Benvenuti Integral

Anna Kolesárová, Jun Li, and Radko Mesiar

Slovak University of Technology, Fac. of Chemical and Food Technology,
Radlinského 9, 812 37 Bratislava, Slovakia
School of Sciences, Communication University of China,
Beijing 100024, China
Slovak University of Technology, Fac. of Civil Engineering,
Radlinského 11, 813 68 Bratislava, Slovakia
{anna.kolesarova,radko.mesiar}@stuba.sk,
lijun@cuc.edu.cn

**Abstract.** Based on the relationship between the Choquet integral and concave integral recently introduced by Lehrer, we propose a new concept of a pseudo-concave Benvenuti integral. The relationship between this new integral and the standard Benvenuti integral is also studied.

**Keywords:** Benvenuti integral, Choquet integral, concave integral, monotone set function, pseudo-addition, pseudo-multiplication.

## 1 Introduction

Few years ago, Lehrer has proposed the concept of a concave integral [5,6] which in the case of supermodular (i.e. concave) measures coincides with the Choquet integral [2]. Both the Choquet and concave integrals can be seen as special instances of decomposition-integrals studied in [3]. Note that these integrals are built by means of the standard arithmetic operations $+$ and $\cdot$ on $[0, \infty]$. The Benvenuti integral was introduced and discussed in 2002 in [1]. It generalizes both the Choquet and Sugeno integrals. When a pseudo-multiplication with a neutral element is considered, then the Benvenuti integral belongs to the class of universal integrals recently introduced by Klement et al. in [4]. The aim of this contribution is to generalize concave integrals using as a background pseudo-arithmetic operations $\oplus$ and $\odot$ considered by Benvenuti et al. in [1], and to define a pseudo-concave Benvenuti integral.

The paper is organized as follows. In the next section, the original Benvenuti integral is recalled, as well as the Choquet, Sugeno and concave integrals. In Section 3, the concept of a pseudo-concave Benvenuti integral is introduced, and its connection with the standard Benvenuti integral is studied. Section 4 contains several examples and the last section brings some concluding remarks.

## 2 Benvenuti's Integral and Some Other Integrals

Let $(\Omega, \mathcal{A})$ be a fixed measurable space. A monotone set function $m \colon \mathcal{A} \to [0, \infty]$ is called a monotone measure whenever $m(\emptyset) = 0$. Recall that a monotone

S. Greco et al. (Eds.): IPMU 2012, Part IV, CCIS 300, pp. 565–570, 2012.

measure $m$ is supermodular whenever $m(A \cup B) + m(A \cap B) \geq m(A) + m(B)$ for all $A, B \in \mathcal{A}$.

For the convenience of the reader we repeat the relevant notions needed for introducing the Benvenuti integral which is based on two pseudo-arithmetical operations.

**Definition 2.1.** *Let $F \in ]0, \infty]$. A binary operation $\oplus : [0, F]^2 \to [0, F]$ is called a pseudo-addition on $[0, F]$ if the following properties are satisfied for all possible elements:*

(A1)  $a \oplus b = b \oplus a$  *(commutativity)*
(A2)  $a \leq a', \ b \leq b' \ \Rightarrow \ a \oplus b \leq a' \oplus b'$  *(monotonicity)*
(A3)  $(a \oplus b) \oplus c = a \oplus (b \oplus c)$  *(associativity)*
(A4)  $a \oplus 0 = 0 \oplus a = a$  *(neutral element)*
(A5)  $a_n \to a, \ b_n \to b \ \Rightarrow \ a_n \oplus b_n \to a \oplus b$  *(continuity).*

The axioms (A2)-(A5) ensure that a pseudo-addition $\oplus$ on $[0, F]$ forms an $I$-semigroup of Mostert and Shields [9]. The general form of the pseudo-addition is commutative. Although the commutativity of $\oplus$ follows from the remaining axioms, we prefer the definition with stated commutativity as in [1].

**Definition 2.2.** *Let $\oplus$ be a given pseudo-addition on $[0, F]$ and let $M \in ]0, \infty]$. A binary operation $\odot : [0, F] \times [0, M] \to [0, F]$ is called a $\oplus$-fitting pseudo-multiplication if the following properties are satisfied for all possible elements:*

(M1)  $0 \odot b = b \odot 0 = 0$  *(zero element)*
(M2)  $a \leq a', \ b \leq b' \ \Rightarrow \ a \odot b \leq a' \odot b'$  *(monotonicity)*
(M3)  $(a \oplus b) \odot c = a \odot c \oplus b \odot c$  *(left distributivity)*
(M4)  $(\sup_n a_n) \odot (\sup_m b_m) = \sup_{n,m} a_n \odot b_m$  *(left continuity).*

Note that we will follow the usual convention to the priority of operations, i.e., $a \odot c \oplus b \odot c$ means $(a \odot c) \oplus (b \odot c)$.

Let $a$ be any element in $[0, F]$, $A \in \mathcal{A}$. Recall that the basic function $b(a, A)$: $X \to [0, F]$ is given by

$$b(a, A)(x) = \begin{cases} a \text{ if } x \in A, \\ 0 \text{ otherwise.} \end{cases} \tag{1}$$

The formal definition of the Benvenuti integral based on $\oplus$ and $\odot$ (see [1], Definition 4.5), can be rewritten as follows.

**Definition 2.3.** *Let $F, M \in ]0, \infty]$. Fix a pseudo-addition $\oplus : [0, F]^2 \to [0, F]$ and a $\oplus$-fitting pseudo-multiplication $\odot : [0, F] \times [0, M] \to [0, F]$. Then for any monotone measure $m : \mathcal{A} \to [0, M]$ and any $\mathcal{A}$-measurable function $f : X \to [0, F]$, the Benvenuti integral $(B) - \int^\oplus f \odot dm$ is given by*

$$(B) - \int^\oplus f \odot dm = \sup \left\{ \bigoplus_{j \in J} a_j \odot m(A_j) \right\}, \tag{2}$$

*where $J$ is a finite set, $a_j \in ]0, F]$, $A_j \in \mathcal{A}$, $A_i \cap A_j \in \{A_i, A_j\}$ for all $i, j \in J$, and $\bigoplus\limits_{j \in J} b(a_j, A_j) \leq f$.*

Obviously, if we consider $M = F = \infty$, $\oplus = +$, $\odot = \cdot$, formula (2) recovers the Choquet integral, i.e.,

$$(B) - \int^+ f \cdot dm = (C) - \int f dm. \tag{3}$$

Note that an alternative form of the Choquet integral is

$$(C) - \int f dm = \int\limits_0^\infty m(f \geq t) dt,$$

where the right-hand side integral is the classical (improper) Riemann integral. Similarly, if we consider $M = F = 1$, $m(X) = 1$, $\oplus = \vee$, $\odot = \wedge$, formula (2) gives the Sugeno integral, i.e.,

$$(B) - \int^\vee f \wedge dm = (S) - \int f dm. \tag{4}$$

Note that an alternative representation of the Sugeno integral is

$$(S) - \int f dm = \bigvee_{t \in [0,1]} (t \wedge m(f \geq t)).$$

The concave Lehrer integral for measurable functions $f: X \to [0, \infty]$ introduced in [6] for a finite space $X$, and in [5] for a general space $X$, is given by

$$(cL) - \int f dm = \sup \left\{ \sum_{j \in J} a_j m(A_j) \right\}, \tag{5}$$

where $J$ is a finite set, $a_j > 0$, $A_j \in \mathcal{A}$ for all $j \in J$, and $\sum\limits_{j \in J} b(a_j, A_j) \leq f$. As it was shown in [5,6],

$$(cL) - \int f dm = (C) - \int f dm$$

for all measurable functions $f: X \to [0, \infty]$ if and only if $m: \mathcal{A} \to [0, \infty]$ is a supermodular monotone measure.

## 3    Pseudo-concave Benvenuti Integral

Inspired by Lehrer's modification of the Choquet integral, we propose the next modification of the Benvenuti integral, extending the original framework of Lehrer.

**Definition 3.1.** *Let $F$, $M \in ]0, \infty]$. Fix a pseudo-addition $\oplus: [0, F]^2 \to [0, F]$ and a $\oplus$-fitting pseudo-multiplication $\odot: [0, F] \times [0, M] \to [0, F]$. Then for any monotone measure $m: \mathcal{A} \to [0, M]$ and any $\mathcal{A}$-measurable function $f: X \to [0, F]$, the pseudo-concave Benvenuti integral $(pcB)$-$\int^{\oplus} f \odot dm$ is given by*

$$(pcB) - \int^{\oplus} f \odot dm = \sup \left\{ \bigoplus_{j \in J} a_j \odot m(A_j) \right\}, \tag{6}$$

*where $J$ is a finite set, $a_j \in ]0, F]$, $A_j \in \mathcal{A}$ for all $j \in J$, and $\bigoplus_{j \in J} b(a_j, A_j) \leq f$.*

It can be shown that the relationship between the Benvenuti integral and the pseudo-concave Benvenuti integral is similar to the relationship between the Choquet integral and the concave integral.

**Proposition 3.1.** *Let $m: \mathcal{A} \to [0, M]$ be a monotone measure. Then the Benvenuti integral and the pseudo-concave Benvenuti integral coincide, i.e., for each $\mathcal{A}$-measurable function $f: X \to [0, F]$ it holds*

$$(B) - \int^{\oplus} f \odot dm = (pcB) - \int^{\oplus} f \odot dm,$$

*if and only if $m$ is a $(\oplus, \odot)$-supermodular monotone measure, i.e., if and only if*

$$\alpha \odot m(A \cup B) \oplus \alpha \odot m(A \cap B) \geq \alpha \odot m(A) \oplus \alpha \odot m(B)$$

*for all $A$, $B \in \mathcal{A}$ and $\alpha \in [0, F]$.*

## 4    Examples

*Example 4.1.* Let $g: [0, F] \to [0, \infty]$ be an increasing bijection and define the operation $\oplus: [0, F]^2 \to [0, F]$ by

$$a \oplus b = g^{-1} \left( g(a) + g(b) \right).$$

Clearly, the operation $\oplus$ is a pseudo-addition. By Example 3.4 in [1], each $\oplus$-fitting pseudo-multiplication $\odot: [0, F] \times [0, M] \to [0, F]$ can be represented as

$$a \odot b = g^{-1} \left( g(a) \cdot \varphi(b) \right),$$

where $\varphi: [0, M] \to [0, \infty]$ is a nondecreasing left-continuous function satisfying the property $\varphi(0) = 0$. Then

$$(pcB) - \int^{\oplus} f \odot dm = g^{-1} \left( (cL) - \int g(f) d\varphi(m) \right), \tag{7}$$

i.e., the pseudo-concave Benvenuti integral is a transform of the standard concave integral. Obviously, if $F = M = \infty$ and $g = \varphi = id_{[0,\infty]}$, then

$$(pcB) - \int^{\oplus} f \odot dm = (cL) - \int f dm,$$

which means that in that case, the standard concave integral is obtained.

*Example 4.2.* Let $g\colon [0,F] \to [0,K]$, $K \in ]0,\infty[$, be an increasing bijection. Then the operation $\oplus\colon [0,F]^2 \to [0,F]$ given by

$$a \oplus b = g^{-1}\left(\min\{K, g(a) + g(b)\}\right)$$

is a pseudo-addition. Modifying Example 3.5 in [1], we obtain that each $\oplus$-fitting pseudo-multiplication $\odot\colon [0,F] \times [0,M] \to [0,F]$ can be represented as

$$a \odot b = g^{-1}\left(\min\{K, g(a) \cdot \varphi(b)\}\right),$$

where $\varphi\colon [0,M] \to \{0\} \cup [K,\infty]$ is a nondecreasing left-continuous function satisfying the property $\varphi(0) = 0$. Similarly as in Example 4.1, formula (7) gives the connection between this type of pseudo-concave Benvenuti integral and the concave integral.

For example, consider $M = F = K = 1$, $g = id_{[0,1]}$ and $\varphi\colon [0,1] \to \{0\} \cup [1,\infty]$ given by

$$\varphi(x) = \begin{cases} 0 & \text{if } x \le 0.5, \\ 2 & \text{otherwise.} \end{cases}$$

Let $X = [0,1]$, $\mathcal{A} = \mathcal{B}([0,1])$ and let $m$ be the Lebesgue measure on $\mathcal{B}([0,1])$. For any $p \in ]0,\infty[$ define $f_p\colon X \to [0,1]$ by $f_p(x) = x^p$. Then

$$(pcB) - \int^{\oplus} f_p \odot \mathrm{d}m = \min\{1, 2^{1-p}\}.$$

*Example 4.3.* Let $\oplus$ be the idempotent pseudo-addition on $[0,F]$, i.e., $\oplus = \vee$. Then for any $\vee$-fitting pseudo-multiplication $\odot\colon [0,F] \times [0,M] \to [0,F]$ it holds

$$(pcB) - \int^{\vee} f \odot \mathrm{d}m = (B) - \int^{\vee} f \odot \mathrm{d}m = \bigvee_{t \in [0,F]} \left(t \odot m(f \ge t)\right),$$

i.e., the pseudo-concave Benvenuti integral and the Benvenuti integral coincide. This fact also follows from Proposition 3.1, because any monotone measure is $(\vee, \odot)$-supermodular, independently of a $\vee$-fitting pseudo-multiplication $\odot$.

# 5  Concluding Remarks

We have generalized the concave Lehrer integral by means of the pseudo-concave Benvenuti integral. Note that following the original Lehrer's approach in [5,6], the concave integral can be introduced equivalently by means of special concave positively homogeneous functionals. As observed in [8], the concavity and positive homogeneity of such functionals is equivalent to the supermodularity and positive homogeneity. Therefore our next research will be focused on the introduction of pseudo-concave Benvenuti integrals by means of special $\oplus$-supermodular and $\odot$-homogeneous functionals.

**Acknowledgement.** The first author acknowledges the support of the project of Science and Technology Assistance Agency under the contract No. APVV–0092-11 and third author acknowledges the support of the project of Science and Technology Assistance Agency under the contract No. APVV–0073–10 and the project VEGA 1/0171/12.

# References

1. Benvenuti, P., Mesiar, R., Vivona, D.: Monotone set functions-based integrals. In: Pap, E. (ed.) Handbook of Measure Theory, vol. II, pp. 1329–1379. Elsevier Science (2002)
2. Choquet, G.: Theory of capacities. Ann. Inst. Fourier 5, 131–292 (1953-1954)
3. Even, Y., Lehrer, E.: Decomposition-Integral: Unifying Choquet and concave integrals (2011), http://www.math.tau.ac.il/~lehrer/papers/decomposition.pdf
4. Klement, E.P., Mesiar, R., Pap, E.: A universal integral as common frame for Choquet and Sugeno integral. IEEE Trans. Fuzzy Syst. 18(1), 178–187 (2010)
5. Lehrer, E., Teper, R.: The concave integral over large spaces. Fuzzy Sets and Systems 159, 2130–2144 (2008)
6. Lehrer, E.: A new integral for capacities. Econom. Theory 39, 157–176 (2009)
7. Mesiar, R., Li, J., Pap, E.: Pseudo-concave Integrals. In: Li, S., Wang, X., Okazaki, Y., Kawabe, J., Murofushi, T., Guan, L. (eds.) NLMUA 2011. AISC, vol. 100, pp. 43–49. Springer, Heidelberg (2011)
8. Li, J., Mesiar, R., Pap, E.: Discrete pseudo-integrals. Working paper (2011)
9. Mostert, P.S., Shields, A.L.: On the structure of semigroups on a compact manifold with boundary. Ann. Math. 65, 365–369 (1957)
10. Sugeno, M.: Theory of Fuzzy Integrals and Its Applications. PhD thesis, Tokyo Institute of Technology (1974)
11. Wang, Z., Klir, G.J.: Generalized Measure Theory. Springer, Boston (2009)

# An Economic Analysis of Coopetitive Training Investments for Insurance Agents

Mahito Okura[*]

Faculty of Economics, Nagasaki University, Japan
okura@nagasaki-u.ac.jp

**Abstract.** The main purpose of this research is to investigate the effects of market demand uncertainty in the coopetitive insurance market. To that end, we build a game-theory model including training investments of insurance agents in an insurance market with demand uncertainty.

We derive the following results from our analysis. First, insurance firms undertake less training investment if it is determined competitively by insurance firms. From this result, we show how some associations in the insurance market coordinate the amount of training investment and produce a higher amount of training investment. Second, we show how the effectiveness of coopetition becomes larger when demand uncertainty is larger. We confirm from that finding that realizing the coopetitive situation is more important if the demand uncertainty in the insurance market is large and that demand uncertainty is an important element in coopetition studies.

**Keywords:** Coopetition, Insurance agent, Game theory.

## 1 Introduction

It is well known that insurance can realize more efficient risk allocation and enhance efficiency. However, because insurance products are invisible and complex, some problems may be encountered. For example, individuals may purchase unnecessary and/or unsuitable insurance products because of their insurance agents' inappropriate activities.[1] Such activities lower consumers' confidence in insurance market, insurance firms, and the insurance industry. Thus, from the perspective of maintaining confidence, the training of insurance agents is one of the most important issues facing insurance firms.

In the real world, training of insurance agents is conducted not only by each insurance firm but also by the insurance industry as a whole. Thus, the insurance market contains both cooperative training and competitive sales systems. In other

---

[*] The author would like to acknowledge financial support by the Ministry of Education, Culture, Sports, Science and Technology in the form of a Grant-in-Aid for Young Scientists (B), 21730339 and 24730362.
[1] Okura (2009b) analyzed the relationship between insurance agents' sales effort and wage schedules by a principal-agent model.

S. Greco et al. (Eds.): IPMU 2012, Part IV, CCIS 300, pp. 571–577, 2012.

words, the insurance market is neither perfectly cooperative nor perfectly competitive, that is "coopetitive". Furthermore, every market, including insurance, has some kinds of uncertainty. For example, the amount of demand is changing every day. If the insurance market faces demand uncertainty, we examine how that affects the effectiveness of the coopetition in an insurance market. To answer the above question, this article builds a game-theory model that combines training investments for insurance agents in an insurance market with demand uncertainty.

The remainder of this article is organized as follows. Section 2 explains why game theory is a powerful tool for analyzing a coopetitive market situation. Section 3 builds the model and derives some results. Concluding remarks are presented in Section 4.

## 2   Methodology

A number of articles apply game theory to coopetition studies. For example, Brandenburger and Nalebuff (1996, 5–8) argue for the usefulness of game theory in understanding a coopetitive situation. Lado *et al.* (1997, 113) show how game theory explains behavior associated with interfirm relationships. Okura (2007, 2008, 2009a) argues that game theory can be a powerful tool to investigate coopetition. Pesamaa and Eriksson (2010, 167) describe how game theory can be a useful tool for analyzing and predicting actors' interdependent decisions. In coopetition studies, there are three advantages of use of game theory.[2]

First, game theory can analyze interactions between firms in an oligopolistic market. It is natural that coopetition cannot be realized in a monopolistic market. Also, we cannot consider coopetition in a perfectly competitive market because the definition of perfect competition precludes strategic choices. Thus, coopetition only arises in oligopolistic markets and game theory is the principal method used for analyzing that market structure.[3] Actually, the insurance market in many countries including Japan can be considered to be oligopolistic. For example, in the case of Japan's insurance industry, there are 83 insurance firms (43 life insurance and 40 nonlife (direct) insurance firms at the end of 2011), which means that game theory can be an appropriate tool to analyze an insurance market with coopetition.

Second, game theory is a rigorous analytical method. In particular, game theory is the primary tool for investigating a multistage process, because it can be treated as an extensive-form game, and the equilibrium of this game can be derived by the backward induction used to compute the equilibrium.

Third, game theory permits us to distinguish much more easily between the cooperative and competitive aspects in a coopetitive market. Coopetitive situations have a tendency to be complex because they contain elements of both cooperation and competition. However, game theory can be used to build a simple model by separating the cooperative and competitive aspects in a coopetitive market situation.

---

[2] The following explanations are a summary of the descriptions in Okura (2007).
[3] For example, Shy (1995, 11) argued that "[...] game theory is especially useful when the number of interactive agents is small."

## 3    The Model

Suppose that there are two insurance firms named insurance firm A and insurance firm B, respectively, in the market. They sell their insurance products through insurance agents. Our model develops the following three-stage game.

In the first stage, both insurance firms competitively decide on the amount of their training investments for insurance agents to maintain market confidence. $k_i$ represents the amount of training investment by the insurance firm $i$ for $i \in \{A, B\}$. The amount of training investment depends on the level that maintains the confidence of the insurance market. The investment function is quadratic and is assumed to be specified by $(1/2)k_i^2$.

In the second stage, the nature determines the situation with regard to confidence in the insurance market. There are three possible cases as follows. The first case can be called the "good" confidence case in which all (potential) consumers are credible to the insurance market. In this case, the form of the demand function is

$$p^G = a - q_A^G - q_B^G, \tag{1}$$

where superscript $G$ means the good confidence case, $a$ denotes the intercept of the demand function that represents insurance market size, $p$ represents the insurance premium, and $q_A$ and $q_B$ are the quantities of insurance products sold by insurance firm $A$ and $B$, respectively. The probability of realizing the good confidence case is $k_A k_B$. The second case is the "bad" confidence case. This case indicates that the activities of the insurance agents of either insurance firm tend to lower confidence in both of them. Although not all insurance agents choose inappropriate activities, it is assumed that (potential) consumers lose confidence not just in individual agents but in the whole insurance market. Thus, the demand function in this case is

$$p^B = \lambda a - q_A^B - q_B^B, \tag{2}$$

where superscript $B$ means the bad confidence case. $\lambda \in (0,1)$ represents the degree of lowering the confidence. In other words, the insurance market is diminished by insurance agents' inappropriate activities. The probability of realizing the bad confidence case is $k_1(1 - k_2) + k_2(1 - k_1)$. The third case can be called the "worst" confidence case. This case indicates that the insurance agents of both insurance firms actively lower confidence in the insurance market. The demand function in this case is

$$p^W = \lambda^2 a - q_A^W - q_B^W, \tag{3}$$

where superscript $W$ means the worst confidence case. The size of the insurance market reduces more than in the bad confidence case because $\lambda \in (0,1)$. The probability of realizing the worst confidence case is $(1 - k_1)(1 - k_2)$.

In the third stage, after both insurance firms observe which case is realized, they simultaneously decide the quantities of insurance products. At that time, the size of the insurance market, represented by $a$, has some uncertainty but is assumed to be distributed by the normal distribution function $N(\mu, \sigma^2)$, where $\mu \equiv E[a]$ represents the mean, and $\sigma^2 \equiv [(a-\mu)^2]$ represents the variance of the size of the insurance market.

Because each insurance firm takes its decisions in the first and third stages, we analyze these stages by backward induction.

First, we consider the third stage.[4] Both insurance firms can choose their quantities of insurance products in accordance with a demand function and its uncertainty. In the good confidence case, both insurance firms are assumed to be risk neutral and their profit functions can be written as

$$\pi_i^G = p^G q_i^G - \frac{1}{2}k_i^2 = \left(a - q_A^G - q_B^G\right)q_i^G - \frac{1}{2}k_i^2, \tag{4}$$

where $\pi_i^G$ represents the profit of insurance firm $i$ in the good confidence case.

From equation (4), we derive the equilibrium quantities of insurance products as

$$q_i^{G*} = \frac{a}{3} = \frac{\mu}{3} + \frac{1}{3}(a-\mu), \tag{5}$$

where the asterisk (*) means that value is the equilibrium value. Substituting equation (5) into equation (4), the equilibrium profit of each insurance firm shows that

$$\pi_i^{G*} = \left\{\frac{\mu}{3} + \frac{1}{3}(a-\mu)\right\}^2 - \frac{1}{2}k_i^2. \tag{6}$$

From equation (6), the equilibrium expected profit of each insurance firm is

$$E\left[\pi_i^{G*}\right] = \frac{1}{9}\left(\mu^2 + \sigma^2\right) - \frac{1}{2}k_i^2. \tag{7}$$

In the bad confidence case, the profit function of each insurance firm can be written as

$$\pi_i^B = p^B q_i^B - \frac{1}{2}k_i^2 = \left(\lambda a - q_A^B - q_B^B\right)q_i^B - \frac{1}{2}k_i^2, \tag{8}$$

where $\pi_i^B$ represents the profit of insurance firm $i$ in the bad confidence case. From equation (8), we derive the equilibrium quantities of insurance products as

$$q_i^{B*} = \frac{\lambda a}{3} = \frac{\lambda \mu}{3} + \frac{\lambda}{3}(a-\mu). \tag{9}$$

Substituting equation (9) into equation (8), the equilibrium profit of each insurance firm becomes

$$\pi_i^{B*} = \left\{\frac{\lambda \mu}{3} + \frac{\lambda}{3}(a-\mu)\right\}^2 - \frac{1}{2}k_i^2. \tag{10}$$

---

[4] The analysis in the third stage originates entirely from Sakai (1991, Chapter 3), which investigated broader cases such as the monopolistic information case.

From equation (10), the equilibrium expected profit of each insurance firm is

$$E\left[\pi_i^{B*}\right] = \frac{\lambda^2}{9}\left(\mu^2 + \sigma^2\right) - \frac{1}{2}k_i^2 . \tag{11}$$

Similarly, the equilibrium quantities of insurance products and expected profits in the worst confidence case can be derived as

$$q_i^{W*} = \frac{\lambda^2 a}{3} , \tag{12}$$

$$E\left[\pi_i^{W*}\right] = \frac{\lambda^4}{9}\left(\mu^2 + \sigma^2\right) - \frac{1}{2}k_i^2 , \tag{13}$$

where $\pi_i^W$ represents the profit of insurance firm $i$ in the worst confidence case.

Next, let us consider the first stage. The expected profit of each insurance firm in the first stage, which is denoted by $E[\Pi_i]$, can be written as

$$E[\Pi_i] = k_A k_B E\left[\pi_i^{G*}\right] + \{(1 - k_A)k_B + k_A(1 - k_B)\}E\left[\pi_i^{B*}\right] + (1 - k_A)(1 - k_B)E\left[\pi_i^{W*}\right]. \tag{14}$$

Substituting equations (7), (11), and (13) into equation (14), we obtain

$$E[\Pi_i] = \frac{\left[k_A k_B + \lambda^2\{(1 - k_A)k_B + k_A(1 - k_B)\} + \lambda^4(1 - k_A)(1 - k_B)\right]\left(\mu^2 + \sigma^2\right)}{9} - \frac{1}{2}k_i^2. \tag{15}$$

From equation (15), the optimal amount of training investment may be derived as

$$k_i^* = \frac{\lambda^2\left(1 - \lambda^2\right)\left(\mu^2 + \sigma^2\right)}{9 - \left(1 - \lambda^2\right)^2\left(\mu^2 + \sigma^2\right)} . \tag{16}$$

From equation (16), the equilibrium expected profit of each insurance firm is

$$E[\Pi_i^*] = \frac{\lambda^4\left(\mu^2 + \sigma^2\right)\left\{18 - \left(1 - \lambda^2\right)^2\left(\mu^2 + \sigma^2\right)\right\}}{2\left\{9 - \left(1 - \lambda^2\right)^2\left(\mu^2 + \sigma^2\right)\right\}} - \frac{1}{2}\left\{\frac{\lambda^2\left(1 - \lambda^2\right)\left(\mu^2 + \sigma^2\right)}{9 - \left(1 - \lambda\right)^2\left(\mu^2 + \sigma^2\right)}\right\}^2 . \tag{17}$$

To evaluate the equilibrium amount of training investment that is denoted in equation (16), the optimal amount of training investment when both insurance firms cooperatively choose their amount of training investment is derived by maximizing total expected profit, defined as

$$E[\tilde{\Pi}^*] = E[\Pi_A^*] + E[\Pi_B^*], \tag{18}$$

where tilde (~) means that value is derived in a cooperative training investments situation. From equation (18), the equilibrium training investment of each insurance firm are derived by

$$\tilde{k}_i^* = \frac{2\lambda^2 (1 - \lambda^2)(\mu^2 + \sigma^2)}{9 - 2(1 - \lambda^2)^2(\mu^2 + \sigma^2)}. \tag{19}$$

By comparing equations (16) and (19), it is easy to derive

$$\tilde{k}_i^* > k_i^*. \tag{20}$$

This equation (20) implies that both insurance firms choose a lesser amount of training investment when they are in competition. In other words, the equilibrium amount of training investment runs into the "prisoners' dilemma" situation because both insurance firms want to be free riders on their rival's training investment when acting competitively. To avoid realizing such Pareto-inferior outcome, it is better if each firm cooperatively chooses its training investments. Thus, in practice, insurance firms train their insurance agents not only for themselves exclusively, but in effect for all the other insurance firms. For example, Japanese insurance agents cannot sell some kinds of insurance products that are risky and complicated unless they have had some training and pass the examination required to demonstrate knowledge of the insurance laws and products. Such training for insurance agents is conducted by some insurance associations such as The Life Insurance Association of Japan and The General Insurance Association of Japan. Moreover, "educational activities" and "enhancement of quality of agents and solicitors" are listed in the activities of The Life Insurance Association of Japan and The General Insurance Association of Japan, respectively.[5] Thus, from the results of our analysis, these associations can be evaluated as "coordinators" seeking to avoid the prisoners' dilemma situation. Because both insurance firms in our model are clearly competitive in the third stage, the game including a coordinator contains both competitive and cooperative aspects. In other words, the existence of insurance associations promotes a coopetitive insurance market and increases incentives to raise training investments by all insurance firms.

Furthermore, we analyze whether such coopetition becomes more effective when demand uncertainty become large. To know how the effectiveness of coopetition changes in accordance with changes in demand uncertainty, we define the following measure, which represents the effectiveness of coopetition in the insurance market.[6]

$$\theta \equiv \frac{\tilde{k}_i^*}{k_i^*} = 1 + \frac{9}{9 - 2(\mu^2 + \sigma^2)(1 - \lambda^2)^2}. \tag{21}$$

In the equation (21), $\theta > 1$ is always satisfied, and means the effectiveness of coopetition is larger if $\theta$ is larger.

To investigate the effect of demand uncertainty on the effectiveness of coopetition, by partially differentiating equation (21) with respect to $\sigma^2$, we obtain

---

[5] These main activities can be confirmed from each association's website. See
http://www.seiho.or.jp/english/about/objective/ and
http://www.sonpo.or.jp/en/about/activity/ (accessed April 30, 2012).

[6] The following results are the same if the effectiveness of the coopetition in the insurance market is defined as $\tilde{k}_i^* - k_i^*$.

$$\frac{\partial \theta}{\partial \sigma^2} = \frac{18\left(1 - \lambda^2\right)^2}{\left\{9 - 2\left(\mu^2 + \sigma^2\right)\left(1 - \lambda^2\right)^2\right\}^2} > 0.$$

(22)

Equation (22) implies that effectiveness of coopetition in the insurance market becomes larger when demand uncertainty increases. This result shows that realizing the coopetitive situation is more important if demand uncertainty in the insurance market is large. From that perspective, we find that demand uncertainty is an important element in coopetition studies.

## 4    Concluding Remarks

This article considered training investments for insurance agents in terms of coopetition. We derived the following results from our analysis. First, insurance firms undertake less training investment if it is determined competitively by insurance firms. From this result, we showed how some associations in the insurance market coordinate the amount of training investment and produce a higher amount of training investment. Second, we showed how the effectiveness of coopetition becomes larger when demand uncertainty is larger. We confirmed from that finding that realizing the coopetitive situation is more important if the demand uncertainty in the insurance market is large. Also, we concluded that demand uncertainty is an important element in coopetition studies.

## References

1. Brandenburger, A.M., Nalebuff, B.J.: Coopetition. Doubleday, New York (1996)
2. Lado, A.A., Boyd, N.G., Hanlon, S.C.: Competition, Cooperation, and the Search from Economic Rents: A Syncretic Model. Academy of Management Review 22(1), 110–141 (1997)
3. Okura, M.: Coopetitive Strategies of Japanese Insurance Firms: A Game-Theory Approach. International Studies of Management and Organization 37(2), 5–69 (2007)
4. Okura, M.: Why Isn't the Accident Information Shared? A Coopetition Perspective, Management Research 6(3), 219–225 (2008)
5. Okura, M.: Coopetitive Strategies to Limit the Insurance Fraud Problem in Japan. In: Dagnino, G.B., Rocco, E. (eds.) Coopetition Strategy: Theory, Experiments and Cases, pp. 240–257. Routledge, London (2009a)
6. Okura, M.: An Analysis of the Unpaid Insurance Benefits Problem in Japan. Journal of Claim Adjustment 2(1), 135–150 (2009b)
7. Pesamaa, O., Eriksson, P.E.: Coopetition among Nature-based Tourism Firms: Competition at Local Level and Cooperation at Destination Level. In: Yami, S., Castaldo, S., Dagnino, G.B., Le Roy, F. (eds.) Coopetition: Winning Strategies for the 21st Century, pp. 166–182. Edward Elgar Publishing, Massachusetts (2010)
8. Sakai, Y.: The Theory of Oligopoly and Information. Toyo Keizai Shinposha, Tokyo (1991) (in Japanese)
9. Shy, O.: Industrial Organization: Theory and Applications. The MIT Press, Cambridge (1995)

# A Coopetitive Approach to Financial Markets Stabilization and Risk Management

David Carfì[1] and Francesco Musolino[2]

[1] University of California at Riverside, California, USA
davidcarfi71@yahoo.it
[2] University of Messina, Italy
francescomusolino@hotmail.it

**Abstract.** The aim of this paper is to propose a methodology to stabilize the financial markets by adopting Game Theory, and in particular the Complete Study of a Differentiable Game and the new mathematical model of Coopetitive Game, proposed recently in the literature by D. Carfì. Specifically, we will focus on two economic operators: a real economic subject and a financial institute (a bank, for example) with a big economic availability. At this purpose, we examine an interaction between the above economic subjects: the Enterprise, our first player, and the Financial Institute, our second player. The unique solution which allows both players to win something, and therefore the only one collectively desirable, is represented by an agreement between the two subjects. So the Enterprise artificially causes an inconsistency between spot and future markets, and the Financial Institute takes the opportunity to win the maximum possible collective (social) sum, which later will be divided with the Enterprise by contract. In fact, the Financial Institute is unable to make arbitrages alone because of the introduction, by the normative authority, of an economic transactions tax (that we propose to stabilize the financial market, in order to protect it from speculations). We propose hereunder two kinds of agreement: a fair transferable utility agreement on the initial interaction and a same type of compromise in a coopetitive context.

**Keywords:** Financial Markets and Institutions, Financing Policy, Risk, Financial Crisis, Games, Arbitrages, Coopetition.

## 1  Introduction

The recent financial crisis has shown that, in order to stabilize markets, it is not enough to prohibit or to restrict short-selling. In fact:

– *big speculators can influence badly the market and take huge advantage from arbitrage opportunities, caused by themselves.*

In this paper (see also [1]), by the introduction of a tax on financial transactions, we propose a method aiming to limit the speculations of medium and big

S. Greco et al. (Eds.): IPMU 2012, Part IV, CCIS 300, pp. 578–592, 2012.

financial operators and, consequently, a way to make more stable the financial markets. Moreover, our aim is attained without inhibiting the possibilities of profits. At this purpose, we will present and study a natural and quite general normal form game - as a possible standard model of fair interaction between two financial operators - which gives to both players mutual economic advantages. Finally, we shall propose an even more advantageous coopetitive model and one its possible compromise solution.

**Note.** Our model could also address the problem of *credit crunch*, which we explain also inspired by the economist G. Ragusa. In the last years, despite the banking world has available a huge amount of money (on Dec. '11 and on Feb. '12 the ECB loaned money to banks at the rate of 1%, respectively 490 and 530 billion euros), there is no available money in the real economy. This phenomenon has begun to show its first sign of life from the second half of '08, and it reached its peak in Dec. '11. The credit crunch is a wide phenomenon: Europe shows a decrease of 1.6% in loans to households and businesses. In Italy, this phenomenon is particularly pronounced, because the decline in loans was even of 5.1% from 2008. *Where's the money loaded by ECB?* Badly, the money remained caged in the world of finance: with some of the money from ECB, banks bought government bonds (so the spread went down); another part of the money is used by the banks to rectify their assets in accordance with EBA requirements (European Banking Authority); the rest of the money was deposited at ECB, at the rate of 0.5% (lower than the rate at which they received it). Moreover, from the second half of '08, the deposits of European banks at ECB are quadrupled. In view of this, our model takes a different dimension and different expectations: in our model, the bank (the Speculator) put money in the real economy by lending to the Enterprise; it eliminates the risk of losing money for the economic crisis and obtains a gain by an agreement with the Enterprise (which gains something too). The credit crunch, by our model, should be gradually attenuated until it disappears.

## 1.1 Methodologies

The strategic game $G$, we propose for modeling our financial interaction, requires a construction on 3 times, say time 0, 1 and 2.

**0)** At time 0, the Enterprise can choose to buy futures contracts in order to hedge the market risk of the underlying commodity, which (the Enterprise knows) should be bought at time 1 in order to conduct its business activities.

**1)** The Financial Institute, on the other hand, acts with speculative purposes on the spot markets (buying or short-selling the goods at time 0) and on the future market (by the opposite action of that performed on the spot market). The Financial Institute may so take advantage of the temporary misalignment of the spot and future prices, created by the hedging strategy of the Enterprise.

**2)** At the time 2, the Financial Institute will cash or pay the sum determined by its behavior in the future market at time 1.

## 1.2 Financial Preliminaries

Here, we recall the financial concepts that we shall use in the present article.

**1)** Any (positive) real number is a *(proper) purchasing strategy*; a negative real number is a *selling strategy*.

**2)** The *spot market* is the market where it is possible to buy and sell at current prices.

**3)** *Futures* are contracts between two parties to exchange, for a price agreed today, a specified quantity of the underlying commodity, at the expiry of the contract.

**4)** *A hedging operation* through futures consists in purchase of future contracts, in order to reduce exposure to specific risks on market variables (in this case on the price).

**5)** A hedging operation is said *perfect* when it completely eliminates the risk of the case.

**6)** *The future price* is linked to the underlying spot price. We assume that:
**6.1)** the underlying commodity does not offer dividends;
**6.2)** the underlying commodity hasn't storage costs and has not convenience yield to take physical possession of the goods rather than future contract.

**7)** The general relationship linking the future price $F_0$, with delivery time $t$, and spot price $S_0$, with sole interest capitalization at the time $t$, is $F_0 = S_0 u^t$, where $u = 1 + i$ is the capitalization factor of the future and $i$ the corresponding interest rate. If not, the arbitrageurs would act on the market until future and spot prices return to levels indicated by the above relation.

# 2   The Game and Stabilizing Proposal

## 2.1   The Description of the Game

We assume that our **first player** is an Enterprise, wich chooses to buy future contracts to hedge against an upwards change of price for the underlying commodity; commodity of which, the Enterprise should buy a certain quantity $M_1$ at time 1, in order to conduct its business. Therefore, the Enterprise can choose a strategy $x \in [0, 1]$, representing the percentage of the quantity of the total underlying $M_1$ that the Enterprise itself will purchase through futures, depending on it wants: to not hedge ($x = 0$); to hedge partially ($0 < x < 1$); to hedge totally ($x = 1$). On the other hand, our **second player** is a Financial Institute operating on the spot market of the underlying asset that Enterprise knows it should buy at time 1. The Financial Institute works in our game also on the futures market:

**1)** taking advantage of possible gain opportunities - given by misalignment between spot prices and future prices of the commodity;

**2)** or accounting for the loss obtained, because it has to close the position of short sales opened on the spot market.

These actions determine the payoff of the Financial Institute. The Financial Institute can therefore choose a strategy $y \in [-1, 1]$, which represents the percentage of the quantity of the underlying $M_2$ that it can buy (in algebraic sense)

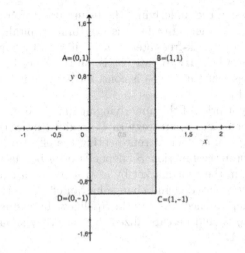

**Fig. 1.** The bi-strategy space of the game

with its financial resources, depending on it intends: to purchase the underlying on the spot market $(y > 0)$; to short sell the underlying on the spot market $(y < 0)$; to not intervene on the market of the underlying $(y = 0)$. In Fig. 1, we illustrate the bi-strategy space $E \times F$ of the game.

## 2.2 The Payoff Function of the Enterprise

The payoff function of the Enterprise, that is the function which represents quantitative relative gain of the Enterprise, referred to time 1, is given by the net gain obtained on not hedged goods $x'M_1$ (here $x' := 1 - x$). The gain related with the not hedged goods is given by the quantity of the not hedged goods $(1 - x)M_1$, multiplied by the difference $F_0 - S_1(y)$, between the future price at time 0 (the term $F_0$) - which the Enterprise should pay, if it decides to hedge - and the spot price $S_1(y)$ at time 1, when the Enterprise actually buys the goods that it did not hedge. So, the payoff function of the Enterprise is defined by

$$f_1(x, y) = F_0 M_1 x' - S_1(y)M_1 x' = (F_0 - S_1(y))M_1(1 - x), \qquad (1)$$

for every bi-strategy $(x, y)$ in $E \times F$, where:

**1)** $M_1$ is the amount of goods that the Enterprise should buy at time 1;

**2)** $x' = 1 - x$ is the percentage of the underlying asset that the Enterprise buys on the spot market at time 1, without any coverage (and therefore exposed to the fluctuations of the spot price of the goods);

**3)** $F_0$ is the future price at time 0. It represents the price established at time 0 that the Enterprise has to pay at time 1 in order to buy the goods. By definition, assuming the absence of dividends, known income, storage costs and convenience yield to keep possession the underlying, the future price after $(t - 0)$ time units is given by $F_0 = S_0 u^t$, where $u = 1 + i$ is the (unit) capitalization factor with rate $i$. By $i$ we mean the risk-free interest rate charged by banks on deposits of other banks, the so-called LIBOR rate. $S_0$ is, on the other hand, the spot price of the underlying asset at time 0. $S_0$ is constant because it is not influenced by our strategies $x$ and $y$.

**4)** $S_1(y)$ is the spot price of the underlying at time 1, after that the Financial Institute has implemented its strategy $y$. It is given by $S_1(y) = S_0 u + nuy$, where $n$ is the marginal coefficient representing the effect of the strategy $y$ on the price $S_1(y)$. The price function $S_1$ depends on $y$ because, if the Financial Institute intervenes in the spot market by a strategy $y$ not equal to 0, then the price $S_1$ changes, since any demand change has an effect on the asset price. We are assuming the dependence $n \mapsto ny$, in $S_1$, linear by assumption. The value $S_0$ and the value $ny$ should be capitalized, because they should be transferred from time 0 to time 1.

**The Payoff Function of the Enterprise.** Therefore, recalling the definitions of $F_0$ and $S_1$, the payoff function $f_1$ of the Enterprise (from now on, the factor $nu$ will be indicated by $\nu$) is given by:

$$f_1(x, y) = -M_1(1 - x)\nu y = -M_1(1 - x)nuy. \tag{2}$$

## 2.3   The Payoff Function of the Financial Institute

The payoff function of the Financial Institute at time 1, that is the algebraic gain function of the Financial Institute at time 1, is the multiplication of the quantity of goods bought on the spot market, that is $yM_2$, by the difference between the future price $F_1(x, y)$ (it is a price established at time 1 but cashed at time 2) transferred to time 1, that is $F_1(x, y)u^{-1}$, and the purchase price of goods at time 0, say $S_0$, capitalized at time 1 (in other words we are accounting for all balances at time 1).

**Stabilizing Strategy of Normative Authority.** In order to avoid speculations on spot and future markets by the Financial Institute, which in this model is the only one able to determine the spot price (and consequently also the future price) of the underlying commodity, we propose that the normative authority imposes to the Financial Institute the payment of a tax on the sale of the futures. So the Financial Institute can't take advantage of price swings caused by itself. We assume that this tax is fairly equal to the incidence of the strategy of the Financial Institute on the spot price, so the price effectively cashed or paid for the futures by the Financial Institute is $F_1(x, y)u^{-1} - \nu y$, where $\nu y$ is the tax paid by the Financial Institute, referred to time 1.

**Remark.** We note that if the Financial Institute wins, it acts on the future market at time 2 in order to cash the win, but also in case of loss it must necessarily

act in the future market and account for its loss because at time 2 (in the future market) it should close the short-sale position opened on the spot market.
The payoff function of the Financial Institute is defined by:

$$f_2(x, y) = y M_2(F_1(x, y)u^{-1} - \nu y - S_0 u),$$   (3)

where:

(1) $y$ is the percentage of goods that the Financial Institute purchases or sells on the spot market of the underlying;

(2) $M_2$ is the maximum amount of goods that the Financial Institute can buy or sell on the spot market, according to its economic availability;

(3) $S_0$ is the price paid by the Financial Institute in order to buy the goods. $S_0$ is a constant because our strategies $x$ and $y$ do not influence it.

(4) $\nu y$ is the normative tax on the price of the futures paid at time 1. We are assuming that the tax is equal to the incidence of the strategy $y$ of the Financial Institute on the price $S_1$.

(5) $F_1(x, y)$ is the price of the future market (established) at time 1, after the Enterprise has played its strategy $x$. The function price $F_1$ is given by $F_1(x, y) = S_1(y)u + mux$, where $u = 1 + i$ is the factor of capitalization of interests. By $i$ we mean risk-free interest rate charged by banks on deposits of other banks, the so-called LIBOR rate. With $m$ we intend the marginal coefficient that measures the influence of $x$ on $F_1(x, y)$. The function $F_1$ depends on $x$ because, if the Enterprise buys futures with a strategy $x \neq 0$, the price $F_1$ changes because an increase of future demand influences the future price. The value $S_1$ should be capitalized because it follows the fundamental relationship between futures and spot prices (see subsection 1.2, no. 7). The value $mx$ is also capitalized because the strategy $x$ is played at time 0 but has effect on the future price at time 1.

(6) $(1 + i)^{-1}$ is the discount factor. $F_1(x, y)$ must be translated at time 1, because the money for the sale of futures are cashed at time 2.

The payoff Function of the Financial Institute. Recalling functions $F_1$ and $f_2$, we have $f_2(x, y) = y M_2 mx$, for each $(x, y) \in E \times F$.

The payoff function of the game is so given, for every $(x, y) \in E \times F$, by:

$$f(x, y) = (-\nu y M_1(1 - x), y M_2 mx).$$   (4)

# 3 Study of the Game

## 3.1 Nash Equilibria

If the two players decide to adopt a selfish behavior, they choose their own strategy maximizing their partial gain. In this case, we should consider the classic Nash best reply correspondences. The best reply correspondence of the Enterprise is the correspondence $B_1 : F \to E$ given by $y \mapsto \max_{f_1(\cdot, y)} E$,

584     D. Carfi and F. Musolino

where $\max_{f_1(\cdot, y)} E$ is the set of all strategies in $E$ which maximize the section $f_1(\cdot, y)$. Symmetrically, the best reply correspondence $B_2 : E \to F$ of the Financial Institute is given by $x \mapsto \max_{f_2(x, \cdot)} F$. Choosing $M_1 = 1$, $\nu = 1/2$, $M_2 = 2$ and $m = 1/2$, which are positive numbers (strictly greater than 0), and recalling that $f_1(x, y) = -M_1 \nu y (1 - x)$, we have $\partial_1 f_1(x, y) = M_1 \nu y$, this derivative has the same sign of $y$, and so:

$$B_1(y) = \begin{cases} \{1\} & \text{if } y > 0 \\ E & \text{if } y = 0. \\ \{0\} & \text{if } y < 0 \end{cases}$$

Recalling that $f_2(x, y) = M_2 m x y$, we have $\partial_2 f_2(x, y) = M_2 m x$ and so: $B_2(x) = \{1\}$ if $x > 0$ and $B_2(x) = F$ if $x = 0$. In Fig.2 we have in red the inverse graph of $B_1$, and in blue that one of $B_2$.

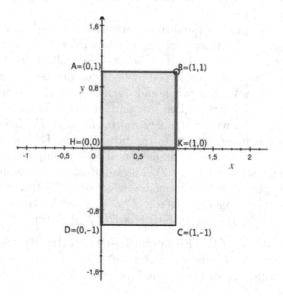

**Fig. 2.** Nash equilibria

**The set of Nash equilibria**, that is the intersection of the two best reply graphs (graph of $B_2$ and the symmetric of $B_1$), is $\{(1, 1)\} \cup [H, D]$.

**Analysis of Nash Equilibria.** The Nash equilibria can be considered quite good, because they are on the weak maximal Pareto boundary. It is clear that if the two players pursue the profit, and choose their selfish strategies to obtain the maximum possible win, they arrive on the weak maximal boundary. The selfishness, in this case, pays well. This purely mechanical examination, however, leaves us unsatisfied. The Enterprise has two Nash possible alternatives: not to hedge, playing 0, or to hedge totally, playing 1. Playing 0 it could both to win or lose, depending on the strategy played by the Financial Institute; opting instead for 1, the Enterprise guarantee to himself to leave the game without any loss and without any win.

**Analysis of Possible Nash Strategies.** If the Enterprise adopts a strategy $x \neq 0$, the Financial Institute plays the strategy 1 winning something, or else if the Enterprise plays 0 the Financial Institute can play all its strategy set $F$, indiscriminately, without obtaining any win or loss. These considerations lead us to believe that the Financial Institute will play 1, in order to try to win at least "something", because if the Enterprise plays 0, its strategy $y$ does not affect its win. The Enterprise, which knows that the Financial Institute very likely chooses the strategy 1, will hedge playing the strategy 1. So, despite the Nash equilibria are infinite, it is likely the two players arrive in $B = (1,1)$, which is part of the proper maximal Pareto boundary. Nash is a viable, feasible and satisfactory solution, at least for one of two players, presumably the Financial Institute.

## 3.2    Cooperative Solutions

The best way for the two players to get both a gain is to find a cooperative solution. One way would be to divide the **maximum collective profit**, determined by the maximum of the collective gain functional $g$, defined by $g(X, Y) = X + Y$, on the payoffs space of the game $G$, i.e the profit $W = \max_{f(E \times F)} g$. The maximum collective profit $W$ is attained at the point $B'$, which is the only bi-win belonging to the straight line $g^{-1}(1)$ (with equation $g = 1$) and to the payoff space $f(E \times F)$. So, the Enterprise and the Financial Institute play $(1,1)$, in order to arrive at the payoff $B'$. Then, they split the obtained bi-gain $B'$ by means of a contract.

**Financial Point of View.** The Enterprise buys futures to create artificially a misalignment between future values and spot prices; misalignment that is exploited by the Financial Institute, which get the maximum win $W = 1$. For a **possible fair division** of $W = 1$, we employ a *transferable utility solution*: finding on the transferable utility Pareto boundary of the payoff space a non-standard Kalai-Smorodinsky solution (non-standard because we do not consider the whole game, but only its maximal Pareto boundary). We find the supremum of maximal boundary, $\sup \partial^* f(E \times F)$, which is the point $\alpha = (1/2, 1)$ and we join it with the infimum of maximal Pareto boundary, $\inf \partial^* f(E \times F)$, which is $(0, 0)$. We note that the infimum of our maximal Pareto boundary is equal to $v^\sharp = (0, 0)$ (the conservative bi-gain of the game). The intersection point $P$, between the straight line of maximum collective win (i.e. $(g = 1)$) and the straight line joining the supremum of the maximal Pareto boundary with its infimum (i.e., the line $Y = 2X$) is the desirable division of the maximum collective win $W = 1$ between the two players. Fig.3 shows the situation. The point $P = (1/3, 2/3)$ suggests that the Enterprise should receive $1/3$, by contract, from the Financial Institute, while at the Financial Institute remains the win $2/3$.

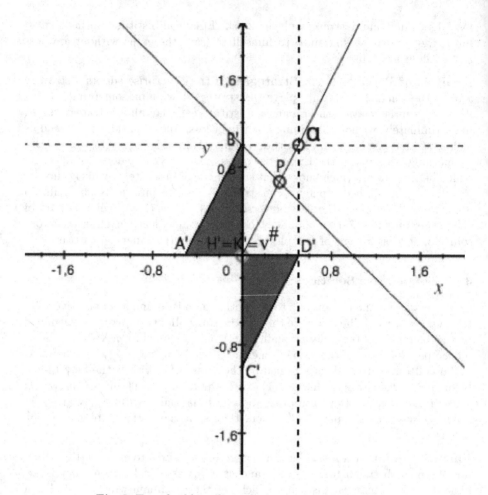

**Fig. 3.** Transferable utility solution: cooperative solution

# 4   Coopetitive Approach

Now we pass to the coopetitive approach. We have two players, the Enterprise and the Financial Institute, each of them has a strategy set in which to choose his strategy; moreover, the two players can cooperatively choose a strategy $z$ in a third set $C$. The two players choose their cooperative strategy $z$ to maximize (in some sense we specify) the gain function $f$.

**The Shared Strategy.** The strategy $z \in [0, A]$ is a shared strategy, which consists in the possibility for the Enterprise to use money borrowed by the Financial Institute from the European Central Bank with a very low interest rate (hypothesis highly plausible given the recent anti-crisis measures adopted by the ECB), rate which, by convention we assume equal to 0. The two players want the loan so that the Enterprise can create an even higher misalignment between spot and futures price, misalignment which will be exploited by the Financial Institute. In this way, both players can get a greater win than that one obtained without a shared strategy $z$. The two players can then choose a shared strategy depending on they want: to not use the money of the ECB ($z = 0$); to use a part of the money of the ECB so that the Enterprise purchases futures ($0 < z < A$); to use totally the money of the ECB so that the Enterprise purchases futures ($z = A$).

**The Payoff Function of the Enterprise.** In practice, to the previous payoff function $f_1$, we must add the action of the Enterprise to buy futures contracts and after sell them. The win of the Enterprise is given by the quantity of futures brought, $zF_0^{-1}$, multiplied by the difference $F_1 u^{-1} - F_0$, between the future price at time 1 when it sell the futures and the future price at time 0 when it buys the futures.

**Remark.** Similarly to what happened to the Financial Institute, also the Enterprise has to pay a tax on the sale of the future contracts. We assume that this tax is equal to the impact of the Enterprise on the price of the futures, in order to avoid speculative acts created by itself.
We have:

$$h_1(x, y, z) = -\nu y M_1(1 - x) + zF_0^{-1}(F_1(x, y, z)u^{-1} - m(x + zA^{-1}) - F_0) \quad (5)$$

where:
   **(1)** $zF_0^{-1}$ is the quantity of futures purchased. It is the ratio between the money $z$ taken on loan from the ECB and $F_0$, the futures price at time 0.
   **(2)** $m(x + zA^{-1})$ is the normative tax paid by the Enterprise on the sale of futures, referred to the time 1. In keeping with the size of $x$, also $zA^{-1}$ is a percentage. In fact $zA^{-1}$ is given by the quantity of future purchased with the strategy $z$ (i.e. $zF_0^{-1}$) multiplied by $F_0 A^{-1}$, that is the total maximum quantity of futures that the Enterprise can buy with the strategy $z$.
   **(3)** $F_1(x, y, z)$ is the price of the future market (established) at time 1, after the Enterprise has played its strategies $x$ and $z$. The price $F_1(x, y, z)$ is given by

$$F_1(x, y, z) = ((S_0 + ny)u^2 + m(x + zA^{-1}))u, \quad (6)$$

where $u = 1 + i$ is the factor of capitalization of interests. By $i$ we mean risk-free interest rate charged by banks on deposits of other banks, the so-called LIBOR rate. With $m$ we intend the marginal coefficient that measures the impact of $x$ and $zA^{-1}$ on $F_1(x, y, z)$. $F_1(x, y, z)$ depends on $x$ and $z$ because, if the Enterprise buys futures with a strategy $x \neq 0$ or $z \neq 0$, the price $F_1$ changes because an increase of future demand influences the future price.
   **(4)** $(1 + i)^{-1}$ is the discount factor. $F_1(x, y, z)$ must be actualized at time 1 because the money for the sale of futures are cashed at time 2.

(5) $F_0$ is the future price at time 0. It represents the price established at time 0 that has to be paid at time 1 in order to buy the goods. It is given by $F_0 = S_0 u^t$, where $u = 1 + i$ is the capitalization factor with rate $i$. By $i$ we mean risk-free interest rate charged by banks on deposits of other banks, the so-called "LIBOR" rate. $S_0$ is, on the other hand, the spot price of the underlying asset at time 0. $S_0$ is a constant because it does not influence our strategies $x$, $y$ and $z$.

**The Payoff Function of the Enterprise.** From now on the value $A$ will be equal to 1 for sake of calculation. Recalling the above point (5), Eq. (5) and Eq. (6), we have (setting $u := 1 + i, x' = 1 - x$)

$$h_1(x,y,z) = -\nu M_1 x' y + z F_0^{-1}[((S_0+ny)u^2+m(x+zA^{-1})u)u^{-1}-m(x+zA^{-1})-S_0u],$$

that is

$$h_1(x,y,z) = -\nu M_1(1 - x)y + F_0^{-1}\nu y z. \tag{7}$$

From now on, the value $F_0$ will be equal to 1, for sake of simplicity.

**The Payoff Function of the Financial Institute.** In the payoff function of the second player, we have to add the strategy $z$ multiplied by $A^{-1}$ (that, as we remember, is equal to 1) to the strategy $x$ played by the Enterprise. Then, we have $h_2(x,y,z) = yM_2m(x + z)$. So, we have

$$h(x,y,z) = (-\nu M_1(1 - x)y, M_2 mxy) + yz(\nu, M_2 m). \tag{8}$$

**The Coopetitive Translating Vectors.** We note immediately, that the new function it is the same payoff function $f$ of the first game,

$$f(x,y) = (-\nu y M_1(1 - x), yM_2 mx),$$

translated by the vector function $v(y, z) := zy(\nu, M_2 m)$. Recalling that $y \in [-1,1]$ and $z \in [0,1]$, we see that the vector $v(y,z)$ belongs to the 2-range $[-1,1](\nu, M_2 m)$.

**Payoff Space.** Concerning payoff space of our game, we note a significant result. But before we state it, observe that, since any shared strategy $z$ is positive, the part of the payoff space $f([0,1]^2)$, where $y$ is greater than 0, is translated upwards, while the part of the game where $y$ is less than 0 is translated downwards. Since our coopetitive game makes sense if and only if the two players will agree and collaborate to maximize their wins with the strategies $x$ and $y$ greater than 0 (it would be paradoxical to choose a strategy $z > 0$ to increase the loss), our significant 3-strategic space is reduced to the cube $Q := [0,1]^3$. Let $S := [0,1]^2$

**Proposition.** *The payoff space $h(Q)$ is union of $h(.,0)(S)$ and $h(.,1)(S)$.*

*Proof.* In fact, we'll show that the shared strategy that maximizes the wins when $y \geq 0$ is always $z = 1$. We'll show that $h(x,y,z) \leq h(x,y,1)$, for every $y \geq 0$ and every $x$ in $E$. Recalling the definition of $h$, we have to show that

$$(-\nu y M_1(1-x), y M_2 mx) + yz(\nu, M_2 m) \leq (-\nu y M_1(1-x), y M_2 mx) + y(\nu, M_2 m),$$

that is $yz(\nu, M_2 m) \leq y(\nu, M_2 m)$ and therefore $yz \leq y$, which is indeed verified for any $y \geq 0$. We can show also that $h(x,y,z) \geq h(x,y,0)$, for every $y \geq 0$ and every $x$ in $E$. Indeed, we have to show that

$$(-\nu y M_1(1-x), y M_2 mx) + yz\nu, M_2 m) \geq (-\nu y M_1(1-x), y M_2 mx),$$

that is $yz(\nu, M_2 m) \geq 0$ and therefore $yz \geq 0$, which is indeed verified for any $y \geq 0$. Since, with $x \in [0,1]$ and $y \in [0,1]$, we have $h(x,y,0) \leq h(x,y,z) \leq h(x,y,1)$, we obtain that all Pareto bi-strategies in $H([0,1]^3)$ are included in the union of the images of $h(.,0)(S)$ and $h(.,1)(S)$. ∎

So, transforming our bi-strategic space $S$ by $f(.,0)$ (in dark green) and $f(.,1)$ (in light green), in the Fig.4 we have the whole payoff space of the our coopetitive game $(h, >)$. If the Enterprise and the Financial Institute play the bi-strategy $(1,1)$, and the shared strategy 1, they arrive at the point $B'(1)$, that is the maximum of the coopetitive game $G$, so the Enterprise wins $1/2$ (amount greater than $1/3$ obtained in the cooperative phase) while the Financial Institute wins even 2 (an amount much greater than $2/3$, value obtained in the first cooperative phase).

**Kalai-Smorodisky Solution.** The point $B'(1)$ is the maximum of the game. But the Enterprise could be not satisfied by the win $1/2$, value that is much more little than the win 2 of the Financial Institute. In addition playing the shared strategy $z = 1$, the Enterprise increases slightly the win obtained in the non-coopetitive game, while the Financial Institute even wins more than double. For this reason, precisely to avoid that the envy of the Enterprise can affect the game, the Financial Institute might be willing to cede part of its win by contract to the Enterprise in order to make more balanced the distribution of money. One way would be to divide the maximum collective profit, determined by the maximum of the function of collective gain $g(X,Y) = X + Y$ on the payoffs space of the game G, i.e the profit $W = \max_S g$. The maximum collective profit is represented with evidence by the point $B'(1)$, which is the only bi-win belonging to the straight line $X + Y = 5/2$ and to the payoff space. So the Enterprise and the Financial Institute play the 3-strategy $(1,1,1)$, in order to arrive at the payoff $B'(1)$ and then split the wins obtained by contract. Practically: the Enterprise buys futures to create artificially (also thanks to the money borrowed from the European Central Bank) a very big misalignment between future and spot prices, misalignment that is exploited by the Financial Institute, which get the maximum win $W = 5/2$. For a possible quantitative division of this

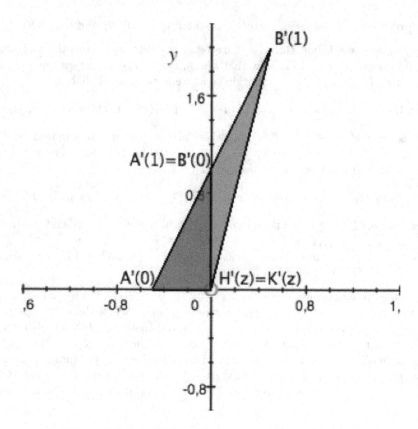

**Fig. 4.** The payoff space of the coopetitive game $h(Q)$

win $W = 5/2$ between the Financial Institute and the Enterprise, we use the transferable utility solution applying the Kalai-Smorodinsky method. We proceed finding the inferior extremum of our game, $\inf \partial^* h(E \times F \times C)$ which is $(-1/2, 0)$ and join it with the superior extremum, $\sup \partial^* h(E \times F \times C)$, according to the Kalai-Smorodinsky method, which is given by $(5/2, 3)$. The coordinates of the point of intersection $P'$ between the straight line of maximum collective win (i.e. $X + Y = 2.5$) and the straight line which joins the supremum with the infimum (i.e. $Y = X + 1/2$) give us the desirable division of the maximum collective win $W = 2.5$ between the two players. In the Fig.5 we make us more aware of the situation. In order to find the coordinates of the point $P'$ is enough to put in a system of equations $X + Y = 2.5$ and $Y = X + 1/2$. Finally we obtain $X = 1$ and $Y = 3/2$. Thus $P' = (1, 3/2)$ suggests as solution that the Enterprise receives 1 (the triple than the win obtained in the cooperative phase of the non-coopetitive game) by contract by the Financial Institute, while at the Financial Institute remains the win $3/2$ (more than double than the win obtained in the cooperative phase of the non-coopetitive game).

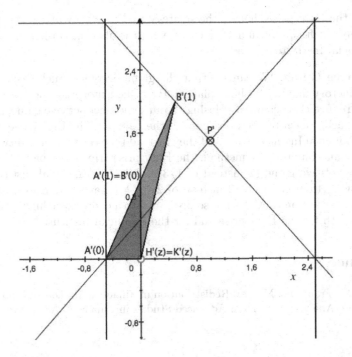

**Fig. 5.** Transferable utility solution in the coopetitive game: cooperative solution

# 5 Conclusions

The games just studied suggests a possible regulatory model providing the stabilization of the financial market through the introduction of a tax on financial transactions. In fact, in this way it could be possible to avoid speculations, which constantly affect modern economy. The Financial Institute could equally gains without burdening on the financial system by unilateral manipulations of traded asset prices. Moreover, by our model, the phenomenon of the credit crunch (which in recent years has put in crisis small and medium enterprises in Europe) should be greatly attenuated.

**Non-coopetitive Game.** The unique optimal solution is the cooperative one above exposed, otherwise the game appears like a sort of "your death, my life". This type of situation happens often in the economic competition and leaves no escapes if either player decides to work alone, without a mutual collaboration. In fact, all non-cooperative solutions lead dramatically to mediocre results for at least one of the two players. Now it is possible to provide an interesting key in order to understand the conclusions which we reached using the transferable utility solution. Since the point $B = (1, 1)$ is also the most likely Nash equilibrium, the number $1/3$ (that the Financial Institute pays by contract to the Enterprise) can be seen as the fair price paid by the Financial Institute to be sure that the Enterprise chooses the strategy $x = 1$, so they arrive effectively to more likely Nash equilibrium $B = (1,1)$, which is also the optimal solution for the Financial Institute.

**Coopetitive Game.** We can see that the game becomes much easier to solve in a satisfactory manner for both players. Both the Enterprise and the Financial Institute reduce their chances of losing than the non-coopetitive game, and even they can easily reach to the maximum of the game: so the Enterprise wins $1/2$ and the Financial Institute wins 2. If they instead take the tranfer utility solution with the Kalai-Smorodisky method, the Enterprise triples the payout obtained in non-coopetitive game ($1$ instead of $1/3$), while the Financial Institute wins more of twice than before ($3/2$ instead of $2/3$). We have moved from an initial competitive situation that was not so profitable to a coopetitive highly profitable situation both for the Enterprise and for the Financial Institute.

# Reference

1. David, C., Francesco, M.: Fair Redistribution in Financial Markets: a Game Theory Complete Analysis. Journal of Advanced Studies in Finance (JASF) 4(II) (2011)

# Global Green Economy and Environmental Sustainability: A Coopetitive Model

David Carfì[1] and Daniele Schilirò[2]

[1] Department of Mathematics
University of California at Riverside
900 Big Springs Road, Surge 231 Riverside, CA 92521-0135, USA
davidcarfi71@yahoo.it
[2] Department DESMaS,
University of Messina,
Via Tommaso Cannizzaro 275, Me 98122, Messina, Italy
danieleschiliro@unime.it

**Abstract.** This paper provides a coopetitive model for a global green economy, taking into account the environmental sustainability. In particular, we propose a differentiable coopetitive game $G$ (in the sense recently introduced by D. Carfì) to represent a global green economy interaction, among a country $c$ and the rest of the world $w$. Our game $G$ is a linear parametric (Euclidean) perturbation of the classic Cournot duopoly. In the paper we offer the complete study of the proposed model and in particular a deep examination of its possible coopetitive solutions.

**Keywords:** Complete analysis of $C^1$ games, coopetitive games, global green economy, environmental sustainability.

## 1 Introduction

A major driver of human impact on Earth's systems is the destruction of biophysical resources. The accelerating carbon emissions, in particular, indicate a mounting threat of climate change with potentially disastrous human consequences. The total environmental impact of a community or of humankind as a whole on the Earth's ecosystems depends on both population (which is increasing) and impact per person, which, in turn, depends in complex ways on what resources are being used, whether or not those resources are renewable, and the scale of the human activity relative to the carrying capacity of the ecosystems involved.

### 1.1 Environmental Sustainability (ES)

Thus, we are facing a problem of environmental sustainability (ES). Goodland in [7] defines ES as the maintenance of natural capital. ES emphasizes the environmental life-support systems without which neither production nor humanity could exist. These life-support systems include atmosphere, water and soil; all of

S. Greco et al. (Eds.): IPMU 2012, Part IV, CCIS 300, pp. 593–606, 2012.

these need to be healthy, meaning that their environmental service capacity must be maintained. So ES can be represented by a set of constraints on the four major activities regulating the scale of the human economic subsystem: the use of renewable and nonrenewable resources on the source side, and the pollution and waste assimilation on the sink side. This is why ES implies that careful resource management be applied at many scales, from economic sectors like agriculture, manufacturing and industry, to work organizations, to the consumption patterns of households and individuals and to the resource demands of individual goods and services.

## 1.2  Geopolitical Situation

Currently, there is no international consensus on the problem of global food security or on possible solutions for how to nourish a population of 9 billion by 2050. Freshwater scarcity is already a global problem, and forecasts suggest a growing gap by 2030 between annual freshwater demand and renewable supply [9]. The increasing dependence on fossil fuels, the problems of security of supply and the best solutions for mitigating climate change require important and urgent measures that must be adopted at a global level. The economic and geopolitical events are changing the international context and also the costs of energy supply in the world industrialized nations. The financial and economic crisis of 2008, in particular, has caused a widespread disillusionment with the prevailing economic paradigm, and it has determined a strong attraction for the green economy.

## 1.3  Green Economy

The green economy is an economy concerned with being:

1. environmentally sustainable, based on the belief that our biosphere is a closed system with finite resources and a limited capacity for self-regulation and self-renewal. We depend on the earths natural resources, and therefore we must create an economic system that respects the integrity of ecosystems and ensures the resilience of life supporting systems;
2. socially just, based on the belief that culture and human dignity are precious resources that, like our natural resources, require responsible stewardship to avoid their depletion;
3. locally rooted, based on the belief that an authentic connection to place is the essential pre-condition to sustainability and justice. The global green economy is an aggregate of individual communities meeting the needs of its citizens through the responsible production and exchange of goods and services.

Thus global green economy growth is compatible with environmental sustainability over time, since it seeks to maintain and restore natural capital.

## 1.4  The Coopetition

This paper applies the notion of coopetition within a macro-global context for environmental problems. The concept of coopetition is a complex construct originally devised by Brandenburger and Nalebuff ([1]) in strategic management at microeconomic level (see [8]). According to this concept, the economic agents (i.e. firms or countries) must interact to find a win-win solution, that indicates a situation in which each agent thinks about both cooperative and competitive ways to change the game. So in our case, each country has to decide whether it wants to collaborate with the rest of the world in getting an efficient global green economy, even if the country is competing in the global scenario.

## 1.5  Our Model

The coopetitive model here suggested is environmentally sustainable, since it should lead to *maintain natural capital*, by using mainly renewable resources. This *ES coopetitive model* also aims at reducing emissions of greenhouse gases, determining the reduction of global pollution, in this way it contributes to the establishment of a sustainable and lasting global green economy. Finally, the model determines a change in the patterns of consumption of households towards goods and human behaviors with a lower environmental impact. So the coopetitive strategy, in our model, consists in implementing a set of policy decisions whose purpose is to be environmental sustainable and to enforce the global green economy. This is why the coopetitive variable in our model is represented by a vector variable whose components guarantee the achievement of the environmental sustainability of a global green economy. Thus, this original ES coopetitive model, applied at the global green economy, aims to enrich the set of tools for environmental policies.

**Win-Win Solutions.** The model provides several possible win-win solutions, strategic situations in which each country takes advantages by cooperating and competing at the same time, more than simply competing without cooperating; this shows the convenience for each country to participate actively to an environmental sustainability program within a coopetitive framework. The model is based on a game theory framework that provides a set of possible solutions in a coopetitive context, allowing us to find bargaining Pareto solutions in a win-win scenario (see also [6]).

**Strategies.** The coopetitive strategies in our ES coopetitive model are:

1. investment in maintenance of natural renewable resources;
2. investment in *green technologies* against pollution (air, water);
3. incentives and taxes to change the patterns of consumption of the households.

# 2    The Model: An ES Coopetitive Model of Economy

The coopetitive model we propose hereunder must be interpreted as a normative model, in the sense that it will show the more appropriate solutions and win-win strategies chosen within a cooperative perspective, under precise conditions imposed by assumption.

## 2.1    Strategies

The strategy sets of the model are:

1. the set $E$ of strategies $x$ of a certain country $c$ - the possible aggregate biological-food production of the country $c$ - which directly influence both payoff functions, in a proper game theoretic approach á la *Cournot*;
2. the set $F$ of strategies $y$ of the rest of the word $w$ - the possible aggregate biological-food production of the rest of the world $w$ - which influence both pay-off functions;
3. the set $C$ of 3-dimensional shared strategies $z$, set which is determined together by the two game players, $c$ and the rest of the world $w$.

**Interpretation of the Cooperative Strategy.** Any vector $z$ in $C$ is the 3-level of aggregate investment for the ES economic approach, specifically $z$ is a triple $(z_1, z_2, z_3)$, where:

1. the first component $z_1$ is the aggregate investment, of the country $c$ and of the rest of the world $w$, in *maintenance of natural renewable resources*;
2. the second component $z_2$ is the aggregate investment, of the country $c$ and of the rest of the world $w$, in *green technologies against pollution*;
3. the third component $z_3$ is the aggregate algebraic sum, of the country $c$ and of the rest of the world $w$, of *incentives (negative) and taxes (positive) to change the patterns of consumption of the households*.

In the model, we assume that $c$ and $w$ define ex-ante and together the set $C$ of all cooperative strategies and (after a deep study of the coopetitive interaction) the triple $z$ to implement as a possible component solution.

## 2.2    Main Strategic Assumptions

We assume that any real number $x$, in the canonical unit interval $E := \mathbb{U} = [0, 1]$, is a possible level of aggregate production of the country $c$ and any real number $y$, in the same unit interval $F := \mathbb{U}$, is the analogous aggregate production of the rest of the world $w$.

**Measure Units of the Individual Strategy Sets.** We assume that the measure units of the two intervals $E$ and $F$ be different: the real unit 1 in $E$ represents the maximum possible aggregate production of country $c$ of a certain biological product and the real unit 1 in $F$ is the maximum possible aggregate production of the rest of the word $w$, of the same good. Obviously these two units represents totally different quantities, but - from a mathematical point of view - we need only a rescale on $E$ and a rescale on $F$ to translate our results in real unit of productions.

**Cooperative Strategy.** Moreover, a real triple (3-vector) $z$, belonging to the canonical cube $C := \mathbb{U}^3$, is the 3-investment of the country $c$ and of the rest of the world $w$ for new low-carbon innovative technologies, in the direction of sustainability of natural resources and for the environmental protection. Also in this case, the real unit 1 of each factor of $C$ is, respectively:

1. the maximum possible aggregate investment in maintenance of natural renewable resources;
2. the maximum possible aggregate investment in green technologies against pollution (air, water);
3. the maximum possible aggregate algebraic sum of incentives and taxes to change the patterns of consumption of the households.

Let us assume, so, that the country and the rest of the world decide together, at the end of the analysis of the game, to contribute by a 3-investment $z = (z_1, z_2, z_3)$. We also consider, as payoff functions of the interaction between the country $c$ and the rest of the word $w$, two *Cournot type* payoff functions, as it is shown in what follows.

### 2.3 Payoff Function of Country $c$

We assume that the payoff function of the country $c$ is the function $f_1$ of the unit 5-cube $\mathbb{U}^5$ into the real line, defined by

$$f_1(x, y, z) = 4x(1 - x - y) + m_1 z_1 + m_2 z_2 + m_3 z_3 = 4x(1 - x - y) + (m|z),$$

for every triple $(x, y, z)$ in the 5-cube $\mathbb{U}^5$, where $m$ is a characteristic positive real 3-vector representing the marginal benefits of the investments decided by country $c$ and by the rest of the world $w$ upon the economic performances of the country $c$.

### 2.4 Payoff Function of the Rest of the World $w$

We assume that the payoff function of the rest of the world $w$, in the examined strategic interaction, is the function $f_2$ of the 5-cube $\mathbb{U}^5$ into the real line, defined by

$$f_2(x, y, z) = 4y(1 - x - y) + (n|z),$$

for every triple $(x, y, z)$ in the 5-cube $\mathbb{U}^5$ , where $n$ is a characteristic positive real 3-vector representing representing the marginal benefits of the investments decided by country $c$ and the rest of the world $w$ upon the economic performances of the rest of the world $w$ itself. Note the symmetry in the influence of the pair $(m, n)$ upon the pair of payoff functions $(f_1, f_2)$.

## 2.5    Payoff Function of the Coopetitive Game

We have so build up a coopetitive gain game $G = (f, \geq)$, with payoff function $f : \mathbb{U}^5 \to \mathbb{R}^2$, given by

$$f(x, y, z) = (4x(1 - x - y) + (m|z), 4y(1 - x - y) + (n|z)) =$$
$$= 4(x(1 - x - y), y(1 - x - y)) + \sum z(m : n),$$

for every triple $(x, y, z)$ in the compact 5-cube $\mathbb{U}^5$, where $(m : n)$ is the 3-family of 2-vectors $((m_i, n_i))_{i=1}^3$ (that is the family $((m_1, n_1), (m_2, n_2), (m_3, n_3))$) and where $\sum z(m : n)$ denotes the linear combination $\sum_{i=1}^3 z_i(m_i, n_i)$, of the family $(m : n)$ by the system of coefficients $z$.

# 3    Study of the Game $G = (p, \geq)$

Fixed a cooperative strategy $z$ in the cube $\mathbb{U}^3$, the game $G(z) = (p_z, \geq)$, with payoff function $p_z$ defined on the square $\mathbb{U}^2$ by $p_z(x, y) = f(x, y, z)$, is the translation of the game $G(0_3)$ by the vector $v(z) = \sum z(m : n)$, so that we can study the game $G(0_3)$ ($0_3$ is the origin of the Euclidean 3-space) and we can translate the various information of the game $G(0_3)$ by the vector $v(z)$. So, let us consider the game $G(0_3)$. This game $G(0_3)$ has been studied by Carfì and Perrone in [3] (see also [2], [4] and [5]). The payoff conservative part (part of the payoff space greater than the conservative bi-value $(0, 0)$) is the canonical 2-simplex $\mathbb{T}$, convex envelope of the origin and of the canonical basis $e$ of the Euclidean plane $\mathbb{R}^2$. This conservative part is represented in fig.1.

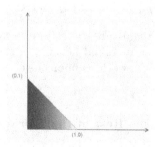

**Fig. 1.** The conservative part of the Cournot payoff space, i.e. the positive part of the image $p_0(\mathbb{U}^2)$

**Dynamical Interpretation of Coopetition.** In what follows we are interested in the trajectory of the dynamic path generated by the above conservative part $\mathbb{T}$ in the co-opetitive evolution determined by the function $f$. The multi-time dynamic path we are interested in is the set-valued function $\gamma : \mathbb{U}^3 \to \mathbb{R}^2 : z \mapsto \Gamma(z)$, where $\Gamma(z)$ is the conservative part of the game $G(z)$. The trajectory is nothing but the union of all configurations determined by the path $\gamma$: what we shall call our coopetitive payoff space.

### 3.1   Payoff Space and Pareto Boundary of the Payoff Space of $G(z)$

The Pareto boundary of the payoff space of the $z$-section normal-form game $G(z)$ is the segment $[e_1, e_2]$, with end points the two canonical vectors of the Cartesian vector plane $\mathbb{R}^2$, translated by the vector $v(z) = \sum z(m : n)$, this is true for all 3-strategy $z$ in the unit cube $\mathbb{U}^3$ (3-dimensional set).

### 3.2   Payoff Space of the Co-opetitive Game $G$

The payoff space of the co-opetitive game $G$, the image of the payoff function $f$, is the union of the family of payoff spaces $(p_z(\mathbb{U}^2))_{z \in C}$, that is the convex envelope of the of points $0$, $e_1$, $e_2$, and of their translations by the three vectors: $v(1,0,0) = (m_1, n_1)$; $v(1,1,0) = \sum_{i=1}^{2}(m_i, n_i)$ and $v(1,1,1) = \sum_{i=1}^{3}(m_i, n_i)$.

**The Construction of the Pareto Maximal Coopetitive Path.** We show, in the following five figures, the construction of the coopetitive payoff space in three steps, in the particular case in which $m = (-1,1,1)$ and $n = (2,1,-1)$, just to clarify the procedure. Moreover we shall consider here only the coopetitive space $S$ generated by the Pareto maximal boundary $\mathbb{M}_2 = [e_1, e_2]$, since the Pareto Maximal boundary of the coopetitive game $G$ is contained in this part $S$.

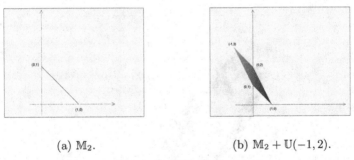

(a) $\mathbb{M}_2$.                    (b) $\mathbb{M}_2 + \mathbb{U}(-1, 2)$.

**Fig. 2.** Step 0 and step 1

**The Pareto Maximal Boundary of the Payoff Space $f(\mathbb{U}^5)$.** The Pareto maximal boundary of the payoff space $f(\mathbb{U}^5)$ of the coopetitive game $G$ is the union of segments $[P', Q'] \cup [Q', R']$, where the point $P'$ is $(0,4)$, the point $Q'$ is $(2,2)$ and the point $R'$ is $(3,0)$.

# 4   Solutions of the Model

## 4.1   Properly Coopetitive Solutions

In a purely coopetitive fashion, the solution of the coopetitive game $G$ must be searched for in the coopetitive dynamic evolution path of the Nash payoff $N' = (4/9, 4/9)$. Let us study this coopetitive dynamical path. We have to start from the Nash payoff $N'$ and then generate its coopetitive trajectory $\mathcal{N} := N' + \mathbb{U}(-1, 2) + \mathbb{U}(1, 1) + \mathbb{U}(1, -1)$. A *purely coopetitive* solution is obtainable by cooperating on the set $C$ and (interacting) competing *á la Nash* in a suitable best compromise game $G(\bar{z})$, where the cooperative strategy $\bar{z}$ is suitably and cooperatively chosen by the two players, by solving a bargaining problem. To be more precise, we give the following definition of properly coopetitive solution.

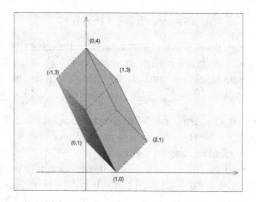

**Fig. 3.** Second step: $\mathbb{M}_2 + \mathbb{U}(-1, 2) + \mathbb{U}(1, 1)$

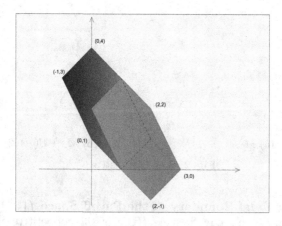

**Fig. 4.** Third and final step: $\mathbb{M}_2 + \mathbb{U}(-1, 2) + \mathbb{U}(1, 1) + \mathbb{U}(1, -1)$

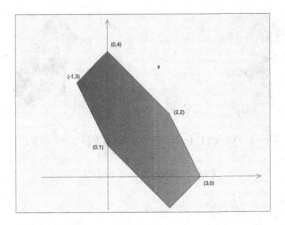

**Fig. 5.** The coopetitive dynamical path of the initial Pareto boundary $\mathbb{M}_2$

**Definition (of purely coopetitive solution.** *We say that a triple* $t = (x, y, z)$ *is a properly coopetitive solution of a coopetitive game* $G = (f, \geq)$ *if its image* $f(t)$ *belongs to the maximal Pareto boundary of the payoff Nash Path of* $G$.

**Interpretation.** The complex game just played was developed with reference to the strategic triple $(x, y, z)$, and the functional relation $f$, which represents a continuous infinite family of games *á la Cournot*, where in each member-game of the family the quantities are the strategies which vary in order to establish the Cournot-Nash equilibrium, and where the vector $z$ allows the game to identify possible cooperative solutions in a competitive environment, thus we have obtained a *pure co-opetitive solution.*

### 4.2   Construction of the Nash Path

As before, we can proceed step by step, as the following 5 figures just show.

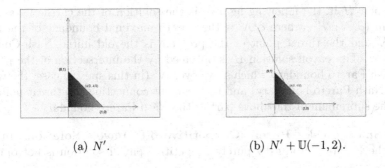

(a) $N'$.                    (b) $N' + \mathbb{U}(-1, 2)$.

**Fig. 6.** Step 0 and step 1

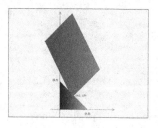 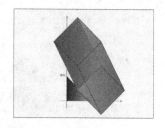

(a) $N' + \mathbb{U}(-1, 2) + \mathbb{U}(1, 1)$.    (b) $N' + \mathbb{U}(-1, 2) + \mathbb{U}(1, 1) + \mathbb{U}(1, -1)$.

**Fig. 7.** Step 2 and step 3

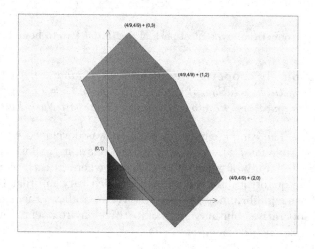

**Fig. 8.** The coopetitive dynamical path of the initial Nash equilibrium $N'$

**Kalai-Smorodinsky Purely Coopetitive Payoff Solution.** The Kalai-Smorodinsky purely coopetitive payoff solution, with respect to the Nash payoff - the point $H$ in the following figure - is the solution of the classic bargaining problem $(\partial^* \mathcal{N}, N')$, where $\partial^* \mathcal{N}$ is the Pareto maximal boundary of the Nash path $\mathcal{N}$ and the threat point of the problem is the old initial Nash-Cournot payoff $N'$. The payoff solution $H$ is obtained by the intersection of the part of the Nash Pareto boundary which stays over $N'$ (in this specific case, the whole of the Nash Pareto boundary) and the segment connecting the threat point $N'$ with the supremum of the above part of the Nash Pareto boundary.

**Kalai-Smorodinsky Purely Coopetitive TU Payoff Solution.** In this game the Kalai-Smorodinsky purely coopetitive payoff solution is not optimal

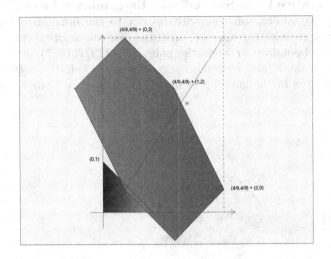

**Fig. 9.** Kalai-Smorodinsky purely coopetitive payoff solution: $H$

with respect to the Transferable Utility approach, indeed the TU Pareto boundary of our Nash path is the straight line

$$N' + (0,3) + \mathrm{span}(1, -1),$$

and the payoff $H$ does not belong to this line. The unique point of intersection among this TU boundary and the segment connecting the threat point $N'$ with the supremum of the Nash Pareto boundary is what we define the *Kalai-Smorodinsky purely coopetitive TU payoff solution*.

### 4.3 Super-Cooperative Solutions

We can go further, finding a Pareto solution obtainable by double cooperation, in the following sense: we assume that in the game the two players will cooperate both on the cooperative 3-strategy $z$ and on the bi-strategy pair $(x, y)$.

**Super Cooperative Nash Bargaining Solution.** The super cooperative Nash bargaining payoff solution, with respect to the infimum of the Pareto boundary, is by definition the point of the Pareto maximal boundary $M$ obtained by maximizing the real functional $h : \mathbb{R}^2 \to \mathbb{R}$ defined by $(X, Y) \mapsto (X - \alpha_1)(Y - \alpha_2)$, where $\alpha$ is the infimum of the Pareto maximal boundary. In our case $\alpha$ is the origin of the plane, so this solution coincide with the medium point $Q' = (2, 2)$ of the segment $[P', (4, 0)]$. This point $Q'$ represents a win-win solution with respect to the initial (shadow maximum) supremum $(1, 1)$ of the pure Cournot game, since it is strongly greater than $(1, 1)$.

**Super Cooperative Kalai-Smorodinsky Bargaining Solution.** The Kalai-Smorodinsky bargaining solution, with respect to the infimum of the Pareto boundary, coincide with the intersection of the diagonal segment [inf $M$, sup $M$] and the Pareto boundary $M$ itself: the point $K = (12/7, 16/7)$, of the segment $[P', Q']$. This point $K$ also represents a good win-win solution with respect to the initial (shadow maximum) supremum $(1, 1)$ of the pure Cournot game.

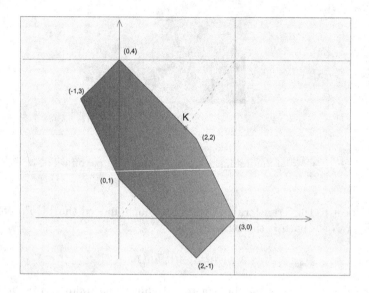

**Fig. 10.** Super-cooperative Kalai-Smorodinsky solution in the payoff space: $K$

**Super Cooperative Kalai-Smorodinsky Transferable Utility Solution.** The transferable utility solutions of our game in the payoff space are all the payoff pairs staying on the straight line $\text{aff}(P', Q') = (0, 4) + \text{span}(1, -1)$, the feasible TU solutions are those belonging to the segment $s = [(0, 4), (3, 1)]$. Note, anyway, that the Kalai-Smorodinsky solution of the bargaining problem $(s, 0_2)$ is again the point $K$: the super cooperative Kalai-Smorodinsky transferable utility solution coincides with the super cooperative Kalai-Smorodinsky bargaining solution.

### 4.4   Sunk Costs

For what concerns the sunk costs, we consider an initial bi-cost $(1, 1)$ necessary to begin the ES approach to the production, so that in a non-coopetitive environment we have a translation by the vector $(-1, -1)$ of the Nash equilibrium payoff $(4/9, 4/9)$. Although we have a bi-loss, in a co-opetitive environment the gain is strictly greater than the absolute value of the bi-loss, thus the new super-cooperative Kalai-Smorodinsky solution $K - (1, 1)$ is greater than the old Nash equilibrium payoff.

# 5   Conclusions

Our coopetitive model has tried to demonstrate which are the win-win solutions of a coopetitive strategic interaction that aims at a policy of Environment Sustainability and to implement a Green Economy. This policy concerns

1. investment in maintenance of natural renewable resources;
2. investment in green technologies against pollution (air, water);
3. incentives and taxes to change the patterns of consumption of the households;

taking into account its sunk costs, and the determination of aggregate output of biological food of any country $c$ in a non-cooperative game *á la Cournot* with the rest of the world.

The *original analytical elements* that characterized our coopetitive model are the following:

1. firstly, we defined $z$ as the cooperative strategy, which is the instrumental 3-vector (3 dimensions) of the ES policy;
2. secondly, we adopted a non-cooperative game *á la Cournot* for establishing an equilibrium bi-level $(x, y)$, that represents the levels of outputs of country $c$ and of the rest of the world $w$;
3. thirdly, we introduced the sunk costs of the ES approach;
4. finally, we suggested not only a pure coopetitive solution, but also two super-cooperative solutions on the coopetitive maximal Pareto boundary of our interaction, adopting the Nash bargaining and the Kalai-Smorodinsky methods, thus obtaining two best compromise solution.

**Acknowledgements.** The authors wish to thank Dr. Eng. Alessia Donato for her valuable help in the preparation of the figures.

# References

1. Branderburger, A.M., Nalebuff, B.J.: Coopetition. Currency Doubleday, New York (1996)
2. Carfì, D.: Payoff space in $C^1$-games. Applied Sciences (APPS) 11, 1–16 (2009)
3. Carfì, D., Perrone, E.: Game complete analysis of symmetric Cournot duopoly. MPRA Paper 35930, University Library of Munich, Germany (2012)
4. Carfì, D., Ricciardello, A.: An Algorithm for Payoff Space in $C^1$-Games. Atti della Accademia Peloritana dei Pericolanti, Classe di Scienze Fisiche Matematiche e Naturali LXXXVIII(1), 1–19 (2010)
5. Carfì, D., Ricciardello, A.: Topics in Game Theory. APPS Monographs - Balkan Society of Geometry (2012)
6. Carfì, D., Schilirò, D.: Crisis in the Euro area: coopetitive game solutions as new policy tools. Theoretical and Practical Research in Economic Fields II(1), 23–36 (2011)

7. Goodland, R.: The concept of environmental sustainability. Annual Review of Ecology and Systematics 26, 1–24 (2005)
8. Schilirò, D.: Knowledge, Learning, Networks and Performance of Firms in Knowledge-Based Economies. In: Prinz, A., Steenge, A., Isegrei, N. (eds.) New Technologies, Networks and Governance Structures, Wirtschaft: Forschung und Wissenschaft Bd. 24, pp. 5–30. LIT-Verlag, Berlin (2009)
9. United Nations, Introduction. Setting the stage for a green economy transition. United Nations Environment Programme, New York (2011)

# Asymmetric R&D Alliances and Coopetitive Games

Daniela Baglieri[1], David Carfì[2], and Giovanni Battista Dagnino[3]

[1] University of Messina
Via dei Verdi 75, 98122, Messina, Italy
dbaglieri@unime.it
[2] Department of Mathematics
University of California at Riverside, USA
davidcarfi71@yahoo.it
[3] University of Catania
Corso Italia 55, 95129, Catania, Italy
dagnino@unict.it

**Abstract.** In this paper we show how the study of asymmetric R&D alliances, that are those between young and small firms and large and MNEs firms for knowledge exploration and/or exploitation, requires the adoption of a coopetitive framework which consider both collaboration and competition. We draw upon the literature on asymmetric R&D collaboration and coopetition to propose a mathematical model for the coopetitive games which is particularly suitable for exploring asymmetric R&D alliances.

**Keywords:** R&D alliances; coopetitive games.

## 1 Introduction

Scholarly attention to co-opetition has increased with the practical significance of collaboration among competitors (Brandenburger and Nalebuff, 1996; Sakakibara, M. 1997; Padula and Dagnino, 2007) and competition among *friends* (for instance, university-industry relationships; see: Carayannis and Alexander, 1999; Baglieri 2009).

**R&D Alliances.** Despite the increased importance of co-opetition, limited research has examined factors that may drive co-opetition, particularly in high technology industries where R&D alliances seem to be growing rapidly. A notable trend is the rapid growth of R&D alliances between large, well-established firms and small, growing firms. We term these alliances asymmetric R&D alliances. These inter-organizational arrangements rise a number of open questions related to the disparately partners bargaining power which affect, among others, alliances outcomes.

(1) Are asymmetric R&D alliances a win-win or win-lose partnerships?
(2) What are the main firms' strategies partners may deploy to *enlarge the pie* and create more value?

S. Greco et al. (Eds.): IPMU 2012, Part IV, CCIS 300, pp. 607–621, 2012.
© Springer-Verlag Berlin Heidelberg 2012

The answers to these questions are important for both larger and smaller firms to better select their partners, the scope and type of alliance, and the resources to be allocated for new product development.

**Coopetitive Games.** This paper aims at developing a mathematical model for the coopetitive games which is particularly suitable for exploring asymmetric R&D alliances. Despite the classic form games involving two players - that can choose the respective strategies only cooperatively or not-cooperatively, in an exclusive way - we propose that players have a common strategy set $C$, containing other strategies (possibly of different type with respect to the previous one) that must be chosen cooperatively. Consequently, for any coopetitive game, we necessarily build up a family of classic normal-form games which determines univocally the given coopetitive game. Thus, the study of a coopetitive game is reconducted to the study of a family of normal-form games in its completeness. In this paper, we suggest how this latter study can be conduct and what could be the concepts of solution of a coopetitive game corresponding to the main firms' strategies, potentially deployed in asymmetric R&D settings.

**Asymmetric R&D Alliances: A Coopetitive Perspective.** Several researchers have clearly indicated the importance of co-opetition for technological innovation.

(1) Jorde and Teece (1990) suggested that the changing dynamics of technologies and markets have led to the emergence of the simultaneous innovation model. For firms to pursue the simultaneous innovation model and succeed in innovation, they should look for collaboration opportunities that allow them to bring multiple technologies and diverse and complementary assets together.

(2) Von Hippel (1987) argued that collaboration for knowledge sharing among competitors occurs when technological progress may be faster with collective efforts rather than through individual efforts and when combined knowledge offers better advantages than solo knowledge. More recent research clearly shows the importance of co-opetition in technological innovation.

(3) Quintana-Garcia and Benavides-Velasco (2004) empirically show that collaboration with direct competitors is important not only to acquire new technological knowledge and skills from the partner, but also to create and access other capabilities based on intensive exploitation of the existing ones.

(4) Similarly, Carayannis and Alexander (1999) argue that co-opetition is particularly important in knowledge intensive, highly complex, and dynamic environments.

**Coopetition among Firms.** Following the seminal work of Nalebuff and Brandenburger (1996), some scholars have studied how firms cooperate in the upstream activities and compete in the downstream activities (Walley, 2007), in order to pursuit several goals:

(1) to integrate complementary resources within the value net (Nalebuff and Brandenburger, 1996; Bagshaw and Bagshaw, 2001; Wilkinson and Young, 2002; Laine, 2002);

(2) to increase the heterogeneity of the resources needed to successfully compete in convergent businesses (Ancarani and Costabile, 2006);

(3) to enhance learning opportunities (Hamel et alii, 1989);

(4) to boost firms R&D capabilities (Valentini et alii, 2004);

(5) to speed up innovation (Hagel III and Brown, 2005).

**Note.** This broad range of goals explains why coopetition is common in several industries:

(1) Sakakibara (1993) describes R&D cooperation among competing Japanese semiconductor firms.

(2) Hagedoorn, Cyrayannis, and Alexander (2001) document an emerging collaboration between IBM and Apple that resulted in an increasing number of alliances between the two for joint technological development.

(3) Albert (1999) points to the coopetitive relationship between Dell Computers and IBM.

(4) Coopetition is common in mature industries too.

(5) Recent works examine coopetition in soft drink and beverage industry (Bonel and Rocco, 2007); in carbonated soft drink industry (Fosfuri and Giarratana, 2006); and in tuna industry (LeRoy, 2006).

Therefore, the idea to working with the enemy is not new, although it has been a *an under researched theme* (Dagnino and Padula, 2002).

**What Is New Here?** What it is new in this paper is the attempt to apply coopetition in a asymmetric R&D alliances setting, theme which has been more investigated in industrial organizational literature that largely explores how increases in cooperative activity in the markets for technology (i.e. licensing) affect levels of competitive activity in product markets. In this paper, we adopt another option which addresses the question how firms manage simultaneously patterns of cooperation and competition in their R&D relationships (firm level) and, thus, how firms enlarge the pie (cooperation) and share the pie (competition). According to a process view, we propose a mathematical model to determine possible suitable behaviors (actions) of partners during their strategic interactions, from both non-cooperative and cooperative point of view.

**Organization of the Paper.** In the first section we introduce the model of coopetitive game of D. Carfi. In the second we apply the complete analysis of a differentiable game (see [1,3,5]) to an asymmetric interaction of two firms. In the last section we study a possible coopetitive extension of that asymmetric interaction to obtain a win-win situation in a R&D coopetitive perspective.

## 2    Coopetitive Games

In this paper we show and apply the mathematical model of a *coopetitive game* introduced by David Carfi in [2] and [4]. The idea of coopetitive game is already used, in a mostly intuitive and non-formalized way, in Strategic Management Studies (see for example Brandenburgher and Nalebuff).

**The Idea.** A coopetitive game is a game in which two or more players (participants) can interact *cooperatively and non-cooperatively at the same time*. Even Brandenburger and Nalebuff, creators of coopetition, did not define, precisely, a *quantitative way to implement coopetition* in the Game Theory context.

The problem to implement the notion of coopetition in Game Theory is summarized in the following question:

*how do, in normal form games, cooperative and non-cooperative interactions can live together simultaneously, in a Brandenburger-Nalebuff sense?*

To explain the above question, consider a classic two-player normal-form gain game $G = (f, >)$ - such a game is a pair in which $f$ is a vector valued function defined on a Cartesian product $E \times F$ with values in the Euclidean plane $\mathbb{R}^2$ and $>$ is the natural strict sup-order of the Euclidean plane itself. Let $E$ and $F$ be the strategy sets of the two players in the game $G$. The two players can choose the respective strategies $x \in E$ and $y \in F$ cooperatively (exchanging information) or not-cooperatively (not exchanging informations), but these two behavioral ways are mutually exclusive, at least in normal-form games: the two ways cannot be adopted simultaneously in the model of normal-form game (without using convex probability mixtures, but this is not the way suggested by Brandenburger and Nalebuff in their approach). There is no room, in the classic normal game model, for a simultaneous (non-probabilistic) employment of the two behavioral extremes *cooperation* and *non-cooperation*.

**Towards a Possible Solution.** David Carfi ([2] and [4]) has proposed a manner to pass this *impasse*, according to the idea of coopetition in the sense of Brandenburger and Nalebuff:

in a Carfi's coopetitive game model, the players of the game have their respective strategy-sets (in which they can choose cooperatively or not cooperatively) and a common strategy set $C$ containing other strategies (possibly of different type with respect to those in the respective classic strategy sets) that *must be chosen cooperatively*. This strategy set $C$ can also be structured as a Cartesian product (similarly to the profile strategy space of normal form games), but in any case the strategies belonging to this new set $C$ must be chosen cooperatively.

### 2.1   The Model for $n$ Players

We give in the following the definition of coopetitive game proposed by Carfi (in [2] and [4]).

**Definition (of $n$-player coopetitive game).** *Let $E = (E_i)_{i=1}^n$ be a finite $n$-family of non-empty sets and let $C$ be another non-empty set. We define $n$-player coopetitive gain game over the strategy support $(E, C)$ any pair $G = (f, >)$, where $f$ is a vector function from the Cartesian product $^\times E \times C$ (here $^\times E$ denotes the classic strategy-profile space of $n$-player normal form games, i.e. the Cartesian product of the family $E$) into the $n$-dimensional Euclidean space $\mathbb{R}^n$ and $>$ is the natural sup-order of this last Euclidean space. The element of the set $C$ will be called cooperative strategies of the game.*

A particular aspect of our coopetitive game model is that any coopetitive game $G$ determines univocally a family of classic normal-form games and vice versa; so that any coopetitive game could be defined as a family of normal-form games. In what follows we precise this very important aspect of the model.

**Definition (the family of normal-form games associated with a coopetitive game).** *Let $G = (f, >)$ be a coopetitive game over a strategic support $(E, C)$. And let $g = (g_z)_{z \in C}$ be the family of classic normal-form games whose member $g_z$ is, for any cooperative strategy $z$ in $C$, the normal-form game $G_z :=$ $(f(., z), >)$, where the payoff function $f(., z)$ is the section $f(., z) : {}^{\times}E \to \mathbb{R}^n$ of the function $f$, defined (as usual) by $f(., z)(x) = f(x, z)$, for every point $x$ in the strategy profile space ${}^{\times}E$. We call the family $g$ (so defined) **family of normal-form games associated with (or determined by) the game $G$** and we call **normal section** of the game $G$ any member of the family $g$.*

We can prove this (obvious) theorem.

**Theorem.** *The family $g$ of normal-form games associated with a coopetitive game $G$ uniquely determines the game. In more rigorous and complete terms, the correspondence $G \mapsto g$ is a bijection of the space of all coopetitive games - over the strategy support $(E, C)$ - onto the space of all families of normal form games - over the strategy support $E$ - indexed by the set $C$.*

Thus, the exam of a coopetitive game should be equivalent to the exam of a whole family of normal-form games (in some sense we shall specify). In this paper we suggest how this latter examination can be conducted and what are the solutions corresponding to the main concepts of solution which are known in the literature for the classic normal-form games, in the case of two-player coopetitive games.

## 2.2   Two Players Coopetitive Games

In this section we specify the definition and related concepts of two-player coopetitive games; sometimes (for completeness) we shall repeat some definitions of the preceding section.

**Definition.** *Let $E$, $F$ and $C$ be three nonempty sets. We define **two player coopetitive gain game carried by the strategic triple** $(E, F, C)$ any pair of the form $G = (f, >)$, where $f$ is a function from the Cartesian product $E \times F \times C$ into the real Euclidean plane $\mathbb{R}^2$ and the binary relation $>$ is the usual sup-order of the Cartesian plane (defined component-wise, for every couple of points $p$ and $q$, by $p > q$ iff $p_i > q_i$, for each index $i$).*

**Remark (coopetitive games and normal form games).** The difference among a two-player normal-form (gain) game and a two player coopetitive (gain) game is the fundamental presence of the third strategy Cartesian-factor $C$. The presence of this third set $C$ determines a total change of perspective with respect to the usual exam of two-player normal form games, since we now have to consider a normal form game $G(z)$, for every element $z$ of the set $C$; we have, then, to study an entire ordered family of normal form games in its own totality, and we have to define a new manner to study these kind of game families.

## 2.3    Terminology and Notation

**Definitions.** *Let* $G = (f, >)$ *be a two player coopetitive gain game carried by the strategic triple* $(E, F, C)$. *We will use the following terminologies:*

1. *the function* $f$ *is called the **payoff function of the game** $G$;*
2. *the first component* $f_1$ *of the payoff function* $f$ *is called **payoff function of the first player** and analogously the second component* $f_2$ *is called **payoff function of the second player**;*
3. *the set* $E$ *is said **strategy set of the first player** and the set* $F$ *the **strategy set of the second player**;*
4. *the set* $C$ *is said the **cooperative strategy set of the two players**;*
5. *the Cartesian product* $E \times F \times C$ *is called the strategy space of the game* $G$.

**Interpretation.** We have:
1. two players, or better an ordered pair $(1, 2)$ of players;
2. anyone of the two players has a strategy set in which to choose freely his own strategy;
3. the two players can/should *cooperatively* choose strategies $z$ in a third common strategy set $C$;
4. the two players will choose (after the exam of the entire game $G$) their cooperative strategy $z$ in order to maximize (in some sense we shall define) the vector gain function $f$.

## 2.4    Normal Form Games of a Coopetitive Game

Let $G$ be a coopetitive game in the sense of above definitions. For any cooperative strategy $z$ selected in the cooperative strategy space $C$, there is a corresponding normal form gain game $G_z = (p(z), >)$, upon the strategy pair $(E, F)$, where the payoff function $p(z)$ is the section $f(., z) : E \times F \to \mathbb{R}^2$, of the payoff function $f$ of the coopetitive game - the section is defined, as usual, on the competitive strategy space $E \times F$, by $f(., z)(x, y) = f(x, y, z)$, for every bi-strategy $(x, y)$ in the bi-strategy space $E \times F$.

Let us formalize the concept of game-family associated with a coopetitive game.

**Definition (the family associated with a coopetitive game).** *Let* $G = (f, >)$ *be a two player coopetitive gain game carried by the strategic triple* $(E, F, C)$. *We naturally can associate with the game* $G$ *a family* $g = (g_z)_{z \in C}$

*of normal-form games defined by* $g_z := G_z = (f(.,z), >)$, *for every* $z$ *in* $C$, *which we shall call* **the family of normal-form games associated with the coopetitive game** $G$.

**Remark.** It is clear that with any above family of normal form games $g = (g_z)_{z \in C}$, with $g_z = (f(.,z), >)$, we can associate:

1. a family of payoff spaces $(\text{im} f(.,z))_{z \in C}$, with members in the payoff universe $\mathbb{R}^2$;

2. a family of Pareto maximal boundary $(\partial^* G_z)_{z \in C}$, with members contained in the payoff universe $\mathbb{R}^2$;

3. a family of suprema $(\sup G_z)_{z \in C}$, with members belonging to the payoff universe $\mathbb{R}^2$;

4. a family of Nash zones $(\mathcal{N}(G_z))_{z \in C}$; with members contained in the strategy space $E \times F$;

5. a family of conservative bi-values $v^\# = (v_z^\#)_{z \in C}$; in the payoff universe $\mathbb{R}^2$.

And so on, for every meaningful known feature of a normal form game. Moreover, we can interpret any of the above families as *set-valued paths* in the strategy space $E \times F$ or in the payoff universe $\mathbb{R}^2$. It is just the study of these induced families which becomes of great interest in the examination of a coopetitive game $G$ and which will enable us to define (or suggest) the various possible solutions of a coopetitive game.

# 3   Solutions of a Coopetitive Game

The two players of a coopetitive game $G$ should choose the cooperative strategy $z$ in $C$ in order that:

1. the reasonable Nash equilibria of the game $G_z$ are $f$-preferable than the reasonable Nash equilibria in each other game $G_{z'}$;

2. the supremum of $G_z$ is greater (in the sense of the usual order of the Cartesian plane) than the supremum of any other game $G_{z'}$;

3. the Pareto maximal boundary of $G_z$ is higher than that of any other game $G_{z'}$;

4. the Nash bargaining solutions in $G_z$ are $f$-preferable than those in $G_{z'}$;

5. *in general, fixed a common kind of solution for any game* $G_z$, *say* $S(z)$ *the set of these kind of solutions for the game* $G_z$, *we can consider the problem to find all the optimal solutions (in the sense of Pareto) of the set valued path* $S$, *defined on the cooperative strategy set* $C$. *Then, we should face the problem of* **selection of reasonable Pareto strategies** *in the set-valued path* $S$ *via proper selection methods (Nash-bargaining, Kalai-Smorodinsky and so on).*

Moreover, we shall consider the maximal Pareto boundary of the payoff space $\text{im}(f)$ as an appropriate zone for the bargaining solutions. The payoff function of a two person coopetitive game is (as in the case of normal-form game) a vector valued function with values belonging to the Cartesian plane $\mathbb{R}^2$. We note that in general the above criteria are multi-criteria and so they will generate multi-criteria optimization problems. In this section we shall define rigorously some kind of solution, for two player coopetitive games, based on a bargaining method, namely a Kalai-Smorodinsky bargaining type. Hence, first of all, we have to precise what kind of bargaining method we are going to use.

**Bargaining Problems.** In this paper we shall use the following definition of bargaining problem.

**Definition (of bargaining problem).** *Let $S$ be a subset of the Cartesian plane $\mathbb{R}^2$ and let $a$ and $b$ be two points of the plane with the following properties:*

*1. they belong to the small interval containing $S$, if this interval is defined (indeed, it is well defined if and only if $S$ is bounded and it is precisely the interval $[\inf S, \sup S]_{\le}$ );*

*2. they are such that $a < b$;*

*3. the intersection $[a, b]_{\le} \cap \partial^* S$, among the interval $[a, b]_{\le}$ with end points $a$ and $b$ (it is the set of points greater than $a$ and less than $b$, **it is not** the segment $[a, b]$) and the maximal boundary of $S$ is non-empty.*

*In this conditions, we call **bargaining problem on $S$ corresponding to the pair of extreme points** $(a, b)$, the pair $P = (S, (a, b))$. Every point in the intersection among the interval $[a, b]_{\le}$ and the Pareto maximal boundary of $S$ is called **possible solution of the problem** $P$. Some time the first extreme point of a bargaining problem is called **the initial point of the problem** (or **disagreement point** or **threat point**) and the second extreme point of a bargaining problem is called **utopia point** of the problem.*

In the above conditions, when $S$ is convex, the problem $P$ is said to be convex and for this case we can find in the literature many existence results for solutions of $P$ enjoying prescribed properties (Kalai-Smorodinsky solutions, Nash bargaining solutions and so on ...).

**Remark.** Let $S$ be a subset of the Cartesian plane $\mathbb{R}^2$ and let $a$ and $b$ two points of the plane belonging to the smallest interval containing $S$ and such that $a \le b$. Assume the Pareto maximal boundary of $S$ be non-empty. If $a$ and $b$ are a lower bound and an upper bound of the maximal Pareto boundary, respectively, then the intersection $[a, b]_{\le} \cap \partial^* S$ is obviously not empty. In particular, if $a$ and $b$ are the extrema of $S$ (or the extrema of the Pareto boundary $S^* = \partial^* S$) we can consider the following bargaining problem $P = (S, (a, b))$ (or $P = (S^*, (a, b))$) and we call this particular problem a *standard bargaining problem on $S$* (or *standard bargaining problem on the Pareto maximal boundary $S^*$*).

**Kalai Solution for Bargaining Problems.** Note the following property.

**Property.** *If $(S, (a, b))$ is a bargaining problem with $a < b$, then there is at most one point in the intersection $[a, b] \cap \partial^* S$, where $[a, b]$ is the **segment joining the two points** $a$ and $b$.*

**Definition (Kalai-Smorodinsky).** *We call **Kalai-Smorodinsky solution** (or **best compromise solution**) of the bargaining problem* $(S, (a, b))$ *the unique point of the intersection* $[a, b] \cap \partial^* S$*, if this intersection is non empty.*

We end the subsection with the following definition.

**Definition (of Pareto boundary).** *We call **Pareto boundary** every subset $M$ of an ordered space which has only pairwise incomparable elements.*

**Nash (proper) Solution of a Coopetitive Game.** Let $N := \mathcal{N}(G)$ be the union of the Nash-zone family of a coopetitive game $G$, that is the union of the family $(\mathcal{N}(G_z))_{z \in C}$ of all Nash-zones of the game family $g = (g_z)_{z \in C}$ associated to the coopetitive game $G$. We call *Nash path of the game $G$* the multi-valued path $z \mapsto \mathcal{N}(G_z)$ and Nash zone of $G$ the trajectory $N$ of the above multi-path. Let $N^*$ be the Pareto maximal boundary of the Nash zone $N$. We can consider the bargaining problem $P_{\mathcal{N}} = (N^*, \inf N^*, \sup N^*)$.

**Definition.** *If the above bargaining problem $P_{\mathcal{N}}$ has a Kalai-Smorodinsky solution $k$, we say that $k$ is **the properly coopetitive solution of the coopetitive game $G$.***

The term "properly coopetitive" is clear:

– *this solution $k$ is determined by cooperation on the common strategy set $C$ and to be selfish (competitive in the Nash sense) on the bi-strategy space $E \times F$.*

**Bargaining Solutions of a Coopetitive Game.** It is possible, for coopetitive games, to define other kind of solutions, which are not properly coopetitive, but realistic and sometime affordable. These kind of solutions are, we can say, *supercooperative*. Let us show some of these kind of solutions.

Consider a coopetitive game $G$ and

1. its Pareto maximal boundary $M$ and the corresponding pair of extrema $(a_M, b_M)$;
2. the Nash zone $\mathcal{N}(G)$ of the game in the payoff space and its extrema $(a_N, b_N)$;
3. the conservative set-value $G^\#$ (the set of all conservative values of the family $g$ associated with the coopetitive game $G$) and its extrema $(a^\#, b^\#)$.

*We call:*

1. **Pareto compromise solution of the game** $G$ the best compromise solution (K-S solution) of the problem $(M, (a_M, b_M))$, if this solution exists;
2. **Nash-Pareto compromise solution of the game** $G$ the best compromise solution of the problem $(M, (b_N, b_M))$ if this solution exists;
3. **conservative-Pareto compromise solution of the game** $G$ the best compromise of the problem $(M, (b^\#, b_M))$ if this solution exists.

**Transferable Utility Solutions.** Other possible compromises we suggest are the following. Consider *the transferable utility Pareto boundary $M$ of the coopetitive game $G$*, that is the set of all points $p$ in the Euclidean plane (universe of payoffs), between the extrema of $G$, such that their sum $^+(p) := p_1 + p_2$ is equal to the maximum value of the addition $+$ of the real line $\mathbb{R}$ over the payoff space $f(E \times F \times C)$ of the game $G$.

**Definition (TU Pareto solution).** *We call **transferable utility compromise solution of the coopetitive game** $G$ the solution of any bargaining problem $(M, (a, b))$, where*

1. *$a$ and $b$ are points of the smallest interval containing the payoff space of $G$*
2. *$b$ is a point strongly greater than $a$;*
3. *$M$ is the transferable utility Pareto boundary of the game $G$;*
4. *the points $a$ and $b$ belong to different half-planes determined by $M$.*

Note that the above forth axiom is equivalent to require that the segment joining the points $a$ and $b$ intersect $M$.

**Win-Win Solutions.** In the applications, if the game $G$ has a member $G_0$ of its family which can be considered as an "initial game" - in the sense that the pre-coopetitive situation is represented by this normal form game $G_0$ - the aims of our study (following the standard ideas on coopetitive interactions) are: 1) to "enlarge the pie"; 2) to share the pie in order to obtain a win-win solution with respect to the initial situation. So that we will choose as a threat point $a$ in TU problem $(M, (a, b))$ the supremum of the initial game $G_0$.

**Definition (of win-win solution).** *Let $(G, z_0)$ be a **coopetitive game with an initial point**, that is a coopetitive game $G$ with a fixed common strategy $z_0$ (of its common strategy set $C$). We call the game $G_{z_0}$ as **the initial game of** $(G, z_0)$. We call **win-win solution of the game** $(G, z_0)$ any strategy profile $s = (x, y, z)$ such that the payoff of $G$ at $s$ is strictly greater than the supremum $L$ of the **payoff core** of the initial game $G(z_0)$.*

**Remark.** The payoff core of a normal form gain game $G$ is the portion of the Pareto maximal boundary $G^*$ of the game which is greater than the conservative bi-value of $G$.

**Remark.** From an applicative point of view, the above requirement (to be strictly greater than $L$) is very strong. More realistically, we can consider as win-win solutions those strategy profiles which are strictly greater than any reasonable solution of the initial game $G_{z_0}$.

**Remark.** In particular, observe that, if the collective payoff function $^+(f) = f_1 + f_2$ has a maximum (on the strategy profile space $S$) strictly greater than the collective payoff $L_1 + L_2$ at the supremum $L$ of the payoff core of the game

$G_{z_0}$, the portion $M(> L)$ of TU Pareto boundary $M$ which is greater than $L$ is non-void and it is a segment. So that we can choose as a threat point $a$ in our problem $(M, (a, b))$ the supremum $L$ of the payoff core of the initial game $G_0$ to *obtain some compromise solution.*

**Standard Win-Win Solution.** A natural choice for the utopia point $b$ is the supremum of the portion $M_{\geq a}$ of the transferable utility Pareto boundary $M$ which is upon (greater than) this point $a$: $M_{\geq a} = \{m \in M : m \geq a\}$.

# 4  An Asymmetric Interaction among Firms

**The Economic Situation.** We consider two economic agents, firms. The second one is already in the market the first one is not. The possible strategies of the first are Enter in the market (E) and Not Enter in market (N). The strategies of the second one are High prices (H) and Low prices (L). The payoff (gains) of the two firms are represented in the following table:

$$
\begin{array}{ccc}
 & H & L \\
E & (4, 2) & (0, 3) \\
N & (0, 3) & (0, 4)
\end{array}
$$

**The Finite Game Associated with the Economic Situation.** The above table defines a bimatrix $M$ and, consequently, a finite loss game $(M, <)$.

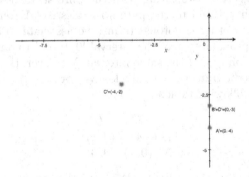

**Fig. 1.** Initial finite payoff space, of the game $(M, <)$

It is evident that the pair of strategies (E, L) is a dominant Nash equilibrium of the game, in other terms its a strict Nash equilibrium (even if the Nash equilibria are two, also (N,L) is a Nash equilibrium). This Nash equilibrium leads to the gain payoff $(0, 3)$. But, we have to do some considerations: 1) the second player could gain much more if the first does not enter; 2) the market offers a potential total gain 6, in correspondence to the bi-strategy (Enter, High prices). We have three questions: a) is it possible for the second player to gain more than 3? b) is it possible that the two firms collectively obtain the total amount offered by the market? c) if the case (b) happens, what is a possible fair division of the total amount among the firms? c) is it possible to enlarge the pie coopetitively? We shall answer to these questions during our study. To do so, first we consider the mixed extension of the game $(M, <)$.

## 4.1   The Mixed Extension

**Scope of the Mixed Extension.** We shall examine the von Neumann extension of the finite game $(M, <)$ to find other possible realistic and applicable economic behaviors and solutions.

**The Extension.** We, firstly, have to imbed (canonically) the finite strategy spaces into the probabilistic canonical 1-simplex of the plane (since there are two strategies for any firm). The strategy Enter (and High prices) shall be transformed into the first canonical vector $e_1$ of the plane and the strategy Non Enter (and Low prices) shall be transformed into the second canonical vector of the plane $e_2$. So our new bistrategy space is the Cartesian square of the canonical 1-simplex of the plane (wich is the convex envelop of the canonical basis $e$ of the plane), $\operatorname{conv}(e)^2$. It is a 2-dimension bistrategy space, since the canonical 1-simplex is 1-dimensional. So we can imbed the simplex in the real line $\mathbb{R}$ and the bi-strategy space into the Euclidean plane $\mathbb{R}^2$. To do this, roughly speaking, we consider the injection associating with the pure strategies Enter and High prices the probability 1 and to the pure strategies Not Enter and Low prices the probability 0. In other (rigorous) terms, we associate to any mixed strategy $(x, 1 - x)$ the probability $x$ of the interval $[0, 1]$ and to any mixed strategy $(y, 1 - y)$ the probability $y$ of the same interval. Moreover, the considered finite loss game $(M, <)$ is the translation by the loss vector $(0, -4)$ of the game $(M', <)$ represented in the following table:

$$
\begin{array}{ccc}
 & H & L \\
E & (-4, 2) & (0, 1) \\
N & (0, 1) & (0, 0)
\end{array}
$$

The mixed extension of the game $(M, <)$ is, thus, the translation, by the same vector $(0, -4)$, of the extension of the game $(M', <)$, so we can study this latter extension.

## 4.2   The Mixed Extension and the Coopetitive Extension

**Formal Description of the Mixed Extension.** The mixed extension of the finite game $(M', <)$ is the infinite differentiable loss-game $G_0 = (f_0, <)$, with strategy sets $E = F = [0, 1]$ and biloss (disutility) function $f_0$ defined, on the Cartesian square $\mathbb{U}^2 := [0, 1]^2$, by $f_0(x, y) = (-4xy, x + y)$, for every bistrategy

$(x, y)$ in $\mathbb{U}^2$. For what concerns the coopetition, we assume that the two firms decide to produce their products in a common industry, *lowing the costs linearly and so obtaining more gain*. We obtain the new payoff function $f : \mathbb{U}^3 \to \mathbb{R}^2$ defined, for every bistrategy $(x, y)$ in $\mathbb{U}^2$ and any cooperative strategy $z$ in the common set $C = \mathbb{U}$, by $f(x, y, z) = (-4xy - z, x + y - z)$. The function $f$ is a coopetitive extension of $f_0$ and it is obtained by a *coopetitive translation*, via the vector function $v : \mathbb{U} \to \mathbb{R}^2$, defined by $v(z) = -z(1, 1)$, for every $z \in C$. The study of this two games $f_0, f$ could be conducted by analytical technics introduced and already applied by D. Carfi in [1,2,3,4,5]. This study is briefly represented in the following figures, in which we show also some possible natural solutions.

In figure 2, we see the payoff space of the game $f_0$. There are infinitely many Nash payoffs: the entire segment $[A', B']$. Note that in a cooperative perspective, all the minimal Pareto boundary under the Nash payoff $B'$ (the core of the game) are rationalizable.

In figure 3, we see two possible extended Kalai solutions $K'$ and $K''$ and the Nash bargaining solution $N'$.

In figure 4, we see two possible extended transferable utility Kalai solutions $H$ and $K$, with respect to the conservative bi-value $B'$ and the infima of the the core and of the game.

In figure 5, we see the entire payoff space of the coopetitive game, that is the image $f(\mathbb{U}^3)$.

In figure 6, we see two possible extended Kalai solutions $H'$ and $H''$, and two possible extended transferable utility Kalai solutions $K'$ and $K''$, having the conservative bi-value $B'$ (sup of the coopetitive Nash path) and the infimum of the partial Nash coopetitive path $B' + [0, 1]v(1)$ as threat points and the infimum of the entire coopetitive game as utopia point.

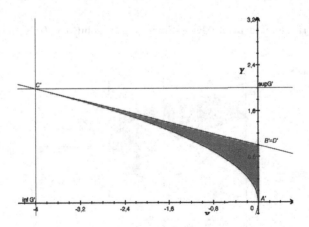

**Fig. 2.** Payoff space of the mixed extension: $f_0(\mathbb{U}^2)$

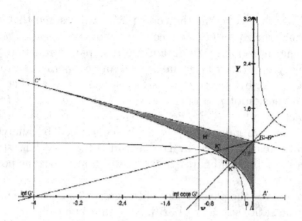

**Fig. 3.** Two Kalai solutions $K', K''$ and the Nash bargaining solution $N$ on payoff space $f_0(\mathbb{U}^2)$

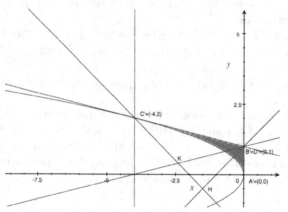

**Fig. 4.** Two transferable utility Kalai-Smorodinsky solutions $H, K$ on payoff space $f_0(\mathbb{U}^2)$

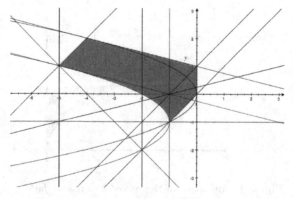

**Fig. 5.** The coopetitive payoff space $f(\mathbb{U}^3)$

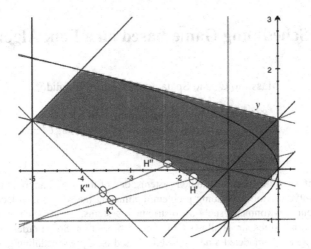

**Fig. 6.** Kalai solutions $H', H''$ and transferable utility Kalai solutions $K', K''$ on coopetitive loss space

**Conclusions.** The sample of coopetitive game, provided in the present contribution, is essentially a *normative model*. It has pointed out the strategies that could bring to win-win solutions, in a *super-cooperative perspective and in a super-cooperative transferable utility perspective, after a coopetitive extension*. At this aim, we use an extended Kalai-Smorodinsky method, appropriate to determine fair partitions, for the *win-win solutions*, on the Pareto boundary and transferable utility Pareto boundary of the coopetitive game. The solutions offered by our coopetitive model show, using Brandenburgher words, how to "enlarge the pie and share it fairly".

# References

1. Carfì, D.: Payoff space in $C^1$-games. Applied Sciences (APPS) 11, 1–16 (2009)
2. Carfì, D.: A Model for Coopetitive Games. MPRA paper 2012 (2012)
3. Carfì, D., Perrone, E.: Game complete analysis of symmetric Cournot duopoly, MPRA paper (2012)
4. Carfì, D., Schilirò, D.: Crisis in the Euro area: coopetitive game solutions as new policy tools, TPREF-Theoretical and Practical Research in Economic Fields, summer issue 2011, pp. 23–36 (2011)
5. Carfì, D., Ricciardello, A.: An Algorithm for Payoff Space in C1-Games. AAPP. LXXXVIII(1) (2010)

# A Job Scheduling Game Based on a Folk Algorithm

Massimo Orazio Spata and Salvatore Rinaudo

STMicroelectronics, Department: IMS – R&D
{massimo.spata,salvatore.rinaudo}@st.com

**Abstract.** In the modern distributed systems, one of the most important targets is to resolve the job scheduling problem, optimizing the solution. In fact, in a concurrent environment such as distributed systems, jobs synchronization access to shared resources allows CPU time optimization. So, in order to solve this problem, we modeled a new scheduler based on a job scheduling game, in which multiple jobs concur to use multiple CPUs as players of this game model. Every single job payoff is related to total job completion time minimization, allowing system throughput maximization. The implemented model provides integration of Nash Equilibrium to MiniMax solution inspired by the "folk theorem" of Game Theory. This new algorithm has been tested, and results validate decrease of Nash Equilibrium inefficiency for the proposed distributed model.

**Keywords:** Scheduling problems, Load Balancing, Game Theory, Folk Theorem, Distributed Systems, Multi-core, Intelligent Complex Systems, Mobile Agents System.

## 1    Introduction

A new network vision is recently born and it has been called Distributed Computing. The new Distributed Computing architecture paradigm allows a higher computation throughput and an easy data sharing, allowing users access in a simple way to distributed computational resources. The main cause for such trend is mass production of cheap, fast and reliable microprocessors [1]. A better throughput on distributed computing environment can be implemented through help of scheduling algorithms [2].

Previous research [2, 3, 4] showing that Nash Equilibrium can be applied to scheduling algorithms helping us to optimize total throughput in such distributed systems. However, Nash Equilibrium solution is not the Pareto optimal solution for each possible input. The Prisoners' Dilemma problem is an example of Nash Equilibrium inefficiency [5, 6, 7].

A new algorithm based on Game Theory has been implemented, merging the Mini-Max algorithm with the Nash Equilibrium solutions, improving Nash Equilibrium efficiency. As the matter of fact, there is an interesting result in game theory - curiously known as the *folk theorem* - which shows how the infinitely repeated Prisoners' Dilemma, under rationality hypothesis, making it possible to obtain an efficient payoff balance for players [5].

S. Greco et al. (Eds.): IPMU 2012, Part IV, CCIS 300, pp. 622–631, 2012.
© Springer-Verlag Berlin Heidelberg 2012

In the follow sections, some concepts of Game Theory with mobile agent are briefly reviewed. Section 3 and Section 4 present the proposed load balancing algorithm and Mobile Agents System designed. Finally, section 5, 6, 7 summarizes the proposed MOS algorithm integration on a Multi-Cores Architecture, main contributions to this paper, experimental results and comments on future directions for this work.

## 2  Related Works

Prior art in relation with this paper is reported in [8] and in [9]. In [8], it is demonstrated that on a Distributed Systems, applying Nash Equilibrium scheduling algorithm, the average waiting time on a queue decreases minimizing the total job completion time.

In [9], three different scheduling algorithms are compared, based on: Nash Equilibrium, Random and MiniMax (Pareto Optimal). The results show that game theory and Nash Equilibrium approach are very similar to a random scheduling strategy. Pareto Optimal (MiniMax) algorithm results in the best scheduling algorithm. In [9] the implemented solution has been applied to a Grid site. Target is maximize Grid site Reputation Index (RI) which quantifies the contributions of the site (intuitively a higher RI would lead to a better reputation of the organization as a whole).

Analysis of the prior art shows that is possible use of Nash Equilibrium solution to job scheduling problems in such distributed systems.

Instead, in this proposed solution model, the job scheduling game implementing a Multi Agent System infrastructure [2, 3, 4] through the JADE framework (a Java Agent Development Framework), with the *FIPA specifications* compliances and through a set of graphical tools that supports the debugging and deployment phases [11].

In the next sections, will be explained the theory on which is based the Agent modeling of the above entities.

## 3  The Multi Agent System Model

Multi Agents System (MAS) are a paradigm which can help us building an intelligent distributed system model. But for a software agent, in order to take decisions, it first has to be able to perceive what is going on around it. So, an intelligent agent must have an equivalent source of information regarding the world in which it lives. Usually, this information comes in through *networks of sensors*. For these reasons, they must be dynamic and have the capability to learn from environments, adapting to different scenarios [11].

### 3.1  Competing agents

Developed MAS model, provides competition between Agents, and players correspond to jobs. The strategy set of each player is the set of initial load for every cpu. Given a strategy for each player, the total load on each cpu is given by the sum of jobs processing times to choose a cpu. So, briefly each agent playing competes with other agents to allocate a cpu.

Usually each player seeks to minimize the total job completion time on its chosen cpu. So, standard objective function for every player (or agent) is minimizing the job completion time on one loaded cpu.

The main entities pertaining to the designed agent's system architecture are: Interpreter Agent, MiniMax Agent, MaxiMin Agent, Nash Agent, Scheduler Agent, *MOS* algorithm.

*Agent's functionality Goal*
To minimize the total jobs completion time, maximizing the throughput [2, 3]

- To send and receive information regarding submitted jobs
- To calculate the input complexity for the job [2]
- To calculate: initial load, the job service rate $\lambda$, and job inter-arrival rate $\mu$  [2]
- To create the payoff matrix with the above parameters as arrays of strategies [2, 3]
- To find the Nash Equilibrium [3, 4]
- To find the MiniMax and MaxiMin solutions [14]
- To compare Nash and MiniMax solutions
- To compare MOS solution with MaxiMin solutions
- To schedule jobs on the selected cpu $C$

*Agent's quality Goal*

- To send computed values to a Scheduler Agent

*Nash Agent*
It is an Agent instantiated for every submitted job and analyzes all the possible Nash Equilibrium solutions. His behavior is defined by NashBehaviour Class.

The target of Nash Agent is analyzing an input file containing payoff matrix for the submitted jobs. The Nash Agent post condition is to invoke start method of FindNashEquilibrium Class in order to find Nash Equilibrium solution for the Prisoners' Dilemma problem.

*MiniMax Agent*
It is an Agent instantiated for every submitted job. The behavior of this Agent is defined by class MiniMaxBehavior. MiniMax Agent target is to return the MiniMax solution for the matrix $M$.

*MaxiMin Agent*
It is an Agent instantiated for every submitted job. The behavior of this Agent is defined by class MaxiMinBehavior. MaxiMin Agent target is to return the MaxiMin solution for the matrix $M$.

*Interpreter Agent*
The target of this Agent is to analyze the input for every job. The Agent behavior is defined by: InterpreterBehaviour Class. This Agent gives a weight to the job input complexity.

*Scheduler Agent*
The target of this Agent is to schedule jobs on the most appropriate cpu *C*, following the matchmaking of *MOS* solution (explained in the next paragraph) values. The Agent behavior is defined by: SchedulerBehaviour Class.

*Modeling Agents with UML Sequence Diagram*
Figure 1 shows the Agent architecture model obtained through the UML Sequence Diagram:

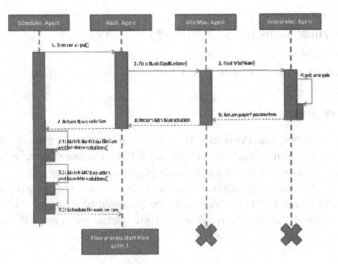

**Fig. 1.** Class Agents UML sequence Diagram

# 4     The Strategic Game Form Model

In [5] a strategic game form *G*, with two players is:

$$(X,Y,E,h)$$

Where:

- *X,Y,E* are sets
- *X* represents available choices for player *I*; idem for *Y* respect to player *II*.
- *E* represents a set of possible strategies for the game
- *h* : *X×Y* → *E*. So *h* is an output function providing results achieved on players' choices, and if player *I* chooses *x* and player *II* chooses *y*, get *h(x,y)* results.

In a game $G$, you need to know the players' preferences for the different elements of $E$. A fast and simple mode to describe these preferences is to use "utility function" $u(x)$ [5, 6, 7]. For example, for player $I$ assume it is given a function $u$ defined in $E$ and with values in $\mathbb{R}$, interpreting $u(e')\geq u(e'')$ as an expression of: player $I$ prefers outcome $e'$ to outcome $e''$.

So, having a game form $(X,Y,E,h)$ and two utility functions (for both players) $(u_1,u_2)$, this is the expression form of the game:

$$(X,Y,E,h,u_1,u_2)$$

Through composition operator $\circ$, let be $f_1=u_1 \circ h$ and $f_2=u_2 \circ h$, we will obtain $(X,Y,f_1,f_2)$ or a strategic form game for two players, as defined in [4].
Where:

- $X,Y$ are sets
- $f_1,f_2 : X \times Y \rightarrow \mathbb{R}$
- A Nash Equilibrium for $G=(X,Y,f_1,f_2)$ is $(x^*,y^*) \in X \times Y$:
  - $f_1(x^*,y^*)\geq f_1(x,y^*)$　$\forall\, x \in X$
  - $f_2(x^*,y^*)\geq f_2(x^*,y)$　$\forall\, y \in Y$　[5]

### 4.1　The Prisoner's Dilemma

In the Game Theory, the Prisoner's Dilemma is a type of non-cooperative game where the only concern of each individual player ("*the Prisoner*") is to maximize his own payoff, without any concern for the other player's payoff.

In this type of game the preference relation effect $>_i$ is that players have an obvious strategy to apply, and this is consequent to the presence of dominant strategies. The other effect of payoff is that the result of strategic interaction is non-efficient for this game [4,5].

*Agent payoff*
Apply the Prisoner's Dilemma model to a specific example and suppose having $m$ players' equivalent to $m$ jobs that must be scheduled on $t$ cpus $C$:

- Possible moves are equivalent to all possible job allocations $j_1, j_2, ..., j_m$ on $C_1, C_2, ..., C_t$
- Total available moves number for every agent is given by $t^m$
- Payoff in our model is equivalent to minimizing job completion time, optimizing system throughput
- Game Matrix $M=\{M_1, ..., M_p\}$ with $i = 1, ..., p$
- A preference relation $>i$ to maximize throughput: where $a,b,c,d$ are parameters representing the 1-minute exponentially average CPU run queue length [3].

For example: given a game with 2 cpus $C_1$ and $C_2$ and 2 jobs $j_1$ and $j_2$. Then, it could be model the game form in strategic mode through a matrix, where rows represent the job strategies which $j_1$ can choose and the columns represent the job strategies which $j_2$ can choose. The following table is a simple Game Matrix $M$ for the Prisoner's Dilemma problem for 2 agents (jobs $j_1$ and $j_2$) and 2 cpus ($C_1$ and $C_2$):

$M$:

|       |       | $j_2$    |          |
|-------|-------|----------|----------|
|       |       | $C_1$    | $C_2$    |
| $j_1$ | $C_1$ | $(c, c)$ | $(a, d)$ |
|       | $C_2$ | $(d, a)$ | $(b, b)$ |

Where, in the case of the Prisoner's Dilemma problem:   $d>c>b>a$.
On the above Game Matrix, Nash Equilibrium will be calculated as [12]:

- set payoff for agents' $j_1$ then the second agent $j_2$ determine best payoff, through the relation preference, between the second component of the two strategies on row 1 $c,d$ and on the row 2 $a,b$;
- set payoff for agents' $j_2$ then the first agent $j_1$ determine best payoff, through the relation preference, between the first component of the two strategies on column 1 $c,d$ and column 2 $a,b$.

In other words, every Nash Agent will do conjectures about other agents' strategies and decide the best strategy for him, ensure that every other Agent does not have other strategies with the highest profit, playing within all matrixes and following Nash Equilibrium solutions for Prisoner's Dilemma problem [5,12].

## 4.2    The Folk Theorem

A well-known result in game theory known as "*The Folk Theorem*" suggests that finding Nash Equilibria in repeated games should be easier than in one-shot games.

"*The Folk Theorem*" for repeated games establish that if the players are patient enough, then any feasible strictly individually rational payoff can be obtained as Equilibrium payoffs. We start with the Nash Folk Theorem which obtains feasible strictly individually rational payoffs as Nash Equilibria of the repeated game [17].

Inspired by "*The Folk Theorem*", h designed a new algorithm which iterates a strategic Game $G$, comparing obtained Nash Equilibrium and MiniMax solutions and then refining with MaxiMin solutions through a Multi Agent System.

## 4.3    MiniMax Algorithm

In Game Theory the MiniMax [13], is a strategy to minimize the maximum possible loss, or alternatively, to maximize the minimum gain (MaxiMin). In zero-sum games, the MiniMax solution is equivalent to the Nash Equilibrium. In the case of study, the Prisoners' Dilemma Game is a non-zero-sum game, so MiniMax Solution, is not necessarily equivalent to Nash Equilibrium Solution.

## 4.4    MOS Algorithm

In order to solve Nash Equilibrium inefficiency, inspired by Folk Theorem of Game Theory, proposed solution is based on a Mobile Agent System, introducing two Agents named MiniMax Agent and MaxiMin Agent, which play against the Nash Agent iterating the strategic Game 2 times. The winner Agent of this iterates Game is the solution of the proposed Algorithm. So, the proposed solution increases the Nash Equilibrium efficiency, finding Pareto optimal solutions where Nash Equilibrium is sub-optimal, as for example in the Prisoner's Dilemma problem, or where Nash Equilibrium not exists at all. Moreover, the proposed algorithm is integrated as a scheduler on a Multi-Cores architecture. Figure 2 shows the the new proposed solution by MOS algorithm for example in a strategic Game where $d>c>b>a$ as in Prisoners' Dilemma problem. Follow the implemented MOS algorithm:

MOS Algorithm

```
For every Matrix M
  Calculate every Nash Equilibrium and select the solutions through
  Nash Agent
  If Nash Equilibrium solution not exists then MiniMax is the temporary
  solution for the initial game matrix
  Calculate every MiniMax and select the solutions through MiniMax
  Agent
  Play a new Game between all the selected Nash and MiniMax Agents
    For every Nash Agent compare his solution with every MiniMax Agent
    solution
      If Nash Agent solution correspond to the MiniMax Agent solution
      and there are not any other solutions then this is the temporary
      solution
      Else for every Nash solution, and for every MiniMax solution
      iterate the Prisoner's Dilemma problem, building a new matrix
      with Nash solution in the first line and MiniMax solution in the
      second line
      Apply Nash Equilibrium solution to the new Matrix and return
      this solution
  Refine obtained solution, playing a new check Game between the
  returned solution and MaxiMin solution applying Nash Equilibrium
  solution to the new Game Matrix.
```

# 5    The Proposed MOS Algorithm Integration on a Multi-cores Architecture

Let's start by looking at MOS integration on a general Multi-Cores architecture. An integration of MOS algorithm into a Multi-Cores architecture is described in figure 2.

To the hardware point of view, this Multi-Cores accelerator looks like an IO unit; it communicates with the CPU using IO commands and DMA memory transfers. To the software point of view, this Multi-Cores accelerator is another computer to which a MOS algorithm sends data and thread to execute.

This Multi-Core architecture has its own memory, called device memory. As with CPUs, access time to the memory is quite slow. Threads run synchronously or asynchronously over the $m$ Cores and the MOS algorithm decide, how to schedule threads on them on the basis of MOS thread scheduling Game. MOS is Agent based software, and agents are players of the thread scheduling game. MOS is essentially a scheduler algorithm that enables to optimize the total system throughput for the threads. It allows concurrent access to the shared General Purpose resources: *Core 1, Core 2, ..., Core m* (red boxes on the above figure 2). The MOS scheduler interact with the Thread Control Unit (blue box on figure 2), transmitting information regarding thread allocation and distributions to the Cores. This Multi-cores architecture is a massive parallel processor that has many cores on it and MOS algorithm requires a parallel programming model, and most importantly, data parallelism. This hardware architecture allows thousands of threads running at the same time in contrast to a general CPU where you have few threads running at the same time, this increase the parallelism to a great extends.

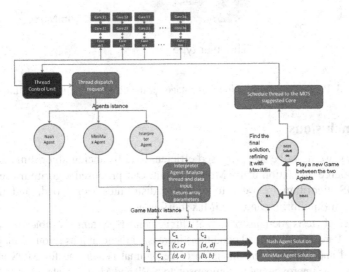

**Fig. 2.** MOS algorithm integration with a multi-core system

# 6    Experimental Results

In this section, we perform an experimental study on the proposed algorithms via simulation. We consider a distributed system setting, which contains 24 cpus. We then analyze the average performance of the algorithms over 500 jobs. The version of the MOS algorithm, implements the Nash and MiniMax technique. Also, the MOS algorithm terminates after a limited number of iterations. Our experiments focus on three metrics, namely: Nash, MiniMax and MOS.

Tests demonstrate the strength of the implemented system. Figure 3 plots the resulting percentage metrics about three algorithms. It shows that the MOS algorithm increases the percentage number of Pareto optimal solution for the game. The gain is more salient reducing the cpu number (by less than 10% in the distributed system). The trade-off is that the required number of executions of the MOS algorithm increases linearly with the number of Game iterations. One interesting side benefit of the MOS algorithm is that it worsens the dispatching overhead as well. A possible explanation is that MOS scheduler computational complexity is $O(n^2)$ in worst case. Thus, in practice, it is reasonable to run a small number of jobs per time (<500). This allows system designers to schedule and distribute the right amount of jobs per time. The Pareto optimal solution percentage for the experimental job simulations is reported in Figure 3:

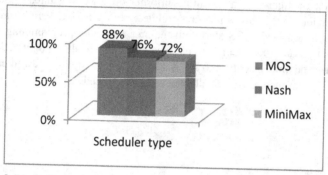

**Fig. 3.** Pareto Optimal solution percentage for the different applied algorithms

# 7    Conclusions

In this paper, we describe our proposed efficient load balancing algorithm and Pareto optimal resource utilization using Mobile Agent. Our proposed algorithm use Mobile Agent MOS algorithm in order to optimize distributes work load, and trying to decrease Nash Equilibrium and MiniMax inefficiency.

Experimental tests demonstrate that implemented system is able to calculate dynamically Pareto Optimal load conditions increasing the total jobs throughput, and with variable load and job/cpu ratio. In figure 6 the optimal percentage for MOS algorithm shows an average improvement in comparison to Nash and MiniMax algorithm.

So, the main target achieved is decreasing significantly MiniMax and Nash Equilibrium inefficiency. According to preliminary results, although our system gives a good result to some extent, there are some points to be modified to reach our target. Therefore we will describe our results in detail in our forthcoming work.

In the near future, this research may be applied to multi-cores systems or to the Smart Grids systems [14, 15, 16]. So, for example using this implemented idea, we are able to predict the behavior of a general distributed system as a *Smart Grid*. Each Agent behaves rationally and only reacts to a price signal, and builds an intelligent Agent-based strategies device system.

# References

1. Myint, C.C., Tun, K.M.L.: A Framework of Using Mobile Agent to Achieve Efficient Load Balancing in Cluster. In: Proceedings of 6th Asia-Pacific Symposium on Information and Telecommunication Technologies, APSITT 2005, November 10, pp. 66–70 (2005), doi:10.1109/APSITT.2005.203632

2. Spata, M.O.: A Nash-Equilibrium Based Algorithm for Scheduling Jobs on a Grid Cluster. In: WETICE 2007, pp. 251–252 (2007)

3. Spata, M.O., Pappalardo, G., Rinaudo, S., Biondi, T.: Agent-Based Negotiation Techniques for a Grid: The Prophet Agents. e-Science 149 (2006)

4. Spata, M.O., Rinaudo, S.: A scheduling Algorithm based on Potential Game for a Cluster Grid. JCIT Journal of Convergence Information Technology (2009)

5. Patrone, F.: Decisori razionali interagenti. Una introduzione alla Teoria dei Giochi - Edizioni PLUS, Pisa (2006) ISBN: 88-8492-350-6

6. Osborne, M.J., Rubinstein, A.: A Course in Game Theory, Par. "Strategic Games", pag. 9,11,14. The MIT Press (July 12, 1994)

7. Nash, J.: Equilibrium points in n-person games. Proceedings of the National Academy of Sciences 36, 48–49 (1950)

8. Ferguson, D., Nikolaou, C., Sairamesh, J., Yemini, Y.: Economic models for allocating resources in computer systems. In: Clearwater, S. (ed.) Market-Based Control: A Paradigm for Distributed Resource Allocation. World Scientific, Hong Kong (1996)

9. Kwok, Y.-K., Song, S., Hwang, K.: Non-Cooperative Grids: Game Theoretic Modeling and Strategy Optimization. Submitted to IEEE Trans. Parallel and Distributed Systems (December 2004)

10. Foundation for Intelligent Physical Agents, FIPA Agent Management Specification & Support for Mobility Specification, Geneva, Switzerland (October 2000), http://www.fipa.org

11. Nash, J.: Equilibrium points in n-person games. Proceedings of the National Academy of Sciences 36, 48–49 (1950)

12. Von Neumann, J.: Zur Theorie der Gesellschaftsspiele. Math. Annalen. 100, 295–320 (1928)

13. Vale, Z.A., Morais, H., Khodr, H.: Intelligent multi-player smart grid management considering distributed energy resources and demand response. In: 2010 IEEE Power and Energy Society General Meeting, pp. 1–7 (2010), doi:10.1109/PES.2010.5590170

14. Mohsenian-Rad, A.-H., Wong, V.W.S., Jatskevich, J., Schober, R.: Optimal and autonomous incentive-based energy consumption scheduling algorithm for smart grid. In: Innovative Smart Grid Technologies (ISGT), pp. 1–6 (2010), doi:10.1109/ISGT.2010.5434752

15. Ibars, C., Navarro, M., Giupponi, L.: Distributed Demand Management in Smart Grid with a Congestion Game. In: First IEEE International Conference on Smart Grid Communications (SmartGridComm), pp. 495–500 (2010), doi:10.1109/SMARTGRID.2010.5622091

16. Aumann, R.J.: Survey of repeated games. In: Aumann, R.J. (ed.) Essays in Game Theory and Mathematical Economics in Honor of Oskar Morgenstern, pp. 11–42. Wissenschaftsverlag, Bibliographisches Institut, Mannheim, Wien (1981)

# Randomized Game Semantics
# for Semi-fuzzy Quantifiers

Christian G. Fermüller and Christoph Roschger

Theory and Logic Group 185.2
Vienna University of Technology

**Abstract.** We first show that randomized payoff in classical evaluation games leads to so-called weak Łukasiewicz logic. A further step of generalization results in Giles's game semantics for full Łukasiewicz logic. Finally we extend the concept of randomization to characterize a family of semi-fuzzy quantifiers embedded into Łukasiewicz logic.

## 1 Introduction

Fuzzy quantification combines the theory of generalized quantifiers [15] with degree based reasoning. As pointed out in Glöckner's monograph [10], there is what can be called an "embarrassment of riches" in modeling vague natural language quantifiers like *many, few, about half*, etc.: the space of candidates for truth functions is simply too complex and large, even if we restrict attention to monadic quantifiers, as we will do here. Glöckner addresses this challenge by focusing on semi-quantifiers first, i.e. quantifiers with classical (bi-valued) scope, and proposes an axiomatically defined scheme for lifting these to fully fuzzy quantification in a later step. Here we want to embed certain semi-fuzzy quantifiers into Łukasiewizc logic, which is not only one of most important formalisms of deductive (mathematical) fuzzy logics in the sense of Hájek [11,12,4], but also allows for a particularly interesting semantic characterization in terms of dialogue games combined with bets on dispersive experiments, introduced by Giles [9,8]. In a sense, this reacts to the mentioned embarrassment of riches by suggesting a bottom-up approach: we start with a convincing and well explored semantic framework for standard first-order Łukasiewicz logic and extend it in a rather lean manner that remains close to its spirit.

Since we do not want to assume familiarity with Giles's game, we begin with the familiar Henkin-Hintikka evaluation game for classical logics and, unlike Giles, introduce many-valued games in reference to that classical game.

## 2 Randomizing Henkin-Hintikka games

As already shown by Hintikka [13], building on an idea of Henkin, the Tarskian notion of truth in a model can be characterized—and in fact generalized—by a two person game played on a first order formula with respect to a given model. We present the classical evaluation game in a slightly unusual terminology that will make the later transition to Giles's game more transparent.

S. Greco et al. (Eds.): IPMU 2012, Part IV, CCIS 300, pp. 632–641, 2012.
© Springer-Verlag Berlin Heidelberg 2012

**The $\mathcal{H}$-Game.** There are two players, say *me* and *you*, who can both act in the roles of either the *attacker* or the *defender* of a formula. The game is played with respect to a given classical first order interpretation $M$, where all domain elements are witnessed by constants. $M$ can thus be identified with an assignment of 0 (*false*) or 1 (*true*) to the variable free atoms of the language. By $v_M(F)$ we denote the truth value to which $F$ evaluates in $M$.

Every state of the game is determined by a sentence (closed formula) $F$ and a *role assignment:* either me or you act as the defender of $F$, the opponent player is the attacker. We will say that player $\mathbf{X}$ *asserts* $F$, if $\mathbf{X}$ is the defender of $F$. The game starts with my assertion of some formula and proceeds according to the following rules corresponding to the form of the currently considered formula.

($R_\wedge$) If I assert $F \wedge G$ then you attack by pointing either to the left or to the right subformula. I then have to assert $F$ or $G$, according to your choice.[1]
($R_\vee$) If I assert $F \vee G$ then I have to assert either $F$ or $G$ at my own choice.
($R_\neg$) If I assert $\neg F$ then our roles are switched and you have to assert $F$.
($R_\exists$) If I assert $\exists x F(x)$ then I have to pick a constant $c$ and assert $F(c)$.
($R_\forall$) If I assert $\forall x F(x)$ then you pick $c$ and I have to assert $F(c)$.

The rules for you defending a formula are completely dual. Role assignment remain unchanged for all state transitions, except for the one explicitly triggered by ($R_\neg$).

Once the game has arrived at an *atomic state*, i.e., at a state where either I or you assert an atomic formula $A$, I win (and you lose) if $v_M(A) = 1$ and I lose (and you win) if $v_M(A) = 0$. We call the game starting with my assertion of $F$ the $\mathcal{H}$-game for $F$ under $M$.

**Theorem 1 (Hintikka).** *A sentence $F$ is true in an interpretation $M$ (in symbols: $v_M(F) = 1$) iff I have a winning strategy in the $\mathcal{H}$-game for $F$ under $M$.*

Our aim is to provide a similarly elegant characterization of *graded truth* for first order fuzzy logics. While game semantics can be generalized to cover a wide range of different many-valued logics (see [5,3,7]) we will stick here to infinite valued Łukasiewicz logic, which is arguably the most important example of a deductive fuzzy logic in the sense of [2].

Łukasiewicz logic $\mathbf{L}$ provides two forms of conjunction: *weak conjunction* ($\wedge$) and *strong conjunction* (&); negation ($\neg$), implication ($\rightarrow$), (weak) disjunction ($\vee$), and standard quantifiers ($\forall$ and $\exists$); specified semantically as follows:

$$v_M(F \wedge G) = \min(v_M(F), v_M(G)) \qquad v_M(F \vee G) = \max(v_M(F), v_M(G))$$
$$v_M(F \& G) = \max(0, v_M(F) + v_M(G) - 1) \qquad\qquad v_M(\bot) = 0$$
$$v_M(\neg F) = 1 - v_M(F) \qquad v_M(F \rightarrow G) = \min(1, 1 - v_M(F) + v_M(G))$$
$$v_M(\forall x F(x)) = \inf_{c \in D}(v_M(G(c))) \qquad v_M(\exists x F(x)) = \sup_{c \in D}(v_M(G(c)))$$

where $D$ is the domain of $M$ (which we identify with the set of constants).

---

[1] Note the duality of the rules for $\wedge$ and $\vee$. A version of conjunction where both conjuncts have to be asserted will be considered for $\mathcal{G}$-games, in Section 3.

There are many good reasons to base $\mathbf{L}$ on the full syntax, as specified above.[2] In particular this nicely fits the general theory of t-norm based fuzzy logics as introduced by Hájek [11,12] and developed into a prolific subfield of mathematical logic by many researchers since, as witnessed by the recent handbook [2]. However, in the vast literature on fuzzy logic and on many-valued logics in general one frequently considers only $\wedge$, $\vee$, and $\neg$ as propositional connectives. We will call this fragment of $\mathbf{L}$, together with the standard quantifiers ($\forall$, $\exists$), *weak Łukasiewicz logic* $\mathbf{L}^w$ here. The restrictions of $\mathbf{L}$ and $\mathbf{L}^w$ to the propositional part will be denoted by $\mathbf{L}_p$ and $\mathbf{L}_p^w$, respectively.

In order to transfer $\mathcal{H}$-games into a many-valued setting we borrow an idea of Giles [9,8] and reformulate the winning condition in a way that will lead to an interesting interpretation of intermediate truth values in terms of expected risks of payments. We conceive of the evaluation of the atomic formula $A$ at the final state of an $\mathcal{H}$-game as a *(binary) experiment* $\mathsf{E}_A$ that either *fails*, meaning $v_M(A) = 0$, or *succeeds*, meaning $v_M(A) = 1$. The experiment $\mathsf{E}_\perp$ always fails. Moreover, we stipulate that I have to pay 1€ to you if I lose the game. Hence winning strategies turn into strategies for avoiding payment.[3] So far this just amounts to an alternative way to present the original game. The main innovation of Giles is to let the experiments $\mathsf{E}_A$ be *dispersive*. This means that $\mathsf{E}_A$ may show different results upon repetition, where the individual trials of the experiment are understood as independent events. (Of course, $\mathsf{E}_\perp$ remains non-dispersive: it simply always fails.) The reader is invited to think about intended applications modeling vague language: while in concrete dialogues competent language users either (momentarily and provisionally) accept or don't accept grammatical utterances upon receiving them, vagueness results in a brittleness or dispersiveness of such highly context dependent decisions. (See, e.g, [16,1].) In order to arrive at 'degrees of truth' for an atomic $A$ in such a model, one assumes that the dialogue partners associate a fixed success probability $\pi(\mathsf{E}_A)$ to the experiment $\mathsf{E}_A$, which may be thought of as (implicitly) answering the question "Do you accept $F$ (at this instance)?" By $\langle A \rangle = 1 - \pi(\mathsf{E}_A)$ we denote the *risk* associated with $A$, i.e., the *expected* (average) loss of money associated with an assertion of $A$. The function $\langle \cdot \rangle$ that maps each atomic sentence into a failure probability of the corresponding experiment is called *risk value assignment*. Note that risk value assignments are in 1-1-correspondence with (many-valued) interpretations via $\langle A \rangle_M = 1 - v_M(A)$.

The setting of randomized payoff for $\mathcal{H}$-games straightforwardly leads to a characterization of weak propositional Łukasiewicz logic $\mathbf{L}_p^w$, as shown in the following theorem.

---

[2] Actually one can define all connectives of $\mathbf{L}$ from just $\rightarrow$ and $\perp$ or alternatively from $\&$ and $\perp$. But neither $\rightarrow$ nor $\&$ can be defined from the remaining connectives.

[3] Note the asymmetry of the payoff scheme: even when the roles of attacker and defender are switched, it is *me*, not *you*, who has to pay upon losing the game. This is necessary to ensure that enforceable payments (inversely) correspond to truth values. Giles's extended game scenario allows one to restore perfect symmetry, as we will see in Section 3.

**Theorem 2.** *A $\mathbf{L}_p^w$-sentence $F$ is evaluated to $v_M(F) = x$ in interpretation $M$ iff in the $\mathcal{H}$-game for $F$ under the corresponding risk value assignment $\langle \cdot \rangle_M$ I have a strategy that limits my expected risk to $(1-x)\, \mathfrak{C}$, while you have a strategy that ensures that my expected risk is not below this value.*

*Proof.* We use $\langle | \, G \rangle^*$ to denote my final expected risk in a game where I am defending and you are attacking $G$ assuming that we both play optimally by employing the usual min-max strategy.[4] If I am the attacker and you are the defender of $G$ this value is denoted by $\langle G \, | \rangle^*$.

If $F$ is atomic then $\langle F \, | \rangle^* = 1 - \langle F \rangle_M$ and $\langle | \, F \rangle^* = \langle F \rangle_M$ and thus my risk is $v_M(F)$ in the former case and $1 - v_M(F)$ in the latter case, as required. Otherwise we argue by induction on the complexity of $F$ that $\langle | \, F \rangle^* = 1 - v_M(F)$.

- If I assert $\neg G$, the game continues with your assertion of $G$ and $\langle | \, \neg G \rangle^*$ reduces to $\langle G \, | \rangle^* = 1 - \langle | \, G \rangle^*$, just like in the truth function for $\neg$.
- If I assert $G \vee H$ then I will pick $G$ or $H$ according to where my associated expected risk is smaller. Therefore $\langle | \, G \vee H \rangle^* = \min(\langle | \, G \rangle^*, \langle | \, H \rangle^*)$, and thus $v_M(G \vee H) = \max(v_M(G), v_M(H)) = 1 - \min(1 - \langle | \, G \rangle^*, 1 - \langle | \, H \rangle^*)$.
- If I assert $G \wedge H$ then you will pick $G$ or $H$ according to where my associated risk, i.e., your expected gain, is higher. Therefore $\langle | \, G \wedge H \rangle^* = \max(\langle | \, G \rangle^*, \langle | \, H \rangle^*)$, corresponding to $v_M(G \wedge H) = \min(v_M(G), v_M(H))$.

The cases where you defend and I attack $F$ are completely dual.  $\square$

Note that we are only interested in *expected* payoffs. Since individual trials of experiments are independent events, truth functionality is preserved. Consider a game for $A \vee \neg A$ for example. While I will finally have to pay either $1\mathfrak{C}$ or nothing, depending on the result of $\mathsf{E}_A$, my optimal expected loss under the risk value assignment corresponding to interpretation $M$ is $\min(\langle A \rangle_M, 1 - \langle A \rangle_M)\mathfrak{C}$, which indeed amounts to $(1 - v_M(A \vee \neg A))\mathfrak{C}$.

There is a slight complication in lifting Theorem 2 to the first order level: in an $[0, 1]$-valued interpretation $M$ witnessing domain elements for quantified sentences may not exist. More precisely, we may have $v_M(\forall x F(x)) < v_M(F(c))$ and $v_M(\exists x F(x)) > v_M(F(c))$ for all constants $c$. For this reason we define the following general notion for games with randomized payoff (as in our new version of the $\mathcal{H}$-game, above, and in $\mathcal{G}$-games, introduced below).

**Definition 1.** *A game with randomized payoff is $r$-valued for player $\mathbf{X}$ if, for every $\epsilon > 0$, $\mathbf{X}$ has a strategy that guarantees that her expected loss is at most $(r + \epsilon)\, \mathfrak{C}$, while her opponent has a strategy that ensures that the loss of $\mathbf{X}$ is at least $(r - \epsilon)\, \mathfrak{C}$. We call $r$ the* risk *for $\mathbf{X}$ in that game.*

This notion allows us to state the generalization of Theorem 2 to $\mathbf{L}^w$ concisely:

---

[4] We assume the reader to be familiar with basic notions of game theory. Formally, we have described a finite zero-sum two person game in extended form with perfect information. Although the payoff is defined in terms of expected payments, probabilities do *not* enter the game itself. The min-max principle induces *pure* optimal strategies. I.e., mixed strategies are not needed to arrive at the (unique) equilibrium.

**Theorem 3.** *A $\mathbf{L}^w$-sentence $F$ is evaluated to $v_M(F) = x$ in interpretation $M$ iff the $\mathcal{H}$-game for $F$ under risk value assignment $\langle \cdot \rangle_M$ is $(1-x)$-valued for me.*

*Proof.* Building on the proof of Theorem 2, it only remains to consider the induction steps for quantified sentences:

- If I assert $\exists x F(x)$, then the game continues with my assertion of $F(c)$ for a constant $c$ picked by me in a manner that minimizes my risk. In fact, since there might possibly be no domain element witnessing the infimum $v_M(\exists x F(x)) = \inf_{c \in D}(v_M(F(c)))$, we can only ensure that, for any given $\delta > 0$, $\langle | \exists x F(x) \rangle^* = \langle | F(c) \rangle^* = 1 - v_M(\exists x F(x)) + \delta$.
- If I assert $\forall x F(x)$, the game continues with my assertion of $F(c)$, where $c$ is chosen by you to maximize my risk. Therefore, analogously, we obtain $\langle | \forall x F(x) \rangle^* = \langle | F(c) \rangle^* = 1 - v_M(\forall x F(x)) - \delta$ for some $\delta > 0$.

The cases where you are the defender of a quantified formula are dual.    □

Note that the value $\epsilon$ mentioned in Definition 1 does not directly correspond to $\delta$ as used in the above proof, but rather results from the accumulation of appropriate $\delta$s. In any case, since our intended applications assume *finite domains*, we may from now on safely ignore the fact that, in general, truth values of statements involving quantifiers are only approximated by expected risk in concrete instances of a game. We nevertheless retain the notion of the *value of a game*, but could actually simplify Definition 1 by dropping all references to $\epsilon$.

## 3   From $\mathcal{H}$-Games to $\mathcal{H}$-Games

Already in the 1970s Robin Giles [9,8] introduced an evaluation game that was intended to provide 'tangible meaning' to reasoning about statements with dispersive semantic tests as they appear in physics. For the logical rules of his game Giles referred not to Henkin or Hintikka, but to Lorenzen's dialogue game semantics for intuitionistic logic [14]. In particular, (essentially) the following rule for implication was proposed:

$(R_\rightarrow)$ If I assert $F \rightarrow G$ then you may attack by asserting $F$, which obliges me to assert $G$. (Analogously if you assert $F \rightarrow G$.)

In contrast to $\mathcal{H}$-games, such a rule introduces game states, where more than one formula may be currently asserted by each of us. Since, in general, it matters whether we assert the same statement just once or more often, game states are now denoted as pairs of multisets of formulas. We call such games $\mathcal{G}$-*games*. A *final state* of a $\mathcal{G}$-game where $\{p_1, \ldots, p_n\}$ is the multiset of atomic assertions made by you and $\{q_1, \ldots, q_m\}$ is the multiset of atomic assertions made by me is denoted by

$$[A_1, \ldots, A_n \mid B_1, \ldots, B_m].$$

Again we assume that a binary experiment $\mathsf{E}_A$ is associated with every atomic $A$ with corresponding risk $\langle A \rangle = 1 - \pi(\mathsf{E}_A)$. We now make payments fully dual and stipulate that I have to pay 1€ to you whenever an instance of an experiment corresponding to one of my atomic assertion fails, while you have to pay me 1€ for each instance of a failing experiment corresponding to one of your atomic assertions. We obtain the following value for the expected total amount of money (in €) that I have to pay to you at the exhibited final state:

$$\langle A_1, \ldots, A_n \mid B_1, \ldots, B_m \rangle = \sum_{1 \leq i \leq m} \langle B_i \rangle - \sum_{\leq j \leq n} \langle A_j \rangle.$$

We call this value briefly my *risk* associated with that state. Note that the risk can be negative in $\mathcal{G}$-games, i.e., the risk values of the relevant propositions may be such that I expect a net payment by you to me.

Interestingly, the logical rules $(R_\wedge)$, $(R_\vee)$, $(R_\forall)$, and $(R_\exists)$ defined in Section 2 remain unchanged for $\mathcal{G}$-games. By adding the above implication rule $(R_\rightarrow)$ and defining $\neg F = (F \rightarrow \bot)$ we arrive at Giles's game for Łukasiewicz logic.

We like to point out that $(R_\rightarrow)$ contains a hidden *principle of limited liability*: the player opposing the defender of $F \rightarrow G$ may (instead of asserting $F$ in return for the opponent's assertion of $G$) explicitly choose not to attack $F \rightarrow G$ at all. This option results in a branching of the game tree. The state $[\Gamma \mid \Delta, F \rightarrow G]$, where $\Gamma$ and $\Delta$ are multisets of sentences asserted by you and me, respectively, and where the exhibited occurrence indicates that you currently refer to my assertion of $F \rightarrow G$, has the two possible successor states: $[F, \Gamma \mid \Delta, G]$ and $[\Gamma \mid \Delta]$. In the latter state you have chosen to limit your liability in the following sense. Attacking an opponent's assertion should never incur an expected (positive) loss, which were the case if the risk associated with asserting $F$ is higher than that for asserting $G$. In such cases a rational player in the attacking role will explicitly renounce an attack on $F \rightarrow G$. For all other logical connectives the principle is ensured by the fact that—in all games considered here—each occurrence of a formula can be attacked at most once. (The attacked occurrence is removed from the state in the transition to a corresponding successor state.)

Another form of the principle of limited liability can be considered for defending moves. In defending any sentence $F$, the defending player has to be able to hedge her (possible) loss associated with the assertions made in defense of $F$ to at most 1€. This is already the case for all logical rules considered so far. However, as shown in [5,6], by making this principle explicit we arrive at a rule for strong conjunction, that is missing in Giles:

$(R_\&)$ If I assert $F\&G$, I have to assert either both $F$ and $G$, or assert $\bot$ instead.

This allows us to characterize strong Łukasiewicz logic **Ł** by a $\mathcal{G}$-game:

**Theorem 4 (essentially Giles, but see also [6]).** *A **Ł**-sentence $F$ is evaluated to $v_M(F) = x$ in interpretation $M$ iff the $\mathcal{G}$-game for $F$ under risk value assignment $\langle \cdot \rangle_M$ is $(1 - x)$-valued for me.*

# 4   (Semi-)Fuzzy Quantifiers and Random Witnesses

As Glöckner emphasizes in his important monograph on fuzzy quantifiers [10], the very concept of generalized quantifiers over $[0, 1]$ poses a challenge that may be termed an *embarrassment of riches*: even when we focus on logical quantifiers of type $\langle 1 \rangle$, i.e., monadic quantifiers like $\exists$ and $\forall$, the space of possible truth functions is too large and complex to support the selection of plausible candidates for linguistically adequate models.[5] We argue that a simple generalization of the game for **Ł**, described in Section 3, allows one to address this challenge by singling out a lean class of quantifiers that nicely fits Giles's idea to provide "tangible meaning" to logical connectives in terms of bets on the results of dispersive experiments. Remember that the only difference between the rules $(R_\forall)$ and $(R_E)$ for defending assertions $\forall x F(x)$ and $\exists x F(x)$, respectively, is that either the defender or the attacker has to pick the constant $c$ that determines the new sentence $F(c)$ that remains to be defended. Because of the randomized setting of $\mathcal{G}$-games, the following rule for a new type of (unary) quantifier $\Pi$ seems natural:

$(R_\Pi)$ If I assert $\Pi x F(x)$ then I have to assert $F(c)$ for a randomly picked $c$.

The random choice refers to a uniform distribution of the domain. Note that, while all kinds of other forms of randomly picking domain elements might be considered in principle, we recall from the literature on generalized quantifiers (see, e.g., [15,18]) that a necessary condition for a quantifier to be called *logical* is the *domain invariance* of its semantics.[6] As will get clear below, this is guaranteed for $\Pi$ (and for the quantifiers considered in Section 5) by insisting on random choices with respect to a uniform distribution.

While $(R_\Pi)$, arguably, makes sense for arbitrary **Ł**-formulas $F$ in the scope of $\Pi$, we will view $\Pi$ as a *semi-fuzzy quantifier* and hence insist on classical formulas in its scope. To explain and motivate this design choice, we point out that Glöckner [10] responses to the above mentioned challenge ("too many" candidates for modeling fuzzy quantifiers) by focusing on semi-fuzzy quantifiers first and employing an axiomatically specified scheme for lifting those semi-fuzzy quantifiers to fully fuzzy quantifiers later. We follow this suggestion and enrich the language of **Ł** by distinguishing between *classical* (two-valued) and (possibly) *fuzzy* formulas already at the syntactic level. More formally, we specify the language for logic **Ł**$(Qs)$, where $Qs$ is a list of (unary) quantifier symbols other than $\forall$ or $\exists$, as follows:

$$\gamma ::= \bot \mid \hat{P}(t) \mid \neg\gamma \mid (\gamma \vee \gamma) \mid (\gamma \wedge \gamma) \mid \forall v\gamma \mid \exists v\gamma$$
$$\varphi ::= \gamma \mid \tilde{P}(t) \mid \neg\varphi \mid (\varphi \vee \varphi) \mid (\varphi \wedge \varphi) \mid (\varphi \to \varphi) \mid (\varphi \& \varphi) \mid \forall v\varphi \mid \exists v\varphi \mid Qv\gamma$$

where $\hat{P}$ and $\tilde{P}$ are meta-variables for classical and for general (i.e., possible fuzzy) predicate symbols, respectively, $Q \in Qs$; $v$ is our meta-variable for object

---

[5] We use the term "linguistically adequate" here for vague determiners like "many", "few", "about half" etc. in the same sense as Glöckner [10], but want to emphasize that this amounts to a much less stringent criterion than empirical adequateness with respect to observable behavior of competent speakers as studied in (formal) semantics of natural language by linguists (see, e.g., [17]).

[6] There is no agreement in the literature on when a generalized quantifier is to be called *logical*. However it is at least clear that invariance with respect to isomorphisms between domains is a necessary condition. See [15] for a discussion of this issue.

variables; $t$ denotes a sequence of terms, i.e. either object variable or a constant symbol, matching the arity of the preceding predicate symbol. Note the scope of the additional quantifiers from $Qs$ is always a classical formula. Otherwise the syntax is as for $\mathbf{L}$ itself.

The following notion supports a crisp specification of truth functions for semi-fuzzy quantifiers over finite interpretations.

**Definition 2.** *Let $\hat{G}(x)$ be a classical formula and $v_M(\cdot)$ a corresponding evaluation function over the finite domain $D$. Then*

$$\operatorname{Prop}_x \hat{G}(x) = \frac{\sum_{c \in D} v_M(\hat{G}(c))}{|D|}$$

Rule $(R_\Pi)$ matches the specification of $\Pi$ by $v_M(\Pi x F(x)) = \operatorname{Prop}_x F(x)$.

**Theorem 5.** *A $\mathbf{L}(\Pi)$-sentence $F$ is evaluated to $v_M(F) = x$ in an interpretation $M$ iff the $\mathcal{G}$-game for $F$ augmented by rule $(R_\Pi)$ is $(1 - x)$-valued for me under risk value assignment $\langle \cdot \rangle_M$.*

Theorem 5 will turn out to be an instance of a more general result to be proved in the next section.

# 5 Proportionality Quantifiers

Remember that in the context of our $\mathcal{G}$-games we have considered *three types of challenges* to the defender $\mathbf{X}$ of a quantified sentence $Q x F(x)$. In each case $\mathbf{X}$ has to assert $F(c)$, but the constant (domain element) is either

**(A)** chosen by the attacker, or
**(D)** chosen by the defender, or
**(R)** chosen randomly.

We will speak of a challenge of type A, D, or R, respectively. The need to variate these three challenges arises when we allow the defender (and possibly also the attacker) of $Q x F(x)$ to bet either *for* or *against* $F(c)$. Betting for $F(c)$ simply means to assert $F(c)$, betting against $F(c)$ is equivalent to betting for $\neg F(c)$ and thus amounts to an assertion of $\bot$ in exchange for an assertion of $F(c)$ by the opposing player. Note that we can view this as follows: $\mathbf{X}$ pays 1€ for a betting ticket regarding $F(c)$ that entitles her to receive whatever payment by her opponent $\mathbf{Y}$ is due for $\mathbf{Y}$'s assertion of $F(c)$ according to the results of associated dispersive experiments made at the end of the game.

By allowing the players to choose between various successor states that result from an attack on $Q x F(x)$ by certain numbers of bets for or against various instances of $F(x)$, where the constants replacing $x$ can be of type A, D, or R, we arrive at a rich set of possible quantifier rules. Here we will only investigate the family of *proportionality quantifiers* $\Pi_m^k$ specified by the following schematic game rule, where $\hat{F}$ is a classical formula:

$(R_{\Pi_m^k})$ If I assert $\Pi_m^k x \hat{F}(x)$ then $k+m$ constants are chosen randomly and I have to pick $k$ of those constants, say $c_1, \ldots, c_k$, and bet for $\hat{F}(c_1), \ldots, \hat{F}(c_k)$, while simultaneously betting against $\hat{F}(c_1'), \ldots, \hat{F}(c_m')$, where $c_1', \ldots, c_m'$ are the remaining $m$ random constants. (Likewise for your assertion of $\Pi_m^k x \hat{F}(x)$.)

Although not mentioned explicitly we emphasize that the principle of limited liability remains in place: after the constants are chosen, I may assert $\bot$ (i.e., agree to pay 1€) instead of betting as indicated above.

We claim that this rule matches the extension of $\mathbf{L}$ to $\mathbf{L}(\Pi_m^k)$ by

$$v_M(\Pi_m^k \hat{F}(x)) = \binom{k+m}{k}(\operatorname{Prop}_x \hat{F}(x))^k (1 - \operatorname{Prop}_x \hat{F}(x))^m.$$

**Theorem 6.** *A* $\mathbf{L}(\Pi_m^k)$*-sentence* $F$ *is evaluated to* $v_M(F) = x$ *in interpretation* $M$ *iff the* $\mathcal{G}$*-game for* $F$ *augmented by rule* $(R_{\Pi_m^k})$ *is* $(1-x)$*-valued for me under risk value assignment* $\langle \cdot \rangle_M$.

*Proof.* Relative to the proof of Theorem 4 (see [9,8,6]) we only have to consider states of the form $\left[ \Gamma \mid \Delta, \Pi_m^k x \hat{F}(x) \right]$. (I.e., we only consider my assertions of proportionally quantified sentences. The case for your assertions of $\Pi_m^k x \hat{F}(x)$ is dual.) For my enforceable risk at such a state we have

$$\left\langle \Gamma \mid \Delta, \Pi_m^k x \hat{F}(x) \right\rangle^* = \langle \Gamma \mid \Delta \rangle^* + \left\langle \mid \Pi_m^k x \hat{F}(x) \right\rangle^*$$

and it remains to show that my optimal way to reduce the exhibited quantified formula to instances as required by rule $(R_{\Pi_m^k})$ results in a risk that corresponds to the specified truth function. In order to do so remember that the principle of limited liability is in place. Moreover remember that $\hat{F}$ is classical. This means that I either finally have to pay 1€ for my assertion of $\Pi_m^k x \hat{F}(x)$ or do not have to pay anything at all for it. The latter is only the case if all my bets for $\hat{F}(c_1), \ldots, \hat{F}(c_k)$, as well as all my bets against $\hat{F}(c_1'), \ldots, \hat{F}(c_m')$, for $c_1, \ldots, c_k$, $c_1', \ldots, c_m'$ as specified in rule $(R_{\Pi_m^k})$ succeed. The probability that this event obtains, i.e., the inverse of my associated risk, is readily calculated to be

$$\binom{k+m}{k} p^k (1-p)^m,$$

where $p = \operatorname{Prop}_x \hat{F}(x)$, which matches the relevant truth function in $\mathbf{L}(\Pi_m^k)$. $\square$

# 6   Conclusion

We have extended Giles's game based semantics for Łukasiewicz logic by considering randomly chosen domain elements as witnessing constants for certain instances of quantified statements. This allows one to specify the meaning of certain semi-fuzzy quantifiers in the spirit of Giles's approach to approximate reasoning. Further extensions are needed to model vague natural language quantifiers like *most, few,* or *about half.* In particular, in order to arrive at linguistically adequate models, one should move from monadic to dyadic quantifiers and moreover incorporate context dependency. Together with other relevant questions, like lifting to fully fuzzy quantifiers, axiomatization, complexity, and the relation to other forms of game semantics, this is a topic for future work.

**Acknowledgments.** This work has been supported by the ESF/Austrian Science Foundation (FWF), Grant 1143-G15 (LogICCC/LoMoReVI).

# References

1. Barker, C.: The dynamics of vagueness. Linguistics & Philosophy 25(1), 1–36 (2002)
2. Cintula, P., Hájek, P., Noguera, C. (eds.): Handbook of Mathematical Fuzzy Logic. College Publications (2011)
3. Cintula, P., Majer, O.: Towards evaluation games for fuzzy logics. In: Majer, O., Pietarinen, A.-V., Tulenheimo, T. (eds.) Games: Unifying Logic, Language, and Philosophy, pp. 117–138. Springer (2009)
4. Esteva, F., Godo, L., Hájek, P., Navara, M.: Residuated fuzzy logics with an involutive negation. Archive for Mathematical Logic 39, 103–124 (2000)
5. Fermüller, C.G.: Revisiting Giles's game. In: Majer, O., Pietarinen, A.-V., Tulenheimo, T. (eds.) Games: Unifying Logic, Language, and Philosophy. Logic, Epistemology, and the Unity of Science, pp. 209–227. Springer (2009)
6. Fermüller, C.G., Metcalfe, G.: Giles's game and the proof theory of łukasiewicz logic. Studia Logica 92(1), 27–61 (2009)
7. Fermüller, C.G., Roschger, C.: From games to truth functions: A generalization of Giles's game
8. Giles, R.: A non-classical logic for physics. Studia Logica 33(4), 397–415 (1974)
9. Giles, R.: A non-classical logic for physics. In: Wojcicki, R., Malinkowski, G. (eds.) Selected Papers on Łukasiewicz Sentential Calculi, pp. 13–51. Polish Academy of Sciences (1977)
10. Glöckner, I.: Fuzzy quantifiers: a computational theory. STUDFUZZ, vol. 193. Springer (2006)
11. Hájek, P.: Metamathematics of Fuzzy Logic. Kluwer Academic Publishers (2001)
12. Hájek, P.: What is mathematical fuzzy logic. Fuzzy Sets and Systems 157(157), 597–603 (2006)
13. Hintikka, J.: Logic, language-games and information: Kantian themes in the philosophy of logic. Clarendon Press, Oxford (1973)
14. Lorenzen, P.: Logik und Agon. In: Atti Congr. Internaz. di Filosofia, pp. 187–194. Sansoni (1960)
15. Peters, S., Westerståhl, D.: Quantifiers in language and logic. Oxford University Press, USA (2006)
16. Shapiro, S.: Vagueness in context. Oxford University Press, USA (2006)
17. Solt, S.: Vagueness in quantity: Two case studies from a linguistic perspective. In: Cintula, P., et al. (eds.) Reasoning under Vagueness - Logical, Philosophical and Linguistic Perspectives. College Publications (2011)
18. van Benthem, J.: Questions about quantifiers. Journal of Symbolic Logic 49(2), 443–466 (1984)

# Algorithms for Payoff Trajectories in $C^1$ Parametric Games

David Carfì[1] and Angela Ricciardello[2]

[1] Department of Mathematics
University of California at Riverside
900 Big Springs Road, Surge 231 Riverside, CA 92521-0135, USA
davidcarfi71@yahoo.it
[2] Department of Mathematics, Faculty of Sciences MM.FF.NN.
University of Messina, Italy
aricciardello@unime.it

**Abstract.** In 2009 ([4]) a new procedure to determine the payoff space of non-parametric differentiable normal form games has been presented. Then, the new procedure has been applied (in [1]) to numerically determine an original type of 3-dimensional representation of the family of payoff spaces in normal-form $C^1$ parametric games, with two players. In this work, the method in [4] has been pointed out and assumed with the aim of realizing an algorithm which (computationally) gives the real geometric representation of the payoff trajectory of normal-form $C^1$-parametric games, with two players. The application of our algorithm to several examples concludes the paper. Our analysis of parametric games, also, allows us to pass from the standard normal-form games to their coopetitive extension, as already illustrated in several applicative papers by D. Carfì.

**Keywords:** Normal form games, critical zone and payoff space.

## 1 Introduction

The great achievement of the game theory arises form the wide variety of fields in which it has been applied, in order to model and analyze a large collection of human and animal behavior as well as economic, political, sociological and psychological ones. Our study pertains to normal-form $C^1$-games in $n$-dimensions, that is $n$-player normal form games whose payoff functions are at least of class $C^1$ and defined on (compact) intervals of the real Euclidean $n$-spaces. This study includes also games whose payoff functions present a parameter varying in a one dimensional set. In [11, 21, 18–20] the authors analyze parametric games, where the parameter set is interpreted as a coopetitive strategy space. Our analysis of parametric games allows us to pass from the standard normal-form games (see, for this classic games, [3, 2, 24, 25]) to their coopetitive extension, as illustrated in several applicative papers by D. Carfì. In particular, in [4], a new procedure to determine the payoff space of non-parametric differentiable games has been

S. Greco et al. (Eds.): IPMU 2012, Part IV, CCIS 300, pp. 642–654, 2012.

presented, then this new procedure has been applied in [1] to numerically determine the payoff space for normal-form $C^1$ parametric games, in two dimensions.
In this work, the method in [4] has been pointed out and assumed with the
aim of realizing an algorithm for the computational representation of the payoff
trajectory in the case of normal-form $C^1$-parametric games. To ease the reader,
in the first section of the paper we bring to mind terminology and some definitions, while in the second part, the method proposed in [4] and applied in the
development of our algorithm, is presented. Moreover, the particular case of two
parametric games is shown in the third section. The application of our algorithm
to several examples concludes the paper.

## 2 Preliminaries and Notations

In order to help the reader and increase the level of readability of the paper,
we recall some notations and definitions about $n$-player games in normal-form,
presented yet in [4, 1].

**Definition 1 (of game in normal-form).** *Let $E = (E_i)_{i=1}^n$ be an ordered
family of non-empty sets. We call n-**person game in normal-form**, upon
the support $E$, each function $f : {}^\times E \to \mathbb{R}^n$, where ${}^\times E$ denotes the Cartesian
product $\times_{i=1}^n E_i$ of the family $E$. The set $E_i$ is called the **strategy set of player**
$i$, for every index $i$ of the family $E$, and the product ${}^\times E$ is called the **strategy
profile space**, or the n-strategy space, of the game.*

**Terminology.** Together with the previous definition of game in normal form,
we have to introduce some terminologies:

- the set $\{i\}_{i=1}^n$ of the first $n$ positive integers is said *the set of players* of the
  game;
- each element of the Cartesian product ${}^\times E$ is said a *strategy profile*, or $n$-
  strategy, of the game;
- the image of the function $f$, i.e., the set $f({}^\times E)$ of all real $n$-vectors of type
  $f(x)$, with $x$ in the strategy profile space ${}^\times E$, is called the *n-payoff space*, or
  simply the *payoff space*, of the game $f$.

Moreover, we recall the definition of Pareto boundary whose main properties
have been presented in [6]. By the way, the maximal boundary of a subset $T$ of
the Euclidean space $\mathbb{R}^n$ is the set of those $s \in T$ which are not strictly less than
any other element of $T$.

**Definition 2 (of Pareto boundary).** *The **Pareto maximal boundary of**
**a game** $f$ is the subset of the n-strategy space of those n-strategies $x$ such that
the corresponding payoff $f(x)$ is maximal in the n-payoff space, with respect to
the usual order of the euclidean n-space $\mathbb{R}^n$. If $S$ denotes the strategy space
${}^\times E$, we shall denote the maximal boundary of the n-payoff space by $\overline{\partial} f(S)$ and
the maximal boundary of the game by $\overline{\partial}_f(S)$ or by $\overline{\partial}(f)$ . In other terms, the*

*maximal boundary* $\overline{\partial}_f(S)$ *of the game is the reciprocal image (by the function* $f$) *of the maximal boundary of the payoff space* $f(S)$. *We shall use analogous terminologies and notations for the* **minimal Pareto boundary.**

# 3  The Method for $C^1$ Games

In this paper, we deal with normal-form game $f$ defined on the product of $n$ compact and non-degenerate intervals of the real line, and such that $f$ is the restriction to the $n$-strategy space of a $C^1$ function defined on an open set of $\mathbb{R}^n$ containing the $n$-strategy space $S$ (which, in this case, is a compact infinite part of the $n$-space $\mathbb{R}^n$). Details are in [4, 17], but in the following we recall some basic notions.

## 3.1  Topological Boundary

We recall that the *topological boundary* of a subset $S$ of a topological space $(X, \tau)$ is the set defined by the following three equivalent assertions:

- it is the closure of $S$ minus the interior of $S$: $\partial S = \bar{S} \backslash \text{int}(S)$;
- it is the intersection of closure of $S$ with closure of its complement: $\partial S = \bar{S} \cap \overline{(X \backslash S)}$;
- it is the set of those points $x$ of $X$ such that every neighborhood of $x$ contains at least one point of $S$ and at least one point in the complement of $S$.

**Note.** Observe that the topological boundary of the support $X$ of the topological space $(X, \tau)$ is empty (in the topological space itself).

The key theorem of our method is the following one, we invite the reader to **pay much attention to the topologies used below.**

**Theorem 1.** *Let* $f$ *be a* $C^1$ *function defined upon an open set* $O$ *of the euclidean space* $\mathbb{R}^n$ *and with values in* $\mathbb{R}^n$. *Then, for every part* $S$ *of the open set* $O$, *the topological boundary of the image of* $S$ *by the function* $f$, **in the topological space** $f(O)$ *(i.e. with respect to the relativization of the Euclidean topology to* $f(O)$, *is contained in the union* $f(\partial_O S) \cup f(C)$, *that is*

$$\partial_{f(O)} f(S) \subseteq f(\partial_O S) \cup f(C),$$

*where: (1)* $C$ *is the critical set of the function* $f$ *in* $S$ *(that is the set of all points* $x$ *of* $S$ *such that the Jacobian matrix* $J_f(x)$ *is not invertible); (2)* $\partial_O S$ *is the topological boundary of* $S$ *in* $O$ *(with respect to the relative topology of* $O$).

**Note.** Observe for example the following trivial case. Let $O$ be the unit open ball $B(0_2, 1)$ of the plane and let $f$ be the immersion of $O$ in the plane. If $S := O$, then $f(S) = O$; the boundary of $f(S)$ in $f(O)$ is empty (since $f(O) = O$), the boundary of $S$ in $O$ is empty too, and the theorem gives the trivial inclusion $\varnothing \subseteq \varnothing$.

**Note.** We note, however, that when $S$ is a compact subset of the open set $O$ (it doesn't matter in what topology...), then the boundaries of $S$ and $f(S)$ in $O$ and $f(O)$ coincides with the boundaries of $S$ and $f(S)$ in $\mathbb{R}^n$.

# 4  Two Players Parametric Games

In this section we shall introduce the definitions of parametric games, as it is employed in the following.

**Definition 3.** Let $E = (E_t)_{t \in T}$ and $F = (F_t)_{t \in T}$ be two families of non empty sets and let $f = (f_t)_{t \in T}$ be a family of functions, where $f_t : E_t \times F_t \to \mathbb{R}^2$, for each $t \in T$. We define **parametric gain game over the strategy pair** $(E, F)$ **and with family of payoff functions** $f$ the pair $G = (f, >)$, where the symbol $>$ stands for the usual strict upper order of the Euclidean plane $\mathbb{R}^2$. We define the **payoff space of the parametric game** $G$ as the union of all the payoff spaces of the game family $g = ((f_t, >))_{t \in T}$, that is, as the union of the payoff family

$$P = (f_t(E_t \times F_t))_{t \in T}.$$

**Dynamics.** We will refer to the above family $g$ as to **the parametric trajectory (or the dynamical path) of the game** $G$, since we can see it as a curve of games:

$$g : T \to g(T) : t \mapsto (f_t, >).$$

## 4.1  Aims of the Paper

Our algorithm gives us

- the dynamical evolution of the payoff family $P$, in the sense of the dynamical evolution (in real time) when we consider the parameter set $T$ as the real time straight-line (this by movies);
- the trace of this parametric trajectory, i.e., the very payoff space of the parametric game $G$.

## 4.2  Payoff Set-Dynamics

We note also that the family $P$ can be identified with the multi-valued path in $\mathbb{R}^2$

$$p : T \to \mathbb{R}^2 : t \mapsto f_t(E_t \times F_t),$$

(multivalued means that to each value $t \in T$ the mappings $p$ associates a subset of the plane, and not one unique single point of it) and that the graph of this path $p$ is a subset of the Cartesian product $T \times \mathbb{R}^2$, on the other hand, the trace of the curve $p$, is a subset of the plane and it is the union of all the values of the multi-valued path $p$.

## 4.3    The Game Framework of the Algorithm

In particular we focus on parametric games in which the families $E$ and $F$ consist of only one set, respectively. In the latter case, we can identify a parametric game with a pair $(f, >)$, where $f$ is a function from a Cartesian product $T \times E \times F$ into the plane $\mathbb{R}^2$, where $T$, $E$ and $F$ are three non-empty sets.

**Definition 4.** *When the triple* $(T, E, F)$ *is a triple of subsets of normed spaces, we define the parametric game* $(f, >)$ *of class* $C^1$ *if the function* $f$ *is of class* $C^1$.

# 5    Numerical Results

In [1], we gave a representation of the payoff space of a parametric game as disjoint union the payoff space family. In this work, we depict the very payoff trajectory (the trace in the plane of the dynamical evolution of the payoff family) of a parametric game. In order to compare the two algorithms, in the following we will analyze the same games illustrated in [1]. In details, we consider a (loss) parametric game $(h, <)$, with strategy sets $E = F = [0, 1]$, parameter set $T = [0, 1]^2$ and biloss (disutility) function $h : T \times E \times F \to \mathbb{R}^2$, whose section $h_{(a,b)} : E \times F \to \mathbb{R}^2$ is defined by

$$h_{(a,b)}(x, y) = (x - (1 - a)xy, y - (1 - b)xy),$$

for all $(x, y) \in E \times F$ and $(a, b) \in [0, 1]^2$.

The above game is the Von Neumann mixed extension of the natural finite game represented by the following bi-matrix

$$\begin{pmatrix} (0, 0) & (0, 1) \\ (1, 0) & (a, b) \end{pmatrix}.$$

Assume, now, that the parameter points $(a, b)$ belong also to the 1-sphere $\mathbf{S}_p^1$, with respect to the $p$-norm, in the Euclidean plane $\mathbb{R}^2$, for some positive real $p$; that is, let us assume $a^p + b^p = 1$, for some positive real $p$. Consider, then, the restriction $g : S \times E \times F \to \mathbb{R}^2$, of the function $h$ to the parameter set $S = \mathbf{S}_p^1 \cap T$. By projecting on the first factor of the product $S \times E \times F$, we can consider, instead of the parametric game $g$, with parameter set $\mathbf{S}_p^1 \cap T$, the equivalent parametric game $(f, <)$, with parameter set $[0, 1]$ and $a$-payoff function $f_a$ defined by

$$f_a(x, y) = (x - (1 - a)xy, y - (1 - (1 - a^p)^{1/p})xy),$$

for all $(x, y) \in E \times F$ and $a \in [0, 1]$. Here, by equivalent parametric game, we mean the existence of the bijection $j : S \to [0, 1] : (a, b) \mapsto a$, whose inverse is the bijection

$$j^{-1} : [0, 1] \to S : a \mapsto (a, (1 - a^p)^{1/p}).$$

## 5.1   The algorithm

The algorithm, applied for the representation of payoff spaces, shows the following main steps.

INPUT: $E \times F = rectangular\{P1 \equiv (x1, y1), P2 \equiv (x2, y1), P3 \equiv (x2, y2), P4 \equiv (x1, y2)\}$; $T = [a_m, a_M]$; $f_{a,1}(x, y)$, $f_{a,2}(x, y)$

PROCESSING:

– TRANSFORMATION OF THE TOPOLOGICAL BOUNDARY: $\forall \overline{a} \in T$ we obtain

$$X = f_{1,\overline{a}}(x1, y) \cup f_{1,\overline{a}}(x, y1) \cup f_{1,\overline{a}}(x3, y) \cup f_{1,\overline{a}}(x, y3)$$

with $x \in [x1, x3]$ and $y \in [y1, y3]$

$$Y = f_{2,\overline{a}}(x1, y) \cup f_{2,\overline{a}}(x, y1) \cup f_{2,\overline{a}}(x3, y) \cup f_{2,\overline{a}}(x, y3)$$

with $x \in [x1, x3]$ and $y \in [y1, y3]$

– EVALUATION OF THE CRITICAL ZONE $CZ$: we solve the equation

$$\partial_1 f_{1,a}(x, y) \cdot \partial_2 f_{2,a}(x, y) - \partial_2 f_{1,a}(x, y) \cdot \partial_1 f_{2,a}(x, y) = 0$$

– TRANSFORMATION OF THE CRITICAL ZONE: $\forall (\overline{x}, \overline{y}) \in CZ$ we obtain

$$f_a(\overline{x}, \overline{y}) = (f_{1,a}(\overline{x}, \overline{y}), f_{2,a}(\overline{x}, \overline{y}))$$

OUTPUT: plots of the payoff trajectory.

## 5.2   Examples

In the following subsections we shall consider the following examples:

1. $f : [0, 1]^3 \to \mathbb{R}^2 : f_a(x, y) = (x - (1 - a)xy, y - axy)$,
   *for all $x, y$ and $a$ in $[0, 1]$.*

2. $f : [0, 1]^3 \to \mathbb{R}^2 : f_a(x, y) = (x - (1 - a)xy, y - (1 - (1 - a^{0.1})^{10})xy)$,
   *for all $x, y$ and $a$ in $[0, 1]$.*

3. $f : [0, 1]^3 \to \mathbb{R}^2 : f_a(x, y) = (x - (1 - a)xy, y - (1 - (1 - a^{0.5})^2)xy)$,
   *for all $x, y$ and $a$ in $[0, 1]$.*

4. $f : [0, 1]^3 \to \mathbb{R}^2 : f_a(x, y) = (x - (1 - a)xy, y - (1 - (1 - a^2)^{0.5})xy)$,
   *for all $x, y$ and $a$ in $[0, 1]$.*

5. $f : [0, 1]^3 \to \mathbb{R}^2 : f_a(x, y) = (x - (1 - xy), y - (1 - (1 - a^{10})^{0.1})xy)$,
   *for all $x, y$ and $a$ in $[0, 1]$.*

6. $g : [0, 1] \times [0, 2]^2 \to \mathbb{R}^2 : g_a(x, y) = (x + y + a, x - y + a^2)$,
   *for all $x, y \in [0, 2]$ and $a \in [0, 1]$.*

7. $h : [-1, 1] \times [0, 2]^2 \to \mathbb{R}^2 : h_a(x, y) = (x + y + a, x - y + |a|)$,
   *for all $x, y \in [0, 2]$ and $a \in [-1, 1]$.*

8. $c : [0, 6] \times [0, 1]^2 \to \mathbb{R}^2 : c_a(x, y) = (x(1 - x - y) + a, y(1 - x - y) - (a - 3)^2/6 + 3/2)$,
   *for all $x, y \in [0, 1]$ and $a \in [0, 6]$.*

## 5.3 What's New in Our Paper

In this work we present a new numerical approach: our algorithm does not represent the disjoint union of the payoff family

$$(f_a(E \times F))_{a \in T}, \tag{1}$$

as we did in [1], but we represent its simple union, that is, the genuine *payoff space of the game G*.

## 5.4 First Game: $(f, <)$ with $p = 1$

Let $E = F = [0, 1]$ be the strategy sets of our parametric game $(f, <)$ and let $a$ be a real number fixed in the interval $[0, 1]$. Consider the $a$-biloss (disutility) function of the parametric game $(f, <)$, defined by

$$f_a(x, y) = (x - (1 - a)xy, y - axy),$$

for all $x, y$ in $[0, 1]$. The critical zone of the function $f_a$, for every $a$ in $[0, 1]$, is the segment

$$\mathcal{C}(f_a) = \{(x, y) \in [0, 1]^2 : 1 - ax - (1 - a)y = 0\}.$$

Figure 1, shows the payoff space of the parametric game $(f, <)$. In particular, we can distinguish the transformations of the strategy topological boundary, in blue, and the transformations of the critical zones in green.

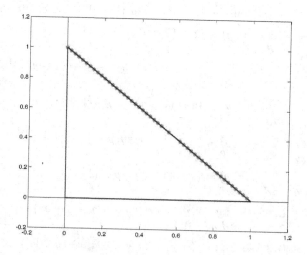

**Fig. 1.** The first game

## 5.5   Second Game: $(f, <)$ with $p = 0.1$

Our second game has strategy sets $E = F = [0, 1]$ and $a$-biloss function $f_a$, given by

$$f_a(x, y) = (x - (1 - a)xy, y - (1 - (1 - a^{0.1})^{10})xy),$$

for all $x, y$ $a$ in $[0, 1]$. The critical zone of the $a$-biloss function is the segment

$$\mathcal{C}(f_a) = \{(x, y) \in [0, 1]^2 : 1 - (1 - (1 - a^{0.1})^{10})x - (1 - a)y = 0\}.$$

Figure 2 shows the payoff space of the game $(f, <)$. In particular, we can distinguish the transformations of the strategy topological boundary in blue and the transformations of the critical zones in green.

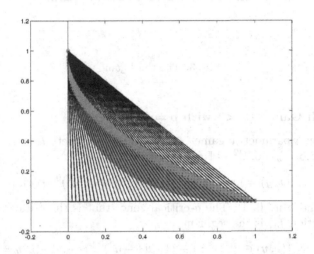

**Fig. 2.** The second game

## 5.6   Third Game: $(f, <)$ with $p = 0.5$

The parametric game $(f, <)$ has strategy sets $E = F = [0, 1]$ and $a$-biloss function

$$f_a(x, y) = (x - (1 - a)xy, y - (1 - (1 - a^{0.5})^2)xy),$$

for all $x, y$ and $a$ in $[0, 1]$. The $a$-critical zone is the segment

$$\mathcal{C}(f_a) = \{(x, y) \in [0, 1]^2 : 1 - (1 - (1 - a^{0.5})^2)x - (1 - a)y = 0\},$$

with $a$ in $T$. Figure 3 illustrates the payoff space of the game $(f, <)$.

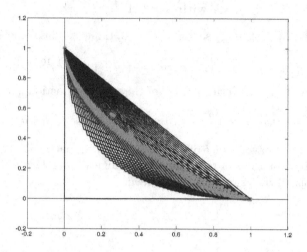

**Fig. 3.** The third game

## 5.7 Fourth Game: $(f, <)$ with $p = 2$

Here we show a parametric game $(f, <)$ with strategy sets $E = F = [0, 1]$ and $a$-biloss function $f_a : [0, 1]^2 \to \mathbb{R}^2$, defined by

$$f_a(x, y) = (x - (1 - a)xy, y - (1 - (1 - a^2)^{0.5})xy),$$

for all $x, y$ and $a$ in $[0, 1]$. The $a$-critical zone (that is the critical zone of the $a$-payoff function $f_a$) is the segment

$$\mathcal{C}(f_a) = \{(x, y) \in [0, 1]^2 : 1 - (1 - (1 - a^2)^{0.5})x - (1 - a)y = 0\}.$$

Figure 4 shows the payoff space of the game $(f, <)$. Note the union of transformations of strategy topological boundary (the topological boundary of the strategy rectangle $E \times F$) in blue and the transformations of critical zones in green.

**Remark.** Strictly speaking, to obtain the payoff space even of a non-parametric game, it is not enough to transform the strategy boundary and the critical zone, indeed the theorem 1 is clear, the *topological boundary of a payoff space* is contained into the union of such transformations; nevertheless, when you have those transformations it is enough to consider, as payoff space, the closed bounded region (we are considering compact strategy spaces) of the plane having that union as topological boundary. For example in the above example, the payoff space is the union of the convex triangle with vertices $(0,0)$, $(0,1)$, $(1,0)$ with the part blue colored.

## 5.8 Fifth Game: $(f, <)$ with $p = 10$

The strategy sets of this fifth game are $E = F = [0, 1]$ and the $a$-biloss function $f_a$ is defined by

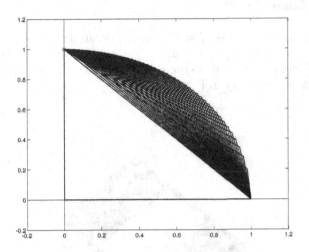

**Fig. 4.** The fourth game

$$f_a(x, y) = (x - (1 - a)xy, y - (1 - (1 - a^{10})^{0.1})xy),$$

for all $x, y$ and $a$ in $[0, 1]$. The $a$-critical zones is the segment

$$\mathcal{C}(f_a) = \{(x, y) \in [0, 1]^2 : 1 - (1 - (1 - a^{10})^{0.1})x - (1 - a)y = 0\},$$

for any $a$ belonging to $T$. We obtain the payoff space represented in Figure 5.

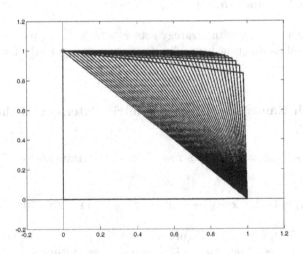

**Fig. 5.** The fifth game

## 5.9    Sixth Game: $(g, <)$

Sixth game has strategy sets $E = F = [0, 2]$, parameter set $T = [0, 1]$ and $a$-biloss function $g_a(x, y) = (x + y + a, x - y + a^2)$, for all $x, y$ in $[0, 2]$ and $a$ in $[0, 1]$. The critical zone is void, so the payoff spaces overlap the transformations of the topological boundary in Figure 6.

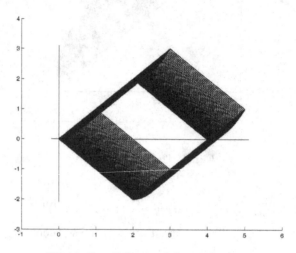

**Fig. 6.** Payoff Space of the sixth game

## 5.10    Seventh Game: $(h, <)$

Here we present a game with strategy sets $E = F = [0, 2]$, parameter set $T = [-1, 1]$ and $a$-biloss function $h_a(x, y) = (x + y + a, x - y + |a|)$, for all $x, y, a$ in $[-1, 1]$.

## 5.11    Eighth Game: $(c, <)$ (A Parametric Extension of the Cournot Game)

The game $(c, <)$ has strategy sets $E = F = [0, 1]$, parameter set $T = [0, 6]$ and $a$-payoff function

$$c_a(x, y) = (x(1 - x - y) + a, y(1 - x - y) - (1/6)(a - 3)^2 + 3/2),$$

for all $x, y$ in $[0, 1]$, $a$ in $[0, 6]$. Figure 8 shows the payoff space, note the transformations of strategy boundary in blue and the transformations of critical zone in green. The game $(c, <)$ (see also [22]) is a parametric extension, by means of the translating vector function $v : [0, 6] \to \mathbb{R}^2 : a \mapsto (a, -(1/6)(a - 3)^2 + 3/2)$ of the classic Cournot kernel $(x, y) \mapsto (x(1 - x - y), y(1 - x - y))$ (see [12–16]).

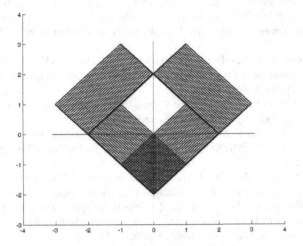

**Fig. 7.** Payoff Space of the seventh game

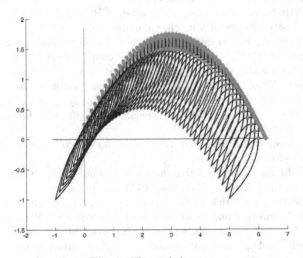

**Fig. 8.** The eighth game

# References

1. Agreste, S., Carfí, D., Ricciardello, A.: An algorithm for payoff space in $C^1$ parametric games. Applied Sciences 14 (2011)
2. Aubin, J.P.: Mathematical Methods of Game and Economic Theory. North-Holland (1986)
3. Aubin, J.P.: Optima and Equilibria. Springer (1995)
4. Carfí, D.: Payoff space of $C^1$ Games. Applied Sciences 11, 35–47 (2009)

5. Carfi, D.: Differentiable game complete analysis for tourism firm decisions. In: Proceedings of the 2009 International Conference on Tourism and Workshop on Sustainable Tourism within High Risk Areas of Environmental Crisis, Messina (April 2009)

6. Carfi, D.: Optimal boundaries for decisions. AAPP LXXXVI(1), 1–12 (2008)

7. Carfi, D.: Complete study of linear infinite games. Proceedings of the International Geometry Center 2(3) (2009)

8. Carfi, D.: A Model for Coopetitive Games. MPRA paper 2012 (2012), http://ideas.repec.org/f/pca735.html

9. Carfi, D.: Decision-form games. In: Communications to SIMAI Congress, vol. 3, pp. 1–12 (2009),http://cab.unime.it/journals/index.php/congress/article/view/307

10. Carfi, D..Francesco, M.: Fair Redistribution in Financial Markets: a Game Theory Complete Analysis. Journal of Advanced Studies in Finance (JASF) 4(II) (2011)

11. Carfi, D., Patanè, G., Pellegrino, S.: A Coopetitive approach to Project Financing. In: Proceedings of International Conference "Moving from Crisis to Sustainability: Emerging Issues in the International Context" (2011)

12. Carfi, D., Perrone, E.: Game Complete Analysis of Bertrand Duopoly. Theoretical and Practical Research in Economic Fields, Association for Sustainable Education, Research and Science 0(1), 5–22 (2011)

13. Carfi, D., Perrone, E.: Game complete analysis of Bertrand Duopoly. MPRA Paper 31302, University Library of Munich, Germany (2011)

14. Carfi, D., Perrone, E.: Asymmetric Cournot duopoly: game complete analysis. MPRA Paper 37093, University Library of Munich, Germany (2012)

15. Carfi, D., Perrone, E.: Game complete analysis of symmetric Cournot duopoly. MPRA Paper 35930, University Library of Munich, Germany (2012)

16. Carfi, D., Perrone, E.: Asymmetric Bertrand duopoly: game complete analysis by algebra system Maxima. MPRA Paper 35417, University Library of Munich, Germany (2011)

17. Carfi, D., Ricciardello, A.: An Algorithm for Payoff Space in $C^1$-Games. AAPP 88(1) (2010)

18. Carfi, D., Schilirò, D.: Coopetitive games and transferable utility: an analytical application to the Eurozone countries (2011) (pre-print)

19. Carfi, D., Schilirò, D.: Crisis in the Euro area: coopetitive game solutions as new policy tools. Theoretical and Practical Research in Economic Fields, summer issue, 1–30 (2011), http://www.asers.eu/journals/tpref.html

20. Carfi, D., Schilirò, D.: A coopetitive model for a global green economy. Proceedings of International Conference "Moving from Crisis to Sustainability: Emerging Issues in the International Context" (2011)

21. Carfi, D., Schilirò D.: A model of coopetitive game and the Greek crisis. In print on AAPP (2012), http://arxiv.org/abs/1106.3543

22. Carfi, D., Trunfio, A.: A non-linear coopetitive game for Global Green Economy. In: Proceedings of International Conference "Moving from Crisis to Sustainability: Emerging Issues in the International Context" (2011), http://ideas.repec.org/f/pca735.html

23. Myerson, R.B.: Game theory. Harvard University press (1991)

24. Osborne, A., Rubinstein, M.J.: A course in Game Theory. Academic press (2001)

25. Owen, G.: Game theory. Academic press (2001)

# Rule-Base Design Using Probabilistic Weights: A Preliminary Analysis of Uncertainty Aspects

Leonardo G. de Melo, Luís Alberto Lucas, and Myriam R. Delgado

Federal University of Technology of Paraná
Av. Sete de Setembro, 3165, Centro
Curitiba, Brazil, CEP 80230-901
lmelo@ufpr.br, {lalucas,myriamdelg}@utfpr.edu.br

**Abstract.** This paper proposes an approach for rule base design that considers most of information obtained from a data set. The proposed method provides fuzzy rules where each consequent label has an associated weight which is determined in a probabilistic way. The paper also presents the method's formalization using crisp and fuzzy relations and their association with the probability theory. The resulting fuzzy system is applied to five instances of a classification problem and its performance is compared to that obtained from a fuzzy classifier provided by the classical Wang-Mendel method. The results show that the proposed design method outperforms the comparison approach.

**Keywords:** Probabilistic fuzzy systems, Automatic rule base design, Wang-Mendel method, Crisp and fuzzy relations, Bayes Theorem, Classification problem.

## 1 Introduction

Since the emergence of fuzzy sets theory [1], it was supposed to be joined with the probability theory to produce better uncertainty handling. There is an extensive discussion about the theme in the literature: some authors agree with such combination [2,3], while others limit to a simple comparison between the theories [4,5].

Some approaches aim to develop hybrid systems for handling uncertainty [2,3]. However, those results are not the first joining these theories. Other authors have also previously succeeded in developing fuzzy techniques with probability theory, including fuzzy random variables [6,7], which give rise to fuzzy probability distributions [8] and the central limit theorem for those types of variables; and the probabilistic fuzzy sets described in [9].

Meghdadi and Akbarzadeh [2] formalized the Probabilistic Fuzzy Logic Systems (PFS). In PFS both types of uncertainty are treated. The rule base comprises fuzzy rules whose consequents are distributed into different fuzzy sets. In the system proposed by [2] the rules have several consequent labels, each one associated with a given probability measure, and the output is a random choice. The PFS proposal inspired the methodology presented in this paper as we also

S. Greco et al. (Eds.): IPMU 2012, Part IV, CCIS 300, pp. 655–664, 2012.

associate probabilistic weights to every possible label in the consequent of each fuzzy rule. However, in this work we provide a simple way to calculate these weights.

## 2   Wang-Mendel Method

The WM approach [10] can be briefly described below. Given a data set $T$, consisting of pairs $(\mathbf{x}_t, y_t)$, $t = 1, ..., |T|$ where $\mathbf{x}_t = (x_1, ..., x_n)$ is the input vector and $y_t$ is the output, a rule $R^t$ is created for each pair $(\mathbf{x}, y)$, considering a fuzzy partition for each fuzzy variable $X_v$, $v = 1, ..., n$, where $L_v$ is the total of linguistic terms in the fuzzy partition of variable $X_v$. The linguistic term $l_v^t$ chosen for each variable $X_v$ in the rule $R^t$ is $l_v^t = \arg\max{(\mu_{l_v}(x_v), l_v = 1, ..., L_v)}$, i.e, $l_v^t$ is associated with the membership function that has the highest membership degree at point $x_v$. An initial rule base $(RB_{complete} = \{R^1, R^2, ..., R^t, ...R^{|T|}\})$ is formed by joining all these fuzzy rules. $RB_{complete}$ may contain redundant and conflicting rules, i.e, there may exist several rules with the same antecedents and different consequents. A final reduced rule base $RB_{reduc}$ is created by reducing $RB_{complete}$. In this case, only a single rule is kept for each possible antecedent (premise), and its consequent (conclusion) is chosen based on the firing strength value $(FS^t = \mu_{l_1^t}(x_1) \mathbf{t} \mu_{l_2^t}(x_2) \mathbf{t} ... \mathbf{t} \mu_{l_n^t}(x_n))$, where $\mathbf{t}$ is a t-norm and $\mu_{l_v^t}(x_v)$ is the membership degree of $x_v$ at the membership function associated with the linguistic term $l_v$ chosen for $X_v$ in the rule $R^t$. The consequent is such that its firing strength is the highest among all the consequents with the same premise.

WM method can be considered one of the simplest ways to generate rules from data. However, during the last phase (i.e, while obtaining the reduced rule-base), it can discard important information concerning conflict and redundancy in data. In this paper we propose an alternative method that considers most of important information available in the data set.

## 3   The Proposed Approach

As in WM method, we also have a data set $T$, consisting of $|T|$ pairs $(\mathbf{x}_t, y_t)$ where $\mathbf{x}_t = (x_1, ..., x_n)$ is the input vector and $y_t$ is the output. Differently from WM that considers every point in $T$ individually, in our proposed approach we focus on every Region of Interest (RoI) resulting from the fuzzy grid partition and most of information available in such region.

Let $\mathbb{X}_v$ be the universe of input variable $X_v$, $v = 1, ..., n$ and $\mathbb{Y}$ be the universe of output variable $Y$. We can define $\mathbb{X} = \mathbb{X}_1 \times \mathbb{X}_2 \times \cdots \times \mathbb{X}_n$, with $T$ given by: $T = \{(\mathbf{x}_t, y_t) \mid \mathbf{x}_t \in \mathbb{X}, y_t \in \mathbb{Y}\}, t = 1, ..., |T|$. Now, assume a fuzzy partition $P_{X_v} = \{A_v^1, A_v^2, \cdots, A_v^{L_v}\}$ for each input variable $X_v$, where $L_v$ is the total of linguistic terms and $A_v^k$ is a fuzzy set representing the $k^{th}$ membership function of $P_{X_v}$. Similarly, consider $P_Y = \{B_1, B_2, \cdots, B_{L_y}\}$ a fuzzy partition for the output variable $Y$. $P_{X_v}$ and $P_Y$ will produce a grid partition in the mapping space $\mathbb{X} \times \mathbb{Y}$, and we define a fuzzy rule $Rule^j$ : IF $X_1$ is $A_1^j$ AND $X_2$ is $A_2^j$ AND $\cdots$ AND $X_n$ is $A_n^j$ then $Y$ is $y^j$ to represent every region of interest ($\text{RoI}^j$, $j = 1, ..., \prod_v L_v$) resulting from this grid partition, where each $\text{RoI}^j$ can be defined as:

$$\text{RoI}^j(\mathbf{x}) = \{\mathbf{x} \mid \mathbf{x} \in \mathbb{X}, \mu_{A_v^j}(\mathbf{x}) > 0, v = 1, \cdots, n\} . \tag{1}$$

Let a fuzzy relation describing the antecedent of Rule$^j$ be defined as:

$$AR^j(\mathbf{x}) = \{(\mathbf{x}, \mu_{AR^j}(\mathbf{x})) \mid \mathbf{x} \in \text{RoI}^j(\mathbf{x}), \ \mu_{AR^j}(\mathbf{x}) = \mu_{A_1^j}(x_1) \mathbf{t} \cdots \mathbf{t} \ \mu_{A_n^j}(x_n)\},$$

where $\mathbf{t}$ is a t-norm. Considering only points in the training set, the height of $AR^j(\mathbf{x})$ becomes $H_{AR^j} = \sup_{\mathbf{x} \in T}(\mu_{AR^j}(\mathbf{x}_t))$, where sup is the supremum operator.

A question that arises is: how to choose the consequent $y^j$ that best represents Rule$^j$ : $AR^j(\mathbf{x}) \to y^j$, considering most of information available in $\text{RoI}^j$ and $T$?

In this paper we propose the use of a weight $w_i^j$ to be associated with every possible label, i.e, $y^j = \{B_1 : w_1^j, \text{ or } B_2 : w_2^j, \text{ or } \cdots \text{ or } B_{L_y} : w_{L_y}^j\}$, where each $w_i^j$ will be calculated in a probabilistic way as detailed below.

Let a discrete crisp relation $S^j$ be given by $S^j(\mathbf{x}_t) = T \cap \text{RoI}^j(\mathbf{x})$. The discrete crisp relation $S_i^j$ can be defined as:

$$S_i^j(\mathbf{x}_t) = \{\mathbf{x}_t \mid \mathbf{x}_t \in S^j(\mathbf{x}_t)), y_t = B_i\}, i = 1, ..., L_Y . \tag{2}$$

In fuzzy classifiers, the association $y_t = B_i$ is easy to achieve as $y_t$ and $B_i$ are labels indicating classes of the application domain. In fuzzy inference systems developed for general purposes, this association can be made considering that the linguistic term $B_i$ to be chosen for each $y$ in $T$ is $B_i = \arg \max (\mu_{B_l}(y_t), l = 1, ..., L_y)$. In other words, $B_i$ is the consequent label associated with the membership function in the output fuzzy partition that has the highest membership degree at point $y_t$.

Generally speaking, when we have an automatic generation algorithm based on a data set and fuzzy partition, every region of interest $\text{RoI}^j$ can be partitioned into different sets or discrete crisp relations ($S_i^j$), each one associated with a consequent label $B_i$ as depicted in Fig 1.

In Fig. 1 we have an example of a fuzzy partition based on trapezoidal membership functions and a total of $n = 2$ input variables.

The aim is to represent every $\text{RoI}^j$ through a single fuzzy rule with a premise $AR^j$ and multiple labels $B_i$ in the consequent, each one associated with a weight ($w_i^j$), $i = 1, .., L_Y$. According to Fig. 1, we can use frequency information to calculate this weight. The more points in $T$ are associated with label $B_i$, the higher is the weight $w_i^j$. Nevertheless, it is not interesting that we consider only $B_i$ frequency because points with the "highest quality" should be the most important ones.

Let $R_i^j$ be a discrete fuzzy relation defined by (3).

$$R_i^j(\mathbf{x}_t) = \{(\mathbf{x}_t, \mu_{R_i^j}(\mathbf{x}_t)) \mid \mathbf{x}_t \in S_i^j(\mathbf{x}_t), \ \mu_{R_i^j}(\mathbf{x}_t) = \mu_{AR^j}(\mathbf{x}_t)\} . \tag{3}$$

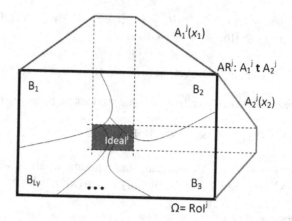

**Fig. 1.** Probability and fuzzy aspects in RoI$^j$: $Ideal^j$ is a crisp relation

We can then define the best region in RoI$^j$, named $Ideal^j$, as a discrete crisp relation given by:

$$Ideal^j(\mathbf{x}_t) = \{\mathbf{x}_t \mid \mathbf{x}_t \in S^j(\mathbf{x}_t), \mu_{R^j}(\mathbf{x}_t) = H_{AR^j}\} \ . \tag{4}$$

The principal goal of our method is to associate $w_i^j$ with the conditional probability $P(B_i | Ideal^j)$, i.e, the weight $w_i^j$ is calculated as the probability of $B_i$, given the evidence $Ideal^j$ in the $j^{th}$ region considered. According to the probability theory we have:

$$w_i^j = P(B_i | Ideal^j) = \frac{P(B_i).P(Ideal^j | B_i)}{P(Ideal^j)} = \frac{P(Ideal^j \cap B_i)}{\sum_i P(Ideal^j \cap B_i)} \ . \tag{5}$$

The main drawback of this approach is the hard decision imposed by the crisp relation $Ideal^j$. If there is not any point associated with $B_i$ in the best region of RoI$^j$, i.e, $Ideal^j \cap B_i = \emptyset$, the weight $w_i^j$ becomes null regardless of all the remaining information associated with $B_i$ (maybe good information) available in that RoI. We can then redefine $Ideal^j$ using a fuzzy relation as that depicted in Fig. 2.

The fuzzy version of $Ideal^j$ can be achieved in different ways. In this paper we assume, for simplicity aspects, $Ideal^j = R^j = \cup R_i^j$. Then we can redefine (4):
$Ideal^j(\mathbf{x}_t) = \{(\mathbf{x}_t, \mu_{R^j}(\mathbf{x}_t)) \mid \mu_{R^j}(\mathbf{x}_t) = \mu_{A_1^j}(x_1) \mathbf{t} \cdots \mathbf{t} \ \mu_{A_n^j}(x_n), \mathbf{x}_t \in S^j(\mathbf{x}_t)\}$,
and (5) becomes:

$$w_i^j = P(B_i | Ideal^j) = \frac{P(R^j \cap B_i)}{\sum_i P(R^j \cap B_i)} \ . \tag{6}$$

According to (2), $B_i$ is directly associated with $S_i^j$, $R^j \cap B_i = R^j \cap S_i^j = R_i^j$, and $w_i^j$ can be defined based on $R_i^j$:

$$w_i^j = P(B_i | Ideal^j) = \frac{P(R^j \cap B_i)}{\sum_i P(R^j \cap B_i)} = \frac{P(R_i^j)}{\sum_i P(R_i^j)} \ . \tag{7}$$

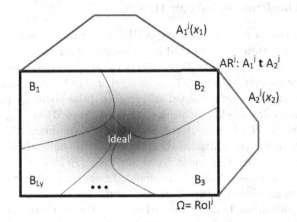

**Fig. 2.** Probability and fuzzy aspects in $RoI^j$: $Ideal^j$ is a fuzzy relation

According to [11] we have $P(x \text{ is } F) = P(F)$, where $P(F)$ is the probability of a fuzzy event defined in the universe $\mathbb{U}$. Assuming a discrete universe such that every point $x \in \mathbb{U}$ is equiprobable, i.e, its probability function is given by $p(x) = 1/|\mathbb{U}|$, we have:

$$P(F) = \sum_{x \in \mathbb{U}} \mu_F(x) p(x) = \frac{\sum_{x \in \mathbb{U}} \mu_F(x)}{|\mathbb{U}|} = \frac{|F|}{|\mathbb{U}|} \, . \tag{8}$$

Assuming that all points in the training set are generated by a uniform distribution, consequently every point $\mathbf{x}_t \in S^j$ is equiprobable, we have, according to (8), $P(R_i^j) = |R_i^j|/|S^j|$. Then, $w_i^j$ is now given by (9).

$$w_i^j = P(B_i|Ideal^j) = \frac{|R_i^j|/|S^j|}{\sum_i |R_i^j|/|S^j|} = \frac{|R_i^j|}{\sum_i |R_i^j|} \, . \tag{9}$$

Equation (9) shows that while defining $w_i^j$, we can consider both quantity and quality information. More specifically, we consider not only the total number of points in $RoI^j$ associated with $B_i$ but also their qualities, both combined in $|R_i^j| = \sum_{\mathbf{x}_t} \mu_{R_i^j}(\mathbf{x}_t)$.

According to [2], a fuzzy system comprised of a rule-base with probabilistic weights is named Probabilistic Fuzzy System (PFS), i.e, the rules have several consequents with different probabilities of occurrence and the output is defined based on a random choice. In [2] the authors do not define a mechanism to calculate the probabilistic weights, our work represents an interesting alternative to perform this task. The inference mechanism to be adopted by a PFS can be that proposed by [12].

## 3.1   The Proposed Algorithm

Despite the possibility of using a PFS in a probabilistic way, in this paper we adopt a deterministic rule that is the basis for many statistical classifiers [13]. Let $B$ denote the object label that takes a value of $B_i$ if an object belongs to group $i$. Let $\mathbf{d}$ be an attribute vector (or any other input data characteristic) associated with an object to be classified and $P(B_i|\mathbf{d})$, the posterior probability of group $i$. The probability of classification error is $P(Error|\mathbf{d}) = \sum_{i \neq c} P(B_i) = 1 - P(B_c)$, if we decide $B_c$. Hence, if the purpose is to minimize the probability of total classification error (misclassification rate), we have the following widely used Bayesian classification rule: $B_c = \arg\max (P(B_i|\mathbf{d})), i = 1, ..., C$, where $C$ is the total of classes being considered. In the following we detail the proposed approach considering $Ideal^j$ instead of $\mathbf{d}$.

The algorithm being proposed as an alternative to the WM method is described in a classification context and it can be summarized in the following steps.

1. Set the number of linguistic terms ($L_Y$ and $L_v$, $v = 1, .., n$) and perform the fuzzy partition of the input space ($\mathbb{X}$) and the output space ($\mathbb{Y}$), based on the expert knowledge or any automatic approach (for example, those based on clustering methods). Let $C = L_y$ be the total of linguistic terms in the output fuzzy partition and $J = \prod_v L_v$ be the total of Regions of Interest $RoI$ resulting from the grid partition.
2. For each region $j$: Associate every point $\mathbf{x} \in T$ with a candidate rule and calculate the compatibility degree of this point with respect to the $RoI^j$, as $\mu_{R_i^j}(\mathbf{x}_t)$ (3).
3. Aggregate redundant rules by combining quantity and quality information through the measure given by $|R_i^j|/\sum_i |R_i^j|$.
4. Obtain each probabilistic weight $w_i^j$ according to (9) and associate it with each $B_i$.
5. Choose $B_c^j$, for each $RoI^j$, as $B_c^j = \arg\max (w_i^j = P(B_i|Ideal^j)), i = 1, ..., C$.

The complete step-by-step description for the proposed algorithm is detailed in the following example.

According to step 1, let $A_1^k$, $k = 1, ..., L_1$, and $A_2^k$, $k = 1, ..., L_2$ be the labels that define the fuzzy partition of the input space $\mathbb{X}_1 \times \mathbb{X}_2$. Consider three regions of interest $RoI^j$, $j = 1, ..., 3$, where $RoI_j$ is given by (1). As described in step 2, let a set of pairs $(\mathbf{x}_t, y_t)$ in the data set $T$ and their membership degree $\mu_{R_i^j}(\mathbf{x}_t)$ such that they provide a set of candidate rules for each $RoI^j$ as those shown in the first three columns of Table 1.

Based on step 3 we aggregate redundant rules and represent them by the overall information $|R_i^j|/\sum_i |R_i^j|$ (fourth column of Table 1). According to step 4, the weights are calculated based on equation 9 and associated with each consequent label (fifth column of Table 1). Finally, according to step 5, we choose the consequent label for each $RoI^j$, as the one associated with the highest probability (those emphasized in the fifth column of Table 1).

**Table 1.** Candidate rules and the final weight calculation

| Columns | | | | |
|---|---|---|---|---|
| 1 | 2 | 3 | 4 | 5 |
| $RoI^j$ | If $x_1$ is and $x_2$ is then $y$ is | $\mu_{R_i^j}(\mathbf{x}_t)$ | $\dfrac{|R_i^j|}{\sum_i |R_i^j|}$ | $B_i:\ w_i^j$ |
| 1 | $A_1^1\quad A_2^1\quad 1$ <br> $A_1^1\quad A_2^1\quad 1$ <br> $A_1^1\quad A_2^1\quad 2$ | 0.8 <br> 0.9 <br> 0.7 | (0.8+0.9)/(0.8+0.9+0.7) <br> (0.7)/(0.8+0.9+0.7) | 1 : 0.708333 <br> 2 : 0.291667 |
| 2 | $A_1^2\quad A_2^2\quad 2$ <br> $A_1^2\quad A_2^2\quad 2$ <br> $A_1^2\quad A_2^2\quad 1$ | 0.9 <br> 0.6 <br> 0.3 | (0.9+0.6)/(0.9+0.6+0.3) <br> (0.3)/(0.9+0.6+0.3) | 2 : 0.8333 <br> 1 : 0.1667 |
| 3 | $A_1^3\quad A_2^3\quad 3$ <br> $A_1^3\quad A_2^3\quad 3$ | 0.5 <br> 0.4 | (0.5+0.4)/(0.5+0.4) | 3 : 1 |

## 4    Experiments and Results

In this section we consider a simple classification problem to test the proposed approach performance. To determine how differently the methods behave when we decrease the "separability" in data, five instances (a, b, c, d, e) of a classification problem are produced with different means ($\mu$) and variances ($\sigma$) in the hyper-Gaussian functions that generate all points, including a testing set and that used to obtain the rule-base (named training set for short). Table 2 shows the parameters used to generate data, i.e, the coordinates $c_1$ and $c_2$ of each ($\mu_i$), $i = 1, ..., 3$ and the standard deviation $\sigma$.

**Table 2.** Instances of the classification problem

| Instance | coordinates $(c_1, c_2)$ for | | | $\sigma$ |
|---|---|---|---|---|
| | $\mu$ of class 1 | $\mu$ of class 2 | $\mu$ of class 3 | |
| a | (10,10) | (10,30) | (30,10) | 9 |
| b | (10,10) | (10,20) | (20,10) | 9 |
| c | (10,10) | (10,30) | (30,10) | 12 |
| d | (10,10) | (10,20) | (20,10) | 12 |
| e | (10,10) | (10,20) | (20,10) | 15 |

Figures 3 and 4 illustrate the points generated for instances a and b and the partition set $P_{X_v} = \{A_v^1, A_v^2, \cdots, A_v^{L_v}\}$, with $L_v = 3$ and $A_v^k$ defined as $A_v^1 = N(10, 15)$, $A_v^2 = N(20, 15)$, $A_v^3 = N(30, 15)$ for both variables.

We use a total of 1000 points for each class, dividing them into five groups of 200 points each. We then apply a cross-validation method (more specifically 5-fold cross validation [14]). The first four groups, totaling 800 points are used for training the algorithms, while the last group forms the testing set. Another group is then used for testing, the remaining for training and so on, until all groups have the chance to participate in the testing phase. The results are presented

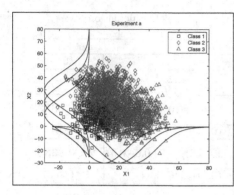 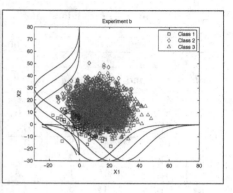

**Fig. 3.** Points distribution for instance a    **Fig. 4.** Points distribution for instance b

**Table 3.** Correct classification percentage ($P_{CO}$)

| Instance | Approach | $Fold_1$ | $Fold_2$ | $Fold_3$ | $Fold_4$ | $Fold_5$ | Average | Std. dev. |
|---|---|---|---|---|---|---|---|---|
| a | WM | 64.67% | 72.50% | 70.67% | 63.67% | 39.17% | 62.13% | 13.38% |
| | Prob | 73.50% | 84.50% | 80.00% | 83.67% | 83.83% | 81.10% | 4.59% |
| b | WM | 52.00% | 41.50% | 57.83% | 39.50% | 49.00% | 47.97% | 7.55% |
| | Prob | 69.17% | 65.83% | 68.33% | 61.83% | 69.83% | 67.00% | 3.26% |
| c | WM | 56.83% | 55.67% | 59.50% | 55.50% | 71.83% | 59.87% | 6.88% |
| | Prob | 64.00% | 72.00% | 77.00 % | 63.83% | 68.83% | 69.13% | 5.58% |
| d | WM | 25.67% | 31.50% | 50.00% | 34.83% | 32.83% | 34.97% | 9.07% |
| | Prob | 61.50% | 61.17% | 55.17% | 59.17% | 63.00% | 60.00% | 3.03% |
| e | WM | 43.17% | 52.17% | 45.00% | 33.50% | 47.50% | 44.27% | 6.91% |
| | Prob | 48.50% | 56.17% | 54.17% | 53.50% | 51.67% | 52.80% | 2.89% |

in Table 3 that compares the efficiencies of the Wang-Mendel algorithm (WM), and the proposed method (Prob). As a criterion for approaches comparison we use the percentage of correct outputs $P_{CO} = PC/PT \cdot 100$ where $PC$ is the total number of test points correctly classified and $PT$ is the total test points.

As the confidence intervals overlap we choose Mack-Skillings statistics "which presents a procedure for testing $H_0$ for block data where one has an equal number $c > 1$ replications for each of the treatment-block combinations" [15]. In this paper, treatments are classifiers ($k = 2$), blocks are instances ($b = 5$) and replications are folds ($c = 5$). The null hypothesis $H_0$ states that all treatments (i.e, classifiers) are equal i.e, there is no statistical difference between them. Mack-Skillings statistics provides MS=28.85 which is greater than the tabular $ms_{0.0491} = 4.034$ at 4,91% significance level i.e, $H_0$ must be rejected, so the classifiers are different and we know (with 95% of confidence) that Probabilistic method outperforms the Wang-Mendel approach.

We must elucidate how the results in Table 3 are obtained. After deriving the fuzzy rules by each method (Table 4), these rules are implemented as a classifier.

**Table 4.** Rule base obtained by WM and probabilistic methods: instances a and b, Fold1

| If X1 is and X2 is | | then Class is | Probabilistic $w_i^j$ | | WM then Class is | |
|---|---|---|---|---|---|---|
| | | | Instance a | Instance b | Instance a | Instance b |
| 1 | 1 | 1 | **0.8341** | **0.5182** | 1 | 1 |
| | | 2 | 0.0852 | 0.2551 | | |
| | | 3 | 0.0807 | 0.2267 | | |
| 1 | 2 | 1 | **0.5088** | 0.3247 | 2 | 2 |
| | | 2 | 0.4652 | **0.5591** | | |
| | | 3 | 0.0260 | 0.1162 | | |
| 1 | 3 | 1 | 0.0996 | 0.1488 | | 1 |
| | | 2 | **0.8982** | **0.7977** | 2 | |
| | | 3 | 0.0022 | 0.0536 | | |
| 2 | 1 | 1 | 0.4863 | 0.3035 | | |
| | | 2 | 0.0161 | 0.1053 | | |
| | | 3 | **0.4977** | **0.5912** | 3 | 3 |
| 2 | 2 | 1 | 0.3129 | 0.2623 | | 1 |
| | | 2 | 0.3205 | 0.3203 | | |
| | | 3 | **0.3666** | **0.4174** | 3 | |
| 2 | 3 | 1 | 0.0599 | 0.1191 | 1 | 1 |
| | | 2 | **0.8910** | **0.6975** | | |
| | | 3 | 0.0491 | 0.1834 | | |
| 3 | 1 | 1 | 0.0843 | 0.1740 | | |
| | | 2 | 0.0043 | 0.0592 | | |
| | | 3 | **0.9114** | **0.7669** | 3 | 3 |
| 3 | 2 | 1 | 0.0363 | 0.1482 | | |
| | | 2 | 0.0651 | 0.1063 | | |
| | | 3 | **0.8986** | **0.7455** | 3 | 3 |
| 3 | 3 | 1 | 0.0189 | 0.0380 | | |
| | | 2 | **0.5436** | **0.6940** | 2 | 2 |
| | | 3 | 0.4375 | 0.2679 | | |

In the case of the proposed method, the rule consequent is defined as the label associated with the highest probabilistic weight (those emphasized in Table 4). After each rule infers its class output associated with its activation degree, these labels are aggregated by the maximum, i.e, the class indicated on system output is that whose rule has the highest activation degree. In the calculus of $P_{CO}$, the actual values are compared with those indicated in the system output.

## 5   Conclusions

In this paper, we proposed a new approach to generate fuzzy rules, using probabilistic weights. The proposed method was presented (including a simple example) with a special attention to its connection with Probability Theory and the definition of a special relation (named Ideal) in each region resulted from the grid partition. The effectiveness of the new method was tested in a classification problem where the proposed algorithm was compared with the classic WM. In the future we intend to test the proposed approach in real problems to evaluate its effectiveness when compared with fuzzy and non-fuzzy based approaches. Though we know that the performance analysis for changing from a crisp relation in $Ideal^j$ to its fuzzy version is necessary, such analysis is out of the scope of this paper and will be considered in a forthcoming work. Other future works include different ways to calculate $Ideal^j$ and a robustness analysis comparing uniform *versus* other probability distributions while generating the data set $T$.

**Acknowledgments.** Myriam Delgado acknowledges the CNPq grant 307735/ 2008-7, Fundação Araucária project 400/09 - 10705 for the partial financial support.

# References

1. Zadeh, L.A.: Fuzzy Sets. Inform. and Control 8, 338–353 (1965)
2. Meghdadi, A., Akbarzadeh, T.M.: Probabilistic Fuzzy Logic and Probabilistic Fuzzy Systems. In: 10th IEEE International Conference on Fuzzy Systems, pp. 1127–1130 (2001)
3. Colettia, G., Scozzafavab, R.: Conditional probability and fuzzy information. Computational Statistics & Data Analysis 51, 115–132 (2006)
4. Laviolette, M., Seaman Jr., J.W.: The efficacy of fuzzy representations of uncertainty. IEEE Transactions on Fuzzy Systems 2, 4–15 (1994)
5. Wilson, N.: Vagueness and Bayesian Probability. IEEE Transactions on Fuzzy Systems 2, 34–36 (1994)
6. Kwakernaak, H.: Fuzzy Random Variables-I. Definitions and Theorems. Inf. Sci. 15, 1–29 (1978)
7. Kwakernaak, H.: Fuzzy Random Variables II. Algorithms and examples for the discrete case. Inf. Sci. 17(3), 253–278 (1979)
8. Taylor, M., Boswell, S.: A central limit theorem for fuzzy random variables. Fuzzy Sets and Systems 24, 331–344 (1987)
9. Hirota, K.: Concepts of probabilistic set. Fuzzy Sets and Systems 5, 31–46 (1981)
10. Wang, L., Mendel, M.: Generating Fuzzy Rules by Learning from Examples. IEEE Trans. Systems Man and Cybernetics 22, 1414–1427 (1992)
11. Pedrycs, W., Gomide, F.: An Introduction to Fuzzy Sets: Analysis and Design. MIT Press (1998)
12. Liu, Z., Li, H.-X.: A Probabilistic Fuzzy Logic System for Modeling and Control. IEEE Transactions on Fuzzy Systems 13, 848–859 (2005)
13. Zhang, G.P.: Neural networks for classification: a survey. IEEE Transactions on Systems, Man and Cybernetics, Part C (Applications and Reviews) 30, 451–462 (2000)
14. Weiss, S., Kulikowski, C.: Computer Systems That Learn. Morgam Kaufmann (1991)
15. Hollander, M., Wolfe, D.: Nonparametric Statistical Methods. John Wiley & Sons (1999)

# Biomedical Diagnosis Based on Ion Mobility Spectrometry – A Case Study Using Probabilistic Relational Modelling and Learning*

Marc Finthammer, Ryszard Masternak, and Christoph Beierle

Dept. of Computer Science, FernUniversität in Hagen, Germany

**Abstract.** Aiming at providing a non-invasive and easy-to-use method for the early detection of bronchial carcinoma, it has been proposed to apply ion mobility spectrometry (IMS) to the breath a person exhales. Extending previous work using such IMS data, we report on a case study using methods of probabilistic relational modelling and learning. By taking additional features of an IMS measurement into account and using refined clustering and modelling methods, inference accuracy is increased.

## 1 Introduction

Ion mobility spectrometry (IMS) provides a means for detecting particular substances in gaseous analytes, and [1] reports on an approach where IMS is applied to the breath a person exhales in order to get a diagnosis whether the person has bronchial carcinoma or not. In [4,3], this application scenario is addressed using probabilistic relational learning (for an overview of the field of probabilistic relational learning see e.g. [5]). In [4,3], the IMS results are first transformed into peaks in a spectrum and then into peak clusters. The relationships among the peak clusters and the diagnosis of bronchial carcinoma are modelled by Markov Logic Networks (MLNs) [12]. Various learning scenarios are presented in [4,3] yielding an accuracy of up to 90% for diagnosing bronchial carcinoma in a given set of IMS measurements.

In this paper, we extend the approach presented in [4,3]. in several ways. We investigate whether taking into account also the height and the extension of a peak, along with its position, has an influence on the inference quality. We refine the clustering of peaks in several ways, and introduce extended modelling approaches. Finally, we present and evaluate a series of IMS learning scenarios and experiments, leading to an accuracy higher than in [4,3], even when using a stricter notion of accuracy that reflects the certainty of a diagnosis. A detailed account of the full case study reported here can be found in [9].

## 2 Ion Mobility Spectrometry and the IMS Database $D_{bc}$

In order to determine chemical substances in gaseous analytes, ion mobility spectrometry (IMS) can be used [1]. This method relies on characterizing substances

---

* The research reported here was partially supported by the DFG (BE 1700/7-2).

S. Greco et al. (Eds.): IPMU 2012, Part IV, CCIS 300, pp. 665–675, 2012.

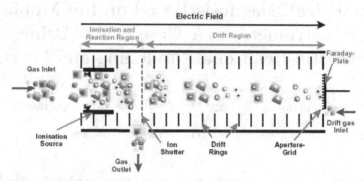

**Fig. 1.** Schematic overview of an ion mobility spectrometer (from [1])

in gases by their ion mobility. Figure 1 illustrates the working principle of an ion mobility spectrometer. After ionisation, ion swarms enter the drift region through an ion shutter. The time needed to pass the drift region is called *drift time*, and the ion mobility is inversely proportional to the drift time. Ion mobility is determined by mapping the drift time to the signal intensity measured at the Faraday plate (cf. Fig. 1). If the gaseous analyte contains various substances, they may reach the Faraday plate at the same time. Therefore, a multi capillary column is used for the pre-separation of different substances [1] so that they enter the spectrometer at different time points, called *retention times*.

Formally, a *drift vector* $S$ is a sequence $S = (z_1, \ldots, z_n)$ of signal intensities $z_i$ measured at the Faraday plate at time points $i \times C$ where $C$ is a fixed time interval. A spectrum $M$ is a sequence $M = (S_0, \ldots, S_m)$ of drift vectors corresponding to distinct retention times $r_{t_0}, \ldots, r_{t_m}$. An IMS spectrum $M$ can be visualized as a heat map on the two dimensions drift time and retention time, while the signal intensity is represented by a colour. One is particularly interested in *peaks* in this heat map as each peak gives information about a particular substance in the analyte. A peak object in a spectrum is characterized by a set of direct or closely related neighbours in the matrix $M$ whose signal value is above a given minimal value; thus, a peak object corresponds to a specific area in the heat map. The determination of peaks in a measurement requires sophisticated processing of the raw spectra (see [1] for details). Peak objects taken from two different measurements that correspond to the same substance occur at corresponding areas in their respective heat maps (cf. Fig. 2)

The experiments described in this paper are based upon an IMS database $D_{bc}$ containing data from 158 persons. The measurements were taken from 82 patients suffering from bronchial carcinoma (denoted by *bc group*), and from 76 persons belonging to a control group (denoted by $\overline{bc}$ *group*) without bronchial carcinoma. Each measurement contains from 3 up to 44 peaks. In summary, there are 2 399 peaks where each peak is characterized by a quintuple $p = (t_D, t_R, h, e_D, e_R)$ with:

- drift time $t_D \in [0, 1.46]$ in ms,
- retention time $t_R \in [0, 3078]$ in s,

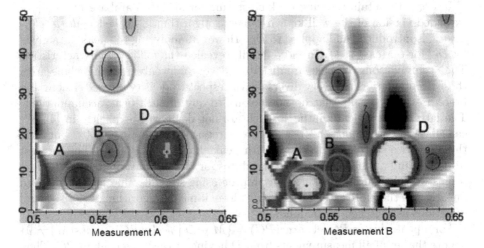

**Fig. 2.** Two different measurements and their corresponding peak object positions

- height (voltage) $h \in [0, 3.7]$ in V,
- drift time extension $e_D \in [0, 0.3]$ in ms,
- retention time extension $e_R \in [0, 3078]$ in s.

Note that the two parameters $e_D$ and $e_R$ determine an elliptical area for the peak which is used in the visualization tool PeakViewer (see Sec. 4).

While the work reported in [4,3] starts with the same IMS database $D_{bc}$, it considers only the first two parameters $t_D$, $t_R$ of a peak, abstracting from the other individual peak characteristics. In the following, we will investigate how these other characteristics can also be taken into account.

## 3   Peak Clustering

Formally, an IMS database $D = \{M_1, \ldots, M_d\}$ is a set of measurements $M_i$ where each measurement is an IMS spectrum $M_i = (S_0^i, \ldots, S_m^i)$. For a spectrum $M$ let $peaks(M)$ denote the set of peaks in $M$, and $peaks(D) = \cup_{M \in D} peaks(M)$. Then a *peak clustering* for $D$ is a partitioning $PC_1, \ldots, PC_p$ of $peaks(D)$, and $peak\_index : peaks(D) \rightarrow \{1, \ldots, p\}$ denotes the mapping that sends each peak $P$ to the index $j$ of the unique *peak cluster* $PC_j$ with $P \in PC_j$. A peak cluster is meant to represent a vague concept of a peak that corresponds to a substance but allows for slight variations in its actual manifestation within a spectrum. Since in the ideal case each peak in a spectrum corresponds to a different substance, we are only interested in peak clusterings that map all peaks within a single measurement to different clusters, i.e., if the restriction $peak\_index_{|peaks(M)}$ is injective for every $M \in D$. As in [4], such a clustering for $D$ is called *(measurement) slicing*. Furthermore, every peak should belong to not more than one cluster, and since we do not even know the number of different substances, the clustering approach should also determine the number of clusters.

In order to obtain a slicing peak clustering for an IMS database $D$, in [4] an extended version of the well-known $k$-means algorithm [8], called *multi-level k-means*, is introduced and applied to $D_{bc}$. However, analyzing the peak data given by $D_{bc}$ for our case study in more detail, revealed the following characteristics: The accumulations of peaks are distributed very unevenly over the whole area, these accumulations are very diverse with respect to density and extension, and there are many peaks that do not belong to any of such peak accumulations. The latter may indicate outliers which are not dealt with explicitly in [4]. We can observe that almost all peaks have a retention time $t_R \leq 600s$, but that there are also some measurements with peaks having $t_R > 3000s$. This suggest to use scaling and normalization procedures for the peak attributes being more sophisticated than in [4] where in a preprocessing step all values are normalized linearly. We therefore extended the multi-level k-means algorithm of [4] in several directions as sketched in the following.

For a peak cluster $PC$ let $meas(PC) = \{M \in D \mid peaks(PC) \cap peaks(M) \neq \emptyset\}$ denote the set of all measurements from $D$ having at least one peak in $PC$. Then

$$pmq(PC) = \frac{1}{|meas(PC)|} \sum_{M \in meas(PC)} |peaks(PC) \cap peaks(M)| \qquad (1)$$

is called *peak-per-measurement quotient* for $PC$. For an upper bound $pmq_{max}$ for these quotients, a clustering $PC_1, \ldots, PC_p$ respects $pmq_{max}$ iff $pmq(PC_i) \leq pmq_{max}$ for every $i = 1, \ldots, p$. Obviously, a clustering is slicing iff it respects $pmq_{max} = 1$. Using these notions, the multi-level k-means approach of [4] recursively splits up any non-slicing peak cluster into separate clusters until the whole clustering is slicing. Instead of using the strong condition resulting from $pmq_{max} = 1$, we relaxed this criterion by using a value slightly greater than 1. E.g., setting $pmq(PC_i) = 1.05$ allows that the average number of peaks from the same measurement in a cluster may be up to 1.05. Subsequently, multiple peaks in a cluster from the same measurement were identified as erroneous and removed, yielding again a slicing cluster. Our experiments described later on showed that this approach resulted in an improved clustering quality.

A further deficiency of the clustering approach used in [4] is that at each level, the number of clusters used for further splitting a non-slicing cluster $PC$ is set to the maximal number of peaks in $PC$ that result from the same measurement; in our experiments, this turned out to be a rather restrictive condition. Instead, we used a scale-space approach (see [7,14]). For each peak in a non-slicing cluster $PC$, appropriate scale-space parameters depending on the distance between peaks are determined. The number $k$ of clusters is then given by the number of maxima in the scale space representation, and the initial value of $k$ is obtained by initially putting all peaks into a single non-slicing cluster. Furthermore, the clustering in [4] does not take explicitly into account outliers, deviations of values caused e.g. by impreciseness of the sensors or by variations of the environment, or the rather diverse distribution of peaks. In order to consider these aspects more closely, we employed various means of normalizing peak attributes when

| | parameters | | | | | results | |
|---|---|---|---|---|---|---|---|---|
| | normali-<br>zation | k-<br>start | pmq<br>max | min.<br>clust. | center | nc | peaks per clust.<br>min/avg/max | J-quality |
| cv2.0 | stat, lin-lin | 20 | 1.4 | 4 | random | 39 | 4/51/156 | 0.2359 |
| cv2.1 | stat, lin-lin | 20 | 1.25 | 4 | random | 42 | 4/51/150 | 0.2857 |
| cv3.0 | dyn, lin-lin | auto | 1.05 | 0.25% | random | 39 | 9/52/147 | 0.4982 |
| cv4.0 | dyn, lin-lin | auto | 1.05 | 0.25% | scale-s | 36 | 9/57/146 | 0.5148 |
| cv4.1c | dyn, lin-lin | auto | 1.05 | 0.25% | scale-s | 46 | 9/43/137 | 0.6193 |
| cv4.1s | dyn, lin-sqr | auto | 1.05 | 0.25% | scale-s | 46 | 9/43/146 | 0.5288 |

**Fig. 3.** Clustering variants (nc - number of clusters)

using them in clustering conditions, and we also used different methods for determining the center of a cluster. An overview of some of the clustering versions used in our case study is given in Fig. 3. The parameter entries on the left hand side of Fig. 3 should be read as follows:

- Normalization: *stat* (all values normalized only once for all iterations), *dyn* (values normalized separately for each iteration), *lin-lin* (X and Y axis normalized linearly), *lin-sqr* (X axis normalized linearly, Y axis normalized using square root)
- *k-start*: number of clusters for first iteration; *auto* (automatically determined from data)
- *min. clust.*: minimal cluster size (number of peaks or percentage of all peaks)
- *center*: method for determining cluster center (*random* or using scale-space approach)

Applying these clustering variants to $D_{bc}$ yielded from 36 to 46 clusters with at least 4 and at most 156 peaks per cluster, with an average number of peaks per cluster ranging rom 43 to 57 (cf. right hand side in Fig. 3). In order to compare these clustering results, we manually generated a reference clustering by exploiting the visual representation provided by the PeakViewer tool (Sec. 4). For each automatically generated clustering, we determined its *J-quality* as its *J-distance* to this reference clustering. For any two partitionings $\mathcal{A}, \mathcal{B}$ of the same set of elements, we define their J-distance $J\text{-}dist(\mathcal{A}, \mathcal{B}) \in [0, 1]$, based upon the well-known Jaccard similarity coefficient $J(A, B) = \frac{|A \cap B|}{|A \cup B|}$ for arbitrary sets $A, B$, by $\delta(\mathcal{A}, \mathcal{B}, 0, |\mathcal{A}| + |\mathcal{B}|)$ with:

$$\delta(\mathcal{A}, \mathcal{B}, d, m) = \begin{cases} \frac{2d}{m} & \text{if } \mathcal{A} = \emptyset \text{ or } \mathcal{B} = \emptyset \\ \delta(\mathcal{A}\backslash A, \mathcal{B}\backslash B, d + J(A, B), m) & \text{otherwise, where } J(A, B) \text{ is} \\ & \text{maximal for } (A, B) \in \mathcal{A} \times \mathcal{B} \end{cases}$$

While clusterings with a higher J-quality generally resulted in a better predicting accuracy, using it in its current form has the disadvantage of treating all clusters identically, i.e., it measures a cluster independently of its relevance. If a peak cluster corresponding to a substance being highly relevant with respect to bronchial carcinoma is poorly generated, it has the same impact on the J-quality as a poorly generated cluster corresponding to an irrelevant substance. This seems to be one of the reasons why there is no strict monotone dependency between J-quality and final prediction accuracy. In fact, using the clustering variant $cv4.1s$ yielded the best predicting accuracy, and this variant is used in the modelling scenarios described in the sequel.

# 4    A Toolbox for Experiments and Their Evaluation

In order to support the systematic experimentation with and the evaluation of different options, we developed a corresponding toolbox. The toolbox contains the PeakViewer system [9] being able to visualize all five peak dimensions $p = (t_D, t_R, h, e_D, e_R)$ and providing facilities in particular for

- choosing appropriate clustering variants, including the setting of which peak attributes should be used for clustering and how these attributes should be scaled and normalized,
- applying the chosen clustering variant, and
- manually determining a reference peak clustering.

The core functionalities of PeakViewer are loading peak data, generating clusters from a training set, classifying the test data, and visualizing all these steps and their results. It provides a powerful GUI and also a command line mode, the latter being useful in particular for performing sequences of tasks like cross validation. FoldCross is a specific tool for automated 10-fold cross validation, and ParamWalk is another subsystem for systematically increasing a chosen clustering parameter and performing 10-fold cross validation for each parameter value.

# 5    Experiments

## 5.1    Relational Probabilistic Modelling and Learning for $D_{bc}$

In our case study, we applied methods of probabilistic relational modelling and learning to (a logic representation of) $D_{bc}$. The logic representation (for convenience, also referred to as $D_{bc}$) involves atomic formulas of the form $bc(M)$ and $pcInM(pc18, M)$, indicating that measurement $M$ belongs to a person with lung cancer, and that peak cluster $pc18$ occurs in measurement $M$, respectively. Using the logic modelling of $D_{bc}$, our aim is to learn a system being able to answer the question whether $bc(M)$ holds or does not hold. For this learning task, we used methods of Inductive Logic Programming (ILP) [10] and Markov Logic Networks [12].

Inductive Logic Programming has been used very successfully in machine learning for inducing first-order hypotheses from examples and background knowledge. For our application scenario we employed the ILP system Aleph [13] for learning bronchial carcinoma diagnosing rules from $D_{bc}$.

*Markov logic* [12] establishes a framework which combines Markov networks [11] with first-order logic to handle a broad area of statistical relational learning tasks. The Markov logic syntax complies with first-order logic except that each formula $F_i$ is quantified by an additional (positive or negative) weight value $w_i$. Semantics are given to sets of Markov logic formulas by a probability distribution over (propositional) possible worlds which is given by a log-linear model defined over weighted ground formulas. The fundamental idea in Markov logic is that first-order formulas are not handled as hard constraints but each formula is softened depending on its weight. These weights induce a kind of priority ordering on the formulas of the knowledge base that determines their respective influence on the probabilities of the log-linear model. A *Markov logic network (MLN) L* is a set of weighted first-order logic formulas together with a set of constants $C$, and the semantics of $L$ is given by a ground Markov network $M_{L,C}$ constructed from $F_i$ and $C$ [12]. The standard semantics of Markov networks [11] is used for reasoning, e.g. to determine the probabilistic inferences of $L$ (see [12] for details). In our case study, we used the Alchemy system that provides a range of learning and inferencing facilities for MLNs [6].

## 5.2  Binary and Probabilistic Accuracy

For grading the quality of the obtained results, one criterium is the *predictive accurracy*. For a system yielding probabilities as answers, turning each probability into a binary value according to a fixed limit (here 0.5), yields what we will call *predictive binary accuracy* (or just *b-accuracy*) defined by

$$a_b(\alpha) = \frac{|TP| + |TN|}{|E_T| + |E_F|}$$

where $TP = \{e \in E_T \mid \alpha(e) \geq 0.5\}$ is the set of true positive and $TN = \{e \in E_F \mid \alpha(e) < 0.5\}$ the set of true negative answers, $E_T$ and $E_F$ are the sets of positive and negative instances, and $\alpha(e)$ is the probability assigned to $e \in E_T \cup E_F$.

However, the notion of b-accuracy that was also used in e.g. [4] has the disadvantage that an answer with a high probability like 0.95 is viewed as being equivalent to an answer with a probability of e.g. 0.65. In order to take the certainty of an answer into account, we propose the notion of *predictive probabilistic accuracy* (or just *p-accuracy*) defined by

$$a_p(\alpha) = \frac{1}{|E_T| + |E_F|}\Big(\sum_{e \in E_T} \alpha(e) + \sum_{e \in E_F}(1 - \alpha(e))\Big)$$

For instance, suppose we have $E_T = \{e_1, e_2, e_3\}$, $E_F = \{e_4, e_5\}$, $\alpha(E_T) = \{0.7, 0.9, 0.4\}$, and $\alpha(E_F) = \{0.45, 0.4\}$. Thus, there is one false negative answer, and the b-accuracy is $a_b = \frac{(1+1+0)+(1+1)}{5} = 0.8$, while the p-accuracy is only $a_p = \frac{(0.7+0.9+0.4)+(0.55+0.6)}{5} = 0.63$.

The p-accuracy measure is closely related to the Brier score [2] and to ROC curves [15]. Note that b-accuray and p-accuray coincide if $\alpha(e) \in \{0, 1\}$ for every instance $e$. In our case study, we used both b-accuray and p-accuray for grading the outcome of a learning scenario.

|         | 2D pos    | 2D      | 3D     | 5D     | 2D+M      |
|---------|-----------|---------|--------|--------|-----------|
| ALEPH-0 | Ah0_2Dpos | Ah0_2D  |        |        |           |
| ALEPH-1 | Ah1_2Dpos | Ah1_2D  | Ah1_3D | Ah1_5D | Ah1_2D+M  |
| ALEPH-2 | Ah2_2Dpos | Ah2_2D  |        |        |           |
| ALEPH-3 | Ah3_2Dpos | Ah3_2D  |        |        |           |
| Alchemy-0 | Ay0_2Dpos | Ay0_2D | Ay0_3D |        |           |

**Fig. 4.** Learning scenarios for structure learning for $D_{bc}$

## 5.3  Learning Scenarios and Inference Results

In [9], a series of modelling and learning experiments was carried out with $D_{bc}$;
Fig. 4 lists an excerpt of these experiments. The first three characters of an
experiment identifier like Ah1_3D specifies the structure learning system (Aleph
or Alchemy) and a set of parameter settings for that system. The remaining
characters stand for the modelling type:

*2D pos* - peaks are modelled with two dimensions, and only positive literals are
  used (in all other modellings, also negative literals are used).
*2D, 3D,* and *5D* - peak modelling with 2, 3, or 5 dimensions.
*2D+M* - modelling of peaks with two dimensions and taking into account the
  number of peaks in a measurement.

For each of the scenarios indicated in Fig. 4, we used the Alchemy system as an
inference tool for checking the diagnosis quality of the learning result. In order to
avoid overfitting or pure coincidence distorting the results, all experiments were
randomized in two different ways. For every experiment, the corresponding peak
clustering was carried out 50 times with slightly modified clustering parameters,

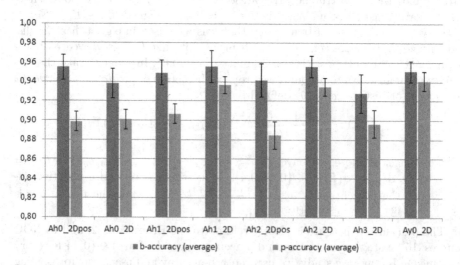

**Fig. 5.** Inference results obtained with Alchemy for various learning experiments

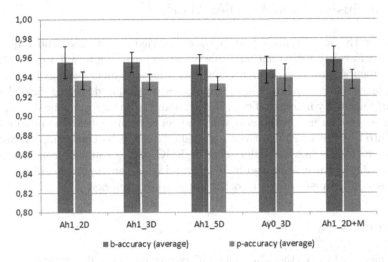

**Fig. 6.** Inference for 2D, 3D, 5D modelling and taking the number of peaks into account

and for each clustering result the subsequent learning and inference steps were carried out using 10-fold cross validation. The resulting diagnosis quality will be presented as a bar chart showing the average results for both b-accuracy and p-accuracy and also indicating the standard deviation. In comparison to the (b-)accuracy results of only up to 90% reported in [4], b-accuracy and even p-accuracy are generally higher. In the following, we will present and further evaluate our findings in more detail under various aspects.

If allowing also negated literals yields an improvement, then this indicates that the missing of a particular substance in the breath a patient exhales constitutes information possibly being relevant for the diagnosis of bronchial carcinoma. Note that for this comparison, Alchemy structure learning must be left out since here all formulas learned may contain negated or non-negated atoms. A graphical representation of the inference quality of the 2D modellings graded by both b-accuracy and p-accuracy is given in Fig. 5. The inference result Ah0_2Dpos[0.9546/0.8985] (where this notation states that for experiment Ah0_2Dpos an average b-accuracy of 0.9546 and an average p-accuracy of 0.8985 was achieved) indicates that Aleph may be able to find good rules with only positive literals, but generally, rules containing both positive and negative literals as in Ah1_2D[0.9555/0.9364] seem to perform better, in particular with respect to p-accuracy.

Whereas the 2D modelling considers only the position of a peak, in 3D and 5D modelling also the height and the extension of peaks is taken into account. Fig. 6 shows that in our $D_{bc}$ case study there is no improvement in the inference results when going to 3D or 5D modelling, but it can be observed that there is a lower standard deviation for both b-accuracy and p-accuracy. Taking into account the number of peaks in a measurement as in Ah1_2D+M[0.9580/0.9369] leads to a slight improvement for both notions of accuracy .

# 6 Conclusions and Further Work

Extending the work reported in [4,3], we carried out a case study applying methods of probabilistic relational modelling and learning to a database of IMS measurements, aiming at inferring whether a measurement belongs to a person having bronchial carcinoma. Using refined clustering and modelling yielded a significantly accuracy increase. There is still room for further refinements; e.g., the relevance of an observed substance with respect to bronchial carcinoma should be taken into account when determinig the quality of a peak clustering (cf. Sec. 3), or other measures like the Brier score or ROC curves could be considered (cf. Sec. 5.2). Our future work also includes employing the approach to larger IMS databases and transferring it to other application scenarios.

# References

1. Baumbach, J.I., Westhoff, M.: Ion mobility spectometry to detect lung cancer and airway infections. Spectroscopy Europe 18(6), 22–27 (2006)
2. Brier, G.W.: Verification of forecasts expressed in terms of probability. Monthly Weather Review 78(1), 1–3 (1950)
3. Finthammer, M., Beierle, C., Fisseler, J., Kern-Isberner, G., Baumbach, J.I.: Using probabilistic relational learning to support bronchial carcinoma diagnosis based on ion mobility spectrometry. International Journal for Ion Mobility Spectrometry 13, 83–93 (2010)
4. Finthammer, M., Beierle, C., Fisseler, J., Kern-Isberner, G., Möller, B., Baumbach, J.I.: Probabilistic Relational Learning for Medical Diagnosis Based on Ion Mobility Spectrometry. In: Hüllermeier, E., Kruse, R., Hoffmann, F. (eds.) IPMU 2010. CCIS, vol. 80, pp. 365–375. Springer, Heidelberg (2010)
5. Getoor, L., Taskar, B. (eds.): Introduction to Statistical Relational Learning. MIT Press (2007)
6. Kok, S., Singla, P., Richardson, M., Domingos, P., Sumner, M., Poon, H., Lowd, D., Wang, J.: The Alchemy System for Statistical Relational AI: User Manual. Department of Computer Science and Engineering. University of Washington (2008)
7. Lindeberg, T.: Scale-space. In: Wah, B.W. (ed.) Wiley Encyclopedia of Computer Science and Engineering. John Wiley & Sons, Inc. (2008)
8. MacQueen, J.B.: Some methods of classification and analysis of multivariate observations. In: Proceedings of the Fifth Berkeley Symposium on Mathematical Statistics and Probability, pp. 281–297 (1967)
9. Masternak, R.: Application of probabilistic relational learning for the analysis of multidimensional, spectrometric data. Master Thesis, Dept. of Computer Science, FernUniversität in Hagen, Germany (2011) (in German)
10. Muggleton, S., De Raedt, L.: Inductive logic programming: Theory and methods. Journal of Logic Programming 19/20, 629–679 (1994)
11. Pearl, J.: Probabilistic Reasoning in Intelligent Systems: Networks of Plausible Inference. Morgan Kaufmann (1988)
12. Richardson, M., Domingos, P.: Markov logic networks. Machine Learning 62(1), 107–136 (2006)

13. Srinivasan, A.: The Aleph Manual (2007),
www.comlab.ox.ac.uk/activities/machinelearning/Aleph/
14. Yu, W., Li, X., Liu, J., Wu, B., Williams, K.R., Zhao, H.: Multiple peak alignment in sequential data analysis: A scale-space-based approach. IEEE/ACM Trans. Comput. Biology Bioinform. 3(3), 208–219 (2006)
15. Zhou, X.-H., McClish, D.K., Obuchowski, N.A.: Statistical Methods in Diagnostic Medicine, 2nd edn. Wiley, Hoboken (2011)

# Conditioning in Decomposable Compositional Models in Valuation-Based Systems

Radim Jiroušek[1] and Prakash P. Shenoy[2]

[1] Faculty of Management at Univ. of Economics, Jindřichův Hradec, Czech Republic
radim@utia.cas.cz
[2] School of Business at University of Kansas
Lawrence, KS, USA
pshenoy@ku.edu

**Abstract.** Valuation-based systems (VBS) can be considered as a generic uncertainty framework that has many uncertainty calculi, such as probability theory, a version of possibility theory where combination is the product $t$-norm, Spohn's epistemic belief theory, and Dempster-Shafer belief function theory, as special cases. In this paper, we focus our attention on conditioning, which is defined using the combination, marginalization, and removal operators of VBS. We show that conditioning can be expressed using the composition operator. We define decomposable compositional models in the VBS framework. Finally, we show that conditioning in decomposable compositional models can be done using local computation. Since all results are obtained in the VBS framework, they hold in all calculi that fit in the VBS framework.

**Keywords:** valuation-based systems, probability theory, possibility theory, Dempster-Shafer belief function theory, Spohn's epistemic belief theory, conditionals, compositional models, decomposable compositional models, conditioning in decomposable compositional models.

## 1 Introduction to Valuation-Based Systems

Valuation-based systems (VBS) were introduced in [9] as a generic uncertainty calculus that has many uncertainty calculi, such as probability theory, a version of possibility theory [2] with the product t-norm, Spohn's epistemic belief theory [11], and D-S belief function theory [1,8], as special cases. In this section, we formally introduce the VBS framework. Most of the material is in this section is taken from [9].

VBS consists of two parts — a static part that is concerned with representation of knowledge, and a dynamic part that is concerned with reasoning with knowledge.

The static part consists of objects called variables and valuations. Let $\Phi$ denote a finite set whose elements are called *variables*. Elements of $\Phi$ are denoted by upper-case Roman alphabets such as $X$, $Y$, $Z$, etc. Subsets of $\Phi$ are denoted by lower-case Roman alphabets such as $r$, $s$, $t$, etc.

S. Greco et al. (Eds.): IPMU 2012, Part IV, CCIS 300, pp. 676–685, 2012.

Let $\Psi$ denote a set whose elements are called *valuations*. Elements of $\Psi$ are denoted by lower-case Greek alphabets such as $\rho$, $\sigma$, $\tau$, etc. Each valuation is associated with a subset of variables, and represents some knowledge about the variables in the subset. Thus, we will say that $\rho$ is a valuation for $r$, where $r \subseteq \Phi$.

We can depict VBS graphically by graphs called valuation networks. Consider a finite set of valuations $\Lambda \subset \Psi$ defining a valuation-based system. A corresponding *valuation network* (VN) is a bi-partite graph with variables and valuations as nodes, and there is an edge between each valuation and the variables in the subset associated with it. An example is shown in Figure 1. In this example, $\Phi = \{D, G, B\}$, $\Lambda = \{\delta, \gamma, \beta\}$, where $\delta$ is a valuation for $\{D\}$, $\gamma$ is a valuation for $\{D, G\}$, and $\beta$ is a valuation for $\{D, B\}$.

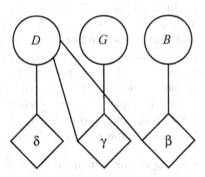

**Fig. 1.** A valuation network

We will identify a subset of valuations $\Psi_n \subset \Psi$, whose elements are called *normal* valuations. Normal valuations are valuations that are coherent in some sense. In probability theory, normal valuations are probability potentials whose values add to one. In D-S belief function theory, normal valuations are basic probability assignment potentials whose values for non-empty subsets add to one (or their corresponding commonality potentials).

The dynamic part of VBS consists of several operators that are used to make inferences from the knowledge encoded in a VBS. We will define three basic operators: combination, marginalization, and removal, and their properties.

**Combination.** The first operator is the *combination* operator $\oplus \colon \Psi \times \Psi \to \Psi_n$, which represents aggregation of knowledge. It has the following properties.

1. *(Domain)* If $\rho$ is a valuation for $r$, and $\sigma$ is a valuation for $s$, then $\rho \oplus \sigma$ is a normal valuation for $r \cup s$.
2. *(Commutativity)* $\rho \oplus \sigma = \sigma \oplus \rho$.
3. *(Associativity)* $\rho \oplus (\sigma \oplus \tau) = (\rho \oplus \sigma) \oplus \tau$.

The domain property expresses the fact that if $\rho$ represents some knowledge about variables in $r$, and $\sigma$ represents some knowledge about variables in $s$, then $\rho \oplus \sigma$ represents the aggregated knowledge about variables in $r \cup s$. The commutativity and associativity properties reflect the fact that the sequence in which knowledge is aggregated makes no difference in the aggregated result. In probability theory, combination of two valuations is pointwise multiplication followed by normalization assuming normalization is possible. If normalization is not possible, this means that the knowledge encoded in $\rho$ and $\sigma$ are completely inconsistent. Henceforth, for the sake of simplicity, we will assume that we don't have inconsistent valuations.

The set of all normal valuations with the combination operator $\oplus$ forms a commutative semigroup. We will let $\iota_\emptyset$ denote the (unique) identity valuation of this semigroup. Thus, for any normal valuation $\rho$, $\rho \oplus \iota_\emptyset = \rho$. It is easy to see that the domain of $\iota_\emptyset$ is $\emptyset$, hence the notation.

The set of all normal valuations for $s$ with the combination operator $\oplus$ also forms a commutative semigroup (which is different from the semigroup discussed in the previous paragraph). Let $\iota_s$ denote the (unique) identity for this semigroup. Thus, for any normal valuation $\sigma$ for $s$, $\sigma \oplus \iota_s = \sigma$.

It is important to note that in most uncertainty calculi, in general, $\rho \oplus \rho \neq \rho$. Thus, it is important to ensure that we do not double count knowledge when double counting matters, i.e., it is okay to double count knowledge $\rho$ that is idempotent, i.e., $\rho \oplus \rho = \rho$. In representing our knowledge as valuations from $\Psi$, we have to ensure that there is no double counting of non-idempotent knowledge.

**Marginalization.** Another operator is marginalization $-X\colon \Psi \to \Psi$, which allows us to coarsen knowledge by marginalizing $X$ out of the domain of a valuation. It has the following properties.

1. (*Domain*) If $\rho$ is a valuation for $r$, and $X \in r$, then $\rho^{-X}$ is a valuation for $r \setminus \{X\}$.
2. (*Normal*) $\rho^{-X}$ is normal if and only if $\rho$ is normal.
3. (*Order does not matter*) If $\rho$ is a valuation for $r$, $X \in r$, and $Y \in r$, then $(\rho^{-X})^{-Y} = (\rho^{-Y})^{-X}$, which we will denote by $\rho^{-\{X,Y\}}$.
4. (*Local computation*) If $\rho$ and $\sigma$ are valuations for $r$ and $s$, respectively, $X \in r$, and $X \notin s$, then $(\rho \oplus \sigma)^{-X} = (\rho^{-X}) \oplus \sigma$.

The domain property is self-explanatory. Marginalization preserves normal (and non-normal) property of valuations. The order does not matter property dictates that when we coarsen knowledge by marginalizing out several variables, the order in which the variables are marginalized does not matter in the final result. Thus, if $\rho$ is a normal valuation for $r$, then $\rho^{-r} = \iota_\emptyset$, which is the only normal valuation for $\emptyset$. Sometimes, we will let $\rho^{\downarrow r \setminus \{X,Y\}}$ denote $\rho^{-\{X,Y\}}$. Thus, the "$-$" notation is useful when we wish to emphasize the variables being marginalized, whereas the "$\downarrow$" notation is useful when we wish to emphasize the variables that remain after the marginalization operation. In probability theory, marginalization of variable $X$ corresponds to addition over the state space of $X$.

Making inferences in VBS means finding the (posterior) marginal of the joint valuation for some variables of interest, i.e., computing $(\oplus \Lambda)^{\downarrow \{Z\}}$, where $\Lambda$ includes valuations that represent observations and independent pieces of evidence, and $Z$ denotes an unobserved variable of interest. When we have many variables in $\Phi$, it may be computationally intractable to compute explicitly the joint valuation $(\oplus \Lambda)$. The local computation property allows us to compute the marginal $(\rho \oplus \sigma)^{-X}$ without having to explicitly compute $\rho \oplus \sigma$. Notice that the combination in $(\rho^{-X}) \oplus \sigma$ is on a smaller set of variables $(r \cup s \setminus \{X\})$ compared to $\rho \oplus \sigma$ (which is on $r \cup s$). By repeatedly using this property for all variables being marginalized in some sequence, we get the so-called variable elimination algorithm for computing marginals. Also, if we wish to compute several marginals, then it is useful to cache the intermediate results in the computation of one marginal so that these can be re-used in the computation of other marginals. A binary join tree is a data structure that is useful for this purpose. For details, see [10].

While the combination and marginalization operators suffice for the problem of making inferences, there is yet another operator, called removal, that is useful for defining conditionals, and for defining the composition operator.

**Removal.** The removal operator $\ominus: \Psi \times \Psi_n \to \Psi_n$ represents removing knowledge in the second valuation from the knowledge in the first valuation. The properties of the removal operator are as follows.

1. (*Domain*): Suppose $\sigma$ is a valuation for $s$ and $\rho$ is a normal valuation for $r$. Then $\sigma \ominus \rho$ is a normal valuation for $r \cup s$.
2. (*Identity*): For each normal valuation $\rho$ for $r$, $\rho \oplus \rho \ominus \rho = \rho$. Thus, $\rho \ominus \rho$ acts as an identity for $\rho$, and we denote $\rho \ominus \rho$ by $\iota_\rho$. Thus, $\rho \oplus \iota_\rho = \rho$.
3. (*Combination and Removal*): Suppose $\pi$ and $\theta$ are valuations, and suppose $\rho$ is a normal valuation. Then, $(\pi \oplus \theta) \ominus \rho = \pi \oplus (\theta \ominus \rho)$.

We call $\sigma \ominus \rho$ the valuation resulting after removing $\rho$ from $\sigma$. Notice that the removal operator cannot be extended as an operator $\ominus : \Psi \times \Psi \to \Psi_n$ because of the identity property, which defines the removal operator as an inverse of the combination operator. In probability theory removal is pointwise division followed by normalization (here, division of any real number by zero results in zero, by definition).

It is important to note that given a normal valuation $\rho$ for $r$, we have a number of (may be different) identity valuations $\iota$ such that $\rho \oplus \iota = \rho$. So far we have explicitly mentioned $\iota_\emptyset$, $\iota_r$ and $\iota_\rho$. However, and it will be shown in Lemma 1, for any $s \subseteq r$, $\iota_{\rho \downarrow s}$ acts also as an identity valuation for $\rho$, i.e.,

$$\rho \oplus \iota_{\rho \downarrow s} = \rho.$$

We reproduce some important results about the removal operator from [9].

**Proposition 1.** *Suppose $\pi$, $\sigma$, $\theta$ are valuations, and $\rho$ is a normal valuation for $r$ and $X \notin r$. Then,*

$$(\pi \oplus \theta) \ominus \rho = (\pi \ominus \rho) \oplus \theta, \tag{1}$$

*and*

$$(\sigma \ominus \rho)^{-X} = \sigma^{-X} \ominus \rho. \tag{2}$$

**Domination.** As defined in the identity property, $\rho \oplus \iota_\rho = \rho$. In general, if $\rho'$ is a normal valuation for $r$ that is distinct from $\rho$, then $\rho' \oplus \iota_\rho$ may not equal $\rho'$. However, there may exist a class of normal valuations for $r$ such that if $\rho'$ is in this class, then $\rho' \oplus \iota_\rho = \rho'$. Following the terminology in [5], we will call this class of normal valuations as valuations that are *dominated* by $\rho$. Thus, if $\rho$ dominates $\rho'$, written as $\rho \gg \rho'$, then $\rho' \oplus \iota_\rho = \rho'$. In probability theory, if $\rho$ and $\rho'$ are normal probability potentials for $r$ such that $\rho(\mathbf{x}) = 0 \Rightarrow \rho'(\mathbf{x}) = 0$, then $\rho \gg \rho'$.

**Composition.** A general definition of the composition operator is as follows. Suppose $\rho$ and $\sigma$ are normal valuations for $r$ and $s$, respectively, and, to avoid composition of conflicting valuations, suppose that $\sigma^{\downarrow r \cap s} \gg \rho^{\downarrow r \cap s}$. The composition of $\rho$ and $\sigma$, written as $\rho \triangleright \sigma$, is defined as follows:

$$\rho \triangleright \sigma = \rho \oplus \sigma \ominus \sigma^{\downarrow r \cap s} \tag{3}$$

Unlike the combination operator, the valuations $\rho$ and $\sigma$ being composed do not have to be distinct. Intuitively, we adjust for the double-counting of the knowledge in $\rho$ and $\sigma$ by removing the knowledge that is double counted.

The most important properties of the composition operator that were proved in [6] are summarized in the following proposition.

**Proposition 2.** *Suppose $\rho$ and $\sigma$ are normal valuations for $r$ and $s$, respectively, and suppose that $\sigma^{\downarrow r \cap s} \gg \rho^{\downarrow r \cap s}$. Then the following statement hold.*

1. Domain: $\rho \triangleright \sigma$ *is a normal valuation for* $r \cup s$.
2. Composition preserves first marginal: $(\rho \triangleright \sigma)^{\downarrow r} = \rho$.
3. Non-commutativity: *In general,* $\rho \triangleright \sigma \neq \sigma \triangleright \rho$.
4. Commutativity under consistency: *If $\rho$ and $\sigma$ have a common marginal for $r \cap s$, i.e.,* $\rho^{\downarrow r \cap s} = \sigma^{\downarrow r \cap s}$, *then* $\rho \triangleright \sigma = \sigma \triangleright \rho$.
5. Non-associativity: *Suppose $\tau$ is a normal valuation for $t$, and suppose* $\tau^{\downarrow (r \cup s) \cap t} \gg (\rho \triangleright \sigma)^{\downarrow (r \cup s) \cap t}$. *Then, in general,*

$$(\rho \triangleright \sigma) \triangleright \tau \neq \rho \triangleright (\sigma \triangleright \tau).$$

6. Associativity under a special condition: *Suppose $\tau$ is a normal valuation for $t$, suppose* $\tau^{\downarrow (r \cup s) \cap t} \gg (\rho \triangleright \sigma)^{\downarrow (r \cup s) \cap t}$, *and suppose* $s \supset (r \cap t)$. *Then,*

$$(\rho \triangleright \sigma) \triangleright \tau = \rho \triangleright (\sigma \triangleright \tau).$$

7. Composition of marginals: *Suppose $t$ is such that* $(r \cap s) \subseteq t \subseteq s$. *Then*

$$(\rho \triangleright \sigma^{\downarrow t}) \triangleright \sigma = \rho \triangleright \sigma.$$

## 2    Conditionals

Suppose $\tau$ is a normal valuation for $t$, and suppose $r$ and $s$ are disjoint subsets of $t$. We call $\tau^{\downarrow (r \cup s)} \ominus \tau^{\downarrow r}$ the *conditional for $s$ given $r$ with respect to $\tau$*. To simplify notation, we will let $\tau(s|r)$ denote $\tau^{\downarrow (r \cup s)} \ominus \tau^{\downarrow r}$. Also, if $r = \emptyset$, let $\tau(s)$ denote $\tau(s|\emptyset)$.

The following proposition is taken from [9].

**Proposition 3.** *Suppose $\tau$ is a normal valuation for $t$, and suppose $r$, $s$, and $u$ are disjoint subsets of $t$. Then the following statements hold.*

1. $\tau(s) = \tau^{\downarrow s}$.
2. $\tau(r) \oplus \tau(s|r) = \tau(r \cup s)$.
3. $\tau(s|r) \oplus \tau(u|r \cup s) = \tau(s \cup u|r)$.
4. *Suppose $X \in s$. Then, $\tau(s|r)^{-X} = \tau(s \setminus \{X\}|r)$.*
5. $\tau(r) \oplus (\tau(s|r)^{-s}) = \tau(r)$.
6. $\tau(s|r)$ *is a normal valuation for $r \cup s$.*

**Lemma 1.** *Suppose $\tau$ is a normal valuation for $t$, and suppose $r \subseteq t$. Then*

$$\tau \oplus \iota_{\tau(r)} = \tau.$$

*Proof.* In the following equations, we use only the associativity and commutativity properties of combination, and property 2 of Proposition 3.

$$\tau \oplus \iota_{\tau(r)} = (\tau(r) \oplus \tau(t \setminus r|r)) \oplus \iota_{\tau(r)} = (\tau(t \setminus r|r) \oplus \tau(r)) \oplus \iota_{\tau(r)}$$
$$= \tau(t \setminus r|r) \oplus (\tau(r) \oplus \iota_{\tau(r)}) = \tau(t \setminus r|r) \oplus \tau(r) = \tau.$$

$\square$

Lemma 1 will help us to prove the following lemma, which expresses conditioning using the composition operator.

**Lemma 2.** *Suppose $\tau$ is a normal valuation for $t$, and suppose $r$ and $s$ are nonempty disjoint subsets of $t$ such that $r \cup s = t$. Then*

$$\tau(s|r) = \iota_{\tau(r)} \triangleright \tau.$$

*Proof.*

$$\iota_{\tau(r)} \triangleright \tau = \iota_{\tau(r)} \oplus \tau \ominus \tau^{\downarrow r} = \tau \ominus \tau^{\downarrow r} = \tau(s|r).$$

$\square$

**Conditional Independence for Variables.** Suppose $\tau$ is a normal valuation for $t$, and suppose $r$, $s$, and $v$ are disjoint subsets of $t$. We say $r$ is *conditionally independent of $s$ given $v$ with respect to $\tau$*, written as $r \perp\!\!\!\perp_\tau s \mid v$, if $\tau^{\downarrow(r \cup s \cup v)}$ factors into valuations $\alpha$ for $r \cup v$ and $\beta$ for $s \cup v$, i.e., $\tau^{\downarrow r \cup s \cup v} = \alpha \oplus \beta$.

Some observations. First, while $\tau$ has to be necessarily normal, valuations $\alpha$ and $\beta$ do not have to be normal. Second, the definition of conditional independence does not involve the removal operator, only the combination and marginalization operators. However, we can characterize conditional independence in terms of conditionals, which are defined using the removal operator. This is done in Proposition 4 below. Third, if $s = \emptyset$, then $r \perp\!\!\!\perp_\tau \emptyset \mid v$ since we can let $\alpha = \tau^{\downarrow(r \cup v)}$ and $\beta = \iota_v$. This property is called *trivial independence* by Geiger and Pearl [3]. Fourth, if $v = \emptyset$, then we say $r$ and $s$ are *independent* with respect to $\tau$, written as $r \perp\!\!\!\perp_\tau s$, if $\tau^{\downarrow(r \cup s)} = \alpha \oplus \beta$, where $\alpha$ is a valuation for $r$ and $\beta$ is a valuation for $s$. Thus, independence is a special case of conditional independence.

The following result is proved in [9].

**Proposition 4.** *Suppose $\tau$ is a normal valuation for $t$, and suppose $r$, $s$, and $v$ are disjoint subsets of $t$. The following statements are equivalent.*

1. $r \perp\!\!\!\perp_\tau s \mid v$.
2. $\tau(r \cup s \cup v) = \tau(v) \oplus \tau(r|v) \oplus \tau(s|v)$.
3. $\tau(r \cup s|v) = \tau(r|v) \oplus \tau(s|v)$.
4. $\tau(r \cup s \cup v) \oplus \tau(v) = \tau(r \cup v) \oplus \tau(s \cup v)$.
5. $\tau(r \cup s \cup v) = \tau(r|v) \oplus \tau(s \cup v)$.
6. $\tau(r|s \cup v) = \tau(r|v) \oplus \iota_{\tau(s \cup v)}$.
7. $\tau(r|s \cup v) = \alpha \oplus \iota_{\tau(s \cup v)}$, *where $\alpha$ is a valuation for $r \cup v$.*

## 3    Decomposable Compositional Models in VBS

In probability theory, inference with Bayesian networks is usually based on the idea of *local computation* of Lauritzen and Spiegelhalter [7]. This idea can be briefly expressed as follows. A Bayesian network is first transformed into a decomposable model (using well-known operations *moralization* and *triangulation* of a directed graph), and the required posterior marginal is then computed by a process exploiting the "tree" structure of decomposable models. Therefore, it is not surprising that we speak about decomposable compositional models in the VBS framework.

The tree structure of decomposable models is expressed as a running intersection property. We say that a sequence of sets $s_1, s_2, \ldots, s_n$ meets *running intersection property* (RIP) if for each $j = 2, 3, \ldots, n$ there exists a $k < j$ such that

$$s_j \cap (s_1 \cup \ldots \cup s_{j-1}) = s_j \cap s_k.$$

Decomposable compositional models are formed by multiple applications of the composition operator. Since it is not always associative (property 5 of Proposition 2), we use the following convention. If we do not specify an order using brackets, the operators will always be performed from left to right, i.e., $\tau^{\downarrow s_1} \triangleright \tau^{\downarrow s_2} \triangleright \tau^{\downarrow s_3} \triangleright \ldots \triangleright \tau^{\downarrow s_n}$ denotes $(\ldots ((\tau^{\downarrow s_1} \triangleright \tau^{\downarrow s_2}) \triangleright \tau^{\downarrow s_3}) \triangleright \ldots \triangleright \tau^{\downarrow s_n})$.

**Definition 1.** *Suppose $\tau$ is a normal valuation for $t$. We say $\tau$ is decomposable if there exists a sequence $(s_1, s_2, \ldots, s_n)$ of subsets of $t$ such that it meets RIP and*

$$\tau = \tau^{\downarrow s_1} \triangleright \tau^{\downarrow s_2} \triangleright \ldots \triangleright \tau^{\downarrow s_n}.$$

*In this case we also say that $\tau$ is decomposable with respect to the sequence $(s_1, s_2, \ldots, s_n)$.*

It is well-known that if a sequence $(s_1, s_2, \ldots, s_n)$ meets RIP, then we can find another sequence starting with, say $s_j$, that also meets RIP. More precisely, for each $j = 1, 2, \ldots, n$ there exists (at least one) permutation $(s_{\ell_1}, s_{\ell_2}, \ldots, s_{\ell_n})$ that meets RIP and such that $s_{\ell_1} = s_j$. Therefore, the following assertion is of great importance.

**Theorem 1.** *If $\tau$ is decomposable with respect to $(s_1, s_2, \ldots, s_n)$, and $(s_{j_1}, s_{j_2}, \ldots, s_{j_n})$ is a permutation of $(s_1, s_2, \ldots, s_n)$ such that it meets RIP, then $\tau$ is decomposable with respect to $(s_{j_1}, s_{j_2}, \ldots, s_{j_n})$, i.e.,*

$$\tau = \tau^{\downarrow s_1} \rhd \tau^{\downarrow s_2} \rhd \ldots \rhd \tau^{\downarrow s_n} = \tau^{\downarrow s_{j_1}} \rhd \tau^{\downarrow s_{j_2}} \rhd \ldots \rhd \tau^{\downarrow s_{j_n}}.$$

*Proof.* The proof of this assertion is based on an important result concerning decomposable graphs, which follows from the results of S. Haberman ([4], Lemma 2.8) saying that the system of subsets (more exactly, *multiset*)

$$\{s_2 \cap s_1, s_3 \cap (s_1 \cup s_2), s_4 \cap (s_1 \cup s_2 \cup s_3), \ldots, s_n \cap (s_1 \cup \ldots \cup s_{n-1})\}$$

does not depend on the selected RIP ordering of the sequence $(s_1, s_2, \ldots, s_n)$. Taking into account the running intersection property, we know that each element of this multiset is an intersection of two sets from the sequence $(s_1, s_2, \ldots, s_n)$. Therefore, the above mentioned property can be expressed as follows: For any pair of distinct sets $s_i, s_j$ from a system $\{s_1, s_2, \ldots, s_n\}$, which can be ordered to meet RIP, the number of times the set $s_i \cap s_j$ appears in the sequence

$$s_{j_2} \cap s_{j_1}, s_{j_3} \cap (s_{j_1} \cup s_{j_2}), s_{j_4} \cap (s_{j_1} \cup s_{j_2} \cup s_{j_3}), \ldots, s_{j_n} \cap (s_{j_1} \cup \ldots \cup s_{j_{n-1}})$$

does not depend on the RIP ordering $(s_{j_1}, s_{j_2}, \ldots, s_{j_n})$.

Suppose $\tau$ is decomposable with respect to $(s_1, s_2, \ldots, s_n)$. Using the definition of composition, we have:

$$\tau = \tau^{\downarrow s_1} \oplus \left( \tau^{\downarrow s_2} \ominus \tau^{\downarrow s_2 \cap s_1} \right) \oplus \left( \tau^{\downarrow s_3} \ominus \tau^{\downarrow s_3 \cap (s_1 \cup s_2)} \right) \oplus \ldots$$

$$\oplus \left( \tau^{\downarrow s_n} \ominus \tau^{\downarrow s_n \cap (s_1 \cup \ldots \cup s_{n-1})} \right)$$

which can be reorganized independently of the RIP ordering (using the properties of combination and removal and Proposition 1) as follows:

$$\tau = \left( \tau^{\downarrow s_1} \oplus \tau^{\downarrow s_2} \oplus \ldots \oplus \tau^{\downarrow s_n} \right)$$

$$\ominus \tau^{\downarrow s_2 \cap s_1} \ominus \tau^{\downarrow s_3 \cap (s_1 \cup s_2)} \ominus \ldots \ominus \tau^{\downarrow s_n \cap (s_1 \cup \ldots \cup s_{n-1})} \qquad \square$$

# 4   Conditioning in Decomposable Compositional Models

In this section, we assume that $\tau$ is a normal valuation for $t$, and that it is decomposable with respect to $(s_1, s_2, \ldots, s_n)$. Suppose we wish to compute the conditional $\tau(t \setminus \{X\} | \{X\})$.

First, we have to find an ordering of $s_1, s_2, \ldots, s_n$ such that it meets RIP, and such that the first set from this ordering contains $X$. We know from Theorem 1 that $\tau$ is decomposable also with respect to this new sequence. Therefore, without loss of generality we can assume that it is $(s_1, s_2, \ldots, s_n)$, which means that we assume $X \in s_1$. Thus, using Lemma 2, we compute

$$\tau(t \setminus \{X\} | \{X\}) = \iota_{\tau(X)} \rhd \tau = \iota_{\tau(X)} \rhd \left( \tau^{\downarrow s_1} \rhd \tau^{\downarrow s_2} \rhd \ldots \rhd \tau^{\downarrow s_n} \right).$$

However, due to property 6 (associativity under a special condition) of Proposition 2, we have

$$\iota_{\tau(X)} \triangleright \left(\left(\tau^{\downarrow s_1} \triangleright \tau^{\downarrow s_2} \triangleright \ldots \triangleright \tau^{\downarrow s_{n-1}}\right) \triangleright \tau^{\downarrow s_n}\right)$$
$$= \left(\iota_{\tau(X)} \triangleright \left(\tau^{\downarrow s_1} \triangleright \tau^{\downarrow s_2} \triangleright \ldots \triangleright \tau^{\downarrow s_{n-1}}\right)\right) \triangleright \tau^{\downarrow s_n}, \qquad (4)$$

because $s_1$, and thus even more $s_1 \cup \ldots \cup s_{n-1}$, contains $\{X\} \cap s_n$. Notice that also the other assumption of associativity under a special condition is fulfilled because

$$\tau^{\downarrow (s_1 \cup \ldots \cup s_{n-1}) \cap s_n} \gg \left(\iota_{\tau(X)} \triangleright \left(\tau^{\downarrow s_1} \triangleright \tau^{\downarrow s_2} \triangleright \ldots \triangleright \tau^{\downarrow s_{n-1}}\right)\right)^{\downarrow (s_1 \cup \ldots \cup s_{n-1}) \cap s_n}.$$

Repeating the idea behind equality (4), we get

$$\iota_{\tau(X)} \triangleright \left(\left(\tau^{\downarrow s_1} \triangleright \tau^{\downarrow s_2} \triangleright \ldots \triangleright \tau^{\downarrow s_{n-2}}\right) \triangleright \tau^{\downarrow s_{n-1}}\right)$$
$$= \left(\iota_{\tau(X)} \triangleright \left(\tau^{\downarrow s_1} \triangleright \tau^{\downarrow s_2} \triangleright \ldots \triangleright \tau^{\downarrow s_{n-2}}\right)\right) \triangleright \tau^{\downarrow s_{n-1}}.$$

Thus, eventually, after repeating this step $(n-1)$ times we get

$$\tau(t \setminus \{X\}|\{X\}) = \iota_{\tau(X)} \triangleright \tau = \left(\iota_{\tau(X)} \triangleright \tau^{\downarrow s_1}\right) \triangleright \tau^{\downarrow s_2} \triangleright \ldots \triangleright \tau^{\downarrow s_n},$$

from which we see that $\tau(t \setminus \{X\}|\{X\})$ is again a decomposable model with respect to $(s_1, s_2, \ldots, s_n)$. Let $\hat{\tau}$ denote $\tau(t \setminus \{X\}|\{X\})$. We can compute the marginal valuations of $\hat{\tau}$ (that are necessary to represent this multidimensional valuation as a compositional model) as follows:

$$\hat{\tau}^{\downarrow s_1} = \iota_{\tau(X)} \triangleright \tau^{\downarrow s_1}$$
$$\hat{\tau}^{\downarrow s_2} = \hat{\tau}^{\downarrow s_2 \cap s_1} \triangleright \tau^{\downarrow s_2}$$
$$\vdots$$
$$\hat{\tau}^{\downarrow s_n} = \hat{\tau}^{\downarrow s_n \cap (s_1 \cup \ldots \cup s_{n-1})} \triangleright \tau^{\downarrow s_n}.$$

Notice that this computation is tractable because, thanks to RIP, at each step $\hat{\tau}^{\downarrow s_i \cap (s_1 \cup \ldots \cup s_{i-1})}$ is easily computable since $s_i \cap (s_1 \cup \ldots \cup s_{i-1})$ must be contained in some $s_k$ for $k < i$.

# 5    Summary and Conclusions

We have described the abstract VBS framework including the composition operator. We have shown that conditioning, which is defined using the combination, marginalization, and removal operators of VBS, can be expressed in terms of the composition operator. We have defined a decomposable compositional model as a special type of a compositional model in the VBS framework. We have shown that for decomposable compositional models, conditional valuations can be computed efficiently using local computation. All of this is done in the abstract VBS framework. Since the VBS framework applies to many different uncertainty calculi, we have effectively defined decomposable compositional models, and efficient computation of conditionals in decomposable compositional models, for any calculi that fits in the VBS framework. For example, because Spohn's epistemic theory fits in the VBS framework, all results described in this paper applies to this calculus.

**Acknowledgements.** This work has been supported in part by funds from grant GAČR 403/12/2175 to the first author, and from the Ronald G. Harper Distinguished Professorship at the University of Kansas to the second author. We are grateful to Milan Studený for valuable discussions and comments.

# References

1. Dempster, A.P.: Upper and lower probabilities induced by a multivalued mapping. Annals of Mathematical Statistics 38, 325–339 (1967)
2. Dubois, D., Prade, H.: Possibility Theory: An Approach to Computerized Processing of Uncertainty. Plenum Press (1988)
3. Geiger, D., Pearl, J.: Logical and algorithmic properties of independence and their application to Bayesian networks. Annals of Mathematics and Artificial Intelligence 2, 165–178 (1990)
4. Haberman, S.J.: The Analysis of Frequency Data. The University of Chicago Press, Chicago (1974)
5. Jiroušek, R.: Composition of probability measures on finite spaces. In: Geiger, D., Shenoy, P.P. (eds.) Uncertainty in Artificial Intelligence: Proceedings of the 13th Conference (UAI 1997), pp. 274–281. Morgan Kaufmann, San Francisco (1997)
6. Jiroušek, R., Shenoy, P.P.: Compositional models in valuation-based systems. Working Paper No. 325, School of Business, University of Kansas, Lawrence, KS (2011)
7. Lauritzen, S.L., Spiegelhalter, D.J.: Local computation with probabilities on graphical structures and their application to expert systems. Journal of Royal Statistical Society, series B 50, 157–224 (1988)
8. Shafer, G.: A Mathematical Theory of Evidence. Princeton University Press, Princeton (1976)
9. Shenoy, P.P.: Conditional independence in valuation-based systems. International Journal of Approximate Reasoning 10, 203–234 (1994)
10. Shenoy, P.P.: Binary join trees for computing marginals in the Shenoy-Shafer architecture. International Journal of Approximate Reasoning 17, 239–263 (1997)
11. Spohn, W.: A general non-probabilistic theory of inductive reasoning. In: Shachter, R.D., Levitt, T.S., Lemmer, J.F., Kanal, L.N. (eds.) Uncertainty in Artificial Intelligence 4 (UAI 1990), pp. 274–281. North Holland (1990)

# Author Index